Kelsey Brodsho

HEALTH LAW

By

Barry R. Furrow
Professor of Law
Widener University

Thomas L. Greaney
Professsor of Law
Saint Louis University
Co-Director, Center for Health Law Studies

Sandra H. Johnson
Professor of Law
Professor of Law in
Health Care Administration, and
Professor of Law in Internal Medicine
Saint Louis University

Timothy Stoltzfus Jost
Newton D. Baker, Baker and Hostetler Professor of Law,
and Professor of Health Services Management and Policy
The Ohio State University

Robert L. Schwartz
Professor of Law
University of New Mexico School of Law
Professor of Pediatrics
University of New Mexico School of Medicine

This book is an abridgement of Furrow, Greaney,
Johnson, Jost & Schwartz's
"Health Law, Volumes 1 & 2, Practitioner Treatise Series".

HORNBOOK SERIES®

WEST GROUP

ST. PAUL, MINN., 2000

TEXT IS PRINTED ON 10% POST
CONSUMER RECYCLED PAPER

Preface to the Second Edition

Health law and policy have changed significantly since the first edition of this book was published a half decade ago. Not surprisingly, therefore, this book is quite different from its first edition. Whole chapters have been dropped and added. A new chapter on ERISA has been added, reflecting ERISA's rise to prominence in the past half decade both as a major impediment to regulating and imposing liability on managed care and as an important grounds for recovery against employee benefits plans for denied services. Our previous chapter on tort rerform has been shortened and moved into the chapter on professional liability and the chapter on health reform has been eliminated, recognizing that the former topic does not seem as urgent as it did a decade or two ago, and that the latter, though more urgent now than ever, cannot seem to get the attention of law makers. Material from the former chapter on liability of managed care organizations, a topic of continuing importance, has been distributed to several other chapters because the subject matter is better handled under other main topics, such as institutional liability, ERISA, and managed care regulation. New sections have been added and others expanded to better cover topics that have emerged in the past half decade as major concerns in health law, such as conversions of not-for-profit entities, physician unions, mergers of physician groups and managed care plans, and regulatory responses to genetic discrimination. Throughout the book, new footnotes have been added and others expanded, recognizing the continued flow of new health law cases, statutes, regulations, and books and articles.

Though much has changed in this hornbook, much also remains the same: concise and thorough analysis of the issues, extensive references to primary and secondary sources, comprehensive subject matter coverage, and easy access through an extensive index and complete authority tables. While the hornbook is written so as to be immediately accessible to students, its authority has been recognized by the Supreme Court (which has twice cited the companion treatise in the past four years) and by hundreds of law review articles, which have cited the hornbook, treatise or casebook by the same authors.

The authors would like to thank our research assistants, Susan Orr, Jennifer Renucci and Allyson Sobel (Barry's research assistants); Ernie C. de Baca, Elicia Montoya, Kari Morrissey, and Laura Schauer (Rob's research assistants); Karie Gill (Tim Greaney's research assistant); Claire Conrad and Joseph Blecha (Rob's handlers), Mary Ann Jauer (Program Coordinator for the Saint Louis University Health Law Center and a good friend); Connie Sweeney (Barry's secretary); Michele Whetzel-Newton (Tim Jost's secretary); and Professor Leslie Mansfield of the University of Tulsa School of Law who have assisted in the preparation of this second edition. We would also like to thank.our Deans: Douglas Ray (Barry's Dean), Robert Desiderio and Alfred Mathewson (Rob's Deans), Gregory Williams (Tim Jost's Dean), and Jeffrey E. Lewis (Tim Greaney and Sandra Johnson's Dean).

*

WESTLAW® Overview

Health Law offers a detailed and comprehensive treatment of basic rules, principles and issues relating to the health law. To supplement the information contained in this book, you can access Westlaw, a computer-assisted legal research service of West Group. Westlaw contains a broad array of legal resources, including case law, statutes, expert commentary, current developments and various other types of information.

Learning how to use these materials effectively will enhance your legal research abilities. To help you coordinate the information in the book with your Westlaw research, this volume contains an appendix listing Westlaw databases, search techniques and sample problems.

THE PUBLISHER

*

Summary of Contents

Table of Contents

Chapter 3. Regulation and Licensure of Health Care Professionals

Chapter 6. The Liability of Health Care Professionals

A. Physician Liability for Patient Injury

B. Physician Obligations to Obtain a Patient's Informed Consent

Chapter 13. Medicare and Medicaid Fraud and Abuse

A. Introduction

B. False Claims and Statements

C. Bribes, Kickbacks, and Much Else

D. Self–Referrals

Chapter 17. Wrongful Birth, Wrongful Life and Wrongful Conception

Chapter 18. Abortion

HEALTH LAW

*

Chapter 1

REGULATION OF HEALTH CARE INSTITUTIONS

Table of Sections

Research References

   Am Jur 2d, Physicians, Surgeons, and Other Healers §§ 131–144, 158–173
   ALR Index: Extended Health Care Facility; Health and Human Services Department;
      Health Care Quality Improvement Act; Health Maintenance Organizations; Health
      Organizations; Health Providers
   ALR Digest: Hospitals and Other Health Care Facilities § 1, 7
   Am Jur Pleading and Practice Forms (Rev), Physicians, Surgeons, and Other Healers
      §§ 11–105

§ 1–1. Introduction to Quality Control Regulation

Even though only licensed health care professionals may practice the "healing arts" within a health care facility,[1] a quality-control system that stopped with the individual professional would be incomplete.[2] Although hospitals, nursing homes and other health care facilities cannot "practice medicine," the quality of the institution itself has a very significant impact on the quality of care received by patients. The scope of institutional quality issues is extensive, ranging from the adequacy of buildings, equipment, maintenance and sanitation through the fiscal and managerial soundness of the operation as well as the selection, training and monitoring of professional staff.

This chapter will review only the two major sources of public quality-control regulation—licensure by the states and federal regulation through the Medicare and Medicaid programs. In addition to these two major sources of public regulation, local governments and other state and federal agencies regulate health care facilities. Furthermore, licensed health care professionals, including the administrators of certain types of facilities, must answer to their own licensure agencies for conduct within health care institutions.

§ 1–1

1. See Chapter 3.

2. There is, of course, energetic debate over the degree to which government regulation is necessary, if at all. See e.g., Timothy S. Jost, The Necessary and Proper Role of Regulation to Assure the Quality of Health Care, 25 Houston L. Rev. 525 (1988); C. Havighurst, Deregu-

lating the Health Care Industry (1982); James Blumstein and Frank Sloan, Redefining Government's Role in Health Care: Is a Dose of Competition What the Doctor Should Order?, 34 Vand. L. Rev. 849 (1981); Rand Rosenblatt, Health Care, Markets, and Democratic Values, 34 Vand. L. Rev. 1067 (1981).

Health care facilities respond as well to quality-control pressures that are considered private in nature, although the line between public regulation and private quality-control mechanisms is not entirely solid. Private accreditation organizations, private litigation for breach by the institution of the appropriate standard of care, and market forces all exert some influence over the quality of health care organizations.

While nearly all institutional health care providers in the United States are regulated on some level by state and federal agencies, the character and scope of that regulation vary. Historical accident and sheer political power certainly explain some differences in the regulatory environment among health care institutions. But many regulatory differences relate to the type of health care provided, the strength of private quality-control mechanisms and the character of the population served by the facility.

A. TAXONOMY OF HEALTH CARE INSTITUTIONS

Any description of health care facilities tends to be incomplete and quickly outdated as the health care industry rapidly responds to changes in health care markets, payment methods and even government quality-control regulation by redesigning and repackaging health care delivery. A major challenge for quality-control regulatory policy is the vast and changing structure of health care facilities. Licensure, for example, will govern only those organizations that fall within the statutory definition of facilities requiring a license. Health care entities that do not fall within the statutory definition will not be subject to state control through licensure.

Regulatory standards and procedures may also differ depending on whether the particular health care service is offered by or within a regulated provider. So, for example, services provided by a hospital may be subject to oversight within the hospital's licensure rather than within a separate licensure system.[3] Hospitals typically offer "intra-institutional" specialty services such as birthing centers, wellness centers, and occupational health testing and rehabilitation programs; and determination of whether the service is "part" of the hospital may be complex.

Beyond the threshold definitional issue, differences among health care organizations often correlate with the nature and scope of federal and state quality-control regulation. For example, nursing homes are subject to a high degree of regulation by both federal and state governments. In contrast, hospitals, home health agencies and other organizations confront a regulatory system that is less aggressive and less comprehensive. The contrast among nursing homes, acute-care hospitals, and home health care agencies illustrates the importance of understanding the distinctions among health care institutions.

§ 1–2. Nursing Homes

Most nursing home residents are chronically rather than acutely ill. The average length of stay for nursing home patients is much longer than the

3. See e.g., 210 ILCS 5/3, requiring a license of providers of ambulatory surgical services, but specifically excluding licensed hospitals from the statutory definition. Similarly, the Joint Commission on Accreditation of Healthcare Organizations requires that such services be assessed and evaluated as part of the accredited hospital's accreditation.

average length of stay for patients in acute care hospitals. The dependency of most nursing home residents in activities of daily living, including eating, dressing, bathing, toileting and transferring is extreme. The level of dependency has been steadily increasing.

The characteristics of the nursing home population, in comparison to that of hospitals, have limited their ability to engage in private litigation to remedy harms suffered as a result of breaches of established standards of care, although such litigation is increasing.[1] Physical injuries such as broken bones and bruises in very frail elderly persons may be caused either by ordinary touching or by poor care or abuse. Causation is, therefore, difficult to prove. The mental impairment of many nursing home patients makes them poor witnesses. Their limited life-span and their disabilities minimize legally recognizable damages for injury or death. They do not suffer lost wages. Their access to private attorneys has been limited because small damage awards discourage contingent fee arrangements and because of the isolation of institutionalization. Because of these limitations, several states have enacted statutes providing for private rights of action for nursing home residents. These statutes generally provide a cause of action for breach of statutory standards and may provide for enhanced damage awards and attorney's fees.[2]

While hospitals developed in the United States as charitable institutions primarily under the direction and control of physicians, nursing homes developed originally as "mom-and-pop" enterprises, in which individuals boarded elderly persons in private homes.[3] Over three-fourths of the privately owned hospitals in the United States are nonprofit. In contrast, approximately three-fourths of private nursing homes are for-profit.[4]

Advances in medical treatment, especially in surgery and technology, which led to greater physician control within the hospital,[5] did not substantially influence nursing home care. Reinforced by external organizations such as the Joint Commission, the medical staff structure plays a critical role in hospital governance.[6] The staff privileges system and medical staff governance

§ 1–2

1. For a discussion of barriers to private litigation by nursing home residents, see generally, Patricia A. Butler, Nursing Home Quality of Care Enforcement: Part I—Litigation by Private Parties, 14 Clearinghouse Rev. 622 (1980); Sandy McNath, The Nursing–Home Maltreatment Case, 21 Trial 52 (Sept. 1985); Patricia Nemore, Protecting Nursing–Home Residents, Trial 54 (Dec. 1985). For a discussion of liability issues in long-term care, see S.H. Johnson, N.P. Terry, and M.A. Wolff, Nursing Homes and the Law: State Regulation and Private Litigation (1985). But see, Marshall Kapp, Malpractice Liability in Long–Term Care: A Changing Environment, 24 Creighton L. Rev. 1235 (1991) and Chapter 7.

2. See e.g., Stiffelman v. Abrams, 655 S.W.2d 522 (Mo.1983) and Harris v. Manor Healthcare Corp., 95 Ill.Dec. 510, 489 N.E.2d 1374 (Ill.1986), both interpreting state statutes creating private rights of action. See generally, David F. Bragg, Dealing with Nursing Home Neglect: The Need for Private Litigation, 39 S.

Tex. L. Rev. 1 (1997); Tracy Lazarus, et al., Don't Make Them Leave Their Rights at the Door: A Recommended Model State Statute to Protect the Rights of the Elderly in Nursing Homes, 4 J. of Contemp. Health Law & Policy 321 (1988).

3. For a detailed economic history of the growth of the nursing home industry see, Catherine Hawes and Charles D. Phillips, "The Changing Structure of the Nursing Home Industry and the Impact of Ownership on Quality, Cost, and Access" in Institute of Medicine, For–Profit Enterprise in Health Care 492 (1986).

4. Institute of Medicine, For–Profit Enterprise in Health Care 134 (1986), also describing other differences between nursing homes and hospitals.

5. See e.g., Paul Starr, The Social Transformation of American Medicine (1982).

6. See discussion of staff privileges in Chapter 4.

of the hospital have not developed to any comparable extent in nursing homes. In addition, while professional nurses dominate direct patient care in hospitals, the role of the registered nurse in the majority of long-term care institutions is that of supervisor with most of the direct patient care rendered by nonprofessional or paraprofessional nurses' aides.

The tradition of dominance of professional control within hospitals has certainly contributed to the development of a strong custom of professional self-regulation in hospitals. Whether through private accreditation, through intra-institutional quality-control mechanisms, or through pressures exerted by professional licensure, such private professionally dominated quality-control mechanisms are stronger than public governmental quality-control regulatory systems for hospitals. In contrast, nursing homes do not have a strong tradition of self-regulation. While the Joint Commission on Accreditation of Healthcare Organizations, the major private accreditation organization for health care facilities, does offer an accreditation program for nursing homes, it is not as widely adopted as the program for hospitals.[7]

Widely-publicized scandals concerning poor patient care have plagued the nursing home industry.[8] Although the number of facilities actually involved in these charges could be small, the public and legislative perception of the industry has been affected by this history. Acute-care hospitals have largely escaped such scandals, while psychiatric hospitals share a history similar to that of nursing homes.[9]

When aggressive nursing home licensure systems first developed in the states, the demand for nursing home care was very high. A strong demand for nursing home spaces leaves a potential nursing home resident or the resident's family with little or no choice among facilities once the essential factors of source of payment (if Medicare, Medicaid or other public assistance) and level of care required are considered. In addition, proximity to family and friends is a significant concern in the selection of a nursing home in light of the typically long stay. Choice is further limited by the short length of time available for placement and the stress accompanying such a severe change. Such constraints on consumer choice limit the power of the market over quality. This market failure in the nursing home context is exacerbated because the resident, who is the actual consumer of services, is often not the one making the choice. Further, the ability of residents to leave one facility for another if a bad choice is made is limited by the physical and mental frailty of many residents.[10] The excess of demand over supply for nursing home care and problems with nursing home transfers had a direct impact on the development of intermediate sanctions as alternative penalties that would not require closing the facility.[11]

7. See discussion in § 1–4.

8. See e.g., F. Moss & V. Halamandaris, Too Old, Too Sick, Too Bad—Nursing Homes in America (1977); M. Mendelson, Tender Loving Greed (1974).

9. See e.g., Cospito v. Heckler, 742 F.2d 72, 83 (3d Cir.1984), cert. denied 471 U.S. 1131, 105 S.Ct. 2665, 86 L.Ed.2d 282 (1985), citing history of abuses in psychiatric hospitals as justification for less favorable regulatory treatment than acute-care hospitals.

10. See e.g., West's Cal. Health & Safety Code § 1325 and Connecticut Gen.Stat.Ann. § 19a–542, identifying transfer trauma as a rationale for the statutory nursing home receivership.

11. See e.g., Jane Beyer, The Need to Change Traditional Entitlement Doctrine Analysis in Decertification of Nursing Homes, 59 N.C.L.Rev. 943 (1981).

§ 1–3. Home Health Care

The organization and delivery of home health care differs significantly from health care delivery in hospitals and in nursing homes, with implications for quality-control regulation. Virtually the full panoply of medical care available in the hospital may be provided in the home, including ventilators, dialysis, and nasogastric feeding. The increasing reliance on home care as a major health care delivery system acting in the relative isolation of individual residences challenges assumptions based on images of home and family. Medicare payment for home health care increased exponentially in the 1990s,[1] although the legislative changes in 1997 to reduce Medicare costs seem to have had a disproportionate impact on home health care.[2]

As with nursing homes, home health does not have a strong history of private accreditation, except for those agencies operating as a service of an accredited hospital. Only in 1988 did the JCAHO issue its first set of standards for freestanding home health agencies, although other accreditation organizations had offered accreditation much earlier.[3]

Further, private litigation has not exerted the level of influence in home health care that it has had over hospital behavior. Litigation by patients receiving home health care faces many of the obstacles, including fragility, small damage awards and isolation, faced by nursing home patients. In fact, there are additional obstacles related to proof of the cause of the injury when care is given by multiple caregivers and to theories limiting the liability of the agency itself.[4] There are some indications, however, that such litigation is becoming more common.

B. PRIVATE ACCREDITATION AND PUBLIC QUALITY CONTROL REGULATION

§ 1–4. Medicare "Deemed Status" for JCAHO Accredited Health Care Providers

The Joint Commission on Accreditation of Healthcare Organizations (JCAHO) is the leading health care facility accreditation organization and dominates the accreditation of hospitals, though it accredits a very wide range of other health care facilities, including home health agencies, nursing homes and laboratories, among others.[1] The Joint Commission currently accredits virtually all U.S. hospitals with more than twenty-five beds. JCAHO accredi-

§ 1–3

1. See Brian E. Davis, The Home Health Care Crisis: Medicare's Fastest Growing Program Legalizes Spiraling Costs, 6 Elder L.J. 215 (1998).

2. Costs: Employment, Prices Fall as Providers React to BBA Provisions, Health Care Daily Report (BNA), November 26, 1999.

3. Other organizations accredit home health care agencies. For example, the National League for Nursing has accredited home health agencies for nearly twenty-five years. Nat'l League for Nursing, Accreditation of

Home Health Agencies and Community Nursing Services (1976). See discussion in § 1–4.

4. See e.g., Sandra H. Johnson, "Liability Issues" in Delivering High Technology Home Care (Maxwell J. Mehlman and Stuart J. Youngner, eds.) (1991).

§ 1–4

1. See Joint Commission on Accreditation of Healthcare Organizations, Committed to Quality: An Introduction to the Joint Commission on Accreditation of Healthcare Organizations (1990), for a description of the Commission's accreditation programs and structure.

tation programs for other types of health care providers have not had a participation level comparable to their hospital accreditation program.

The JCAHO, and the many other private voluntary accreditation organizations in the health care system, represent a classic form of self-regulation. The professionals and institutions participating in such programs both establish the standards of quality and inspect and enforce those standards against participating facilities. The governing board of the JCAHO, for example, includes members appointed by the American Medical Association, the American Hospital Association, the American College of Surgeons, the American College of Physicians and the American Dental Association.[2] The JCAHO differs, however, from other examples of self-regulation in that it has been dominated not by representatives of the health care facilities it accredits, but by representatives of the physicians who practice within those facilities. For this reason, the JCAHO might better be understood as an example of cross-regulation, in this instance regulation of hospitals or other health care organizations by doctors,[3] bringing with it some degree of cross-purposes.[4] In practice, at least in relation to its hospital accreditation program, the JCAHO is viewed by the hospital industry as an external regulator rather than a collegial consultative actor.[5]

Critics have described the JCAHO inspection process as inadequate, however, and have attacked both the control exercised by provider groups[6] and the conflict of interest present in the JCAHO's marketing of consulting services to accredited facilities.[7] This view argues that the wide acceptance of the JCAHO hospital program is a result of the providers' largely unchallenged control over both standards and surveillance. In responding to such criticisms, the JCAHO has identified its goal as assisting hospitals in improving their performance: "We keep as many institutions as possible within the pale of our influence, so we can keep lifting them up. You get more things fixed with a cooperative arrangement."[8] Individual hospitals complain that government inspectors, in contrast to the JCAHO surveyors, exaggerate minor or temporary problems.[9]

---

2. Timothy S. Jost, The Joint Commission on Accreditation of Hospitals: Private Regulation of Health Care and the Public Interest, 24 B.C. L. Rev. 835 (1983); James S. Roberts, et al., A History of the Joint Commission on Accreditation of Hospitals, 258 J.A.M.A. 936 (1987).

3. The Commission's Board is dominated by representatives of organizations of physicians, but the Commission establishes advisory committees with broader participation for their accreditation programs. The Professional Technical Assistance Committee for the home care accreditation program, for example, includes representatives from the American Association of Retired Persons, the Visiting Nurses Association, the National Association of Area Agencies on Aging and the Health Care Financing Administration, among others. 58 Fed.Reg. 35007 (June 30, 1993).

4. See generally, Emily Friedman, Accreditation Redesign Evolving, 30 Med.World News 24 (June 26, 1986).

5. See e.g., Donna Ojanen Thomas, How to Survive an Accreditation Review, 50 RN 17 (1987); Michael Abramowitz, On the Road with a Hospital Inspector: How Well Does a Private Agency Survey the Nation's Health Care Centers, Washington Post, August 27, 1991, at 20B.

6. Walt Bogdanich, Prized by Hospitals Accreditation Hides Perils Patients Face, Wall St. Journal, p. 1 col. 1 (Oct. 12, 1988), concluding that the JCAHO fails to act decisively and is subject to a "fundamental" conflict.

7. Brian McCormick, GAO Faults Public, Private Hospital Accreditation, 34 Am. Med.News June 10, 1991 at 8.

8. Walt Bogdanich, Prized by Hospitals Accreditation Hides Perils Patients Face, Wall St. Journal, p. 1 col. 1 (Oct. 12, 1988).

9. Id.

Critics also attack the limitations of JCAHO accreditation standards. JCAHO standards, like government quality-control standards, had emphasized structural indicators that demonstrate the capacity to provide quality care, rather than clinical indicators used to examine the quality of care actually provided. JCAHO standards have established professional control of the organization, for example, through a hospital's medical staff, as itself an indicator of quality. Other examples of structural standards include requirements of written policies, adequate equipment and minimum staffing. Responding to criticism of their standards, JCAHO has adopted an "Agenda for Change," to develop clinical indicators for use in accreditation. This project has moved the JCAHO toward a continuous quality improvement (CQI) model rather than a quality assurance model.[10] The CQI model of quality control tends to increase the flexibility of managers and providers in terms of structure and process and tends to emphasize performance outcomes.[11]

Criticism of the limitations of JCAHO accreditation standards still occurs, despite JCAHO's movement toward a continuous quality improvement model. In July of 1999, the Office of Inspector General released four reports assessing JCAHO's role in hospital quality oversight.[12] The reports conclude that although the Joint Commission surveys provide an important vehicle for reducing risk and fostering improvement in hospital care, the surveys are unlikely to detect substandard patterns of care or individual practitioners with questionable skills. In addition, the reports determine that the hospital review system, led by JCAHO, has been shifting toward a collegial model that could result in insufficient attention to regulatory approaches intended to protect patients from poor care. In response to the reports, the Health Care Financing Administration, who is responsible for overseeing the "deemed status" of JCAHO, offered a detailed plan that would strengthen oversight of JCAHO, as well as balance the collegial and regulatory approaches to hospital quality oversight.

The most controversial quality-control issue concerning private accreditation is the fusing of private accreditation with public regulation.[13] This occurs, for example, when private accreditation is used as a substitute for public regulation. Most states have to a greater or lesser degree incorporated JCAHO accreditation into their hospital licensure standards.[14] JCAHO accreditation is a prerequisite for payment by some health insurance plans; is required in practice for a hospital to be approved for a residency program; and may be a

10. See e.g., Mary T. Koska, New JCAHO Standards Emphasize Continuous Quality Improvement, 65 Hospital 41 (Aug. 5, 1991).

11. Dennis S. O'Leary, Accreditation in the Quality Improvement Mold—A Vision for Tomorrow, Quality Review Bulletin March 1991 at 71.

12. See Department of Health and Human Services Office of Inspector General, Report No. OEI–01–97–00050, *The External Review of Hospital Quality: A Call for Greater Accountability*, (July 1999), which provides a summary of the three parallel reports.

13. See generally, Timothy S. Jost, The Necessary and Proper Role of Regulation to Assure the Quality of Health Care, 25 Houston

L. Rev. 525 (1988); David Lawrence, Private Exercise of Governmental Power, 61 Ind. L.J. 647 (1986).

14. See e.g., Alaska Stat. § 18.20.080(a) (hospitals); Official Code Georgia Ann. § 31–7–3(b) (health facilities); Iowa Code Ann. § 135J.2 (hospices); Md. Health Gen. Code Ann. § 8–403 (alcohol and drug abuse treatment programs); Md. Health Gen. Code Ann. § 10–504(1) (mental health facilities); Vernon's Ann. Missouri Stat. § 630.705(3), (6) (mental hospitals); N.C. Gen. Stat. § 131E–138(g) (home health agencies); Ohio Rev. Code § 3727.02(a) (hospitals).

prerequisite for other benefits.[15] In recognition of the broad acceptance of JCAHO within the hospital industry, JCAHO standards have been found relevant to proof of the standard of care in corporate negligence cases against hospitals;[16] as a source of judicially enforced procedural requirements for staff privileges;[17] and as a legal standard for the duty to provide emergency care.[18] JCAHO standards have also figured prominently in constitutional challenges to the adequacy of care provided in public institutions.[19]

Under the Medicare statute, JCAHO accredited hospitals are deemed to meet most requirements for Medicare certification.[20] No regular federal inspection is required of JCAHO-accredited hospitals, although the government may perform validation surveys. An accredited hospital that is found as a result of a validation survey to be out of compliance with Medicare standards is subject to termination from the Medicare program.[21]

The federal Medicare program relies on private parties to carry out other quality-control functions of the federal program. For example, the federal government contracts with private Utilization and Quality Peer Review Organizations for the review of services provided Medicare beneficiaries.[22] The government also contracts with private corporations to act as Medicare carriers and intermediaries to implement Medicare standards for coverage of services.[23] What distinguishes the acceptance of JCAHO accreditation as adequate for certification as a Medicare provider is that the government and JCAHO do not have a contractual relationship governing JCAHO's accreditation of Medicare participating facilities. The statutory requirement that accreditation organizations apply for deemed status and that the proposed acceptance of a particular organization be published in the Federal Register seems to have opened the possibility of negotiation over essential points, however.[24] The conditions established in the recognition of deemed status for JCAHO accreditation for home health agencies approach the detail and incentives of a contractual relationship.[25]

15. See e.g., West's Cal.Bus. & Prof. Code § 2089.5(e)(3) (approved training for physicians); West's Ann.Ind.Code §§ 20–12–30–5.7 (approved training for physicians); Haw. Rev. Stat. §§ 393–7(c)(6)(C) (mandated insurance benefits for detoxification services); Nev.Rev. Stat. § 608.156 (mandated insurance benefits for drug and alcohol rehabilitation services). See also, City of Akron v. Akron Center for Reproductive Health, 462 U.S. 416, 103 S.Ct. 2481, 76 L.Ed.2d 687 (1983), declaring unconstitutional an Ohio statute requiring that all abortions be performed in a Joint Commission-accredited hospital.

16. See Chapter 7.

17. See e.g., Lake Hospital and Clinic v. Silversmith, 551 So.2d 538 (Fla.App.1989).

18. See e.g., Thompson v. Sun City Community Hospital, Inc., 688 P.2d 605 (Ariz. 1984).

19. Woe by Woe v. Cuomo, 559 F.Supp. 1158 (E.D.N.Y.1983); 729 F.2d 96, 106–107 (2d Cir.1984), cert. denied 469 U.S. 936, 105 S.Ct. 339, 83 L.Ed.2d 274 (1984); 638 F.Supp. 1506 (E.D.N.Y.1986) (describing JCAHO standards

and procedures); 801 F.2d 627 (2d Cir.1986) (reversing permanent injunction but affirming preliminary injunction). The ultimate settlement of the case included a requirement that the facility maintain accreditation by the Commission. Foe v. Cuomo, 700 F.Supp. 107 (E.D.N.Y.1988), cert. denied 498 U.S. 972, 111 S.Ct. 441, 112 L.Ed.2d 424 (1990).

20. 42 U.S.C.A. §§ 1395x(e), 1395bb; 42 C.F.R. § 488.5. Medicare conditions of participation, including deemed status for private accreditation, apply to Medicaid certification as well for some providers. See e.g., 42 C.F.R. § 440.70 (home health agencies); § 440.10(a)(3)(iii) (hospitals); § 440.40(a)(ii) (swing-bed skilled nursing facilities within hospitals).

21. 42 U.S.C.A. § 1395cc(b); 42 C.F.R. § 488.6.

22. See § 3–24.

23. See § 11–3.

24. 42 U.S.C.A. § 1395bb.

25. 58 Fed. Reg. 35007 (June 30, 1993).

The Medicare statute permits the Department of Health and Human Services to accept private accreditation in lieu of federal certification if the accreditation organization provides reasonable assurances that its accreditation program for that type of facility meets federal standards.[26] Under this provision, the Health Care Financing Administration has allowed JCAHO accreditation deemed status for home health agencies.[27] In recognizing deemed status for JCAHO accreditation of home health agencies, the Department conditioned continued recognition on several factors including release of JCAHO survey reports to the Health Care Financing Administration routinely and to the public upon request;[28] reporting by JCAHO to the Office of Inspector General of any complaints it receives concerning fraud and abuse; and service as a witness in any adverse action taken by the government against a home health agency using JCAHO accreditation for certification. JCAHO also agreed to perform an annual unannounced survey of home health agencies seeking deemed status by virtue of accreditation. This conditional recognition of deemed status for JCAHO accreditation of home health agencies represents a quite detailed and specific evaluation of JCAHO's comparability to federal regulation. The adoption of certain procedures, such as the annual unannounced survey rather than the usual triennial announced survey, for providers seeking to use accreditation for certification purposes may result in a more effective survey system for home health care than the federal government has been able to provide.

Until 1988, clinical laboratories in hospitals accredited by the Joint Commission or laboratories accredited by other federally-approved accreditation organizations were deemed to meet federal requirements. In 1988, the Clinical Laboratory Improvement Amendments required private accreditation organizations to apply for federal approval under standards set by the Department of Health and Human Services in order to allow the specific accreditation program to substitute for federal inspection.[29]

Criticism of federal deference to JCAHO for certification of Medicare provider hospitals has continued. Some government studies have questioned the reliability of JCAHO procedures and the comparability of JCAHO standards and federal Medicare standards,[30] although the Health Care Financing Administration maintains that JCAHO accreditation and Medicare certification for hospitals are substantially equivalent.[31] In general, there is little empirical research that directly relates indicators of quality to JCAHO accred-

26. 42 U.S.C.A. § 1395bb; 58 Fed. Reg. 61816–01 (Nov. 23, 1993).

27. 58 Fed.Reg. 35007 (June 30, 1993). See also, GAO, Home Health Care: HCFA Properly Evaluated JCAHO's Ability to Survey Home Health Agencies (1992). The Department has also allowed accreditation by the Community Health Accreditation Program, a subsidiary of the National League for Nursing, deemed status for home health agencies. 57 Fed. Reg. 22773 (May 29, 1992).

28. But see, 58 Fed. Reg. 61816–01 (Nov. 23, 1993).

29. 42 U.S.C.A. § 263a(e); 57 Fed.Reg. 33992 (July 31, 1992), to be codified at 42 C.F.R. §§ 493.501–493.511.

30. See e.g., GAO, Health Care: Hospitals with Quality of Care Problems Need Closer Monitoring, (GAO/HRD–91–40, May 9, 1991); GAO, Health Care: Actions to Terminate Problem Hospitals from Medicare are Inadequate (GAO/HRD–91–54, Sept. 5, 1991).

31. State survey agencies regularly conduct follow-up surveys of JCAHO accredited hospitals to validate the Commission's performance. HCFA must report the results of this validation process annually to Congress. 42 U.S.C.A. § 1395ll(b).

itation status.[32] In addition, some critics argue that the federal government simply abdicates its responsibility to monitor the quality of services it purchases by relying on private accreditation.[33]

Critics also have argued that while private accreditation may be appropriate for some types of health care providers, it is unacceptable for others. In 1981, for example, the Health Care Financing Administration proposed accepting JCAHO accreditation of nursing homes in lieu of federal Medicare certification.[34] Consumer advocates and members of Congress opposed the proposal, and it was withdrawn.[35]

Still, there are advantages to be gained by some relationship between private accreditation and government regulation. Standards developed by organizations dominated by the industry itself are more acceptable and may be more easily enforced as they are more likely to fall within the custom of the trade. Some argue that private organizations can change and improve standards more rapidly and more responsively than can the government, which is bound by administrative requirements in the standard-setting process.[36] In addition, the JCAHO is cited by some for its leadership role in encouraging institutional policies protective of individual patients. At base, however, the adherence of the federal government to deference to JCAHO accreditation, with the adjustments in federal monitoring of the accreditation process described previously, continues because it costs the government less than direct regulation. A quality-control survey and enforcement system for Medicare hospitals would cost, by some estimates, at least $59 million annually in additional staff and training.[37] Although Medicare funds actually bear part of the cost of JCAHO accreditation because of the prospective payment system's foundation in historical hospital costs,[38] most of the cost of JCAHO accreditation lies outside the Medicare program, allowing the federal government indirectly to shift the cost of its quality-control duty to the provider itself.[39]

32. See e.g., U.S. Congress, Office of Technology Assessment, The Quality of Medical Care: Information for Consumers 197–200 (1988); Timothy S. Jost, Medicare and the Joint Commission on Accreditation of Healthcare Organizations, 57 J. of Law & Contemp. Probs. 15 (1994), summarizing the available empirical research.

33. See e.g., JCAHO Slow to Change, 12 People's Medical Society Newsletter 1 (Feb. 1992).

34. 47 Fed.Reg. 23,404 (May 27, 1982).

35. Opposition to the proposal led to the commission by Congress of a study of nursing home care by the Institute of Medicine. The IOM study generated the substantial changes incorporated in OBRA of 1987. Institute of Medicine, Improving the Quality of Care in Nursing Homes 1–2 (1986). The Deficit Reduction Act of 1984 (P.L. 98–369) allows HCFA to recognize deemed states for accredited nursing homes, but it has not done so.

36. Testimony of Thomas Morford, Hospital Accreditation and Compliance with Medicare's Conditions of Participation, Hearings before the Subcommittee on Health of the House Committee on Ways and Means, 101st Congress, 2d Sess. 25 (1990).

37. Estimate by the Health Care Financing Administration in 1991, reported in General Accounting Office, Health Care: Hospitals with Quality-of–Care Problems Need Closer Monitoring 25 (GAO/HRD–91–40, May 9, 1991).

38. Terry S. Coleman, Legal Aspects of Medicare & Medicaid Reimbursement, 28–34 (1990).

39. Current federal Medicare law prohibits direct user fees for survey and certification purposes for skilled nursing facilities. 42 U.S.C.A. § 1395aa(e). But see discussion of Clinical Laboratory Improvement Amendments in § 1–15.

§ 1–5. Challenges to Private Accreditation Process or Standards

The interrelation of JCAHO accreditation and federal certification for Medicare or Medicaid raises an issue of unconstitutional delegation of governmental authority. In *Cospito v. Heckler*,[1] the Third Circuit upheld the constitutionality of a provision of the Medicare and Medicaid statutes requiring that inpatient psychiatric hospitals for persons under the age of 21 be JCAHO accredited in order to participate in the federal programs. Under the relevant statutes, loss of Commission accreditation resulted in the loss of federal certification for reimbursement for care and the loss of government benefit payments made directly to the individual patients themselves. In reviewing the claim of unconstitutional delegation of governmental authority, the court first concluded that the statutory standards were adequately directive to survive a challenge based on unconstitutional delegation of legislative authority to an administrative agency.[2] Then, reading the retained authority of the Department very broadly, the court concluded that the statute did not, in fact, delegate the Secretary's authority to the Commission. Although *Cospito* relies on an expansive reading of the Secretary's retained authority under the statute at issue in the case, the holding of *Cospito* is actually more persuasive in the context of the current boundaries for deemed status for JCAHO accreditation. In 1984, Congress removed the accreditation requirement for such psychiatric facilities.[3]

Plaintiffs may pursue constitutional claims against private accreditation associations only if they are able to prove state action. In *St. Agnes Hospital v. Riddick*,[4] for example, a Catholic hospital challenged the denial of accreditation for its residency program in obstetrics and gynecology by the Accreditation Council for Graduate Medical Education (ACGME). The state of Maryland required graduation from a residency program accredited by ACGME, or its equivalent, as a condition of licensure for medical doctors. The District Court held, though ambiguously, that there was no state action in the ACGME's revocation of St. Agnes' accreditation. Though the court's holding is not absolutely clear, it is consistent with other cases in analogous situations.[5]

Under the common law of most states, purely private associations bear some duty toward applicants for membership in terms of the fairness of the procedures used by the association. In fact, the requirement of "fundamental fairness" in regard to staff privileges decisions has as its basis the common law of private associations.[6] Some courts have reviewed the rules of private accreditation under the common law of private associations to assure that they are not arbitrary or capricious or in violation of the public interest.[7] Few have reviewed the merits of particular standards under the common law.[8]

§ 1–5

1. 742 F.2d 72 (3d Cir.1984), cert. denied 471 U.S. 1131, 105 S.Ct. 2665, 86 L.Ed.2d 282 (1985).

2. See § 1–11.

3. Pub.L. §§ 2340(a) & (b).

4. 748 F.Supp. 319 (D.Md.1990). See also, McKeesport Hospital v. The Accreditation Council for Graduate Medical Education, 24 F.3d 519 (3d Cir. 1994).

5. See e.g., National Collegiate Athletic Ass'n v. Tarkanian, 488 U.S. 179, 109 S.Ct. 454, 102 L.Ed.2d 469 (1988).

6. See e.g., Siqueira v. Northwestern Memorial Hospital, 87 Ill.Dec. 415, 477 N.E.2d 16 (Ill.App.1985).

7. See e.g. Pinsker v. Pacific Coast Society of Orthodontists, 116 Cal.Rptr. 245, 526 P.2d 253 (Cal.1974).

C. STATE AND FEDERAL AUTHORITY TO REGULATE

§ 1–6. State Regulation

The source of the state's power to regulate health care institutions is the police power, which is retained by the states in our federal system. Under the police power, the state's regulation of health care institutions must further health, safety and the general welfare. In reviewing legislation challenged as lying beyond the scope of the state's police power, courts will uphold the legislation if its contribution to health, safety and general welfare is at least fairly debatable. Challenges to health care facility regulations arguing that the regulations are beyond the scope of the police power have not succeeded.[1]

Licensure is the primary mechanism chosen by state legislatures to regulate health care facilities, though certification is also sometimes used. In addition to its regulation of health care providers through licensure, the state also regulates health care providers through the enforcement of the requirements of the federal-state Medicaid program. The state's authority under Medicaid, however, is dependent upon and subject to the federal authority.[2] Under the Medicaid statute the federal Department of Health and Human Services holds the formal authority to sanction providers, although in practice the state agency often carries out the enforcement actions.[3] The states apply federal standards and use federally-approved survey instruments in inspecting Medicaid facilities.[4] The federal government retains the authority to perform validation surveys, often called "look behind" surveys, to monitor the state inspections.[5] If the Department concludes in its own inspection of a facility that the facility does not meet federal Medicaid standards, the Department may levy sanctions independent of the state agency.[6]

§ 1–7. Federal Regulation

While the states have authority to regulate health care facilities under their police power, the federal government's primary authority arises from its financing authority exercised as purchaser of health care.[1] The federal govern-

8. See e.g., Marjorie Webster Junior College v. Middle States Association, 432 F.2d 650 (D.C.Cir.1970), cert. denied 400 U.S. 965, 91 S.Ct. 367, 27 L.Ed.2d 384 (1970).

§ 1–6

1. See for example, State ex rel. Eagleton v. Patrick, 370 S.W.2d 254 (Mo.1963); Hoffman v. Moore, 420 N.Y.S.2d 771 (N.Y.App.Div.1979); People v. Casa Blanca Convalescent Homes, Inc., 206 Cal.Rptr. 164 (Cal.App.1984).

2. In order to participate in the Medicaid program, the state must submit a state plan that meets federal standards. 42 U.S.C.A. § 1396a(a).

3. 42 U.S.C.A. § 1395m.

4. 42 U.S.C.A. § 1396r(g)(2)(C).

5. 42 U.S.C.A. § 1395i–3(g)(3)(A); 42 U.S.C.A. § 1396r(g)(3)(A), providing for validation surveys; 42 U.S.C.A. § 1395i–3(g)(3)(D); 42 U.S.C.A. § 1396r(g)(3)(D), providing for special compliance surveys.

6. 42 U.S.C.A. § 1395i–3(g)(3)(A); 42 U.S.C.A. § 1396r(g)(3)(A); 42 U.S.C.A. § 1395i–3(g)(3)(D); 42 U.S.C.A. § 1396r(g)(3)(D).

§ 1–7

1. In an exception to the more common reliance on the financing authority, a major federal quality-control regulatory program governing clinical labs applies to all clinical laboratories. 42 U.S.C.A. § 263a. The federal authority for this program is not its financing power but its authority under the commerce clause. 57 Fed. Reg. 7002, 7121 (February 28, 1992).

ment, as purchaser, regulates through provider certification. In order to receive payments under Medicare or Medicaid, the major current federal health care programs,[2] an institutional provider must be certified and must sign a provider agreement with the Health Care Financing Administration for Medicare and with the state Medicaid agency for Medicaid. The federal government has used its purchasing power to require facilities to meet standards that go beyond the particular federal health care program used as the touchstone for its authority to regulate. For example, the Social Security Act now requires that providers receiving Medicare payments meet standards concerning the screening, treatment and discharge of any patient, including patients who are not Medicare beneficiaries, presenting at the facility's emergency room.[3]

Federal regulation of health care providers through its health care benefit programs takes two forms. The first encompasses regulation that determines payment issues, including amount and methods of payment as well as coverage of particular services.[4] The second form of federal health care regulation more directly regulates the quality of services through standard-setting and survey and enforcement processes. Of course, the two are not entirely separable. Coverage standards and decisions may have a substantial impact on the quality of care received by patients.[5] Utilization review of medical services undoubtedly relates directly to quality as excessive or inappropriate treatment provides only poor quality of care.[6] It is important, however, to distinguish payment regulation from quality regulation.

D. ESTABLISHING REGULATORY STANDARDS

§ 1–8. Introduction

State and federal regulators, as administrative agencies, are bound by the procedural requirements of the relevant administrative procedures act.[1] These acts typically include mandated procedures for the development and promulgation of standards. The substantive standards developed by the regulatory agency must not be arbitrary and capricious and must fall within the agency's statutory authority.[2] Regulated providers also may challenge substantive standards under constitutional principles, including vagueness and unconstitutional delegation.

§ 1–9. Procedural Requirements for Promulgating Standards

The statutes providing for quality-control regulation of health care institutions typically include only broad outlines of the substantive standards with which the institutions must comply. The statute typically authorizes the regulatory agency to provide more detailed standards in regulations promulgated under the relevant administrative procedures act. In addition, for

2. See Chapters 11 and 12.

3. See Chapter 10.

4. See Chapters 11 and 12.

5. See e.g., Eleanor D. Kinney, In Search of Bureaucratic Justice: Home Health Benefits in the 1980s, 42 Admin. L. Rev. 251 (1990).

6. See § 9–10.

§ 1–8
1. See e.g., 5 U.S.C.A. §§ 500–701. Most states also have adopted an administrative procedures act in some form. Vernon's Ann. Mo. Stat. § 536; Mass.Gen. Laws Ann. ch. 30A.
2. See § 1–10.

inspection-based quality-control regulatory systems, documents such as the survey instrument, which functions as an inspection checklist, and other guidelines provided by the agency to the surveyors are equally important in describing accurately the substantive standards applicable to the provider.[1]

A continuing dispute in the promulgation of federal regulatory standards is whether rules and standards issued by the agency have legislative effect, and so must be promulgated under the notice and comment requirements of § 553 of the Administrative Procedures Act.[2] If instead, the rules are interpretative or procedural, the agency can issue them without following the notice and comment requirements. Whether agency rules or guidelines are interpretative/procedural or instead legislative is never entirely clear.

This issue has been litigated for decades in the context of many federal programs, but litigation has been particularly active in relation to nursing home regulation.[3] In 1989, the District Court for the District of Columbia held that HCFA was not required to promulgate legislative rules to implement OBRA of 1987 and that HCFA did not have to provide notice and an opportunity to comment on rules that restated the language of the statute.[4] In other cases reviewing rules under OBRA of 1987, district courts in Texas and Louisiana held that preadmission screening criteria issued by HCFA were legislative rules requiring notice and comment,[5] and a district court in Idaho held that the same rules did not require notice and comment.[6] The Seventh Circuit recently considered the claim that the inspection manual used in Medicaid inspections of nursing homes was "regulation" and, therefore, required notice and comment prior to implementation. The District Court had dismissed the plaintiff trade association's claim, but the Court of Appeals reversed, holding that the District Court should review the plaintiffs Administrative Procedures Act claim. The court held, however, that substantive challenge to the manual was premature. The Seventh Circuit decision was reversed by the Supreme Court in a 5 to 4 decision.[7] One commentator has accurately described litigation over the required procedures for promulgation of administrative rules as "often proxies for profound ideological differences over the subject of the rule or policy."[8]

§ 1–9

1. See e.g., Estate of Smith v. Heckler, 747 F.2d 583 (10th Cir.1984), reviewing substantive standards incorporated within the federal survey instrument used for Medicaid certification. See Eleanor D. Kinney, Rule and Policy Making for the Medicaid Program: A Challenge to Federalism, 51 Ohio St. L. J. 855 (1990).

2. 5 U.S.C.A. § 553.

3. See e.g., Estate of Smith v. Bowen, 675 F.Supp. 586 (D.Colo.1987).

4. Gray Panthers Advocacy Committee v. Sullivan, 1989 WL 97937 (D.D.C.1989), affirmed, appeal denied and remanded 1990 WL 278659 (D.C.Cir.1990). The court also stated that it could not in advance of the issuance of interpretative guidelines judge whether those guidelines were actually legislative and required notice and comment or whether those guidelines were interpretative or procedural and exempt from the notice and comment requirements.

5. Texas Health Care Association v. Bowen, 710 F.Supp. 1109 (W.D.Tex.1989); Rayford v. Bowen, 715 F.Supp. 1347 (W.D.La.1989).

6. Idaho Health Care Association v. Sullivan, 716 F.Supp. 464 (D.Idaho 1989).

7. Illinois Council on Long Term Care Inc. v. Shalala, 143 F.3d 1072 (7th Cir. 1998), aff'd 2000 WL 22341 (February 29, 2000.

8. Eleanor D. Kinney, Rule and Policy Making for the Medicaid Program: A Challenge to Federalism, 51 Ohio St. L.J. 855 (1990).

E. SUBSTANTIVE REVIEW OF STANDARDS

§ 1–10. Arbitrariness

Plaintiffs may challenge regulatory standards as being arbitrary and capricious or inconsistent with the authority granted the agency by the statute. Generally, this standard for judicial review of agency rulemaking presents a formidable barrier to plaintiffs challenging regulatory standards on a substantive basis. In *Estate of Smith v. Heckler*,[1] however, the Tenth Circuit Court of Appeals held that the Secretary of the Department of Health and Human Services had a duty to "develop and implement a system of nursing home review and enforcement which focuses on and ensures high quality patient care." Plaintiffs in the case argued that the survey instrument, and not the conditions of participation described in the statute, was the source of the failure of the Secretary to meet this duty. The plaintiffs argued, and the Tenth Circuit agreed, that the survey instrument was "facility-oriented" rather than "patient-oriented" and that the "facility-oriented" survey instrument resulted in an enforcement system that required only "paper compliance" with federal standards. The court held that the Department's use of "facility-oriented" measurements in the survey instrument was arbitrary and capricious. The district court on remand ordered the Secretary to develop a new survey instrument which, after one unsatisfactory attempt, eventually was developed.[2]

§ 1–11. Unconstitutional Delegation

Standards also may be challenged as an unconstitutional delegation of legislative authority to an administrative agency. The recognized complexity of setting quality standards allows the legislature to confer broad, though not entirely unfettered, discretion to the agency. Plaintiffs have not generally succeeded in this claim under the federal delegation doctrine.[1] Challenges to state regulatory standards have been more successful under state delegation doctrine, though the success rate for such claims is not high.[2]

§ 1–12. Vagueness

Statutory and administrative quality-control standards may also be challenged as unconstitutionally vague. In judging whether a standard gives the provider adequate notice of its substantive requirements, the proper focus is

§ 1–10

1. 747 F.2d 583 (10th Cir.1984). See Holland, Smith v. O'Halloran: Nursing Home Reform in the Courts, 13 Colo. L. Rev. 2248 (1984), for further information on the background of this litigation; Alan E. Schabes, "Long Term Care Surveys" in Long Term Care Handbook (1991). See also, Hillburn v. Maher, 795 F.2d 252 (2d Cir.1986), cert. denied 479 U.S. 1046, 107 S.Ct. 910, 93 L.Ed.2d 859 (1987), affirming district court's order to state agency to enforce Medicaid standards requiring skilled nursing facilities to provide particular services; Valdivia v. California Department of Health Services, 1992 WL 226316 (E.D.Cal.

1992), concerning the state's compliance with federal requirements under OBRA of 1987.

2. The Secretary published new regulations, which directed the survey process until OBRA 1987 took effect in 1990. 54 Fed. Reg. 5316 (Feb. 2, 1989).

§ 1–11

1. See e.g., Cospito v. Heckler, 742 F.2d 72 (3d Cir.1984), cert. denied 471 U.S. 1131, 105 S.Ct. 2665, 86 L.Ed.2d 282 (1985).

2. See e.g., High Ridge Management Corporation v. State, 354 So.2d 377 (Fla.1977); Jones v. Cabinet for Human Resources, 710 S.W.2d 862 (Ky.App.1986).

on the clarity of the regulation rather than the statute standing alone. Here again, however, such claims are rarely successful.[1]

F. SPECIFIC FEDERAL REGULATORY STANDARDS

§ 1–13. Nursing Homes

Partly as a result of the litigation in *Estate of Smith v. Heckler*[1] and partly as a result of ongoing disputes between Congress and the Health Care Financing Administration, HCFA commissioned the Institute of Medicine of the National Academy of Sciences to conduct a study on federal enforcement of quality standards for nursing homes.[2] The study examined the appropriate standards for quality measurement in nursing homes; the survey and inspection process; and the enforcement mechanisms required for implementation of standards. Many recommendations made by the report of the study were incorporated into the Medicare and Medicaid regulation of nursing homes through the Omnibus Budget Reconciliation Act of 1987. The Act made significant changes in standards, a process of change that continues.

One of the changes brought about by OBRA was the addition of a residents' rights provisions of the federal statute.[3] A Residents' Bill of Rights has been a familiar part of nursing home regulatory standards since the 1970s. As of the late 1970s, more than half of the states and the District of Columbia had such provisions in the licensure statutes applicable to nursing homes.[4] Although the federal Medicare and Medicaid regulations have included residents' rights requirements for many years, the Omnibus Budget Reconciliation Act of 1987 elevated and strengthened the position of these requirements in the survey enforcement process under Medicare and Medicaid.[5] In addition, the inclusion of intermediate sanctions within the federal programs may make it more likely that the residents' rights provisions will be enforced.

While the substantive content of residents' rights provisions varies among the states and between federal statutes, residents' rights generally have addressed similar concerns relating to participation in medical treatment decisionmaking; privacy; dignity; access to visitors and services; the ability to pursue grievances; the selection of a physician; and transfer and discharge rights. The federal residents' rights provisions also established significant

---

§ 1–12

1. See e.g., People v. Casa Blanca Convalescent Homes, Inc., 206 Cal.Rptr. 164 (Cal.App. 1984); State v. Brenner, 486 So.2d 101 (La. 1986); Levine v. Whalen, 384 N.Y.S.2d 721, 349 N.E.2d 820 (N.Y.App.1976).

§ 1–13

1. 747 F.2d 583 (10th Cir.1984).

2. Institute of Medicine, Improving the Quality of Care in Nursing Homes 2 (1986).

3. For a comprehensive review of nursing home standards see, Patricia Nemore, Nursing Home Law, 215 PLI/Est 163 (August 3–4, 1992); Toby S. Edelman, The Nursing Home

Reform Law: Issues for Litigation, 24 Clearinghouse Review 545 (October 1990).

4. A.B.A., Model Recommendation: Intermediate Sanctions for Enforcement of Quality of Care in Nursing Homes (1981). See Beverly Enterprises–Florida v. McVey, 739 So.2d 646 (Fla.App.1999), holding that state residents' rights provisions were not unconstitutional and not unconstitutionally vague.

5. 42 U.S.C.A. § 1395i–3(d); 42 U.S.C.A. 1396r(d); 42 C.F.R. pt. 483. See also, Toby S. Edelman, The Nursing Home Reform Law: Issues for Litigation, 24 Clearinghouse Review 545 (October 1990); Sandra H. Johnson, "Residents' Rights Under OBRA of 1987" in Long Term Care Handbook (1991).

requirements for the protection and management of residents' personal funds.[6]

One of the most notable provisions in the federal residents' rights provisions applicable to nursing homes is the limitation on the use of physical and chemical restraints.[7] Nothing short of a revolution has occurred in the perception of the acceptability of the routine application of physical restraints in nursing homes,[8] spurred in part by the new federal standards.[9] It is fair to say that the standard of care for the use of restraints in nursing facilities has undergone a significant change. The restrictive view in the federal guidelines on the use of restraints is consistent with these developments. Over the past few years, empirical research regarding the use of restraints repeatedly has rejected the customary use of such devices.[10] According to these investigations, restraints do not necessarily reduce injuries and may instead cause or increase the likelihood of injury and of misdiagnosis of underlying medical conditions. Furthermore, the fear of liability for failure to use restraints is inflated.[11]

The current federal statute provides that residents "have the right to be free from ... any physical or chemical restraints imposed for purposes of discipline or convenience and not required to treat the residents' medical symptoms." The statute requires that restraints may be used only to ensure the physical safety of the resident or other residents and only when ordered by a physician in a written order specifying the "duration and circumstances"[12] for which restraints may be used. The final regulations on the use of physical restraints do not clarify these requirements as they merely repeat the statutory language.[13] The Guidance to Surveyors issued by the Health Care Financing Administration of the Department of Health and Human Services for use in the survey process includes much more detail, defining physical and chemical restraints as well as other important concepts.[14]

The facility is not absolved from regulatory liability by the mere presence of a doctor's written order for restraints since the facility's duty extends beyond securing such documentation. There is a potential for conflict, of course, between the facility's medical director and the resident's attending

---

6. 42 U.S.C.A. § 1395i–3(c)(6); 42 U.S.C.A. § 1369r(c)(6).

7. 42 U.S.C.A. §§ 1395i–3(c)(1)(A)(ii); 42 U.S.C.A. § 1396r(c)(1)(A)(ii); 42 C.F.R. § 483.13.

8. See e.g., R. Guttman et al., Report of the Council of Scientific Affairs, Use of Restraints for Patients in Nursing Homes, 8 Archives of Family Medicine 101 (Mar–Apr 1999).

9. See e.g., Lois Evans, Neville Strumpf, et al., Restraint–Free Care: From Dream to Reality, Geriatric Nursing 122 (May/June 1990). See also, Physical and Chemical Restraints in Nursing Facilities: An Introduction for Residents' Advocates, Nursing Home Law Letter, National Senior Citizens Law Center (June 1992), reprinted in Patricia Nemore, Nursing Home Law, 215 PLI/Est. 163 (1992); N.G. Castle, Physical Restraints in Nursing Homes: A Review of the Literature Since The Nursing Home Reform Act of 1987, 55 Medical Care Research Review 139 (June 1998).

10. See e.g., Lois Evans, Neville Strumpf, Tying Down the Elderly: A Review of the Literature on Physical Restraint, 37 J. Am. Geriatric Society 65 (1989).

11. Sandra H. Johnson, The Fear of Liability and the Use of Restraints in Nursing Homes, 18 Law, Medicine & Health Care 263 (Fall, 1991); Marshall Kapp, Nursing Home Restraints and Legal Liability: Merging the Standard of Care and Industry Practice, 13 J. Leg. Med. 1 (1992).

12. 42 U.S.C.A. §§ 1395i–3(c)(1)(A)(ii)(II); 42 U.S.C.A. § 1396r (c)(1)(A)(ii)(II).

13. 42 C.F.R. § 483.13.

14. See e.g., State Operations Manual, Provider Certification Transmittal No. 250 (April 1992) p–76 to p–78; "Additional Guidance" (October 1992). These manuals are frequently updated.

physician, whom the resident has the right to select under the federal statute.[15]

The restrictions on the use of restraints have been relatively well-accepted after some initial resistance on the part of nursing homes. In addition to concerns over potential liability, facilities were concerned that decreased use of restraints would require increased staffing. Reports indicate, however, that increased staff has not been required as a prerequisite to a lower incidence of physical restraint.[16]

OBRA of 1987 also made significant additions to the rights of residents regarding transfer and discharge,[17] even though the permissible reasons for discharge under the Act did not change significantly from those established in earlier regulations.[18] The current allowable reasons for transfer or discharge include a resident's return to health so that he or she no longer requires the facility's services; the resident's failure to pay allowable charges; the closing of a facility; the inability of the facility to meet the resident's needs; and endangerment of the safety or health of individuals in the facility by the presence of the resident.

The federal statute requires that the facility notify the resident, and the family or legal representative of the resident if known, of the reasons for the transfer or discharge and of his right to appeal the transfer or discharge through an appeals process established by the state. The facility must provide the notice thirty days in advance of the transfer or discharge unless the resident's presence in the facility endangers the health and welfare of others; the resident has experienced such a marked degree of improvement that more immediate transfer or discharge is appropriate; the resident has urgent medical needs requiring transfer or discharge; or the resident has not resided in the facility at least thirty days.[19] The facility is required to prepare the resident for discharge.

The state must establish a "fair mechanism" for hearing appeals of transfers and discharges contested by the resident.[20] The Health Care Financing Administration has established minimum requirements for the fair hearing process, requiring that the state use the Medicaid fair hearing process.[21] The regulations apply to both Medicaid and non-Medicaid payees. Importantly for representation of facilities and residents, the regulations require the states to allow public access to the transfer and discharge hearings decisions. The resident's remedies under the federal statute may be limited to the state appeals process. At least two cases have held that the statutory transfer provisions did not create a private right of action for residents challenging an

15. 42 U.S.C.A. § 1395i–3(c)(1)(A)(i); 42 C.F.R. § 483.40.

16. See e.g., Mary Tinetti, et al., Mechanical Restraint Use Among Residents of Skilled Nursing Facilities, 265 JAMA 468 (Jan. 23/30, 1991); Charles D. Phillips, et al., Reducing the Use of Physical Restraints in Nursing Homes: Will It Increase Costs?, 83 Am. J. Public Health 342 (1993).

17. 42 U.S.C.A. § 1395i–3(c)(2); 42 U.S.C.A. § 1396r(c)(2). 42 C.F.R. § 483.12. Kathleen Knepper, Involuntary Transfers and Discharges of Nursing Home Residents under

Federal and State Law, 17 J.Leg. Med. 215 (1996).

18. See 42 C.F.R. §§ 405.1121(k)(11) and 442.311(c).

19. 42 U.S.C.A. § 1395i–3(c)(2)(B); 42 U.S.C.A. § 1396r(c)(2)(B).

20. 42 U.S.C.A. § 1395i–3(e)(3); 42 U.S.C.A. § 1396r(e)(3).

21. 42 C.F.R. § 483.204(b), 57 Fed. Reg. 56450–01 to be codified at 42 C.F.R. § 483.200 et seq.

inappropriate transfer.[22] The resident may have a contractual claim under the nursing home admission agreement, however.[23]

Of course, the resident may have rights in transfer and discharge beyond those provided in the federal statute. For example, although the U.S. Supreme Court consistently held that nursing home residents had no constitutional protections in the context of decisions that would ultimately lead to transfer or discharge,[24] some cases were settled under consent decrees that provided significant protections to residents.[25] Litigation may continue to expand residents' rights under the statute. In addition, the state may have adopted more expansive transfer and discharge rights in the facility licensure statute.[26]

§ 1–14. Clinical Laboratories

In one of its more controversial and massive[1] regulatory efforts, the Department of Health and Human Services has set standards under the Clinical Laboratory Amendments of 1988 for the performance of laboratory tests in a wide variety of settings, including doctors' offices.[2] Proposed regulations issued by the Department in 1990 generated 60,000 comments.[3] In a subsequently issued "final rule with comment period," the Department established standards for thousands of laboratory procedures.[4] The Department subsequently issued technical correcting amendments[5] and a new final rules.[6]

Undoubtedly, regulatory standard-setting under CLIA is complex and tests the ability of a public regulatory system to respond to rapid changes in technology. Whether HCFA will be able to respond to changes in a timely fashion remains unclear. HCFA has established a Clinical Laboratory Advisory Committee which will review specific procedures and recommend changes to HCFA. The substantial changes during the course of rulemaking under CLIA foreshadow the nature of this continuing and highly charged regulatory standard-setting process.

22. Nichols v. St. Luke Center of Hyde Park, 800 F.Supp. 1564 (S.D.Ohio 1992); Chalfin v. Beverly Enterprises, 741 F.Supp. 1162 (E.D.Pa.1989).

23. Chalfin v. Beverly Enterprises, 741 F.Supp. 1162 (E.D.Pa.1989). For a discussion of private claims under nursing home agreements, see Charles Lattanzi, Nursing Home Contracts: Is It Time for Bad Faith to Come Out of Retirement?, 6 J. L. & Health 61 (1991/1992).

24. O'Bannon v. Town Court Nursing Center, 447 U.S. 773, 100 S.Ct. 2467, 65 L.Ed.2d 506 (1980); Blum v. Yaretsky, 457 U.S. 991, 102 S.Ct. 2777, 73 L.Ed.2d 534 (1982).

25. See e.g., Blum v. Yaretsky, consent decree reported at [1980] Medicare and Medicaid Guide (CCH) ¶ 30,418 at 9,644 (S.D.N.Y. Oct. 17, 1979).

26. See e.g., Michigan Compiled Laws Ann. § 333.21702 et seq.; West's Fla. Stat. Ann. § 400.022(i)(p).

§ 1–14

1. The Health Care Financing Administration expected 180,000 laboratories to register under CLIA. Diane M. Gianelli, Physicians Clamor To Claim Their Labs Exempt From CLIA, 36 Am. Med. News 1 (June 7, 1993).

2. 42 U.S.C.A. § 263a(b).

3. 57 Fed. Reg. 7187, 7189 (Feb. 28, 1992), modified at 59 Fed. Reg. 682–01 (Jan. 6, 1994).

4. 57 Fed. Reg. 7001 and 7187 (Feb. 28, 1992), to be codified at 42 C.F.R. § 493.1 et seq. This list was updated at 58 Fed. Reg. 39860–01 (July 26, 1993).

5. 58 Fed. Reg. 5212–01, 7140 to 7142 (Feb. 28, 1992).

6. 58 Fed. Reg. 5215–01 (Jan. 19, 1993), with technical corrections at 58 Fed. Reg. 39154–01 (July 22, 1993). The Department issued additional final rules with opportunity to comment in December 1994 and in May 1997 (59 Fed. Reg. 62606 and 62 Fed. Reg. 25855).

G. ENFORCEMENT

§ 1–15. Variation by Type of Institution

Every state requires that both hospitals and nursing homes obtain and maintain an operating license from the state in order to conduct business. Most states require the same of home health agencies. Each health care provider—whether hospital, nursing home, home health agency or other—receiving payment for services through Medicare or Medicaid must be certified to participate in those programs. The enforcement environment varies considerably among different types of health care institutions and as well among the states. Even if statutes and regulations apply similar standards and enforcement processes to particular categories of health care institutions, serious differences emerge from disparities in funding for enforcement and priorities set as a matter of internal policy within the enforcement agency. Variations in enforcement posture or attitude also produce very significant differences for regulated health care facilities.

a. *Hospitals*

Both the federal and state regulation of hospitals rely primarily on a self-regulatory, consultative model, deferring substantially to the standards and enforcement process of the private Joint Commission on Accreditation of Healthcare Organizations.[1] Deficiencies in the enforcement of regulatory standards for hospitals simply have not attracted substantial public attention or attention in the legal literature.

b. *Nursing Homes*

In contrast, regulatory standards and enforcement in regard to nursing home care consistently have produced eye-catching headlines and have generated a substantial body of legal literature. Nursing home enforcement on both the federal and state levels over the past ten years or so has adopted an enforcement-oriented, rather than a consultative, approach toward regulation.[2] Enforcement of nursing home standards tends to consume the bulk of the budget of the state health care facility regulatory agencies, reflecting the priority given to public regulation of nursing homes.[3]

c. *Home Health Care*

Licensure of home health agencies, unlike state licensure of nursing homes, has rested on an undeveloped, bare-bones system, generally falling among the lowest of priorities for state enforcement agencies. Much state licensure activity with regard to home health agencies has been merely a response to federal requirements for Medicare payments to such agencies, rather than a regulatory priority. Federal enforcement of Medicare standards

§ 1–15

1. See discussion of accreditation in § 1–4.

2. See e.g., Timothy S. Jost, Enforcement of Quality Nursing Home Care in the Legal System, 13 Law, Medicine & Health Care 160 (1985); Institute of Medicine, Improving the Quality of Care in Nursing Homes 147–149; Patricia Day & Rudolf Klein, The Regulation of

Nursing Homes: A Comparative Perspective, 65 Milbank Q. 303 (1987).

3. Institute of Medicine, Improving the Quality of Care in Nursing Homes 318, 331 (1986). Still, the General Accounting Office has reported that state enforcement is lax. Enhanced HCFA Oversight of State Programs Would Better Ensure Quality, (GAO/HEHS–00–6), November 1999.

historically has been less aggressive. With the granting of deemed status to private accreditation for home health agencies,[4] the federal government has taken a significant step toward placing home health agencies within the self-regulatory enforcement environment enjoyed by hospitals.[5] Home health agencies have been subject to increased scrutiny in recent years, however.[6]

d. Clinical Laboratories

One of the more controversial regulatory enforcement programs is the federal regulation of clinical laboratories under the Clinical Laboratory Improvement Amendments of 1988.[7] Most of the controversy in the enforcement process arises from the fact that CLIA requires that individual private physicians, who perform certain on-site laboratory tests at their offices, subject their offices to on-site inspections under the Act.[8] The Act also applies to clinical laboratories within other facilities, including Medicare and Medicaid certified facilities.[9]

CLIA does provide for deemed status for federally-approved private accreditation programs[10] and for an exemption from the requirements of the Act for a laboratory licensed by and located in a state that has a state licensing and inspection program approved by the Department of Health and Human Services.[11] Clinical laboratories pay a "user fee" for the federal inspection and certification process or for their registration if privately accredited and exempt from federal inspection.[12] The user fees were intended to pay entirely for the enforcement costs of CLIA.

§ 1–16. Procedural Requirements

a. Introduction

Institutional licensure and certification under Medicare and Medicaid are each administrative systems. As such, the legal issues raised relating to procedural requirements during the course of enforcement actions are generally quite similar to those discussed elsewhere in relation to professional licensure.[1]

b. Judicial Review

Access to judicial review of administrative action regarding health care facilities is limited by the administrative law doctrine of exhaustion of

---

4. See discussion of deemed status in § 1–4.

5. For discussions of the quality of home care see, Marshall Kapp, Improving Choices Regrading Home Care Services: Legal Impediments and Empowerments, 10 St. Louis U. Pub. L. Rev. 441 (1991); House Select Comm. On Aging, The "Black Box" of Home Care Quality (reprint of report produced by the American Bar Association Commission on Legal Problems of the Elderly), 99th Cong., 2d Sess. (1986).

6. Gina M. Reese and Joseph H. Hafkenschiel, Hot Topics in Home Health Care, 20 Whittier L. Rev. 365 (1998).

7. Pub. L. 100–578, codified at 42 U.S.C.A. § 263a.

8. 42 U.S.C.A. § 263a(a).

9. Id.

10. 42 U.S.C.A. § 263a(e). See § 1–4. The Joint Commission on Accreditation of Healthcare Organizations, The American Association of Blood Banks, and the American Osteopathic Association have all been granted deemed status. 63 Fed. Reg. 17429–02 (April 9, 1998).

11. 58 Fed. Reg. 5212–01, (Jan. 19, 1993), correction at 58 Fed. Reg. 48323–01 (Sept. 15, 1993), to be codified at 42 C.F.R. § 493.614.

12. 57 Fed. Reg. 31664–01 (July 17, 1993), with technical corrections and revisions at 58 Fed. Reg. 5215–01 (Jan. 19, 1993).

§ 1–16

1. See §§ 3–13 through 3–18.

administrative remedies. Providers contesting sanctions under Medicare, for example, generally must exhaust administrative remedies prior to seeking judicial review of the Department's decision to sanction.[2] Several courts have allowed providers to contest penalties without exhausting administrative remedies, however, in cases in which the provider was not seeking judicial review of the substantive administrative decision.[3] Evidence not submitted during the administrative process may not be admissible for judicial review.[4] The scope of judicial review over agency adjudicatory action generally is limited to the substantial evidence standard.[5]

c. Unannounced Inspections

Regulatory enforcement requires that inspectors or surveyors have access to the health care facility. Inspections have raised a number of issues relating to constitutional requirements for searches.[6] For example, facilities have challenged particular demands for records as unconstitutionally overbroad.[7]

The most important question arising under the Fourth Amendment requirements for searches are those relating to warrantless searches. Standard routine surveys or inspections are often announced in advance and consensual. But an important part of the enforcement process is the ability of the agency to perform unannounced inspections.[8] In the context of licensure, the constitutional limitations placed on warrantless unannounced inspections are assessed in the context of the licensee's advanced knowledge that acceptance of a license or conduct of a licensed business involves regulatory oversight. Although accepting a license does not amount to consent for unconstitutional searches, the status of the facility as a licensed business has the effect of granting the government enforcement agency broader authority to conduct warrantless searches than in other situations. Similarly, acceptance of federal financing for services results in broader governmental authority for unannounced inspection.[9]

An unannounced search must be related to a legitimate government purpose, and the government must also show that advance notice of an

2. 42 U.S.C.A. § 1395cc(h); 42 U.S.C.A. § 405(g). See e.g., Dallas Healthcare, Inc. v. Health and Human Services Commission, 921 F.Supp. 426 (N.D.Tex.1996); Northwest Healthcare, L.P. v. Sullivan, 793 F.Supp. 724 (W.D.Tex.1992); Livingston Care Center v. United States, 934 F.2d 719 (6th Cir.1991), cert. denied 502 U.S. 1003, 112 S.Ct. 636, 116 L.Ed.2d 654 (1991); Americana Healthcare Corp. v. Schweiker, 688 F.2d 1072 (7th Cir. 1982), cert. denied 459 U.S. 1202, 103 S.Ct. 1187, 75 L.Ed.2d 434 (1983).

3. See e.g., Wayside Farm, Inc. v. U.S. Department of Health and Human Services, 863 F.2d 447 (6th Cir.1988).

4. See e.g., Ringwald v. Division of Health of Missouri, 537 S.W.2d 552 (Mo.1976); Zieverink v. Ackerman, 437 N.E.2d 319 (Ohio App. 1981).

5. See e.g., Clay County Manor v. State, 849 S.W.2d 755 (Tenn.1993); Jones v. Cabinet for Human Resources, 710 S.W.2d 862 (Ky. App.1986).

6. In addition to the constitutional claims, facilities have challenged the agency's access to patient records as violative of the patients' right to privacy and the facility's duty to protect the patients' privacy rights. See S. Johnson, N. Terry and M. Wolff, Nursing Homes and the Law: State Regulation and Private Litigation §§ 2–6, 2–7. See also, Robbins v. Budke, 739 F.Supp. 1479 (D.N.M.1990).

7. Much of the litigation on the state level regarding the scope of searches arose in New York as a result of aggressive investigations of nursing homes by a special prosecutor for nursing homes. See e.g., People v. Doe, 410 N.Y.S.2d 233 (N.Y.Sup.1978); Sigety v. Hynes, 372 N.Y.S.2d 771 (N.Y.Sup.1975).

8. See e.g., 42 U.S.C.A. § 1395i–3(g)(2)(A); 42 U.S.C.A. § 1396r(g)(2)(A).

9. See e.g., U.S. v. Brown, 763 F.2d 984 (8th Cir.1985), cert. denied 474 U.S. 905, 106 S.Ct. 273, 88 L.Ed.2d 234 (1985); U.S. v. Griffin, 555 F.2d 1323 (5th Cir.1977).

inspection would be impractical in the sense of allowing regulated providers to temporarily remedy or disguise violations.[10] Facilities refusing unannounced inspections may be subject to penalty.[11]

d. Due Process

Health care providers[12] are entitled to due process[13] in the imposition of government penalties relating to licensure or certification under Medicare or Medicaid, if the penalties result in the deprivation of property. Revocation of the operating license clearly results in the deprivation of property and triggers due process requirements.[14] Termination of the Medicare or Medicaid provider agreement, in contrast, may or may not result in the deprivation of a protectible property interest.[15] Other penalties do not result in the deprivation of property. For example, reducing a facility's license to a conditional license, in effect placing the facility on probation,[16] and publicly listing a facility as a violator of state standards[17] may not deprive the provider of a property interest protected by the due process clause.

The nature of the procedure required prior to the imposition of penalty relates to the importance of the private interest, the length of the deprivation, the likelihood of error and the nature of the government interests involved.[18]

---

10. U.S. v. Biswell, 406 U.S. 311, 92 S.Ct. 1593, 32 L.Ed.2d 87 (1972). Several states have also considered the constitutionality of unannounced inspections. See e.g., Clay County Manor v. State of Tennessee, 849 S.W.2d 755 (Tenn.1993); Blue v. Koren, 72 F.3d 1075 (2d Cir. 1995).

11. See e.g., Urban v. Reidy, 142 A.2d 133 (R.I.1958); Uzzillia v. Commissioner of Health, 367 N.Y.S.2d 795 (N.Y.App.Div.1975), appeal dismissed 375 N.Y.S.2d 97, 337 N.E.2d 605 (N.Y.App.1975); Clay County Manor v. State of Tennessee, 849 S.W.2d 755 (Tenn.1993).

12. Residents of a sanctioned nursing home, do not have a constitutional right to due process prior to sanction of the facility. See e.g., O'Bannon v. Town Court Nursing Center, 447 U.S. 773, 100 S.Ct. 2467, 65 L.Ed.2d 506 (1980); Kelly Kare, Ltd. v. O'Rourke, 930 F.2d 170 (2d Cir.1991), cert. denied 502 U.S. 907, 112 S.Ct. 300, 116 L.Ed.2d 244 (1991). But see, Haymons v. Williams, 795 F.Supp. 1511 (M.D.Fla.1992), holding that beneficiaries were entitled to notice and hearing prior to termination of provider.

13. Administrative agencies also generally must abide by their own statutory procedure, by their own rules of operation and by the requirements of the relevant administrative procedures act. See e.g., Aurelia Osborn Fox Memorial Hospital Society v. Whalen, 391 N.Y.S.2d 20 (N.Y.App.Div.1977); Valley View Convalescent Home v. Department of Social and Health Services, 599 P.2d 1313 (Wash.App. 1979). But see, Grove School v. Department of Public Health, 112 Ill.Dec. 364, 513 N.E.2d 973 (Ill.App.1987); State ex rel. St. Michael's v. Department of Admin., Division of Hearings and Appeals, 404 N.W.2d 114 (Wis.App.1987).

14. See e.g., Thompson v. Division of Health of Missouri, 604 S.W.2d 802 (Mo.App. 1980); Robinson v. Kentucky Health Facilities, 600 S.W.2d 491 (Ky.App.1980).

15. See e.g., Cohen v. Bane, 853 F.Supp. 620 (E.D.N.Y.1994); MEDCARE HMO v. Bradley, 788 F.Supp. 1460 (N.D.Ill.1992); Plaza Health Laboratories, Inc. v. Perales, 878 F.2d 577 (2d Cir.1989); Kelly Kare, Ltd. v. O'Rourke, 930 F.2d 170 (2d Cir.1991), cert. denied 502 U.S. 907, 112 S.Ct. 300, 116 L.Ed.2d 244 (1991); and Geriatrics, Inc. v. Harris, 640 F.2d 262 (10th Cir.1981).

16. In Altenheim German Home v. Turnock, 902 F.2d 582, 583 (7th Cir.1990), Judge Posner writing for a unanimous panel seems to imply that merely placing a facility on a conditional license may not result in a deprivation of property, although the state did not contest plaintiff's assertion that it did. In Somerset House v. Turnock, 900 F.2d 1012 (7th Cir. 1990), another Seventh Circuit panel noted that the trial court had held that placing a facility on conditional license, standing alone, did not amount to a deprivation of property.

17. See e.g., Somerset House v. Turnock, 900 F.2d 1012, 1015 (7th Cir.1990), noting but not reviewing on appeal trial court's application of the "stigma plus" standard, under which damage to reputation does not amount to a deprivation of property, but that damage to reputation plus change in legal status would result in deprivation of property and trial court's holding that removal from eligibility for QUIP funding provided to facilities exceeding state standards satisfied requirement of change in legal status.

18. See e.g., Mathews v. Eldridge, 424 U.S. 319, 96 S.Ct. 893, 47 L.Ed.2d 18 (1976).

Revocation of license generally requires substantial pre-revocation procedural protections.[19] Pre-penalty hearings, allowing oral presentation of evidence and cross-examination of witnesses, are not necessarily required, as a matter of constitutional law, for imposition of intermediate sanctions such as suspension of admissions,[20] notification to the public of violation,[21] and placement of facility on conditional licensure status.[22]

A pretermination hearing generally is not constitutionally required for termination of the Medicare or Medicaid provider agreement where the health and safety of the residents is in serious jeopardy.[23] Even in the absence of such serious justification, a pretermination hearing may not be required as the courts generally do not find that the interests of the provider in continued funds weigh very heavily against other government interests.[24] Nor does termination of the provider agreement generally satisfy the requirement of irreparable injury to justify a preliminary injunction against termination.[25]

The Medicare and Medicaid statutes do authorize immediate termination of the provider agreement if the health and safety of the residents are in serious jeopardy.[26] The provision for immediate termination of the provider agreement necessarily has been controversial.[27] At least one court has rejected the Department's claim that it has the authority to terminate the provider agreement immediately even when the health and safety of the residents is not in immediate jeopardy.[28] The intermediate sanctions provision enacted under the Omnibus Reconciliation Act of 1987, gave the Department authority to choose to impose intermediate sanctions in lieu of immediate termination when the health and safety of the residents is not in immediate jeopardy. The Department continues to pursue termination in certain cases, however.

19. See e.g., Thompson v. Division of Health of Missouri, 604 S.W.2d 802 (Mo.App. 1980); Robinson v. Kentucky Health Facilities, 600 S.W.2d 491 (Ky.App.1980).

20. See generally, Clay County Manor v. State of Tennessee, 849 S.W.2d 755 (Tenn. 1993).

21. See e.g., Somerset House v. Turnock, 900 F.2d 1012 (7th Cir.1990).

22. See e.g., Altenheim German Home v. Turnock, 902 F.2d 582 (7th Cir.1990).

23. Americana Healthcare Corp. v. Schweiker, 688 F.2d 1072 (7th Cir.1982), cert. denied 459 U.S. 1202, 103 S.Ct. 1187, 75 L.Ed.2d 434 (1983).

24. See e.g., Northwest Healthcare, L.P. v. Sullivan, 793 F.Supp. 724 (W.D.Tex.1992); Geriatrics Inc. v. Harris, 640 F.2d 262 (10th Cir. 1981). But see, MEDCARE HMO v. Bradley, 788 F.Supp. 1460 (N.D.Ill.1992).

25. See e.g., Wayside Farm, Inc. v. U.S. Department of Health and Human Services, 863 F.2d 447 (6th Cir.1988); Claridge House,

Inc. v. United States Department of Health and Human Services, 795 F.Supp. 1393 (S.D.Ohio 1991); Northwest Healthcare, L.P. v. Sullivan, 793 F.Supp. 724 (W.D.Tex.1992).

26. 42 U.S.C.A. § 1395i–3(h)(2)(A)(i); 42 U.S.C.A. § 1396r(h)(3)(B)(i).

27. See e.g., Americana Healthcare Corp. v. Schweiker, 688 F.2d 1072 (7th Cir.1982), cert. denied 459 U.S. 1202, 103 S.Ct. 1187, 75 L.Ed.2d 434 (1983), involving consolidation of litigation challenging procedure by several nursing homes.

28. Claridge House, Inc. v. U.S. Department of Health and Human Services, 795 F.Supp. 1393 (S.D.Ohio 1991). See also, Columbus West Health Care Co. v. Sullivan, 1989 WL 119415 (S.D.Ohio 1989). But see, Northern Health Facilities, Inc. v. U.S., 39 F.Supp.2d 563 (D.Md.1998), and Lake County Rehabilitation Center, Inc. v. Shalala, 854 F.Supp. 1329 (N.D.Ind.1994) (holding that the Secretary of Health and Human Services has the authority to terminate a facilities participation in the Medicare and Medicaid programs absent findings of immediate jeopardy).

§ 1–17. Enforcement Sanctions

a. *Intermediate Sanctions*

Enforcement that depends on all-or-nothing sanctions—whether revocation of license or termination of the provider agreement—is often ineffective in the health care setting. Such sanctions are likely to become empty threats and rarely applied because of the substantial negative consequences generated by causing a health care provider to cease operation. Closing a substandard nursing home, for example, through revocation or denial of its operating license or termination of its provider agreement is not always a successful enforcement event because it disrupts the lives and may injure the health of the residents and may aggravate a shortage of nursing home beds. License revocation and decertification also threaten serious economic harm to the facility's owners and so ordinarily are accompanied by procedures that are time-consuming, often delaying enforcement and making heavy demands on the inspection and legal services resources of the enforcement agencies.

The limitations of single-sanction enforcement systems have been documented in several health-care settings;[1] but state and federal regulation of nursing homes provides the most well-developed and sophisticated demonstration of intermediate sanctions.[2] The Institute of Medicine study of state licensure enforcement systems concluded that intermediate sanctions were an important part of an effective enforcement system and recommended that the federal government adopt intermediate sanctions for the enforcement of nursing home standards and mandate that states receiving federal funds for nursing home care have intermediate sanctions available under state law.[3] Congress responded affirmatively in the Omnibus Budget Reconciliation Act of 1987 by including intermediate sanctions for the federal government and mandating the enactment of intermediate sanctions for state agencies.[4] The Act also provided intermediate sanctions for home health agencies[5] and for clinical laboratories.[6] With the federal mandate and the consolidation in several states of health care facility licensure statutes, the availability of intermediate sanctions for enforcement against all regulated health care providers has expanded.[7]

Intermediate sanctions more precisely relate the severity of sanctions to the severity of violations and may be imposed more quickly and efficiently. Although the state statutes vary and the federal statute differs from typical

§ 1–17

1. See e.g., U.S.Dept. of Health and Human Services, Office of Inspector General, Home Health Aide Services for Medicare Patients, Sept. 1987 at 9.

2. See e.g., Institute of Medicine, Improving the Quality of Care in Nursing Homes 146–168 (1986); Sandra H. Johnson, State Regulation of Long–Term Care: A Decade of Experience with Intermediate Sanctions, 13 Law, Medicine & Health Care 173 (1985); Sandra H. Johnson, Quality–Control Regulation of Home Health Care, 26 Hous. L. Rev. 901, 936–950 (1989).

3. Institute of Medicine, Improving the Quality of Care in Nursing Homes 146–168 (1986).

4. See e.g., 42 U.S.C.A. § 1395i–3(h)(2)(B); 42 U.S.C.A. § 1396r(h)(2); 57 Fed. Reg. 39278–01 (Aug. 28, 1992), applying to skilled nursing

facilities. See Claridge House v. U.S. Department of Health and Human Services, 795 F.Supp. 1393 (S.D.Ohio 1991). See also, Andrew A. Skolnick, After Long Delay, Federal Regulations for Enforcing Nursing Home Standards May Be Issued This Year, 269 J.A.M.A. 2348 (May 12, 1993).

5. 42 U.S.C.A. § 1395bbb(f); 42 U.S.C.A. § 1396t(j).

6. 42 U.S.C.A. § 263a(h).

7. With the creation of intermediate sanctions, some courts have required enforcement agencies to use intermediate sanctions rather than more serious sanctions in particular cases. See e.g., Villines v. Division of Aging, 722 S.W.2d 939 (Mo.1987). But see, Lake County Rehabilitation Center v. Shalala, 854 F.Supp. 1329 (N.D.Ind.1994); Claridge House, Inc. v. U.S. Department of Health and Human Services, 795 F.Supp. 1393 (S.D.Ohio 1991).

state statutes in some respects, there is enough similarity to allow generalization in discussing these sanctions. Two of the more common intermediate sanctions are civil fines and receiverships.[8]

b. Civil Penalties

Among the most effective of the intermediate sanctions is the civil fine.[9] With an appropriate range, the amount of the fine can be adjusted to reflect the severity of the particular violation and the compliance history of the facility.[10] Civil fines increase the cost and decrease the benefit of violations. Unlike civil litigation,[11] however, civil monetary penalties do not ordinarily compensate the victim of substandard care.[12] The most serious threat to the effectiveness of civil fines is persistent, systemic delay, which may occur if the civil penalty system is not well-designed.[13] Civil fines can be effective with facilities that have repeated violations if the statute allows amplified penalties and the agency develops a method for aggressively monitoring repeated violations.[14]

c. Receiverships and Temporary Management

In a receivership, the provider retains ownership of the facility, but a court-appointed receiver controls and manages the facility.[15] The receivership can maintain a facility in operation while the residents are safely transferred. A receivership can in some circumstances upgrade a seriously substandard facility for continued operation under the previous or new owners. In implementing receiverships, the most important statutory provisions are those that specify the grounds for the appointment of a receiver, that provide the funds necessary for the receivership and that set a termination date for the

---

8. Other intermediate sanctions include: the public monitor, which allows the agency to appoint a person to monitor a troubled facility's performance often on a daily basis on-site (see e.g., N.M. Stat. Ann. § 24–1–5.2(A)(1)(b); Alaska Stat. § 18.20.310(a)(6); 42 U.S.C.A. § 1395i–3(h)(2)(B)(iii); 42 U.S.C.A. § 1396r(h)(2)(A)(iii)); suspension of admissions, which results in a bar on new admissions and has an increasing economic effect on the facility as time passes (see e.g., N.M. Stat. Ann. § 24–1–5.2(A)(1)(e); Ariz. Rev. Stat. § 36–427(c)); and denial of payment, which operates in a similar fashion to suspension of admissions (see e.g., 42 U.S.C.A. § 1395i–3(h)(2)(B)(i); 42 U.S.C.A. § 1396r(h)(2)(A)(i)). In addition, some states have criminally prosecuted nursing home providers for violation of certain standards involving abuse or neglect of patients. See e.g., State v. Brenner, 486 So.2d 101 (La.1986); State v. Chadderton, 832 P.2d 481 (Wash.1992).

9. See e.g., N.M. Stat. Ann. § 24–1–5.2(A)(2) (health facilities); Tenn. Code Ann. § 68–11–804 (nursing homes); Conn. Gen. Stat. Ann. §§ 19a–524 to 19a–528 (health facilities). See also, People v. Casa Blanca Convalescent Homes, Inc., 206 Cal.Rptr. 164 (Cal. App.1984), applying fines provision of the unfair business practices statute to nursing home violations.

10. See e.g., People v. Casa Blanca Convalescent Homes, Inc., 206 Cal.Rptr. 164 (Cal. App.1984), upholding fine of $167,500 for multiple serious violations.

11. See discussion of private right of action in § 1–2.

12. But see, Gentry v. Department of Public Health, 475 N.W.2d 849 (Mich.App.1991), appeal denied 478 N.W.2d 99 (Mich.1991); Kizer v. County of San Mateo, 279 Cal.Rptr. 318, 806 P.2d 1353 (Cal.1991).

13. See e.g., Vernon's Ann. Mo. Stat. § 198.067(2), providing that only a court can levy a fine, thus requiring extensive resources for implementation.

14. See generally, Sandra H. Johnson, State Regulation of Long–Term Care: A Decade of Experience with Intermediate Sanctions, 12 Law, Medicine & Health Care 175–177 (1985).

15. See e.g., Arkansas Code Ann. § 20–10–908; West's Ann. Cal. Health & Safety Code § 1325; West's Colorado Rev. Stat. Ann. § 25–3–108; D.C. Code § 32–1412; West's Florida Stat. Ann. § 400.126; 210 ILCS 45/3–503. The federal statutes provide for "temporary management," which appears analogous to a receivership in function, though temporary management may be imposed administratively. See e.g., 42 U.S.C.A. § 1395i–3(h)(2)(B)(iii); 42 U.S.C.A. § 1396r(h)(2)(A)(iii).

receivership.[16] Absent statutory provision for nursing home receiverships, some courts have appointed a receiver under their equitable powers.[17]

Statutory receivership requires court appointment, although the appointment may be ex parte in certain circumstances.[18] The court monitors the receivership, with prior court approval required of certain expenditures, and approves the final accounting.[19] Because the receivership generally completely removes control over the facility during the time of the receivership, the facility owners may assert a claim that taking of property has occurred. In *Birnbaum v. State*,[20] the court characterized the owners' precipitous closing as an illegal act that posed a danger to public safety. Thus, as a situation analogous to a nuisance, no taking occurred in the government's action to prevent the dangerous activity.[21] The court also relied upon a line of cases in which courts have found no taking when highly regulated businesses have been required to continue operation at a loss.[22] Even if a taking is found, it is likely that most of the nursing home statutes contain provisions for some compensation in the form of public aid for patient care[23] or, even in some cases, fair rental value for the building.[24] In addition, nursing homes receive direct economic advantage from state regulation in the form of limits on competition through state regulation of nursing home supply.[25]

H. HEALTH PLANNING AND CERTIFICATE OF NEED

§ 1–18. Introduction

From the mid 1970s until the early 1980s the primary federal and state regulatory strategy for controlling health care costs was to constrain the supply of health care resources through health planning, primarily through certificate of need programs that required hospitals to obtain government approval for capital investments. Although the federal government has now largely abandoned this strategy, certificate of need programs and health planning are still very much alive in the majority of the states. Although

16. For studies of nursing home receiverships, see Sandra H. Johnson, Nursing Home Receiverships: Design and Implementation, 24 St. Louis U. L. J. 681 (1981); Sandra H. Johnson, State Regulation of Long–Term Care: A Decade of Experience with Intermediate Sanctions, 12 Law, Medicine & Health Care 173, 177–179 (1985).

17. See e.g., In re Brookhollow Associates, 575 F.2d 1003 (1st Cir.1978); Toler v. Lula Toler Convalescing Home, 364 S.W.2d 680 (Ark.1963); People v. Abbott Manor Nursing Home, 421 N.Y.S.2d 451 (N.Y.App.Div.1979), affirmed 436 N.Y.S.2d 614, 417 N.E.2d 1002 (N.Y.App.1980).

18. See e.g., Vernon's Ann. Mo. Stat. § 198.108.

19. See e.g., D'Guardia v. Piffath, 579 N.Y.S.2d 447 (N.Y.App.Div.1992); Birnbaum v. State, 543 N.Y.S.2d 23, 541 N.E.2d 23 (N.Y.App.1989); People v. Abbott Manor Nursing Home, 490 N.Y.S.2d 411 (N.Y.App.Div. 1985). See also, Reivitz v. Healthcare Management, Inc., 419 N.W.2d 574 (Wis.App.1987).

20. 543 N.Y.S.2d 23, 541 N.E.2d 23 (N.Y.App.1989).

21. The court relied on Keystone Bituminous Coal Ass'n. v. DeBenedictis, 480 U.S. 470, 107 S.Ct. 1232, 94 L.Ed.2d 472 (1987). But see, Lucas v. South Carolina Coastal Council, 505 U.S. 1003, 112 S.Ct. 2886, 120 L.Ed.2d 798 (1992).

22. See e.g., Brooks–Scanlon Co. v. Railroad Comm'n, 251 U.S. 396, 40 S.Ct. 183, 64 L.Ed. 323 (1920); Gibbons v. United States, 660 F.2d 1227 (7th Cir.1981); Continental Air Lines v. Dole, 784 F.2d 1245 (5th Cir.1986).

23. Good Shepherd Health Facilities v. Department of Health, 789 P.2d 423 (Colo.App. 1989).

24. McKinney's—N.Y. Pub. Health Law § 2810(2)(b).

25. See e.g., Birnbaum v. State, 543 N.Y.S.2d 23, 541 N.E.2d 23 (N.Y.App.1989).

health planning receives little attention in many health law courses, it still is a very important area of practice for many health lawyers.[1]

Constricting supply seems an odd approach to controlling costs. Artificial constriction of supply ought to increase rather than decrease prices. Yet health planning as a cost-control strategy is founded on a plausible hypothesis that demand for medical treatment (unlike the demand for other commodities) increases as supply increases, and without lowering costs. The argument supporting this hypothesis unfolds as follows: First, patients understand neither the causes of nor the solutions to their medical problems, and therefore must trust physicians to decide what medical care to purchase. Realizing this, hospitals, at least under cost-based reimbursement, compete primarily to attract physicians, rather than patients, and make any capital expenditures that will increase their attractiveness to physicians. Physicians—believing that if there is a beneficial treatment, the patient should receive it—admit patients to the hospital or prescribe tests or treatment to the extent of available supply.

Because of the interplay of these factors, the demand for care will always expand to the limits of the supply. As the price need not fall for demand to increase, the cost of medical care will correspondingly rise. This theory, first proposed by Milton Roemer, and thus identified as Roemer's law, is aphorized as "A bed built is a bed filled is a bed billed."[2]

One regulatory strategy for discouraging such excessive capital investment is to require health care institutions to demonstrate a "need" to expand or to acquire new health technology in order to obtain the state's consent for a purchase. This consent is granted through a "certificate of need" (CON). The health planning process defines "need" by first discerning the appropriate level of demand for health services and then determining the amount of health resources needed to meet this demand. Both demand and supply are determined using a scientific and political process described below. The permitted level of health resources supply is then allocated among institutional health providers through a certificate of need program. Finally, providers ration among their patients the beds and technology permitted them so that only those who truly "need" services will receive them.

§ 1–18

1. Probably the best source of information on health planning law currently available is Elena Salerno Flash, Hillary T. Fraser, & Sally T. True, Certificate of Need Regulation, in I. Health Care Corporation Law, (Mark A. Hall, ed., 1999). The American Health Planning Association publishes regularly a National Director of Health Planning, Policy, and Regulatory Agencies, which provides up to date information on the state of health planning.

2. See Milton Roemer, Bed Supply and Hospital Utilization: A Natural Experiment, 35 Hosp. 37 (Nov. 1, 1961). See, further describing the theory, Judith R. Gelman, Competition and Health Planning: An Issues Paper, 101–09 (1982); Paul L. Joskow, Controlling Hospital Costs 57–71 (1981); James F. Blumstein &

Frank A. Sloan, Health Planning and Regulation through Certificate of Need: An Overview, 1978 Utah L. Rev. 3, 4–5; Randall Bovbjerg, Problems and Prospects for Health Planning: The Importance of Incentives, Standards, and Procedures in Certificate of Need, 1978 Utah L. Rev. 83, 85–97; Sallyanne Payton & Rhonda M. Powsner, Regulation Through the Looking glass: Hospitals, Blue Cross, and Certificate-of-Need, 79 Mich. L. Rev. 203, 253, 268–77 (1980). Note that the key to this hypothesis is full insurance reimbursement for capital costs. As long as hospitals can expect insurers to reimburse them fully for any capital expenditures, they have no incentive not to spend money to enhance their size and therapeutic capacity. To the extent that insurers have switched to reimbursement policies that do not fully reimburse capital costs, however, the hypothesis may no longer be valid.

Though Roemer's law is the principal justification for health planning as a cost-control strategy, others have emerged.[3] First, health planning could reduce the cost of health care by eliminating duplication and promoting consolidation of services to achieve economies of scale. The health planning process could permit, for example, only one hospital to install a particular kind of equipment, but also require the hospital to share it. A second hospital would then be permitted to install (and required to share) a different piece of expensive technical equipment. Health planning could also eliminate excess hospital beds through closings and consolidations. Use of the certificate of need process to tightly control the construction of nursing home beds can limit access to nursing homes (which generally have much less excess capacity than hospitals) and thus have a significant impact on state Medicaid budgets, which finance a high percentage of nursing home care. Some have even argued that health planning could be used to respond to the excesses of managed care.[4]

Most studies have found that CON has had little effect on controlling the cost of hospital care.[5] This appears to be true because the bulk of hospital costs are labor costs, which are not directly affected by CON. There is some evidence that controlling the diffusion of new technology through CON can have a positive effect on cost,[6] although other studies have found that CON decisionmaking processes can result in an oversupply of technology.[7] Evidence is clearer that CON can control nursing home costs, as the high occupancy rates in nursing homes make more possible control of demand through control of supply.[8] There is also some evidence that CON can slow technology diffusion, though the results of studies on this are conflicting.[9] There is little evidence of a surge in health care construction or costs following CON repeal.[10]

§ 1–19. History of Federal Health Planning Efforts

The most important federal health planning initiative has clearly been the National Health Resources Planning and Development Act (NHRPDA),[1]

3. Robert B. Hackney, New Wine in Old Bottles: Certificate of Need Enters the 1990s, 18 J. Health Pol., Pol'y & L 927 (1993) catalogues alternative purposes for health planning programs.

4. Thaddeus J. Nodzenski, Regulating Managed Care Coverage: A New Direction for Health Planning Agencies, 7 Ann. Health L. 1 (1998).

5. Policy Analysis, Inc., and Urban Systems Research and Engineering, Inc., Evaluation of the Effects of Certificate of Need Programs. Volume 1, Executive Summary (1981); Christopher J. Conover & Frank A. Sloan, Does Removing Certificate-of-Need Lead to a Surge in Health Care Spending? 23 J. Health Pol., Pol'y & L. 455 (1998); Charles E. Begley, et al., Factors That May Explain Interstate Differences in Certificate of Need Decisions, Health Care Fin. Rev., June 1982 at 87; Frank A. Sloan & Bruce Steinwald, Effects of Regulation on Hospital Costs and Input Use, 23 J. L. & Econ. 81 (1980).

6. Ann Lawthers–Higgins, et al., The Impact of Certificate of Need on CT Scanning In Massachusetts, 9 Health Care Management Rev. Summer 1984 at 71.

7. Clark C. Havighurst & Robert S. McDonough, The Lithotripsy Game in North Carolina: New Technology under Regulation and Deregulation, 19 Indiana L. Rev 989 (1986).

8. Judith Feder & William Scanlon, The Shortage of Nursing Home Beds, 4 J. Health Pol., Pol'y & L. 725 (1980); Judith R. Lave, Cost Containment Policies in Long Term Care, 22 Inquiry 7 (1985). But see discussion in § 1–2.

9. See, Connover & Sloan, supra note 5 at 475–76.

10. *Id.*

§ 1–19

1. Pub. L. 93–641, 88 Stat. 2225 (1974) (formerly codified at 42 U.S.C.A. §§ 300k to 300n–6) (repealed 1986).

which in 1974 replaced most of the earlier federal planning programs. The NHRPDA, the result of a complex and lively political debate, created a series of agencies at the federal, state, and local levels, and gave them a variety of planning and regulatory functions.

At the federal level it created a National Council on Health Planning and Development, to, among other things, aid the Secretary of the then Department of Health, Education and Welfare to develop standards and goals for the appropriate supply, distribution, and organization of health resources.[2] The statute also articulated federal health planning priorities.[3] These, significantly, did not explicitly include cost control until 1979.

However, the most important impact of the NHRPDA was at the state and local level. The country was to be divided up into health service areas (of which there were eventually over 200), which were to be served by Health Systems Agencies (HSAs).[4] The HSAs could be nonprofit private corporations, public regional planning bodies, or units of local government, but had to have independent governing boards which represented provider and consumer interests, with a majority of consumers. The HSAs were to develop health systems plans (HSPs) and annual implementation plans (AIPs), and to review and make recommendations concerning applications for certificates of need (CONs) and proposals for federal funding (PUFFs).

At the state level, two new agencies were to be created, a State Health Planning and Development Agency (SHPDA), which was to be a state agency; and the Statewide Health Coordinating Council (SHCC), which was to be composed largely of HSA representatives.[5] The SHPDA was to review the state health plan (SHP), to pass on CON applications, and to review the appropriateness of existing health services. The SHCC was to develop the final SHP, and to advise the SHPDA. CON approval was required for new institutional health services, including capital expenditures in excess of $150,-000. States that did not comply with the federal requirements would not only lose their health planning funds, but would also suffer loss of federal funding for other health care programs.

The NHRPDA was substantially amended in 1979.[6] The thrust of the 1979 amendments was to attempt to make health planning a tool to encourage competition. In particular, HMOs were singled out for favorable treatment under the 1979 amendments. In the early 1980s, federal funding for health planning was cut and then eliminated. On November 14, 1986 the NHRPDA was repealed.[7] Because many states continue to operate CON programs that resemble the model established by the NHRPDA, it is important to be aware of its history.

2. 42 U.S.C.A. § 300k–3 (repealed 1986).

3. 42 U.S.C.A. § 300k–2 (repealed 1986).

4. 42 U.S.C.A. §§ 300l to 300l–5 (repealed 1986).

5. 42 U.S.C.A. §§ 300m to 300m–6 (repealed 1986).

6. Health Planning and Resources Development Amendments of 1979, Pub. L. No. 96–79, 93 Stat. 592.

7. Pub. L. No. 99–660, Tit. VII, § 701(a), 100 Stat. 3743, 99 (1986) (effective January 1, 1987).

§ 1–20. State Certificate of Need Statutes

a. Introduction

With the demise of the federal health planning program in 1986, several states totally eliminated health planning.[1] A number of other states had abolished health planning earlier in the 1980s and the mid–1990s in the face of diminished federal interest in, and funding of, health planning.[2] Most states, however, (about three dozen as of this writing) have retained certificate of need programs.[3] The reasons why states have retained CON programs are complex and varied, but among the most important are the ability CON gives states to control Medicaid costs by limiting nursing home beds, the control CON gives states over proliferation of new medical technology, and the fear of rapid expansion of some health care services upon deregulation.

b. Facilities Covered

Starting from the common framework of the NHRPDA, state health planning statutes have diverged dramatically over the past half decade. Most states that have retained CON programs still apply CON requirements comprehensively to health care facilities, generally defined as in the former federal health planning regulations[4] to include hospitals, skilled nursing facilities, kidney disease treatment centers, intermediate care facilities, rehabilitation facilities, and ambulatory surgical facilities.[5] In addition, many states apply CON requirements to a variety of other health care entities, including home health agencies, hospices, substance abuse treatment centers, freestanding ambulatory treatment centers, community mental health centers, and intermediate care facilities for the mentally retarded. A number of state statutes, however, explicitly exclude from coverage physician's offices[6] or independent clinical laboratories.[7] Other states exclude hospitals that serve underserved populations.[8] Finally, mobile imaging units that are used by hospitals may not be covered if the technology is not acquired by a the hospitals themselves.[9]

§ 1–20

1. California, Colorado, South Dakota, and Wyoming.

2. Arizona, Idaho, Kansas, Minnesota, New Mexico, North Dakota, Texas, Utah and Vermont. Others have sharply limited or sunset their programs.

3. See Alabama Code §§ 22–4–1 to 22–4–17; Alaska Stat. §§ 18.07.031–18.07.111; Ark. Code Ann. §§ 20–8–101—20–8–112; Conn. Gen. Stat. Ann. §§ 19a–630, 19a–638—19a–639d, 19a–408.031—19a–408.0455; Del. Code tit. 16, §§ 9301–9311; Official Code Georgia Ann. §§ 31–6–1 to 31–6–70; Haw. Rev. Stat. §§ 323D–41—323D–83; 20 ILCS 3960/1–3960/19; West's Ann. Ind. Code §§ 16–29–1–1—16–29–5–1; Iowa Code Ann. §§ 135.61–135.83; Ky. Rev. Stat. §§ 216B.010–216B.135.15; Me. Rev. Stat. Ann. tit. 22, §§ 301–324; Md. Code, Health–General §§ 19–101 to 19–124; Mass. General Laws Ann. ch. 111, §§ 25B–25H; Miss. Code §§ 41–7–171 to 41–7–209; Vernon's Ann. Missouri Stat. §§ 197.300–197.366; Mont. Code Ann. §§ 50–5–301 to 50–5–310; Neb. Rev. Stat. §§ 71–5801 to 71–5872; Nev. Rev. Stat. §§ 439A.010–439A.120; N.H. Rev. Stat. Ann. §§ 151–C:1—151–C:15; N.J. Stat. Ann. §§ 26:2H–1–26:2H–11.1; McKinney's—N.Y. Pub. Health Law §§ 2802, 2803; N.C. Gen. Stat. §§ 131E–175 to 131E–199; Ohio Rev. Code §§ 3702.51–3702.68; Okla. Stat. Ann. tit. 63, §§ 1–851 to 1–859, 1–880.1–1–880.11; Or. Rev. Stat. §§ 442.015–442.347; Pa. Stat. tit. 35, §§ 448.101–448.712, 448.901–448.904b; R.I. Gen. Laws §§ 23–15–1 to 23–15–10; S.C. Code Ann. §§ 44–7–110 to 44–7–230; Tenn. Code Ann. §§ 68–11–101 to 68–11–125; Va. Code §§ 32.1–102.1—32.1–102.12; 32.1–122.01—32.1–122.08; West's Rev. Code Wash. Ann. §§ 70.38.015 to 70.38.920; W.Va. Code §§ 16–2D–1 to 16–2D–13; Wis. Stat. Ann. §§ 150.01–150.86.

4. Former 42 C.F.R. § 123.401 (repealed).

5. See e.g., Maryland Code, Health–General § 19–101(f); Mich. Comp. Laws Ann. § 333.22205; Or. Rev. Stat. § 442.015(14); West's Rev. Code Wash. Ann. § 70.38.025.

6. Ala. Code § 22–21–260(5); Official Code Ga.Ann. § 31–6–47(4); Ky. Rev. Stat. § 216B.020(2)(a); Tenn. Code Ann. § 68–11–102(5)(B)(iii).

7. Hawaii Rev. Stat. § 323D–54(2).

8. Official Code Ga. Ann. 31–6–47(16) (for certain types of projects); Ky. Rev. Stat. § 216B.020(2).

Some state statutes explicitly cover HMOs,[10] while others states explicitly exclude them from coverage, at least if certain requirements are met.[11] These exclusions were prompted by the 1979 federal CON amendments, which prohibited states from regulating HMOs under CON, in a belief that HMOs represented an independent competitive strategy for reducing the cost of health care which should not be interfered with by CON.

Finally, some states have only retained CON requirements for specific types of facilities, most commonly nursing homes.[12] This strategy makes some sense, as nursing home industry growth directly impacts state government health care (Medicaid) costs, and certificate of need, as was noted above, has been relatively successful in controlling nursing home costs. Further, states that have abolished certificate of need have experienced some of their most dramatic health care industry growth in the nursing home sector.

c. Cost Thresholds

Covered health care entities must obtain planning approval to carry out certain activities, commonly including construction of a new facility, capital investments whose cost exceeds a certain threshold, acquisition of new equipment costing more than a certain amount, increase or decrease of bed capacity beyond a specified number or percentage of existing capacity, and addition of new services the operating cost of which exceeds a stipulated amount.[13] Unless statutes are written to cover all new equipment and facilities, no matter how acquired, CON statutes are easily evaded.

The threshold amounts for capital expenditures before CON approval is required currently vary from $500,000 in Arkansas, Oklahoma and Maine to over $9,000,000 in Massachusetts, with most states in the $1,000,000 to $2,000,000 range.[14] Approval thresholds for major medical equipment are generally lower, most commonly in the $400,000 to $1,500,000 range. New service annual operating cost thresholds cluster in the $150,000 to $1,000,000 range. Bed capacity increases or decreases commonly require approval when they exceed the lesser of 10 beds or 10% of capacity.[15]

A number of state statutes explicitly list new services that a health care entity cannot purchase or begin to offer without obtaining planning approval.

9. See Commission for Health Economics Control in Kentucky v. Medical Consultants Imaging Co., 844 S.W.2d 437 (Ky.App.1992) (mobile single photon emission computed tomography (SPECT) unit acquired by independent company not covered even though unit would be used by hospitals.).

10. See Mich. Comp. Laws Ann. § 333.22227.

11. Maryland Code, Health–General § 19–116; West's Rev. Code Wash. Ann. § 70.38.111(1); W.Va. Code § 16–2D–4(b). These statutes generally track former 42 U.S.C.A. § 300m–6(b).

12. These states include Arkansas (which also covers home health agencies), Indiana, Oklahoma (also substance abuse centers), Montana (also renal dialysis, ambulatory surgi-cal centers, and lithotripsy), Wisconsin, Nebraska, Oregon, and Louisiana. A number of the states that abolished certificate of need retained moratoria on nursing home construction.

13. See e.g. Hawaii Rev. Stat. § 323D–43; Pa. Stat. tit. 35, § 448.701.

14. See Elena Salerno Flash, Hillary T. Fraser, & Sally T. True, Certificate of Need Regulation, in I. Health Care Corporation Law, (Mark A. Hall, ed., 1999), 1999 Supp. at 90–91 (1998 data from American Health Planning Ass'n). A number of states index threshold amounts for inflation from a base amount in a base year.

15. Maryland Code, Health–General § 19–115(h).

These are generally high cost tertiary services or facilities such as burn units, cardiac catheterization services, neonatal intensive care units, open heart surgery, or organ transplantation.[16] Alternatively, some statutes specifically exclude from approval requirements other investments or equipment, such as equipment used solely for research purposes,[17] expenditures unrelated to patient care (as for fire safety equipment or parking facilities),[18] or outpatient services. Other statutes provide for "nonsubstantive" review for projects unlikely to result in significant increases in health care expenditures.[19] While a few states require approval before the acquisition of an existing facility can proceed,[20] most states only require notification of the purchase if it will not itself lead to increased costs.[21] A few states also explicitly require a certificate of need prior to the relocation[22] or closure of a facility.[23] This permits the state an opportunity to protect access to care for inner city residents by preventing health care facilities from fleeing to the suburbs.

d. CON Procedures

Certificate of need statutes commonly set out procedures for obtaining a certificate of need. Most statutes contemplate a reactive process, under which the certificate of need agency or commission reviews and passes on individual CON applications as they are filed. A number of states, however, provide in addition for combined or batched review of certain projects, permitting the CON agency to consider together applications for similar projects periodically on a comparative basis and thus to focus more on planning considerations and less exclusively on a single CON request.[24] Other states provide similarly for applications to be considered in standard review cycles.[25]

Once the application is filed, several states require the planning agency to determine on an expedited basis whether a CON application is compete and ready for review.[26] After a completed application is filed, the agency or committee responsible for CON review generally has a limited amount of time to consider the application. Some statutes also make provision for simplified review for particular projects or emergency review.[27]

Although all states provide for CON review by administrative agencies, the nature of the administrative process differs somewhat. Some statutes seem to rely heavily on review of written documents and comments.[28] Though

16. Official Code Ga. Ann. § 31–6–2(5); Mich. Comp. Laws Ann. § 333.22203(11); Miss. Code § 41–7–191(1)(d); Tenn. Code Ann. § 68–11–106(a)(4).

17. Mich. Comp. Laws Ann. § 333.22243; W.Va. Code § 16–2D–4(c). These statutes resemble former 42 U.S.C.A. 300m–6(h).

18. Ky. Rev. Stat. § 216B.015(14);. West's Rev. Code Wash. Ann. § 70.38.105(4)(d).

19. Ky. Rev. Stat. § 216B.095.

20. See e.g., Haw.Rev.Stat. 323D–71–83 (approval of conversion of non-profits to for-profits).

21. Maryland Code, Health—General § 19–115(j)(5)(ii).

22. See e.g., Maryland Code, Health—General § 19–115(g).

23. W.Va.Code § 16–2D–3(b). Compare Tenn. Code Ann. § 68–11–106(a)(7), which re-

quires a CON to discontinue any obstetrical or maternity service.

24. Ky.Rev. Stat. § 216B.062(2); Mich. Comp. Laws Ann. § 333.22229; Pa. Stat. tit. 35, § 448.702(i); West's Rev. Code Wash. Ann. § 70.38.115(7).

25. Me. Rev. Stat. Ann. tit. 22, § 307(6–A); R.I. Gen. Laws § 23–15–6.

26. Official Code Ga. Ann. § 31–6–43 (within 10 days); Iowa Code Ann. § 135.66 (within 15 days); Pa.Stat. tit. 35 § 448.702(b) (45 days).

27. Iowa Code Ann. § 135.67; Me. Rev. Stat. Ann. tit. 22 § 308.

28. See e.g., Official Code Ga. Ann. § 31–6–44.

statutes normally require public notice of proposals,[29] some statutes seem to contemplate a public hearing, much like a rule-making hearing, in which public input will be solicited.[30] Others seem to contemplate an administrative hearing of a more adjudicative nature, with representation by counsel and written findings of facts and conclusions of law.[31] Most statutes provide for decisionmaking on the record and prohibit ex parte contacts before a decision is rendered.[32] Because CON applications involve particular facts and interests of great value, quasi-judicial hearings are inevitable. Because, however, what is ultimately at stake is planning to serve the health care needs of the public generally, an argument can be made for permitting broad public participation and for not making the proceedings too "judicial" in nature. Provision is usually afforded for reconsiderations and administrative appeals of CON initial decisions.[33]

e. CON Criteria

Many state statutes set out criteria by which CON proposals are to be evaluated.[34] These often reflect those criteria provided under the former federal law[35] and rules[36], which mandated consideration of, inter alia, state health plans; long-range plans of the entity seeking the CON; the needs of the population served by the entity including the needs of special, medically undeserved populations; the availability of less costly alternatives; the financial feasibility of the project and its affect on costs; the availability of resources for the project; the special needs and circumstances of HMOs; the quality of care provided by the applicant in existing facilities; and the effect of the project on competition. Alternatively, some state statutes require the state CON agency to promulgate standards for review of CON proposals.[37] Some state statutes permit the CON agency to impose conditions on CONs,[38] others prohibit the CON agency from imposing conditions on grants.[39]

State CON statutes make available judicial review of agency CON decisions to persons who have participated in the administrative proceedings.[40] Finally, statutes also make available civil and criminal penalties or injunctive relief where projects are undertaken without a CON where one is legally required.[41]

---

29. See e.g., Me. Rev. Stat. Ann. tit 22 § 307; N.C. Gen. Stat. § 131E–185(a1)(4); S.C. Code 44–7–200.

30. Iowa Code Ann. § 135.66(3)(b); Me. Rev. Stat. Ann. tit. 22, § 307(2–B); N.C. Gen. Stat. § 131E–185(a1)(2); S.C. Code § 44–7–210(B).

31. Ky. Rev. Stat. § 216B.085; Maryland Code Health–General § 19–118(f); Miss. Code § 41–7–197(2); Mich. Comp. Laws Ann. § 333.22232(2). Pa. Stat. tit. 35, § 448.704, provides for hearings initially before the HSA and for further hearings on reconsideration before the Department of Health.

32. See e.g., tit. 35 Pa. Stat. § 448.702(f)(2).

33. Official Code Ga. Ann. § 31–6–44; N.C. Gen. Stat. § 131E–188; S.C. Code § 44–7–210(D).

34. Official Code Ga. Ann. § 31–6–42; Iowa Code Ann. § 135.64; Me. Rev. Stat. Ann. tit.

22, § 309(2); N.C. Gen. Stat. § 131E–183; Pa. Stat. tit. 35, § 448.707; W.Va. Code § 16–2D–6.

35. 42 U.S.C.A. § 300n–1(c) (repealed 1986).

36. 42 C.F.R. § 123.412 (repealed).

37. See e.g., S.C. Code § 44–7–190.

38. Mich. Comp. Laws Ann. § 333.22231(1)(c), (2); W.Va. Code § 16–2D–9(c), (d).

39. Pa. Stat. tit. 35, § 448.702(e)(1).

40. Official Code Ga. Ann. § 31–6–44(i); Me. Rev. Stat. Ann. tit. 22, § 311; N.C. Gen. Stat. § 131E–188. But see N.H. Rev. Stat. Ann. § 151–C:10 (providing only for appeal by a person who had submitted an application for a CON).

41. See e.g., Pa. Stat. tit. 35, § 448.603(e), (f); W.Va. Code § 16–2D–13.

§ 1–21. Litigation Involving Certificate of Need Issues

Because certificate of need cases by definition involve interests of great value, denial of a CON frequently results in litigation. Because expansion of or offering a new health care service by an institution pursuant to a CON can often have serious effects on its competitors, grant of a CON also leads often to litigation. The volume of CON litigation has continued unabated over a decade since the demise of the federal program. From 1982 through mid–1988 case-law developments relating to CON were tracked by The Guide to Health Planning Law, published by the Western Center for Health Planning, an excellent source for those litigating in the area.

Early in the history of the CON program, cases involving the constitutionality of CON,[1] the relationship between the federal and state health planning programs,[2] and the relationship between health planning and the antitrust laws were common.[3] Today cases generally focus on statutory interpretation and issues of administrative law, though constitutional issues are still raised from time to time.[4] Among the issues most frequently litigated are:

a. whether a project or entity is subject to CON review;

b. whether criteria or health plans have been properly adopted and properly applied by the CON agency or council;

c. whether a CON decision is otherwise substantively correct;

d. whether administrative procedures were properly followed by the CON applicant or agency (including the taking of actions within prescribed time limits); and

e. whether a person has a right to or standing to seek judicial review or whether judicial review is otherwise appropriate.

Cases tend to turn on technicalities of state CON or administrative law and to be highly specific to the facts of the particular case. Seldom do they involve issues of broad applicability beyond the particular state, or even beyond the particular CON application at issue.

§ 1–21

1. See e.g., Montgomery County, Maryland v. Califano, 449 F.Supp. 1230 (D.Md.1978), affirmed 599 F.2d 1048 (4th Cir.1979); North Carolina ex rel. Morrow v. Califano, 445 F.Supp. 532 (E.D.N.C.1977), affirmed 435 U.S. 962, 98 S.Ct. 1597, 56 L.Ed.2d 54 (1978); Goodin v. Oklahoma ex rel. Okla. Welfare Comm., 436 F.Supp. 583 (W.D.Okla.1977); Merry Heart Nursing and Convalescent Home v. Dougherty, 330 A.2d 370 (N.J.Super. App.Div.1974); Attoma v. State Dep't of Social Welfare, 270 N.Y.S.2d 167 (N.Y.App.Div.1966).

2. See e.g., Harrisburg Hosp. v. Thornburgh, 616 F.Supp. 699 (M.D.Pa.1985) (NHRPDA did not supersede state planning law), affirmed without op. 791 F.2d 918 (3d Cir.1986) (NHRPDA did not supersede state planning law); Greater St. Louis Health Sys. Agency v. Teasdale, 506 F.Supp. 23 (E.D.Mo. 1980) (state CON law fatally inconsistent with federal law).

3. See e.g., North Carolina v. P.I.A. Asheville, Inc., 740 F.2d 274 (4th Cir.1984) (en banc), cert. denied 471 U.S. 1003, 105 S.Ct. 1865, 85 L.Ed.2d 159 (1985); Hospital Bldg. Co. v. Trustees of Rex Hosp., 691 F.2d 678 (4th Cir.1982), cert. denied 464 U.S. 890, 104 S.Ct. 231, 78 L.Ed.2d 224 (1983); 791 F.2d 288 (4th Cir.1986); Huron Valley Hosp. v. City of Pontiac, 650 F.Supp. 1325 (E.D.Mich.1986), affirmed 849 F.2d 262 (6th Cir.1988), cert. denied 488 U.S. 942, 109 S.Ct. 367, 102 L.Ed.2d 357 (1988).

4. See e.g. See St. Luke Hosp. v. Health Policy Bd. 913 S.W.2d 1 (Ky.App.1996); In re Regulations Governing the State Health Plan, 637 A.2d 1246 (N.J.1994); Gordon v. Allen, 482 S.E.2d 66 (Va.App.1997). One recent case held that it was unconstitutional for the state to require a CON for physician's offices that perform abortions in response to political pressure. Planned Parenthood of Greater Iowa v. Atchison, 126 F.3d 1042 (8th Cir.1997).

Health planning requires significant expertise in and knowledge of health care, economics, and local geography. Health planning decisions can have far reaching effects on the public. It is therefore appropriate that courts generally defer to the agency decision as long as it is supported by substantial evidence and not arbitrary or illegal.

Administrative procedure issues abound in CON cases. Several cases have held under specific state statutes that the CON agency loses jurisdiction to act on CON applications and must approve them automatically if action is not taken within statutory time limits.[5] CON denials have also been affirmed, however, where the applicant failed to appeal in a timely manner,[6] or failed to submit proper documentation with the application.[7] Courts will reject the CON agency decision under state administrative law where it is not supported by findings or reasons.[8]

Judicial review of administrative decisions involving CONs is refused where the decision below is not final,[9] or where the party seeking review had not exhausted remedies in the administrative proceedings below.[10] Cases frequently involve the standing of competitors to seek judicial review. While standing is usually recognized,[11] there are cases denying standing where the competitor was not a party below,[12] or where the competitor seeks review of a particular decision which state law grants competitors no standing to challenge, such as an agency decision finding a proposed expenditure non-reviewable[13] or delaying consideration of a proposal.[14] Competitors often have much at stake in CON decisions and should be afforded review, but it is unfair to both the applicant and the agency to permit judicial review at the instance of competitors who did not make their case before the agency below. Finally, standing is occasionally afforded others, such as residents,[15] to challenge CON decisions.

5. Laurel Wood v. Department of Human Resources, 452 S.E.2d 334 (N.C.App.1995); In re Good Samaritan Medical Center, 572 N.E.2d 849 (Ohio App.1991); HCA Crossroads Residential Centers, Inc. v. North Carolina Dep't. of Human Resources, 398 S.E.2d 466 (N.C. 1990); Health Services Management, Inc. v. Missouri Health Facilities Review Comm., 791 S.W.2d 732 (Mo.App.1990).

6. Gummels v. North Carolina Dept. of Human Resources, 392 S.E.2d 113 (N.C.App. 1990).

7. Humhosco, Inc. v. Department of Health and Rehab. Services, 561 So.2d 388 (Fla.App. 1990). The court also held that the agency was not estopped from raising this issue because it had failed to note the absence of the required documents in a required statement of omissions letter sent the applicant after the application was received. Id., 561 So.2d at 391–92.

8. In re Valley Hosp., 573 A.2d 203 (N.J. Super. App.Div.1990); Matter of Bloomingdale Convalescent Center, 558 A.2d 19 (N.J.Super. App.Div.1989).

9. Merle West Medical Center v. State Health Planning and Dev. Agency, 764 P.2d 613 (Or.App.1988) (decision that proposed bed conversion was subject to CON review not reviewable final order).

10. Community Psychiatric Centers v. North Carolina Dep't of Human Resources, 405 S.E.2d 769 (N.C.App.1991).

11. See e.g., St. Joseph Hosp. v. Department of Health, 887 P.2d 891 (Wash.1995); In re Valley Hosp., 573 A.2d 203 (N.J. Super. App.Div.1990).

12. See e.g., HCA Crossroads Residential Centers, Inc. v. North Carolina Dept. of Human Resources, 392 S.E.2d 398 (N.C.App. 1990).

13. Powers v. Commonwealth Dep't of Health, 570 A.2d 1350 (Pa.Comwlth.1990).

14. West County Care Center, Inc. v. Missouri Health Facilities Review Comm., 773 S.W.2d 474 (Mo.App.1989).

15. See e.g., Stewart v. Commonwealth, Dep't of Health, 593 A.2d 14 (Pa. Comwlth.1991).

Chapter 2

FEDERAL TAX EXEMPTION OF HEALTH CARE INSTITUTIONS

Table of Sections

Research References

Am Jur 2d, Corporations §§ 173–175
ALR Index: Exemptions and Exclusions; Taxation
ALR Digest: Taxes § 132
Am Jur Legal Forms 2d, Corporations § 74:880
20 Am Jur Trials 255, Preparing a Federal Income Tax Case for Trial; 13 Am Jur Trials
    1, Defending Federal Tax Evasion Cases

§ 2–1. Introduction

Tax exemption can refer both to exemption from state and local taxes (such as sales tax, real estate tax and state corporate income tax) and from the federal corporate income tax. Requirements for exemption from state and local taxes vary considerably among the states. Cases reviewing tax exemption under state or local law are cited in this section to the extent they are relevant to policy issues for federal tax exemption.

Although a great range of organizations qualify for tax-exempt status under one of the more than twenty major subsections of section § 501(c), the most desirable of the categories is the § 501(c)(3) status because it alone allows contributions to the exempt organization to be tax deductible to the donor. Tax-exempt status under § 501(c)(3) may also qualify the organization for other important benefits, such as the ability to issue tax-exempt bonds.

Tax exemption is now commonly viewed as a public subsidy to the exempt organization, especially when "revenue enhancement" is a government priority. One study estimates the value of exemption from the federal corporate income tax for hospitals at $1.6 billion and the full federal subsidy, including the impact of the deductibility of contributions, at over $4 billion.[1] This view of tax exemption as subsidy raises two questions: Does the benefit to the public in general, not to the hospital, of tax exemption and the nonprofit corporate structure offset the loss of revenue? Is the exemption fair to the exempt organization's competitors? The literature on the impact and value of the nonprofit form of organization[2] and the tax exemption for health care institutions[3] is abundant and growing.

Reflecting increased scrutiny of tax exemption for hospitals, the Internal Revenue Service has adopted a more aggressive posture toward enforcement of the standards of tax exemption. The Internal Revenue Service and the Department of Health and Human Services now also coordinate enforcement efforts relating to patient dumping and fraud and abuse.[4]

The following sections address several major legal issues concerning the tax exemption of health care entities.[5] The first focuses on the basic require-

§ 2–1

1. John Copeland and Gabriel Rudney, Federal Tax Subsidies for Not–for–Profit Hospitals, Tax Notes, 3/26/90 p. 1559. See also, Margaret A. Potter, Taxation of Nonprofit Hospitals: A Cost Impact Model, 37 Hospital & Health Services Administration 89 (1992), for a computerized model that analyzes the potential tax liability of a tax-exempt hospital.

2. See e.g., Nina J. Crimm, An Explanation of the Federal Income Tax Exemption for Charitable Organizations, 50 Fla. L. Rev. 419 (1998); Mark A. Hall and John D. Colombo, the Donative Theory of the Charitable Tax Exemption, 1991 Ohio St. L. J. 1379; Henry Hansmann, The Role of Nonprofit Enterprise 89 Yale L.J. 835 (1980); Henry Hansmann, The Rationale for Exempting Nonprofit Organizations from Corporate Income Taxation, 91 Yale L.J. 54 (1981); Evelyn Brody, Of Sovereignty and Subsidy: Conceptualizing the Charity Tax Exemption, 23 J. Corp. L. 585 (1998).

3. See e.g., Institute of Medicine, National Academy of Sciences, For–Profit Enterprise in Health Care (1986); Robert C. Clark, Does the Nonprofit Form Fit the Hospital Industry? 93

Harv.L.Rev. 1416 (1980); Etzioni and Doty, Profit in Not–for–Profit Corporations: The Example of Health Care, 91 Political Science Quarterly 433 (1976); In Sickness and In Health (J. Seay and B. Vladeck, eds. 1988); David Falcone and David G. Warren, The Shadow Price of Pluralism: The Use of Tax Expenditures to Subsidize Hospital Care in the United States, 13 J. Health Policy, Politics and Law 735 (1988); Douglas M. Mancino, Income Tax Exemption of the Contemporary Nonprofit Hospital, 32 St. Louis U. L. J. 1015 (1988); Mark A. Hall and John D. Colombo, The Charitable Status of Nonprofit Hospitals: Toward a Donative Theory of Tax Exemption, 66 Wash. L. Rev. 307 (1991).

4. General Couns. Mem. 39862 (Dec. 4, 1991); IRS Audit Guidelines for Exempt Organizations, Department of Treasury, Internal Revenue Service § 331.1.

5. Tax-exempt health care organizations also are prohibited from engaging in lobbying, to any substantial degree, as are all federally tax-exempt organizations. Treas. Reg. § 1.501(c)(3)–1(b)(3); § 1.501(c)(3)–1(c)(3); § 1.501(c)(3)–1(d)(2). See generally, Laura

ments for tax-exempt status, including the requirement of charity care. The next five sections focus on issues relating to the distribution of benefits from transactions. The last sections review tax-exempt issues for particular structures for health care delivery.[6]

A. TAX–EXEMPT PURPOSES

§ 2–2. Organizational   and   Operational   Tests   Under § 501(c)(3)

Section 501(c)(3) of the Internal Revenue Code provides for tax exemption for corporations that are "organized and operated exclusively for religious, charitable, scientific ... or educational purposes." In order to qualify for § 501(c)(3) status, the entity must meet an "organizational test" as well as an "operational test."[1] The organizational test under § 501(c)(3) requires that the organization's articles of incorporation specify that the organization is limited to exempt purposes.[2] The articles also must specify that the assets of the exempt organization will be distributed in a particular manner upon dissolution.[3] The operational test requires that the entity be operated "primarily" for exempt purposes.[4] The operational test also prohibits distribution of earnings to private shareholders or individuals.[5]

§ 2–3. Charitable Purposes

a. Federal

The most prominent general requirement for federal § 501(c)(3) tax-exempt status is that the health care institution serve charitable purposes.[1] The standards for the satisfaction of this requirement have evolved over time. Although there is some dispute over the matter and the Internal Revenue Service has not itself been consistent in its position, the promotion of health, standing alone, does not satisfy the requirements of charitable purpose for federal tax exemption.[2] In the last few years, the provision of uncompensated charity care has been a major focus of the inquiry concerning community benefit.

In 1956, the Internal Revenue Service issued a Revenue Ruling[3] that

Brown Chisolm, Politics and Charity: A Proposal for Peaceful Coexistence, 58 G.W. L. Rev. 308 (1990); Miriam Galston, Lobbying and the Public Interest: Rethinking the Internal Revenue Code's Treatment of Legislative Activities, 71 Tex. L. Rev. 1269 (1993); Developments in the Law—Political Activity of Nonprofit Corporations, 105 Harv. L. Rev. 1656 (1992).

6. Corporate and governance issues for nonprofit health care organizations are discussed in Chapter 5.

§ 2–2

1. Treas. Reg. § 1.501(c)(3)–1(a).

2. Treas. Reg. § 1.501(c)(3)–1(b). The regulation addresses specific provisions in detail.

3. Treas. Reg. § 1.501(c)(3)–1(b)(4).

4. Although the statute requires that the exempt organization be organized and operated

"exclusively" for exempt purposes, this requirement has been interpreted by the Service to require less than exclusive dedication to exempt purposes. Treas. Reg. § 1.501(c)(3)–1(c). See § 2–8.

5. Treas. Reg. § 1.501(c)(3)–1(c)(2). See discussion in § 2–5.

§ 2–3

1. Treas. Reg. § 1.501(c)(3)–1(d)(2).

2. See generally, John D. Colombo, Are Associations of Doctors Tax Exempt? Analyzing Inconsistencies in the Tax–Exemption of Health Care Providers, 9 Va. Tax. Rev. 469 (1990); Geisinger Health Plan v. Commissioner, 985 F.2d 1210 (3d Cir.1993).

3. A Revenue Ruling is the IRS Commissioner's view of the law concerning a particular issue. A Revenue Ruling may be given some

required a tax-exempt hospital to "be operated to the extent of its financial ability for those not able to pay for the services rendered."[4] In 1958, the Tax Court upheld denial of exempt status to a hospital that allocated between 2% and 5% of its revenue to indigent care.[5] In 1969, however, the Service issued a Revenue Ruling stating that "the promotion of health is considered to be a charitable purpose." An illustration included in this Revenue Ruling indicated that a hospital that operated an emergency room open to all regardless of ability to pay; that admitted all persons from the community who were able to pay; and that otherwise transferred indigent patients would satisfy the requirement of charity.[6] In *Simon v. Eastern Kentucky Welfare Rights Organization*,[7] the Supreme Court considered a suit challenging the 1969 Revenue Ruling, but held that the plaintiff organization lacked standing. As recently as 1983, a Revenue Ruling concluded that a hospital that transferred indigent patients and that did not operate an emergency room because the health planning agency had concluded that the service was not needed in the area satisfied the requirement of a charitable purpose.[8]

A focus on levels of charity care as a *quid pro quo* for the exempt status, as a matter of public policy making, has intensified in the last decade. In addition, the drive toward cost containment and reductions in government health care programs has increased the demand for uncompensated care and constrained a hospital's capacity for cost shifting. The emphasis of the Internal Revenue Service, in response to these factors, has changed considerably over that evident in the 1983 Revenue Ruling, although the 1969 and 1983 Revenue Rulings remain the foundation for the Service's inquiry into the level of charity care provided.

The Internal Revenue Manual, which provides instructions to IRS personnel conducting audits, directs the specialists to investigate the satisfaction by the hospital of the "community benefit" standard of § 501(c)(3) status. The Manual relies upon the 1969 Revenue Ruling to identify five criteria, including whether the hospital operates a full-time emergency room treating patients regardless of ability to pay and whether the hospital's non-emergency care services are open to everyone in the community who has the ability to

deference by the courts though not to the same degree as an administrative regulation. There is some variation among the circuits on this point, however. See e.g., Johnson City Medical Center v. U.S., 999 F.2d 973 (6th Cir.1993); Indiana National Corp. v. U.S. 980 F.2d 1098 (7th Cir.1992). Salomon, Inc. v. U.S., 976 F.2d 837 (2d Cir.1992); Corbin v. U.S., 760 F.2d 234 (8th Cir.1985); Eastern Kentucky Welfare Rights Organization v. Simon, 506 F.2d 1278 (D.C.Cir.1974). See also, Deborah A. Geier, Commentary: Textualism and Tax Cases, 66 Temple L. Rev. 445 (1993). A General Counsel Memorandum is an internal IRS memorandum explaining various IRS positions on the tax law. Some courts have accorded GCMs some deference, although it may be more accurate to describe that deference as a willingness to be persuaded by the Commissioner's legal argument. See e.g., Idaho First National Bank v. Commissioner, 997 F.2d 1285 (9th Cir.1993). A Private Letter Ruling is a written statement

issued by the IRS in response to a taxpayer's inquiry about the tax consequences of a specific transaction. As with any administrative agency, Internal Revenue Service positions and policies may or may not accurately state the law as viewed by a court. Court cases on the specific issues discussed in this chapter are infrequent, however.

4. It has been argued that the reference to the hospitals' financial ability to provide free care means that no minimum amount of uncompensated care is required. See e.g., Robert S. Bromberg, The Charitable Hospital, 20 Cath. U. 237 (1970).

5. Lorain Avenue Clinic v. Commissioner, 31 T.C. 141 (1958).

6. Rev. Rul. 69–545.

7. 426 U.S. 26, 96 S.Ct. 1917, 48 L.Ed.2d 450 (1976).

8. Rev. Rul. 83–157.

pay.[9] The Manual allows a hospital to operate without an emergency room under certain circumstances,[10] but directs the auditors to give "careful consideration" to other services and activities, including the level of charity care. In coordinating its activities with those of the Department of Health and Human Services, the Service's Manual describes the requirements of the Emergency Medical Treatment and Labor Act[11] and directs the specialist to examine reports filed, records maintained and actions taken under the requirements of that Act. The Manual also requires the examiner to determine whether the proportion of the hospital's patient population that receives Medicaid reflects the proportion of Medicaid recipients in the community. Even with the detail developed by the Service in its instructions to specialists performing hospital audits, the standards and judgment as to whether the hospital satisfies the community benefit standard are not terribly precise.[12]

There have been many proposals for change in federal law relating to charity care as a condition of tax exemption. For example, the General Accounting Office recommended that Congress consider linking tax exemption to a certain level of care provided to Medicaid patients, free care provided to the poor and efforts to improve the health status of underserved portions of the community. The report studied hospitals in California, Florida, Iowa, Michigan and New York and concluded that many hospitals enjoyed tax benefits out of proportion to the amount of charity care they provided.[13] Associations of nonprofit hospitals responded to the report challenging the data on which it was based.[14]

b. State Tax Exemption

The states also have become more aggressive in scrutinizing exemptions from state real estate and sales taxes in relation to the provision of charity care.[15] In fact, thus far, the most significant impact of the change in the policy focus analysis of the relation of tax exemption and charity care has come on the state level.

The leading case in the area of state tax exemption is *Utah County v. Intermountain Health Care, Inc.*,[16] in which the Utah Supreme Court declared tax exemption of the hospital to be unconstitutional under the Utah Constitution. The Utah Constitution allowed tax exemption only if the organization

---

9. The other criteria require the hospital to have a governing board composed of active members who are "civic leaders" rather than administrators and doctors; to maintain corporate separateness if the hospital is part of a multi-entity system; and to make admission to the medical staff open to all qualified physicians in the area, consistent with the size and nature of the facilities. Internal Revenue Manual 7(10)69, HB 333.1(1)(c).

10. Internal Revenue Manual 7(10) 69, HB 333.1(4).

11. See §§ 10–2 through 10–12.

12. See Geisinger Health Plan v. Commissioner, 985 F.2d 1210, 1217 (3d Cir.1993).

13. General Accounting Office, Rep., Nonprofit Hospitals: Better Standards Needed for the Exemption GAO/HRD–90–84 (May 1990). See also, Alice A. Noble et al., Charitable Hos-

pital Accountability: A Review and Analysis of Legal and Policy Initiatives, 26 J.L. Med. & Ethics 116 (1998).

14. See e.g., Catholic Hospitals Challenge GAO Report on Tax–Exempt Hospitals, 90 Tax Notes Today 159–7 (9/1/90).

15. See e.g., Atrium Village, Inc. v. Board of Review, 417 N.W.2d 70 (Iowa 1987); Care Initiatives v. Board of Review, 500 N.W.2d 14 (Iowa 1993); Rideout Hospital Foundation, Inc. v. County of Yuba, 10 Cal.Rptr.2d 141 (Cal. App.1992); Board of Supervisors v. Group Health Association, 414 S.E.2d 602 (Va.1992).

16. 709 P.2d 265 (Utah 1985). See also, Allentown Hospital–Lehigh Valley Hospital Center v. Board of Assessment Appeals, 611 A.2d 793 (Pa.Cmwlth.1992). But see, Callaway Community Hospital Association v. Craighead, 759 S.W.2d 253 (Mo.App.1988).

was a charitable organization. The majority and dissenting opinions in this case cover the waterfront of the dispute over how to measure charity care and how much charity care is required, as well as arguments over the general structure and behavior of nonprofit hospitals. The majority concluded that the amount of charity care provided was inadequate to justify exemption from state taxation. Subsequent to the case, the voters in Utah rejected a constitutional amendment that would bar taxation of hospitals, and the hospital agreed to expand its charitable services to an amount in excess of the taxes it would otherwise owe in order to retain its exempt status.[17]

Similar disputes have occurred in other states and cities, as to local taxes, as well.[18] For example, hospitals in Pennsylvania have been particularly embattled, with at least one hospital agreeing to pay several million dollars in lieu of taxes.[19]

§ 2–4. Private Inurement

Section 501(c)(3) provides that "no part of the net income of the exempt organization shall [inure] to the benefit of any shareholder or private individual." The prohibition against private inurement requires that net earnings of a not-for-profit organization are dedicated to the organization's exempt purposes and are not distributed to "insiders" such as directors, officers, managers or those who have a close relationship to the organization.[1] Tax-exempt health care organizations must maintain an excess of revenue over expenses in order to stay in operation, but instead of distributing this margin among shareholders or owners, the tax-exempt organization must use the retained earnings to further exempt purposes. Violation of the inurement prohibition may result in either intermediate sanctions under § 4958 of the Internal Revenue Code[2] or revocation of the hospital's exemption.[3]

In the past, the Internal Revenue Service has taken the position that physicians, whether employees or simply members of the hospital medical staff, "enjoy a close professional working relationship with the tax-exempt hospital and, therefore," have a personal and private interest in the activities of the hospital of the sort that are subject to the inurement prohibition. In Revenue Ruling 97–21, however, the IRS acknowledged that physicians are not necessarily insiders or disqualified persons for purposes of inurement

---

17. As reported in Health Lawyers News Report, May 1988 at 4.

18. For a review of initiatives in several states, see Alice A. Noble, et al., Charitable Hospital Accountability: A Review and Analysis of Legal and Policy Issues, 26 J.L. Med. & Ethics 116 (1998).

19. Leigh Page, Pennsylvania Hospitals Facing Fight Over Tax Exempt Status, 34 American Medical News 1 (July 22, 1991), describing agreement by hospital to pay $11 million over 10 years in lieu of city taxes. See also, G. J. Simon, Jr., Non–Profit Hospital Tax Exemptions: Where Did They Come From and Where Are They Going?, 31 Duq. L. Rev. 343 (1993), including a review of Pennsylvania law on nonprofit hospitals; Developments in the Law–Nonprofit Corporations, 105 Harvard L.

Rev. 1612 (1992), analyzing actions by local governments regarding nonprofit status.

§ 2–4

1. See, United Cancer Council v. Commissioner, 165 F.3d 1173 (7th Cir.1999), in which the 7th Circuit narrowed the scope of the insider concept for purposes of the private inurement doctrine.

2. See § 2–6.

3. The IRS revoked tax-exempt status, for example, in a case in which it found the price set for the sale of a tax-exempt hospital was not fair market value for that type of provider. The Tax Court opinion provides a detailed analysis of the transaction. Anclote v. Commissioner of Internal Revenue, T.C. Memo. 1998-273 (1998), aff'd 190 F.3d 541 (11th Cir. 1999).

solely by virtue of being recruited or holding medical staff membership in an exempt hospital.[4] The determination is to be made on a case-by-case basis. If the physician is not deemed to be an insider, physician compensation packages, recruitment subsidies and physician-hospital joint ventures are still subject to scrutiny under the private benefit proscription.[5]

It is the position of the Internal Revenue Service that there is no de minimis exception to the private inurement doctrine.[6] The prohibition against private inurement, therefore, extends to inurement that is merely incidental.

§ 2–5.   Private Benefit

The Internal Revenue Service also applies a private benefit restriction on the activities of § 501(c)(3) providers. Although private inurement and private benefit are quite similar, the Service has distinguished the two. The constraint on private benefit is not limited to insiders, as in the private inurement doctrine. The private benefit doctrine applies to any individual. In addition, while private inurement is not allowed, tax-exempt organizations may provide benefits to private individuals as long as such benefits are incidental. Private benefit is allowed to occur and is tolerated without penalty as long as the amount is insubstantial[1] and the benefit is "a necessary concomitant of the activity which benefits the public at large; in other words, the benefit cannot be achieved without necessarily benefiting certain private individuals."[2] The Service, for example, consistently has recognized that tax-exempt hospitals must offer competitive compensation in recruiting management and medical personnel in order to achieve their exempt purposes.[3] However, the IRS and the courts have become much more aggressive in examining recruitment and compensation packages.[4]

§ 2–6.   Excess Benefit

The 1996 Taxpayer Bill of Rights added a provision to the Internal Revenue Code that permits the IRS to impose intermediate sanctions on individuals who engage in excess benefit transactions. Under § 4958 of the Internal Revenue Code, excess benefit transactions between tax-exempt organizations and disqualified persons are subject to a two-tier penalty tax. An excess benefit transaction is defined in the Code as any transaction in which an economic benefit provided by a tax-exempt organization directly or indirectly to, or for the use of, any disqualified person exceeds the value of consideration received by the organization in exchange for the benefit.[1] Excess benefit transactions include transactions involving payment of unreasonable compensation, non-fair market value transactions, as well as revenue-sharing

4. See § 2–7.

5. See § 2–5.

6. See e.g., General Couns. Mem. 35855 (June 21, 1974); General Couns. Mem. 39862 (Dec. 2, 1991).

§ 2–5

1. See e.g., General Couns. Mem. 39862 (Dec. 2, 1991).

2. General Couns. Mem. 37789 (Dec. 18, 1978).

3. See e.g., General Couns. Mem. 35268 (March 14, 1973); General Couns. Mem. 37789

(Dec. 18, 1978); General Couns. Mem. 39798 (April 24, 1986). But see, General Couns. Mem. 39862 (Dec. 2, 1991), in which hospital arguments that prohibition of sales of stream of income would hamper the hospital's ability to compete for physicians were rejected. See also, Chapter 15 on fraud and abuse concerns.

4. See § 2–7 and 2–8.

§ 2–6

1. 26 U.S.C.A. § 4958(c)(1)(A).

arrangements under which a disqualified person receives payment based on the exempt organization's income. The excess benefit subject to tax under § 4958 is generally the excess of the value of the benefit provided to the disqualified person over the value of goods or services rendered.

A disqualified person, defined as a person who is in a position to exercise substantial influence over the organization, is subject to a first-tier tax of 25% of the excess benefit.[2] An organization manager, typically a trustee, director or officer of the organization, is subject to a first-tier tax equal to 10% of the excess benefit if he knowingly participates in the excess benefit transaction.[3] A 200% excise tax is imposed on a disqualified person if there is no correction of the excess benefit transaction within a specified period of time.[4]

The proposed regulations implementing § 4958 of the Internal Revenue Code provide that a compensation arrangement is presumed to be reasonable, and a transfer of property, a right to use property, or any other benefit or privilege is presumed to be at fair market value if three criteria are satisfied.[5] First, the arrangement must be approved by a board of directors or trustees that was composed entirely of individuals unrelated to, and not subject to the control of, the disqualified person involved in the arrangement. Second, the board must have obtained and relied upon appropriate data as to comparability. And third, the board must have adequately documented the basis for its determination. If these three criteria are satisfied, penalty excise taxes can only be imposed if the IRS develops sufficient contrary evidence to rebut the probative value of the evidence put forth by the parties to the transaction.[6]

Intermediate sanctions may be imposed by the IRS in lieu of, or in addition to, revocation of an organization's tax-exempt status.[7] In general, intermediate sanctions are the sole sanction to be imposed if the excess benefit transactions do not rise to the level that warrants revocation of tax-exempt status. In practice, revocation of tax-exempt status, with or without the imposition of excise taxes, is an appropriate sanction only when the organization no longer operates as a charitable organization under § 501(c)(3).[8]

Intermediate sanctions, which provide an alternative to revocation of exemption for violations of § 501(c)(3)'s prohibition against private inurement, are viewed as the most significant development in the law of tax-exempt organizations in 30 years. Section 4958 of the Internal Revenue Code is likely to transform the application of the private inurement and private benefit doctrines, as well as change the manner in which tax-exempt healthcare organizations approach business dealings with physicians.

§ 2–7. Physician Recruitment

In 1997, the Internal Revenue Service released final Physician Recruitment Guidelines in Revenue Ruling 97–21. This Ruling is the final version of

---

2. 26 U.S.C.A. § 4958(a)(1).

3. 26 U.S.C.A. § 4958(a)(2).

4. 26 U.S.C.A. § 4958(b).

5. 63 Fed. Reg. 41486, 41492 (Aug. 4, 1998).

6. Id.

7. H. Rep. 104–506, 104th Congress, 2d sess. (1996).

8. Id. at 59. See Carolyn D. Wright, First Intermediate Sanctions Petitions Now Available, Tax Notes Today, Dec. 3, 1999, reporting on IRS actions.

a proposed ruling, Announcement 95–25, which itself broadened the scope of the Hospital Physician Recruitment Guidelines developed in connection with the IRS' 1994 closing agreement with tax-exempt Hermann Hospital.[1] Revenue Ruling 97–21 provides exempt hospital governing boards with precedential guidance as to whether the hospital violates the requirements for exemption under § 501(c)(3) upon providing certain types of physician recruitment incentives.

Unlike the proposed revenue ruling, Rev. Rul. 97–21 distinguishes between a tax-exempt hospital recruiting a physician to its medical staff to perform services for or on behalf of the hospital, and one recruiting a physician to provide services to the community, but not necessarily for or on behalf of the hospital. If the hospital recruits a physician to its medical staff, the operational test is satisfied upon the hospital's showing that the physician is compensated reasonably for the services provided. In contrast, if the physician is being recruited to provide services in the community, the operational test is satisfied if (1) the recruitment furthers the hospital's exempt purposes, (2) the recruitment does not result in private inurement, (3) the hospital does not engage in any substantial activity that causes it to be operated for the benefit of a private interest, or (4) the hospital refrains from engaging in unlawful activities. The Final Ruling suggests that the IRS will not approve cross-town recruiting where the hospital is recruiting the physician as a source of referrals.

In Rev. Rul. 97–21, the IRS seems to suggest that exempt hospitals may provide significant recruitment incentives, as long as the incentives are reasonably related to the hospital's exempt purpose, the amount is reasonable, and any private benefit to the physician is outweighed by the public purpose served. In addition, Rev. Rul. 97–21 indicates that physician compensation packages must be in writing, negotiated at arms' length, and in conformity with guidelines established by the exempt hospital's board of directors.

Compensation packages that include signing bonuses, professional liability insurance reimbursement, mortgage guaranty, moving expenses, subsidized office space for a limited time, start-up financial assistance and net income guarantees are permissible under the Ruling. Commentators suggest that the ruling should not be read as prohibiting arrangements other than those listed. Nor does it necessarily indicate that the incentives listed will always be proper or that they are unlimited in amount or duration.[2]

While the five scenarios examined in Revenue Ruling 97–21 are helpful, like any case illustration their usefulness is limited. If an exempt hospital's situation is not the mirror image of one of the scenarios enumerated in the Ruling, the hospital's governing board must use their judgment in determining whether a recruitment incentive is reasonable.

§ 2–7

1. See generally, Gerald M. Griffith, IRS Guidance on Physician Recruitment: From the Seeds of Hermann Hospital to the Proposed and Final Rulings and Beyond, 30 J. Health & Hosp. L. 75 (1997); Bruce Shih and Daniel Settlemayer, IRS Revenue Ruling Released on Physician Recruitment: Still Plenty of Leeway, 9 Health Lawyer 1 (1997).

2. *See* Doris L. Martin, *IRS Issues Revenue Ruling on Physician Recruitment by Hospitals*, 4 N.Y. Health L. Update 1 (1997).

Rev. Rul. 97–21 does not directly address physician retention incentives. Therefore, these incentives should be scrutinized under the existing standards for physician compensation packages.[3]

§ 2–8. Physician Compensation

The Service has addressed the boundaries of acceptable compensation packages. In so doing, the Service has set some general standards, although the ultimate determination of excess compensation depends on the circumstances of the particular case.[1] Generally, compensation must relate directly to the actual benefit created by the compensation package for the tax-exempt hospital in relation to its exempt purpose. The compensation must also be reasonable.[2] Compensation is reasonable if it is "such [an] amount as would ordinarily be paid for like services by like enterprises under like circumstances."[3]

Physicians can be, but are not necessarily, "disqualified persons" under Internal Revenue Code § 4958, which imposes excise taxes on excess benefit transactions.[4] If a physician is deemed to be a disqualified person, however, the compensation is presumed to be reasonable if the requirements enumerated in the section are satisfied. If the requirements are not satisfied, or if the IRS can successfully rebut the presumption, an excise tax of 25% of the excess benefit will be imposed on the physician.[5]

Gross revenue compensation arrangements are permissible only if adequate safeguards against private inurement are in place.[6] Generally, the arrangement must contain contractual limits[7], and the individual's entire compensation package, including the revenue-based payments, must represent reasonable compensation for the services actually performed.[8] In addition, the revenue-sharing plan must not act as a profit-sharing device.[9] The package must divide the risk of loss and the potential for gains in a way that does not favor the physician or place greater risk on the exempt hospital.[10] And finally, the arrangement must in some way promote the exempt purpose of the hospital and not merely provide an economic incentive for the physician.[11]

In an unreleased private letter ruling, the IRS recently ruled that a gainsharing arrangement under which a hospital financially rewarded physicians who improved services and reduced costs would not adversely affect the hospital's exempt status under § 501(c)(3).[12] The hospital and a physician group wanted to improve clinical outcomes and the quality of care while reducing costs. Savings from reduced costs were to be used to fund an incentive award pool, and awards to physicians were to be consistent with fair

---

3. *See* § 2–8.

§ 2–8

1. Treas. Reg. § 1.513–1.
2. Treas. Reg. § 1.513–1(d)(2).
3. Treas. Reg. § 1.162–7(b)(3).
4. *See* § 2–6.
5. *See* § 2–6.
6. IRS Continuing Profession Education Exempt Organization Teacher and Instruction Program Textbook, 1995 Edition (August 1994) [hereinafter IRS EO Program Textbook].

7. IRS EO Program Textbook, *supra* note 4.
8. Rev. Rul 69–383, 1969–2 C.B. 113; General Couns. Mem. 39,862 (Dec. 2, 1991).
9. See § 2–8.
10. IRS EO Program Textbook, supra note 4.
11. Id.
12. *IRS Okays Gainsharing Arrangement in Unreleased Letter Ruling*, 1999 Tax Notes Today 128–39.

market value.[13] The IRS concluded that the program would not affect the hospital's § 501(c)(3) status because the incentive pool was not to be funded unless the physician group provided quality care to the satisfaction of patients and the hospital realized "tangible costs savings."

§ 2–9. Unrelated Business Taxable Income

An exempt hospital may engage in business ventures that are not directly related to the exempt purposes of the organization provided that the hospital is operated primarily for exempt purposes, does not violate the inurement proscription and does not jeopardize its ability to achieve its exempt purposes. Income realized from such unrelated business endeavors is taxable, however.

An "unrelated trade or business" is that which is regularly carried on and "not substantially related to the exercise of the organization of its charitable purpose or function."[1] The regulations provide that a trade or business is related to the organization's exempt purpose and not taxable if it has a substantial "causal relationship to the achievement of exempt purposes (other than through the production of income)" and "contributes importantly to the accomplishment of the exempt purposes of an organization."[2] The production of income, even if this revenue is devoted entirely to the exempt purpose, does not itself satisfy the requirement of a substantial relationship.[3]

The Service has justified the unrelated business income tax as a means of preventing unfair competition between tax-exempt and for-profit providers.[4] Thus, part of the analysis of whether income from a business venture is unrelated business taxable income focuses on the impact of the activity on competitors by inquiring whether the activity at issue is one generally offered by commercial enterprise. The categorization of a business activity of an exempt organization as related or unrelated to the exempt purpose of the organization follows very few bright-line rules. Approaches to the question of exempt purposes within the context of unrelated business income differ substantially from those used in the context of the qualification of an entity for exempt status itself. This is most apparent in the treatment of alternative delivery systems.[5]

An issue of unrelated business income often arises when hospitals sell services, which they routinely provided to their own patients or employees,[6] to others outside those groups. For example, hospital pharmacies could sell pharmaceuticals to the general public.[7] These efforts may be commendable uses of excess capacity and may produce income that would be used to

13. Id.

§ 2–9

1. Treas.Reg. § 1.513–1.

2. Treas.Reg. § 1.513–1(d)(2).

3. Treas.Reg. § 1.513–1(d)(2).

4. Treas. Reg. § 1–513–1(b). See also, Private Letter Rul. 8125007.

5. See §§ 2–10 through 2–12.

6. Services provided for the convenience of patients or employees do not produce unrelated business taxable income. See e.g., Rev. Rul. 69–267 and 69–268.

7. See e.g., Rev. Rul. 68–374, 1968–1 C.B. 242; 68–375, 1968–2 C.B. 245; 68–376, 1968–2 C.B. 246; 85–110, 1985–2 C.B. 166; Carle Foundation v. United States, 611 F.2d 1192 (7th Cir.1979), cert. denied, 449 U.S. 824, 101 S.Ct. 85, 66 L.Ed.2d 27 (1980); Hi–Plains Hospital v. United States, 670 F.2d 528 (5th Cir.1982), cited in Internal Revenue Manual 333.8(3). The Manual also addresses medical research, laundry services, and medical office buildings. Internal Revenue Manual 7(10)69, HB 333.8(6), (7) and (8).

accomplish the hospital's exempt purposes. Income produced through such efforts, however, is subject to taxation as unrelated business income unless it falls within established exceptions.[8]

Income produced by the provision of laboratory services to persons other than the hospital's patients is ordinarily taxable; however, if the services provided are highly sophisticated and not offered by commercial laboratories in the area, the sale of services satisfies a community need. Income is not taxable under those circumstances. If the services enable the hospital to provide medical education and training, they may relate substantially to one of the hospital's exempt purposes.[9] If the sale of services meets either of these criteria and is produced in a volume related to these criteria, income will not be taxable.[10]

The regulations on unrelated business activities also limit the amount of such activity that the exempt organization may undertake in relation to its exempt activities. There is no specific amount of unrelated business that is acceptable, though the amount must be insubstantial in relation to the activities of the organization.[11] The indeterminate limit on the volume of unrelated business activities has been a part of the motivation behind corporate reorganization in health care, through which unrelated business activities can be separately incorporated.[12]

B. JOINT VENTURES

§ 2–10. Physician–Hospital Joint Ventures

The inurement principle also applies to physician-hospital joint ventures.[1] In a 1991 General Counsel Memorandum, which revoked and reversed the Service's position in three earlier private letter rulings, the Service concluded that three joint ventures violated the proscription against private inurement.[2] Each of the joint ventures involved the sale of a "stream of income" from a hospital service department, such as outpatient surgery or obstetrics/gynecology, to a separate partnership or corporation in which both the hospital and physician members of the hospital's medical staff had ownership interests. The partnership or corporation provided no services to the hospital itself.

The Service examined the flow of income to the physician joint venturers in relation to the benefit received by the hospital in furtherance of its exempt purposes. The Service concluded that there was little relation between the

---

8. There are also several statutory exceptions to the unrelated business income tax. These include, for example, some services provided to small hospitals (I.R.C. § 501(e) and 513(e)) and passive income, such as interest and dividends (I.R.C. § 512(b)). See Joseph C. Mandarino, Recent Changes to The Internal Revenue Code May Require Tax–Exempt Hospitals to Restructure Ownership of Certain Activities, 7 Annals Health L. 159 (1998).

9. See e.g., St. Luke's Hospital of Kansas City v. United States, 494 F.Supp. 85 (W.D.Mo. 1980).

10. See e.g., Private Letter Ruling 8125007. See also, Revenue Rulings 68–376; 85–109; 85–

110, cited in the Internal Revenue Manual 7(10)69, HB 333.8(2).

11. Treas. Reg. § 1.501(c)(3)–1(b)(1)(iii); § 1.501(c)(3)–1(c)(1); § 1.501(c)(3)–1(e).

12. See generally, General Couns. Mem. 39598 (Dec. 8, 1986).

§ 2–10

1. The Manual includes a section specifically addressing joint ventures. Internal Revenue Manual 7(10)69, HB 333.4.

2. General Couns. Mem. 39862 (Dec. 2, 1991).

joint venture and the hospital's exempt purpose. The Service believed that the hospitals developed the joint venture as a way of securing admissions from the physician participants and as a way of pre-empting competition. Although the G.C.M. distinguishes permissible incentive compensation plans,[3] it concluded that the sale of stream of income is *"per se "*inurement.

In addition to examining whether the joint venture resulted in the inurement of net earnings to "insiders," the Service considered whether the private benefit created on behalf of the physician participants violated the requirement that the hospital operate exclusively for exempt purposes. The G.C.M. distinguished the problem of private benefit from that of inurement by identifying the scope of the private-benefit analysis as including persons who may not qualify as insiders under the standards for private inurement and by allowing private benefit that is incidental in amount. In contrast, any amount of private inurement results in immediate sanctions[4] or revocation of the exemption. The analysis for private benefit to individuals is otherwise comparable to that for inurement. In fact, it is difficult to distinguish the two requirements. Any private benefit created in the course of the operation of the exempt institution must be incidental to the achievement of exempt purposes in the sense that the community benefit is not attainable without benefitting private individuals. The private benefit must also be insubstantial in comparison to the public benefit realized through the specific transaction or agreement.[5] In regard to the joint ventures described above, the Service concluded that they violated the prohibition against private benefit because the value realized by the physician participants greatly outweighed any benefit to the public. The Service rejected obtaining admissions and avoiding competition as beneficial to the public.[6] Community benefits do include projections of expansion of health care resources; the addition of new providers; cost containment; and improved treatment.[7]

A third issue that relates to the exempt purpose of the hospital is the requirement that the joint venture not jeopardize the hospital's ability to accomplish its purpose. The Service has abandoned its position that the exempt organization may not participate as a general partner in a limited partnership. Instead, the partnership is examined for its satisfaction of charitable purpose, for the benefit to non-exempt partners and for adequate protection against financial loss to the exempt organization.[8] An agreement may jeopardize the hospital's ability to accomplish its exempt purpose if it limits the hospital's decisionmaking authority in a manner inconsistent with the accomplishment of the exempt purpose or presents an unacceptable financial risk.[9]

3. Citing General Couns. Mem. 39674 (June 17, 1987).

4. See §§ 2–4 and 2–5.

5. Citing General Couns. Mem. 37789 (Dec. 18, 1978).

6. The Service also specifically modified an earlier G.C.M. that suggested that obtaining referrals related to an exempt hospital's achievement of exempt purposes. See General Couns. Mem. 39732 (May 27, 1988).

7. See e.g., Private Letter Ruling 9323030 (June 11, 1993), concluding that participation

in general partnership with for-profit corporation to construct and operate rehabilitation center satisfied exempt purposes in satisfying a quantified community need for rehabilitation services. The Service reserved comment on whether participation by physicians in the joint venture would affect its exempt status.

8. See generally, General Couns. Mem. 39862 (Dec. 2, 1991).

9. See e.g., Private Letter Rul. 9024085 (June 15, 1990); Private Letter Rul. 9308034 (February 26, 1993); Private Letter Rul. 9323030 (June 11, 1993).

C. TAX EXEMPTION OF ALTERNATIVE DELIVERY SYSTEMS

§ 2–11. Whole Hospital Joint Ventures

Tax-exempt organizations may engage in business activities jointly with for-profit organizations. Section 501(c)(3) requires that the exempt entity be organized and operated "exclusively" for exempt purposes, but the regulations interpret that standard as requiring the exempt organization engage "primarily in activities that accomplish one or more . . . exempt purposes" and further state that the exempt organization violates this standard if "more than an insubstantial" amount of its activities are not in furtherance of exempt purposes.[1] In addition, § 501(c)(3) requires that the exempt entity comply with the private inurement and private benefit doctrines discussed above.

As tax-exempt hospital systems seek to contain costs and compete for managed care contracts, whole hospital joint ventures between exempt hospitals and for-profit hospital corporations are growing steadily. As a result of this growth, the IRS released Revenue Ruling 98–15, which is designed to give the health care industry guidance on tax exemption issues associated with the formation of joint ventures between tax-exempt hospitals and for-profit companies.

In the Revenue Ruling, the IRS analyzes two fact situations involving the contribution of all of an exempt organization's operating assets to a limited liability company (LLC) jointly owned by the contributing exempt organization and a for-profit company. In the Ruling, the IRS confirms the previous position that allows a § 501(c)(3) organization to form and participate in a partnership and retain its exempt status if the partnership furthers a charitable purpose, and the partnership arrangement permits the exempt organization to act exclusively in furtherance of its exempt purpose and only incidentally for the benefit of the for-profit partner.

Revenue Ruling 98–15 also emphasizes the IRS's position that the tax-exempt entity must retain control over the joint venture. Characteristics of a whole hospital joint venture which indicate inadequate control include fifty percent board governance, management by a subsidiary of the for-profit partner, a management company's unilateral right to renew the contract, and broad powers not reserved by the governing board.

The application of Revenue Ruling 98–15 is limited to the specific fact situations addressed. As such, it provides a safe harbor for an exempt organization that structures its whole hospital joint ventures in a manner identical to the approved scenario. An exempt organization must use its judgment when deciding whether arrangements falling outside of the Ruling will jeopardize their exempt status. Although Revenue Ruling 98–15 only discusses the whole hospital joint venture, health care organizations can use the Ruling for general guidance in structuring other types of joint ventures.[2]

---

§ 2–11

1. 26C.F.R. § 1.501(c)(3)–1(c).

2. Bruce Shih and Daniel Settlemayer, Joint Ventures Rev. Rul. 98–15: Don't Apply Blindly, 10 Health Lawyer 8 (1998).

§ 2–12. Structure of Alternative Delivery Systems

Managed care became a key concept of health care delivery in the cost-conscious 1980s and gained momentum in the 1990s. It has taken on a wide variety of forms and organizations, all intended to manage consumer use of health care services. Managed care continues to dominate as a method of cost control, and the forms and structure of managed care programs continue to develop. Among the most prominent players in managed care programs are the alternative delivery systems (ADS). The most familiar of these are health maintenance organizations (HMOs), independent practice associations (IPAs), and preferred provider organizations (PPOs), although the organization of ADS is not at all static and new permutations appear constantly. In addition, managed care entities have played a large role in the development of integrated delivery systems.

HMOs, IPAs and PPOs have all attempted to achieve tax exempt status under § 501(c)(3). These organizations may be tax exempt under other sections of § 501(c).[1] Still, the § 501(c)(3) status is preferable for the same reasons that hospitals protect their § 501(c)(3) status.

The structures of HMOs, IPAs and PPOs are detailed elsewhere in this text.[2] Some structural characteristics, however, are particularly important for their qualification for § 501(c)(3) status.

An HMO delivers both office-based primary care and hospital-based acute care to its subscribers who pay a predetermined, per capita premium regardless of the amount or cost of medical services actually used. HMOs usually contract with health care facilities for institution-based health care, such as inpatient hospital services for their members, and pay the hospitals on a capitation, per diem or fee-for-service basis. HMOs either directly provide primary care services through employee physicians or contract with individual physicians or physician associations. HMOs generally fit within three models. In the staff model, physicians are direct employees of the HMO. In the group model, physicians are members of a partnership or corporation that contracts with the HMO to provide services to subscribers on a capitation basis. The physicians' partnership or corporation generally pays its member physicians a salary and incentives. Both the staff model and group model typically are located in a center or clinic operated by the HMO. The third HMO model is the IPA model.[3] The IPA contracts on behalf of its physician members with the HMO for services provided by the individual doctors in their own offices. Preferred provider organizations are least amenable to a single description, although they generally are associations of providers organized to negotiate fees, including discounts, with payers. The treatment of an HMO that is part of an integrated delivery system relates primarily to the HMO's structure,

---

§ 2–12

1. See e.g., I.R.C. § 501(c)(4). Section 501(c)(4) entities are exempt from federal corporate taxation, but cannot raise capital through tax-exempt bonds. See also, Private Letter Rul. 9412002 (Mar. 25, 1994), reviewing HMO's qualification for tax treatment as an insurance company.

2. See Chapter 9.

3. The Internal Revenue Service describes a fourth model of HMO, the "network" model. In this type of organization, the HMO contracts with a network of two or more independent practice associations. See e.g., General Couns. Mem. 39829 (Aug. 30, 1990). The tax treatment of such an HMO is most likely to follow that of the IPA-model HMO.

although the specific relationship between the HMO and the § 501(c)(3) entities in the integrated delivery system may have an impact.

§ 2–13.   Tax Exemption of HMOs, IPAs, and PPOs

A staff model HMO, which provides health services directly to subscribers/members, received § 501(c)(3) status in *Sound Health Association v. Commissioner*.[1] In addition to providing services to subscribers/members, the HMO in *Sound Health* offered emergency medical services at its clinic to all persons regardless of ability to pay. It had informed ambulance services of the availability of this service. In addition, it had provided free obstetrical care to patients of a family clinic on a referral basis. Finally, it instituted a program of reduced or waived membership fees for indigent persons. This fee waiver program was to be supported by private charitable contributions raised for that purpose. The IRS had denied the HMO its exemption because "preferential treatment will be accorded to . . . members-subscribers" in violation of the prohibition against private benefit and because the prepayment of medical services was a "form of insurance," and so not exempt under § 501(c)(3). The Tax Court reversed, holding that rendering medical care was a charitable purpose and that the HMO could satisfy the qualifications to which hospitals were held, relying on the availability of emergency treatment and the fee waiver program. The Tax Court held that "[i]f the charitable hospital can, except for emergency cases, restrict its treatment to paying patients, the Association should be able to restrict itself to paying members." The Court was not persuaded by the IRS' claim that the HMO offered a "form of insurance" through spreading the risk of the costs of treatment among subscribers, because this risk-spreading benefit was a public benefit available to a large number of potential subscribers. In 1981, the Service "acquiesced" in *Sound Health Association*,[2] but noted that it had not argued that the HMO provided insurance, but rather that the risk-spreading benefitted only the members of the HMO.

Not until fifteen years later did a federal circuit court review the satisfaction of the requirements of § 501(c)(3) by a health maintenance organization. In *Geisinger Health Plan v. Commissioner*,[3] a case with implications for the IRS policy toward hospitals as well,[4] the Third Circuit reversed a Tax Court decision granting an IPA-model HMO § 501(c)(3) status.[5] The Court of Appeals noted that there is no "clear test" for the charitable status

§ 2–13

1. 71 T.C. 158 (1978). HMOs generally qualify for exempt status under § 501(m) of the Internal Revenue Code, but that status is not as desirable as § 501(c)(3).

2. General Couns. Mem. 38735 (May 29, 1981).

3. 985 F.2d 1210 (3d Cir.1993).

4. See § 2–3.

5. The IRS had denied tax exempt status to the HMO, as it had earlier IPA-model HMOs. See e.g., General Couns. Mem. 39057 (November 9, 1983). The HMO contracted with an IPA for primary care services, performed utilization review, and paid specialists on a fee-for-service basis. The HMO argued that its method of operation eliminated the need for new capital expenditures and duplicative construction. The IRS denied the exemption because the HMO, unlike the HMO in Sound Health Association, did not provide emergency services, did not operate a fee waiver program, did not provide for enrollment by Medicaid or Medicare beneficiaries, and would limit membership in the beginning to a defined group of persons. In addition, the board of the HMO consisted of members of the IPA, indicating that it was operated for the private purposes of the physicians. See also, Rev. Rul. 86–98 and General Couns. Mem. 39829 (Sept. 10, 1990).

of hospitals[6] and rejected any "strict, multi-factor test" for § 501(c)(3) status of health maintenance organizations.[7] The court held that the Geisinger Health Plan (GHP) did not meet the requirements of § 501(c)(3) because the HMO itself provided no health care services open to members of the general public regardless of their ability to pay; nor did it conduct research or educational programs for the public.

Because its services were for members only, GHP was found to exist primarily for the private benefit of its members and not for the public's benefit. The Third Circuit held the offer of below-market subsidized fees to be irrelevant, in contrast to the opinion of the Tax Court in *Sound Health*, which had found fee discounts relevant though not determinative. In the view of the Third Circuit, the discounted fees did not overcome GHP's restriction of services to subscribers only. The court also found that the subsidized dues program was to be offered to only a "minuscule" number and so could not offset the HMO's primary benefit to private individuals as opposed to the general public.

Although the Third Circuit rejected any requirement that an HMO exempt under § 501(c)(3) operate an emergency room, it did adhere to the formal requirement that the HMO directly provide services to the public—whether research, public education or health care. The pure IPA-model HMO cannot meet this threshold formal requirement.

The Third Circuit's view that subsidized or free memberships are irrelevant, because they leave the HMO a subscribers-only entity, should be challenged. After all, free or greatly discounted subscriptions are in effect the equivalent of free medical care, because an HMO subscription operates as a voucher for free health care from an HMO physician, including the primary care that indigent persons most often lack. An adjustment in this position would not, however, change the ultimate result in *Geisinger* because it would not meet the requirement that the HMO offer direct services and because the court found the number of subsidized memberships to be seriously inadequate.

The Internal Revenue Service issued a new chapter in its Exempt Organizations Guidelines Handbook, which guides the IRS examinations of tax-exempt organizations. The new chapter describes the Service's approach to tax exemption for HMOs.[8] In this document, the Service divides HMOs into "provider HMOs," which provide services at locations it actually owns or leases, and "arranger HMOs," which provide services through physician contracts at locations owned by the physicians. The categorization does not exactly mirror the traditional categories of HMOs. The guidelines generally state that the provider HMOs will be examined under the principles of Sound Health. The arranger HMO must satisfy the requirements of Geisinger.[9]

Both independent practice associations and preferred provider organizations have sought § 501(c)(3) status unsuccessfully.[10] The Service denied

6. Geisinger at 1216.

7. Geisinger at 1219.

8. Internal Revenue Manual, Chapter 27, Health Maintenance Organizations.

9. See generally, Phillip G. Royalty, Recent Developments Affecting Tax–Exempt HMOs, Tax Notes Today, Oct. 28, 1999.

10. But see, University Affiliated Health Care, Inc., IRS Exemption Ruling, 1995 WL

§ 501(c)(3) status to an IPA because it merely served physicians as an "alternative method to the direct billing and collection of fees from patients" and, in negotiating on behalf of physician members, was "akin to a collective bargaining representative." The IPA had not indicated a willingness to assume fees of indigent patients.[11] The Service resolved the tax status of PPOs by reference to its analysis of IPA-model HMOs.[12]

§ 2–14. HMOs Within Integrated Delivery Systems

An HMO may seek § 501(c)(3) status on a stand-alone basis or as an integral part of an integrated delivery system. If tax-exempt status is sought on the stand-alone basis, the HMO itself must satisfy the community benefit standard.[1] If, however, it is unable to satisfy the community benefit test on its own, an HMO within an integrated delivery system may qualify vicariously if it is able to satisfy the two rigorous requirements of the Third Circuit's integral part doctrine.

The inclusion of a health maintenance organization within an integrated delivery system will allow § 501(c)(3) status for the HMO if it is deemed to be an "integral part" of the integrated delivery system. Under the integral part doctrine, a subsidiary organization may obtain tax exemption vicariously through a tax-exempt parent organization if the subsidiary's activities advanced the exempt purposes of the exempt parent organization. In *Geisinger Health Plan*, the health maintenance organization argued that it met the standards for 501(c)(3) status as an "integral part" of a system consisting of 501(c)(3) organizations.[2] Geisinger argued that it qualified for 501(c)(3) status if it provides an essential service to the 501(c)(3) entities in the system or to the direct beneficiaries (i.e., the patients) of the system's 501(c)(3) entities The Third Circuit in *Geisinger* remanded the case to the Tax Court for resolution of the HMO's "integral part" argument.

On remand, the Tax Court applied a two-prong test to determine whether the HMO qualified for exemption under the integral part doctrine.[3] The two prongs were (1) whether the HMO's activities were carried on under the supervision and control of an exempt affiliated organization; and (2) whether the activities could be regularly carried on by the exempt organization without constituting an unrelated trade or business.[4] The Tax Court held that the HMO had not sustained its burden of proving that it was an integral part of its exempt parent's activities. It failed to prove that operating a non-staff-model HMO serving individuals other than patients of the related hospitals would not be an unrelated trade or business if conducted by its parents.

In affirming the Tax Court's holding against the HMO, the Third Circuit took a somewhat different approach to the integral part doctrine.[5] The court stated that a subsidiary may qualify for tax-exempt status as an integral part of its § 501(c)(3) parent if: (1) it is not carrying on a trade or business which

79630 (I.R.S.), preferred provider organization obtained § 501 (c)(3) exempt status.

11. General Couns. Mem. 38894.

12. General Couns. Mem. 39799 (Oct. 25, 1989).

§ 2–14

1. See § 2–3(a).

2. Geisinger Health Plan v. Commissioner, 985 F.2d 1210 (3d Cir.1993).

3. Geisinger Health Plan v. Commissioner, 100 T.C. 394 (1993).

4. Id. at 402–404.

5. Geisinger Health Plan v. Commissioner, 30 F.3d 494 (3d Cir.1994).

would be an unrelated trade or business if carried on by the exempt parent, and (2) its relationship to its parent somehow enhances the subsidiary's own exempt character so that when this "boost" provided by the parent is added to the contributions made by the subsidiary, the subsidiary would be entitled to 501(c)(3) status.[6] Focusing on whether HMO's affiliation with the integrated delivery system enhanced the HMO's exempt nature, the Third Circuit found that by virtue of the affiliation, the HMO did not serve a broader patient base in the community than if it were unaffiliated. The court, therefore, concluded that the HMO failed to receive the requisite boost needed to satisfy the integral part doctrine.[7]

§ 2–15.   Tax Exemption of Integrated Delivery Systems

The Internal Revenue Service has granted § 501(c)(3) status to vertically integrated delivery systems (IDS). The application for one of the first to receive exemption described the following organization.[1] Loma Linda University Medical Center, a § 501(c)(3) organization, is the sole corporate member of the Friendly Hills Healthcare Network (Network). The Network acquired both an acute care hospital and several clinics providing primary care. The Network acquired the assets of a medical group through purchase and donation by the physician owners of the medical group.[2] The Network financed its purchase of assets in part through tax-exempt bonds. The Network was governed by a ten-member board of directors, only two of which could be members of the medical group. The medical group reorganized into a new medical group and, although the group did not own any of the assets of the Network, it contracted with the Network to provide all professional medical services for the Network's enrollees. The medical group was to be paid on a capitated basis, with the amount established in arms-length negotiations and related to competitive rates and reasonable compensation.

The Network operated the acute-care hospital with an open medical staff and would operate an emergency room and clinics providing treatment to all urgent cases without regard to ability to pay and would provide other treatment to indigent patients on a discount basis. The Network also would participate in Medicare and Medi–Cal. The Network would also conduct significant medical research and health education programs. The stated goal of the reorganization of the separate parts into one integrated delivery system was to "enhance the accessibility, quality and cost-efficiency of services rendered to the [community]." According to IRS counsel, several factors in the acquisitions and the operation of the IDS itself raised significant issues. Fundamentally, the Service viewed its task as balancing the community benefit provided by the IDS against the "very substantial private benefits" provided the physicians in the payment of a "fairly high price" by the

---

6.   Id. at 501.

7.   Id. at 502; see also, Laverne Wood & Peter Grant, The Third Circuit's Integral Part Test in Geisinger Health Plan: Implications for Integrated Delivery Systems, 10 Exempt Org. Tax. Rev. 1351 (1994).

§ 2–15

1.   See e.g., Friendly Hills Healthcare Network Qualifies for (c)(3) Exemption, 93 Tax

Notes Today 40–113 (February 19, 1993), which includes the text of the IRS letter.

2.   See generally, Kenneth L. Levine, Guidelines on Donations of Medical Practices to Tax–Exempt Hospitals, 92 Tax Notes Today 233–113 (November 20, 1992).

Network for the acquisition of their practices.[3] The Service considered that the acquisition was part purchase and part donation. In addition, the Service reviewed the participation of the physicians in the governance of the Network and established a "20–percent safe harbor" of physician membership on the board. Limitations on compensation to the physicians for services rendered were also important. Finally, the Service attempted to transfer the standards for the exemption of hospitals to this foundation-model integrated delivery system. The service required that the acute care hospital maintain an open medical staff, but did not require that the clinics have an open medical staff. In subsequent determinations, the IRS has also considered whether the integrated delivery system has an open emergency room, and whether Medicare and Medicaid patients are treated in a nondiscriminatory manner.

Subsequent to the Friendly Hills Network determination, the IRS stated that they will be more flexible regarding the twenty percent physician board limitation for integrated delivery systems.[4] Under the new approach, an exempt integrated delivery system could be governed by a board of directors with more than twenty percent physician representations without jeopardizing the organization's exemption as long as the majority of the voting members of the board is comprised of independent community members and the organization has in place a substantial conflict of interest policy.[5] In fact, the IRS determined that one physician network was entitled to tax exempt status under § 501(c)(3) even though the governing board of the organization was composed entirely of physicians.[6]

The IRS has granted § 501(c)(3) status to numerous integrated delivery systems following the foundation model and to others organized with different structures. The top concerns of the Service have remained the satisfaction of community benefit standard; private inurement and private benefit; and the details of the purchase of medical practices.

D. CONCLUSION

§ 2–16. Conclusion

Tax exemption for health care providers has changed tremendously over the past several years. The fundamental theory underlying exempt status for hospitals has shifted and has focused upon a single rationale, the provision of charity care. Economic and political pressures for increased revenue and for the relief of duties previously met by government funding programs have placed tax-exempt status under close scrutiny. In addition, the shift away from hospital-based care and toward newer structures for delivering a broader range of health care have tested the reach of the traditional requirements of tax-exempt status for hospitals and emerging organizational forms.

---

3. Sale of the assets of a § 501(c)(3) organization also raises exemption issues. See e.g., Psychiatric Center Contests Loss of Exempt Status for Sale of Hospital At Less Than Fair Market Value, 92 Tax Notes Today 83–70 (April 17, 1992).

4. Statement by Marcus Owens, Exempt Organizations Division Director, made at the Annual Healthcare Tax Law Institute Conference on April 26, 1996.

5. William S. Painter, Recent Legislation, Cases, and Other Developments Affecting Health Care Providers and Integrated Delivery Systems, SB51 ALI–ABA 97 (1997).

6. See, *C.H. Wilkinson Physician Network Qualifies for (c)(3) Exemption*, 14 Exempt Org. Tax Rev. 309 (1996).

Chapter 3

REGULATION AND LICENSURE OF HEALTH CARE PROFESSIONALS

Table of Sections

Research References

Am Jur 2d, Physicians, Surgeons, and Other Healers §§ 26–130

ALR Index: Medical Certificates; Medical Practice Act; Medical Schools

ALR Digest: Hospitals and Other Health Care Facilities § 7; Physicians and Surgeons §§ 1–11

Am Jur Pleading and Practice Forms (Rev), Physicians, Surgeons, and Other Healers §§ 11–105

§ 3–1. Introduction

Licensing requirements for the health care professions[1] are governed by state law through the states' authority under the police power to protect the health, safety and general welfare of the community. Licensing statutes govern entry into the licensed professions, disciplinary actions and the delivery of health care services by unlicensed persons. These statutes are implemented by boards dominated by the regulated professions. In fact, the licensing of health professionals in the United States is often described as a system of professional self-regulation, even though the boards usually include lay members; are governed by procedures and standards set by the legislature; and make decisions subject to review by the courts.[2]

Licensure is only one part of a much broader quality-control configuration that includes among its more powerful components certification by voluntary professional boards[3] and the credentialing system for clinical staff

§ 3–1

1. A very wide range of health care professionals commonly require a license under state law. For example, the state of California requires a license for chiropractors (§ 1000–5); clinical laboratory technologists (§ 1261.5); clinical laboratory bioanalysts (§ 1260); cytotechnologists (§ 1270); dentists (§ 1634); physicians and surgeons (allopathic) (§ 2050); podiatrists (§ 2461); speech pathologists (§ 2532); physical therapists (§ 2630); vocational nurses (§ 2859); registered nurses (§ 2732); midwives (§ 2507); psychologists (§ 2903); hearing aid dispensers (§ 3350); physician assistants (§ 3519); osteopathic physicians (§ 3600–5); respiratory therapists (§ 3701); psychiatric technicians (§ 4510); and clinical social workers (§ 4996), among others. In addition, California statutes provide that research psychoanalysts (§ 2529); spectacle lens dispensers (§ 2559.1); and others be registered with the state in order to practice. Finally, California provides for certification for drugless practitioners (§ 2500); nurse-midwives (§ 2746); and nurse-anesthetists (§ 2829). [All references are to Cal. Bus. & Prof. Code.]

2. David Orentlicher, The Role of Professional Self Regulation, in Regulation of The Healthcare Professions 129 (Timothy S. Jost, ed. 1997). See also, Kenneth Meier, Regulation: Politics, Bureaucracy, and Economics 179 (St. Martin's Press 1985), describing occupational licensure in general: "For all intents and purposes the subsystem usually has only one advocacy coalition, the coalition dominated by the occupation. A second advocacy coalition is possible when one occupation conflicts with another, when a member of the macropolitical system seeks to intervene, or when a well-organized consumer movement exists. In general, however, the regulated and the regulator operate in isolation."

3. See §§ 14–5 to 14–15.

privileges within hospitals and other institutions.[4] These two private quasi-regulatory processes also are controlled in great degree by the professions whose members submit themselves for review.

Allocation of substantial power to the medical professions furthers the public interest, it is argued, because the lay public is incapable of adequately evaluating the quality of medical services.[5] In economic terms, the market for professional health care services is characterized by market failure: consumers are incapable of assessing quality due to imperfect information and there is a high risk of negative externalities or danger to the consumer or third parties. It is this market failure that provides the rationale for restrictive licensure and peer review regulation for the health care professions.

Professional self-regulation, including the licensure systems in health care, has been strongly criticized.[6] Professional entry requirements are viewed as homogenizing treatment approaches through mandating uniformity in professional education.[7] The authority to define and implement restrictions on the delivery of health care services by unlicensed and competing licensed individuals, gives the dominant health care professions anticompetitive control over their markets, raising the cost of health care.[8] Critics argue that the restrictive entry and practice controls of professional licensure, as implemented by the profession-dominated agencies and as supported by the judicial deference afforded these administrative agencies, do not produce an adequate gain in the quality of health care services to offset their negative effects.[9]

Licensing systems govern discipline of the licensed practitioners, in addition to controlling entry and scope of practice. Critics of the dominance of the medical professions in disciplinary matters argue that the professions are ineffective in monitoring the behavior and competence of their colleagues and too often yield to fraternal leniency. Both the rate of disciplinary actions and the penalties assessed in cases of professional misconduct or incompetence have been criticized.[10] Still, licensing generally is viewed as an important player in quality control while it is understood that it is as well a significant public concession to the professions.[11]

A. ENTRY REQUIREMENTS

4. See Chapter 4 and §§ 14–15 to 10–22.

5. See e.g., Sabastier v. State, 504 So.2d 45 (Fla.App.1987).

6. Classic attacks on occupational licensure include the work of Walter Gellhorn (see e.g., Individual Freedom and Governmental Restraints (Louisiana State University Press 1956) and The Abuse of Occupational Licensing, 44 U. Chi. L. Rev. 6 (1976)) and that of Milton Friedman (see e.g., Capitalism and Freedom (University of Chicago Press 1962)).

7. See e.g., Milton Friedman, Capitalism and Freedom (University of Chicago Press 1962); Reuben Kessel, Price Discrimination in Medicine, 1 J. L. and Economics 20 (1959); Dorsey, Occupational Licensing and Minorities, 7 Law and Human Behavior 171 (1983).

8. See § 3–8.

9. See e.g., Leffler, Physician Licensure: Competition and Monopoly in American Medicine, 21 J. L. & Econ. 165 (1978); Symposium on Professional Regulation, 7 Law and Human Behavior (1983); Law and Polan, Pain and Profit: The Politics of Malpractice (1978); and Derbyshire, Medical Licensure and Discipline in the United States (1969).

10. See e.g., Frances H. Miller, Medical Discipline in the Twenty–First Century: Are Purchasers the Answer?, 70 Law & Contemp. Probs. 31 (1997); Report of the Inspector General, Department of Health and Human Services 1990.

11. See, e.g., Timothy S. Jost, Oversight of the Quality of Medical Care: Regulation, Management or The Market, 37 Ariz. L. Rev. 825 (1995).

§ 3–2. Specific Requirements and the Influence of Professional Organizations

Licensure statutes generally set minimum requirements and qualifications for each of the licensed health professions. Typical prerequisites for licensure include graduation from an approved educational program, acceptable performance on a standardized examination and a review of personal history for character issues.[1] Some state statutes still include a citizenship requirement, but such requirements probably violate the U.S. Constitution.[2]

Entry requirements for licensed health care practitioners have been criticized as discriminating against minorities;[3] as raising the price of services;[4] as inappropriately restricting access of individuals to the occupational market;[5] and as slowing innovation in health care by mandating uniformity in education.[6] The general justification for licensure entry requirements is the same as that used for licensure in general: entry requirements contribute to the quality of health care; and the expertise of the regulatory system, rather than consumer choice in the market, is required for effective quality control. The history of the minimum educational requirement for physician licensure in the United States presents a picture of both facets of licensure entry requirements.[7] After the states enacted licensure requirements for physicians in the 1870s and 1880s, the American Medical Association began a campaign to establish standards for medical education and to assure that only graduates of medical schools meeting those standards were allowed to sit for state licensing examinations. With the Flexner Report, sponsored by the AMA and funded by the Carnegie Foundation, the AMA gained, and has retained, control over accreditation of medical schools[8] and, thus, over the major prerequisite for state licensure examinations.

The National League of Nursing, the American Nurses Association and other nurse organizations have supported and actively lobbied for increased educational requirements for nursing, focusing on proposals to set the baccalaureate degree as the minimum educational requirement.[9]

The vision of nursing as an educated occupation was first advocated by Florence Nightingale in the late 1850s and was supported by a post-Civil War women's movement and the growth of the modern hospital. The early schools of nursing, with the first founded in 1873, were all hospital-based and

§ 3–2

1. See e.g., Vernon's Ann. Mo. Stat. § 334.031; S.H.A. 225 ILCS 60/9.

2. Application of Griffiths, 413 U.S. 717, 93 S.Ct. 2851, 37 L.Ed.2d 910 (1973).

3. See e.g., Stuart Dorsey, Occupational Licensing and Minorities, 7 Law and Human Behavior 171 (1983).

4. See e.g., Reuben Kessel, Price Discrimination in Medicine, 1 J. Law and Economics 20 (1959).

5. See e.g., Walter Gellhorn, The Abuse of Occupational Licensing, 44 U. Chi. L. Rev. 6 (1976).

6. Hogan, The Effectiveness of Licensing, 7 Law & Human Behavior 130 (1983).

7. For extensive histories of the movement toward licensure of physicians and the influence of the American Medical Association, see Reuben Kessel, The A.M.A. and the Supply of Physicians, 36 Law & Contemp. Prob. 267 (1970); Paul Starr, The Social Transformation of American Medicine (1987).

8. The American Medical Association currently also controls accreditation of educational programs for some non-physician health care providers. See e.g., Conn. Gen. Stat. Ann. § 20–12a(b)(1); Ark. Stat. Ann. § 72–2008.

9. Bonnie Bullough, The Law and The Expanding Nursing Role 203–210 (1980); Emily Friedman, The Troubled Past of an "Invisible" Profession, 264 J.A.M.A. 2851 (Dec. 12, 1990).

provided unpaid labor to the hospitals. In fact, all of the nursing services provided in hospitals through the 1920s were provided by unpaid student nurses.

Early campaigns for licensure and registration of nurses in the 1890s were led by nurse educators, typically from the upper and middle classes and educated in teaching hospitals. Increased entry requirements were opposed by the "professed nurses," who were of the lower classes, were relatively untrained and viewed the move toward licensure as a maneuver intended to put them out of business. By 1923, 48 states had enacted licensure statutes. Nursing had its own "Flexner Report" in the Goldmark Report and the report of the Committee on the Grading of Nursing Schools, both produced in the 1920s, which identified oversupply and undertraining as major problems in nursing.

Only in 1965 did the American Nurses Association advocate the baccalaureate degree as the minimum educational requirement for licensure. Currently, in most states, graduates of hospital-based nursing diploma schools still are able to sit for the required entry examination and receive a license. The move by the ANA toward increased educational entry requirements for nursing has been viewed by some as relating more to concerns over class status, recognition and respect than over quality. It has also been opposed by registered nurses holding associate degrees, by the hospital-based schools of nursing and by licensed practical nurses.[10]

B. UNAUTHORIZED PRACTICE

§ 3–3. Background

The state medical practice acts define the practice of medicine quite broadly and indeterminately. These statutes prohibit any but licensed physicians, and other licensed health care professionals when acting within the bounds of their own licensure, from practicing medicine. This statutory prohibition falls upon two distinct groups: individuals unlicensed for any of the health professions and licensed health care professionals. Enforcement of the statutory prohibition often includes disciplinary or criminal action against a licensed physician for aiding the unauthorized practice of medicine.[1]

§ 3–4. Unlicensed Practitioners

a. Services Offered to the Public

Statutes prohibiting the unauthorized practice of medicine, or another health care profession, typically include a threshold "holding out" requirement: the individual charged with the unauthorized practice of medicine must have held himself or herself out as offering services defined in the statute as the province of licensed professionals. At a minimum, this provision prohibits representing oneself as holding a license that one does not in fact possess and

10. Emily Friedman, The Troubled Past of an "Invisible" Profession, 264 J.A.M.A. 2851 (Dec. 12, 1990).

§ 3–3

1. See e.g., Bryce v. Board of Medical Quality Assurance, 229 Cal.Rptr. 483 (Cal.App. 1986).

from using a licensed title.[1]

While the statutes could be read to require some active public representation of an offer of services, the courts have resisted such a narrow interpretation.[2] The "holding out" requirement appears to be an attempt to distinguish health care services provided by family members and close friends from those provided by strangers. While some state statutes do not apply unless a fee has been paid to the practitioner, not all have such a requirement,[3] and so it is not accurate to view the reach of the unauthorized practice prohibition as extending only to "commercial" or "business" relationships.

b. Consent of the Patient

In some cases the unlicensed person has taken affirmative steps of disclosure and claimed in his or her defense that the individuals using the services actually knew that the practitioner was not licensed to provide health care services.[4] Defenses based on the consent of the person using the services generally have not succeeded. The medical practice act, as an exercise of the state's police power to protect the general health and welfare of the public, simply is viewed as empowering the state to prohibit certain activities even if undertaken with the knowledgeable consent of the individuals involved.[5]

There is demand in the marketplace for health services offered by unlicensed providers and for nontraditional services provided for the improvement of health.[6] It is not unusual for the patients or clients of the practitioner charged with the unauthorized practice of medicine to join in litigation on behalf of the practitioner, claiming a legal right to access to the services they desire, usually without success.[7]

§ 3–5. Defining the Prohibited Activities

The heart of litigation over violations of the prohibition against the unauthorized practice of medicine is the interpretation and application of the statutory definition of the practice of medicine to a particular set of activities. Statutory definitions of the practice of medicine vary among the states. Generally, however, the definitions tend to be quite broad.[1]

The plain language of some of the medical practice acts may be interpreted to reach such commonplace services as the sale of books on healing and the sale of nutritional supplements. At least one court has distinguished these activities from the practice of medicine in that the simple sale of books, vitamins and diet substances does not involve the seller in the diagnosis of the

§ 3–4

1. See e.g., State Department of Health v. Hinze, 441 N.W.2d 593 (Neb.1989); State v. Howard, 337 S.E.2d 598 (N.C.App.1985), review denied, appeal dismissed 341 S.E.2d 581 (N.C.1986); Williams v. State, 453 So.2d 1051 (Ala.Civ.App.1984).

2. State ex rel. Medical Licensing Board v. Stetina, 477 N.E.2d 322 (Ind.App.1985).

3. See e.g., West's Ann. Cal. Business & Professions Code § 2052.

4. See e.g., People v. Jihan, 130 Ill.Dec. 422, 537 N.E.2d 751 (Ill.1989) (The court did not consider the release in deciding whether the Medical Practice Act had been violated.) See also, Board of Medical Quality Assurance v. Andrews, 260 Cal.Rptr. 113 (Cal.App.1989).

5. See e.g., Board of Medical Quality Assurance v. Andrews, 260 Cal.Rptr. 113 (Cal.App. 1989).

6. David M. Eisenberg et al., Unconventional Medicine in the United States, 328 New Eng. J. Med. 246 (1993).

7. See § 3–7.

§ 3–5

1. See e.g., West's Ann. Ind. Code 25–22.5–1–1.1.

conditions of particular individuals nor in the prescription of a particular item for a particular condition.[2] A similar distinction was made by a court rejecting a claim by a defendant that the medical practice act was unconstitutionally vague in that it would reach the use of home remedies.[3] In contrast, one court viewed its state medical practice act as potentially prohibiting such activities as the self-injection of insulin, ear piercing and tattooing.[4]

The medical practice acts have been held to reach "any activity customarily performed by a licensed practitioner, such as diagnosis, treatment, or prescribing medications"[5] and so to prohibit supervision of severe fasting at a "health sanctuary;"[6] recommendation of vitamins and food supplements to correct a physical ailment;[7] provision of "celestial water" and "special pillows" to cure stomach pains;[8] use of "herbal tumor removal" for the treatment of cancer;[9] and the use of colonic irrigation.[10] In all of these cases, the unlicensed provider of services "prescribed" particular activities or substances for the relief of conditions or ailments identified through some type of diagnostic test, including commonly used medical tests such as blood or urine analysis and more unconventional tests such as iridology, or through patient-reported symptoms.

Prohibitions against the unauthorized practice of medicine may reach the utilization review practices of managed care health plans[11] if the utilization review function is characterized as the practice of medicine. Such review of treatment decisions in managed is often performed, at least at initial levels, by nonphysicians, leading to arguments that utilization review is the practice of medicine and so may be performed only by licensed physicians.[12] At least one court has held that utilization review is the practice of medicine. In Murphy v. Board of Medical Examiners,[13] the Arizona Court of Appeals held that the Arizona medical board had jurisdiction over a physician providing pre-treatment certification as medical director of a health insurance plan. Dr. Murphy had disagreed with a patient's primary care physician and surgeon and had refused to authorize surgery. The surgeon performed the surgery despite the refusal and was proven correct in the diagnosis. The court stated that "Dr. Murphy substituted his medical judgment for theirs and determined that the surgery was 'not medically necessary.' There is no other way to characterize

2. State v. Howard, 337 S.E.2d 598 (N.C.App.1985), review denied, appeal dismissed 341 S.E.2d 581 (N.C.1986).

3. People v. Ray, 74 Ill.Dec. 677, 456 N.E.2d 179 (Ill.App.1983).

4. Miller v. Medical Association of Georgia, 423 S.E.2d 664 (Ga.1992). See also, Hicks v. Arkansas State Medical Bd., 537 S.W.2d 794, 795 (Ark.1976).

5. Board of Medical Quality Assurance v. Andrews, 260 Cal.Rptr. 113 (Cal.App.1989).

6. Id.

7. Foster v. Georgia Board of Chiropractic Examiners, S.E.2d 877 (Ga. 1987), the Georgia legislature has since amended OCGA § 43–9–16 to provide that chiropractors may recommend the use of vitamins, minerals or food supplements; State v. Miller, 542 N.W.2d 241 (Iowa 1995); State Department of Health v. Hinze, 441 N.W.2d 593 (Neb.1989).

8. State v. Hoffman, 733 P.2d 502 (Utah 1987).

9. State v. Howard, 337 S.E.2d 598 (N.C.App.1985), review denied, appeal dismissed 341 S.E.2d 581 (N.C.1986).

10. See e.g., State v. Nelson, 317 S.E.2d 711 (N.C.App.1984); State ex rel. Medical Licensing Board v. Stetina, 477 N.E.2d 322 (Ind. App.1985), appeal after remand 513 N.E.2d 1234 (Ind.App.1987).

11. See Chapter 9.

12. For a review of state law on this issue, Comment, Is Utilization Review the Practice of Medicine?, 19 J. Legal Med. 431 (1998) including descriptions of state statutes and attorneys general opinions.

13. 949 P.2d 530 (Ariz.App.1997).

Dr. Murphy's decision: it was a 'medical' decision." Another appellate court, however, reached a somewhat different decision. In Morris v. District of Columbia Board of Medicine, the appellate court held that a physician, licensed in Maryland but not in the District, was not engaged in the unauthorized practice of medicine in the District when he acted as medical director of a health plan and participated in treatment certification decisions.[14] The court specifically noted, however, that its decision was very fact-sensitive and depended on the details of the actual function of the physician. In Morris, the medical director participated only in post-treatment certification; participated in the committee that actually reviewed the individual cases, but was not a voting member of the committee; and reviewed the committee's decisions, but only for "clarity."

a. Judicial Deference

The courts afford the boards' broad deference in exercising the police power of the state in defining the practice of medicine. The courts allow the boards, within the authority granted through the relevant statute, broad discretion in designating certain activities as permissible or impermissible. The justification for this deferential posture lies in the classic and traditional allocation of authority in an administrative system: the agency has the advantage of special expertise and has more flexibility in accommodating change; the courts are limited in their ability to resolve conflicts among a large number of competing interests and to design a cohesive regulatory strategy.[15]

b. Vagueness in the Definition of the Prohibited Practice

Medical practice acts generally provide that a violation of the statutory prohibition against the unauthorized practice of medicine is a misdemeanor or felony.[16] In addition, a licensed health care provider who aids and abets an unlicensed individual in the practice of medicine may be subject to disciplinary measures such as license revocation.[17] In cases of serious injury or death, related criminal charges such as involuntary manslaughter or reckless homicide may be proven.[18]

Both unlicensed practitioners and licensed professionals have litigated claims that the state medical practice acts are unconstitutionally vague, but with little success. The defendant challenging a statute as unconstitutionally vague must overcome a presumption against unconstitutionality; and almost without exception the courts have rejected such claims in this context.

The standard applied in a vagueness challenge is whether the statute is clear enough to give the ordinary person notice that his or her behavior will violate the statute.[19] Hypothetical cases in which the application of the statute

---

14. 701 A.2d 364 (D.C.App.1997).

15. See e.g., R. Stewart, The Reformation of American Administrative Law, 88 Harv. L. Rev. 1667 (1975).

16. 225 ILCS 60/49; West's Ann. Cal. Business & Professional Code § 2052.

17. Minn. Stat. Ann. § 147.091(1), subd. 1(i); Official Code Ga. Ann. § 43–34–37(a)(9).

18. See e.g., Graham v. State, 480 N.E.2d 981 (Ind.App.1985), cert. denied 479 U.S. 1007, 107 S.Ct. 646, 93 L.Ed.2d 702 (1986).

19. State v. Southworth, 704 S.W.2d 219, 223–224 (Mo.1986), holding that "practice of medicine" and "practice of midwifery" are both terms of common usage and not vague; People v. Rosburg, 805 P.2d 432 (Colo.1991), holding that "practice of midwifery" not vague, as the term midwifery is a term of common usage.

is either unclear or plainly unintended do not prove that the statute is unconstitutionally vague if the defendant's actual activities clearly fall within the reach of the statute.[20] Only very recently have challengers claiming unconstitutional vagueness met with any success.

In *Miller v. Medical Association of Georgia*, the Georgia Supreme Court in a one-page opinion held that an amendment to the medical practice act of Georgia violated constitutional requirements of due process.[21] The amendment, challenged by the Georgia Nurses Association, provided that only doctors, dentists, podiatrists, and veterinarians could perform any "surgery, operation, or invasive procedure in which human or animal tissue is cut, pierced or otherwise altered by the use of any mechanical means, laser, ... medication administered by injection ...".[22] Although the opinion is silent on the legislative history of the amendment, the Georgia legislature apparently enacted the amendment at the urging of the Medical Association of Georgia to prohibit optometrists from using lasers to correct vision problems. The impact on nursing practice went unnoticed until after the act was signed by the governor.[23] In holding the amendment unconstitutional, the court stated that the amendment was "so wide-ranging in its impact that [the court] cannot possibly make one interpretation of the statute that we would be certain would render it constitutional."[24] Included among the activities that might be illegal under the restriction, according to the court, were self-injection of insulin, ear-piercing, tattooing and insertion of intravenous lines by licensed nurses.

Despite the legislative history of the Georgia amendment, it is not so very different from definitions of the scope of practice of medicine that have been upheld in previous cases.[25] Its only significant departure from the norm is the failure to preserve an exception for nursing practice.

In one other state has the medical practice act been held void for vagueness. The Illinois Supreme Court held that the term "midwifery" in a 1985 medical practice act, which had been repealed prior to the opinion but after the criminal conviction of a lay midwife for the unauthorized practice of medicine, was unconstitutionally vague.[26] The statute prohibited the "practice

20. See e.g., People v. Ray, 74 Ill.Dec. 677, 456 N.E.2d 179 (Ill.App.1983); State v. Hoffman, 733 P.2d 502, 505 (Utah 1987); Bowland v. Municipal Court, 134 Cal.Rptr. 630, 636, 556 P.2d 1081, 1087 (Cal.1976). See also, State Board of Nursing and State Board of Healing Arts v. Ruebke, 913 P.2d 142 (Kan.1996), in which the Kansas Supreme Court reversed a lower court's holding that the medical practice act and nursing practice act were unconstitutionally vague, in a challenge by a lay midwife; the state Supreme Court, however, held that the statutes did not prohibit lay midwifery.

21. 423 S.E.2d 664 (Ga.1992). The statute at issue has since been repealed. Ga. L. 1993, p. 349.

22. Official Code Ga. Ann. 43–34–1 (repealed 1993).

23. "Georgia Legislature Rushed Into a Mistake" Atlanta Constitution, May 28, 1992, Page A/1.

24. Miller v. Medical Association of Georgia, 423 S.E.2d 664 (Ga.1992).

25. See e.g., State ex rel. Medical Licensing Board v. Stetina, 477 N.E.2d 322 (Ind.App. 1985).

26. People v. Jihan, 130 Ill.Dec. 422, 537 N.E.2d 751 (Ill. 1989), reviewing Illinois Medical Practice Act of 1985. But see, State v. Kimpel, 665 So.2d 990 (Ala.Crim.App.1995), holding statute was not unconstitutionally vague when the statute's words and meaning are clear on its face as prohibiting a narrowly defined class of conduct, the practice of nurse midwifery; People v. Rosburg, 805 P.2d 432 (Colo.1991), holding that the term "midwifery" was a term of common usage and, therefore, not unconstitutionally vague.

of midwifery" without a license. The state had argued that defendant had practiced midwifery because she delivered a child. The court found the state's use of the term delivery to be "as vague as that of 'midwifery,' " connoting a "major role in physically removing or extracting a baby from its mother's womb." "Assisting at childbirth" was a broader term, in the view of the court, and perhaps not the practice of midwifery. The ambiguity in scope made the statute unconstitutionally vague.[27]

The opinions in these cases may be idiosyncratic. The cases may reflect unstated disapproval of the legislative history of the particular acts. More recent challenges based on vagueness have not succeeded.[28]

§ 3–6.　Nonconforming Approaches to Health Care

a. *Introduction*

The states have adopted a variety of approaches to deal with nontraditional, nonconforming or innovative approaches to health care. Some states do provide licenses to non-allopathic non-osteopathic practitioners, such as the naturopathic and homeopathic practitioners discussed below. Others explicitly remove certain practices from the jurisdiction of the licensure board, as in the registration system for naturopathy in the District of Columbia.[1] In a few instances, the state legitimizes the nonconforming practice but requires that standard disclosure and consent forms be signed by the patient.[2]

Nonconforming practices, whether new and innovative or traditional and currently not popular, may instead be subsumed within the scope of practice of licensed providers, such as medical doctors, but prohibited to any unlicensed practitioner. One example of this last phenomenon is the incorporation of assistance at childbirth within the practice of medicine. Capture of alternative practice approaches by the licensed professions is not an altogether satisfactory resolution of regulatory or consumer concerns: it may raise the cost of the care; the involvement of a provider trained in one of the mainstream professions may change the nature of the services provided; and licensed professionals practicing non-mainstream medicine may themselves be subject to discipline.[3]

---

27. See also, Peckmann v. Thompson, 745 F.Supp. 1388 (C.D.Ill.1990), reviewing Illinois Medical Practice Act of 1987, reversed on issuance of summary judgment, 966 F.2d 295 (7th Cir.1992).

28. See e.g., State Board of Nursing v. Ruebke, 913 P.2d 142 (Kan.1996), holding statutes defining healing arts and practice of nursing were not unconstitutionally vague.

§ 3–6

1. Described in Douglass v. District of Columbia, 1987 WL 15696, n. 2 (D.D.C.1987).

2. See e.g., Clark v. Department of Professional Regulation, 463 So.2d 328 (Fla.App. 1985).

3. In re Guess, 382 S.E.2d 459 (N.C.App. 1989) (appeal by licensee of disciplinary action; action set aside for lack of proof of harm to the public); 393 S.E.2d 833 (N.C.1990), cert. denied 498 U.S. 1047, 111 S.Ct. 754, 112 L.Ed.2d 774

(1991) (appeal by licensee of disciplinary action; action upheld); Guess v. Board of Medical Examiners, 1991 WL 352536 (E.D.N.C.1991) (action by licensee for declaratory judgment and injunctive relief against penalty based on unconstitutionality of statute; relief denied due to lack of jurisdiction); Fuller v. Board of Medical Examiners, 1991 WL 352537 (E.D.N.C. 1991) (claim for injunctive relief by Guess's patients based on constitutional right to obtain homeopathic treatment; action denied); Guess v. Board of Medical Examiners, 967 F.2d 998 (4th Cir.1992) (consolidated appeal of Guess's and patients' claims before the district court) (Guess's claims were in part barred by *res judicata* and the patient's derivative claims were moot due to the court's lack of jurisdiction to review Guess's claims.)

The interest in alternative or complementary medicine and non-conforming practices has increased dramatically.[4] In 1992, the National Institute of Health created the Office of Alternative Medicine (OAM) to fund research on alternative therapies.[5] Whether the deferential posture of the courts toward the very restrictive regulation of non-conforming practice will change as a result of new research on such practices remains to be seen.[6]

b. Homeopathy and Naturopathy

Many of the cases litigating the unlicensed practice of medicine involve services that in the view of a nonbeliever might be considered outright quackery. But others involve practices that, if not accepted by the mainstream health care professions, at least have a foundation in a discipline that at one time enjoyed a sometimes substantial degree of legitimacy. Two examples of this latter category include cases involving the practice of naturopathy and homeopathy.

Naturopathy is "a system of therapeutics in which neither surgical nor medicinal agents are used" in favor of "natural (nonmedicinal) forces."[7] Statutory definitions of naturopathy include that of the state of Washington, which defines naturopathy as "the art and science of the diagnosis, prevention, and treatment of disorders of the body by stimulation or support, or both of the natural processes of the human body. * * * The practice of naturopathy includes manual manipulating, the prescription, administration, dispensing and use, except for the treatment of malignancies or neoplastic disease, of nutrition and food science, physical modalities, homeopathy, certain medicines of mineral, animal, and botanical origin, hygiene and immunization, common diagnostic procedures, and suggestion."[8]

The practice of naturopathy has been prosecuted as the practice of medicine by unlicensed providers in several cases. Many states, including Utah, Oregon, Washington and Kansas, permit and regulate the practice of naturopathy in some way.

During the two decades after the Civil War, homeopathic medicine, which is based on the principle that likes are cured by likes and which emphasizes

---

4. David M. Elsenberg et al., Unconventional Medicine in the United States, Vol. 28 New Eng. J. Med. 246 (1993); Charles Marwick, Complementary Medicine Congress Draws a Crowd, 274 JAMA 106 (1995).

5. David M. Elsenberg et al., Unconventional Medicine in the United States, Vol. 28 New Eng. J. Med. 246 (1993).

6. At least one state has significantly narrowed the authority of its licensure board in restricting the practice of alternative medicine N.C.Stat. § 90–14(a)(6). See e.g., Lori B. Andrew, The Shadow Health Care System: Regulation of Alternative Health Care Providers, 32 Hous. L. Rev. 1273 (1996); Kathleen M. Boozang, Western Medicine Opens the Door to Alternative Medicine, 24 Am. J. L. & Med. 185 (1998); Michael H. Cohen, A Fixed Star in Health Care Reform: The Emerging Paradigm of Holistic Healing, 27 Ariz. St. L. J. 79 (1995).

7. Stedman's Medical Dictionary 1025 (25th ed. 1992).

8. West's Rev. Code Wash. Ann. § 18.36A.040. Practitioners of naturopathy have been convicted for the illegal practice of medicine (State v. Howard, 337 S.E.2d 598 (N.C.App.1985), review denied, appeal dismissed 341 S.E.2d 581 (N.C.1986); Williams v. State ex rel. Medical Licensure Commission, 453 So.2d 1051 (Ala.Civ.App.1984); Reisinger v. Commonwealth, State Board of Medical Education and Licensure, 399 A.2d 1160 (Pa. Cmwlth.1979)) and for illegally practicing chiropractic (Feingold v. Commonwealth, State Board of Chiropractic, 568 A.2d 1365 (Pa. Cmwlth.1990)). See also, State Department of Health v. Hinze, 441 N.W.2d 593 (Neb.1989); and State v. Maxfield, 564 P.2d 968 (Idaho 1977). Utah Code Ann. § 58–12–22. Or. Rev. Stat. § 685.010 et seq. (Amended 1993 Oregon Laws Ch. 42 (S.B.).) West's Rev. Code Wash. Ann. § 18.36A.010 et seq. Kan. Stat. Ann. 65–2872a.

close attention to patient reporting of symptoms, enjoyed great popularity in the United States,[9] with several states licensing practitioners of homeopathy.[10] By the turn of the century, however, the popularity of homeopathy peaked. Currently at least two states, Arizona[11] and Nevada,[12] license practitioners of homeopathy.[13] Both statutes define homeopathy in terms of the administration of substances of animal, vegetable, chemical or mineral origin, ordinarily in microdosages.[14] In other states, the practice of homeopathy has been held to be the practice of medicine, and therefore an illegal practice for any but licensed physicians.[15]

c. Midwifery

The question of whether the practice of midwifery falls within the practice of medicine, and, therefore, is prohibited to any but licensed providers,[16] may be the single most frequently litigated unauthorized practice question. At least three distinct groups of providers are involved in providing assistance at childbirth: doctors, nurses and lay midwives. Several states have statutes that specifically authorize assistance at childbirth by lay midwives.[17] In others, the medical practice act may specify that lay midwifery is illegal, while some states specifically license or certify nurse-midwives.[18]

Licensure of nurse-midwives does not necessarily resolve all issues concerning the delivery of childbirth services. Regulatory restrictions on the practice of nurses acting as midwives may limit the type of services available.[19] For example, in *Leigh v. Board of Registration in Nursing*,[20] the Supreme Court of Massachusetts upheld discipline of a nurse providing midwifery services in the mother's home under the nurse practice act which prohibited participation of nurse midwives in home births. The court rejected the licensee's argument that she was providing midwifery rather than nurse-midwifery services. In *Leggett v. Tennessee Board of Nursing*,[21] however, the court held that the Board of Nursing had no authority over a nurse providing lay midwifery services without satisfying the educational and other requirements set down by the board for nurse-midwives. The court based its decision on both the medical practice act and the nurse practice act. The Tennessee medical practice act specifically exempted midwifery from the unauthorized

9. Paul Starr, The Social Transformation of American Medicine 98–99 (1982).

10. Id. at 106.

11. Ariz. Rev. Stat. § 32–2901 et seq.

12. Nev. Rev. Stat. § 630A.010 et seq.

13. See also, Conn. Gen. Stat. Ann. ch. 370 § 20–8; establishing a homeopathic medical examining board.

14. Ariz. Rev. Stat. § 32–2901; Nev. Rev. Stat. § 630A.040.

15. See e.g., Sabastier v. State, 504 So.2d 45, 46 (Fla.App.1987).

16. See § 3–10.See e.g., Alaska Stat. § 08.65.050; Ark. Code Ann. 17–85–102; N.H. Rev. Stat. Ann. § 326–D:4; S.C. Code Ann. § 40–33–50; Tex. Rev. Civ. Stat. Ann. Art. 4512i.

17. See e.g., Vernon's Ann. Missouri Stat. § 334.010.

18. See e.g., Ala. Code § 34–19–4; Ariz. Rev. Stat. § 36–752; Conn. Gen. Stat. § 20–86c; Utah Code Ann. § 56–44a–301. See also, People v. Rosburg, 805 P.2d 432 (Colo.1991), holding that licensure of nurse midwives and prohibition of lay midwifery does not violate lay midwives' right to equal protection; Hunter v. State, 676 A.2d 968 (Md.1996), court concluded that the legislative history of provisions for certification of nurse midwives required the conclusion that the statute permitted only registered nurses certified by the board as nurse midwives to provide midwifery services.

19. See e.g., Lori B. Andrews, The Shadow Health Care System: Regulation of Alternative Health Care Providers, 32 Hous. L. Rev. 1273 (1996).

20. 481 N.E.2d 1347 (Mass.1985).

21. 612 S.W.2d 476 (Tenn.App.1980).

practice of medicine, and the nurse practice act had no specific provision for nurse-midwives. The court concluded that "given that some couples will continue to decide on home deliveries," the restriction of midwifery services to licensed nurses, who were forbidden by regulation from assisting at home births, was "contrary to the goal of promoting public health,"[22] although its ruling was based on the statutory scheme enacted by the legislature and is not to be read as a restriction on the state's authority to prohibit lay midwifery.

In several cases, the courts have attempted to examine the specific actions taken by midwives in assisting at childbirth to discern whether these activities are in fact the practice of medicine and, therefore, subject to prosecution as the unauthorized practice of medicine. In *Leigh v. Board of Registration in Nursing*,[23] for example, the court held that "ordinary assistance in the normal cases of childbirth"[24] was not the practice of medicine, but that using "obstetrical instruments when a physician is unavailable and [prescribing] drugs" does constitute the practice of medicine.[25] In State Board of Nursing and State Board of Healing Arts v. Ruebke, the Supreme Court of Kansas held that lay midwifery was permitted as it was neither the unauthorized practice of medicine nor the unauthorized practice of nursing.[26]

The statutory use of the term "midwifery" has been attacked as unconstitutionally vague repeatedly and usually unsuccessfully.[27] The restriction of midwifery has also attracted intense litigation asserting a right to choose the type of childbirth assistance services desired.[28] Claims of rights to provide or receive midwifery services have generally failed.[29]

§ 3–7. Right to Choose or Provide A Particular Form of Treatment

Patients have attempted to claim a constitutional right to choose a particular form of health care treatment in the face of statutory prohibitions against the provision of health care services they desire. These claims have been singularly unsuccessful,[1] except in the cases of access to abortion or

22. Id. at 481.

23. 481 N.E.2d 1347 (Mass.1985).

24. Citing Commonwealth v. Porn, 82 N.E. 31 (Mass.1907).

25. Id. at n. 12.

26. 913 P.2d 142 (Kan.1996). The court held that even if midwifery were considered the practice of medicine, the defendant was exercising delegated authority from a physician with whom she worked.

27. See e.g., Bowland v. Municipal Court, 134 Cal.Rptr. 630, 556 P.2d 1081 (Cal. 1976); State v. Southworth, 704 S.W.2d 219 (Mo. 1986); People v. Rosburg, 805 P.2d 432 (Colo. 1991); Smith v. State ex rel. Medical Licensing Board, 459 N.E.2d 401 (Ind.App.1984). But see People v. Jihan, 130 Ill.Dec. 422, 537 N.E.2d 751 (Ill.1989) and Peckmann v. Thompson, 745 F.Supp. 1388 (C.D.Ill.1990).

28. See § 3–7; See also, Dale Walker, A Matter of the Quality of Birth: Mothers and Midwives Shackled by the Medical Establishment and Pennsylvania Law, 23 DuQuesne L.

Rev. 171 (1984); Debra Evenson, Midwives: Survival of An Ancient Profession, 7 Women's Rts. L. Rep. 313 (1982); Kathleen Whitby, (Note) Choice in Childbirth: Parents, Lay Midwives, and Statutory Regulation, 30 St. Louis U. L. J. 985 (1986).

29. See e.g., People v. Rosburg, 805 P.2d 432 (Colo.1991); Leigh v. Board of Registration in Nursing, 506 N.E.2d 91 (Mass.1987). But see, Northrup v. Superior Court, 237 Cal.Rptr. 255 (Cal.App.1987).

§ 3–7

1. See e.g., State v. Howard, 337 S.E.2d 598, 603 (N.C.App.1985), review denied, appeal dismissed 341 S.E.2d 581 (N.C.1986); Bowland v. Municipal Court, 134 Cal.Rptr. 630, 556 P.2d 1081 (Cal. 1976); Leigh v. Board of Registration in Nursing, 481 N.E.2d 1347 (Mass. 1985); State v. Southworth, 704 S.W.2d 219 (Mo.1986); Guess v. Board of Medical Examiners, 967 F.2d 998 (4th Cir.1992); Majebe v. North Caroling Board, 416 S.E.2d 404 (N.C.

contraceptives which implicate the heightened constitutional status of reproductive decisionmaking.[2]

For example, patients have attempted to claim a constitutional right to choose a midwife for childbirth assistance. These claims have consistently failed even when made in the context of the women's right to privacy in reproductive decisionmaking, the lack of empirical evidence of better outcomes with commonly used obstetrical technology, and the substantial history of conflict between medical and other approaches to childbirth.[3] Claims of rights to provide midwifery services have also generally failed.[4]

Similarly, although the right to practice is a property right protected by due process,[5] courts have consistently held that a practitioner has no constitutional right to practice in a particular manner or to provide particular services.[6] Many states do specifically exempt from the prohibition against the unlicensed practice of medicine some defined religious practices. For example, most states exempt Christian Science practitioners from the reach of the medical practice act.[7] Some states provide a broader exemption for religious practices.[8] Practitioners claiming that their services are protected by a First Amendment right to practice their religion, in the absence of a statutory exemption for their activities, have generally not been successful.[9]

C. SCOPE OF PRACTICE

§ 3–8. Licensed Health Professionals Generally

A licensed non-physician health care provider may be prosecuted for violation of the prohibition against the unauthorized practice of medicine. The licensed professional, in contrast to the unlicensed practitioner, will have a defense against prosecution to the extent that the actions identified as the

App. 1992, review denied 421 S.E.2d 355 (N.C. 1992); Mitchell v. Clayton, 995 F.2d 772 (7th Cir.1993); Ohio College of Limited Medical Practice et al. v. Ohio State Medical Board et. al., 670 N.E.2d 490 (Ohio App.1995), review denied, appeal dismissed 666 N.E.2d 566 (Ohio 1996). But see, Andrews v. Ballard, 498 F.Supp. 1038 (S.D.Tex.1980).

2. See Chapter 18.

3. See e.g., Leigh v. Board of Registration in Nursing, 481 N.E.2d 1347 (Mass.1985); Hunter v. State, 676 A.2d 968 (Md.1996). See also, Chris Hafner–Eaton and Laurie K. Pearce, Birth Choices, the Law, and Medicine: Balancing Individual Freedoms and Protection of the Public's Health, 19 J. Health Pol. Pol'y & L. 813 (1994); David M. Smolin, The Jurisprudence of Privavy in a Splintered Supreme Court, 75 Marq. L. Rev. 975 (1992); Lisa C. Ikemoto, The Code of Perfect Pregnancy: At the Intersection of the Ideology of Motherhood, The Practice of Defaulting to Science, and the Interventionist Mindset of Law, 53 Ohio State L. Rev. 1205 (1992).

4. See e.g., People v. Rosburg, 805 P.2d 432 (Colo.1991); Leigh v. Board of Registration in

Nursing, 481 N.E.2d 1347 (Mass.1985). But see, Northrup v. Superior Court, 237 Cal.Rptr. 255 (Cal.App.1987).

5. See § 3–12.

6. See e.g., In re Guess, 393 S.E.2d 833 (N.C.1990); Majebe v. North Carolina Board, 416 S.E.2d 404 (N.C.App.1992), review denied 421 S.E.2d 355 (N.C.1992); Williams v. State ex rel. Medical Licensure Commission, 453 So.2d 1051 (Ala.Civ.App.1984); Idaho Association of Naturopathic Physicians v. United States Food and Drug Administration, 582 F.2d 849 (4th Cir.1978), cert. denied 440 U.S. 976, 99 S.Ct. 1547, 59 L.Ed.2d 795 (1979).

7. See e.g., Hawaii Rev. Stat. § 453–2; Mass. Gen. L. Ann. Ch. 112, § 7; Md. Code Ann., Health Occ. § 14–102; Wis. Stat. Ann. § 448.03.

8. See e.g., Idaho Code § 54–1804(f); Neb. Rev. Stat. § 71–1, 103(3); West's Ann. Cal. Bus. & Prof. Code § 2063; La. Rev. Stat. Ann. § 37:1291; Colo. Rev. Stat. § 12–36–106.

9. See e.g., State v. Cantrell, 558 A.2d 639 (Vt.1989); Board of Medical Quality Assurance v. Andrews, 260 Cal.Rptr. 113 (Cal.App.1989).

unauthorized practice of medicine fall within the legitimate scope of practice allowed under his or her license.

The disciplinary board charged with supervising the licensure of physicians generally has the primary responsibility for enforcing the prohibition against the unauthorized practice of medicine by health care providers licensed in the other health care professions. In addition, boards governing non-physician licensed professionals, such as nurses, pharmacists and others, will enforce any statutory prohibitions that exist concerning the unlicensed practice of that particular profession. Unproductive conflicts arise between licensure boards governing different licensed health care professions in setting boundaries on authorized scope of practice. The recent growth in the participation of licensed non-physician health care providers in health care delivery in response to increased cost-containment pressures,[1] especially in managed care,[2] and in response to expanded training and role identification for non-physician health care providers has contributed to the incidence of these clashes. Some states, therefore, have created a joint board consisting of members of each of the licensed professions and have allocated to that joint board or superboard some authority for delineating and monitoring the scope of practice of the regulated professions.[3]

Regulation of the scope of practice of non-physician licensed health care professionals raises many of the same legal and policy issues as does the enforcement of the prohibition against the unauthorized practice of medicine against unlicensed providers.[4] For example, there is an inherent degree of vagueness, though usually not viewed as reaching the level of unconstitutionality,[5] in a definitional approach to scope-of-practice delineations among the licensed health care professions. A vagueness challenge may in fact be more difficult for a licensed health practitioner because the courts will use professional custom to resolve ambiguities and will charge the licensed practitioner with knowledge of such custom.[6]

Statutory definitions of the scope of practice of the licensed professions include terms that are quite general. For example, "diagnosis" is ordinarily included in the definition of the practice of medicine, while a typical nursing practice act includes "nursing diagnosis" within the practice of nursing[7] and statutes governing the practice of physician assistants may prohibit the physician assistant from making a "final diagnosis"[8] or a "definitive diagnosis." The function or process of diagnosis remains the same whether performed by physician, nurse or physician assistant.[9]

§ 3–8

1. Barbara J. Safriet, Health Care Dollars and Regulatory Sense: The Role of Advanced Practice Nursing, 9 Yale Journal on Regulation 417 (1992); Tom Christoffel, Hiring on the Cheap: Health Care Costs, The Eclipse of Physicians and Change in Licensing Laws, 4 St. Louis U. P. L. Forum 57 (1984).

2. See Group Health Plan v. State Board of Registration for the Healing Arts, 787 S.W.2d 745 (Mo.App.1990).

3. See e.g., Idaho Code § 54–1402(d); Vernon's Ann. Mo. Stat. § 334.104.3.

4. William M. Sage and Linda H. Aiken, Regulating Interdisciplinary Practice, in Regu-

lating the Healthcare Professions, 71 (Timothy S. Jost, ed. 1997).

5. See § 3–5.

6. See e.g., Jacobs v. United States, 436 A.2d 1286 (D.C.App.1981).

7. See e.g., Vernon's Ann. Mo. Stat. § 335.016(8)(b).

8. Va. Code § 54.1–2952.

9. Several authors have noted the lack of a reasoned definition for the term diagnosis as used in these statutes. See e.g., Sadler & Sadler, Recent Developments in the Law Relating to the Physician's Assistant, 24 Vand. L. Rev.

Licensing boards, acting within the broad reach of the police power, currently are not required to prove that limitations on scope of practice are grounded in empirical research assessing the risk presented by the provision of services by one particular practitioner as compared to another.[10] At the same time, the conflict between the stated licensure goal of protection of the public health and the externality of anticompetitive market control is close to the surface in the turf battles among licensed health professionals.

§ 3–9. The Practice of Nursing

Nursing practice acts parallel the medical practice acts in establishing entry requirements, disciplinary grounds and procedures, and definitions of the scope of practice of nursing. The legal issues relating to entry requirements and professional discipline in nursing do not differ from those applicable to medicine. The professions do differ, however, in their legitimate scope of practice under the licensure statutes.

Although nurse licensure statutes formerly presented nursing as a practice that required the supervision or direction of a licensed medical doctor,[1] the nursing practice acts enacted in the 1970's adopted a broader definition of the practice of nursing and legally established the profession as providing an independent practice and exercising independent judgment.[2] Nurse practice acts continue to expand the scope of practice of nursing.[3]

With the expansion of the practice of nursing, the jurisdictional claims of medicine and nursing have overlapped as the "practice of medicine" and the "practice of nursing" can involve the same functions.[4] For example, while the practice of medicine includes the function of diagnosis, the practice of nursing includes the function of "nursing diagnosis."[5]

Considering a general nurse practice statute in *Sermchief v. Gonzales*, the Supreme Court of Missouri described a "nursing diagnosis:" "a nurse undertakes only a nursing diagnosis, as opposed to a medical diagnosis, when she or he finds or fails to find symptoms described by physicians standing orders and

1193 1203–1204 (1971) and Audrey Ennen, (Note) Interpreting Missouri's Nursing Practice Act, 26 St. Louis U. L. J. 931, 945–946 (1982). See also, Sermchief v. Gonzales, 660 S.W.2d 683 (Mo.1983), (practice of nursing and medicine); Barry v. State Medical Board, 1990 WL 126292 (Ohio App.1990) (practice of physician assistant and nurse); Medical Society of New Jersey v. New Jersey Department of Law and Public Safety, 575 A.2d 1348 (N.J.1990), (overlap between practice of medicine and practice of physical therapy).

10. See generally, concerning risk assessment in scope-of-practice regulation, Sandra H. Johnson, Regulatory Theory and Prospective Risk Assessment in the Limitation of Scope of Practice, 4 J. Leg. Med. 447 (1983).

§ 3–9

1. See e.g., Vernon's Ann. Mo. Stat. § 335.010.2 (1969), as cited in Sermchief v. Gonzales, 660 S.W.2d 683 (Mo.1983).

2. See e.g., Elizabeth Harrison Hadley, Nurses and Prescriptive Authority: A Legal and Economic Analysis, 15 Am. J. L. & Med. 245 (1989).

3. See e.g., Vernon's Ann. Mo. Stat. § 334.104, authorizing collaborative practice arrangements between doctors and nurses allowing nurses to administer and dispense drugs. See also, William M. Sage, Staffing National Health Care Reform: A Role for Advanced Practice Nurses, 26 Akron L. Rev. 187 (1992).

4. The Committee on Nursing of the American Medical Association in its report, Medicine and Nursing in the 1970s's—A Position Statement, stated that "the same act may be clearly the practice when performed by a physician and the practice of nursing when performed by a nurse." Approved by the A.M.A. Board of Trustees and House of Delegates, June, 1970, 13 J.A.M.A. 1881 (1970).

5. See e.g., Vernon's Ann. Mo. Stat. § 334.155(b).

protocols for the purpose of administering courses of treatment prescribed by the physician in such orders and protocols." Beyond that foray, however, the court refused to "draw that thin and elusive line that separates the practice of medicine and the practice of professional nursing in modern day delivery of health services." Rather, the court referred to legislative intent to expand the scope of authorized nursing practices in the Missouri statute, and held that the acts of the nurses at issue in the case clearly fell within the legislative intent of the statute.[6]

The nurse practitioner statutes typically require that the nurse practitioner have completed more advanced education and training than is required for licensure as a registered nurse. Nurse practitioners, which include nurse anesthetists, nurse midwives and clinical nurse specialists, among others are also referred to as advanced practice nurses.

A significant variant in the advanced practice statutes occurs in the relationship with the physician. While nurse practice acts enacted in the 1970's signaled a move toward the independent practice of nursing, the legal recognition of advanced practice nursing in the 1990's has caused nurse practitioners to reestablish close working relationships with physicians. Some advanced practice nursing statutes provide that the nurse practitioner practice under the supervision of a physician.[7] Others recognize advanced practice nursing in collaboration with licensed physicians,[8] and still others describe advanced nursing practice without reference to the participation of a supervisory or collaborative physician.[9]

§ 3–10. Physician Assistants

Physician assistants (PAs) perform functions delegated to them by a physician. Physician assistants may function in the absence of specific statutory authority because the medical practice acts allow a physician to utilize or employ an assistant to perform delegated tasks.[1] The permissible scope of delegation, in the absence of specific statutory delineation, depends on the prevailing custom of the medical profession relating to the degree of supervision and control to be exercised by the delegating physician[2] and the expertise of the doctor who, because of the nature of delegation, may delegate only functions within the doctor's own competence. The drive for professionalization by physician assistants and the market advantages of a specific legal status for practice, among other factors, have led most states to provide for

6. See also, Professional Health Care, Inc. v. Bigsby, 709 P.2d 86 (Colo.App.1985).

7. See e.g., Cal. Bus. & Prof. Code § 2746.5 (certificate authorizes nurse midwife to practice nurse midwifery "under the supervision of a licensed physician and surgeon who has current practice or training in obstetrics"); Cal. Bus. & Prof. Code § 2836.1(d) (requiring physician supervision for the furnishing of drugs or devices by nurse practitioner).

8. See e.g., Mo. V.A.M.S. § 334.104 (authorizing collaborative practice arrangements in the form of written agreements, protocols or standing orders, but describing the prescriptive authority of the nurse practitioner as delegated).

9. See e.g., Md. Health Occup. § 8–601 (recognizing nurse midwives).

§ 3–10

1. See e.g., Minn. Stat. Ann. § 147.091, subd. 1(i); West's Colo. Rev. Stat. Ann. § 12–36–106(5)(a); Ariz. Rev. Stat. § 32–1401; Del. Code. Ann. tit. 24, § 1703.

2. See e.g., Jacobs v. United States, 436 A.2d 1286 (D.C.App.1981). See also, State Board of Nursing and State Board of Healing Arts v. Ruebke, 913 P.2d 142 (Kan.1996), holding that lay midwife worked within delegated practice.

licensure, certification or registration of physician assistants with established entry criteria and a specified permissible scope of delegation.

Statutory definitions of the scope of practice of physician assistants usually provide that PAs may not exercise independent judgment or diagnose the patient's condition,[3] although the states may vary on the nature of the diagnostic activity allowed the PA.[4] The self-identification of PAs as dependent practitioners does not necessarily mean that functions of a physician assistant are narrower than those of a nurse practitioner.[5] Just as with nursing, the scope of practice of physician assistants has experienced substantial expansion.[6]

Physician assistants are required to act under the supervision of a licensed physician, but the level of supervision required varies among the states.[7] Some states provide for the required supervision in greater detail.[8] Some set specific limits on the number of PAs that any one physician may employ[9] or require prospective approval of the board for the specific practice setting of the individual PA.[10]

Most states, including California,[11] Minnesota[12] and West Virginia,[13] provide specific requirements for PA's prescriptive authority. In California, for example, the supervising physician who delegates prescriptive authority must adopt a written protocol that specifies all criteria for the use of the particular drug or device.[14] In addition, the medical record of any patient cared for by the PA for whom the supervising physician's prescription has been transmitted must be reviewed within seven days.[15] The California statute also places restrictions on PAs ability to prescribe Schedule II through Schedule V controlled substances.[16]

D.　DISCIPLINE

§ 3–11.　Background

Discipline is designed to improve the quality of health care services through rehabilitating, retraining or removing incompetent providers from the practice before patients are injured. Although protection of the public health provides the rationale for licensure, disciplinary actions under the licensing statutes do not require that injury to any particular patients be proven.[1] In seeking to prevent injuries, licensure resembles somewhat the

---

3. See § 3–9.

4. See e.g., S.D. Codified Laws § 36–4A–22; Alaska Stat. § 08.64.170; Va. Code Ann. § 54.1–2952.

5. For example, an opinion issued by the Attorney General of Arizona concluded that a physician assistant had authority to order a radiography exam and that a nurse practitioner did not have that authority. Ariz. Att'y Gen. Op. No. 182–034 (Mar. 10 1982).

6. See e.g., Ariz. Rev. Stat. § 32–2501(9), authorizing PAs to perform minor surgery.

7. See e.g., Alaska Stat. § 08.64.170; Hawaii Rev. Stat. § 453–2(4); West's Rev. Code Wash. Ann. § 18.71A.020(2); 225 ILCS 95/4.

8. See e.g., Conn. Gen. Stat. Ann. § 20–12a(a)(7).

9. See e.g., N.Y. Educ. Law § 6542; Ariz. Rev. Stat. § 32–2533; Colo. Rev. Stat. § 12–36–106.

10. See e.g., W.Va. Code § 30–3–16(b), (g); Oregon Rev. Stat. § 677.515(1)(b).

11. Cal. Bus. & Prof. Code § 3502.1.

12. Minn Stat. Ann. § 147A.09.

13. W. Va. Code § 30–3–16(*l*).

14. Cal. Bus. & Prof. Code § 3502.1(a)(2).

15. Cal. Bus. & Prof. Code § 3502.1(d).

16. Cal. Bus. & Prof. Code § 3502.1(b)(2).

§ 3–11

1. See e.g., Colorado v. Hoffner, 832 P.2d 1062 (Colo.App.1992).

credentialing process in hospitals,[2] but with the advantage of reaching directly into the private extra-institutional practice of the licensed provider. As compared to malpractice litigation, disciplinary action may more directly prevent patient injuries, but it does not compensate injured patients.[3]

All members of the licensed health care professions are subject as a condition of licensure to disciplinary control by the legislatively designated agency or board. It is discipline of physicians, however, that attracts the most public scrutiny.

In a 1990 study of disciplinary actions from 1985–1989, the Office of Inspector General reported that disciplinary actions against physicians by medical licensing agencies were impeded by limitations on agency authority; limitations on sharing of information with other agencies; standards of proof calling for clear and convincing evidence; lack of clear-cut standards for competent medical care; and inadequate communication of agencies across state lines. Understaffing and case backlogs were also serious problems. The majority of disciplinary actions are based on the improper use of drugs or alcohol (57%); with many fewer involving incompetence (11.5%). An interesting observation in the OIG report is that the majority of disciplinary actions involve behavior in the doctor's office rather than in a hospital setting. As to penalties assessed, the OIG reported that a significant number of disciplinary actions resulted in "private" remedies, such as a private letter of concern, reprimand or warning.[4]

§ 3–12. Procedural Requirements

The licensing board, like all adjudicative administrative agencies, must follow the procedures required by its enabling statute and other applicable statutes such as the state's administrative procedures act. Failure to comply with statutory procedural requirements will result in judicial rejection of the board's decision and remand.[1] In addition, a licensee has a property right in the license[2] and so is guaranteed due process for any action restricting that

2. See Chapter 4. See also, Nat Hershey, An Alternative to Mandatory Licensure of Health Professionals, 50 Hospital Progress 71 (Mar. 1969) and Institutional Licensure for Health Professionals?, 57 Hospital Progress 75 (Sept. 1976), recommending increased reliance on hospital credentialing process over licensure.

3. See generally, on the relationship between discipline and malpractice, Walter Gellhorn, Medical Malpractice Litigation (U.S.)— Medical Mishap Compensation (N.Z.), 73 Cornell L. Rev. 170 (1988); Law and Polan, Pain and Profit: The Politics of Malpractice (1978); Derbyshire, Medical Licensure and Discipline in the United States (1969).

4. Report of the Inspector General, Department of Health and Human Services 1990. See also, James Gray and Eric Zicklin, Why Bad Doctors Aren't Kicked Out of Medicine, 69 Medical Economics 126 (Jan. 20, 1992), detailing limitations on the effectiveness of medical disciplinary systems using information gathered in interviews with state licensure boards.

For a more recent review of the disciplinary process see, Timothy S. Jost, et al., Consumers, Complaints, and Professional Discipline: A Look at Medical Licensure Boards, 3 Health Matrix 309 (1993).

§ 3–12

1. See for example, Lopez v. New Mexico Board of Medical Examiners, 754 P.2d 522 (N.M.1988). But see, Ramirez v. Ahn, 843 F.2d 864 (5th Cir.1988), cert. denied 489 U.S. 1085, 109 S.Ct. 1545, 103 L.Ed.2d 849 (1989).

2. See e.g., Dent v. State of West Virginia, 129 U.S. 114, 9 S.Ct. 231, 32 L.Ed. 623 (1889); Wills v. Composite State Board of Medical Examiners, 384 S.E.2d 636 (Ga.1989). See also, Telang v. Commonwealth of PA, 714 A.2d 1109 (Pa.Cmwlth.1998); Abrahamson v. Department of Professional Regulation, 154 Ill.Dec. 870, 568 N.E.2d 1319 (Ill.App.1991), reversed on other grounds 180 Ill.Dec. 34, 606 N.E.2d 1111 (Ill. 1992); Mishler v. Nevada State Board of Medical Examiners, 896 F.2d 408 (9th Cir. 1990); Fleury v. Clayton, 847 F.2d 1229 (7th

license. Constitutional due process claims may involve both the United States Constitution and the constitution of the state. The licensee may waive his or her procedural rights through an explicit and knowing consent to procedural irregularities.[3]

§ 3–13. Adequate Notice

A fundamental constitutional requirement of due process is that the one in danger of loss of a property right receive adequate notice of the charges against him or her. Questions of adequate notice in disciplinary actions usually involve claims that the notice was inadequate in content, rather than timeliness, and so did not inform the licensee of the deficiencies at issue in the disciplinary action. Courts have remanded proceedings in which the hearing examined issues not specified in the notice to the licensee.[1] Courts have tolerated deficiencies in notice if the deficiencies are cured prior to the hearing.[2]

§ 3–14. Delay in Prosecution

Disciplined physicians have argued that substantial delay between the event that is the basis of the disciplinary action and the prosecution of the action unfairly prejudices the licensee. Courts have been unusually consistent in rejecting such claims,[1] with two notable exceptions. First, courts have found delay relevant in cases in which the board revoked a license some time after issuance, not based on any dishonesty in the application or violation of professional standards by the licensee, but based on administrative errors of the agency in originally issuing the license. The courts resolve this issue through the doctrine of estoppel.[2] Secondly, some courts have been receptive to arguments by physicians charged with sexual misconduct with patients that delay in prosecution required dismissal of charges.[3]

§ 3–15. Right to Discovery

All agree that the board has a duty to disclose exculpatory information to the licensee, but jurisdictions differ on the question of broader access to evidence. In *Wills v. Composite State Board*,[1] the Supreme Court of Georgia relied on both statutory interpretation and due process to hold that the

Cir.1988). But see, Burkhalter v. Texas State Board of Medical Examiners, 918 S.W.2d 1 (Tex.App.1996); Pittenger v. Department, 596 A.2d 1227 (Pa.Cmwlth.1991); contra In re Magee, 362 S.E.2d 564 (N.C.App.1987).

3. See e.g., Pritchard v. Catterson, 401 S.E.2d 475 (W.Va.1990).

§ 3–13

1. See e.g., Dhabuwala v. State Board for Professional Medical Conduct, 651 N.Y.S.2d 249 (N.Y.App.Div.1996); Celaya v. Department, 560 So.2d 383 (Fla.App.1990); Wagman v. Florida, 590 So.2d 12 (Fla.App.1991); Willner v. Department, 563 So.2d 805 (Fla.App.1990): In re Magee, 362 S.E.2d 564 (N.C.App.1987).

2. See e.g., In re Jones, 590 N.E.2d 72 (Ohio App.1990); Arkansas State Medical Board v. Leipzig, 770 S.W.2d 661 (Ark.1989).

§ 3–14

1. See e.g., Lawrence v. DeBuono, 673 N.Y.S.2d 773 (N.Y.App.Div.1998); Gropp v. D.C. Board, 606 A.2d 1010 (D.C.App.1992); Rojas v. Sobol, 563 N.Y.S.2d 284 (N.Y.App.Div. 1990); Wills v. Composite State Board, 384 S.E.2d 636 (Ga.1989). But see, Lopez v. New Mexico, 754 P.2d 522 (N.M.1988).

2. See e.g., Arceo v. Selcke, 168 Ill.Dec. 275, 589 N.E.2d 675 (Ill.App.1992); Krakow v. Department, 586 So.2d 1271 (Fla.App.1991).

3. See § 3–23.

§ 3–15

1. 384 S.E.2d 636 (Ga.1989). See also, Board v. Spinden, 798 S.W.2d 472 (Mo.App. 1990).

licensee has a right to access to the investigative file, triggered by a request for exculpatory material. The relevant Georgia statute specifically prohibited access to investigative materials for "any purpose other than a hearing before the board." The court also relied on the grave nature of disciplinary action to find a constitutional right to such documents. But a New York appellate court denied access to such a file, viewing the licensee's request as a "fishing expedition."[2]

§ 3–16. Right to a Hearing

With few exceptions, due process also guarantees a hearing prior to final disciplinary action.[1] Courts have held that full evidentiary hearings are not required when the disciplinary action is based on criminal conviction for a crime that provides grounds for disciplinary action;[2] on findings of other state agencies (such as the state Medicaid agency);[3] and on disciplinary penalties levied in other states based on grounds available in the state prosecuting the subsequent disciplinary action.[4]

§ 3–17. Combination of Functions

One of the more startling experiences for practitioners subject to disciplinary action is the frequent combination of functions in the process. For example, the office of attorney general may be responsible for investigating or prosecuting the case before the board while attorneys from the same state office may serve as legal counsel to the board and ultimately may represent the board in litigation over challenges to the board's decision. Members of the disciplinary board may also be involved in various stages of the disciplinary proceedings, including both proceedings to decide whether to pursue the case and the final fact-finding and penalty phase.

The United States Supreme Court in *Withrow v. Larkin*[1] reviewed and upheld as constitutional the combination of functions in the disciplinary process of the state of Wisconsin. These disciplinary proceedings involved the disciplinary board in both investigative and adjudicative functions. The board initially held a nonadversarial investigative hearing to determine whether the proscribed conduct occurred. The licensee and his attorney were permitted to and did attend this hearing, although they were not afforded the opportunity to present evidence or cross-examine witnesses. Subsequently, the board held a full adversarial hearing to determine whether violations that would support

---

2. Rojas v. Sobol, 563 N.Y.S.2d 284 (N.Y.App.Div.1990). See also, Smith v. Department of Registration, 120 Ill.Dec. 360, 523 N.E.2d 1271 (Ill.App.1988).

§ 3–16

1. Pre-sanction hearings are not usually required in cases involving immediate suspension for patient safety. See discussion in § 1–17.

2. See e.g., Denier v. State Board of Medicine, 683 A.2d 949 (Pa.Cmwlth.1996); Galang v. State, 484 N.W.2d 375 (Wis.App.1992); Paiano v. Sobol, 572 N.Y.S.2d 440 (N.Y.App.Div. 1991); Dragan v. Commissioner, 530 N.Y.S.2d 896 (N.Y.App.Div.1988).

3. See e.g., Camperlengo v. Barell, 578 N.Y.S.2d 504, 585 N.E.2d 816 (N.Y.App.1991);

Choi v. State, 550 N.Y.S.2d 267, 549 N.E.2d 469 (N.Y.App.1989). Collateral estoppel may bar a licensee from challenging facts found in proceedings of other state agencies. See e.g., Abraham v. Ambach, 522 N.Y.S.2d 318 (N.Y.App.Div.1987).

4. See e.g., In the Matter of Cole, 476 A.2d 836 (N.J. Super. App.Div.1984); McKay v. Board, 788 P.2d 476 (Or.App.1990); Tandon v. State Board of Medicine, 705 A.2d 1338 (Pa. Cmwlth.1997).

§ 3–17

1. 421 U.S. 35, 95 S.Ct. 1456, 43 L.Ed.2d 712 (1975).

license suspension or revocation had been committed. The Court held that the combination of investigative and adjudicative functions, as occurred in the case before the court, would not, "without more," violate due process. The Court noted that, in challenging the combination of functions, the plaintiff must overcome "a presumption of honesty and integrity in those serving as adjudicators." But the Court did state that the circumstances of a particular case may produce an intolerably high and unconstitutional risk of unfairness.

Courts, in applying the *Withrow* standard, have generally upheld the apparent blending of investigative, prosecutorial and adjudicative functions.[2] In an unusual decision, however, the Supreme Court of Pennsylvania in *Lyness v. Commonwealth* held the structure of the state's disciplinary process unconstitutional, parting company with the United States Supreme Court.[3]

The Pennsylvania Supreme Court specifically rejected the *Withrow* analysis. In particular, the court rejected the analogy drawn in *Withrow* between the disciplinary process under challenge and the single judge in criminal proceedings presiding at a probable cause hearing and the subsequent trial. The Pennsylvania court noted that the right of the criminal defendant to a jury trial guaranteed that the defendant, unlike the defendant in disciplinary proceedings, could interpose a jury between himself or herself and the possibly tainted judge. The Pennsylvania Supreme Court turned to and based its holding of unconstitutionality on its interpretation of the Constitution of the State of Pennsylvania, which in the view of the court, demands a higher standard of procedural fairness than does the U.S. Constitution.

§ 3–18. Scope of Judicial Review

Once the administrative process is complete,[1] the disciplined licensee may seek judicial review. The available scope of review over the outcome itself is limited to whether the decision is supported by substantial evidence on the record. The courts do not provide a *de novo* review. With a narrow scope of review, the courts usually uphold the decisions of the boards,[2] although courts

2. See e.g., Clausing v. State of Washington, 955 P.2d 394 (Wa.App.1998); DeBlanco v. Ohio State Medical Board, 604 N.E.2d 212 (Ohio App.1992) (individual attorney prosecuting cases did not participate in board's deliberations or advise board); Ogg v. Louisiana Board of Chiropractic Examiners, 602 So.2d 749 (La. App.1992) (assistant attorney general was both prosecutor and general counsel to the board but did not participate in the board's deliberations). See also, Berezoski v. Ohio State Medical Board, 549 N.E.2d 183 (Ohio App.1988) (attorney hearing examiner did not participate in investigation).

3. 605 A.2d 1204 (Pa.1992). See also, Quinn v. Louisiana Department of Health and Hospitals, 691 So.2d 299 (La.Ct.App.1997), commingling of prosecutorial and adjudicative functions violates both the letter of the LA Admin. Proc. Act and the due process goals it is designed to further.

§ 3–18

1. The administrative principal of exhaustion of remedies does not apply in every case.

Exceptions to the exhaustion of remedies doctrine can be made if: the administrative remedy is inadequate; the complainant will suffer irreparable injury; the agency has acted in excess of its authority, or pursuit of an administrative remedy is futile. Pet v. Department, 542 A.2d 672 (Conn.1988); Wills v. Composite State Board, 384 S.E.2d 636 (Ga.1989); Group Health Plan v. State Board of Registration, 787 S.W.2d 745 (Mo.App.1990); Johnson v. Department of Public Health 710 A.2d 176 (Conn. App.1998); Thompson v. New Hampshire Board of Medicine, 719 A.2d 609 (N.H.1998).

2. See e.g., Bevacqua v. Sobol, 579 N.Y.S.2d 243 (N.Y.App.Div.1992), affirmed without opinion 569 N.Y.S.2d 604, 572 N.E.2d 45 (N.Y.App. 1991); Davis v. Psychology Examining Board, 431 N.W.2d 730 (Wis.App.1988); Dharmavaram v. Department of Professional Regulation, 159 Ill.Dec. 692, 576 N.E.2d 361 (Ill.App.1991); El Gabri v. Rhode Island Board of Medical Licensure, 1998 WL 961165 (R.I.Super.).

have on occasion rejected agency decisions.[3] The fact-specific nature of the inquiry—whether the administrative adjudication is supported by substantial evidence on the record—makes it difficult to generalize in a way that will predict the outcome of judicial review. At least one court has admonished the agency to write a decision that clearly sets out the board's rationale.[4] Courts that have rejected the agency's decision as lacking adequate support on the record have closely examined the written reasons provided by the board, apparently demanding a close match between "reasons" and "motivation," rejecting generalizations that the provider is simply a "bad apple." The reviewing court may also look for identity between the stated rationale for the board's decision and the evidence on the record.[5]

Courts may also review the penalty assessed against the licensee. Penalties may be challenged as disproportionate to the violation.[6] The disciplinary board is limited by the statutory authority granted to the agency by the statute.[7]

§ 3–19. The National Practitioner Data Bank

Through the Health Care Quality Improvement Act of 1986,[1] which included provisions granting limited immunity to persons or organizations participating in peer review activities,[2] Congress established the National Practitioner Data Bank to improve the availability of information concerning disciplinary actions among the states and staff privileges actions among health care institutions and in exchange for the statutory immunity granted under the Act.[3] The Data Bank is operated by the Department of Health and Human Services through contract with a private corporation. The Data Bank became operational in 1990.

State medical and dental licensing boards are required to report to the Data Bank certain disciplinary actions taken on grounds related to the professional competence or professional conduct of the licensed professional.[4]

3. See e.g., Abraham v. Ambach, 522 N.Y.S.2d 318 (N.Y.App.Div.1987); Bettencourt v. Board, 558 N.E.2d 928 (Mass.1990); Gard v. State Board, 747 S.W.2d 726 (Mo.App.1988); Gingo v. State Medical Board, 564 N.E.2d 1096 (Ohio App.1989); Hoover v. The Agency for Health Care Administration, 676 So.2d 1380 (Fla.Dist.Ct.App.1996).

4. Enu v. Sobol, 576 N.Y.S.2d 378 (N.Y.App.Div.1991).

5. Morris v. Board of Registration in Medicine, 539 N.E.2d 50 (Mass.1989), cert. denied 493 U.S. 977, 110 S.Ct. 503, 107 L.Ed.2d 506 (1989).

6. For cases rejecting the assessed penalty, see Bernal v. Department, 517 So.2d 113 (Fla. App.1987), affirmed 531 So.2d 967 (Fla.1988); Sarosi v. Sobol, 553 N.Y.S.2d 517 (N.Y.App. Div.1990); Arceo v. Selcke, 168 Ill.Dec. 275, 589 N.E.2d 675 (Ill.App.1992). For cases accepting the assessed penalty, see Cassella v. Commonwealth, 547 A.2d 506 (Pa.Cmwlth. 1988); Grimberg v. Department, 542 So.2d 457 (Fla.App.1989); Morrissey v. Sobol, 575 N.Y.S.2d 960 (N.Y.App.Div.1991); Dharmavar-

am v. Department, 159 Ill.Dec. 692, 576 N.E.2d 361 (Ill.App.1991); Manyam v. Sobol, 583 N.Y.S.2d 613 (N.Y.App.Div.1992); Hidalgo v. Sobol, 574 N.Y.S.2d 605 (N.Y.App.Div.1991); Beldengreen v. Sobol, 572 N.Y.S.2d 113 (N.Y.App.Div.1991); Gropp v. D.C. Board, 606 A.2d 1010 (D.C.App.1992); Starr v. State Board of Medicine, 720 A.2d 183 (Pa.Cmwlth.1998).

7. See e.g., Turner v. Department, 591 So.2d 1136 (Fla.App.1992); Willner v. Department, 563 So.2d 805 (Fla.App.1990).

§ 3–19

1. 42 U.S.C.A. § 11101 et seq.; 54 Fed. Reg. 42,722, codified at 45 C.F.R. Pt. 60 et seq. For a comprehensive legislative history of the Act, see Bernard Reams, The Health Care Quality Improvement Act of 1986: A Legislative History of Pub. L. 99–660 (1990).

2. See § 14–22.

3. For an assessment of the operation of the Data Bank since 1990, see 110 Public Health Reports (July/August, 1995).

4. 42 U.S.C.A. § 11132. The act provides that an action is *not* considered to be based on

In addition, medical and dental professional societies must report certain adverse actions taken against members to the state medical or dental licensure board, which must then send a copy of the report to the Data Bank.[5] While hospitals must query the Data Bank at least every two years for each member of their medical staff,[6] state licensure boards are not required to make a query of the Data Bank but may do so.[7]

Individual practitioners may request their own records from the Data Bank and are to receive a copy from the Data Bank of each report at the time it is made. Practitioners reported to the Data Bank may dispute any report made against them. The basis for the dispute is limited to the factual accuracy of the report and whether the report was filed in accordance with the Data Bank's requirements. Practitioners may not contest the merits of the malpractice claim or settlement or the basis of the adverse action against the practitioner's clinical privileges, licensure or accreditation status. The Secretary of Health and Human Services is charged with reviewing and resolving disputes.[8]

Only state licensure boards, health care entities required to query the Data Bank, individual practitioners as to their own records and researchers using nonidentifiable data are permitted access to information in the Data Bank.[9] The general public does not have access to the information in the Data Bank, although consumer organizations have lobbied for such access.[10] Neither malpractice insurers nor third-party payers are permitted access to the Data Bank, although there are reports that these entities may be requiring physicians to request and turn over their own Data Bank records as a condition of receiving coverage or reimbursement.[11]

Controversy surrounding the scope of the mandated reporting to the Data Bank has arisen in connection with reports required of health care institutions concerning privileges actions[12] and of malpractice insurers concerning malpractice payments.[13] The Department of Health and Human Services has interpreted the statutory reporting requirements for state licensure boards in a manner that is not entirely without controversy. State licensing boards must report revocation, suspension, censure, reprimand, probation and sur-

---

professional competence or professional conduct if it is based primarily on the physician's association with a professional society or association; competitive behavior such as fees or advertising; participation in a prepaid group health plan or other delivery system; or the physician's association with, employment or supervision of a "particular class" of health care practitioner. 42 U.S.C.A. § 11151(9).

5. 42 U.S.C.A. § 11132.

6. 42 U.S.C.A. § 11135(a).

7. 42 U.S.C.A. § 11137(a).

8. The National Practitioner Data Bank Guidebook Supplement (August 1992), written by the Department of Health and Human Services, provides examples of cases in which the Secretary resolved disputes in favor of the practitioner. A 1995 Report by the U.S. Department of Health and Human Services indicated that only approximately 6% of pro-

fessional liability reports and 10% of adverse action reports are disputed.

9. 42 U.S.C.A. § 11136.

10. Mark Kadzielski, The National Practitioner Data Bank: Big Brother or Paper Tiger? Health Span (July/August 1992) p. 8. See also, 110 Public Health Reports (July/August 1995); Public Citizen Releases Listing of Disciplined Docs, 6 No.6 Cal. Health L. Monitor 8 (1998). Attorneys for plaintiffs in malpractice suits can access the Data Bank only if plaintiff can prove that the defendant health care entity failed to make a query on the practitioner defendant.

11. Brian McCormick, Debate on Data Bank Reveals Physicians' Frustrations, 34 American Medical News 5(1) (July 8, 1991).

12. See § 14–22.

13. 42 U.S.C.A. § 11131. See also, Mark Kadzielski, The National Practitioner Data

render of the license and must also report revisions to adverse license actions, such as reinstatement of the license. In contrast, state licensing boards are not to report denial of an initial application; fines or other monetary penalties unless these are accompanied by reportable licensure actions; settlement agreements imposing a monitor for a specific period, unless the monitoring "constitutes a restriction of the practitioner's license or is considered to be a reprimand."[14] There is some speculation that state licensure boards are designing penalties to avoid the reporting requirement of the act.[15]

Individual health care professionals are not required to make reports to the Data Bank. These licensed professionals may have a duty under state law, however, to report information relating to unprofessional conduct of a licensee to the appropriate state licensure board.[16]

E. SUBSTANTIVE GROUNDS FOR DISCIPLINE

§ 3–20. Generally

Statutory grounds for discipline may be found in general statutes applicable to all professions licensed by the state;[1] or in sections applicable to all licensed health care professions;[2] or in statutory provisions applicable only to particular health care professions.[3] The majority of bases for discipline do not vary significantly among the states. Common grounds for discipline include incompetence;[4] gross negligence;[5] aiding and abetting the unlicensed practice of the profession;[6] conviction of a felony or other crime related to the attributes required for the practice of the profession;[7] unlawful sale of drugs;[8] impairment due to drugs or alcohol;[9] and professional discipline in another state on grounds that would constitute grounds in the state taking action.[10] In addition, most states include a generic prohibition against "unprofessional

Bank: Big Brother or Paper Tiger? HealthSpan (July/August 1992).

14. Department of Health and Human Services, National Practitioner Data Bank Guidebook Supplement (August 1992).

15. Leigh Page, Reasons Unclear Why Licensure Actions Shifted, 34 American Medical News 3(2) (May 27, 1991). See also, Fitzhugh Mullan et al., The National Practitioner Data Bank: Report From the First Year, 268 J.A.M.A. 73 (1992), analyzing the reports to the Data Bank.

16. See e.g., McKinney's—N.Y. Pub. Health Law § 230(11)(a). See also, James Gray and Eric Zicklin, Why Bad Doctors Aren't Kicked Out of Medicine, 69 Medical Economics 126 (Jan. 20, 1992), comparing the effectiveness of reporting requirements in three states.

§ 3–20

1. See e.g., McKinney's—N.Y. Educ. Law § 6509.

2. See e.g., West's Ann. Cal. Bus. & Prof. Code § 725 and § 726.

3. See e.g., 225 ILCS 60/22 (governing physicians); 225 ILCS 65/25 (governing nursing).

4. West's Ann. Cal. Bus. & Prof. Code § 2761(a)(1); West's Ann. Cal. Bus. & Prof. Code § 2234(d); 225 ILCS 65/25(b)(4); McKinney's—N.Y. Educ. Law § 6509(2).

5. West's Ann. Cal. Bus. & Prof. Code § 2761(a)(1); West's Ann. Cal. Bus. & Prof. Code § 2234(b); 225 ILCS 65/25(b)(14); McKinney's—N.Y. Educ. Law § 6509(2).

6. West's Ann. Cal. Bus. & Prof. Code § 2761(a)(2), (d); West's Ann. Cal. Bus. & Prof. Code § 2264; McKinney's—N.Y. Educ. Law § 6509(6); 225 ILCS 60/22(32).

7. West's Ann. Cal. Bus. & Prof. Code § 2761(a)(2), (f); West's Ann. Cal. Bus. & Prof. Code § 2236(a); 225 ILCS 65/25; McKinney's—N.Y. Educ. Law § 6509(5).

8. West's Ann. Cal. Bus. & Prof. Code § 2237; 225 ILCS 65/25(b)(8); 225 ILCS 60/22(17).

9. West's Ann. Cal. Bus. & Prof. Code § 2762; West's Ann. Cal. Bus. & Prof. Code § 2239; 225 ILCS 65/25(b)(9); McKinney's—N.Y. Educ. Law § 6509(3); 225 ILCS 60/22(7).

10. West's Ann. Cal. Bus. & Prof. Code § 2761(a)(2), (k); West's Ann. Cal. Bus. & Prof.

conduct," which may form the basis for discipline.[11]

Some states have enacted more unusual grounds for disciplinary action. For example, Illinois specifically provides for disciplinary action against licensed physicians for abandonment of a patient;[12] commission of child abuse or neglect;[13] and failure to report to the licensing agency any "adverse judgment, settlement, or award arising from a liability claim related to acts or conduct similar to acts or conduct which would constitute grounds for action" under the statute.[14] New York provides for disciplinary action against any licensed professional for "refusing to provide professional service to a person because of such person's race, creed, color, or national origin."[15] The California statute regulating discipline for physicians lists a number of medical treatments or activities as "unprofessional conduct" and a basis for disciplinary action. These include willful failure to comply with statutory informed consent requirements for sterilization procedures;[16] prescribing, dispensing, administering or furnishing liquid silicone for breast implant;[17] and violation of statutory restrictions on the use of laetrile or amygdalin.[18]

Disciplinary grounds involving "immoral" activities or those evidencing "moral turpitude" on the part of the practitioner are common. State statutes generally limit discipline for immoral actions to those that relate to the licensee's qualifications or ability to function in the licensed profession.[19] Due process standards require that the grounds for professional discipline "have a rational connection with the applicant's fitness or capacity to practice."[20] Acts that have been held to relate sufficiently to the licensee's professional performance include tax fraud,[21] knowingly receiving child pornography,[22] and sexual activity with a patient.[23]

§ 3-21. Judicial Review of Grounds for Disciplinary Action

While the statute sets out grounds for discipline, the administrative agency may interpret the statutory standards through agency rules or promulgated regulations. In establishing its own statement of disciplinary grounds, as a function of interpreting the statute, the agency must remain within the authority delegated by the legislature in the licensing statute.[1] This limitation

---

Code § 2305; 225 ILCS 65/25(b)(10) (1992); McKinney's—N.Y. Educ. Law § 6509(5)(b).

11. See for example, 225 ILCS 60/22(5) and (38); 225 ILCS 65/25(b)(7); McKinney's—N.Y. Educ. Law § 6509(9).

12. 225 ILCS 60/22(16).

13. 225 ILCS 60/22(23). Also included among disciplinary grounds for nurses. 225 ILCS 65/25(b)(12).

14. 225 ILCS 60/22(36).

15. McKinney's—N.Y. Educ. Law § 6509(6).

16. West's Ann. Cal. Bus. & Prof. Code § 2250.

17. West's Ann. Cal. Bus. & Prof. Code § 2251.

18. West's Ann. Cal. Bus. & Prof. Code § 2258.

19. See e.g., West's Ann. Cal. Bus. & Prof. Code § 2761; 225 ILCS 60/22(20).

20. Schware v. Board of Bar Examiners of New Mexico, 353 U.S. 232, 77 S.Ct. 752, 1 L.Ed.2d 796 (1957), referring specifically to discipline of attorneys.

21. See e.g., In re Kindschi, 319 P.2d 824 (Wash.1958).

22. See e.g., Bevacqua v. Sobol, 579 N.Y.S.2d 243 (N.Y.App.Div.1992).

23. See § 3-23.

§ 3-21

1. See e.g., Jordan v. Department, 522 So.2d 450 (Fla.App.1988); Casey v. State Board of Registration for Healing Arts, 830 S.W.2d 478 (Mo.App.1992); Medical Society v. New Jersey Department, 575 A.2d 1348 (N.J.1990); Merritt v. Department, 654 So.2d 1051 (Fla. App.1995).

on agency discretion is generally more effective when the statute is more specific.[2]

The scope of judicial review for challenges to the rationality or advisability of the agency's or the legislature's standards is limited to examining whether the standard is arbitrary. While the standard of review makes it likely that most claims of arbitrariness will fail, some do succeed.[3]

§ 3–22. Constitutional Challenges

Licensees also have challenged substantive licensure requirements as unconstitutional under due process and equal protection. In order to be successful in this claim, the licensee must prove that the particular requirement is not reasonably related to protection of the public health and welfare.[1] This due-process analysis parallels the deferential review of the scope of the state's authority under the police power.

Claims that licensure disciplinary standards violate equal protection generally have not met with success. Several courts have held that the practice of medicine or other health care profession does not constitute a "fundamental right" for constitutional purposes and so will satisfy equal protection scrutiny if there is a rational basis for the regulation.[2] Licensees have been equally unsuccessful in identifying classifications that would heighten the equal protection scrutiny applied to the challenged standard.[3]

Because licensure penalties are punitive, the statute and regulations must be clear enough to give licensees adequate notice of the prohibited behavior. Licensees subject to disciplinary action may challenge the grounds for discipline as being void for vagueness. Courts have upheld standards relating to sexual abuse, competency, morality and habitual intemperance, among others, against vagueness challenges.[4]

§ 3–23. Specific Grounds for Discipline

Three particular grounds for professional discipline deserve special attention. Disciplinary actions based on the incompetency of the practitioner may not constitute the majority of licensure actions,[1] but in many ways this basis for discipline goes to the heart of the entire enterprise. The issue of impairment due to drugs or alcohol does form the basis of the majority of

2. See e.g., Arkansas State Nurses Assoc. v. Arkansas State Med. Board, 677 S.W.2d 293 (Ark.1984); New Mexico Bd. of Pharmacy v. New Mexico Bd. of Osteopathic Medical Examiners, 626 P.2d 854 (N.M.App.1981).

3. See e.g., Arkansas State Nurses Association v. Arkansas State Medical Board, 677 S.W.2d 293 (Ark.1984).

§ 3–22

1. See e.g., State v. Liggett, 576 P.2d 221 (Kan.1978).

2. See e.g., State v. Liggett, 576 P.2d 221, 228 (Kan.1978); Jones v. State Board of Medicine, 555 P.2d 399 (Idaho 1976), cert. denied 431 U.S. 914, 97 S.Ct. 2173, 53 L.Ed.2d 223 (1977).

3. State v. Liggett, 576 P.2d at 228–230.

4. See e.g., Haley v. Medical Disciplinary Board, 818 P.2d 1062 (Wash.1991) and Adams v. Texas, 744 S.W.2d 648 (Tex.App.1988) (standard on sexual abuse not vague); Rathle v. Grote, 584 F.Supp. 1128 (M.D.Ala.1984) and Braun v. Board of Dental Examiners, 702 A.2d 124 (Vt.1997) (competency standard not vague); Abrahamson v. Department of Professional Regulation, 154 Ill.Dec. 870, 568 N.E.2d 1319 (Ill.App.1991) (morality standard not vague), reversed on other grounds 180 Ill.Dec. 34, 606 N.E.2d 1111 (Ill.1992); Colorado v. Hoffner, 832 P.2d 1062 (Colo.App.1992) (standard on "habitual intemperance" not vague). See also, § 3–6.

§ 3–23

1. See §§ 3–1 and 3–11.

disciplinary actions.[2] The issue of sexual activity with patients generates a disproportionate number of appellate cases and has attracted wide public and professional attention.

a. Proof of Incompetency or Negligence

In some situations, medical licensure boards have attempted to define specific practice standards prospectively through rules and regulations. The board then adjudicates individual cases under the promulgated rules or regulations to determine whether a violation of those standards has occurred in a particular case. This prospective regulatory approach has been especially common in relation to the inappropriate prescription of narcotics,[3] one of the more common grounds for disciplinary action.[4]

Deviation from professional practice standards must be proven by the disciplinary agency. Where specific standards of practice have not been promulgated by the board, courts have sometimes required testimony of expert witnesses as to the standard of care[5] even though the board is dominated by medical professionals and as a specialized administrative agency is expected to use its own expertise in resolving a case.[6] With the addition of non-professional or consumer members to the licensure boards, it is likely that at least some members of the board do not have sophisticated expertise in the medical disciplines. If these board members are to participate as full members of the board in the decisionmaking process, expert witnesses may be useful.[7]

Legal issues relating to the qualification of expert witnesses in these disciplinary proceedings are similar to those arising in medical malpractice cases, although the boards are accorded more discretion in admitting the testimony of expert witnesses than is allowed in jury trials.[8] Proceedings of Peer Review Organizations are admissible on the issue of breach of professional standards of care.[9] Proceedings before other state agencies might be used to determine the question of incompetency in some narrow cases.[10]

b. Impairment Due to Abuse of Drugs or Alcohol

"Impairment" is a term of art in professional licensure.[11] It is also a central term in the federal Americans with Disabilities Act,[12] which prohibits

---

2. See § 3–11.

3. See e.g., Casey v. State Board of Registration for Healing Arts, 830 S.W.2d 478 (Mo. App.1992); Brost v. Ohio State Medical Board, 581 N.E.2d 515 (Ohio 1991); United States v. Clinical Leasing, 930 F.2d 394 (5th Cir.1991), cert. denied 502 U.S. 864, 112 S.Ct. 188, 116 L.Ed.2d 149 (1991); Eaves v. Board of Medical Examiners, 467 N.W.2d 234 (Iowa 1991); Caldwell v. Department, 684 N.E.2d 913 (Ill.App. 1997).

4. Report of the Inspector General, Department of Health and Human Services 1990. See Symposium Issue, Appropriate Management of Pain, 24 J.Law, Med. & Ethics (winter 1996) for effect on access to treatment for pain.

5. See e.g., Devous v. Wyoming State Bd. of Med. Examiners, 845 P.2d 408 (Wyo.1993).

6. See e.g., Arlen v. State, 399 N.E.2d 1251 (Ohio 1980), holding that expert testimony not required to establish standard of care; In re Williams, 573 N.E.2d 638 (Ohio 1991), holding

that expert testimony not required but that board's finding not supported by substantial evidence.

7. See e.g., Andrew L. Hyams, Expert Psychiatric Evidence in Sexual Misconduct Cases Before State Medical Boards, 18 Am. J. Law & Medicine 171, 195–197 (1992). See also, Levinson v. Connecticut Board of Chiropractic Examiners, 560 A.2d 403 (Conn.1989).

8. See e.g., Enu v. Sobol, 576 N.Y.S.2d 378 (N.Y.App.Div.1991); People v. Brown, 770 P.2d 1373 (Colo.App.1989).

9. See e.g., Pritchard v. Catterson, 401 S.E.2d 475 (W.Va.1990).

10. Choi v. State, 550 N.Y.S.2d 267, 549 N.E.2d 469 (N.Y.App.1989).

11. Sandra Johnson, Regulatory Responses to Professional Misconduct: Sexual Misconduct, Controlled Substances and Impairment, in Regulation of the Health Care Professions 45, 49 (Timothy S. Jost ed., 1997).

discrimination against persons who have a physical or mental impairment or a record of such impairment or are viewed as having such impairment.[13] Title II of the ADA applies to the licensing functions of the professional licensure boards of the states.[14] The Act reaches the application, examination and admissions functions as well as the disciplinary functions, including the impaired physician programs offered by the medical boards.[15]

Early cases involving physician impairment under the ADA indicate some latitude for board actions in the context of discipline.[16] In discipline cases, there usually is evidence of misconduct or malpractice or increased risk, and the courts have nearly uniformly ruled that the licensee is not qualified to practice in such cases.[17] Exclusion from the profession does not violate the ADA if the licensee is not qualified to practice and no reasonable accommodations can be made.[18]

Impaired health care providers present a serious threat to the quality of health care services. Impairment due to drug or alcohol is a common ground for discipline among the states.[19] Estimates of the incidence of physician impairment due to alcoholism or drug dependency vary.[20] Statutory provisions regarding the use of drugs or alcohol by physicians or other health care providers generally require that the excessive use result in some impairment of functions,[21] although some specify that danger or injury to the licensee may be sufficient.[22] Courts reviewing disciplinary action based on chemical dependency have been willing, however, to presume impairment from dependency.[23]

Although impairment due to drugs or alcohol provides grounds for disciplinary action under the state licensing statutes, most states have established programs designed to provide rehabilitative, non-disciplinary interventions for impaired doctors, nurses and other health professionals.[24] The rehabilitative approach to impairment naturally emerges from the recent emphasis on chemical dependency as an illness rather than a failure in character, especially in professionals. It also responds to perceived concerns

12. 42 U.S.C. § 12101 et. seq. (1990).

13. 42 U.S.C. § 12102(2) (1990).

14. See e.g., Alexander v. Margolis, 921 F.Supp. 482 (W.D.Mich.1995); Medical Society of New Jersey v. Jacobs, 1993 WL 413016 (D.N.J.).

15. See Johnson, supra note 11, at 49.

16. Id. at 61.

17. See e.g., Firman v. Department of State, 697 A.2d 291 (Pa.Cmwlth.1997) distinguishing conduct from status.

18. Id.

19. See §§ 3–11.

20. See e.g., W.E. McAuliffe, et al., Alcohol Use and Abuse in Random Samples of Physicians and Medical Students, 81 Am.J. Public Health 177 (1991); W.E. McAuliffe, et al., Psychoactive Drug Use Among Practicing Physicians and Medical Students, 315 New Eng. J. Med. 805 (1986); A. Krakowski, Stress and the Practice of Medicine: Physicians Compared with Lawyers, 42 Psychother Psychosom 143

(1984); R.D. Moore, et al., Youthful Precursors of Alcohol Abuse in Physicians, 88 Am. J. Med. 332 (1990); Karl Gallegos and Janetta Kelly, Trends in Physician Drug Abuse: Prevention and Control, 10 Addiction & Recovery 28 (1990); Patrick Hughes, et al., Prevalence of Substance Abuse Among U.S. Physicians, 267 J.A.M.A. 2333 (May 6, 1992); William J. Mandell, An Approach to the Impaired Physician, 20 Physician Executive (May 1994).

21. See e.g., 225 ILCS 65/25(b)(9).

22. See e.g., West's Ann. Cal. Bus. & Prof. Code § 2762 (discipline when use is "dangerous * * * to [the licensee] * * * or to the public").

23. See e.g., O'Brien v. Commissioner of Education, 523 N.Y.S.2d 680 (N.Y.App.Div. 1988). See also, Charles Winick, Social Behavior, Public Policy, and Nonharmful Drug Use, 69 Milbank Quarterly 437 (1991).

24. See e.g., McKinney's–N.Y. Pub. Health Law § 230(17)-(18).

that a punitive disciplinary approach pushes impaired health care providers undercover, risking greater injury to the public. It is hoped that the availability of a program of non-punitive rehabilitation encourages a higher rate of reporting and self-reporting of impaired physicians, as physicians who voluntarily enter such programs avoid disciplinary actions.[25]

Some studies of physician treatment programs indicate relapse rates of 10% to 20%.[26] Other studies indicate relapse rates ranging from 30% to 57%, though severity and duration of relapse may vary.[27]

c. *Sexual Activity With Patients*

The number of disciplinary actions for sexual misconduct is increasing rapidly, nearly tripling between 1990 and 1995, though medical licensure boards have been criticized as less than effective in their performance in this area. Estimates of the incidence of sexual activity by physicians with patients vary, falling between 5% to 10% of practicing physicians. These estimates are viewed by some as understated.[28]

Sexual activity by physicians with patients may generate legal claims against the physician for malpractice[29] or may result in criminal prosecution, either under general sexual assault statutes or under recently enacted more specific statutes.[30] Patients may also pursue proceedings before professional associations, such as the American Psychiatric Association, of which the practitioner is a member. Sexual misconduct also provides grounds for disciplinary action. Most of the research and legislation on physician-patient sexual activity concerns sexual relations between patients and psychiatrists or other psychotherapists, as opposed to physicians in other practice settings. Because of the intense and intimate emotional relationship encouraged in psychotherapy,[31] ethical norms against sexual activity by psychotherapists

25. See e.g., Carol Morrow, Doctors Helping Doctors, Vol. 14 No. 6 Hastings Center Report 32 (Dec. 1984). A focus on rehabilitation rather than punishment may be meeting more resistance in the nurse discipline. See H. Lippman and S. Nagle, Addicted Nurses: Tolerated, Tormented or Treated?, 55 RN 36 (1992).

26. See e.g., M ..F. Fleming, Physician Impairment: Options for Intervention, 50 American Family Physician 41 (July 1994); B. Schneidman, Editorial: The Philosophy of Rehabilitation for Impaired Physicians, 82 Federation Bulletin 124 (1995).

27. See e.g., K.L. Sprinkle, Physician Alcoholism: A Survey of the Literature, 81 Federation Bulletin, 113 (1994).

28. Sexual Misconduct in the Practice of Medicine, 266 J.A.M.A. 2741 (Nov. 20 1991), stating that the incidence is believed to be underreported; Nanette Gartrell, et al., Physician-patient Sexual Contact: Prevalence and Problems, 157 Western J. of Med. 139 (August, 1992); Catherine S. Leffler, Sexual Conduct Within the Physician–Patient Relationship: A Statutory Framework for Disciplining the Breach of Fiduciary Duty, 1–SPG Widener L. Symp. J. 501 (1996).

29. Linda Jorgenson, Rebecca Randles, and Larry Strasburger, The Furor Over Psychotherapist–Patient Sexual Contact: New Solutions to an Old Problem, 32 William and Mary Law Review 645 (1991), [hereinafter Jorgenson et al.] providing a comprehensive review of causes of action against psychotherapists and their employers.

30. See e.g., Mich. Comp. Laws Ann. § 750.520b(1)(f)(iv); Minn. Stat. Ann. § 609.342(1)(g); West's Ann. Cal. Business & Professional Code § 729. See Larry Strasburger, Linda Jorgenson, and Rebecca Randles, Criminalization of Psychotherapist–Patient Sex, 148 Am. J. of Psychiatry 859 (July 1991); Jordana B. Glasglow (Note), Sexual Misconduct by Psychotherapists: Legal Options Available to Victims and a Proposal for Change in Criminal Legislation, 33 B.C. L. Rev. 645 (1992). See e.g., People of the State of Illinois v. Burpo, 647 N.E.2d 996 (Ill.1995).

31. See e.g., Jorgenson, et al., 652–657, discussing transference and countertransference in the therapeutic context. See also, Simmons v. United States, 805 F.2d 1363, 1365 (9th Cir.1986) (referring to transference as contributing to heightened vulnerability and injury).

with patients have uniformly condemned such conduct.[32]

In late 1991, the House of Delegates of the American Medical Association adopted the report of the Council on Ethical and Judicial Affairs opinion concerning all physician-patient sexual conduct. The Council concludes that "sexual contact or romantic relationship concurrent with the physician-patient relationship is unethical." The Council adopts the theory of emotional engagement, identified as occurring during the course of psychotherapy and as supporting the stamping of all sexual activity between current patients and psychotherapists as unethical, and extends the same analysis to the physician-patient relationship in other contexts.[33]

Courts have accepted the argument that it is the *special* relationship between psychotherapist and patient that makes sexual activity between the two unethical and that sexual activity between non-psychotherapist physicians and patients is not unethical unless there is specific evidence of misconduct.[34] Some courts have distinguished cases involving psychotherapists, in which sexual activity was held to be properly the subject of disciplinary penalty or malpractice claim, from those involving physicians in other practices, relying on "the greater propensity of psychiatric patients to develop strong emotional dependence upon their physicians ... and, correspondingly, the greater possibility for emotional exploitation of the patient."[35]

Courts may find the distinction between psychotherapists and other physicians attractive because it supports the still generally held view that sexual contact by lawyers with their clients is not necessarily unethical,[36] but that sexual conduct between lawyers in certain practices, such as matrimonial law, and clients is unethical.[37]

The ethical standing of sexual activity between a physician and a *former* patient is more controversial. In a survey in which 94% of doctors stated that they opposed sexual contact with current patients, only 37% opposed sexual contact with former patients.[38] The 1991 Opinion of the AMA Council on

32. See Jorgenson, et al., 647–648, citing codes or policies of several professional organizations.

33. Sexual Misconduct in the Practice of Medicine, 266 J.A.M.A. 2741 (Nov. 20, 1991).

34. Such specific evidence would include sexual assaults during the course of treatment such as fondling or penetration during physical examination. See e.g., Kim v. Sobol, 580 N.Y.S.2d 581 (N.Y.App.Div.1992). At least one statute specifically provides that a patient is presumed to be incapable of consenting to such sexual activity. See e.g., West's Fla.Stat.Ann. § 458.331(j).

35. Zipkin v. Freeman, 436 S.W.2d 753, 755 (Mo.1968), referring to "the transference phenomenon;" Gromis v. Medical Board of California, 10 Cal.Rptr.2d 452 (Cal.App.1992), quoting *Zipkin*, and distinguishing California cases involving psychotherapists.

36. See e.g., American Bar Association Formal Ethics Opinion 92–364 "Sexual Relations With Clients," providing that sexual relations with clients in situations of special vulnerability are unethical; California Rule 3–120 "Sexual

Relations with Client" prohibiting attorneys from demanding sexual relations as a condition of professional representation; employing coercion, intimidation, or undue influence in entering sexual relations with a client; or continuing a sexual relationship with a client when it causes incompetence in providing legal representation. See also, Sandra H. Johnson, Judicial Review of Disciplinary Action for Sexual Misconduct in the Practice of Medicine, 270 J.A.M.A. 1596 (Oct. 6, 1993); Linda M. Jorgenson and Pamela K. Sutherland, Fiduciary Theory Applied to Personal Dealings: Attorney–Client Sexual Contact, 45 Ark. L. Rev. 459 (1992); John M. O'Connell (Note), Keeping Sex Out of the Attorney–Client Relationship: A Proposed Rule, 92 Colum. L. Rev. 887 (1992).

37. American Academy of Matrimonial Lawyers, Bounds of Advocacy/Standards of Conduct Rule 2.16 (1991). See also, Abed Awad, Attorney–Client Sexual Relations, 22 J. Legal Prof. 131 (1998).

38. Nanette Gartrell, et al., Physician-patient Sexual Contact: Prevalence and Problems, 157 Western J. of Med. 139 (August 1992).

Ethical and Judicial Affairs states that the minimum duty of a physician in cases in which a "true romantic relationship" develops is to terminate the professional relationship, although subsequent sexual activity may still be unethical under certain circumstances.[39] Even in the case of psychotherapists, sexual activity with former patients is not generally viewed as invariably unethical,[40] although whether the therapist terminated the professional relationship may be at issue.[41]

The enforcement of licensure restrictions against sexual activity by physicians with current patients or former patients has presented numerous conflicts. Administrative processes may present an advantage over criminal actions because of the range of sanctions, the lower burden of proof and the longer period after the event during which the victim may make a legally reviewable complaint.[42] Even so, the effectiveness of the disciplinary system in handling improper sexual activity has been criticized.[43]

Complaints of inappropriate sexual conduct by patients against physicians frequently present issues of the relative credibility of the patients and the doctors involved, often as to whether the events in fact occurred. Courts generally rely on the findings of the trier of fact as to credibility.[44] State licensing boards responding to a survey reported the use of expert testimony in limited cases to address specific issues of credibility, including inferences raised by substantial delay in filing a complaint and evaluation of the complainant's psychiatric history in relation to the reliability of the complaint.[45] Empirical research indicates that patients who have reported sexual contact with their physicians experience the same emotional and emotionally-related physical injuries as do the victims of sexual assault and that reporting by the patient might also be delayed by referrals for treatment to physicians sympathetic to the offending physician.[46] This empirical research should also

39. Opinions of the Council on Ethical and Judicial Affairs § 8.14 (1992).

40. See e.g., Paul S. Appelbaum and Linda Jorgenson, Psychotherapist–Patient Sexual Contact After Termination of Treatment: An Analysis and a Proposal, 148 Am. J. Psychiatry 1466 (Nov. 1991). See also, 740 ILCS 140/1, providing that a former patient has a cause of action against a therapist for sexual contact occurring within one year of terminating therapy.

41. Pundy v. Department of Professional Regulation, 155 Ill.Dec. 945, 570 N.E.2d 458 (Ill.App.1991), and Morris v. State Board of Psychology, 697 A.2d 1034 (Pa.Cmwlth.Ct. 1997), upholding disciplinary penalty when psychiatrist-patient relationship had not been clearly terminated; Yero v. Department of Professional Regulation, 481 So.2d 61 (Fla.App. 1985), no violation when relationship had been clearly terminated.

42. Jorgenson, et al., 728, recommending licensure remedies as "one of the quickest, most effective means of dealing with psychotherapist misconduct."

43. Sexual Misconduct in the Practice of Medicine, 266 J.A.M.A. 2741, reporting that the rate of disciplinary actions does not parallel the number of accusations, even though the

rate of false accusations appears to be extremely low.

44. See e.g., Bassim v. Sobol, 577 N.Y.S.2d 521 (N.Y.App.Div.1991), appeal dismissed in part, denied in part 583 N.Y.S.2d 185, 592 N.E.2d 793 (N.Y.App.1992); Andreski v. Commissioner, 552 N.Y.S.2d 701 (N.Y.App.Div. 1990). But see, In the Matter of Wang, 441 N.W.2d 488 (Minn.1989); Lieberman v. Department of Professional Regulation, 573 So.2d 349 (Fla.App.1990); Larocca v. State Board of Registration for the Healing Arts, 897 S.W.2d 37 (Mo.App.1995).

45. See Andrew L. Hyams, Expert Psychiatric Evidence in Sexual Misconduct Cases Before State Medical Boards, 18 Am. J. of Law & Med. 171. See also, Reddy v. State Board for Professional Medical Conduct, 686 N.Y.S.2d 520 (N.Y.App.Div.1999); Perez v. Missouri State Board, 803 S.W.2d 160 (Mo.App.1991), rejecting claim of laches in case in which patient filed complaint five years after activity ended, noting that issue was "only significant as it goes to ... credibility" and deferring to hearing commission on the issue of credibility.

46. See review of the research in Sexual Misconduct in the Practice of Medicine, 266 J.A.M.A. 2741 (Nov. 20, 1991).

be considered in the balancing of interests performed when the licensee complains of unfair delay in the pursuit of disciplinary action.

Some agencies address complaints concerning sexual contact under generic statutory grounds for discipline, such as those referring to unprofessional conduct or acts indicating moral turpitude.[47] Others penalize only sexual contact that is exploitative of the physician-patient relationship.[48] State agencies with more specific statutes or regulations[49] have not avoided definitional problems on review. Some specific statutes prohibit sexual activity with "patients," raising an inference that the statute intended to distinguish between sexual conduct with current patients and with former patients. The definition of "patient" and the boundary of a physician-patient relationship may leave room for interpretation.[50] Statutes specifically prohibiting sexual activity between physicians and current patients do not address circumstances identified by the AMA Council on Ethical and Judicial Affairs,[51] in which sexual activity with a former patient would be unethical.

Specific statutes authorizing discipline for sexual activity with patients may be narrowly interpreted. In *Gromis v. Medical Board of California*,[52] for example, the California Court of Appeal rejected discipline of a physician who had sexual intercourse with a current patient. The court held that there was no evidence in the record to support the board's conclusion that the sexual activity was "substantially related to the qualifications, functions, or duties of the occupation for which a license was issued," as specifically required by the California statute, because there was no proof that the doctor had induced consent through his status nor that his medical decisionmaking and judgment regarding the patient was compromised. The appellate court also rejected the trial court's finding that the sexual activity met the statutory standard for discipline since it arose out of the patient-physician relationship and injured the patient.

Disciplinary sanction for activities, such as billing fraud or tax fraud, which relate less directly to the practice of medicine, have been held to relate substantially to the licensee's fitness for practice.[53] The Opinion of the Council of Ethical and Judicial Affairs explains that sexual relations may detract from

47. See e.g., Heinecke v. Department of Commerce, 810 P.2d 459 (Utah App.1991); Pundy v. Department of Professional Regulation, 155 Ill.Dec. 945, 570 N.E.2d 458 (Ill.App. 1991); Perez v. Missouri State Board, 803 S.W.2d 160 (Mo.App.1991); Haley v. Medical Disciplinary Board, 818 P.2d 1062 (Wash. 1991). See also, Gladieux v. Ohio State Medical Board, 1999 WL 770959 (Ohio App.1999), upholding disciplines absent specific statutory provision, against physician who had sexual relations with the mothers of several of his pediatric patients. See also, Board of Physician Quality Assurance v. Banks, 729 A.2d 376 (Md. 1999), upholding discipline against physician, under general statutory provision relating to unprofessional conduct, for sexual harassment of hospital employee.

48. See e.g., Wyo. Stat. § 33–26–402(a)(vii).

49. See e.g., Ariz. Rev. Stat. § 32–1401(25)(z); West's Colo. Rev. Stat. Ann. § 12–36–117(1)(r); West's Fla. Stat. Ann. § 458.331(1)(j).

50. See e.g., Levin v. Idaho State Board of Medicine, 987 P.2d 1028 (Idaho 1999); Haley v. Medical Disciplinary Board, 818 P.2d 1062 (Wash.1991). See also, Heinecke v. Department of Commerce, 810 P.2d 459 (Utah App.1991).

51. The position of the Council is that sexual contact with former patients is unethical if the "sexual contact occurred as a result of the use or exploitation of trust, knowledge, influence, or emotions derived from the former professional relationship." Sexual Misconduct in the Practice of Medicine, 266 J.A.M.A. 2741 (Nov. 20, 1991).

52. 10 Cal.Rptr.2d 452 (Cal.App.1992).

53. See e.g., Haley v. Medical Disciplinary Board, 818 P.2d 1062 (Wash.1991), analogizing sexual activity with a patient to tax fraud in its relationship to the licensee's qualifications to continue in the practice of medicine.

the goals of the physician-patient relationship and may obscure the physician's objective judgment concerning the patient's health care. It does not limit the prohibition of sexual activity to situations where such a negative impact has in fact occurred.[54]

It has been argued that physician-patient sexual activity is protected constitutionally by a right of privacy.[55] This argument is assailable on two grounds. First, the presumption of consent by the patient to the sexual activity may be questioned in light of the AMA Opinion and other research.[56] Second, the only absolute restriction in the AMA Opinion on a doctor engaging in sexual activity with a current patient is that the doctor first terminate the physician-patient relationship. While this may be a burden on sexual activity, ordinarily the burden will not be unreasonable.

F. THE MEDICARE UTILIZATION AND QUALITY CONTROL PEER REVIEW ORGANIZATION PROGRAM

§ 3–24. Introduction

The Medicare Utilization and Quality Control Peer Review Organization (PRO or QRO) Program is the federal government's primary tool for assuring that services provided to Medicare beneficiaries are medically necessary, of a quality that meets professionally recognized standards of health care, and provided in an appropriate setting.[1] It is intended both to protect the health and safety of Medicare beneficiaries and to control the cost of the Medicare program.

The initial Medicare law, adopted in 1965, did little to regulate the medical necessity, appropriateness, and quality of services provided to Medicare beneficiaries. It required only hospital-based utilization review committees to assure appropriate utilization of services,[2] state licensure to assure that physicians were minimally qualified,[3] and accreditation by the Joint Commission on Accreditation of Hospitals to secure the quality of hospitals.[4] By the early 1970s, however, it became apparent that further controls were needed to limit excessive utilization of Medicare services.[5] Out of this concern

---

54. Code of Medical Ethics, Current Opinions of the Council on Ethical and Judicial Affairs of the American Medical Association 9.04 (1992).

55. In the Matter of Pons, 1991 WL 245003 (Ohio App.1991); reversed by Ohio Supreme Court 614 N.E.2d 748 (Ohio 1993), but without discussion of constitutional issue.

56. See e.g., Final Report of the Task Force on Sexual Abuse of Patients, Commissioned by the College of Physicians and Surgeons of Ontario (Nov. 25, 1991). See also, West's Fla. Stat. Ann. § 458.331(1)(j), establishing a legal presumption that sexual activity during the course of medical treatment is not consensual.

§ 3–24

1. 42 U.S.C.A. § 1320c–3(a)(1). Much of the material in this section is drawn from Timothy Stoltzfus Jost, Administrative Law Issues In-

volving the Medicare Utilization and Quality Control Peer Review Organization (PRO) Program: Analysis and Recommendations, 50 Ohio St. L. J. 1 (1989).

2. Pub. L. 89–97, § 1861(k), 79 Stat. 285, 318–19.

3. Pub. L. 89–97, § 1861(r), 79 Stat. 285, 321.

4. Pub. L. 89–97, § 1865, 79 Stat. 285, 326–27.

5. See Social Security Amendments of 1972, Senate Finance Committee Report, No. 1230, 92d Cong. 2d Sess., 254–69 (1972); Medicare & Medicaid, Problems Issues and Alternatives, Staff of Senate Comm. on Finance, 91st Cong. 2d Sess., 105–09 (Feb. 9, 1970).

grew the Professional Standards Review Organization (PSRO) program, which used regional nonprofit physicians groups to review the use of medical services by beneficiaries of federal medical assistance programs, including Medicare.[6] Though the primary emphasis of PSROs was on utilization review, they also conducted Medical Care Evaluation Studies (later Quality Review Studies) aimed at improving the quality of medical care. PSROs never succeeded in meeting the expectations of their supporters or overcoming the criticisms of their detractors. The 1982 Tax Equity and Fiscal Responsibility Act (TEFRA) abolished the PSRO program, creating in its stead the PRO program.[7]

The PRO program was intended to be a leaner and more effective program than its predecessor. The 195 PSRO regions were trimmed to fifty-four (now fifty-three) statewide areas. The old system of grant-funding was replaced by biennial (now triennial) contracts, to be awarded by competitive bidding. Ineffective PROs were to be terminated. PROs could no longer delegate utilization review functions to hospitals, as had the PSROs. Though PROs were initially to be physician sponsored organizations (as were the old PSROs), the statute allows HHS to turn to other organizations, including insurance companies or Medicare fiscal intermediaries, to form PROs if initial physician-sponsored contractors prove ineffective. Unlike PSROs, PROs could be for-profit entities. Finally, the PROs were given enhanced sanction and payment denial authority to carry out their responsibilities.[8]

In the year following the creation of the PRO program (before it was in fact implemented) Congress adopted the prospective payment system (PPS) for Medicare based on diagnosis-related groups (DRGs).[9] This system ended the prior cost-related reimbursement system, under which Medicare had reimbursed hospitals the costs they incurred in caring for Medicare patients, and substituted for it a program that paid hospitals primarily on a lump-sum per hospitalization basis. The PROs were given the assignment of policing the undesirable hospital behavior DRG reimbursement could encourage: premature discharge of patients, underservice of hospitalized patients, and gaming of the system by either transferring patients between hospitals or units within hospitals or by assigning improper DRGs.

There are currently forty-two PROs serving the fifty-three PRO areas. They consist of both "physician sponsored," organizations (composed of at least 20% of the physicians practicing in the review area, or are composed of 10% of the physicians in the area and are otherwise representative of the state physician community)[10] and "physician access" organizations, usually insurance companies, having a sufficient number of physicians available to carry on review functions.[11] PROs must include on their boards at least one consumer

6. Pub. L. No. 92–603, § 249F, 86 Stat. 1329, 1429–1445.

7. Pub. L. 97–248, § 143, 96 Stat. 324, 382.

8. See Joseph A. Cislowski, Congressional Research Service Report for Congress, The Peer Review Organization Program, 4–5 (1987); Kathleen N. Lohr, Peer Review Organizations: Quality Assurance in Medicare, 7, 14–15 (1985); Peter Melette, The Changing Focus of Peer Review Under Medicare, 20 U. Rich. L.

Rev. 315 (1986) (describing the changes from the PSRO to PRO program).

9. Pub.L. 98–21, Title VI, 97 Stat. 65, 149–172.

10. HHS Office of Inspector General, The Utilization and Quality Control Peer Review Organization (PRO) Program, An Exploration of Program Effectiveness, 3 (1989); 42 C.F.R. § 462.102.

11. 42 C.F.R. § 462.103.

representative.[12] The PROs vary significantly in size, the largest having hundreds of employees and annual budgets of millions of dollars. The budget for the PRO program for FY 1999 was $411 million.

PROs are delegated review responsibility under three year contracts with HHS.[13] The contracts are drafted to conform to a "Scope of Work." The PROs are currently governed by the Sixth Scope of Work.[14] HHS may terminate a PRO that has substantially failed to carry out its contract.[15] The PRO program is supervised by the Office of Clinical Standards and Quality of the Health Care Financing Administration (HCFA) of HHS.

The primary task of the PROs is to review and improve the quality of health care services provided to Medicare beneficiaries.[16] PROs focus their review primarily on care provided to beneficiaries by doctors in hospitals. Since the late 1980s PROs have also reviewed care provided by Medicare managed care organizations.[17]

The nature of PRO review changed radically in the early 1990s. During the first three scopes of work (through 1992), Indeed, PRO's currently often refer to themselves as quality review organizations or QROS. PROs regularly received from fiscal intermediaries (the insurance companies and other entities that handle Medicare reimbursement to providers) data on bills paid for services rendered to Medicare beneficiaries. The PRO selected a sample of these cases for review and requested medical records on these cases from the hospitals, which were reviewed at the hospital, or at the PRO office. Once medical records fitting these sample criteria were identified and copied, they were reviewed by professional reviewers (usually nurses) applying criteria screens to identify utilization or quality problems. Each inpatient hospital discharge was reviewed for quality problems using HCFA's generic quality screens, for necessity and appropriateness using PRO discharge and admission criteria screens, and for DRG validation. Care provided outside of the hospital setting was only reviewed for quality, and not for utilization problems.

Under the Fourth, Fifth, and Sixth Scopes of Work, the nature of PRO review changed dramatically. The Health Care Quality Improvement Program (HCQIP), implemented with the Fourth Scope of Work, has relied much less on review of individual cases and much more on identification of patterns of practice using large data sets. It has also relied less on focused review of particular cases, and more on cooperative projects directed at improving care generally. It explicitly eschews a punitive approach to quality oversight, focusing instead on research and education.[18]

12. 42 U.S.C.A. § 1320c–1(3).

13. 42 U.S.C.A. § 1320c–2(c)(3).

14. http: // www.hcfa.gov / quality / qlty–5b.htm. A brief summary of this document was published in the Federal Register at 64 Fed. Reg. 36021 (1999).

15. 42 U.S.C.A. § 1320c–2(c)(6). Such a termination is not subject to judicial review. 42 U.S.C.A. § 1320c–2(f). Pennsylvania Peer Review Organization v. United States, 50 B.R. 640, Medicare & Medicaid Guide (CCH), ¶ 34,-992 (Bkrtcy.Pa.1985).

16. PROs also review Medicaid cases for states that contract for such assistance, 42

U.S.C.A. § 1320c–7 and review for private payers, 42 U.S.C.A. § 1320c–3(a)(11).

17. Current provisions requiring PRO review of Medicare + Choice organizations (subject to waiver for organizations that have "consistently maintained an excellent record of quality assurance and compliance." are found at 42 U.S.C.A. § 13952–22(g)(3).

18. Wilma M. Hopman, Uniform Clinical Data Set: A Comprehensive Clinical Information System, in Health Care: Innovation, Impact and Challenge (S. Mathwin Davis, ed.); Stephen F. Jencks & Gail R. Wilensky, The Health Care Quality Improvement Initiative: A

Under the Sixth Scope of Work, each PRO must participate in National Quality Improvement Projects.[19] Projects are currently underway working with six clinical areas: acute myocardial infarction, heart failure, pneumonia, stroke/transient ischemic attack/atrial fibrillation, diabetes and breast cancer. The PROs are responsible for using HCFA supplied baseline data and data that they themselves collect to design and implement quality improvement projects in these areas.[20] They are responsible for designing and implementing their own local quality improvement projects that respond to local issues or opportunities, including at least one project aimed at care in settings other than acute care or Medicare+Choice plans, and one involving disparities in care received by disadvantaged groups.[21] PROs are also to carry out quality improvement projects in conjunction with Medicare+Choice plans.[22] HCFA has claimed impressive success for PRO quality of care initiatives to date.[23]

Though PROs prefer to present themselves to health care professionals and providers as partners for quality improvement, they have a darker side. The PROs also provide the medical expertise that HCFA needs to police the quality and necessity of care provided to Medicare beneficiaries. In this capacity, the PROs, often quite reluctantly, have to take on the role of quality enforcers. Thus PROs are required to investigate complaints by Medicare beneficiaries about the quality of Medicare-covered services, including services provided by Medicare+Choice organizations.[24] PROs are responsible for reviewing cases where hospitals inform patients that their care is not, or is no longer, covered by Medicare.[25] PROs must review the use of assistants for cataract surgery and validate assignment of DRGs in some cases.[26] They may sanction practitioners who have failed in a substantial number of cases to comply with statutory obligations to provide medically necessary care of a quality complying with professionally recognized standards or who have grossly and flagrantly violated such obligations in one or more instances.[27] And under the Sixth Scope of Work, PROs are required to a Payment Error Prevention Program (PEPP), which providers have viewed as an attempt to enlist PROs in fraud and abuse policing.[28] PROs are still viewed by some in the provider community, therefore, not only as allies in quality improvement, but also as potential adversaries.

New Approach to Quality Assurance in Medicare, 268 JAMA 900, 900–01 (1992).

19. Sixth Scope of Work, ¶ C.3.A.1.

20. Id.

21. Id. at ¶ C.3.B.2.

22. Id. at C.3.B.3.

23. See Health Care Financing Administration, PRO Results: Bridging the Past with the Future, Sept. 1998, at http://www.hcfa/gov/quality/3k1.htm. See also Linda Prager, Quality Improvement Project

Paying Off for Patients, 41 Am. Med. News, June 15, 1998 at 9.

24. 42 U.S.C.A. § 1320c–3(a)(14).

25. 42 U.S.C.A. § 1320c–3(e).

26. Fourth Scope of Work, § C.3.5.b.

27. 42 U.S.C.A. § 1320c–5(b); 42 C.F.R. Part 1004.

28. Sixth Scope of Work, supra note 14, at C.3.B.4. See Vida Foubister, Physicians Peeved by PRO's Punitive Posture, 42 Am.Med. News, July 12, 1999 at 8.

Chapter 4

PROFESSIONAL RELATIONSHIPS IN THE HEALTH CARE ENTERPRISE

Table of Sections

Sec.

F. QUALITY ASSURANCE AND RISK MANAGEMENT

G. MEDICAL INFORMATION AND RECORDS: CONFIDENTIALITY AND DISCLOSURE

———————

Research References

Am Jur 2d, Labor and Labor Relations §§ 1094–1102; Physicians, Surgeons, and Other
    Healers §§ 150–157
ALR Index: Extended Health Care Facility; Health Care Quality Improvement Act;
    Physicians and Surgeons
ALR Digest: Hospitals and Other Health Care Facilities § 1
Am Jur Legal Forms 2d, Physicians and Surgeons §§ 202:51–202:56
38 POF2d 445, Vicarious Liability of Physician for Negligence of Another; 25 POF2d
    411, Nurse's Failure to Give Physician Timely Notice of Patient's Condition

§ 4–1. Introduction

This chapter presents current legal issues in both the traditional and more contemporary forms of professional relationships in health care delivery, including staff privileges, hospital-based practice contracts, and employment.[1]

§ 4–1

1. The antitrust implications of staff privileges are discussed extensively at §§ 14–15 to

The structure of professional relationships, particularly within hospitals, has changed drastically in the last decade. Cost containment, the legitimization and encouragement of competition in health care delivery and the increased professional identity in health care administration each have worked to diminish the professional hegemony previously enjoyed as a given by physicians in the hospital setting. Still, physicians often hold considerable leverage over the institutions in which they practice. It once may have been accurate to generalize the hospital as a "physicians' cooperative" operated primarily for the benefit of the doctors; however, any generalization today about the relative power of physicians and the health care organizations within which they practice will be limiting if not entirely inaccurate. Hospitals and physicians now organize their relationships using a number of different forms. Still, staff privileges, which is the first relationship we study below, forms the background framework.

A.　STAFF PRIVILEGES

§ 4–2.　Background

A physician or other health care professional[1] may admit or treat patients in a particular hospital only if the practitioner has admitting or clinical privileges at that hospital. The Joint Commission on Accreditation of Healthcare Organizations defines clinical privileges as "[p]ermission to provide medical or other patient care services in the granting institution, within well-defined limits, based on the individual's professional license and his/her experience, competence, ability and judgment."[2] To provide patient care service independently within a hospital, physicians must be admitted to membership in the hospital's medical staff.[3]

Hospital privileges are critical to the practice of most physicians and many other independent health care practitioners. At the same time, hospitals[4] generally have become more restrictive in their granting and monitoring of privileges for several reasons, including the hospital's potential liability for

14–22.

§ 4–2

1. Health care professionals who are not physicians may hold some form of staff and clinical privileges. Many of the issues raised are identical to those discussed throughout this chapter. See e.g., Clemons v. Fairview Medical Center, Inc., 480 So.2d 1211 (Ala.1985), whether by-laws guarantee pre-termination procedures to physical therapist holding privileges. Others relate specially to the limited licensure of non-physician providers. See e.g., Spiro v. Highlands General Hospital, 489 So.2d 802 (Fla.App.1986), contract for services beyond scope of license illegal and unenforceable. Most of the litigation involving staff privileges for nonphysician practitioners involves claims of violation of antitrust laws. See §§ 10–16 to 10–25.

2. Joint Commission on Accreditation of Healthcare Organizations, Accreditation Manual for Hospitals, MS. 1.1.2.

3. Accreditation Manual for Hospitals, MS. 1.1.1.

4. Although it is the "hospital" that is responsible for staff privileges decisions, the medical staff and the administration and the governing board each have roles to play, delineated in the corporate and medical staff by-laws and in accreditation and hospital licensure standards, with the governing board retaining ultimate decisionmaking authority. Conflicts between hospitals and their medical staffs have received substantial attention. Also important to consider in evaluating hospital staff privileges processes are conflicts between administration and the governing board. See e.g., John D. Blum, Hospital–Medical Staff Relations in the Face of Shifting Institutional Business Strategies: A Legal Analysis, 14 U. Puget Sound L. Rev. 561 (1991).

failure to adequately monitor the quality of physicians practicing within the hospital[5] and the connection between the practice patterns of the physician and the financial risk borne by the hospital. The high stakes for both parties in credentialing decisions make the area ripe for litigation.

Physicians may invoke judicial review of negative credentialing decisions under a variety of statutory, constitutional or common law theories. For example, physicians may pursue claims under federal antitrust statutes,[6] under state statutes specifically governing staff privileges,[7] and under federal or state anti-discrimination statutes,[8] among others. Doctors subject to credentialing processes that meet a minimum requirement of state action may claim certain constitutional protections.[9] In addition, each state has developed a common law basis for judicial review of staff privileges decisions.[10]

§ 4–3. Exhaustion of Internal Procedures

The law relevant to judicial review of staff privileges operates from a starting point of deference to the institution's judgment and an interest in avoiding excessive litigation, though there are some exceptions.[1] As part of this judicial deference to staff privileges decisions, courts generally have established a requirement that persons suing to challenge adverse credentialing decisions must exhaust procedures available within the institution prior to filing suit. Failure to exhaust internal procedures may result in summary judgment in favor of the hospital.

The application of an exhaustion requirement to staff privileges reflects deference to the expertise of the health care institution as well as concern with minimizing litigation by allowing the institution to correct its own errors and decreasing the cost of litigation by encouraging the development of a factual record prior to trial.[2] Plaintiffs challenging a staff privileges decision as illegal under federal antidiscrimination statutes, however, generally are not required to exhaust institutional procedures.[3]

§ 4–4. Public v. Private Institutions

A threshold question in many credentialing cases requires characterizing

---

5. See Chapter 7.

6. See §§ 14–15 to 10–22.

7. States often require as a condition of licensure that hospitals establish a credentialing process for the medical staff. A few states have established very specific procedural and substantive standards for hospital credentialing decisions, which are idiosyncratic to the particular state. For example, New York provides for a review of adverse private credentialing decisions. McKinney's—N.Y. Pub. Health Laws § 2801–b. Physicians must submit their challenges to the administrative agency prior to filing suit. See e.g., Saha v. Record, 575 N.Y.S.2d 986 (N.Y.App.Div.1991); Shapiro v. Central General Hospital, Inc., 581 N.Y.S.2d 430 (N.Y.App.Div.1992).

8. See §§ 4–20 through 4–23.

9. See §§ 4–4 and 4–5.

10. See §§ 4–6, 4–7 and 4–8.

§ 4–3

1. See discussion of anti-discrimination statutes at § 4–20 and of antitrust considerations at §§ 14–15 to 10–22.

2. See e.g., Eufemio v. Kodiak Island Hospital, 837 P.2d 95 (Alaska 1992); Soentgen v. Quain & Ramstad Clinic, 467 N.W.2d 73 (N.D. 1991); Garrow v. Elizabeth General Hospital and Dispensary, 401 A.2d 533 (N.J.1979). But see, Keskin v. Munster Medical Research Foundation, 580 N.E.2d 354 (Ind.App.1991); Franson v. Massena Memorial Hospital, 977 F.Supp. 160 (N.D.N.Y.1997).

3. See e.g., Chowdhury v. Reading Hospital and Medical Center, 677 F.2d 317 (3d Cir. 1982), cert. denied 463 U.S. 1229, 103 S.Ct. 3569, 77 L.Ed.2d 1411 (1983), exhaustion not required for claim under Title VI; Doe v. St. Joseph's Hospital of Fort Wayne, 788 F.2d 411 (7th Cir.1986), exhaustion not required for claim under Title VI or Title VII.

the credentialing decision at issue as either a decision involving state action[1] and so supporting constitutional claims by the aggrieved practitioner, or as a private decision in which such claims are not available. One approach to the question of whether the particular credentialing decision involves state action is to analyze the character of the hospital.

Entities owned and operated by federal, state or local governments represent purely public institutions and clearly are subject to constitutional claims by practitioners.[2] Similarly, hospitals entirely owned and operated by non-governmental entities, even though they receive government funds for care delivered under state or federal health care programs, such as Medicare or Medicaid or as loans for capital improvements or expansion, are generally considered private institutions for purposes of credentialing litigation.[3] As private institutions, they are not subject to constitutional claims.

The financial crisis experienced by state and local public hospitals in the 1980s resulted in a privatization effort which produced "hybrid" hospitals that assume one of several organizational structures. For example, such hospitals may be owned by a governmental entity but managed by a private management firm under contract with the government; or the hospital may be owned and controlled by a separately incorporated not-for-profit "public benefits" corporation; or the governmental entity may contract with a hospital owned and operated by private parties for the satisfaction of the government's duty to provide health care for the indigent public.[4]

Several courts have reviewed the question of the appropriate characterization of such facilities as public or private for purposes of credentialing challenges. Some courts have examined the facility's credentialing process to identify whether there is control of credentialing decisions by governmental entities. In *Kiracofe v. Reid Memorial Hospital*,[5] for example, the court examined a situation in which the city held title to the land on which the hospital stood. The city also appointed four board members, and the hospital's by-laws stated that it was owned by "the people." The court concluded that there was no state action because the government did not attempt to participate in or influence the hospital's decision to terminate the plaintiff's staff privileges. This approach is consistent with the traditional analysis of possible

§ 4–4

1. The question of state action for purposes of constitutional claims against hospitals for credentialing decisions should not be confused with the "state action doctrine" applicable to antitrust claims. See discussion at §§ 10–2 and 10–19.

2. See e.g., Northeast Georgia Radiological Associates, P.C. v. Tidwell, 670 F.2d 507 (5th Cir.1982); Hutton v. Memorial Hospital, 824 P.2d 61 (Colo.App.1991); Huellmantel, M.D. v. Greenville Hospital System, 402 S.E.2d 489 (S.C.App.1991); Ezekwo v. NYC Health & Hospitals Corp., 940 F.2d 775 (2d Cir.1991), cert. denied 502 U.S. 1013, 112 S.Ct. 657, 116 L.Ed.2d 749 (1991); Engelstad, M.D. v. Virginia Municipal Hospital, 718 F.2d 262 (8th Cir. 1983); Alonso v. Hospital Authority of Henry County, 332 S.E.2d 884 (Ga.App.1985); Finley v. Giacobbe, 79 F.3d 1285 (2d Cir. 1996).

3. See e.g., St. Mary's Hospital v. Radiology Professional Corporation, 421 S.E.2d 731 (Ga. App.1992); Richardson v. St. John's Mercy Hospital, 674 S.W.2d 200 (Mo.App.1984); Long v. Houston Northwest Medical Center, 1991 WL 19837 (Tex.App.1991); Mahmoodian v. United Hospital Center, 404 S.E.2d 750 (W.Va. 1991), cert. denied 502 U.S. 863, 112 S.Ct. 185, 116 L.Ed.2d 146 (1991); Stiller v. La Porte Hospital, 570 N.E.2d 99 (Ind.App.1991); Babcock v. St. Francis Medical Center, 543 N.W.2d 749 (Neb.Ct.App.1996).

4. See e.g., E. Richard Brown, Public Hospitals on the Brink: Their Problems and Their Options, 7 J. Health Politics, Policy and Law 927, 939–941 (1983). See also, Walter L. Metcalfe, Jr., Indigent Health Care In St. Louis: An Innovative Solution to an Intractable Problem, 32 St. Louis U. L.J. 1075 (1988).

5. 461 N.E.2d 1134 (Ind.App.1984).

state action in private institutions, in which the courts examine the specific attributes of government participation in a particular institution. In this approach, the court will find state action only when there is a nexus between the participation of the government and the credentialing decision.[6]

Other courts have relied more on the degree of general control provided for in the structure of the public-private enterprise. In *Jatoi v. Hurst–Euless–Bedford Hospital Authority*,[7] the Fifth Circuit found state action in a situation in which the Hospital Authority had leased the hospital to a private organization for day-to-day operations, including credentialing decisions, but had provided financial support and had retained control over the operation of the hospital. Relying on *Jatoi*, the Tenth Circuit also found state action on the part of a publicly owned hospital leased to and operated by a private management corporation under a contract that provided that the private corporation had responsibility for medical staff privileges decisions.[8]

A few jurisdictions have held that certain hospitals, which would have been considered private hospitals under traditional analysis, are "quasi-public" hospitals and so are subject to due process requirements in their credentialing actions.[9] Jurisdictions vary in the factors that determine the hospital's status as "quasi-public". For example, New Mexico and Arizona have reviewed the staffing decisions of private hospitals based on the fact that the hospitals had monopolies in particular areas, and thus were not subject to economic controls.[10] Other courts rely on other factors, including the nature and extent of public funding, and whether the hospital was part of a government plan to provide hospital facilities to the public.[11]

Another related line of cases does not use the "quasi-public" categorization. Instead these jurisdictions base judicial review of the merits of private hospitals' staffing decisions on the reasoning that hospitals have a fiduciary duty to act for the public good.[12]

The exercise of distinguishing between public and private hospitals is important if the decisions of public hospitals are subject to greater procedural requirements or closer judicial scrutiny if challenged. Some courts, however, have suggested that the traditional public-private distinction has become meaningless, at least for the issue of minimum procedural requirements. This view is based on the applicability of the common-law "fundamental fairness"

6. See also, Weston v. Carolina Medicorp Inc., 402 S.E.2d 653 (N.C.App.1991), review denied 409 S.E.2d 611 (N.C.1991); Canady v. Providence Hospital, 903 F.Supp. 125 (D.D.C. 1995).

7. 807 F.2d 1214 (5th Cir.1987), cert. denied 484 U.S. 1010, 108 S.Ct. 709, 98 L.Ed.2d 660 (1988). See also, Ahmed v.Berkshire Medical Center, Inc., 1998 WL 157016 (D.Mass.).

8. Milo v. Cushing Mun. Hosp., 861 F.2d 1194 (10th Cir.1988).

9. See e.g., Silver v. Castle Memorial Hospital, 497 P.2d 564 (Hawaii 1972); Peterson v. Tucson General Hospital, Inc., 559 P.2d 186 (Ariz.App.1976); Kelly v. St. Vincent Hospital, 692 P.2d 1350 (N.M.App.1984).

10. Peterson v. Tucson General Hospital Inc., 559 P.2d 186 (Ariz.App.1976); Kelly v. Vincent Hospital, 692 P.2d 1350 (N.M.App. 1984).

11. Bricker v. Sceva Speare Memorial Hospital, 281 A.2d 589 (N.H.1971); Silver v. Castle Memorial Hospital, 497 P.2d 564 (Hawaii 1972).

12. Woodard v. Porter Hospital, Inc., 217 A.2d 37 (Vt.1966); Sussman v. Overlook Hospital Association, 222 A.2d 530 (N.J.Super. Ch. Div.1966), affirmed 231 A.2d 389 (N.J.Super. App.Div.1967); Greisman v. Newcomb Hospital, 192 A.2d 817 (N.J.1963), although the court also took into account the hospital's public funding and monopoly in the area.

doctrine[13] and the federal Health Care Quality Improvement Act[14] to private credentialing decisions.[15]

§ 4–5.   Procedural Requirements for Credentialing Processes

The denial, revocation or limitation of staff privileges is ordinarily viewed as a deprivation of a property interest.[1] Thus, public hospitals, "quasi-public" hospitals and private hospitals where there is state action in credentialing decisions,[2] must meet constitutional due process requirements in their credentialing procedures. Generally, courts have held that procedural due process requires, at a minimum, adequate notice, adequate opportunity for a hearing, the right to introduce evidence and the right to confront and cross-examine witnesses.[3]

Due process may not apply in cases in which an exclusive contract for services is involved.[4] In *Hutton v. Memorial Hospital*,[5] for example, the Colorado Court of Appeals held that a physician denied staff privileges at a municipal hospital was not entitled to a hearing when the denial was based on the existence of an exclusive contract for services in the applicant physician's area of practice rather than a qualitative evaluation of the applicant.[6]

Due process requirements may also be diminished in cases in which there is a threat to public safety. Such a balancing of the public interest against the potential injury to the claimant would support summary suspension with a post-suspension hearing.[7]

Private credentialing procedures, although not governed by constitutional due process requirements, generally must meet requirements of "fundamental fairness," a common-law doctrine developed to govern access to private

13. See § 4–5.

14. 42 U.S.C.A. § 11101 et seq. See also, § 10–25.

15. See e.g., Mahmoodian v. United Hospital Center, 404 S.E.2d 750 (W.Va.1991). cert. denied 502 U.S. 863, 112 S.Ct. 185, 116 L.Ed.2d 146 (1991); Allison v. Centre Community Hospital, 604 A.2d 294 (Pa.Cmwlth.1992).

§ 4–5

1. See e.g., Greenwood v. New York, 163 F.3d 119 (2d Cir. 1998), holding that clinical staff privileges guaranteed by state law at a state hospital are a property interest protected by the Due Process Clause of the Fourteenth Amendment. See also, Shaw v. Hospital Authority of Cobb County, 507 F.2d 625 (5th Cir.1975), appeal after remand 614 F.2d 946 (5th Cir.1980), holding that arbitrary refusal to grant privileges to podiatrists implicated the practitioner's liberty interests; Ezekwo v. NYC Health & Hospital Corporation, 940 F.2d 775 (2d Cir.1991), cert. denied 502 U.S. 1013, 112 S.Ct. 657, 116 L.Ed.2d 749 (1991), holding that plaintiff had a property interest in becoming chief resident. But see, Bloom v. Hennepin County, 783 F.Supp. 418 (D.Minn.1992), holding no property interest exists where contract read in conjunction with by-laws provided no

procedural guarantees for revocation of privileges; Kattar v. Three Rivers Area Hospital Authority, 1999 WL 402419 (W.D.Mich.), holding physician who was an employee of professional corporation did not show that he held a property interest in his position protected by due process.

2. See § 4–4.

3. See e.g., Huellmantel v. Greenville Hospital System, 402 S.E.2d 489, 491 (S.C.App. 1991). See also South Carolina Department of Labor, Licensing and Regulation v. Girgis, 503 S.E.2d 490 (S.C.Ct.App.1998).

4. See §§ 4–9 to 4–11.

5. 824 P.2d 61 (Colo.App.1991). See also, Bryan A. Liang, An Overview and Analysis of Challenges to Medical Exclusive Contracts, 18 J. Leg. Med. 1 (1997); and Engelstad v. Virginia Municipal Hospital, 718 F.2d 262 (8th Cir. 1983). But see, Northeast Georgia Radiological Associates v. Tidwell, 670 F.2d 507 (5th Cir. 1982).

6. See also § 4–11.

7. See e.g., Caine v. Hardy, 943 F.2d 1406 (5th Cir.1991), cert. denied 503 U.S. 936, 112 S.Ct. 1474, 117 L.Ed.2d 618 (1992).

associations that "control important economic interests."[8] Under the rubric of fundamental fairness, courts have required hospitals to provide adequate notice and an adequate opportunity to respond to charges.[9] Courts may establish other procedural requirements as well.[10]

In addition to the common-law doctrine of fundamental fairness, the Health Care Quality Improvement Act of 1986 (HCQIA) has also influenced the design of internal staff privileges procedures.[11] The HCQIA immunizes "professional review bodies" and individuals participating in "professional review actions" from damages arising from antitrust or other types of claims.[12] In order to qualify for this immunity, the professional review body must be composed of individuals who are not in "direct economic competition with the physician involved."[13] In addition, the HCQIA requires that a professional review action must meet the four standards set forth in the Act. A professional review action must be taken (1) in reasonable belief that the action was in furtherance of quality health care; (2) after a reasonable effort to obtain the facts of the matter; (3) after adequate notice and hearing procedures are afforded to the physician involved or after such other procedures as are fair to the physician under the circumstances, and; (4) in the reasonable belief that the action was warranted by the facts known after reasonable effort to obtain the facts.[14] The Act establishes a rebuttable presumption that actions falling within the definition of "peer review actions" meet these tests; the presumption, however, may be rebutted by a "preponderance of the evidence."[15] In immunizing professional review actions, the HCQIA provides an incentive for private hospitals, which are not governed by constitutional due-process requirements, to adhere to the set of federal standards enumerated in the Act. The HCQIA, however, does not either explicitly or implicitly afford aggrieved physicians a cause of action when a hospital fails to follow the Act's prescribed peer review process.[16]

State hospital licensure statutes also may establish minimum procedural requirements in some detail.[17] Some courts have relied on such statutes to imply a duty, enforceable in a private action by a physician, on the part of both public and private hospitals to provide internal procedures that satisfy such criteria.[18]

---

8. Rosenblit v. Fountain Valley Regional Hospital, 282 Cal.Rptr. 819, 825 (Cal.App. 1991); Goodstein v. Cedars–Sinai Medical Center, 78 Cal.Rptr.2d 577 (Cal.App.1998). See also, Siqueira v. Northwestern Memorial Hospital, 87 Ill.Dec. 415, 477 N.E.2d 16 (Ill.1985).

9. See e.g., Mahmoodian v. United Hospital Center, 404 S.E.2d 750 (W.Va.1991), cert. denied 502 U.S. 863, 112 S.Ct. 185, 116 L.Ed.2d 146 (1991).

10. See e.g., Rosenblit v. Fountain Valley Regional Hospital and Medical Center, 282 Cal. Rptr. 819 (Cal.App.1991).

11. 42 U.S.C.A. § 11112(a).

12. See e.g., Brader v. Allegheny General Hospital, 167 F.3d 832 (3d Cir. 1999). See also, § 10–25.

13. 42 U.S.C.A. § 11112(a)(3)(iii).

14. 42 U.S.C.A. § 11112(a).

15. Id.

16. Wayne v. Genesis Medical Center, 140 F.3d 1145 (8th Cir.1998).

17. See e.g., R.I. General Laws § 23–17–23, specifically requiring that procedures meet JCAHO standards; McKinney's–N.Y. Public Health Law § 2801–b, requiring written statement of reasons; Official Code Georgia Ann. § 31–7–7, setting time limits for action by public hospitals on applications.

18. See e.g., Lawler v. Eugene Wuesthoff Memorial Hospital Association, 497 So.2d 1261 (Fla.App.1986); Lake Hospital and Clinic v. Silversmith, 551 So.2d 538 (Fla.App.1989); Spunberg v. Columbia/JFK Medical Center, Inc., 1997 WL 868607 (Fla.Cir.Ct.).

Beyond the minimum requirements of due process, fundamental fairness and the Health Care Quality Improvement Act, all hospitals must comply with their own medical staff by-laws as they relate to the administration of the staff privileges system. Some courts have viewed compliance with the procedural guarantees of the by-laws as an integral part of minimum fairness to the practitioner[19] or as a matter of right under state law requiring that licensed hospitals have medical staff by-laws.[20] Others have founded mandatory compliance with by-laws on the public's interest in the administration of hospitals.[21] Many courts have adopted the position that the medical staff by-laws represent a contract[22] between the institution and physicians holding staff privileges at the facility[23] at least for the purpose of setting out procedural guarantees,[24] although some have resisted such a conclusion.[25]

The requirement that hospitals comply with their medical staff by-laws does not always require that doctors be accorded all of the procedures described in those by-laws. The medical staff member may waive specific procedures during the course of the proceedings.[26] Releases executed as a part

19. See e.g., Rao v. St. Elizabeth's Hospital, 94 Ill.Dec. 686, 488 N.E.2d 685 (Ill.App.1986).

20. See e.g., St. Mary's Hospital v. Radiology Professional Corporation, 421 S.E.2d 731 (Ga.App.1992), rejecting claim that by-laws formed a contract, but holding that physician had claim in tort based on hospital's duty under state statute to have by-laws governing medical staff.

21. See e.g., Balkissoon v.Capitol Hill Hospital, 558 A.2d 304 (D.C.App.1989); Owens v. New Britain General Hospital, 643 A.2d 233 (Conn.1994).

22. The rationale on which the courts base a conclusion that physicians have an enforceable right to procedures required in the by-laws may affect the statute of limitations for the cause of action. The courts vary on this question. See e.g., Eufemio v. Kodiak Island Hospital, 837 P.2d 95 (Alaska 1992), rejecting a statute of limitations for appeals from administrative hearings or arbitration decisions and adopting the statute of limitations for contract claims; Stringer v. Board of Trustees, 233 N.W.2d 698 (Mich.App.1975), applying statute of limitations for injuries to persons or property.

23. See e.g., Bartley v. Eastern Maine Medical Center, 617 A.2d 1020 (Me.1992), holding that by-laws "may constitute an enforceable contract between the medical center and its staff physicians"; Katz v. Children's Hospital, 602 N.E.2d 598 (Mass.App.1992), assuming for purposes of argument that the by-laws created "contractual rights" in the plaintiffs; Rees v. Intermountain Health Care, 808 P.2d 1069 (Utah 1991), upholding jury verdict in favor of plaintiff physician, noting that claim was "essentially breach of contract" for violation of by-laws. See also §§ 4–9 to 4–12 and 4–13.

24. See e.g., Saint Louis v. Baystate Medical Center, 568 N.E.2d 1181 (Mass.App.1991), stating: "To the extent that hospital by-laws

have elements of contract, it is that doctors not be stripped of privileges without the process prescribed by the by-laws;" Eyring v. East Tennessee Baptist Hospital 950 S.W.2d 354 (Tenn.App.1997), holding that the bylaws adopted by hospital setting forth the procedures for depriving a physician of staff membership or clinical privileges served as an enforceable contract.

25. See e.g., Tredrea v. Anesthesia & Analgesia, P.C., 584 N.W.2d 276 (Iowa 1998), holding that medical staff by-laws did not create contractual rights for continued staff privileges in the absence of a specific statement to that effect. Murdoch v. Knollwood Park Hospital, 585 So.2d 873 (Ala.1991), stating, in dicta, that the court was "not convinced" that the by-laws created a binding contract with the doctor; St. Mary's Hospital v. Radiology Professional Corp., 421 S.E.2d 731 (Ga.App.1992), holding that by-laws "themselves confer no contractual rights" but holding that plaintiff would have tort claim, as opposed to contract claim against hospital; Keskin v. Munster Medical Research Foundation, 580 N.E.2d 354 (Ind. App.1991), stating that "staff by-laws do not always constitute a contract between Hospital and its staff"; Robles v. Humana Hospital, 785 F.Supp. 989 (N.D.Ga.1992), holding that by-laws were not contractual, but that hospital was required to adhere to procedures provided for in by-laws. See also, § 4–11.

26. Rao v. St. Elizabeth's Hospital, 94 Ill. Dec. 686, 488 N.E.2d 685 (Ill.App.1986), holding that physician waived right to notice by consenting to continuing the hearing despite lack of notice on specific charges; St. Mary's Hospital of Athen, Inc. v. Cohen, 456 S.E.2d 79 (Ga.Ct.App.1995), holding physician, by his silence, waived right to insist on compliance with procedural requirements of medical staff by-laws. But see, Rees v. Intermountain Health

of application for staff privileges may be enforceable under certain circumstances.[27] In addition, procedures provided for in the medical staff by-laws may not apply to situations in which a facility revokes staff privileges as part of the process of instituting an exclusive contract with other physicians for medical services.[28] Finally, a contract between the physician and the hospital usually displaces procedures provided for in the by-laws.[29]

§ 4–6. Scope of Judicial Review of the Merits of Private Credentialing Decisions

In the absence of specific statutes setting statutory criteria for credentialing and implicitly or explicitly authorizing more substantial review,[1] courts will review the proceedings in a particular case to assure substantial compliance with procedures required by the private institution's by-laws, but the majority of courts will go no further.[2] The justification for judicial unwillingness to review private credentialing decisions on the merits rests primarily in conventional arguments of deference to expertise, with the courts yielding to medical judgment in credentialing decisions. In addition, the emergence of direct liability on the part of hospitals for failure to engage in an effective credentialing process supports wide latitude for credentialing decisions.[3] Finally, statutory limited immunity for participants in peer review[4] may indicate a public policy of deference to the peer review process.[5] Both the economic and non-economic injury suffered by physicians through negative privileges decisions and the potential for anti-competitive behavior, however, must be balanced against these reasons for non-review.[6]

The line between judicial review limited to assuring compliance with the medical staff by-laws and judicial review of the merits of the decision can be very fine. For example, in *Rao v. St. Elizabeth's Hospital*,[7] the physician plaintiff claimed that the immediate suspension of his staff privileges violated the hospital's medical staff by-laws. Under the by-laws, certain administrators

---

Care, 808 P.2d 1069 (Utah, 1991), holding that doctor's silence was not an intentional and voluntary waiver.

27. Some applications for privileges include a release from liability. The courts appear willing to enforce such releases, although only within the most narrow construction the clauses can bear. See e.g., Keskin v. Munster Medical Research Foundation, 580 N.E.2d 354 (Ind. App.1991), holding that a broad release applied only to persons providing information to hospital and not to claims that hospital violated its own by-laws; Stitzell v. York Memorial Osteopathic Hospital, 754 F.Supp. 1061 (M.D.Pa. 1991), construing broadly drafted exculpatory clause to immunize only good faith actions and not to apply to violations of procedural requirements of by-laws and 768 F.Supp. 129 (M.D.Pa.1991), holding that settlement agreement resolving physician's legal claim controlled physician's rights and did not require a hearing; Everett v. St. Ansgar Hospital, 974 F.2d 77 (8th Cir.1992), stating in dicta that exculpatory clause waived right to sue for breach of contract except in case of bad faith; Rees v. Intermountain Health Care, 808 P.2d 1069 (Utah 1991), holding that release of hos-

pital and medical staff from good faith acts in evaluating privileges application applies only to defamation suits.

28. See § 4–11.

29. See § 4–11.

§ 4–6

1. See e.g., §§ 4–20 through 4–23.

2. See e.g., Eufemio v. Kodiak Island Hospital, 837 P.2d 95 (Alaska 1992); Vakharia v. Swedish Covenant Hospital, 987 F.Supp. 633 (N.D.Ill.1997); Brinton v. IHC Hospitals, Inc., 973 P.2d 956 (Utah 1998).

3. See § 7–4.

4. See § 4–26.

5. See generally, Mahmoodian v. United Hospital Center, 404 S.E.2d 750 (W.Va.1991), cert. denied 502 U.S. 863, 112 S.Ct. 185, 116 L.Ed.2d 146 (1991).

6. See §§ 14–15 to 10–22 discussion antitrust considerations.

7. 94 Ill.Dec. 686, 488 N.E.2d 685 (Ill.App. 1986).

and committees had authority to immediately suspend privileges "whenever action must be taken immediately in the best interest of patient care in the Hospital." The court rebuffed plaintiff's argument that the court, even in limiting its review to compliance with the by-laws, should review whether the best interest of patient care actually required summary suspension of his privileges. The court in rejecting plaintiff's argument stated that the determination of whether patient care required immediate suspension "would seem to fall within the ambit of judgment best exercised by hospital authorities" and was "properly a medical [decision] to be addressed to the discretion of the medical professionals."

This approach limits judicial enforcement of the by-laws to procedural protections only and could be viewed as inconsistent with a position that the medical staff by-laws form a contract with members of the medical staff. Most courts, however, have maintained both that the by-laws are contractual and that review is limited to compliance with procedural provisions.[8]

In *Stiller v. La Porte Hospital*,[9] in contrast, the Indiana court reviewed the sufficiency of the evidence presented to the hospital's board. In its view, the court was merely assuring that the hospital complied with its by-laws, which provided that the governing board of the hospital would affirm the recommendation of the executive committee if "the findings, conclusions, and report and recommendation of the Executive Committee are supported by substantial and reliable evidence." The court limited its review: it would not judge credibility of witnesses; it would not "reweigh" the evidence; and "[o]nly where there is a total failure of evidence or where the judgement is contrary to uncontradicted evidence" would it reverse the hospital's decision. In addition, the court held that it would "only look to the evidence most favorable to the [hospital]." The court upheld the hospital's decision as supported by sufficient evidence.[10]

§ 4–7. Legitimate Grounds for Staff Privileges Decisions

Hospitals base staff privileges decisions on a variety of factors in addition to the standards most obviously related to competency and quality of care. The courts generally have approved the use of a wide range of other criteria for staff privileges decisions.[1]

8. See e.g., Katz v. Children's Hospital, 602 N.E.2d 598 (Mass.App.1992); Saint Louis v. Baystate Medical Center, 568 N.E.2d 1181 (Mass.App.1991).

9. 570 N.E.2d 99 (Ind.App.1991).

10. See also, Mahmoodian v. United Hospital Center, 404 S.E.2d 750 (W.Va.1991), cert. denied 502 U.S. 863, 112 S.Ct. 185, 116 L.Ed.2d 146 (1991), holding that a court is to review credentialing decisions for substantial compliance with procedural requirements in by-laws rather than the "merits" but that "an inherent element of 'fair hearing procedures' is a requirement of sufficient evidence to support the hospital's decision."

§ 4–7

1. See e.g., Weston v. Carolina Medicorp, Inc., 402 S.E.2d 653 (N.C.App.1991), review

denied 409 S.E.2d 611 (N.C.1991), upholding summary suspension and revocation of privileges for failure to comply with hospital's policies on patients with HIV; Everhart v. Jefferson Parish Hosp. Dist. No. 2, 757 F.2d 1567 (5th Cir.1985), holding that ability to work with others was reasonably related to quality medical care and so denial of privileges on that basis did not violate a doctor's right to substantive due process; Paskon v. Salem Memorial Hospital District, 806 S.W.2d 417 (Mo.App. 1991), cert. denied 502 U.S. 908, 112 S.Ct. 302, 116 L.Ed.2d 245 (1991), upholding revocation of privileges for failure to maintain federal narcotics license; Mahmoodian v. United Hospital Center, 404 S.E.2d 750 (W.Va.1991), cert. denied 502 U.S. 863, 112 S.Ct. 185, 116 L.Ed.2d 146 (1991), reviewing case law on legitimacy of by-laws concerning disruptive prac-

One of the more controversial grounds for credentialing decisions to emerge in the past few years is the practice of economic credentialing.[2] There is some dispute over the definition of "economic credentialing" because a single factor may relate both to cost and to quality. This is especially true in situations of overutilization of medical procedures, including diagnostic procedures.[3]

Although complaints against the use of economic factors emerge from a wide range of medical staff situations, they are currently most prevalent in the institution and administration of exclusive contracts and closed medical staffs. In these contexts, the courts have directly considered the issue and have generally viewed cost-control as a legitimate basis for decisions relating to the structure of the medical staff.[4]

§ 4–8. Illegitimate Grounds for Staff Privileges Decisions

State statutes may establish permissible and impermissible criteria for staff privileges decisions. The majority of the states have provisions within their hospital licensure statutes, applying to both public and private hospitals, that prohibit a hospital from excluding particular groups of practitioners. State law may prohibit exclusion of physicians based on the type of medical degree they have earned (i.e., M.D. or D.O.), for example.[1] Or, such statutes may require that hospitals afford clinical privileges to non-physician practitioners such as nurse midwives.[2]

State statutes also may set substantive standards for the credentialing process. For example, the New York statute provides that it is an "improper practice" for a hospital to take an adverse action against a doctor's staff privileges, including an application for privileges, without providing written reasons that relate to "patient care, patient welfare, the objectives of the institution or the character or competency of the applicant."[3] New York courts have held that physicians have a cause of action under the statute[4] for

titioners and upholding hospital's revocation of privileges; Todd v. Physicians & Surgeons Community Hospital, 302 S.E.2d 378 (Ga.App. 1983), upholding right of hospital to amend its by-laws to require membership in the American Medical Association or American Dental Association.

2. See generally, John D. Blum, Economic Credentialling: A New Twist in Hospital Appraisal Process, 12 J. Leg. Med. 427 (1991); Mark Hall, Institutional Control of Physician Behavior: Legal Barriers to Healthcare Cost Containment, 137 U. Pa. L. Rev. 431 (1988); John D. Blum, Hospital–Medical Staff Relations in the Face of Shifting Institutional Business Strategies: A Legal Analysis, 14 U. Puget Sound L. Rev. 561 (1991); Judith E. Orie, Economic Credentialing: Bottom–Line Medical Care, 36 Duq. L. Rev. 437 (1998).

3. See e.g., Rao v. St. Elizabeth's Hospital, 94 Ill.Dec. 686, 488 N.E.2d 685 (Ill.App.1986); Knapp v. Palos Community Hospital, 80 Ill. Dec. 442, 465 N.E.2d 554 (Ill.App.1984), appeal after remand 126 Ill.Dec. 362, 531 N.E.2d 989 (1988).

4. See § 4–10.

§ 4–8

1. 1 See e.g., Vernon's Ann. Tex. Civ. St. art. 4495b; Ohio Rev. Code § 3701.351; West's Fla. Stat. Ann. § 395.0191.

2. See e.g., Ohio Rev. Code § 3701.351.

3. McKinney's—N.Y. Public Health Law § 2801–b. See also, Maryland Code, Health–Gen. Ann. § 19–319(e)(1) & (2)(i).

4. McKinney's N.Y. Public Health Law § 2801–c. But see, Del Castillo v. Bayley Seton Hospital, 569 N.Y.S.2d 168 (N.Y.App.Div. 1991), holding physician had no cause of action under the statute when privileges were terminated pursuant to a contract, but that physician stated a claim for breach of contract. See also, Medical Center Hospitals v. Terzis, 367 S.E.2d 728 (Va.1988), holding that identical statute does not allow substantive review of the merits of the privileges decision.

improper practices.[5]

Courts reviewing staff privileges decisions under constitutional due process standards or under judicially created doctrines, such as the public fiduciary standard for hospitals, may reject grounds for staff privileges decisions. For example, the New Jersey Supreme Court has held that a hospital, as a public fiduciary, may base denials of staff privileges on the hospital's need for the specialty and other factors related to utilization but may not base the granting of privileges on whether the applicant doctor is associated professionally with other physicians currently members of the hospital's medical staff.[6]

Finally, hospitals are subject to federal and state anti-discrimination statutes that prohibit discrimination on the basis of gender, race, age, national origin, disability or other factors. These statutes may apply both to employment and to staff privileges decisions.[7]

B. PHYSICIAN–HOSPITAL CONTRACTS FOR PHYSICIAN SERVICES

§ 4–9. Background

Physician-hospital contracts for medical services are not new. For many years, physicians have provided hospital-based medical services, such as anesthesiology, pathology, radiology and emergency medicine, under contract with hospitals. Physicians have long worked under contract as administrators of medical staffs or departments within hospitals or as members of full-time closed staffs. Hospital-physician contracting has come to the forefront as hospitals seek increased control over contracting physicians, stimulated by strategic responses to changes in the market for hospital services and in payment practices. Physician-hospital contracts, especially contracts that make the physician or physician group the exclusive provider of particular services for the hospital, are the most frequent targets of complaints about "economic credentialing."[1]

Perspectives on the value and purpose of exclusive contracts are at odds. The American Hospital Association identifies several reasons for exclusive contracting: to ensure coverage of needed services; to allocate coverage responsibilities equitably; to provide optimal patient services; and to ensure performance of hospital administrative functions. Most physicians initially viewed exclusive contracting as a particularly strong form of "economic credentialing," because cost was usually an explicit factor in a hospital's deciding to institute exclusive contract and in the selection from among competing physician groups. Physician organizations such as the American Medical Association and the American College of Radiology provided early litigation support in battles over the impact of physician-hospital contracts

5. See e.g., Lipsztein v. Mount Sinai Hospital, 565 N.Y.S.2d 812 (N.Y.App.Div.1991); Saha v. Record, 575 N.Y.S.2d 986 (N.Y.App.Div. 1991). See also, Gelbard v. Genesee Hospital, 680 N.Y.S.2d 358 (N.Y.App.Div.1998).

6. Desai v. St. Barnabas Medical Center, 510 A.2d 662 (N.J.1986).

7. See §§ 4–20 through 4–23.

§ 4–9

1. See §§ 4–7 and 4–10.

upon the security of traditional staff privileges.[2] In fact, litigation over exclusive contracts has become so bitter and counterproductive that several attempts are being made to create non-litigious dispute mechanisms.[3] Exclusive, and non-exclusive, contracting for physician services by a hospital has continued to increase. Of course, physician groups holding the contracts may find them quite advantageous as compared to independent practice.

Legal issues raised by contracts between physicians and physician groups are common to contract law generally. For example, physician-hospital contracts are susceptible to formation problems, for reasons familiar to health care lawyers.[4] This section does not discuss the contract issues common to any contract for services. Rather, it reviews only those legal issues that are peculiar to the health care environment.

§ 4–10. Hospital's Authority to Determine Structure of Medical Staff

A challenge to the hospital's authority to restructure the delivery of medical services requires an analysis of two issues. First, the court examines whether the hospital has authority within its by-laws to effect such a change in the manner it did. Second, the same courts choose to review the rationale supporting the hospital decision.

a. Governance Authority to Restructure

The courts generally have read corporate and medical staff by-laws broadly in affirming the right of the hospital to restructure its medical staff.[1] For example, in *Bartley v. Eastern Maine Medical Center*,[2] the court held that corporate by-laws specifying that the board was to have the "necessary authority and responsibility" to engage in the "general management" of the hospital provided the board the authority to execute an exclusive contract for emergency medical services.[3]

In the absence of specific procedures established in the corporate or medical staff by-laws, the hospital may design an internal process for the decision to institute an exclusive contract. The choice of procedures may have serious implications. Procedures outside of the medical staff peer review

---

2. Mary T. Koska, Review Exclusive Contracts in Light of Recent Challenges, 66 Hospitals 38 (April 20, 1992).

3. See e.g., Mary T. Koska, Review Exclusive Contracts in Light of Recent Challenges, 66 Hospitals 38(3) (April 20, 1992). But see, Vakharia v. Little Company of Mary Hospital and Health Care Centers, 917 F.Supp. 1282, 1302 (N.D.Ill.1996).

4. See e.g., Ingraffia v. NME Hospitals, 943 F.2d 561 (5th Cir.1991); Dowling v. UHS of Delaware, 1992 WL 37698 (E.D.La.1992); Kramer v. Kent General Hospital, 1992 WL 91130 (Del.Super.1992); St. Mary's Hospital v. Radiology Professional Corporation, 421 S.E.2d 731 (Ga.App.1992); Gleicher, Friberg & Associates v. University of Health Sciences, 166 Ill. Dec. 460, 586 N.E.2d 418 (Ill.App.1991).

§ 4–10

1. The hospital must comply with any statutory requirements. One response to the increase in exclusive contracts has been efforts to pass legislation prohibiting economic credentialing. Mary T. Koska, Review Exclusive Contracts in Light of Recent Challenges, 66 Hospitals 38 (April 20, 1992).

2. 617 A.2d 1020 (Me.1992).

3. See also, Williams v. Hobbs, 460 N.E.2d 287 (Ohio App. 1983); Hutton v. Memorial Hospital, 824 P.2d 61 (Colo.App.1991). Keskin v. Munster Medical Research Foundation, 580 N.E.2d 354 (Ind.App.1991). But see, Vakharia v. Little Company of Mary Hospital and Health Care Centers, 917 F.Supp. 1282, 1302 (N.D.Ill. 1996).

process may not have the advantage of statutory immunity available for peer review, for example.[4]

The procedure used by the hospital to restructure the staff also may strengthen the hospital's position if the decision is challenged in litigation. Internal procedures used in the restructuring seemed to have influenced court decisions in favor of the hospital. Internal procedures that appear to have triggered a favorable review include a board resolution stating that it was "the policy of [the hospital] that the hospital may enter into exclusive contracts;"[5] a finding by the medical staff's fair hearing committee that a full-time staff was justifiable and that the chief of the department could make that decision;[6] the establishment of a task force to recommend a structure for provision of services;[7] and the formal involvement of physician administrators.[8]

The courts have not generally required that the hospital's decision to restructure the provision of services have the ratification or approval of the medical staff. Instead, several courts have viewed the hospital's corporate by-laws, rather than the medical staff by-laws, as controlling. Viewing the corporate by-laws as the source of authority for the medical staff by-laws makes the medical staff by-laws dependent upon, rather than equal to, the corporate by-laws.[9] Nor have courts interpreted statutes specifying that a licensed hospital have an organized medical staff as requiring that the hospital gain the staff's approval.[10] Evidence of support for the exclusive agreement among the medical staff in general, however, certainly strengthens the hospital's position.

b. Rationale for Restructuring

The rationale supporting the hospital's use of exclusive agreements for the provision of physician services may be relevant for a number of reasons. If the standard of review established in the jurisdiction allows review of the merits of privileges decisions, for example, the court will examine the reasons for the decision to restructure.[11] The reasons underlying actions related to exclusive contracts also may affect statutory immunity.[12] Finally, the reasons for the termination of privileges will influence whether procedural requirements ordinarily applicable to the hospital's revocation of medical staff privileges apply to the plaintiff. Several cases distinguish between adverse

4. See e.g., Szczerbaniuk v. Memorial Hospital, 129 Ill.Dec. 454, 536 N.E.2d 138 (Ill. 1989). But see, Ray v. St. John's Health Care Corp., 582 N.E.2d 464 (Ind.App.1991).

5. Hutton v. Memorial Hospital, 824 P.2d 61 (Colo.App.1991).

6. Katz v. Children's Hospital Corp., 602 N.E.2d 598 (Mass.App.1992).

7. See e.g., Mateo–Woodburn v. Fresno Community Hospital, 270 Cal.Rptr. 894 (Cal. App.1990); Strauss v. Pennisula Regional Medical Center, 916 F.Supp. 528 (D.Md.1996).

8. See e.g., Katz v. Children's Hospital Corp., 602 N.E.2d 598 (Mass.App.1992).

9. See e.g., Katz v. Children's Hospital Corp., 602 N.E.2d 598 (Mass.App.1992);

Strauss v. Pennisula Regional Medical Center, 916 F.Supp. 528 (D.Md.1996).

10. See e.g., Keskin V. Munster Medical Research Foundation, 580 N.E.2d 354 (Ind. App.1991); Strauss v. Pennisula Regional Medical Center, 916 F.Supp. 528 (D.Md.1996).

11. See e.g., Bloom v. Hennepin County, 783 F.Supp. 418 (D.Minn.1992); Lewin v. St. Joseph Hospital, 146 Cal.Rptr. 892 (Cal.App. 1978); Redding v. St. Francis Medical Center, 255 Cal.Rptr. 806 (Cal.App.1989). But see, Keskin v. Munster Medical Research Foundation, 580 N.E.2d 354 (Ind.App.1991); Katz v. Children's Hospital Corp., 602 N.E.2d 598 (Mass. App.1992).

12. See e.g., Keskin v. Munster Medical Research Foundation, 580 N.E.2d 354 (Ind.

staff privileges decisions grounded on the incompetence or the character of the physician from those based on other concerns in justifying a holding that the physician was not entitled to procedures provided for in medical staff by-laws.[13]

Typically, hospitals have justified exclusive contracts as important for the quality of the medical care provided patients. Quality concerns are an acceptable justification for the use of exclusive contracts. Recognized quality issues include evidence of problems in adequate coverage of patients' needs[14] and evidence of hostility or disputes among members of the department[15] as well as more generally stated concerns for quality.[16] In some situations, the hospital's duty to provide emergency treatment may support a decision to contract for medical services.[17] Cost considerations have been explicit in at least a few cases involving restructuring of the provision of medical services; and the courts generally have accepted cost control as a legitimate interest of the hospital justifying such a decision.[18]

Although some courts have examined the general rationale for the hospital's decision to provide for needed services under an exclusive contract, they have resisted reviewing the merits of the hospital's choice of one provider over another as the exclusive provider of services or one particular form of exclusive contract over any other.[19] This is consistent with the general posture of deference to the hospital's decisions in individual medical staff situations, although the reason for deference here does differ from that accorded other staff privileges decisions. Judicial deference regarding the institutional decision to exclusively contract for medical services is not related to respect for the greater expertise of the medical staff in medical questions. Instead, the courts are deferring primarily to the administrative authority and business judgment of the hospital.

§ 4–11. Impact of Contracts on Revocation or Reduction of Staff Privileges

When a hospital adopts an exclusive agreement, the action will have an impact on physicians who currently hold privileges as well as those who will receive privileges under the exclusive contract. A current physician's privileges may be reduced or revoked. A physician who receives privileges under

App.1991); Ray v. St. John's Health Care Corp., 582 N.E.2d 464 (Ind.App.1991).

13. See e.g., Mateo–Woodburn v. Fresno Community Hospital, 270 Cal.Rptr. 894 (Cal. App.1990); Bloom v. Hennepin County, 783 F.Supp. 418 (D.Minn.1992).

14. See e.g., Mateo–Woodburn v. Fresno Community Hospital, 270 Cal.Rptr. 894 (Cal. App.1990).

15. See e.g., Saint Louis v. Baystate Medical Center, 568 N.E.2d 1181 (Mass.App.1991).

16. See e.g., Keskin v. Munster Medical Research Foundation, 580 N.E.2d 354 (Ind. App.1991); Katz v. Children's Hospital Corp., 602 N.E.2d 598 (Mass.App.1992).

17. See e.g., Bloom v. Hennepin County, 783 F.Supp. 418 (D.Minn.1992), holding that public hospital serves the public interest in exclusively contracting for emergency room

medical services with the purpose of providing coverage for patients regardless of ability to pay. See also, Owens v. Nacogdoches County Hospital Dist., 741 F.Supp. 1269 (E.D.Tex. 1990), finding that hospital's staffing of emergency obstetric services only with private on-call physicians inevitably led to patient dumping in violation of federal statute. See §§ 12–2 through 12–12.

18. See e.g., Bartley v. Eastern Maine Medical Center, 617 A.2d 1020 (Me.1992); Alonso v. Hospital Authority of Henry County, 332 S.E.2d 884 (Ga.App.1985). But see, Ray v. St. John's Health Care Corp., 582 N.E.2d 464 (Ind.App.1991).

19. See e.g., Keskin v. Munster Medical Research Foundation, 580 N.E.2d 354 (Ind. App.1991); Engelstad v. Virginia Municipal Hospital, 718 F.2d 262 (8th Cir.1983).

the exclusive contract may sign a contract that alters rights afforded under the medical staff bylaws.

a. Staff Privileges Held Prior to Restructuring

Restructuring of the medical staff through an exclusive contract will have an adverse impact on privileges held by physicians prior to the contract. Hospitals have argued that such an impact does not trigger procedures required in the medical staff by-laws for revocation of privileges. In several cases, defendant hospitals have argued that "staff privileges" and "clinical privileges" are distinct things, and that denial of access to the hospital for the purpose of practicing medicine does not amount to denial or revocation of membership on the medical staff. Plaintiff physicians, on the other hand, have argued that restrictions on their ability to practice within the hospital operated as a "constructive revocation" of their staff privileges.[1]

The courts' reactions to this argument have varied. In *Lewisburg Community Hospital v. Alfredson,*[2] the court considered the case of a radiologist who had practiced at the defendant hospital under a contract that provided that termination of the contract would not cause automatic termination of "staff appointment." The hospital terminated Alfredson's contract and entered into an exclusive contract with another group of providers. Upon termination of the contract, the hospital informed Alfredson that he remained a member of the medical staff and could attend medical staff meetings, but could not use hospital equipment or personnel and could not charge any fees for interpreting diagnostic film produced on hospital equipment. The court rejected the hospital's argument that it had not reduced or revoked Alfredson's staff privileges. The court instead read the medical staff by-laws to provide that clinical privileges were part of staff privileges. The court relied on provisions that required that applications for staff privileges include the scope of clinical privileges requested and that medical staff members may exercise only those privileges granted. The court held that because the hospital's action had made Alfredson's staff privileges meaningless, Alfredson was entitled to the procedures provided for in the by-laws.

In many other cases, however, courts have been willing to draw a distinction between staff privileges and clinical privileges.[3] Typical of these cases, which appear to form a majority, is *Dutta v. St. Francis Regional Medical Center, Inc.*[4] in which the court considered the claim of a radiologist. The hospital had entered an exclusive agreement with another radiologist. The hospital did not revoke plaintiff's staff privileges or her clinical privileges. Rather, the hospital denied her access to the hospital's radiology facilities. The court rejected plaintiff's claim that she was entitled to a hearing under the medical staff by-laws, finding that the hospital's barring her from its radiology facilities did not affect her "status as a member of the medical staff or her opportunity to exercise clinical privileges" as she still had authority to admit and prescribe treatment for patients even though she could not "ad-

§ 4-11

1. See e.g., Bartley v. Eastern Maine Medical Center, 617 A.2d 1020 (Me.1992).

2. 805 S.W.2d 756 (Tenn.1991).

3. See e.g., Bartley v. Eastern Maine Medical Center, 617 A.2d 1020 (Me.1992); Engelstad v. Virginia Mun. Hosp., 718 F.2d 262 (8th Cir.1983); Bryant v. Glen Oaks Medical Center, 650 N.E.2d 622 (1995).

4. 850 P.2d 928 (Kan.App.1993), affirmed, 867 P.2d 1057 (Kan.1994). See also, Richter v. Danbury Hospital, 1998 WL 321853 (Conn.Super.).

minister treatment personally." The medical staff by-laws provided for a hearing when the physician's "exercise of clinical privileges" was adversely affected; however, the section describing the conduct of the hearing specified that the purpose of such a hearing was to resolve "on an intra-professional basis, matters bearing on professional competency and conduct." Relying primarily on this latter section, the court held that plaintiff was not entitled to a hearing because the hospital had made no claim that Dutta's services were incompetent or unacceptable. The court distinguished *Alfredson* on the basis of differences in language in the by-laws.

An alternative analysis accepts that revocation has occurred but examines the reason for the action against privileges to determine whether the hospital must follow the procedures identified in the medical staff by-laws. In *Volcjak v. Washington County Hospital Association*,[5] a hospital terminated an anesthesiologist's clinical privileges, without providing him a hearing, when it entered an exclusive contract with a group of anesthesiologists. The hospital claimed that the medical staff bylaws did not apply when a physician's privileges were terminated as a result of a decision to enter into an exclusive contract, and that the bylaws only required due process procedures when a physician was formally accused of professional misconduct. The court held against the hospital, noting that the by-laws did not state that they did not apply in cases of exclusive contracting. Further the court stated that while the hospital "characterized its decision to enter an exclusive contract as a 'business decision,' the undisputed facts showed that allegations of inadequate 'quality of care' involving the [plaintiff] and his department ... were the primary and exclusive reasons for the hospital's decision." The court held that an adverse action with respect to the anesthesiologist's privileges was taken by the hospital in the course of resolving the problems raised by the HCFA report, and the anesthesiologist, therefore, was entitled to the due process requirements contained in the medical staff bylaws.

Absent similar evidence, the courts are likely to view the decision as one belonging to the governing board of the hospital rather than to its medical staff. Therefore, the decision would not be governed by procedures described in the medical staff by-laws.[6] Physicians holding privileges prior to the exclusive contract do not have a right to continue practicing at the hospital or to be included in the exclusive contract.[7]

b. Staff Privileges Held Under Contract

If the aggrieved physician is one who has practiced at the hospital under contract, the claim to protections afforded in the medical staff by-laws is most frequently analyzed as a matter of interpretation of the physician-hospital contract.[8] An agreement that provides for simultaneous termination of privileges through termination of the contract may also eliminate the right to due

5. 723 A.2d 463 (Md. Ct. Spec. App. 1999).

6. See e.g., Bartley v. Eastern Maine Medical Center, 617 A.2d 1020 (Me.1992); Mateo–Woodburn v. Fresno Community Hospital, 270 Cal.Rptr. 894 (Cal.App.1990).

7. Major v. Memorial Hospitals Association, 71 Cal.App.4th 1380, 84 Ca. Rptr.2d 510 (Cal. App. 1999).

8. See e.g., St. Mary's Hospital v. Radiology Professional Corp., 421 S.E.2d 731 (Ga.App. 1992); Anne Arundel General Hospital, Inc. v. O'Brien, 432 A.2d 483 (Md.App.1981); Strauss v. Pennisula Regional Medical Center, 916 F.Supp. 528 (D.Md.1996).

process of a physician practicing in a public hospital.[9] In some cases, the courts have instead interpreted the scope of the medical staff by-laws in a way that does not extend procedural protections to the contract physician.[10]

Medical staff by-laws provisions designed to protect staff privileges when a physician-hospital contract has been terminated have met with mixed success. For example, in *Bloom v. Hennepin County*,[11] the District Court reviewed a by-laws provision that stated that "medical staff membership shall also be completely separate and independent of any employment agreements." The court noted that plaintiff and defendant disagreed on the meaning of this provision, with plaintiff physician arguing that staff privileges continued after contract termination and the defendant hospital arguing that the provision allowed a physician's privileges to be terminated even if the contract were not. The court held that the by-law's procedural requirements applied only when privileges were restricted or revoked by "corrective action" based on quality problems and not when, as in plaintiff's case, the contract between plaintiff and the exclusive provider of services was terminated.[12] In contrast, a Florida appellate court held that an amendment to the medical staff by-laws effectively modified a pre-existing physician-hospital contract for the director of pathology services.[13] This amendment provided that termination of a contract for medico/administrative services would not affect the doctor's staff privileges in any way. The court found consideration for the amendment in the hospital's "retention of the benefits bestowed upon it by the Joint Commission on Accreditation of Hospitals."

Termination of physician contracts may also give rise to claims of tortious interference with contractual or business relationships. A claim of tortious interference with contractual relationships allows a plaintiff to seek legal and equitable relief if a defendant improperly interferes with the plaintiff's contractual relationship with a third party. This cause of action generally requires an improper, intentional interference with a known contractual relationship, which causes the plaintiff injury, though jurisdictions do differ in the basic elements of this claim. A plaintiff may bring a claim of interference with business relationships, even in the absence of a contract. Both of these claims arise in a great number of staff privileges cases, particularly those involving contracts, usually with little success.[14] Such a claim has been successful in some cases, however, due to unusual circumstances.[15]

9. See e.g., Bloom v. Hennepin County, 783 F.Supp. 418 (D.Minn.1992). But see, Northeast Georgia Radiological Associates v. Tidwell, 670 F.2d 507 (5th Cir.1982).

10. See e.g., Bartley v. Eastern Maine Medical Center, 617 A.2d 1020 (Me.1992).

11. 783 F.Supp. 418 (D.Minn.1992).

12. See also, Bartley v. Eastern Maine Medical Center, 617 A.2d 1020 (Me.1992), holding that similar provision did not apply to plaintiff because only employment and access to practice within the hospital were terminated while privileges were not.

13. Hospital Corporation of Lake Worth v. Romaguera, 511 So.2d 559 (Fla.App.1986).

14. See e.g., Gillum v. Republic Health Corp., 778 S.W.2d 558 (Tex.App.1989); Carson v. Northwest Community Hospital, 139 Ill.Dec. 194, 548 N.E.2d 579 (Ill.App.1989); Bloom v. Hennepin County, 783 F.Supp. 418 (D.Minn. 1992); Hutton v. Memorial Hospital, 824 P.2d 61 (Colo.App.1991); Jackson v. Radcliffe, 795 F.Supp. 197 (S.D.Tex.1992); Saint Louis v. Baystate Medical Center, 568 N.E.2d 1181 (Mass.App.1991); St. Mary's Hospital of Athens, Inc. v. Radiology Professional Corp., 421 S.E.2d 731 (Ga.App.1992); Stitzell v. York Memorial Osteopathic Hospital, 754 F.Supp. 1061 (M.D.Pa.1991); Gonzalez v. San Jacinto Methodist Hospital, 880 S.W.2d 436 (Tex.App.1994); Sullivan v. Baptist Memorial Hospital–Golden Triangle, Inc., 722 So.2d 675 (Miss. 1998).

15. American Medical International, Inc. v. Scheller, 590 So.2d 947 (Fla.App.1991); Saha v. Record, 575 N.Y.S.2d 986 (N.Y.App.Div.1991)

C. EMPLOYMENT–AT–WILL

§ 4–12. Employment–At–Will

Doctors, nurses, administrators and others working in private health care facilities without an employment contract or under a contract that does not provide for a particular term of employment or does not require cause for termination, are generally subject to the doctrine of employment-at-will. At-will employment allows both employer and employee to terminate their relationship for no cause, subject to the restrictions of anti-discrimination or other statutes.[1] This doctrine varies considerably among the states but some generalizations can be made.

§ 4–13. Exceptions

An at-will employee may have a claim for wrongful discharge if his or her situation falls within one of the exceptions to at-will employment in the jurisdiction. In none of these exceptions has there developed a position that health care workers should have the benefit of special exceptions from the at-will doctrine.

Implied contract, the most commonly accepted exception to the at-will doctrine, allows an employee handbook or personnel manual to reach the level of an enforceable contract. Under this exception, the courts review the handbook or manual and the manner in which it has been used in relation to the plaintiff employee to determine whether it represents a contract between the parties and whether that contract prohibits discharge of the employee. State courts vary in the circumstances under which they will declare that a handbook or manual has created a contract right to continued employment.[1] Although many states have concluded that medical staff by-laws are contractual in nature for purposes of the procedures required upon revocation or limitation of staff privileges,[2] the courts have not been particularly receptive to arguments that the medical staff by-laws create an implied contract that regulates or prohibits discharge from employment of an otherwise at-will employee.[3]

The "public policy" exception, a second well-accepted exception to the at-will doctrine, allows for a claim of wrongful discharge where the plaintiff is discharged for conduct that is protected by a specific state mandate. The public policy exception generally is quite narrow, requiring the plaintiff to identify a statute or other state law that specifically protects the activity that was the cause for dismissal.[4] Courts have refused to recognize a public policy

and Robles v. Humana Hospital Cartersville, 785 F.Supp. 989 (N.D.Ga.1992).

§ 4–12

1. See e.g., §§ 4–16 and 4–20.

§ 4–13

1. See e.g., Duldulao v. St. Mary of Nazareth Hospital Center, 106 Ill.Dec. 8, 505 N.E.2d 314 (Ill.1987); Hrehorovich v. Harbor Hospital Center, 614 A.2d 1021 (Md.App.1992); Helland v. Kurtis A Froedtert Memorial Lu-

theran Hospital, 601 N.W.2d 318 (Wis.App. 1999); Sides v. Duke University, 328 S.E.2d 818 (N.C.App.1985); Doyle v. Holy Cross Hospital, 682 N.E.2d 68 (Ill.App.1997).

2. See §§ 4–5 and 4–6.

3. See e.g., Engelstad v. Virginia Municipal Hospital, 718 F.2d 262 (8th Cir.1983). See also, § 4–11.

4. Spierling v. First American Home Health Services, Inc., 737 A.2s 1250 (Super. Ct.

exception to at-will employment for health care professionals who claim that they were discharged, in contravention of state statutes generally relating to quality of care, for criticizing or taking steps to improve the quality of patient care at the employing institution.[5] Courts also have not been receptive under the public policy exception to claims of wrongful discharge where the professional employee's actions were based on personal moral principles.[6]

In cases involving public hospitals,[7] however, at-will employees may be able to claim the protection of the First Amendment for such statements.[8] In addition, such statements and activities may be protected under the National Labor Relations Act.[9] Health care professionals working as at-will employees or otherwise may find certain actions based on individual moral principles protected in limited circumstances under state statutes governing advance directives for treatment.

A third exception, which incorporates a duty of good faith and fair dealing within at-will relationships, is less widely accepted and varies more among the states. Under this implied duty, a hospital employer was liable for wrongful discharge where it failed to investigate charges against the employee before discharge.[10] The courts generally have not extended this exception to health care workers as a special group.[11] One court, in fact, refused to extend the duty to a doctor at-will employee because the doctor, as a well-educated individual, and the hospital were equals in terms of bargaining power.[12]

D. NATIONAL LABOR RELATIONS ACT

§ 4–14. Application to Hospitals

Although the National Labor Relations Act originally covered non-profit hospitals, the Taft–Hartley amendments of 1947 excluded non-profit hospitals from the statute's definition of employer. The National Labor Relations Board refused to exercise jurisdiction over for-profit hospitals as well until 1967. In 1974, the Health Care Amendments to the Act repealed the statutory exclusion of non-profit hospitals, and the NLRB extended its jurisdiction to all hospitals thereafter.[1] The NLRA provides protection for "employees" who

Pa. 1999); McQuary v. Bel Air Convalescent Home, Inc., 684 P.2d 21 (Or.App.1984).

5. See e.g., Hrehorovich v. Harbor Hospital Center, 614 A.2d 1021 (Md.App.1992), holding that health code enacted with purpose of promoting a quality health care system did not constitute the statutory mandate required for the public policy exception.

6. See e.g., Warthen v. Toms River Community Memorial Hospital, 488 A.2d 229 (N.J.Super.1985), cert. denied, 501 A.2d 926 (N.J.1985); Farnam v. CRISTA Ministries, 807 P.2d 830 (Wash.1991).

7. See § 4–4.

8. See e.g., Waters v. Churchill, 511 U.S. 661, 114 S.Ct. 1878, 128 L.Ed.2d 686 (1994), setting standards for First Amendment claims by government employees in case involving nurse's claim that discharge was based on statements concerning the quality of patient care. See also, Tiernan v. Charleston Area Medical Center, Inc., 506 S.E.2d 578 (W.Va. 1998).

9. See §§ 4–15 through 4–18.

10. Crenshaw v. Bozeman Deaconess Hospital, 693 P.2d 487 (Mont.1984).

11. See e.g., Hrehorovich v. Harbor Hospital Center, 614 A.2d 1021 (Md.App.1992).

12. Aung v. Fontenot, 1992 WL 57471 (Tex.App.1992).

§ 4–14

1. See generally, Mark H. Grunewald, The NLRB's First Rulemaking: An Exercise in Pragmatism, 41 Duke L. J. 274 (1992). See also, Cathy Schatz Glaser, Labor Relations in the Health Care Industry—The Impact of the 1974 Health Care Amendments to the National Labor Relations Act, 54 Tulane L.R. 417 (1980).

engage in union or protected concerted activity. Although there are some narrow exceptions, professionals, skilled workers and lesser skilled workers in health care settings are all covered by the Act.[2] Those protections, however, do not extend to "supervisors" as defined in the Act.[3] In addition, several issues have arisen that are particular to union organizing and collective bargaining in the health care setting.

§ 4–15. Definition of Bargaining Units

One of the most hotly contested issues in the application of NLRA standards to union activity in hospitals is the definition of bargaining units. The NLRB delineates and certifies bargaining units, which describe the particular group of employees to be included in a representation election and in collective bargaining with the employer. The interests of management and labor diverge in the definition of bargaining units with the employer preferring larger units of employees with heterogenous, and therefore conflicting, interests and the union preferring smaller groups with common interests. The definition of bargaining units is particularly difficult in health care institutions where the work force tends to be heterogeneous in training and function.[1]

After years of defining bargaining units on a case-by-case basis, the National Labor Relations Board in 1989 issued a rule concerning bargaining units in acute-care hospitals.[2] The Board's rule recognizes only the following units: physicians, registered nurses, other professional employees, medical technicians, skilled maintenance workers, clerical workers, guards and other nonprofessional employees. Under the NLRB's rule, units must have a minimum of six employees for certification.[3]

The Supreme Court upheld both the rulemaking authority of the Board and the rule itself.[4] In a unanimous opinion, the Court held that the rule was not arbitrary and capricious, noting that the Board retained the authority to depart from the rule under extraordinary circumstances.[5] Litigation under the

2. For the past twenty years, The National Labor Relations Board maintained that interns and residents are not employees under the Act. Cedars–Sinai Medical Center, 223 N.L.R.B. 251 (1976) and N.L.R.B. v. Committee of Interns and Residents, 566 F.2d 810 (2d Cir.1977), cert. denied, 435 U.S. 904, 98 S.Ct. 1449, 55 L.Ed.2d 495 (1978), holding that despite Board's position that house staff is not covered by the Act, the Act preempts state collective bargaining statute covering house staff. In late 1999, however, the Board ruled in a 3 to 2 decision that interns and residents were employees and were protected by the NLRA. Boston Medical Center Corp. and House Officers Ass'n/Comm. Of Interns and Residents, 330 NLRB No. 30, Nov. 26, 1999. The Board also holds that members of the religious order that owns and operates a hospital are not members of bargaining units in that hospital. See e.g., St. Anthony Center, 220 N.L.R.B. 1009, 90 L.R.R.M. 1405 (1975); St. Rose De Lima Hospital, Inc., 223 N.L.R.B. 1511, 92 L.R.R.M. 1181

(1976); Mercy Hospital of Buffalo, 266 N.L.R.B. 944, 113 L.R.R.M. 1076 (1983).

3. See, Chris Phan, Physician Unionization: The Impact on the Medical Profession, 20 J. Legal Med. 115 (1999).

§ 4–15

1. See discussion in American Hospital Association v. NLRB, 899 F.2d 651 (7th Cir. 1990), affirmed, 499 U.S. 606, 111 S.Ct. 1539, 113 L.Ed.2d 675 (1991).

2. See Mark H. Grunewald, The NLRB's First Rulemaking: An Exercise in Pragmatism, 41 Duke L. J. 274 (1992) for a very detailed "legislative" history of the rule, including discussions at Board meetings and testimony at hearings.

3. 29 C.F.R. § 103.30.

4. American Hospital Association v. NLRB, 499 U.S. 606, 111 S.Ct. 1539, 113 L.Ed.2d 675 (1991).

5. Id. at 1546, 499 U.S. at 617.

"extraordinary circumstances" provision of the rule has begun.[6] Little empirical research has been completed to evaluate the effect of the bargaining unit rule in acute-care hospitals.[7]

§ 4–16. Physicians' Unions

In response to restrictions imposed by managed health care programs, an increasing number of physicians are seeking out unions. For many physicians, however, the ability to unionize has been limited by their status as self-employed or independent contractors. For example, in 1997, the UFCW Local 56 sought NLRB certification to be a bargaining representative for 400 New Jersey "primary care and specialty physicians" employed by a for-profit HMO. The physicians stated that they hoped such representation would help them regain control of patient care decisions. The NLRB Regional Director found the physicians to be independent contractors, for the HMO did not have substantial control "with respect to the physical conduct in the performance of services" the doctors provide.[1] Newly proposed legislation, however, may allow independently practicing physicians to bargain collectively against HMOs.[2]

Physicians' ability to unionize may also be hindered if the courts find that physicians are supervisory employees.[3] Physicians may be classified as supervisors because of their role in directing nurses, technicians and other members of the health care staffs. If this occurs, physicians will not qualify for protection under the NLRA, so their employer would not have to recognize the union nor bargain with it. Factors the courts have considered in determine status as an employee include the degree of skill needed for the job, the authority to hire and discharge workers, the control over compensation for fellow workers, any entrepreneurial interest in the venture, and whether the premises where the services are performed are controlled by the employer.[4]

A growing number of physicians are engaged in true employer-employee relationships. The NLRB has determined that physicians employed by hospitals would be designated "professional employees." Under the NLRA, these physicians, therefore, are allowed to form their own unions. The American Medical Association has recently taken steps towards forming a national labor union for physicians.[5]

---

6. See Marc Mandelman, NLRB Rulemaking on Health Care Collective Bargaining Units: Predictability, But At What Cost?, 9 Hofstra Labor L.J. 483 (1992), for a review of the rulemaking and this early litigation.

7. See e.g., Michael H. LeRoy, Joshua L. Schwarz, Karen S. Koziara, The Law and Economics of Collective Bargaining for Hospitals: An Empirical Public Policy Analysis of Bargaining Unit Determinations, 9 Yale J. Reg. 1 (1992).

§ 4–16

1. *Regional Director Finds HMO Physicians are Independent Contractors*, 100 Daily Labor Report 1 (1999).

2. See H.R.1304, introduced by Rep. Tom Campbell.

3. See § 4–14.

4. See Chris Phan, Physician Unionization: The Impact on the Medical Profession, 20 J. Legal Med. 115 (1999).

5. AMA Begins Formation of Body to Help Physicians Form Local Bargaining Unit, BNA Health Care Daily Report, Sept. 13, 1999.

§ 4–17. Nurses' Unions

Nursing unions began seeking recognition under the NLRA immediately following the 1974 amendments. In the 1970's and 1980's, the NLRB developed a special test for determining whether nurses were to be considered supervisors or employees. Under the "patient care" test, the NLRB often found that a nurse's supervisory authority was not exercised in the interest of the employer, but rather in the interest of the patient.[1] Recently, however, the granting of protection to professional nurses has become uncertain due to the Supreme Court's decision in *NLRB v. Health Care & Retirement Corp. of America*.[2] In *Health Care*, the Court rejected the NLRB's patient care test. The Court held that nurses could not be excluded from supervisory status based on the argument that an interest in patient care was separate from the interests of the employer.[3] The majority of the Court found no basis for the distinction. While the decision in *Health Care* will not result in the elimination of all unions in the field of nursing, it could be used to exclude a large number of individual nurses from protection under the NLRA.

Subsequent to the Supreme Court's decision in *Health Care*, the NLRB abandoned the patient care test and returned to the traditional analysis for determining supervisory status of nurses. In *Providence Hospital & Alaska Nurses Association*, the Board stated that if an employee performed any of the twelve functions listed in the NLRA's definition of a "supervisor," it would then determine if the employee satisfied the "functions in the interest of the employer" and "exercises independent judgment" requirements.[4] The Board went on to conclude that since the charge nurses in *Providence Hospital* did not exercise independent judgment in the performance of their duties, they were not supervisors. Therefore, the charge nurses could not be excluded from protection under the NLRA.[5] While the protection of professional nurses under the NLRA is still uncertain, the analytical approach set forth in *Providence Hospital* would result in a more careful determination of when nurses are truly exercising supervisory authority. The Sixth Circuit, however, has reaffirmed that staff nurses are supervisors and admonished the NLRB for its continued rulings that such nurses are protected by the Act as employees.[6]

§ 4–18. Conditions of Employment

Collective bargaining generally focuses on wages, benefits, hours and related work conditions. Concerns of workers in health care facilities often include other attributes of the work environment as well. Collective bargaining for professional employees in health care has involved issues of professional development and issues relating to patient care.[1] Early studies of collective

§ 4–17

1. See Children's Habilation Center, Inc. v. NLRB, 887 F.2d 130, 134 (7th Cir.1989); NLRB v. Res–Care Inc., 705 F.2d 1461 (7th Cir.1983).

2. 511 U.S. 571 (1994).

3. Id. at 576–580.

4. 1996 WL 46343, 320 NLRB No. 49 (1996).

5. Id.

6. Integrated Health Services of Michigan v. NLRB, 191 F.3d 703 (6th Cir.1999). But see, NLRB v. Hilliard Development Corp., 187 F.3d 133 (1st Cir.1999), and, NLRB v. Gran Care Inc., 170 F.3d 662 (7th Cir.1999), affirming an NLRB decision that nurses were not supervisors.

§ 4–18

1. See Marina Angel, Professionals and Unionization, 66 Minn. L.R. 383 (1982), for a

bargaining by nurses revealed that union members viewed such professional issues as important in collective bargaining.[2]

The NLRA reaches these concerns. The Act provides that it is an unfair labor practice to terminate the employment of a person for engaging in concerted action to improve the terms and conditions of employment.[3] Under this section, employees who join together to protest conditions in the facility may be entitled to reinstatement if discharged. For example, the courts have ordered reinstatement for a nurse who participated in preparing a report critical of the hospital for the Joint Commission on Accreditation of Healthcare Organizations[4] and for employees who complained to a local newspaper about working conditions and patient care.[5]

§ 4–19. Strikes

Strikes by health care professionals, particularly strikes by nurses, have been approached as an ethical as well as a legal issue by the professions. For example, until it changed its position in 1968, the American Nurses Association held the position that strikes by nurses were unprofessional.[1] Public disapproval of strikes against health care institutions may limit organizing efforts in health care.[2]

When Congress amended the NLRA in 1974 to protect organizing and collective bargaining in not-for-profit private hospitals, it included several provisions to minimize the disruptive effects of work stoppages in health care facilities. These provisions require, for example, that labor organizations give advance notice of the date and time of any strike or picketing activity to the health care institution and the Federal Mediation and Conciliation Service.[3]

E. ANTI–DISCRIMINATION STATUTES

§ 4–20. Special Issues for the Health Care Setting

Although hospitals generally enjoy judicial deference in structuring and monitoring their medical staffs, they are subject to a variety of anti-discrimi-

classic analysis of the issues presented by unionization of professionals.

2. See e.g., Allen M. Ponak, Unionized Professionals and the Scope of Bargaining: A Study of Nurses, 34 Ind. & Lab.Rel.Rev. 396 (1981); Eleanor G. Feldbaum, Collective Bargaining in the Health Sector: A Focus on Nurses, 4 J.Health and Hum.Resources Ad. 148 (Fall, 1981). Under 29 U.S.C.A. § 158(d), employers may have to bargain in good faith over some of these issues.

3. 29 U.S.C.A. § 157.

4. Misericordia Hospital Medical Center v. NLRB, 623 F.2d 808 (2d Cir.1980).

5. NLRB v. Mount Desert Island Hospital, 695 F.2d 634 (1st Cir.1982); Community Hospital of Roanoke Valley, Inc. v. NLRB, 538 F.2d 607 (4th Cir.1976).

§ 4–19

1. See e.g., James L. Muyskens, Nurses' Collective Responsibility and the Strike Weapon, 7 J.Med. & Phil.J. 101 (Feb. 1982); Robert Veatch and David Bleich, Interns and Residents on Strike, 5 Hastings Center Rep. 709 (1975).

2. Michael H. LeRoy, Joshua L. Schwarz, Karen S. Koziara, The Law and Economics of Collective Bargaining for Hospitals: An Empirical Public Policy Analysis of Bargaining Unit Determinations, 9 Yale J. Reg. 1 (1992).

3. 29 U.S.C.A. § 158(g). 29 U.S.C.A. § 183(a) provides for the Director of the Federal Mediation and Conciliation Service to establish an impartial board of inquiry to investigate issues and make a written report to the parties involved in the dispute, including recommendation for settlement. This can be done when the Director is of the opinion that a strike, if permitted to occur or continue, will substantially interrupt the delivery of health care in the locality concerned. See also, Federal Mediation and Conciliation Service—Assistance in Health Care Industry, 29 C.F.R. Pt. 1420.

nation statutes that treat health care institutions no differently than other enterprises. Litigation alleging illegal discrimination in staff privileges and related contracting decisions has been infrequent thus far. Such litigation may increase with the exemption of civil rights claims from the immunity provided peer review decisions under the Health Care Quality Improvement Act.[1]

Two particular issues do arise in the application of anti-discrimination statutes to health care workers. First, the coverage of an anti-discrimination statute may be questioned because the work relationships in health care settings often do not conform to traditional formal employment relationships. Second, concerns for the quality of patient care and patient safety are played out in the proof of whether illegal discrimination or legitimate peer review occurred. This section reviews these two issues for the major federal anti-discrimination statutes,[2] including Title VI[3] and Title VII[4] of the Civil Rights Act of 1964, the Age Discrimination in Employment Act,[5] Section 504 of the Rehabilitation Act[6] and the Americans with Disabilities Act.[7]

§ 4–21. Existence of an Employment Relationship

Title VII prohibits discrimination "with respect to ... compensation, terms, conditions or privileges of employment."[1] Title VII requires that plaintiff prove an employment relationship,[2] but it does not require that plaintiff be the employee of the defendant as that term is often understood.

Standards for finding an employment relationship sufficient for a claim under Title VII include a common law "control" test and, alternatively, a "hybrid" test requiring some degree of control by defendant over plaintiff's work combined with a certain economic relationship between the two. Finally,

§ 4–20

1. 42 U.S.C.A. § 11101 et seq. See § 10–25.

2. Most states also have anti-discrimination statutes that will apply to the situations discussed in this section. See e.g., Ohio Rev. Code § 4112 et seq. (Anderson); McKinney's—N.Y. Exec. Law § 296 et seq. Some cities also have local ordinances that would be relevant to these issues. Los Angeles, Cal., Municipal Code art. 5.8 §§ 45.80–93; San Francisco, Cal., Municipal ordinance art. 38, §§ 3801–3816. In some circumstances, state anti-discrimination statutes have exerted more control than the federal statutes. See § 4–22. Other related federal statutes include the Equal Pay Act 29 U.S.C.A. § 206(d).

3. 42 U.S.C.A. §§ 2000d–2000d–4, prohibiting programs which receive federal financial assistance from discriminating against program participants based on race, color or national origin.

4. 42 U.S.C.A. §§ 2000e et seq., prohibiting discrimination in employment practices based on race, color, religion, sex or national origin.

5. 29 U.S.C.A. §§ 621 et seq., prohibiting discrimination in employment practices based on age.

6. 29 U.S.C.A. § 794, prohibiting programs which receive federal financial assistance from

discriminating against otherwise qualified people just because they are handicapped. The Act also requires affirmative action on behalf of handicapped individuals. 29 U.S.C.A. § 793 (applying to federal contractors) and 29 U.S.C.A. § 791(b) (applying to the federal government).

7. 42 U.S.C.A. §§ 12101 et seq., prohibiting discrimination in employment, public services, and "public accommodations and services operated by private entities" based on a person's disability.

§ 4–21

1. 42 U.S.C.A. § 2000e–2(a)(1).

2. Because the Age Discrimination in Employment Act uses language nearly identical to that of Title VII, the analysis developed in Title VII cases is generally applicable to ADEA cases, such as in the determination of whether an employment relationship exists. See e.g., Patel v. Lutheran Medical Center, 753 F.Supp. 1070 (E.D.N.Y.1990); Kuck v. Bensen, 647 F.Supp. 743 (D.Me.1986), amended, 649 F.Supp. 68 (1986), noting that the ADEA allows for proof of an employment relationship by the common law control test or the economic realities test discussed below.

plaintiff may satisfy the Title VII requirement of an employment relationship if defendant controls the plaintiff's employment opportunities. The application of these standards is not at all clear,[3] and there is no one dominant test.[4] Even within circuits, the minimum standard may be unclear.[5]

The common law control test is familiar from institutional liability litigation.[6] This test is the most difficult for plaintiff. It is unlikely that a hospital with an open staff exerts sufficient control under this standard to allow plaintiff to meet the requisite employment relationship in relation to physicians with staff privileges; however, the test may be met in some physician-hospital contracts.[7]

The less restrictive test requires that plaintiff prove some degree of control by the defendant as well as an economic relationship that mimics employment. Factors relevant for the finding of control include whether the plaintiff works under the supervision of another and the degree of skill required for the job. Economic factors include the method of payment to the plaintiff; whether the plaintiff receives retirement benefits; whether the defendant pays social security taxes; whether leave is available; the length of service; the provision of equipment by the defendant; the manner of termination; and whether the plaintiff's work is an integral part of defendant's business.[8]

A third route for establishing the necessary employment relationship is met if the plaintiff is dependent upon the defendant for employment opportunities or if the plaintiff is susceptible to the discrimination the statute was intended to eliminate. In *Sibley Memorial Hospital v. Wilson*,[9] the Circuit Court of Appeals for the District of Columbia held that the hospital defendant and the plaintiff nurse were in an employment relationship under the statute. The defendant hospital had not employed or contracted with the nurse but had contacted a nurse registry on behalf of a hospital patient for a private duty nurse. The hospital had, however, refused plaintiff's services because of

3. See e.g., Doe v. St. Joseph's Hospital, 788 F.2d 411 (7th Cir.1986), holding that it was premature to dismiss plaintiff's claim on the pleadings because of the uncertainty over the kind of employment relationship required by Title VII; Vakharia v. Swedish Covenant Hospital, 765 F.Supp. 461 (N.D.Ill.1991). But see, Mitchell v. Frank R. Howard Memorial Hospital, 853 F.2d 762 (9th Cir.1988), cert. denied, 489 U.S. 1013, 109 S.Ct. 1123, 103 L.Ed.2d 186 (1989), dismissing plaintiff's claim holding that the pleadings were insufficient to state a claim under Title VII for failure to prove the existence of an employment relationship.

4. The Equal Employment Opportunity Commission, which enforces Title VII on behalf of the government, has issued a policy statement concerning the criteria for an employment relationship, applicable to both Title VII and the ADEA; however, the Commission policy statement does not have the force of law. E.E.O.C. Compliance Manual, "Control by Third Parties Over the Employment Relation-

ship Between an Individual and His/Her Direct Employer."

5. See e.g., Ikpoh v. Central DuPage Hospital, 1992 WL 211074 (N.D.Ill.1992), noting that "[a]lthough it is clear that the strict common law test, the most restrictive of the three, is not favored in this circuit, there is some confusion as to whether the hybrid test or the economic realities test is the proper Seventh Circuit standard."

6. See Chapter 7.

7. See §§ 4–9 through 4–11.

8. The EEOC includes several more factors in its policy statement on this hybrid test. EEOC Compliance Manual, "Independent Contractors and Independent Businesses."

9. 488 F.2d 1338 (D.C.Cir.1973). But see, Vakharia v. Swedish Covenant Hospital, 765 F.Supp. 461 (N.D.Ill.1991), discussing whether the court in *Sibley* relied upon the hospital's control over the nurse's access to patients or upon the nurse-patient association.

his gender.[10]

The courts have not uniformly found an employment relationship between a hospital and physician with traditional staff privileges,[11] but many have.[12] Physician-hospital contracts in which the hospital exercises some degree of control over the physician's practice will contribute toward the establishment of an employment relationship for Title VII purposes.[13] In one case, the court relied upon the operation of a physician referral service by the hospital as a touchstone for the satisfaction of the requirement of an employment relationship.[14] In others, courts have found that the hospital's allegedly discriminatory revocation or denial of privileges or rejection of a proposal for services interfered with the doctor's employment with another medical services organization.[15] In a traditional staff privileges context, defendant's control over access to the hospital's facilities clearly has some direct impact on the ability of plaintiff to secure patients. If the physician-patient or nurse-patient relationship is viewed as an employment opportunity, the hospital's control over the professional's access to patients is likely to satisfy the required employment relationship.[16]

Title VI of the Civil Rights Act of 1964[17] and Section 504 of the

10. But see, Shrock v. Altru Nurses Registry, 810 F.2d 658 (7th Cir.1987), holding no employment relationship between a nurse and a referral agency for purposes of Title VII.

11. See e.g., Mitchell v. Frank R. Howard Memorial Hospital, 853 F.2d 762 (9th Cir. 1988), cert. denied, 489 U.S. 1013, 109 S.Ct. 1123, 103 L.Ed.2d 186 (1989); Diggs v. Harris Hospital–Methodist, Inc., 847 F.2d 270 (5th Cir.1988), cert. denied, 488 U.S. 956, 109 S.Ct. 394, 102 L.Ed.2d 383 (1988); Ikpoh v. Central DuPage Hospital, 1992 WL 211074 (N.D.Ill. 1992); Amro v. St. Luke's Hospital, 39 F.E.P. 1574, 1986 WL 766 (E.D.Pa.1986).

12. See e.g., Bender v. Suburban Hospital, 998 F.Supp. 631 (D.Md.1998), holding that doctor with staff privileges was not an employee; Doe v. St. Joseph's Hospital, 788 F.2d 411 (7th Cir.1986); Mallare v. St. Luke's Hospital, 699 F.Supp. 1127 (E.D.Pa.1988), concluding that the plaintiff pled sufficient facts to reach the jury on the issue; Vakharia v. Swedish Covenant Hospital, 765 F.Supp. 461 (N.D.Ill.1991), holding that the hybrid test was met in the case of an anesthesiologist where the "independence and self-determination" of the ordinary physician was diminished because of the hospital's control over her practice and her inability to maintain a private practice outside of the hospital in that specialty; Ross v. Beaumont Hospital, 678 F.Supp. 680 (E.D.Mich.1988), holding that the doctor's service as chair of committees, participation in progressive discipline and the fact that the plaintiff's entire livelihood was based at the hospital satisfied the Title VII requirement of an employment relationship. See also, Christopher v. Stouder Memorial Hospital, 936 F.2d 870 (6th Cir. 1991), cert. denied, 502 U.S. 1013, 112 S.Ct. 658, 116 L.Ed.2d 749 (1991).

13. See e.g., Mousavi v. Beebe Hospital for Sussex County, 674 F.Supp. 145 (D.Del.1987), affirmed, 853 F.2d 919 (3d Cir.1988). Physician–hospital contracts may also assist the plaintiff in establishing an "employer" covered by Title VII. But see Cilecek v. Inova Health System Services, 115 F.3d 256 (4th Cir.1997). Only employers who have fifteen or more employees fall within the coverage of Title VII. Plaintiffs who are employees of entities such as physician corporations or partnerships, with fewer than fifteen employees may be able to sue a large entity, e.g., the hospital that contracts with the plaintiff's employer, by proving that the hospital and the plaintiff's employer are integrated enterprises. To do this, the plaintiff must prove there is an interrelation of operations; common management; centralized control of personnel policy and a degree of common ownership or financial control. See e.g., Baker v. Stuart Broadcasting Co., 560 F.2d 389 (8th Cir.1977); EEOC v. Financial Assurance, Inc., 624 F.Supp. 686 (W.D.Mo. 1985).

14. Ikpoh v. Central DuPage Hospital, 1992 WL 211074 (N.D.Ill.1992); Pao v. Holy Redeemer Hospital, 547 F.Supp. 484 (E.D.Pa. 1982).

15. LeMasters v. Christ Hospital, 777 F.Supp. 1378 (S.D.Ohio 1991); Gomez v. Alexian Brothers Hospital of San Jose, 698 F.2d 1019 (9th Cir.1983).

16. In its policy statement on the existence of the employment relationship, the EEOC adopts the position that interference with an employment relationship, rather than some other type of business opportunity, is required.

17. 42 U.S.C.A. §§ 2000d–2000d–4.

Rehabilitation Act,[18] unlike Title VII, the ADEA and the Americans with Disabilities Act, reach only entities that receive federal funding.[19] Receipt of Medicare, Medicaid or Hill–Burton funds or other federal funding brings a hospital within the reach of Title VI.[20] For some time, § 504 of the Rehabilitation Act was interpreted to apply only to specific programs or activities within an institution that received federal funds. After amendment by Congress, however, the Act clearly applies to the entirety of an institution that receives federal funds.[21]

Although few cases have reviewed the specific application of Title VI to staff privileges decisions, they generally have held that Title VI does not extend to credentialing decisions.[22] In so holding, the courts have relied on a portion of the statute that limits federal enforcement action in the context of employment discrimination to situations in which the primary objective of the federal funding is providing employment.[23] The claim of discrimination in staff privileges could still succeed, despite this narrow reading of Title VI, if plaintiff were an intended beneficiary of federal funding received by defendants.[24]

The Department of Health and Human Services has authority to enforce the requirements of Title VI, independent of suit by a private plaintiff. In *United States v. Harris Methodist Fort Worth*,[25] the Fifth Circuit Court of Appeals reviewed several legal issues arising in the context of an investigation by the Department of the hospital's practices regarding staff privileges. Although the appellate court prohibited the Department from proceeding further because the scope of the search was unreasonable, it did discuss the applicability of Title VI to government investigation of staff privileges decisions. The Fifth Circuit held that decisions affecting staff privileges for non-employee physicians were covered by Title VI because those physicians are persons who "participate in" a federally-funded program by directly caring for the hospital's patients.

The court in *Harris Methodist* distinguished on several grounds the earlier cases holding that Title VI does not cover staff privileges decisions. First, the court supported the exclusion of private actions challenging staff

18. 29 U.S.C.A. § 794.

19. 42 U.S.C.A. § 2000d; 29 U.S.C.A. § 794.

20. 42 U.S.C.A. § 2000d–4a; Linton v. Commissioner of Health and Environmental, 779 F.Supp. 925, 934 (M.D.Tenn.1990); United States v. Harris Methodist Fort Worth, 970 F.2d 94, 97 (5th Cir.1992).

21. Civil Rights Restoration Act of 1987, Pub. L. No. 100–259, 102 Stat. 28 (1988). See e.g., Lussier v. Dugger, 904 F.2d 661 (11th Cir.1990).

22. Doe v. St. Joseph's Hosp., 788 F.2d 411, 420 (7th Cir.1986); Vuciecevic v. MacNeal Memorial Hosp., 572 F.Supp. 1424, 1430 (N.D.Ill. 1983); Vakharia v. Swedish Covenant Hosp., 824 F.Supp. 769 (N.D.Ill.1993).

23. 42 U.S.C.A. § 2000d–3. But see, 45 C.F.R. § 80.5(e), requiring that institutional assurances of compliance with Title VI, in the case of "hospital construction grants," include assurances of non-discrimination in relation to physicians' staff privileges in the entire hospital and in "facilities operated in conjunction therewith."

24. See e.g., Chowdhury v. Reading Hospital and Medical Center, 677 F.2d 317 (3d Cir. 1982), cert. denied, 463 U.S. 1229, 103 S.Ct. 3569, 77 L.Ed.2d 1411 (1983), assuming for purposes of appeal that plaintiff physician had a private cause of action for denial of staff privileges as an intended beneficiary of the federal funding, but remanding to the trial court for resolution of the issue after more complete development of the record. But see, Vuciecevic v. MacNeal Memorial Hospital, 572 F.Supp. 1424 (N.D.Ill.1983), and Doe v. St. Joseph's Hospital of Fort Wayne, 788 F.2d 411 (7th Cir.1986), each rejecting an intended beneficiary claim.

25. 970 F.2d 94 (5th Cir.1992).

privileges decisions from the reach of Title VI, citing the courts' general reluctance to "second-guess hospitals' administrative and health care decisions" as well as their "visceral aversion to permitting anti-discrimination legislation to further doctors' individual interests." Second, the court stated that a finding of an employment relationship in staff privileges sufficient for a claim under Title VII supported a finding of no private right of action for discrimination in staff privileges under Title VI. The Fifth Circuit cited in support of its position legislative history indicating that the employment exclusion of Title VI was intended to correlate with the coverage of employment discrimination under Title VII of the same Act. The court read the earlier Fifth Circuit case of *Diggs v. Harris Hospital—Methodist*,[26] in which the court had concluded that the physician was not an employee under Title VII, as consistent with its decision in this case to include staff privileges decisions within Title VI.

§ 4–22. Proving Race, Age, and Sex Discrimination

Litigation of claims of illegal discrimination against health care professionals generally is similar to litigation of such claims in other settings and health care has not generally been viewed as unique. Judicial deference to medical judgment common in litigation challenging staff privileges actions under common law theories[1] is inappropriate, in cases brought under the federal anti-discrimination statutes. The decisions must be reviewed on the merits without according the benefit of any presumption in favor of defendant's decision.

Only a few appellate cases have reviewed evidence of problems of quality of care in discrimination claims. For example, in *Davis v. West Community Hospital*,[2] the Fifth Circuit affirmed a case in which the district court had dismissed a claim under Title VII on the grounds that the hospital had a legitimate, nondiscriminatory reason for terminating plaintiff's staff privileges.

To the extent that physician recruitment programs satisfy the threshold requirement of an employment relationship, they are susceptible to claims of age discrimination or race discrimination.[3] Such programs often target financial support toward physicians who will increase the patient flow to the hospital. If the market criteria are expressed or applied in a manner that excludes physicians by age, years out of medical school, race, gender or other discriminatory criteria, there may be a violation of the ADEA or Title VII.

§ 4–23. Proving Discrimination Based on Handicap or Disability

a. Scope of the Americans with Disabilities Act of 1990 (ADA)

26. 847 F.2d 270 (5th Cir.1988), cert. denied, 488 U.S. 956, 109 S.Ct. 394, 102 L.Ed.2d 383 (1988).

§ 4–22

1. See § 4–6.

2. 786 F.2d 677 (5th Cir.1986). See also, Flanagan v. Aaron E. Henry Community Health Services Center, 876 F.2d 1231 (5th Cir.1989); Mallare v. St. Luke's Hospital of Bethlehem, 699 F.Supp. 1127 (E.D.Pa.1988); Mousavi v. Beebe Hospital, 674 F.Supp. 145 (D.Del.1987).

3. See e.g., Ikpoh v. Central DuPage Hospital, 1992 WL 211074 (N.D.Ill.1992).

The ADA prohibits discrimination against individuals with disabilities by employers (Title I), public entities (Title II), and private entities that provide public accommodations and/or services (Title III).[1] The purposes of the ADA include providing "a clear and comprehensive national mandate for the elimination of discrimination against individuals with disabilities"[2] and "clear, strong, consistent, enforceable standards addressing discrimination against individuals with disabilities."[3] Section 504 of the Rehabilitation Act of 1973 also prohibits discrimination based on disability.[4]

The Rehabilitation Act prohibits discrimination based "solely" on the disability of "an otherwise qualified individual."[5] The Americans with Disabilities Act prohibits discrimination "against a qualified individual with a disability because of the disability of such individual in regard to ... terms, conditions, and privileges of employment."[6] This difference in language may be at issue in particular cases where the claimant argues multiple motives for the discrimination.[7] The two statutes are closely related, and cases interpreting § 504 will be relevant for the ADA.[8]

Although the Rehabilitation Act and the Americans with Disabilities Act cover employment discrimination, their coverage of non-employment staff privileges decisions has not been clearly established. The analysis of the existence of an employment relationship under Title VII is probably transferrable to the same questions with respect to § 504 and to the ADA.[9] Because the Equal Employment Opportunity Commission enforces both Title VII and the ADA in relation to employment discrimination, transfer of the analysis from Title VII may be likely. Under Title VII, relationships in which the defendant exercises a sufficient degree of control over the plaintiff's activities and has certain economic relationships with plaintiff will meet the statutory definition of employment.[10] Health care professionals whose only relationship with a hospital is traditional staff privileges may not meet the statutory standard for employment.[11]

b. *Definition of Disability Under the ADA*

The Supreme Court decided a series of cases in 1999 which substantially narrowed the definition of disability as it had been developed in case law

§ 4–23

1. 42 U.S.C.A. § 12101 et seq.

2. 42 U.S.C.A. § 12101 (b) (1).

3. 42. U.S.C.A. § 12101 (b) (2).

4. 29 U.S.C.A. § 794. One federal circuit has ruled that the Rehabilitation Act does not reach employment discrimination, but the holding misconstrues the statute and has been rejected implicitly and explicitly by several cases. Trageser v. Libbie Rehabilitation Center, 590 F.2d 87 (4th Cir.1978).

5. 29 U.S.C.A. § 794(a)

6. 42 U.S.C.A. § 12111 et seq.

7. Howe v. Hull, 874 F.Supp. 779 (D.Ohio 1994).

8. 42 U.S.C.A. § 12201(b). *See also*, Wendy Parmet, Discrimination and Disability: The Challenge of the ADA, 18 Law, Medicine & Health Care 331 (1990).

9. *See e.g.*, Karen Rothenberg, The AIDS Project: Creating a Public Health Policy— Rights and Obligations of Health Care Workers, 48 Md. L. Rev. 93 (1989); Note, Hospitals and AIDS Discrimination: Applicability of Federal Discrimination Laws to HCWs and Staff Physicians, 6 J. Contemp. Health L. and Pol'y 193 (1990).

10. Christopher v. Stouder Memorial Hospital, 936 F.2d 870 (6th Cir.1991).

11. See e.g. Alexander v. Rush North Shore Medical Center, 101 F.3d 487 (7th Cir. 1996); Pamintuan v. Nanticoke Memorial Hospital, 1997 WL 129338 (D.Del.); Vakharia v. Swedish Covenant Hospital, 190 F.3d 799 (7th Cir.1999) (all holding that staff privileges did not meet statutory definition of employment).

under the ADA. In *Murphy v. United Parcel Service,*[12] the Court held that the determination of whether a person's impairment substantially limits a major life activity should be made with reference to any mitigating measures. Murphy was fired from his position as a driver of commercial vehicles when his employer learned that his unmedicated blood pressure exceeded Department of Transportation requirements. However, Murphy's blood pressure was within the established parameters when he was properly medicated. The Court held that there was no substantial limitation on a major life activity when Murphy took his medication, and therefore he was not disabled under the ADA, and could not suffer from illegal discrimination under the ADA. On the same day, the Court also decided *Sutton v. United Air Lines,*[13] wherein the Court held that severely myopic individuals, whose eyesight can be corrected to 20/20 or better with the use of corrective lenses, also do not have a disability under the ADA.[14]

The importance of these Supreme Court decisions is that they provide a basis on which to bar the entire ADA claim. If a plaintiff is not "disabled" under the Act, the case is dismissed and there is no opportunity for the plaintiff to prove that he or she could perform the job; i.e., that he or she is "otherwise qualified" for the position.

c. *Discrimination Based on HIV*

The applicability of § 504 to persons who are HIV positive or who have AIDS has been tested in many cases.[15] In *School Board of Nassau County v. Arline,*[16] the United States Supreme Court considered the application of § 504 to a teacher who had tuberculosis. The Court's opinion established a framework for analyzing the application of § 504 in the context of transmissible disease that has been adopted consistently in cases involving HIV.[17] The Court held that the plaintiff teacher was handicapped within the meaning of § 504 because the medical condition "gave rise both to a physical impairment *and* to contagiousness." In a footnote, the Court stated that it did not consider and did not resolve the potential extension of its holding to persons who are seropositive for HIV but who do not have the medical conditions associated with AIDS. Since *Arline,* however, several cases have held that § 504 prohibits discrimination against both persons who are only HIV positive and those who have AIDS.[18]

12. 527 U.S. 516, 119 S.Ct. 2133 (1999).

13. 527 U.S. 471, 119 S.Ct. 2139 (1999).

14. See also, Albertsons, Inc. v. Kirkingburg, 527 U.S. 555, 119 S.Ct. 2162 (1999).

15. See Lawrence O. Gostin, The AIDS Litigation Project: A National Review of Court and Human Rights Commission Decisions, Part II: Discrimination, 263 Journal of the American Medical Association 2086 (April 18, 1990), for a review of reported and unreported cases and settlements under state statutes as well as under the federal statutes.

16. 480 U.S. 273, 107 S.Ct. 1123, 94 L.Ed.2d 307 (1987).

17. After *Arline,* Congress amended the Rehabilitation Act to provide that the Act's prohibition of employment discrimination does not apply to persons with contagious diseases who present a "direct threat to the health or safety of other individuals or who, by reason of the currently contagious disease or infection, is unable to perform the duties of the job." 29 U.S.C.A. § 706(8)(D) (1993). This amendment was generally viewed as "codifying *Arline.*" See e.g., AIDS Policy & Law, 3/23/88 (BNA); Lawrence O. Gostin, The AIDS Litigation Project: A National Review of Court and Human Rights Commission Decisions, Part II: Discrimination, 263 JAMA 2086 (April 18, 1990).

18. See e.g., Chalk v. United States District Court, 840 F.2d 701 (9th Cir.1988), on remand, 814 F.Supp. 844 (N.D.Cal.1992); Severino v. North Fort Myers Fire Control District, 935 F.2d 1179 (11th Cir.1991); Harris v. Thigpen, 941 F.2d 1495, 1524 (11th Cir.1991).

The definition of disability under the ADA includes both persons with AIDS and persons who are asymptomatic HIV positive. In *Bragdon v. Abbott*,[19] a patient infected with HIV brought suit against a dentist who refused to fill a cavity in her tooth in his dental office, but offered to perform the procedure at a hospital, if she paid the additional expenses. The patient asserted that she had a disability under the ADA and was illegally discriminated against by the dentist. The Court held that HIV is an "impairment from the moment of infection"[20] and therefore asymptomatic HIV constitutes an impairment. The Court further held that this impairment substantially limited one of her major life functions (reproduction), and therefore met the definition of disability under the ADA. In this regard the Court stated:

> It cannot be said as a matter of law that an 8% risk of transmitting a dread and fatal disease to one's child does not represent a substantial limitation on reproduction.... When significant limitations result from the impairment, the definition [of disability] is met even if the difficulties are not insurmountable.[21]

In *Arline*, the Supreme Court also set a standard for the determination of whether a person handicapped by a contagious disease is "otherwise qualified" for the position at issue. The Court relied on an amicus brief filed by the American Medical Association arguing that the question requires "findings of facts, based on reasonable medical judgments given the state of medical knowledge, about (a) the nature of the risk (how the disease is transmitted), (b) the duration of the risk (how long is the carrier infectious), (c) the severity of the risk (what is the potential harm to third parties) and (d) the probabilities the disease will be transmitted and will cause varying degrees of harm."[22] The Court also stated that the courts "should normally defer to the reasonable medical judgments of public health officials."[23] In adopting a medical or scientific basis for the determination of whether a particular individual is otherwise qualified for the position, the Court rejected a standard based on mere perceptions or fears of transmissibility.

Under the *Arline* analysis of § 504, policies concerning health care workers with HIV or AIDS must consider the actual risk of transmission to patients in the particular circumstances under consideration.[24] Under the ADA, whether the individual employee presents a "direct threat" to health or safety in the workplace is a legitimate qualification standard.[25] The regulations incorporate the *Arline* standards in defining "direct threat."[26]

Risk assessment continues to be a critical issue in litigation involving HIV under the ADA or Section 504.[27] The *Arline* decision elevated expert opinion concerning risk. Thereafter, guidelines issued by the Centers for Disease Control and by professional medical organizations were referenced frequently

19. Bragdon v. Abbott, 524 U.S. 624, 118 S.Ct. 2196 (1998). See § 10–22.

20. Id. at 2204.

21. *Id.* at 2206.

22. *Arline*, 480 U.S. at 288.

23. Id.

24. See e.g., Doe v. Attorney General, 941 F.2d 780 (9th Cir.1991), on remand 814 F.Supp. 844 (N.D.Cal.1992).

25. 42 U.S.C.A. § 12113(b).

26. 29 C.F.R. § 1630.2(r).

27. See generally, Leonard Glantz, Wendy Mariner & George Annas, Risky Business: Setting Public Health Policy for HIV-infected Health Care Professionals, 70 Milbank Q. 43 (1992); Sidney D. Watson, Eliminating Fear Through Comparative Risk: Docs, AIDS and the Anti–Discrimination Ideal, 40 Buffalo L. Rev. 739 (1992).

in court decisions and provided a touchstone for the assessment of risk in relation to HIV.[28] Individual cases, however, continued to evidence a very low tolerance for risk of transmission in the health care workplace.[29] The Supreme Court's recent decision in Bragdon v. Abbott includes a significant discussion of risk assessment in relation to HIV. The lack of deference to professional association policies may undermine the favorable position that had been created in *Arline*.

The risk of HIV transmission from patients to health care workers also raises legal and public policy issues. Both the risk of transmission and the fear of transmission have an impact on the availability and quality of health care for persons with AIDS. Studies continue to indicate that the risk of transmission from patient to health care provider is smaller, though more substantial in circumstances in which HIV-infected blood could enter the body through a needle stick or other method, than the risk of transmission from health care worker to patient. Still, the health care institution has a duty to provide a safe workplace for its employees and may be liable to health care workers who contract AIDS from patients.[30]

Health care employers may be liable to health care employees who experience an occupational exposure to HIV. Tort claims against health care employers face a number of obstacles, however. Employees included within the coverage of workers' compensation may be restricted to that system, which limits the losses covered, unless the worker can prove that he or she fits within an exception to that coverage. Beyond the workers' compensation limitation, tort actions will face difficulties in proving causation and in proving negligence. Proof of causation requires that the health care worker eliminate other possible sources of the infection.[31]

F.   QUALITY ASSURANCE AND RISK MANAGEMENT

§ 4–24.   Introduction

While professional licensing and credentialing, discussed in the last chapter, may assure that those entering the medical profession possess minimal qualifications, these processes are much less effective at removing from practice those who cease to be qualified, and even less useful for assuring that patients receive health care of optimal quality. Of alternative means of assuring quality, among the most important are the quality assurance, quality improvement, and risk management systems that exist within hospitals and other health care institutions.

Most hospitals employ two distinct but closely related systems to oversee the quality of care: risk management and quality assurance or quality improvement. The goals of an effective risk management program are to

---

28.   See e.g., Mary Anne Bobinski, Risk and Rationality: The Centers for Disease Control and the Regulation of HIV–Infected Workers, 36 St. Louis U.L.J. 213 (1991).

29.   See e.g., Doe v. University of Maryland Medical System Corp., 50 F.3d 1261 (4th Cir. 1995); Bradley v. Univ. of Texas M.D. Anderson Cancer Center, 3 F.3d 922 (5th Cir. 1993).

30.   The Occupational Safety and Health Act, 29 U.S.C.A. § 651 et seq., governs hospitals and other health care institutions.

31.   See e.g., Goins v. Mercy Center for Health Care Services, 667 N.E.2d 652 (Ill. 1996); Madrid v. Lincoln County Med. Center, 909 P.2d 14 (N.M.App.1995).

eliminate the causes of loss experienced by the hospital and its patients, employees, and visitors; lessen the operational and financial effects of un-avoidable losses; and cover inevitable losses at the lowest cost. As such, risk management is concerned not only with the quality of patient care delivered by a hospital, but also with the safety and security of the hospital's employees, visitors, and property. The risk manager also administers claims against the hospital if injuries occur and oversees the hospital's insurance programs, determining which risks the hospital ought to insure against and which it ought to retain through self-insurance or high deductible reinsurance. Finally, the risk manager must be concerned with public and patient relations, as dissatisfied patients are more likely to sue for medical errors.

The most important tool of the risk manager is the incident report. Hospitals require incident reports on occurrences that have resulted or could result in hospital liability or patient dissatisfaction. Examples include sudden deaths, falls, drug errors or reactions, injuries due to faulty equipment, injuries to hospital employees or visitors, threats of legal action, and unex-plained requests from attorneys for medical records. Department heads and supervisors are usually responsible for filing incident reports, which are usually prepared by nurses. Incident reports are directed to the hospital risk manager, who investigates them as necessary. The risk manager also informs appropriate administrative and medical staff, and when necessary, the hospi-tal's insurer, about reported incidents. By compiling data from incident reports, the risk manager can identify problem areas within the hospital and thus help prevent errors and injuries. Incident reports also assist in claim management, permitting the hospital to avoid costly lawsuits by quickly coming to terms with injured patients in cases in which liability seems clear, and facilitating early coordination with an attorney to plan a defense where litigation seems unavoidable. Some malpractice insurance contracts include reservation of rights clauses, which permit the insurer to refuse to pay unreported claims, underscoring the importance of incident reports.

Health care institution quality assurance or improvement programs are directly concerned with assessing and improving the quality of patient care. Quality assurance or improvement has historically focused more narrowly on patient care than does risk management, though this narrow focus may be changing. It is more comprehensive than risk management, however, in that it considers a wide variety of quality concerns, not just discrete mishaps.

The most significant tools of traditional institutional quality assurance programs have been the committees that oversee the quality of various institutional functions. Common hospital committees include a surgical case review committee, which oversees the quality and necessity of surgery; an infections committee, which evaluates patients' infections, oversees the dis-posal of infectious material, and monitors the use of antibiotics; a drug usage committee, which observes the use of drugs; a pharmacy and therapeutics committee, which monitors the availability and handling of drugs; a medical records committee, which assures the quality and completeness of medical records; a utilization review committee, which assures that patients are not admitted inappropriately or hospitalized too long; and a medical audit com-mittee, which reviews the quality of care provided in the hospital as a whole or in certain departments. Some hospitals also have an overall quality control committee which coordinates quality assurance efforts throughout the hospital.

Two other committees that are very important to quality assurance processes are the medical staff executive and credentials committees. The former serves as the cabinet of the medical staff, and in this capacity oversees all efforts of the medical staff to ensure quality. The credentials committee passes on applications for medical staff appointments and reappointments, and establishes and reviews physician clinical privileges, i.e., it determines which doctors can practice in the hospital and what procedures they may perform. As such, these committees have a vital role in assuring the quality of care provided by the hospital.

Some committees, such as the credentials and executive committees, are medical staff committees; i.e., they are composed of and answerable to physicians who practice in the hospital. Others, such as the quality assurance or infections control committees, are likely to be hospital committees, answerable to the hospital administration and to include other professionals besides physicians. In many hospitals, committees play an active role in assuring the quality of care; in others they exist primarily to meet accreditation requirements, and do little.

The nature of quality assurance has changed dramatically in the recent past, however, with health care institutions, under the encouragement of the JCAHO, moving toward using continuous quality improvement or total quality management programs. These programs emphasize improving the total system of care delivery, rejecting the traditional emphasis of both risk management and quality assurance on identifying and sanctioning specific instances of substandard care.[1] They are based on industrial quality improvement models. Though these models vary significantly in their details, they generally focus on widespread data collection and analysis to identify areas where improvement is possible, on creation of a culture in which collaborative efforts to improve quality are enthusiastically embraced, and on service to the customer. Though these programs have changed the philosophy and focus of quality improvement activities within hospitals, they have not, by and large, supplanted the committee structure through which quality assurance activities have traditionally been pursued, nor have they had a significant impact on the peer review litigation with which this section is concerned.

Traditionally risk management has been outcome oriented—it has operated primarily by reacting to bad outcomes. Quality assurance has been more process oriented—including retrospective review of substandard medical practice and concurrent review of the care process (as with proctoring of doctors with probationary staff privileges). Risk management has been predominantly a management function; quality assurance predominantly a clinical function.

§ 4–24

1. See Troyen A. Brennan and Donald M. Berwick, New Rules: Regulation, Markets and the Quality of American Health Care (1996); Donald M. Berwick, et al., Curing Health Care: New Strategies for Quality Improvement (1990); Gerald Hickson, et al., Development of an Early Identification and Response Model of Malpractice Prevention, 1997 L. & Contemp. Probs. 7; Timothy Stoltzfus Jost, Oversight of the Quality of Medical Care: Regulation, Management, or the Market? 37 Ariz.L.Rev. 825 (1995); Donald M. Berwick, Continuous Improvement as an Ideal in Health Care, 320 New Eng. J. Med. 53 (1989); Donna D. Fraiche, Implementing Total Quality Management: The Role of the Medical Staff, Med. Staff. Couns. Summer 1993 at 51.

Increasingly, however, the functions have become less distinct, with quality assurance committees, for example, reviewing incident reports, or risk management departments engaging in criteria-based screening of patient charts to identify adverse patient occurrences.

§ 4–25. Legal Requirements and Stimuli for Risk Management and Quality Assurance

Though the primary reason most hospitals pursue risk management and quality assurance is to assure high quality patient care and protect their patients from harm, there are also a variety of legal requirements or incentives that encourage these efforts. First, the threat of medical malpractice litigation is a powerful incentive for hospitals to develop risk management and quality assurance programs. As will be discussed further in Chapter 7, hospitals that fail to conform to industry standards governing the credentialing and monitoring of the performance of physicians may be liable in many states to patients who are injured through the negligence of those physicians. Further, there is a widespread belief, supported by some empirical evidence, that effective risk management and quality assurance or improvement programs can reduce claim and claim settlement costs.[1]

The accreditation standards of the JCAHO offer another powerful incentive for hospitals to establish risk management and quality assurance programs. Many states tie institutional licensure to JCAHO accreditation, and accreditation permits a hospital to be deemed eligible for participation in the Medicare program.[2] JCAHO accreditation standards are also looked to by the courts of some states as setting standards of care to which hospitals must conform to avoid liability for negligence.[3]

The Joint Commission Accreditation Manual has included quality assurance requirements since the 1960s. As quality oversight theory and technology has evolved, so have Joint Commission requirements. The Joint Commission, for example, was an early leader in pushing hospitals to develop continuous quality improvement programs. More recently the Joint Commission's ORYX initiative has begun to integrate data-driven, continuous quality performance measurement systems into the Joint Commission hospital accreditation program as a supplement to traditional standards-based assessments.[4] The Joint Commission has also started requiring hospitals to monitor, and under some circumstances report, sentinel events, i.e. "unexpected occurrences involving death or serious physical or psychological injury, or risk thereof."[5]

Hospitals that participate in the Medicare program but are not JCAHO accredited must comply with the Medicare Conditions of Participation, which

§ 4–25

1. Laura L. Morlock & Faye E. Malitz, Do Hospital Risk Management Programs Make a Difference?: Relationships Between Risk Management Program Activities and Hospital Malpractice Claims Experience, 54 Law & Contemp. Prob., Spring 1991 at 1; Orley H. Lindgren, et al., Medical Malpractice Risk Management Early Warning Systems, 54 Law & Contemp. Prob. Spring 1991 at 23.

2. 42 U.S.C.A. § 1395bb.

3. See e.g., Pedroza v. Bryant, 677 P.2d 166, 170–71 (Wash.1984), and Chapter 7 infra.

4. wwwb.jcaho.org/perfmeas/oryxqa.html.

5. wwwb.jcaho.org/sentinel/se_pp.html.

also require that the hospital have a quality assurance program.[6] Nursing homes that participate in the Medicare or Medicaid program must also have a quality assessment and assurance committee, which must meet quarterly to identify quality issues and to develop and implement plans to correct quality deficiencies.[7] The confidentiality of information generated in this process is protected by federal statute,[8] and the Missouri Supreme Court has recently held the records of such committees to be immune under this statute from state grand jury discovery.[9]

A number of states have adopted explicit statutes or regulations requiring hospitals to have risk management or quality assurance programs as a condition of licensure.[10]

Most states, however, have chosen to rely on laws that encourage, rather than require, risk management and quality assurance or improvement by protecting participants in these processes. All states currently have statutes extending at least some protection to peer review participants in health care institutions. These statutes first make information created in the quality assurance peer review processes confidential, usually insulating it from discovery in litigation and from introduction in evidence. Second, they protect peer review decisionmakers and persons who provide information to the peer review process from civil liability claims brought by persons who receive negative reviews in the quality assurance process. Finally, a much smaller number of statutes protect risk management documents from discovery or risk managers from liability.

Statutes immunizing quality assurance participants and processes recognize the quasi-independent status of the medical staff in the modern hospital. They acknowledge the fact that hospitals depend on physicians to carry out quality assurance or quality improvement peer review, yet have only a limited ability to compel physicians to participate constructively in the process. They realistically recognize that physicians will be more willing to participate candidly and conscientiously in peer review if they:

> 1) can be reasonably protected from being sued by other physicians whose care they criticize,

> 2) can be assured that suggestions intended as constructive criticism will not reappear as evidence denouncing a colleague in a subsequent malpractice suit against that colleague, and

> 3) can be shielded from public airing of their private critiques of the performance of another professional.

Legislatures have been less willing to immunize risk management information and participants in risk management programs. In the first instance, risk management incident reports are usually generated by hospital employees, who are unlikely to incur personal liability for reporting and have a clear duty as employees to report. Incident reports are common in business general-

---

6. 42 C.F.R. § 482.21.

7. 42 U.S.C.A. §§ 1395i–3(b)(1)(B), 1396r(b)(1)(B).

8. 42 U.S.C. § 1395i–3(b)(1)(B).

9. State ex rel Boone Retirement Center v. Hamilton, 946 S.W.2d 740 (Mo.1997).

10. See U.S. General Accounting Office, Health Care: Initiatives in Hospital Risk Management 20—37 (1989); Arlene J. Diosegy, Risk Management in Health Care Facilities Law 389, 391 n.4 (Anne M. Dellinger, ed. 1991).

ly, usually generated for business reasons. They are not usually protected from discovery in other contexts. Moreover, incident reports are often among the best available sources of information as to what happened in a particular accident, and thus policy-makers are loathe to shield them from discovery.

§ 4–26. The Peer Review Discovery Immunity and Evidentiary Privilege

The issue of access by litigants to medical peer review materials has generated a surprising volume of litigation. The most common context in which such documents are sought is in malpractice litigation where the plaintiff either seeks evidence of physician negligence in the plaintiff's own case or in similar instances involving other patients, or is attempting to show that a hospital is guilty of corporate negligence for not undertaking adequate peer review of a physician it has privileged. Peer review documents are also commonly sought when a physician seeks review of adverse peer review actions or sues peer reviewers under theories such as defamation, interference with a business relationship, or antitrust. Finally, peer review documents are often also requested by regulatory agencies, such as state professional licensure boards, seeking evidence of physician incompetency.

State statutes immunizing peer review documents from discovery or introduction into evidence date from the late 1960s and the 1970s. There was some common law development of the privilege prior to the adoption of these statutes. The leading case adopting a medical peer review privilege in the absence of a statute was *Bredice v. Doctors Hospital, Inc.*[1] In *Bredice,* a malpractice case, the plaintiff sought discovery of all of the minutes and reports of the hospital administrative or medical staff committees that had reviewed the circumstances of the death of the plaintiff's deceased. The Court, applying the policies supporting protection from discovery discussed above, found a qualified peer review privilege and denied the plaintiff discovery of the requested documents.

A judicially-created, public-policy based immunity from discovery of peer review documents has been recognized in a few other cases.[2] However, most courts that have been asked to recognize such a privilege where it is not established by statute have refused to do so.[3] Cases denying the privilege acknowledge a strong public policy in favor of affording litigants free and open access to relevant information, and a reluctance to create new privileges not recognized by legislation or court rules. Courts have been particularly loathe to establish a privilege where the litigant seeking discovery was the person

§ 4–26

1. 50 F.R.D. 249 (D.D.C.1970), affirmed 479 F.2d 920 (D.C.Cir.1973).

2. See, e.g. Weekoty v. United States, 30 F.Supp.2d 1343 (D.N.M.1998); Segal v. Roberts, 380 So.2d 1049 (Fla.App.1979); Dade County Medical Ass'n v. Hlis, 372 So.2d 117 (Fla.App.1979); Oviatt v. Archbishop Bergan Mercy Hosp., 214 N.W.2d 490 (Neb.1974).

3. See e.g., Memorial Hosp. v. Shadur, 664 F.2d 1058 (7th Cir.1981); Syposs v. United States, 63 F.Supp.2d 301 (W.D.N.Y.1999); Burrows v. Redbud Community Hosp. Dist., 187 F.R.D. 606 (N.D.Cal.1998); Ott v. St. Luke

Hosp., 522 F.Supp. 706 (E.D.Ky.1981); Robinson v. Magovern, 83 F.R.D. 79 (W.D.Pa.1979); Hutchinson v. Smith Laboratories, Inc., 392 N.W.2d 139 (Iowa 1986); Wesley Medical Center v. Clark, 669 P.2d 209 (Kan.1983); Nazareth Literary & Benevolent Inst. v. Stephenson, 503 S.W.2d 177 (Ky.1973); Cronin v. Strayer, 467 N.E.2d 143 (Mass.1984); State ex rel. Chandra v. Sprinkle, 678 S.W.2d 804(Mo.1984); Bay Area Health Dist. v. Griffin, 698 P.2d 977 (Or.App.1985); Davison v. St. Paul Fire & Marine Ins. Co., 248 N.W.2d 433 (Wis.1977).

reviewed in the peer review process.[4] Though the universal statutory recognition of peer review privileges and immunities makes the question of a common law privilege largely moot, the issue still arises from time to time in situations in which, for a variety of reasons, the statutory protection does not fit the particular case in which a privilege is sought.[5]

Peer review statutes vary in the protection they afford peer review information.[6] The most common approach is to both immunize information from discovery and to privilege it against introduction into evidence. Such statutes commonly state that information is privileged and confidential and immune from subpoena, discovery, or admission into evidence.[7] Some statutes, however, only protect peer review information from discovery,[8] on the one hand, or, on the other, from admission in evidence.[9] Other statutes merely state that the information is confidential.[10] Courts strictly applying nonspecific statutes have alternatively held peer review information to be discoverable, though not admissable,[11] or immune from discovery, though not privileged.[12]

State peer review protection statutes have been generally upheld against a variety of state constitutional challenges. Due process and equal protection challenges have routinely been turned back upon a finding that the statutes are rationally related to a legitimate state interest.[13]

Statutes vary considerably as to the specificity with which they designate the committees and functions they are intended to cover. While some statutes generally refer to "peer review committees"[14] or "organized committees of hospital medical staffs",[15] others provide exhaustive lists of committees to which they are meant to apply. Medical societies are often covered by peer review protection statutes,[16] and newer statutes explicitly cover HMOs or group practices.[17] Courts have generally been quite willing to cast the peer review privilege net widely within hospitals, bringing within the coverage of peer review protection statutes, for example, pharmacy and therapeutic committees,[18] infection control committees,[19] surgical conference committees,[20] and

4. See e.g., Memorial Hosp. v. Shadur, 664 F.2d 1058 (7th Cir.1981); Robinson v. Magovern, 83 F.R.D. 79 (W.D.Pa.1979).

5. See e.g., Hutchinson v. Smith Laboratories, Inc., 392 N.W.2d 139 (Iowa 1986) (statute does not apply retroactively, common law privilege will not be applied to protect material antedating the statute); Matter of Parkway Manor Healthcare Ctr., 448 N.W.2d 116 (Minn. App.1989) (neither statute nor common law immunize nursing home quality assurance material).

6. See American Medical Association, A Compendium of State Peer Review Immunity Laws (1988), for a comprehensive review of all state immunity laws. See also, Don Harper Mills, Medical Peer Review: The Need to Organize a Protective Approach, 1 Health Matrix 67 (1991).

7. E.g., Conn.Gen.Stat.Ann. § 19a–17b; W.Va.Code § 30–3C–3.

8. E.g., Ariz. Rev. Stat. § 36–445.01(A); La. Stat.Ann.—Rev. Stat. § 22:2021.

9. E.g., Mont. Code Ann. § 50–16–205; Or. Rev. Stat. § 41.675.

10. E.g., Mich. Comp. Laws Ann. § 333.21515.

11. Willing v. St. Joseph Hosp., 126 Ill.Dec. 197, 531 N.E.2d 824 (Ill.App.1988).

12. Coburn v. Seda, 677 P.2d 173 (Wash. 1984).

13. Lilly v. Turecki, 492 N.Y.S.2d 286 (N.Y.App.Div.1985); Jenkins v. Wu, 82 Ill.Dec. 382, 468 N.E.2d 1162 (Ill.1984); Gates v. Brewer, 442 N.E.2d 72 (Ohio App.1981); Eubanks v. Ferrier, 267 S.E.2d 230 (Ga.1980).

14. Iowa Code Ann. § 147.135.

15. Ark. Code Ann. § 16–46–105(a).

16. Though some statutes specify that a medical society must contain a certain percentage of physicians in the area to be protected. See e.g., West's Ann.Cal. Civ. Code § 43.7(b) (25%).

17. See La. Stat. Ann.—Rev. Stat. § 13:3715.3(A); Minn. Stat. Ann. § 145.61(5).

18. Good Samaritan Hosp. v. American Home Products Corp., 569 So.2d 895 (Fla.App. 1990).

a conference committee involving an entire department.[21]

Where the question has been raised as to inclusion of a particular committee, courts have looked to hospital by-laws[22] and Joint Commission[23] requirements. Courts have been most resistant to bringing within the coverage of peer review protection statutes hospital administrative officers[24] or governing boards[25] and, to a lesser extent, credentials committees.[26] Courts have also been reluctant to extend the coverage of these statutes to entities other than hospitals, such as nursing homes[27] or utilization review contractors,[28] when these entities are not explicitly covered by the statutes.

Most statutes delineate generally the material they intend to immunize. Protected material is commonly described by language such as the "proceedings and records"[29]; "proceedings, minutes, records, and reports,"[30] or "proceedings and records."[31] Persons who testify at committee proceedings are also commonly shielded from having to reveal the content of their testimony.[32] However, peer review protection statutes frequently specify that information, documents, or records available from other sources are not immunized merely because they have been presented to or considered by a peer review committee.[33]

Courts will readily protect the core material that peer review statutes intend to keep confidential—the deliberations of peer review committees, documents prepared explicitly for them, and testimony heard by them.[34] However, courts generally permit discovery of documents prepared outside of peer review committees for other purposes, but incidentally shared with the committee,[35] or information about committees or their processes that are not sensitive in nature.[36] Information routinely prepared or accumulated by hospi-

19. In re "K", 561 A.2d 1063 (N.H.1989); Cofone v. Westerly Hosp., 504 A.2d 998 (R.I. 1986).

20. In re S–88–08–1940A, 573 N.Y.S.2d 814 (N.Y.Sup.1991).

21. County of Los Angeles v. Superior Court, 274 Cal.Rptr. 712 (Cal.App.1990).

22. Shelton v. Morehead Memorial Hosp., 347 S.E.2d 824, 827 (N.C.1986); Coburn v. Seda, 677 P.2d 173, 178 (Wash.1984).

23. Trinity Med. Ctr. v. Holum, 544 N.W.2d 148 (N.D.1996); In re "K", 561 A.2d 1063, 1066–67 (N.H.1989); Coburn v. Seda, 677 P.2d 173, 178 (Wash.1984).

24. See e.g., Santa Rosa Memorial Hosp. v. Superior Court, 220 Cal.Rptr. 236, 245–47 (Cal. App.1985).

25. Hinson v. Clairemont Community Hosp., 267 Cal.Rptr. 503, 512–14 (Cal.App. 1990); Shelton v. Morehead Memorial Hosp., 347 S.E.2d 824, 829–30 (N.C.1986). But see, Lake Hosp. and Clinic v. Silversmith, 551 So.2d 538, 541–42 (Fla.App.1989) (holding that records of board of directors were protected by statute).

26. See Manthe v. VanBolden, 133 F.R.D. 497 (N.D.Tex.1991) (records of credential's committee not protected).

27. In re Parkway Manor Healthcare Ctr., 448 N.W.2d 116 (Minn.App.1989).

28. State ex re. Tennill v. Roper, 965 S.W.2d 945 (Mo.App.1998).

29. West's Fla.Stat.Ann. § 395.0193(7).

30. Ark.Code.Ann. § 16–46–105.

31. W.Va.Code § 30–3C–3.

32. West's Ann.Cal.Evid. Code § 1157(b); Hawaii Rev. Stat. § 624–25.5(a).

33. See West's Fla.Stat.Ann. § 395.0115(7); W.Va. Code § 30–3C–3.

34. Brownwood Regional Hospital v. Eleventh Court of Appeals, 927 S.W.2d 24 (Tex. 1996); Memorial Hosp.—The Woodlands v. McCown, 927 S.W.2d 1 (Tex.1996). See also, Frank v. Trustees of Orange County Hosp., 530 N.E.2d 135, 137–38 (Ind.App.1988) (even private conversations of peer reviewers outside of committee context privileged as probing them might reveal content of committee deliberations.)

35. See Jacksonville Medical Ctr., Inc. v. Akers, 560 So.2d 1313 (Fla.App.1990).

36. See, arguing that expansive recognition of exceptions to the peer review privilege has eviscerated the protection afforded by the Illinois Act, Pamela McKinney, The Peer Review

tal administrators for administrative purposes, for example, has been held disclosable.[37] Guidelines or criteria applied by peer review committees,[38] final decisions of committees affecting staff privileges,[39] and lists of committee members[40] have also been refused protection. Statements to peer review committees by physicians who are defendants in malpractice litigation and who were the subject of committee review has occasionally been revealed.[41] Hypothetical questions of witnesses with access to privileged material have also been permitted where committee deliberations themselves are not probed.[42]

The most frequently litigated coverage issue is whether the statutes immunize files prepared in the physician credentialing process. The courts are split on this question, with some courts holding that such files are prepared in anticipation of peer review and thus protected by the privilege,[43] other courts viewing credentials applications as administrative material, prepared by the applicant doctors themselves rather than by peer review committees, and thus subject to discovery.[44] Where credentials files contain both peer review and non-peer review material, in camera review has been required to identify non-privileged material for disclosure.[45]

Peer review statutes are also commonly subject to a number of explicit exceptions that recognize instances where absolute confidentiality of the peer review process might be broken. The broadest exception is that found in the District of Columbia statute, which codified *Bredice*[46]and permits discovery

Privilege: A Dying Cause? 25 Journal of Health and Hospital Law 201 (1992).

37. Brown v. Superior Court, 214 Cal.Rptr. 266 (Cal.App.1985); Marsh v. Lake Forest Hosp., 116 Ill.Dec. 612, 519 N.E.2d 504 (Ill. App.1988); Barnes v. Whittington, 751 S.W.2d 493 (Tex.1988). See also, Ekstrom v. Temple, 142 Ill.Dec. 910, 553 N.E.2d 424, 428–29 (Ill. App.1990) (in camera review necessary to determine if infection control documents prepared for peer review or administrative purposes.)

38. Willing v. St. Joseph Hosp., 126 Ill.Dec. 197, 201–02, 531 N.E.2d 824, 828–29 (Ill.App. 1988); Kalish v. Mount Sinai Hosp., 270 N.W.2d 783, 786 (Minn.1978) (though guidelines were not admissable in evidence).

39. Richter v. Diamond, 91 Ill.Dec. 621, 483 N.E.2d 1256 (Ill.1985); Moretti v. Lowe, 592 A.2d 855, 858 (R.I.1991); Anderson v. Breda, 700 P.2d 737, 741–42 (Wash.1985).

40. Ekstrom v. Temple, 142 Ill.Dec. 910, 553 N.E.2d 424, 429 (Ill.App.1990) but see, Cedars–Sinai Medical Center v. Superior Court of Los Angeles County, 16 Cal.Rptr.2d 253 (Cal.App.1993) (denying discovery of the identities of review committee members under California law).

41. Romero v. Cohen, 679 N.Y.S.2d 264 (Sup.Ct. 1998); Carroll v. Nunez, 524 N.Y.S.2d 578, 579–80 (N.Y.App.Div.1988). But see, Spinks v. Children's Hosp. Nat'l Medical Ctr., 124 F.R.D. 9 (D.D.C.1989) (requiring a showing of "extraordinary necessity" even though

information might be outside the scope of statutory privilege).

42. Eubanks v. Ferrier, 267 S.E.2d 230 (Ga.1980); Wheeler v. Central Vt. Medical Ctr., Inc., 582 A.2d 165 (Vt.1989).

43. McGee v. Bruce Hospital System, 439 S.E.2d 257 (S.C.1993); Cruger v. Love, 599 So.2d 111 (Fla.1992); Humana Hosp. Desert Valley v. Superior Court, 742 P.2d 1382 (Ariz. App.1987); Snell v. Superior Court, 204 Cal. Rptr. 200 (Cal.App.1984); Tarpon Springs Gen. Hosp. v. Hudak, 556 So.2d 831 (Fla.App.1990); Parker v. St. Clare's Hosp., 553 N.Y.S.2d 533 (N.Y.App.Div.1990); Carroll v. Nunez, 524 N.Y.S.2d 578 (N.Y.App.Div.1988).

44. Manthe v. VanBolden, 133 F.R.D. 497, 502–03 (N.D.Tex.1991); Hill v. Sandhu, 129 F.R.D. 548, 550–51 (D.Kan.1990); Hinson v. Clairemont Community Hosp., 267 Cal.Rptr. 503, 508–10 (Cal.App.1990); Pritchard v. Swedish American Hosp., 136 Ill.Dec. 605, 545 N.E.2d 129 (Ill.App. 1989); Willing v. St. Joseph Hosp., 126 Ill.Dec. 197, 531 N.E.2d 824 (Ill.App.1988).

45. See e.g., Jacksonville Medical Ctr., Inc. v. Akers, 560 So.2d 1313, 1316 (Fla.App.1990) (credentials file submitted to in camera review to expunge notes written on application by members of peer review committee).

46. Bredice v. Doctors Hospital, Inc., 50 F.R.D. 249 (D.D.C.1970), affirmed 479 F.2d 920 (D.C.Cir.1973).

upon a showing of "extraordinary necessity."[47] Another exception found in several statutes permitting access to "the statements made by any person in attendance at such a meeting who is a party to an action or proceeding the subject matter of which was reviewed at such meeting",[48] has also been interpreted as not to permit discovery of credentialing information in malpractice actions.[49]

Most litigation concerning exceptions to peer review confidentiality statutes has involved attempts to gain access to the records either by state regulatory agencies or by physicians who have been denied staff privileges or had their privileges revoked. Several statutes explicitly permit access to peer review records by state professional or institutional licensure agencies.[50] A recent California court decision permits access to peer review records in criminal proceedings.[51] In other states, courts have interpreted peer review protection statutes as only barring access to records in civil, as opposed to administrative proceedings, and thus as not precluding access by regulatory agencies.[52] Where statutes do not permit regulatory agencies access to peer review data, however, courts have refused discovery by such agencies.[53]

Many statutes also contain specific exceptions permitting access to peer review documents by physicians whose staff privileges are denied or revoked in the peer review process,[54] presumably out of a concern that permitting deprivation of valuable privileges through secret processes is unfair and may violate due process.[55] A few courts have denied physicians access to peer review data where no explicit exception is found in the statute, however.[56] More commonly, courts have refused access to peer review information by physicians suing peer review committees or their members in tort, noting that the records are only available in judicial review or mandamus actions.[57] This interpretation effectively transforms the statutes from discovery immunity to civil liability immunity statutes.

47. D.C. Code Ann. § 32–505. See also N.H.Rev.Stat.Ann. § 151:13–a (permitting discovery in a proceeding alleging "repetitive malicious action and personal injury brought against a physician * * * ").

48. McKinney's—N.Y.Pub.Health Law § 2805–m.

49. Parker v. St. Clare's Hosp., 553 N.Y.S.2d 533 (N.Y.App.Div.1990).

50. Ariz.Rev.Stat. § 36–445.01(A); Ark. Code Ann. § 16–46–105; West's Colo.Rev.Stat. Ann. § 25–3–109(4)(a); Iowa Code Ann. § 147.135.

51. In re Search Warrant, No. 13489 (Calif. SuperCt., Jan. 2. 1998) reported in BNA Health Care Daily, March 23, 1998.

52. Commissioner of Health Serv. v. Kadish, 554 A.2d 1097, 1099 (Conn.App.1989), certification denied 563 A.2d 1355 (Conn.1989); Mercy Hosp. v. Department of Professional Regulation, Bd. of Medical Examiners, 467 So.2d 1058, 1059–60 (Fla.App.1985); Commissioner of Health Serv. v. William W. Backus Hosp., 485 A.2d 937, 939 (Conn.Super.1984); Unnamed Physician v. Commission on Medical Discipline, 400 A.2d 396, 402 (Md.1979).

53. Beth Israel Hosp. Ass'n v. Board of Registration in Medicine, 515 N.E.2d 574 (Mass.1987); Petition of Atty. Gen., 369 N.W.2d 826 (Mich.1985).

54. See Ariz. Rev. Stat. § 36–445.01; La. Stat.Ann.—Rev.Stat. § 13:3715.3(A); N.H. Rev. Stat.Ann. § 151:13–a(II).

55. See Jenkins v. Wu, 82 Ill.Dec. 382, 468 N.E.2d 1162, 1167–68 (Ill.1984). See also Hayes v. Mercy Health Corp., 739 A.2d 114 (Pa.1999) (interpreting Pennsylvania peer review statute to permit access to records of doctor challenging privilege suspension).

56. Parkway Gen. Hosp. Inc. v. Allinson, 453 So.2d 123, 126 (Fla.App.1984).

57. California Eye Institute v. Superior Court, 264 Cal.Rptr. 83, 85 (Cal.App.1989); Knapp v. Palos Community Hosp., 126 Ill.Dec. 362, 531 N.E.2d 989, 995–96 (Ill.App.1988). See also Irving Healthcare System v. Brooks, 927 S.W.2d 12 (Tex.1996) (discovery refused in tort case because peer review statute contains no exception for statements made to committee with malice).

State peer review privileges are not binding on federal courts deciding cases under federal laws, and have been rejected in cases involving the Emergency Medical Treatment and Active Labor Act,[58] the antitrust laws,[59] the Protection and Advocacy for Individuals with Mental Illness Act;[60] and the Federal Tort Claims Act.[61] Federal courts have also refused to either apply state peer review privileges or to recognize a federal peer review privilege in cases involving the Health Care Quality Improvement Act.[62]

Litigants in a number of cases have asserted that the peer review privilege has been waived, either because privileged information has been inappropriately shared with persons not legally entitled to it,[63] or because information has been appropriately disclosed (e.g., to a doctor denied staff privileges) and is now sought in other contexts.[64] Although a few courts have found that disclosure waives the privilege (treating disclosed information as a secret which once revealed cannot again be hidden),[65] more hold that peer review information is privileged as a matter of public policy, and does not become available for all purposes just because it is disclosed under special circumstances.[66]

Before a waiver issue can be resolved it is often necessary to determine whether the person or entity who has allegedly waived the privilege is in fact entitled to assert it. Does the privilege belong to the hospital, persons engaged in the peer review process, a doctor whose work has been reviewed, or all of the above? Courts tend to allow a doctor whose care has received an adverse review to assert the privilege whether or not it is asserted by the committee or its members.[67] It has been held, however, that a physician who received an adverse review cannot sue for breach of confidentiality if the hospital chooses to make the review public.[68]

When a dispute arises as to applicability of the privilege to particular materials, courts normally insist on in camera review.[69] A mere assertion of

58. Burrows v. Redbud Community Hosp. Dist., 187 F.R.D. 606 (N.D.Cal.1998).

59. Pagano v. Oroville Hosp. 145 F.R.D. 683 (N.D.Cal.1993).

60. Pennsylvania Protection and Advocacy, Inc. v. Houstoun, 1999 WL 1045152 (E.D.Pa. 1999).

61. Syposs v. United States, 63 F.Supp.2d 301 (W.D.N.Y.1999), but see Weekoty v. Unites States, 30 F.Supp.2d 1343 (D.N.M.1998) (applying state peer review privilege in Federal Tort Claims Act case).

62. Patt v. Family Health Systems, Inc. 1999 WL 1034225 (E.D. Wisc. Nov. 10, 1999); Pickett v. Woodland Heights Gen. Hosp., 1997 WL 394822 (E.D.Tex. June 18, 1997); Johnson v. Nyack Hospital, 169 F.R.D. 550, 560 (S.D.N.Y.1996); Robertson v. Neuromedical Center, 169 F.R.D. 80, 84 (M.D.La.1996).

63. Franco v. District Court, 641 P.2d 922, 931 (Colo.1982); McGlynn v. Grinberg, 568 N.Y.S.2d 481, 482–83 (N.Y.App.Div.1991); Straube v. Larson, 600 P.2d 371, 376 (Or. 1979), appeal after remand 699 P.2d 206 (Or. App.1985).

64. Henry Mayo Newhall Memorial Hosp. v. Superior Court, 146 Cal.Rptr. 542, 547–48 (Cal.App.1978).

65. See e.g., Whitman v. United States, 108 F.R.D. 5, 6–8 (D.N.H.1985). Cf. Baltimore Sun Co. v. University of Md. Medical Sys. Corp., 584 A.2d 683, 687–88 (Md.1991) (press permitted access to otherwise privileged records disclosed in judicial proceeding).

66. Virmani v. Presbyterian Health Serv. Corp. , 515 S.E.2d 675 (N.C.1999); Emory Clinic v. Houston, 369 S.E.2d 913, 914 (Ga.1988), on remand 374 S.E.2d 236 (Ga.App.1988); Zajac v. St. Mary of Nazareth Hosp. Ctr., 156 Ill.Dec. 860, 571 N.E.2d 840, 846–47 (Ill.App. 1991).

67. Humana Hosp. Desert Valley v. Superior Court, 742 P.2d 1382, 1389 (Ariz.App.1987).

68. Amid v. Hawthorne Community Medical Group, 261 Cal.Rptr. 240, 245 (Cal.App. 1989).

69. See e.g., Hurst v. Creasman, 1989 WL 151660 (M.D.N.C.1989); Jacksonville Medical Ctr., Inc. v. Akers, 560 So.2d 1313, 1316 (Fla. App.1990); State ex rel. Grandview Hosp. and

the privilege without supporting affidavits or in camera review is generally insufficient.[70]

§ 4–27. Confidentiality of Risk Management Material

For reasons noted above, few of the statutes that protect the confidentiality of quality assurance materials also protect risk management materials. A few state statutes explicitly immunize risk management incident reports from discovery.[1] Others, on the other hand, explicitly exclude incident reports from the protection of the peer review privilege.[2] Most state statutes, however, do not expressly address the issue of immunity of risk management materials from discovery or introduction into evidence, leaving them unprotected except insofar as they come within the scope of the peer review or some other privilege.

Where state statutes do not explicitly immunize incident reports from discovery, courts have been reluctant to stretch quality assurance peer review privileges to cover them.[3] Cases rejecting attempts to bring risk management materials within statutory immunity tend to note that incident reports deal with factual matters and are the kind of safety information that any company might compile for business purposes. A public policy based immunity for risk management materials has also been rejected for similar reasons.[4] Several courts have held, however, that risk management data collected for peer review quality assurance or safety committees are within the protection of the statutory peer review privilege.[5]

Since legislatures and courts have been reluctant to protect risk management materials explicitly through statutory privileges, hospitals seeking protection tend to argue that these documents are covered either by the attorney–client evidentiary privilege or by the work product discovery immunity. Courts are split on whether incident reports are covered by the attorney-client (or insurer-insured) privilege, with the result often depending on how the court views the facts. Where the court perceives documents to have been prepared predominantly for business loss control purposes, the privilege has been rejected.[6] Where, however, the report was filed with an attorney or

Medical Center v. Gorman, 554 N.E.2d 1297 (Ohio 1990). See also State ex rel. Good Samaritan Medical Center–Deaconess Hosp. Campus v. Maroney, 365 N.W.2d 887, 893 (Wis.App. 1985) (authorizing in camera review of documents by malpractice screening panel in prelitigation arbitration proceedings.)

70. Ekstrom v. Temple, 142 Ill.Dec. 910, 553 N.E.2d 424, 428–29 (Ill.App.1990).

§ 4–27

1. Kan. Stat. Ann. § 65–4925(a)(2); Mass. Gen.Laws Ann. ch. 111, § 205(b); Tenn. Code Ann. § 63–6–219(c).

2. Ark. Code Ann. § 16–46–105(c); Mass. Gen.Laws Ann. ch. 111 § 204(b).

3. See Columbia/HCA Healthcare Corp. v. Eighth Judicial District, 936 P.2d 844 (Nev. 1997); Cochran v. St. Paul Fire and Marine Ins. Co., 909 F.Supp. 641 (W.D.Ark.1995); John C. Lincoln Hosp. and Health Center v. Superior Court, 768 P.2d 188 (Ariz.App.1989);

Dunkin v. Silver Cross Hosp., 158 Ill.Dec. 35, 573 N.E.2d 848 (Ill.App.1991); Wiener v. Memorial Hosp. for Cancer and Allied Diseases, 453 N.Y.S.2d 142 (N.Y.Sup.1982).

4. St. Louis Little Rock Hosp., Inc. v. Gaertner, 682 S.W.2d 146 (Mo.App.1984).

5. Dorris v. Detroit Osteopathic Hosp. Corp., 594 N.W.2d 455 (Mich.1999); Gallagher v. Detroit–Macomb Hosp. Ass'n, 431 N.W.2d 90 (Mich.App.1988). Further, interrogatories demanding disclosure of extensive information relating to the peer review processes for which otherwise disclosable reports were prepared may be rejected as conflicting with the peer review privilege. See State ex rel. Lester E. Cox Medical Centers v. Darnold, 944 S.W.2d 123 (Mo. 1997).

6. Sakosko v. Memorial Hosp., 118 Ill.Dec. 818, 522 N.E.2d 273 (Ill.App.1988); St. Louis Little Rock Hosp., Inc. v. Gaertner, 682 S.W.2d 146 (Mo.App.1984); Clark v. Norris, 734 P.2d 182 (Mont.1987).

insurer for litigation purposes, the privilege may apply.[7]

A more common argument is that incident reports are litigation work product, immunized from discovery. Here again, the courts are split depending on their view of incident reports. Where incident reports are seen primarily as business documents, not prepared specifically for litigation, they are not protected.[8] Where courts view them as investigative reports, formulated for litigation defense, they are protected.[9] The work product immunity, however, unlike the peer review or attorney client privileges, is qualified, it only protects the documents from discovery absent a showing that there is a special need or unique hardship requiring access to the information, which is not available through other means.

Data collected through quality improvement or quality management programs that are run administratively rather than through traditional peer review committees may very well be treated like incident reports, and thus be subject to discovery.

§ 4–28. Protection of Participants in the Peer Review and Risk Management Processes From Liability

Physicians who have been censured by the peer review process have frequently retaliated by suing participants in that process. The most frequent ground for such suits is defamation, based on allegations that either comments made in the peer review process or the conclusion of that process defamed the reputation of the censured physician. Some of these suits also allege business torts, such as interference with a business relationship or with an economic expectancy. Cases are also brought claiming a conspiracy by competitors to violate the antitrust laws by excluding the censured physician from competition.

The serious threat which such litigation poses to the peer review process is immediately apparent. If such litigation is allowed, physicians will refuse to participate at all in the quality assurance process, or, where the hospital can compel them to participate, will not participate candidly and conscientiously. To protect the peer review process from this threat, courts and legislatures have afforded peer review committee members and those who testify before peer review committees protection from liability. Recognizing, however, that peer review actions can have very serious consequences for the censured professional, and are not always motivated by good will, protection from liability is commonly qualified, not absolute.

Even in the absence of statutory provisions, a number of courts have protected participants in the peer review process from defamation liability by recognizing a peer review privilege. Most frequently courts have established a

---

7. Sierra Vista Hosp. v. Superior Court, 56 Cal.Rptr. 387 (Cal.App.1967); Enke v. Anderson, 733 S.W.2d 462 (Mo.App.1987).

8. Columbia/HCA Healthcare Corp. v. Eighth Judicial Dist., 936 P.2d 844 (Nev.1997); Sims v. Knollwood Park Hosp., 511 So.2d 154 (Ala.1987); Sakosko v. Memorial Hosp., 118 Ill.Dec. 818, 522 N.E.2d 273 (Ill.App.1988); Shotwell v. Winthrop Community Hosp., 531 N.E.2d 269 (Mass.App.1988); State ex rel.

Faith Hosp. v. Enright, 706 S.W.2d 852 (Mo. 1986); St. Louis Little Rock Hosp., Inc. v. Gaertner, 682 S.W.2d 146 (Mo.App.1984); Vandenburgh v. Columbia Memorial Hosp., 457 N.Y.S.2d 591 (N.Y.App.Div.1982); Barnes v. Whittington, 751 S.W.2d 493 (Tex.1988).

9. See e.g., Mlynarski v. Rush Presbyterian–St. Luke's Medical Ctr., 157 Ill.Dec. 561, 572 N.E.2d 1025 (Ill.App.1991).

qualified privilege, protecting statements made in good faith, without malice, for a proper purpose to an appropriate committee or person.[1] A few courts, however, have recognized an absolute privilege, treating peer review proceedings as quasi-judicial in nature.[2] Persons participating in the peer review process have also successfully defended defamation actions where their statements were considered to be statements of opinion rather than of fact,[3] or where their statements were substantially true.[4] Quasi-judicial immunity has also been recognized where a doctor was involved in a state medical board peer review proceeding.[5]

Virtually all of the states have now adopted statutes offering some protection from liability to participants in the peer review process.[6] These statutes protect from liability both those who testify before and participate as members in peer review committees. They also may protect the hospital itself as to actions taken pursuant to the peer review process.[7] As with peer review confidentiality statutes, these statutes normally identify the committees whose members, employees, consultants and witnesses they afford protection.

The key issue raised by peer review liability protection statutes and the cases interpreting them is whether the protection they afford is qualified or absolute. The issue is important, of course, not just because absolute immunity offers protection in the rare situations where qualified immunity would not, but because absolute immunity affords the possibility of disposing of the lawsuit by a motion to dismiss, while qualified immunity often permits the plaintiff to raise evidentiary issues that must be tried.

A few statutes offer absolute immunity from liability to participants in the peer review process.[8] More provide qualified immunity, protecting actions taken "in good faith" or "without malice" and statements made with "reasonable belief" or which were not false and known to be false.[9] These statutes

§ 4–28

1. Spencer v. Community Hosp., 42 Ill.Dec. 272, 408 N.E.2d 981 (Ill.App.1980); Garrow v. Elizabeth Gen. Hosp. & Dispensary, 401 A.2d 533 (N.J.1979); Raymond v. Cregar, 185 A.2d 856 (N.J.1962); Bainhauer v. Manoukian, 520 A.2d 1154 (N.J.Super. App.Div.1987); Mayfield v. Gleichert, 484 S.W.2d 619 (Tex.Civ.App. 1972).

2. Franklin v. Blank, 525 P.2d 945 (N.M.App.1974). But see DiMiceli v. Klieger, 206 N.W.2d 184 (Wis.1973) (refusing to treat peer review proceedings as quasi-judicial or to consider communications to them as absolutely privileged.)

3. Gill v. Hughes, 278 Cal.Rptr. 306, 311 (Cal.App.1991).

4. Franklin v. Blank, 525 P.2d 945 (N.M.App.1974); Kinney v. Daniels, 574 F.Supp. 542 (S.D.W.Va.1983).

5. Ostrzenski v. Seigal, 177 F.3d 245 (4th Cir. 1999).

6. A few states also offer statutory immunity to risk managers, see e.g., West's Fla.Stat. Ann. § 395.041(11). One statute also protects the employment status of "whistle-blowers"

within a health care institution. Or.Rev.Stat. § 441.057.

7. Eyring v. Fort Sanders Parkwest Med. Ctr. Inc., 991 S.W.2d 230 (Tenn.1999).

8. Ariz. Rev. Stat. § 36–445.02; Idaho Code § 39–1392c; N.H.Rev.Stat.Ann. § 151:13–a. California courts initially applied in peer review proceedings a statute that afforded an absolute privilege in official proceedings, but when a more specific statute was enacted recognizing only a qualified immunity, applied it instead. See Hackethal v. Weissbein, 154 Cal.Rptr. 423, 592 P.2d 1175 (Cal.1979).

9. See e.g., Ala.Code § 6–5–333 (action taken "without malice and in a reasonable belief that such action * * * is warranted by the facts made known to him."); West's Fla.Stat. Ann. § 395.0115(5) ("action taken without intentional fraud"); McKinney's—N.Y. Public Health Law § 2805–j (providing information "in good faith and without malice"); Tenn. Code.Ann. § 63–6–219(b)(2), (statements made "unless such information is false and the person providing it had actual knowledge of such falsity."); W.Va.Code § 30–3C–2 (immunity for persons providing information unless such "information is false and the person providing

often specify further that immunity is only available for actions taken within the scope of the committee's function or for actions related to its purposes.[10] Some states provide absolute immunity for persons who testify before peer review committees, but only qualified immunity to their members.[11]

In contrast to discovery immunity statutes, which are often interpreted restrictively to protect the plaintiff's rights to information, liability immunity statutes tend to be interpreted broadly to protect the peer review process.

Courts have upheld peer review immunity statutes against constitutional attack[12], and applied them retroactively to pending litigation.[13] In states where statutes afford absolute immunity, such as Illinois, courts have repeatedly turned back attempts to establish liability.[14] In states that recognize only qualified immunity, courts have refused to imply malice or fraud[15] and have insisted that intent to injure or malicious conduct be specifically pleaded and proved.[16] Courts have maintained that the plaintiff bears the burden of proof of all elements of the case,[17] and permitted summary judgment where proof was not forthcoming.[18]

A few statutes award costs and reasonable attorney's fees to a prevailing defendant sued for conducting or participating in peer review.[19] This to some extent compensates a defendant afforded only a qualified privilege who must litigate unfounded claims of malice or bad faith.

Professional liability insurance policies of physicians participating in peer review coverage may very well not cover the costs of defending an action brought by a physician injured through the process, particularly if the obligatory claims of malice or bad faith are made in the complaint. It is essential, therefore, that health care institutions agree to defend and to indemnify for litigation costs participants in the peer review process.

such information knew, or had reason to believe, that such information was false" and for review organizations, their members, agents, and employees who assist the committee "in the absence of malice and gross negligence.") The Arizona statute offers immunity for quality assurance actions taken without malice, and then defines malice as "evil intent and outrageous, oppressive, or intolerable conduct that creates a substantial risk of tremendous harm to others." Ariz.Rev.Stat. §§ 36–2401(3)–2402(B). See Smith v. Farha, 974 P.2d 563 (Ka. 1999) (allowing defamation suit alleging malice to proceed despite peer review protection claim).

10. N.J.Stat.Ann. § 2A:84A–22.10(e)(2): Pa.Consolidated Stat.Ann. title 63 § 425.4.

11. La.Stat.Ann.—Rev.Stat. 13:3715.3.

12. See e.g., Jenkins v. Wu, 82 Ill.Dec. 382, 468 N.E.2d 1162 (Ill.1984).

13. Seglin v. Old Orchard Hosp., 139 Ill. Dec. 241, 548 N.E.2d 626 (Ill.App.1989); Levy v. McKiel, 133 Ill.Dec. 405, 541 N.E.2d 242 (Ill.App.1989); Rodriguez–Erdman v. Ravenswood Hosp. Medical Center, 114 Ill.Dec. 576, 516 N.E.2d 731 (Ill.App.1987).

14. Cardwell v. Rockford Memorial Hosp. Ass'n, 144 Ill.Dec. 109, 555 N.E.2d 6 (Ill.1990), cert. denied 498 U.S. 998, 111 S.Ct. 556, 112

L.Ed.2d 563 (1990); Carson v. Northwest Community Hosp., 139 Ill.Dec. 194, 548 N.E.2d 579 (Ill.App.1989); Rodriguez–Erdman v. Ravenswood Medical Ctr., 114 Ill.Dec. 576, 516 N.E.2d 731 (Ill.App.1987).

15. Soentgen v. Quain & Ramstad Clinic, P.C., 467 N.W.2d 73, 79 (N.D.1991); McKeel v. Armstrong, 386 S.E.2d 60 (N.C.App.1989).

16. Gilbert v. Board of Medical Examiners, 745 P.2d 617 (Ariz.App.1987); Adkins v. Sarah Bush Lincoln Health Ctr., 110 Ill.Dec. 947, 511 N.E.2d 1267 (Ill.App.1987); Veldhuis v. Allan, 416 N.W.2d 347 (Mich.App.1987); Jacobs v. Frank, 573 N.E.2d 609 (Ohio 1991); Meistrell v. McPhail, 788 P.2d 1387 (Okla.App. 1989).

17. See e.g., Gannon v. Santa Ana–Tustin Community Hosp., 257 Cal.Rptr. 110 (Cal.App. 1989).

18. Soentgen v. Quain & Ramstad Clinic, P.C., 467 N.W.2d 73 (N.D.1991).

19. West's Fla.Stat.Ann. § 395.0115(8)(a); Haw. Rev. Stat. § 671D–12 (if "claim, or the claimant's conduct during the litigation of the claim, was frivolous, unreasonable, without foundation, or in bad faith").

Some health care institutions have gone further, attempting through their medical staff by-laws to get physicians seeking staff privileges to agree not to sue should privileges be denied or subsequently withdrawn, but the enforceability of such releases is questionable.[20] Courts may be more amenable to enforcing a by-law requiring a physician who loses an unfounded suit challenging the peer review process to pay the defendant's costs and attorney's fees.

Participants in the peer review process are also protected from liability by the Health Care Quality Improvement Act. Because this statute was adopted primarily to address antitrust liability, it is discussed below in chapter 14.

G. MEDICAL INFORMATION AND RECORDS: CONFIDENTIALITY AND DISCLOSURE

§ 4–29. Introduction

Every time a person consults a medical professional, is admitted to a health care institution, or receives a medical test, a medical record is created or an entry is made in an existing record. Billions of such records exist in the United States, most of which will be retained from 10 to 25 years. These records contain very personal information—revelations to psychotherapists or documentation of treatment for alcoholism, venereal disease, or AIDS, for example—the disclosure of which could prove devastating to the patient.[1] Yet most records are available to many users for legitimate—and also often questionable—purposes. One commentator estimated that an average of 75 persons have access to any patient record.[2] With the growth of electronic databases, third party utilization review, managed care organizations, and government oversight, review of patient records has continued to expand.[3] As a result, the tension between the need for confidentiality of patient records and multiple claims to access is no longer easily resolved by professional ethics and institutional management practices, but is increasingly being litigated. Yet patient information in medical records has less legal protection than credit histories or other private information.[4] With the rapid expansion of large managed care organizations and networks, the dissemination of patient information has increased rapidly.[5] The protection of patient confiden-

---

20. Compare Westlake Community Hosp. v. Superior Court, 131 Cal.Rptr. 90, 551 P.2d 410 (Cal.1976) (Holding by-law waiving right to suit void) with De Leon v. St. Joseph Hosp., Inc., 871 F.2d 1229 (4th Cir.1989), cert. denied 493 U.S. 825, 110 S.Ct. 87, 107 L.Ed.2d 52 (1989) (enforcing such a provision absent willful, wanton, or gross misconduct).

§ 4–29

1. Institute of Medicine, Health Data in the Information Age: Use, Disclosure, and Privacy (1994); Office of Technology Assessment, U.S. Congress, Protecting Privacy in Computerized Medical Information (1993) (www.wws.princeton.edu/ōta/ns20/alpha_f.html.

2. American College of Hospital Administrators, Medical Confidentiality, Can it be Protected? 2–3 (1983).

3. Courts allow insurers access to hospital records for purpose of review. See e.g., Pyramid Life Ins. Co. v. Masonic Hosp. Ass'n of Payne County, Oklahoma, 191 F.Supp. 51 (W.D.Okl.1961) (access to patient-insured records allowed).

4. See Janlori Goldman, Institute for Health Care Research and Policy, Georgetown University, The State of Health Privacy: An Uneven Terrain (www.healthprivacy.org/resources.)

5. National Committee for Quality Assurance and the Joint Commission on Accreditation of Healthcare Organizations, Protecting Personal Health Information: A Framework for Meeting the Challenges in a Managed Care Environment (1998) (www.ncqa.org/confide/tablcont.htm).

tiality has become an important goal for regulators concerned about the potential abuses of electronic information.[6]

§ 4–30. Standards for Medical Record Keeping

Hospitals and other providers keep patient medical records to document the treatment given a patient, the plan of future treatment, and communication between the patient's physician and other providers treating that patient. The record is a data base containing factual information about a patient's health status and recording medical opinions based on that information. It is an essential part of a patient's continued treatment.[1] It also documents a patient's consent to medical treatment.[2] An institutional failure to keep proper records may be malpractice, if treating physicians lack essential information and as a result incorrectly treat a patient.[3]

Patient medical records are mandated by a variety of agencies and organizations that accredit, certify, or otherwise regulate hospitals.[4] The Joint Commission on Accreditation of Healthcare Organizations, whose voluntary certifications have become a benchmark for hospital quality, requires the maintenance of adequate medical records.[5] The JCAHO requires that a record be documented accurately, adequately, and in a timely manner, with information readily available and accessible for prompt retrieval, but stored and maintained in a confidential and secure manner. The Medicare program also requires hospitals to be certified as Medicare providers.[6] One "condition of participation" for certification of non-accredited hospitals involves medical record requirements.[7] State licensing agencies typically also require that hospitals maintain medical records for patients to better evaluate the care provided.[8]

Most medical records contain the same categories of information, including patient identification data, a medical history, reports of tests or procedures, informed consent documents, diagnostic and therapeutic orders, and clinical observations by physicians and nurses. Financial information will also typically be included—including information regarding patients' employers, insurance companies, and other responsible parties.[9]

6. See generally Bernard Lo, Confidentiality of Patient Information in a Changing Health Care System, in Protecting the Confidentiality of Patient Information in a Rapidly Changing Health Care System: Summary of a National Conference, Appendix F(1998).

§ 4–30

1. See e.g., Schwarz v. Board of Regents, 453 N.Y.S.2d 836 (N.Y.App.Div.1982) (physician sanctioned for failure to keep accurate patient records, leading to their unavailability to physicians for later treatments).

2. See e.g., Brown v. Sims, 538 So.2d 901 (Fla.App.1989), corrected 538 So.2d 901, 14 Fla. L.Weekly 1047 (Fla.App.3d Dist. 1989), review pending 547 So.2d 635 (Fla.1989), quashed in part 574 So.2d 131 (Fla.1991), vacated in part 579 So.2d 276 (Fla.App.3d Dist. 1991) (stressing the importance of a complete medical record prior to surgery).

3. See e.g., Thomas v. United States, 660 F.Supp. 216 (D.D.C.1987).

4. See Adele A. Waller, et al., Medical Records: Current Issues and Emerging Trends in 1992 Health Law Handbook, 271 et seq. (Alice G. Gosfield, Ed. 1992).

5. See Joint Comm'n on Accreditation of Healthcare Orgs., Accreditation Manual for Hospitals [hereinafter JCAHO Manual].

6. See 42 C.F.R. Pt. 482.

7. See 42 C.F.R. §§ 482.24, 482.61.

8. See e.g., West's Ann.Cal. Health & Safety Code § 1457; McKinney's—N.Y. Pub. Health Law § 4165.

9. The JCAHO requires these elements in the record, see JCAHO Manual at 81–86. Medicare requires these general elements, plus a patient's past history, family history, progress notes, discharge summary. 42 C.F.R. § 482.24

§ 4-31.   Patient Access to Medical Records

Medical records have traditionally been viewed by courts as the property of the institution or practitioner that creates and maintains them.[1] Some courts have recognized a limited property right of the patient in the information in the records.[2] A patient has a right to review his or her own records, or obtain a copy, in some jurisdictions, as a right of access or privacy.[3] However, a provider may still deny a patient access to medical records in a number of jurisdictions, particularly as to psychiatric patients.[4] A person undergoing a medical or psychological examination for employment purposes is arguably not a "patient" within the meaning of state record access statutes, nor is the person in a doctor-patient relationship. Courts have defined "patient" broadly for purposes of obtaining access to medical records, noting that such record statutes are intended to promote, not restrict, patient access.[5]

a.   Sources of a Right of Access

A patient's right of access to his or her medical record has gained ground over the past decade.[6] Half of the states have now enacted statutes permitting patients access to their medical records, whereas in 1978 only seven states had such legislation.[7] The American Hospital Association (AHA) and the American Medical Association (AMA) have also articulated policies in favor of patient's right of access to medical records.[8] Such policies may often be relied upon by courts in developing a common law right of access. While patients have gained ground in terms of access to their medical records, state statutes are subject to a variety of exceptions that limit patient access.[9] Some statutes, for example, only provide access subsequent to discharge[10]; others permit the institution to provide only a summary of the records[11]; and others require the

(1990). States vary in the degree of detail they specify for medical records, with some listing requirements in detail, Haw. Rev.Stat. § 622-58, and others simply describing broad areas, West's Fla. Stat. Ann. §§ 395.016.

§ 4.31

1. See generally, Tom Christoffel, Health and the Law: A Handbook for Health Professionals 331 (1985); McGarry v. J.A. Mercier Co., 262 N.W. 296 (Mich.1935). Specific rules on ownership are also articulated in state statues, e.g., Tenn. Code Ann. § 68-11-304.

2. See e.g., Bishop Clarkson Mem. Hosp. v. Reserve Life Ins. Co., 350 F.2d 1006 (8th Cir. 1965); Pyramid Life Ins. Co. v. Masonic Hospital Ass'n, 191 F.Supp. 51 (D.Okl.1961).

3. Pierce v. Penman, 515 A.2d 948 (Pa.Super.1986); People v. Bickham, 414 N.E.2d 37 (Ill.App.1980); Application of Striegel, 399 N.Y.S.2d 584 (N.Y.Sup.1977).

4. See e.g., Cynthia B. v. New Rochelle Hosp. Medical Ctr., 470 N.Y.S.2d 122, 458 N.E.2d 363 (N.Y.App.1983).

5. Cleghorn v. Hess, 853 P.2d 1260 (Nev. 1993).

6. Wheeler v. Commissioner of Social Services of the City of New York, 662 N.Y.S.2d 550 (N.Y.App.Div.1997) (plaintiff has presump-

tive right to records for purposes of litigation); Mantica v. N.Y.State Dept. of Health, 679 N.Y.S.2d 469 (N.Y.App.Div.1998) (government medical records presumptively subject to disclosure, and statutory privilege of confidentiality of such records belongs exclusively to patient and patient may not be denied access to his or her own health care information based on that privilege.)

7. For a useful survey of the state statutes see Health Privacy Project, The State of Health Privacy: An Uneven Terrain, Institute for Health Care Research and Policy, Georgetown University (July 1999) http://www.healthprivacy.org).

8. See American Hosp. Ass'n, A Patient's Bill of Rights (1973); American Medical Ass'n, Current Opinions of the Judicial Council of the American Medical Association § 7.02 (1984).

9. Cornelio v. Stamford Hospital, 717 A.2d 140 (Conn.1998) (patients' right of access to their health records is limited to those specified by statute.)

10. West's Colo.Rev.Stat.Ann. §§ 25-1-801 & 802; Conn.Gen.Stat.Ann. § 4-104; Me.Rev. Stat.Ann. tit. 22, § 1711.

11. West's Ann.Cal. Health & Safety Code § 25256; Or. Rev. Stat. § 192.525; Minn. Stat. Ann. § 144.335.

patient to show good cause for access.[12] Absent statutory authority, a number of courts have permitted patients access to records under a property theory[13] or a fiduciary theory.[14] Some courts, however, continue to deny patients access to their records.[15]

Many doctors argue that patients should not have access to their records, or should have access only under tight controls. They contend that patients cannot understand the information found in the records, may become anxious and upset by what they find, and may rely on medical information to engage in harmful self-treatment.[16] They argue that patient access to medical information may violate confidences of third parties and discourage physician frankness in recording, and will impose administrative costs on institutions. Patient advocates argue in response that greater access will improve patient understanding of and compliance with treatment, physician-patient relations, and continuity of care. Patient advocates further contend that patients cannot give informed authorization for disclosure of records to others if they do not know the contents of their own records, and thus access is important. The prevailing view is that patients are helped rather than harmed by disclosure. The model of a collaborative physician-patient relationship[17], and the recognition of the role that patient knowledge often plays in treatment, has strengthened the arguments of advocates for enhanced patient access to records.[18]

b. *Retention of Records*

Medical records must be retained for lengthy periods of time, pursuant to state and federal law, typically from seven to ten years. The Medicare program, for example, requires that hospital keep their records for at least five years.[19] State laws generally mandate lengthy periods of retention,[20] with specific provision for certain records such as x-rays.[21] Given the long tail in malpractice cases, with injury sometimes not materializing until years after treatment, and the importance of records for purposes of accreditation, Medicare review and other oversight purposes, lengthy storage is prudent for most providers even without specific statutory mandates.

c. *Discovery of Records*

A patient's medical condition and treatment may be an issue in a variety of civil lawsuits. Records from several providers may be needed to get a complete understanding of the issues involving patient treatment. In such a situation, a defendant can always simply request the records from the plain-

---

12. Miss. Code § 41–9–65.

13. Wallace v. University Hosp. of Cleveland, 164 N.E.2d 917 (Ohio Com.Pl.1959), modified, 170 N.E.2d 261 (Ohio App.1960), appeal dismissed, 172 N.E.2d 459 (Ohio 1961).

14. Hutchins v. Texas Rehabilitation Comm'n, 544 S.W.2d 802 (Tex.Civ.App.1976); Emmett v. Eastern Dispensary and Casualty Hosp., 396 F.2d 931 (D.C.Cir.1967).

15. Gotkin v. Miller, 379 F.Supp. 859 (E.D.N.Y.1974), affirmed 514 F.2d 125 (2d Cir. 1975).

16. Cynthia B. v. New Rochelle Hospital Medical Center, 470 N.Y.S.2d 122, 458 N.E.2d 363 (N.Y.App.1983).

17. See generally, Chapter 6, infra for discussions of informed consent.

18. See, Privacy Protection Study Commission, Personal Privacy in an Information Society, 285, 297 (1977) [hereinafter Personal Privacy]; Loren Roth, et al., Patient Access to Records: Tonic or Toxin? 137 Am.J.Psychiatry 592 (1980).

19. 42 C.F.R. § 482.24(b)(1)(1990).

20. See e.g., N.M. Stat. Ann. § 14–6–2A (10 years from last discharge); Tenn. Code Ann. § 68–11–305(a) (10 years).

21. See e.g., N.M. Stat. Ann. § 14–6–2c (4 years after exposure).

tiff.[22] If information is not disclosed informally, formal discovery devices may be used, including request for production of documents,[23] or a request for a medical authorization by the plaintiff to release medical records. Third party discovery tools, including subpoenas, are also available to obtain medical records. Such subpoenas require the appearance of a record custodian, typically instructing her to bring documents listed in the subpoena.

d. Medical Records at Trial

Medical records will at times pose unique evidentiary issues of admissibility during a trial. As documents subject to the governing rules of evidence in state or federal courts, they may contain privileged information,[24] may be protected by the attorney work-product rule[25], or have been prepared in anticipation of litigation. They may be objected to as hearsay, as containing out of court statements being offered for the truth of the matter asserted,[26] although the business records exception to the hearsay rule is likely to cover most uses of the medical records.[27] Other hearsay exceptions—statements made for medical diagnosis and treatment,[28] declarations against interest,[29] spontaneous utterances—open the door to much of the contents of a medical record.

Medical records may be more likely than other documentary material to require *in camera* inspection by the trial judge, to minimize the risk of inadvertent disclosure of damaging confidential medical information. Criminal cases involving sexual offenses, for example, often require special judicial protections to avoid disclosure of confidential medical information.[30]

e. Alteration or Spoliation of Records

Medical records play a pivotal role in insurance claims, civil litigation involving medical testimony, and medical malpractice cases. By the time an action comes to trial, memories may have dimmed as to what actually occurred at the time of patient injury, leaving the medical record as the most telling evidence. The ability of a provider to retrieve a medical record is therefore vital. If a record is lost or misplaced, whether innocently or

---

22. Under the Federal Rules of Civil Procedure, in fact, Rule 26 requires that a party, without a formal discovery request, shall provide to other parties

(B) a copy of, or a description by category and location of, all documents, data compilations, and tangible things in the possession, custody, or control of the party that are relevant to disputed facts alleged with particularity in the pleadings.

This duty to disclose needed information, without formal discovery, was intended by drafters and the Supreme Court to speed the exchange of basic information, including medical records. See Michael J. Wagner, Too Much, Too Costly, Too Soon? The Automatic Disclosure Amendments to Federal Rule of Civil Procedure 26, 29 Tort & Ins.L.J. 468 (1994).

23. Fed.R.Civ.P. 34.

24. In Jaffee v. Redmond, 518 U.S. 1(1996), the Supreme Court ruled that conversations and notes between a patient and therapist are confidential and that the traditional doctor/patient privilege required that they be protected from compelled disclosure.

25. See Sierra Vista Hosp. v. Superior Court, 56 Cal.Rptr. 387 (Cal.App.1967); Verini v. Bochetto, 372 N.Y.S.2d 690 (N.Y.App.Div. 1975).

26. See generally, McCormick on Evidence, §§ 246, 313 (E. Cleary 3d ed. 1984).

27. The Business Records exception, for example, Fed.R.Evid. 803(6), and its state counterparts, allows admissibility of records made in the regular course of business, following a regular practice, by a properly authorized employee.

28. Fed.R.Evid. 803(4).

29. Fed.R.Evid. 803, 804.

30. Commonwealth v. Bishop, 617 N.E.2d 990 (Mass.1993).

otherwise, a hospital might be liable in a separate action to a patient whose claim against a third party hinged on evidence in that record.[31]

Because either documentation of inadequate care or inadequate documentation of care may result in liability, physicians are sometimes tempted to destroy records or to alter them to reflect the care they wish in retrospect they had rendered. There is nothing wrong with correcting records, so long as corrections are made in such a way as to leave the previous entry clearly readable and the new entry clearly identified as a corrected entry. Premature disposition of records can also result in negligence liability in some states.[32] While a separate action for the negligent maintenance of records is not permitted in most states, failure to maintain or store records may be medical malpractice.[33] In some jurisdictions, absence of essential medical records in a malpractice case creates a rebuttable presumption that the defendant was negligence and that this caused the plaintiff's injuries, absent excuse.[34] Conscious concealment, fabrication, or falsification of records may result in some states in either an inference of awareness of guilt,[35] which the jury will be charged to consider; imposition of punitive damages; or the tolling of the statute of limitations. Such alteration of records is also sufficient justification for a malpractice insurer to drop a physician from coverage.[36] Some states have also recognized a tort of intentional spoliation, imposing liability for the tortious act of despoiling records.[37]

A physician or nurse who fails to properly maintain patient records is subject to sanctions, including loss of license[38] and revocation of right to participate in federal programs such as Medicare or Medicaid.[39]

§ 4–32. Provider Duties to Maintain Confidentiality

a. Sources of Duties

The original source of a physician's duty to maintain the confidentiality of patient information is the Hippocratic Oath, which provides in part:

> Whatever, in connection with my professional practice, or not in connection with it, I see or hear in the life of men, which ought not to be spoken abroad, I will not divulge, as reckoning that all such should be kept secret.

31. See Fox v. Cohen, 40 Ill.Dec. 477, 406 N.E.2d 178 (Ill.App.1980); Bondu v. Gurvich, 473 So.2d 1307 (Fla.App.1984).

32. Fox v. Cohen, 40 Ill.Dec. 477, 406 N.E.2d 178 (Ill.App.1980).

33. Brown v. Hamid, M.D., 856 S.W.2d 51, 57 (Mo.1993).

34. Sweet v. Providence in Washington, 895 P.2d 484(Alaska 1995).

35. This evidentiary inference is traceable back to Pomeroy v. Benton, 77 Mo. 64 (1882) (inference, omnia praesumuntur contra spoliatorem: "all things are presumed against a wrongdoer"); Pisel v. Stamford Hosp., 430 A.2d 1, 15 (Conn.1980); Moore v. General Motors, 558 S.W.2d 720 (Mo.App.1977); Thor v. Boska, 113 Cal.Rptr. 296 (Cal.App.1974).

36. See e.g., Mirkin v. Medical Mutual Liability Ins. Soc'y of Maryland, 572 A.2d 1126 (Md. Spec. App. 1990).

37. Smith v. Superior Court for County of Los Angeles, 198 Cal.Rptr. 829 (Cal.App.1984) (first case to recognize the tort explicitly); rejecting spoliation as a cause of action, Trevino v. Ortega, 969 S.W.2d 950 (Tex.1998). See generally, Thomas G. Fischer, Annotation, Intentional Spoliation of Evidence, Interfering with Prospective Civil Action, As Actionable, 70 A.L.R.4th 984 (1989).

38. See e.g., Weber v. Colorado State Board of Nursing, 830 P.2d 1128 (Colo.App.1992) cert. denied (Dec. 1, 1992).

39. See e.g., Koh v. Perales, 570 N.Y.S.2d 98 (N.Y.App.Div.1991), appeal denied 575 N.Y.S.2d 455, 580 N.E.2d 1058 (N.Y.App.1991).

At the heart of this duty is the notion that patients will be candid in discussing their problems with a physician if they have an expectation of confidentiality. The American Medical Association's Principles of Medical Ethics elaborate on this duty:

> Confidentiality. The information disclosed to a physician during the course of the relationship between physician and patient is confidential to the greatest possible degree. The patient should feel free to make a full disclosure of information to the physician in order that the physician may most effectively provide needed services. The patient should be able to make this disclosure with the knowledge that the physician will respect the confidential nature of the communication. The physician should not reveal confidential communications or information without the express consent of the patient, unless required to do so by law.[1]

Courts have referred to both the Hippocratic oath and the AMA Principles as sources for a common law duty of confidentiality. One court even described the physician's duty as an express warranty of confidentiality, based on the ethical standards of the profession.[2]

b. Statutory Immunities

Several federal and state statutes protect the confidentiality of medical information. Most notable among these are amendments to the Drug Abuse and Treatment Acts and Comprehensive Alcohol Abuse and Alcoholism Prevention, Treatment, and Rehabilitation Act[3] (and their implementing regulations[4]), which impose rigorous requirements on the disclosure of information from alcohol and drug abuse treatment programs. The Federal Privacy Act of 1994 prohibits federal agencies, including federal hospitals, from disclosing information in a system of records without the consent of the person "to whom the record pertains."[5] Some state statutes also provide civil penalties for disclosure of confidential information in medical records generally,[6] or disclosure of particular kinds of information involving categories of patients, such as HIV-infected patients,[7] or alcohol and substance abuse patients.[8]

The Health Insurance Portability and Accountability Act of 1996 was enacted to establish a uniform standard for the transmission of health information data between payers and providers.[9] The proposed Medical Privacy standards, in the absence of timely legislation by Congress, aims to protect electronic health information, but not solely paper based records.[10]

c. Privileges

The confidentiality of medical information is protected by a variety of legal devices. Almost every state has either a physician-patient or psychother-

§ 4–32

1. American Medical Ass'n, Current Opinions of the Judicial Council of the American Medical Association (1984).

2. See Hammonds v. Aetna Casualty & Surety Co., 243 F.Supp. 793 (N.D.Ohio 1965).

3. 42 U.S.C.A. §§ 290dd–3, 390ee–3.

4. 42 C.F.R. Part 2 (1985).

5. 5 U.S.C.A. § 552a(b).

6. See 740 ILCS 110/15; West's Fla. Stat. Ann. § 395.018; Haw. Rev. Stat. § 324–34.

7. West's Ann.Cal. Health & Safety Code § 199.21(d).

8. 20 ILCS 305/8–102.

9. Pub.L.No. 104–191, 110 Stat 1936 (1996).

10. See Department of Health and Human Services, Proposed Rules, Standards for Privacy of Individually Identifiable Health Information, 45 CFR 160–165 (1999) (hereafter Privacy Standards).

apist privilege,[11] an evidentiary device that prohibits either the discovery of medical records or their admissibility at trial.[12] The privilege is a right, held by the patient, to withhold information disclosed to a physician with an expectation of confidentiality. The information disclosed must be needed for treatment, and extraneous information is not privileged from discovery.[13] A health care provider will typically assert the privilege to protect itself from future liability for disclosing confidential information, subject to the patient's voluntary waiver of the privilege later.[14]

The U.S. Supreme Court recognized the psychotherapist-patient privilege in Jaffee v. Redmond, holding that a statement that the defendant police officer made to a licensed social worker in course of psychotherapy, and notes taken by the therapist, were protected from compelled disclosure. The Court stated that: "[e]ffective psychotherapy depends on an atmosphere of confidence and trust, and therefore the mere possibility of disclosure of confidential communications may impede the development of the relationship necessary for successful treatment. The privilege also serves the public interest, since the mental health of the Nation's citizenry, no less than its physical health, is a public good of transcendent importance."

The physician-patient privilege plays only a limited role in protecting confidential patient information. First, it is only a testimonial privilege, not a general obligation to maintain confidentiality: although it may permit a doctor to refuse to disclose medical information in court, it does not require the doctor to keep information from employers, insurers, or other physicians.[15] Second, it is a statutory privilege, or one created through judicial rulemaking, and does not exist in all jurisdictions. According to the Privacy Protection Study Commission, forty-three states have some form of testimonial privilege, yet some of these are only applicable to psychiatrists. Absent such a statute, courts are unwilling to find a privilege, since it did not exist at the common law. Third, as a privilege created by state statute, it does not apply in non-diversity federal court proceedings.[16] Fourth, the privilege is subject to many exceptions in most states. In California, it is subject to twelve exceptions, including cases where the patient is a litigant, criminal proceedings, will contests, and physician licensure proceedings. State privilege statutes often cover only physicians, who today deliver only about 5 percent of health care, and not nurses or other providers.[17] Finally, the privilege applies only to confidential disclosures made to a physician in the course of treatment and is easily waived by the patient. Implied waivers are readily found by the courts, for example, where the patient puts his or her physical or mental health at issue in a lawsuit,[18] or fails to object to admission of testimony.[19]

11. 518 U.S. 1 (1996) (strong dissent in part objecting to over-broad grant of privilege to include social workers).

12. See e.g., Vernon's Ann. Mo. Stat. § 491.060(5).

13. See e.g., People v. Capra, 269 N.Y.S.2d 451, 216 N.E.2d 610 (N.Y.App.1966) (privilege did not protect the discovery of drugs on the defendant by physician during examination).

14. See e.g., Greene v. New England Mut. Life Ins. Co., 437 N.Y.S.2d 844 (N.Y.Sup.1981).

15. Brandt v. Medical Defense Assocs., 856 S.W.2d 667 (Mo.1993) (ex parte communica-

tions with plaintiff's treating physician's is outside the scope of the statutory physician-patient privilege).

16. Personal Privacy, supra § 4–31 note 16, at 284.

17. See e.g., Belichick v. Belichick, 307 N.E.2d 270 (Ohio App.1973).

18. See e.g., Hoenig v. Westphal, 439 N.Y.S.2d 831, 422 N.E.2d 491 (N.Y.App.1981).

19. See, Cope v. Cope, 40 Cal.Rptr. 917 (Cal.App.1964).

§ 4–33. Liability for Breaches of Confidentiality

a. Invasion of Privacy

State courts have imposed a duty of confidentiality upon providers, as either expressed or implied in state licensure or privilege statutes.[1] Several common law theories have also been advanced to impose liability on professionals who disclose medical information. Four major theories have been used: invasion of privacy; breach of a fiduciary duty to maintain confidentiality; violation of statutes defining physician conduct; and breach of implied contract.[2]

The tort of invasion of privacy is limited to actions that would be highly offensive to the ordinary person.[3] It is generally held to include four distinct claims: appropriation of the plaintiff's name or likeness; unreasonable and offensive intrusion upon the seclusion of another[4]; public disclosure of private facts; and publicity which places the plaintiff in a false light in the public eye.[5] Public disclosure of private facts is the subclaim of the tort of invasion of privacy that most clearly fits the medical record release situation,[6] although some cases have involved unauthorized use of patient photographs for medical instruction, or by newspaper.

Such a right to privacy of medical information, based upon a common law right of privacy, is subject to privileges based upon patient consent, judicial compulsion,[7] and other legal mandates including a duty to warn third parties of danger.[8]

b. Implied Statutory Actions

Many states have enacted statutory provisions specifically addressing the confidentiality of HIV or AIDS status. In such cases, a cause of action may be implied from the breach by a defendant of the statute. A release of information as to a patient's HIV status, for example, to an employer or insurer, in violation of a statute, may trigger liability.[9] Even information released pursuant to a subpoena may breach confidentiality if the subpoena is not precise in enumerating what is sought, particularly in the case of HIV or AIDS status.[10]

---

§ 4–33

1. See McCormick v. England, 494 S.E.2d 431 (S.C.App.1997); Berry v. Moench, 331 P.2d 814 (Utah 1958); Felis v. Greenberg, 273 N.Y.S.2d 288 (N.Y.Sup.1966). For a good general discussion, see Lawrence O. Gostin, 80 Corn.L.Rev. 451 (1995).

2. See Lonette E. Lamb, Note, To Tell or Not to Tell: Physician's Liability for Disclosure of Confidential Information About a Patient, 13 Cumb.L.Rev. 617 (1983).

3. The tort owes its origins to an article by Samuel Warren and Louis Brandeis, The Right of Privacy, 4 Harv.L.Rev. 193 (1890), and was later developed by William Prosser into a four-fold tort, as restated in Restatement (Second) of Torts § 652A (1977).

4. Ted LeBlang, Invasion of Privacy: Medical Practice and the Tort of Intrusion, 18 Washburn L.J. 205 (1979).

5. W. Page Keeton, Prosser and Keeton on the Law of Torts § 117 at 851–66 (5th ed. 1984). The Restatement (Second) Torts §§ 652A to 652E, adopts the same categories.

6. See e.g., Berthiaume's Estate v. Pratt, 365 A.2d 792 (Me.1976) (unauthorized use of photograph of dying patient for documentation in medical record, held to be intrusion into seclusion).

7. See United States v. Westinghouse, 638 F.2d 570 (3d Cir.1980).

8. See § 4–34 infra.

9. Doe v. Roe, 599 N.Y.S.2d 350 (N.Y.App. Div.1993).

10. In Arnett v. Baskous, 856 P.2d 790 (Alaska 1993), the plaintiff sued his physician for releasing his medical records to the district attorney, pursuant to a subpoena, one day earlier than the subpoena directed. The court rejected the claim, since the deviation from the order was minor.

c. *Other Theories*

A provider's disclosure of confidential information obtained in a confidential relationship may give rise to a tort action.[11] The courts speak of a public policy that demands that "doctors obey their implied promise of secrecy."[12] Courts have implied such a duty from the patient's statutory privilege to exclude the doctor's testimony in litigation,[13] from the obligations of the medical license in the state granting that license,[14] and from specific statutory exceptions for certain disclosures, such as gunshot wounds. The Ohio Supreme Court has upheld such a duty, recognizing the tort of breach of confidentiality.[15] The plaintiff must show "unconsented, unprivileged disclosure to a third party of nonpublic information that the defendant has learned within a confidential relationship." Id. at 1455.

A state may also by statute specifically prohibit disclosure of patient confidences, subject on to certain exceptions.[16] Some statutes allow damages for a breach of the statute. Thus in *Renzi v. Morrison*,[17] the court held that a therapist who voluntarily disclosed a psychiatric patient's confidential communication, while a witness for the patient's spouse in divorce proceedings, could be liable under Illinois law. If medical information is disclosed as a result of a patient have placed his medical condition at issue in litigation, he has waived confidentiality.[18]

A breach of contract action[19] requires a specific agreement to protect confidential information, and damages may be difficult to assess.[20] However, some courts have been willing to imply a contract to maintain confidentiality.[21] Where an accurate disclosure of information is made in good faith for a

11. Eckhardt v. Charter Hospital of Albuquerque, Inc., 953 P.2d (C.A.N.M. 1997) (therapist disclosed confidential information to patient's husband); Crippen v. Charter Southland Hospital, Inc., 534 So.2d 286 (Ala.1988); Horne v. Patton, 287 So.2d 824 (Ala.1973) (doctor under a duty not to make extra-judicial disclosures of the doctor-patient relationship); MacDonald v. Clinger, 446 N.Y.S.2d 801 (N.Y.App. Div.1982); see Alan B. Vickery, Note, Breach of Confidence: An Emerging Tort, 82 Colum.L.Rev. 1426 (1982).

12. Hammonds v. Aetna Cas. & Sur. Co., 243 F.Supp. 793, 796 (D.Ohio 1965).

13. See e.g., Berry v. Moench, 331 P.2d 814 (Utah 1958); Hammonds v. Aetna Cas. & Sur. Co., 243 F.Supp. 793 (D.Ohio 1965).

14. See e.g., In re Conduct of Lasswell, 673 P.2d 855 (Or.1983); Simonsen v. Swenson, 177 N.W. 831 (Neb.1920) ("This information the physician is bound, not only upon his own professional honor and the ethics of his high profession, to keep secret, but by reason of the affirmative mandate of the statute itself.").

Professional regulations were similarly cited in Hammonds v. Aetna Cas. & Sur. Co., 243 F.Supp. 793 (D.Ohio 1965), in Doe v. Roe, 400 N.Y.S.2d 668 (N.Y.Sup.1977), and in Clark v. Geraci, 208 N.Y.S.2d 564 (N.Y.Sup.1960).

15. Biddle v. Warren General Hospital, 715 N.E.2d 518 (Ohio 1999).

16. See Or. Rev. Stat. § 677.190(5) disqualifying or otherwise disciplining a physician for "wilfully or negligently divulging a professional secret."

17. 188 Ill.Dec. 224, 618 N.E.2d 794 (Ill. App.1993).

18. Aufrichtig v. Lowell, 609 N.Y.S.2d 214 (N.Y.App.Div.1994).

19. In Doe v. Roe, 400 N.Y.S.2d 668 (N.Y.Sup.1977), the court upheld an action for breach of an express oral contract by the physician to maintain confidentiality of the plaintiff's HIV-positive status; "a cause of action may be asserted for breach of an express promise to preserve the confidentiality of a patient's medical condition"; Noel v. Proud, 367 P.2d 61 (Kan.1961); Hammonds v. Aetna Cas. & Sur. Co., 237 F.Supp. 96 (D.Ohio 1965) and Hammonds v. Aetna Cas. & Sur. Co., 243 F.Supp. 793 (D.Ohio 1965); Doe v. Roe, 400 N.Y.S.2d 668 (N.Y.Sup.1977).

20. Implied contract claims were allowed in Horne v. Patton, 287 So.2d 824 (Ala.1973), in Hammonds v. Aetna Cas. & Sur. Co., 243 F.Supp. 793 (D.Ohio 1965), and in Doe v. Roe, 400 N.Y.S.2d 668 (N.Y.Sup.1977) (psychiatrist).

21. See Horne v. Patton, 287 So.2d 824, 832 (Ala.1973).

legitimate purpose, courts are generally reluctant to impose liability.[22] However, where a legislature has enacted a complex statutory scheme protecting confidential information, particularly on HIV or AIDS status, the courts have been more willing to allow claims.

Other claims have included medical malpractice[23] and defamation.[24]

§ 4–34. Provider Duties to Disclose Patient Information to Third Parties

Access to medical records is sought by third parties for a variety of reasons—by treating providers providing follow-up care, by insurance companies with obligations to bill, by law enforcement authorities.[1] Law enforcement agencies for example often seek access to medical information. A moderate-size Chicago hospital reported that the FBI requested information about patients as often as twice a month. Attorneys seek medical records to establish disability, personal injury, or medical malpractice claims for their clients. Though they most commonly will ask for records of their own clients, they may also want to review records of other patients to establish a pattern of knowing medical abuse by a physician or the culpability of a hospital for failing to supervise a negligent practitioner. Life, health, disability and liability insurers often seek medical information, as do employers and credit investigators. Disclosure of information from medical records may occur without a formal request. Though secondary users of medical information commonly receive information pursuant to patient record releases, they have been known to seek and compile information surreptitiously.[2] Another study found that 51% of doctors and 70% of medical students discuss confidential information at parties. These secondary disclosures of medical information are of great importance to patients, since disclosure can result in loss of employment, denial of insurance or credit, or, at a minimum, severe embarrassment.

The volume of requests for medical information is impressive. The director of the medical record department of a 600 bed university hospital testified to the Privacy Protection Study Commission that his hospital received 2,700 information requests a month: 34% from third-party payers; 37% from other physicians; 8% in the form of subpoenas; and 21% from other hospitals, attorneys, and miscellaneous sources. An attorney for the Mayo Clinic testified to the same Commission that the clinic receives 300,000 requests a year, 88% related to reimbursement.[3]

22. See Klipa v. Board of Educ., 460 A.2d 601 (Md.Spec.App.1983).

23. Clark v. Geraci, 208 N.Y.S.2d 564 (N.Y.Sup.1960) (rejecting argument).

24. Gilson v. Knickerbocker Hosp., 116 N.Y.S.2d 745 (N.Y.App.Div.1952) (rejecting argument).

§ 4.34

1. See generally, Lawrence Gostin, Health Information Privacy, 80 Cornell L. Rev. 451 (1995); Institute of Medicine, Committee on Regional Health Data Networks, Health Data in the Information Age (1994) (www.nap.edu/readinroom/).

2. See Personal Privacy, supra § 4–31 note 18 at 286 (1977). Employers increasingly breach confidentiality by using records from their own employee-assistance programs (EAPs) to cut down on use of their medical and mental health benefits, often by firing employees whose problems could prove expensive over time. See Ellen E. Schultz, If You Use Firm's Counselors, Remember Your Secrets Could Be Used Against You, Wall St.J., C1, C6 (May 26, 1994).

3. Personal Privacy, supra § 4–31 note 18, at 280. On handling the disclosure of medical information, see J. Bruce, Privacy and Confidentiality in Health Care (1984); W. Roach, et al., supra note 83, at 59–116. On disclosure of

The federal and state governments may seek medical record information for a variety of purposes: workplace investigations, Fraud and Abuse prosecutions, and other investigations. The Supreme Court in *Whalen v. Roe*[4] upheld government action to secure and maintain personal medical information in circumstances where the government demonstrated adequate safeguards against public disclosure of that information. *Whalen* was a challenge by a group of physicians and patients to the constitutionality of a New York statute requiring physicians to forward to the state copies of prescriptions for drugs prone to abuse. The Court held that New York's statutory scheme and security measures illustrated proper concern and protection for the individual's privacy interest in such information.[5] States also obtain patient medical information under statutes authorizing its collection. Thus, hospitals, employers, insurers, and other recipients of medical data must report information concerning occupational accidents and illnesses, worker's compensation, child abuse, sexual assault, venereal and other communicable diseases, and abortions.[6]

a. Patient Consent

Medical information is needed by professional and non-professional medical staff in medical institutions for a variety of purposes, from treatment to quality assurance. Patients may expressly consent to the release of medical information in their records. Some states by statute expressly authorize such records' release upon consent of the patient.[7] Patient consent to release of information may also be presumed from the circumstances. Providers treating the patient have access to the record, with consent presumed from acceptance of the treatment. When a patient is transferred from one provider to another, disclosure of information is needed for continuity of care.[8] Emergency treatment likewise presumes patient consent. Patients may also be held to waive their right to confidentiality, for example by putting their mental or physical state at issue in a legal proceeding.[9]

Access to records is also sought routinely for a variety of medical evaluation and support purposes. For example, in-house quality assurance committees, JCAHO accreditation inspection teams, and state institutional licensure reviewers all must review medical records to assess the quality of hospital care. Consent for in-house use of patient information is typically implied from the patient's agreement to treatment.[10] Patient records may be

records of non-litigants in litigation, see Harold L. Hirsh, The Great Wall About Nonparty Patient Medical Records is Crumbling, 31 Med.Trial Tech.Q. 434 (1985).

4. 429 U.S. 589, 97 S.Ct. 869, 51 L.Ed.2d 64 (1977).

5. Whalen has been held to support the government's right to compel surrender of employee health records to OSHA. See e.g., General Motors Corp. v. Director of the Nat. Inst. for Occupational Safety and Health, 636 F.2d 163 (6th Cir.1980).

6. See e.g., West's Fla. Stat. Ann. § 322.126 (requiring driver disabilities to be reported to the Dept. of Highway Safety); id., § 385.202 (requiring reporting of cancer patient records).

7. See West's Ann. Cal. Civ. Code § 56.12.

8. See Vernon's Ann. Tex. Civ. Stat. art. 4495b, § 5.08(h)(7); West's Ann. Cal. Civ. Code § 56.10(c)(1). The COBRA Anti–Dumping legislation requires that a hospital transferring a patient from its emergency room to another hospital to transmit patient records. 42 U.S.C.A. § 1395dd(c)(2)(B). See also Chapter 12.

9. See Britt v. Superior Court, 143 Cal. Rptr. 695, 574 P.2d 766 (Cal.1978); Orr v. Sievert, 292 S.E.2d 548 (Ga.App.1982).

10. Some states authorize such disclosure by state. See e.g., West's Ann. Cal. Civ. Code § 56.10(c)(1); West's Fla. Stat. Ann. § 395.3025.

essential for effective review of quality within an institution, and some states by statute authorize access to patient records.[11] Absent statutory authorization, however, providers should be careful to protect patient information not needed for internal quality control.

Release of patient information to outside review organizations or licensing boards depends on state law. Some statutes explicitly allow state boards to review patient records in order to investigate provider misconduct.[12] Given judicial deference to the value of patient confidentiality, however, providers may be at risk if they disclose patient information absent statutory or judicial support. The Medicare program provides that providers must allow Peer Review Organizations (PROs) access to records that relate to treatment of Medicare patients.[13]

Third party payers are the most common requesters of medical records outside the treatment setting. Information may be released to payers with the patient's consent, with most insurers requiring patients to authorize the release of information when they file claims for payment. Some states provide by statute for disclosure without patient authorization to determine insurer responsibility for payment.[14]

Medical researchers frequently use information from medical records. If researchers are affiliated with the institution holding the records, access is routinely granted; if they are external to the institution, a request to review records may be reviewed more carefully, but will often be granted.[15]

b. Statutory Disclosures

State public health laws require medical professionals and institutions to report a variety of medical conditions and incidents: venereal disease, contagious diseases such as tuberculosis,[16] wounds inflicted by violence, poisonings, industrial accidents,[17] abortions,[18] drug abuse,[19] child abuse,[20] abuse of others, such as the elderly or disabled.[21] The justification for overriding patient interests in confidentiality is the state's interest in preserving the public health, under the exercise of its police powers. Such surveillance is a central component of public health assessment.[22]

c. Duties to Warn Third Parties

A provider's duty to maintain confidentiality may conflict with a duty to disclose information to third parties in order to warn them of a risk of violence, a contagious disease, or some other risk. Such a duty to disclose may

11. Ill.Compiled St. Ann. Ch. 735 ILCS 5/8–2101.

12. Nev. Rev. Stat. § 629.061 (1991); see Nach v. Department of Professional Regulation, 528 So.2d 908 (Fla.App.1988); In re Board of Medical Review Investigation, 463 A.2d 1373 (R.I.1983).

13. 42 C.F.R. § 476.102 (1993).

14. West's Ann. Cal. Civ. Code § 56.10(c)(2).

15. See Angela R. Holder, The Regulation of Human Subjects Research § 23.05, in Treatise on Health Care Law (Michael G. MacDonald et al., Eds. (1992)).

16. McKinney's—N.Y. Pub. Health Law § 2101 (communicable disease).

17. See e.g., Minn. Stat. Ann. § 144.34.

18. See e.g., Minn. Stat. Ann. § 145.413.

19. See e.g., West's Ann. Cal. Health & Safety Code § 11164.

20. West's Fla. Stat. Ann. § 415.511 (child abuse).

21. See West's Fla. Stat. Ann. § 415.101; Ky. Rev. Stat. § 209.030.

22. Sandra Roush et al., Mandatory Reporting of Diseases and Conditions by Health Care Professionals and Laboratories, 282 J.A.M.A. 164 (1999).

be based on a statute, such as a child abuse or venereal disease reporting act, or on the common law duty of psychotherapists to warn identifiable persons threatened by their patients. Duties to disclose may conflict with duties to protect confidentiality, posing interpretative problems for the courts.[23] In spite of these worries, physicians and other health professionals have in many jurisdictions an affirmative obligation by statute or common law to disclose confidential information in order to protect third parties against hazards created by their patients.

The obligations of health professionals normally extend only to the patients with whom they have a legal relationship, either under an implied or an express contract. This duty may extend to former patients as well where a risk is discovered after the relationship ends, for example with implanted medical devices that are later found to create safety risks.[24] Requirements of confidentiality of the physician-patient relationship militate against disclosure generally, and disclosure may expose the physician to expansive liability. Courts have therefore been reluctant to expand duties to warn too broadly, generally refusing to require physicians to advise their patients not to drive if their condition might create a risk to third parties[25]; examples include patients with avision or drowsiness problems that leads to an accident.[26] Even though a statute may require notification of state officials of a patient's health problem, this does not create a duty on the part of the physician to unforeseeable third parties.[27]

1. Psychiatric Dangerousness. The risk created by a dangerous patient provides a clear example of judicially imposed duties to warn third parties. Failures by psychotherapists to warn third parties have been the source of substantial litigation.[28] The duty to warn first appeared in the psychiatric context, beginning with *Tarasoff v. Regents of the University of California*.[29] The duty to warn in *Tarasoff* involved a specific, readily identified individual.[30] Some courts have limited the duty to warn to such a situation,[31] or have

23. See State v. Andring, 342 N.W.2d 128 (Minn.1984).

24. See, e.g., Harris v. Raymond, 715 N.E.2d 388 (Ind.1999)(temporamandibular joint implants could rupture; court held that physician who has implanted such devices has a duty to warn his or her current and former patients of such safety issues).

25. Calwell v. Hassan, 925 P.2d 422 (Kan. 1996)(physician has no duty to warn patient with sleep disorder not to drive); Praesel v. Johnson, 967 S.W.2d 391 (Tex.1998)(physician has no duty to third parties to warn epileptic patients not to drive); Witthoeft v. Kiskaddon, 733 A.2d 623 (Pa.1999)(ophthalmologist's failure to notice Department of Transportation of patient's vision disorder does not create a private cause of action). Contra, Duvall v. Goldin, 362 N.W.2d 275 (C.A.Mich. 1984).

26. See Estate of Witthoeft v. Kiskaddon, 733 A.2d 623 (Pa. 1999), where an ophthalmologist failed to inform either his patient or the Pennsylvania Department of Transportation of the patient's poor visual acuity, and later injured the plaintiff while driving. The court refused to create a private action from the

violation of the Pennsylvania statute requiring notification of the Registry of Motor Vehicles of a patient's poor vision. See also Calwell v. Hassan, 925 P.2d 422 (Kan.1996), where the court found that a physician treating an outpatient for a drowsiness condition did not have duty to prevent harm to others.

27. Praesel v. Johnson, 967 S.W.2d 391 (Tex. 1998)(no common law duty on physician to third parties to warn epileptic patients not to drive; and statute allowing physicians to inform state of identity of patient with epilepsy for possible license revocation does not support negligence per se).

28. See for example, Davis v. Lhim, 335 N.W.2d 481 (Mich.App.1983), remanded 366 N.W.2d 7 (Mich.1985), where the court held that a psychiatrist owes a professional duty of care to those who could be foreseeably injured by his patient.

29. 131 Cal.Rptr. 14, 551 P.2d 334 (Cal. 1976).

30. See also, McIntosh v. Milano, 403 A.2d 500 (N.J.Super.Law Div.1979); Hedlund v. Superior Court of Orange County, 194 Cal.Rptr.

rejected the duty to warn obligation.[32] Other jurisdictions, however, have expanded the duty to include readily identifiable individuals who would be at risk of the patient's violence,[33] or even whole classes foreseeably at risk.[34] In some states, statutes attempt to spell out third parties who must be informed, typically in mental health situations.[35] The Tarasoff duty has been accepted by most states, with only Virginia and Texas explicitly rejecting Tarasoff.[36]

2. Contagious Diseases. The risk of contagion is another example of a duty to disclose confidential patient information.[37] A long line of cases involve risks of disease or infection. Physicians have been held liable for failing to warn the daughter of a patient with scarlet fever, a wife about the danger of infection from a patient's wounds, a neighbor about the patient's smallpox.[38] Family members are foreseeable third parties, as are neighbors.[39] Courts have cited to the Restatement (Second) Torts, § 324A, which provides in part that one who provides services to another may be liable to a third person for harm resulting from his failure to exercise reasonable care, if the "the harm is suffered because of reliance of the other or the third person upon the undertaking." In the case of communicable diseases, courts have included in the class of persons at risk anyone who is physically intimate with the patient. As one court said, "[p]hysicians are the first line of defense against the spread of communicable diseases, because physicians know what measures must be

805, 669 P.2d 41 (Cal.1983); Lipari v. Sears, Roebuck & Co., 497 F.Supp. 185 (D.Neb.1980).

31. Brady v. Hopper, 570 F.Supp. 1333 (D.Colo.1983), affirmed 751 F.2d 329 (10th Cir. 1984).

32. State v. Tarbutton, 407 A.2d 538 (Del.Super.1979); Cole v. Taylor, 301 N.W.2d 766 (Iowa 1981); Shaw v. Glickman, 415 A.2d 625 (Md.Spec.App. 1980).

33. Emerich v. Philadelphia Center for Human Development, Inc., 720 A.2d 1032 (Pa. 1998) (mental health professional owes duty to warn a third party of threats of harm); Estate of Morgan v. Fairfield Family Counseling Center, 673 N.E.2d 1311 (Ohio 1997) (when psychotherapist knows or should know that his outpatient poses a serious risk of harm to others, therapist has duty to exercise best professional judgment to prevent such harm); Turner v. Jordan, 957 S.W.2d 815 (Tenn.1997) (psychiatrist owed nurse duty to protect her from violent patient); Bradley v. Ray, 904 S.W.2d 302 (Mo.C.A. 1995) (psychologist owes common law duty to child to warn appropriate authorities that client presents serious danger of future violence); Almonte v. N.Y. Medical College, 851 F.Supp. 34 (D.Conn.1994) (duty of psychiatrist to control student who was pedophile and was studying to become a child psychiatrist); Bardoni v. Kim, 390 N.W.2d 218 (Mich.App.1986).

34. Lipari v. Sears, Roebuck & Co., 497 F.Supp. 185 (D.Neb.1980).

35. See e.g., 740 ILCS 110/12. For affirmative obligations to warn, see Ariz. Rev. Stat. § 36–517.02; Ky. Rev. Stat. § 202A.400.

36. See Thapar v. Zezulka, 994 S.W.2d 635 (Texas 1999) (no duty warn third parties of patient threats, given Texas confidentiality statute); Nasser v. Parker, 455 S.E.2d 502 (Va. 1995); Evans v. U.S., 883 F.Supp. 124 (S.D.Miss.1995) (finding no duty in Mississippi law). See generally Bradley v. Ray, 904 S.W.2d 302 (Mo.App.1995) for a list of cases.

37. See, e.g., Troxel v. A.I. Dupont Institute, 675 A.2d 314 (Sup.Ct.Pa. 1996) (duty of physician to take steps to prevent spread of cytomegalovirus by warning mother that she should avoid contact with pregnant women); Bolieu v. Sisters of Providence in Washington, 953 P.2d 1233 (Alaska 1998) (residential health facility owed duty to spouses of nursing assistants to minimize spread of staph infections). See Tracy A. Bateman, Annotation, Liability of Doctor or Other Health Practitioner to Third Party Contracting Contagious Disease from Doctor's Patient, 3 ALR 5th 370(1992).

38. See Gammill v. United States, 727 F.2d 950, 954 (10th Cir.1984) (physician may be found liable for failing to warn a patient's family, treating attendants, or other persons likely to be exposed to the patient of the nature of the disease and the danger of exposure). See generally Tracy A. Bateman, Annotation, Liability of Doctor or Other Health Practitioner to Third Party Contracting Contagious Disease from Doctor's Patient, 3 A.L.R. 5th 370 (1992); 61 Am.Jur.2d Physicians and Surgeons § 245 (1981); 70 C.J.S. Physicians and Surgeons § 88 (1987).

39. See Freese v. Lemmon, 210 N.W.2d 576 (Iowa 1973).

taken to prevent the infection of others."[40] The cases tend to involve specific identifiable third parties.[41]

Duties to warn patients of medical risks may arise out of medical knowledge of how diseases are communicated. While contagious diseases are the most obvious example of risks to third parties when a physician fails to warn either the patient or those intimate with the patient, one court has stretched the concept to require warnings to third parties exposed to the same disease vector as the patient. Thus, a physician treating a patient with Rocky Mountain Spotted Fever has been held to a duty to warn members of his family, not because the disease is contagious, but because the infected ticks that transmit the disease "cluster," increasing the risk to those likely to be exposed. Risks to family members become foreseeable risks if one family member is infected. Since early detection leads to a high cure rate, and the disease is fatal in 40 percent of the cases absent early detection, the risk is a substantial one.[42] A physician may be expected to warn family members about the risk of contagion as the result of treatment.[43]

The courts have moved beyond family members to include then unknown third parties, imposing on treating physicians a duty to inform patients or to warn third parties when deadly illnesses such as AIDS or highly contagious ones such as hepatitis are involved. In Reisner v. Regents of the University of California,[44] the patient, Jennifer, a 12–year old girl, received a transfusion contaminated with HIV antibodies during surgery. The physician learned of the contamination, continued to treat Jennifer but never told her or her parents about the tainted blood. Three years later, she started to date Daniel Reisner and they had sexual relations. Two years later, the doctor finally told Jennifer she had AIDS and Jennifer told Daniel. Jennifer died a month later. Daniel then learned he was HIV positive.

The defendants argued they owed no duty to Daniel, who was an unidentified third party at the time Jennifer was infected with HIV. The court cited *Tarasoff* and other cases that had imposed a duty to warn either the patient or third parties about risks, holding that the defendants had a duty to warn a contagious patient to take steps to protect others.

> One the physician warns the patient of the risk to others and advises the patient how to prevent the spread of the disease, the physician has fulfilled his duty—and no more (but no less) is required. . . .
>
>   . . . We need not decide in this case what the result would be if someone infected by Daniel sued the doctor who failed to warn Jennifer,

40. DiMarco v. Lynch Homes–Chester County, 583 A.2d 422 (Pa.1990); see also, Troxel v. A.I.Dupont Institute, 675 A.2d 314 (Pa.Super.1996); Shepard v. Redford Community Hospital, 390 N.W.2d 239 (Mich.App. 1986).

41. Knier v. Albany Medical Ctr. Hosp., 500 N.Y.S.2d 490 (N.Y.Sup.1986) (no duty to warn public that person has contagious disease).

42. Bradshaw v. Daniel, 854 S.W.2d 865 (Tenn.1993).

43. Tenuto v. Lederle Laboratories, 687 N.E.2d 1300 (N.Y.App.1997) (physician gave dose of oral poliomyelitis vaccine manufactured by Lederle to a five month old girl, and failed to ask the girl's father if he had previously been vaccinated against polio, and to warn the parents of the risk for contact polio. The risk were known since 1961 and were described in the package inserts and the PDR. The court held that the physician "knew or should have known that his comprehensive services necessarily brought into play the protection of the health of plaintiffs, who relied upon his professional expertise in providing advice and other forms of medical services.).

44. 37 Cal.Rptr.2d 518 (C.A.Cal., 2d App. Dist. 1995).

and the fact that a duty is owed to Daniel does not mean it will be extended without limitation. However, the possibility of such an extension does not offend us, legally or morally. Viewed in the abstract ... we believe that a doctor who knows he is dealing with the 20th Century version of Typhoid Mary ought to have a very strong incentive to tell his patient what she ought to do and not do and how she ought to comport herself in order to prevent the spread of her disease.

In DiMarco v. Lynch Homes—Chester County,[45] the sexual partner of a patient sued her physicians, who had assured her that she would not contract hepatitis. The plaintiff Janet Viscichini, a blood technician, went to the Lynch Home to take a blood sample from one of the residents. During the procedure, her skin was accidentally punctured by the needle she had used to extract blood. When she learned that the patient had hepatitis, she sought treatment from Doctors Giunta and Alwine. They told her that if she remained symptom free for six weeks, she would not be infected by the hepatitis virus. She was not told to refrain from sexual relations for any period of time following her exposure to the disease, but she practiced sexual abstinence until eight weeks after the exposure. Since she had remained symptom-free during that time, she then resumed sexual relations with the plaintiff. She was later diagnosed as suffering from hepatitis B in September; in December, the plaintiff was similarly diagnosed.

The court cited Restatement (Second) Torts, § 324A, which provided in part that one who provides services to another may be liable to a third person for harm resulting from his failure to exercise reasonable care, if the "the harm is suffered because of reliance of the other or the third person upon the undertaking." The court allowed the action, concluding that the class of persons at risk included any one who is physically intimate with the patient.

When a physician treats a patient who has been exposed to or who has contracted a communicable and/or contagious disease, it is imperative that the physician give his or her patient the proper advice about preventing the spread of the disease. ... Physicians are the first line of defense against the spread of communicable diseases, because physicians know what measures must be taken to prevent the infection of others.

Other jurisdictions have allowed actions for the negligent infliction of emotional distress where a contagious disease is misdiagnosed.[46]

3.   Genetic Information. Increased knowledge of genetic defects and their possible transmission promises to expand the duties of physicians and other health care professionals to warn and protect not only patients but also third parties. The Human Genome Project holds the promise of understanding the genetic sources of many inheritable illnesses, and that knowledge brings added responsibility by physicians to discuss these factors with patients.[47] Malpractice suits have been brought for negligent genetical testing and

45.   583 A.2d 422 (S.C. Pa. 1990).

46.   Chizmar v. Mackie, 896 P.2d 196 (Alaska 1995) (physician tested patient for HIV virus, reported a false positive result).

47.   See generally Leroy Hood & Lee Rowen, Genes, Genomes and Society, in Genetic Secrets: Protecting Privacy and Confidentiality in the Genetic Era (Mark A. Rothstein ed., 1997). For a full law review symposium devoted to genetic technology, see Genetic Technology: Social Values and Personal Autonomy in the 21st Century, 34 Wake Forest 557 (1999).

counseling for decades, usually as wrongful life and wrongful death suits.[48] The new genetic knowledge expands these obligations to include duties to warn patients, or their children, of possible transmissible diseases that may require monitoring or prophylactic measures. Genetically transmissible risks elevate a physician's duty to warn beyond imminent contagious diseases to latent genetic defects that may or may not materialize over a long period of time. The so-called breast cancer gene provides an example of such a duty. A woman who possesses the gene might want to step up self-monitoring, mammograms and other early detection approaches. When physicians err in analyzing patients' genetic histories, the consequences can be serious. Many of the wrongful birth/wrongful life cases involve negligence by a genetic counselor or physician in advising parents as to their risks in having genetically impaired children. Courts have split in their willingness to impose duties on physicians for such errors.

In Pate v. Threlkel,[49] the court held that a physician owes a duty to the children of a patient to warn the patient of a genetically transmittable condition. In 1987, Marianne New received treatment for medullary thyroid carcinoma, a genetically transferable disease. Three years later, In 1990, Heidi Pate, New's adult daughter, learned that she also had medullary thyroid carcinoma. She sued, arguing that the physician had a duty to warn her of this risk . The court refused to impose a duty to warn such third parties directly on the physician, assuming that a warning to the patient would be reasonable.warning.

> Our holding should not be read to require the physician to warn the patient's children of the disease. In most instances the physician is prohibited from disclosing the patient's medical condition to others except with the patient's permission.[ ] Moreover, the patient ordinarily can be expected to pass on the warning. To require the physician to seek out and warn various members of the patient's family would often be difficult or impractical and would place too heavy a burden upon the physician. Thus, we emphasize that in any circumstances in which the physician has a duty to warn of a genetically transferable disease, that duty will be satisfied by warning the patient.

The court failed to consider the possibility that a patient might not want to warn her children, or that other events would make it unlikely that the children would receive a warning.

Safer v. Pack[50] involved an early failure by a physician to warn the daughter of a man who died of multiple polyposis of the colon. The physician treated the father surgically for the colon cancer, but he died at age forty-five. The plaintiff Donna Safer was ten years old at the time of her father's death, and her sister was seventeen. Twenty-six years later, Donna began to experience lower abdominal pain. Examinations and tests revealed a cancerous blockage of the colon and multiple polyposis. In March, Ms. Safer underwent a total abdominal colectomy with ileorectal anastamosis, and chemotherapy treatment. She then sued Dr. Pack for his failure to warn of the risk to Donna

48. See generally Chapter 17.

49. 661 So.2d 278 (Fla. 1995). See also Safer v. Pack, 677 A.2d 1188 (Sup.Ct., A.D.N.J. 1996) (duty of physician to warn members of immediate family of patient of genetic condition, multiple polyposis).

50. 677 A.2d 1188 (Sup.Ct, App.Div, 1996).

Safer of polyposis. They argued that multiple polyposis was a hereditary condition that, if undiscovered and untreated, invariably leads to metastatic colorectal cancer, and that the genetic component of this disease was "known at the time Dr. Pack was treating Mr. Batkin and that the physician was required, by medical standards then prevailing, to warn those at risk so that they might have the benefits of early examination, monitoring, detection and treatment, that would provide opportunity to avoid the most baneful consequences of the condition." The court held that the children of a patient fall with the "zone of foreseeable risk" for purposes of warning of inheritable diseases.

> We see no impediment, legal or otherwise, to recognizing a physician's duty to warn those known to be at risk of avoidable harm from a genetically transmissible condition. In terms of foreseeability especially, there is no essential difference between the type of genetic threat at issue here and the menace of infection, contagion or a threat of physical harm. ... [ ] The individual or group at risk is easily identified, and substantial future harm may be averted or minimized by a timely and effective warning.

The court rejected the limits on the duty to warn imposed by the Florida Supreme Court in Pate, which limited the duty of the physician to informing the patient, extending the duty to warn not only the patient but members of the immediate family. As to young children at risk, the court required that "reasonable steps" should be taken to ensure that the genetic information reached them.[51]

d. AIDS Confidentiality and Reporting

Special characteristics of AIDS and of the AIDS epidemic present new and unique challenges to health care workers trying to understand their general duty to keep confidences and their specific obligations, by contrast, to disclose medical information as part of their duty to warn others.[52] First, widespread continuing fear of AIDS and ignorance about how it is spread, combined with a history of prejudice and discrimination against gay men among whom AIDS has been most common, have amplified concerns of privacy and confidentiality. If information about a person's AIDS infection or HIV positivity reaches employers, insurers, schools, family, or acquaintances, it may have disastrous consequences. Many therefore argue that maintenance of the strictest confidentiality is essential if voluntary AIDS testing programs are to succeed—that

---

51. The court acknowledged the possibility of family conflict over such information, citing to Sonia M. Suter, Whose Genes Are These Anyway? Familial Conflicts Over Access to Genetic Information, 91 Mich. L.Rev. 1854 (1993).

52. See among the many sources on confidentiality and disclosure of AIDS-related information, Lawrence O. Gostin and James G. Hodge, Piercing the Veil of Secrecy in HIV/ AIDS and Other Sexually Transmitted Diseases: Theories of Privacy and Disclosure in Partner Notification; 5 Duke J.Gender L. & Pol'y 9 (1998); Lawrence O. Gostin and James G. Hodge, The "Names" Debate: The Case For National HIV Reporting in the U.S., 61 Alb.

L.Rev. 679(1998); Association of State and Territorial Health Officials, Guide to Public Health Practice: AIDS Confidentiality and Anti–Discrimination Principles (1988); Lawrence O. Gostin, Hospitals, Health Care Professionals, and AIDS: The "Right to Know" the Health Status of Professionals and Patients, 48 Md.L.Rev. 12 (1989); Donald H. Hermann & Rosalind D. Gagliano, AIDS, Therapeutic Confidentiality, and Warning Third Parties, 48 Md. L.Rev. 55 (1989); Richard North and Karen H. Rothenberg, The Duty to Warn "Dilemma"—A Framework for Resolution, 4 AIDS & Pub.Policy J. 133 (1989).

any risk of disclosure will discourage persons who may possibly be HIV infected or who have AIDS or ARC from seeking testing and counseling.[53]

Second, the fact that the HIV virus cannot be spread through casual contact, unlike many other contagious diseases, limits the need for disclosure of information about infection. The fact that the rate of infection through heterosexual genital intercourse is very low (about .001 per exposure) may argue against a duty to warn heterosexual partners, since it is unlikely that casual heterosexual partners will be infected; or may argue in favor of a warning, since it is possible that longer term partners may have not yet been infected. The possibility of transmission to unborn children may also argue for warning potentially infected persons who may potentially bear children.

Third, the fact that AIDS is presently incurable makes prevention more essential. A conflict is immediately evident: strict confidentiality may encourage persons who may be infected to come forward to be tested and thereafter modify their behavior voluntarily to avoid infecting others; but limited disclosure may better protect persons who may be exposed to possible infection. Availability of treatment modalities that may slow the infection process strongly argues for increased awareness of HIV-positivity by those infected, in order to get early treatment.

The states have adopted a variety of legislative and administrative approaches to confidentiality and disclosure of information regarding HIV-positivity, ARC, and AIDS status.[54] Most states have adopted statutes mandating strict confidentiality of AIDS-related information.[55] The range of allowable exceptions to such confidentiality requirements is quite broad, however. All states now require physicians to report AIDS cases to state public health authorities,[56] and a number also require reporting of cases of asymptomatic HIV infection, usually anonymously.[57] Other states have adopted laws permitting disclosure of HIV test results to persons at risk of HIV infection from sexual or needle sharing contacts with the infected person.[58] The physician is protected from liability whether he discloses or chooses not to disclose the information.[59]

Health care workers have an obligation in some states by statute to counsel HIV-infected patients to take special precautions to avoid infecting others and to tell their sexual or needle-sharing partners to seek testing, counseling, and treatment. If patients indicate, however, that they will not do

53. See generally, Lawrence O. Gostin and James G. Hodge, Piercing the Veil of Secrecy in HIV/AIDS and Other Sexually Transmitted Diseases: Theories of Privacy and Disclosure in Partner Notification; 5 Duke J.Gender L. & Pol'y 9 (1998).

54. For detailed summaries of state law and AIDS litigation, see Lawrence O. Gostin, The AIDS Litigation Project, 263 J.A.M.A. 1961 (1990); State AIDS Reporter (M.J. Rowe & C.C. Ryan eds.); and Larry Gostin, Public Health Strategies for Confronting AIDS: Legislative and Regulatory Policy in the United States, 261 J.A.M.A. 1621 (1989). See Doe v. Marselle, 675 A.2d 835 (Conn.1996) (cause of action allowed against physician for "willful" violation of confidentiality statute).

55. See West's Ann. Cal. Health & Safety Code § 199.21; West's Fla. Stat. Ann. § 381.004(3).

56. Lawrence O. Gostin, The AIDS Litigation Project, 263 J.A.M.A. 1961 (1990).

57. West's Ann. Cal. Health & Safety Code § 199.21(j).

58. See Official Code Ga. Ann. § 38–723(g) (disclosure to spouse, sexual partner or child permitted under some circumstances); McKinney's—N.Y. Pub. Health Law § 2782(4)(a) & (b).

59. See West's Ann. Cal. Health & Safety Code § 199.25(c).

so, the health care worker's obligation to warn others is defined by the law of the particular state.[60] A number of states permit public health authorities to engage in contact tracing or partner notification with respect to persons with AIDS or who are HIV-infected.[61] Five different approaches to contact tracing have been identified: 1) solicitation of the names of all sexual and needle-sharing contacts of AIDS-and HIV-infected persons with subsequent notification of all identified contacts (with offers for testing and counselling); 2) limited contact tracing focusing on high risk or especially vulnerable groups who are likely to be unaware of the risk of infection (heterosexual contacts of individuals with AIDS); 3) voluntary contact tracing: infected persons are asked to notify potentially infected persons voluntarily and assistance is offered to those who want help in notifying others; 4) notification in special circumstances, as to rescue or emergency personnel potentially infected in the line of duty; 5) notification of specific persons in specific situations, such as those exposed to infected blood.[62] Colorado has been particularly active in contact tracing, and claims that its program has resulted in the identification and treatment of a number of individuals who would not otherwise have been aware of their HIV positive status.[63] Contact tracing usually depends on voluntary disclosure of sexual and needle-sharing partners by the infected person and may be ineffective in situations where the infected person refuses to notify others voluntarily.

One particular situation in which the disclosure of the identity of HIV-infected persons has been frequently sought is where a person who has become HIV-infected through tainted blood seeks disclosure of the identity of the donor who donated the infected blood, either to assist in establishing negligence on the part of the blood service or to permit a suit against the donor. These cases have tended to deny discovery, relying on various privacy, physician patient privilege, or discovery protection theories and on the importance of protecting the identity of blood donors to encourage voluntary blood donations.[64]

Hospitals and other institutional providers face similar tensions in deciding whether to warn patients about exposure to HIV-infected staff. While little evidence exists that HIV is transmitted from provider to patient,[65] some courts have been willing to find a duty to warn that overrides state and

60. The AMA has taken a position on this question:

> Where there is no statute that mandates or prohibits reporting of seropositive individuals to public health authorities and it is clear that the seropositive individual is endangering an identified third party, the physician should (1) attempt to persuade the infected individual to cease endangering the third party; (2) if persuasion fails, notify authorities; and (3) if authorities take no action, notify and counsel the endangered third party.

HIV Blood Test Counseling: A.M.A. Physician Guidelines (1988).

61. See e.g., S.C. Code § 44–29–90; Tenn. Code Ann. § 68–10–101.

62. See Karen H. Rothenberg, et al., The AIDS Project: Creating a Public Health Poli-

cy—Rights and Obligations of Health Care Workers, 48 Md.L.Rev. 94, 181–183 (1989).

63. See Partner Notification for Preventing Immunodeficiency Virus (HIV) Infection—Colorado, Idaho, South Carolina, Virginia, 260 J.A.M.A. 613 (1988).

64. See Krygier v. Airweld, Inc., 520 N.Y.S.2d 475 (N.Y.Sup.1987). See Richard C. Bellow & Daryl J. Lapp, Protecting the Confidentiality of Blood Donors' Identities in AIDS Litigation, 37 Drake L.Rev. 343 (1988).

65. The studies to date have found no evidence of transmission from provider to patient, with the possible exception of the Kimberly Bergalis case. See e.g., Ban Mishu et al., A Surgeon with AIDS: Lack of Evidence of Transmission to Patients, 264 J.A.M.A. 467 (1990) (study of 2160 patients of Nashville surgeon).

federal confidentiality laws. Thus in *Amaral v. Gordon*,[66] a medical group was held potentially liable for damages for its failure to warn its patients that a staff gynecologist was HIV-positive, even though it faced criminal penalties by statute for each disclosure. In *Estate of Behringer v. The Medical Center at Princeton*[67] the court held that the hospital had an obligation to disclose that a staff otolaryngologist (ENT) and plastic surgeon was suffering from AIDS. The hospital developed a special informed consent for HIV-positive providers, and a new policy for HIV-positive workers that barred them from patient care situations where they might pose risks to patients. The *Behringer* court analyzed informed consent in terms of the material risks faced by a patient. While conceding that the risk of transmission of HIV from provider to patient was very low,[68] the court saw the risks as including extended uncertainty for a patient exposed to a surgical accident involving a surgeon with AIDS.[69] One state has tried to balance the competing claims of warning and confidentiality by statute.[70] Other states have imposed a duty on physicians to disclose their HIV-positive status when seeking a patient's consent to perform invasive medical procedures, and a claim for the negligent infliction of emotional distress will lie absent such disclosure.[71]

§ 4–35. Quality of Care and Outcome Data

The Health Care Quality Improvement Act of 1986 (HCQIA86) forces providers to collect information on physicians when granting staff privileges to these physicians. The goal of the reporting system is to spot the incompetent practitioner. The physician's record is central in two ways to this process. It must accurately reflect all Data Bank information, so that peer review committees can confidently engage in credentialing decisions without fear of subsequent civil litigation. The record must also be constantly updated to reflect malpractice settlements and disciplinary actions taken against physicians, which must be reported to the Data Bank. The evolution of quality assurance in health care entities has moved toward continuous quality improvement, a method of constantly evaluating and changing health care with quality parameters in mind.[1] Continuous quality improvement requires a focus on comparative data as to effectiveness of medical procedures, feedback and education of physicians, and development of practice guidelines that embody the research findings. Hospitals and managed care organizations actively engage in programs to promote high quality and effective practice, through implementation of clinical algorithms, outcome based studies, application of quality control principles from industry, and large scale analysis of practice patterns across plans.[2] These programs of outcomes management are

66. No. 126484 (Los Angeles County, Cal.Super.Ct. 1990) (digested in *Insurance & Liability*, Hospitals, July 20, 1990, at 22–23).

67. 592 A.2d 1251 (N.J.Super.Law Div. 1991).

68. The court observed that the actual risk of transmission is small, in the range of 1/130,-000 to 1/4,500. But it also found that the cumulative risk to surgical patients would be much higher.

69. 592 A.2d 1251, 1278 (N.J.Super.Law Div.1991).

70. Ky. Rev. Stat. § 202A.400.

71. Doe v. Noe, 1997 WL 789854 (Ill.App. 1997).

§ 4–35

1. William Fifer, The Evolution of Quality Assurance Systems in Health Care—A Personal Retrospective, 4 The Medical Staff Counselor 11 (1990).

2. For a summary of many of these current outcome-based research projects, see LuAnn Heinen et al., 7 Health Affairs 145–150 (1988).

now being implemented in hospitals and managed care organizations under pressure from JCAHO and the federal government.

The change in focus within health care institutions toward quality improvement has implications for medical recordkeeping. First, practice parameters are used for education, screening, quality assurance and risk management. Such parameters provide a much brighter standard of care in the case of a bad patient outcome than do the more diffuse evidence of standards in tort cases. The AMA tells physicians to be aware of such guidelines, and document in the medical record their reasons for deviating from such guidelines in particular cases, to avoid a claim of negligence. A notation in the record when the guideline is followed also helps to track the patient's treatment and management.[3] The rapid acceleration of information gathering by health care institutions is likely to lead to disclosure of such comparative success rates and outcome data where available.[4]

Systematic accumulation of outcome data is changing the standard of care for hospitals. The rapid acceleration of information gathering by health care institutions is likely to have two legal effects. First, it will lead to demands for disclosure of such comparative success rates and outcome data where available.[5] Informed consent doctrine might be invoked by an injured patient, who argues that comparative data as to the physician's success rates was desirable risk information for the patient.[6] Second, a patient injured in the hospital might argue that the hospital was negligent in retaining a physician on the medical staff, if outcome data complied by the hospital reveals that the physician was at the very bottom of the staff profile.[7] A health care provider may in the future have a duty to gather such information carefully, as the standard of care evolves toward systematic data collection of outcomes, and to regularly monitor the outcomes of individual physicians.[8] A properly designed utilization review process within an institution will produce data as to unnecessary procedures, high error rates, and other early warnings of problems with a staff physician. The existence of such a process will give a hospital actual notice of a problem, leading to liability.[9] A hospital is also under a duty to restrict the clinical privileges of staff physicians who are incompetent to handle certain procedures, and to detect concealment by a staff doctor of medical errors.[10] While some courts have limited this duty to only those situations where a hospital has learned of physician insufficiencies,[11] others have talked of "negligent supervision" in terms of an affirmative duty to detect problems.[12] Such data is closer to sophisticated computerized incident reporting than to peer review activities, driven by hospital administrative recordkeeping rather than medical staff committee actions. Nor do peer

---

3. American Medical Association, Legal Implications of Practice Parameters (1990).

4. See generally, Aaron D. Twerksi and Neil B. Cohen, Comparing Medical Providers: A First Look at the New Era of Medical Statistics, 58 Brook. L. Rev. 5, 12–13 (1992).

5. *Id.*

6. See Chapter Six, § 6–11d.

7. See Chapter Seven, § 7–9a.

8. See e.g., Gonzales v. Nork, No. 228566 (Sup.Ct., Sacramento Cty., Cal., Nov. 19, 1973).

9. Cronic v. Doud, 119 Ill.Dec. 708, 523 N.E.2d 176 (Ill.App.1988), appeal denied 125 Ill.Dec. 214, 530 N.E.2d 242 (Ill.1988).

10. Cronic v. Doud, 119 Ill.Dec. 708, 523 N.E.2d 176 (Ill.App.1988), appeal denied 125 Ill.Dec. 214, 530 N.E.2d 242 (Ill.1988); Corleto v. Shore Mem. Hosp., 350 A.2d 534 (N.J.Super.Law Div. 1975).

11. Albain v. Flower Hosp., 553 N.E.2d 1038 (Ohio 1990).

12. Oehler v. Humana, Inc., 775 P.2d 1271 (Nev.1989).

review statutes cover such regularized data collection, which is not done for specific committee meetings, but as a routine part of administrative data gathering. Such outcome data would be invaluable to a plaintiff's lawyer under a range of malpractice theories.

§ 4–36. Electronic Health Information

Computer recordkeeping is increasingly common in storing and retrieving medical records.[1] Sensitive health care data are stored, transferred and used with the ease that only modern computers could allow.[2] Given the sheer volume of data collected on each patient, the movement to computerize patient records is being pushed along by pressures from the federal and state governments as well as hospital desires for efficiency.[3] As health care has blossomed into a complex industry, the organizations involved, from employers to drug companies and managed organizations, have a compelling interest in data to control their costs, increase revenues and improve performance. Information has as a result become a central aspect of the health care enterprise.[4]

Violations of health information privacy fall into three major groups. First, medical record information is abused or misappropriated.[5] Legal protections for the alteration of the computerized medical record are less stringent than those for release of medical records generally.[6] New computer development may add confidential information to these porous patient files. For example, the increased use of e-mail messages from patients to their physicians can lead to the storage of these messages in the file, allowed the patient's own words to be easily accessed. Patients may reveal too much in light of the casual and conversational attributes of e-mail messaging.[7] Data security measures and sanctions against misuse can reduce this problem.[8] Second, health information may be used by institutions for marketing and

§ 4–36

1. See generally, James G. Hodge, Lawrence O. Gostin, and Peter D. Jacobson, Legal Issues Concerning Electronic Health Information: Privacy, Quality, and Liability, 282 J.A.M.A. 1466 (1999); Terri Arnold, Let Technology Counteract Technology: Protecting the Medical Record in the Computer Age, 15 Hastings Comm. & Ent.L.J. 455 (1993); Off. of Tech. Assessment, U.S. Congress, Protecting Privacy in Computerized Medical Information (1993); Denise C. Andreson, The Computerization of Health Care: Can Patient Privacy Survive? 26 J. Health and Hosp. Law 1 (1993); John D. Rootenberg, Computer–Based Patient Records: The Next Generation of Medicine?, 267 J.A.M.A. 168 (1992); Off. of Tech. Assessment, U.S. Congress, Policy Implications of Medical Information Systems 50–51 (1997).

2. Committee on Maintaining Privacy & Security in Health Care Applications of the National Information Infrastructure, National Research Council, For the Record: Protecting Electronic Health Information 25 (1997) (noting that more than half of hospitals were investing in electronic medical records and the market would grow into a \$\$1.5 billion indus-

try by 2000); Lawrence O. Gostin, Health Information Privacy, 80 Cornell L.Rev. 451 (1995); David M. Studdert, Direct Contracts, Data Sharing and Employee Risk Selection: New Stakes for Patient Privacy in Tomorrow's Health Insurance Markets, 25 Am.J.Law & Med. 233 (1999).

3. Indiana has expressly authorized retention of medical records in computer files. See West's Ann. Ind. Code §§ 34–3–15.5–1 et seq.

4. Paul Starr, Health and the Right to Privacy, 25 Am.J.L. & Med. 194, 196 (1999).

5. Id. at 196–197.

6. Terri Finkbine Arnold, Let Technology Counteract Technology: Protecting the Medical Record in the Computer Age, 15 Hastings Com. & Ent. L.J. 455 (1993).

7. Alissa R. Spielberg, Online Without a Net: Physician–Patient Communication by Electronic Mail, 25 Am.J.Law & Med 267, 274 (1999).

8. Latanya Sweeney, Weaving Technology and Policy Together to Maintain Confidentiality, 25 J.Law, Med & Ethics 98 (1997).

other commercial purposes, for example by selling patient prescription information to direct mail companies.[9] Some of these uses may be valuable and the costs to patients small. Third, organizations may abuse confidential patient health information in substantial and serious ways that result in discrimination, loss of employment, insurance or other welfare benefits.[10]

The Institute of Medicine has recommended that all providers adopt a computer-based patient record as the standard.[11] Personally identifiable health information about individuals is available in electronic form in health databases and online networks. Such computerization of records aims to improve efficiency in health care delivery. It is likely that a standardized online database for all patients will become the national norm.[12] This movement toward medical record computerization creates serious computer security and confidentiality issues.[13] A third party with a modem and a computer can in theory download confidential patient information, opening the door to even wider proliferation of sensitive information about individuals. This raises privacy concerns about individually identifiable health information and the quality and reliability of that information.[14] A computer security system can offer substantial confidentiality protections compared to traditional medical records because fewer access points are available to a computer; each person's access can be restricted to limited information; and information can be monitored through individual access codes. Computer storage can be designed with safeguards such as passwords, access codes, and selective "need to know" requirements for certain portions of a patient's file. Unauthorized access to computer files can also be traced through audit systems more easily than can such access to paper records.[15] Informed consent doctrine could be redefined to require both the physician and the institution to discuss some of these informational risks with patients.[16]

General principles are needed to guide the design of electronic health information protections. One such framework has been offered to guide patient privacy policies, proposing eleven principles.[17] First, health care organizations should remove all personal identifiers to the fullest extent possible consistent with maintaining the usefulness of the information. Second, priva-

9. Id. at 197.

10. Id. at 198.

11. Institute of Medicine, The Computer–Based Patient Record: An Essential Technology for Health Care (Richard S. Dick and Elaine B. Steen, eds. 1991); see also, General Accounting Office, Committee on Governmental Affairs, U.S. Senate, Medical ADP Systems: Automated Medical Records Hold Promise to Improve Patient Care (January 1991).

12. The American Medical Record Association has changed its name to the American Health Information Management Association, acknowledging the role of information management and the computerization of health records. HHS to Study National Computer Billing System, 46 Healthcare Fin. Mgmt. Ass'n. 7 (1992).

13. See generally, Lawrence O. Gostin, Joan Turek–Brezina, Madison Powers, and Rene Kozloff, Privacy and Security of Health Information in the Emerging Health Care System, 5 Health Matrix 1 (1995); Wendy E. Parmet, Public Health Protection and the Privacy of Medical Records, 16 Harv. C.R.–C.L. L.Rev. 265 (1981); Diane B. Lawrence, Strict Liability Computer Software and Medicine: Public Policy at the Crossroads, 23 Tort & Ins.L.J. 1 (1991).

14. See Hodge et al., supra n.1.

15. See generally, Benjamin Wright, Electronic Health Care Information—Record Keeping and Privacy Aspects (1993).

16. See generally, Frances H. Miller, Health Care Information Technology and Informed Consent: Computers and the Doctor-Patient Relationship, 31 Ind.L.Rev. 1019 (1998).

17. Health Privacy Working Group, Principles for Health Privacy (1999) (www.healthprivacy.org).

cy protections should follow the data, binding all subsequent recipients. Third, an individual should have the right to access his or her own health information and to supplement it. Fourth, individuals should be given notice about the use and disclosure of their information and their rights. Fifth, health care organizations should implement security safeguards for storage, use and disclosure of health information. Sixth, personally identifiable health information should not be disclosed without patient authorization except in limited circumstances. Seventh, health care organizations should establish policies and review procedures as to the collection, use and disclosure of such information. Eighth, such organizations should use an objective and balanced process to review the use and disclosure of personally identifiable health information for research. Ninth, such information should not be disclosed to law enforcement officials absent a warrant or court order. Tenth, protections should enhance existing laws prohibiting discrimination. Eleventh, effective remedies for violations of privacy protections should be established.

§ 4–37. Federal Standards for Privacy of Individually Identifiable Health Information

The Department of Health and Human Services (HHS) has proposed standards for protection of privacy of individual health information.[1] The Health Insurance Portability and Accountability Act[2] (HIPAA) required Congress to enact comprehensive legislation to protect electronic health data by August 21,1999, or if Congress failed to act, the Department of Health and Human Services(DHHS) must develop regulations. DHHS recommended that legislation to protect health information should adopt five principles: (1) boundaries: such information should be disclosed only for health purposes, with few exceptions allowed; (2) security: health information should not be distributed without patient authorization and recipients of such information must protect it; (3) consumer control: persons are entitled to access and amend their health records and to be told of purposes for which it is to be used or disclosed; (4) accountability: those improperly handling such information should be subject to criminal penalties and civil actions; (5) public responsibility: individual privacy interests must yield to national priorities in public health, prevention of health care fraud, medical research, and law enforcement.[3]

The proposed standards aim to provide "enhanced protections for individually identifiable health information."[4] The public is concerned about the use of sensitive health care information both by the health care system and also outside that system. State laws protect this information, but the protection is variable and has large gaps.[5] State laws have failed to keep up with advances

§ 4–37

1. Department of Health and Human Services, Proposed Rules, Standards for Privacy of Individually Identifiable Health Information, 45 CFR 160–165 (1999) (hereafter Privacy Standards).

2. Pub.L.No. 104–191, 110 Stat. 2033.

3. See generally James G.Hodge, The Intersection of Federal Health Information Privacy and State Administrative Law: The Protection of Individual Health Data and Workers' Compensation, 51 Adm.L. Rev. 117 (1999).

4. Summary, Privacy Standards.

5. See Health Privacy Project, The State of Health Privacy: An Uneven Terrain, Institute for Health Care Research and Policy, Georgetown University (July 1999) (http://www.healthprivacy.org).

in health care information technology.[6] The Standards continue to call for federal legislation, for several reasons. First, the HIPAA limits the application of the rules to health plans, health care clearinghouses, and any health care provider who transmits health information in electronic form. This does not include many entities who receive, use and disclose health care information outside of this system of protection. Second, HIPAA did not provide for enforcement authority such as a private right of action for individuals to sue.

Protected health information encompasses individual identifiable health information maintained or transmitted by covered entities which is in or has been in electronic form.[7] The rule applies to the information, not particular records. Protected information is defined to mean individually identifiable health information that is or has been electronically maintained or electronically transmitted by a covered entity, as well as such information when it takes other forms. The example given is that of protected information read from a computer screen and discussed orally, printed, photographed or otherwise duplicated.[8] Paper records are not be covered.[9] The goal of protection is "to define and limit the circumstances in which an individual's protected health information may be used or disclosed by others ... to make the use and exchange of protected health information relatively easy for health care purposes, and more difficult for purposes other than health care."[10] Information transactions[11] are defined to include health claims or other encounter information, health care payment and remittance advice, coordination of benefits, health claims status, enrollment and disenrollment, plan eligibility, premium payments, referral certification and authorization, first report of injury, health claims attachments, and other transactions as the Secretary of HHS adopts.

Covered entities are barred from using or disclosing health information except under the Rule's exceptions.[12] Such information can be used with individual authorization.[13] Such information could be used without authorization for treatment, payment, and health care operations.[14] For example, providers could refer to a medical record, disclose information to other providers as need to consult about diagnosis or treatment, and as part of referrals. Claims and payment are also disclosable.[15] Information could also be

---

6. Id., Executive Summary.

7. Health insurance is defined in § 1171(4) of the Act as "any information, whether oral or recorded in any form or medium, that is created or received by a health care provider, health plan, public health authority, employer, life insurer, school or university, or health care clearinghouse; and that relates to the past, present, or future physical or mental health or condition of an individual, the provision of health care to an individual, or the past, present, or future payment of the provision of health care to an individual."

8. Medical Standards at 46.

9. Medical Standards at 17.

10. Id.

11. Id., § 1173(a)(1).

12. "Health plan" is defined in § 1171 as "an individual plan or group health plan that provides, or pays the cost of, medical care."

This includes group health plans, health insurance issuers, health maintenance organizations, Part A or B of the Medicare program; Medicaid; Medicare supplemental policies, long term care policies, employer welfare benefit plans, health care programs for active military personnel, veterans health care programs, CHAMPUS, the Indian Health Service program, Federal Employees Health Insurance Benefits Program, state child health plans, Medicare Plus Choice organization, and any other individual plan or group health plan that provides or pays for the cost of health care.

13. Medical Standards Proposed § 164.508.

14. Id. at § 164.506(a). The terms "treatment", "payment", and "health care operations" are defined in proposed § 164.504.

15. Id. at p. 53.

used without authorization for public and public policy-related purposes, such as public health, research, health oversight, law enforcement, and use of coroners.[16] Covered entities could also use and disclose protected health information when required to do so, e.g., mandatory reporting under state law or pursuant to a search warrant. Protected information must be disclosed by entities only to (1) permit individuals to inspect and copy protected information about them[17] and (2) FOR enforcement of this rule.[18] The rules do not require a different level of protection depending on the sensitivity of the information, since the assumption is that all protected information should have effective protection from inappropriate use regardless of sensitivity.

The rule replaces pro forma authorization by individuals with regulatory protections, to create a sphere of privacy protection broader than that which presently exists. The preamble states that "[o]ur proposal is based on the principle that a combination of strict limits on how plans and providers can use and disclose identifiable health information, adequate notice to patients about how such information will be used, and patients' rights to inspect, copy and amend protected health information about them, will provide patients with better privacy protection and more effective control over the dissemination of their information than alternative approaches to patient protection and control."[19]

The Privacy Standards are based on a principle of "minimum necessary" in order to restrict the use of information to the minimum amount needed to accomplish the purpose for which it is used or disclosed, considering practical and technological limitations.[20] The rule proposes that individuals be able to request of a covered entity that protected health information is restricted from further use or disclosure for treatment, payment and health care operations. The entity does not have to agree to the restriction; but the rules would enforce any restrictions contractually agreed upon.[21]

Individual authorizations for use or disclosure of information must be voluntary, and may not be obtained as a condition of treatment or payment.

To implement these rules, institutions must appoint a privacy official, develop a training program, implement safeguard to protect privacy information from intentional or accidental misuse, provide a complaints system, and develop a system of sanctions for employees and business partners violating the procedures established.[22] The HIPAA authorizes the Secretary of HHS to impose civil monetary penalties up to $25,000 for each year for each provision violated. Criminal penalties are graduated, increasing if the offense is committed under false pretenses or with intent to sell the information or reap other gains.

16. Id. at proposed § 164.510. National priority items include: oversight of the health care system; public health functions; research; judicial and administrative proceedings; law enforcement; emergency circumstances; information to next-of-kin; identification of a deceased person; government health data systems; facility patient directories; banks to process health care payments and premiums; management of active duty military and other special classes; other laws that mandate disclosure.

17. § 164.514.

18. § 164.522.

19. Id. at 18.

20. Id., proposed § 164.596(a).

21. Id., proposed § 164.506(c).

22. Id., proposed § 164.518.

The proposed Standards have been criticized on several grounds. The major criticism is that doctors, hospitals, and plans could freely share patient information without consent so long as the purpose was treatment, payment and health care purposes generally. A physician in a hospital system could examine the records of patients with similar conditions without their consent, and he or she could also consult the records of people in the same family or household without approval to aid, for example, in diagnosing contagious conditions.[23] And patients would have no right to learn who had received access to their record without consent. A second criticism is that law enforcement officials could receive information based solely on an administrative subpoena which does not require judicial approval. Third, as noted in the Standards themselves, under HIPAA, patients may not be given the right to sue civilly for violations of their privacy rights.

§ 4–38. Conclusion

The obvious benefits of computerized record keeping have propelled medical records to a central position in health care delivery.[1] A standardized database of patient information has the potential to promote efficiency, further competition, and allow providers to better track patient outcomes. Only a computerized record, in spite of its confidentiality dimensions, can further such goals. The legal issues raised by such computerization are not unique, but the proliferation of access to such data through computers requires early attention to the implementation of the Privacy Standards, which provides safeguards to restrict access to such patient information. Standardized computer records will be the central feature in any future health care or health insurance system involving networks of providers and aggregated buyers of health care all operating under the mantle of increased efficiency and cost saving imperatives. Protecting patient privacy is essential to maintain confidence in the health care system.[2]

23. See Geri Aston, Cheers and Jeers Greeting Clinton's Privacy Proposal, 42 Am. Med. News 1, 29 (1999) (quoting Paul Appelbaum).

§ 4–38

1. Institute of Medicine, The Computer–Based Patient Record: An Essential Technology for Health Care (1997) (www.nap.edu/readingroom/.)

2. Janlori Goldman, Protecting Privacy to Improve Health Care, 17 Health Affairs 47 (1998).

Chapter 5

HEALTH CARE BUSINESS ASSOCIATIONS

Table of Sections

Research References

Am Jur 2d, Physicians, Surgeons, and Other Healers §§ 200–301
ALR Index: Extended Health Care Facility; Health Maintenance Organizations; Health Providers; Medical Service Organization
ALR Digest: Hospitals and Other Health Care Facilities § 7
Am Jur Legal Forms 2d, Arbitration and Award § 23:11; Physicians and Surgeons §§ 202:51–202:56

§ 5–1. Introduction

This chapter deals with the variety of organizational forms that health care enterprises may adopt. Each kind of business association carries with it a distinct body of law that affects such important aspects of the enterprise as liability, dissolution, governance and authority to bind the organization. In addition, the business form adopted may materially assist the enterprise in complying with other bodies of law affecting health care providers, such as fraud and abuse, tax exemption, certificate of need, antitrust, and professional licensing laws.

For the attorney advising health care clients, the selection of a business form is more of an art than a science. Often a complex, multivariate choice is presented in which achieving a client's goals in one area may entail accepting certain trade-offs and risks in others. Further, a hallmark of modern business law is the flexibility that statutory schemes now permit business organizations. Increasingly, entities may adapt "plain vanilla" statutory forms to meet their particular business needs or regulatory requirements. Thus, careful planning and counseling regarding the matrix of risks and benefits associated with the various possible business forms is required.

Below we discuss the principal forms of business associations commonly employed by health care enterprises: for-profit corporations, not-for-profit corporations, professional corporations, partnerships, limited liability companies and joint ventures.[1] Finally, we conclude with an analysis of the organizational forms commonly used in structuring modern healthcare enterprises.

---

§ 5–1

1. Not discussed herein is the sole proprietorship which lacks separate statutory treatment and is generally governed by common-law rules of agency, contract and property.

A. FOR–PROFIT CORPORATIONS

§ 5–2. Characteristics of the For–Profit Form

The corporation has emerged, principally during the last century, as the dominant form of business organization in the United States. In terms of aggregate volume of business transactions, corporations account for almost 90% of the nation's commerce and virtually all large business organizations have adopted the corporate form. The reasons for the enormous popularity of the corporate form are found in four fundamental characteristics the law imbues upon these artificial entities: limited liability, continuity of existence and transferability of ownership, centralized management, and separate legal existence.

Limited Liability for Investors

Subject to certain statutory and common-law limitations, investors are not liable for the obligations of the corporation. While shareholders' investments in the entity become assets of the corporation and thus are available for satisfying corporate debts and obligations, the personal assets of investors are protected from claims against the corporation. It may initially appear that the gains from limited liability are illusory because creditors will simply demand higher interest rates or extra security from corporations, thus reducing the net benefits of this feature of corporate existence. Nevertheless, by shifting risks to a better risk bearer, the form creates benefits. In effect, by giving up potential earnings, investors buy insurance against personal liability.[1] In addition, limited liability eliminates potentially enormous transaction costs that would be incurred if creditors had to check the credit worthiness of (or ultimately bring collection suits against) numerous, geographically-disbursed investors.[2]

Continuity of Existence and Transferability of Ownership

Corporate existence continues despite changes in the identity of those owning shares. Moreover, shareholders are free to transfer their full interests in shares during their lifetimes and ownership passes to their estates upon death. The principal benefits of these features are promotion of liquidity and the consequent spur to creating a market for corporate ownership. By lowering transaction costs and facilitating transfers, this characteristic of corporate existence encourages capital formation.[3] Indeed, the growth of the modern corporation is in large part attributable to the ready access to large amounts of investment capital that free transferability affords.

§ 5–2

1. See Robert Charles Clark, Corporate Law 8 (1986).

2. Id.; see also Frank H. Easterbrook & Daniel R. Fischel, The Economic Structure of Corporate Law (1991). Recent scholarship has questioned the efficiency gains from limited liability and argued for eliminating limited liability for the benefit of tort claimants. See e.g., Henry Hansmann & Reinier Kraakman, Toward Unlimited Shareholder Liability for Corporate Torts, 100 Yale L.J. 1879 (1991); cf. Frank H. Easterbrook & Daniel R. Fischel, Limited Liability and the Corporation, 52 U. Chi. L. Rev. 89 (1985).

3. For closely held corporations, however, the marketability of ownership interests may be promoted by permitting shareholders to agree to limit their freedom and consequently state statutes permit entities voluntarily to adopt certain restrictions on transferability.

Centralized Management

Corporate statutes centralize managerial power chiefly by granting to the board of directors ultimate power to manage the corporation. This feature encourages efficient specialization of functions among those involved in the business. Investors need not have expertise or the ability to manage the affairs of the corporation while managers need not have capital to invest. The formal link between ownership and governance in corporations is provided by statutory requirements that the board of directors be selected by shareholders and that certain actions require shareholder approval. The common law reinforces directors' obligations to shareholders by establishing fiduciary duties binding the board to serve exclusively the interests of the corporation. In most large corporations, however, both shareholders and directors play a relatively passive role and management as a practical matter is vested in officers and employees. Although officers and employees are at least nominally bound by fiduciary duties, agency law, and the direct supervision by those above them in the corporate organization, many feel these controls are ineffective. Thus, despite its other benefits, the separation of ownership from control may foster exploitation of shareholders. Academic commentary has long debated the extent to which corporate managers are free to pursue their own interests unconstrained by shareholder preferences. The "market for corporate control" is widely regarded as placing limits on the ability of slothful or corrupt managers to harm shareholder interests.[4]

Separate Legal Existence

For the most part, the law treats corporations as separate legal entities. Statutes confer on them powers to sue and be sued, to own property, and to have essentially the same powers as those possessed by individuals in conducting business. This feature produces efficiency benefits by reducing transaction costs and inefficiencies associated with carrying on businesses through agents. The corollary to this principle is that the principal obligations of persons working for the corporation are to maximize the wealth of the owners (the shareholders) and serve the interests of the corporation.

The characteristics discussed above that define corporate existence and explain the popularity of the corporate business form also serve to illuminate many of the basic problems that corporate law seeks to address. As Dean Clark's insightful analysis suggests, the fundamental tensions of corporate law derive from these characteristics.[5] Thus, one central issue involves the abuse of limited liability, i.e., the use of the corporate shield in ways that benefit certain groups unfairly while not furthering its basic purposes or functions. Secondly, abuse of free transferability of shares arises in a variety of settings in which securities are traded on the basis of false, fraudulent or inadequate information. A third recurring theme in corporate law concerns the abuse of managerial power, i.e., selfish use of centralized management

---

4. See Adolf A. Berle & Gardiner C. Means, The Modern Corporation and Private Property (rev. ed. 1967). For a variety of views on the effect of separation of ownership from control, see Michael C. Jensen & William H. Meckling, Theory of the Firm: Managerial Behavior, Agency Costs and Ownership Structure, 3 J. Fin. Econ. 305 (1976); Frank H. Easterbrook &

Daniel R. Fischel, The Economic Structure of Corporate Law (1991); Victor Brudney, Corporate Governance, Agency Costs and the Rhetoric of Contracts, 85 Colum. L. Rev. 1403 (1985).

5. Robert Charles Clark, Corporate Law 32–33.

authority by directors or managers who are careless, indolent or subject to conflicts of interest. Finally, treatment of the corporation as a separate legal entity poses a variety of thorny issues regarding the extent to which the corporation should possess basic rights associated with separate entities (such as freedom of speech) and whether limits should be placed upon the extent of the corporation's powers.

As noted, corporations are creatures of statute and every state has multiple corporate statutes (or sub-parts thereof) that deal with specialized corporate entities such as not-for-profit corporations, professional corporations, public corporations and closely-held corporations. One difficulty, discussed below, is that corporate law has generally failed to make meaningful distinctions along what is perhaps the most economically-significant axis: i.e., between close corporations and publicly traded corporations. Although many states have adopted close corporations statutes and the common law has sometimes observed the distinction, the law for the most part has treated these very different institutions under the same body of law.[6]

Close corporations (or "closely held corporations" as they are sometimes called) are those having only a small number of shareholders, whose shares are not publicly traded and which are usually of relatively small size. In health care, most professional corporations are closely held. It can be seen that in close corporations the four fundamental characteristics of corporate existence are usually not present or their effects are significantly diluted as economic relationships within such entities are more closely analogous to partnerships than they are to publicly traded corporations. For example, management in these entities usually remains in the hands of shareholders, who themselves are likely to be the principal directors, officers or employees of the corporation. Hence, ownership and control typically are not separated in close corporations. In addition, continuity of existence and transferability of shares may be quite limited, as the economic fortunes of closely held corporations are often intimately bound to the fortunes of its individual owners. Limited liability can also be illusory in the close corporation because creditors will often insist on personal guarantees from shareholders.[7]

§ 5–3. Formation of the Corporation

Although incorporation has been greatly simplified under most modern corporation statutes, close attention must be paid to the choice of the state of incorporation and a number of important details in that process. This selection may take on considerable significance because the law of the state of incorporation governs most issues concerning the internal affairs of the corporation and because the substantive laws of the states differ in many respects. The process of incorporating entails compliance with a number of requirements that vary considerably from state to state. Care must be taken

---

6. The leading commentary on the subject has aptly summarized the law's treatment of close corporations as follows:

> [T]he norms in the corporation statutes were designed largely to protect shareholders and investors in publicly held corporations where there is a separation of management from ownership and a very real danger to the investing public. In all probability, the legis-

latures in enacting these norms did not think of close corporations at all.

F. Hodge O'Neal & Robert B. Thompson, O'Neal's Close Corporations § 5.06, at 20 (3d ed. 1987).

7. See generally discussion of close corporations infra § 5–9.

to comply with the specific statutory requirements of the jurisdiction in which the corporation is being formed.

a. The Articles of Incorporation

The articles of incorporation, sometimes referred to as the "certificate of incorporation" or the "corporate charter," refers to the document required to be filed with the Secretary of State in order to form a corporation under state law. Although the various jurisdictions differ, most statutes require that the articles contain at a minimum the following information: the name of the corporation; the duration of the corporation's existence (which may be perpetual); the purposes of the corporation; the number of shares authorized to be issued and a specification of the rights and preferences of such shares; the number of directors and the names and addresses of the initial board of directors and each incorporator; and the addresses of the registered office of the corporation and its registered agent.[1]

Beyond assuring compliance with these relatively straightforward statutory directives, attention must be paid to a number of discretionary provisions that may be included in the articles of incorporation. Many state statutes provide that certain important aspects of corporate governance are subject to statutory rules only if the corporation elects to "opt in," or conversely that a statutory provision applies unless the corporation elects to "opt out." In most circumstances this election must be expressly stated in the articles of incorporation although in some instances inclusion in the bylaws is sufficient. In order to avoid application of the default provision in the statute, jurisdictions may require a specific election in the articles concerning the following issues of corporate governance: shareholders' preemptive rights to acquire new shares,[2] cumulative voting,[3] greater (or sometimes lesser) quorums for shareholder voting,[4] indemnification of directors,[5] and limitations on director liability for monetary damages for breaches of fiduciary duties.[6] In addition, most statutes allow corporations to impose certain restrictions regarding corporate governance if specifically adopted in the articles of incorporation or the bylaws.[7]

Although modern statutes permit the articles to designate a corporate purpose "to engage in any lawful business,"[8] some corporations elect to adopt a narrower purpose clause. This is usually done to assure investors that their

---

§ 5–3

1. See e.g., 805 Ill. Comp. Stat. Ann. 5/2.10; West's Fla. Stat. Ann. § 607.0202. The Revised Model Business Corporation Act ("RMBCA") simplifies many requirements regarding the articles by providing that every corporation has perpetual duration unless a shorter period is chosen (§ 3.02) and that the corporation's purpose is that of engaging in "any lawful business" unless a more limited purpose is set forth in the articles (§ 3.01(a)).

2. See e.g., RMBCA § 6.30; Vernon's Ann. Tex. Bus. Corp. Act art. 3.02.

3. See e.g., RMBCA § 7.28; 15 Pa. Cons. Stat. Ann. § 1106; Md. Code, Corporations & Ass'ns, § 2–104.

4. See e.g., RMBCA § 7.25; Ariz. Rev. Stat. § 10–032; Official Code Ga. Ann. § 14–2–727.

5. See e.g., RMBCA § 8.52; McKinney's— N.Y. Bus. Corp. Law § 723; West's Colo. Rev. Stat. Ann. § 7–3–101.5; West's Ann. Ind. Code § 23–1–37–9.

6. See e.g., Del. Code tit. 8, § 102(b)(7).

7. See e.g., RMBCA § 8.02 (corporation may prescribe qualifications for directors in articles or bylaws); RMBCA § 8.03 (specifying or fixing number of board members or permitting variable range of board members); RMBCA § 8.06 (articles may provide for staggered terms for directors).

8. See also RMBCA § 3.01 (corporation has purpose to engage in any lawful business unless a more limited purpose is specified).

capital will be devoted to a specified, limited range of business activities. A limited purpose clause may also serve to assure compliance with statutory regulations restricting the permissible scope of the entity's businesses (for example, statutes limiting the types of businesses professional corporations can engage in or requiring the corporation to specify professions it will engage in).[9]

As to the powers of the corporation, the statutes generally enumerate a broad list of specific powers that every corporation shall possess, but additional powers are also found in nonstatutory corporate law.[10] As a general matter, enumeration of powers in the articles may be a risky undertaking as it may give rise to an inference that unlisted powers were denied.[11]

b. The Ultra Vires Doctrine

Under early common law, transactions by a corporation that were beyond the purposes or powers of the corporation were deemed *"ultra vires"* and hence void under the rather formalistic view that the corporation lacked legal power to enter into the transaction. That approach was gradually eroded by a series of cases applying a variety of doctrines to avoid inequitable results, essentially making such actions voidable rather than void.[12] The most important developments in this area, however, have been statutory, as modern statutes limit the applicability of the doctrine to a narrow range of circumstances. Thus, most states now specifically provide that no corporate acts shall be invalid "on the ground that the corporation lacks or lacked power to act."[13] The only exceptions are for: suits by shareholders against corporations to enjoin *ultra vires* acts (often with the proviso that affected parties are present in the litigation and it is "equitable" to enjoin the act); proceedings against the corporation by officers or directors of the corporation; and proceedings by the state attorney general to dissolve the corporation or enjoin a corporate act.[14] In some circumstances, such as where the state statute is ambiguous or the corporation has not assumed the full range of corporate powers permitted by the statute, *ultra vires* issues have also been raised.

In regard to health care providers, the issue of *ultra vires* corporate action has arisen where hospitals have entered lines of business not embraced by the statement of purposes in their articles of incorporation. For example, an association of retail florists and a floral company claimed that a county hospital operating a gift and floral shop was acting *ultra vires*.[15] As competitors of the corporation, plaintiffs lacked standing; however, the court held that plaintiffs had standing as taxpayers to sue a public corporation under Alabama law. The statute under which the hospital board was originally

9. See infra § 5–22.

10. The Revised Model Act contains broad provisions not contained in most statutes. See e.g., RMBCA § 3.02 (corporation "has the same powers as an individual to do all things necessary and convenient to carry out its business and affairs"); RMBCA § 3.02(15) (powers to make certain donations and political contributions).

11. See Robert W. Hamilton, Corporations Including Partnerships & Limited Partnerships 201–202 (6th ed. 1998).

12. See e.g., Goodman v. Ladd Estate Co., 427 P.2d 102 (Or.1967) (doctrines of estoppel and unjust enrichment mitigate strict application of ultra vires doctrine); see generally Arthur R. Pinto & Douglas M. Branson, Understanding Corporate Law 15–16 (1999).

13. RMBCA § 3.04.

14. See e.g., RMBCA § 14.30; see also 711 Kings Highway Corp. v. F.I.M.'s Marine Repair Serv. Inc., 273 N.Y.S.2d 299 (N.Y.Sup.1966).

15. Alabama State Florists Ass'n v. Lee County Hosp. Bd., 479 So.2d 720 (Ala.1985).

incorporated authorized any and all acts "necessary and incidental to the operation, maintenance and improvement of the hospital." Relying in part on federal tax rulings finding floral and gift shops substantially related to the exempt purposes of nonprofit hospitals, the court concluded that the operation of the shop was not *ultra vires*. In a similar case, a nonprofit hospital corporation that created a separate corporation to provide laundry service for itself and other neighboring hospitals did not engage in an *ultra vires* act where its articles of incorporation empowered it to do all things "necessary, convenient, useful or incidental" to achieve the hospital's ultimate purpose.[16]

c. *Corporate Bylaws*

Most state statutes require that corporations adopt bylaws which constitute their formal rules of internal governance. Bylaws need not be filed with the Secretary of State and most states have no specific requirements regarding their content.[17] Depending on the jurisdiction, bylaws may be adopted by incorporators, the board of directors or, in certain cases, shareholders. Incorporators or initial directors typically adopt initial bylaws at the formation of the corporation. Usually either shareholders or directors may amend or repeal bylaws though sometimes this power must be specifically reserved to the shareholders in the articles of incorporation.[18] Valid bylaws have the force of law and are binding on corporate directors, officers and employees, although courts have recognized hospital bylaws adopted by "custom and acquiescence" without a formal meeting.[19] Where bylaws are inconsistent with the articles of incorporation, the articles control.

The Joint Commission on Accreditation of Healthcare Organizations (JCAHO) mandates that hospital bylaws include specific provisions concerning: the hospital's role and purpose; the responsibility and duties of board members and criteria and selection process for choosing them; organizational structure, including the authority of officers and committees of the board and other matters; requirements for establishment of a medical staff; the definition of "conflicts of interest;" and relationships between the board and others responsible for governance.[20] The JCAHO requires that hospitals also have a second set of bylaws, "medical staff bylaws," which must be adopted and approved by the medical staff and the board.

Likewise, the Medicare program imposes certain conditions that must be set forth in the medical staff bylaws, including a description of the organization of the medical staff, specifications of the privileges and duties in each

---

16. Arkansas Uniform & Linen Supply Co. v. Institutional Services Corp., 700 S.W.2d 358 (Ark.1985).

17. A few states mandate that certain information be included in the bylaws if not contained in the articles, see e.g., West's Ann. Cal. Corp. Code § 212; others list examples of information that may be included, see e.g., Minn. Stat. Ann. § 302A.181.

18. See e.g., West's Ann. Cal. Corp. Code § 211 (amendment by "outstanding shares" or by the board); cf. West's Ann. Ind. Code § 23–1–39–1 (by directors unless otherwise provided). The Revised Model Business Corporation Act permits the board to amend or repeal bylaws unless the articles reserve such power

exclusively to shareholders; but in any event shareholders may amend or repeal bylaws regardless of the board's power. RMBCA § 10.20.

19. In re Osteopathic Hosp. Ass'n of Delaware, 195 A.2d 759 (Del.1963); but cf. O'Leary v. Board of Directors, Howard Young Medical Ctr., Inc., 278 N.W.2d 217 (Wis.App.1979) (bylaws cannot be adopted by "custom and acquiescence" where bylaws and other indicia of corporate intent mandate formal meetings and adherence to specified procedures).

20. Joint Commission on Accreditation of Healthcare Organizations, Comprehensive Accreditation Manual for Hospitals: The Official Handbook GO–7 (1997).

category of the medical staff, standards for selection for membership on the medical staff, and rules governing specific medical requirements.[21]

d. Promoters, Pre–Incorporation Transactions and Defective Incorporation

Promoters are those persons who organize a variety of business relationships on behalf of the corporation prior to incorporation. These steps frequently involve entering into contracts with employees, investors, landlords and suppliers. Although the incorporation process has been greatly simplified, promoters nevertheless often make these commitments before the formal incorporation of the business. A frequently litigated issue has been whether the promoter of the subsequently-formed corporation should be liable on such contracts. As a general matter, promoters are personally liable for pre-incorporation contracts even after the corporation comes into existence unless evidence of a contrary intent is present.[22] The sometimes draconian effect of this doctrine may be avoided where promoters can demonstrate that a novation occurred and that the parties intended that the corporation adopt the obligation upon formation and discharge the promoter.[23] The general rule that the corporation is not automatically bound shields it from liability unless it explicitly or implicitly adopts the contracts or obligations of its promoters.[24]

Another important common law doctrine concerns the possibility of promoter liability where the parties to a contract mistakenly believe a corporation to have been formed. Courts responded to the harsh result of holding promoters liable in such circumstances with the *"de facto* corporation*"* doctrine, which provides that where a good faith attempt to incorporate was made and there was actual use of the corporate form, *de jure* corporation status would be attributed to the corporation except as against challenges by the state. However, many states have abolished the *de facto* corporation doctrine; in these jurisdictions only actual incorporation (evidenced by simply filing the articles with the Secretary of State) will establish of corporate existence.[25]

For health care institutions, failure to comply with regulatory requirements will not necessarily deny them corporate existence as long as proper incorporation procedures have been undertaken. Where, for example, a professional corporation failed to obtain a certificate of registration from a state medical licensing board and had not met minimum paid-in capital under state corporate law, the court nevertheless found that a valid medical corporation existed because the entity had received its certificate of incorporation from the state.[26] The court interpreted the other statutory provisions as establishing conditions of doing business and not inconsistent with valid incorporation.

21. See 42 C.F.R. § 482.22(c); see also id. at § 482.22(c)(5) (bylaws must require physical examinations for certain patients admitted to the hospital).

22. Quaker Hill, Inc. v. Parr, 364 P.2d 1056 (Colo.1961); Medical Management Resources, Inc. v. Waxman, 1987 WL 4733 (E.D.Pa.1987) (cardiologist entering into pre-incorporation contract personally liable where both sides were aware he was contracting on behalf of a corporation to be formed) (dictum). See generally Restatement (Second) of Agency § 326.

23. Medical Management Resources Inc. v. Waxman, 1987 WL 4733 (E.D.Pa.1987) (post-incorporation renewal of contract by corporation would probably bar further promoter liability) (dictum).

24. McArthur v. Times Printing Co., 51 N.W. 216 (Minn.1982).

25. See. e.g., Robertson v. Levy, 197 A.2d 443 (D.C.App.1964).

26. Birt v. St. Mary Mercy Hosp. of Gary, Inc., 370 N.E.2d 379 (Ind.App.1977).

§ 5–4. Disregarding the Corporate Entity

a. *The Doctrine of "Piercing the Corporate Veil"*

As noted earlier, one of the fundamental attributes of corporate existence is that the corporation is looked upon as a distinct legal entity with the corollary tenet that shareholders are shielded from personal liability for corporate obligations. Nevertheless, courts sometimes apply common law principles to "pierce the corporate veil" and hold shareholders personally liable for corporate debts or obligations. Unfortunately, despite the enormous volume of litigation in this area, the case law fails to articulate any sensible rationale or policy that explains when corporate existence should be disregarded. Indeed, courts are remarkably prone to rely on labels or characterizations of relationships (such as "alter ego," "instrumentality," or "sham") and the decisions offer little in the way of predictability or rational explanation of why enumerated factors should be decisive.

Courts invoking the piercing doctrine frequently cite the venerable principle that the corporate legal entity may not be used "to defeat the public convenience, justify wrong, protect fraud or defend crime."[1] Factors relevant to applying this rather elastic precept are numerous and not entirely consistent. According to an empirical study of veil-piercing cases, the following were the factors most frequently mentioned by the courts: domination and control by the shareholder of the corporate entity; common officers and directors between corporate shareholders and corporate subsidiaries; lack of substantive separation between the entities; undercapitalization of the corporation; failure to follow corporate formalities; and misrepresentation by the corporate entity.[2] Other circumstances are also often cited as explaining veil piercing jurisprudence. For example, it is commonly believed that courts are less likely to disregard the corporate entity for plaintiffs whose dealings with the corporation are voluntary, such as contract creditors. Such creditors, it is argued, can anticipate risks and bargain for personal guarantees or higher prices or interest rates in their dealings with the corporation.[3]

Veil piercing is reserved almost exclusively for close corporations and corporate groups (i.e., corporate entities owning other corporations). Courts rarely, if ever, pierce publicly traded entities to reach shareholders, unless the shareholder is another corporation. Courts are more likely to disregard the corporate entity when liability is directed at sibling corporations, but are less inclined to do so when the plaintiff seeks to get to a subsidiary by disregarding a parent corporation.[4]

Finally, an important factor in veil piercing cases is the legal or regulatory setting in which claims arise. Piercing often takes place in the context of

---

§ 5–4

1. United States v. Milwaukee Refrigerator Transit Co., 142 Fed. 247, 255 (C.C.Wis.1905).

2. Robert B. Thompson, Piercing the Corporate Veil: An Empirical Study, 76 Cornell L. Rev. 1036, 1063 (1991); see also Laya v. Erin Homes, Inc., 352 S.E.2d 93 (W.Va.1986) (listing 19 factors considered by courts in determining whether to pierce the corporate veil).

3. See, e.g., Arthur R. Pinto & Douglas M. Branson, Understanding Corporate Law 49–50

(1999). Somewhat surprisingly, however, empirical research suggests that courts pierce the corporate veil more frequently in contract cases than tort cases. Robert B. Thompson, Piercing the Corporate Veil: An Empirical Study, 76 Cornell L. Rev. 1036, 1068–70 (1991). On the efficiency benefits of limited liability for corporations see supra § 5–2 n.2.

4. Robert B. Thompson, Piercing the Corporate Veil: An Empirical Study, 76 Cornell L. Rev. 1036, 1056–57 (1991).

regulatory or statutory policies such as tax law, workers' compensation or Medicare regulations. Courts appear to look to whether piercing helps accomplish the goals of these statutes more than any other factor in determining whether to disregard separate corporate existence. Although not all statutory policies give rise to equal enthusiasm for piercing, as a general matter, courts appear to be more willing to pierce the corporate veil to enforce clear statutory policies.[5]

b. Veil Piercing in the Health Care Industry

Courts have addressed attempts to disregard the corporate entity in the health care industry in a number of contexts. Neither the fact that health care services are being provided nor that providers render care through complex corporate structures will by itself support piercing the corporate veil. However, where recognition of the corporate entity interferes with clearly articulated public policy, courts are more willing to find liability on the part of shareholders.

The separate corporate status of a subsidiary hospital will normally shield the corporate parent from liability even where the parent shares officers, pays salaries of some employees, and has some management control over the affairs of the subsidiary.[6] In cases involving hospital systems with multiple corporate entities, courts are usually reluctant to pierce the corporate veil even where the parent exercises extensive control over the subsidiary and its name is prominently displayed in the advertising, signs and literature of the subsidiary hospital.[7] By the same token, courts have refused to recognize defensive use of piercing, holding entities liable for the obligations attaching to corporate status where traditional piercing factors are absent.[8] In addition, physician-shareholders practicing medicine in legitimate professional corporations or under employment contracts with health care institutions have avoided personal liability for contracts and negligence where the corporate entity followed corporate formalities and did not mislead or defraud third parties.[9]

In most jurisdictions, the fact that a health care entity is "thinly" capitalized will not by itself allow voluntary creditors to pierce the corporate veil. Evidence of fraud or injustice resulting from recognition of the corporate entity is usually required.[10] In cases involving other traditional piercing

---

5. Professor Thompson's analysis suggests that although courts are less willing to pierce in the context of certain statutes such as federal income tax and workers' compensation laws, they pierce more readily in other contexts, including situations involving the Medicare statute. Id. at 1060–62 (piercing in four of seven Medicare cases, compared to an overall rate of 40% for all statute-related cases). See infra § 5–4(b). See also Robert Charles Clark, Corporate Law 91–92 (1986).

6. See e.g., Boafo v. Hospital Corp. of Am., 338 S.E.2d 477 (Ga.App.1985).

7. See, e.g., Humana, Inc. v. Kissun, 221 Ga.App. 64, 471 S.E.2d 514 (1996), reversed on other grounds 479 S.E.2d 751 (1997) (traditional agency principles may create liability where there are insufficient grounds to pierce); see also Ritter v. BJC Barnes Jewish Christian

Health Systems, 987 S.W.2d (Mo. App. E.D. 1999) (refusing to hold parent entity liable on agency, veil-piercing, vicarious liability or apparent authority theories despite extensive control over subsidiary hospital's operations).

8. Associated Hosp. Services, Inc. v. State, 588 So.2d 356 (La.1991) (state not required to disregard separate corporate identity of hospital service corporation owned by hospital members in assessing state sales tax on transactions between members and the corporation).

9. See Ize Nantan Bagowa, Ltd. v. Scalia, 577 P.2d 725 (Ariz.App.1978).

10. See North Arlington Medical Bldg., Inc. v. Sanchez Constr. Co., 471 P.2d 240 (Nev. 1970); United States v. Healthwin–Midtown Convalescent Hosp. & Rehabilitation Ctr., Inc., 511 F.Supp. 416 (C.D.Cal.1981), affirmed 685 F.2d 448 (9th Cir.1982).

factors such as failure to observe corporate formalities and commingling corporate and non-corporate assets or business affairs, courts have been reluctant to pierce absent manifest injustice or outright fraud. A representative case is *Ize Nantan Bagowa, Ltd. v. Scalia,*[11] in which a physician employed by a corporation providing emergency room care to hospitals was unable to pierce the corporate veil to recover her salary and severance pay. The court refused to allow the plaintiff to reach the personal assets of a shareholder despite his having transferred assets out of the corporation and created a second, separate corporation to operate a family practice clinic. It emphasized the absence of proof that the incorporation of the clinic was designed to defraud plaintiff and the fact that the corporation's insolvency resulted from its inability to successfully bid for renewal of its hospital contracts.[12]

Cases involving government claims against providers who were overpaid by the Medicare and Medicaid programs illustrate the importance attributed to statutory policy in certain veil-piercing cases. In a leading case, *United States v. Pisani,*[13] the government sought to recover Medicare overpayments made to a corporation owned by a single physician/shareholder. The Third Circuit pierced the corporate veil, holding the physician personally liable despite the absence of fraud. Although some of the traditional factors militating in favor of disregard of the corporate entity were also present, the court stressed the clear legislative purpose embodied in the Medicare law that providers may only be reimbursed for the reasonable costs of their services. This purpose would be easily circumvented if providers could freely submit inflated cost reports, pocket the money through distributions or repayment of loans from a corporation and avoid personal liability. In other cases, courts have pierced the corporate veil despite the absence of any traditional factors where failure to do so would allow providers to avoid the strong statutory objective of preventing abuse of the Medicare and Medicaid program.[14]

§ 5–5. Corporate Fiduciary Duties

Corporate law imposes fiduciary duties upon those who govern corporations, namely directors, officers and controlling shareholders. The purpose of these duties is to ameliorate the inefficiencies and inequities resulting from the separation of ownership and management in the corporate enterprise. Despite the benefits flowing from specialization, risks of managerial sloth, opportunism and negligence occur whenever corporate officers and directors have small personal stakes in the financial success of the corporation and are not adequately policed by the mechanisms of "corporate democracy" such as shareholder voting or by the market for corporate control. For these reasons, corporate fiduciary duties obligate directors, officers and others to act in the best interests of the corporation. However, in interpreting these duties, courts have been acutely sensitive to dangers inherent in judicial interference with

---

11. 577 P.2d 725 (Ariz.App.1978).

12. Id. at 729. See also First Downtown Dev. v. Cimochowski, 613 So.2d 671 (La.App.), writ denied 615 So.2d 340 (La.1993) (declining to pierce the corporate veil where sole shareholder's failure to disclose his intentional breach of contract was not fraud).

13. 646 F.2d 83 (3d Cir.1981).

14. United States v. Normandy House Nursing Home, Inc., 428 F.Supp. 421 (D.Mass. 1977); see also United States v. Arrow Medical Equip. Co., 1990 WL 210601 (E.D.Pa.1990).

managerial discretion and have been extremely reluctant to second-guess business judgments. Traditionally, the law has held that the fiduciary duties of officers and directors embrace two basic obligations: a duty of care and a duty of loyalty.

§ 5–6.　The Duty of Care

a.　*The Traditional Formulation of the Doctrine*

The duty of care sets forth a standard of diligence and competence for officers and directors in performing their functions of managing the corporation's affairs. It expresses a generalized obligation to exercise proper care and to act in good faith and after sufficient investigation when exercising managerial responsibilities. For directors, failure to meet the standard can mean personal liability for the entire amount of the damages sustained by the corporation.[1]

The majority of states have codified the standard of care for directors of corporations; these statutes are generally consistent with the language of both the old and revised model acts, which in turn are consistent with formulations established under common law. Typically, these statutes require that directors perform their functions [1] in good faith, [2] in a manner they reasonably believe to be in the best interest of the corporation, and [3] with the care an ordinarily prudent person in a like position would exercise under similar circumstances.[2]

b.　*The Business Judgment Rule*

The duty of care articulated in statutory and common law bears little relation to the actual standard against which director conduct is measured. Application of the common law business judgment rule—a rebuttable presumption that in performing their duties directors are acting honestly and rationally and that their decisions are informed—has operated to bar findings of liability for directors where their activities seem to violate the negligence standard of the traditional formulation. According to some commentary, the effect of the business judgment rule has been to establish a process-oriented due care test. As long as the director acts in good faith, with due care to inform herself of the facts relevant to the decision, she will not be found liable even if the decision would not meet the standard of the "ordinarily prudent person."[3]

The practical result has been that liability for damages under the duty of care has rarely been found and then usually only where some suggestion of self-dealing has been present.[4] Thus, although the statutory standard may

---

§ 5–6

1. See Smith v. Van Gorkom, 488 A.2d 858 (Del.1985).

2. See e.g., RMBCA § 8.30(a); Del. Code tit. 8, § 145; McKinney's—N.Y. Bus. Corp. Law § 71; ALI, Principals of Corporate Governance § 4.01(a) (adopting standards essentially identical to RMBCA). The formulation derives from Selheimer v. Manganese Corp. of Am., 224 A.2d 634 (Pa.1966). See also Aronson v. Lewis, 473 A.2d 805 (Del.1984). See generally Litwin v. Allen, 25 N.Y.S.2d 667 (N.Y.Sup.1940).

3. See Charles Hansen, The ALI Corporate Governance Project: Of the Duty of Due Care and the Business Judgment Rule, A Commentary, 41 Bus. Law. 1237 (1986); see generally, Robert W. Hamilton, Corporations Including Partnerships & Limited Partnerships (6th ed. 1998).

4. See Joy v. North, 692 F.2d 880, 885 (2d Cir.1982), cert. denied 460 U.S. 1051, 103 S.Ct. 1498, 75 L.Ed.2d 930 (1983) ("While it is often stated that corporate directors and officers will be liable for negligence in carrying out their

seem to imply a simple negligence standard, no cases hold officers or directors liable for such failures. Several states have enunciated other formulations such as gross negligence[5] or have required proof of fraud or *ultra vires* actions.[6] Finally, despite the apparent leniency which courts apply in interpreting the duty, a large number of states have passed laws allowing shareholders to elect to eliminate or limit the liability of directors for breaches of the duty of care by so providing in the corporation's articles of incorporation.[7]

c. The Duty to Make Informed Judgments

The business judgment rule does not apply to uninformed decisions. In an important decision, *Smith v. Van Gorkom*,[8] the Delaware Supreme Court held directors personally liable for business judgments that the court concluded were the result of uninformed decisions. The court applied a standard of gross negligence to the conduct of inattentive directors reviewing a takeover bid for their company. It found that board members had breached their duty to make an informed decision by failing to inquire about the role of the company's president in forcing the company's sale, failing to question the basis for the negotiated price and arriving at their decision in a hurried manner.

d. Supervisory Responsibilities

Most state statutes explicitly permit directors to reasonably rely on information presented by officers, legal counsel and others to whom they delegate responsibility.[9] This protection is limited by the qualification that directors are not acting in good faith if they have knowledge concerning the matters in question such that reliance on others is unwarranted.[10] Thus, as an example, it has been suggested that a hospital director who relies upon facially erroneous submissions by management or advocates a course of action as an accommodation to a personal friend runs afoul of the duty of care standard.[11]

Although the general duty of care would seem to imply a corresponding duty to take adequate steps to supervise management, some courts have been remarkably reluctant to sanction directors for mere inattention to the activities of officers. For example, in one Delaware case, the court invoked the business judgment rule to shield directors who failed to detect antitrust violations by executives even though the board had not undertaken any meaningful monitoring of the affairs of lower level corporate employees.[12] The extreme passivity contemplated for directors with regard to oversight by this case, however, may not reflect either the prevalent legal standard or good

corporate duties all seem agreed that such a statement is misleading * * * [corporate officers and directors are] rarely, if ever * * * found liable for damages."). See generally Robert Charles Clark, Corporate Law 123–36 (1986).

5. See Aronson v. Lewis, 473 A.2d 805 (Del. 1984).

6. See Gearhart Indus., Inc. v. Smith Int'l, Inc., 741 F.2d 707, 721 (5th Cir.1984) (applying Texas law).

7. See, e.g., Del. Corp. L. 8, § 102(b)(7); RMBCA § 2.02(b)(4). See also infra § 5–8.

8. 488 A.2d 858 (Del.1985).

9. See, e.g., Ala. Code § 10–2A–73; West's Ann. Cal. Corp. Code 5309; see also RMBCA § 8.30(b).

10. See RMBCA § 8.30(c).

11. Robert J. Burdett, Director Liability: A Guide to Preventing Trouble in the Hospital Boardroom 30–36 (1991).

12. Graham v. Allis–Chalmers Mfg. Co., 188 A.2d 125 (Del.1963) (Board has "no duty to install and operate a corporate system * * * to ferret out wrong doing.").

business practice.[13] Indeed, in the case of *In Re Caremark International, Inc., Derivative Litigation*,[14] Delaware seems to have narrowed the leeway suggested by earlier cases. In approving a settlement of a shareholder derivative suit against a corporation that had paid over $250 million in fines and damages for violations of the fraud and abuse laws, the Chancellor found that directors have a responsibility to assure that adequate methods exist for reporting and monitoring compliance with statutes and regulations. A "sustained or systemic failure of the board to exercise oversight" may indicate an absence of good faith and breach of the duty of care, although the court acknowledged the standard for liability was "quite high" and specifics may be governed by business judgment rule principles.[15] On the facts before it, the court suggested that the corporation's efforts to comply with antikickback laws and assure compliance with its policies did not amount to such a failure.

Where management engages in outright fraud and the facts suggest that directors have breached the standard of gross negligence in failing to detect misappropriation of corporate funds, director liability has been imposed.[16] Even where such failure to supervise constitutes a breach of the duty of care, however, the court must further find that the negligent supervision was a proximate cause of the loss to the corporation.[17]

e. The Duty of Care in Health Care Corporations

There are relatively few cases applying the duty of care in the health care context. Nevertheless, it is clear that directors of hospitals assume no lesser fiduciary burdens than directors of any other corporation.[18] Thus, a hospital director may not bargain away his duties or accept the position of director as a "dummy" or accommodation to another person.[19] In addition, in the leading case of *Stern v. Lucy Webb Hayes National Training School for Deaconesses and Missionaries*, the district court imposed liability on trustees of a not-for-profit hospital who failed to use diligence in supervising and inquiring into the actions of those making financial decisions on behalf of the hospital and who failed to perform their fiduciary duties to act in good faith to oversee the hospital's financial affairs.[20]

In most decided cases, however, the business judgment rule has protected good faith judgments by boards of directors. For example, retroactive bonus payments to members of a hospital medical staff were found not to constitute a violation of board members' fiduciary duties where the payments bore some reasonable relation to the value of services rendered in the past.[21] Likewise, it is clear that the business judgment rule will protect managers and directors

13. See ALI, Principles of Corporate Governance § 4.01, at 217–18 ("the corporate director should be concerned that the corporation has a program looking toward compliance" with applicable laws and that "maintains procedures for monitoring such compliance.").

14. 698 A.2d 959 (Del.Ch.1996).

15. Id. at 971.

16. See Francis v. United Jersey Bank, 432 A.2d 814 (N.J.1981).

17. Id.

18. Ray v. Homewood Hosp., 27 N.W.2d 409 (Minn.1947); Stern v. Lucy Webb Hayes Nat'l Training School for Deaconesses & Missionaries, 381 F.Supp. 1003 (D.D.C.1974). See also discussion of fiduciary duties of directors of nonprofit corporations infra § 5–14.

19. Ray v. Homewood Hosp., 27 N.W.2d 409 (Minn.1947).

20. Stern v. Lucy Webb Hayes Nat'l Training School for Deaconesses & Missionaries, 381 F.Supp. 1003 (D.D.C.1974); see §§ 5–14–5–15, infra.

21. Beard v. Achenbach Memorial Hosp. Ass'n, 170 F.2d 859 (10th Cir.1948).

who commit honest errors or make mistakes in judgment involving everyday commercial matters even though the errors may be so gross as to demonstrate the unfitness of the individual to manage the corporation's affairs.[22]

It is at least arguable that the duty of care for directors of hospitals and other health care institutions should encompass somewhat broader responsibilities than those imposed on most business directors, given the heightened obligations imposed by licensure, accreditation and regulatory requirements.[23] The conventional formulation of the duty of care—whether a director has acted "with the care of ordinarily prudent persons in a like position and under similar circumstances"—suggests that courts should consider public interest responsibilities embraced by these regulations.[24] While this approach implies a somewhat higher standard of care than that applied to directors of ordinary commercial enterprises, the business judgment rule would still safeguard most actions of hospital directors. As discussed below, the case for elevated fiduciary standards is even stronger for directors of non-for-profit entities.

§ 5–7. The Duty of Loyalty

The fiduciary duty of loyalty (sometimes called a duty of "fair dealing")[1] holds that directors and officers must act in a manner that promotes the welfare of the corporation and not their own individual interests. The law's fundamental concern here rests with the potential harms arising from transactions involving conflicts of interest. The common law applies closer scrutiny to these transactions than it does to negligent behavior examined under the duty of care and the business judgment rule affords no protection in duty of loyalty cases.

At the same time, the cases recognize that self-interested transactions are sometimes beneficial (and indeed may be essential) to the welfare of the corporation. Therefore, both statutory and common law principles countenance certain self-dealing and related transactions when they are "fair" to the corporation. We discuss below the kinds of transactions that have been scrutinized under the duty of loyalty and related principles.

a. Self-Dealing

Transactions involving "self-dealing" involve the most fundamental conflict of interest. The classic case involves a director acting in his management

22. Para–Medical Leasing, Inc. v. Hangen, 739 P.2d 717 (Wash.App.1987); Nursing Home Bldg. Corp. v. DeHart, 535 P.2d 137 (Wash. App.1975).

23. For example, the JCAHO defines the responsibilities of the governing board to include responsibility "for establishing policy, maintaining quality patient care, and providing for institutional management and planning." Joint Commission on Accreditation of Healthcare Organizations, Accreditation Manual for Hospitals, G.B. 1.1 et seq. Likewise, state licensure provisions typically require governing boards to exercise control over the operations and management of a hospital. See e.g., West's Ann. Ind. Code § 16–21–2–5; Iowa Code Ann. § 135B.11.

24. Historically, somewhat higher fiduciary standards have been applied to certain businesses, such as banking. See Litwin v. Allen, 25 N.Y.S.2d 667 (N.Y.Sup.1940); see also Bates v. Dresser, 251 U.S. 524, 530–31, 40 S.Ct. 247, 249–50, 64 L.Ed. 388 (1920).

§ 5–7

1. The ALI employs the "duty of fair dealing" terminology to include the obligation of directors and officers under the duty of loyalty, ALI, Principles of Corporate Governance §§ 5.06–5.09, the fiduciary duties of controlling shareholders, §§ 5.10–5.14, and duties involving transfer of control in which a director or officer is interested, §§ 5.15–5.16.

capacity and on behalf of the corporation, who engages in a transaction in which he (or another entity in which he has a strong personal or financial interest) is on the other side of the transaction. Although the concepts of "self-dealing" or "conflict of interest" are rarely defined in the statutes, the case law has applied self-dealing analysis to situations in which (1) a director engages in a transaction in which he deals directly with the corporation of which he is a director (e.g., an entity owned or controlled by the director, or in which he has a significant financial interest, transacts business with the corporation of which he is a director) or (2) a director has an indirect interest creating the conflict (e.g., his immediate family has a strong financial interest in, or the director is on the board of an entity dealing with, the director's corporation).[2]

Although early common law treated such transactions as automatically voidable at the election of the corporation without regard to fairness, modern statutes follow the rule that conflict of interest transactions are not voidable "solely" because of a conflict of interest if any one of three requirements are met: (1) the transaction is ratified or approved by the board of directors (or committee thereof) after full disclosure and without participation of interested directors; (2) the transaction is ratified or approved by the shareholders (excluding participation of shares owned or controlled by interested directors); or (3) the transaction is fair to the corporation.[3] Importantly, these statutes do not validate all transactions meeting one or more of these requirements; instead, they simply remove the impediment of automatic voidability arising from the conflict of interest position of a director.[4]

Where disinterested approvals are not possible, a searching "intrinsic fairness" test is applied. As the Delaware Supreme Court recently characterized the inquiry, "interested directors bear the burden of proving the entire fairness of the transaction in all its aspects, including both the fairness of the price and the fairness of the directors' dealings."[5] A self-interested transaction found to be fair to the corporation, even though it has not received shareholder or director approval (or that has been approved by interested directors), will thus not constitute a violation of the duty of loyalty. On the other hand, conflict of interest transactions approved by disinterested directors might still not be allowed to stand if the court determines they are not fair to the corporation, although a more lenient level of scrutiny may apply.[6]

A few decisions have examined self-dealing involving health care institu-

2. The RMBCA adopted a detailed and complex codification of the conflict of interest problem in Subchapter F. RMBCA §§ 8.61–8.63.

3. See, e.g., Delaware Code tit. 8, § 144; N.C. Gen. Stat. § 55–8–31; S.C. Code § 33–8–310; Ohio Rev. Code § 1701.60.

4. See Official Comment to § 8.31 of RMBCA.

5. Oberly v. Kirby, 592 A.2d 445, 469 (Del. 1991); see also Weinberger v. UOP, Inc., 457 A.2d 701 (Del.1983).

6. See ALI, Principles of Corporate Governance § 5.01 (summarizing the modern view that "if transactions are fair, they will be al-

lowed to stand, even in the absence of approval by disinterested directors, and if transactions are approved by disinterested directors under fair procedures, they will normally be subjected to a much lighter level of scrutiny"). The standard for transactions approved by neutral entities in Delaware may be even more lenient. See Oberly v. Kirby, 592 A.2d 445 (Del.1991)(transactions receiving disinterested approvals scrutinized under the business judgment rule); see also Rosenblatt v. Getty Oil Co., 493 A.2d 929 (Del.1985); Puma v. Marriott, 283 A.2d 693 (Del.Ch.1971).

tions. In *Gilbert v. McLeod Infirmary*,[7] the court voided a sale of land by a hospital to one of its director, finding the director had failed to establish that the price was fair to the corporation. In *Stern v. Lucy Webb Hayes National Training School for Deaconesses and Missionaries*,[8] the district court condemned self-dealing by interested hospital trustees who had participated in the hospital's decisions regarding an investment contract, the deposit of funds in non-interest bearing accounts and other financial matters. Although applying these principles in the context of nonprofit corporations,[9] these cases for the most part apply conventional corporate self-dealing analysis. Thus, corporate board members would be well-advised to fully disclose conflict of interest transactions and seek approvals from disinterested directors or shareholders with all conflicted directors not participating.[10] It should be remembered, however, that disinterested approvals do not necessarily guarantee that self-dealing will pass judicial scrutiny. Hence transactions should be "fair" to the corporation, evidenced by full disclosure of material information and objective appraisals.

b. *Corporate Opportunities*

The corporate opportunity doctrine refers to the fiduciary obligation of directors to refrain from profiting from business opportunities that belong to the corporation. Courts may hold directors who usurp corporate opportunities without consent of the corporation liable for all profits they realize from the stolen business or for the lost profits of the corporation. In some cases, courts have imposed a constructive trust on the purloined business. The central issue of what constitutes a "corporate opportunity" varies among the jurisdictions. The narrowest conception embraces those areas in which the corporation has an interest or an expectancy arising out of an existing right.[11] A growing number of jurisdictions have adopted an alternative formulation, the so-called "line of business" test, which attempts to evaluate the proximity of the new business opportunity to the businesses in which the corporation is already engaged. A third approach combines the "line of business" test with an assessment of the fairness under the circumstances of allowing the interested officer or director to take personal advantage of the opportunity.[12]

Although not entirely a distinct step analytically, courts next ask the closely-related question of whether the opportunity may be taken by the corporate insider. It is well-established that directors may take advantage of the opportunity if the corporation elects not to act on the opportunity itself[13] and that the corporation may ratify the usurpation of a corporate opportunity in certain circumstances. However, courts are split as to whether directors and officers may seize a corporate opportunity simply on the basis that the corporation is financially unable to undertake the opportunity.[14] The case law

7. 64 S.E.2d 524 (S.C.1951).

8. 381 F.Supp. 1003 (D.D.C.1974).

9. See infra § 5–16.

10. See Robert J. Burdett, Jr., Director Liability: A Guide to Preventing Trouble in the Hospital Boardroom 99–101 (1991) (recommending adoption of a written conflict of interest policy, inclusion of the policy in corporate bylaws, use of routine, periodic disclosure questionnaires and other steps to avoid conflict of interest challenges).

11. See Burg v. Horn, 380 F.2d 897 (2d Cir.1967).

12. See Miller v. Miller, 222 N.W.2d 71 (Minn.1974).

13. See Zidell v. Zidell, Inc., 560 P.2d 1086 (Or.1977).

14. Compare A.C. Petters Co. v. St. Cloud Enters., Inc., 222 N.W.2d 83 (Minn.1974), with Klinicki v. Lundgren, 695 P.2d 906 (Or.1985).

is also less than clear as to the circumstances permitting appropriation of corporate opportunities.[15]

The corporate opportunity doctrine was applied in the health care context in *Quinn v. Cardiovascular Physicians, P.C.*[16] In that case, two of the three physician-shareholders of a professional corporation terminated the entity's business activities and transferred its assets to a second corporation. The Supreme Court of Georgia held that the third shareholder, who was left out of the newly-formed corporation, might have a reasonable expectation that the first corporation's contract to perform cardiology services at a hospital would continue or be renewed. Moreover, the court refused to find that no corporate opportunity existed because the first corporation was unable to exploit the opportunity in view of the actions of the two physicians. A question of fact existed as to whether the claimed inability was "nothing more than the result of the refusal by [the two shareholders] to perform medical services on behalf of the first corporation."[17] The remedy in corporate opportunity cases is to deny the wrongdoers the fruits of their actions. For example, an Illinois court imposed a constructive trust upon a corporation set up by a physician to compete with another professional corporation of which he was an officer.[18]

c. Loans to Directors

Most jurisdictions take a stricter stance against corporate loans to directors than other interested transactions. For example, several states flatly prohibit all such transactions.[19] Others, including the Revised Model Business Corporation Act, require approvals from shareholders or directors and that the loan benefits the corporation.[20] The apparent rationale for stricter treatment of loans than other self-dealing transactions is the difficulty in detecting unfair transactions and the uncertainty of the value of the director's promise.

d. Fairness Obligations of Controlling Shareholders and Oppression of Minority Shareholders

In addition to officers and directors, controlling shareholders owe fiduciary duties to the corporation and to its shareholders. Minority shareholders are at risk of being injured by a variety of transactions such as the issuance of new shares, share repurchases, transactions between parent corporations and partially-owned subsidiaries, and a variety of others. The obligation of majority shareholders is usually characterized in terms of "fairness" or "intrinsic fairness" to minority interests.[21] The case law generally places the burden on

15. See ALI, Principles of Corporate Governance § 5.05 at 400–401. The commentary has pointed out that the law has generally failed to take into account important dissimilarities between closely held corporations and publicly traded corporations, especially the vastly different motivations and roles of directors in the two kinds of entities. See e.g., Robert Charles Clark, Corporate Law 242–43 (1986). See also Pat K. Chew, Competing Interests in the Corporate Opportunity Doctrine, 67 N.C. L. Rev. 435 (1989); Victor Brudney & Robert Charles Clark, A New Look at Corporate Opportunities, 94 Harv. L. Rev. 997 (1981).

16. 326 S.E.2d 460 (Ga.1985).

17. Id. at 464.

18. Patient Care Services v. Segal, 337 N.E.2d 471 (Ill.App.1975).

19. See e.g., D.C. Code § 29–304(6) (allowing loans to employees but not officers and directors). See also 6 Zolman Cavitch, Business Organizations: With Tax Planning § 127.05[3].

20. RMBCA § 8.32; see also Alaska Stat. § 10.06.485 (prohibiting loans to directors without approval of two-thirds of voting shares); N.D. Cent. Code § 10–19.1–89(c), (d) (board must determine that a loan to an officer who is also an employee is in the best interests of the corporation).

21. See Jones v. H. F. Ahmanson & Co., 81 Cal.Rptr. 592, 599, 460 P.2d 464, 471 (Cal. 1969).

controlling shareholders to prove that transactions with a controlled corporation are fair; however, approval by disinterested minority shareholders will shift the burden to the party challenging the transaction to prove that a waste of corporate assets has occurred.[22] Thus, in situations in which controlling shareholders attempt to "cash out" minority interests through merger transactions, an "intrinsic fairness" test is used. In these circumstances, courts require that both fair dealing and fair price be demonstrated.[23] The fiduciary duty of majority shareholders rests on conflict of interest principles because either the parent corporation or the controlling shareholders engage in self-dealing when they establish a price at which shares will be purchased.

In contrast to the cases just discussed in which the duty of loyalty is clearly implicated because majority shareholders are engaged in self-interested transactions, many cases in this area involve more subtle grievances. Minority shareholders in close corporations often claim that the majority is attempting to "freeze" them out by denying them corporate offices and salaries. For shareholders financially dependent on their salaries from the corporation and without prospect of selling their shares, the "freeze out" is obviously a highly effective weapon. However, courts are generally disinclined to interfere with internal corporate affairs such as selection of officers, directors, or employees or salary or dividend policies.

Nevertheless, some courts have dealt with the problem by recognizing a fiduciary obligation owed by majority shareholders to the minority in close corporations. Massachusetts has pioneered in this area, adopting a rule that examines certain transactions affecting minority shareholders under the lens of a strict fiduciary standard ("utmost good faith and loyalty").[24] Close scrutiny is justified by the close practical similarities between close corporations and partnerships. Courts stress the need for stronger fiduciary bonds where co-shareholders are interdependent, minority shareholders are at risk of unfair actions by the majority and there is no market for the stock of the corporation. Thus in *Wilkes v. Springside Nursing Home, Inc.*,[25] the Massachusetts Supreme Court found that the majority had acted in bad faith and in violation of their heightened fiduciary duties to a minority owner of a nursing home when they removed him from his salaried position in an apparent attempt to freeze him out.

§ 5–8. Immunity, Indemnity and Insurance

Although the case law does not appear to place excessively onerous fiduciary obligations on corporate directors, the perception that even a small risk of devastating personal liability may deter individuals from serving on corporate boards has led to a variety of measures designed to protect board

22. Rosenblatt v. Getty Oil Co., 493 A.2d 929 (Del.1985). See also ALI, Principles of Corporate Governance § 5.10, at 437–47.

23. Weinberger v. UOP, Inc., 457 A.2d 701 (Del.1983). Likewise, where a parent's control of a subsidiary's operation causes a benefit to the parent that excludes and is detrimental to minority shareholders, a similar analysis is applied. Sinclair Oil Corp. v. Levien, 280 A.2d 717 (Del.1971). See also Speiser v. Baker, 525 A.2d 1001 (Del.Ch.1987).

24. Donahue v. Rodd Electrotype Co., 328 N.E.2d 505 (Mass.1975) (share repurchase by close corporation subject to "equal opportunity rule"; corporation must provide all shareholders equal access to "market" for shares created by repurchase).

25. 353 N.E.2d 657 (Mass.1976); see also Quinn v. Cardiovascular Physicians, P.C., 326 S.E.2d 460 (Ga.1985); Zidell v. Zidell, Inc., 560 P.2d 1091 (Or.1977); Comolli v. Comolli, 246 S.E.2d 278 (Ga.1978).

members. The trade-off for encouraging wider participation on boards, of course, is the risk of diluting the prophylactic effect on board behavior that the fiduciary duties are intended to provide.

Over forty states have enacted statutes allowing shareholders to limit through their articles of incorporation the liability of corporate directors for monetary damages for breaches of the duty of care.[1] These statutes typically exclude from the exemption certain acts or omissions, e.g. those that constitute: (1) a breach of a director's duty of loyalty, criminal activity, or willful or wanton misconduct; (2) intentional misconduct or transactions from which directors derived an improper personal benefit; or (3) lack good faith.[2] Some states have extended the protection to corporate officers[3] and others have placed caps on liability that cover almost all derivative suits against directors.[4] Statutes governing nonprofit organizations provide similar protection although most apply only to uncompensated directors.[5] Nonprofit exemption statutes also differ in that they are self-executing: no adoption by the corporation or its members is usually required.[6]

The second major shield for corporate officers and directors is found in laws mandating or permitting the corporation to defend and indemnify them for liabilities resulting from the performance of their duties. Most statutes provide for mandatory indemnification: the corporation must indemnify directors in litigation in which they are "successful on the merits or otherwise." Under some statutes, indemnification is not required where the director is less than "wholly successful"[7] in litigation and the corporation may limit mandatory indemnification by provision in the articles of incorporation.[8] Indemnification statutes also provide for permissive indemnification against litigation expenses and damages, subject to appropriate authorization from the corporation (acting through a majority of disinterested directors, shareholders or, in certain circumstances, based on the opinion of independent legal counsel).[9] However, permissive indemnification is generally subject to a variety of statutory standards such as the requirement that the director have acted in good faith and in a manner he reasonably believed to be consistent with the best interests of the corporation; in the case of criminal actions, statutes usually require that the officer or director have had no reasonable cause to believe his conduct was unlawful.[10]

Finally, because the coverage provided by indemnification is not complete and because of the risk that the corporation may be unable to indemnify its officers and directors due to bankruptcy, the purchase by corporations of director and officer (D & O) insurance has gained widespread acceptance. To

§ 5–8

1. The first state to do so was Delaware. See Del. Code tit. 8, § 102(b)(7). See 6 Zolman Cavitch, Business Organizations: with Tax Planning § 127.02 App. (1989).

2. See e.g., Del. Code tit. 8, § 102(b)(7); 15 Pa. Cons. Stat. Ann. § 513.

3. See e.g., Md. Code, Corporations & Ass'ns 2–405.2; N.J. Stat. Ann. § 14A:2–7.

4. See, e.g, Haw. Rev. Stat. § 415–48.5; Utah Code Ann. § 16–10a–841.

5. See e.g., Mass. Gen. L. Ann. ch. 231, § 85W; McKinney's—N.Y. Not-for-Profit Corp. Law § 720a. Some nonprofit statutes

reach officers. See e.g., Or. Rev. Stat. § 65.369; and others cover all uncompensated volunteers, see e.g., S.D. Codified Laws § 47–23–29.

6. See e.g., McKinney's—New York Not-for-Profit Corp. Law § 720a; but see Mich. Comp. Laws Ann. § 450.2209.

7. See e.g., RMBCA § 8.52.

8. See e.g., RMBCA § 8.52.

9. See e.g., Del. Code tit. 8, § 145(a)-(d).

10. See e.g., Del. Code tit. 8, § 145(a); see also RMBCA § 8.51.

avoid claims that a corporation's purchase of insurance for its directors and officers itself constitutes a breach of fiduciary duties (especially with regard to non-indemnifiable events), most states have enacted enabling laws.[11] These statutes typically allow for the purchase of insurance against claims arising out of the directors' or officers' responsibilities to the corporation, whether or not the corporation would have the power to indemnify against such liabilities. However, the protection afforded by D & O insurance is itself often less than complete. Many states forbid by statute or common law certain categories of coverage, such as for criminal acts. Moreover, in practice, insurance policies often exclude a variety of claims that are of particular importance to hospital directors and some insure only on a "claims made" (rather than occurrence) basis.[12]

§ 5–9.   Statutory Close Corporations and Subchapter S Corporations

Close corporations tend to more closely resemble partnerships than publicly traded corporations in that they usually have a relatively small number of shareholders who are often involved directly in the management of the business (and who may serve as directors, officers or employees). Moreover, because as a matter of practical economics the fortunes of the enterprise are often tied to the individuals comprising its management and the absence of a market for the shares of such entities, minority shareholders may find themselves vulnerable to the whims of the majority.

As discussed earlier, much of general corporate law is premised on economic attributes that do not apply to close corporations.[1] It is thus important for investors in close corporations to tailor carefully relationships among the parties and the structure of the entity in order to protect their interests and to deal with problems that may arise. For example, a number of potential difficulties can be dealt with by contractual arrangements: shareholders may enter into "buy-sell" agreements to avoid disputes upon changes in ownership; they may enter into voting trusts or other shareholder agreements to prevent deadlocks; and they may assure themselves of employment through contractual arrangements.[2] Likewise, they may adjust the governance or capital structure of the corporation to protect their rights by various means such as by issuing separate classes of stock,[3] adopting cumulative voting for directors[4] or adopting supermajority voting requirements.[5]

Although modern statutes allow considerable flexibility in designing financial and governance arrangements that meet the needs of investors in such enterprises, considerable advanced planning and foresight are required. Many states have adopted "integrated" or statutory close corporations laws that are designed to offer a "plain vanilla" statutory structure that is more

11.   See e.g., Del. Code tit. 8, § 145(g).

12.   See Robert J. Burdett, Jr., Director Liability: A Guide to Preventing Trouble in the Hospital Boardroom 60–63 (1991).

§ 5–9

1.   See supra § 5–2.

2.   See generally Robert W. Hamilton, Business Organizations: Unincorporated Business and Closely Held Corporations, §§ 8.27–8.33

(1996). David R. Herwitz, Business Planning: Materials on the Planning of Corporate Transactions (3d ed. 1987); Robert Charles Clark, Corporations 761–84 (1986).

3.   RMBCA § 6.01(a); Lehrman v. Cohen, 222 A.2d 800 (Del.1966).

4.   RMBCA § 7.28.

5.   RMBCA §§ 7.25 & 7.26.

suitable to the needs of these entities than is the general corporation statute. These laws typically place restrictions on the number and kinds of shareholders such entities may have[6] and impose certain other restrictions. For example, close corporations are required to provide notice on share certificates and in their articles of incorporation that the rights of shareholders may differ materially from those of shareholders of other corporations.[7] These statutes offer important benefits to small business. They enable closely-held entities to avoid unnecessary corporate formalities, assume governance structures more appropriate for their size and may also help avoid circumstances that lead to deadlocks and oppression of minority interests.

Another option for closely held enterprises is to elect to be treated as a "Subchapter S corporation" under Federal tax laws. In Subchapter S corporations, income and losses "flow through" the corporation to shareholders who are taxed pro rata based on their individual ownership interests. Thus, like partners, owners of S corporations avoid the "double tax" applicable to corporations (i.e., corporate income taxation at the entity level and taxes on dividends and other distributions at the individual level). However, the Internal Revenue Code places a number of important limitations upon the kinds of entities that may qualify: the corporation must have fewer than 35 shareholders; all shareholders must be U.S. citizens; the corporation may issue only one class of stock (though it may have voting and non-voting classes); shareholders must be persons and not partnerships or corporations; and the corporation may not be part of an "affiliated group" (defined as a group of corporations with 80% or more common ownership).[8] However, the requirements that shareholders may not be corporations or partnerships makes the Subchapter S option impossible for many complex health care organizations.

§ 5–10. The Corporate Practice of Medicine Doctrine

The corporate practice of medicine doctrine prohibits corporations and other business entities from engaging in the practice of medicine. It has been applied to prohibit corporations from hiring physicians to provide medical treatment for their employees; insurers from directly offering health care services; hospitals and clinics from hiring doctors; and partnerships with lay partners from engaging in medical practice. Although modern case law is scarce and a few states have specifically rejected the doctrine, it is still widely observed by health care entities establishing new enterprises. Even in jurisdictions in which the law appears to be moribund, many lawyers advise clients to avoid risks by structuring arrangements so that direct corporate control of physician activities is not present.

The doctrine has been persuasively and caustically criticized for inhibiting the use of profit-seeking business forms, discouraging innovation in health care organization and cost control and solidifying professional sovereignty over consumers.[1] The doctrine's anachronistic effects in today's health care

---

6. See, e.g., Model Stat. Close Corp. Supp. § 3 (corporations with no more than 50 shareholders may convert to close corporation; no limit on new corporations); Ala. Code § 10–2A–301(1)(b) (permitting articles of incorporation to set forth shareholder qualifications).

7. See, e.g., Mont. Code Ann. § 35–9–201.

8. I.R.C. § 1361(b)(1).

§ 5–10

1. See e.g., Mark A. Hall, Institutional Control of Physician Behavior: Legal Barriers to Health Care Cost Containment, 137 U. Pa. L. Rev. 431, 509, 518 (1988) ("puzzling doctrine

marketplace are striking. Its tendency to impose barriers to hierarchical control of doctors and to efficient management practices clashes directly with competition-driven impulses to establish greater institutional control over provider practices. On the other side, the central focus of the corporate practice doctrine may have greater resonance as the public and policymakers become increasingly concerned that managed care is usurping physician discretion by substituting the judgments of nonprofessionals for those of providers of care.[2]

a. Sources of the Doctrine and its Flawed Rationale

Only a handful of states expressly prohibit corporate practice by statute.[3] In other states, courts have fashioned the doctrine from two sources: (1) state licensing and medical practice acts that bar unlicensed persons from practicing medicine, and (2) a variety of policy arguments.[4]

The statutory foundations of the doctrine are dubious at best. It is true, as courts invoking the doctrine emphasize, that corporations possess no medical license to practice medicine, nor could they because such entities cannot attend medical school, be tested, or possess the requisite moral qualifications to do so.[5] However, if these characteristics are prerequisite to practicing medicine, then corporations cannot engage in medical practice; conversely, it could be argued that if employees' activities are attributable to corporations, their licensed status should be attributed as well.[6] Remarkably, courts interpreting the doctrine expansively have simultaneously read statutes allowing "persons" to obtain licenses to refer only to natural persons, while interpreting prohibitions against "persons" practicing medicine to include corporations as well as natural persons.[7]

Courts relying on policy arguments to justify the corporate practice of medicine doctrine emphasize several concerns: first, corporate practice creates

---

* * * clouded with confused reasoning and * * * founded on an astounding series of logical fallacies."); Henry B. Hansmann, Reforming Nonprofit Corporation Law, 129 U. Pa. L. Rev. 497, 538–40 (1981); Comment, Adam M. Freiman, The Abandonment of the Antiquated Corporate Practice of Medicine Doctrine: Injecting a Dose of Efficiency Into The Modern Health Care Environment, 47 Emory L.J. 697 (1998).

2. See Andre Hampton, Resurrection of the Prohibition on the Corporate Practice of Medicine Doctrine: Teaching Old Dogma New Tricks, 66 U. Cinn. L.Rev. 489 (1998)(arguing that the doctrine can help correct conflict of interest problems associated with physician risk-sharing).

3. West's Ann. Cal. Bus. & Prof. Code § 2400; West's Colo. Rev. Stat. Ann. § 12–36–134; Ohio Rev. Code § 1701.03; Wis. Stat. Ann. § 448.08.

4. See Comment, Adam M. Freiman, The Abandonment of the Antiquated Corporate Practice of Medicine Doctrine: Injecting a Dose of Efficiency Into The Modern Health Care Environment, 47 Emory L.J. 712 (1998) (citing estimates that thirty-seven states have statutory or common law prohibitions or authority

implying such prohibitions, but most are rarely enforced).

5. See e.g., Dr. Allison, Dentist, Inc. v. Allison, 196 N.E. 799, 800 (Ill.1935) (medical practice requires more than mere knowledge or skill, but "personal characteristics, such as honesty, guided by an upright conscience and a sense of loyalty to clients or patients, even to the extent of sacrificing pecuniary profit, if necessary * * * No corporation can qualify. It can have neither honesty nor conscience.").

6. See Mark A. Hall, Institutional Control of Physician Behavior: Legal Barriers to Health Care Cost Containment, 137 U. Pa. L. Rev. 431, 512 (1988). States rejecting the corporate practice doctrine have followed this line of argument. See State Electro–Medical Inst. v. State, 103 N.W. 1078 (Neb.1905); State ex rel. Sager v. Lewin, 106 S.W. 581 (Mo.App.1907); see also Bartron v. Codington County, 2 N.W.2d 337 (S.D.1942).

7. See Mark A. Hall, Institutional Control of Physician Behavior: Legal Barriers to Health Care Cost Containment, 137 U. Pa. L. Rev. 431, 512 (1988); Alanson W. Willcox, Hospitals and the Corporate Practice of Medicine, 45 Cornell L. Rev. 432, 437 (1960).

divided loyalties and risks commercial exploitation of patients;[8] second, physicians employed by business entities will be subject to lay control in practicing their profession;[9] third, the physician-patient relationship, which relies on trust and confidence, will be undermined by corporate practice;[10] and, fourth, corporate practice tends to "commercialize" the professions.[11]

These policy concerns assume the desirability of absolute physician sovereignty and harken back to a time in which medical judgments prevailed independent of cost ramifications.[12] As suggested above, most cases relying on such arguments predate contemporary market conditions in which many physicians are, in fact, hired as employees by hospitals, corporations and clinics; managed care demands greater control over provider practices; and increasing specialization requires close affiliation with institutional entities.[13] Moreover, the numerous exceptions carved out by statute and common law raise doubt as to purported policy justifications for expansive application of the doctrine. With the corporate practice doctrine hollowed out by exceptions, the existence of any underlying policy rationale is dubious.

Perhaps the most telling shortcoming of purported policy-based rationales for the doctrine is the tendency to overlook the linkage between organized medicine's ethical prescriptions in this area and the financial interests of practitioners. A number of ethical canons, including those barring corporate practice of medicine, have been found to have anticompetitive effects.[14] The adverse economic consequences of these ethical norms must be weighed against any social benefits flowing from interpreting the doctrine.

b. *The Case Law*

In its most straightforward application, the corporate practice of medicine doctrine prohibits persons without medical licenses, including corporations and their lay employees, from actually practicing medicine. This aspect of the doctrine is not controversial; it is a logical and necessary corollary to licensure and medical practice acts. Many of the early cases invoking the doctrine involved instances of shady practitioners, quackery and commercial exploitation under the corporate banner. The doctrine also reflects a policy preference for preventing avoidance of liability.[15]

---

8. See e.g., Parker v. Board of Dental Examiners, 14 P.2d 67 (Cal.1932).

9. See e.g., Garcia v. Texas State Bd. of Medical Examiners, 384 F.Supp. 434 (W.D.Tex. 1974), affirmed 421 U.S. 995, 95 S.Ct. 2391, 44 L.Ed.2d 663 (1975).

10. See e.g., State ex rel. Standard Optical Co. v. Superior Court, 135 P.2d 839 (Wash. 1943).

11. See e.g., Bartron v. Codington County, 2 N.W.2d 337 (S.D.1942).

12. See Paul Starr, The Social Transformation of American Medicine (1982); Mark A. Hall, Institutional Control of Physician Behavior: Legal Barriers to Health Care Cost Containment, 137 U. Pa. L. Rev. 431, 516 (1988).

13. See John Wiorek, The Corporate Practice of Medicine Doctrine: An Outmoded Theory in Need of Modification, 8 J. Legal Med. 465, 489 (1987).

14. Ethical prescriptions of the American Medical Association prohibiting lay interference, contract medicine, or physicians dispensing services "under terms or conditions which tend to interfere with or impair the free and complete exercise" of medical judgment and skill, were successfully challenged by the Federal Trade Commission. See In re American Medical Ass'n, 94 F.T.C. 701 (1979), affirmed 638 F.2d 443 (2d Cir.1980), affirmed by equally divided court 455 U.S. 676, 102 S.Ct. 1744, 71 L.Ed.2d 546 (1982). See generally Chapter 10.

15. For example, the California Supreme Court has applied the doctrine to uphold its finding that a dentist had "aided and abetted" his corporation in unlawfully practicing dentistry. Parker v. Board of Dental Examiners, 14 P.2d 67 (Cal.1932).

Judicial interpretations have expanded the reach of the doctrine far beyond instances of actual practice of medicine by unlicensed persons or direct control over medical decisions by corporate entities. Illegal corporate practice has been found where corporate entities hire professionals or receive payment for services rendered by professionals.[16] Thus, one of the most common applications of the doctrine has been to bar lay entities such as department stores, employers with "industrial medicine" programs and medical products franchisees from employing professionals.[17] For example, in *California Association of Dispensing Opticians v. Pearle Vision Center, Inc.*,[18] a California court upheld a preliminary injunction against a corporation operating retail ophthalmic dispensing outlets. The court noted the defendant's control over the practice of optometry by its franchisees in respect to both treatment decisions and business operations, and applied corporate practice principles to bar lay control over healing arts practitioners. Similar reasoning has led courts to find that participation by a lay co-partner in a medical clinic constituted the unlicensed practice of medicine. Given the power of each general partner to participate in the control of the business and bind other partners, one court found illegal practice and held the lay co-partner lacked any legally cognizable interest in the clinic.[19]

The corporate practice doctrine has been applied in a variety of contexts. For example, courts have invoked the doctrine to refuse to enforce a non-competition agreement between a corporation and its former employee,[20] to support judgments in *quo warranto* actions by state attorneys general against corporations operating clinics providing fixed-fee medical services[21] and to strike down corporate health plans contracting with insureds to pay for medical services in exchange for pre-paid premiums when they receive treatment from a plan-approved physician.[22] Occasionally the corporate practice of medicine doctrine has provided a shield against liability. Some courts have held hospitals and HMOs not responsible for the negligence of physician-employees, reasoning that because corporations cannot practice medicine or direct the practice of physicians in their employ, they cannot be liable for the latter's professional malpractice.[23]

The cases usually draw no distinction between situations in which lay persons or entities provide purely administrative tasks in support of professional services and those in which they make "professional" judgments or in some sense dictate treatment decisions. Thus, sufficient predicate for illegal practice of medicine has been found where lay corporations or other entities

16. People by Kerner v. United Medical Serv., 200 N.E. 157 (Ill.1936).

17. See e.g., Obuchowski v. Dental Comm'n, 178 A.2d 537 (Conn.1962) (lay-controlled laboratory may not employ dentist); State Bd. of Optometry v. Gilmore, 3 So.2d 708 (Fla.1941)(department store prohibited from employing physician and optometrist); People by Kerner v. United Medical Serv., 200 N.E. 157 (Ill.1936) (corporation may not employ physician).

18. 191 Cal.Rptr. 762 (Cal.Ct.App.1983).

19. Morelli v. Ehsan, 737 P.2d 1030 (Wash. Ct.App.1987), reversed on other grounds 756 P.2d 129 (Wash.1988). See also Flynn Bros., Inc. v. First Medical Assocs., 715 S.W.2d 782

(Tex.App.1986); Early Detection Center, Inc. v. Wilson, 811 P.2d 860 (Kan.1991).

20. Dr. Allison, Dentist, Inc. v. Allison, 196 N.E. 799 (Ill.1935).

21. See, e.g., People by Kerner v. United Medical Serv., 200 N.E. 157 (Ill.1936).

22. People ex rel. State Bd. of Medical Examiners v. Pacific Health Corp., 82 P.2d 429 (Cal.1938).

23. See, e.g., Moon v. Mercy Hosp., 373 P.2d 944 (Colo.1962); Rosane v. Senger, 149 P.2d 372 (Colo.1944). See also Williams v. Good Health Plus, Inc.-HealthAmerica Corp. of Texas, 743 S.W.2d 373 (Tex.App.1987).

employ physicians,[24] make decisions affecting financial matters or management,[25] hire nurses and exercise the rights and duties of a general partner.[26] In perhaps the most extreme application of this reasoning, a court allowed a county to refuse payment to a corporate clinic owned and operated entirely by physicians.[27] The premise of this holding appears to have been that potential harms flowing from divided allegiances (serving the interest of the corporation and patients) are sufficient to invoke the doctrine.

While most courts have refused to distinguish between a physician's professional service and a lay person's administrative duties, the doctrine is usually not applied where a physician affiliates with a corporate entity as an "independent contractor" rather than an employee.[28] Consequently, the common practice in states in which the doctrine is still recognized is for hospitals to engage physicians as independent contractors or, in many instances, to contract with professional corporations or partnerships rather than to employ physicians.[29] However, some courts have found that corporate practice has occurred where a corporate clinic or hospital merely collected fees on behalf of a physician.[30] Moreover, the Attorney General of California has rejected the distinction and would apply the corporate practice doctrine to independent contractors.[31]

On the other side of the coin, jurisdictions that specifically reject the doctrine or construe it narrowly appear to permit lay persons or entities to freely make contracts, hire physicians as salaried employees and perform a broad range of administrative or supervisory functions. These states interpret their medical practice statutes to prohibit corporations or lay employees only from becoming directly involved in diagnosing illness and treating patients.[32] In Berlin v. Sarah Bush Lincoln Health Center,[33] the Illinois Supreme Court construed its rarely-enforced corporate practice ban not to reach reached employment of physicians by hospitals. The court's decision rested on its view that the "public policy concerns which support the corporate practice doctrine [are] inapplicable to a licensed hospital in the modern health care industry."[34] At the same time, however, it declined to overturn prior case law, noting that the doctrine was "entirely appropriate to a general corporation possessing no licensed authority to offer medical services to the public."[35]

24. People by Kerner v. United Medical Servs., 200 N.E. 157 (Ill.1936).

25. Parker v. Board of Dental Examiners of California, 14 P.2d 67 (Cal.1932); People ex rel. State Bd. of Medical Examiners v. Pacific Health Corp., 82 P.2d 429 (Cal.1938).

26. See Morelli v. Ehsan, 737 P.2d 1030 (Wash.App.1987), reversed on other grounds 756 P.2d 129 (Wash.1988).

27. Bartron v. Codington County, 2 N.W.2d 337 (S.D.1942).

28. See Group Health Ass'n v. Moor, 24 F.Supp. 445 (D.D.C.1938).

29. See Jeffrey F. Chase–Lubitz, The Corporate Practice of Medicine Doctrine: An Anachronism in the Modern Health Care Industry, 40 Vand. L. Rev. 445, 473 (1987).

30. See e.g., Watt v. Texas State Bd. of Medical Examiners, 303 S.W.2d 884 (Tex.Civ. App.1957).

31. 65 Cal. Op. Att'y Gen. 223 (Apr. 7, 1982) (lay-controlled industrial medical corporations contracting with independent contractor-physicians on fixed fee basis to treat employees and perform pre-employment examinations constitute violation of state medical practices act).

32. State Electro–Medical Inst. v. State, 103 N.W. 1078 (Neb.1905) (corporation incapable of practicing medicine because impersonal entities cannot diagnose or treat diseases); see also State ex rel. Sager v. Lewin, 106 S.W. 581 (Mo.App.1907).

33. 688 N.E.2d 106 (1997).

34. Id. at 776.

35. Id.

c. Exceptions and Nonenforcement

The case law presents a misleading picture of the actual importance of the corporate practice doctrine, however, because there are a large number of judicial and statutory exceptions that make it possible to avoid the law's draconian effects. Moreover, the doctrine is rarely enforced even in jurisdictions with relatively clear precedent.

Some states have enacted statutes that remove health maintenance organizations and certain clinics from the reach of the doctrine.[36] State health care reform legislation has endorsed employment of physicians, although some statutes require that hospitals expressly agree not to interfere with the professional judgments of physicians in their employ.[37] In addition, courts have created exemptions for medical schools and not-for-profit hospitals that employ physicians.[38] Virtually all jurisdictions allow not-for-profit hospitals to provide services through salaried physicians,[39] permit corporations to employ residents and interns,[40] and sanction the practice of medicine through professional corporations.[41] Another important limitation is provided by judicial rulings that the doctrine does not reach independent contractor arrangements between hospitals or other entities and providers. As discussed below, many integrated systems comply with the letter, if not the spirit, of the doctrine by establishing "captive professional corporations" in which a corporation supplying physician services is "owned" by a physician shareholder who has in fact ceded control to the lay-controlled integrated system.[42]

Courts seize on both legislative action and inaction to avoid applying the doctrine. For example, the Supreme Court of Kansas construed a corporate practice statute to permit employment of physicians by hospitals based on licensure laws that require hospitals to provide "physician services" and the absence of any likelihood of injury to the public from such arrangements.[43] Similarly, to justify limiting the doctrine, the Illinois Supreme Court relied heavily on the fact that the legislature had enacted laws requiring hospitals to provide various medical services.[44] The dissent stressed that the majority had ignored sixty years of legislative acquiescence in the doctrine and that nothing in the legislation cited compelled or assumed that hospitals would employ physicians. States with more firmly-embedded corporate practice prohibitions, however, have tended to resist arguments premised on implied legislative repeal.[45]

---

36. See e.g., Ala. Code § 27–21A–23(a); Del. Code tit. 16, § 9112.

37. See e.g., Mont. Code Ann. § 37–3–322(23)(c)(i).

38. See People ex rel. State Bd. of Medical Examiners v. Pacific Health Corp., 82 P.2d 429 (Cal.1938). See generally Patricia F. Jacobson, Prohibition Against Corporate Practice of Medicine: Dinosaur or Dynamic Doctrine?, in 1993 Health Law Handbook 67 (Alice G. Gosfield ed.) (collecting cases and administrative actions creating exceptions to the doctrine).

39. See e.g., Complete Serv. Bureau v. San Diego County Medical Soc'y, 272 P.2d 497 (Cal. 1954); People ex rel. State Bd. of Medical Examiners v. Pacific Health Corp., 82 P.2d 429 (Cal.1938).

40. Rush v. Akron Gen. Hosp., 171 N.E.2d 378 (Ohio Ct. App.1957); see also Albany Medical College v. McShane, 499 N.Y.S.2d 376, 489 N.E.2d 1278 (N.Y.App.Div.1985).

41. See infra §§ 5–27.

42. See infra § 5–27.

43. St. Francis Regional Medical Center, Inc. v. Weiss, 869 P.2d 606 (Kan.1994); see also Rush v. City of St. Petersburg, 205 So.2d 11 (Fla.Dist.Ct.App.1967) (approving hospital employment because it did not affect the physician-patient relationship).

44. Berlin v. Sarah Bush Lincoln Health Center, 688 N.E.2d 106 (Ill.1997); see supra § 5–10b.

In summary, the corporate practice doctrine is founded on questionable policy grounds and lacks coherent justification in the contemporary health services delivery environment. In applying the doctrine, courts have invoked a number of exceptions, but the plain language of established case law in many jurisdictions often permits little leeway for avoiding the doctrine's effects. Although almost unanimous in condemning the corporate practice doctrine, the commentary is somewhat split as to how much practical effect it still possesses. There is a prevailing perception that corporate practice prohibitions are widely ignored and that employment relationships are commonly entered into even in states with medical practice prohibitions still on the books. At the same time, in view of the practical necessity of solidifying hierarchical arrangements between entities in evolving managed care systems[46] and the possibility that even ambiguous restrictions on corporate employment of physicians may hinder the growth of managed care, the doctrine appears ripe for reexamination.

d. Fee Splitting Prohibitions

Many states that do not prohibit the corporate practice of medicine forbid physicians to engage in the somewhat analogous practice known as "fee splitting." Fee splitting prohibitions are rooted in the same ethical concerns that spawned the corporate practice doctrine. The medical practice acts of many states empower their state boards of medicine to discipline physicians for fee-splitting, typically in statutory provisions that also prohibit bonuses, kickbacks or rebates for patient referrals for services.[47] These statutes usually do not define "fee splitting" and are often vague about the requisite connection to patient referrals, and much of the law that has developed in this area is found in administrative decisions of state medical practice boards. These laws have been invoked to challenge a variety of contemporary arrangements pursuant to which physicians sell their practices and/or contract with independent firms to provide management, billing, contracting and other administrative services.[48]

Read literally, the prohibition on splitting fees with any other person or entity might seem to bar physicians from sharing profits with other shareholders in a corporate entity. However, states not recognizing the corporate practice of medicine doctrine do not interpret fee splitting laws to prohibit professional corporations or corporate ownership of physician practices. A number of jurisdictions, have nevertheless questioned arrangements such as those provided by physician management companies, pursuant to which a for-profit firm avoids ownership of physician practices but shares earnings under contractual commitments to provide management and other services in return

45. Conrad v. Med. Board of California, 48 Cal.App.4th 1038, 55 Cal.Rptr.2d 901 (1996) (statute allowing hospital district to contract with physicians did not implicitly permit physician employment).

46. See N.M. Op. Att'y Gen. No. 87–39 (July 30, 1987) ("Many of the earlier decisions in this area may not be germane to the health care environment today. A market demand for integrated health care delivery has emerged in recent years").

47. E.g., Fla. Stat. Ann. § 458.331(1)(i). See generally, Richard O. Jacobs & Elizabeth Goodman, Splitting Fees or Splitting Hairs? Fee Splitting and Health Care–The Florida Experience, 8 Annals Health L. 239, 241 (1999)(thirty six states have laws prohibiting fee-splitting or kickbacks).

48. See discussion of MSOs infra, § 5–50a.

for a percentage of revenues. In Florida, for example, an appellate court upheld a state board ruling that a contract between a physician management company and a physician group constituted illegal feel splitting.[49] Under the arrangement, the group was to pay thirty percent of its net income in return for services that included fostering practice expansion through marketing, creation of a preferred provider network, negotiation of managed care contracts and affiliations with other networks. The board found that paying a specified percentage of net income without regard to the cost of providing those services constituted a fee split and further that establishing networks and providing marketing services was a referral within the meaning of the statute.[50] A central issue in the analysis appears to have been the nexus between the division of fees and provisions encouraging referrals.[51] In a subsequent case, the Florida Board found no illegal fee splitting where a physician group split its net revenues with a physician management company up to a cap of $10,000 per month.[52] The Board stressed that the cap and the absence of any obligation that the practice management company add patients to the practice removed risk that the arrangement was undertaken for referrals. Viewed in this light, courts may distinguish fee splitting that directly implicates physician judgements about their patients' care, as in the case of those relating to referrals, from those splits arising from a division of services.

B.   NOT–FOR–PROFIT CORPORATIONS

§ 5–11.   Distinguishing Characteristics

Despite their considerable size and importance to the American economy, not-for-profit[1] corporations are governed by a regime of law that is frequently obscure and fails to distinguish among the variety of not-for-profit corporations or between such entities and their for-profit counterparts. Commentators have emphasized that legal principles governing fiduciary duties and responsibilities are not clearly drawn and that helpful precedent in this area is sparse.[2]

49. Phymatrix Management Co. v. Bakarania, 1999 WL 424411 (Fla.Dist.Ct.App.1999). See also Physician Practice Management: North Carolina Suits Challenge Medpartners' Clinic Agreements as Illegal Fee Splitting, 8 Health L. Rep. 471 (March 25, 1999).

50. In re: Petition for Declaratory Statement of Magan L. Bakarania, M.D., 20 F.A.L.R. 395 (1997).

51. See Richard O. Jacobs & Elizabeth Goodman, Splitting Fees or Splitting Hairs? Fee Splitting and Health Care–The Florida Experience, 8 Annals Health L. 239, (1999); see also Practice Management Associates, Inc. v. Orman, 614 So.2d 1135 (Fla.Dist.Ct.App.1993); but cf. Crow v. Agency for Health Care Administration, 669 So.2d 1160 (Fla.Dist.Ct.App. 1996).

52. Florida: State Board Approves Management Contract that Splits Income Without Ties to Referrals, 8 Health L. Rep. 1313 (Aug. 12, 1999).

§ 5–11

1. Although statutes and commentary frequently employ the term "nonprofit" to describe these entities, the term "not-for-profit" more accurately depicts the reality that such institutions may seek and earn profits as long as they are used in fulfilling the organization's missions. See Robert S. Pasley, Organization and Operation of Non–Profit Corporations—Some General Considerations, 19 Clev. St. L. Rev. 239, 241 (1970).

2. See Thomas H. Boyd, Note, A Call to Reform the Duties of Directors Under State Not–for–Profit Corporation Statutes, 72 Iowa L. Rev. 725 (1987) ("directors' duties and responsibilities particularly ambiguous and obscure, leaving courts with insufficient guidance on what law to apply"); Alan C. Geolot, Note, The Fiduciary Duties of Loyalty and Care Associated with the Directors and Trustees of Charitable Organizations, 64 Va. L. Rev. 449 (1978).

As a general matter, the case law tends to adopt the same standards applicable to for-profit fiduciaries except to the extent that it recognizes special obligations of not-for-profit directors to obey the charitable purposes of the institution and to guard its assets.[3] On the statutory side, the picture is not much clearer. Although almost all states have not-for-profit corporation statutes, many fail to set forth any express, general standard of conduct governing directors' duties, while the majority of jurisdictions adopt broad formulations borrowed from the general corporate laws[4] without drawing any distinctions between for-profit and not-for-profit corporations or among the diverse kinds of organizations adopting the not-for-profit form.[5]

Adding to the complexity is the fact that other statutory commands, most notably the federal tax laws, play a vital role in establishing the fiduciary duties and responsibilities of those running not-for-profit corporations.[6] For example, the requirement that no part of the net earnings of exempt organizations "inures to the benefit of any private shareholder or individual"[7] operates to prohibit self-dealing by directors. In addition, private foundations must include provisions in their articles of incorporation prohibiting them from "engaging in any act of self-dealing."[8] Given the potentially devastating consequences of violating federal tax laws, directors of not-for-profit organizations undoubtedly pay closer attention to the obligations created by these laws than to the duties imposed by corporate law. Finally, a variety of other laws, including securities, bankruptcy and antitrust, differentiate between the two kinds of corporate forms.[9] In many instances, these laws afford somewhat favored treatment to not-for-profit organizations, creating additional incentives to adopt that form.

The central feature distinguishing for-profit and not-for-profit corporations is the so-called "nondistribution constraint."[10] Although permitted to retain earnings, not-for-profit corporations are forbidden to distribute those earnings to persons controlling the corporation either directly through dividends or indirectly through payments to employees, creditors, directors or others. While not-for-profit corporations may have "members" who are empowered to vote in limited circumstances and to elect directors, they may not receive distributions of profits in any form.[11]

---

3. See, e.g., Oberly v. Kirby, 592 A.2d 445, 472–73 (Del.1991)("Although principles of corporate law generally govern the activities of such a corporation, its fiduciaries have a special duty to advance its charitable goals and protect its assets.").

4. For statutory formulations of the duty of care for not-for-profit fiduciaries, See, e.g., West's Ann. Cal. Corp. Code §§ 5231, 7231; Conn. Gen. Stat. Ann. § 33–447(d); 805 Ill. Comp. Stat. Ann. § 105/108.85; La. Stat. Ann.—Rev. Stat. § 12:226(A).

5. Attempts to rectify these problems are found in the scholarship of Professor Henry B. Hansmann, see Reforming Nonprofit Corporation Law, 129 U. Pa. L. Rev. 497 (1981); The Evolving Law of Nonprofit Organizations: Do Current Trends Make Good Policy?, 39 Case W. Res. L. Rev. 807 (1988–1989); and in the revised model act promulgated by the American Bar Association, Revised Model Nonprofit

Corporation Act (1988) (hereinafter, "RMNCA").

6. See Chapter 2 for an analysis of the federal tax code treatment of not-for-profit organizations.

7. I.R.C. § 501(c)(3).

8. I.R.C. § 508(e)(1)(B). See also id. at § 4941 (specifying prohibited forms of self-dealing for foundations).

9. See Comment, Developments in the Law—Nonprofit Corporations, 105 Harv. L. Rev. 1578, 1582–83 (1992).

10. See Henry B. Hansmann, Reforming Nonprofit Corporation Law, 129 U. Pa. L. Rev. 497, 500 (1981).

11. The Revised Act defines "members" as persons having the right to vote for the election of directors pursuant to the corporation's

The absence of corporate shareholders compels unique governance rules for nonprofit entities for several reasons. First, it forecloses the possibility of a capital market that might help to police the activities of fiduciaries. Second, there is no class of financially interested individuals who could be expected to bring lawsuits to enforce fiduciary duties in the courts.[12] Further, to the extent that not-for-profit corporations operate in sectors of the economy in which competition is attenuated, the disciplining effect of the marketplace upon directors and officers may also be lessened.

Some states draw a number of important distinctions between not-for-profit corporations having members, or "mutual benefit corporations," and those that serve a public or charitable purpose, so-called "public benefit corporations."[13] Public benefit corporations under state law usually qualify as 501(c)(3) charitable entities,[14] have self-perpetuating boards of directors and do not have members to whom they may distribute assets on dissolution; some state laws also apply a higher standard of conduct to directors of these entities. Mutual benefit corporations such as trade associations and certain mutual insurance companies have members who may be entitled to receive distributions of assets on dissolution. Though not required under statutory law, members may have rights to vote to choose directors and on other matters.[15]

§ 5–12. Directors, Members and Corporate Governance

State nonprofit corporation laws customarily provide that members elect the board of directors of not-for-profit corporations, but at the same time allow considerable room for varying this practice through provision in the articles.[1] Hence, many boards are "self-perpetuating," i.e. successor directors are chosen by existing members of the board. In some cases, selection of directors may be vested in entities outside the formal structure of the corporation, such as a religious order. At least one state attempts to ensure that not-for-profit hospitals serve their public interest responsibilities by requiring each institution to select at least forty percent of its directors from specified consumer groups.[2]

Formal criteria for membership varies widely among not-for-profits and is a matter that should be carefully drafted in corporate articles or bylaws. Common membership criteria in hospitals include: donations to or affiliation with the hospital or its sponsor, selection by the governing board or outside entity, or election by existing members. Although typically not addressed in

---

articles or bylaws, RMNCA § 1.40(21), and contains provisions protecting members' rights in circumstances. See, e.g., RMNCA § 10.03 (amendments of articles by directors and members); § 10.21 (amendments of bylaws).

12. Members' standing to enforce fiduciary duties in not-for-profit corporations is discussed infra § 5–18.

13. The RMNCA and the California Code are among the statutes that rely on this distinction. Both apply public benefit organization rules to religious organizations, but relax the regulatory oversight to the latter to some degree. See James J . Fishman & Stephen

Schwarz, Nonprofit Organizations 69–72 (1995).

14. See supra Chapter 2.

15. See supra note 11.

§ 5–12

1. See, e.g., RMNCA § 2.02. Failure to follow proper procedures in electing board members has been found to constitute grounds for enjoining a hospital board's action. Bedford County Hosp. v. County of Bedford, 304 S.W.2d 697 (Tenn.App.1957).

2. W.Va. Code § 16–5B–6a.

the charter or bylaws, in extraordinary circumstances members may be removed for cause.[3]

Battles for control of not-for-profit hospitals have not been uncommon. Often the complaint is that board members have abandoned the original mission of the entity through proposed transfers of assets or shifts in business operations.[4] In these disputes, courts carefully scrutinize the allocation of powers contained in the articles and bylaws, while at the same time attempting to honor the expectations of the parties.

For example, in one extraordinary case, a lay board sought to perpetuate its control over a hospital whose members were staff physicians.[5] Resisting the physician-members' attempt to amend the articles, the board appointed a large number of new members to defeat the proposal and adopt an alternative making the board self-perpetuating. The court granted the physicians' requested relief, finding that the directors had violated their fiduciary duties to the corporation by their precipitous actions recruiting new members and soliciting their proxies without giving the physician members an opportunity to also solicit proxies. In a Delaware case, the articles of an osteopathic hospital provided that members elected the board and also empowered the board select physicians for membership; however, nonphysician members could only be selected with the concurrence of a majority of the members.[6] When the lay board attempted to amend the bylaws to make themselves members, the court overturned what it found to be a facially valid bylaw amendment[7] because it upset settled expectations among physician members that they would be able to vote on admission of lay members.

§ 5–13. Articles of Incorporation and Bylaws

For the most part, the articles of incorporation and bylaws of not-for-profit corporations are governed by statutory requirements similar to those applicable to for-profit corporations. As suggested above, the articles and bylaws establish rules of succession and the authority of members and directors. Moreover, these documents are often critical in situating control and fixing governance rules in a manner that best preserves the organization's original charitable purpose and assures continuity of control.

For hospitals owned by or affiliated with religious organizations, the articles often specifically reserve certain powers to a designated entity of the church. For example, the articles of incorporation of Catholic hospitals cus-

---

3. Grace v. Grace Inst., 268 N.Y.S.2d 901 (N.Y.App.Div.1966), reversed on other grounds 279 N.Y.S.2d 721, 226 N.E.2d 531 (N.Y.App. Div.1967) (board had power to remove member of corporation who had breached duty to corporation by pattern of vexatious litigation).

4. See infra, §§ 5–17, 5–21.

5. Hatch v. Emery, 400 P.2d 349 (Ariz.Ct. App.1965).

6. In re Osteopathic Hosp. Ass'n of Delaware, 191 A.2d 333 (Del.Ch.1963), affirmed 195 A.2d 759 (Del.1963). See also Oberly v. Kirby, 592 A.2d 445 (Del.1991)(reconciling conflicting factual recitations in cases involving Osteopathic Hospital Association).

7. Apparently the court interpreted the governance structure contained in the articles to give the board broad powers of amendment. 191 A.2d at 335–36. However, in Oberly v. Kirby, 592 A.2d 445 (Del.1991), the Delaware Supreme Court invalidated a similar attempt by a board to amend the bylaws to permit it to elect members because the articles in that case vested members with powers analogous to those of shareholders' and because the delegation to the board contained in the articles, although expansive, did not mention powers to elect members.

tomarily reserve powers in an order or other affiliated organization of the Church. These generally include fundamental matters such as: appointment of directors, amendments of the bylaws and articles, and decisions regarding organic changes (e.g., dissolution, mergers or sales of significant assets).

§ 5–14.   The Fiduciary Duties of Not–For–Profit Directors

Historically, courts have applied a variety of fiduciary standards to the actions of directors of not-for-profit corporations. The older view, reflected today in the common law of a few states, treated not-for-profit corporations as constructive trusts and their directors as trustees.[1] Under this approach, directors may be liable for simple negligence in performing their duties and subject to an absolute ban on self-dealing or other transactions involving conflicts of interest. Trust characterization is traceable to the donative nature of most early not-for-profit corporations. Courts reasoned that entities receiving funds on the condition that they be used exclusively for a specific mission should be treated as trusts in favor of donors.[2]

Most courts today, however, apply the same fiduciary standards applicable to for-profit directors. The shift from trust treatment is explained by the practical similarities between for-profit and not-for-profit corporations and public policy factors such as encouraging individuals to serve as directors.[3] Although the ready equation of for-profit and not-for-profit fiduciary responsibilities has drawn academic criticism,[4] the for-profit standard has prevailed in modern statutes as well. For example, the Revised Model Nonprofit Corporation Act provides that a "director shall not be deemed to be a trustee with respect to the corporation."[5] An important qualification of the foregoing must be made with regard to not-for-profit organizations that receive donations subject to a charitable trust. In this circumstance, the directors will be bound by the stricter standard applicable to trusts. Thus where the trust forbids a sale, the corporation must seek approval to sell its assets and may require cy pres approval as to how it will use the proceeds of the sale.[6]

§ 5–14

1. See, e.g., Brown v. Concerned Citizens for Sickle Cell Anemia, Inc., 382 N.E.2d 1155 (Ohio 1978); Lynch v. John M. Redfield Found., 88 Cal.Rptr. 86 (Cal.App.1970); see generally Thomas H. Boyd, Note, A Call to Reform the Duties of Directors Under State Not–For–Profit Corporation Statutes, 72 Iowa L. Rev. 725, 733–34 (1987).

2. Another, less common, approach going to the other extreme is found in case law refusing to scrutinize charitable directors' activities closely in deference to the volunteer nature of directors' participation. See Lizabeth Moody, State Statutes Governing Directors of Charitable Corporations, 18 U.S.F. L. Rev. 749, 754 (1984).

3. See Stern v. Lucy Webb Hayes Nat'l Training School for Deaconesses & Missionaries, 381 F.Supp. 1003, 1013 (D.D.C.1974).

4. See, e.g., Henry B. Hansmann, Reforming Nonprofit Corporation Law, 129 U. Pa. L. Rev. 497, 569–73 (1981); Alan C. Geolot, Note, The Fiduciary Duties of Loyalty and Care Associated with the Directors and Trustees of Charitable Organizations, 64 Va. L. Rev. 449 (1978); Howard Oleck, NonProfit Corporations, Organizations and Associations (5th ed. 1988).

5. RMNCA § 8.30(e).

6. See Michael W. Peregrine, Charitable Trust Laws and the Evolving nature of the Nonprofit Hospital Corporation, 30 J. Health & Hosp. L. 11 (1997); Evelyn Brody, The Limits of Charity Fiduciary Law, 57 Md. L.Rev. 1400, 1465–66 (1998). These principles have been applied in cases involving conversions of not-for-profit entities, see infra § 5–21, and are sometimes applied under the rubric of directors "duty of obedience," see infra § 5–17.

§ 5–15. The Duty of Care

a. *The Common Law Standard*

Not–for–profit hospital boards and officers are subject to essentially the same standard of care that is applied to all corporate directors and officers. As noted above, not-for-profit statutes closely parallel the general corporate law, which gives judges considerable flexibility in interpreting the duty of care.[1] Courts have applied the relatively lenient for-profit standard, requiring gross negligence or willful misconduct[2] in the few decisions concerning alleged breaches by not-for-profit hospital directors.[3] The corporate standard has been widely applied to not-for-profit corporations of all kinds.[4] Indeed, the most prominent case applying the stricter trustee standard of care may well have involved an abuse constituting gross negligence.[5] While the business judgment rule is not explicitly incorporated in not-for-profit statutes (just as it is not in general corporate statutes), courts have embraced the concept to absolve not-for-profit directors of responsibility for business judgments that involve no conflict of interest, are reasonably informed and meet minimal standards of good faith. In addition, the case law recognizes no special treatment for not-for-profit directors merely because they are not compensated, serve primarily for fundraising purposes, or perform other special roles on the board. The general rule is that all directors must be active, functioning members and are held to the standard of care of an ordinarily prudent person in a like position under similar circumstances.[6] Even statutes differentiating among the various kinds of not-for-profit corporations have generally applied the same standard of care to directors of all such corporations.[7]

Hospital boards have not always escaped personal liability for their actions even under the lenient corporate standard. In *Stern v. Lucy Webb Hayes National Training School for Deaconesses and Missionaries*,[8] members of the governing board of Sibley Memorial Hospital were sued in a class action alleging that certain board members breached their duty of care by acquiescing in or approving the deposit of hospital funds in low-interest or no-interest accounts in banks with which some board members were affiliated. Although applying the heightened "gross negligence" standard and disclaiming any intention to penalize board members for "mere mistakes of judgment," the court found a breach of the duty of care.[9] The principal violation lay in the

---

§ 5–15

1. See, e.g., West's Ann. Cal. Corp. Code § 309 (for-profit), §§ 5231, 7231 (not-for-profit); Minn. Stat. Ann. § 302A.251(1) (for-profit), § 317A.251(1) (not-for-profit); N.J. Stat. Ann. § 14A:6–14 (for-profit), § 15A:6–14 (not-for-profit).

2. See discussion of duty of care for general business corporations supra § 5–6.

3. Stern v. Lucy Webb Hayes Nat'l Training School for Deaconesses & Missionaries, 381 F.Supp. 1003, 1013–14 (D.D.C.1974); Beard v. Achenbach Memorial Hosp. Ass'n, 170 F.2d 859, 862 (10th Cir.1948); See generally Daniel L. Kurtz, Board Liability: Guide for Nonprofit Directors 22 (1988) ("after years of debate on this matter, there is now broad agreement" that the corporate standard is to be applied).

4. See, e.g., John v. John, 450 N.W.2d 795, 806 (Wis.App.1989), cert. denied 498 U.S. 814, 111 S.Ct. 53, 112 L.Ed.2d 28 (1990); Midlantic Nat'l Bank v. Frank G. Thompson Found., 405

A.2d 866 (N.J.Super. Ch. Div.1979); Stern v. Lucy Webb Hayes Nat'l Training School for Deaconesses & Missionaries, 381 F.Supp. 1003 (D.D.C.1974).

5. Lynch v. John M. Redfield Found., 88 Cal.Rptr. 86 (Cal.App.1970) (noninvestment of substantial funds for five years).

6. See Ray v. Homewood Hosp., 27 N.W.2d 409 (Minn.1947); Midlantic Nat'l Bank v. Frank G. Thompson Found., 405 A.2d 866 (N.J.Super. Ch. Div.1979).

7. See, e.g., McKinney's—N.Y. Not–for–Profit Corp. Law § 717(a); West's Ann. Cal. Corp. Code §§ 5231, 7231; but see West's Ann. Cal. Corp. Code § 9241 (differing standard of care for directors of religious not-for-profit corporations).

8. 381 F.Supp. 1003 (D.D.C.1974).

9. One leading commentator has suggested that the court's decision on the duty of care issue was influenced by the duty of loyalty

failure of certain board members to diligently supervise and inquire into the activities of those making investment decisions. The board's supervisory derelictions (which included nonattendance of meetings of committees charged with management supervision) were held to constitute a violation of the duty of care.[10]

However, in most cases in which courts have examined the actions of hospital officers and directors, the duty of care has been found satisfied. For example, one court held the duty was not breached by a not-for-profit hospital's payment of questionable retroactive "incentive bonuses," finding such payments were not "reckless or extravagant conduct" and hence did not violate the duty.[11] Notably, these cases explicitly or implicitly invoke the business judgment rule, often justifying judicial deference to management decisions on the basis of the nature of the decision being challenged.[12] In opposing a number of conversions of nonprofit hospitals and health plans attorneys general have alleged that directors of the nonprofit corporations had breached their fiduciary duty of care.[13] Most of these cases have been resolved without going to final judgement on the merits, but the precedent that has developed underscores the difficulties inherent in establishing a breach of the duty. For example, a Michigan court ruled against the attorney general's challenge to a nonprofit hospital's conversion as part of a joint venture with Columbia/HCA based on the hospital's board alleged breached its fiduciary duty of care.[14] The court found that the board fulfilled its responsibilities by performing due diligence, but disapproved the arrangement on other grounds.[15]

Application of the business judgment rule in the context of not-for-profit corporations, however, raises several questions. First, it is not clear how the rule would apply to "non-business" discretionary judgments, such as those involving adherence to the charitable goals of the entity. Second, given the special responsibilities of not-for profit fiduciaries and the absence of other

violations also present in the case. Evelyn Brody, the Limits of Charity Fiduciary Law, 57 Md. L.Rev. 1400, 1442 (1998).

10. 381 F.Supp. at 1013–14. The court also found the directors' conduct breached the duty of loyalty. See § 5–16a. In a widely reported case involving, inter alia, the amount of compensation paid to the president of Adelphi University, the New York State Board of Regents removed the university's board of directors for breaching the duty of care in failing to inform themselves and exercise the requisite due care in approving excessive salary and other lavish forms of compensation. Panel of New York State Bd. of Regents, Report and Recommendation or Committee to Save Adelphi v. Diamondopoulos (Feb. 5, 1997).

11. Beard v. Achenbach Memorial Hosp. Ass'n, 170 F.2d 859 (10th Cir.1948). See also Edson v. Griffin Hosp., 144 A.2d 341 (Conn.Super.1958). See generally, discussion of the business judgment rule for general business corporations, supra § 5–6b.

12. Beard v. Achenbach Memorial Hosp. Ass'n, 170 F.2d 859 (10th Cir.1948) ("ill success or bad judgment" not amounting to gross negligence not actionable); Edson v. Griffin Hosp., 144 A.2d 341 (Conn.Super.1958). See also, Scheuer Family Foundation, Inc. v. 60 Assocs., 582 N.Y.S.2d 662 (N.Y.App.Div. 1st. Dept.1992) (no business judgment rule protection where conflicts of interest exist).

13. See Lawrence E. Singer, The Conversion Conundrum: The State and Federal Response to Hospitals' Changes in Charitable Status, 23 AM. J.L. & MED. 221, 222 (1997); Michael Peregrine, J. Health L. ; Naomi Ono, Boards of Directors Under Fire: An Examination of Nonprofit Board Duties in the Health Care Environment, 7 Ann. Health L. 107 (1998).

14. Kelley v. Michigan Affiliated Healthcare Sys., Inc., No. 96–838–CZ (Mich. Ct. Cl., Sept. 5, 1996).

15. Id.; see also Fair Care Foundation v. District of Columbia Dept. of Ins. And Securities Regulation, 716 A.2d 987 (D.C.1998)(approving conversion despite questions raised about integrity and competence of board and officers).

methods of ensuring their faithfulness, one may question whether the almost blanket protection afforded by the rule is appropriate. It is conceded that application of the rule serves to foster an appropriate level of risk-taking by management and encourages volunteers to serve on the boards of not-for-profit institutions. Nevertheless, in view of the absence of market controls and the nature of the selection process for not-for-profit fiduciaries (which is often not directed at finding capable business managers), the mechanical application of the rule deserves closer attention.[16]

b. The Duty of Care Under the Revised Model Nonprofit Corporation Act

The Revised Model Nonprofit Corporation Act (RMNCA) with its Reporter's commentary provides one of the most complete expositions of the duty of care. Although closely modeled on the standard of the Revised Model Business Corporation Act, the flexibility embodied in the language of the Act may afford not-for-profit directors even greater protection than their counterparts serving on for-profit corporate boards.[17]

The RMNCA states the basic standard of care as follows:

A director shall discharge his or her duties as a director, including his or her duties as a member of a committee:

(1) in good faith;

(2) with the care an ordinarily prudent person in a like position would exercise under similar circumstances; and

(3) in a manner the director reasonably believes to be in the best interests of the corporation.[18]

c. Analysis of the Duty of Care in the Not–For–Profit Context

Embedded in the concept of "care" are several underlying principles. First, a director must take steps to reasonably inform herself of the affairs and activities of the corporation. This entails devoting the necessary time and attention to the affairs of the corporation; assuring that she is supplied with adequate information; and/or instituting appropriate controls, monitoring and law compliance activities. To some extent, however, these requirements are mitigated by the "like position" and "similar circumstances" language employed in the RMNCA and other statutory formulations.[19] If interpretive principles such as those suggested by the official commentary become widely accepted, a risk arises that not-for-profit directors may find shelter behind their lack of experience and lack of capacity for their positions. Indeed, critics

---

16. See Official Comment to the RMNCA § 8.30 ("it may seem anomalous to apply business judgment rule to non-profit corporations"; rule operative only if compliance with § 8.30 not established). One text suggests renaming the rule "the best judgment rule" to emphasize its focus on directors' duty to make informed decisions in good faith. James J. Fishman & Stephen Schwarz, Nonprofit Organizations 186 (1995).

17. Adoption of fiduciary standards applying the degree of "good faith and diligence, care and skill" which "ordinary and prudent men" would exercise under similar circum-

stances is usually seen to implicate the for-profit standard, although contrary interpretations are possible. See, e.g., Brown v. Concerned Citizens for Sickle Cell Anemia, Inc., 382 N.E.2d 1155 (Ohio 1978); see generally Thomas H. Boyd, Note, A Call to Reform the duties of Directors Under State Not–for–Profit Corporation Statutes, 72 Iowa L. Rev. 725, 738 (1987).

18. RMNCA § 8.30(a).

19. See generally Daniel L. Kurtz, Board Liability: Guide for Nonprofit Directors 24–31 (1988) (closely analyzing language of RMNCA).

have emphasized that director and officer behavior should be more closely monitored because the risk of mismanagement is greater given the absence of a capital market or SEC disclosure requirements.[20]

Advocates of more stringent duty of care standards for not-for-profit officers and directors stress that such rules would result in wider dissemination of information and adoption of prophylactic procedures by not-for-profit boards. In addition, stricter judicial scrutiny would foster more careful selection of competent members to supervise those functions. On the other hand, the costs associated with holding not-for-profit directors to a stricter standard are not insignificant. Board members might become unduly conservative and unwilling to take risks, while certain individuals who provide fundraising or other specialized services might be discouraged from serving as directors.[21]

§ 5–16.   The Duty of Loyalty

a.   Common Law and Statutory Standards

The duty of loyalty applicable to not-for-profit directors closely parallels the duty imposed on for-profit directors and officers. Directors must pursue the interests of the corporation when acting in their corporate capacity and are prohibited from serving their own interests at the expense of those of the corporation. A breach of that duty removes the director's action from the protection of the business judgment rule. Under modern statutes and common law, however, transactions between a corporation and a director or officer, or between a corporation and another entity in which one of its directors or officers has an interest, are neither void nor voidable if: (1) the conflict of interest is disclosed and the transaction is approved by a majority of disinterested directors; (2) the conflict is disclosed to members and the transaction is approved by a majority of disinterested members; or (3) the transaction is "fair" to the corporation.[1]

As with for-profit corporations, duty of loyalty violations fall generally into two broad categories; self-dealing transactions and usurpation of corporate opportunities. The former category usually involves transactions in which a director or officer has a personal pecuniary interest in a transaction in which the corporation also has an interest;[2] however, it applies in certain instances in which a director pursues the interest of a third party.[3] Courts have set aside transactions in which officers or directors have breached their duty of loyalty by engaging in unauthorized self-dealing,[4] or dealings with a director's related organization or company.[5] The cases generally hold that the

---

20. See, e.g., Developments in the Law—Nonprofit Corporations, 105 Harv. L. Rev. 1578, 1602 (1992).

21. See Alan C. Geolot, Note, The Fiduciary Duties of Loyalty and Care Associated with the Directors and Trustees of Charitable Organizations, 64 Va. L. Rev. 449, 465 (1978).

§ 5–16

1. See supra § 5–7.

2. See, e.g., Fowle Memorial Hosp. Co. v. Nicholson, 126 S.E. 94 (N.C.1925) (lease of hospital to directors); Gilbert v. McLeod Infir-

mary, 64 S.E.2d 524 (S.C.1951) (sale of property by not-for-profit corporation to its trustees).

3. See, e.g., Collins v. Beinecke, 504 N.Y.S.2d 72, 495 N.E.2d 335 (N.Y.App.1986); Societa Operaia Di Mutuo Soccorso Villalba v. Di Maria, 122 A.2d 897 (N.J.Super. Ch. Div. 1956).

4. See Mountain Top Youth Camp, Inc. v. Lyon, 202 S.E.2d 498 (N.C.App.1974).

5. See Old Settlers Club of Milwaukee County v. Haun, 13 N.W.2d 913 (Wis.1944) (securities transaction undertaken through a director's brokerage firm); Blankenship v.

duty reaches all "interested" directors, even if they did not vote for or participate in the conflicting decision; holding stock in or sitting on the board of the other corporation is sufficient to establish the conflict.[6]

In self-dealing transactions, application of the strict trustee standard would hold any transaction between the trust and trustee voidable regardless of the reasonableness or fairness of the transaction. Although strains of this approach are sometimes detectable in duty of loyalty cases involving not-for-profit directors,[7] the modern trend has been to apply the more lenient corporate standard. Thus, most statutes and courts permit interested director transactions to be validated by a fully-informed majority of disinterested directors or, in the case of mutual benefit nonprofit corporations, fully-informed members. Such approval also brings the transaction within the business judgment rule for purposes of duty of care evaluations.[8] When an independent committee is not available, the interested director assumes the burden of proof of demonstrating the transaction's inherent fairness to the corporation.[9] Self-interested transactions involving directors of not-for-profit hospitals have been struck down where no disinterested approval was obtained and the transaction lacked indicia of fairness.[10] Perhaps because it is relatively easy to "sanitize" self-dealing transactions, courts are prone to deal severely with situations in which interested insiders do not scrupulously adhere to disclosure and approval standards. For example, in Boston Children's Heart Foundation v. Nadal–Ginard,[11] a distinguished physician who was president and board member of a foundation whose by-laws allowed him to set his own compensation, failed to disclose to the board that he was receiving substantial compensation from another entity for performing much of the same work for which he was being paid by the foundation. The First Circuit found that he had violated his fiduciary duties by not disclosing to the board all material information about his compensation and refused to consider the doctor's contention that his overall salary was fair and reasonable.

Allegations of breaches of fiduciary duty of loyalty have figured prominently in several challenges to conversions of not-for-profit entities. In Butterworth v. Anclote Manor Hospital,[12] for example, a state attorney general challenged a conversion of a nonprofit hospital whose assets were purchased by a for-profit entity, the sole shareholders of which were the directors and corporate members of the nonprofit. The assets were purchased for $6.3 million; two years later, the converted, for-profit hospital was sold for more than $29 million. A challenge by former policyholders of Blue Cross and Blue

Boyle, 329 F.Supp. 1089 (D.D.C.1971) (excessive cash from union welfare fund maintained at bank controlled by union rather than being invested).

6. Oberly v. Kirby, 592 A.2d 445, 468 (Del. 1991).

7. See, e.g., Old Settlers Club of Milwaukee County v. Haun, 13 N.W.2d 913 (Wis.1944).

8. Oberly v. Kirby, 592 A.2d 445 (Del. 1991).

9. Oberly v. Kirby, 592 A.2d 445 (Del. 1991).

10. See, e.g., Stern v. Lucy Webb Hayes Nat'l Training School for Deaconesses & Missionaries, 381 F.Supp. 1003 (D.D.C.1974)

discussed supra § 5–15a; Gilbert v. McLeod Infirmary, 64 S.E.2d 524 (S.C.1951); Fowle Memorial Hosp. Co. v. Nicholson, 126 S.E. 94 (N.C.1925); Warren v. Reed, 331 S.W.2d 847 (Ark.1960).

11. 73 F.3d 429 (1st Cir.1996).

12. 566 So.2d 296 (Fla.Dist.Ct.App.1990). See also Fair Care Foundation v. District of Columbia Dept. of Ins. And Securities Regulation, 716 A.2d 987 (D.C.App.1998)(rejecting claims that board's decision was infected by conflicts of interest and issues going to members integrity).

Shield of Ohio resulted in a settlement in which the board chairman and other trustees returning $6.8 million in compensation and retirement benefits they received after approving a merger with Columbia/HCA Healthcare Corporation.[13] Stories of self-dealing, lucrative consulting contracts, and excessive severance packages for insiders of the nonprofit entity became increasingly common as the conversion phenomenon began to gather steam.[14] While several abuses were uncovered and resolved without reaching final judgment, commentators have pointed out that claimed breaches of fiduciary duties may be difficult to establish given the corporate standard that courts apply to such transactions.[15]

Clear statutory guidance is often lacking as many statutes do not specifically address the loyalty standard[16] and most others say little about what constitutes a breach of the duty. For the most part, these statutes follow the pattern of establishing when self-interested transactions may avoid the rule of automatic voidability. The RMNCA goes somewhat further, defining the duty as requiring that directors act in good faith and "in a manner the director reasonably believes to be in the best interests of the corporation."[17] In addition, it specifically delineates circumstances in which a conflict exists.[18] Other statutes, however, set definitive standards with respect to certain transactions. For example, a majority of states flatly ban loans to officers and directors of not-for-profit corporations.[19] The basis for this ban is the potential for abuse and the difficulty in distinguishing between appropriate and inappropriate loans.[20]

The second important category of transaction covered by the duty of loyalty involves actions by directors or officers appropriating or usurping business opportunities that belong to the corporation. Under this so-called "corporate opportunity doctrine," activities that fall within a corporation's "line of business" or that otherwise in fairness belong to the corporation may not be taken by insiders without first offering it to the corporation.[21] In the

13. See Ohio: Former Blues Resolves Two Lawsuits Arising from Filed Columbia Merger, 7 BNA Health Law Reptr. 10 (January 1, 1998)(reporting settlement of Lesser v. Blue Cross and Blue Shield of Ohio (Ohio Ct. Comm Pls, No. 332396, Dec. 17, 1997).

14. See Lawrence E. Singer, The Conversion Conundrum: The State and Federal Response to Hospitals' Changes in Charitable Status, 23 Am. J.L. & Med. 221, 222 (1997); Naomi Ono, Boards of Directors Under Fire: An Examination of Nonprofit Board Duties in the Health Care Environment, 7 Ann. Health L. 107 (1998); Eleanor Hamburger et al., The Pot of Gold: Monitoring Health Care Conversions Can Yield Billions of Dollars for Health Care, 29 Clearinghouse Rev. 473 (1995) ..

15. Lawrence E. Singer, The Conversion Conundrum: The State and Federal Response to Hospitals' Changes in Charitable Status, 23 Am. J.L. & Med. 221, 222 ("establishing a breach can be difficult given the sometimes subtle nuances and reasonable characterizations that can be attached to signing bonuses and other forms of executive compensation that legitimately may be a component of the

conversion process"). See also Fair Care Foundation v. District of Columbia Dept. of Ins. And Securities Regulation, 716 A.2d 987 (D.C.App.1998)(approving conversion despite questions raised about self-dealing by board and officers).

16. As noted, many courts apply corporate principles to nonprofit corporations even in the absence of specific statutory guidance. Oberly v. Kirby, 592 A.2d 445 (Del.1991).

17. RMNCA § 8.30(a)(3).

18. See RMNCA § 8.31(d).

19. See, e.g., Haw. Rev. Stat. § 415B–70; Iowa Code Ann. § 504A.27; McKinney's—N.Y Not–for–Profit Corp. Law § 716; RMNCA § 8.32. In this regard most states apply a stricter standard than that applicable to for-profit corporations.

20. RMNCA § 8.32, Official Comment (stating, however, that advances of money from petty cash and for corporate purposes are not loans within the meaning of this section).

21. See discussion of corporate opportunity doctrine, supra § 5–7b.

context of not-for-profit corporations, however, this doctrine has rarely been found applicable.[22] Historically, most donative not-for-profit organizations lacked authority under their articles or did not possess the financial where-withal to enter into business opportunities outside their principal mission. Hence, directors were free to pursue business opportunities that presented themselves. However, in today's market, with not-for-profit corporations routinely involved in commercial enterprises, the rationale for the doctrine would seem to require strict adherence by directors and officers to the limitations it imposes.

b. Analysis of the Duty of Loyalty in the Not–For–Profit Context

A vigorous debate has developed concerning the wisdom of applying the for-profit standard to self-dealing transactions involving not-for-profit organizations. Professor Hansmann has argued for a flat prohibition in certain circumstances against all self-dealing transactions (subject to a few limited exceptions regarding reasonable salaries and expenses and other matters).[23] Under this view, "commercial" not-for-profit corporations, like hospitals, are subject to greater abuse by insiders than for-profits because they are typically subject to fewer controls such as the market for corporate control and derivative lawsuits by shareholders. In addition, a blanket rule would offer a bright line that would be readily understood by all and easily enforced. Critics of this approach point out that a strict duty of loyalty may force directors to forego opportunities that would benefit the corporation and may ultimately deter participation on not-for-profit boards.[24] Proponents of the strict fiduciary duty respond that commercial not-for-profits have the option of choosing the lesser fiduciary duties by converting to the for-profit form if the not-for-profit duties are too constraining.[25]

§ 5–17. The Duty of Obedience

A third fiduciary obligation—and one uniquely applicable to not-for-profit directors—is sometimes referred to as the duty of obedience. This duty, which is actually an extension of the obligations of charitable trustees to administer trusts in a manner faithful to the wishes of the creator of the trust, essentially ensures that those running a not-for-profit corporation adhere to the broad dictates of the corporation's "mission" or other statement of purpose.[1] How-

22. For a well reasoned case applying the doctrine to a not-for-profit organization, see Northeast Harbor Golf Club, Inc. v. Nancy Harris, 661 A.2d 1146 (Me. 1995). Cf. Mile–O–Mo Fishing Club, Inc. v. Noble, 210 N.E.2d 12 (Ill.App.1965).

23. See Henry B. Hansmann, Reforming Nonprofit Corporation Law, 129 U. Pa. L. Rev. 497, 569–74 (1981).

24. See, e.g., RMNCA § 8.31, Official Comment ("many individuals are elected to nonprofit boards because of their ability to enter into or cause an affiliate to enter into a transaction with and for the benefit of the corporation."). See also Comment, Developments in the Law—Nonprofit Corporations, 105 Harv. L. Rev. 1578, 1604 (1992) (stricter standard

should apply only to public benefit corporations which lack external controls).

25. Henry B. Hansmann, The Evolving Law of Nonprofit Organizations: Do Current Trends Make Good Policy?, 39 Cas. W. Res. L. Rev. 807, 821 (1989).

§ 5–17

1. The principal authority identifying this duty as a separate and distinct obligation of trustees is Daniel L. Kurtz, Board Liability: Guide for Nonprofit Directors 84–90 (1988). For the view that this problem should be analyzed under the duty of care, see Evelyn Brody, The Limits of Charity Fiduciary Law, 57 Md. L.Rev. 1400 (1998).

ever, the case law often affords considerable latitude in determining how broadly-phrased purposes or "missions" may be fulfilled.[2]

The charitable purpose or mission protected by the duty is usually expressed in the corporate charter or bylaws. Although the donor's original purpose guides the inquiry, courts frequently inquire into the past activities of the organization for evidence of that purpose.[3] Nevertheless, courts will frequently grant directors leeway in exercising discretion by interpreting the language of the charter to permit it to adapt to contemporary conditions or finding express or implied powers to sell an institution or radically change the nature of its business.[4] The general rule, however, seems to be that directors must follow clearly-stated charitable objectives even if other alternatives exist that are more profitable, efficient or even more needed by the community.[5] Thus, courts have refused to allow a significant modification of the original charitable purpose on dissolution of the corporation or when business realities had forced a significant change in the location or nature of the not-for-profit enterprise.[6]

For example, in *Queen of Angels Hospital v. Younger*,[7] a not-for-profit corporation sponsored by the Franciscan Sisters leased a hospital it had been operating for forty-four years to a proprietary organization with the intention of using the proceeds to operate medical clinics providing free medical care to the community. The court found that the articles of the corporation (describing Queen of Angels as a "hospital") and its history established that its assets were held in trust for the purpose of operating a hospital. While this did not preclude the corporation from engaging in other activities in addition to operating a hospital, it did bar the abandonment of the original purpose in favor of clinics. Notably, the court chose to ignore language in the hospital's corporate purpose clause suggesting broader charitable purposes, stating that although the corporation was entitled to do many things besides operating a hospital, essential to all those other activities was the continued operation of a hospital.[8] However, while some older cases like *Queen of Angels* cases apply charitable trust principles to enforce a strict duty of obedience on directors, others apply the "substantial departure" test more flexibly to permit boards to allow nonprofit entities to adapt to changing conditions.[9] Not surprisingly, attorneys general challenging conversions of not-for-profit hospitals and health plans have invoked the former standard.[10]

---

2. See In re Multiple Sclerosis Serv. Org., 505 N.Y.S.2d 841, 496 N.E.2d 861 (N.Y.App. 1986).

3. Id.; Queen of Angels Hosp. v. Younger, 136 Cal.Rptr. 36 (Cal.App.1977).

4. See, e.g., City of Paterson v. Paterson Gen. Hosp., 235 A.2d 487 (N.J.Super. Ch. Div. 1967); Holden Hosp. Corp. v. Southern Illinois Hosp. Corp., 174 N.E.2d 793 (Ill.1961).

5. See Daniel W. Coyne & Kathleen Russell Kas, the Not–for–Profit Hospital as a Charitable Trust: To Whom Does Its Value Belong?, 24 J. Health & Hosp. L. 48 (1991).

6. See, e.g., Attorney Gen. v. Hahnemann Hosp., 494 N.E.2d 1011 (Mass.1986); Queen of

Angels Hosp. v. Younger, 136 Cal.Rptr. 36 (Cal. App.1977).

7. 136 Cal.Rptr. 36 (Cal.App.1977).

8. Id. (citing Holt v. College of Osteopathic Physicians and Surgeons, 394 P.2d 932 (Cal. 1964)).

9. E.g., Taylor v. Baldwin, 247 S.W.2d 741 (Mo.1952); City of Paterson v. Paterson General Hospital, 235 A.2d 487 (N.J. Super. Ct. Ch. Div. 1967).

10. See Michael W. Peregrine, Charitable Trust Laws and the Evolving nature of the Nonprofit Hospital Corporation, 30 J. Health & Hosp. L. 11 (1997)(reviewing theories pursued by states in challenging conversions).

Furthermore, even a valid amendment of the not-for-profit entity's charitable purpose will not necessarily relieve the board's obligations. In the *Hahnemann Hospital* case,[11] the board of a nonprofit charitable corporation amended its articles to add new purposes. The court held that while the amendment would permit funds obtained after the amendment to be devoted to the new purpose, any such use of prior unrestricted gifts would constitute a breach of the directors' fiduciary duties.

§ 5–18. Standing

The question of who should have standing to enforce fiduciary duties is a critical issue in not-for-profit corporate governance. Shareholders of for-profit corporations (and their attorneys) have financial incentives to police the activities of directors through derivative litigation and third party actions. Lacking shareholders, not-for-profit corporations are deprived of this class of potential plaintiffs. Although some not-for-profits have members, these individuals often do not have strong incentives to uncover and challenge breaches of fiduciary duties. Moreover, other important differences from for-profit corporations, such as the absence of both a capital market and disclosure obligations under securities regulation, militate in favor of a permissive rule of standing for private parties.

Most statutes grant standing to enforce fiduciary duties to state attorneys general.[1] Where statutory authority is unclear, courts have analogized not-for-profit corporations to charitable trusts to find the attorney general has the power to bring actions against directors.[2] In the case of mutual benefit corporations, some cases hold that the attorney general is the exclusive enforcer of these duties.[3] It is doubtful, however, that attorneys general have adequate incentives or resources to act as the only monitors of fiduciary behavior. Thus some jurisdictions allow others to enforce the duties.

A number of statutes[4] and court decisions[5] have vested standing in members and directors of not-for-profits. On rare occasions, standing is recognized for donors and others with a "special interest."[6] Statutes allowing members to bring derivative actions on behalf of not-for-profit corporations often impose procedural requirements analogous to those applicable to shareholders' derivative suits,[7] as well as additional requirements such as minimum

11. Attorney Gen. v. Hahnemann Hosp., 494 N.E.2d 1011 (Mass.1986).

§ 5–18

1. See, e.g., N.Y. Not–for–Profit Corp. Law § 720; but cf. RMNCA § 6.30.

2. See, e.g., Lopez v. Medford Community Ctr., Inc., 424 N.E.2d 229 (Mass.1981); cf. State ex rel. Butterworth v. Anclote Manor Hosp., Inc., 566 So.2d 296 (Fla.App.1990).

3. Voelker v. Saint Louis Mercantile Library Ass'n, 359 S.W.2d 689, 698 (Mo.1962).

4. See, e.g., RMNCA § 6.30(a); N.Y. Not–for–Profit Corp. Law § 623(a). Some statutes provide for derivative suits by members representing a specified minimum number or percentage of votes. RMNCA § 6.30.

5. See, e.g., John v. John, 450 N.W.2d 795 (Wis.App.1989), cert. denied 498 U.S. 814, 111 S.Ct. 53, 112 L.Ed.2d 28 (1990) (allowing directors to sue co-director); Jackson v. Stuhlfire, 547 N.E.2d 1146 (Mass.App.1990) (allowing members of non-profit to bring suit).

6. See, e.g., Jones v. Grant, 344 So.2d 1210 (Ala.1977); but cf. Associate Students of University of Oregon v. Oregon Inv. Council, 728 P.2d 30 (Or. 1986) (denying standing to student scholarship recipients challenging university investment policies) . .

7. See, e.g., RMNCA § 6.30(c); McKinney's—N.Y. Not–for–Profit Corp. Law § 623(d).

member participation needed to initiate an action.[8] In recognition of the fact that some not-for-profit corporations lack members to bring suits, some courts have permitted co-directors to sue other directors to enforce fiduciary duties.[9]

Most jurisdictions have been extremely reluctant to grant standing to other parties. Although a few cases recognize such rights for those with a "special relationship" to the corporation, such as patients of a charitable hospital[10] and students of a not-for-profit college, outsiders to the corporation rarely have standing.[11] Critics of the "special relationship" line of cases argue that permissive standing rules lead to excessive litigation and that such groups are not likely to have significant additional information so as to increase the probability of meritorious litigation.[12] A number of cases have also denied donors standing to enforce fiduciary duties, holding that donation of unrestricted funds neither creates a charitable trust nor sufficient "special interest" to justify standing.[13]

§ 5–19. Conversions of Not–For–Profit Entities: Policy Issues

The massive migration to the for-profit sector by nonprofit health care firms (described by one scholar as the "largest redeployment of charitable assets in the Anglo–American world since Henry VII closed the monasteries in 1536–1540"[1]) has stirred considerable controversy. Although conversions of nonprofit entities had occurred for many years, state attorneys general began aggressively monitoring them in the mid-nineties after several well-publicized episodes involving allegations of self-dealing and enormous undervaluations attracted national attention. Acting under their authority to protect charitable assets and to ensure that they are used for proper charitable purposes, attorneys general have challenged a large number of transactions involving not-for-profit hospitals and Blue Cross/Blue Shield organizations, with settlements that have established charitable foundations controlling over $9 billion in assets.[2] On the legislative front, over thirty states have enacted statutes governing conversions;[3] in addition, some states have enacted laws designed to assure greater community benefits from entities enjoying tax-exempt status.[4] The state of the law, however, is very much in flux, as few cases have

---

8. See, e.g., RMNCA § 6.30(a)(i) (requiring 5% of the voting power or 50 members, whichever is less, to initiate an action). For criticism of these requirements, see Comment, Developments in the Law—Nonprofit Corporations, 105 Harv. L. Rev. 1578, 1605 (1992).

9. John v. John, 450 N.W.2d 795 (Wis.App. 1989), cert. denied 498 U.S. 814, 111 S.Ct. 53, 112 L.Ed.2d 28 (1990); RMNCA § 6.30(a)(ii).

10. Stern v. Lucy Webb Hayes Nat'l Training School for Deaconesses & Missionaries, 367 F.Supp. 536, 540–541 (D.D.C.1973), opinion supplemented by 381 F.Supp. 1003 (D.D.C. 1974).

11. See Jones v. Grant, 344 So.2d 1210 (Ala.1977); cf. Miller v. Alderhold, 184 S.E.2d 172 (Ga.1971) (student standing rejected).

12. See Comment, Developments in the Law—Nonprofit Corporations, 105 Harv. L. Rev. 1605, 1606–1609 (1992) (proposing in-

creased penalties for breaches of fiduciary duties through imposition of fines on directors in lieu of expanding the class of persons with standing to sue).

13. See, e.g., Denckla v. Independence Found., 193 A.2d 538 (Del.1963); Holden Hosp. Corp. v. Southern Illinois Hosp. Corp., 174 N.E.2d 793 (Ill.1961).

§ 5–19

1. James J. Fishman, Checkpoints on the Conversion Highway: Some Trouble Spots in the Conversion of Nonprofit Health Care Organizations to For-profit Status, 23 J. Corp. L. 701 (1998).

2. Laurie Larson, How Does Your Foundation Grow?, 51 Trustee 11 (1998).

3. See infra § 5–22.

4. See infra § 5–23.

proceeded to final decision and the legal precedent governing not-for-profit entities is sparse.

Conversions of hospitals to for-profit status attracted national attention with the aggressive acquisition and joint-venture strategy pursued by Columbia/HCA Healthcare Corporation and a few other publicly traded hospital corporations.[5] Significant numbers of not-for-profit hospitals were acquired in the 1990's, a phenomenon undoubtedly attributable to financial pressures facing many community hospitals as well as to the need to be more efficient and raise capital to compete in the era of managed care.[6] Whether because of the legal entanglements of Columbia/HCA and other large for-profit hospital corporations, or because of the heightened legal scrutiny being applied to such transactions, the pace of acquisitions appears to have slowed considerably.[7] Health Maintenance Organizations have converted in far greater proportions than hospitals: over one-third of all HMOs have converted (compared to one percent of all nonprofit hospitals), bringing over two-thirds of all HMOs to for-profit status.[8] HMOs' greater receptivity to the for-profit form is explained by the fact that HMOs do not enjoy the same community-based support as do not-for-profit hospitals and by the increasing strictures placed by states and the IRS on them to retain on their tax exempt status.[9] Probably the greatest foment has occurred over the conversion of Blue Cross and Blue Shield plans to the for-profit form. As a result of a large number of mergers the total number of independent Blue plans has declined to 52 (from 69 in 1995 and 128 in 1975).[10] Other Blues that have not converted to the for-profit form have also been involved in controversial transactions. Many have switched from charitable to mutual benefit nonprofit corporate forms while others have undertaken various "restructurings" involving joint ventures or asset sales that left the not-for-profit entity as a greatly diminished charitable enterprise.

A heated and largely unresolved policy debate has arisen over the societal effects of conversions in the health care sector. Proponents of conversions stress that not-for-profit entities such as hospitals do not return social benefits in the form of charity care or community service commensurate with the tax relief they receive and that for profit entities provide comparable or better care at lower net costs.[11] Other arguments have been advanced in favor

---

5. Founded in 1987, Columbia grew to control 350 hospitals by 1996, acquiring approximately 30 not-for-profit hospitals per year in 1995 and 1996. Id.; Bruce Japsen, Another Record Year for Dealmaking: Activity Among Medium Size Companies Fuels Continued Drive Toward Consolidation, Mod. Healthcare, Dec. 23, 1996 at 37.

6. Between 1990 and 1996, 192 of the more than 5,000 not-for-profit hospitals in the United States converted to for profit status; in 1996, the total number of conversions was sixty. General Accounting Office, Not–For–Profit Hospitals: Conversion Issues Prompt Increased State Oversight, GAO/HEHS–98–24 (1997).

7. In 1998, the number of for-profit hospitals declined by two (to 1,329) and the number of beds in those hospitals dropped by 1,013, to 182,403. Modern Healthcare, January 1, 1999; see also, David A. Hyman, Hospital Conversions: Fact, Fantasy, and Regulatory Follies, 23 J. Corp. L. 741 (1998).

8. James J. Fishman & Stephen Schwarz, Nonprofit Organizations: Cases and Materials (1998 Supp.) at 4.

9. See id. On the tax status of HMOs, see Chapter 2.

10. Chris Rauber, Can't Shake the Blues: Nation's Blues Plans Gain Market Share But Post Another Year of Billion Dollar Losses, Mod. Healthcare, March 22, 1999 at 14. See also, Consumers Union, Conversion and Preservation of Charitable Assets of Blue Cross and Blue Shield Plans: How States have Protected or Failed to Protect the Public's Interest available at http://www.consumersunion.org/health/bcbs15wc998.htm (describing Blue Cross and Blue Shield conversions, actual and contemplated, in twenty-five states).

11. See Note, "First, Do No Harm": An Analysis of the Nonprofit Hospital Sales Acts, 45 UCLA L. Rev 503 (1997)(summarizing economic theories and empirical evidence); David

of conversions, including placing tax-exempt entities on the tax rolls; assuring an efficient redeployment of capital; ending the myth that nonprofits supply more charity care or other social benefits than for-profit counterparts; and facilitating consolidation and reduction of capacity.[12] Opponents of conversions marshal empirical evidence pointing in the opposite direction, such as the reduced levels of charity care provided by hospitals undergoing conversion.[13] They also argue that the numerous health care market imperfections are most efficiently addressed by not-for-profit firms which are less likely to exploit consumer ignorance for their own economic benefit.[14] Careful analysis of the available evidence counsels agnosticism. It is, for example, not clear whether and to what extent not-for-profits supply "better" or less costly care; nor is it known whether the corporate organizational form is the cause of any such benefits.[15] On the other hand, there is no doubt that many nonprofit entities shoulder significant burdens in providing and cross subsidizing care and that undoing existing structures would cause massive disruptions. As one leading researcher summarized the policy implications of the learning in this area, the "debate over for profit health care is fueled as much by values as by evidence."[16]

§ 5–20. Mechanics of Conversions of Not–For–Profit Corporations

The term "conversion" is used rather loosely in the literature and the law. As a general matter, the rubric might include any transaction in which the assets and/or control of a not-for profit entity comes under the control of a for-profit entity. This definition would embrace not only mergers and asset acquisitions but joint ventures and other contractual arrangements pursuant to which assets formerly devoted to not-for-profit purposes come to be controlled by an independent for-profit firm. The issue of central importance for legal and policy analyses is whether, upon conversion, assets are deployed for the original, charitable purposes to which they were originally dedicated or to some acceptably close substitute purpose.

A. Hyman, Hospital Conversions: Fact, Fantasy, and Regulatory Follies, 23 J. Corp. L. 741 (1998); Malik M. Hasan, Let's End the Nonprofit Charade, 334 New Eng. J. Med. 1055 (1996); Gary Claxton et al., Public Policy Issues in Nonprofit Conversions: An Overview, Health Aff. Mar.-Apr. 1997.

12. See Bradford H. Gray, Conversion of HMOs and Hospitals: What's at Stake?, Health Affairs, Mar.-Apr., 1997, 29, 33–34;

13. Nonprofit Conversions: Charity Care Declined at Calif. Hospitals Following

Conversion to For-profit Status 7 Health Care Policy Rept. (May 1999)(hospital charity care declined at California nonprofit hospitals that converted to for-profit corporations). Consumers Union, "White Knights or Trojan Horses?" (May 10, 1999). See also, John Copeland, Nonprofit Versus For–Profit Hospitals, 18 Exempt Org. Tax Rev. 35 (1997) (comparing for profit and nonprofit hospitals based on net effect on taxes forgiven or paid; hospital costs; and community

benefits); Gary J. Young et al., Does the Sale of Nonprofit Hospitals Threaten Health Care for the Poor, Health Aff., Jan–Feb 1997, at 137 (examining effects of acquisitions on the provision of uncompensated care").

14. Bradford H. Gray, Conversion of HMOs and Hospitals: What's at Stake?, 16 Health Affairs 29 (Mar.-Apr.,1997); Mark Schlesinger, et al., Charity and Community: The Role of Nonprofit Ownership in a Managed Health Care System, 21 Health Pol. Pol'y & L. 712 (1996). See also, M. Gregg Bloche, Should the Government Intervene to Protect Non Profits?, 17 Health Affs. 7 (Sept.-Oct., 1998).

15. See M. Gregg Bloche, Should the Government Intervene to Protect Non Profits?, 17 Health Affs. 7 (Sept.-Oct., 1998).

16. Bradford H. Gray, Conversion of HMOs and Hospitals: What's at Stake?, 16 Health Affairs 29 (Mar.-Apr.1997).

There are several kinds of conversions:

Conversions in Place. A conversion in place is perhaps the simplest and most direct form of conversion. It has been used by HMOs and other managed care entities principally because it allows contractual commitments to remain unchanged. Typically, the transition is effected simply by an amendment to the nonprofit corporation's articles of incorporation which deletes all nonprofit provisions and adds powers and purposes to conduct for-profit activities. Only a handful of states permit conversions in place and, even where allowed, complexities may arise in the transfer of fixed assets.[1]

Mergers. A conversion may also occur by merger of a nonprofit corporation into a for-profit entity. Often the nonprofit establishes a new for-profit corporation to which it contributes its assets in exchange for cash, notes, and stock. Thereafter, the nonprofit corporation merges into the for-profit corporation. In the case of charitable entities, a foundation or new nonprofit corporation is created to receive the cash or stock from the surviving corporation.

Drop-down conversions. In a drop-down conversion, the not-for-profit transfers some or all of its assets and liabilities to a wholly or partially owned subsidiary in exchange for stock and/or notes. This arrangement allows the for-profit subsidiary to raise capital through the equity market. Because the original not-for-profit entity remains in existence, it is sometimes argued that no conversion has taken place and no legal obligation (such as transferring assets to charity) attaches.

Asset Sales. In a sale of assets, the not-for-profit corporation sells its operating assets to a for-profit corporation typically in return for stock, notes, or cash. Foundations are usually established to hold these assets for charitable purposes. In contrast to a conversion in place, an asset sale requires that the for-profit obtain appropriate state licenses.

Joint Ventures and Leases. The not-for-profit may establish a shared interest in a new joint venture entity by contributing health care assets. The for-profit entity typically contributes cash or other financial assets. Where the parties wish to share control, as in a "whole hospital joint venture," the for profit entity contributes a sum equal to the value of half the value of the hospital and contributes the remainder to the not-for-profit entity which can devote those sums to charitable purposes.

§ 5–21. Legal Issues Raised by Conversion of Not–For–Profit Corporations

a. *IRS Regulation*

Most conversions in the health care sector involve entities that are tax exempt under section 501(c) of the Internal Revenue Code. However, the Internal Revenue Service's authority in these situations is limited and has not been interpreted to restrict conversions as long an entity remains properly organized as a nonprofit entity and continues to pursue an exempt purpose.[1]

§ 5–20

1. See Douglas M. Mancino, Taxation of Hospitals and Health Care Organizations 21–28 (1995 & 1998 Supp.) (listing Arizona, California, Pennsylvania, Utah and Virginia as permitting conversions in place).

§ 5–21

1. John Colombo, A Proposal for an Exit Tax on Nonprofit Conversion Transactions, 23

The Internal Revenue Service has the authority to prevent private inurement which may contribute to ensuring an adequate purchase price. With the enactment of intermediate sanctions authority, the IRS now has greater flexibility and capacity to monitor conflicts of interest;[2] however, it still lacks legal authority to require advance approval except for joint ventures between for-profit and nonprofit organizations. Consequently, regulation of conversions has been governed principally by state common law and statutes.

b. State Nonprofit Corporation Law

Conversion to for-profit status may raise a number of issues under nonprofit corporation law. First, the fiduciary duties of the board of the converting corporation require that in making the conversion decision, board members exercise due care, make an informed decision, act with undivided loyalty and assure that the charitable or other purposes specified in the corporation's organizing documents are followed.[3] Although attorneys general have often relied upon breaches of one or more of these duties as a basis for challenging conversions, this approach has been accurately characterized as "a relatively weak weapon in the arsenals of attorneys general and community activists."[4]

State nonprofit corporation law also strictly regulates the disposition of assets. Conversions that entail the disappearance of the not-for-profit entity raise issues of compliance with laws governing dissolution of such entities. Under section 501(c)(3) of the Internal Revenue Code, the nonprofit's articles of association must state that upon dissolution, the organization's assets are to be distributed for one or more exempt purposes or to a governmental body for a public purpose. Similarly, under state corporate law public benefit corporations or charities must transfer their assets on dissolution to 501(c)(3) entities, to charities, or to other entities for similar uses.[5] By contrast, mutual benefit organizations may distribute their assets to members upon dissolution unless provided otherwise in their certificates of incorporation or bylaws.[6] A number of the challenges to conversions have turned on (1) whether a dissolution had in fact occurred, so as to trigger the requirement of disposition of the assets to a charitable enterprise, and (2) whether the not-for-profit corporation was a public benefit corporation and hence bound by such obligations on dissolution, or whether it was a mutual benefit corporation and not so bound.

In Blue Cross and Blue Shield of Missouri v. Angoff,[7] the court confronted a "reorganization" by Blue Cross and Blue Shield of Missouri (BCBSMO) pursuant to which it had transferred over 80 percent of its most valuable, managed care assets to a for-profit subsidiary. The court found that BCBSMO

J. Corp. L. 779 (1998). James J. Fishman, Checkpoints on the Conversion Highway: Some Trouble Spots in the Conversion of Nonprofit Health Care Organizations to For-profit Status, 23 J. Corp. L. 701 (1998)

2. See Ch. 2.

3. See discussion of fiduciary duties in nonprofit corporations supra §§ 5–15–5–17.

4. Lawrence E. Singer, The Conversion Conundrum: The State and Federal Response to Hospitals' Changes in Charitable Status, 23 AM. J.L. & MED. 221, 236(1997.

5. RMNCA § 14.06(7). However some states adopt a much looser standard, essentially allowing assets to be transferred to organizations engaged in "substantially similar" activities to those engaged in by the dissolving corporation. See, e.g., 805 Ill. Comp. Stat. 105/112.16 (1997); Ore. Rev. Stat. § 61.530 (1997).

6. RMNCA § 14.06.

7. 1998 WL 435697 (Mo.App. W.D.1998).

had thereby abandoned its nonprofit purposes of offering nonprofit health plans and hence exceeded its legal authority.[8] The court's holding appears to rest on a conclusion that the magnitude of the change amounted to such a radical departure as to constitute an abandonment of defendant's purposes, despite the fact that it continued to hold substantial assets and conduct significant business in furtherance of its nonprofit purposes. In a number of other situations involving claims of abandonment of nonprofit purposes, parties have reached settlements after legislative interventions clarified the legal responsibilities of the converting entity.[9]

As noted above, not all nonprofit corporations are charitable. The RMBCA and many states establish two kinds of nonprofit corporations: public benefits corporations (which include charities) and mutual benefit corporations. The distinction is of profound significance for conversion transactions because characterization as a mutual benefit nonprofit may permit the surviving entity to avoid distributing any assets to a charitable foundation. A number of courts have held that Blue Cross plans were charitable corporations. Though highly fact specific, these cases have generally found charitable or public benefit purposes after examining statements contained in the companies' articles of incorporation, activities undertaken since incorporation, the composition of boards of directors, and public statements.[10] By contrast, a Texas court concluded that Blue Cross and Blue Shield of Texas (BCBST) was not a charitable corporation and therefore did not fall within the Texas Attorney General's charitable trust jurisdiction.[11] Consequently, the court held that the company could merge with Illinois Blue Cross–Blue Shield (an Illinois mutual insurance company) without dedicating any of its assets to charitable purposes. In reaching its decision, the Texas court relied on a variety of factors that indicated how BCBST actually operated, such as that it was regulated as an insurance company; provided no charity care or other traditionally charitable services; did not receive charitable gifts or contributions; charged competitive market prices for its product; and operated for the benefit of its policy holders, not the public at large.[12] Inclusion of language within the articles of incorporation indicating a charitable purpose has normally mandated the imposition of a charitable trust of some type on the assets—even where subsequent operations have little or no resemblance to traditional charitable activities. In the Texas case, however, operational

---

8. Id.

9. See, e.g., Ga. Code Ann. Sec. 33–20–1 et seq.; see generally, Nichole J. Starr, The Conversion and Settlement of Georgia Blue: Are Consumer Groups Still Singing the Blues? 32 J. Health L. 115 (1999). In California, the State Department of Corporations initially determined that Blue Cross would not have to make a payment to a charitable foundation after it transferred its assets to a for-profit subsidiary. After legislation was introduced that would require public benefit corporations to maintain and increase charitable contributions in proportions to assets held, the parties agreed to a substantial settlement which ultimately led to the creation of two foundations with assets in excess of $2 billion. E. Hamburger et al., The Pot of Gold:Monitoring Health

Care Conversions Can Yield Billions of Dollars for Health Care, Clearinghouse Rev., Aug.-Sept. 1995 (describing settlement of conversions in California).

10. See, e.g., Blue Cross and Blue Shield of Kansas v. Nixon, CV–197–330 (Cr. Ct. Mo., 1998); In the Matter of the Application of Blue Cross & Blue Shield of New Jersey, Inc. for Conversion to a Domestic Mutual Insurer, Cas. No. A–004505–96T1); and State of Ohio v. Blue Cross & Blue Shield Mutual of Ohio, Case No. 311, 632).

11. Morales v. Blue Cross and Blue Shield of Texas, No. 96–13907 (D. Ct. Travis City, TX) (Sept. 18, 1998).

12. Id.

factors seem to have played a decisive role in the court's characterization of the entity as a mutual benefit corporation.

c. *Charitable Trust Law*

Although charitable corporations such as nonprofit hospitals are not themselves charitable trusts, their assets may be impressed with a charitable trust.[13] In such cases, the requirements of the charitable trust doctrine must be met. The assets of the charitable trust must be dedicated to the original purposes of the settlor and, whenever those purposes become impossible to pursue the trustees must dedicate the charitable assets to a purpose that resembles the original intent of the settlor as closely as possible.[14] Because most conversions change the purpose of charitable corporations they must comply with the common law doctrine of *cy pres*. Under the doctrine, which applies to both charitable corporations and charitable trusts, a court may find that it is impossible, impractical, or illegal to carry out the donor's intent and that, in addition to the specific charitable purposes outlined in the trust instrument, the donor implied a general charitable intent beyond the one specifically mentioned.[15] Where the court so finds, *cy pres* principles mandate that the trustees dedicate the charitable assets to a purpose that resembles the original intent of the settlor as closely as possible.

In the context of conversions two kinds of *cy pres* questions may arise. The "front end" *cy pres* issue is whether the board of the charitable corporation has legal authority to decide to sell assets without the approval of a court (or in some cases, of the attorney general).[16] If, for example, a hospital received restricted donations (i.e., donations impressed with an actual trust), court approval is required. On the other hand, receipt of unrestricted donations would in most states not prohibit the hospital board from selling the charitable assets; however, some courts would restrict the use of any proceeds received before the corporation amended its corporate purposes. The "back end" *cy pres* issue arises with respect to use of the proceeds from the sale and requires judicial approval where the board would devote those proceeds to purposes other than the ones specified in the hospital corporation's charter.

13. A charitable trust is "a fiduciary relationship with respect to property arising as a result of a manifestation of an intention to create it and subjecting the person by whom the property is held to equitable duties to deal with the property for a charitable purpose." Restatement (Second) of Trusts § 348 (1959). For example, where courts find that a hospital represented itself to donors, the state and the public that it was a hospital, a charitable trust may be imposed on its assets. See, e.g., Queen of Angels v. Younger, 66 Cal.App.3d 359 (1977).

14. The Restatement of Trusts provides:

[I]f property is given in trust to be applied to a particular charitable purpose, and it is or becomes impossible or impracticable or illegal to carry out the particular purpose, and if the settlor manifested a more general intention to devote the property to charitable purposes, the trust will not fail but the court will direct the application of the property to some charitable purpose which falls within the general charitable intention of the settlor.

Restatement (Second) of Trusts § 399 (1959); see also id. at § 372 (fiduciary duty of trustees to assure that charitable assets continue to be devoted to the charitable purpose).

15. Austin W. Scott & William F. Fratcher, Scott on Trusts § 348.1(4th ed. 1989). Under the closely related doctrine of deviation, a court may allow the breach of an administrative restriction on charitable assets where compliance with the restriction is impossible or impractical, or where compliance with the restriction would defeat the intended purpose of the gift.

16. Evelyn Brody, The Limits of Charity Fiduciary Law, 57 Md. L.Rev. 1400 (1998).

How strictly courts will interpret the "impossibility" and "impracticability" requirements appears to vary. A narrow approach would require that the assets be devoted to the identical purposes specified in the trust: thus proceeds from a hospital sale could not be used for preventative care or subsidized charitable care unless primary and secondary hospital services were "impossible."[17] It can be seen that such a strict application of the impossibility standard might foreclose alternative uses for funds unless bankruptcy were imminent, and further, that funds could not be used for alternative health care services unless there was no possibility of funding hospital services. A leading commentator has aptly criticized this approach: "Why should the wishes of the long-ago donors of what is now a small percentage of financial resources force the duplication of hospital services?"[18] In some circumstances, courts may avoid draconian results by interpreting the donor's intent broadly to permit additional uses for the funds or to invoke the doctrine of "deviation" which permits minor deviations from the gift's restrictions to achieve the donor's ultimate intent.[19]

Most states give the state attorney general authority to enforce provisions of a charitable trust, either by common law precedent or statute. Thus, transactions that involve material changes in the use of charitable assets of a nonprofit would be subject to oversight by state attorneys general. In appropriate cases, the attorney general could file suit to enforce the interests of the public and the charitable beneficiaries in the operations of the nonprofit.[20]

§ 5–22. State Statutes Regulating Conversions of Not–For–Profit Entities

A number of states have enacted statutes governing the process and setting standards for regulatory approvals of conversions of not-for-profit entities.[1] Several political and legal factors have contributed to the rapid

---

17. See James J. Fishman, Checkpoints on the Conversion Highway: Some Trouble Spots in the conversion of Nonprofit Health Care Organizations to For–Profit Status, 23 Iowa J. Corp. L. 701, 731 (1998)(comparing California's "strict constructionist view of cy pres" which requires proceeds from hospital sales to be used to carry out the hospital's original purpose to New York's more liberal approach which allows for distribution to organizations engaged in "substantially similar activities" and leaves it up to the board of directors to determine to whom distributions should be made, citing Queen of Angels Hosp. v. Younger, 136 Cal. Reporter 36 (1977) and In re Multiple Sclerosis Service Org., 496 N.E.2d 861 (N.Y.App.1986)).

18. Evelyn Brody, The Limits of Charity Fiduciary Law, 57 Md. L. Rev. 1400, 1470 (1998).

19. See M. Greg Bloche, Corporate Takeover of Teaching Hospitals, 65 S. Cal. L.Rev. 1035, 1043 (1992) (urging that courts recognize that technological and market pressures on hospitals constitute unforseen circumstances that would permit the use of proceeds involving restricted funds to apply to research or teaching).

20. James J. Fishman & Steven Swarz, Nonprofit Organizations 245 (1995).

§ 5–22

1. See Cal. Corp. Code §§ 5913–5919 (West 1999); Colo. Rev. Stat. § 10–16–324 (1998); 1997 Conn. Acts 188 (Reg. Sess.); 1998 Conn. Acts. 36 (Reg. Sess.); D.C. Code Ann. §§ 32–551 to 32–560 (1998); Ga. Code Ann. §§ 31–7–400 to 31–7–412, 31–7–89.1 (1999); Haw. Rev. Stat. §§ 323D–1 to 323D–12 (1998); La. Rev. Stat. Ann. §§ 40:2115.11 to 40:2115.22 (West 1998); Md. Code Ann. State Gov't. §§ 6.5–101 to 6.5–307 (1999); Md. Code Ann. Health–Gen. § 19–327 (1998); Neb. Rev. Stat. §§ 71–20,102 to 71–20,114 (1998); N.H. Rev. Stat. Ann. §§ 7:19 et seq. (1997); Ohio Rev. Code Ann. §§ 109.35, 109.35, 109.99 (Anderson 1997); Or. Rev. Stat. §§ 65.800–65.815 (1997); R.I. Gen. Laws §§ 23–17.14–1 to 23.17.14–31 (1997); S.D. Codified Laws § 47–24–17 (Michie 1999); Va. Code Ann. §§ 55–531 to 55–533 (Michie 1999); Wash. Rev. Code §§ 70.44.007, 70.44.300 (1998); Wis. Stat. §§ 50.35, 165.40 (1999).

adoption of statutory remedies in this area. First, the pace and size of conversions of hospitals, HMOs and Blue Cross plans has captured widespread public attention.[2] A number of these transactions generated concern among policymakers about the laxity of governmental oversight especially where gross undervaluation of the assets of the nonprofit entity resulted in enrichment of buyers and sometimes unconscionable benefits to insiders of the former nonprofit entity.[3] These episodes persuaded many legislators that managers of nonprofit enterprises engaged in conversions were not adequately safeguarding the charitable interests at stake and that existing legal standards and procedures were inadequate to protect community assets devoted to charitable purposes.

The states' legislative response seems to reflect several somewhat inconsistent objectives. Although states have not prohibited conversions outright, many of the legislative efforts seem designed to discourage conversions by placing extensive regulatory obstacles in their path and granting supervising authorities considerable discretion in evaluating them. This approach reflects the view that not-for-profit entities provide special benefits to the community in the form of charity care, higher quality, and cross subsidization of services that would not otherwise be available through the private sector.[4] In addition, critics of conversions point to the uncertainty and complexity of valuation of nonprofit assets and argue that an unregulated and non-public process is unlikely to produce a "fair" valuation. A second rationale for conversion statutes is the need to protect the corpus of charitable assets from diversions caused by undervaluations or self-dealing by interested fiduciaries. This approach is neutral on the desirability of conversions but stresses the lax supervision by state regulators and the absence of interested monitors in the forms of members or stakeholders to trigger legal remedies.

Most statutes place a variety of procedural requirements upon converting entities. As a conditions precedent for completing conversion transactions these statutes generally share the common element of assuring that some form of prior notification will occur, that information needed by the reviewing authority will be provided, and in some cases that public disclosure of the details of the transaction will be made. Some statutes go further and specify specific substantive standards and require that the reviewing authority gather and evaluate evidence in these areas. To the extent that the statutes lack such specificity, traditional concepts of fiduciary duties, charitable trust law and nonprofit corporation law presumably apply to the regulators' review. Unfortunately, most statutes do not clarify the nature of the legal claim or entitlement to the proceeds of the charitable sale and simply assume that

2. See, e.g., Greg Jaffe & Monica Langley, Generous to a Fault? Fledgling Charities Get Billions From Sale of Nonprofit Hospitals, Wall St. J. (Nov. 6, 1996) at A1; [Insert Title] Health Aff. March–April, 1997 (describing restructuring of Blue Cross in California resulting in charitable foundations with $3.2 billion in assets; calculating number of conversions of acute care hospitals at 59 in 1995).

3. See John D. Colombo, A Proposal for An Exit Tax on Nonprofit conversion Transactions, 23 J. Corp. L. 779 (1998) (estimating actual value of assets of California's Healthnet

HMO to be approximately 500% higher than originally estimated by the organization and funding of charitable foundations on conversion of PacifiCare Health Systems at less than 1% of actual value of the enterprise).

4. See discussion of policy issues raised by conversions, supra § 5–19. See also Comment, First, Do No Harm: An Analysis of the Nonprofit Hospital Sale Acts, 45 UCLA L. Rev. 502 (1997); Robert Kuttner, Columbia/HCA and the Resurgence of the For Profit Hospital Business (Pt. 1), 335 New Eng. J. Med. 362 (1996).

economic benefits of conversion should flow back to the nonprofit entity.[5] Although the National Association of Attorneys General has proposed a comprehensive model act to govern conversions, it has yet to gain widespread support in the states.[6]

a. Procedural Provisions of Nonprofit Conversion Statutes

Conversion statutes typically require mandatory notification and reporting to the state attorney general of impending transactions and provide for waiting periods of various duration to enable the attorney general to complete his evaluation.[7] Some statutes apply specifically to hospitals or health care facilities[8] while others govern all health care facilities and service plans.[9] Another difference is that some statutes specify that review is triggered by transactions involving "all or substantially all" of the not for profits assets,[10] while others employ a vaguer standard such as whether "a material amount of the assets of the public benefit corporation,"[11] and still others require a minimum percentage of ownership to trigger review.[12] Some statutes also require public notice of conversion transactions,[13] which may include public hearings and public disclosure of supporting documents,[14] and grant subpoena power to relevant regulatory authorities.[15] Finally, an important aspect of the procedural requirements under many statutory schemes is mandatory affirmative approval from the regulatory authority before the conversion can be undertaken.[16] Alternative approaches provide that if the regulator fails to act within a specified period, the conversion is deemed approved.[17] Some statutes provide for post-approval monitoring and mandatory annual reporting of activities,[18] while others prohibit or place limits on subsequent conversions of not-for-profit entities by the for-profit acquirer[19] or bar persons from acquiring ownership or voting power in another not-for-profit entity.[20]

5. Relying on a recapture theory, Professor Colombo has proposed an "exit tax" which would require nonprofit entities to surrender the value of appreciation of the economic assets of the entity where the converted enterprise has not needed the tax exemption to operate or where partnership principles would so dictate. His proposal usefully advances normative and policy justifications for the tax and suggests pragmatic means for imposing it. See John D. Colombo, A Proposal for An Exit Tax on Nonprofit Conversion Transactions, 23 J. Corp. L. 779 (1998).

6. Nat'l Ass'n of Attorneys General, Model Act for Nonprofit Healthcare Conversions (hereinafter "Model Conversion Act"). See NAAG Issues Model Conversion Guidelines Requiring Notification, Approval of State A.G., Health L. Rep. (BNA), April 9, 1998). The act is closely analyzed in Kevin F. Donahue, Crossroads in Hospital Conversions: A Survey of Nonprofit Hospital conversion Legislation, 8 Annals H.L. 39 (1999).

7. See, e.g., Cal. Corp. Code § 5915 (West Supp. 1997). A few states require notice to other entities such as the state department of health, see, e.g., R.I. Gen. Laws § 23–17–14, or the corporation or charitable trust commissioner, see, e.g., N.H. Rev. Stat. § 7:19.6 (III).

8. See, e.g., Neb. Rev. Stat. § 71–20, 102 (1998).

9. See, e.g., Cal. Health and Safety Code § 1399.72.

10. E.g., Va. Code Ann. § 55–531. See also Or. Rev. Stat § 65.803(a)(i) ("significant amount" of nonprofit assets).

11. See Cal. Corp. Code § 5914 (1998).

12. See, e.g., Neb. Rev. Stat. § 71–20, 103 (regulating acquisitions resulting in at least a 20% change in ownership of a hospital or resulting in the purchaser holding a cumulative 50% or greater share of ownership or control); Ga. Code Ann. § 31–7–400(2)(A) (50% of assets with a five year look-back).

13. See, e.g., Neb. Rev. Stat. § 71–20, 107.

14. Wisc. Stat. § 165.40(3)(b); see also Model Conversion Act § 8.01 (all documents considered public records).

15. See, e.g., Neb. Rev. Stat. § 71–20, 106.

16. Cal. Corp. Code § 5914; Md. Code Ann., State Gov't § 6.5–102; Ohio Rev. Code Ann. § 109.34(b).

17. See, e.g., Neb. Rev. Stat. § 71–20, 107.

18. See, e.g., Me. Rev. Stat. Ann. Tit. 24, § 2329 (1997).

19. See, e.g., R.I. Gen. Laws § 23–17.14–19 (1998).

b. *Substantive Review of Community Impact, Valuation and Other Factors*

Statutes specifying the criteria to be used in reviewing conversion transactions often set forth a laundry list of factors to be considered by the regulating authority. Typical factors include: whether the terms of the transaction are "fair and reasonable;" whether the transaction will result in inurement to any private person or entity; whether the proposed use of the transaction's proceeds is consistent with the charitable trust on which the assets are held; the effect on the availability or accessibility of health care to the affected community; whether the transaction is in the public interest; whether the seller exercised due diligence in deciding to sell and negotiating the terms of the sale; and whether the procedures used by the seller, including use of expert assistance, were fair.[21] As a general matter, these statutes mandate only that the attorney general or other reviewing authority consider the impact of the conversion and do not require disapproval, regardless of the magnitude of the problem.[22] A more prescriptive legislative approach has been to require that the parties to the transaction specify certain facts and plans, such as the amount of indigent care the for-profit entity expects to provide.[23]

Perhaps the most important substantive issue covered by the statutes is valuation. Reviewers are required to assess the fair market value of the assets to be sold or transferred, as well as whether management contracts under the acquisition are for reasonably fair value. Beyond broad requirements that the nonprofit entity receive "fair value,"[24] or "reasonably fair value,"[25] the statutes generally attempt to bolster the reviewing authority's ability to evaluate the assets transferred and the compensation received. For example, many jurisdictions require that a fairness evaluation from an independent expert.[26] An important question not resolved by many statutes is whether the reviewer should require or encourage the seller to receive the highest possible value.[27] Another important issue specifically addressed by only a few statutes[28] is whether charitable assets are placed at unreasonable risk, e.g., where the financing arrangements or resulting joint venture agreement imposes risk on the nonprofit entity.

Finally, the statutes provide a variety of remedies. Transactions not approved can be voided and states often are given the power to revoke licenses if purchasers fail to uphold commitments.[29] The procedural provisions discussed above provide some assurance of effective monitoring of legal obli-

20. Colo. Rev. Stat. Ann. § 10–16–324 (1999).

21. See, e.g., Cal. Corp. Code § 5917; Haw. Rev. Stat. § 323D–77 (1998). Cf. Model Conversion Act § 5.02 ("optional" provisions for states deeming it appropriate to consider conversion's impact on health delivery and access).

22. Neb. Rev. Stat. § 71–20,109; Or. Rev. Stat § 65–811.

23. See, e.g., R.I. Gen. Laws § 23–17.14–6(a)(21).

24. See, e.g., Md. Code Ann. State Gov't., § 6.5–301(1999).

25. Haw. Rev. Stat. § 323 D–76.

26. Neb. Rev. Stat. § 71–20,108(5).

27. For contrasting views on this point, compare Kevin F. Donahue, Crossroads in Hospital Conversions: A Survey of Nonprofit Hospital Conversion Legislation, 8 Annals H.L. 39 (1999), with Colin T. Moran, Why Revlon Applies to Nonprofit Corporations, 53 Bus. Law. 373 (1998).

28. See, e.g., Neb. Rev. Stat. § 71–20,-108(6).

29. Conn. Gen. Stat. Ann. § 19a–486a; Neb. Rev. Stat. § 71–20, 102–13.

gations that has been lacking in this area for some time. They assure timely provision of information to enable the regulator to make an informed judgment and require that sellers will disclose processes and data supporting the fairness of negotiations. Critics have pointed out, however, that statutes incorporating new substantive standards have created an open-ended regulatory regime and have placed substantial burdens upon authorities such as attorneys general who are ill-equipped to assume such broad regulatory responsibilities. All statutes listing substantive criteria appear to take the "laundry list" approach. That is, they specify a large number of criteria for the attorney general to review and apparently leave it to her discretion to evaluate the degree and seriousness of abuses and the nature of remedies to be required. While some states provide that the regulator may contract with experts regarding issues of valuation or the effects of the merger on the local community and that the expenses of such expert advice should be borne by the applicant, this is, at best, only a partial solution to the problems posed by the laundry list approach.[30] In addition, critics note that many of the specified standards, such as the adequacy of community health facilities and "public interest" and fairness standards, are highly subjective and run the risk of political manipulation.[31] To give one example, defining the "community" for purposes of assessing community benefit, will require analysis of the geographic scope of services of existing providers, the need both present and projected in the area for such services, and the availability of alternative sources of care. Finally, valuation of assets is an extremely complex and uncertain task. There is no consensus on appropriate valuation procedures and valuation of nonprofit HMOs and health care plans is fraught with difficulty.[32]

§ 5–23. State Community Benefits Statutes

In the early 1990s, policymakers began to consider imposing specific community benefit requirements on nonprofit hospitals, HMOs and other organizations that enjoy tax exempt status.[1] However, proposals introduced in Congress in the early 1990s failed to garner support.[2] Responding to the perceived shortage of charity care provided by some not-for-profit hospitals and the opportunity to obtain higher tax revenues from those entities not providing adequate charity care, a number of states enacted community benefit laws. There are two basic types of such statutes. First, planning and reporting laws, adopted by four states, require that nonprofit hospitals assess

30. Colo .. Rev. Stat. Ann. § 6–19–406; Haw. Rev. Stat. Ann. § 432C–3.

31. Comment, First, Do No Harm: An Analysis of the Nonprofit Hospital Sale Acts, 45 UCLA L. Rev. 503 (1997); Robert Kuttner, Columbia/HCA and the Resurgence of the For Profit Hospital Business (Pt. 1), 335 New Eng. J. Med. 362 (1996).

32. See Theresa McMahon, Fair Value? The Conversion of Nonprofit HMOs, 30 U.S.F.L. Rev. 355 (1996). Comment, First, Do No Harm: An Analysis of the Nonprofit Hospital Sale Acts, 45 UCLA L. Rev. 503 (1997); see also Robert Kuttner, Columbia/HCA and the Resurgence of the For Profit Hospital Business (Pt. 1), 335 New Eng. J. Med. 362 (1996)

(describing the difficulty in ascertaining whether purchase price will establish a foundation adequate to perpetuate a hospital's historic commitment to community services).

§ 5–23

1. The Clinton Administration proposed requiring community benefit needs assessment and planning requirements in its health reform proposals in 1993. See Health Security Act, H.R. 3600, 103d Cong. 3d Sess. (1993) § 7601. See generally Chapter 2.

2. See Tax-exempt Status of Hospitals and Establishment of Charity Care Standards, Hearing Before House Committee on Ways and Means, 102d Cong. 1st Sess. (1991).

the health care needs of their communities, develop community benefit plans responsive to community needs, and periodically report detailed information.[3] Massachusetts has gone further, applying its voluntary guidelines to both hospitals and health maintenance organizations.[4] As a general matter, these statutes require that hospitals reaffirm or formulate a mission statement reflecting policies that are in the public interest and meet their responsibilities to the community. They also mandate a needs assessment which includes a process for consulting community leaders and conducting planning ascertainment efforts in the community. Finally, most statutes require public disclosure and opportunity for community comment on the hospital's proposals. Some statutes, like Indiana's, undertake to define community benefit, establishing as evaluative benchmarks: unreimbursed cost to hospitals or providing charity care; government sponsored indigent care; donations of time, money and equipment; community and professional education; government-sponsored program services; research; and subsidized health services.[5]

The second form of community benefit law is more prescriptive. This approach, adopted by Texas, Pennsylvania and Utah, requires hospitals to provide a minimum amount of community benefit in addition to imposing planning and reporting requirements discussed above.[6] These statutes, which are generally tied to state property tax exemptions, define in some detail the types of charitable activities that will count and specify minimum community benefits requirements. For example, the Pennsylvania statute requires that public charities provide a minimum amount of community service according to one of seven statutory standards. One standard mandates that the charity provide uncompensated goods or services equal to five percent of the institution's costs, or maintain open admissions policy and provide uncompensated goods and services equal to at least 75% of net operating income, but not less than 3% of total operating expenses.[7] Administration of these statutes obviously requires detailed definitions of the goods and services that will fulfill the statutory requirements as well as methodologies for defining the community served and quantifying the care or goods provided.

C. PROFESSIONAL CORPORATIONS

§ 5–24. Introduction and Overview

Historically, professionals organized their businesses principally as sole proprietorships or partnerships. However, since its development in the early 1960s, the professional corporation business form has gained widespread acceptance. Although the initial popularity of professional corporations was largely attributable to certain favorable federal tax consequences once associated with incorporation,[1] the continuing adoption of this form of business

3. See Cal. Health & Safety Code §§ 127340–127365; Indiana Enrolled Act No. 1023, 108 Leg. 2d Reg. Sess. (1994); N.Y. Pub. Health L. § 2803–1.

4. Attorney General of Massachusetts, Community Benefit Guidelines for Nonprofit Acute Care Hospitals (June, 1994).

5. Ind. Code Ann. § 16–182.

6. 10 Pa. Cons. Stat. Ann. §§ 371–85; 25 Tex. Admin. Code §§ 13.11–20; Utah State Tax Commission, Nonprofit Hospital and Nursing Home Charitable Property Tax Standards.

7. Pa. Cons. Stat. Ch. 10 § 375.

§ 5–24

1. Significant tax benefits formerly accrued from incorporation because corporations received preferential treatment over partners and the self-employed with respect to certain benefits such as contributions to qualified re-

organization bespeaks other administrative and legal advantages. Professional corporations are creatures of state statutory law. Every state and the District of Columbia has enacted such a statute, although some refer to the form as a "professional association" rather than a professional corporation. Despite the promulgation of a model act in the late 1970s,[2] state statutes continue to vary widely in many important respects.

§ 5–25. Quasi–Corporate Forms

Several forms of business associations are available for professionals desiring to secure some of the benefits of incorporation without adhering to the requirements of professional corporation statutes. For the most part, these forms are somewhat antiquated relics of the era preceding professional incorporation and offer only limited benefits to professionals doing business today.[1] Moreover, the dearth of case law regarding these forms tends to make each somewhat of a risky proposition.

One such form is the common law business association. Often called joint stock associations, these unincorporated business enterprises enable parties to divide ownership interests by issuing shares of stock. Several state constitutions specifically define "corporations" to include unincorporated associations possessing corporate characteristics.[2] However, uncertainties about regulation, personal liability and federal tax treatment[3] have greatly diminished the prevalence of this business form. Under the statutory formulation in some states, the joint stock company or association is treated as a corporation in all essential aspects.[4]

§ 5–26. Professional Corporation Statutes: Scope and Interpretation

It is important to bear in mind several things when evaluating or interpreting professional corporation statutes. First, these statutes do not operate in a vacuum—they must be interpreted in conjunction with the state's general corporation law, as well as a variety of regulatory laws that govern professional conduct. Second, the ethical concerns that for many years forestalled acceptance of professional corporations have had a profound influence on the laws ultimately adopted and their interpretation by courts. Indeed,

tirement plans. Following passage of the Economic Recovery Tax Act, Pub. L. No. 97–34, 95 Stat. 172 and the Tax Equity and Fiscal Responsibility Act of 1982, Pub. L. No. 97–248, 96 Stat. 324, this disparity between corporate and non-corporate entities was largely eliminated although corporations and their employees still enjoy the advantage of being able to deduct certain fringe benefits. See Karen M. Maycheck, Shareholder Liability in Professional Legal Corporations: A Survey of the States, 47 U. Pitt. L. Rev. 817, 817 (1986).

2. Model Professional Corporation Supplement, Model Business Corporation Act (1984) [hereinafter MPCS]. See generally, Changes in the Model Business Corporation Act—Professional Corporation Supplement, 33 Bus. Law. 929 (1978).

§ 5–25

1. See, e.g., N.Y. Const. art. X, § 4 and Wash. Const. art. XII, § 5 (joint stock companies); N.J. Stat. Ann. §§ 42:3–9 to 3–11 (partnership associations); Mass. Gen. Laws Ann. Ch. 182, §§ 1–14 ("Massachusetts Trust").

2. See, e.g., N.Y. Const. art. X, § 4 and Wash. Const. art. XII, § 5.

3. To qualify for corporate tax treatment without formal incorporation, a business entity must appear more like a corporation than a partnership or a trust. Treas. Reg. § 301.7701–2(a)(2).

4. See, e.g., McKinney's—N.Y. Gen. Ass'ns Law Arts. 2,3. See generally 17 Berrien C. Eaton, Jr., Business Organizations—Professional Corporation & Associations § 9.02, at 9–10, n.15 (1970).

never far from the surface is a fundamental tension between the corporate form, with its institutionalized hierarchies, agency relationships and liability rules and the concept of professionalism which embraces autonomy and direct responsibility for patient welfare.

Most states' professional corporation statutes are designed to deal almost exclusively with issues peculiar to incorporation by professionals such as liability for malpractice, state licensure requirements and the role of lay persons in the organization. Consequently, the statutes usually supplement and incorporate by reference the substance of the general business corporation act of the state. Typically, a professional corporation statute will provide that the state's business corporation law will apply except as to those provisions that conflict with the professional corporation statute.[1] Questions frequently arise as to which statute takes precedence. Some jurisdictions expressly resolve all conflicts in favor of their professional corporation law.[2] Where statutory guidance is lacking, the general rule of statutory construction suggests that the more specific statute, usually the professional law, should prevail.

Conflicts also may arise between a professional corporation statute and state laws regulating health care professionals. Professional corporation statutes usually state that they do not amend laws applicable to qualifications to practice or to limit the powers of licensing boards.[3] However, where possible conflicts arise, inconsistencies between professional corporation statutes and other legal regimes are generally resolved in favor of the former where they are more specific and do not entrench on issues closely linked to qualifications to practice.[4]

As a general matter, courts will treat the professional corporation exactly like any other corporation.[5] Unless a professional corporation statute provides otherwise, corporate law governing agency relationships, liability, corporate formalities and fiduciary duties applies.[6] Professional corporations are also subject to the same basic organizational and governance principles regulating relationships among shareholders, officers and directors. Like general business corporation statutes, professional corporation statutes afford little in the way of disclosure regulation. Moreover, owing to the small size and localized nature of most offerings in the professional context, state and federal securities laws rarely intrude.[7]

§ 5–26

1. See, e.g., Del. Code tit. 8, § 618; West's Ann. Cal. Corp. Code § 13403.

2. See, e.g., West's Ind. Code § 23–1.5–2–1; MPCS § 2.

3. See, e.g., 805 Ill. Comp. Stat. Ann. §§ 10/4, 10/8.

4. See, e.g., N.M. Op. Att'y Gen. No. 69–63 (conflict between state dental practice act and professional corporation act regarding permissible name under which persons may practice dentistry resolved in favor of latter); Calif. Op. Att'y Gen. No. 69–95 (restricting power of state board to issue certificate of registration to corporation not complying with professional corporations law).

5. Peters v. Golds, 366 F.Supp. 150 (E.D.Mich.1973).

6. See, e.g., Allstate Ins. Co. v. Horowitz, 461 N.Y.S.2d 218 (N.Y.City Civ.1983); Streb v. Abramson–Caro Clinic, 401 So.2d 410 (La. App.), cert. denied 403 So.2d 69 (La.1981); Peters v. Golds, 366 F.Supp. 150 (E.D.Mich. 1973).

7. Federal securities laws and most state blue sky laws contain private offering exemptions which would be applicable to most professional corporations. See 15 U.S.C.A. § 77c(a)(11), § 77d(2); Ohio Rev. Code § 1707.03(O)(2). Additionally, some blue sky laws expressly exempt professional corporations and associations. See, e.g., Ky. Rev.Stat. § 292.400; see generally, Berrien C. Eaton, Jr.,

§ 5–27. Restrictions on Rendering Professional Services and Corporate Practice

Most statutes provide that professional corporations can only render professional services related to the specific professions governed by the statute. Thus, professional corporations may not branch out into unrelated income-generating businesses. However, generally recognized exceptions include investments in real estate, mortgages and securities when such activities are related to the professional service that the corporation is authorized to provide as well as services ancillary thereto.[1]

In furtherance of goals of maintaining supervisory control over professional qualifications and practices and reducing risks of diluting professional norms under the corporate form, professional corporation laws impose a variety of restrictions.[2] A host of requirements designed to assure professional accountability are also common. These provisions generally mandate that licensed professionals occupy positions of corporate control typically requiring that all or a majority of the board be comprised of physicians.[3]

One may question whether absolute prohibitions of lay persons serving as officers or directors of professional corporations serve the public interest or are needed to protect professional values. As many publicly traded corporations have learned, outside directors can provide expertise in matters such as finance, management and accounting; in addition, they may bring a neutral or even skeptical viewpoint on certain matters. In recognition of these considerations, the Revised Model Act requires that only one-half of the directors and one-half of principal officers be licensed professionals.[4]

In states recognizing the corporate practice of medicine doctrine, integrated systems typically avoid the restriction of the law by establishing "captive professional corporations." Under these arrangements, in order to provide physician services the system contracts with a professional corporation, the stock of which is owned by a single physician (or group). Typically that physician (who may also be an employee of the professional corporation) enters into a contractual arrangement, sometimes called a "shareholder control agreement" pursuant to which the physician-shareholder agrees to hold the stock for the benefit of the parent system corporation.[5] Additional agreements may also exist, such as a management services agreement through which the parent system controls the day-to-day operations of the professional corporation and employment agreements between the system and the physician-shareholder. States have shown no willingness to look through these

Business Organizations: Professional Corporations & Associations § 9.04[21] (1970).

§ 5–27

1. See, e.g., Vernon's Ann. Mo. Stat. § 356.061.

2. See, e.g., Del. Code tit. 8, § 610; 805 Ill. Comp. Stat. Ann. § 10/11. However, the Model Professional Corporation Supplement permits ownership by partnerships if all partners are "qualified persons" and by professional corporations authorized by state law to render a professional service articulated in the articles. See MPCS § 20.

3. See, e.g., McKinney's—N.Y. Bus. Corp. Law § 1508; West's Colo. Rev. Stat. Ann. § 12–36–134(1)(d); 805 Ill. Comp. Stat. Ann. § 10/10; Ariz. Rev. Stat. § 10–907; West's Colo. Rev. Stat. Ann. § 12–36–134(1)(f); Ohio Rev. Code § 1785.07; MPCS § 22.

4. MPCS § 30. See generally, discussion of the corporate practice of medicine supra § 5–10.

5. Charles F. Kaiser & Marvin Friedlander, Corporate Practice of Medicine, IRS Exempt Organizations: CPE Text for FY 2000, Ch. F, 1999 TNT 169–17 (Sept. 1, 1999).

arrangements and many have explicitly acknowledged that they recognize that beneficial ownership in a professional corporation can be held by a non-physician.[6]

§ 5–28. Transferability of Ownership

Another fundamental aspect of corporate existence, free transferability of ownership interests, causes special problems in the professional setting. Because transfers to non-professionals are seen as potentially undermining professional discretion or otherwise impinging on professional relationships, most statutes limit transfers of ownership of shares in professional corporations. Some states regulate voluntary and involuntary transfers by requiring that they be accompanied by a statement from the appropriate professional regulatory body stating that the buyer or recipient of the shares possesses all requisite licenses.[1] Typically the only exception to this rule is where the transfer follows the death, disability, or disqualification of a shareholder.[2] When ownership of professional shares falls into the hands of non-professionals, some statutes specify a "reasonable" time within which shares must be sold to a licensed professional or be reacquired by the corporation.[3] Failure to maintain shares pursuant to the requirements of the statute may result in the involuntary change of status to that of a general business corporation.[4]

§ 5–29. Ethical Standards and Confidentiality

Virtually all state statutes provide that the professional relationship is not altered by incorporation.[1] Such language is understood as mandating that the same ethical standards and privileges apply to professionals practicing in the corporate form as to those employing other business forms. Thus, practicing professionals—whether associated with a corporation or a partnership—remain subject to the regulation and discipline of their respective professional regulatory boards.[2] Furthermore, the corporate entities themselves are often subject to regulatory control.[3]

Some statutes also single out specific professional standards and privileges and apply them to professional corporations and their members. Two items so treated are limitations on who may render "professional" services and the duty of patient confidentiality.[4] As in non-corporate practice, only licensed professionals, or those under the supervision of licensed professionals, may perform professional services.[5] Some statutes have also expressly extended the duty of confidentiality to the corporation.[6]

---

6. The IRS requires such assurances from the state attorney general before approving 501(c)(3) status for professional corporations. Apparently such assurances have been routinely provided. Id.

§ 5–28

1. See, e.g., R.I. Gen. Laws § 7–5.1–3.

2. See supra § 5–23.

3. See, e.g., Ala. Code § 10–4–389 (within 30 days of disqualification, or 6 months of death); Alaska Stat. §§ 10.45.210, 10.45.220; MPCS § 23.

4. See, e.g., Del. Code tit. 8, § 615.

§ 5–29

1. See, e.g., Alaska Stat. § 10.45.140(a); MPCS § 32; Petition of Bar Ass'n of Hawaii,

516 P.2d 1267 (Hawaii 1973); Feinstein v. Attorney–General, 366 N.Y.S.2d 613, 326 N.E.2d 288 (N.Y.App.1975). See Karen M. Maycheck, Shareholder Liability in Professional Legal Corporations: A Survey of the States, 47 U. Pitt. L. Rev. 817, 834–35 (1986).

2. MPCS § 64.

3. See, e.g., West's Colo. Rev. Stat. Ann. § 12–36–134(3); Zimmerman v. Hogg & Allen, P.A., 209 S.E.2d 795 (N.C.1974).

4. See, e.g., MPCS §§ 13, 32.

5. See, e.g., Del. Code tit. 8, § 607; 805 Ill. Comp. Stat. Ann. § 10/7; West's Ann. Ind. Code § 23–1.5–2–5; MPCS § 13(a). Such re-

§ 5–30. Limited Liability

Limitation of personal liability for shareholders remains an important advantage of the professional corporation. Virtually all professional corporation statutes provide limited liability for the ordinary business obligations of the corporation (e.g., business debts, negligence unassociated with professional services, bankruptcy).[1] In addition, many statutes also protect shareholders from liability for the professional torts of their fellow shareholders or employees not under their supervision or direction. A contrasting approach is to remove the corporate shield for all actions growing out of professional malpractice or wrongdoing; under these statutes individual liability is extended to all shareholders as in a partnership.[2]

Courts have recognized the state policy in affording protection to shareholders and have rejected challenges to limited liability for professional corporations.[3] However, corporate existence has been disregarded where traditional veil-piercing factors are present, such as undercapitalization or failure to follow corporate formalities.[4] Thus, while the professional corporate form enables professionals to shield personal assets from the potentially devastating financial impact of personal liability for certain corporate obligations, this protection is subject to numerous exceptions and is no stronger than that applicable to private corporations.

The refusal of almost all states to extend limited liability to instances of providers' own professional negligence or misconduct rests on the strong insistence on accountability that underlies traditional notions of professional responsibility and the malpractice law of most jurisdictions. Most states attempt to accommodate these two objectives by restricting limited liability to professional services personally rendered by the professional or in some cases rendered under the supervision of the professional and extending personal liability to those who have direct control over the tortfeasor.[5] The cases applying agency principles reach similar results even with statutes which limit liability to the actor.[6] A number of statutes remove doubt about the corporation's liability in such circumstances by expressly imposing liability up to the full value of the corporation's property.[7] As noted above, a number of states

quirements do not apply to services for which no license is required. See, e.g., MPCS § 13(b).

6. See, e.g., MPCS § 32; West's Colo. Rev. Stat. Ann. § 12–36–134(5).

§ 5–30

1. See, e.g., La. Stat. Ann.—Rev. Stat. § 12:907; Nev. Rev. Stat. § 89.060. See § 26a infra.

2. See, e.g., Ariz. Rev. Stat. § 10–905; Nelson v. Patrick, 326 S.E.2d 45 (N.C.App.1985); Zimmerman v. Hogg & Allen, P.A., 209 S.E.2d 795 (N.C.1974). Some states limit co-shareholder liability where the corporation maintains malpractice insurance at a statutorily specified level. See, e.g., West's Colo. Rev. Stat. Ann. § 12–36–134(1)(g).

3. See, e.g., We're Associates Co. v. Cohen, Stracher & Bloom, P.C., 490 N.Y.S.2d 743, 480

N.E.2d 357 (N.Y.App.1985); Petition of Bar Ass'n of Hawaii, 516 P.2d 1267 (Hawai'i 1973).

4. See United States v. Lorenzo, 768 F.Supp. 1127 (E.D.Pa.1991); see also Ize Nantan Bagowa, Ltd. v. Scalia, 577 P.2d 725 (Ariz. App.1978); see generally § 5–4 supra.

5. See, e.g., Del. Code tit. 8, § 608; McKinney's—N.Y. Bus. Corp. Law § 1505(a); Boyd v. Badenhausen, 556 S.W.2d 896 (Ky.1977) (doctor held liable for the negligence of his staff in failing to provide patient with test results).

6. See Connell v. Hayden, 443 N.Y.S.2d 383 (N.Y.App.Div.1981). Restatement (Second) of Agency §§ 344, 350, 351, 356 & 358 (1958).

7. See, e.g., 805 Ill. Comp. Stat. Ann. § 10/8; N.J. Stat. Ann. § 14A:17–8; 15 Pa. Cons. Stat. Ann. § 2925.

specify that shareholders remain personally liable for the professional activities of professional employees or co-shareholders even where shareholders have no personal involvement in rendering the service.[8] In addition, some professional corporation statutes condition limited liability or corporate status upon maintenance of a statutorily-designated security (i.e., malpractice insurance or a surety bond).[9]

The boundary line establishing personal liability differs among the various jurisdictions. Many states specifically distinguish activities that do not involve professional relationships and limit liability in such circumstances.[10] A few statutes reserve limited liability for those transactions in which the shareholder has not "personally participated."[11] As to statutes that are silent concerning the liability of innocent shareholders, there is little guidance in the case law.[12] However, the fact that the professional corporation statute incorporates by reference the general corporate law of the state "unless inconsistent" with the professional corporation statute would seem to militate in favor of insulating such shareholders from liability.

Jurisdictions attempt to accommodate the desire for limited liability and the need for professional accountability by eliminating limited liability for professional services personally rendered by the professional or, in some cases, rendered under the supervision of the professional.[13] Statutes commonly extend personal liability to those who have direct control over the tortfeasor. The cases applying agency principles reach similar results even with statutes which limit liability to the actor.

D. PARTNERSHIPS

§ 5–31. Introduction and Overview

Except for sole proprietorships, partnerships are by far the most common form of business enterprise in the United States. There are three principal kinds of partnerships: (1) general partnerships, governed by state statutes, almost all of which are closely modeled on the Uniform Partnership Act (UPA) or the Revised Uniform Partnership Act (RUPA);[1] (2) limited partnerships, governed by statutes modeled on either the Uniform Limited Partnership Act (ULPA) or its successor adopted in 1975 and revised in 1985, the

8. See, e.g., West's Colo. Rev. Stat. Ann. § 12–36–134(1)(g).

9. See, e.g., West's Colo. Rev. Stat. Ann. § 12–36–134(1)(g) (joint and several liability for all shareholders except when corporation carries professional liability insurance meeting state requirements); S.D. Codified Laws §§ 47–11A–8 to 12, §§ 47–11B–17 to 21, §§ 47–11C–17 to 21.

10. See, e.g., Or. Rev. Stat. § 58.185(7) (no personal liability for debts or contractual obligations of corporation).

11. See, e.g., Hawaii Rev.Stat. § 415A–11.

12. See 4A Zolman Cavitch, Business Organizations: with Tax Planning § 82.03[1], at 82–

82 n.15 (1989); see also Birt v. St. Mary Mercy Hosp., 370 N.E.2d 379 (Ind.App.1977).

13. See, e.g., Ariz. Rev. Stat. § 10–905; Conn. Gen. Stat. Ann. § 33–182; Mich. Comp. Laws Ann. § 450.226; Or. Rev. Stat. § 58.185.

§ 5–31

1. Despite its widespread adoption since it was drafted in 1914, the UPA has been criticized for being confusing, not terribly well-drafted and prone to setting statutory presumptions that run counter to the expectations of most persons entering into partnerships. RUPA, which was adopted in 1994 and amended in 1996, modernizes much of the language of the older act and adds a number of new concepts. It has not as yet achieved widespread acceptance.

Revised Uniform Limited Partnership Act (RULPA);[2] and (3) Limited Liability Partnerships, governed by statutes following the Model Limited Liability Partnership Act.[3] Partnerships are not a unitary phenomenon. Like corporations, they vary considerably in size and complexity, ranging from simple, two-person "handshake" agreements to large, publicly-traded limited partnerships with complex agreements evidencing the understandings of the parties.

A hallmark of the partnership form is flexibility. The statutes allow parties to vary many statutory standards to suit their particularized needs. Partnership statutes are sometimes conceptualized as setting forth only a "model contract" that can be freely altered, preferably through a written partnership agreement. Under this view, statutory rules ideally should reflect what most persons entering into partnerships would regard as implicit in their partnership agreements.[4] However, the somewhat antiquated UPA contains many provisions that probably do not reflect the preferences of most people entering into partnerships. Because the sometimes-draconian statutory standards of the UPA will otherwise govern in states that have not adopted the RUPA, the importance of a written agreement cannot be overemphasized.

Another important feature of partnerships is the "flow through" of taxable income and losses to partners under federal and state tax laws. Unlike C corporations, partnerships are not taxed as an entity, hence there is no double taxation of enterprise income.[5] Additional advantages over the corporate form include informality and lower organizational and operational costs in terms of state taxes and fees. The principal disadvantage of the form is the absence of limited liability: general partners may be personally liable for partnership debts. Another potential risk is the agency power vested in all general partners that enables them to bind the partnership and thus create both partnership and individual liabilities. In some cases this may impose unacceptable risks for partners who fear being bound by obligations they cannot prevent.

1. GENERAL PARTNERSHIPS

§ 5–32. Formation and Partnership Agreements

Creation of a general partnership does not require a written agreement or formal filing with the state.[1] In determining whether a partnership has been formed, courts look to whether the intent of the parties was to form "an association of two or more persons to carry on as co-owners a business for profit,"[2] as the UPA defines a general partnership. The act establishes a

---

2. State statutes governing limited partnerships exhibit far less uniformity than their general partnership counterparts because many states have not yet adopted RULPA and the version ultimately adopted often varies in important respects from the model act on which it is based.

3. Limited Liability Partnerships are discussed infra § 5–45.

4. See Alan R. Bromberg & Larry E. Ribstein, Bromberg & Ribstein on Partnership, § 6.07 (1992); Donald J. Weidner, Three Policy Decisions Animate Revision of Uniform Partnership Act, 46 Bus. Law. 427, 468 (1991).

5. Partnerships are reporting entities, however, and must generally file income tax returns even though no income tax need be paid.

§ 5–32

1. Some matters, however, may require filing or state approvals. For example, entities doing business under a fictitious name may be required to notify local or state authorities. See, e.g., Ohio Rev. Code § 1329.10(B).

2. UPA § 6(1).

number of positive and negative presumptions, the most important being that sharing of profits constitutes prima facie evidence of a partnership, unless the profits are received as payment of debts, rent, wages, annuities for surviving partners, interest on a loan, or consideration for sale of the goodwill of property or businesses.[3]

Importantly, partnership status may be inferred from various circumstances including the parties' intent and their economic relationship. Neither the parties' characterization of the entity nor their subjective intent, however, is determinative. Thus, the existence of a medical partnership has been inferred from physicians' filing for a certificate under a fictitious-name statute, the fact that their professional liability endorsement recited that they were insured "individually and as co-partners" and from adoption of the term "partner" by some of the physicians in the group.[4] Moreover, courts have held that partnership relationships exist as a matter of law where the statutory test is satisfied despite express disclaimers by participants of any intent to function as a partnership.[5] In addition, the cases sometimes recognize "partnerships by estoppel" where a person makes a representation to another that she is a partner in an existing partnership or with persons who are not actual partners and where there has been reliance by the third party.[6]

In numerous instances, the UPA provides that statutory terms apply "subject to any agreement" between partners, thus affording the opportunity to adopt rules suitable to the parties' particular needs. RUPA goes even further, allowing parties to agree on all matters not specifically mandated by the act.[7] The critical importance of the partnership agreement lies in its role in establishing customized rules respecting governance, financial arrangements, membership, dissolution and a host of other matters. Moreover, the provisions of the partnership agreement may have important financial ramifications with respect to other laws, such as tax liability.[8]

§ 5–33. Management and Internal Governance

The UPA provides that partners have equal rights to manage the partnership and that all disputes as to ordinary matters are to be resolved by majority vote, with each partner having one vote regardless of the size of his capital contribution, profit participation or other factors.[1] Certain matters, such as admission of new partners, require unanimous consent,[2] as do

---

3. UPA § 7(4); see also id. § 7(2)(joint tenancy, tenancy in common, tenancy by the entireties, joint property, common property or part ownership do not by themselves establish a partnership), § 7(3) (sharing of gross returns does not by itself establish partnership).

4. Van Dyke v. Bixby, 448 N.E.2d 353 (Mass.1983); cf. John P. Harris, M.D., Inc. v. Parmley, 480 So.2d 500 (La.App.1985).

5. See Martin v. Peyton, 158 N.E. 77 (N.Y.App.1927).

6. UPA § 16. See Kaplan v. Gibson, 385 S.E.2d 103 (Ga.App.1989) (finding sufficient evidence to support existence of an "ostensible partnership" between members of a medical professional corporation based on defendants' having repeatedly held themselves out as part-

ners; no error in trial court's omission of instruction requiring detrimental reliance on the representation).

7. RUPA § 103.

8. The partnership agreement may allocate income, losses, gains and other tax items among the parties, and these agreements will be given effect for federal tax purposes, provided the allocations are considered to have "substantial economic effect" within the meaning of I.R.C. § 704(b) and the regulations issued thereunder.

§ 5–33

1. UPA § 18(e), (h).

2. UPA § 18(g).

agreements that contradict the terms of the partnership agreement.[3] Many rules affecting internal governance can be altered by mutual agreement. For example, day-to-day management may be vested in committees, voting power can be allocated according to a formula reflecting contributions to the firm (or other factors) and supermajorities may be required to provide assurance that drastic changes will not occur without the consent of a substantial proportion of the voting interests.

§ 5–34. Allocation of Profits and Losses; Compensation to Partners

Absent an agreement, partners have no entitlement to compensation for services performed for the partnership, even if one partner performs a disproportionate amount of work or supplies an extraordinary benefit.[1] However, each partner is entitled to the return of his capital contributions,[2] and to indemnification for payments and liabilities incurred in the ordinary course of partnership business or incurred to preserve its business or property.[3]

On the division of profits and losses, the default setting of the UPA produces results that may be contrary to the expectations of the parties. Absent an agreement to the contrary, partners share equally in profits and are equally liable for losses (including losses of capital by the other partners), regardless of their capital contributions or the value of other services provided by them.[4]

Finally, each partner is an agent for the partnership and is empowered to bind the partnership in accordance with the statutory formulation which is based on principles of actual and apparent authority.[5] However, the UPA limits this authority by proscribing certain actions[6] and providing that acts in contravention of a restriction on partners' authority shall not bind the partnership to persons having knowledge of the restriction.[7]

§ 5–35. Fiduciary Duties

a. The Duty of Care

Although the UPA contains no specific duty of care provision, courts frequently invoke partners' fiduciary duties in sweeping terms.[1] The case law contains occasional suggestions that partners may owe each other a duty of due care, measured by the ordinarily prudent person standard.[2] The rationale for holding partners to a strict or at least modest fiduciary duty of care rests on the closely interdependent relationship of partners (e.g., the ability of each

---

3. UPA § 18(h).

§ 5–34

1. UPA § 18(f). The sole exception to this general principle is that surviving partners are entitled to compensation for services provided in winding up a dissolved partnership's affairs. Id.

2. UPA § 18(a).

3. UPA § 18(b).

4. UPA § 18(a).

5. UPA § 9.

6. See UPA § 9(3) (partner may not assign partnership property in trust for creditors, dis-

pose of goodwill of the business, undertake any action that would make it impossible to carry on the ordinary business of the partnership, confess a judgment, or submit a partnership claim to arbitration).

7. UPA § 9(4).

§ 5–35

1. See Meinhard v. Salmon, 164 N.E. 545 (N.Y.App.1928).

2. See, e.g., Rosenthal v. Rosenthal, 543 A.2d 348 (Me.1988).

partner to bind the partnership) and the assertion that partners expect no lesser obligation of care and diligence than that imposed on agents or corporate directors. However, the limited case law on the subject suggests a less exacting fiduciary standard for alleged mismanagement, one that invokes business judgment rule-like principles and usually holds partners liable only where bad faith or fraud is proved.[3] RUPA specifies a standard of "gross negligent or reckless conduct, intentional conduct, or intentional misconduct, or a knowing violation of law,"[4] but only prohibits waivers that "unreasonably restrict" the duty of care.[5]

b. The Duty of Loyalty

Partners' duty of loyalty is far more solidly rooted in the statutes and common law than is the duty of care. Statutory sources include the UPA's provisions requiring that every partner must account to the partnership "for any benefit, and hold as trustee any profits derived by him without the consent of the other partners";[6] vesting equal management powers in all partners;[7] and establishing a duty to provide full and truthful information to other partners on demand.[8] The cases have rigorously applied this duty, suggesting occasionally heightened, trustee-like obligations (perhaps beyond those applicable to corporate directors).[9] Behavior caught by this fiduciary obligation includes self-dealing transactions, takings of corporate opportunities and competition with the partnership.[10] At a minimum, these actions require the informed consent of the partners.

Partners may, of course, engage in outside businesses that do not compete with the partnership.[11] Indeed, they may do so without having to share income derived from such activities with the partnership even where the business is the result of experience, contacts or know-how attributable to their participation in the partnership.[12] However, this freedom may be limited by express or implied agreement among the partners. For example, a physician in a medical partnership who also served as a hospital administrator was found to have violated his fiduciary duties by keeping secret the fact that he was being paid for his hospital duties and not treating that income as partnership income.[13] The court emphasized that although the administrative work was known to partners and the hospital did not compete with the partnership, in pooling their talents in a partnership, the physicians agreed that all would devote their full time and effort to the partnership and that outside employment required approval of the partners.

3. See, e.g., Washington Medical Ctr., Inc. v. Holle, 573 A.2d 1269 (D.C.App.1990); Bane v. Ferguson, 890 F.2d 11 (7th Cir.1989). See generally Alan A. Bromberg & Larry R. Ribstein, Bromberg & Ribstein on Partnership § 6.07, at 6:85 (1992).

4. RUPA § 404(c).

5. RUPA § 103(b)(4).

6. UPA § 21. Although the title of this section is "Partner Accountable as a Fiduciary," that is the only time the word "fiduciary" is used in the UPA.

7. UPA § 18(e).

8. UPA § 20.

9. See, e.g., Meinhard v. Salmon, 164 N.E. 545 (N.Y.App.1928).

10. See, e.g., Washington Medical Ctr., Inc. v. Holle, 573 A.2d 1269 (D.C.App.1990); Olivet v. Frischling, 164 Cal.Rptr. 87 (Cal.App.1980); Menos v. Hodges, 499 S.W.2d 427 (Mo.1973).

11. See, e.g., Truman v. Martin, 321 N.W.2d 420 (Neb.1982).

12. See Alan R. Bromberg & Larry E. Ribstein, Bromberg & Ribstein on Partnership § 6.07, at 6:84 (1992).

13. Weller v. Simenstad, 127 N.W.2d 794 (Wis.1964).

The fiduciary standards generally prohibit the same kind of self-dealing and taking of partnership opportunities as those forbidden to corporate directors.[14] However, these transactions may also raise separate issues of non-disclosure or incomplete disclosure where they are undertaken without the knowledge or informed consent of other partners.[15] The fiduciary principle has also been invoked frequently where parties deal in bad faith or offend a court's sense of fairness in undertaking transactions that affect other partners. For example, causing dissolutions in order to take advantage of corporate opportunities to the exclusion of some partners or exercising management control in a way that treats other partners unfairly have been found to violate the high standard of loyalty expected of partners.[16] Although partners are bound to each other by the strongest of fiduciary duties, the exercise of contractual rights to terminate a partnership or expel a partner without cause will be upheld absent evidence of bad faith.[17]

Again RUPA takes a decidedly more permissive approach, specifying a set of duties that are the exclusive obligations of partners to each other. These duties include prohibitions against self-dealing, competing with the partnership and failing to account for "profits, property or benefits" properly owed to the partnership.[18] However these duties are waivable where conduct is specifically identified and approved or ratified by other partners.[19]

§ 5–36. Liability to Third Parties

Partnerships are liable for wrongful and tortious acts of employees and partners committed within the scope of their employment or business. In addition, as discussed above, the partnership may be bound by its partners and agents under agency principles. A partnership may even be treated as an entity under criminal statutes and held accountable independent of the liability of its members.[1]

The UPA distinguishes two types of partnership liability. It makes partners jointly and severally liable for wrongful acts and omissions and breaches of trust (e.g., torts), but only jointly liable for all other debts and obligations of the partnership (e.g., contracts).[2] The most important consequences of the distinction are (1) generally, exhaustion of partnership assets is required before individual assets may be reached for joint liability but not

14. Menos v. Hodges, 499 S.W.2d 427 (Mo. 1973); Alan R. Bromberg & Larry E. Ribstein, Bromberg & Ribstein on Partnership § 6.07 (1992); see generally §§ 5–6—5–7 supra.

15. UPA §§ 20, 21. See, e.g., Jennison v. Bierer, 601 F.Supp. 1167 (D.Vt.1984).

16. See, e.g., Russell v. Truitt, 554 S.W.2d 948 (Tex.Civ.App.1977).

17. St. Joseph's Regional Health Center v. Munos, 326 Ark. 605, 934 S.W.2d 192 (1996).

18. RUPA § 404(b).

19. RUPA § 103(b). See also id. § 404(e) (partner does not violate duty merely because his conduct furthers his own interests).

§ 5–36

1. See, e.g., People v. Smithtown Gen. Hosp., 399 N.Y.S.2d 993 (N.Y.Sup.1977).

2. UPA §§ 13–15. Some states make all liability joint and several, See, e.g., Vernon's Ann. Mo. Stat. § 358.150; N.C. Gen. Stat. § 59–45. Joint and several liability may also be created in contract actions by agreement by some or all partners to undertake a separate obligation or by statutes or procedural rules for joint obligors. See Alan R. Bromberg & Larry E. Ribstein, Bromberg & Ribstein on Partnership, § 510(d) at 5:79. RUPA provides that partners are jointly and severally liable for all partnership obligations but requires that creditors must seek satisfaction out of partnership assets before they can pursue the assets of individual partners. RUPA §§ 306, 307.

for joint and several liability; and (2) a judgment against one partner extinguishes claims against other partners in joint liability but not in joint and several liability.[3] Thus, where liability is joint but not several and service of all partners is impractical, unjoined partners may not be bound. Joint and several liability, on the other hand, permits plaintiffs to proceed against individual partners for the full amount of the partnership obligation.[4] Liability extends, however, only to the period during which a person was a partner and new partners are liable for obligations preceding their admission only to the extent of their partnership interest.[5] RUPA, by contrast, makes all liability joint and several and requires that judgment creditors exhaust partnership assets before proceeding against partners individually.[6]

The consequences of these liability rules are an important factor affecting the desirability of the partnership form. Under joint and several liability, torts committed by the partnership subject all partners to liability in their individual capacities so that innocent partners may be liable for their partners' negligence. Thus, where a jury finds one partner guilty of medical malpractice and a second partner not guilty, judgment is nevertheless entered against the second partner under joint and several liability.[7] In some jurisdictions, the rule extends to punitive damages as well.[8] Joint and several partnership liability also "passes through" to partners whose partnership is a general partner in a second partnership.[9]

2. LIMITED PARTNERSHIPS

§ 5–37. Distinguishing Characteristics

Every state has adopted a limited partnership statute, although as noted above, there is considerable diversity among them. The principal differences between limited and general partnerships are (1) for "limited partners," liability for partnership obligations is restricted to their investment in the partnership while "general partners" assume full personal liability as in a general partnership; (2) the law restricts limited partners' rights to participate in the control of the business; (3) interest in a limited partnership may be more freely assigned than in general partnerships and many kinds of withdrawals do not necessarily cause dissolution of the partnership; and (4) in order to achieve limited partnership status, partners must first file a certificate with governmental authorities. Except as otherwise provided in state limited partnership statutes, the law of general partnerships governs limited partnerships.[1]

§ 5–38. Formation and Basic Requirements

Under most statutes, the limited partnership must have at least one general partner and at least two partners; where the latter requirement is

3. See Alan R. Bromberg & Larry E. Ribstein, Bromberg & Ribstein on Partnership at § 5.08(b), at 5:55.

4. Id. at § 5.08(b) (1992).

5. UPA § 17.

6. RUPA §§ 506(a), 307(d).

7. Zuckerman v. Antenucci, 478 N.Y.S.2d 578 (N.Y.Sup.1984).

8. See, e.g., Rogers v. Hickerson, 716 S.W.2d 439 (Mo.App.1986).

9. Head v. Henry Tyler Construction Corp., 539 So.2d 196 (Ala.1988).

§ 5–37

1. RULPA § 1105; ULPA § 6(2).

otherwise satisfied, one person may be both a general and a limited partner.[1] Corporations, partnerships, limited partnerships, trusts, estates and associations may be either partners or general partners under RULPA.[2] Some statutes impose various requirements respecting the name of the firm, such as forbidding use of any limited partner's name.[3] Where persons have failed to substantially comply[4] with filing requirements, the limited partnership is not recognized as a legal entity and limited partners risk personal liability, though the statutes commonly provide protection for those who in good faith believed that a limited partnership had been created.[5]

A written partnership agreement is not required by law, but given the nature of the enterprise, it is almost indispensable for documenting the parties' understandings. Indeed, modern statutes are in large part premised on the assumption that the parties have a written agreement. The basic definition of limited partnerships is essentially the same as for general partnerships: an association of two or more persons to carry on a business as co-owners for profit. An important consideration in deciding whether to adopt the form is that limited partnership interests may be treated as securities under federal and state securities regulation and hence filing and accounting costs may be high if no exemption is available.

§ 5–39.   Relationships Among Partners: Management, Powers, and Duties

As in general partnerships, partners may agree upon a wide range of rules governing their internal affairs including allocations of contributions, distributions and losses; management through specialized committees, and other matters. However, in contrast to the UPA, the RULPA and modern acts set more realistic default rules to apply in the absence of an agreement among the partners. For example, profits and losses are allocated *pro rata* according to capital contributions of the partners[1] and limited partners may assign full limited partnership interests unless otherwise agreed.[2]

General partners in limited partnerships have essentially the same rights and powers as partners in general partnerships to act as agents. While limited partners risk losing their limited liability status when they participate in control, they may nevertheless have actual or apparent authority to act for the partnership. Partnership agreements commonly limit the authority of limited partners to act for the firm, though there is no prohibition on granting them actual authority to bind the partnership.[3]

Management power is vested exclusively in the general partners who possess the same powers to bind the partnership as apply under the UPA.[4]

§ 5–38

1. RULPA § 101(7).

2. RULPA § 101 (6), (11).

3. See, e.g., ULPA § 5(a)(1); but see Del. Code tit 6, § 17–102(3) (allowing use of limited partners' names).

4. See, e.g., 59 Pa. Cons. Stat. Ann. § 512.

5. See, e.g., RULPA §§ 201(b), 304.

§ 5–39

1. RULPA § 503.

2. RULPA § 702. ULPA allows assignment of full limited partnership interests only if all partners agree or if the certificate so provides. ULPA § 19(1).

3. See Mery v. Universal Sav. Ass'n, 737 F.Supp. 1000 (S.D.Tex.1990). See generally, Alan R. Bromberg and Larry E. Ribstein, Bromberg & Ribstein on Partnership, § 14.01.

4. RULPA permits the partnership agreement to establish separate classes of management authority and place other controls on management powers. RULPA § 405.

Despite restrictions on control activities, limited partners are not barred under modern statutes from voting on all matters.[5] Older statutes enumerate certain actions that exceed the powers of the general partners, such as confessing judgments or admitting new general partners or limited partners without specific authorization in the certificate.[6] Unanimous consent is required to permit the general partners to engage in the forbidden actions. RULPA affords greater latitude in this area by simply providing that the powers of general partners are limited by the Act and provisions of the partnership agreement.[7]

In principle, partners are bound by the same broadly-stated fiduciary responsibilities that apply to general partnerships. Although the statutes give little guidance in this area, the common law suggests that a somewhat heightened standard applies to general partners given their plenary powers of management and the relatively passive role played by limited partners.[8] RULPA grants limited partners the right to initiate derivative suits if general partners refuse to do so or if an effort to cause those general partners to do so is not likely to succeed.[9]

§ 5–40. Limited Liability and Participation in Control by Limited Partners

The defining attribute of limited partnerships is the protection from personal liability they afford limited partners. However, limited partners lose this protection when they take part in the control of the business. ULPA and case law based on older statutes do not give clear guidance as to what constitutes sufficient "participation in control" so as to jeopardize limited liability status. For example, courts found that limited partners who appointed managers, voted on matters of significance or served as officers stepped over the line and were personally liable.[1] Uncertainty surrounding the critical issue of potential personal liability inhibited adoption of the limited partnership form, and ultimately gave rise to RULPA which contains clearer standards and significantly liberalizes the protection afforded to limited partners who participate to some degree in the control of the business. First, RULPA establishes certain "safe harbors," i.e., activities and powers of limited partners that do not by themselves constitute participation in the control of the business. These provisions give limited partners the flexibility to advise and consult with general partners, attend meetings, serve as officers, agents or employees and, under certain conditions, vote upon or otherwise approve or

---

5. RULPA provides that the partnership agreement may grant to all or a group of limited partners the right to vote on matters. RULPA § 302. See also § 303(b)(6) and discussion of liability of limited partners infra § 5–40.

6. ULPA § 9(1).

7. RULPA § 403; see also RULPA §§ 301(b)(1), 401 (allowing admission of new general and limited partners pursuant to partnership agreement or with written consent).

8. See Russell v. Truitt, 554 S.W.2d 948 (Tex.Civ.App.1977); Bassan v. Investment Exch. Corp., 524 P.2d 233 (Wash.1974).

9. RULPA § 1001.

§ 5–40

1. See, e.g., Holzman v. De Escamilla, 195 P.2d 833 (Cal.App.1948); Delaney v. Fidelity Lease, Ltd., 526 S.W.2d 543 (Tex.1975); but cf. Frigidaire Sales Corp. v. Union Properties, Inc., 562 P.2d 244 (Wash.1977)(no liability absent reliance by creditors on limiteds being general partners). See Annotation, Liability of Limited Partner Arising from Taking Part in Control of Business under Uniform Limited Partnership Act, 79 A.L.R.4th 427 (1990).

disapprove management actions.[2] Perhaps more importantly, the act limits the class of potential plaintiffs exclusively to "persons who transact business with the limited partnership reasonably believing, based upon the limited partner's conduct, that the limited partner is a general partner."[3] This provision, which effectively shields much managerial activity from challenge, is based on the recognition that there is no sound policy ground for holding limited partners liable where business creditors did not rely on the status of the partners. Academic commentary has questioned the need for control-based liability for limited partners[4] and one state has abandoned it entirely.[5]

The two features of limited partnerships just discussed—limited liability and the absence of control for limited partners—may have significant ramifications in connection with regulation by licensing agencies. For example, one court has construed a state nursing home licensure requirement that all persons constituting a licensee bear the full responsibilities of a licensee to bar limited partnerships from holding a license to operate a nursing home.[6] In addition, prohibitions on exercising control may prevent limited partnerships from fulfilling statutory or regulatory responsibilities. In one interesting case, a hospital district became a limited partner in a venture to construct a medical office building.[7] The court found that a lease executed by the general partners binding the district in its capacity as limited partner violated state constitutional prohibitions against debt by a loan. The court went on to hold the limited partnership agreement void because, as a limited partner, the hospital district could not object to the lease without "participating in control"; hence, under limited partnership law it could not prevent itself from becoming a party to an *ultra vires* act.

Finally, an important aspect of limited partnership statutes is the extent to which they permit corporations to act as general partners. These provisions permit persons to set up limited partnerships and insulate any participant from significant liability exposure by forming corporations to act as the general partner. Courts have upheld such arrangements as not inconsistent with the purpose of the limited liability statutes, noting that third parties were free to inquire and bargain over the entity constituting the general partner. However, courts will pierce the veil of corporate general partners to hold shareholders, officers or directors liable where the traditional piercing factors such as undercapitalization, fraud or "alter ego" conduct so dictate.[8]

---

2. RULPA § 303(b).

3. RULPA § 303(a).

4. Joseph J. Basile, Limited Liability for Limited Partners: An Argument for Abolition of the Control Rule, 38 Vand. L. Rev. 1199 (1985).

5. Official Code Ga. Ann. § 14–9–303.

6. Windsor Park Nursing Home v. Trussell, 247 N.Y.S.2d 189 (N.Y.Sup.1964).

7. Black v. First Federal Sav. & Loan Ass'n of Fargo, 830 P.2d 1103 (Colo.App.1992), aff'd sub nom. LaPlata Medical Ctr. Assocs., Ltd. v.

United Bank of Durango, 857 P.2d 410 (Colo. 1993).

8. Delaney v. Fidelity Lease Ltd., 526 S.W.2d 543 (Tex.1975); Frigidaire Sales Corp. v. Union Properties Inc., 562 P.2d 244 (Wash. 1977). See generally John J. Ratigan, Note, Piercing the Veil of the Corporate General Partner in the Hybrid Limited Partnership: A Suggested Remedy for Inequitable Conduct, 17 Suffolk L.R. 949 (1983).

E. LIMITED LIABILITY COMPANIES AND LIMITED LIABILITY PARTNERSHIPS

§ 5–41. Distinguishing Characteristics

The limited liability company (LLC) is a hybrid business organization of recent origin in the United States that possesses some of the most advantageous characteristics of the partnership and corporate forms. Although likely to prove attractive to many large and small businesses, it is important to bear in mind that the LLC is still at an incipient stage of development. With no uniform statute and little case law, adoption of the LLC form entails some risks and uncertainties.[1]

The most important features of LLCs are:

- LLCs shield all owners and managers from liability for the debts of the entity.
- LLCs can receive partnership treatment for tax purposes.
- LLCs can be designed to assure continuity of existence.
- Most LLC statutes permit free transferability of ownership.
- There is no requirement for control by a board of directors, but centralized management is possible.
- The LLC form eliminates many restrictions that render unattractive other options for closely-held businesses such as limited partnerships, S Corporations and statutory close corporations. LLC statutes generally place no ceiling on the permissible number of owners, permit different classes of ownership and allow for ownership by certain entities and persons prohibited by other forms (e.g., nonresident aliens, corporations and certain trusts).

§ 5–42. Principal Features of LLC Statutes

All fifty states and the District of Columbia have enacted LLC statutes.[1] Although a Uniform LLC Act has been promulgated, most are based to some extent on the Wyoming LLC Act and the statutes vary in many important respects. While it is impossible to canvass the provisions of the statutes here we discuss below some of the more important aspects of the laws that affect health care providers.

a. Formation and Financing

Creation of a limited liability company requires filing of articles of organization with the state. Conducting business prior to filing can result in joint and several liability for owners for debts and liabilities incurred prior to filing.[2] Although there is no limit on the number of members (owners) in an LLC, most statutes require multiple members, a factor that might prove

---

§ 5–41

1. See generally, Larry E. Ribstein & Robert R. Keating, Ribstein and Keatinge on Limited Liability Companies (1992 & Supp.); see also, Carol Goforth, The Rise of the Limited Liability Company: Evidence of a Race Between the States, But Heading Where?, 45 Syracuse L.Rev. 1193 (1995); Richard L. Parker, Corporate Benefits Without Corporate Taxation: Limited Liability Company and Limited Partnership Solutions to the Choice of Entity Dilemma, 29 S.D. L. Rev. 399 (1992).

§ 5–42

1. The first LLC statute, adopted originally in 1977 was Wyoming's, Wyo. Stat. § 17–15–101 et seq., followed by Florida's in 1982, West's Fla. Stat. Ann. ch. 608.401 et seq.

2. See, e.g., Ala. Code § 10–12–14(b). Filing and issuance of the articles is often treated as conclusive evidence that the LLC has been legally organized. Id. at § 10–12–14(a).

bothersome for professionals in solo practice, especially because of professional requirements that all members be licensed professionals.[3]

In most states, members may contribute property, services, promissory notes or almost anything of value to purchase a membership interest.[4] Members of an LLC are not required to recognize gain or loss when they contribute property to an LLC in exchange for an economic interest in the entity.[5] Although members cannot be held personally liable for the LLC's debts, many statutes provide that members are personally liable to the LLC for failing to make agreed-upon contributions.[6]

b. Management and Governance

LLC statutes permit flexibility concerning management. Most allow members to elect in the articles of organization to vest management authority with elected managers; absent such a choice, statutes usually provide that management will be by the LLC members, with voting rights in proportion to their interests in the LLC's profits.[7] Few statutes address the fiduciary duties of the managers, but those that do seem to contemplate application of the same duties that apply to corporate directors.[8]

c. Transferability of Interests

Members' financial rights are freely assignable unless otherwise agreed. However, statutes commonly permit restrictions on management rights of transferees where unanimous consent of other members is lacking.[9]

d. Continuity of Life: Dissolution and Disassociation of Members

Most statutes fix the maximum duration of an LLC at no more than thirty years.[10] In addition, automatic dissolution of the LLC is usually imposed upon the occurrence of certain events including death, retirement, resignation or bankruptcy of a partner. The disadvantageous aspects of this feature can be overcome by providing in the articles of organization that members have the right to continue the LLC and obligating them through contractual commitments to exercise that right within a specified period.[11]

§ 5–43. Federal Tax Classification

Although a central issue for entities considering adopting the LLC form initially was whether owners will be subject to double taxation as is the case

---

3. See, e.g., West's Fla. Stat. Ann. § 608.405 (two or more members required); Wyo. Stat. § 17–15–106(same).

4. See, e.g., Va. Code § 13.1–1002; Md. Code, Corporations & Ass'ns § 4A–101(f).

5. See I.R.C. § 721(a).

6. See, e.g., Wyo. Stat. § 17–15–121(a).

7. See, e.g., Utah Code Ann. § 48–2b–125.

8. See Colo. Rev. Stat. Ann. § 7–80–406 (manager shall perform duties "in good faith, in a manner he reasonably believes to be in the best interest of the limited liability company, and with such care as an ordinarily prudent person in a like position would use under similar circumstances"). Ratification of conflict of interest transactions by managers is likely to be impossible because manager-members are

not "disinterested." See Robert R. Keatinge et al., The Limited Liability Company: A Study of the Emerging Entity, 47 Bus. Law 375, 391 (1992) (predicting that consent by all members to each conflict transaction will be required absent an agreement to the contrary).

9. See, e.g., S.H.A. 805 ILCS 180/30–5 (requiring unanimous consent for transferee to participate in the management of the business); Utah Code Ann. § 48–2b–131(1) (consent by nontransferring members receiving majority of profits required to approve transfer of all rights and privileges).

10. See, e.g., West's Colo. Rev. Stat. Ann. § 7–80–204(b); Minn. Stat. Ann. § 322B.20.

11. Edward J. Roche et al., Limited Liability Companies Offer Pass–Through Benefits Without S Restrictions, 74 J. Tax'n 248 (1991).

with corporations or whether it will obtain pass-through treatment as a partnership, the IRS now allows firms to "check-the-box" and simply elect to be taxed either as a partnership or corporation.[1]

§ 5–44. Professional LLCs

Most early LLC statutes were silent on whether professionals could avail themselves of the form. However, a growing number of states now provide that LLCs may be used to conduct any lawful business or any business that a partnership or individual may conduct.[1] Moreover, some statutes specifically authorize professionals to practice in the LLC form.[2]

Several states have adopted separate statutory subchapters for professional limited liability companies, or professional limited companies (PLCs), as they are sometimes called.[3] In general, these laws blend many of the limitations and other provisions of professional corporation statutes with the basic LLC statutory framework. For example, these statutes usually provide that PLCs may be organized only for the purpose of engaging in a specific profession, while allowing the entity to have additional purposes of doing "all lawful things which may be incidental to or necessary or convenient in connection with" the practice of the profession.[4] Statutes enumerating the professions eligible to practice as PLCs generally embrace a fairly wide range of health care providers.[5] Some statutes allow multiple professions to practice in a single entity, but these provisions are likely to track the requirements set by professional corporations statutes.

PLC statutes are careful to preserve professional regulatory requirements and explicitly disclaim any intention to alter professional ethical responsibilities or the relationship between professional and client or patient.[6] These provisions purport not to modify liability standards for professionals rendering professional services, and impose personal liability for negligent or wrongful acts of members or persons under their supervision and control. However, members' liability is limited for non-professional debts and obligations and for the professional errors of other members.[7] In addition, some statutes provide that management powers within the PLC may not be held by persons not

---

§ 5–43

1. Classification of Organizations for Federal Tax Purposes, Treas. Reg. § 301.7701–1. Under the so-called Kitner Regulations, Treas. Reg. § 301.7701–2(a)(1)(as amended in 1983) an unincorporated entity had to meet certain criteria to be classified as a corporation rather than a partnership for federal tax purposes.

§ 5–44

1. See, e.g., Ala. Code § 10–12–3; Official Code Ga. Ann. § 14–11–201; Md. Code, Corporations & Ass'ns § 4A–201 (excluding business of insurers); Wyo. Stat. § 17–15–103 (excluding banking and insurance).

2. See, e.g., Ala. Code § 10–12–4; Ark. Code Ann. § 4–32–103; Minn. Stat. Ann. § 319A.03; N.C. Gen. Stat. § 57c–2–01.

3. Ariz. Rev. Stat. § 29–841; Iowa Code Ann. § 490A.1501; Mont. Code § 35–8–1301 et seq.; N.H. Rev. Stat. Ann. ch. 304–D; N.D.

Cent. Code § 10–31–02.1; Va. Code § 13.1–1100.

4. Iowa Code Ann. § 490A.1502; cf. Va. Code § 13.1–110.

5. See, e.g., Iowa Code Ann. § 490A.1501; Va. Code § 13.1–1102; Va. Code § 54.1–2900 et seq.

6. For example, the Iowa statute states: "This subchapter does not modify any law applicable to the relationship between an individual practicing a profession and a person receiving professional services, including, but not limited to, any liability arising out of such practice and any law respecting privileged communications." Iowa Code Ann. § 490A.1507.

7. See, e.g., Va. Code § 13.1–1109; Ariz. Rev. Stat. § 29–846.

licensed to render the same professional service that the company was organized to render.[8]

Most PLC statutes seek to assure that all individuals holding membership interests are licensed to practice the profession of the professional limited company. The Iowa statute, for example, forbids transfers to nonqualifying individuals and establishes a mechanism for required purchase of membership interests by the PLC upon the death of a member, transfer of a member's interest by operation of law, and other events.[9] Some states' limited liability company statutes do not explicitly require professionals' ownership of the stock for the LLC to employ professionals.[10] Licensure requirements for members and restrictions on the scope of permissible businesses can restrict the use of PLCs for organizing vertically integrated health delivery systems.

§ 5–45. Limited Liability Partnerships

The Limited Liability Partnership (LLP) is a business form that shares many of the characteristics of partnerships with some of the characteristics of LLCs. LLPs are essentially general partnerships that limit partners' personal liability for certain actions when the partners file a registration and comply with certain requirements. As a general matter, the rules applicable to general partnerships respecting management, financial rights, transfer and dissolution operate as default rules for LLPs.[1] Like LLCs, many of these provisions can be adjusted by agreement, usually through provisions in the partnership agreement. As partnerships, LLPs must observe the necessary requirements for formation of general partnerships with the additional, and relatively simple, requirement of filing an LLP registration.

An important difference from LLC statutes, and a subject of some variation among the state LLP laws, is the extent to which the form provides limited liability. Most LLP statutes limit partners' personal liability only with respect to certain categories of claims. The statutes typically limit liability for negligence, misconduct or wrongful acts (whether in tort, contract or otherwise), but not for most contract liability.[2] Many of the more recently-enacted statutes provide for limited liability for all kinds of liability.[3] Although most statutes appear to anticipate, either explicitly or implicitly, that corporate veil-piercing standards will apply to LLPs, there are open questions as to whether LLPs might nevertheless be pierced more readily in the professional context where there is less than adequate capitalization for potential malpractice claims or where notification to clients was inadequate.[4]

F. STRUCTURING HEALTH CARE ENTERPRISES

8. See, e.g., Va. Code § 13.1–1118.

9. Iowa Code Ann. § 490A.1512.

10. E.g., Ark. Code Ann. § 4–32–101 to –1316 (1996); Ga. Code Ann. § 4–11–100 to –1109 (1994); Md. Code Ann. Corps. & Ass'ns §§ 4A–101 to –1103 (1993).

§ 5–45

1. Larry E. Ribstein, Unincorporated Business Entities § 1301 (1996). Most states have adopted LLP statutes, see Bromberg & Larry E. Ribstein, Bromberg & Ribstein on Limited Liability Partnerships and the Revised Uniform Partnership Act (1995 & Supp.).

2. See, e.g., Del Code tit. 6, sec. 1515(b).

3. See, e.g., N.Y. McKinney's Cons. Laws, ch. 39, Partnership Law sec. 26. See also, Amendments to Add Limited Liability Partnership Provisions to Uniform Partnership Act (1996).

4. See Larry E. Ribstein, Unincorporated Business Entities § 1301 D (1996).

§ 5–46. Introduction

Since the late 1970's, health care organizations have adapted to the changing environment by adopting complex organizational structures and entering into a variety of affiliations with other entities. Today a large number of hospitals are multi-corporate entities, often combining for-profit and not-for-profit units, and almost all engage in some form of joint venture or alliance with physicians, suppliers or other hospitals. For their part, physicians have increasingly abandoned solo practice in favor of group arrangements (in both corporate form and partnerships), networks of various kinds, and employment relationships. In addition, a striking proportion of physicians have acquired ownership interests in joint ventures offering ancillary services. For many hospitals, insurers, physicians and other providers seeking closer working arrangements, "integrated delivery systems" became a popular organizational response.

Organizational arrangements undertaken by health care enterprises span the range of business forms discussed in the preceding sections of this chapter and the factors to be considered in choosing a business form include virtually all the subjects discussed in this book. Attorneys counseling on these matters must reconcile clients' multiple objectives with an almost infinite array of possible organizational structures. As mentioned at the outset, legal counseling here is more art than science and trade-offs and risks need to be appreciated and clearly articulated. While an analysis of the enormous range of organizational arrangements is beyond the scope of this book, we discuss below the principal legal considerations that figure prominently in matching choice of organizational form and health care clients' objectives.

§ 5–47. Complex Health Care Organizations

Today most acute care hospitals[1] do business as part of a multi-corporate organization in which various functions or related services are performed through separate legal entities. Large hospitals frequently operate as subsidiaries of holding companies in which supportive or ancillary activities are performed by affiliated corporations, foundations or partnerships. Designing an appropriate corporate structure depends on the particular legal, business, regulatory and tax environment in which the hospital operates and the objectives of the particular institution.

Adoption of complex corporate forms entails costs and risks as well as advantages. Obviously, restructuring an entity generates legal, accounting and administrative expenses that may be substantial. In addition, ongoing administrative burdens may be created. For example, it is important to observe formalities such those involved in appointing successor directors and holding meetings required under corporate law in order to avoid risks that the corporate veil will be pierced in the event of a sizeable judgment against a corporate affiliate. For the same reason, an affiliated entity must be adequately capitalized for the risks it incurs. Likewise, it may be helpful from the

---

§ 5–47

1. The analysis in the text generally applies as well to a number of other health care enterprises, especially those operating entities such as nursing homes, psychiatric and substance abuse hospitals, ambulatory care centers, laboratories and other ancillary service providers.

perspective of avoiding veil-piercing to select some directors not affiliated with the corporate group. A complex corporate structure also necessitates careful and periodic monitoring of the organizational structure and making appropriate changes. Reimbursement principles, statutes, common law, and administrative regulations that once made the corporate design beneficial may turn suddenly to the entity's disadvantage. As a general proposition, the more complex the structure, the more costly the task of assuring that the organization is in compliance with new laws and is still reaping the advantages associated with the structure.

Hospitals face a wide array of alternatives for structuring their enterprises. First, the hospital may choose between for-profit or not-for-profit forms. As discussed above, the not-for-profit form offers access to tax-exempt financing, donations from the community, tax-exempt status and often a reservoir of good will in the local community. The for-profit form affords the opportunity to secure access to investment capital and freedom to invest in a wide variety of enterprises. Most organizational structures discussed below are equally available to for-profit and not-for-profit entities. That is, not-for-profits may elect a multi-corporate form, operate for-profit subsidiaries, participate as general or limited partners, and engage in joint ventures.

In addition, it is possible to arrange affiliated entities in separate corporations. The internal corporate structures of hospitals vary considerably, but three principal models of organization may be identified. First, hospitals may establish wholly-owned subsidiary corporations to perform functions or provide services. Second, the hospital corporation may establish sibling corporations, which are separate corporate entities but whose initial directors are appointed by the hospital corporation. Finally, hospitals may create a parent holding company which holds all the shares or is the sole member of the hospital corporation and a number of other corporate entities providing services to the hospital.

The parent holding company model has achieved the widest acceptance because it centralizes control while insulating to a considerable extent affiliated corporations for purposes of veil-piercing analysis, reimbursement, regulatory requirements and other matters discussed above. The limitations of the parent-subsidiary model are that the direct control exercised by parents over subsidiaries has led regulators and payers to treat the entities as one. The sibling corporation model would seem to offer even greater insulation because the hospital does not directly control the affiliates. However, the principal drawback of establishing sibling corporations is that once control over the sister entity has been surrendered, there is no guarantee that it will continue to serve exclusively the interests of the hospital. Of course, control may be exerted by the hospital by reserving the right to appoint or approve new directors and establishing intertwined methods of financing. However, such control devices may weaken claims that the entities are not closely related for regulatory purposes including Medicare cost-based payment rules and may risk disregard of the corporate entity in liability suits.

§ 5–48. Joint Ventures and Other Alliances Between Health Care Organizations

Hospitals commonly enter into shared services agreements with each other to share costs of everything from laundry services to acquisitions of complex equipment. Physicians and hospitals frequently jointly own and operate entities offering ancillary services as well as medical office buildings and equipment. Hospitals and physicians often integrate to form entities that negotiate for provider contracts with payers, or in the case of HMOs, actually perform the insurance function themselves. In anticipation of negotiating with health alliances, hospitals, insurers and physicians have begun to form integrated delivery systems to link most primary and acute care provider services in a single business unit.

These arrangements are often loosely designated as "joint ventures,"[1] a term that has come to describe virtually any kind of arrangement by which entities cooperate for a business purpose. In fact, there is a seemingly endless array of structural arrangements that these cooperative enterprises may adopt. The business forms employed include all the entities described in this chapter as well as conventional contracting and leasing arrangements. An analysis of the structural alternatives and their suitability for various kinds of health care enterprises, though beyond the scope of this book, is treated in numerous other sources.[2] The task is essentially one of attempting to address the myriad of potential legal problems and varying business objectives by devising an appropriate organizational structure.

§ 5–49. Integrated Systems

Changes in health care financing and the prospect of legislative reform unleashed a torrent of reorganization and innovation in health care delivery in the 1990s. First, horizontal integration—combinations of providers competing at the same level of care—increased significantly. For example, physicians have formed group practices, HMOs, "clinics without walls"[1] and other arrangements that entail varying degrees of clinical and administrative integration. Hospitals have likewise combined in increasing numbers, merging with other hospitals as well as forming joint ventures and informal alliances with hospitals for shared management, purchasing or joint operation or ownership of facilities and equipment. Perhaps even more striking, however, has been the explosive growth of vertical integration through which "integrated delivery systems" have developed to offer hospital, physician and ancillary health care services as well as to provide management and information support services to providers. In some cases the integration extends beyond

---

§ 5–48

1. In common law, "joint ventures" are partnerships undertaken for a fixed term or purpose. See, e.g., Meinhard v. Salmon, 164 N.E. 545 (N.Y.App.1928). See also Harry G. Henn, Agency–Partnership and Other Unincorporated Business Enterprises 585 (2d ed. 1985).

2. An excellent compendium of structural arrangements and analysis of their legal implications is Gerald R. Peters, Healthcare Integration: A Legal Manual for Constructing Integrated Organizations (1995).

§ 5–49

1. The clinic without walls (or "group practice without walls") is an entity formed by sole practitioners or physician groups. The physicians or groups practice at multiple sites and usually retain ownership of practice assets and purchase their own supplies. Depending upon the amount of integration desired, the entity operates a central office providing or contracting with others such as medical services organizations, see § 5–49a, to provide marketing, billing and other services for the physicians. In some instances the clinic without walls is organized without creating a separate legal entity and is done through joint contracting with third parties. See James G. Wiehl, Benefits and Detriments of Various Structural Models in Integrated Health Care Delivery Systems Manual para. 410 (Alan Fine, ed. 1993); Kenneth L. Levine, The Tax Status of Vertically Integrated Health Care Delivery Systems, 26 J. Health & Hosp. L. 257, 269 n. 4 (1993).

combining providers' services to include operating an HMO or other insurance plan.

The impetus behind the growth in integrated delivery systems is not hard to discern. With payers insisting on capitated contracts or effective management of utilization and with most health reform proposals strongly supporting such arrangements, providers need organizational structures that enable them to agree upon and implement such arrangements. Integrated systems also facilitate pooling of capital, spreading of financial risk, realizing economies of scale and aligning goals of physicians and hospitals. Finally, integration fosters a "seamless" system that ideally promotes quality of care by providing a comprehensive continuum of care from prevention through treatment and follow-up.[2] At the same time, many integrated systems have proven unsuccessful as they have been unprepared to take on the insurance role and have not developed information systems capable of dealing with financial and case management problems.[3]

We discuss below several models of organizational arrangements designed to realize the advantages of greater provider integration. There is considerable diversity among actual systems within each model, however, and many forms represent transitional arrangements for providers moving toward more complete and formal integration.[4]

a. Management Services Organizations

Management services organizations (MSOs) are entities formed to provide management services and other assistance to affiliated physicians, physician groups or other entities such as "clinics without walls."[5] Sometimes also referred to as "managed services organizations" or "medical service organizations," these entities generally entail either acquisition or management of physician practices by an entity not controlled by physicians, usually a hospital or hospital-physician joint venture. MSOs perform a variety of functions for physicians including billing and collection, personnel management, and group purchasing. In addition, they supply the administrative and information services necessary for managed care contracting such as utilization review, management information systems, facility design, and negotiation services. One variant, the so-called "turn-key" MSO, offers a full range of facilities and support services needed by physician practices including practice space, equipment, and ancillary personnel. Turn-key MSOs often acquire and lease back the tangible assets of existing physician practices. Subject to the

2. F. Kenneth Ackermann, III, The Movement Toward Vertically Integrated Regional Systems, 17 Health Care Mgt.Rev. 81 (No. 3, 1992).

3. See Edric B. Engert & Douglas W. Emery, Integrated Delivery Systems: Non Fait Accompli, 7 Managed Care Q. 29 (1999); James C. Robinson, The Future of Managed Care Organization, 18 Health Affs. 7 (1999).

4. A number of sources are available describing the structural alternatives involved in integrating delivery of health care and the legal issues they present. See, e.g., Gerald R. Peters, Healthcare Integration: A Legal Manual for Constructing Integrated Organizations (1995); Andrew J. Demetriou & Thomas Dutton, Health Care Integration: Structural and

Legal Issues (BNA Health L. & Bus. Series No. 1300, 1996); Integrated Delivery Systems, 20 Topics in Health Care Financing (Paul R. De-Muro, ed.) (Spring, 1994); Carl H. Hitchner et al., Integrated Delivery Systems: A Survey of Organizational Models, 29 Wake Forest L.Rev. 273 (1994); Integrated Health Care Delivery Systems Manual (Alan Fine, ed. 1993). See generally Anthony D. Shaffer & Peter A. Pavarini, Resolving Conflicting Laws and Policy in Integrated Delivery Systems, 12 J. L. & Health 85 (1998).

5. Carl H. Hitchner et al., Integrated Delivery Systems: A Survey of Organizational Models, 29 Wake Forest L.Rev. 273 (1994)

governance rules adopted in setting up the MSO, the entity will usually have authority to contract with managed care entities.

Many, MSOs are hospital subsidiaries or separate corporations or joint ventures in which hospitals and physicians share ownership. While the for-profit corporate form is most often chosen, MSOs are also organized as partnerships, nonprofit corporations and limited liability companies. Many view the MSO as a transitional vehicle that assists hospitals and physicians in taking the initial steps necessary to participate in managed care contracting. Physicians surrender little in the way of autonomy and reap some benefits of collective practice management and economies of scale for managed care contracting. Hospitals are able to obtain closer ties and affiliations with primary care physicians, thereby assuring an adequate referral base for hospital services.

Several important legal constraints limit the desirability and usefulness of the MSO. First, it is highly unlikely that MSOs operated as subsidiaries or joint ventures of hospitals will be eligible for tax exempt status because they provide more than incidental benefit to physicians whose practices they manage. The hospital's tax exempt status might be threatened where its investment in the MSO does not fall within its charitable purpose or where private inurement or private benefit issues are raised.[6]

Because the MSO cannot require referrals to a specific hospital, its utility in assisting and in planning for capitated contracts is limited. The activities of the MSO may also raise issues under state and federal self-referral, fraud and abuse and anti-kickback laws. Medicare fraud and abuse issues arise when any remuneration is given with an intent to induce the referral of services covered by the Medicare or Medicaid programs as would be the case if the value of management services received exceeds the payment made by the physician group or if a purpose for the arrangement is to induce physician referrals. Finally, of considerable significance in this area is the effect of the Stark laws.[7] MSOs negotiating managed care contracts and supplying practice support services to physicians must establish that the charges for those services are consistent with fair market value, commercially reasonable, and are not tied to referrals.[8]

Where the corporate practice of medicine doctrine is recognized, MSOs managing physician practices must be careful not to undertake activities that would interfere with the physicians' professional judgment.[9] Particularly problematic are paying for goodwill in connection with the acquisition of physician practices and providing management services in exchange for compensation based on a percentage of the practice's net revenues.[10] Antitrust law issues may pose problems for many MSOs. Because the arrangements involve no risk sharing and very little financial integration among physicians, the group might run afoul of antitrust price fixing rules unless the MSO operates

6. See Chapter 2.

7. The Act prohibits referrals from physicians to an entity with which the physician or an immediate family member has a financial relationship and prohibits billings by entities pursuant to prohibited referrals. See Chapter 13.

8. See Leonard C. Homer, How New Federal Laws Prohibiting Physician Self–Referrals Affect Integrated Delivery Systems, 11 Health-Span 21 (No. 4, April, 1994).

9. See supra § 5–10.

10. Carl H. Hitchner et al., Integrated Delivery Systems: A Survey of Organizational Models, 29 Wake Forest L.Rev. 273 (1994)

solely as a "messenger" leaving decisions on whether to accept managed care contracts to the discretion of the individual physicians.[11]

Another important version of the MSO model is the investor-owned Physician Practice Management Company (PPMC). PPMCs are for-profit entities that acquire tangible and certain intangible assets of physician practices, usually in return for cash and stock in the company. Physicians usually remain in professional corporations or other entities and deliver services pursuant to long term MSO management services agreements with the PPMC for which the PPMC receives a management fee. Through public offerings of a substantial part of the equity in the company, PMPCs provide access to capital markets for practice expansion and development and also offer physicians with opportunities to cash out their interests. Although initially enjoying spectacular success in the stock market, a number of publicly traded PPMCs have suffered significant financial setbacks and have spawned lawsuits alleging violations of fee-splitting, securities, anti-kickback and other laws.[12]

b. Physician–Hospital Organizations

Physician-hospital organizations (PHOs) link hospitals, physician groups, and sometimes other provider entities to form a network capable of contracting with third party payers to provide a reasonably comprehensive package of services. Although such physician-hospital ventures may be established by contract, PHOs are typically separate legal entities controlled by governing boards consisting of both physician and hospital representatives. A delicate task for PHOs is to develop governance structures that satisfy all participants concerned with getting their voice heard in the entity's decisionmaking while avoiding risks of deadlock.[13] When formed by contractual agreement, the provider network operates through a single agent empowered to represent all providers in managed care contract negotiations, sometimes with the legal capacity to bind them under a power of attorney.[14]

Although the PHO may bring together a large number of geographically-dispersed providers, it does not entail full integration because physicians and hospitals continue to function separately and hierarchical organizational structures are not established.[15] In essence, the PHO operates as a negotiating agent on behalf of hospitals and physicians. Some PHOs are "open" to all members of the hospital staff, while others are "closed" and apply credentialing standards beyond those required for staff membership. In the latter case, membership is limited to physicians meeting quality and cost criteria, and usually an ongoing review of members' performance is required. The appeal of PHOs in contracting with HMOs is that they are able to reduce the transac-

---

11. See Chapter 14.

12. See Alan S. Gassman & Scott P. Swope, Exposure of Offers and Directors of Practice Management Companies, 1 Health Care Fraud & Abuse Newsletter 27 (Dec. 1998). On PPMCs and fee-splitting, see supra § 5–10d.

13. While physicians or physician entities may or may not have an ownership interest in the PHO, as a practical matter significant physician input into the affairs of the PHO is usually necessary. Commonly relied upon means for assuring physician input include board membership and bylaw provisions re-

quiring physician approvals for specified transactions. However, impasses may arise from certain structural arrangements such as when governance boards have equal representation of physicians and the hospital.

14. Carl H. Hitchner et al., Integrated Delivery Systems: A Survey of Organizational Models, 29 Wake Forest L.Rev. 273 (1994).

15. Carl H. Hitchner et al., Integrated Delivery Systems: A Survey of Organizational Models, 29 Wake Forest L.Rev. 273 (1994).

tion costs of securing agreements and offer a package of quality and utilization controls that govern both medical and hospital services.

The PHO model of organization entails relatively little functional integration among participants. Because the PHO does not invest in physicians' tangible assets, it requires a relatively small capital investment compared to other forms of integration. Therefore, the form usually does not entail significant risks under the corporate practice of medicine doctrine because the lay entity does not have control over professional discretion. Typically, the PHO entity enters into managed care agreements and shares the profits and risks of capitated contracts. These arrangements may be sufficiently integrated to avoid per se price fixing characterization under the antitrust laws.[16] However, they may trigger requirements under state law that the entity obtain licensure as an HMO or an insurance company.[17]

c. *Foundation Model Systems*

It has become common to refer to the "medical foundation model" as a distinct kind of integrated delivery system even though the foundation—a nonprofit corporation providing physician services—is but one element in the integrated system.[18] Under this model, the nonprofit foundation controls and manages the hospitals and medical facilities in the network; employs or contracts with physicians and other professionals to provide services; and contracts with payers or consumers to provide services. Usually the foundation is an affiliate or subsidiary of a hospital or the parent of a health system and often owns and operates medical entities and clinics offering the full range of both primary and specialized physician services. In some cases, the foundation may own or be affiliated with its own HMO, in which case it is comparable to the fully integrated delivery systems that combine financing and delivery discussed in the next section.

The advantages of the foundation-model system lie in its extensive coordination and integration of provider services and its ability to help physicians obtain access to capital while also enabling them to retain autonomy over patient care matters. For example, foundations supply a variety of support and other services, such as fund raising, administrative, information, and negotiating services that link the functions of its provider affiliates. Where state corporate practice of medicine law does not pose an obstacle, the typical medical foundation contracts with affiliated physician groups or employs physicians directly and agrees to supply equipment, supplies, and personnel needed in their practice. In contrast to the MSO, the foundation-model system usually owns or operates one or more hospitals, outpatient clinics as well as the equipment, practice locations, medical records, and

16. On the other hand, PHOs lacking significant risk-sharing may be construed as illegal horizontal agreements under Section 1 of the Sherman Act. See infra Chapter 14.

17. See, e.g., Cal. Health & Safety Code § 1345(f) (HMO license required of any person who undertakes to arrange for the provision of health services to subscribers or to reimburse for such services in return for a prepaid or periodic charge); see generally, Hitchner et al., supra note 3, at 297. See generally Chapters 3 & 9.

18. The terminological confusion emanates from the practice in states such as California where physicians and hospitals have established foundations to avoid the corporate practice of medicine problems, with the resulting IDS often being referred to as a "foundation." See Gerald R. Peters, Organizational and Business Issues Affecting Integrated Delivery Systems, 20 Topics in Health Care Financing 1, 1 (Spring, 1994).

supplies of the medical practices of its affiliated physicians. Moreover, there is considerably greater integration of the hospitals with the foundation-model and so, a much stronger likelihood that the system will be able to secure tax exempt status.

A variety of corporate organizational structures may be employed by medical foundations. Under the independent foundation-model, the foundation is established as an independent entity with the majority of its board or membership comprised of community leaders or other nonproviders. Under this approach, hospitals and physicians sacrifice some measure of control in exchange for fundraising capability and community support.[19] Another variation is the controlled foundation-model, in which the hospital is the sole corporate member and controls the governing board and policies of the foundation while physician groups are subsidiaries of the foundation. While maximizing hospital control, this approach does not insulate the hospital from liability and requires extensive efforts to assure physicians that their interests will not be ignored. A third option is to share control over the system. One variation makes the foundation, hospital, and physician entities subsidiaries of a corporate parent (e.g., a holding company) that oversees the operations of all subsidiaries including the foundation.[20]

Foundation-model integrated delivery systems have achieved some success in surmounting legal obstacles that may plague other kinds of networks. For example, the Internal Revenue Service has issued several rulings finding foundation-model systems have met their requirements for tax exempt status. Particularly relevant from the Service's perspective were: the fact that a foundation has an independent board of directors; operation of an acute care hospital with an open medical staff and open emergency room; participation in Medicare and Medicaid programs; provision of charity care or participation in medical research and health education programs; the reasonableness of physician compensation; and avoidance of private inurement or private benefit.[21]

Foundations acquiring physician practices may avoid problems under anti-kickback laws, if they establish that the purchase price does not constitute remuneration intended to induce referrals. This will turn on whether the sale may fit within the very narrow safe harbor regulation or, in the alternative, whether a variety of factors (e.g., whether consideration paid exceeded fair market value and whether payment included payment for goodwill) suggest that the payment was not made in exchange for or to induce referrals.[22] Likewise, the foundation must assure that physician compensation

19. The Friendly Hills Healthcare Network, which was the subject of the first IRS ruling on the tax exempt status of integrated networks, was formed when the Loma Linda University Medical Center formed a foundation governed by a 10–member board drawn from the community not more than two of whom were doctors affiliated with the network. Friendly Hills Healthcare Network, 7 Exempt Org.Tax Rev. 490 (1993).

20. This model is viewed as especially well-suited for situations in which one or a few medical groups account for the lion's share of a hospital's volume and the hospital seeks to achieve long-lasting vertical integration. See Robert A. Nelson, A Future Model for Integrated Health Care, 39 Med.Group Mgmt. 96, 100 (1992).

21. See Chapter 2; John D. Colombo, Health Care Reform and Federal Tax Exemptions: Rethinking the Issues, 29 Wake Forest L.Rev. 215 (1993).

22. Id.; Hitchner et al., supra note 3, at 299–300.

is not a means simply to distribute earnings and is the product of arm's length bargaining that results in reasonable compensation.[23]

Where the corporate practice of medicine doctrine presents a problem, foundations generally contract with multi-specialty groups. However, even these arrangements must ensure that physicians retain adequate control over their practices to avoid characterization as an employment relationship.[24] As to antitrust issues, foundations in which providers lack formal or de facto control over the operation of the entity should not be characterized as a horizontal agreement and hence would be far more likely to pass muster. When characterized as a horizontal agreement, the amount of integration and risk sharing usually present in foundation-model systems would likely prevent treatment as per se price fixing.[25]

d. Full Integration

The fully integrated system is one that combines comprehensive, integrated service delivery with the insurance function. Prototypical examples are those HMOs which employ staff physicians (staff model HMOs) or contract with group practice physicians (group model HMOs) *and* own their own hospital for provision of acute care services.[26] These arrangements are fully integrated in several respects. First, individuals must obtain all covered health services from the HMO; any services received from non-HMO providers are paid for out-of-pocket. Thus, patients are closely bound to the HMO for their care. Second, physicians are employees or are paid through capitated payments and other financial incentives that serve to align their incentives with those of the HMO. Essentially, both the HMO and its providers are at risk for overutilization. Finally, internalization of the insurance function within the entity enables the HMO to design and market to employers and individuals a single and complete package that integrates all provider and insurance services. In sum, the combination of functions and the alignment of consumer and provider interests are most complete in this kind of organization. Nevertheless, other integrated systems that combine delivery and insurance functions (such as a foundation operating an HMO) may approximate this form of integration, depending upon how completely providers' allegiances are tied to the integrated system.

23. See Gen.Couns.Mem. 39862.

24. See Hitchner et al., supra note 3; see § 5–10.

25. See § 14–35.

26. For analysis of HMOs and the laws affecting their operations see Chapter 9.

Chapter 6

THE LIABILITY OF HEALTH CARE PROFESSIONALS

Table of Sections

A. PHYSICIAN LIABILITY FOR PATIENT INJURY

B. PHYSICIAN OBLIGATIONS TO OBTAIN A PATIENT'S INFORMED CONSENT

Sec.

6–25.   Conclusion.

Research References

Am Jur 2d, Physicians, Surgeons, and Other Healers §§ 200–301

ALR Index: Individual Liability; Joint and Several Liability; Malpractice By Medical or Health Professions

ALR Digest: Hospitals and Other Health Care Facilities §§ 4–6

Am Jur Pleading and Practice Forms (Rev), Physicians, Surgeons, and Other Healers §§ 241–855

26 POF3d 185, Discovery Date in Medical Malpractice Litigation; 25 POF3d 313, Toxic Torts: Proof of Medical Monitoring Damages for Exposure to Toxic Substances; 16 POF3d 189, Negligent Infliction of Emotional Distress by Health Care Provider

44 Am Jur Trials 317, Forensic Document Examination in Medical Malpractice Cases; 39 Am Jur Trials 261, Planning and Producing A "Day-in-the-Life" Videotape in a Personal Injury Lawsuit; 38 Am Jur Trials 1, Professional Liability for Failure To Report Child Abuse; 23 Am Jur Trials 479, Determining the Medical and Emotional Bases for Damages; 16 Am Jur Trials 471, Defense of Medical Malpractice Cases; 15 Am Jur Trials 373, Discovery and Evaluation of Medical Records

A.   PHYSICIAN LIABILITY FOR PATIENT INJURY

Litigation over patient injury caused by health care professionals can be found in early English and American law. The application of both contract and negligence principles against physicians for medical failures can be found as early as 1375, in *Stratton v. Cavendish*, where the King's Bench considered the botched surgery performed by Dr. Swanlon on the hand of the plaintiff. The court compared the surgeon's error to that of a smithy: "If a smith undertakes to cure my horse, and the horse is harmed by his negligence or failure to cure in a reasonable time, it is just that he should be liable".[1] The court talks of both negligence and of a physician's failure to cure, an apparent reference to warranty concepts.

Medical litigation against physicians has increased dramatically over the past fifty years. Several explanations for the increase have been offered. First, medical practice has changed: it has become more dependent on technologies—surgery, drugs, and diagnostic tools—as medicine tackles more illnesses with a wider range of intrusive treatments; the availability of third party financing for health care has made such treatments available to more people; and the end result of more intrusive treatment is more patient injury. Second, malpractice litigation has also become easier: modern rules of pleading and practice make suing easier; modern urban juries are less sympathetic to physicians; and more physicians are willing to testify against their colleagues at trial. Such changes have increased both the frequency of litigation and the severity of the awards against physicians.

---

1. William Carleton, Stratton v. Swanlon: The Fourteenth–Century Ancestor of the Law of Malpractice, The Pharos 20 (Fall 1982). The earliest recorded American case is Cross v. Guthery, 1 Am. Dec. 61 (1794) (husband permitted to sue surgeon for damages resulting from an unskillful operation on his wife, causing her death). For a critique of the development of the American jurisprudence of malpractice, see Theodore Silver, One Hundred Years of Harmful Error: The Historical Jurisprudence of Medical Malpractice, 1992 Wis. L. Rev. 1193 (1992).

The substance of malpractice law is also evolving: new causes of action have developed—for example, mental distress, strict products liability; new damages have been recognized, such as "loss of a chance"; limitations on proof, such as the locality rule, have been abrogated or limited in many states. No one change is a watershed event, but the cumulative effect has been to improve a plaintiff's chances of winning against a physician.

§ 6–1. The Contract Between Patient and Physician

A physician-patient relationship is normally a prerequisite to a professional malpractice suit against a doctor. When for example a doctor employed by an insurance company examines an individual for the purpose of qualifying him for insurance coverage, the usual rule has been that a doctor owes no duty to the individual to treat or to disclose problems discovered during the examination.[1] Pre-employment physicals likewise do not give rise to the relationship, given the absence of a therapeutic purpose,[2] nor do examinations by an insurer's physician of a claimant against the insurer as the result of injuries from an automobile accident.[3] The physician must normally consent, expressly or impliedly, before the doctor-patient relationship is created.[4]

Some courts treat the existence or absence of a contractual doctor-patient relationship as simply a factor to be weighed in determining liability, but not a dispositive one by itself, refusing to exempt physician from general rules of negligence law.[5] Thus in *Daly v. United States*[6] the court upheld an action against the Federal government for the failure of a V.A. radiologist to disclose abnormalities in the plaintiff's chest x-rays, which the physician had discovered during a preemployment physical. Workplace examinations of employees may also give rise to a physician-patient relationship, requiring the physician to disclose any findings that might threaten the examinee's health.[7]

a. Express and Implied Contract

The physician-patient relationship can be considered initially as a contractual one. Physicians in private practice may contract for their services as they see fit, and retain substantial control over the extent of their contact with patients. Physicians may limit their specialty, their scope of practice, their geographic area, and the hours and conditions under which they will see patients. They have no obligation to offer services that a patient may require that are outside the physician's competence and training; or services outside the scope of the original physician-patient agreement, where the physician has limited the contract to a type of procedure, to an office visit, or to consultation only. They may transfer responsibility by referring patients to other specialists. They may refuse to enter into a contract with a patient or to treat patients, even under emergency conditions.[8]

§ 6–1

1. Saari v. Litman, M.D., 486 N.W.2d 813 (Minn.App.1992).

2. Ney v. Axelrod, 723 A.2d 719 (Pa.Super.Ct.1999)

3. Martinez v. Lewis, 942 P.2d 1219 (Colo. App.1997)

4. St. John v. Pope, 901 S.W.2d 420, 423 (Tex.1995).

5. Pope v. St. John, 862 S.W.2d 657, 659 (Tex.App.—Austin 1993).

6. 946 F.2d 1467 (9th Cir.1991).

7. Webb v. T.D., et al., 951 P.2d 1008 (Mont.1997) (relying on Green v. Walker, 910 F.2d 291, 296 (5th Cir.1990)).

8. Hiser v. Randolph, 617 P.2d 774, 776 (Ariz.App.1980).

Physicians may also expressly contract with a patient for a specific result.[9] Courts will sometimes allow parol evidence to fill in the terms of these contracts, where the patient has signed other consent forms.[10] Once the physician-patient relationship has been created, however, physicians are subject to an obligation of "continuing attention."[11] Termination of the physician-patient relationship, once created, is subject in some jurisdictions to a "continuous treatment" rule to determine when the statute of limitations is tolled.[12] Treatment obligations cease if the physician can do nothing more for the patient.[13] After surgery, where follow-up care is needed, a surgeon must continue to care for the patient until the threat of post-operative complications is past.[14]

When a patient goes to a doctor's office with a particular problem, she is offering to enter into a contract with the physician. When the physician examines the patient, she accepts the offer and an implied contract is created. The physician is free to reject the offer and send the patient away, relieving herself of any duty to that patient.[15]

An express written contract is rarely drafted for specific physician-patient interactions.[16] An implied contract is usually the basis of the relationship between a physician and a patient. A physician who talks with a patient by telephone may be held to have an implied contractual obligation to that patient if medical advice is given.[17] A physician such as a pathologist who renders services to a patient but has not expressly contracted with him is bound by certain implied contractual obligations—to properly perform his or her medical function. Conducting laboratory tests, reviewing the results of tests performed by others, preparing reports, billing the patient—any of these steps may be sufficient to create a contractual relationship even if the physician has never met or examined the patient.

Consultation by a treating physician with another physician by telephone will not usually create a physician-patient relationship.[18] The concern is that such informal conferences will be deterred by the fear of liability.[19] If the telephone call is to an on-call specialist, the specialist will be held to have a duty to the patient if he or she (1) participates in the patient's diagnosis; (2)

---

9. Stewart v. Rudner, 84 N.W.2d 816, 822–23 (Mich.1957).

10. Murray v. University of Pa. Hosp., 490 A.2d 839 (Pa.Super.1985) (court allowed parol evidence to show the existence of an oral agreement to guarantee the prevention of future pregnancies by a tubal ligation).

11. Ricks v. Budge, 64 P.2d 208 (Utah 1937).

12. Sander v. Geib, Elston, Frost Professional Association, 506 N.W.2d 107, 114 (S.D. 1993) (relationship must be based on "on-going, continuous, developing and dependent relationship").

13. See Jewson v. Mayo Clinic, 691 F.2d 405 (8th Cir.1982). Accord Wells v. Billars, 391 N.W.2d 668 (S.D.1986).

14. Shirk v. Kelsey, 186 Ill.Dec. 913, 617 N.E.2d 152 (Ill.App. 1 Dist.1993).

15. See e.g., Childs v. Weis, 440 S.W.2d 104 (Tex.Civ.App.1969).

16. Jones v. Malloy, 412 N.W.2d 837, 841 (Neb.1987). See Tisdale v. Pruitt, 394 S.E.2d 857 (S.C.App.1990) (for judicial difficulties with contextual consent).

17. Weaver v. University of Michigan Board of Regents, 506 N.W.2d 264 (Mich.App. 1993).

18. See e.g., Lopez v. Aziz, 852 S.W.2d 303 (Tex.App.—San Antonio 1993).

19. See Reynolds v. Decatur Memorial Hosp., 660 N.E.2d 235, 240 (Ill.App. 4 Dist. 1996) ("It would have a chilling effect upon practice of medicine. It would stifle communication, education and professional association, all to the detriment of the patient.").

prescribes a course of treatment[20]; and (3) owes a duty to the hospital and/or health plan of which he is a part, to provide such care.[21] Absent such proof, no contract will be found by most courts.[22] Simply answering a professional inquiry or being asked if the physician wants to be brought into the case is not sufficient.[23] If the original physician arranges for another to "cover" her patient, with the patient's agreement, the original physician is not vicariously liability for any malpractice of the covering doctor.[24] If, however, a physician evaluates information provided by a nurse and makes a medical decision as to a patient's status, a doctor-patient relationship may be established.[25]

Physicians who practice in institutions provide health care within the limits of the health plan coverage or their employment contracts with the institution. The initial contact between the physician and the patient is preceded by an express contract spelling out the details of the relationship. Physicians who are members of a health maintenance organization have a duty to treat plan members, as part of their contractual obligation to the HMO. In these situations, the express contract is between the physician and the HMO, and the subscriber and the HMO, with an implied contract between the subscriber and the treating physician.[26] Members of a hospital staff may also be expressly bound to treat patients, particularly in the emergency room when they are on call.[27] They have waived their rights to refuse to treat particular patients, as a result of their contractual obligations to the hospital. Certain contractual obligations therefore flow from the employment setting, binding physicians to treat individual patients. The traditional contractual relationship may also include obligations, such as completing a variety of benefit forms for a patient. If these forms are not properly and timely completed, and a patient suffers an economic detriment, courts have held that a suit for breach of contract will lie.[28]

b. *Specific Promises and Warranties of Cure*

A contract claim may have several advantages for the plaintiff. The statute of limitations is typically longer than for a tort action. The plaintiff need not establish the medical standard of care and thus may not need to present expert testimony. A contract claim may be viable even when the doctor has made the proper risk disclosure, satisfying the requirements of the tort doctrine of informed consent. Finally, a contract claim offers a remedy to

20. Cogswell v. Chapman, 672 N.Y.S.2d 460 (N.Y.App.Div.1998)

21. See Wheeler v. Yettie Kersting Memorial Hospital 866 S.W.2d 32 (Tex.App.1993)(physician on-call evaluated patient information and made a decision to transfer the patient to another hospital; sufficient to create physician-patient relationship); see also McKinney v. Schlatter, 692 N.E.2d 1045 (Ohio App.1997); .

22. St. John v. Pope, 901 S.W.2d 420, 423 (Tex.1995).

23. Reynolds v. Decatur Memorial Hospital, 660 N.E.2d 235 (Ill.App.Ct.1996); Oja v. Kin, 581 N.W.2d 739 (Mich.App.1998); Ortiz v. Shah, 905 S.W.2d 609 (Tex.App.1995).

24. McKay v. Cole, 625 So.2d 105 (Fla.App. 3 Dist.1993).

25. Wheeler v. Yettie Kersting Memorial Hospital, 866 S.W.2d 32 (Tex.App.1993).

26. Hand v. Tavera, 864 S.W.2d 678, 679 (Tex.App.1993)("... [W]hen a patient who has enrolled in a prepaid medical plan goes to a hospital emergency room and the plan's designated doctor is consulted, the physician-patient relationship exists and the doctor owes the patient a duty of care."). For a discussion of these overlapping contractual obligations, see generally Susan M. Wolf, Toward a Systemic Theory of Informed Consent in Managed Care, 35 Houston L.Rev. 1631 (1999); E. Haavi Morreim, Balancing Act: The New Medical Ethics of Medicine's New Economics 139 (1991).

27. Hiser, 617 P.2d at 777.

28. Chew v. Meyer, M.D. P.A., 527 A.2d 828 (Md.App.1987).

the plaintiff who underwent the procedure because of the enticements of the physician.

The contract between physician and patient can be breached in a variety of ways. The physician may promise to use a certain procedure and then use an alternative procedure,[29] may promise to do a procedure and then allow another physician to operate,[30] or contract to perform a procedure and then simply not do it, to the patient's detriment.[31] In *Zehr v. Haugen*,[32] for example, defendant physician agreed to perform a surgical sterilization on the plaintiff, failed to do so properly, and the wife became pregnant and bore a healthy child. The court allowed not only a negligence suit, but also both breach of contract and warranty claims.

A breach may also be found where the doctor promises a particular result which fails to occur. The classic case is *Guilmet v. Campbell*,[33] where the physician treated the patient for a bleeding ulcer. The doctor had allegedly told the patient prior to the operation:

> Once you have an operation it takes care of all your troubles. You can eat as you want to, you can drink as you want to, you can go as you please. Dr. Arena and I are specialists, there is nothing to it at all—it's a very simple operation. You'll be out of work three to four weeks at most. There is no danger at all in this operation. After the operation you can throw away your pill box.[34]

The patient suffered serious after effects, and the jury found for the plaintiff on a breach of contract theory. Such cases are understandably rare, since few physicians would promise a patient a guaranteed result for most medical procedures.[35] But an express contract may be made, and the physician will under the right facts be held to have warranted the result.[36]

A contract claim allows the plaintiff to assert an "expectation" interest, placing the aggrieved party in the position she would have been in had the contract been fully performed. Thus a plaintiff has been allowed to assert a contract claim for failure to perform a tubal ligation, resulting in the birth of a healthy child; the damages claimed may include the costs of raising the child and providing for a college education.[37]

---

29. See Moser v. Stallings, 387 N.W.2d 599 (Iowa 1986) (plastic surgeon did not perform chin implant as part of cosmetic surgery on plaintiff, after telling patient that implant would be a part of the procedure; court in dicta suggested that patient might have had a contract claim); Stewart v. Rudner, 84 N.W.2d 816 (Mich.1957) (physician broke promise to perform Caesarean section).

30. See e.g., Labarre v. Duke Univ., 393 S.E.2d 321 (N.C.App.1990), review denied 399 S.E.2d 122 (N.C.1990).

31. Zehr v. Haugen, 871 P.2d 1006 (Ore. 1994)(failure to permit tubal ligation as agreed states a claim for breach of contract).

32. 855 P.2d 1127 (Or.App.1993).

33. 188 N.W.2d 601 (Mich.1971).

34. Id. at 606.

35. One emerging area in which warranties are being offered is that of fertility treatment. Fertility clinics in Minnesota and California have begun to offer a guarantee that their patients will have patients, or they will get their money back. See Stephen L. Cohen, Should Health Care Come With a Warranty? The New York Times 12 (November 10, 1996).

36. In Haase v. Starnes, 915 S.W.2d 675 (Ark.1996), the defendant advertised "We guarantee you a full, growing head of hair for the rest of your life" and "Transplants guaranteed to grow for the rest of your life". Plaintiff suffered an infection during treatment, creating a scar that left him unable to sustain hair transplants. The court held that the trial court had erred in granting summary judgment.

37. Zehr v. Haugen, 871 P.2d 1006 (Ore. 1994).

The existence of a contract or warranty claim is a question of law for the court.[38] Courts will sometimes allow contract claims, but then define the "contract" restrictively. Courts typically distinguish "therapeutic assurances" from express warranties to effect a cure.[39] Statements of opinion by a physician as to the result of a procedure will not impose contractual liability even if incorrect.[40] Other courts have imposed evidentiary burdens, requiring proof by clear and convincing evidence.[41] Even if the burden of proof is not elevated from the preponderance test to clear and convincing evidence, the jury will be instructed that they must find that the physician "clearly and unmistakably [gave] a positive assurance [that he or she would] produce or * * * avoid a particular result * * *."[42] In some states, the Statute of Frauds specifically requires agreements guaranteeing therapeutic results to be in writing and signed to be enforceable.[43]

§ 6–2. Basic Principles of Malpractice Liability

The liability of health care providers is governed by general negligence principles. Malpractice is usually defined as unskillful practice resulting in injury to the patient, a failure to exercise the "required degree of care, skill and diligence" under the circumstances.[1] A physician is not a guarantor of good results, nor is he required to exercise the highest degree of care possible. As one court said, "The physician will not be held to a standard of perfection nor evaluated with benefit of hindsight."[2] A physician's inability to pass certification and licensure examinations is not relevant to his or her negligence in performing a particular procedure.[3] However, jury instructions that allow for an "error in judgment" by a physician are increasingly rejected by the courts as unduly favorable to defendants.[4] The courts are not tolerant of accordion-like defenses that grant doctors too much discretion and mislead the jury.

The standard of care by which the conduct of both general practitioners and specialists is measured is treated as national by most state courts. A good statement is found in *Hall v. Hilbun*:

> The duty of care * * * takes two forms: (a) a duty to render a quality of care consonant with the level of medical and practical knowledge the physician may reasonably be expected to possess and the medical judgment he may be expected to exercise, and (b) a duty based upon the adept

38. Hawkins v. McGee, 146 A. 641, 643 (N.H.1929).

39. Ferlito v. Cecola, 419 So.2d 102 (La. App.1982)(the court held that a dentist's statement that crown work would make the plaintiff's teeth "pretty" did not constitute a guarantee).

40. Anglin v. Kleeman, 665 A.2d 747 (N.H.1995)(statement to patient awaiting knee surgery to treat basketball injury that the operation could give the patient "knee that was stronger than ... before" not a warranty).

41. See Burns v. Wannamaker, 315 S.E.2d 179 (S.C.App.1984), affirmed and modified 343 S.E.2d 27 (S.C.1986).

42. Scarzella v. Saxon, 436 A.2d 358 (D.C.App.1981).

43. See e.g., West's Ann. Ind. Code 16–915– 1–4; 40 Penn. Statues s. 1301.606. See also Powers v. Peoples Community Hosp. Auth., 455 N.W.2d 371 (Mich.App.1990).

§ 6–2

1. Bardessono v. Michels, 91 Cal.Rptr. 760, 764, 478 P.2d 480, 484 (Cal.1970).

2. Wainwright v. Leary, 623 So.2d 233, 237 (La.App.1993). See also Murray v. U.S., 36 F.Supp.2d 713 (E.D.Va.1999)(applying Virginia Law).

3. Beis v. Dias, 859 S.W.2d 835 (Mo.App. 1993).

4. See Deyo v. Kinley, 565 A.2d 1286 (Vt. 1989).

use of such medical facilities, services, equipment and options as are reasonably available.[5]

Most jurisdictions have moved from the locality rule to a national standard for specialists, due to concerns about a "conspiracy of silence"[6], unfair limitations on the use of experts, and recognition of the national basis of medical education and practice.[7] The standard of practice for general practitioners, interns and residents is still based on the local community or a similar community in most jurisdictions,[8] although some courts have broadened the national standard to apply to all physicians, including general practitioners.[9] Many jurisdictions, like *Hall*, also allow evidence describing the practice limitations under which the defendant labors.[10] *Hall's* "resource component" allows the trier of fact to consider the facilities, staff and other equipment available to the practitioner in the institution, following the general rule that courts should take into account the locality, proximity of specialists and special facilities for diagnosis and treatment.[11] The standard of care governs a physician's conduct during the period when the patient is under his or her care; this includes follow-up care to ensure that a patient obtains medical records and information as requested.[12]

The standards for evaluating the delivery of professional medical services are not normally established by either judge or jury. The medical profession itself sets the standards of practice and the courts enforce these standards in tort suits. Defendants trying to prove a standard of care normally present expert testimony describing the actual pattern of medical practice, without any reference to the effectiveness of that practice. Most jurisdictions give professional medical standards conclusive weight, so that the trier of fact is not allowed to reject the practice as improper.[13] In tort litigation not involving professionals, courts are willing to reject customary practice if they find the practice dangerous or out-of-date.[14] On rare occasions, the courts have allowed the case to proceed in spite of agreement that the defendant satisfied the

5. 466 So.2d 856, 872–73 (Miss.1985). Hall was followed in Turner v. Temple, 602 So.2d 817 (Miss.1992).

6. See e.g., Trull v. Long, 621 So.2d 1278 (Ala.1993). Some courts require that the plaintiff prove such a conspiracy of silence in the particular case before an instruction will be allowed. See e.g., Thibodeaux v. Aetna Cas. & Sur. Co., 216 So.2d 314 (La.App.1968).

7. See e.g., Bates v. Meyer, 565 So.2d 134 (Ala.1990).

8. See e.g. Bahr v. Harper–Grace Hospitals, 528 N.W.2d 170 (Mich.1995).

9. Sheeley v. Memorial Hospital, 710 A.2d 161, 166 (R.I.1998)("The appropriate standard of care to be utilized in any given procedure should not be compartmentalized by a physician's area of professional specialization or certification. On the contrary, we believe the focus in any medical malpractice case should be the procedure performed and the question of whether it was executed in conformity with the recognized standard of care, the primary concern being whether the treatment was administered in a reasonable manner.")

10. Vergara v. Doan, M.D., 593 N.E.2d 185, 187 (Ind.1992) ("availability of facilities may be considered").

11. See Blair v. Eblen, 461 S.W.2d 370 (Ky. 1970); Restatement (Second) of Torts, § 299A, cmt. g (1977) ("Allowance must be made also for the type of community in which the actor carries on his practice. A country doctor cannot be expected to have the equipment, facilities, experience, knowledge or opportunity to obtain it, afforded him by a large city.").

12. Dunning v. Kerzner, 910 F.2d 1009 (1st Cir.1990).

13. See e.g., Holt v. Godsil, 447 So.2d 191 (Ala.1984); Senesac v. Assoc. in Obstetrics and Gynecology, 449 A.2d 900 (Vt.1982). See generally Morris, Custom and Negligence, 42 Colum. L. Rev. 1147 (1942).

14. See Joseph H. King Jr., In Search of a Standard of Care for the Medical Profession—the "Accepted Practice" Formula, 28 Vand. L. Rev. 1213, 1236 (1975).

customary practice of her specialty, where evidence is presented that the defendant was aware of dangers in the standard practice.[15] Other cases that reject customary practice as a categorical defense, such as *Helling v. Carey*,[16] involve a readily understandable therapy or diagnostic procedure. In such cases, some courts have allowed the trier of fact to weigh without expert testimony the relative risks of using the procedure or omitting it. Most jurisdictions, however, have been reluctant to follow *Helling* in replacing the established medical standard of care with a case-by-case judicial balancing.[17] Others have noted that proof of "ordinary care" can prevail over a defense of compliance with custom.[18]

The standard of care is not, however, always a bright line practice. The standard in *Hall* for judging the defendant's conduct was "minimally competent physicians in the same specialty".[19] This minimal competence test seems less demanding than standard jury instructions in other states that require comparison to "the average practitioner in the class to which he or she belongs".[20] "Average" suggests a mid-point in the range of practitioners, while "minimal" places the defendant's conduct distinctly lower on a scale of practice. Such semantic differences are important in jury instructions, since a jury is likely to both notice and understand the difference as a matter of ordinary language. The standard of care must be at least compliance with available technology at the time the diagnosis or treatment was offered to the patient, without the benefit of hindsight.[21]

a. Sources of Standards of Practice

The standard of care applied in a tort suit or hospital peer review process has not been derived historically from an external authority such as a government standard. In the medical profession, as in other professions, standards have developed in a complicated way through the interaction of leaders of the profession, professional journals and meetings, and networks of colleagues. Neither the Food and Drug Administration, the National Institutes of Health, the Department of Health and Human Services nor state licensing boards have had much to do with shaping medical practice. Most clinical policies develop from a flow of reports in the literature, at meetings, and in peer discussions. Over a period of time, hundreds of separate comments come together to form a clinical policy. If this becomes generally

---

15. See e.g., Toth v. Community Hosp., 292 N.Y.S.2d 440, 239 N.E.2d 368, 369 (N.Y.App. 1968).

16. 519 P.2d 981 (Wash.1974), reaffirmed in Gates v. Jensen, 595 P.2d 919 (Wash.1979).

17. Other states that have considered Helling have rejected the Washington courts' position. See Barton v. Owen, 139 Cal.Rptr. 494 (Cal.App.1977) (claims physicians negligently acted in treatment of brain abscess).

18. See Nowatske v. Osterloh, 543 N.W.2d 265 (Wis.1996), where the court noted that "customary conduct is not dispositive and cannot overcome the requirement that physicians exercise ordinary care.... We recognize that in most situations there will be no significant difference between customary and reasonable practices. In most situations physicians, like other professionals, will revise their customary practices so that the care they offer reflects a due regard for advances in the profession. An emphasis on reasonable rather than customary practices, however, insures that custom will not shelter physicians who fail to adopt advances in their respective fields and who consequently fail to conform to the standard of care which both the profession and its patients have a right to expect.

19. Hall, 466 So.2d at 871.

20. Zintek v. Perchik, 471 N.W.2d 522, 530 (Wis.App.1991).

21. See Klisch v. Meritcare Medical Group, Inc. 134 F.3d 1356 (8th Cir. 1998).

accepted, it becomes "standard practice."[22] A national standard of practice does not exist for many procedures and tools, and the "highest and best" practice may not be the safest or most effective in the long run. Substantial regional variations exist in the use of many procedures, with no apparent differences in outcome (life expectancy, morbidity, days missed from work).[23] Different practice styles exist in different regions, and even within states, based on a local concept of good practice.

The development and proliferation of clinical practice guidelines is one of the transforming forces in current medical practice.[24] American physicians and specialty groups have expended substantial efforts on standard setting in recent years, specifying treatments for particular diseases. Clinical practice protocols (also referred to as practice parameters or guidelines[25]) have been developed by specialty societies such as the American Academy of Pediatrics; by the government, through the National Institutes of Health; and by individual hospitals in the clinical setting.[26] The development of practice standards and guidelines by national medical organizations is accelerating the process of moving all medical practice toward national standards. Such guidelines provide a particularized source of standards against which to judge the conduct of the defendant physician, and their production by national medical specialty societies and the government will be influential.[27] Such guidelines are sets of suggestions, described in decision rules, based on current medical consensus on how to treat a certain illness or condition. The Institute of Medicine has defined clinical guidelines as "systematically developed statements to assist practitioner and patient decisions about appropriate health care for specific clinical circumstances." They are standardized specifications for using a procedure or managing a particular clinical problem." Such guidelines may be

22. See generally David Eddy, Clinical Policies and the Quality of Clinical Practice, 307 New Eng. J. Med. 343 (1982).

23. See the work of John Wennberg for elaboration of practice variation. He first discussed the concept of variation in health care delivery between regions in John Wennberg and A. Gittlesohn, Small Area Variations in Health Care Delivery 182 Science 1102 (1973). See also "The Paradox of Appropriate Care," 258 JAMA 2568 (1987). For a review of the literature, including Wennberg's work, up to 1987, see Pamela Paul–Shaheen, Jane Deane Clark, and Daniel Williams, "Small Area Analysis: A Review and Analysis of the North American Literature," 12 J. Health Politics, Policy and Law 741 (1987) (very extensive bibliography).

24. A outpouring of writing on practice guidelines has occurred over the past several years. See generally Arnold J. Rosoff, The Role of Clinical Practice Guidelines in Health Care Reform, 5 Health Matrix 369 (1995); Institute of Medicine, Clinical Practice Guidelines: Directions For A New Program 8 (Marilyn J. Field & Kathleen N. Lohr eds., 1990); John Ayres, The Use and Abuse of Medical Practice Guidelines, 15 J. Legal Med. 421, 436–38 (1994); Office of Technology Assessment, U.S.

Congress, OTA–H–608, Identifying Health Technologies That Work: Searching For Evidence 145–47 (1994); Mark A. Hall and D. Sophocles Dadakis, Institution–Specific Protocols Emerge: Character of Guidelines Evolves, Concern Lingers Over Protection (February 1996).

25. See e.g., Institute of Medicine, Clinical Guidelines: Directions for a New Program 2–4–2–22, M. Field and K. Lohr, Eds. (1990).

26. The Agency for Health Care Policy and Research (AHCPR) within HCFA, for example, has the responsibility of developing guidelines for clinical practice through the Department's Medical Treatment Effectiveness Program. This program supports research, data development, and other activities to develop and review clinically relevant guidelines, standards of quality, performance measures, and medical review criteria, in order to improve the quality and effectiveness of health care services. See Pub. L. No. 101–239 (1990).

27. See Eleanor D. Kinney and Marilyn M. Wilder, Medical Standard Setting in the Current Malpractice Environment: Problems and Possibilities, 22 U.C. Davis L. Rev. 421, 448 (1989); John C. West, The Legal Implications of Medical Practice Guidelines, 27 J. Health & Hosp. L. 97 (1994).

quality-oriented, reducing variations in practice with improving patient care[28]; they may also be cost-reducing, promoting a lower cost approach to care.

Clinical pathways share many common attributes with practice guidelines. They are interdisciplinary plans of care that outline the ideal sequence and timing of interventions for patients with a particular diagnosis, procedure, or symptom. They are designed to reduce delays and resource use while maintaining quality of care. They guide care of patients with a highly predictable course of illness, and have been developed for high-volume, high-cost or high-risk diagnoses or procedures. Pathways are intended for use in hospitals or for cases as they move from hospital to home. They cover longer periods of treatment, presenting a kind of map of treatment to guide physicians and support staff, while also educating patients as to the sequence of treatment. They also allow a way to track patient outcomes and document whether or not a patient's outcomes were achieved. Critical pathways are specific: they describe what will happen to a patient every day that the patient is in the hospital. This specificity includes not only traditional nursing functions, but also medication and treatments that can be ordered only by a physician. An example of such a critical pathway is one developed by University Hospitals of Cleveland for patients chronically dependent on a ventilator, to reduce the costs of caring for this population, based on a retrospective chart review of ventilator-dependent patients and projected reimbursement by third-party payers to the hospital for the patients. The pathway is developed with the patient's physician to fit the patient's needs. Other pathways include one developed by Johns Hopkins Hospital for patients undergoing a radical, retropubic prostatectomy (removal of the prostate gland).[29]

A widely accepted clinical standard may be presumptive evidence of due care, but expert testimony will still be required to introduce the standard and establish its sources and its relevancy.[30] The source of the study will determine the weight to be given it.[31] They can also be used to impeach the opinion of a medical expert.[32] Medical societies that develop guidelines may even expose themselves to liability if poorly crafted guidelines lead to injury, or if they fail to keep the guidelines up-to-date as the medical knowledge advances.[33]

28. Guidelines for the proper use of beta blockers are one example. See, e.g., Francois P. Sarasin et al., Successful Implementation of Guidelines for Encouraging the Use of Beta Blockers in Patients After Acute Myocardial Infarction, 106 Am.J.Med.499(1999).

29. See generally Donna D. Ignatavicius and Kathy A. Hausman, Clinical Pathways for Collaborative Practice 10 (1995); Karen Butler, Health Care Quality Revolution: Legal Landmines for Hospitals and the Rise of the Critical Pathway, 58 Alb. L. Rev. 843 (1995).

30. See generally Kinney and Wilder, id.; Gwen M. Schockemoehl, Admissibility of Written Standards as Evidence of the Standard of Care in Medical and Hospital Negligence Actions in Virginia, 18 U. Rich. L. Rev. 725 (1984); Maxwell J. Mehlman, Assuring the Quality of Medical Care: The Impact of Outcome Measurement and Practice Standards, 18 Law, Med. & Health Care 368 (1990).

31. See generally Physician Payment Review Commission, Annual Report to Congress 1990 15, Legal Impediments to Physician Efforts to Increase Appropriateness of Care (1990).

32. See Roper v. Blumenfeld, 706 A.2d 1151, 1156 (N.J.Super.A.D.1998)(defendant allowed to use 1992 Parameters of Care for Oral and Maxillofacial Surgery: A Guide of Practice, Monitoring and Evaluation to examine his expert and cross examine the plaintiff's expert; the Parameter established that the injury suffered by the plaintiff was a known complication of the procedure.).

33. Mark R. Chassin, Standards of Care in Medicine, 25 Inquiry 437 (1988).

Clinical guidelines raise difficult legal questions, since they potentially offer an authoritative and settled statement of what the standard of care should be for a given treatment or illness. A court has several choices when such guidelines are offered in evidence. Such a guideline might be evidence of the customary practice in the medical profession. A doctor practicing in conformity with a guideline would be shielded from liability to the same extent as one who can establish that she or he followed professional custom. The guideline acts like an authoritative expert witness or a well-accepted review article. Using guidelines as evidence of professional custom, however, is problematic if they are ahead of prevailing medical practice. A guideline could also serve as a defense, representing the practice of at least a "respectable" minority of the relevant profession.[34]

Guidelines have already had an effect on settlement patterns, according to surveys of malpractice lawyers.[35] Plaintiffs have used such guidelines to their advantage in malpractice cases, particularly the guidelines of the American College of Obstetricians and Gynecologists (ACOG).[36]

Such guidelines provide a particularized source of standards against which to judge the conduct of the defendant physician. A widely accepted clinical standard may be presumptive evidence of due care, but expert testimony will still be required to introduce the standard and establish its sources and its relevancy. A guideline could thus be treated as negligence per se or at least a rebuttable presumption that could then be countered with evidence. The American Medical Association (AMA) now opposes direct adoption of practice guidelines as a legal standard. The AMA urges instead that they be offered only as evidence of the customarily observed professional standard of practice and that their degree of authority depend on the degree of their acceptance among medical practitioners. Such guidelines however often lack specificity, such as a guideline developed by the American College of Physicians which states that routine chest X-rays do not need to be performed at hospital admission "unless the medical history or symptoms and signs of chest disease in the judgment of the physician" require it. By leaving so much to physician judgment, the standard fails to provide a bright line evidentiary standard for a liability suit.

Professional societies also attach disclaimers to their guidelines, thereby undercutting their defensive use in litigation. The American Medical Association, for instance, calls its guidelines "parameters" instead of protocols to indicate a large sphere of physician discretion, and further suggests that all guidelines contain disclaimers stating that they are not intended to displace physician discretion. Such guidelines therefore cannot be treated as conclusive.[37]

34. See generally Andrew L. Hyams, David W. Shapiro, and Troyen A. Brennan, Medical Practice Guidelines in Malpractice Litigation: An Early Retrospective, 21 J.Health Pol., Pol'cy & Law 289 (1996).

35. Id.

36. See, e.g., Miles v. Tabor, M.D., 443 N.E.2d 1302 (Mass.1982) (obstetrician's failure to initiate resuscitation of infant immediately after delivery violated ACOG guidelines);

Green v. Goldberg, 630 So.2d 606 (Fla.Dist.Ct. App.1993)((ACOG bulletin on breast cancer treatment used to support expert testimony); Basten v. U.S., 848 F.Supp. 962 (M.D.Ala. 1994)(ACOG guidelines requiring that alpha-fetoprotein screening be offered and that acceptance or rejection be documented.) See generally Andrew L. Hyams et al, id at 296–299.

37. See Mark R. Chassin, Standards of Care in Medicine, 25 Inquiry 437 (1988).

Medical knowledge about evidence-based medicine has accumulated at a staggering rate. Between 1966 and 1995, the number of clinical research articles based on randomized clinical trials jumped from about 100 per year to 10,000 annually.[38] Web-based databases have proliferated to help physicians gain efficient and use-friendly access to this proliferation of guidelines and other medical information.[39] The National Guideline Clearinghouse[40] offers free access by physicians and others to the current clinical practice guidelines, with instantaneous searches of the database. A search produces all guidelines on a given subject, along with an appropriateness analysis of each guideline.[41] The Clearinghouse provides a standardized abstract of each guideline, and grades the scientific basis of its recommendations and the development process for each. Full text or links to sites with the guidelines are provided. Readers are given synopses to produce a side-by-side comparison of guidelines, outlining where those agree and disagree, and physicians can access electronic mail groups to discuss development and implementation. These guidelines must pass certain entry criteria to be included: they must be current, contain systematically developed statements to guide physician decisions, have been produced by a medical or other professional group, government agency, health care organization or other private or public organization; and they must show that they were developed through systematic search of peer-reviewed scientific evidence. The benefits: easy search features, database comprehensiveness and Internet location make this the most powerful tool to date. Various appropriateness tests have been developed to evaluate guidelines.[42] The problem with such guidelines, ironically, given their power to set the standard of care in a malpractice case, is that they do not have much effect in changing physician behavior. Physician adherence to guidelines appears to be hindered by inertia, lack of awareness, and external barriers such as lack of time or difficulty of use.[43]

Other Internet based services are available on a commercial basis. One example is MDConsult, a commercial database available by subscription that makes available hundreds of medical textbooks and treatises, as well as easy access to clinical practice guidelines. Subscribership in such commercial sites, designed to be user-friendly, has grown geometrically over the past two years, as physicians look for easy research access to data about patient problems. A survey by MDConsult of physician subscribers found that physicians were accessing the website for a fast and easy way to check the literature while treating patients, allowing for immediate answers; to keep up and to expand a physician's knowledge base about particular conditions. Physicians felt that

38. Mark R. Chassin, Is Health Care Ready for Six Sigma Quality? 76 the Milbank Quarterly 565, 574 (1998).

39. See generally Barry R. Furrow, Broadcasting Clinical Guidelines on the Internet: Will Physicians Tune In? 25 Am.J.Law & Med. 403 (1999).

40. http://www.guideline.gov.

41. The Clearinghouse was created to deal with the criticism that guidelines published in peer-reviewed medical literature do not adhere to established methodological standards. See Terrence M. Shaneyfelt, Michael F. Mayo-Smith, and Johann Rothwangl, Are Guidelines Following Guidelines? The Methodological

Quality of Clinical Practice Guidelines in the Peer–Reviewed Medical Literature, 281 J.A.M.A. 1900 (1999).

42. See Paul G Shekelle and David L. Schriger, Evaluating the Use of the Appropriateness Method in the Agency for Health Care Policy and Research Clinical Practice Guideline Development Process, 31 Health Services Research (1996).

43. See Michael D. Cabana et al, Why Don't Physicians Follow Clinical Practice Guidelines? A Framework for Improvement, 282 J.A.M.A. 1458 (1999).

the immediacy of access to a comprehensive website improved their informational base and therefore their quality of practice.

Medscape is another commercial site that provides a full range of online resources for physicians. It offers a journal scan on the newest research findings, free access to abstracts on MEDLINE, access to drug searching through First DataBank, the largest Web-based drug and disease database, access to clinical practice guidelines, treatment updates, full text articles in many journals, and a clinical management series n the form of interactive e-med texts. A subscriber can also set up an email account to get specific information sent on a regular basis on specific topics. These commercial services in particular offer a busy physician quick and painless access, quite efficiently to both journals and guidelines, as well as to new literature and comments by experts.

The location of current information on the Internet facilitates its ease of access to physicians, and its link to other commercial sites makes it easy to connect to, no matter what portal a physician uses to access medical information databases on the Web. Failure to access such data bases is likely to become an important piece of evidence in a malpractice suit, since it is evidence that a physician has failed to stay current in his or her field of practice. A physician relying on a contraindicated drug, an outdated surgical technique, or an inappropriate description of risk factors in getting a patient's informed consent may be attacked by the plaintiff using the results of a computer search.[44]

Medical practice guidelines or practice protocols can be raised as an affirmative defense by a physician in a malpractice suit to show compliance with accepted practice. Several states have legislated the use of practice guidelines, offering tort immunities in exchange for following such guidelines.[45] Physicians are immunized from suit if they practice in accordance with such standards.[46] Checklists are provided in these statutes to guide physicians

---

44. See Warrick v. Giron, 290 N.W.2d 166 (Minn.1980).

45. Florida, Maine, Minnesota, and Kentucky also allow the use of practice parameters by physicians as an affirmative defense. See Ky. Rev. Stat. Ann. S342.035 (Michie 1995) indicating that "[a]ny provider of medical services under this chapter who has followed the practice parameters or guidelines developed or adopted pursuant to this subsection shall be presumed to have met the appropriate legal standard of care in medical malpractice cases regardless of unanticipated complication that may develop or be discovered after". id. See Minn. Stat. § 62J.34(3)(a) (1994) (providing an absolute defense for providers). Maine, Florida and Vermont also have adopted this approach, and several other states—e.g., Colorado, Pennsylvania, Rhode Island, Virginia, and Hawaii— also have considered or are considering adoption of guidelines legislation. Maryland, by contrast, under Md. Code Ann., [Health–Gen.] s19–1606 (1995), has mandated that practice parameters are not admissible into evidence in any legal proceeding under the statute.

46. Medical Liability Demonstration Project, Me. Laws, 24 § 2971–78 (1989). The Maine statute provides:

> * * * [I]n any claims for professional negligence against a physician or the employer of a physician participating in the project in which a violation of standard of care is alleged, only the physician or the physician's employer may introduce into evidence as an affirmative defense the existence of the practice parameters and risk management protocols developed pursuant to the project.

The law was premised on concerns that physicians practiced too much "defensive medicine" in response to liability fears, ordering tests primarily to protect themselves from subsequent suits. If given some protection in the liability area, they could change their practice patterns without fear of liability. The Maine legislation includes physicians in emergency medicine, anesthesia, and obstetrics and gynecology. Physicians who elect to participate can assert compliance with established practice parameters and risk management protocols as an affirmative defense in any malpractice suit

such as obstetricians and trauma physicians on what to do for patients with certain conditions.[47] Such reforms, its proponents say, will reduce physician malpractice premiums by solidifying the standard of care, reducing practice variation, and reducing the risk of suits against providers.[48] Critics of practice guidelines generally worry that physician flexibility will be lost in trying new approaches, that regulation will increase, and that physician quality will diminish as the practice of medicine becomes less attractive.[49]

Telemedicine. The possibilities of telemedicine go far beyond access to large medical databases. A physician in a rural area could get the assistance of a large medical center in diagnosing a patient's problems; such a physician might also be able to track a patient at home to monitor vital signs and symptoms. As Bradham et al write,

> Through telemedicine, patients and doctors in rural or economically depressed areas might immediately access specialized services that their communities lack, thereby increasing convenience, diagnostic ability, and the overall quality of local medical care. Further, telemedicine technologies might allow hospitals to release patients sooner by permitting clinicians to monitor patient progress remotely, which in turn would reduce costly hospital stays.[50]

Telemedicine has not yet advanced beyond the trial stage in most areas, although it is likely to provide improved access to diagnosis and consultation by rural physicians in particular.

b. Proving the Plaintiff's Case by Expert Testimony

The standard or customary practice by those in the defendant doctor's specialty or area of practice is normally established through the testimony of medical experts. In any jurisdiction, plaintiffs, to withstand a motion for a directed verdict, must 1) qualify their medical witnesses as experts; 2) satisfy the court that the expert's testimony will assist the trier of fact; and 3) have the witnesses testify based upon facts that support their expert opinions. The expert ideally should be in the same specialty as the defendant, but an expert

---

brought against them, during the five years of the demonstration project. The practice parameters and risk management protocols will be developed by advisory committees in each of the practice areas. Outside experts will not be able to challenge the standard, and the physician is not bound by the standard in a case in which he deviated from the protocol. The project will not take effect until 50% in any specialty elect to participate. See Smith, Maine's Liability Demonstration Project—Relating Liability to Practice Parameters, 18 State Health Legislation Report 1 (1990).

47. See also The Florida Health Plan, 1992 Fl. Laws ch. 92–33, § 408.02; The HealthRight Act (MnCare), 1992 Minn. Laws 549; Vermont Health Care Reform Act, Vt. Stat. Ann. tit. 18 § 9403 et seq.

48. For a discussion of the politics of the Maine Treatment Guidelines, see Edward Felsenthal, Cook Care: Maine Limits Liability for Doctors Who Meet Treatment Guidelines, Wall St. J. May 3, 1993, at A1.

49. See for these criticisms and others, Robert H. Brook, Practice Guidelines and Practicing Medicine: Are They Compatible?, 262 JAMA 3027 (1989).

50. Douglas D. Bradham, Sheron Morgan, and Margaret E. Dailey, The Information Superhighway: A Critical Discussion of its Possibilities and Legal Implications, 30 Wake Forest L. Rev. 145, 147(1995) (discussing existing telemedicine projects around the United States). See also Daniel McCarthy, The Virtual Health Economy: Telemedicine and the Supply of Primary Care Physicians in Rural America, 21 Am. J.L. & Med. 111 (1995); Robin Elizabeth Margolis, Law and Policy Barriers Hamper Growth of Telemedicine, 11 No. 10 HealthSpan 14 (1994) (noting among other problems complicated conflict-of-law problems that might arise with a out-of-state physician giving a telemedicine consultation). See also Second Invitational Consensus Conference on Telemedicine and the National Information Infrastructure, 1 Telemedicine J. 321 et seq. (1995).

can be qualified even if he does not practice in the same specialty as the defendant.[51] If an expert has only limited experience with a complex medical procedure, or offers an opinion beyond the scope of his expertise, he may be disqualified.[52] However, the fact that the expert has never treated a disease such as the plaintiff's does not bar the testimony, so long as the expert had general experience with the problem and its causation.[53] The test is whether the witness will aid the trier of fact. Courts have applied very flexible standards in qualifying medical experts, noting that "fields of medicine overlap and more than one type of practitioner may perform the diagnosis or treatment"[54].

A plaintiff must offer proof that the defendant physician breached the legally required standard of care and was thus negligent.[55] Expert testimony is needed to establish both the standard of proper professional skill or care and a failure by the defendant to conform. The expert does not have to testify explicitly that the conduct was "malpractice," since the trier of fact can draw inferences from the proven facts.[56] More than one expert may testify as to a issue of breach of the standard of care or causation; for example, in a case of silicone gel breast implants, a plastic surgeon may testify as to the governing standard of care, while a pathologist is better qualified to testify as to the damages caused by the implant.[57] The expert must however be able to say that the defendant's failure breached a general medical practice; a simple statement that the expert would have done differently may not be sufficient.[58] The testimony must be based "upon a reasonable degree of medical and scientific certainty" to satisfy most state courts.[59]

The abolition of the locality rule in most states eases the plaintiff's burden of proof, broadening the plaintiff's choices of available experts. Plaintiff's experts normally must be in the same specialty as the defendant. Under some circumstances, however, courts have allowed physicians in other specialties to testify, so long as the alleged negligence involves matters within the knowledge of every physician. A general surgeon can testify as to the standard of care of a plastic surgeon performing elective surgery, as to general surgical issues such as whether nerves in the forehead should have been protected.[60] The test is whether the witness, because of medical education, can properly assess the actions of the defendant.[61] The expert must be familiar with the standard of care in the area where the defendant practices.[62] The standard of care may be based upon the expert's own practice and education.

51. See e.g., Lambert v. Shearer, 616 N.E.2d 965, 974 (Ohio App.1992) ("There is absolutely no restriction in the law that only treating physicians can testify in medical malpractice cases.").

52. See e.g., Meunier v. Minnesota Dept. of Revenue, 503 N.W.2d 125 (Minn.1993).

53. Harmon v. Patel, 186 Ill.Dec. 944, 617 N.E.2d 183 (Ill.App. 1 Dist.1993).

54. Id., 616 N.E.2d at 974. See e.g., Guerrero v. Smith, 864 S.W.2d 797 (Tex.App.1993) (surgeon testified for plaintiff against defendant M.D. who used homeopathic medicine, injuring plaintiff).

55. Id.

56. Campbell v. Palmer, 568 A.2d 1064, 1067 (Conn.App.1990) (radiologist testified for plaintiff as to what he and his peers would do).

57. Chambers v. Ludlow (M.D.), 598 N.E.2d 1111 (Ind.App.1992).

58. Maurer v. Trustees of the Univ. of Pa., 614 A.2d 754, 762 (Pa.Super.1992) (expert "did not testify to anything more than his own personal standard of care").

59. Carter v. Johnson, 187 Ill.Dec. 52, 617 N.E.2d 260, 264 (Ill.App. 1 Dist.1993).

60. Hauser v. Bhatnager, 537 A.2d 599 (Me.1988).

61. See e.g., Bremner v. Charles, 859 P.2d 1148 (Or.App.1993).

62. Kobialko v. Lopez, M.D., 160 Ill.Dec. 90, 576 N.E.2d 1044 (Ill.App.1991).

Clinical practice guidelines or parameters provide a ready-made particularized standard that an expert can use as a benchmark against which to test a defendant's conduct. An expert need not be board certified in the subject of the suit, so long as he has the appropriate education and experience.[63] The liberal view is that an expert need not possess a medical degree so long as he has the medical knowledge.[64] Some jurisdictions adopt a narrower view, often by statutory limits, requiring that the expert have the practical experience of practice in the same area as the defendant.[65]

Experts may base their testimony on their knowledge, education and experience.[66] They may also rely on outside studies in the research literature, and in some cases even admit such outside materials. In *Young v. Horton*,[67] for example, the court allowed into evidence four medical journal articles that had concluded that a majority of patients forget that they gave informed consent to their doctors prior to surgery. The medical expert then testified based both on his experience with informed consent and on the articles' conclusions.[68]

The basis of an expert's testimony may be subject to a new level of scrutiny based on Supreme Court decisions as to scientific evidence. The admissibility of "novel" scientific evidence is often a thorny issue in environmental and toxic tort cases, although rarely in malpractice cases. The standard for evaluating such evidence had long been held to be established by the Court in Frye v. United States,[69] where the Supreme Court considered the polygraph test and its limitations. The Court held that expert opinion based on a scientific technique is inadmissible unless the technique is "generally accepted" as reliable in the relevant scientific community. In Daubert v. Merrell Dow Pharmaceuticals, Inc.,[70] the Court again considered the admissibility of scientific evidence, in this case epidemiological and other evidence of birth defects caused by mothers' ingestion of Bendectin. The Court rejected the *Frye* test of "general acceptability" as a threshold test of admissibility of novel scientific evidence, holding that the Federal Rules of Evidence, particularly Rule 702, make the trial judge the gatekeeper of such evidence, with the responsibility to assess the reliability of an expert's testimony, its relevance, and the underlying reasoning or methodology. Expert testimony must have a valid scientific connection to the issues in the case, and be based on "scientifically valid principles". The scientific evidence must pertain to scientific knowledge defined as falsifiable scientific theories capable of empirical testing.

The Supreme Court followed Daubert with the Joiner and Kumho cases. In General Electric Company v. Joiner,[71] the Court held that abuse of discretion is the standard for review of a district court's decision to admit or exclude scientific evidence. The Court has extended the Daubert factors to all expert testimony, not just scientific testimony, in Kumho v. Carmichael.[72] The Court held that Daubert's gatekeeping role for federal courts, requiring an

63. Hanson v. Baker, 534 A.2d 665 (Me. 1987).

64. Thompson v. Carter, 518 So.2d 609, 614 (Miss.1987) (toxicologist allowed to testify as to side effects of a drug prescribed by defendant physician).

65. See Bell v. Hart, 516 So.2d 562 (Ala. 1987) (pharmacist and toxicologist testimony disallowed).

66. See Fed. R. Evid. 703, 704.

67. 855 P.2d 502 (Mont.1993).

68. Id.

69. 293 F. 1013 (App.D.C.1923).

70. 509 U.S. 579 (1993).

71. 522 U.S. 136 (1997)

72. 526 U.S. 137, 119 S.Ct. 1167 (1999)

inquiry into both relevance and reliability, applies not only to scientific testimony but to all expert testimony. The Court noted that this was a flexible test, not a checklist, and it is tied to the particular facts of the case. But "some of these factors may be helpful in evaluating the reliability even of experience-based expert testimony …"[73] The use of the Daubert test is to "make certain that an expert, whether basing testimony upon professional studies or personal experience, employs in the courtroom the same level of intellectual rigor that characterizes the practice of an expert in the relevant field."[74] The trial judge is a gatekeeper to decide whether experts are allowed to testify. Under the three cases, the judge is to apply factors such as the presence of peer review and the rate of error in determining if an expert is reliable.

This caselaw may impose a higher level of scrutiny by the trial judge on the typical malpractice expert, particularly in cases involving institutional liability, where the expert may testify about a system design in a hospital or a salary incentive system in a managed care system. It remains to be seen how the trilogy will affect judicial screening of malpractice experts. It is clear, however, that in state courts, since Daubert, Joiner, and Kumho, expert reports are being challenged with increasing frequency.[75] Experts may have to be careful to base opinions on a theory that has independent indicia of reliability or has been peer reviewed. Literature support is more likely to be required as a basis of expert opinion. Expert testimony will be subjected to a motion in limine to test whether the Daubert and Kumho factors are satisfied. One analyst has contended that the real use of these cases is to give the trial judge the right to decide if an expert is honest.[76]

State courts may accept or reject these tests for evaluating scientific evidence. In Reese v. Stroh,[77] the Washington Supreme Court considered the use of Prolastin, protein replacement therapy, for emphysema. The treatment, while FDA-approved, lacked statistical proof of efficacy. The court held that "[a]n expert opinion regarding application of an accepted theory or methodology to a particular medical condition does not implicate Frye." They also declined to accept the Daubert test, finding that it was unnecessary to do so. They held that an expert's practical experience and acquired knowledge is sufficient without further proof of statistical efficacy. Since the defendant did not argue that the theory or methodology involved in Prolastin therapy lacked acceptance in the scientific community, an expert opinion regarding application of an accepted theory to a particular medical condition does not implicate Frye.[78]

73. Id. at 1176.

74. Id.

75. See, e.g., Checchio v. Frankford Hospital–Torresdale Division, et al., 717 A.2d 1058 (Pa.Super.1998).

76. Michael Gottesman, From Barefoot to Daubert to Joiner: Triple Play or Double Error?, 40 Ariz. L. Rev. 753, 759 (1998).

77. 907 P.2d 282 (Wash.1995).

78. Id. at 286. State courts continue to reject the Daubert approach to expert testimony in malpractice cases. See Swain v. Battershell, 983 P.2d 873 (Mont.1999)(Daubert does

not govern admissibility of expert opinion about informed consent); Waitek v. Dalkon Shield Claimants Trust, 934 F.Supp. 1068((N.D.Iowa 1996)(Daubert does not apply to gynecologist's expert testimony, because he based his opinions on experience and training); Collins v. Commonwealth, 951 S.W.2d 569, 574–575(Ky.1997)(Daubert not triggered because doctor's expert testimony involved basic female anatomical findings that "did not involve any novel scientific techniques or theories"). See generally Katherine M. Atikian, Note and Comment, Nasty Medicine: Daubert v. Merrell Dow Pharmaceuticals, Inc. Applied

c. Other Methods of Proving Negligence

Plaintiffs will normally use their own experts to establish a standard of care, defendant's deviation from it, and causation, as was done in *Hall*. Negligence can also be established by other methods.

1. Examination of Defendant's Expert Witnesses. The plaintiff may establish the standard of care through cross examination of expert witnesses for the defendant in rare cases.[79] While this may be sufficient to surmount a motion for a directed verdict, it is unlikely to present the trier of fact with a strong and convincing statement of physician negligence.

2. Drug Company Warnings. The Physician's Desk Reference Manual (PDR)[80], and pharmaceutical package insert instructions and warnings, contain statements of uses and risks mandated by the Food and Drug Administration. Physicians rely on the PDR when making decisions about drug dosages and administration. The courts have been willing to permit evidence of both PDR warnings and package inserts to establish the standard of care for use of the particular drug, typically when they are supported by expert testimony.[81] The PDR and inserts however do not establish the standard of care as a matter of law, so that a physicians' failure to adhere to them would not be negligence without expert testimony.

The PDR may also be used to show that a standard of care did not exist for a particular use of a drug.[82]

3. Common knowledge in situations where a layperson could understand the negligence without the assistance of experts. Normally, expert testimony is required to establish malpractice, on the assumption that professional misconduct involves scientific understanding beyond the level of lay people. The "common knowledge" exception relaxes this requirement when the errors are obvious to anyone.[83] Common examples of such a relaxation of expert testimony requirements include situations where a foreign instrument is found in a patient's body following surgery or where the injury is to a part of the body unrelated to the condition for which the patient sought treatment.[84] A physician's obvious or admitted ignorance of an illness or a procedure may also create a duty to investigate and consult another physician.[85]

---

to a Hypothetical Medical Malpractice Case, 27 Loy. L.A. L. Rev. 1513 (1994).

79. Porter v. Henry Ford Hosp., 450 N.W.2d 37 (Mich.App.1989). See also McDermott v. Manhattan Eye, Ear & Throat Hosp., 255 N.Y.S.2d 65, 203 N.E.2d 469 (N.Y.App. 1964).

80. *Physician's Desk Reference* (1999).

81. Morlino v. Medical Center, 706 A.2d 721 (N.J.1998)(PDR could be considered as to side effects of an antibiotic given to pregnant patient whose fetus then died); Bowman v. Songer, 820 P.2d 1110 (Colo.1991) (admission of the excerpt from the Physicians' Desk Reference is proper to aid the jury in determining whether physician's actions were consistent with standard of care). See also Thompson v. Carter, 518 So.2d 609 (Miss.1987) (use of pack-

age insert as prima facie evidence of proper use of Bactrim).

82. Maurer, 614 A.2d at 762.

83. Therrell v. Fonde, 495 So.2d 1046 (Ala. 1986); Hastings v. Baton Rouge General Hosp., 498 So.2d 713 (La.1986); Bauer v. Friedland, 394 N.W.2d 549 (Minn.App.1986).

84. Bauer v. White, 976 P.2d 664 (Wash.App.1999)(surgical pins left in patient; no need for expert testimony to establish that this was negligence); see also Pruett v. Williams, 623 So.2d 1115 (Ala.1993). Many of the res ipsa loquitur cases involve such circumstances, allowing the drawing of a permissive inference by the trier of fact of negligence.

85. Largess v. Tatem, 291 A.2d 398 (Vt. 1972).

4. Negligence per se, as when the defendant physician violated a clearly articulated practice within the specialty. Courts will not only relax requirements of expert testimony in rare cases of "common knowledge" errors by defendants, but will impose negligence per se where the errors were so obvious and violative of the standard of care as to leave no room for disagreement. Thus, a doctor who orders radiology and other tests on a pregnant plaintiff, injuring the fetus, has been held to be negligent per se.[86] Overprescribing of drugs in a pattern that bears no relationship to particular patient needs has also prompted judicial standard setting.[87]

5. Substantive use of a learned treatise. At the common law, a treatise could be used only to impeach the opponent's experts during cross-examination. It could only undercut the expert's testimony, not function substantively to build the plaintiff's case. The concern was hearsay, since the author of the treatise was not available for cross-examination as to statements contained in the treatise. Federal Rule of Evidence (FRE) 803(18)[88] creates an exception to the hearsay rule, so that the learned treatise can be used for substantive purposes, so long as the treatise is accepted as reliable. An expert must be on the stand to explain and assist in the application of the treatise.[89] The treatise must be declared reliable by the trial court, after a motion by the moving lawyer to use the treatise substantively under FRE 803(18) or its state equivalent.[90]

6. An admission by the defendant that he or she was negligent. A defendant may make an extrajudicial admission that is sufficient to serve as direct expert testimony, and may even admit his own culpability while testifying.[91] A plaintiff may meet his burden of proof by either of these categories of admissions. Thus, in Grindstaff v. Tygett,[92] the defendant described a delivery in the hospital records as a "tight midforceps rotation". In his deposition, when asked what this phrase meant, he described the rotation as "[o]ne in which you would have to apply excessive pressure to effect the maneuver."[93] This was held to be sufficient to submit the case to the jury.[94]

Extrajudicial admissions may create an inference of negligence sufficient to eliminate the need for expert testimony. Thus in Hill v. McCartney,[95] a dentist while drilling hit the plaintiff's jaw or gum, causing immediate swelling. The dentist, becoming distraught, cried out: "Oh, don't worry about it. I will take care of you. I have malpractice insurance ... I did something

86. See Deutsch v. Shein, 597 S.W.2d 141 (Ky.1980) (defendant negligent per se in ordering radiology and other tests on the pregnant plaintiff, injuring the fetus).

87. In United States v. Zwick, 413 F.Supp. 113 (N.D.Ohio 1976) (an action for injunctive relief brought by the United States against a physician who had prescribed over 3,800,000 doses of anorectic controlled substances in a three year period).

88. Fed. R. Evid. 803(18).

89. Tart v. McGann, 697 F.2d 75 (2d Cir. 1982).

90. Warren v. Everist, 706 So.2d 593 (La. App.1998); Maggipinto v. Reichman, 481 F.Supp. 547 (E.D.Pa.1979). See also Comment,

Substantive Admissibility of Learned Treatises and the Medical Malpractice Plaintiff, 71 Nw. U. L. Rev. 678 (1977).

91. Meena v. Wilburn, 603 So.2d 866 (Miss. 1992) (physician admitted he breached his duty in his answer to the complaint, in the opening statement, in testimony, by his lawyer's objections, and during the debate over jury instructions.)

92. 698 S.W.2d 33 (Mo.App.1985).

93. Id. at 34.

94. Id.

95. 590 N.W.2d 52 (Iowa App.1998).

freaky to you. I fucked you up."[96] The court held that this was sufficient to deny a motion for summary judgment by the defendant and let the jury decide on negligence.

An implicit admission of culpability can also be found through evidence of intimidation by defendant of plaintiff's expert witnesses, which a jury is allowed to consider as defendant's consciousness of the weakness of his case, creating a permissible inference of guilt.[97]

A defendant's expert testimony as to the standard of care may raise a sufficient question of fact for the trier of fact to withstand a motion for a directed verdict, even thought it is not an admission of liability.[98]

7. Testimony by the plaintiff. In a rare case, the plaintiff himself is a medical expert, qualified to evaluate the defendant physician's misconduct.[99] Such a plaintiff may of course testify as to the standard of care and the defendant's breach of it.

§ 6–3. Altering the Burden of Proof

In the typical malpractice case, the plaintiff must introduce expert testimony as to the standard of care or face a nonsuit. The courts have developed several doctrines that ease the plaintiff's burden of proof, shifting either the burden of production of evidence or the burden of persuasion onto the defendant.

a. *Res Ipsa Loquitur*

The best known of these evidentiary devices is the doctrine of *res ipsa loquitur* (Latin for "The thing speaks for itself"), which eliminates the plaintiff's need to present expert testimony as to negligence of the defendant. *Ybarra v. Spangard*[1] states the requirements for applying the doctrine in a medical malpractice case.

> The doctrine of *res ipsa loquitur* has three conditions: "(1) the accident must be of a kind which ordinarily does not occur in the absence of someone's negligence; (2) it must be caused by an agency or instrumentality within the exclusive control of the defendant; (3) it must not have been due to any voluntary action or contribution on the part of the plaintiff."[2]

The doctrine, like the "common knowledge" exception to the requirement that a plaintiff prove the case by expert testimony, is invoked in situations where a lay jury could draw inferences from the accident as to the defendant's fault.[3] In Prosser's words, "[t]here are * * * medical and surgical errors on which any lay[person] is competent to pass judgment and conclude from common experience that such things do not happen if there had been proper skill and care."[4]

96. Id. at 54.

97. See Meyer v. McDonnell, 392 A.2d 1129, 1134 (Md.App.1978).

98. See e.g., Gemme v. Goldberg, 626 A.2d 318, 326 (Conn.App.1993).

99. Lamont v. Brookwood Health Serv., 446 So.2d 1018 (Ala.1983).

§ 6–3

1. 154 P.2d 687 (Cal.1944).

2. Id. at 689.

3. See also Nixdorf v. Hicken, 612 P.2d 348 (Utah 1980).

4. W. Page Keeton et al., Prosser & Keeton on the Law of Torts § 39, at 256 (5th ed. 1984).

The common *res ipsa loquitur* situation is a patient who enters the hospital for surgery and suffers an injury to another portion of the body.[5] Another frequent error is the failure to remove surgical tools or sponges from a patient's body after surgery.[6] When foundational facts of the doctrine are established, whether by expert testimony[7] or by common experience of laypersons, the plaintiff need not present expert testimony on the standard of care. The doctrine thus creates in most cases a weak inference of negligence. While a plaintiff can prove too much, and lose access to the doctrine, courts distinguish situations in which evidence of cause of injury is so strong and extensive as to leave nothing for inference[8] and those which establish cause but still raise only an inference as to defendant's negligence.[9] Mere introduction of evidence to support specific negligence allegations does not render the doctrine inapplicable. If the defendant's uncontroverted evidence is that she complied with the standard of care, then some courts will not allow an instruction on res ipsa loquitur. If medical testimony establishes multiple possible causes for the bad outcome, then the doctrine is not applicable.[10] If the defendant intentionally created the risk to the patient to avoid a more significant risk, res ipsa is not available.[11] If the bad outcome would have occurred despite the exercise of the highest degree of care by the physician, such as the risk that a staph infection may enter a surgical wound, a res ipsa instruction may not be given.[12] Where the patient is under the exclusive control of one physician, the inference does not apply against another physician lacking such control.[13]

The requirement of control by the defendant is interpreted liberally by most courts. The defendant must simply be under a duty that he cannot delegate to another, such as "a surgeon who allows a nurse to count the sponges."[14] The requirement of exclusive control in medical malpractice may be satisfied by concurrent or joint control[15], or based in part on vicarious liability.[16] The res ipsa doctrine may also apply when responsibility is unallocated, as in *Ybarra*.[17]

Res ipsa loquitur is a rule of circumstantial proof, often justified by the helplessness of surgical patients; the control over instrumentalities and information by health care providers; the difficulties in proving causation where a plaintiff is unconscious during surgery; and judicial suspicion at times that

5. Born v. Eisenman, 962 P.2d 1227 (Nev. 1998); Graham v. Thompson, 854 S.W.2d 797 (Mo.App.1993).

6. Fieux v. Cardiovascular & Thoracic Clinic, 978 P.2d 429 (Or.App.1999); Schorlemer v. Reyes, 974 S.W.2d 141 (Tex.App.1998); Coleman v. Rice, 706 So.2d 696 (Miss.1997).

7. See Cherry v. Herques, 623 So.2d 131 (La.App.1993); Bearfield v. Hauch, 595 A.2d 1320 (Pa.Super.1991).

8. See Ollman v. Wisconsin Health Care Liability Ins., 505 N.W.2d 399 (Wis.App.1993).

9. See Farr v. Wright, M.D., 833 S.W.2d 597 (Tex.App.1992).

10. Storniolo v. Bauer, 574 N.Y.S.2d 731 (N.Y.App.Div.1991).

11. Wagner v. Deborah Heart & Lung Center, 588 A.2d 860 (N.J.Super.App.Div.1991).

12. Mahan v. Bethesda Hosp., Inc., 617 N.E.2d 714 (Ohio App.1992).

13. Wright v. Carter, 622 N.E.2d 170 (Ind. 1993).

14. W. Page Keeton et al., Prosser and Keeton on the Law of Torts § 39, at 249–50 (5th ed. 1984).

15. Sammons v. Smith, 353 N.W.2d 380, 387–88 (Iowa 1984).

16. Frost v. Des Moines Still College of Osteopathy and Surgery, 79 N.W.2d 306, 313 (Iowa 1956).

17. See Joan Teshima, Annotation, Applicability of Res Ipsa Loquitur in Cases of Multiple Medical Defendants—Modern Status, 67 A.L.R.4th 544 § 9 (1989 & Supp.).

professionals may protect each other by not being forthcoming. If the defendant's experts testify that the bad result is an irreducible risk of the procedure, the doctrine is usually not applicable.[18]

In most states, *res ipsa loquitur* operates to create an inference of negligence. That is, the jury may infer that the defendant was in some way negligent, but it is not compelled to conclude negligence. It can reject the inference as well as accepting it. A few states treat *res ipsa* as a rebuttable presumption, so that a plaintiff who proves a *res ipsa* case should win unless the defendant comes forward with some evidence to rebut the presumed negligence.[19] A few states have developed a version termed "conditional RIL", in which expert testimony as to the probable causes of the injury can establish an inference of negligence.[20] Some jurisdictions refuse to apply the doctrine in medical malpractice cases, out of concern that doctors might be held liable for rare bad outcomes, whether or not they were related to any negligence by the defendant.[21] Some states have even eliminated the availability of *res ipsa loquitur* by statute as part of malpractice reform packages, on the theory that it unfairly helps the plaintiff to the doctor's detriment, by eliminating proof of fault by the physician.[22]

b. Shifting the Burden of Persuasion

Courts have in rare situations used a variety of burden-shifting devices to ease the plaintiff's burden of proof. *Res ipsa loquitur*, as applied in *Ybarra*, supra, obviated the plaintiff's need to prove error by the defendants with particularity. In a few cases, courts have shifted the burden of persuasion onto the defendants, requiring that they present evidence that exonerates themselves, or face liability. The rule in such cases approximates strict liability in its impact on the defendants, and is typically found in surgical cases where the causal connections are difficult to trace, multiple parties are involved, and the injury is outside the scope of the surgery.[23] Such shifts in the burden of proof are sometimes granted in "missing witness" instructions, where the court allows the jury to presume negligence and causation from the mere absence of a crucial piece of evidence.

c. Strict Liability

The doctrine of strict liability (or implied warranty) has not been applied to medical services. While the courts have noted that the policy arguments in favor of the imposition of strict liability apply to the provision of medical services, they have found the countervailing considerations to be more convincing, resisting strict liability (or implied warranty) as applied to a health care professional or institution.[24] In spite of the policy justifications for

18. Tappe v. Iowa Methodist Medical Center, 477 N.W.2d 396 (Iowa 1991).

19. See generally Dan B. Dobbs, Torts and Compensation: Personal Accountability and Social Responsibility for Injury, 173–174 (1985); W. Page Keeton et al. Prosser and Keeton on the Law of Torts, §§ 39–40 (5th ed. 1984).

20. Spidle v. Steward, 37 Ill.Dec. 326, 402 N.E.2d 216 (Ill.1980).

21. Kapsch v. Stowers, 434 S.E.2d 539 (Ga. App.1993). Even in such cases, however, the courts will allow proof by circumstantial evidence of the facts upon which the expert witness relies.

22. Office of Technology Assessment, Impact of Legal Reforms on Medical Malpractice Costs 70 (1993).

23. See e.g., Estate of Chin v. St. Barnabas Medical Center, 734 A.2d 778(N.J.1999), applying Anderson v. Somberg, 338 A.2d 1 (N.J. 1975).

24. Hoven v. Kelble, 256 N.W.2d 379 (Wis. 1977).

applying strict liability to medical services, the courts have been reluctant to do so, considering the uncertainties of medical practice, fears of cost increases, and the risk of slowing medical innovation.[25] The Pennsylvania Supreme Court in Cafazzo v. Central Medical Health Services[26] argued that the policy reasons for strict liability were not present: providers are already subject to suit for the quality or quantity of services provided; incentives for safety are already provided as to medical devices and drugs by federal regulation; providers have little or no control over the circulation of defective products; and the provider as a "deep pocket" able to distribute the costs of compensating injuries "would further endanger the already beleaguered health care system". The court concluded: "In short, medical services are distinguished by factors which make them significantly different in kind from the retail marketing enterprise at which 402A is directed."[27]

In Porter v. Rosenberg,[28] the court considered a strict liability claim against the physician for a breast implant. The court rejected strict liability in the case but opened the door slightly to a judicial "essence of the transaction" test for future cases. "[i]f distributing products is part of the health care provider's business and the sales or distribution aspect in the particular transaction between the health care provider and the patient predominates over the services aspect an action in strict liability may lie against the health care provider.[29]

The courts often have distinguished between medicine and other "commercial" enterprises, noting that health care providers who use products during the course of treatment are providing services and are not "sellers"[30] In Johnson v. Sears,[31] the court allowed a plaintiff to plead strict liability against a hospital for alleged defects in mechanical and administrative services.[32]

25. Id. at 391.

26. 668 A.2d 521 (Pa.1995). One federal case, interpreting earlier Pennsylvania law, allowed a suit against a hospital on a Restatement (Second) Torts, § 402A theory. In *Karibjanian v. Thomas Jefferson University Hospital*, 717 F.Supp. 1081 (E.D.Pa.1989), the plaintiff alleged that her husband died as the result of exposure in 1956 to the substance Thorotrast, a form of thorium dioxide, with which he was injected during a diagnostic medical procedure called a cerebral arteriography. The court denied the hospital's motion to dismiss. Cafazzo effectively clarifies Pennsylvania law, and renders *Karibjanian* obsolete.

27. Id at 526.

28. 650 So.2d 79, 83 (Fla.App. 4 Dist.1995)

29. Such examples might include a nutrition doctor selling diet products or a dentist selling electric toothbrushes. Some manufacturers may rely solely or mainly on utilizing health care professionals for distribution of their products and the health care professional may rely on selling the product as part of its business as additional profit separate from provision of other medical services.

30. See In re Breast Implant Product Liability Litigation, 503 S.E.2d 445 (S.C.1998)(summarizing caselaw of other states rejecting strict liability). For a detailed analysis that rejects strict liability for both physicians and hospitals, see Tanuz v. Carlberg, 921 P.2d 309 (N.M.App. 1996 (surgical insertion of temporomandibular joint implants); Parker v. St. Vincent Hospital, 919 P.2d 1104 (N.M.App.1996)(hospitals not distributors or suppliers of product); Parker v. E.I. Du Pont de Nemours & Co., 909 P.2d 1 (N.M.App.1995)(analysis of strict liability principles and medical devices).

31. 355 F.Supp. 1065, 1067 (E.D.Wis.1973).

32. Other courts have extended Johnson. See Grubb v. Albert Einstein Medical Center, 387 A.2d 480, 490 (Pa.Super.1978), the defendant physician used a plug cutter to remove a bone plug from the vertebrae of the plaintiff; as a result of a series of errors, the patient was rendered a quadriplegic. The court held that § 402A of the Restatement, (Second) Torts was applicable to the hospital.

Use of medical devices and drugs by physicians as part of diagnosis and treatment increases the likelihood of judicial willingness to go beyond negligence-based theories. Physicians are increasingly dependent upon diagnostic machinery, computer-assisted tests, and drugs and medical devices. Strict liability and breach of warranty theories, as well as negligence, are likely to be attractive doctrines to apply, by analogy to the products liability area generally.[33] Most courts still continue to apply the service-sale distinction, however, rejecting strict liability theories.[34]

Strict liability, in the guise of vicarious liability, may be imposed on physicians who supervise medical students or residents on the support staff, as well as nurses and allied health professionals. In Brown v. Flowe[35], the defendant was a member of the faculty of the East Carolina University School of Medicine, with clinical privileges. The treating doctor was a fourth year resident at the hospital, without clinical privileges. The defendant controlled her "manner of performance" during surgery, advising her to apply steady pressure to insert a trocar into the decedent's abdomen, leading to her death. The court held that the faculty physician was vicariously liable, following the Hospital Bylaw requirement that "only a licensed physician with clinical privileges shall be directly responsible for a patient's diagnosis and treatment". The Affiliation Agreement provided that medical students and house shall "shall be responsibly involved in patient care under the supervision of the Dean and the faculty of the School of Medicine."

§ 6–4. Other Theories of Liability

a. Negligent Infliction of Mental Distress

A separate claim for emotional distress may exist where the plaintiffs, either as "bystanders" or as "direct" plaintiffs, have experienced emotional distress as a result of medical treatment. The claims often involve institutional or provider insensitivity or rudeness to particularly vulnerable plaintiffs. Some courts require proof of physical injury or evidence that plaintiff was in the "zone of danger"[1] as a prerequisite to this action, to safeguard against fraudulent claims.[2] Such physical injury can often be proved simply by evidence that the plaintiff experienced depression, nightmares, stress and anxiety.[3] Other jurisdictions have eliminated the requirement of physical injury.[4] Other courts, while allowing a damage claim for distress, maintain that the mental distress is not an independent cause of action, but simply a

---

33. Alan Kahan and Jeffrey N. Gibbs, Reuse of Disposable Medical Devices: Regulatory and Liability Issues, 2 HealthSpan 12 (1985).

34. Dove v. Ruff, M.D., 558 N.E.2d 836, 838 (Ind.App.1990).

35.   496 S.E.2d 830 (N.C.App.1998); see also Hebert v. LaRocca, 704 So.2d 331, 338 (La. App. 3 Cir.1997) (held that a physician in fellowship training "is to follow the instruction and direction of the teaching physician, is to perform those tasks assigned to him and to do so under the direct supervision and control of the teaching physician, and is to report anything which appears improper or out of the ordinary to the teaching physician.")

§ 6–4

1. Jones v. Howard Univ., 589 A.2d 419 (D.C.App.1991).

2. See e.g., Hammond v. Central Lane Communications Center, 816 P.2d 593 (Or. 1991).

3. See e.g., Love v. Cramer, 606 A.2d 1175 (Pa.Super.1992).

4. Bolton v. Caine, 584 A.2d 615 (Me.1990) (physician's failure to inform patient of possible presence of cancerous lesions); Homer v. Long, 599 A.2d 1193 (Md.App.1992) (allegation psychiatrist seduced wife thereby causing breakup of marriage).

negligence action.[5] The typical case involves "bystanders" who witness injury to a loved one. *Dillon v. Legg* was the first case to articulate a general test of foreseeability of harm, a primary guideline being whether the distress resulted from the "sensory and contemporaneous observance of the accident."[6] Parents would thus need to "observe" the accident or trauma in jurisdictions following the *Dillon* approach.[7] The California Supreme Court repudiated the *Dillon* "foreseeability" approach in *Thing v. La Chusa*[8], limiting recovery to situations where the plaintiff (1) is closely related to the injury victim; (2) is present at the scene of the injury producing event at the time it occurs and is then aware that it is causing injury to the victim; and (3) as a result suffers serious emotional distress—a reaction beyond that which would be anticipated in a disinterested witness and which is not an abnormal response to the circumstances.[9]

The United States Supreme Court, in Consolidated Rail Corporation v. Gottshall,[10] developed a standard for evaluating the negligent infliction of mental distress under the Federal Employers' Liability Act (FELA). The Court adopted the common law "zone of danger" test, which limits recovery to those plaintiffs who sustain a physical impact as a result of the defendant's negligent conduct or who are placed in immediate risk of physical harm by that conduct.[11] The foreseeability analysis of Dillon v. Legg[12] was rejected by the court as too open-ended, as limiting liability inconsistently, forcing judges to make "highly subjective" determinations.[13]

If a contractual relationship forms the basis for liability for emotional distress, some courts have relaxed the observation requirement, holding that foreseeability is not required.[14]

The application of the tort of negligent infliction of mental distress often reveals hospital failures to provide sensitive, appropriate care.[15] Some courts impose liability because of the vulnerability of the plaintiffs, coupled with the "crass insensitivity" of the medical staff.[16] Vulnerability, plus breach by a health care provider of fiduciary obligations to patients, may also lead to a distress claim.[17] The courts have expanded fiduciary obligations arising out of professional relationships to justify emotional distress damages. The vulnerable plaintiff facing a hostile or rude health care provider is a unifying theme in these cases. Special relationships, such as the parent-child relationship, or

---

5. Burgess v. Superior Court, 9 Cal.Rptr.2d 615, 831 P.2d 1197 (Cal.1992). Some states have neither explicitly accepted nor rejected the doctrine of negligent infliction of emotional distress. See Pierce v. Caday, 422 S.E.2d 371 (Va.1992).

6. Dillon v. Legg, 69 Cal.Rptr. 72, 441 P.2d 912 (Cal.1968).

7. Some jurisdictions continue with the older zone of danger test, requiring that a bystander actually be at risk before recovery is permitted. Boucher v. Dixie Medical Center, 850 P.2d 1179 (Utah 1992).

8. 257 Cal.Rptr. 865, 771 P.2d 814 (Cal. 1989).

9. See e.g., Johnson v. Ruark Obstetrics and Gynecology Assoc., 395 S.E.2d 85 (N.C. 1990).

10. 512 U.S. 532 (1994).

11. Id. at 546.

12. 441 P.2d 912 (Cal.1968).

13. 512 U.S. at 551.

14. See e.g., Newton v. Kaiser Hospital, 228 Cal.Rptr. 890 (Cal.App.1986).

15. Oswald v. LeGrand, 453 N.W.2d 634 (Iowa 1990).

16. See also Wargelin v. Sisters of Mercy Health Corp., 385 N.W.2d 732 (Mich.App. 1986).

17. See e.g., Carey v. Lovett, 622 A.2d 1279 (N.J.1993); Rowe v. Bennett, 514 A.2d 802 (Me.1986).

vulnerable contexts, such as childbirth, trigger judicial willingness to allow a separate distress claim.[18]

Patients exposed to providers or blood materials in the health care setting have sued for the negligent infliction of emotional distress, based on their fear of contagion of the HIV virus. Courts have resisted such claims. In K.A.C. v. Benson,[19] the plaintiff sued a physician who had performed two gynecological examinations of her during a period when he suffered from AIDS and had open sores on his hands and forearms as a result of dermatitis. Shortly after the second examination, the Minnesota Department of Health contacted 336 patients on whom Dr. Benson had performed one or more invasive procedures while gloved, but while suffering from exudative dermatitis. None of the patients tested HIV positive, but over 50 sued him and the Clinic where he worked. The plaintiff argued that she was in the 'zone of danger' for purposes of a claim of negligent infliction of emotional distress. The court wrote:

> This court has long recognized that a person within the zone of danger of physical impact who reasonably fears for his or her own safety during the time of exposure, and who consequently suffers severe emotional distress with resultant physical injury may recover emotional distress damages whether or not physical impact results.[] However, a remote possibility of personal peril is insufficient to place plaintiff within a zone of danger for purposes of a claim of negligent infliction of emotional distress. Consequently, we hold that a plaintiff who fails to allege actual exposure to HIV is not, as a matter of law, in personal physical danger of contracting HIV, and thus not within a zone of danger for purposes of establishing a claim for negligent infliction of emotional distress. Id. at 559.

The majority of jurisdictions considering this issue have agreed that the plaintiff must allege actual exposure to HIV to recover emotional distress damages.[20]

b. Intentional Torts.

The intentional infliction of emotional distress is available in settings where the physician's conduct can be described as "outrageous". This "outrage" tort requires a finding of intent on the part of the physician to cause emotional distress; conduct that was extreme and outrageous and "utterly intolerable in a civilized community"; plaintiff's distress caused by the physician's conduct; and the distress suffered by the plaintiff was severe. A finding of "outrageous" requires such acts by a physician as the intentional fondling of a patient during physical examinations in a sexually suggestive manner.[21] Such a claim is difficult to establish and is treated restrictively by courts.

c. Physician Duties to Be Patient Advocates

Solo practice, once the norm in American medical practice, is disappearing. By 1996, more than a third of physicians were located in group practices

18. See Jacoves v. United Merchandising, 11 Cal.Rptr.2d 468 (Cal.App.1992).

19. 527 N.W.2d 553 (Minn.1995)

20. See, e.g., Burk v. Sage Products, Inc., 747 F.Supp. 285 (E.D.Pa.1990); Ordway v. County of Suffolk, 583 N.Y.S.2d 1014 (N.Y.Sup.Ct.1992); Carroll v. Sisters of St. Francis Health Serv., Inc., 868 S.W.2d 585 (Tenn.1993); Johnson v. West Virginia Univ. Hosp., 413 S.E.2d 889 (W.Va.1991). See also John R. Austin, HIV/AIDS and the Health Care Industry Liability: An Annotated Bibliography, 27 J. Marshall L.Rev. 513 (1994).

21. McQuay v. Guntharp, 963 S.W.2d 583 (Ark.1998)

of three or more and another third were employees or contractors. The reorganization of the health care industry has pushed physicians into group practices and employment in health care institutions or managed care organizations or alliances with hospitals in integrated delivery systems. The large health care corporation, long resisted by the medical profession, has come into its own. Health care is more constrained by explicit financial limits. Institutions that provide health care—such as hospitals or nursing homes—and entities that pay for health care—including insurers and self-insured employers—now oversee the work of the medical professionals who practice within them or whose care they purchase. The emergence of managed care organizations that both pay for and provide care gives lay managers even greater control over medical practice, in the name of both cost containment and quality of care.

The use of prospective payment systems and the expansion of managed care organizations have imposed substantial constraints on the formerly open-ended fee-for-service system of American health care. Physicians in the past could order tests, referrals and hospitalization for patients with little resistance from either insurers or employers who may have footed the premium bill. Cost-constrained systems now create tensions between cost control and quality of care. Heavy pressure is put on physicians to reduce diagnostic tests, control lengths of stay in hospitals, and trim the fat out of medical practice. As physicians experience outside utilization review, limits in drug formularies as to what may be prescribed, and constraints on specialist and hospital referrals, they feel caught between duties to patients and duties to the institutions in which they now operate. They are faced with a possible obligation to be a patient advocate against the cost-conserving tendencies of the managed care organizations employing them.[22] The contours of this obligation are not clear, but some form of duty seems to be taking shape in the courts.

A physician may have an obligation to assist patients in obtaining payment for health care. At a minimum, this means that the doctor must promptly advise the patient or direct him to an appropriate institutional office for further information. No court has yet held that a physician must actively assist a patient in obtaining funding for a procedure that the physician feels is necessary. No court would require a physician to pay out of his own pocket for a treatment that a patient needs; there is no "duty to rescue" in the sense of a physician's financial obligation to support his patient. However, the *Wickline* case and others support the argument that a physician operating within a constrained reimbursement structure and an institutional bureaucracy is expected to be familiar with limits on payment.[23]

In Wickline v. State,[24] the plaintiff claimed that California's Medi–Cal, through its utilization review, refused to grant her a needed eight days of hospitalization after surgery and complications, instead agreeing to pay for only four. She ended up having to have her right leg amputated. Her surgeon

22. For a discussion of the theory of payment incentives and new ideas for paying physicians, see James C. Robinson, Blended Payment Methods in Physician Organizations Under Managed Care, 282 J.A.M.A. 1258(1999).

23. See also the discussion in Chapter 9 of utilization review, and the ERISA preemption caselaw now developing, discussed in ¶ 8–8.

24. 239 Cal.Rptr. 810 (Cal.App.1986)

had filled out the proper government forms to request the extra eight days, and this request was denied. He was angry, but also felt that a four day stay was within the standard of care, and the experts agreed. It was also clear that if he or the plaintiff's other treating physicians wanted to, they could have again requested the additional days, and in that case the Medi–Cal program would most likely have granted them. The court noted in dicta that third party payers could be liable when "medically inappropriate decisions result from defects in the design or implementation of cost containment mechanisms as, for example, when appeals made on a patient's behalf for medical or hospital care are arbitrarily ignored or unreasonably disregarded or overridden."[25] They then articulated a limited duty for a physician as patient advocate: "However, the physician who complies without protest with the limitations imposed by a third party payer, when his medical judgment dictates otherwise, cannot avoid his ultimate responsibility for his patient's care. He cannot point to the health care payer as the liability scapegoat when the consequences of his own determinative medical decisions go sour."[26] In language prescient of the ERISA litigation that hit the federal courts ten years later, the court worried about the effects of cost containment on physician judgment, even though such cost sensitivity is essential to control health care inflation. "It is essential", they wrote, "that cost limitation programs not be permitted to corrupt medical judgment."[27]

Later cases have held that external utilization review bodies can be held liable for negligent review if a patient suffers harm through denial of care, and that treating physicians will be held jointly and severally liable if they fail to act to protect their patient's interests. In Wilson v. Blue Cross of Southern California,[28] the court limited *Wickline* but expanded potential liability of outside reviewers. Wilson needed extended psychiatric hospitalization, according to his physicians. He was discharged however, and committed suicide. While the court held that the physician in this case did not have an obligation to appeal the negative denial, the court was clear that a doctor could be jointly liable under the right set of facts.

Some courts have allowed plaintiffs to plead a duty of a physician to assist patients in finding other sources of funding for expensive procedures. In Wilson v. Chesapeake Health Plan, Inc.,[29] the plaintiff pleaded a variety of theories against the specialist, the managed care plan, and the hospital.[30] The plaintiff Hugh Wilson, a thirty one year old employee of the city of Baltimore, developed liver disease. He was a member of a prepaid health plan, the Chesapeake Health Plan, Inc.(Chesapeake). Dr. Cooper, a Maryland gastroenterologist to whom Wilson was referred by his primary care physician, diagnosed Wilson as having non-alcoholic cirrhosis of the liver. Mr. Wilson and his wife were informed that this condition would be fatal without a liver transplant. Cooper reassured Wilson that a liver transplant would be covered

25. Id. at 819.

26. Id.

27. Id at 820.

28. 271 Cal.Rptr. 876, 222 Cal.App.3d 660 (1990).

29. Circuit Court, Baltimore, Maryland 1988 (No. 88019032/CL76201).

30. The facts are taken in part from the court's description in Presbyterian University Hospital v. Wilson, 654 A.2d 1324 (Md. C.A. 1995), where the Maryland court of appeals held that the trial court was justified in finding that hospital had sufficient contacts with Maryland to justify exercise of specific personal jurisdiction without violating due process.

under his HMO coverage. Chesapeake however decided that such a transplant was not a covered service under the subscriber agreement. Dr. Cooper contacted Dr. Starzl, the head of the transplant service at Presbyterian University Hospital (PUH) in Pittsburgh, Pennsylvania. Despite Mr. Wilson's lack of insurance coverage, Dr. Starzl agreed to admit Mr. Wilson and told Dr. Cooper to have Mr. Wilson come to PUH the following Monday. As Dr. Starzl testified: "My honest assessment at the time was ... that Dr. Cooper was laboring under a dictate, a decision by the governance group of this HMO that they would not allow transplantation coverage. And that Dr. Cooper took it upon himself to say to the system, I am not going to go with this, I am going to try to sneak the patient out. That was my impression. And that, on the other end, I told him, Dr. Cooper, I am going to take the patient, and carry on the battle." The Wilsons arrived in Pittsburgh two days later.

Upon his arrival, Mr. Wilson was refused admittance to PUH because the credit administrator had informed the admitting office that coverage for Mr. Wilson's liver transplant had not been confirmed. After being refused admittance, the Wilsons were provided accommodations at a hostel connected with PUH. The administrator then participated in protracted discussions with Chesapeake and Mr. Wilson's union, the International Brotherhood of Electrical Workers' (IBEW), to discuss the possibility of providing coverage for Mr. Wilson's liver transplant.

Due to deteriorating health, Mr. Wilson was admitted to the emergency room at PUH under his insurance three days later. At Dr. Starzl's urging, Mrs. Wilson returned to Baltimore to work further on the financing problem, and she then only then learned that the Maryland Medical Assistance Program would pay for the procedure once the Wilsons had spent down their savings. During this period a second liver became available, but it was also thrown away. Mr. Wilson died before Mrs. Wilson could obtain Maryland MA coverage and despite the fact that two suitable livers had become available to PUH for transplant during the time Mr. Wilson was in Pittsburgh.

Count 16 of the plaintiff's complaint alleged that Dr. Cooper and the health plan

> knew or should have known that staff and resources existed ... to assist the Wilsons in determining the scope of coverage provided by their HMO, other insurers, and alternative funding sources, but they failed to utilize such resources, alert plaintiffs to the existence of such resources or advise them of the need to identify a funding source. (Complaint, p. 33).

The trial court refused to dismiss this count in the complaint. The plaintiff then settled with Dr. Cooper and the Chesapeake Health Plan, and the case went to trial against Presbyterian Hospital. The plaintiff obtained a multi-million dollar jury verdict in the case.

The specialist, Dr. Cooper, was not an expert on the Maryland Medical Assistance program and eligibility, but it was not difficult to determine eligibility. The managed care organization, even if did not cover a procedure, could offer financial advice to subscribers as to reimbursement options. The central office of the managed care organization should be expected to know in the intricacies of its own coverage of subscribers, as well as other sources for funding if the plan's coverage is limited.

Few other cases have considered a duty such as that proposed in *Wilson*. But a physician may be held liable for knowledge of an insurer's rules under some circumstances. In Ferguson v. New England Mutual Life Insurance Co.,[31] the patient and her husband sued the physician and the insurer where benefits were denied for medically unnecessary and inappropriate services. The physician had assured the plaintiffs through his staff that the prescribed treatment would be covered by their insurance policy. The court extended implied contract law to include physician knowledge of the insurer's rules. Since HMO contracts often prohibit the physician from charging the beneficiary for denied payments, one can argue for an obligation on the physician to advocate for the patient and to have "full knowledge of the scope of the insured's coverage."

An analogous line of caselaw can also be found in the insurance benefit cases, where a plaintiff is denied insurance coverage because a physician neglected to complete benefit forms. In Murphy v. Godwin,[32], the plaintiff's family doctor neglected to complete a medical form they needed to obtain health insurance. As a result, their application was declined by the insurance company. The court held:

> Although it is well known that physicians usually accommodate patients by filling in the forms required by them for various reasons connected with insurance, the question of a doctor's legal duty toward his patients with respect to completing insurance forms is apparently novel. The existence of such a duty may be found, however, by reference to established tort theory and recognized incidents of the doctor-patient relationship.

> In the absence of special circumstances it was Dr. Godwin's duty to recognize his unique position as the treating physician who alone could comply with the insurance requirement without the expense and delay of a further examination. * * *

A physician who simply examines a person for purposes of employment by a third party and not treatment is generally not obligated to complete insurance forms.[33]

Given the high cost of health care and the limitations on coverage of high-cost procedures in some policies, the courts appear to be willing to expand the duties on both physicians and institutional providers to learn about sources of financing and assist the patient to obtain coverage.

§ 6–5. Defenses to a Malpractice Suit

a. *The Respectable Minority Exception*

Given a range of possible approaches to medical treatments, and disagreement within medical specialties as to the best approach, the courts have developed a variety of defenses to give physicians some leeway in defending

---

31. 554 N.E.2d 1013(Ill.App. 1 Dist.1990).

32. 303 A.2d 668 (Del.Super.1973).

33. See, e.g. Ahnert v. Wildman, 376 N.E.2d 1182 (Ind.App.1978) (" ... to impose a duty of filling out insurance forms on a doctor who has only consented to examine a patient for a third party, and has not undertaken to treat or advise that patient and is not paid by him, would be inconsistent with the very nature of the limited relationship. No case has gone so far as to saddle an examining physician with such a burden. And neither do we.")

their deviation from customary medical practice. A "two schools of thought" or "respectable minority" defense is generally recognized in most states: "[a] physician who undertakes a mode or form of treatment which a reasonable and prudent member of the medical profession would undertake under the same or similar circumstances shall not be subject to liability for harm caused thereby to the patient."[1] This "respectable minority" rule allows for variation in clinical judgment: " * * * a physician does not incur liability merely by electing to pursue one of several recognized courses of treatment."[2] If a defendant establishes that distinctive practices are supported by a minority within the professional group, the judge may direct a verdict for the defendant rather than leaving the issue to the jury.[3] However, where the plaintiff presents testimony that a defendant's practices, while once acceptable practice, are becoming obsolete, the jury will be allowed to find the defendant negligent.[4] Courts are restricting the operation of this defense in some jurisdictions, acknowledging that it may allow too easy an excuse for a physician.[5] In the words of the Colorado Supreme court, "[t]he customary or prevailing practice may not be adequate or objectively reasonable in light of all the facts and circumstances."[6]

States that instruct on "two schools of thought" often impose restrictions on the defense. The size of the respectable minority may be specified in jury instructions.[7] Pennsylvania, for example, requires that a school of thought, to be a defense, must be adopted by a "considerable number of reputable and respected physicians."[8] In the typical case, the minority approach is followed by at least a few doctors, and is often the "best available" for a certain problem.[9] The burden is on the defendant to establish two schools of thought, through the use of expert testimony or the medical literature.[10] Where the malpractice is a failure to properly diagnose, as for example whether the patient had a localized or a generalized infection, the "two schools of thought" or "alternative means of treatment" instruction may not be appropriate where there is only one agreed approach to each type of infection.[11]

The "honest error in judgment" doctrine is a corollary of the "respectable minority" rule. The respectable minority rule allows for a choice between alternative approaches to diagnosis or treatment; the honest error in judgment doctrine allows for a range of uncertainty in choosing between alterna-

§ 6–5

1. Henderson v. Heyer–Schulte Corp., 600 S.W.2d 844 (Tex.Civ.App.1980).

2. Downer v. Veilleux, 322 A.2d 82, 87 (Me. 1974).

3. Hamilton v. Hardy, 549 P.2d 1099 (Colo. App.1976).

4. See e.g., Henderson v. Heyer–Schulte Corp., 600 S.W.2d 844 (Tex.Civ.App.1980).

5. See United Blood Services, a Div. Of Blood Systems, Inc. v. Quintana, 827 P.2d 509 (Colo.1992)(overruling Hamilton v. Hardy, 549 P.2d 1099(Colo.App.1976).

6. State Board of Medical Examiners v. McCroskey, 880 P.2d 1188, 1194(Colo.1994).

7. In Ourada v. Cochran, 449 N.W.2d 211 (Neb.1989), the court rejected a jury instruction that seemed to give the jury too much leeway to reject the plaintiff's experts' testimony.

8. See e.g., Jones v. Chidester, 610 A.2d 964 (Pa.1992). This "considerable number" test is also found in Harris v. Buckspan, 984 S.W.2d 944, 952 (Tenn.App. 1998).

9. See e.g., Leech v. Bralliar, 275 F.Supp. 897 (D.Ariz.1967).

10. Gala v. Hamilton, 715 A.2d 1108 (Pa.1998)("considerable number" does not require numerical certainty, and is a flexible standard that allows the jury to assess the evidence based on expert testimony as well as the medical literature.)

11. See Hutchinson v. Broadlawns Medical Center, 459 N.W.2d 273 (Iowa 1990).

tive treatments.[12] A typical jury instruction reads: "a [physician] is not a guarantor of a cure or a good result from his treatment and he is not responsible for an honest error in judgment in choosing between accepted methods of treatment."[13] The doctrine has been soundly criticized for misleading the jury into thinking that a mistake is acceptable, confusing the jury as to the burden of proof.[14] Where a physician departs from standard practice, she cannot excuse herself from a bad result by arguing it was simply the exercise of her judgment; "... a physician who fails to abide by an objective standard of care is subject to liability even if the failure results from the exercise of judgment."[15]

b. Clinical Innovation

A defense of clinical innovation allows physicians to vary standard treatments to suit the needs of a particular patient, where the patient presents a particular problem or a desperate situation.[16] Courts that have allowed such a defense characterize the physician's decision as judgmental rather than experimental:

> Therapeutic innovation has long been recognized as permissible to avoid serious consequences. The everyday practice of medicine involves constant judgmental decisions by physicians as they move from one patient to another in the conscious institution of procedures, special tests, trials and observations recognized generally by their profession as effective in treating the patient or providing a diagnosis of a diseased condition. Each patient presents a slightly different problem to the doctor. A physician is presumed to have the knowledge and skill necessary to use some innovation to fit the peculiar circumstances of each case.[17]

Physicians often argue that their deviation from a standard of care is clinical innovation, and that surgery in particular must be allowed to innovate. Courts have resisted such arguments.[18] Such experiments are acceptable to the courts typically when conventional treatments are largely ineffective or where the patient is terminally ill and has little to lose by experimentation with potentially useful treatments.[19] Organ transplantation often involves

---

12. Crego v. Carp, 685 A.2d 950 (N.J.Super.Ct.1996); Haase v. Garfinkel, 418 S.W.2d 108, 114 (Mo.1967).

13. This was rejected in Ouellette v. Subak, 391 N.W.2d 810, 816 (Minn.1986). In Ouellette, the court held that this instruction is misleading and subjective. The court proposed an instruction that focused the jury's attention on both the diagnostic work up and its adequacy, and on the accepted nature of the treatment choice. In Klisch v. Meritcare Medical Group, Inc., 134 F.3d 1356 (8th Cir. 1998), the court followed Ouellette, nothing that the phrase "professional judgment" must be used in Minnesota jury instructions, to suggest an objective standard of analysis, rather than "best judgment". See McKersie v. Barnes Hosp., 912 S.W.2d 562 (Mo.App. E.D.1995) (failure of emergency room intern to diagnose appendicitis was negligence rather than mere honest error of judgment.)

14. Teh Len Chu v. Fairfax Emergency Med. Assocs., 290 S.E.2d 820 (Va.1982); accord Watson v. Hockett, 727 P.2d 669 (Wash.1986).

15. Aiello v. Muhlenberg Regional Medical Center, 733 A.2d 433 (N.J.1999).

16. Brook v. St. John's Hickey Memorial Hosp., 380 N.E.2d 72 (Ind.1978) (the plaintiffs alleged that Dr. Fischer was negligent in choosing an injection site which had not been specifically recommended by the medical community and that this choice of an unusual injection site was a medical experiment.).

17. Id. at 76.

18. See e.g., Edenfield v. Vahid, 621 So.2d 1192, 1196 (La.App.1993), writ denied 629 So.2d 1171 (La.1993).

19. See Barrier R. Cassileth et al., Survival and Quality of Life Among Patients Receiving Unproven as Compared with Conventional Cancer Therapy, 324 New Eng. J. Med. 1180 (1991).

therapeutic innovation. The classic case is *Karp v. Cooley*,[20] where Dr. Denton Cooley was sued for the wrongful death of Haskell Karp, after he had implanted the first totally mechanical heart in Mr. Karp, who died some 32 hours after the transplant surgery. The court directed a verdict for Dr. Cooley on the issue of experimentation, holding that the experimental treatment was therapeutic and therefore justified.

New surgical procedures and treatments, other than drugs and medical devices, fall into a regulatory gap. Drugs and medical devices are carefully regulated by the Food and Drug Administration through licensing.[21] Human experimentation generally, if the institution is funded by the federal government in whole or part, is governed by regulations of the Department of Health and Human Services. The regulations require the institution sponsoring the research to establish Institutional Review Boards (IRBs) to evaluate research proposals before any experimentation begins, in order to determine whether human subjects might be "at risk" and if so, how to protect them.[22] It is generally not difficult to determine whether a new drug or device is being used experimentally. It is often very difficult to determine whether a particular surgical procedure is experimental. Surgeons tend to view themselves as artists rather than scientists, custom-tailoring a treatment for a patient's ailment.

A defense such as clinical innovation is problematic, even if it is often viewed favorably by both physicians and the courts[23]. Clinicians are unlikely to be trained scientists, and will not engage in the same kind of systematic record keeping and publication of results as will a trained researcher. Medical researchers have criticized clinical "experiments," calling instead for randomized scientifically valid trials.[24] Most clinical innovation falls somewhere between standard practice and experimental research. Much of this innovation is unregulated by the government.[25] The absence of controls over experimentation has worried some commentators, who have argued that the patient's informed consent is not a sufficient protection against untested procedures. Such experimentation has been termed "nonvalidated practice," since the most salient attribute of a novel practice is the lack of suitable validation of its safety and efficacy.[26]

It is generally not difficult to determine whether a new drug or device is being used experimentally. It is often very difficult to determine whether a

20. 493 F.2d 408 (5th Cir.1974).

21. See the Federal Food, Drug, and Cosmetic Act, 21 U.S.C.A. § 301 et seq.

22. See 45 C.F.R. § 46.101(a).

23. See, for example, Edenfield v. Vahid, 621 So.2d 1192, 1196 (La.App.1993), where the defendant surgeon attempted to repair the plaintiff's anal fistula with a Prolene suture, and the plaintiff ended up incontinent. Such a suture was an unconventional choice, and the medical panel considered its use below the standard of care. One of the experts stated, however, that trends change through "mavericks" trying different techniques: "Unless this something different is so dramatic that [sic] would result in loss of life or limb then I would say more power to him, somebody has got to

try something different and show us that here are other ways of doing things.... the result wasn't ideal, but to consider that a malpractice, no."

24. Dr. Gordon H. Guyatt et al., Determining Optimal Therapy—Randomized Trials in Individual Patients, 314 New Eng. J. Med. 889 (1986).

25. Office of Technology and Assessment, Pub. No. OTA–H–405, Unconventional Cancer Treatments (1990). See Gerald Burke, High Tech, Low Yield: Doctors' Use of Medical Innovation, 4 J.Am.Health Policy 48 (1994).

26. For a good discussion of the problem, see Dale H. Cowan and Eva Bertsch, Innovative Therapy: The Responsibility of Hospitals, 5 J. Leg. Med. 219 (1984).

particular surgical procedure is experimental. Surgeons tend to view themselves as artists rather than scientists, custom-tailoring a treatment for a patient's ailment. Such attitudes can produce bad results. In Felice v. Valleylab,[27] the physician, a third year general surgical resident, used an electrosurgical unit (ESU) to perform a circumcision procedure, although she admitted that she had been taught to perform circumcisions with a scalpel as the standard technique. She testified that the ESU was a new technique that might produce better results. She burned the child's penis so badly that it had to be amputated. The court held that the surgeon's behavior fell below the standard of care in her modification of a familiar technique without knowing the potential risks and by failing to consult with supervising personnel about such risks.

The courts seem willing to tolerate clinical innovation so long as a patient is properly informed as to the innovative and untested nature of the procedure.[28] Where the patient is terminally ill, even more radical experimentation is tolerated, given the cost-benefit ratio for even a procedure with a slight chance of success.

c. Good Samaritan Acts

The purpose of Good Samaritan statutes is to encourage physicians and other providers to offer emergency aid voluntarily, by immunizing them from tort action for any negligent harm they might cause the victim.[29] This reduced standard of care for medical rescuers tries to strike a balance, avoiding a penalty to the hasty physician caught in an unexpected treatment setting, while promoting rescue by providing tort immunity.[30] The malpractice crisis of 1974 undoubtedly played a role in the push by state legislatures to enact such laws. They are an interesting example of a protective response to a low risk of suit. Most physicians have little idea as to whether the state in which they practice has a Good Samaritan law, or what its terms might be. Nor can evidence be found to establish that such laws have encouraged emergency treatment.[31]

Forty-nine states and the District of Columbia have adopted Good Samaritan legislation to protect health care professionals who render emergency aid from civil liability for damages for any injury they cause or enhance. The statutes take a variety of forms. West's Ann.Cal.Bus. & Prof.Code § 2395, for example, states, in relevant part:

27. 520 So.2d 920 (La.App. 3 Cir.1987). In Tramontin v. Glass, 668 So.2d 1252 (La.App. 1996), the same surgeon, using the same device, the ESU, burned the breast of a patient on whom she was performing breast augmentation surgery. In this case the use was not experimental, and the jury found for the defendant.

28. Friter v. Iolab Corporation, 607 A.2d 1111 (Pa.Super.1992) (hospital could be liable for failure to obtain patient's informed consent to implantation of intraocular lens).

29. Robert A. Mason, Good Samaritan Laws—Legal Disarray: An Update, 38 Mercer L. Rev. 1439 (1987).

30. Marshall Shapo, The Duty to Act: Tort Law, Power, & Public Policy 28 (1977).

31. In a study over twenty years ago, the American Medical Association found that the existence of Good Samaritan legislation made no difference to the willingness of physicians to stop and assist. 51.5% said they would stop to furnish emergency aid if the statutes were in effect, and 48.8% if no statute was in effect. Law Dept. of the AMA, 1963 Professional Liability Survey, 189 JAMA 859 (1964).

No licensee, who in good faith renders emergency care at the scene of an emergency, shall be liable for any civil damages as a result of any acts or omissions by such person in rendering the emergency care.

"The scene of an emergency" as used in this section shall include, but not be limited to, the emergency rooms of hospitals in the event of a medical disaster. * * *[32]

Some states grant statutory immunity from suit to emergency medical personnel unless gross negligence is shown.[33] Hospital-based emergency assistance by a physician is often protected where the physician is not on duty at the time of the call for help, did not have notice of the patient's injury, and did not charge a fee.[34] Some statutes protect health care professionals, while others protect all Good Samaritans, without regard to their profession.[35]

Such statutes clearly protect physicians outside the hospital who render true emergency aid to a stranger in need.[36] Most litigation over the use of the statutes as a statutory defense to a malpractice suit has arisen over care in the hospital setting. When a physician responds to an emergency call in the hospital, but has no legal duty to respond, he is considered a medical volunteer.[37] If his contract of employment imposes no duty to render emergency treatment, or the physician is not on duty at the time of the call for help, the Good Samaritan Act applies.[38] The status of the physician may matter; a consulting specialist may be under a different duty to render care than an on-call physician in an emergency room.[39] However, some courts have construed Good Samaritan Acts strictly in the hospital setting.[40] Most states have also imposed the requirement that the physician have no pre-existing duty of care to the patient.[41]

The majority of state statutes exclude medical services rendered in the hospital from the coverage of the statutes, either by excluding emergency services provided in the ordinary course of work or services that doctors render to those with whom they have a doctor-patient relationship or to whom they owe a pre-existing duty.[42] Where medical personnel render emergency aid as part of their duties to assist, some states distinguish salaried emergency medical personnel from those receiving fees or compensation for services by holding them only to a gross negligence standard.[43] The determina-

---

32. West's Ann.Cal.Business and Professional Code § 2395.

33. Mallory v. City of Detroit, 449 N.W.2d 115 (Mich.App.1989).

34. See Hirpa v. IHC Hospitals, Inc., 948 P.2d 785(Utah 1997); Villamil v. Benages, 628 N.E.2d 568 (Ill.App.1993); Gordin v. William Beaumont Hosp., 447 N.W.2d 793 (Mich.App. 1989).

35. California, for example, has Good Samaritan statutes for nurses, rescue team members, police officers, fire fighters, anyone who performs CPR, anyone giving aid at a boating accident, and anyone trying to remove food from someone's throat in a restaurant. See full list in Perkins v. Howard, M.D., 283 Cal.Rptr. 764, 767 n. 2 (Cal.App.1991).

36. See e.g., McCain v. Batson, 760 P.2d 725 (Mont.1988).

37. McKenna v. Cedars of Lebanon Hosp., 155 Cal.Rptr. 631 (Cal.App.1979).

38. See Hirpa v. IHC Hospitals, Inc., 948 P.2d 785 (Utah 1997); Gordin v. William Beaumont Hosp., 447 N.W.2d 793 (Mich.App.1989).

39. See e.g., Deal v. Kearney, 851 P.2d 1353 (Alaska 1993).

40. Beckerman v. Gordon, 618 N.E.2d 56, 57 (Ind.App. 2 Dist.1993).

41. Perkins v. Howard, M.D., 283 Cal.Rptr. 764 (Cal.App.1991).

42. Guerrero v. Copper Queen Hosp., 537 P.2d 1329 (Ariz.1975) (statute not applicable to services in hospital).

43. Tatum v. Gigliotti, 565 A.2d 354 (Md. App.1989), cert. granted 569 A.2d 705 (Md. 1990), affirmed 583 A.2d 1062 (Md.1991).

tion of an emergency is a fact question for the trier of fact,[44] and the courts have been generous in their definition of emergency even when a treatment crisis has stabilized.[45] For example, the subjective belief of the physician that he is responding to an emergency can be considered by the trier of fact.[46]

Indigent care immunity statutes extend Good Samaritan immunity beyond emergencies to the treatment of the indigent generally.[47] The threat that a poor patient will sue a physician is quite low,[48] but some states have considered immunity for physicians and nurses who care for indigent patients. While Good Samaritan statutes simply hope for more provider willingness to help someone in distress in exchange for a qualified immunity from suit, indigent care statutes create a quid pro quo. The District of Columbia, for example, has amended its Good Samaritan Act to provide immunity for volunteer physicians, nurse-midwives and nurses providing obstetrical care.[49] Other states have imposed a statutory duty of rescue on bystanders generally.[50]

If the purpose of Good Samaritan statutes is to encourage emergency aid, they might instead impose a civil or criminal penalty on those who fail to offer such assistance? That is the case in many European countries, and—on the books—in Vermont, which imposes a $100 fine for failure to render aid under some circumstances.[51]

d. *Contributory Fault and Assumption of the Risk*

Patients, through their own mistakes or lifestyle choices, often enhance or even cause their own injuries. People don't take their doctor's advice; they fall off their diets, stop exercising, start and continue smoking, or act in a variety of ways counterproductive to their health.[52] Very few tort cases have

---

44. Pavlov v. Community Emergency Medical Serv., 491 N.W.2d 874 (Mich.App.1992); Roberts v. Myers, M.D., 155 Ill.Dec. 135, 569 N.E.2d 135 (Ill.App.1991).

45. See e.g., Breazeal v. Henry Mayo Newhall Memorial Hosp., 286 Cal.Rptr. 207 (Cal. App.1991).

46. Bryant v. Bakshandeh, M.D., 277 Cal. Rptr. 379 (Cal.App.1991).

47. See 16 State Health Legislation Report (May 1988).

48. See Sara Rosenbaum and Dana Hughes, The Medical Malpractice Crisis and Poor Women, in Prenatal Care, Reaching Mothers, Reaching Infants (Institute of Medicine, National Academy Press, Wash.D.C. 1988).

49. D.C. Code § 2–1345. For a discussion and critique of this act, see generally Bridget A. Burke, Using Good Samaritan Acts to Provide Access to Health Care for the Poor: A Modest Proposal, 1 Annals of Health Law 139 (1992).

50. Minn. Stat. Ann. § 604.05.

51. See 12 Vt.Stat.Ann. § 519. See generally Jean Elting Rowe and Theodore Silver, The Jurisprudence of Action and Inaction in the Law of Tort: Solving the Puzzle of Nonfea-

sance and Misfeasance from the Fifteenth Through the Twentieth Centuries, 33 Duquesne L. Rev. 807 (1995); Saul Levmore, Waiting for Rescue: An Essay on the Evolution and Incentive Structure of the Law of Affirmative Obligations, 72 Va.L.Rev. 879 (1986).

52. See Matthews v. Williford, 318 So.2d 480 (Fla.App.1975) (patient ignored medical warnings to stop smoking, lose weight and go to hospital to be evaluated for chest pains); Smith v. Hull, 659 N.E.2d 185 (Ind.App. 1995)(bald plaintiff underwent hair implants and scalp reduction; he had signed consent forms and been told to wait on scalp reduction until his hair implants fell out, but insisted on proceeding with surgery. The court held that "Smith's desire to sport a full head of hair motivated him to pursue remedies that he knowingly undertook at his own peril." It upheld the trial court's instructions on contributory negligence. For a general discussion of life style choices and policy choices and the problem of scapegoating, see Robert L. Schwartz, Life Style, Health Status, and Distributive Justice, 3 Health Matrix 195 (1993)("If all of those whose life style choices have health consequences were required to bear the full burden of those consequences, there would be few of us (and few diseases or injuries) that would not be implicated.")

considered a patient's lifestyle choice as a defense to a malpractice claim, but the issue has surfaced in several recent cases.[53] Several tort doctrines interact in issues of mitigation: avoidable consequences, the particularly susceptible victim, aggravation of preexisting condition, comparative negligence, and proximate cause. The doctrine of avoidable consequences denies recovery to the plaintiff for any portion of the harm that by the exercise of ordinary care he could have avoided.[54] It comes into play when the injured party's carelessness occurs after the defendant's legal wrong has been committed.[55] Pretreatment habits however are not considered in weighing fault, although they may be relevant to causation. Contributory or comparative negligence in contrast operates when the injured party's carelessness occurs before defendant's wrong has been committed or concurrently with it. Failure to follow medical advice, for example by not stopping smoking so that a wound could heal, is evidence of the plaintiff's comparative negligence.[56] The doctrine of the particularly susceptible victim counteracts avoidable consequences by allowing the jury to consider the vulnerabilities of the plaintiff; it, however, may in some cases be mitigated by the doctrine of aggravation of a preexisting condition.

The doctrines of avoidable consequence and preexisting condition can be distinguished by understanding that the injured person's conduct is irrelevant to the consideration of the doctrine of aggravation of a preexisting condition. A defendant whose acts aggravate a plaintiff's preexisting condition is liable only for the amount of harm actually caused by the negligence.[57] If a physician's duty includes the obligation to prevent a patient from engaging in self-damaging conduct, contributory negligence may not be a defense,[58] although these cases are fact-sensitive and often are allowed to go to the jury.[59]

The courts put the burden of proof as to proper segregation of damages on the defendant as to aggravation and mitigation.[60] Such cases raise fundamental questions about the limits of medicine and the role of patients in their own illnesses. Addictive behaviors like compulsive eating and smoking are not easily abandoned. Allowing a jury to consider such behaviors is problematic, allowing the defense a chance to present an unattractive plaintiff as weak and undeserving.[61] Courts have resisted such a temptation to allow evidence of

53. Ostrowski v. Azzara, 545 A.2d 148 (N.J. 1988). Ostrowski is followed in D'Aries v. Schell, 644 A.2d 134 (N.J.Super.Ct., App.Div. 1994), where the court articulates the chronology for evaluating the plaintiff's conduct: (1) the pre-treatment period; (2) the treatment period during which the malpractice occurred; and (3) the post-malpractice period.

54. See Bryant v. Calantone, 669 A.2d 286 (N.J.Super.Ct., App.Div.1996).

55. Restatement (Second) of Torts, § 465 comment c. (1974).

56. Healthsouth Sports Medicine and Rehabilitation Center of Boca Raton, Inc. v. Roark, 723 So.2d 314 (D.C.App. Fla. 1998) (smoking against doctor's advice); Wyatt v. U.S., 939 F.Supp. 1402 (E.D.Mo.1996) (smoking during hospital treatment).

57. Ostrowski, 545 A.2d at 156.

58. Tobia v. Cooper Hospital University Medical Center, 643 A.2d 1 (N.J.1994).

59. In Hobart v. Shin, 705 N.E.2d 907 (Ill. 1998), the court allowed the physician to raise the patient's contributory negligence as an affirmative defense. The patient was being treated for depression. She was hospitalized and treated with Koxepin, and then discharged once she no longer showed symptoms of depression. Two weeks later she became depressed again, and refused to contact her doctors because she did not want to be rehospitalized . She checked into a hotel room and took a lethal dose of Koxepin.

60. Ostrowski, 545 A.2d at 156.

61. See Sawka v. Prokopowycz, 306 N.W.2d 354 (Mich.App.1981), where the plaintiff sued the defendant for his failure to diagnose lung cancer. The court rejected the claim that the plaintiff's continued smoking and failure to

plaintiff behavior, recognizing that "[s]ick people deserve the same care whether they smoke, drink, drive too fast, or engage in socially unacceptable behavior."[62]

Patient non-compliance with physician instructions often causes treatment failures.[63] The theory of contributory negligence is typically invoked when a patient fails to follow a physician's instructions after a procedure is performed, or while in the hospital;[64] fails to see the physician[65] or another provider[66] as instructed; or makes an intentional and material misrepresentation as to her medical condition.[67] In *Butler v. Berkeley*,[68] the plaintiff removed the nasogastric tube that had been inserted to prevent wounds from being contaminated by food after plastic surgery. This action might have caused the infection that the patient then developed, and the court granted summary judgment for the surgeon on grounds of contributory negligence.[69]

The failure of a patient to follow a treating physician's warnings about behavior can also be considered by the jury under contributory negligence instructions. In Cobo v. Raba,[70] a physician who suffered from depression was treated by the defendant Dr. Raba. Dr. Cobo refused drug treatment for chronic depression, refused to allow the defendant to take notes, and insisted on psychoanalysis as the only mode of treatment. During this period he engaged regularly in unprotected homosexual intercourse with prostitutes, in spite of regular admonitions by the defendant as to the risks, including unprotected sex with a drug-addicted prostitute in a San Francisco bathhouse; he abused alcohol and drugs, and when he became HIV-positive, he substantially delayed his treatment. The court held that the plaintiff's conduct was "clearly active and related directly to his physical complaint,"and the jury should be allowed to evaluate it through a contributory negligence instruction.

Courts are reluctant to apply contributory negligence too liberally.[71] One common requirement is that the patient's negligence must be contemporaneous with that of the physician.[72] Non-cooperation with the physician's orders will mitigate damages, but not relieve the physician of responsibility.[73] In *Weil v. Seltzer*,[74] the defendant argued that the patient was contributorily negligent in failing to discover that the medications given him over a twenty year period were steroids rather than antihistamines as told by the defendant; the court strongly rejected this argument. The court also rejected the assumption of the risk defense, since there was no evidence that the plaintiff knew of the danger

return for further examination as instructed were contributory negligence.

62. Lambert v. Shearer, 616 N.E.2d 965, 976 (Ohio App.1992). See also Matthews v. Williford, 318 So.2d 480 (Fla.App.1975).

63. Joan Stephenson, Noncompliance May Cause Half of Antihypertensive Drug "Failures", 282 J.A.M.A. 313 (1999).

64. See also Ray v. Wagner, 176 N.W.2d 101, 104 (Minn.1970).

65. Hoffart v. Hodge, 567 N.W.2d 600 (Neb.App.1997).

66. Cox v. Lesko, 953 P.2d 1033 (Kan.1998) (patient's failure to under physical therapy after shoulder suggested, as the surgeon prescribed, is comparative fault.).

67. See e.g., Sorina v. Armstrong, 589 N.E.2d 1359 (Ohio App.1990).

68. 213 S.E.2d 571 (N.C.App.1975).

69. Id. See also Musachia v. Rosman, 190 So.2d 47 (Fla.App.1966).

70. 495 S.E.2d 362 (N.C.1998).

71. See e.g., Windisch v. Weiman, 555 N.Y.S.2d 731 (N.Y.App.Div.1990).

72. George Washington Univ. v. Waas, 648 A.2d 178 (D.C.App.1994)(and cases cited).

73. See discussion in Durphy v. Kaiser Foundation Health Plan of Mid–Atlantic States, Inc., 698 A.2d 459 (1997).

74. 873 F.2d 1453 (D.C.Cir.1989).

of prolonged steroid use and voluntarily accepted the risks.[75] Courts tend to find that physicians have special fiduciary obligations to patients, due to their skill and knowledge, and it is their responsibility to deal with patient behaviors as part of treating them.[76]

Almost all American jurisdictions have adopted comparative fault, simplifying the issue by eliminating the harsh all-or-nothing effect of contributory negligence. Courts in comparative fault jurisdictions are likely to be more willing to allow evidence of plaintiffs' contributions to their injuries.[77]

The doctrine of assumption of the risk is a viable defense even in many comparative fault jurisdictions. Assumption of the risk is rarely argued except in cases of obvious defects of which the patient should have been aware, such as hazards in the hospital room.[78] The problem of assumption of the risk, in the sense of a conscious explicit assumption of medical risks, blends into the issues of informed consent and waivers of liability. One example of this blending is *Schneider v. Revici*.[79] The Second Circuit considered whether a patient undergoing unconventional treatment for breast cancer after signing a consent form had waived all her rights to sue or assumed the risk of injury from the treatment. The court held that the consent form was not clear and unequivocal as a covenant not to sue, but that the doctrine of assumption of risk was available as a total bar to recovery, based on the language of the signed consent form and the patient's general awareness of the risks of treatment.[80] Such a recognition of the legitimate scope of express assumption of the risk is arguably proper, since it extends the patient's decisionmaking power, even to choose unconventional therapies.[81]

Another defense, related to defenses like comparative fault and assumption of the risk, is that of illegal conduct as a bar to recovery. This defense is invoked when a plaintiff's injuries are due in part to his own illegal conduct in causing his own injury. An example is a plaintiff, addicted to drugs, who dies or suffers injury from his addiction, which a physician or pharmacist arguably should have detected.[82]

e. *Exculpatory Clauses*

Waivers of liability and other attempts at exculpating health care providers from liability are treated with disfavor by the courts. The case of Tunkl v. Regents of the University of California[83] provides the starting point for any analysis of waivers of liability in the health care setting. *Tunkl* involved the validity of a waiver signed by an indigent patient in exchange for free care at the UCLA hospital, releasing the hospital from liability for any negligence

---

75. Id.

76. *See* Lambert v. Shearer, 616 N.E.2d 965 (Ohio App.1992).

77. See generally Victor Schwartz, Comparative Negligence (2nd ed. 1986); William Prosser and Page Keeton, *Torts* sec. 67 (5th ed. 1984). The court in McIntyre v. Balentine, 833 S.W.2d 52 (Tenn.1992), lists only four states remaining without comparative fault: Alabama, Maryland, North Carolina, and Virginia.

78. See e.g., Charrin v. Methodist Hosp., 432 S.W.2d 572 (Tex.Civ.App.1968) (plaintiff tripped over television cord in hospital room;

she knew it was there, having previously pointed it out to the staff).

79. 817 F.2d 987, 995 (2d Cir.1987).

80. Id. at 995.

81. See generally Maxwell Mehlman, Fiduciary Contracting: Limitations on Bargaining Between Patients and Health Care Providers, 51 Univ.Pitt.L.Rev. 365 (1990).

82. Pappas v. Clark, 494 N.W.2d 245 (Iowa App.1992).

83. 32 Cal.Rptr. 33, 383 P.2d 441 (Cal. 1963).

suffered by the patient. The California Supreme Court held that such an agreement between a hospital and an entering patient was invalid. The Court applied a six factor test to determine if the agreement did not involve "the public interest."

    1.   It concerns a business of a type generally thought suitable for public regulation.

    2.   The party seeking exculpation is engaged in performing a service of great importance to the public, which is often a matter of practical necessity for some members of the public.

    3.   The party holds himself out as willing to perform this service for any member of the public who seeks it, or at least for any member coming within certain established standards.

    4.   As a result of the essential nature of the service, in the economic setting of the transaction, the party invoking exculpation possesses a decisive advantage of bargaining strength against any member of the public who seeks his services.

    5.   In exercising a superior bargaining power the party confronts the public with a standardized adhesion contract of exculpation, and makes no provision whereby a purchaser may pay additional reasonable fees and obtain protection against negligence.

    6.   [A]s a result of the transaction, the person or property of the purchaser is placed under the control of the seller, subject to the risk of carelessness by the seller or his agents.[84]

The court held that the UCLA release fell into the category of agreements that affected the public interest. It held that the agreement met all the conditions.

    Courts are generally hostile to attempts by health care providers to limit their liability by contract. The typical case involves a poor plaintiff like Tunkl asked to trade off his common law right to sue in exchange for low cost or free treatment.[85] The special nature of medical care—the vulnerability of patients, the anxious state they are often in when entering the hospital—makes the courts uncomfortable with allowing total waivers of liability.[86] The majority of courts considering the question have followed Tunkl.[87] The only exception courts find acceptable is an exculpatory agreement for treatments involving experimental procedures as the patient's last hope for survival.[88] Short of a complete waiver of a right to sue, hospitals or doctors may be able to constrain a patient's right to sue in tort, for example by agreeing to waive a right to sue for punitive damages, by agreeing on liquidated damages, or by agreeing that an action would be brought in the local state court. One court

---

84. Id. at 37, 383 P.2d at 445–46.

85. See, e.g., Eelbode v. Chec Medical Centers, Inc., 984 P.2d 436 (Wash.App.1999)(rejecting release); Cudnik v. Beaumont Hospital, 525 N.W.2d 891 (Mich.App.1994)(patient receiving radiation therapy for prostate cancer signed agreement; court held it to be "invalid and unenforceable as against public policy."); Ash v. New York Univ. Dental Center, 564 N.Y.S.2d 308 (N.Y.App.Div.1990); Emory Univ. v. Porubiansky, 282 S.E.2d 903 (Ga.1981).

86. Broemmer v. Abortion Serv., 840 P.2d 1013 (Ariz.1992) (abortion clinic's printed agreement to arbitrate, presented to patient when she arrived at clinic to undergo abortion, held to be adhesion contract).

87. Cudnik v. William Beaumont Hospital, 525 N.W.2d 891 (Mich.App.1994).

88. See Colton v. New York Hospital, 414 Y.Y.S.2d 866 (1979).

has rejected a pre-injury agreement that releases a medical researcher from liability for negligent conduct during medical research as against public policy.[89]

Agreements to arbitrate medical malpractice disputes are generally upheld as exempt from attack as contracts of adhesion. Some managed care systems, such as Kaiser Permanente in California, require that plan members submit any malpractice claim to arbitration. Even with partial waivers, the courts are careful to scrutinize the relationship for elements of unconscionability and for lack of clarity in explaining the waiver to a patient.[90] A standardized arbitration agreement will be examined to consider whether the patient had the chance to questions the terms of the agreement; whether hidden or ambiguous terms could be found; whether the patient had to sign in order to get necessary treatment; that the liability of one party was greatly limited; or whether the arbitration process itself was unequal and one-sided.[91] While complete waivers are suspect, a partial waiver might be effective if carefully executed and properly presented to the patient.[92] Arbitration is viewed as less costly, quicker and removes from the crowded court dockets some malpractice cases.

The problem of waivers often arises in institutional informed consent and arbitration settings. Courts will allow evidence of the habitual practice of a physician or clinic to establish that they in fact made the required disclosures.[93] The cases suggest the importance of institutional routine in proving that a patient received information affecting his rights.

Some physicians—such as obstetricians and emergency physicians—have curtailed their services in response to liability insurance concerns. Indigent patients create a special problem, since these patients create a liability risk, yet physicians cannot recover their liability insurance costs because there is no compensation for their services. They cannot also ask the patients to waive their common law rights to sue for negligence, following cases like *Tunkl*. State legislatures, often as part of malpractice reform packages, have responded to this dilemma by providing immunity from tort liability for certain categories of physician services.[94] In particular, physicians or other health professionals who provide free health care services have been granted tort immunity if they provided uncompensated care, unless the care was grossly negligent.[95]

---

89. Vodopest v. MacGregor, 913 P.2d 779, 789 (Wash.1996)(research on high altitude sickness).

90. See Abramowitz v. N.Y. Univ. Dental Center, 494 N.Y.S.2d 721 (N.Y.App.Div.1985).

91. Coon v. Nicola, 21 Cal.Rptr.2d 846 (Cal. App.1993); Buraczynski v. Eyring, 919 S.W.2d 314 (Tenn.1996)(The court held arbitration agreements are not per se void, but must be examined "to determine if they are contracts of adhesion, and if so, whether they contain such unconscionable or oppressive terms as to render them unenforceable. They upheld the agreement).

92. Colton v. New York Hosp., 414 N.Y.S.2d 866 (N.Y.App.1979).

93. Crawford v. Fayez, 435 S.E.2d 545 (N.C.App.1993)(testimony of five former patients sufficient to show doctor's "habit" of warning patients about side effects of infertility drug).

94. See 16 State Health Legislation Report (May 1988).

95. Ariz. Rev. Stat. § 12–571; West's Fla. Stat. Ann. § 768.13; Official Code Ga. Ann. § 51–1–29.1; Ill. Rev. Stat. ch. 111, ¶ 4405; Me. Rev. Stat. Ann. tit. 24, § 2904; S.C. Code § 33–55–210; Va. Code § 54–276.12.

f. Partial Limitations on the Right to Sue

Courts are more willing to allow partial limitations on a patient's right to sue under special circumstances. One such example is *Shorter v. Drury*.[96] *Shorter* arose out of the bleeding death of a hospital patient who, for religious reasons, refused a blood transfusion after a bungled dilation and curettage perforated her uterus. Shorter, a Jehovah's Witness, had signed a release which provided that she relieved the hospital " * * * from any responsibility whatever for unfavorable reactions or any untoward results due to my refusal to permit the use of blood or its derivatives"[97] and further stated "I fully understand the possible consequences of such refusal on my part."[98] The court allowed the release to be given legal effect, but not a complete bar to recovery; the jury found for the plaintiff but reduced plaintiff's wrongful death damages by 75 percent based on an assumption of risk by the Shorters that Mrs. Shorter would die from bleeding. The court upheld the release, on the grounds that it was not against public policy; it did not exculpate the physician from all negligence, but only the risks created by refusal to accept blood transfusions. The court also allowed the jury instruction on assumption of the risk. It allowed the partial release in part because of fears that patients with particular religious beliefs might be refused treatment, and obviated the need for the hospital to get a court order.

Shorter allows a partial waiver in the health care setting, under a special set of circumstances. The issue is important for two reasons. First, providers would like to limit their liability exposure in order to keep malpractice premiums under control. Second, economists and other reformers of the tort system advocate the use of contracts that allocate risk by agreement. Michigan for example by statute created an option of arbitration for patients entering hospitals, allowing patients to choose arbitration for any malpractice claims.[99] Similarly, living wills and durable powers of attorney allow a patient to control the extent of treatment, while protecting the treating doctor from liability for complying with the patient's refusal of treatment. The contract approach to allocating the risks of health care has been advocated by many commentators, as a way to extend consumer sovereignty, save resources, and offer more choices to both providers and patients.[100] Such reliance on provider-patient contracts has also been criticized, as inevitably risking dominance by the stronger party and creating one-sided contracts that do not protect patient interests.[101]

§ 6–6. Causation Problems: Delayed, Uncertain, or Shared Responsibility

a. The Discovery Rule

Statutes of limitations governing tort suits generally require that suit be filed within a period of time, usually two or three years, after the injury or

---

96. 695 P.2d 116 (Wash.1985), cert. denied 474 U.S. 827, 106 S.Ct. 86, 88 L.Ed.2d 70 (1985).

97. Id. at 119.

98. Id.

99. M.C.L.A. § 600.5040 et seq.

100. William H. Ginsburg et al., Contractual Revisions to Medical Malpractice Liability, 49 Law & Contemp. Probs. 253 (1986); Clark

Havighurst, Reforming Malpractice Law Through Consumer Choice, 3 Health Affairs 63 (1984); Richard A. Epstein, Medical Malpractice: The Case For Contract, 1976 Am. B. Found. Res. J. 87.

101. See Maxwell J. Mehlman, Fiduciary Contracting: Limitations on Bargaining Between Patients and Health Care Providers, 51 U. Pitt. L. Rev. 365 (1990).

malpractice occurs. The problem that often arises in the medical setting is that the injury is latent, or hidden, often for some time, for example where a surgical sponge has left in a plaintiff's abdomen during surgery or when a disease like cancer with a long latency period develops.[1] A tort action may accrue at four points: (1) when the defendant breaches his duty; (2) when the plaintiff suffers initial injury; (3) when the plaintiff becomes aware of the injury; and (4) when the plaintiff discovers the causal link between injury and the defendant's breach of duty.[2] If a misdiagnosis causes a subsequent injury that is difficult to date precisely, the statute of limitations runs from the date symptoms attributable to the new injury are obvious to the plaintiff.[3] A plaintiff who is aware of the defendant's negligence and waits to sue until she determines whether additional injuries may result is barred under the discovery rule.[4]

A few states continue to hold that a cause of action accrues when the right to bring an action arose, and this was when the medical error or misdiagnosis had occurred.[5] The latency of many medical problems, and difficulties in discovering that a physician made an error, led many courts toward a more flexible rule. The modern "discovery rule" provides an exception to the rule of repose of a statute of limitations, offering the plaintiff a fair remedy when a cause of action was not discoverable within the statutory period.[6] It typically provides that the statute of limitations begins to run when the plaintiff knows or reasonably should know that she has been injured and her injury was caused by another's conduct. The majority position as to the plaintiff's knowledge is that the limitations period begins to run when the plaintiff discovers, or in the exercise of due diligence reasonably should discover, her cause of action against the defendant.[7] Some states by statute have more elaborate tests; Texas for example, has a two year statute of limitation which runs from either the date of the tort, the last date of the relevant course of treatment, or the last date of relevant hospitalization.[8]

A patient, armed with notice of an injury caused by the wrongful conduct of a health care provider, must then inquire further to determine whether the wrong was actionable. Plaintiffs who refuse to recognize or act on their legal

§ 6–6

1. Ayers v. Morgan, 154 A.2d 788 (Pa. 1959).

2. Weidman v. Wilkie, 660 N.E.2d 157 (Ill. App.1995); Colbert v. Georgetown University, 641 A.2d 469 (D.C.App.1994); Bryant v. Crider, 434 S.E.2d 161 (Ga.App.1993).

3. Van Dusen v. Stotts, 712 N.E.2d 491(Ind.1999)(two year statute of limitations held unconstitutional as applied to the facts of case; plaintiff neither knew nor had reason to know he had cancer within two years after misdiagnosis); Walker v. Melton, 489 S.E.2d 63 (Ga.App.1997).

4. Morton v. National Medical Enterprises, 725 A.2d 462 (D.C.App.1999).

5. See e.g., Smith v. Danek Medical, Inc., 47 F.Supp.2d 698 (W.D.Va.1998)(describing Virginia law; Bryant v. Crider, 434 S.E.2d 161 (Ga.App.1993) (under Georgia statute of limi-

tations, statute runs from the date that the injury occurred and "had physically manifested itself").

6. In Martin v. Richey, 711 N.E.2d 1273 (Ind.1999), the Supreme Court of Indiana struck down the two year medical malpractice statute of limitations as unconstitutional as it applied to the plaintiff, given the latency period of her cancer. The statute was an occurrence test, tolling the statute when the negligent act occurred rather than was discovered by the plaintiff. The court found that the application of the statute to her "would require her to file a claim before she was aware of the malpractice and the resulting injury and would impose an impossible condition on her access to the courts and pursuit of a tort remedy".

7. Ware v. Gifford Memorial Hosp., 664 F.Supp. 169 (D.Vt.1987).

8. Vernon's Ann. Texas Civ.St. Art. 4590i, section 10.01.

rights risk barring their recovery.[9] At this point, the statute of limitations begins to run.[10] Where the patient lacks knowledge of the medical condition and is repeatedly assured by the alleged tortfeasor that all is well, justice requires that the action accrue when the wrongdoing is discovered.[11] Some courts hold that the statute begins to run once the plaintiff is aware that he has been injured, even if the injury later becomes much worse.[12] If the plaintiff has the means of discovering the facts, by using her general knowledge or asking the physician, the discovery rule may not be available.[13] These issues are usually resolved by the jury.

b. Basic Causation Tests

Tests for causal connections between the plaintiff's injury and the defendant's negligence are usually described by the courts in terms of the "but for" test. "But for" the defendant's conduct, the plaintiff would not have suffered injury. The plaintiff must present testimony that the defendant's acts or omissions probably caused the plaintiff's injuries.[14] However, in cases of multiple tortfeasors, missed diagnoses, or preexisting injuries or underlying disease, the "but for" test does not provide the trier of fact with sufficient guidance. In these cases, damage rules such as the "loss of a chance" doctrine and rules governing joint and several liability are used to resolve the causal responsibility issues.[15] Proximate cause instructions allow the trier of fact flexibility in imposing duties on defendants in more complex situations. For example, a physician charged with failing to report child abuse may be liable when the child is injured or killed.[16] The courts instruct the jury that they may find the defendant liable " . . . if the injury is the natural and probable consequence of the original negligent act or omission and is such as might reasonably have been foreseen as probable."[17]

Proximate cause instructions continue to be given in most states. At least one state, California, has rejected instructions on proximate cause as unduly confusing to the jury, adopting instead the "substantial factor" test. In *Mitchell v. Gonzales*[18], the California Supreme Court in effect mandated a jury instruction that asks a jury to determine where the defendant's conduct was a "substantial factor" in bringing about harm, allowing a jury to find against the defendant even if their conduct was only a contributing factor. This "substantial factor" test has been around for 25 years,[19] but the influence of

---

9. Id.

10. Gara v. Semerad, 131 Ill.Dec. 945, 539 N.E.2d 298 (Ill.App.1989).

11. Bussineau v. President and Directors of Georgetown College, 518 A.2d 423 (D.C.App. 1986).

12. Fries v. Chicago & Northwestern Transp., 909 F.2d 1092 (7th Cir.1990) (plaintiff noticed decline in hearing, although medical diagnosis of hearing loss occurred several years later).

13. Taylor v. Tukanowicz, 435 A.2d 181 (Pa.Super.1981).

14. Ulmer v. Ackerman, 621 N.E.2d 1315, 1319 (Ohio App. 3 Dist.1993)("There is no mandatory technical requirement to use a particular work such as 'probable' or 'probability' to state the obvious.")

15. See Ryne v. Garvey, 621 N.E.2d 1320 (Ohio App. 2 Dist.1993).

16. In Stecker v. First Commercial Trust Company, 962 S.W.2d 792 (Ark.1998), the administrator of a child's estate sued doctor for medical negligence and failure to report suspected child abuse as required under Arkansas statute. Evidence that the child's life could have been saved if doctor had reported potential abuse presented question for jury on issue of proximate cause for purposes of medical malpractice claim.

17. Id. at 796

18. 1 Cal.Rptr.2d 913, 819 P.2d 872 (Cal. 1991).

19. See Restatement, (Second) Torts § 431 (1974).

California on tort law evolution is likely to push other states to replace the confusing proximate cause instructions with the "substantial factor" test. This would be in line with other reforms of damage rules. The "substantial factor" has come to be used in lieu of the "but for" test in jury instructions where multiple medical actors and concurrent causation are involved. [20]

c. *Multiple Defendants*

Allocating responsibility among several tortfeasors is complicated. In the typical malpractice case, multiple defendants are considered joint rather than separate tortfeasors either when the parties act together to commit the wrong or when their acts, if independent of each other, unite to cause a single injury. The courts have considered factors such as whether each defendant has a similar duty; whether the same evidence will support an action against each; the indivisible nature of the plaintiff's injury; and identity of the facts as to time, place or result.[21] Concurrent causation instructions are required to help the trier of fact sort out the causation complexities. In Zigman v. Cline,[22], the plaintiff was rendered a paraplegic after an complicated surgery "to correct the severe and normally fatal injuries ... suffered in an automobile accident". Without the surgery he would have died; but a possibility existed that the surgeon erred in his choice of technique in repairing the plaintiff's torn aorta. The court held that the jury should have been instructed as to concurrent causation where a defendant's negligence combines with plaintiff's physical condition.

The increased use of alternative medicine by patients may increase liability exposure for the physician. Joint and several liability is likely to hook the physician firmly if injury is the end result of a continuum of care that includes alternative practitioners. For example, in Samuelson v. McMurtry,[23] the plaintiff was treated by physicians and a chiropractor. His problems began with a boil under his arm, treated by Dr. Holland. The next day he returned to the hospital with a fever and inflammation around the boil and was treated by Dr. McMurty. Eight days later, he went to the hospital emergency room with complaints of back pain. The next day he twice returned to the emergency room. On the first visit he was seen by Dr. Holland but on the second visit he was discouraged by hospital personnel from seeing a physician. The next day, he went to see Dr. Totty, a chiropractor, with complaints of intense back and chest pain and he was treated twice that day by Dr. Totty. The next day he died of pneumonia, "which had not been diagnosed by any of the health care providers." He could have been treated within 6–12 hours of his death. The court held that all practitioners who treat a patient for the same ailment are bound: "There can be little doubt that the participation of all potentially responsible persons as parties in the original action would have resulted in a fuller and fairer presentation of the relevant evidence and would have enabled the jury to make a more informed and complete determination of liability."[24]

Another doctrine with occasional application to medical liability cases is the joint enterprise theory. This theory requires (1) a mutual understanding

20. See Vincent By Staton v. Fairbanks Mem. Hosp., 862 P.2d 847 (Alaska 1993).

21. For an application of these tests, see Riff v. Morgan Pharmacy, 508 A.2d 1247 (Pa.Super.1986).

22. 664 So.2d 968 (Fla.App. 4 Dist.1995).

23. 962 S.W.2d 473 (Tenn.1998).

24. Id. at 476.

for a common purpose between two or more parties, and (2) a right of each party to some voice in the direction and control of the means to carry out the common purpose.[25] For example, where a hospital and a physician group together have a joint voice in the direction and control of a resident physician, they may both have joint control over such a resident for the common purpose of patient care. An equal right of control usually is not required.[26]

§ 6–7. Damage Innovations

a. *The General Rule*

The normal approach to proof of causation and damages is to require the plaintiff to show that absent defendant's negligence, plaintiff would have lived a normal life. Where the plaintiff has an illness such as cancer, with a limited chance of survival, and a doctor's failure to diagnose reduces his chances of survival even further, many courts have refused to allow an action. In the words of one court, "[h]ealth care providers could find themselves defending cases simply because a patient fails to improve or where serious disease processes are not arrested because another course of action could possibly bring a better result."[1] The normal elements of damages, including lost wages, medical expenses past and future, impaired earning capacity, and pain and suffering, are allowed where the negligence of the provider is proved by a preponderance of the evidence.[2] Punitive damages will rarely be recoverable in a malpractice case, although intentional, wanton, or reckless conduct will typically support a claim.[3] Normally, a punitive damage claim against a physician requires evidence as to the physician's financial condition, so the court can decide whether the amount would have a deterrent effect without being excessive.[4]

b. *The "Loss of a Chance" Doctrine*

Where a physician is negligent in diagnosing a disease, and the resulting delay reduces the plaintiff's chances of survival (even though the chance of survival was below fifty percent before the missed diagnosis), a strong argument can be made that the physician should be responsible for the value of the chance that the plaintiff lost,[5] so long as the initial act of the physician

---

25. See Murphy v. Keating, 283 N.W. 389, 392 (Minn.1939).

26. Dang v. St. Paul Ramsey Medical Center, 490 N.W.2d 653 (Minn.App.1992).

§ 6–7

1. Gooding v. University Hosp. Bldg., 445 So.2d 1015 (Fla.1984). See also Pillsbury–Flood v. Portsmouth Hosp., 512 A.2d 1126 (N.H. 1986) ("Causation is a matter or probability, not possibility").

2. See generally Dan B. Dobbs, Remedies (1978).

3. Dempsey v. Phelps, 700 So.2d 1340 (Ala.1997)(doctor acted "wantonly" in treating a children's infection, ignoring obvious symptoms); Smith v. Schulte, 671So.2d 1334 (Ala. 1996)(recognizing validity of punitive damages but reducing award from $4.5 million to $2.5 million); see also Graham v. Columbia–Presby-

terian Medical Center, 588 N.Y.S.2d 2 (N.Y.App.Div.1992).

4. Adams v. Murakami, 284 Cal.Rptr. 318, 813 P.2d 1348 (Cal.1991).

5. The leading law review article, often relied upon by courts adopting the doctrine, is Joseph H. King, Jr., Causation, Valuation and Chance in Personal Injury Torts Involving Preexisting Conditions and Future Consequences, 90 Yale L.J. 1353 (1981). Professor King takes another look at the doctrine in light of judicial struggles in Joseph H. King, "Reduction of Likelihood" Reformulation and Other Retrofitting of the Loss-of-a-Chance Doctrine, 28 U.Mem.L.Rev. 491 (1998). See also Nancy Levit, Ethereal Torts, 61 Geo. Wash. L. Rev. 136 (1992); Darrell L. Keith, Loss of Chance: A Modern Proportional Approach to Damages in Texas, 44 Baylor L. Rev. 759(1992); Lisa Perrochet, Sandra J. Smith

was itself negligent. First, the loss of an improved chance of survival or improvement in condition, even if the original odds were less than fifty percent, is an opportunity lost due to negligence. Much treatment of diseases is aimed at extending life for brief periods and improving its quality rather then curing the underlying disease. Much of the American health care dollar is spent on such treatments, aimed at improving the odds. In the words of the Delaware Supreme Court, "[i]t is unjust not to remedy such a loss."[6] Second, immunizing whole areas of medical practice from liability by requiring proof by more than fifty percent that the negligence caused the injury fails to deter negligence conduct. As Judge Posner wrote in DePass v. U.S., "A tortfeasor should not get off scot-free because instead of killing his victim outright he inflicts an injury that is likely though not certain to shorten the victim's life."[7]

Courts have wrestled with the concept of loss of a chance or increased risk over the past twenty years, adopting one of several approaches to the problem. First, the traditionalists have refused to budge in considering loss chances below fifty percent. A minority of jurisdictions either expressly reject the loss of a chance theory or have simply continued to adhere to the traditional strict causation standard.[8] Their justifications include a fear that the jury is forced to speculate as to the causes of plaintiff's ultimate injury, with only disputed expert probabilities to guide them[9]; that the jury will be misled and impressed by the probabilistic evidence; and that in many cases statistical evidence will be either unavailable or based on inadequate evidence.[10]

A second approach is the "pure" lost chance approach, also called the "increased risk" or "relaxed causation" approach by some courts.[11] If a plaintiff can prove that the defendant's negligence decreased the plaintiff's chance, no matter how slight, he can recover full damages from the trier of fact.[12] Some courts have recognized the theory by classifying the destruction or reduction of a chance for recovery as an independent, compensable harm. These courts concentrate on the causal relationship between the negligent conduct and the statistical loss or reduction in the patient's chances for

and Ugo Colella, Lost Chance Recovery and the Folly of Expanding Medical Malpractice Liability, 27 Tort & Ins. L.J. 615(1992) (50–state survey of the doctrine's acceptance or rejection in the courts).

6. U.S. v. Cumberbatch, 647 A.2d 1098, 1102 (Del.1994)(loss of a chance doctrine not actionable in a statutory wrongful death case, which permits survivors to assert only their statutory claim, not that of the decedent.)

7. 721 F.2d 203, 208 (7th Cir.1983)(Posner,J. dissenting). For a strong statement of the deterrence rationale, see Holton v. Memorial Hospital, 679 N.E.2d 1202, 1212(Ill.1997).

8. See e.g., Jones v. Owings, 456 S.E.2d 371 (S.C.1995)("Legal responsibility in this approach is in reality assigned based on the mere possibility that a tortfeasor's negligence was a cause of the ultimate harm . . [] This formula is contrary to the most basic standards of proof which undergird the tort system); Kilpatrick v. Bryant, 868 S.W.2d 594 (Tenn.1993); Kramer

v. Lewisville Memorial Hospital, 858 S.W.2d 397 (Tex.1993). Cooper v. Sisters of Charity of Cincinnati, Inc. 272 N.E.2d 97 (1971).

9. Kramer v. Lewisville Memorial Hospital, 858 S.W.2d 397, 405(Tex.1993)("Below reasonable probability, however, we do not believe that a sufficient number of alternative explanations and hypotheses for the cause of the harm are eliminated to permit a judicial determination of responsibility. . . . The more likely than not standard is thus not some arbitrary, irrational benchmark for cutting off malpractice recoveries, but rather a fundamental prerequisite of an ordered system of justice.")

10. Leubner v. Sterner, 493 N.W.2d 119 (Minn.1992).

11. Weymers v. Khera, 563 N.W.2d 647, 653 (Mich.1997)(discussing the various approaches).

12. Thompson v. Sun City Community Hosp., 688 P.2d 605 (Ariz.1984).

recovery. They apply the traditional evidentiary standard to this new kind of compensable interest.[13] Most courts have relaxed one of the two traditional legal standards for a prima facie case of causation. Some have employed a standard which allows a plaintiff to meet his burden by proving that the defendant's negligence eliminated a substantial possibility of recovery or survival.[14] Other courts have held that a plaintiff has met his burden by showing that the defendant's negligence increased the risk of harm or injury.[15] Courts in these jurisdictions require that the jury find that the conduct was a "substantial factor" in causing the injury.[16] Another judicial approach to these calculations is to treat the loss of a chance as a wrong separate from wrongful death, and allow the jury to set a dollar amount based on all the evidence, without mechanically applying a percentage to a total damage award.[17]

The third approach is that of proportional "loss of a chance", adopted by many courts that have considered the issue.[18] The leading case is *Herskovits v. Group Health Cooperative*, where the court considered the consequences of a physician's missed diagnosis of lung cancer on the plaintiff's future.[19] The court found that the plaintiff's chances of survival dropped from 39 percent to 25 percent, and that such a loss of a chance to survive was the proximate cause of his death. In the court's words, " * * * [t]o decide otherwise would be a blanket release from liability for doctors and hospitals any time there was less than a 50 percent chance of survival, regardless of how flagrant the negligence."[20]

The calculation of damages in proportional lost chance cases has proved troubling to the courts, as has proof of the probabilities. One judicial struggle with alternative approaches to calculation can be found in *Boody v. U.S.*[21] The court sets out the three possible alternatives for the determination of damages for loss of a chance:

> First, the court or jury without explicit guidance, could arrive at a compensation figure * * * A second method would provide full compensation for the loss of life regardless of the decedent's less than even chance of survival * * * [The third] approach is to compensate plaintiffs for what

---

13. Mayhue v. Sparkman, 653 N.E.2d 1384 (Ind.1995)(rejects lost chance but lightens plaintiff's burden of proving causation.); Note, The Loss of a Chance Theory in Medical Malpractice Cases: An Overview, 13 Am. J. Trial Advoc. 1163 (1990).

14. See e.g., Hicks v. United States, 368 F.2d 626 (4th Cir.1966) (if any substantial possibility of survival existed and if defendant's conduct destroyed it, the defendant is answerable). State decisions so holding include Mayhue v. Sparkman, 627 N.E.2d 1354 (Ind.App.1994).

15. One of the leading cases is Hamil v. Bashline, 392 A.2d 1280(Pa.1978)(following Restatement (Second) Torts, s. 323).

16. See e.g., Snead v. United States, 595 F.Supp. 658 (D.D.C.1984) (District of Columbia law applied to a physician who failed to obtain a pap smear during a gynecological exam that could have disclosed cancer).

17. See Smith v. State of Louisiana, 676 So.2d 543 (1996), where the court held that

> * * * the method we adopt today in this decision, is for the factfinder—judge or jury—to focus on the chance of survival lost on account of malpractice as a distinct compensable injury and to value the lost chance as a lump sum award based on all the evidence in the record, as is done for any other item of general damages.

18. Alberts v. Schultz, 975 P.2d 1279 (N.M. 1999); Roberts v. Ohio Permanente Medical Group, Inc., 668 N.E.2d 480 (Ohio 1996); Delaney v. Cade, 873 P.2d 175 (Kan.1994).

19. Herskovits v. Group Health Cooperative, 664 P.2d 474 (Wash.1983).

20. Id. at 477.

21. Boody v. United States, 706 F.Supp. 1458 (D.Kan.1989).

they lost: the approximate percentage chance of living or surviving for a fixed period of time.[22]

The court in *Boody* found the first approach flawed due to its lack of guidance to the decisionmaker, being little more than the pulling from a hat of an arbitrary figure. The second approach was rejected because the plaintiff is compensated for a percentage of harm that the defendant did not cause or would have occurred naturally. The third approach was favored by the *Boody* court and by those that have accepted the analysis as set out by King. The court found two advantages to the third approach: "[First], it apportions damages in direct relation to the harm caused; it neither over compensates plaintiffs or unfairly burdens defendants with unattributable fault. Second, the percentage method gives juries and judges concrete guidelines on how to measure damages."[23]

Other courts have argued that the third approach gives a false sense of accuracy. The court in *Borgren v. U.S.*,[24] for example, rejected the third approach adopted in *Boody*, concluding that there is little difference between the first and third method, since the decisionmaker confronts a highly subjective decision in either case. "We are unconvinced that the mathematical discounting of the subjective value of human life somehow makes the approach any more precise and more accurate than the approach we have chosen."[25] For this reason the court in *Borgren* adopted the first approach in awarding damages.[26]

The amount of damages available to the plaintiff in lost chance cases is generally equal to the percent of a chance lost as a result of the physician's negligence, multiplied by the total amount of damages that would be awarded.[27] The problem of an uncertain future is compounded in these cases, since by definition the plaintiff has a less than fifty percent survival rate in any case. The final problem is the uncertainty, particularly in cancer cases, given small variations in survival and recurrence rates, making it difficult to say in many cases that the extent of a later cancer was more probably than not caused by the physician's failure to diagnose.

Lost chance cases require calculations that assume a probability of loss and an ultimate outcome if the defendant's treatment had been faultless. One example of an "ultimate outcome" charge is found in the New Jersey Model Jury Charges(Civil)[28]:

22. Id. at 1464.

23. Id. at 1465. The Kansas Supreme Court followed the Boody approach in recognizing the loss of a chance doctrine, in Delaney v. Cade, 873 P.2d 175, 187 (Kan.1994) (requiring as a threshold test that "the resulting injury or lessened degree of recovery suffered by the plaintiff as the result of the malpractice must be substantial").

24. 723 F.Supp. 581 (D.Kan.1989).

25. Id. at 583.

26. In the case of Donnini v. Ouano, 810 P.2d 1163 (Kan.App.1991), the Kansas appellant court addressed application of the theory of loss of chance but did not comment on the calculation of damages.

27. McKellips v. Saint Francis Hosp., 741 P.2d 467, 476 (Okl.1987). In McKellips, 741 P.2d at 476 the court adopted the third approach. As an illustration the court gave the following example:

Jury determines from statistical findings combined with the specific facts relevant to the patient, the patient originally had a 40% chance of cure and the physician's negligence reduced the chance of cure to 25%, (40% − 25%) 15% represents the patients loss of survival. If the total amount of damages proved by the evidence is $500,000, the damages caused by defendant is 15% x $500,000 or $75,000. 741 P.2d at 476.

28. 4th Ed. § 5.36E. See generally Fischer v. Canario, M.D., 670 A.2d 516, 524–526 (N.J. 1996).

If you find that defendant has sustained his/her burden of proof, then you must determine based on the evidence what is the likelihood, on a percentage basis, that the plaintiff's ultimate injuries (*condition*) would have occurred even if defendant's treatment was proper. When you are determining the amount of damages to be awarded to the plaintiff, you should award the total amount of damage. Your award should not be reduced by your allocation of harm. The adjustment in damages which may be required will be performed by the Court.

Loss of a chance and increased risk are grounded in the same justifications of deterring negligent conduct and compensating for real harms that happen to fall below the fifty percent threshold of traditional tort doctrine. Increased risk allows recovery for harm that has not yet occurred, while loss of a chance requires the plaintiff to wait until the condition occurs and then sue.[29]

c. *Future Harm as an Element of Damages*

A different kind of damage claim is raised by physician errors that increase the likelihood of future harm to the plaintiff. Some jurisdictions have allowed recovery for the increased risk of future injury and also for the plaintiff's anxiety that such a risk may materialize in the future.[30] The best discussion of such claims can be found in *Petriello v. Kalman*,[31] where the Connecticut Supreme Court overruled its previous caselaw, considerably expanding the range of damages recoverable in cases of possible future injury. The plaintiff, in her sixteenth week of pregnancy, experienced back pain and vaginal bleeding. She was diagnosed by her obstetrician as having had a missed abortion. He performed a dilation and curettage to remove the dead fetus from the plaintiff's uterus. He used excess force, perforating her uterus and drawing part of her small intestine into her vagina. He then called on a general surgeon to assist. The surgeon repaired the damage by a bowel resection, removing a foot of the plaintiff's intestine and connecting the two ends. The experts agreed that the plaintiff now faced a future risk of bowel obstruction, with one expert estimating the risk as ranging from eight (8%) to sixteen (16%) percent.

The court allowed two distinct damage claims. First, it held that the jury was properly instructed that " * * * it might award the plaintiff damages for her fear of the increased risk that she will someday suffer from a bowel obstruction."[32] Second, it held that "a plaintiff who has established a breach of duty that was a substantial factor in causing a present injury which has resulted in an increased risk of future harm is entitled to compensation to the extent that the future harm is likely to occur."[33] The court defined "likely to occur" as meaning merely a "increased likelihood."

Fear of future harm, or phobic claims, require medical testimony to show that the plaintiff does have a predisposition to or phobia about cancer or a future disease.[34] Future harm damages raise a different set of uncertainty

29. See generally U.S. v. Anderson, 669 A.2d 73 (Del.1996).

30. In re Englert, 596 So.2d 541 (La.1992).

31. 576 A.2d 474 (Conn.1990).

32. Id. at 481.

33. Id. at 484.

34. Coffin v. Board of Supervisors, 620 So.2d 1354 (La.App.1993). Several federal courts have recognized such a damage claim. See e.g., Gilliam v. Roche Biomedical Laboratories, Inc., 989 F.2d 278 (8th Cir.1993); Sterling

problems for the courts: instead of trying to calculate uncertain percentages for what was lost in lost chance cases, the courts must predict the likelihood that a harm will materialize. The two situations are similar, however, in fundamental ways. As medicine refines its ability to diagnose and treat, and as long-term epidemiological and clinical studies proliferate, it is no accident that plaintiffs feel they have been injured when a physician misses a diagnosis or treatment. The very language of probability has come to permeate modern medicine, as greater predictive capabilities have emerged. So long as expert witnesses can testify based on reasonable scientific bases as to probabilities, courts are likely to develop damage doctrines that incorporate this medical knowledge.[35] The loss of a chance doctrine is clearly applicable if a physician negligently fails to diagnose AIDS, or improperly performs the tests for the HIV virus.[36]

If a health care provider exposes a patient to the HIV-virus, through a needle stick, a surgical procedure, or some other means, several states have recognized a cause of action for AIDS phobia. If a person is exposed to the HIV virus, but does not show signs of AIDS, damages for emotional harm may be asserted until such time as tests confirm no further risk of HIV-positivity.[37] The plaintiff must show that her fear of developing AIDS is a reasonable result of the defendants' wrongful conduct. Most jurisdictions require a showing of "actual exposure" both the presence of HIV and a scientifically recognized channel of transmission.[38] The Illinois Supreme Court in *Majca* described the arguments as follows: an actual exposure test will incorporate new scientific evidence as to modes of transmission of the HIV virus; it prevents a plaintiff from recovering damages based on lack of information, and reduces the level of misinformation and fear in the general public; it provides an objective standard, ensuring stability, consistency, and predictability in disposing of these claims.[39]

Other courts have allowed a lower burden of proof, requiring only proof of a possible channel of transmission without evidence of HIV infection, or evidence only of a source of the HIV-virus without proof of a mode of transmission.[40] Compensation for a "window of anxiety" has been allowed even if the plaintiff has not been able to prove that the source of the HIV-virus existed.[41]

v. Velsicol Chemical Corp., 855 F.2d 1188 (6th Cir.1988).

35. See also In re Englert, 596 So.2d 541 (La.1992).

36. See Richard C. Herman, AIDS: Malpractice and Transmission Liability, 58 U. Colo. L. Rev. 63 (1986).

37. Brown v. N.Y.C. Health and Hospitals Corporation, 648 N.Y.S.2d 880 (N.Y.App.Div. 1996); Stephanie B. Goldberg, AIDS Phobia: Reasonable Fears or Unreasonable Lawsuits?, A.B.A. J. 88 (June 1992).

38. See Majca v. Beekil, 701 N.E.2d 1084 (Ill.1998)(and cases cited); Brzoska v. Olson, 668 A.2d 1355 (Del.1995).

39. Majca v. Beekil, 701 N.E.2d 1084, 1089–90 (Ill.1998)

40. Faya v. Almaraz, 620 A.2d 327 (Md. C.A.1993)(plaintiffs learned that their surgeon was HIV-positive when he operated on them; fear of acquiring AIDS not unreasonable even though no channel of transmission was stated.)

41. Hartwig v. Oregon Trail Eye Clinic, 580 N.W.2d 86 (Neb.1998)(recovery for damages for the mental anguish of reasonably fearing AIDS resulting from a physical injury such as a needle stick, when it is unknown if the source was contaminated; damages are for at least a "window of anxiety"—that period from the time of possible exposure to the point when a plaintiff knows or should know that he or she is not infected.).

§ 6–8. Conclusion

Malpractice law, like tort law generally, rarely does more than mirror the state of development of the fields it judges. As medicine has become more national in education and practice, the locality rule gave way to a national test for knowledge and skill. As computerized data bases and clinical practice guidelines have proliferated, physicians are held to more demanding, but often more predictable and accessible, clinical standards of practice. With increased certainty as to the acceptable ranges of diagnosis and treatment, a physician's ability to defend is improved by her ability to show compliance with a clearly articulated practice. As medical research continues to elaborate data as to survival rates from various diseases, such as cancers, with different treatment approaches, the courts will respond with damage doctrines that recognize that plaintiffs have lost something when a chance for recovery is dissipated.

The state and federal courts in common law actions will continue to respond to advances in medical practice by using them as a standard for evaluating physician conduct. As elastic standards of practice are tightened by the developing of clinical practice guidelines, courts will be less tolerant of medical error. Future medical practice will be treated as just another accident-producing activity, as courts narrow the applicability of defenses and force medical enterprises to internalize their accident costs as products liability law has required of manufacturers. The development of enterprise liability for health care institutions has become a real possibility.[1]

B. PHYSICIAN OBLIGATIONS TO OBTAIN A PATIENT'S INFORMED CONSENT

§ 6–9. The Doctrine of Informed Consent

a. Origins of the Informed Consent Doctrine

The doctrine of informed consent developed out of strong judicial deference to individual autonomy, reflecting a prevalent belief in American jurisprudence that an individual has a right to be free from nonconsensual interference with his or her person, and a basic moral principle that it is wrong to force another to act against his or her will. This principle was articulated in the medical context by Justice Cardozo in often quoted language in *Schloendorff v. Society of New York Hospital*[1]: "Every human being of adult years and sound mind has a right to determine what shall be done with his own body * * *."

Informed consent doctrine has guided medical decisionmaking by setting boundaries for the doctor-patient relationship. It has become one of the forces altering the attitudes of a new generation of doctors toward their patients, and its requirements are now reflected in consent forms that health care institutions require patients to sign upon admission and before various procedures are performed. It has also provided the starting point for federal regulations on human experimentation.[2]

§ 6–8

1. See the discussion of enterprise liability in Chapter 7.

§ 6–9

1. 105 N.E. 92, 93 (N.Y.App.1914).
2. A useful reference work, providing substantial discussion of all dimensions of in-

Informed consent has been until recently an unnatural graft onto medical practice. As Jay Katz wrote in *The Silent World of Doctor and Patient*[3], " * * * disclosure and consent, except in the most rudimentary fashion, are obligations alien to medical thinking and practice." The function of disclosure historically was to get patients to agree to what the doctors wanted. The judicial development of informed consent into a distinct doctrine can be roughly divided into three periods, according to Katz. During the first period, up to the mid-twentieth century, courts built upon the law of battery and required little more than disclosure by doctors of their proposed treatment. The second period saw an emerging judicial belief that doctors should disclose the alternatives to a proposed treatment and their risks, as well as of risks of the proposed treatment itself. The third period, from 1972 to the present, has seen legislative retrenchment and judicial inertia.[4]

b. *Battery as a Basis for Suit*

Patient autonomy in medical decisionmaking is the underlying principle in all consent cases, whether based in battery or negligence. The doctrine of battery protects a patient's physical integrity from harmful contacts and her personal dignity from unwanted bodily contact. The doctrine requires only that the patient show that she was not informed of the very nature of the medical touching, typically a surgical procedure. Physical injury is not necessary. When a surgeon, in the course of surgery, removes or operates upon an organ other than the one he and the patient discussed, a battery action lies. The most obvious medical battery cases, e.g., where a surgeon amputates the wrong leg, can be readily brought as a negligence case. If the patient is not aware that the physician is going to perform a particular procedure, she has not consented and a claim for battery may be brought.[5] When a patient and physician have agreed on a particular treatment, and the physician does not follow the agreement, a patient may be awarded dignitary damages on a battery-based theory whether or not the procedure was successful.[6]

The procedural and other advantages of a battery-based action tip the scales substantially in the favor of the patient. First, the focus is on the patient's right to be free from a touching different from that to which she consented. The physician has few defenses to a battery. Second, the plaintiff need not prove through expert testimony what the standard of care was; the proof is only that the particular physician failed to explain to the patient the nature and character of the particular procedure. Third, to prove causation, the plaintiff need only show that an unconsented-to touching occurred. Under a negligence theory the plaintiff must show that he would have declined a procedure if he had known all the details and risks.[7] Use of a battery theory

formed consent, including the federal law as it pertains to human subject experimentation, is Fay A. Rozovsky, Consent to Treatment: A Practical Guide (1990).

3. Jay Katz, The Silent World of Doctor and Patient 1 (1984).

4. A review of the status of informed consent law in the U.S. can be found in Jon F. Merz, Informed Consent Does Not Mean Rational Consent: Cognitive Limitations on Decision–Making, 11 J. Legal Med. 321 (1990).

5. Blanchard v. Kellum, 975 S.W.2d 522 (Tenn.1998)(plaintiff's claim that she did not authorize extraction of all thirty-two of her teeth during a single office visit was a battery claim).

6. Lugenbuhl v. Dowling, 701 So.2d 447 (La.App.1997) (court rejected battery basis of informed consent, but allowed dignitary damages for physician's imposition of unwanted procedure on plaintiff).

7. See generally Kohoutek v. Hafner, 383 N.W.2d 295 (Minn.1986). In Chouinard v. Mar-

therefore reduces the need for medical testimony, rendering irrelevant physicians' beliefs about what patients should know and might want as therapy. Most states permit a battery approach to informed consent only in cases where consent is totally absent to the given procedure. Pennsylvania is the only state that continues to treat a physician's failure to get a patient's informed consent to surgery as a battery, rendering the defendant liable for all injuries the plaintiff suffers from the invasion. A plaintiff need not show that a reasonable person in his place, having been properly advised by his doctor, would not have consented to surgery.[8] Malpractice reform in the states has often included abrogation of the battery basis of informed consent.[9]

Battery theory normally applies when the surgery is completely unauthorized. Fraud and deceit in obtaining a patient's consent has always sounded in battery,[10] although the burden of proving fraudulent inducement is a heavy one.[11] One advantage of the battery-based action in informed consent is the possibility of getting punitive damages, even where actual damages are small. Punitive damages have been criticized as unfair and out of control in tort litigation generally. In malpractice cases, courts are not willing to allow such damages except under extreme circumstances. Deceit and breach of fiduciary obligations by a physician are examples of causes of action that may justify such damages. Total disregard of the patient's desires is sufficient to provoke a court into allowing punitive damages.[12] A few jurisdictions continue to treat informed claims generally as battery-based, even if the patient consented to a procedure but was simply not given full and accurate information about some aspects of the treatment.[13]

Punitive damages are typically awarded as part of the damage claims for an intentional tort such as battery.[14] The focus is on the reprehensible nature of defendant's conduct, which may be reckless or motivated by malice or fraud. Even gross negligence in a malpractice suit usually will not suffice. The circumstances surrounding a tortious act may, however, warrant an inference of a wilful or wanton attitude, or reckless disregard of the patient's wishes.[15]

jani, 575 A.2d 238 (Conn.App.1990), the plaintiff sued the defendant surgeon, claiming that the surgeon had performed bilateral breast surgery although the plaintiff had consented only to surgery on her left breast. She admitted that if the surgeon had asked, she would have consented to the surgery on her right breast. The court applied battery doctrine, holding that plaintiff did not need to present either expert testimony nor testify that she would not have consented if the surgeon had asked.

8. Gouse v. Cassel, 561 A.2d 797, 800 (Pa.Super.1989), affirmed in part, reversed in part 615 A.2d 331 (Pa.1992); Moure v. Raeuchele, 563 A.2d 1217 (Pa.Super.1989).

9. See Rubino v. DeFretias, 638 F.Supp. 182 (D.Ariz.1986).

10. In Perna v. Pirozzi, 457 A.2d 431 (N.J. 1983).

11. See Tonelli v. Khanna, 569 A.2d 282 (N.J.Super.App.Div.1990), certification denied 583 A.2d 344 (N.J.1990).

12. Tisdale v. Pruitt, 394 S.E.2d 857 (S.C.App.1990).

13. Shadrick v. Coker, 963 S.W.2d 726, 729(Tenn.1998)(surgeon performed laminectomy and disc excision on plaintiff, using pedicle screws to help fuse vertebra; he failed to tell the plaintiff that such screws were experimental and not approved by the F.D.A., instead characterizing procedure as "routine".

14. For an excellent discussion of punitive damages generally, see Dan B. Dobbs, Ending Punishment in "Punitive Damages": Deterrence—Measured Remedies, 40 Ala. L. Rev. 831 (1989).

15. See also Strauss v. Biggs, 525 A.2d 992 (Del.1987).

c. Negligence as a Basis of Suit

A judicial sense that medical judgment should be allowed more leeway has led to a movement away from battery to negligent nondisclosure over the years, given battery's lack of what Marcus Plant has called " * * * 'elbow room' in which to establish a defense."[16] Negligent nondisclosure allows many more defenses, covering primarily situations where surgery was authorized but the consent was uninformed.[17] Inadequate consent due to a physician's failure to disclose material information is analyzed under negligence concepts.[18]

§ 6–10. Standards of Disclosure

The phrase "informed consent" first appeared in a California case, *Salgo v. Leland Stanford Jr. University Board of Trustees*.[1] *Salgo* held that even a written consent is ineffective if the patient failed to understand material information about the procedure to be undergone. Such information included the nature of the procedure and its risks. Once the courts moved from a battery-based approach, in which the patient lack of consent made out a prima facie case, to negligence, they had to locate a source of a standard of disclosure and a test for measuring its adequacy. Three choices were available. First, the standard for disclosure of material information could be set by professional practice, applying the traditional medical malpractice rule. Second, balancing the patient's autonomy interests against the possibility that some patients might want too much information or might lie after the fact about the importance of the missing information to their decision, the standard could be set by what a reasonable patient would want to know. Third, a pure subjective standard could be chosen, asking what the particular patient considered important.

a. Physician–Based Standard

The professional disclosure standard, measuring the duty to disclose by the standard of the reasonable medical practitioner similarly situated,[2] requires expert testimony to establish the content of a reasonable disclosure. This professional standard is justified by three arguments. First, it protects good medical practice—the primary duty of physicians is to advance their patients' best interests. Physicians should not have to concern themselves with the risk that an uninformed lay jury will later decide they acted improperly.[3] Second, a patient-oriented standard, the courts fear, would force doctors to spend unnecessary time discussing every possible risk with their patients, thereby interfering with the flexibility that physicians need to decide on the best form of treatment.[4] Third, only physicians can accurately evaluate

---

16. Marcus Plante, An Analysis of "Informed Consent", 36 Fordham L.Rev. 639 (1968).

17. Fay A. Rosovsky, Consent to Treatment, A Practical Guide, § 1.2 (1990).

18. Lugenbuhl v. Dowling, 701 So.2d 447 (La.1997)(doctor failed to tell patient that he would not use mesh as promised to repair a hernia if he found operative conditions to be different from what he had expected; this constituted a failure to provide material information).

§ 6–10

1. 317 P.2d 170 (Cal.App.1957).

2. See Robinson v. Bleicher, 559 N.W.2d 473(Neb.1997); Aronson v. Harriman, 901 S.W.2d 832(Ark.1995); Smith v. Weaver, 407 N.W.2d 174 (Neb.1987).

3. Woolley v. Henderson, 418 A.2d 1123 (Me.1980).

4. David W. Louisell and Harold Williams, 2 Medical Malpractice: Physicians and Related Professions, § 22:06 (Charles W. Benton et al., eds. 1984).

the psychological and other impact that risk would have on particular patients. These concerns are often overstated, and are well-rebutted in the landmark case of *Canterbury v. Spence*.[5] However, more than twenty-five states, either by judicial decision[6], or by statute[7], have adopted this standard.

These jurisdictions ordinarily require the plaintiff to offer medical testimony to establish 1) whether a reasonable medical practitioner in the same or similar community would make this disclosure, and 2) that the defendant did not comply with this community standard.[8] Expert testimony is essential, since determination of what information needs to be disclosed is viewed as a medical question.

b. *Reasonable Patient Standard*

The reasonable patient standard, as held in *Canterbury*, makes the "reasonable patient" the measure of the scope of disclosure. This standard has won over several states in the last few years, approaching a majority position.[9] The South Dakota Supreme Court in *Wheeldon*, in following *Canterbury*, expressed the concern that medical practice might conflict with patient needs. "We agree that the right to know—to be informed—is a fundamental right personal to the patient and should not be subject to restrictions by medical practices that may be at odds with the patient's information needs. * * * Materiality, therefore, is the cornerstone upon which the physician's duty to disclose is based."[10] This view of patient decisionmaking has been characterized as "patient sovereignty", entitling a patient to sufficient information to make an informed health care decision.[11]

The effect of a patient-oriented disclosure standard is to ease the plaintiff's burden of proof, since the trier of fact could find that a doctor acted unreasonably in failing to disclose, in spite of unrebutted expert medical testimony to the contrary. The question of whether a physician disclosed risks that a reasonable person would find material is for the trier of fact, and technical expertise is not required.[12] In *Savold v. Johnson*,[13], the South Dakota Supreme Court held that expert testimony as to informed consent information was not needed where a factual dispute exists as to whether any information of the material risks was given at all. Expert testimony is still needed, however, to clarify the treatments and their probabilities of risks.[14] Experts may also be necessary to testify that the risk was one that the physician should have been aware of as a generally recognized risk within the medical community.[15] Five states by statute have mandated a disclosure standard that

5.   464 F.2d 772 (D.C.Cir.1972).

6.   See e.g., Fain v. Smith, 479 So.2d 1150 (Ala.1985); The Florida Bar; Re Standard Jury Inst.—Civil, 459 So.2d 1023 (Fla.1984).

7.   See e.g., Ala. Code § 6–5–484.

8.   Robinson v. Bleicher, 559 N.W.2d 473, 478 (Neb.1997)(locality standard is applicable).

9.   See e.g., Korman v. Mallin, 858 P.2d 1145 (Alaska 1993)(adopting what the court finds to be the "modern trend"); Carr v. Strode, 904 P.2d 489 (Hawai'i 1995).

10.   Wheeldon v. Madison, 374 N.W.2d 367, 375 (S.D.1985). See also Festa v. Greenberg, 511 A.2d 1371 (Pa.Super.1986).

11.   Backlund v. University of Washington, 975 P.2d 950, 956 (Wash.1999)

12.   Pedersen v. Vahidy, 552 A.2d 419 (Conn.1989); Cooper v. Roberts, 286 A.2d 647 (Pa.Super.1971).

13.   443 N.W.2d 656 (S.D.1989).

14.   Cross v. Trapp, 294 S.E.2d 446, 455 (W.Va.1982).

15.   Febus v. Barot, M.D., 616 A.2d 933 (N.J.Super. App.Div.1992).

does not require expert testimony.[16] Given the current state and national mood in support of legislative limitations on common law tort remedies, it may be expected that the common law of informed consent will continue to be constrained by legislative action.

c. Subjective Patient Standard

The pure subjective standard has not been adopted by the courts because of deep-rooted fears that the patient, with hindsight, will say that the information not disclosed was indeed important to her and that she would have declined treatment. However, a patient may still testify as to what she would or would not have done if fully informed. Such testimony is an inextricable part of the whole informed consent issue in many cases and will be allowed.[17]

§ 6–11. Factors to Be Disclosed

a. Diagnosis

The health care provider must disclose a variety of factors to satisfy the elements of informed consent as articulated by most courts. A physician must first describe the diagnosis, including the medical steps preceding diagnosis, including tests and their alternatives. Since disclosure of diagnosis is so basic to the physician-patient relationship, few cases have talked about a physician's failure to discuss it. Where the diagnosis is uncertain, however, an issue of disclosure might arise. Thus in one case, the court held that a physician's failure to reveal Pap smear results violated a duty of disclosure.[1]

b. Nature and Purpose of Treatment

The nature and purpose of the proposed treatment must be discussed. The probability of success, as a core element of the purpose of a treatment, is rarely discussed by the courts. However, the production of comparative outcomes data by the government, insurers, and providers makes more likely a requirement in the future that probabilities of success and failure be disclosed.

c. Risks and Outcomes

The risks of the treatment are perhaps the most important information for a patient to consider. Risks must be material to a patient's decisionmaking in order to be disclosed.[2] Courts often state that remote risks can be omitted,[3] as can those commonly known by patients.[4] Risks of drug side-effects however are singled out for disclosure by some courts, even if the risk of side-effect is small.[5]

16. See e.g., Iowa Code Ann. § 147.137.

17. See e.g., Bourgeois v. McDonald, 622 So.2d 684 (La.App.1993), writ denied 629 So.2d 1177 (La.1993).

§ 6–11

1. Steele v. St. Paul Fire & Marine Ins., 371 So.2d 843 (La.App.1979), writ denied 374 So.2d 658 (La.1979).

2. Harbeson v. Parke Davis, 746 F.2d 517 (9th Cir.1984).

3. See e.g., Shinn v. St. James Mercy Hosp., 675 F.Supp. 94 (W.D.N.Y.1987).

4. See generally Kissinger v. Lofgren, 836 F.2d 678, 681 (1st Cir.1988) (risks of infection from operations should be known to every patient).

5. Cunningham v. Charles Pfizer & Co., 532 P.2d 1377, 1381 (Okl.1974) (duty to disclose "even though the chances of the adverse reaction occurring are statistically small.").

The threshold of disclosure, as the *Canterbury* court suggests, varies with the product of the probability and the severity of the risk.[6] Thus a five percent risk of lengthened recuperation or a treatable infection[7] might be ignored, while a one percent risk of paralysis, as in *Canterbury*, or an even smaller risk of death, should be disclosed.[8] The focus is on the particular patient, rather than an abstract analysis of risks generally, and in particular on the particular medical susceptibilities of that patient.[9] Such medical conditions as allergies to medications are part of the routine medical workup, and risk assessment must factor in such vulnerabilities. The physician should be adequately informed about the particular situation of the patient, in order to tailor risk disclosure to the particular physical vulnerabilities of that patient.[10] The difference between a temporary and a permanent risk can be critical.[11] Risks of improper performance of an appropriate procedure, due to an error in administration of a test or drug dosage, do not ordinarily have to be disclosed. While negligence may be possible with any treatment or test, it is not part of normal disclosure obligations.[12]

Probabilities of various risks must be disclosed by physicians in a fashion that accurately informs the patient. Thus, one court has held that if a physician tells a patient that the risks of a particular surgical procedure are increased by fifty percent by smoking, the physician must also discuss with the patient the base probability of the average risk to an average patient.[13] Some courts have moved beyond a rote compliance with informed consent procedures, often holding physicians responsible to provide more sophisticated and accurate information.[14] Others resist any requirement that a physician give percentages for risks of surgical procedures.[15]

The duty to disclose the risks of treatment may be expanded if the patient inquires more specifically as to particular risks, under both the reasonable patient and the reasonable physician standards. A patient's request puts the physician on notice as to a patient's particular worries, and a standard disclosure is no longer a defense in such cases.[16]

d. *Disclosure of Skill or Status Risks*

Comparative data as to outcomes and success rates in hospitals and of particular medical specialties is proliferating. A variety of systems for evaluat-

6. Canterbury v. Spence, 464 F.2d 772, 789 n. 85 (D.C.Cir.1972).

7. Fischer v. Wilmington Gen. Hosp., 149 A.2d 749 (Del.Super.1959) (no need to disclose small risk of hepatitis infection from blood transfusion).

8. Ashe v. Radiation Oncology Associates, 1998 WL 430632 (Tenn.App.1998)(risk of paralysis a jury question); Cobbs v. Grant, 104 Cal.Rptr. 505, 502 P.2d 1 (Cal.1972) (disclosure of risk of death is necessary).

9. See Fay A. Rozovsky, Informed Consent: A Practical Guide 45 (1983).

10. Hartke v. McKelway, 707 F.2d 1544, 1549 (D.C.Cir.1983), cert. denied 464 U.S. 983, 104 S.Ct. 425, 78 L.Ed.2d 360 (1983).

11. See, e.g., Johnson v. Brandy, 1995 WL 29230 (Ohio App.1995) (risk of scalp numbness after scalp-reduction surgery for baldness not described as permanent risk, but only tempo-

rary; consent form held to be inadequate disclosure). %

12. See, e.g., Gilmartin v. Weinreb, 735 A.2d 620 (N.J.Super.A.D.1999)(doctor prescribed colchicine, and patient was given an overdose; no requirement that such a possibility of improper dosage be disclosed).

13. Korman v. Mallin, 858 P.2d 1145 (Alaska 1993).

14. See e.g., Distefano v. Bell, 544 So.2d 567 (La.App.1989), writ denied 550 So.2d 650 (La.1989).

15. Kennedy v. St. Charles General Hospital Auxiliary, 630 So.2d 888, 892 (La.App. 1993), writ denied 634 So.3d 863 (La.1994).

16. Korman v. Mallin, 858 P.2d 1145 (Alaska 1993).

ing and improving the quality of health care has evolved over the past two decades.[17] Hospitals and managed care organizations have been actively engaged in programs to promote high quality and effective practice, through implementation of clinical algorithms, outcome-based studies, application of quality control principles from industry, and large scale analysis of practice patterns across plans.[18] Outcomes management proposes that the evaluation of the quality of care be an analysis of outcomes rather than an analysis of the process of care. The rapid acceleration of information gathering by health care institutions is likely to lead to disclosure of such comparative success rates and outcome data where available.[19]

Informed consent doctrine can be interpreted to require a physician to disclose differential success rates, forcing the physician into the awkward position of presenting his or her "batting average". Production of comparative outcome data on both hospitals and physicians for certain procedures, as mandated by the federal government and some states, raises the possibility that disclosure of such success rates may be required.[20] Codman, the medical pioneer of outcome studies, argued as long ago as 1913 that institutions and surgeons should disclose their successes and failures so that the public could choose the best provider.[21] Progress has been slow in the face of medical resistance.

Informed consent doctrine can encompass the requirement that a physician disclose differential success rates, forcing physicians to present their "batting averages". One early decision suggested that physicians should disclose both the general statistical success rate for a given procedure and their particular experience with that procedure.[22] But courts have not generally been willing to mandate specific performance data by physicians under informed consent obligations. Incompetence need not be disclosed.[23] Production of comparative outcome data on both hospitals and physicians for certain procedures raises the possibility that disclosure of such success rates may be required.[24] While outcome information is not sufficiently well developed at

17. Timothy S. Jost, Health System Reform: Forward or Backward With Quality Oversight? 271 J.A.M.A. 1508 (1994).

18. See 7 Health Affairs 145–150 (1988).

19. See Aaron D. Twerksi and Neil B. Cohen, Comparing Medical Providers: A First Look at the New Era of Medical Statistics, 58 Brook. L. Rev. 5, 12–13 (1992) (as statistical validity of data is established, it will become part of litigation).

20. Two states—Pennsylvania and New York—now release physician-specific data. See Linda Oberman, Rating Doctors—Penn. Joins Trend In Releasing Physician–Specific Mortality Data, A.M.A. News 2, 34 (Dec. 7, 1992).

21. Duncan Newhauser, Ernest Amory Codman, M.D. and End Results of Medical Care, 6 Intern. J. Tech.Ass. in Health Care 307 (1990).

22. Hales v. Pittman, 576 P.2d 493 (Ariz. 1978) (discussing the battery count of the plaintiff's complaint).

23. Wachter.v United States, 689 F.Supp. 1420 (D.Md.1988)(applying Maryland and federal law)

24. Newsday, Inc. v. New York Department of Health, 1991 WL 285624 (N.Y.Sup.1991). On December 4, 1990, the Department of Health issued a press release announcing the result of its study of the death rates of cardiac surgery patients in New York hospitals. Thirty hospitals provided heart surgery data from operations performed by 126 cardiac surgeons. The names and individual mortality rates of each of the surgeons were reported to the participating hospitals, and the press release stressed that the reason for disseminating this information was that both patients and referring physicians were expected to use this information to help them decide which institution was best for cardiac procedures. Patients were expected to get from their doctor or hospital:

1. The performance history of each hospital.

2. The performance record of individual surgeons.

present for this purpose, the rapid acceleration of information gathering by health care institutions is likely to lead to disclosure of such comparative success rates and outcome data where available.[25]

The most remarkable decision to date addressing a duty to disclose performance data is Johnson v. Kokemoor.[26] The plaintiff Donna Johnson sued Dr. Richard Kokemoor on a theory of failure to obtain informed consent to surgery. The jury found for the plaintiff on her informed consent counts. The plaintiff, experiencing severe headaches, had a CT scan. Her family physician then referred her to the defendant, a neurosurgeon in the Chippewa Falls area. Dr. Kokemoor then diagnosed an enlarging aneurysm at the rear of the plaintiff's brain and recommended surgery to clip the aneurysm.[27] He performed this surgery in October of 1990, clipping the aneurysm. But as a result of the surgery, the plaintiff was rendered an incomplete quadriplegic, unable to walk or to control her bowel and bladder movements. Her vision, speech and upper body coordination are also partially impaired.

The central issue at trial was whether Dr. Kokemoor "overstated the urgency of her need for surgery and overstated his experience with performing the particular type of aneurysm surgery which she required." Plaintiff asked the defendant about his experience, and he answer that he had performed the surgery she required "several" times, amplifying that by "several," he meant "dozens" and "lots of times."

The Wisconsin Supreme Court viewed the case as presenting three related questions: first, whether the defendant should have disclosed his own experience with the particular procedure; second, whether he should have compared the morbidity and mortality rates among experienced surgeons with those lacking experience, such as himself; and third, whether he should have referred the plaintiff to a tertiary care center staffed by more experienced surgeons. The court held that evidence as to all three issues were material to informed consent in the case.

The court noted that the defendant lacked experience with posterior circulation aneurysms, which were much more difficult than anterior circulation aneurysms that he had performed. He also understated the risks. "According to the plaintiff's witnesses, the defendant had told the plaintiff that her surgery carried a two percent risk of death or serious impairment and that it was less risky than the angiogram procedure she would have to undergo in preparation for surgery. The plaintiff's witnesses also testified that

---

3. The risk of mortality for patients based on their individual risk factors."

A reporter made a FOIL request to the Department for the release of the patient mortality rankings of the individual surgeons comprising the study, and the request was denied upon the ground that disclosing the information would violate the Personal Privacy Protection Law (Public Offices Law Article 6–A) as an unwarranted invasion of the physicians' personal privacy. The court rejected this argument, finding that "[n]o doctor subject to such scrutiny could have any reasonable expectation that the government would withhold from its citizens the patient mortality rate of the doctor. Furthermore, even if there was a legiti-

mate privacy expectation, the interest of the public outweighs it."

25. See Timothy S. Jost, Oversight of the Quality of Medical Care: Regulation, Management, or the Market/ 37 Ariz. L.Rev. 825 (1995); Aaron D. Twerksi and Neil B. Cohen, Comparing Medical Providers: A First Look at the New Era of Medical Statistics, 58 Brook. L. Rev. 5, 12–13 (1992) (as statistical validity of data is established, it will become part of litigation).

26. 545 N.W.2d 495 (Wis.1996).

27. The defendant acknowledged at trial that the aneurysm was not the cause of the plaintiff's headaches.

the defendant had compared the risks associated with the plaintiff's surgery to those associated with routine procedures such as tonsillectomies, appendectomies and gall bladder surgeries.[26"] The performance data for the best surgeons revealed a morbidity and mortality rate of just over ten percent, closer to fifteen percent on average, and for a surgeon with the defendant's limited experience, "closer to the thirty percent range." The defendant maintained that his disclosure was adequate, that he told her that her risks were greater because of the location of the aneurysm. His own experts, however, testified that if a patient asked about their experience, they would reveal their experience and compare it to other physicians performing similar operations.

It appeared that the defendant explicitly misrepresented his experience to the plaintiff, in response to a direct question from her. He responded that he had operated on aneurysms comparable to her aneurysm "dozens" of times. The court noted this, and indicated its reluctance to fashion a bright line test requiring disclosure of comparative performance. However in this case the data was available, the defendant had reviewed it, and misrepresented the risks to the plaintiff. The defendant admitted that he had not shared with the plaintiff information from articles he reviewed prior to surgery. Considering this conduct by the defendant, the Court wrote:

> Had a reasonable person in the plaintiff's position been made aware that being operated upon by the defendant significantly increased the risk one would have faced in the hands of another surgeon performing the same operation, that person might well have elected to forego surgery with the defendant. Had a reasonable person in the plaintiff's position been made aware that the risks associated with surgery were significantly greater than the risks that an unclipped aneurysm would rupture, that person might well have elected to forego surgery altogether. In short, had a reasonable person in the plaintiff's position possessed such information before consenting to surgery, that person would have been better able to make an informed and intelligent decision.

The Court then concluded that "informed consent requires disclosure of all of the viable alternatives and risks of the treatment proposed" which would be material to a patient's decision, particularly when different physicians have substantially different success rates with the same procedure. Assuming that a reasonable person in the patient's position would consider such information material, it should be admissible.[27]

> We caution, as did the court of appeals, that our decision will not always require physicians to give patients comparative risk evidence in

---

26. The defendant testified at trial that he had informed the plaintiff that should she decide to forego surgery, the risk that her unclipped aneurysm might rupture was two percent per annum, cumulative. Since he informed the plaintiff that the risk accompanying surgery was two percent, a reasonable person in the plaintiff's position might have concluded that proceeding with surgery was less risky than non-operative management.

27. The court relied on the few discussions in the recent legal literature that have ad-

dressed these issues of provider comparisons based on empirical data. See Aaron D. Twerski & Neil B. Cohen, Comparing Medical Providers: A First Look at the New Era of Medical Statistics, 58 Brook.L.Rev. 5,6 (1992)(arguing for physician responsibility to "identify and correlate risk factors and to communicate the results to patients". See also Douglas Sharrott, Provider–Specific Quality-of-Care Data: A Proposal for Limited Mandatory Disclosure, 58 Brook.L.Rev. 85 (1992).

statistical terms to obtain informed consent. Rather, we hold that evidence of the morbidity and mortality outcomes of different physicians was admissible under the circumstances of this case.

The court left such disclosure to a case-by-case analysis, recognizing that the basic issue in such cases is "less a question of how a physician chooses to explain the panoply of treatment options and risks necessary to a patient's informed consent than a question of assessing whether a patient has been advised that such options and risks exist."

The duty to disclose performance data in *Johnson* is an expansion of prior common law approaches to disclosure, limited to a specific set of circumstances: a procedure about which performance data was available; a plaintiff who asked the physician specific questions about risks and track records. As the court itself noted, "it was the defendant himself who elected to explain the risks confronting the plaintiff in statistical terms." He then misrepresented the statistical risks deliberately for the sake of his own benefit, that is, a chance to perform the surgery.[28] He concealed a secret, lying to induce a patient to have surgery with him.

Johnson raises interesting questions for the future. Most courts have resisted requirements that specific percentages of risks be disclosed, arguing that medicine is an inexact science.[29] However, at least one other court has suggested that the physician should disclose both the general statistical success rate for a given procedure, and his or her particular experience with that procedure.[30] The *Johnson* case starts at a safe point—a physician withholding valuable information, keeping a secret to the patient's detriment. But there is no reason why such information should not be disclosed as a mandatory obligation, if it is available, whether or not the patient asked. The next step is to require the accumulation of such data, or risk a negative presumption at trial where informed consent is an issue and such comparative data was not available. *Johnson* has become the case to discuss in recent state court decisions, although state courts are still proving resistant to expanded duties of disclosure of competence or performance. In Whiteside v. Lukson[31], the surgeon had never performed a laparoscopic cholecystectomy on a human, although he had practiced the procedure on a pig during a hands-on demonstration. He did not inform the plaintiff of his inexperience, and she ended up with a damaged bile duct during the operation. The court acknowledges that

---

28. The court also upheld a duty to refer a patient to more experienced surgeons nearby, noting that once you concede a duty to share comparative risk data as part of obtaining a patient's informed consent, "an ensuing referral elsewhere will often represent no more than a modest and logical next step."

Given the difficulties involved in performing the surgery at issue in this case, coupled with evidence that the defendant exaggerated his own prior experience while downplaying the risks confronting the plaintiff, the circuit court properly exercised its discretion in admitting evidence that a physician of good standing would have made the plaintiff aware of the alternative of lower risk surgery with a different, more experienced surgeon in a better-equipped facility.

29. Kennedy v. St. Charles General Hospital Auxiliary, 630 So.2d 888, 892 (La.App. 1993).

30. See Hales v. Pittman, 576 P.2d 493 (Ariz.1978) (discussing the battery count of the plaintiff's complaint). Contra, see Foard v. Jarman, 387 S.E.2d 162 (N.C.1990)(lack of experience in performing the procedure need not be disclosed). See generally Paul D. Rheingold, The Admissibility of Evidence in Malpractice Cases: The Performance Records of Practitioners, 58 Brook.L.Rev.75, 80 (1992); Aaron D. Twerksi and Neil B. Cohen, Comparing Medical Providers: A First Look at the New Era of Medical Statistics, 58 Brook. L. Rev. 5, 12–13 (1992).

31. 947 P.2d 1263 (Wash.App. Div. 3 1997)

conflicts of interest[32], experience[33], and HIV status[34] had been required to be disclosed in other jurisdictions.[35] But it concludes that the expansive view would do too much:

> In theory, the physician's own health, financial situation, even medical school grades, could be considered material facts a patient would want to consider in consenting to treatment by that physician. . . . [W]e conclude that a surgeon's lack of experience in performing a particular surgical procedure is not a material fact for purposes of finding liability predicated on failure to secure an informed consent.[36]

In another recent case, Ditto v. McCurdy,[37] two patients underwent breast implant procedures and had complications, and sued the cosmetic surgeon. They argued among other claims that the surgeon's experience should have been disclosed to them, since he was not certified as a plastic surgeon, but only as an otolaryngologist, facial surgeon, and cosmetic surgeon. The court concluded that "[u]nder the circumstances of the present case, we decline to hold that a physician has a duty to affirmatively disclose his or her qualifications or the lack thereof to a patient.[38] The court preferred to leave such disclosure requirements to the legislature.

Disclosure of a physician's physical condition, e.g. an addiction like alcoholism, or a contagious condition, e.g., HIV-positivity, raises troubling legal issues.[39] Certainly an alcoholic surgeon may have an impairment that might seriously affect performance and thus success rate. In Hidding v. Williams,[40] the plaintiff sued on an informed consent theory, alleging in part that the physician had failed to disclose that he was a chronic alcoholic. The court held that such a failure to inform violated Louisiana informed consent requirements. This raises a difficult causation question, since alcoholism may not always impair a physician's performance.[41] The real issue is how the physician is likely to perform generally, regardless of an impairment or other personal characteristic. However, the fact that alcohol abuse might on some occasions create risks for patients does seem at first glance to mandate disclosure. Disclosure creates the risk that a patient will refuse the physician's care because of the status or the addiction, rather than looking at the particular case and the risks posed. The physician will then be stigmatized on the basis of personal information not previously known, and now used against

---

32. Moore v. Regents, 51 Cal.3d 120, 271 Cal.Rptr. 146

33. Johnson v. Kokemoor, 545 N.W.2d 495(1996).

34. Faya v. Almaraz, 620 A.2d 327(Md.1993). See discussion at pp. infra.

35. They cited to William J. McNichols, Informed Consent Liability in a "Managerial Information" Jurisdiction, 48 Okla. L. Rev. 711 I(1996); Judith F. Daar, Informed Consent: Defining Limits Through Therapeutic Parameters, 16 Whittier L. REv. 187(1995). They noted that some jurisdictions had defined material fact to include physician conflicts of interest (Hidding v. Williams, 578 So.2d 1192 (La.App. 1991); HIV status; and lack of experience (Johnson v. Kokemoor).

36. Id. at 1265. See also Abram v. Children's Hosp. of Buffalo, 151 A.D.2d 972, 542

N.Y.S.2d 418 (N.Y.App.Div.1989), appeal dismissed by, 552 N.Y.S.2d 930, 552 N.E.2d 178 (1990)(qualifications need not be disclosed).

37. 947 P.2d 952 (Hawai'i 1997)

38. Id. at 958.

39. See Copithorne v. Framingham Union Hosp., 520 N.E.2d 139 (Mass.1988) for failure to disclose surgeon's sexual problems to staff and patients.

40. 578 So.2d 1192 (La.App.1991).

41. Ornelas v. Fry, 727 P.2d 819 (Ariz.App. 1986) (court refused to allow evidence as to alcoholism of anesthesiologist as a separate claim of negligence, absent a showing that the physician was impaired at the time of the procedure.).

him. On the other hand, alcoholism might be argued as most similar to other risks that a physician might present to a patient, such as a surgeon's wound infection rates or a loss of ability with age. The principle of informed consent, requiring disclosure of all risks material to a patient's decision, appears elastic enough to include these addiction risks.

One escape clause may be the reasonable patient standard, which presumes a patient who will not overreact to addictions or to extremely remote risks. The contagious status of a physician, such as an HIV-positive surgeon, raises even more extreme problems of disclosure, since the disease of AIDS is fatal at present. Arguably a patient would therefore like to know about a physician's status. On the other hand, it can be argued that no material risk is created, given the very low possibility that the virus will be communicated from provider to patient. The emerging case law has focussed on the probability of infection and the severity of it, concluding that even though little evidence supports provider to patient transmission of AIDs, the provider should disclose his or her HIV-positive status.[42] In Estate of Behringer v. The Medical Center at Princeton[43] the court held that the hospital had an obligation to disclose that a staff otolaryngologist (ENT) and plastic surgeon was suffering from AIDS. The knowledge that the surgeon had AIDS led patients to seek transfer or other care, with a high level of cancellation resulting. The hospital developed a special informed consent for HIV-positive providers, and a new policy for HIV-positive workers that barred them from patient care situations where they might pose risks to patients.[44]

The *Behringer* court analyzed informed consent in terms of the material risks faced by a patient, and the conflict of interest faced by HIV-positive or AIDS physicians who know that disclosure might cost them patients and income. While conceding that the risk of transmission of HIV from provider to patient was very low,[45] the court saw other risks as part of the bundle of risks, including the risk of extended uncertainty for a patient exposed to a surgical accident involving a surgeon with AIDS. A surgical accident such as a scalpel cut " * * * may subject a previously uninfected patient to months or even years of continual HIV testing,"[46] with the accompanying "anxiety of waiting for test results, and the possible alterations to life style and child-bearing during the testing period, even if those results ultimately are negative."[47] This is sufficient to be a material risk, since " * * * the risk of accident and implications thereof would be a legitimate concern to the surgical patient, warranting disclosure of this risk in the informed-consent setting."[48]

The court held that the duty to warn third party cases would surely subsume this informed consent duty.[49] A patient can demonstrate not only

42. The studies have found no evidence of transmission from provider to patient, with the possible exception of the Bergalis case. See e.g., Ban Mishu et al., A Surgeon with AIDS: Lack of Evidence of Transmission to Patients, 264 JAMA 467 (1990) (study of 2160 patients of Nashville surgeon).

43. 592 A.2d 1251 (N.J.Super. Law Div. 1991).

44. See e.g., Donald H.J. Hermann and Rosalind D. Gagliano, AIDS, Therapeutic Confidentiality, and Warning Third Parties, 48 Md. L. Rev. 55 (1989).

45. The court observed that the actual risk of transmission is small, in the range of 1/130,-000 to 1/4,500. But it also found that the cumulative risk to surgical patients would be much higher.

46. 592 A.2d at 1278.

47. Id. at 1280.

48. Id.

49. Gordon G. Keyes, Health Care Professionals with AIDS: The Risk of Transmission Balanced Against the Interests of Professionals

that the information about a provider's HIV status is material to his decision, and that he would have made a different decision had he been given the facts.[50]

The implications of the Behringer decision are far-reaching.[51] The disclosure of a contagious status that exposes a patient to a risk of death is similar to other disabilities that might cause a fatal medical error. If HIV-positivity or AIDS must be disclosed, then surely so must alcoholism in a surgeon. A provider's performance can be affected by fatigue, depression, anger, and other psychological states with potentially lethal risks to the patient. We don't presently require disclosure of the various forces that affect providers, and it is hard to imagine how this could be done. If a court is to avoid singling out AIDS as presenting unique risks to a patient, then vastly expanded disclosure obligations may well be next.

The American Medical Association (AMA) and the American Dental Association (ADA) have taken the position that HIV infected professionals should abstain from performing risky invasive procedures, or should disclose their sero-positive status to their patients.[52] The burden is placed on the individual professional. The calculation of the professional organizations appears to be that some patients will stick with the provider because they value their relationship with the professional, or the professional's reputation for quality. But why should the professional disclose his status, if he knows it? He may see his practice diminish or disappear as patients spread the word. If a hospital or managed care organization finds out, they may restrict his practice and cut his income. It is more likely that they will invoke a general contractual provision and restrict his privileges, or in the case of a managed care organization, remove him from panel membership. The infected provider therefore has little incentive to disclose and substantial incentives to remain silent.[53]

While the theory and application of informed consent doctrine by the courts seems to justify disclosure of HIV positive status, the efficacy of the doctrine in actually inducing providers to so act is unclear at best. HIV status does not pose unique risks: the risk of either contagion or death is inherent in a range of provider-created risks. A better way to frame the risks for the courts is to think of such status risks as better regulated by threshold screening of providers for staff privileges, by institutional policies to promote safer health care delivery, and by use of tort law to set a standard of unreasonable risk creation.[54] Methods of achieving such threshold screening to protect patients against high-risk providers include staff privilege limitations, the threat of a negligence suit against a provider who is truly a "typhoid surgeon", and professional self-restraint by physicians who become aware that they are high-risk providers.[55] Informed consent doctrine seems ill-suited

and Institutions, 16 J.C. & U.L. 589, 603 (1990).

50. Id. at 658.

51. See also Faya v. Almaraz, 620 A.2d 327 (Md.App.1993).

52. Olson and Howard–Martin, Controversy Brews Over Guidelines For AIDS–Infected Health Care Workers, HealthSpan 8, 13–15, April 1991.

53. Id.

54. Norman Daniels in HIV–Infected Health Care Professionals: Public Threat or Public Sacrifice?, 70 Milbank Quart. 3 (1992).

55. Leonard H. Glantz et al., Risky Business: Setting Public Health Policy for HIV–Infected Health Care Professionals, 70 The Milbank Quart. 43, 72–73 (1992).

to carry such additional baggage—it is unfair to providers, moves doctrine into an area of risk with no clear stopping point or bright line, and is simply not justified by a risk analysis.[56]

e. Alternatives

Doctors should also disclose alternative methods of diagnosis or treatment that are generally acknowledged within the medical community as feasible;[57] their risks and consequences; and their probability of success. Some courts have held that alternatives should be disclosed, even if the alternative is more hazardous,[58] or the physician is not capable of performing the procedure or evaluating its risk.[59] Such alternatives might include availability to diagnostic tools such as CT scanners and better equipped facilities.[60] Courts may however er limit disclosure by concluding that some alternatives are not legitimate treatment options.[61] Such disclosure is mandated by statute in some states.[62]

Alternatives must be discussed, unless an alternative is not considered to be within the standard of care.[63] The definition of treatment has been construed broadly to include diagnostic options and choices of hospitals for performing a procedure. Physicians must disclose diagnostic procedures that might assist patients in making an informed decision about treatment. In Martin v. Richards,[64] the court held that it was for the jury to decide whether the physicians' failure to inform the parents of a minor patient of the availability of a CAT scan to detect intracranial bleeding and the unavailability of a neurosurgeon at the hospital to operate caused the patient's brain damage. In Vachon v. Broadlawns Medical Foundation,[65] the plaintiff suffered severe multiple trauma injuries and the issue was whether his transfer to a university hospital two hours away instead of to closer trauma hospitals was reasonable. The court held that the decision to transfer was part of treatment and raised an issue of reasonable care.

When a practitioner of alternative medicine convinces a patient to forego conventional medical treatment in favor of alternative therapy, it has been held that the patient must give informed consent to such a choice. In Charell v. Gonzalez,[66] the patient had a hysterectomy and was then persuaded to forego chemotherapy and radiation recommended by the treating physicians, in favor of a special diet of six coffee enemas a day recommended by an alternative medicine practitioner. The defendant did not warn the patient of the risk. The jury found that the plaintiff had assumed 49% of her injuries,

56. See Mark Barnes et al., The HIV–Infected Health Care Professional: Employment Policies and Public Health, 18 Law, Med. & Health Care 311, 324 (1990).

57. See e.g., Teilhaber v. Greene, 727 A.2d 518 (N.J.Super.1999); Moore v. Baker, 989 F.2d 1129 (11th Cir.1993).

58. Gemme v. Goldberg, 626 A.2d 318, 326 (Conn.App.1993).

59. See Holt v. Nelson, 523 P.2d 211 (Wash.App.1974).

60. Martin v. Richards, 531 N.W.2d 70 (Wis.1995)(failure to inform parents of patient that a CG scanner was available to diagnose head injuries, and that facility lacked neurosurgeon to treat intracranial bleeding.)

61. See Lienhard v. State, 431 N.W.2d 861 (Minn.1988).

62. See Wisc.St.Ann. 448.30.

63. See Morris v. Ferriss, 669 So.2d 1316 (La.App. 4 Cir.1996)(physician did not have to advise patient that psychiatric treatment was an alternative treatment for epileptic partial complex seizures, since it was not accepted as feasible); Lienhard v. State, 431 N.W.2d 861 (Minn.1988) (managing pregnancy at home rather than in hospital not a choice between alternative methods of treatment; disclosure therefore not required).

64. 500 N.W.2d 691 (Wis.App.1993).

65. 490 N.W.2d 820 (Iowa 1992).

66. 251 A.D.2d 72(N.Y.App.Div.1998)

but the defendant was also responsible for a substantial portion of the damages of blindness and severe back problems.

f. Prognosis if Treatment or Test Is Declined

A physician may in some jurisdictions have to disclose to the patient not only the consequences of treatment, but also the results of inaction. In *Truman v. Thomas*,[67] Dr. Thomas failed to explain to his patient, Rena Truman, the consequences of her persistent refusal to undergo a pap smear. Dr. Truman saw her as a patient for five years, and often said to her, "You should have a pap smear". She always declined, either not wanting to pay for it or simply not wanting to undergo any more tests. Dr. Thomas is quoted as saying: "We are not enforcers, we are advisors" in justifying his failure to explain the purpose of the test and the consequences of cervical cancer. The California Supreme Court held that a physician has a duty to disclose to a patient the consequences of a failure to decline a test or procedure viewed as valuable by a doctor.

> If a patient indicates that he or she is going to decline the risk-free test or treatment, then the doctor has the additional duty of advising of all material risks of which a reasonable person would want to be informed before deciding not to undergo the procedure.[68]

This "right to an informed refusal" requires a physician to indicate the risks of refusing a procedure or diagnostic test, attempting to force the patient to explicitly make the tradeoff. It requires that the doctor spend a valuable commodity—time—in order to maximize the patient's choices. The doctor controls information otherwise unavailable to patients; from this control flows an obligation to use that information to help patients avoid medical hazards and even to help a patient preserve a tort right to sue the physician. In *Truman*, the court says the "fiducial qualities" of the physician-patient relationship mandate disclosure, given patient ignorance. The courts are increasingly talking in terms of these fiduciary obligations.

The dissent in *Truman* talks about "how far a doctor should go in selling his services without alienating the patient from all medical care."[69] Physicians are exposed to conflicting incentives with regard to testing patients, as is illustrated by new genetic diagnostic technologies.[70]

The *Truman* doctrine, applied to new technologies of genetic screening, raises new problems. The purpose of these tests is to assess whether the patient will develop a particular condition. However, the presence of particular genetic structures and the development of clinically relevant disease is not straightforward for diseases such as heart disease, hypertension, mental illness, or cancer. An abnormal gene may not result in clinical disease. In Huntington's chorea, for example, the time of onset varies from early child-

67. 165 Cal.Rptr. 308, 611 P.2d 902 (Cal. 1980).

68. Id. at 312, 611 P.2d at 906.

69. Truman, 165 Cal.Rptr. at 316, 611 P.2d at 910.

70. David Blumenthal and Richard Zeckhauser, Genetic Diagnosis: Implications for Medical Practice, 5 Intl. J. Tech. Assess. in Health Care 579, 585 (1989). See Bruce J.

Hillman et al., Frequency and Costs of Diagnostic Imaging in Office Practice—A Comparison of Self–Referring and Radiologist–Referring Physicians, 323 New Eng. J. Med. 1604 (1990) (finding that physicians who self-referred patients for diagnostic imaging performed imaging from 2 ½ to 11 times as often as the physician who referred patients to outside radiologists).

hood to the seventies. Thus, patients need to know a great deal about the likelihood of a disease developing before they can face the anxiety produced by a positive test result indicating the presence of a genetic marker for a disease.[71] The disclosure mandated by *Truman* is uncertain in such situations, depending on the standard of disclosure mandated by informed consent requirements in that state.

g. *Prognosis With Treatment*

Patients with diseases such as cancer face a reduced life expectancy even with the best medical treatment. In such cases, patients would presumably like to know as much as possible about their life expectancy for a variety of reasons—estate planning, goodbyes to family and friends, facing death for personal and religious reasons. What is the standard of disclosure if the patient does not explicitly demand the statistics on life expectancy from the treating physician? In Arato v. Avedon,[72] the California Supreme Court was faced with an informed consent suit by the family of a patient who had died of pancreatic cancer. The family alleged that the physicians had failed to obtain the patient's informed consent to pancreatic cancer treatments. They contended that the physicians had a duty as a matter of law to disclose statistical life expectancy data to patients. This data, the family argued, was material both to Mr. Arato's treatment decision and to his nonmedical interests in putting his business and financial affairs in order before his early death. The court rejected this claim as a matter of law, concluding that the jury under a general reasonable patient instruction had ample guidance in evaluating the reasonableness of the disclosures made. The plaintiff had never asked about life expectancy in the course of seventy visits and several months. The treating physicians, lacking direct questions from Arato, justified their lack of disclosure of statistical data to Mr. Arato primarily on the basis of a therapeutic privilege claim: they wanted to avoid creating anxiety in him, depriving him of a hope of cure. Disclosure would have created a "a medically inadvisable state" according to Dr. Avedon. Mr. Arato then underwent a series of painful, prolonged courses of radiation and chemotherapy. He died more than year after initial surgery that discovered the cancer.

The plaintiffs claimed that the mortality data was material to Mr. Arato's decision to undergo the course of therapy, which he might well have declined; and that lacking knowledge of the likelihood of an early death, Arato failed to order his business and financial affairs. The Supreme Court was reluctant to require that specific information be disclosed in the medical contexts.[73] The court trusted the jury to decide what is "material information", rather than issuing a bright line test.

The Arato case is troubling on several grounds, even though it appears to do little more than support the existing reasonable patient instruction in California. First, the court ignored the fact that many patients may want to avoid bad news. The plaintiff's apparent avoidance of information about the possible timetable of his death—his refusal to specifically ask the physicians about life expectancy—is quite predictable for a middle-aged patient. A

71. Aliza Kolker, Advances in Prenatal Diagnosis: Social–Psychological and Policy Issues, 5 Intl. J. Tech. Assess. in Health Care 601, 608 (1989).

72. 858 P.2d 598 (Cal.1993).

73. Id. at 606.

physician may have to be a good therapist to help a patient work through the fear of death.[74] Second, the court made too much of the therapeutic privilege, allowing defense testimony that the standard of disclosure was not to reveal such data unless the patient asked. The better informed consent position is that information disclosure does not turn on what the patient specifically asks to hear about. How sophisticated, after all, must the patient be about statistical life expectancy? About courses of experimental therapy? At what point is the encouragement of patient hope a wrong in and of itself, unfair to the patient, family and to financial assets that may be wasted without planning in the shadow of death? Informed consent law has a number of bright line disclosure requirements in many jurisdictions, including disclosure of risks in probability form, alternatives to therapy, and soon. Third, the court dwelt on the fact that probabilities might not govern the specific patient's prognosis. But they missed the point of the use of such probabilities: while the patient might have lived longer, he might also have died sooner. This is all the more reason to lay out a specific timetable immediately for a patient, since death requires preparation.

h. *Disclosure of Conflicts of Interest*

Medical professionals are in a position of dominance over their patients. The relationship is inherently unequal. The physician has superior knowledge produced by long years of training and practice, expertise the patient cannot have; the physician is less concerned about the patient's health than is the patient; the patient is often anxious and ill-equipped to process complex medical information; and the physician can usually get another patient more easily than the patient can obtain another doctor. Patients are thus vulnerable, and this vulnerability imposes on physicians a "trust", a fiduciary obligation justified by the physician's dominant position in the relationship.

The fee-for-service treatment setting poses substantial conflicts of interest, in which the physician's treatment decision may be affected by his financial interests in treating a particular patient. The possibility of economic pressures clouding physician judgment are systemic in medical practice.[75] Providers may for example have incentives to keep patients even if their own facilities are inadequate.[76] The more modern version of this conflict of interest arises with self-referrals by physicians to their own diagnostic facilities. The emergence of fraud and abuse regulations recognizes that physicians are likely to over refer, given the economic benefits that accrue to them sending patients to their own facilities.

---

74. See generally Jay Katz, The Silent World of Doctor and Patient 213–229 (1984) (arguing that dire prognosis must be disclosed in spite of patient anxiety; for a physician to remain silent is to strip the patient of all control, in favor of physician control.)

75. See generally Marc A. Rodwin, Medicine, Money & Morals: Physicians' Conflicts of Interest (1993); and The Organized American Medical Profession's Response to Financial Conflicts of Interest: 1890–1992, 70 Milbank Q. 703 (1992); see also David Hilifiker, Facing Our Mistakes, 310 New Eng. J. Med. 118, 119 (1984). For examples of negligent failures to

refer, see e.g., Larsen v. Yelle, 246 N.W.2d 841 (Minn.1976) (physician in general practice liable for failing to refer patient with fractured wrist to orthopedic specialist); Ison v. McFall, 400 S.W.2d 243 (Tenn.App.1964). See also Principles of Medical Ethics of the American Medical Association § 8 (requiring doctor to seek consultation "whenever it appears that the quality of medical services may be enhanced thereby.").

76. See Entin, DRGs, HMOs, and PPOs: Introducing Economic Issues in the Medical Malpractice Case, 20 Forum 674 (1985).

Recent cases have used fiduciary concepts to define physician duties to disclose possible conflicts of interest or other information important to a patient in assessing physician motivations. In Moore v. Regents of the University of California,[77] the plaintiff Moore underwent treatment for hairy-cell leukemia at the Medical Center of the University of California at Los Angeles (UCLA Medical Center). Moore first visited UCLA Medical Center shortly after he learned that he had hairy-cell leukemia. His physician, Dr. Golde, hospitalized Moore and withdrew blood and bone marrow aspirate. Dr. Golde did not disclose his preexisting research and economic interests in the cells before obtaining consent to the medical procedures by which they were extracted. The defendants, including Dr. Golde, were aware that Moore's cell line was of great commercial value. The court characterized the cause of action as either a breach of fiduciary duty to disclose facts material to a patient's consent, or in the alternative, as the performance of medical procedures without the patient's consent. The court noted the potentially conflicting loyalties of a physician with a patient in whom he has a research interest: "This is because medical treatment decisions are made on the basis of proportionality—weighing the benefits to the patient against the risks to the patient. * * * a physician who adds his own research interests to this balance may be tempted to order a scientifically useful procedure or test that offers marginal, or no, benefits to the patient."[78] Interests extraneous to a patient's health might skew the physician's judgment, and this is something a patient would like to know in deciding on treatment at the hands of this physician.

In *Moore*, the court explicitly used both fiduciary duty and informed consent doctrine in order to impose an obligation on the physicians to disclose their research and economic interests.[79] A physician must now rescue a patient from the physician's own mixed motivations and conflicts of interest between the patient's good and his own. Commentators have contended that the *Moore* nondisclosure cause of action will fail to reach third parties who benefit from the plaintiff's cell line.[80] One commentator has advocated use of the common law tort of invasion of privacy, in particular the appropriateness of likeness for commercial purposes.[81]

Physicians may at times want to try a new or innovative approach to a patient's problems. The line between innovation and experimentation is a fine one, and may require disclosure to the patient of the novelty of a new treatment approach. In Estrada v. Jaques,[82] the court considered the conflicts that a physician may experience in such an approach: "The psychology of the doctor-patient relation, and the rewards, financial and professional, attendant upon recognition of experimental success, increase the potential for abuse and

---

77. 271 Cal.Rptr. 146, 793 P.2d 479 (Cal. 1990), cert. denied 499 U.S. 936, 111 S.Ct. 1388, 113 L.Ed.2d 444 (1991).

78. Id. at 163, 793 P.2d at 496.

79. See also Lambert v. Park, 597 F.2d 236 (10th Cir.1979); Ostojic v. Brueckmann, 405 F.2d 302, 304 (7th Cir.1968); Margaret S. v. Edwards, 488 F.Supp. 181, 207 (E.D.La.1980); Estrada v. Jaques, 321 S.E.2d 240 (N.C.App. 1984). See Mary Anne Bobinski, "Autonomy and Privacy: Protecting Patients From Their Physicians," 55 Pitt.L.Rev. 291 (1994).

80. See e.g., Anne T. Corrigan, A Paper Tiger: Lawsuits Against Doctors For Non–Disclosure of Economic Interests in Patients' Cells, Tissues and Organs, 42 Case W.Res. L.Rev. 565 (1992).

81. Restatement (Second) of Torts § 652A (1977). Melanie Williams Havens, The Spleen That Fought Back, 20 The Brief 11, 40 (1990).

82. 321 S.E.2d 240 (N.C.App.1984).

strengthen the rationale for uniform disclosure."[83] The questions raised by Estrada are difficult to answer. What should be disclosed to a patient about to undergo an experimental procedure? That this is the first time this team has attempted this procedure? That the literature lacks support at present for it? That the surgeons and radiologists will benefit financially or in career recognition if the procedure succeeds? Must the motivations of the team be clearly disclosed to the patient? It can be argued that the physicians' motivations should not even matter, so long as the patient and the physicians believe that the new procedure offers a better chance for the patient.[84]

Managed care opponents have argued for years that payment arrangements to physicians employed in managed care settings should be disclosed to patients. These payment arrangements include capitation, salary holdback funds, and other financial arrangements designed to affect primary care physicians in their role as gatekeepers to specialists and hospitals. The argument is that such incentives may create a conflict of interest for physicians in which they benefit economically from offering less care to their patients.[85] Federal law requires such disclosure by plans of a certain size to patients, and recent federal and state task forces have recommended that patients be informed generally about physician compensation schemes.[86]

In Neade v. Portes,[87] the plaintiff argued that the physician had breached his fiduciary duty to the decedent by failing to disclose the incentives that operating in his managed care plan. Anthony Neade suffered from a cardiac condition, showing symptoms of coronary artery blockage. He underwent a thallium stress test which Dr. Portes incorrectly interpreted as negative, but continued to have chest pain on several occasions. Dr. Porte refused to allow him to undergo an angiogram, even though two other examining physicians recommended this test and hospitalization. Neade suffered a massive myocardial infarction caused by coronary artery blockage and died.

The plaintiff noted that the contracts between the providers and the HMO provided a capitation fee and a "Medical Incentive Fund" to be used for purposes that included certain tests and referrals to medical specialists.

---

83. Id. at 255.

84. See Edmund D. Pellegrino and David C. Thomasma, A Philosophical Basis of Medical Practice 260 (1981).

85. The evidence for underutilization under managed care is equivocal at best, in spite of much editorializing by the courts. See, e.g., Pantilat, Chesney and Lo, Effect of Incentives on the Use of Indicated Services in Managed Care, 170 West.J.Med. 137 (1999)(managed care appears to produce consistent modest underutilization compared to fee-for-service scenarios, though physician underutilize services under all financial incentives and utilization review.); Hadley, Mitchell, Sulmasy, and Bloche, Perceived Financial Incentives, HMO Market Penetration, and Physicians' Practice Styles and Satisfaction, 34 Health Services Research 1(1999)(general concern that use of financial incentives to influence physician use of resources may have negative effect, but more research is needed before firm conclusions can be drawn). Referral patterns are affected by the form of plan reimbursement and physician compensation. Whether that is bad is another question, since the very purpose of such incentives is to reduce the level of unnecessary health care. See generally Alan L. Hillman, Mark V. Pauly, and J.J. Kerstein, How Do Financial Incentives Affect Physicians, Clinical Decisions and the Financial Performance of Health Maintenance Organizations? 321 N.E.J.M. 86(1989).

86. See 42 CFR 417.479(1996) generally. Advisory Committee on Consumer Protection and Quality in the Health Care Industry, Consumer Bill of Rights and Responsibilities Report to the President of the United States (1997); State of California Managed Health Care Improvement Task Force, Improving Managed Health Care in California: Findings and Recommendations (1998).

87. 237 Ill.Dec. 788, 710 N.E.2d 418 (Ill. App.1999),

Money left in the fund at the end of the 12–month contract period would be split 60–40 between defendants and Chicago HMO. She argued that a fiduciary relationship existed between Dr. Portes and Neade pursuant to which Dr. Portes had a duty to act in good faith and in the best interest of Neade. This duty was breached by his refusal to authorize further testing of Neade, refusing to allow specialists to examine Neade, failing to disclose to Neade defendants' financial relationship with Chicago HMO, including the Medical Incentive Fund, and entering into a contract with Chicago HMO which put defendants' financial well-being in direct conflict with Neade's physical well-being. Plaintiff argued that had she known of Dr. Portes's financial interest in refusing to authorize additional treatment for decedent, she would have sought a second opinion.

The court noted the integration of care in the managed care setting, making physicians both care givers and cost managers. As gatekeepers, physicians decide on further tests, referrals and hospitalization. And they are paid a bonus for controlling referrals, arguably creating an incentive to limit use of services. The court cited Moore for the proposition that a physician has a fiduciary relationship to his patient and an action lies for breach of that duty to disclose material facts. It noted other cases that had rejected such a claim against a physician.[88] The court however concluded that a claim for breach of a fiduciary duty may be pleaded separate from a malpractice claim, drawing support from statutory prohibitions against self referral[89], American Medical Association opinions[90] and cases for breach of duty against attorneys.

The court found that a breach-of-fiduciary-duty claim could proceed against the physician. He had refused further testing, access to specialists, had failed to disclose incentives not to treat ad the conflict of interest that resulted.

In so holding, we do not intend to open the floodgates of litigation, and we caution that not every claim for medical negligence will also set forth a claim for breach of fiduciary duty. In this case, however, we find that plaintiff's claim for breach of fiduciary duty is not duplicative of her medical

88. D.A.B. v. Brown, 570 N.W.2d 168, 169 (Minn.App.1997); Spoor v. Serota, 852 P.2d 1292 (Colo.App.1992); Awai v. Kotin, 872 P.2d 1332 (Colo.App.1993) (claim for breach of fiduciary duty against psychologist properly dismissed as duplicative of negligence claim); Garcia v. Coffman, 946 P.2d 216 (N.M.App. 1997)(claim that chiropractor designed treatment programs to generate income was not claim separate from fraud claim); Hales v. Pittman, 576 P.2d 493 (1978)(no breach of trust claim where malpractice claim provides adequate remedy).

89. Health Care Worker Self–Referral Act (225 ILCS 47/1 et seq. (West 1996))(prohibits a health care worker from referring a patient for health services to an entity in which he is an investor and in which he does not provide direct services, unless the health care worker discloses his investment interest to the patient. 225 ILCS 47/20(b)(7) (West 1996).

90. Current Opinions of the Council on Ethical and Judicial Affairs of the American Medical Association (Current Opinions) (1996–1997 edition). Section 8.132 of Current Opinions provides:

"Physicians must not deny their patients access to appropriate medical services based upon the promise of personal financial reward, or the avoidance of financial penalties. Because patients must have the necessary information to make informed decisions about their care, physicians have an obligation to assure the disclosure of medically appropriate treatment alternatives, regardless of cost.

Physicians must assure disclosure of any financial inducements that may tend to limit the diagnostic and therapeutic alternatives that are offered to patients or that may tend to limit patients' overall access to care. Physicians may satisfy this obligation by assuring that the managed care plan makes adequate disclosure to patients enrolled in the plan." (Emphasis added.) Current Opinions, § 8.132 (1996–97).

negligence claim. It is conceivable that a trier of fact could find both that Dr. Portes was within the standard of care and therefore not negligent in relying on the thallium stress test and the EKG in deciding that an angiogram was not necessary and also that Dr. Portes did breach his fiduciary duty in not disclosing his financial incentive arrangement and, as a proximate result thereof, Neade did not obtain a second opinion, suffered a massive coronary infarction, and died.

Such a cause of action raises challenging problems for the practice of medicine. If a health plan uses a complex mix of salary-holdbacks, feedback, and bonuses, how much information should a patient be told? How much does a patient want to know? Information about such complex payment systems would be better disclosed at the time a subscriber selects his or her managed care plan, rather than making it part of informed consent discussions at the time of treatment.[91] Even the most sophisticated patient would have difficulty in assessing the effect on her physician's behavior of different modes of payment and bonuses, and it adds a complicated layer to discussions about the risks of medical procedures. Physicians can however be trained to better communicate some of these issues of incentives and restrictions on tests and referrals.[92]

§ 6–12. Statutory Duties of Disclosure

a. Advance Directives

The Patient Self–Determination Act became law as part of the Omnibus Budget Reconciliation Act of 1990, and applies to hospitals, skilled nursing facilities, home health agencies, hospice programs, and HMOs with Medicare or Medicaid funding. It requires each facility covered by the act to provide each patient with written information pertaining to:

> (i) an individual's rights under State law (whether statutory or as recognized by the courts of the State) to make decisions concerning * * * medical care, including the right to accept or refuse medical or surgical treatment and the right to formulate advance directives * * * and
>
> (ii) the written policies of the provider or organization respecting the implementation of such rights.[1]

Institutions must document in each patient's record whether the patient signed an advance directive, assure that the state law is followed in the institution, and provide for education of both the staff and the public concerning living wills and durable powers of attorney.[2]

b. COBRA Anti–Dumping Disclosures

Hospitals have disclosure obligations imposed by the COBRA patient anti-dumping act of 1985.[3] The act, aimed to protect patients against transfer from

91. See William M. Sage, Physicians As Advocates, 35 Houston L.Rev.1529 (1999)

92. Wendy Levinson et al., Resolving Disagreements in the Patient–Physician Relationship: Tools for Improving Communication in Managed Care, 282 J.A.M.A. 1477 (1999).

§ 6–12

1. 42 U.S.C.A. § 1395cc (a)(1), (f)(1)(A) (West 1993).

2. Susan M. Wolf et al., "Special Report—Sources of Concern About the Patient Self-Determination Act," 325 New Eng.J.Med. 1666 (1991).

3. 42 U.S.C.A. §§ 1395cc (a)(1)(I), (N),

a hospital for financial reasons, or "dumping", requires that transfers be discussed with the patient and agreed to prior to any transfer. The disclosure requirements are triggered when a hospital seeks to transfer a patient whose emergency medical condition has not stabilized. The hospital may not transfer unless " * * * the individual * * * after being informed of the hospital's obligation under this section and the risk of transfer, in writing requests, transfer to another medical facility * * * "[4]

c. *Other Mandated Disclosures*

Many states by statute have mandated disclosure of specific risks. Iowa and Georgia for example require that the physician disclose the known risks of death, brain damage, quadriplegia, paraplegia, loss of organ function, disfiguring scars.[5] Pennsylvania requires that a woman who is being treated for breast cancer must be informed of "medically accepted alternatives to radical mastectomy."[6] Most state statutes simply impose a physician-based standard of disclosure, without specifically enumerating what kinds of risks must be disclosed.[7] In all states where statutes define the scope of disclosure, disclosure of the required risks satisfies informed consent requirements. Compliance has been held in Texas, for example, to create a presumption of proper disclosure, which can be rebutted only by showing invalidity of the consent form (a forged signature), or lack of capacity.[8]

§ 6–13. Negligent Misrepresentation

If a physician manipulates the disclosure process to get a patient to undertake a procedure, some jurisdictions have allowed an action for negligent misrepresentation.[1] The tort of negligent misrepresentation provides a remedy for false information negligently given a person who relies to his detriment thereon, as specified in section 311 of the Restatement (Second) of Torts:

> (1) One who negligently gives false information to another is subject to liability for physical harm caused by action taken by the other in reasonable reliance upon such information, where such harm results (a) to the other, or (b) to such third persons as the actor should expect to be put in peril by the action taken.

> (2) Such negligence may consist of failure to exercise reasonable care (a) in ascertaining the accuracy of the information, or (b) in the manner in which it is communicated.[2]

1395dd . For discussions of the operation of EMTALA, and its impact on emergency medicine, see Chapter 10.

4. 42 U.S.C.A. § 1395dd(c)(1)(A)(I).

5. Iowa Code Ann. § 147.137 ; see also Official Code Ga. Ann. § 31–9–6.1 setting forth a specific list of medical procedures.

6. 35 Penn. Stat. 5641.

7. See e.g., Ala. Code § 6–5–484.

8. Earle v. Ratliff, 998 S.W.2d 882 (Tex. 1999)

§ 6–13

1. Bloskas v. Murray, 646 P.2d 907 (Colo.1982)(Colorado Supreme Court recognized a separate action for negligent misrepresentation in a malpractice suit, based in a physician's failure to disclose critical information to a patient. The physician had reassured the patient and his wife that his fear about amputation following an ankle replacement procedure was unfounded. The court found that the negligent misrepresentation count was not subsumed under the informed consent theory.

2. Restatements (Second) of Torts § 311.

Comment a indicates that the action is suited to situations where "it is part of the actor's business or profession to give information upon which the safety of the recipient or a third person depends."[3] The action is typically recognized in business transactions involving money losses.[4] It may also apply to the physician-patient relationship. Since patients rely on the assurances of their physicians, they may be influenced by statements that are outside the scope of the physician's duty to disclose under informed consent principles. A physician's representations that he had more experience than was in fact the case, or his assurance that a patient's worries about a particular risk were unfounded, would be enough.

§ 6–14.　Causation and Damage Complexities

Causation is established in an informed consent case if the plaintiff can prove a link between the failure of a doctor to disclose and the patient's injury—first that the risk not disclosed in fact materialized, and second that a patient would have declined treatment if he had received full information about that risk.[1] Two tests of causation have emerged: the objective reasonable patient test and the subjective particular patient test. The former asks what a reasonable patient would have done. The latter asks what the particular patient would have done.

The majority of American jurisdictions have adopted the objective test of causality, because of their apparent discomfort with the risks of plaintiff self-serving testimony.[2] Courts are concerned with a patient's hindsight testimony that he or she would have foregone the treatment, testimony which the court feared would be " * * * hardly * * * more than a guess, perhaps tinged by the circumstance that the uncommunicated hazard has in fact materialized."[3] The fear is of self-serving testimony. As Judge Robinson wrote in *Canterbury*, "It places the physician in jeopardy of the patient's hindsight and bitterness."[4] While the patient's testimony is admissible, it is not dispositive, and will be evaluated by the trier of fact for its reasonableness. Most courts consider such testimony to be helpful to the trier of fact.[5]

The objective test requires that the risk must be "material" to a reasonable patient in the shoes of the plaintiff. Under this standard, a patient's testimony is not needed to get the issue of causation to the jury. The testimony may be admissible and relevant on causation, but is not dispositive.

3. Restatement (Second) of Torts § 311 comment a.

4. Fitzgerald v. Edelen, 623 P.2d 418 (Colo. App.1980).

§ 6–14

1. Pennsylvania does not require proof that a causal relationship exists between the physician's failure to disclose and the patient's consent, allowing recovery regardless of causation. It is the only state that continues to base informed consent causes of action on battery, but with limited application to surgical and other invasive procedures. See Boutte v. Seitchik, 719 A.2d 319 (Pa.Super.1998).

2. See e.g., Backlund v. University of Washington, 975 P.2d 950, 956 (Wash.1999); Cunningham v. United States, 683 F.2d 847 (4th Cir.1982); Otwell v. Bryant, 497 So.2d 111 (Ala.1986); Hartke v. McKelway, 707 F.2d 1544 (D.C.Cir.1983), cert. denied 464 U.S. 983, 104 S.Ct. 425, 78 L.Ed.2d 360 (1983).

See generally Fay A. Rozovsky, Consent to Treatment 78–80 (§ 1.15.4, "Causation in Negligent Consent") (1990); Arnold J. Rosoff, Informed Consent: A Guide for Health Care Providers 151–153 (1981).

3. Canterbury v. Spence, 464 F.2d 772, 790 (D.C.Cir.1972).

4. Id. at 790.

5. Phelps v. Dempsey, 656 So.2d 377 (Ala. 1995).

The jury can decide without it "what a reasonable person in that position would have done."[6] The objective test asks the jury to put themselves in the place of a reasonable person, rather than the particular person. Factors to be considered include the medical condition and age of the patient and risk factors involved in the treatment and alternatives.[7] A jury is unlikely to find causation in these cases, unless (1) the doctor was clearly negligent, so no reasonable person would have agreed to the treatment; (2) the doctor offered an experimental procedure which a person might refuse in spite of the doctor's urgings; (3) the jury ignores its instructions and applies a subjective standard.[8]

One jurisdiction has adopted a "modified objective standard", asking the trier of fact to adopt the viewpoint of the actual patient acting rationally and reasonably, in deciding what is significant to the patient's decision.[9]

A few jurisdictions have adopted the subjective causation test, arguing that such a test better reflects the right of each patient to make a risk assessment before treatment.[10] The jury in most tort cases is asked to put themselves in the shoes of a particular plaintiff, particularly as to pain and suffering awards. In that sense, judicial rejection of the particular patient test seems unreasonable. However, it can be argued that a jury's empathetic attempt to understand the plaintiff's pain in a personal injury case is quite different from the jury's collective attempt to second guess the plaintiff's decision whether or not to undergo the diagnosis or treatment proposed by the doctor. European courts, perhaps because the judges are the trier of fact in most civil cases, are more protective of patient autonomy. The German Federal Supreme Court has adopted a subjective test of causality, for example, with a heavy burden on the physician to show that the particular patient would have undergone the procedure even with information, "lest the right of the patient to receive proper disclosure is being undermined."[11]

Damages in an informed consent case are usually straightforward: if the court finds that a physician has breached his duty to disclose a risk which a reasonable practitioner would have disclosed to a patient (or a reasonable patient would have found material), and further concludes that the operation would not have taken place if the risk had been disclosed, then if the risk materializes and the patient suffers harm, the physician is liable for resulting damages.

§ 6–15. Exceptions to a Duty to Disclose

a. Emergencies

The common law has long recognized the right of a doctor in a true emergency to act without patient consent, so long as he acts in conformity with customary practice in such emergencies.[1] Where the patient is uncon-

6. See Gouse v. Cassel, 615 A.2d 331, 333 (Pa.1992).

7. Backlund v. University of Washington, 975 P.2d 950, 958 (Wash.1999)

8. See Steele v. St. Paul Fire & Marine Ins., 371 So.2d 843 (La.App.1979), cert. denied 374 So.2d 658 (La.1979).

9. Bernard v. Char, 903 P.2d 667 (Hawai'i 1995).

10. See e.g., Leyson v. Steuermann, 705 P.2d 37 (Hawai'i App.1985).

11. See Dieter Giesen, International Medical Malpractice Law (1988) at p. 349, citing to BGH, 7 Feb. 1984 (VI ZR 174/82).

§ 6–15

1. Jackovach v. Yocom, 237 N.W. 444 (Iowa 1931). It continues to be treated as axiomatic in cases such as Wright v. Johns Hopkins

scious and treatment is needed promptly, courts agree that informed consent can be dispensed with. Some courts hold that consent is implied or presumed in these situations. What constitutes an emergency situation is often unclear, but the courts tend to err on the side of permitting emergency treatment without formal consent. Patient disorientation from trauma or medication may be sufficient to render him incompetent to consent.[2] Other courts, however, have held that the emergency-treatment exception cannot be allowed to override the refusal of treatment by a patient who is capable of providing consent. Consent must be obtained even if the physician is persuaded that the patient's life is threatened. In the often chaotic setting of emergency rooms, medical staff may not be able to obtain the consent of a family member. But when a competent patient refuses to consent, treatment may not be forced on the patient.[3]

b. Implied Consent

Where the patient has consented to a procedure to remedy his condition, he is presumed to have consented to all steps necessary to correct it, even though the procedure used varies from that specifically authorized.[4] However, if the alternative procedure is part of the repertoire of treatment for the patient's illness, then it would seem that the doctor should advise the patient of the possibility of this procedure as well as the intended one. If the doctor extends a surgical procedure in order to remedy a problem discovered during the operation, a court may apply the "extension doctrine"[5] to dispense with the patient's consent to the additional procedure. Today it is more likely that a court will demand that a physician discuss the possibility of an extension of the operation where it might be anticipated. Nor will the correction of a minor problem be justified by this doctrine.[6] The emergency doctrine can then protect physicians in rare situations where a true problem is found during surgery.

c. Patient Waivers

Suppose a patient, trusting his doctor to do the best for him, says, "I don't want to know a thing, Doctor, just do what you think is best". Should the doctor be able to use this as a defense? It appears that the patient is exercising self-determination in choosing a veil of ignorance.[7] Patients may under some circumstances want to waive their right to receive medical information. They may simply want to trust the physician to do what is best; they may be intimidated by the medical environment or lack confidence in their own ability to process risk information. Some have argued that a patient's waiver should not be readily granted, and that patients should be

Health Systems Corporation, 728 A.2d 166 (Md.C.A.1999).

2. See e.g., King v. Our Lady of the Lake Regional Med. Center, 623 So.2d 139 (La.App. 1993) (patient's sister properly signed release, given her brother's disorientation prior to gallbladder surgery.)

3. Shine v. Vega, 709 N.E.2d 58, 64–65 (Sup.Jud.Ct.Mass.1999)

4. Kennedy v. Parrott, 90 S.E.2d 754 (N.C. 1956).

5. See Arnold J. Rosoff, Consent to Medical Treatment, § 17.05[2], p. 17–47 in Treatise on Health Care Law (Michael G. MacDonald et al. Eds., Vol. III, 1992).

6. See e.g., Lloyd v. Kull, 329 F.2d 168 (7th Cir.1964).

7. See e.g., Henderson v. Milobsky, 595 F.2d 654 (D.C.Cir.1978). Alan Meisel, The "Exceptions" to the Informed Consent Doctrine: Striking a Balance Between Competing Values in Medical Decisionmaking, 1979 Wis. L. Rev. 413, 453–60.

forced to converse about risks for their own therapeutic benefit.[8] Legally, however, patients may waive their right to give an "informed" consent, either by statute[9] or by judicial ruling.[10] Such a waiver must be made freely and with full information, making it difficult in operation to determine how much the patient must know before disclosure stops. Some hospitals have tried a two part form in which the patient can explicitly decline further information from the provider, after the first step—basic explanation of the procedure—was disclosed. This two-step process, favored by some commentators,[11] has a basic problem: it shifts the burden onto the patient to ask, and asks the patient to trust that the doctor has performed the cost-benefit calculation as a proxy for the patient. While doctors must be agents for patients in assessing the merits of medical procedures, given the kind of background knowledge needed to practice medicine, such a waiver process reinforces attitudes of medical paternalism and annoyance at the time spent giving information. As a result, such a two-step process, while it may satisfy some courts, does not comport with the spirit of informed consent.

d. Blanket Authorizations

Consent forms are often written with overbroad language, either authorizing whatever treatment is necessary for the patient's condition, or stating that all risks have been explained to the patient. Since the purpose of informed disclosure is to specifically inform patients of risks and get their knowledgeable consent, courts have been understandably unwilling to read such clauses broadly.[12] Broad consent language in a form has evidentiary value, but a patient may claim that the oral disclosure was inadequate to inform,[13] or that the patient's delegation to the physician was ambiguous, not including the full scope of the procedure.[14]

e. Therapeutic Privilege

The therapeutic privilege allows a physician to withhold information from a patient when the patient may suffer damage.[15] The underlying concern is that patients may be upset by disclosure of unpleasant information, and thereby rendered unable to make a rational treatment decision, or they may even suffer psychological damage.[16] Such risk disclosure should be avoided

8. See e.g., Mark Strasser, Mill and the Right to Remain Uninformed, 11 J. Med. & Philosophy 265 (1986); contra, see David E. Ost, The "Right" Not to Know, 9 J. Med. & Philosophy 301, 306–07 (1984).

9. See e.g., Alaska Stat. § 09.55.556(b)(2) (Supp. 1989).

10. See Stover v. Association of Thoracic and Cardiovascular Surgeons, 635 A.2d 1047, 1055 (Pa.Super.1993) ("Once the physician has disclosed the risks and alternatives attendant to a surgical procedure, the patient is perfectly free to relinquish her right to make a choice. That course of action in itself constitutes her choice."). In Arato v. Avedon, 23 Cal.Rptr.2d 131, 858 P.2d 598 (Cal.1993), the court noted that the plaintiff "studiously avoided confronting these ultimate issues", i.e., his statistical life expectancy; the physicians therefore assumed that he did not want further informa-

tion. The defenses of waiver and therapeutic privilege overlap in this case, in which the California Supreme Court refused as a matter of law to mandate a disclosure as to life expectancy.

11. See Paul S. Appelbaum et al., Legal Theory and Clinical Practice 183 (1987); Arnold J. Rosoff, Informed Consent: A Guide for Health Care Providers 294 (1981). See also Oregon's informed consent statute, Or. Rev. Stat. § 677.097(2) (Supp. 1990).

12. Wells v. Van Nort, 125 N.E. 910 (Ohio 1919).

13. See e.g., Bourgeois v. McDonald, 622 So.2d 684 (La.App.1993).

14. Cross v. Trapp, 294 S.E.2d 446 (W.Va. 1982).

15. Canterbury, 464 F.2d at 789.

16. Canterbury, 464 F.2d at 789.

when it would be "menacing" to the patient.[17] Thus a physician, for example concerned that a patient with hypertension could be further injured by a discussion of a frightening litany of risks, could invoke the privilege to say nothing.[18]

Given physician unhappiness with requirements of disclosure generally, the therapeutic privilege exception threatens in theory to swallow the informed consent doctrine whole. In analyzing risks to be disclosed, some courts have talked of the need to avoid scaring a patient away from a "needed" procedure, recognizing the effect of disclosure of risks on the patient's choices, which might be contrary to the physician's desire to treat.[19] Little evidence can be found to support this hypothesis that patients can be harmed by the disclosure of risks, although certainly they might be made anxious.[20] Critics have strongly criticized the exception,[21] but physicians continue to maintain that they need the privilege to protect patients from themselves.[22] The privilege is rarely invoked to dismiss a case, although often mentioned in dicta, but many state statutes incorporate the privilege.

f. Contributory Negligence

It is arguable that a plaintiff might be contributorily negligent in some circumstances in discussing a medical problem with a physician, for example by giving the physician inaccurate information. This could be a defense to an informed consent action. In Brown v. Dibbell,[23] the court held that a patient is expected to exercise ordinary care, and must therefore "tell the true and give complete and accurate information about personal, family and medical histories to a doctor to the extent possible in response to the doctor's requests for information".[24] It does not mean that the patient must go further and independently seek information about the diagnosis or treatment. A patient is entitled to trust her physician and to assume that the information disclosed is accurate.

§ 6–16. Institutional Consent Forms

Consent forms are universally used in health care institutions, where most health care is provided. Hospitals use them at several points in a patient's progress through the institution—upon admission, when a generic form is signed; and before surgery or anesthesia, when more detailed forms may be offered. These forms operate as a legal surrogate for consent, sometimes memorializing an actual physician-patient discussion, sometimes acting simply as a fiction. The courts have had little to say about consent forms. A

17. Id.

18. See e.g., Nishi v. Hartwell, 473 P.2d 116 (Hawai'i 1970).

19. Pedersen v. Vahidy, 552 A.2d 419 (Conn.1989).

20. See 1 President's Comm'n for the Study of Ethical Problems in Medicine & Biomedical & Behavioral Research, Making Health Care Decisions 99–102 (1982).

21. Margaret Somerville, Therapeutic Privilege: Variation on the Theme of Informed Consent, 12 Law, Med. & Health Care 4 (1984). See also Elizabeth G. Patterson, The Therapeutic Justification for Withholding Medical Information: What You Don't Know Can't Hurt You, or Can It?, 64 Neb. L. Rev. 721 (1985).

22. See Arnold J. Rosoff's study in Informed Consent: A Guide for Health Care Providers at 313, 346. Rosoff surveyed 800 physicians nationally by mail, asking "Have you ever seen a patient's therapy seriously hindered by his anxiety upon learning sensitive information concerning his case and/or treatment?" 72% responded affirmatively.

23. 595 N.W.2d 358 (Wis.1999).

24. Id. at 368.

consent form, or other written documentation of the patient's verbal consent, is treated in many states as presumptively valid consent to the treatment at issue, with the burden on the patient to rebut the presumption.[1]

If a physician discusses treatment choices and risks with a patient but neglects to obtain the patient's written consent, he or she risks a patient argument as to the extent of risk disclosure. If the trier of fact finds that a reasonable person in the patient's position would not have declined the procedure, then the causal relationship between the failure and the patient's harm is not proven.[2]

The majority view is that the hospital has no duty to obtain a patient's consent to surgery, nor to conduct any kind of inquiry into the quality of the plaintiff's consent.[3] In *Petriello v. Kalman*[4], the Connecticut Supreme Court held that a hospital had no duty to obtain a patient's consent to surgery, nor to conduct any kind of inquiry. The plaintiff had suffered a miscarriage, and the treating physician scheduled the plaintiff for a dilation and curettage to remove the fetus. A hospital nurse medicated the plaintiff before the procedure, without getting the plaintiff's signature on the consent form. While this violated a hospital policy requiring completion of such forms, the court rejected any duty on the part of the hospital. Such a duty is resisted by the courts on the grounds that the responsibility belongs to the attending physician: "This contention is unsound, however, because it equates the signing of the form with the actuality of informed consent, which it is the sole responsibility of the attending physician to obtain."[5] Even the adoption of a hospital regulation that physicians must obtain informed consent is not sufficient to shift the burden of obtaining such consent from the physician to the institution.[6]

A duty on the hospital and its staff to ensure that patient consent is properly obtained by attending physicians has been found only in special circumstances.[7] Institutional responsibility to ensure that a patient's informed consent is obtained exist only in two limited areas: documentation of patient consent for the record and experimental therapies. If a nurse fails to obtain a properly executed consent form and make it part of the patient record, the hospital may be liable for this failure as a violation of its own internal procedures.[8] If a hospital participates in a study of an experimental procedure, it must ensure that the patient is properly informed of the risks of the procedure.[9] A clinic owned and operated by physicians is distinguishable from

§ 6–16

1. See West's Fla. Stat. Ann. § 766.103(4); Ga. Code § 88–2906.1(b)(2); Idaho Code § 39–4305.

2. Capel v. Langford, 734 So.2d 835 (La. App.1999).

3. See e.g., Winters v. Podzamsky, 190 Ill. Dec. 203, 621 N.E.2d 72, 76 (Ill.App.1993) ("[t]he hospital fulfills its obligations to the patient by requiring the signed consent form before allowing surgery to be performed * * *. Any inadequacy of the physician's explanation cannot be imputed to the hospital.").

4. 576 A.2d 474 (Conn.1990).

5. Petriello, 576 A.2d at 478. See also Johnson v. Sears, Roebuck & Co., 832 P.2d 797, 799 (N.M.App.1992).

6. Kelly v. Methodist Hospital, 664 A.2d 148 (Pa.Super.1995).

7. Brownfield v. Daniel Freeman Marina Hosp., 256 Cal.Rptr. 240 (Cal.App.1989) (rape victim not told about morning-after pill for contraception).

8. See, e.g., Butler v. South Fulton Medical Center, Inc., 452 S.E.2d 768, 772 (Ga.App.1994).

9. Kus v. Sherman Hospital, 644 N.E.2d 1214 (Ill.App.1995)(intraocular lens implantations); Friter v. Iolab Corp., 607 A.2d

a hospital, and may be liable for a physician's failure to disclose complications of a procedure to a patient.[10] When a physician uses a device or drug for "off-label" uses on a patient not part of a research trial, the hospital has no duty to inform the patient of the use of the device or drug.[11]

Imposing a duty on a hospital or other institutional provider to obtain informed consent is defensible on several grounds. First, the hospital will work harder to make sure that consent is properly obtained. Given the unwillingness of some physicians to pursue a patient's informed consent in the hospital setting, and the possibility that such consent will be overlooked because of scheduling or other conflicts, the hospital is the logical locus for insuring that a proper informed consent is obtained. Second, in other areas of the law, courts have been sympathetic to an expansion of the role of the hospital, and its corresponding obligations to supervise staff, to establish proper procedures, and to hire properly.[12] Third, the deference to physicians that has been part of the caselaw of hospital-physician relationships is diminishing as courts recognize that the delivery of health care is a team operation in which support is vital to the proper care of patients in the hospital.[13] Fourth, the impetus to complete written records in health care institutions for reimbursement and monitoring purposes has increased the responsibility of the institution to guarantee completeness of records. Written consent forms predominate in institutional settings, given bureaucratic pressures for a complete patient record, a desire to protect against litigation, and a sense that something is better than nothing. They are often reduced to little more than a bureaucratic formality that the institution hopes will erect a defense shield against malpractice suits.[14] Such forms can however be improved to better facilitate doctor-patient conversation and risk disclosure. The task of accomplishing this should fall upon the hospital and its administrative staff.

§ 6–17. Limits on Consent Doctrine

a. *Patient Decisionmaking Limitations*

The courts have struggled to articulate general principles to guide physicians in obtaining patients' informed consent, while researchers have uncovered a spectrum of practical difficulties in obtaining that consent. First, patients often have trouble understanding what they are told, or remembering it. It has been suggested that doctors " * * * test the patients' comprehension of that information * * *."[1] One might even require that the patient pass a

1111(Pa.Super.1992)(same). Contra, see Kershaw v. Reichert, 445 N.W.2d 16 at 17 (N.D. 1989);

10. Trousdale v. City of Faith Hospital, Inc., 892 P.2d 678 (Okla.App.1995).

11. Femrite v. Abbott Northwestern Hospital, 568 N.W.2d 535 (Minn.App.1997); In re Orthopedic Bone Screw Products Liability Litigation, 1996 WL 107556 (E.D.Pa.1996)("a physician is free to use a medical device for an off-label purpose, if, in the physician's best medical judgment, he or she believes that use of the device will benefit the patient"; Klein v. Biscup, 673 N.E.2d 225 (1996).

12. See generally Chapter 7.

13. See Cathy J. Jones, Autonomy and Informed Consent in Medical Decisionmaking: Toward a New Self–Fulfilling Prophecy, 47 Wash. & Lee. L. Rev. 379, 429 (1990).

14. See Charles W. Lidz et al., Informed Consent: A Study of Decisionmaking in Psychiatry 326 (1985).

§ 6–17

1. Cathy J. Jones, Autonomy and Informed Consent in Medical Decisionmaking: Toward a New Self–Fulfilling Prophecy, 47 Wash. & Lee. L. Rev. 379, 429 (1990).

comprehension test before a procedure could be performed. Such feedback has been designed into some consent forms and research protocols.[2] But in clinical practice, as opposed to research settings, courts do not discuss the need to assess patient understanding. Courts simply presume patient comprehension in most cases, absent a showing of legal incompetence.

Second, patient decisionmaking about medical choices often appears irrational, even when information is correctly and fully presented. Patients may undervalue low probability risks because of the difficulty of thinking probabilistically. For example, teenagers may feel invulnerable to a range of harms. Patients may be anxious about treatments for irrational reasons such as fears of the knife or phobic feelings about diseases such as cancer.

Third, patients may have a bias to the near future, giving disproportionate weight to getting benefits and avoiding pain in the short term. One researcher suggests that a scale for comparing risks is needed to help patients compare the odds of a risk of a medical procedure with other life risks they regularly face in driving or flying.[3]

Fourth, patients may refuse treatment because of a belief structure that does not make sense, for reasons that may be socially acceptable (religious belief) or not (depression).[4] While occasionally such patients may be incompetent and a court order can be obtained to compel treatment, such patients may also be legally competent.

Fifth, patients may react to the way choices are framed and articulated, so-called "framing effects". For example, patients told that a given procedure has an 80% survival rate will react differently from those told it has a 20% mortality rate. Patients choose surgery over radiation therapy for lung cancer when outcomes are expressed in terms of the probability of survival rather than the probability of death.[5]

b. The Nature of Physician Practice

Obtaining informed consent requires time for discussion. As physicians feel increased pressure to see more patients, particularly in the managed care setting, full disclosure and open discussion is less likely to occur. Jay Katz's model of conversation in the therapeutic context is based upon the physician-patient relation in specialty practices such as oncology. Where the physician engages in relatively few procedures, and sees a patient over several visits, it is plausible to advocate an extended conversation about detailed risks and alternatives. Such conversations can be easily recorded, videotaped or otherwise memorialized in writing, achieving both patient consent and physician protection.

The primary care setting, however, poses a severe challenge to the model of conversation. The primary care physician does more procedures to more

2. See Robert Miller and Henry S. Willner, The Two–Part Consent Form, 290 New Eng. J. Med. 964 (1974); Henry G. Grabowski et al., Increasing the Likelihood that Consent is Informed, 12 J. Applied Behav. Anal. 283 (1979).

3. See Ronald A. Howard, Microrisks for Medical Decision Analysis, 5 Intl. J. Tech. Assess. in Health Care 357 (1989) (arguing for use of a unit, the microprobability or micromort, to present risks to patients).

4. See generally Dan W. Brock and Steven A. Wartman, When Competent Patients Make Irrational Choices, 322 New Eng. J. Med. 1595 (1990).

5. Barbara J. McNeil et al., On the Elicitation of Preferences for Alternative Therapies, 306 New Eng. J. Med. 1259, 1261 (1982).

patients, spending less time with each patient. He is less likely to be fully up-to-date as to drug and treatment alternatives and side-effects, and never sure when disclosure may safely stop. Listing risks may leave out some that turn out with hindsight to have been critical to the particular patient. Discussing risks without also properly balancing the benefits and alternatives for the patient may not properly inform his decision. A full and comprehensive discussion may not be adequate if in fact the patient does not understand, even though he says he does. The task of informed consent begins to look like it can never be completed satisfactorily.[6] Brody proposes a "transparency" standard, in which " * * * the physician discloses the basis on which the proposed treatment, or alternative possible treatments, have been chosen; and (2) the patient is allowed to ask questions suggested by the disclosure of the physician's reasoning, and those questions are answered to the patient's satisfaction."[7] This relaxed standard aims to render the physician's thinking transparent to the patient, to avoid provider tendencies to present shopping lists of risks to satisfy what is perceived as the law's requirements.

c. The Utility of Communication

Any improved model of informed consent aims to preserve patient autonomy, but also to reduce the risk of a lawsuit directed at the physician. Improved conversations with patients may produce more effective care by eliciting patient cooperation and reducing unnecessary procedures, and may also reduce the risk of malpractice suits by disgruntled patients. If poor communication between physician and patient is the most common cause of malpractice suits, then any increase in physician-patient conversation, it is argued, will reduce the frequency of such suits.[8]

The law of informed consent is highly variable, and at the same time it lacks specificity as a guide to physicians. One commentator has proposed that explicit contracts between providers and patient groups might better serve the doctrine, allowing specific guidelines to be developed by agreement. This would allow the law to be tailor-made to the different settings in which risks arise, contextualizing consent.[9] Contextualization would advance the aim of cost-effectiveness and would also be desirable in its own right. Each goal seeks to improve the informed consent dialogue, and the doctrine that regulates it, by tailoring the law's requirements more carefully to the different settings in which risks arise and are discussed, assessed, and acted upon.

§ 6–18. A Comparative Perspective

An examination of the law of informed consent in other countries yields some surprises for the American lawyer. Courts in most European countries have accepted the principle that patients are entitled to information about medical treatments.[1] The British continue their paternalistic view of the

---

6. Howard Brody, Transparency: Informed Consent in Primary Care, Hastings Center Report 5, 7 (Sept/Oct 1989).

7. Id. at 7.

8. For a good discussion of the patient decision-making paradigm, see Jon F. Merz, On A Decision–Making Paradigm of Medical Informed Consent, 14 J. Leg. Medicine 231 (1993). See also Marlynn L. May and Daniel B.

Stengel, Who Sues Their Doctors? How Patients Handle Medical Grievances, 24 Law & Soc. Rev. 105 (1990).

9. Peter H. Schuck, Rethinking Informed Consent, 103 Yale L.J. 899, 906 (1994).

§ 6–18

1. For a detailed account of informed consent on a comparative basis, see Dieter Giesen,

doctor-patient relationship, while Australia has moved toward a more patient-centered test for disclosure. The British, in Sidaway v. Bethlem Royal Hospital Governors,.[2] applied the reasonable physician standard of disclosure. The plaintiff had persistent pain in the shoulders and neck. Her surgeon advised an operation on her spinal column, failing to inform her of the 1% chance of spinal cord damage that could cause great pain and paralysis. The majority ruled that the test in England for a physician's duty to disclose the risks of treatment is the same as that applicable to diagnosis and treatment: accepted medical practice, as established by the physician's peers. Deference to the medical profession is a judicial recognition of the importance of upholding the power of the English medical profession. In a country where limited resources are committed to the National Health Service, commentators have argued that this approach to informed consent keeps patients uninformed and therefore undemanding. This conserves medical resources, since patients will not be familiar with alternative expensive treatment options.[3]

The view of the Australian High Court in *Rogers v. Whitaker*[4] is more liberal than that of *Sidaway*. Both courts began with the *Bolam* principle, which states that a doctor is not liable "if he acts in accordance with a practice accepted at the time as proper by a responsible body of medical opinion"—in other words, a "reasonable practitioner" test of medical disclosure.[5] However, the High Court noted that Australian courts have rejected the *Bolam* test, holding instead that medical practice is only a guide for the court. The Court distinguished between the duty of a physician to diagnose and treat, and the duty to provide information to patients.

> The law should recognize that a doctor has a duty to warn a patient of a material risk inherent in the proposed treatment; a risk is material if, in the circumstances of the particular case, a reasonable person in the patient's position, if warned of the risk, would be likely to attach significance to it or if the medical practitioner is or should reasonably be aware that the particular patient, if warned of the risk, would be likely to attach significance to it.[6]

The patient in *Rogers* asked about the risk of loss of sight in her good eye, as the result of a surgical procedure on her bad eye. Even though the risk that developed—sympathetic ophthalmia—only occurred once in every 14,000 procedures, it was a material risk to the patient.

§ 6–19. Conclusion

Informed consent is valuable to the plaintiff's lawyer for a simple reason: it may allow her to win a tough case without expert medical testimony that the defendant erred in treating or diagnosing. If an informed consent claim is allowed, the defendant may be liable for all injurious consequences of specific

International Medical Malpractice Law 252–406 (§§ 20–31) (1988).

2. 1 All ER 643 check (H.L. 1985).

3. See Frances H. Miller, Informed Consent for the Man on the Clapham Omnibus: An English Cure for the "American Disease"?, 9 W. New Eng. L. Rev. 169 (1987); Robert Schwartz and Andrew Grubb, Why Britain Can't Afford Informed Consent, 16 Hastings Center Report 22 (1986).

4. ALJR 47 (High Court of Australia 1992).

5. Bolam v. Friern Hosp. Management Committee, 1 W.L.R. 582 (1957).

6. Id. at 11.

undisclosed risks, without the plaintiff having either to allege or prove substandard practice.[1]

The interests otherwise at stake in informed consent discussions are varied. Patients may want to be treated as coequal decisionmakers by their doctor; or they may be ambivalent, with a strong desire to yield to the doctor's professional judgment. The doctor may be most comfortable with a relationship based primarily on the patient's deference to expert judgments, or may seek genuinely to engage the patient in joint decisions. The medical institution—hospital, clinic, HMO—as a bureaucracy struggling to cope with regulations, may perceive consent forms as just another burdensome record-keeping problem. Finally, when a medical accident occurs, the patient's lawyer sees in informed consent another litigation theory, another chance of recovery even though negligent diagnosis or treatment cannot be shown. In the conflict among and convergence of these interests informed consent doctrine is found.

Legal doctrine often shifts the balance of power in existing relationships. In the medical relationship, informed consent in theory moves the patient toward collaboration with the doctor in treatment. Equality in decisionmaking thus reallocates power, reducing the doctor's paternalistic grip on treatment decisions. Respect for patient autonomy is a normative goal in its own right. The doctrine has been valuable for the norm it upholds—the goal of personal autonomy, the protection of individual choice in the widest possible range of situations.[2] The deference that others extend to a patient's decisions, even when they appear irrational, preserves individual autonomy, which has meaning only when respected by others. This model leads into complicated ethical issues, but it remains a baseline for evaluating the way doctors approach patients.[3]

Evidence to prove a strong effect on medical behavior is lacking at present, but some studies support a mild trend toward more open medical disclosure, including disclosure of bad prognoses.[4] A 1961 survey found that 90% of physicians preferred not to tell patients of a cancer diagnosis.[5] Fifteen years later 97% of doctors said they routinely disclosed cancer diagnoses.[6]

§ 6–19

1. See Harnish v. Children's Hosp. Medical Center, 439 N.E.2d 240 (Mass.1982).

2. Professor Alexander Capron argues that informed consent serves six salutary functions. It can:

    1) protect individual autonomy;

    2) protect the patient's status as a human being;

    3) avoid fraud or duress;

    4) encourage doctors to carefully consider their decisions;

    5) foster rational decision-making by the patient; and

    6) involve the public generally in medicine.

Alexander Capron, Informed Consent in Catastrophic Disease Research and Treatment, 123 U.Penn.L.Rev. 340, 365–76 (1974).

3. For a good discussion, see Daniel Callahan, Autonomy: A Moral Good, Not a Moral Obsession, 14 The Hastings Center Report 40 (1984); Joel Feinberg, Autonomy, Sovereignty, and Privacy: Moral Ideals in the Constitution?, 58 Notre Dame L. Rev. 445 (1983); Joel Dyer, Informed Consent and the Non-autonomous Person, 4 IRB 1 (1982).

4. See President's Commission for the Study of Ethical Problems in Medicine and Biomedical and Behavioral Research, Making Health Care Decisions 72–76 (1982).

5. Donald Oken, What to Tell Cancer Patients: A Study of Medical Attitudes, 175 JAMA 1120 (1961).

6. Dennis H. Novak et al., Changes in Physicians' Attitudes Towards Telling the Cancer Patient, 241 JAMA 897 (1979). Many of these studies have however been faulted for inadequate methodologies. See Alan Meisel and Loren Roth, Toward an Informed Discussion of Informed Consent: A Review and Critique of

Informed consent doctrine has focused on the scope of disclosure: low-percentage risks, treatment alternatives, and so on. These elements of disclosure are important, but more important is the comprehension of the patient. While the fact that a litany of risks was disclosed is easy to establish as an evidentiary matter at trial, it is much harder to evaluate true communication from a judicial perspective. Informed consent doctrine as applied in tort cases can only take us so far in promoting physician-patient communication.

C. REFORMING THE TORT SYSTEM FOR MEDICAL INJURIES

As medical practice has become more dependent upon technologies such as surgery, drugs, and diagnostic tools, litigation against health care providers has increased. After World War II, as malpractice insurance coverage became increasingly expensive, the frequency of claims against physicians and hospitals came to be viewed as a source of medical cost inflation. In the 1960s the Federal government began to take on responsibility for financing health care through the Medicare and Medicaid programs, and quality of care and cost issues raised by malpractice became national concerns. By the 1970s, malpractice had become visible. The magnitude of the increase in litigation is illustrated by the fact that 80% of the malpractice suits filed between 1935 and 1975 were filed in the last five years of that forty year period.

§ 6–20. The Sources of the Malpractice "Crisis"

Increases in malpractice litigation in the United States over the past four decades have been attributed to several factors.[1] First, the increase was related to higher levels of medical treatment, paid for in large part by the new Medicare and Medicaid programs of the 1960s. Increasing access to health care increases the number of people who might suffer iatrogenic injuries— more encounters, more negligent injuries.[2] The hazards of complex health care are substantial. As the Harvard Medical Practice study discovered in surveying medical injuries in New York hospitals, approximately one percent of all hospital patients suffer injury due to negligently provided care.[3]

Second, medical technologies of diagnosis and treatment increased the complexity of medical treatment, and the side effects of potent new instrumentalities such as drugs increased patient injury along with benefits.[4] Providers had more opportunity to make mistakes as a side effect of managing the complexity of modern health care. Technological innovations involve a

the Empirical Studies, 25 Ariz. L. Rev. 265, 340 (1983).

§ 6–20

1. The problem is not uniquely American, even if the overall level of litigation in the U.S. is higher than other countries. Canada has experienced an increased growth rate in frequency of claims between 1971 and 1990. See Donald N. Dewees, Michael J. Trebilcock, and Peter C. Coyle, The Medical Malpractice Crisis: A Comparative Empirical Perspective, 54 Law & Contemp. Prob. 217, 218 (1991).

2. Michael Saks, Do We Really Know Anything About the Behavior of the Tort Litigation System—and Why Not? 140 U.Penn. L.Rev. 1147, 1181 at n. 95 (1992).

3. Harvard Medical Practice Study, Patients, Doctors, and Lawyers: Medical Injury, Malpractice Litigation, and Patient Compensation in New York, Exec.Summ. 3–4 (1990) (hereafter Harvard Study).

4. Dep't of Health, Educ. & Welfare, Report of the Secretary's Commission on Medical Malpractice (Gov't Printing Office 1973).

learning curve—the rate of maloccurrence will be higher early in the introduction of a new medical device, drug, or technology.[5]

A third factor, some have argued, is the creation of unrealistic patient expectations. Emerging technologies of modern medicine held out the prospects of remarkable new treatments for patients. Patients, motivated by unrealistic expectations as to what physicians can deliver, sued when disappointed by their outcomes.[6] Malpractice suits from this perspective are attributable to a groundswell of consumer assertiveness and insistence on rights, driven by rising and often unrealistic expectations as to entitlements to security and well-being.[7] The malpractice crisis is thus nourished by a "litigious society", with "a flawed system" that promotes litigation.[8] Others have noted that evidence for this "litigiousness" based on consumer expectations is overblown,[9] poorly supported by research findings, and probably nonexistent.[10]

Increases in the size of jury verdicts, a verifiable phenomenon, reflect both health care cost inflation and jury disapproval of negligent physicians. Group and managed care practice, given their institutional trappings, create less sympathy for the "trusted, family physician", increasing patient willingness to sue.[11] Realistically, however, the primary reason for increases in the size of verdicts is a "combination of inflation, and increases in real income, real medical costs and life expectancy."[12]

A fourth contributor to a perception of a malpractice crisis is physician anger. Physicians are angry because malpractice litigation focuses on the errors of specific individual providers. This personalization of liability produces anger and anxiety in physicians.[13] The legal system has become the lightning rod for changes physicians find unwelcome.[14] Recent empirical evidence has cast doubt on many of the assumptions of critics of the tort system.[15]

5. Mark Shroder and Burton A. Weisbrod, Medical Malpractice, Technological Change, and Learning–by–Doing, II Advances in Health Economics and Health Services Research 185 (1990) (Eds. Richard M. Schiffler, Louis F. Roniter).

6. The 1973 Commission on Medical Malpractice, after describing the forces that led to more patient injury, shifted the blame back to patients. See note 4, *supra*.

7. See also Lawrence Friedman, Total Justice (1985).

8. See Derek Bok, "A Flawed System", Harvard Mag. 38 (May–June 1983).

9. Mark Galanter, "Reading the Landscape of Disputes: What We Know and Don't Know (and Think We Know) About Our Allegedly Contentious and Litigious Society", 31 UCLA L.Rev. 4, 70–72 (1983); Michael Saks, In Search of the "Lawsuit Crisis", 14 L., Med. & Health Care 77 (1986).

10. Michael Saks, Do We Really Know Anything About the Behavior of the Tort Litiga-

tion System—and Why Not? 140 U.Penn. L.Rev. 1147–1289 (1992).

11. More claims are made against physicians who practice in groups. See E. Kathleen Adams and Stephen Zuckerman, Variation in the Growth and Incidence of Medical Malpractice Claims, 9 J. Health Pol., Pol'y & Law 475, 485 (1985). Patients may " * * * receive (or may feel they receive) lower quality care from group physicians is that these doctors spend less time with each individual patient." Id.

12. Mark Cooper, The Verdict Is In: Jury Awards Unchanged Over 30 Years: A Research Report by Citizen Action, at ii(Apr. 1995).

13. The American Law Institute, Reporters' Study, Enterprise Responsibility for Personal Injury, Vol. II: Approaches to Legal and Institutional Change (April 15, 1991) at 113 et seq. (hereafter ALI Study), at p. 289.

14. W. John Thomas, The Medical Malpractice "Crisis": A Critical Examination of a Public Debate, 65 Temp. L. Rev. 459 (1992).

15. See § 9–5(e), infra.

a. The Nature of the Insurance Industry

Any serious analysis of a malpractice "crisis" must begin with the insurance industry. The increase in the frequency of litigation against health care professionals and institutions coincided in the 1970s with a crisis of malpractice insurance availability. The most visible manifestation of the malpractice crisis in the 1970s and again in the 1980s was the size of increase in premiums for malpractice insurance purchased by health care professionals and institutions. Several insurance carriers dropped out of the malpractice market during the 1970s, while others raised their malpractice premiums precipitously to compensate for investment losses.[16] The insurance market shrank, rates rose, and physicians and hospitals felt the pinch. In the mid–1970s state legislatures passed a first wave of reform legislation, and new insurance entities, such as physician-owned insurance companies, were created. The malpractice problem, as measured by the rate of increase of insurance premiums, seemed to stabilize. Then in the 1980s a new round of premium increases and large visible jury verdicts reignited the debate. The insurance "crisis" thus began with a rapid escalation in the costs to physicians and health care providers generally of malpractice insurance, as well as costs to product manufacturers, municipalities, and anyone who carried liability insurance.[17]

Most health care providers buy insurance to protect themselves from medical malpractice claims.[18] Medical malpractice insurance is sold by several types of insurers—commercial insurance companies, health care provider owned companies, and joint underwriting associations. Many large hospitals self-insure for medical malpractice losses rather than purchasing insurance, and a few physicians practice without insurance.[19]

Malpractice insurance is written as either an occurrence or claims-made policy. Under an occurrence policy, the insurance company is liable for any incidents that occurred during the period the policy was in force, regardless of when the claim may be filed. A claims-made policy provides for coverage for malpractice incidents for which claims are made while the policy is in force.[20] To cover claims filed after a claims-made policy has expired, health care providers can purchase insurance known as "tail" coverage.

Medical malpractice insurance policies usually have a dollar limit on the amount that the insurance company will pay on each claim (per occurrence) and a dollar limit for all claims (in aggregate) for the policy period, which is usually one year. Insurance companies usually have minimum and maximum levels of coverage they will write which may vary depending on the risk or physician's specialty. Malpractice insurance coverage may be purchased in

---

16. See M. Hassan, How Profitable Is Medical Malpractice Insurance? 28 Inquiry 74 (1991).

17. See "The Insurance Crisis: Now Everyone is in a Risky Business", Business Week 88 (March 10, 1986).

18. U.S. General Accounting Office, Medical Malpractice: No Agreement on the Problems or Solutions 66–72 (1986). Much of the following discussion is based on the GAO report, and cross references are therefore omitted. See also Frank A. Sloan, Randall R. Bovbjerg, and Penny B. Githens, Insuring Medical Malpractice (Oxford University Press 1991).

19. Joint underwriting associations, nonprofit pooling arrangements created by state legislatures to provide medical malpractice insurance to health care providers in the states in which they are established, are an important source of coverage in some states.

20. Premiums for claims-made policies are generally lower and increase each year during the initial 5 years of the policy because the risk exposure is lower. However, usually after 5 years, the premiums mature or stabilize. Most policies now written for medical malpractice insurance are for claims-made policies.

layers, given the maximum limits of coverage companies will write for individual risks. If the health care provider desires additional coverage above the company's maximum limits, additional coverage may be purchased from one or more other insurance companies. The first layer of coverage is commonly known as basic coverage; the liability coverage above the basic level is known as excess coverage. Umbrella policies usually cover professional, personal, and premises liability in a single policy up to a specified limit. Generally, umbrella policies provide coverage when the aggregate limits of underlying policies have been exhausted.

Insurance depends on actuarially accurate predictions of both the severity of damage awards and the frequency of litigation within a distinct insurance market. Insurers set their rates at a premium level that generates funds to cover losses occurring during the period, the administrative costs of running the company, and an amount for unknown contingencies, the reserve, which may become a profit if not used. The profit may be retained as capital surplus or returned to stockholders as dividends. Ratemaking attempts to predict future claims and expenses are based on past experience. Ratemaking is very complicated, particularly in the malpractice market. First, changes in the legal and economic environment affect the number (frequency) of claims or the dollar amount (severity) of losses. Inflation increases the average severity of claims, and changes in legal theories may increase the frequency and severity of claims. Second, use of historical statistics to predict future losses is based on the law of large numbers—as the number of insured physicians and hospitals increases, actual losses will approach expected losses. The medical malpractice insurance market is small, making the statistical base for making estimates of future losses relatively small. As a result, it is difficult to set accurate premium prices. The "long tail" of malpractice insurance (the long length of time that may elapse after an injury occurs before a claim is filed and settled) is a further complicating factor because the data base used for estimating future losses may not reflect current actual losses. Many claims are filed in the second, third, or later year after treatment.

Malpractice insurance rates for physicians vary by specialty and geographic location and generally increase proportionate to the amount and complexity of surgery performed. Rates may vary from state to state and within a state. For rating purposes, insurance companies usually group physician specialties into distinct classes. Each class represents a different level of risk for the company. The number of and composition of rating classes may vary from company to company. For example, the St. Paul Company uses 8 rating classes for physicians, whereas the Medical Liability Mutual Insurance Company of New York uses 19. Rates are typically determined based on the claims experience of the rating class rather than on the experience of the individual physician. Some insurance companies assess a surcharge, in addition to the standard rate, for physicians with an unfavorable malpractice claims experience. Malpractice insurance rates for hospitals are frequently based on the malpractice loss experience (in terms of numbers of claims filed and the amount per paid claim) of the individual hospital.[21]

---

21. For example, in determining its rates, the St. Paul Company includes a factor to adjust its standard rates for the individual hospital's historical malpractice loss experi-ence. Most hospitals have sufficient claims to make risk rating credible. See Frank A. Sloan and Mahmud Hassan, Equity and Accuracy in Medical Malpractice Insurance Pricing, 9 J.

The market for malpractice insurance fails to satisfy many of the economist's conditions for an ideal insurance market. The ideal market consists of a pooling by the insurer of a large number of homogeneous but independent random events. The auto accident insurance market is perhaps closest to fulfilling this condition, since the large numbers of events involved make outcomes for the insurance pool actuarially predictable. Malpractice lacks these desirable qualities of " * * * large numbers, independence, and risk beyond the control of the insured."[22] The pool of potential policyholders is small, as is the pool of claims, and a few states have most of the claims. The awards vary tremendously, with 50% of the dollars paid out on 3% of the claims. In small insurance programs, a single multimillion dollar claim can have a tremendous effect on total losses and therefore average loss per insured doctor.

Second, losses are not independent, since neither claims against an individual doctor nor against doctors as a group are independent; multiple claims against a doctor relate usually to some characteristic of his practice or his technique, and a lawyer can use knowledge gained in one suit in another. Claims and verdicts against doctors generally reflect social forces—shifts in jury attitudes and legal doctrine. Social and legal attitudes toward medicine recently have been in flux. Given the long tail, or time from medical intervention to the filing of a claim, the impact of these shifts is increased.

Finally, the problems of moral hazard and adverse selection distort the market. Moral hazard characterizes the effect of insurance in reducing an insured's incentives to prevent losses, since he is not financially responsible for losses. Adverse selection occurs when an insurer attracts policy holders of above-average risk, ending up with higher claim costs and lower profits as a result. This may occur because a competing insurer has attracted away lower risk policyholders through the use of lower rates and selective underwriting.[23]

Another contributor to the malpractice crisis is the way the insurance industry does business.[24] The cyclical nature of interest rates, as a measure of return on investments, plays a central role in insurers' pricing decisions. The insurance industry engages in cash-flow underwriting, in which insurers invest the premiums they collect. When interest rates and investment returns are high, insurance companies accept riskier exposures to acquire more investable premium and loss reserves. The insurance industry managed to be profitable from 1976 to 1989. If underwriting and investment results during this period are combined, investment gains more than offset losses. The Government Accounting Office concluded of the insurance "crisis" of the early 1980s that "[t]he underwriting losses resulted, in part, from the industry's cash flow underwriting pricing strategy in which companies sacrificed underwriting gains in an attempt to attract more business and thereby

Health Economics 289 (1990); Helen R. Burstin, Stuart R. Lipsitz, I. Steven Udvarhelyi and Troyen A. Brennan, The Impact of Hospital Financial Performance on Quality of Care, 270 JAMA 845 (1993).

22. Patricia M. Danzon, Medical Malpractice: Theory, Evidence, and Public Policy 90 (1985) (hereafter Danzon).

23. Danzon at 91. See also Kenneth S. Abraham and Lance Liebman, Private Insurance, Social Insurance, and Tort Reform: Toward A New Vision of Compensation for Illness and Injury, 93 Col.L.Rev. 75, 101–105 (1993).

24. Kenneth Abraham, Making Sense of the Liability Insurance Crisis, 48 Ohio St.L.J. 399 (1987)(arguing that underwriting cycle and insurer strategies contribute to liability crises generally.)

enhance investment gains.''[25] This underwriting strategy creates instability in the market. If interest rates and investment yields drop, insurance companies must raise their premiums and drop some lines of insurance, in order to compete, since losses have to be paid.[26]

b. Insurance Availability and Cost: Some Evidence

Malpractice insurance costs are not a major cost for either hospitals or doctors generally; less than one percent of the total American health care bill goes to pay for malpractice insurance. Real premiums rose at about 5% annually between 1974 and 1986, with some evidence of a faster rate of increase after 1980. Since malpractice recoveries are largely used to pay plaintiff medical bills, and since health care cost inflation has exceeded the general rate of inflation, damage awards have grown progressively larger, with corresponding premium increases.[27] However, medical malpractice rates stabilized in 1988 and 1989, and by 1989 insurance companies had begun to reduce their rates.[28] Malpractice insurance has generally ranked in the middle of a list of insurance types, in terms of underwriting profit rates.[29] During the 1980's insurers earned a profit, although malpractice was less profitable than other lines of insurance such as worker's compensation or automobile insurance.[30]

Medical malpractice insurance premiums constitute a serious problem only for those medical specialties and geographic locations that are particularly fraught with malpractice litigation. For surgical specialties and obstetrics, particularly in five states—California, Florida, Illinois, Michigan, and New York—the problem has been acute. And for young doctors, medical school professors, and physicians with below-average incomes, increases in malpractice premiums can consume a significant percentage of gross income. The insurance affordability problem therefore is concentrated in certain areas of medicine. For physicians and hospitals generally the shock effect of sudden rapid increases in premium costs has caused a strong reaction by providers.[31]

§ 6–21. Responses to the Crisis

The response to the perceived "crisis" in malpractice litigation and insurance availability over the past twenty years has been twofold. First, the availability of insurance has been enhanced by changes in the structure of the insurance industry. Second, provider lobbies and insurers have lobbied with substantial success at the state level for legislation to impede the ability of

25. Government Accounting Office, Insurance: Profitability of Medical Malpractice and General Liability Lines (1987). See also Stephen Zuckerman, Randall R. Bovbjerg, and Frank A. Sloan, Effects of Tort Reforms and Other Factors on Medical Malpractice Insurance Premiums, 27 Inquiry 167, 181 (1990).

26. J. Robert Hunter and Thomas C. Borzilleri, The Liability Insurance Crisis, 22 Trial 42, 43 (1986).

27. See Zukerman et al., supra n. 24 at 178.

28. In late 1991 the nation's largest provider of medical malpractice insurance announced a rate freeze in all forty-two states in which it provides insurance until January 1992. Even in New York, where insurance carriers have claimed to be particularly hard-hit by the medical malpractice crisis, premiums leveled off.

29. Mahmud Hassan, How Profitable Is Medical Malpractice Insurance? 28 Inquiry 74 (1991).

30. Id. at 79.

31. In 1984 such an upward swing occurred, following a four to six year "soft" market. See DataWatch, Malpractice Insurance Costs and Physician Practice 1983–1986, 9 Health Affairs 176 (1990); James R. Posner, Trends in Medical Malpractice Insurance, 1970–1985, 49 Law & Contemp. Probs. 37 (1986).

plaintiffs to bring tort suits; to restrict the size of awards; and to more clearly delineate the standard of care required. It was hoped by reformers in the 1970's that state legislation which aimed to reform the tort system would thereby obviate the crisis in availability and affordability in malpractice insurance.[1]

a.   Benchmarks for Evaluating Reforms

The crisis atmosphere in the 1970s and 1980s has led to a variety of legislative acts their proponents hoped would ease the pain of the crisis. Such malpractice reform proposals can be evaluated by three overall standards. First, do the reforms improve the operation of the tort system for compensating victims of medical injuries? Second, will the reforms create incentives for the reduction of medical error and resulting injury to patients? Third, are changes likely to encourage insurers to make malpractice insurance more available and affordable?

The debate over reform of the tort system is reminiscent of the earlier debate over automobile no-fault insurance in the sixties, and the goals against which to measure reform efforts are similar.[2]

b.   Improving Insurance Availability for Physicians

Two major changes, beginning in the mid–70s, have increased the availability of medical malpractice insurance. First, new sources of insurance have emerged. A variety of new sources of insurance have been created either by states or by providers. Joint underwriting associations, reinsurance exchanges, hospital self-insurance programs, state funds, and provider owned insurance companies have sprung into being. Second, the type of policy offered has changed. Medical malpractice insurers changed in the late seventies to writing policies on a claims-made rather than an occurrence basis. The claims-made policy covers claims made during the year of the policy coverage, avoiding the predictability problem of the occurrence policy. Claims-made policies can create problems for insured physicians, particularly if they are not careful to keep coverage intact when they change policies or employers.[3]

c.   Altering the Litigation Process

Starting in the 1970s, states enacted tort reform legislation. Tort reform measures were intended by their proponents to reduce either the frequency of malpractice litigation or the size of the settlement or judgment. If the frequency and severity of tort litigation was thereby reduced, the legislative expectation was then that insurers would lower premiums for insurance, as

---

§ 6–21

1. For summaries of the reform legislation, see Glenn Robinson, The Medical Malpractice Crisis of the 1970's: A Retrospective, 49 Law & Contemp.Prob. 5 (Spring 1986); and Randall Bovbjerg, Legislation on Medical Malpractice: Further Developments and a Preliminary Report Card, 22 U.C. Davis L.Rev. 499 (1989).

2. An influential report by the Institute of Medicine of the National Academy of Sciences in 1978 proposed six criteria for judging the effect of various reforms on the tort system: access to compensation; scope and depth of compensation; procedures for resolving claims; costs and financing; incentives for injury

avoidance; relationship to other methods of compensation and quality assurance mechanisms. Institute of Medicine, Beyond Malpractice: Compensation for Medical Injuries 29–30 (1978). See also U.S. General Accounting Office (GAO), Medical Malpractice: No Agreement on the Problems or Solutions (1986).

3. See Langley v. Mutual Fire, Marine, and Inland Insurance Company, 512 So.2d 752 (Ala.1987). See generally William L. Hutton, Physicians' Suits Against Medical Malpractice Insurers: An Analysis of Current Issues in Professional Liability Insurance Litigation, 11 J.Leg.Med. 225 (1990).

their exposure decreased.[4] These measures can be subdivided into four groups: those affecting the filing of malpractice claims; those limiting the award recoverable by the plaintiff; those altering the plaintiff's burden of proof through changes in evidence rules and legal doctrine; and those changing the role of the courts, usually in the direction of substitution of an alternative forum.

1. Common Tort Reforms

(a.) Reducing the Filing of Claims

If the frequency of litigation is lowered, it is reasonable to assume that insurance companies will have to pay out less money, which in turn should lower premiums. Several reforms are intended to either bar certain claims that could previously have been brought, or create disincentives for the bringing of suits.

(1) Shortened statutes of limitations. Over forty states have now modified their statutes of limitations, in response to the criticism that long statutes of repose complicate insurance prediction of claims and result in uncertainty in portfolio management.[5] States have reduced the time period, typically by requiring that claims be brought within a short time, for example within two years of the injury or one year from the time that the injury should have been discovered with due diligence.

(2) Controlling legal fees. More than twenty states have regulated attorney fees in a variety of ways, including establishing rigid contingency fee structures or requiring judicial review of the "reasonableness" of the fees.[6] The intended effect of these statutes has been to make lawyers more selective in screening out nonmeritorious claims, thus eliminating excessive litigation.[7]

(3) Payment of costs for frivolous claims. Under these statutes or court rules, a malpractice claimant found to have acted frivolously in suing must reimburse the provider for reasonable legal fees, witness fees, and court costs.[8]

(b.) Limiting the Plaintiff's Award

If the previous reforms aim to cut down on the number of cases in court, the next category of reforms is designed to reduce the overall size of the award.

(1) Elimination of the ad damnum clause. This clause, as part of the initial pleading, states the total monetary claim requested by the plaintiff, an amount presumably inflated beyond the level of actual damages

---

4. Drucilla Barker, The Effects of Tort Reform on Medical Malpractice Insurance Markets: An Empirical Analysis, 17 J. Health Pol., Pol., & Law 143 (1992).

5. See Office of Technology Assessment (U.S. Congress), Impact of Legal Reforms on Medical Malpractice Costs, Appendix A (Table A–4) (1993) (hereafter OTA Impact).

6. See e.g., Ariz.Rev.Stat. § 12–568; West's Ann.Cal.Bus & Prof.Code § 6146; Delaware Code 18, § 6865.

7. Danzon found that contingent fees tend to result in equalizing plaintiff attorney compensation to that of the defense bar (whose income is not controlled), and that controls reduce not only lawyers' income, but also plaintiff compensation. Danzon, at 198.

8. See e.g., Ala.Code § 16–22–309; Ill.Rev. Stat. § 607–14.5.

suffered. Thirty-two states have legislated to eliminate the ad damnum clause.[9]

(2) Periodic Payments. Provisions allow or require a court to convert awards for future losses from a single lump sum payment into periodic payments over the period of the patient's disability or life.[10] Such a mode of payment is intended to eliminate a windfall payment to heirs if the injured party dies.

(3) Collateral source rule modifications. The collateral source rule has operated to prevent the trier of fact from learning about other sources of compensation (such as medical insurance) which the plaintiff might possess. The rule arguably permits double recovery. The modifications have either required the court to inform juries about payments from other sources to the patient, or to offset against the award some or all of the amount of payment from other sources. Seventeen states have modified this rule.[11]

(4) Limits on liability. The most powerful reform in actually reducing the size of malpractice awards has been a dollar limit, or cap, on awards. Caps may take the form of a limit on the amount of recovery of general damages, typically pain and suffering; or a maximum recoverable per case, including all damages. Indiana has a $500,000 limit per claim,[12] Nebraska $1 million[13], South Dakota a limit of $500,000 for general damages[14], California $250,000 on recovery for noneconomic damages, including pain and suffering.[15] One interesting reform proposal has been to "schedule" pain and suffering awards, rather than capping them, to narrow the range of variability in jury awards.[16]

(c.) Altering the Plaintiff's Burden of Proof

Several reforms have altered evidentiary rules or legal doctrine to increase the plaintiff's burden of proof.

(1) Res ipsa loquitur. Res ipsa loquitur was judicially expanded during the 1970's by a number of state courts, creating an inference of negligence (or in three states a presumption) even where expert testimony was needed to establish the "obviousness" of the defendant's negligence. Ten states now have barred the use of the doctrine or limited its operation.

(2) Expert witness rules. The plaintiff is normally required to present expert medical testimony as to the standard of care, the defendant's deviation from it, causation, and damages. Some states have now adopted specific requirements that plaintiff experts be qualified in the particular

9. See e.g., Iowa Code Ann. § 619.18; Kan. Stat.Ann. § 60–208; La.Stat.Ann.—Rev.Stat. § 40:1299.41(E); Me.Rev.Stat.Ann. Tit. 21, § 2901.

10. See e.g., Mich.Comp.Laws Ann. § 600.6307; Minn.Stat.Ann. § 549.25; N.H.Rev.Stat.Ann. § 507–C:7; McKinney's—N.Y.Civ.Pract.Law §§ 5031–5039.

11. See e.g., Ky.Rev.Stat. § 411.188; Official Code Ga.Ann. § 51–12–1; West's Colo.Rev. Stat.Ann. § 13–21–111.6; West's Ann.Cal.Civ. Code § 3333.1.

12. West's Ann.Ind.Code § 16–9.5–2–2.

13. Neb.Rev.Stat. § 44–2825.

14. S.D.Codified Laws § 21–3–11.

15. West's Ann.Cal.Civ.Code § 3333.2.

16. See Randall Bovbjerg, Frank Sloan, and James Blumstein, Valuing Life and Limb in Tort: Scheduling "Pain and Suffering," 83 Nw. Univ.L.Rev. 908 (1989).

specialty at issue or devote a large percent of their practice to the specialty. The intent of these reforms is to reduce the ability of the plaintiff to use a so-called "hired gun", a forensic doctor who has never practiced, or no longer practices, in the area of the defendant physician.

(3) Standards of care. The standard of care has evolved judicially from a locality rule to a national standard in most states, not only as to specialists, but also as to general practitioners. Malpractice reform efforts in some states have redefined the standard by statute to resurrect the locality rule (local, similar, state) that governs the litigation, in part to subsidize rural practitioners, to limit the use of forensic experts from other states, and in effect to make cases hard to prove. Another development that may spread is creation of an affirmative defense by a physician who complies with medical practice guidelines. Several states have passed legislation to immunize physicians from suit if they practice in accordance with such standards,[17] issuing checklists to guide physicians such as obstetricians and trauma physicians on what to do for patients with certain conditions. Such a standard of care reform, its proponents hope, will reduce physician malpractice premiums by solidifying the standard of care.[18]

(d.) Changing the Judicial Role

The role of the jury as trier of fact has been perceived by critics of the tort system as introducing bias against defendants and causing delay in compensating plaintiffs. Some argue that development of either screening or alternative dispute resolution devices (ADRs) will speed resolution of cases and screen out frivolous claims more effectively than common law litigation. These reforms are important, because they set up a complicated parallel track for disputes which reduces the judicial role.

(1) Pretrial screening devices. Twenty-five states have implemented screening panels.[19] These panels are intended to rule on the merits of the case before it can proceed to trial and to speed settlement of cases by pricing them in advance of trial. Screening panel laws vary significantly from state to state, but usually require that all cases be heard by the panel before the plaintiff is entitled to trial. A plaintiff is not prevented from filing suit after a panel's negative finding, but the panel's decision is admissible as evidence at trial. The panels range in size from three to

---

17. Florida, Maine, Vermont, Minnesota, and Kentucky allow the use of practice parameters by physicians as an affirmative defense. See Ky. Rev. Stat. Ann. S342.035 (Michie 1995) indicating that "[a]ny provider of medical services under this chapter who has followed the practice parameters or guidelines developed or adopted pursuant to this subsection shall be presumed to have met the appropriate legal standard of care in medical malpractice cases regardless of unanticipated complication that may develop or be discovered after". id. See Minn. Stat. § 62J.34(3)(a) (1994) (providing an absolute defense for providers); Fl. St. § 408.02. Several other states—e.g., Colorado, Pennsylvania, Rhode Island, Virginia, and Hawaii—also have considered or are considering adoption of guidelines legislation. Maryland, by contrast, under Md. Code Ann., [Health–Gen.] s19–1606 (1995), has mandated that practice parameters are not admissible into evidence in any legal proceeding under the statute. Maine passed the first such law as a demonstration project. See generally Ch. 931, Maine Gen. Laws (signed in 1990); Smith, Maine's Liability Demonstration Project—Relating Liability to Practice Parameters, 18 State Health Legislation Report 1 (1990).

18. For a look at the Maine Guidelines, see U.S. General Accounting Office, Medical Malpractice: Maine's Use of Practice Guidelines to Reduce Costs (1993).

19. See e.g., West's Colo.Rev.Stat.Ann. §§ 13–22–401 to 409; Haw.Rev.Stats. §§ 671–11 to 20. See OTA Impact 90–91 (1993).

seven members, and often include a judge or a lay person, at least one lawyer, and one or more health care providers from the defendant's specialty or type of institution. The panel conducts an informal hearing in which it hears testimony and reviews evidence. The finding of the panel may cover both liability and the size of the award.[20] Proponents have contended that such panels are less formal and less time consuming, and therefore less expensive as a way of resolving claims. Better informed panel members, including health care professionals, may also reach more accurate decisions than a lay jury could.[21]

The concerns as to the panels are that they will delay dispute resolution, will favor the provider, and will be ignored unless their use is mandatory.

(2) Arbitration. While screening panels supplement jury trials, arbitration is intended to replace them. Thirteen states have laws promoting arbitration of malpractice disputes.[22] The expected advantages of arbitration include diminished complexity in fact-finding, lower cost, fairer results, greater access for smaller claims, and a reduced burden on the courts.[23] No state requires compulsory arbitration. Like screening panels, the arbitration process uses a panel to resolve the dispute after an informal presentation of evidence. The panel typically consists of a doctor, a lawyer and a layperson or retired judge. The arbitration panel, however, uses members trained in dispute resolution and has the authority to make a final ruling as to both provider liability and damages. The process is initiated only when there is an agreement between the patient and the health care provider to arbitrate any claims.

2. Judicial Responses to Legislative Reform

Reforms have been challenged on a variety of state and federal constitutional bases and under the common law.[24] State supreme courts have struck down tort reform legislation over the past few years, particularly caps on non-economic damages.[25]

(a.) Equal Protection

Tort reform legislation enacted in the states since the 1970s has generally survived constitutional challenge. The major federal challenges have been based on denial of equal protection and violation of substantive due process guarantees under the 14th Amendment. These challenges have been aimed at state statutes imposing special procedural barriers or damage limitations against medical malpractice claimants, thus singling them out as a class. The courts have generally held that states may discriminate in social and economic matters so long as there is a "rational relationship" between the classification and a permissible state objective. Most state reforms have been held to pass the rational basis test, as they arguably serve the valid state purposes of

20. For a detailed discussion of such panels, see Jean Macchiaroli, Medical Malpractice Screening Panels: Proposed Model Legislation to Cure Judicial Ills, 58 Geo.Wash.L.Rev. 181 (1990).

21. For a summary of the empirical findings, see OTA Impact 105–111 (1993).

22. Ala.Code § 6–5–485; West's Colo.Rev. Stat.Ann. § 13–64–403; Maine Rev.Stat.Ann. Tit. 24, § 2701. See OTA Impact 38–42 (1993).

23. See GAO Report at 139–40.

24. For a review of the constitutional principles, see Richard Turkington, Constitutional Limitations on Tort Reform, 32 Villanova L. Rev. 1299 (1987).

25. See William C. Smith, Prying Off Tort Reform Caps, 85 A.B.A.J. 28 (Oct.1999) for a useful chart of court actions.

reducing health and insurance costs and assuring adequate health care delivery.[26]

Most state courts that have considered caps have rejected equal protection challenges.[27] The courts have been deferential to reform legislation, upholding statutes by applying the rational basis test.[28] Others backed away from earlier statements of intensified review.[29] A few jurisdictions have held a reform provision unconstitutional on Equal Protection grounds, applying a more rigorous and intense level of scrutiny.[30] One court has rejected the legislative finding of a medical malpractice crisis, sufficient to justify legislation reforms as rational.[31] By 1991, however, some state courts were showing a renewed willingness to overturn caps on constitutional grounds.[32]

(b.) Due Process

Federal constitutional guarantees of due process insure that state action will not deprive a citizen of "life, liberty, or property without due process of law." A cause of action is considered to be property protected by the Due Process clause.[33] Compensation schemes that eliminate or restrict a patient's ability to bring a negligence action can therefore be challenged as a taking of the patient's property—his right to sue—without due process of law. The North Dakota Supreme Court, in *Arneson v. Olson*,[34] found that the state's Medical Malpractice Act violated substantive due process requirements, concluding that "the cumulative effect of the limitation of the application of the Act to only one category of health-care professionals" violates due process.

Attacks on contingency fee limits, however, have not been successful.[35] One study concluded that attorney fee controls affect severity of claims, but not premiums, a result that is opposite the intended effect.[36]

(c.) State Constitutional Provisions

State constitutional law may also be invoked to challenge tort reforms. The right to trial by jury can be asserted to challenge administrative mechanisms that aim to either supplant a jury's resolution of the plaintiff's claims, or to replace the jury completely. Elective arbitration, as in Michigan, substitutes for the common law jury, and screening panels condition the right to a trial upon submission of a claim to the panel. Jury right attacks have

26. See e.g., Etheridge v. Medical Center Hospitals, 376 S.E.2d 525 (Va.1989) (Virginia Supreme Court upheld the state's $750,000 cap on malpractice awards).

27. See e.g., Bagley v. Shortt, 410 S.E.2d 738, 739 (Ga.1991) ($250,000 cap on punitive damages constitutional); Davis v. Omitowoju, 883 F.2d 1155 (3d Cir.1989).

28. Hoffman v. Powell, 380 S.E.2d 821 (S.C.1989).

29. Compare Leiker v. Gafford, 778 P.2d 823 (Kan.1989), with Farley v. Engelken, 740 P.2d 1058 (Kan.1987).

30. See e.g., Austin v. Litvak, 682 P.2d 41 (Colo.1984).

31. See Boucher v. Sayeed, 459 A.2d 87 (R.I.1983).

32. See e.g., Clark v. Container Corp. of Am., Inc., 589 So.2d 184, 198 (Ala.1991) (stat-ute structuring damage awards violated right to jury trial).

33. See Logan v. Zimmerman Brush Co., 455 U.S. 422 (1982).

34. 270 N.W.2d 125, 137 (N.D.1978).

35. See e.g. *Roa v. Lodi Medical Group*, 695 P.2d 164 (Cal.1985) where the California Supreme Court upheld a statutory limitation on contingency fees. Plaintiff's due process argument was that the statute impermissibly infringes on the right of medical malpractice victims to retain counsel in malpractice actions. The court noted that statutory limits on attorney fees were common around the country, having been extensively regulated.

36. Stephen Zukerman, Randall R. Bovbjerg, and Frank Sloan, Effects of Tort Reforms and Other Factors on Medical Malpractice Insurance Premiums, 27 Inquiry 167, 180 (1990).

generally not been successful where the right to a jury trial was not completely abrogated for malpractice claims.[37]

Caps on damages have also been attacked as violating a plaintiff's right to a jury trial, or as invading the province of the jury as trier of fact. Recent court decisions in Ohio and Oregon have concluded that a right to jury trial is violated by statutory caps.[38] Some recent decisions have found little evidence of a crisis created by malpractice litigation and have rejected damage caps as unconstitutional. Alabama has held its cap on damage awards unconstitutional as violating the Equal Protection guarantees of the state constitution, concluding that the correlation between the damages cap and the reduction of health care costs was "indirect and remote".[39] South Dakota rejected its malpractice damages cap as a violation of substantive Due Process, noted that insurance premium increased were primarily due to insurance industry mismanagement.[40]

Any administrative substitute for the tort system aims to replace the civil system, including the right to a jury trial, must face a more substantial constitutional challenge. State provisions, whether involving compulsory or elective arbitration or mediation, still allow for the jury to ultimately decide the factual questions. When the jury is removed altogether from the process, as in a Worker's Compensation type system, constitutional problems become more severe. Worker's Compensation systems have uniformly been held constitutional as not impermissibly burdening a plaintiff's right to a jury. The arguments for their constitutionality have been that workers impliedly consented to the statutory scheme when they accepted employment and that the system imposes a quid pro quo, or tradeoffs on both parties (strict employer liability for exclusivity of the worker's remedy).[41]

One argument that has succeeded in a few states is that challenged reforms violate the state's "Open Courts" requirement, which provide that citizens have access to the courts in all cases. Thus in *Lucas v. United States*[42], the court held that the Texas cap of $500,000 on liability violated the Texas constitution.[43]

The constitutional themes that the courts sound in these cases, evaluating reform schemes that restrict plaintiffs' common law rights, are as follows:

—the legislation fails to provide plaintiffs with a substitute remedy to obtain redress for injuries. The court in *Lucas* noted and rejected the defendants' arguments of a general benefit;

—caps are arbitrary, given the differences in injuries among victims;

37. See Keyes v. Humana Hospital Alaska, Inc., 750 P.2d 343 (Alaska 1988).

38. Lakin v. Senco Products, Inc., 987 P.2d 463 (Ore.1999)(legislating capping noneconomic loss "interferes with the resolution of a factual issue, i.e., noneconomic damages, that Article I, section 17, commits to the jury."); Ohio ex. Rel. Ohio Academy of Trial Lawyers v. Sheward, 715 N.E.2d 1062(Ohio 1999)(reform act declared unconstitutional as an improper usurpation of judicial power and intrusion upon exclusive authority of the judiciary in violation of Ohio Constitution). Contra, see Pulliam v. Coastal Emergency Services of Richmond, Inc., 509 S.E.2d 307 (Va.1999); Tull v. United States, 481 U.S. 412, 426 n. 9 (1987).

39. Smith v. Schulte, 671 So.2d 1334(Ala.1995).

40. Knowles v. U.S., 544 N.W.2d 183 (S.D. 1996).

41. See e.g., New York Central Railroad Co. v. White, 243 U.S. 188, 37 S.Ct. 247, 61 L.Ed. 667 (1917).

42. 757 S.W.2d 687 (Tex.1988).

43. See also Neagle v. Nelson, 685 S.W.2d 11, 12 (Tex.1985).

—the burden of reducing the social costs of high premiums is forced onto only one category of injured parties;

—a special group of defendants is being singled out for special favorable attention.

(d.) Common Law Arguments

Arbitration and elective no-fault systems involve a contract between a provider and the patient, stipulating the method of resolution of the claim for medical injury. Plaintiffs challenging this provision argue that the provider had superior power and information, or that coercion was exercised in implementing the contract. The contracts can therefore be attacked as voidable either by statute or common law doctrine, but courts have upheld such provisions.[44]

(e.) Encroachment on the Judicial Function

Many of the reform statutes circumvent existing judicial procedures. Screening panels in particular involve a sharing of judicial power with lay decision-makers. The panels can be viewed either as providing merely an expert assessment of the merits of a case, or as improperly performing quasi-judicial functions vested by the state constitution in the judiciary alone.[45] Courts in other states have upheld medical panel review statutes, finding that panel decisions are advisory, operating often as little more than an expert opinion at trial.[46]

§ 6–22.   The Effects of Reform: A Preliminary Assessment

The Robert Wood Johnson Foundation, the federal government, and others have funded several major studies to determine the effects of reform. The results of these studies are solidifying our understanding of the benefits and the limits of reform.[1]

a.   Caps on Awards and Statutes of Limitations

Caps on damage awards and reductions in the amount of time the plaintiff has to file suit have proved effective in lowering the amount paid to plaintiffs, by almost 40% according to one study of closed insurance company claims.[2] Limits on payments through caps generally have produced savings per claim, which insurers are passing on to physicians through lower premiums.[3]

---

44. Morris v. Metriyakool 344 N.W.2d 736 (Mich.1984). See also Buraczynski v. Eyring, 919 S.W.2d 314 (Tenn.1996)(holding that arbitration agreements between physicians and patients are not per se void as against public policy.)

45. Keyes v. Humana Hospital Alaska, Inc., 750 P.2d 343 (Alaska 1988). In Wright v. Central Du Page Hosp. Ass'n, 347 N.E.2d 736 (Ill.1976), the court held that having a panel with lay member on it improperly usurped a judicial function. See generally Jean Macchiaroli, Medical Malpractice Screening Panels: Proposed Model Legislation to Cure Judicial Ills, 58 Geo.Wash.L.Rev. 181 (1990).

46. See Parker v. Children's Hospital of Philadelphia, 394 A.2d 932 (Pa.1978).

§ 6–22

1. An excellent overview of state reforms and their impact can be found in U.S. Congress, Office of Technology Assessment, Impact of Legal Reforms on Medical Malpractice Cases (1993). For a look at reform in Indiana, which adopted many of the reforms discussed above, see Randall R. Bovbjerg and Joel M. Schumm, Judicial Policy and Quantitative Research: Indiana's Statute of Limitations for Medical Practitioners, 31 Ind.L.Rev.1051(1998).

2. See Frank A. Sloan, Paula M. Mergenhagen, and Randall R. Bovbjerg, Effects of Tort Reforms on the Value of Closed Medical Malpractice Claims: A Microanalysis, 14 J.Health Pol., Pol., & Law 663 (1989).

3. Indiana has proved to be an exception to this. Indiana's reforms, among the most strin-

Shortening statutes of limitations also lowers premiums by reducing the number of claims against physicians, although severity of claims is not affected.[4]

b. Pretrial Screening Panels

The use of screening panels reduced obstetrics/gynecology premiums by about 7% the year after they were introduced and about 20% in the long run, suggesting that panels are better at screening OBG cases for non-meritorious claims or encouraging settlement.[5] Another study concluded that only screening panels displayed a statistically significant connection to lower malpractice insurance premiums.[6] A 1988 study of Maryland arbitration panels concluded that the panel system had reduced the number of claims requiring formal adjudication in the courts and decreased the average length of time for resolution. They also were more likely to find in favor of claimants.[7]

c. Other Reforms

Studies have concluded that statutory caps reduce claims severity by almost twenty five percent, collateral source offsets by 11 to 18%, and screening panels had no consistent effect.[8]

Arbitration reduced claim severity by 20%, compared to states without such statutory arbitration. A study of the Michigan experience confirmed Danzon's findings that arbitration claims were closed slightly more quickly, with lower claims costs, and slightly lower recovery.[9] A California study looking at a group of Los Angeles area hospitals participating in an arbitration experiment found that hospitals employing voluntary arbitration had 63% fewer claims; closed claims 22% faster; and realized net savings on closed

gent in the country, include a cap, mandated medical review before trial, and a state-run insurance fund to pay large claims. Indiana payouts are higher than in states with caps, for a number of reasons related to insurer assessment of claims, the role of the defense lawyers, and other considerations. See Eleanor D. Kinney and William P. Gronfein, Indiana's Malpractice System: No–Fault by Accident? 54 Law and Contemporary Problems 169 (1991); William P. Gronfein and Eleanor D. Kinney, Controlling Large Malpractice Claims: The Unexpected Impact of Damage Claims, 16 J.Health Politics, Policy & Law 441 (1991)(the authors suggest that the most reasonable explanation is the way in which the Patient Compensation Fund operates; PCF bases decisions on amount of damage and not liability).

4. See Zukerman et al., Effects of Tort Reforms and Other Factors on Medical Malpractice Insurance Premiums, 27 Inquiry 167 (1990).

5. Zukerman, id. at 176.

6. Frank A. Sloan, State Responses to the Malpractice Insurance "Crisis" of the 1970's: An Empirical Assessment, 9 J.Health Pol., Pol., & Law 629 (1985).

7. See Laura Morlock and Malitz, Nonbinding Arbitration of Medical Malpractice Claims:

A Decade of Experience with Pretrial Screening Panels in Maryland (1988); Sandra S. Thurston, Medical Malpractice Dispute Resolution in Maryland, 1 Courts, Health Science & The Law 81 (1990).

8. Patricia Danzon updated her earlier studies, based upon analysis of claims nationally over the decade 1975 to 1984, for 49 states in some years, based on data from insurance companies that insured approximately 100,000 physicians. Id. She found that the severity of claims rose twice as fast as the Consumer Price Index, a fact related to the fact that health care prices rose faster than consumer prices generally; claim severity continues to be higher in urbanized states, consistent with earlier studies, and is also higher in states "with a high ratio of surgical specialists relative to medical specialists;" Id. at 76. Severity is less in states with larger elderly populations, a fact related to the low wage loss of the elderly and the low potential for damages in a tort suit; and no correlation was found between the number of lawyers per capita and claim severity.

9. Applied Social Research, Inc., Evaluation: State of Michigan Medical Malpractice Arbitration Program—Summary Report 5, 6, 12 (October, 1984).

claims of 62%—41% for loss payments and 21% for investigation and defense costs, as compared to those hospitals not employing voluntary arbitration.[10]

The results reflect to some extent the limits of the studies and the relative novelty of the reforms such as panels or arbitration at the time studied. Time will tell whether procedural reforms requiring an elaborate administrative structure will mature and prove effective. But any ultimate conclusions as to the merits and nature of reform still depend upon the goals sought for the system. Some of the reforms, such as caps and collateral source offset, appear to have slowed the growth of awards in some states. Some reforms, such as statutes of repose, reduce claims filings over the longer term. The claims-made insurance policy and mutual insurance companies may also be a more efficient way of allocating risk and protecting insurance availability.

§ 6–23. The Rationale for an Alternative System

Several reform proposals would substitute an alternative compensation system for the present tort system. The automobile accident debate of the sixties first focused attention on the problems of common law litigation—the costs of fact finding; the delays involved in court proceedings; unevenness in payments, whereby small claims are overpaid and large claims underpaid; the insufficiency of awards getting to plaintiffs after legal fees and administrative costs. To these criticisms, the malpractice crisis has added the psychological costs to physicians of being sued and the alleged added social[1] and economic[2] costs of defensive medicine. The rationales for an alternative compensation system for medical injuries are based upon a broad critique of the current common law jury system as it operates in malpractice cases.[3]

The first common criticism is that the administrative costs of the malpractice system are too high. The critics contend that too little of the malpractice premium dollar goes to the plaintiff in a malpractice suit, noting that the portion of the health insurance premium dollar that goes to a claimant is much higher that the amount returned by the tort system. This criticism fails to observe, however, that first party insurance provides for a contractually specified payment to the insured under specific conditions. Liability insurance by contrast protects the insured against claims of negligence, while also paying compensation to third parties not involved in the insurance contract. The triggering condition for such payment, and the amount, requires a lengthy inquiry by claims adjusters and often by courts and lawyers. Damages are complex and include the uncertainty of future losses. As one commentator observes, "[a] tort law and insurance system may cost 'too much' for the benefits achieved, but they are very different benefits from those of health insurance, so simple comparisons do not advance

10. Duane H. Heintz, Medical Malpractice Arbitration: A Viable Alternative, 34 Arbitration Journal 12 (December 1979).

§ 6–23

1. Ann G. Lawthers, A. Russell Localio, Nan M. Laird, Stuart Lipsitz, Liesi Hebert, and Troyen A. Brennan, Physicians' Perceptions of the Risk of Being Sued, 17 J. Health Pol., Pol., & Law 463 (1992).

2. The American Medical Association has estimated that defensive medicine added $11.7 billion to the cost of physicians' services in 1985. Martin Hatlie, Professional Liability: The Case for Federal Reform, 263 JAMA 584 (1990).

3. The American Medical Association/Specialty Tort Reform Proposal: A Fault–Based Administrative System 1 in Kirk B. Johnson et al., 1 Courts, Health Science & The Law 6–8 (1990).

thoughtful policy. Perhaps provider negligence is dealt with more efficiently and more fairly under a third-party system."[4]

Second, the standard critique observes that compensation is not effectively achieved for many medical injuries. This criticism has substantial validity. Small damage claims are effectively denied any compensation for injuries caused by medical negligence, for two reasons. First, the potential recovery, and the resulting attorney's potential contingency fee, may not be large enough to attract the services of an attorney, particularly if the complexity of the case requires a substantial investment of attorney time. Second, many potential claims are simply never brought to a lawyer by a patient. Compensation does indeed seem to be poorly served by the tort system, in the sense that deserving claims are either neither filed or fail to receive compensation sufficient to cover expenses. The Harvard Study found that while hospitalized patients had a 1% chance of a negligent adverse event, only a tiny fraction of those injuries resulted in claims being filed.[5] The Harvard Team surveyed a representative sample of 31,000 patients hospitalized in New York state in 1984, to ascertain the level of iatrogenic injury and separate out injuries traceable to a provider's negligence from pure "accidents." They found that the incidence of adverse events suffered by hospitalized patients was 3.7%, with 28% of these due to negligence. About 1% of all hospitalized patients suffered a negligent medical injury.[6] If this finding were extrapolated to the United States as a whole, 150,000 iatrogenic deaths occur every year, with more than half due to negligence, and about 30,000 nonfatal disabilities every year.[7] The authors also found that negligence is related to more serious injury: 23% of impairments lasting less than six months were negligently caused, 34% of negligently caused permanent disabilities were, and 51% of deaths. "Two-thirds of the injuries produced by grave negligence were fatal, six times the mortality rate from non-negligent iatrogenic injuries."[8] Poor, elderly, or minority patients suffered higher negligence rates, with age and insurance strong determinants of negligent injury[9]. Hospitals varied in negligence from 1% to 60%.[10] Teaching hospitals had lower rates of negligence, while hospitals with significant numbers of minority patients had higher levels of negligence.[11]

The authors of the Harvard study concluded that too few claims are filed for negligently caused injuries.[12] Once they adjusted for claims filed for nonnegligent injuries, they found that the chances that a claim would be filed by a patient with an identifiable negligent injury increases from 1 in 7.6 to 1 in fifty.[13] If only one in fifty claims for a verifiable negligent injury are filed, then the system certainly does undercompensate injured patients. Americans may in fact file fewer tort claims than the British.[14]

---

4. Frank Sloan et al., Effects of Tort Reforms on the Value of Closed Medical Malpractice Claims; A Microanalysis, 14 J. Health Politics, Policy and Law 663, 680 (1989).

5. The latest chronicle of the Harvard New York Study is found in Paul C. Weiler et al., A Measure of Malpractice: Medical Injury, Malpractice Litigation, and Patient Compensation (1993).

6. Id. at 43.

7. Id. at 55–56.

8. Id. at 45.

9. Id. at 56.

10. Id. at 47.

11. Id. at 49–50.

12. Id. at 62.

13. Id. at 72–73.

14. See Richard A. Posner, Explaining the Variance In the Number of Tort Suits Across U.S. States and Between the United States and

Jury awards in malpractice cases, when a claim is actually brought, are modest, failing in most case to adequately compensate plaintiffs' injuries.[15]

Third, critics argue that juries are inefficient. They are forced to decide causal questions when even the medical experts are uncertain as to why illnesses strike and what appropriate medical treatment should have been. Jurors only see the medical issues once, and can never develop "an institutional memory" to decide a string of cases. Costs are therefore higher, since issues must be developed de novo in each trial. And uncertainty for participants is enhanced by the lack of articulated reasons for a jury verdict. This inefficiency leads to higher insurance costs for physicians and providers, as well as high administrative costs due to excess litigation. This view of the jury also subsumes a deep distrust of lay jurors by professional, who suspect strong biases against physicians. The jury however turns out to be a surprisingly reliable decisionmaking institution, suggesting that this criticism is overstated.[16] The jury is quite accurate in weeding out nonmeritorious claims.[17] One study concluded that jurors assess liability and value damage in the same way as do judges, lawyers, physicians, and other professionals.[18]

Fourth, the role of malpractice judgments in setting proper levels of deterrence is unclear. The AMA critique argues that physicians do not get accurate signals, since most patients do not file a claim, as a result of uncertainty as to the causes of the injury.[19] The California study of 1977 found that only about 10% of negligently injured patients sought compensation. Even for those with major permanent injuries, only about one in six filed suit.[20] Other critics argue that the system overdeters, citing defensive medical practices as one example of overreaction. The tradeoff of system costs versus deterrence effect is difficult to calculate. Danzon[21] has argued that "if the number of negligent injuries is, generously, 20 percent lower than it otherwise would be because of the incentives for care created by the malpractice system, the system is worth retaining, despite its costs."[22]

Critics also argue that physicians are haphazardly exposed to litigation, regardless of their practice or skill. Physicians believe that claim filings and

England, 26 J.Legal Stud. 477, 487–88(1997)(after controlling for factors like income, urbanization, and education).

15. Frank A. Sloan & Thomas J. Hoerger, Uncertainty, Information and Resolution of Medical Malpractice Disputes, 4 J.Risk & Uncertainty 403 (1991); D. Dewees et al., Exploring the Domain of Accident Law 422–23(1996)(jurors undercompensate the most severe injuries).

16. Neil Vidmar, Medical Malpractice and the American Jury 11–12(1995); Randall R. Bovbjerg et al., Juries and Justice: Are Malpractice and Other Personal Injuries Created Equal?, 54 Law and Contemporary Problems 5 (1991); Michael Saks, Do We Really Know Anything About the Behavior of the Tort Litigation System—and Why Not? 140 U.Penn. L.Rev. 1147, 1239 (1992).

17. Randall R. Bovbjerg, Medical Malpractice: Research and Reform, 79 Va. L. Rev. 2155, 2163–66(1993).

18. Neil Vidmar & Jeffrey J. Rice, Assessments of Noneconomic Damage Awards in Medical Negligence: A Comparison of Jurors with Legal Professionals, 78 Iowa L.Rev. 883, 896–901(1993).

19. Saks, id. at 1188. A 1995 study found that among 220 women who suffered an adverse birth outcome, such as death or serious and permanent injury to the infant, none filed a malpractice claim. Frank A. Sloan & Chee Ruey Hsieh, Injury, Liability, and the Decision to File a Medical Malpractice Claim, 29 L. & Soc'y Rev. 413, 430(1995)

20. See California Medical Ass'n & California Hosp. Ass'n, Report on the Medical Insurance Feasibility Study (Don H. Mills, ed., 1977).

21. Patricia Danzon, Medical Malpractice: Theory, Practice, and Public Policy 225–227 (1985).

22. Id. at 225.

jury awards bear little relationship to physician negligence. Since jury awards cast a long shadow over the settlement process, irrational jury awards dilute or cancel any deterrent effect of successful plaintiff suits. If awards are largely random, then why should providers reform their practices? In fact, malpractice suits do not appear to be simply random events that unfairly single out physicians. Physicians usually win cases when they have met community standards of practice, and lose them when their care was indefensible.[23] Payment is made in most cases where the patients is judged to have received substandard care.[24] The tort system has a high probability of awarding injuries caused by substandard care (true positives), but also compensates claims that physician reviewers would describe as undeserving (false positives). The burden of persuasion in a jury trial is not the same as the burden imposed by a physician reviewer examining insurance closed claims; contrary to legal theory as to the burden of proof, the tort system intentionally tolerates a higher level of false positives than would physician reviewers in order to insure that the true positives are more often awarded.[25] It appears that few spurious claims are in fact filed.[26]

Tort litigation has a substantial psychological impact on physicians in excess of the diluted financial incentives created.[27] As Saks observes, "[w]here a deterrence system directly touches only a fraction of the cases it is intended to have impact upon, it needs to find a way to make up for the reduced probability that any potential injurer will feel its effects."[28] Physicians overestimate the risk of being sued and the size of feared judgments.[29] The sheer unpleasantness of being sued also deters, although it has been argued that the lack of clarity as to the locus of negligence in most cases does not provide useful feedback to a provider.[30]

The litigation process is neither as arbitrary nor as unfair as critics suggest.[31] The jury turns out to be a surprisingly reliable decisionmaking

23. Mark I. Taragin et al., The Influence of Standard of Care and Severity of Injury on the Resolution of Medical Malpractice Claims, 117 Ann. Internal Med. 780 (1992); Frederick W. Cheney, Karen Posner, Robert A. Caplan, and Richard J. Ward, Standard of Care and Anesthesia Liability, 261 JAMA 1599 (1989); Henry S. Farber and Michelle J. White, Medical Malpractice: An Empirical Examination of the Litigation Process, 22 Rand J. of Econ. 199 (1991).

24. See Frederick W. Cheney et al., Standard of Care and Anesthesia Liability, 261 JAMA 1599 (1989).

25. See also Frank A. Sloan and Chee Ruey Hsieh, Variability in Medical Malpractice Payments: Is the Compensation Fair?, 24 Law & Soc'y Rev. 997 (1990) (In closed claim review, cases where expert panel agreed that defendant was at fault were more likely to result in payment to claimant).

26. Paul C. Weiler, Fixing the Tail: The Place of Malpractice in Health Care Reform, 47 Rutgers L.Rev. 1157, 1162(1995).

27. See generally Peter A. Bell, Legislative Intrusions into the Common Law of Medical Malpractice: Thoughts About the Deterrent Effect of Tort Liability, 35 Syracuse L.Rev. 939 (1984).

28. Saks, supra n.14 at 1286.

29. A.G. Lawthers et al., Physicians' Perceptions of the Risk of Being Sued, 17 J.Health Politics, Policy & Law 463 (1992) (physicians overestimate the rate of suit for malpractice at three times the actual rate. This perceived risk suggests that physician do respond to the messages sent by litigation.). See also Paul C. Weiler, et al., Proposal for Medical Liability Reform, 267 JAMA 2355, 2356 (1992).

30. Norman G. Poythress, Richard Wiener, and Joseph E. Schumacher, Reframing the Medical Malpractice Tort Reform Debate: Social Science Research Implications for Non-Economic Reforms, 16 Law & Psychology Rev. 65, 72 (1992).

31. Other studies have provided recent useful data on this issue. Frank A. Sloan, et al., Medical Malpractice Experience of Physicians: Predictable or Haphazard? 262 JAMA 3291 (1989).

institution.[32] Lawyers are good screens for frivolous cases. The real problem is that too many potential claims are never filed, leading to underdeterrence of substandard medical practice.[33]

Fifth, critics contend that society pays too much, given the increase in the number of malpractice claim filings and the severity of the awards. Malpractice premiums have increased, and the costs of medical insurance rose from $60 million in 1960 to nearly $5 billion in 1985, with only 16 to 40 cents of each dollar paid ending up in the plaintiff's pocket, in contrast to a worker's compensation system where it is closer to 55% to 70%.[34] The practice of defensive medicine has also been claimed to add substantially to the nation's health care bill, with the AMA's estimate as high as $12 billion.[35]

Sixth, critics claim that access is impaired. Physicians in obstetrics have left practice, it is claimed in part because of their high malpractice premiums. While it is true that many rural areas are now left without obstetricians, it is usually because physicians won't relocate to rural areas due to lack of amenities and lower incomes. Rising premium costs have cut into physician incomes in a few specialties such as obstetrics, contributing to an alteration in physician practice patterns. Critics claim that access to care has suffered, with the malpractice system the culprit. Some states such as Virginia have enacted special legislation just to "solve" the "obstetrics" problem, primarily created by a threat by insurers to leave the state and thereby leave obstetricians without any coverage for malpractice. Evidence suggests however that income trends have held steady, for a complex mix of reasons.[36] Patient access to health care may have suffered at least in some specialties, due to insurance availability and also physicians' often unsupported anxieties about tort litigation.[37] Poor patients in fact are significantly less likely to sue for malpractice than middle class patients; indeed, they may sue only 10% as often as wealthier patients.[38] Physician misperceptions and anxiety have produced protective legislation that cannot be rationally justified.[39] Such misperceptions may also deter physicians from caring for the poor.

32. Saks, supra n. 14 at 1239.

33. See Winsor C. Schmidt, D. Alex Heckert, and Alice A. Mercer, Factors Associated with Medical Malpractice: Results from a Pilot Study, 7 J. Contemp. Health Law & Policy 157, 180 (1991).

34. See Paul C. Weiler et al., A Measure of Malpractice: Medical Injury, Malpractice Litigation, and Patient Compensation 106 (1993).

35. The AMA came up with a figure of $11.7 billion in defensive medicine costs for physician services in 1985. Given health care inflation, that figure, if accepted as a baseline, would approach $20 billion today. Martin Hatlie, Professional Liability: The Case for Federal Reform, 263 JAMA 584 (1990).

36. Fear of malpractice suits has also affected the willingness of physicians to treat Medicaid patients, although little evidence exists that poor patients sue more than other patients. The IOM study noted that while " * * * the causal relationships between professional liability issues, changes in obstetrical practice, and access to care for low-income women cannot be precisely documented, the mere perception among physicians that low-income women pose professional liability problems constitutes a barrier to care." IOM Study II at 65.

37. Margo L. Rosenbach and Ashley G. Stone, DataWatch, Malpractice Insurance Costs and Physician Practice, 1983–1986, 9 Health Affairs 176, 185 (1990)(the most common practice impact of increasing malpractice premiums was discontinuation of obstetric services).

38. See Helen R. Burstin et al., Do the Poor Sue More? A Case–Control Study of Malpractice Claims and Socioeconomic Status, 270 JAMA 1697 (1993).

39. See Karen H. Rothenberg, Myth and Reality: The Threat of Medical Malpractice Claims by Low Income Women, 20 Law, Medicine & Health Care 403 (Winter 1992).

§ 6–24. No–Fault Reforms

No-fault reform proposals aim to eliminate or reduce some of these perceived flaws of the current system.[1] Such proposals can be categorized in light of their combination of key attributes. These attributes, or variables, are categorized by one analyst as follows:[2] (1) the compensable event, (2) the measure of compensation, (3) the payment mechanism, (4) the forum used to resolve disputes, and (5) the method of implementing the new rights and responsibilities. The compensable event may be fault, cause, or loss. The measure for such compensation might be full tort damages, full out-of-pocket losses, partial out-of-pocket damages, scheduled damages. The payment mechanism might be third-party insurance, first-party insurance, social insurance, or a Patient Compensation fund. The forum for resolution of disputes over medical injuries could include a trial by jury, expert review panels, bench trials, binding arbitration, administrative panels, or insurance company determination. Finally, methods of implementing a reform of the malpractice system include either legislation or contract. Any of these variables could be combined to create a new system. The state reforms enacted over the past twenty years have tended to focus on damages reform and alternative dispute resolution.

a. State No–Fault Reforms

Florida and Virginia have implemented limited no-fault programs, to address only birth-related neurological injuries.[3] The impact of escalating premiums on the specialty of obstetrics and the severity of obstetric injuries led these states to focus on this narrow category of malpractice claims.[4] The state of Virginia led the states in implementing a no-fault system for obstetric mishaps.[5] A claim under this Act excludes all other tort remedies, with the exception of a suit "against a physician or a hospital where there is clear and convincing evidence that such physician or hospital intentionally or willfully

---

§ 6–24

1. One of the best recent treatments of malpractice reforms, with excellent notes, is Paul Weiler's Medical Malpractice on Trial (Cambridge, Mass.: Harvard University Press 1991). For an excellent overview of reform proposals, see Randall R. Bovbjerg and Frank A. Sloan, No–Fault for Medical Injury: Theory and Evidence, 67 Univ.Cin.L.Rev. 53 (1998).

2. Kenneth Abraham, Medical Liability Reform: A Conceptual Framework, 260 JAMA 68–72 (1988).

3. For a report on the administrative experience of Florida and Virginia, see Randall R. Bovbjerg, Frank A. Sloan and Peter J. Rankin, Administrative Performance of "No-Fault" Compensation for Medical Injury, 60 Law & Contemp.Prob. 71(1997).

4. Other states are considering no-fault plans, among them Utah and New York. Utah's plan is broader than Virginia and Florida's, proposing pilot projects at selected state hospitals for no-fault compensation for injuries suffered by patients within those hospitals. See

Kenneth Jost, Fault–Free Malpractice, ABA Journal 46 (January 1994).

5. Effective January 1, 1988, the state enacted the "Birth–Related Neurological Injury Compensation Act", creating a compensation fund for neurologically damaged newborns. The critical definition for compensation purposes in the Virginia statute is "[b]irth-related neurological injury". This is defined as "injury to the brain or spinal cord of an infant caused by the deprivation of oxygen or mechanical injury occurring in the course of labor, delivery or resuscitation in the immediate post-delivery period in a hospital which renders the infant permanently nonambulatory, aphasic, incontinent, and in need of assistance in all phases of daily living. This definition shall apply to live births only."

The Florida system, passed a year after Virginia's, is similar. The discussion will therefore focus on the Virginia statute. West's Fla.Stat. Ann. § 766.303 (1991). As of August 1993, the OTA Report reported that 69 claims had been filed under the program. OTA Report, supra § 9–3, n.1, at 45.

caused or intended to cause a birth-related neurological injury", provided that such suit is filed prior to and in lieu of payment of an award.[6]

It was predicted that the eligibility provisions for brain damage would apply to approximately forty live births in the state each year. In fact, only a handful of claims have qualified each year under the statute. The definition is so narrow that only the most severe injuries are covered, and most of those eligible die as infants.[7] The assessment of these state reforms is that they achieved their objective of keeping obstetrical liability coverage for physicians affordable, while taking the most expensive obstetrical cases out of the tort system and resolving them quickly through an informal process. A number of families were compensated who would not have succeeded in the tort system, but only a handful are ever compensated, in part because so few ever pursue a claim. They are "so limited in both scope and scale that the programs cannot achieve many of the broader goals often plausibly ascribed to no-fault."[8]

b. *Medical Adversity Insurance*

Medical adversity insurance, first proposed by Clark Havighurst and Lawrence Tancredi, is a system whereby a patient experiencing a medical outcome which is on a list of avoidable outcomes would be automatically compensated for certain expenses and losses, and foreclosed from any other recovery for those outcomes.[9] Litigation or arbitration could be pursued for outcomes not covered by the policy. The lists of adverse outcomes would be developed by panels of doctors, lawyers, and consumers. These outcomes would be clearly described to reduce the potential for claims disputes. The panels would also establish the amounts of compensation for lost wages. Pain and suffering awards could vary based on the temporary or permanent nature of the injury. Panels would periodically review covered outcomes and compensation in order to make adjustments reflecting changes in medical practice and costs.

When the adverse outcome first occurred, the patient or provider would file the claim with the insurer, who would decide whether the injury was covered. If so, it would make prompt payment. Disputes would be resolved through the courts or arbitration. The plan as proposed would experience rate insurance premiums paid by providers, in order to create incentives for the providers to improve the quality of care, thereby reducing their exposure for the adverse outcomes listed. Provider experience under the plan would also be used to strengthen peer review within hospitals. The original Havighurst–

---

6. Both the Virginia $750,000 cap on damages and the Birth–Related Neurological Injury Compensation Act were responses to the availability of malpractice insurance in the state. In 1986, both St. Paul and Virginia Insurance Reciprocal had declared moratoria on new obstetric coverage, and PHICO had terminated coverage for all physicians in groups of less than 10. Enactment of the Act in particular led to expansion of malpractice coverage by a new carrier, and the offering of larger policies by another.

7. See Stephen Klaidman, Medical Malpractice in Virginia, 1 Courts, Health Science and the Law 75 (1990); David D. Duff, Compensation for Neurologically Impaired Infants: Medical No–Fault In Virginia, 27 Harv.J.Legis. 391 (1990).

8. Randall R. Bovbjerg and Frank Sloan, supra n. 1 at 121–22.

9. See Clark C. Havighurst and Lawrence R. Tancredi, "Medical Adversity Insurance—A No–Fault Approach to Medical Malpractice and Quality Assurance", 51 Milbank Mem. Fund Q. 125 (Spring 1973).

Tancredi proposal assumed that legislation would be needed to effectuate the plan.[10]

c. Contractual Approaches to Liability

Private contracts rather than legislation can be used to implement a compensation system.[11] The Medical Adversity approach above could be handled by contract, for example. Under the contractual approach, providers would voluntarily contract with insurers to cover certain outcomes, which would then be paid on a no-fault basis. Patients would also contract with the providers to accept those amounts listed in the policy. This would allow more flexibility, with variations possible in both covered events and compensation amounts among providers. Noncovered injuries could be handled through the courts or arbitration.

Contract proposals allow for a wide range of consumer options. Plaintiffs and providers could agree in advance to alternative dispute resolution, such as arbitration. They could agree to enterprise liability, such as the Medical Adversity Insurance proposal of Tancredi. They could agree to a variation in the standard of care or liability to be applied to resolve the dispute. And damages could be limited by agreement.[12] Such proposals are popular with free market economists and some academics, but implementation has proved difficult. Only arbitration has been subject to consumer-provider contract agreements, as exemplified by the Michigan elective arbitration system for hospital patients.[13]

d. The A.M.A. Fault–Based Administrative System

The American Medical Association has proposed an administrative fault-based system for resolving malpractice claims, premised upon physician negligence.[14] The proposal aims to better compensate small claims, and to enhance quality by strengthening state medical board's credentialing and disciplinary functions.[15] The heart of the proposal is an administrative system,

---

10. Lawrence R. Tancredi, "Designated Compensable Events: A No–Fault Approach to Medical Malpractice", 10 L.Med. & Health Care 200 (1982); Clark C. Havighurst, "Reforming Malpractice Law Through Consumer Choice", 3 Health Affairs 63 (1984); Lawrence R. Tancredi, Designing a No–Fault Alternative, 49 Law. & Contemp. Probs. 277 (1986). A newer version of the Tancredi concept is called "accelerated-compensation events" (ACEs). The central idea, as with medical adversity insurance, is that lists of medically caused injuries should be drawn up, covering those injuries that should not normally occur and are avoidable if good care is given. These lists are based on professionally selected classes of bad outcomes that medical professionals consider avoidable on a probabilistic basis. Laurence R. Tancredi and Randall R. Bovbjerg, Rethinking Responsibility for Patient Injury: Accelerated–Compensation Events, A Malpractice and Quality Reform Ripe for a Test, 54 Law & Contemp.Prob. 147 (1991). The newest proposal for a selective no-fault system limited to obstetric maloccurrences is Randall R. Bovbjerg, Laurence R. Tancredi, and Daniel S. Gaylin,

Obstetrics and Malpractice: Evidence on the Performance of a Selective No–Fault System, 265 JAMA 2836 (1991).

11. See Jeffrey O'Connell, No–Fault Insurance for Injuries Arising from Medical Treatment: A Proposal for Elective Coverage, 24 Emory L.J. 35 (1975).

12. See generally OTA Report, § 9–3, note 1, at 47–48.

13. See § 9–2 c.2(d.) for a discussion of the Michigan Arbitration Act.

14. The full text of the AMA proposal can be found in AMA/Specialty Society Medical Liability Project, Tort Reform Codification: Model Medical Liability and Patient Protection Act, 1 Courts, Health Science and the Law 87 (1990) (hereafter Courts). The proposal is sharply criticized in Randall R. Bovbjerg, Reforming a Proposed Tort Reform: Improving on the American Medical Association's Proposed Administrative Tribunal for Medical Malpractice, 1 Courts 19 (1990).

15. Antoinette D. Paglia, Taking the Tort out of Court—Administrative Adjudication of

similar to Worker's Compensation, which sets up a review process in several layers: (1) the pre-hearing and initial hearing state; (2) the final decision of the Board; and (3) judicial review.

e. Federal Legislative Proposals

The only Federal no-fault program now in operation covering a health care related injury is the National Childhood Vaccine Injury Act of 1986. It covers solely those individuals injured or killed by vaccines. The program requires a petition to the U.S. Claims Court and an adjudication by that court. The petitioner must elect to accept or reject the judgment of the court. Acceptance bars any tort suit against the manufacturer. The federal government will pay compensation to those who develop specified symptoms or reactions to a vaccine within specified periods of time and suffer a vaccine-related injury that lasts for at least six months.[16]

Proposals at the federal level have surfaced in the past few years with greater frequency. The Bush administration introduced the Health Care Liability Reform and Quality of Care Improvement Act of 1991, through Senator Orrin Hatch.[17] This proposal is more ambitious than other proposals in requiring that all covered malpractice claims be submitted for final resolution to a public or private dispute resolution service certified by the Secretary of Health and Human Services.[18]

f. Enterprise Liability

Enterprise liability, also referred to as "organizational liability" by the American Law Institute,[19] changes the locus of liability for patient injuries without other significant alterations to the rules of proof and damages. The idea is not new;[20] developments in vicarious liability and corporate negligence have moved the locus of much medical liability from independent contractor physicians to the hospital.[21] This proposal, as articulated by the American Law Institute, would make a hospital liable for physician negligence that injures patients within the hospital:[22]

Medical Liability Claims: Is It the Next Step? 20 Sw.U.L.Rev. 41 (1991).

16. See 42 U.S.C.A. § 300aa–1 et seq., Pub.L. 99–660, tit. III, § 311(a), 100 Stat. 3756 (Nov. 14, 1986). For an account of the program, and its current operation, by a Special Master who handles petitions filed under the Act, see Denis J. Hauptly and Mary Mason, The National Childhood Vaccine Injury Act: The Federal No–Fault Compensation Program That Gives a Booster for Tort Reform, 37 Fed.Bar News & J. 452 (1990).

17. S. 1123, 102d Cong, 1st Sess (May 22, 1991). Senator Orrin Hatch sponsored not only the administration bill, but also a bill drafted by the American Medical Association, S. 489, entitled Ensuring Access Through Medical Liability Reform Act of 1991. S. 489 contains mandatory provisions and elective provisions, with a focus on alternative dispute resolution.

18. For a detailed discussion of S. 1232, see Clark C. Havighurst and Thomas B. Metzloff, Commentary: S. 1232—A Late Entry in the Race for Malpractice Reform, 54 Law & Contemp.Prob. 179 (1991).

19. The American Law Institute, Reporters' Study, Enterprise Responsibility for Personal Injury, Vol.II: Approaches to Legal and Institutional Change (April 15, 1991) at 113 et seq. (hereafter ALI Study). The proposal is developed more fully in Kenneth S. Abraham and Paul C. Weiler, Enterprise Medical Liability and the Evolution of the American Health–Care System, 108 Harv.L.Rev. 381 (1994). For a taxonomy of enterprise liability, see Barry R. Furrow, Enterprise Liability and National Health Care Reform, 39 St. Louis U. L.J. 79 (1994).

20. See generally George Priest, The Invention of Enterprise Liability: A Critical History of the Intellectual Foundations of Modern Tort Law, 14 J.Leg.Stud. 461 (1985).

21. See Chapter 7. See also Arthur Southwick, Hospital Liability: Two Theories Have Been Merged, 4 J.Legal Med. 1 (1983).

22. ALI Study at 114.

* * * we would exculpate doctors from personal liability for negligence (and thus eliminate their need to purchase insurance against such liability), on the condition that the hospital assume such liability and provide the insurance, a change that would leave untouched the patient's present entitlement to recover for injuries caused by the doctor's negligence.[23]

Such channeling of liability to the hospital is justified by several arguments. First, insurers would have an improved ability to price insurance, since difficulties in pricing for individual physicians in high-risk specialties will be eliminated; in most other areas of tort law, from environmental to products risks, business enterprises bear the cost of insuring against liability. Second, by eliminating the insurance problems inherent in the fragmented malpractice market, specialties such as obstetrics would no longer face onerous burdens, nor will physicians have to face premiums that fluctuate excessively from year to year. Third, physicians would be freed from the psychological stress inflicted by being named defendants in malpractice suits. Fourth, administrative and litigation costs would be reduced by having only one defendant, rather than the multiplicity of providers named in the typical malpractice suit.[24] Fifth, patterns of poor medical practice would be deterred by placing liability on institutions rather than individuals,[25] since organizations have superior data collecting abilities and management tools for managing risks.[26] The application of this model to managed care makes considerable sense, given the increasing integration of managed care plans and networks.[27]

The critique of such enterprise liability begins with its impact on the autonomy of physicians. Physicians fear that such liability will force them from the status of autonomous practitioners into the status of employees for large health care institutions, with attendant loss of power.[28] Indeed, the ALI proposal acknowledges that enterprise liability will treat physicians as staff physicians in managed care settings.[29] However, such forces are already in operation, evidenced by the rapid growth of managed care organizations, the purchase of group medical practices by hospitals, and other forces that reduce the financial autonomy of physicians, in exchange for other benefits. The issue for health care reform in the next decade will be how to implement such

---

23. Id. at 115.

24. Id. at 119.

25. See ALI Study, pp. 121–126. See generally Lewis A. Kornhauser, An Economic Analysis of the Choice Between Enterprise and Personal Liability for Accidents, 70 Cal.L.Rev. 1345 (1982); Alan O. Sykes, The Economics of Vicarious Liability, 93 Yale L.J. 1231 (1984). Hospital review still tends to focus on individual mistakes, however. See generally Sanford E. Goldman and Thomas G. Rundell, PROS and the Health Care Quality Improvement Initiative: Insights from 50 Cases of Serious Medical Mistakes, 50 Medical Care Review 123 (1993); Haya R. Rubin, William H. Rogers, Katherine L. Kahn, Lisa V. Rubenstein and Robert H. Brook, Watching the Doctor–Watchers: How Well Do Peer Review Organizations Methods Detect Hospital Care Quality Problems? 267 JAMA 2349 (1992).

26. Physician profiling has become commonplace by insurers and providers to track provider behavior. See David W. Emmons et

al., Data on Employee Physician Profiling, Data on Employee Physician Profiling, 26 J.Health and Hosp. Law 73 (March 1993); see also John H. Eichhorn et al., Standards for Patient Monitoring During Anesthesia at Harvard Medical School, 256 J.A.M.A. 1017 (1986).

27. William M. Sage, Enterprise Liability and the Emerging Managed Health Care System, 60 Law & Contemp.Probs. 159 (1997).

28. The position of the American Medical Association's House of Delegates is summed up by Richard Corlin, MD: "One proposal Clinton's made that is absolutely nonnegotiable is enterprise liability, which means if you work for an HMO and get sued, you could get fired. This will lead to a firestorm like nothing they've ever seen. If they want a doctor strike, this is the best way to do it." American Medical News 7 (May 17, 1993).

29. ALI Study at 118.

a liability approach in a changing health care environment where care is as likely to be delivered through loose networks of providers as through hospitals. The benefits of deterrence and risk management may be substantial if enterprise liability is applied to managed care organizations, now organized vertically.[30]

The federal reform proposals may also risk much higher compensation costs, because of increased levels of claims filed. The California study in the 1970s estimated that a no-fault system in California could increase malpractice premiums 300% higher than the tort system's insurance costs.[31] A critique of the Harvard New York study likewise concluded that the costs of a no-fault system could be greater than the present tort system, when the costs of many more claims and system administrative costs are combined.[32] From the insurance industry perspective, these proposals are worrisome, since there seems to be far more malpractice in the world than is ever detected or litigated. A no-fault system may set off an avalanche of litigation, depending upon the design of the system, methods of discussing misadventures to the injured patient, and other structural issues, as yet unresolved.[33] Patients are also more likely to sue their HMO or hospital than their personal physician. If a compensation system rewards many more claimants, particularly small ones, in a more evenhanded and rapid fashion than does the current tort system, it will be an improvement. It is however debatable whether it will be a cheaper system.[34]

Some critics have therefore proposed that we move directly to a social insurance scheme that moves financing out of the private insurance market and into the taxation structure of the government.

g. *Social Insurance*

The last set of proposals draws upon the experience of the United States with the Worker's Compensation System, and that of other countries with pervasive social welfare systems. Such a major reform would achieve the advantages of the other three proposals, plus the advantage of a pure insurance system funded out of general tax revenues.

The programs share common characteristics: programs are established on the premise that society is better able to bear the cost of adverse outcomes than the injured party; compensation is usually predetermined and limited in amount and duration; benefits are scheduled, that is, a standard formula is applied to the same types of injuries; an administering agency processes and validates claims and makes payment of the benefits; determination of fault is usually irrelevant; compensation is essentially automatic for covered losses; and general tax revenues would fund a "pure" social insurance system.

30. See generally William M. Sage, Enterprise Liability and the Emerging Managed Health Care System, 60 Law & Contemp. Probs. 159(1997)(arguing for federalized managed care liability).

31. California Medical and Hospital Associations, Report on the Medical Insurance Feasibility Study (1977).

32. See Maxwell Mehlman, Saying "No" to No–Fault: What the Harvard Malpractice Study Means for Medical Malpractice Reform (New York State Bar Association 1990).

33. Proposals of this type raise difficult questions. Why should a provider come forward to inform a patient that he has suffered a compensable injury? Is the doctor in charge of the case likely to admit error, so that the hospital can present its offer to the patient? If not how can the hospital encourage staff doctors to come forward?

34. See generally Paul C. Weiler et al., A Measure of Malpractice: Medical Injury, Malpractice Litigation, and Patient Compensation (1993). See also Paul C. Weiler, The Case for No–Fault Liability, 52 Md.L.Rev. 908 (1993).

New Zealand's Accident Compensation Act, adopted in 1972 and effective in 1974, removed all damage claims for accidental injuries from the tort system.[35] All New Zealand residents were covered at all times, with the compensation available including payment for loss of earnings (80% of average weekly earnings at the time of the accident, with a limit of about $340 U.S. dollars per week); reasonable costs of medical treatment; lump sums for permanent disability and pain and suffering and payments to a dependent spouse (with limits on the lump sums), payment to dependents for loss of support, and a variety of other expenses. The Accident Compensation Corporation administered the program. An injured person filed a claim with the Corporation, which then decided whether the claim is covered and if so, how much should be paid. The decision could be appealed to the courts. Forty percent of the claims for medical injury were denied, and awards were generally processed promptly. Under the 1972 Act, providers helped patients to collect compensation, gaining an incentive to help their patients qualify for compensation under the no-fault system to avoid direct liability.[36] This scheme was soundly criticized for its lack of deterrence of medical malpractice and its failure to distinguish among classes of victims.[37] The system has now been substantially limited as to benefits paid to accident victims, as the result of a change in government and its response to rapidly escalating payout costs.[38] The new Act, in effect in 1992, creates a Medical Misadventure Account to finance benefits to victims of malpractice.[39] Unlike the previous Act, which lumped accident victims together, this new Account creates a means of finance of compensation by premiums paid by certified health professionals. Experience rating is also applied to health professionals. The Act appears to resurrect the malpractice suit. Under the 1972 Act, the claimant had to establish "medical, surgical, dental, or first aid misadventure".[40] This proved difficult to apply. The new Act now requires that claimants establish "medical error"[41], which requires proof of negligence. The burden on the claimant has thereby been increased, while the deterrent effect of the new Act is also enhanced by the introduction of experience rating.[42]

35. Accident Compensation Act, 1982, No. 181, 1982 N.Z. Stat. 1552 (consolidating and amending the 1972 Accident Compensation Act and amendments).

36. See Accident Compensation Corporation, Accident Compensation Coverage—The Administration of the Accident Compensation Act 9 (7th Ed.1983); GAO Malpractice Report at 155. Ellen K. Solender, New Zealand's No-Fault Accident Compensation Scheme Has Some Unintended Consequences: A Caution to U.S. Reformers, 27 The International Lawyer 91 (1993). For a critical perspective on the above reform proposals, see Richard Mahoney, New Zealand's Accident Compensation Scheme: A Reassessment, 40 Am.J.Comp.L. 159 (1992).

The Swedes and the Finns have also created a self-contained, separate patient compensation scheme. See Marilyn Rosenthal, Dealing with Medical Malpractice: The British and Swedish Experience (1988); Oldertz, The Swedish Patient Insurance System—Eight Years of Experience, 52 Med.-Legal J. 43 (1983); Timothy S. Jost, Quality Assurance in Medical Practice: An International Comparative Study (1990).

37. Mahoney, id. at 161. See, on the deterrent effects or their lack, Craig Brown, Deterrence in Tort and No-Fault: The New Zealand Experience, 73 Cal.L.Rev. 976 (1985) and Richard Miller, The Future of New Zealand's Accident Compensation Scheme, 11 U.Haw.L.Rev. 1 (1989).

38. See generally Richard Mahoney, supra n. 40 at 160.

39. Accident Rehabilitation and Compensation Insurance Act 1992, No. 13.

40. 1982 Act, § 2(1), 1982 N.Z.Stat. 1560.

41. 1992 Act, § 5(10)(a): medical error is defined as "the failure of a registered health professional to observe a standard of care and skill reasonably to be expected in the circumstances."

42. For a critique of the new Act, see Richard S. Miller, An Analysis and Critique of the

§ 6–25. Conclusion

Reform of the tort system for medical injuries makes sense only if reform is combined with changes in the reimbursement of health care. Competition among managed care systems is intensifying, and the consumers of health care now include both individual users and sponsors (large employers, governments, and other institutions that purchase health care on behalf of employees). The marketing of good quality care is becoming as important as important as the marketing of cost-effective care.[1] Managed care organizations are adopting systems that provide incentives for good outcomes, as a response to accreditation pressures and consumer demands.[2]

The irony of malpractice reform is that today both political parties are aligned behind legislation that makes it easier to sue managed care organizations. The earlier mood of crisis over too much tort litigation has given way to a cry for easier suits against managed care organizations for their alleged harm to patients. The politics of reform is entering a new phase, but reform continues to ignore the limitations of tort suits generally in terms of too few claims and uneven awards.[3] Tort reform has been based on anecdote and special interest pleading, failing to respond to the real limitations of tort litigation in compensating severely injured patients. The objective studies of the tort system and of reform have concluded that the American medical liability system is a "a system of few trials, low win rates, declining verdicts, and rare punitive awards."[4] As a quality control system, the tort system is doing poorly, and reforms should concentrate on improving the rate of filings for legitimate claims. It is the irony of tort reform that we need more rather than less malpractice litigation.

1992 Changes to New Zealand's Accident Compensation Scheme, 52 Maryland L.Rev. 1070 (1993).

§ 6–25

1. See Alain Enthoven, Managed Competition of Alternative Delivery Systems, 13 J. Health Pol., Poly. and Law 305 (1988).

2. See generally Barry R. Furrow, Regulating the Managed Care Revolution: Private Accreditation and a New System Ethos, 43 Vill. L.Rev. 501 (1998).

3. See Andrews–Clarke v. Travelers Insurance Company, 984 F.Supp. 49 (D.Mass.1997) for an extended critique of ERISA preemption and its effect of foreclosing valid tort claims.

4. Deborah J. Merritt and Kathryn A. Barry, Is the Tort System in Crisis? New Empirical Evidence, 60 Ohio St. L.J. 315, 398(1999).

Chapter 7

THE LIABILITY OF HEALTH CARE INSTITUTIONS

Table of Sections

A. TORT LIABILITY OF HOSPITALS

Research References

    Am Jur 2d, Physicians, Surgeons, and Other Healers §§ 200–301

    ALR Index: Enterprise Liability; Malpractice By Medical or Health Professions

    ALR Digest: Hospitals and Other Health Care Facilities §§ 4–6

    26 POF3d 185, Discovery Date in Medical Malpractice Litigation; 25 POF3d 313, Toxic Torts: Proof of Medical Monitoring Damages for Exposure to Toxic Substances; 16 POF3d 189, Negligent Infliction of Emotional Distress by Health Care Provider; 15 POF3d 181, Hospital Liability for Negligent Retention of Staff Physician; 14 POF3d 433, Hospital Liability for Negligent Selection of Staff Physician; 6 POF2d 647, Hospital's Failure to Supervise Private Physician Using Hospital Facilities

    44 Am Jur Trials 317, Forensic Document Examination in Medical Malpractice Cases; 39 Am Jur Trials 261, Planning and Producing A "Day-in-the-Life" Videotape in a Personal Injury Lawsuit; 38 Am Jur Trials 1, Professional Liability for Failure To Report Child Abuse; 23 Am Jur Trials 479, Determining the Medical and Emotional Bases for Damages; 19 Am Jur Trials 431, Defending Hospital–Negligence of Physician–Employee; 16 Am Jur Trials 471, Defense of Medical Malpractice Cases; 15 Am Jur Trials 373, Discovery and Evaluation of Medical Records

A. TORT LIABILITY OF HOSPITALS

§ 7–1. The Development of Hospital Liability

The modern hospital—with its operating theaters, its complex diagnostic equipment and laboratories, its large staffs of nurses, doctors, and support personnel—has come to symbolize the delivery of medical care. It was not always so. For centuries, in Europe and in America, hospitals tended the sick and the insane but made no attempt to treat or cure. They were supported by the philanthropy of the wealthy and by religious groups. In the 1870's it could be said that only a small minority of doctors practiced in hospitals, and even they devoted only a small portion of their practice to such work. Before 1900, a person seeking medical care did not consider hospitalization, since doctors made house calls and even operated in the home. By the late 1800's, however, developments in medical knowledge moved the hospital toward a central position in health care. The development of antiseptic and aseptic techniques reduced the previously substantial risk of infection within hospitals; the growing scientific content of medicine made hospitals a more attractive place for medical practice. Therapeutic and diagnostic improvements came to be identified with hospital doctors. These doctors, the product of the modernization of medicine, discovered that the hospital was well suited to their practice needs. Control over the hospital began to shift from the trustees to the doctors during the early 1900's.[1] The hospital became the doctor's workshop, providing facilities to support services provided by independent physician professionals.[2] The liability of the hospital was limited to maintaining the facilities, providing adequate equipment and supplies, and hiring, supervising,

---

§ 7–1

   1. For an excellent extended discussion of the history of the hospital, see Paul Starr, The Social Transformation of American Medicine (1982), particularly Chapter 4.

   2. Schloendorff v. Society of New York Hosp., 105 N.E. 92 (N.Y.App.1914), overruled by Bing v. Thunig, 163 N.Y.S.2d 3, 143 N.E.2d 3 (N.Y.App.1957).

and retaining employed staff such as nurses. As the hospital evolved, physicians became increasingly dependent upon hospital affiliation. By 1975, no doctor would consider practicing without the resources that a hospital offered, and 25 percent of the 330,000 active physicians practiced fulltime in a hospital.

The traditional relationship of doctor to hospital was that of independent contractor rather than employee. The hospital was therefore not regularly targeted as a defendant in a malpractice suit. Only if the doctor whose negligence injured a patient was an employee could the hospital be reached through the doctrine of vicarious liability. The hospital was independently liable only if it were negligent in its administrative or housekeeping functions, for example causing a patient to slip and fall on a wet floor, but was otherwise immune from liability.[3]

Most hospitals prior to 1940 were protected from suit either by charitable or governmental immunity, the result of legislative concerns about the fiscal fragility of many hospitals in a time before government reimbursement of health care was extensive. Hospitals as charitable institutions were also exempted from the general rule that a corporation is responsible for the acts of its employees. In the 1950's, however, courts began to observe the increasing importance of the hospital in providing health care and supervising their staffs.[4] As medicine has grown more commercial, the courts have been less willing to grant a special subsidy in the form of immunities to nonprofit institutions.

a. Charitable Immunity

The doctrine declaring charitable institutions immune from liability can be traced to 1876, in the case of *McDonald v. Massachusetts Gen. Hosp.*[5] The court concluded that a charity patient, negligently operated upon by a student doctor, could not hold the hospital responsible, reasoning that the public and private donations supporting a charitable hospital constituted a trust fund which should not be diverted. The fear was that a single large judgment could destroy a hospital and that the threat might deter potential patrons. Liability insurance was not generally available to cover a hospital's risk exposure.

The trend over the past few decades in most states has been to impose tort liability on all hospitals, regardless of their corporate form or their origins. The charitable immunity doctrine disappeared with remarkable speed from American law. The case of *President and Directors of Georgetown College v. Hughes*,[6] was a watershed case eliminating immunity. In another famous case, *Bing v. Thunig*,[7] the court noted that the prevalence of liability insurance has calmed fears that a charity would be devastated by an adverse negligence judgment. Since that case, over 30 jurisdictions have abrogated charitable immunity, while the remainder retain immunity to the extent of

---

3. See e.g., Jones v. City of New York Hosp., 134 N.Y.S.2d 779 (N.Y.Sup.1954), reversed on other grounds 143 N.Y.S.2d 628 (N.Y.App.Div.1955) (hospital responsible for all administrative acts).

4. See for example Bing v. Thunig, 163 N.Y.S.2d 3, 143 N.E.2d 3 (N.Y.App.1957) (noting that the modern hospital employs a large staff of physicians, nurses, interns, administra-

tive and manual workers, and charges for its services like any corporation).

5. 120 Mass. 432 (1876), overruled by Colby v. Carney Hosp., 254 N.E.2d 407 (Mass.1969).

6. 130 F.2d 810 (D.C.Cir.1942).

7. 163 N.Y.S.2d 3, 143 N.E.2d 3 (N.Y.App. 1957).

statutory ceilings on recoverable damages, or only up to available coverage, or only as to charity care.[8] Partial immunity exists in some states, for example, beyond the coverage limits of liability insurance held by the hospital[9], or as to charity or non-paying patients[10], or where the hospital has no non-charitable assets[11], or where the patient is a "beneficiary" of the hospital[12]. One state court has held that a nonprofit hospital does not qualify as a charity under an immunity statute unless it proves that its funds come mainly from public and private charity.[13] Another state applies an eight factor test to charities, including hospitals, and has continued to apply immunity to hospitals that meet the factors.[14]

b. Sovereign Immunity

Governmental immunity has proved more resistant to elimination by the courts. Such immunity is held by the government or a sub-unit acting in its sovereign capacity. State courts have split on governmental immunity, with some eliminating it, others leaving it to the legislatures, and others retaining immunity in various forms.[15] The Federal Tort Claims Act (FTCA)[16] defines the extent to which the Federal government can be sued. Section 2680 provides for an exception to the Federal government's waiver of immunity for claims based upon "the exercise or performance or the failure to exercise or perform a discretionary function or duty on the part of a federal agency or an employee of the Government, whether or not the discretion involved be abused." Immunity in some cases turns on whether the negligent party was a government employee or an independent contractor.[17]

§ 7–2. Vicarious Liability

Judicial and legislative actions that abrogated immunities have left most hospitals responsible for the torts of their employees, including doctors, under the principle of vicarious liability. The hospital came to be viewed as an enterprise liable for the acts of its employees, and physicians became liable for the acts of their employees, a partner, or another physician working jointly. A master-servant relationship, a partnership, or a joint venture could lead to liability.

The fundamental principle of agency law is vicarious liability, i.e., the master (employer) is responsible for the torts of his servant (employee) even

---

8. See e.g., Weiss v. Goldfarb, 713 A.2d 427 (N.J.1998); Etheridge v. Medical Center Hospitals, 376 S.E.2d 525 (Va.1989).

9. Etheridge v. Medical Center Hospitals, 376 S.E.2d 525 (Va.1989).

10. Cutts v. Fulton–DeKalb Hospital Authority, 385 S.E.2d 436 (Ga.App.1989).

11. Fulton–DeKalb Hosp. Auth'y v. Alexander, 388 S.E.2d 372 (Ga.App.1989).

12. Johnson v. Mountainside Hosp., 571 A.2d 318 (N.J.Super.App.Div.1990), certification denied 584 A.2d 248 (N.J.1990).

13. Child v. Central Maine Medical Ctr., 575 A.2d 318 (Me.1990).

14. George v. Jefferson Hospital Association, 987 S.W.2d 710 (Ark.1999)(the factors are: (1) whether the organization's charter lim-

its it to charitable purposes; (2) whether the charter contains a "not-for-profit" limitation; (3) whether the goal is to break even; (4) whether it has earned a profit; (5) whether any profit or surplus must be used for charitable purposes; (6) whether it depends on contributions and donations for its existence; (7) whether it provides its services free to those unable to pay; and (8) whether the directors and officers receive compensation. These are applied flexibly in light of the operation of modern hospitals.

15. See e.g., Vernon's Ann.Texas.Civ.Prac. & Rem.Code § 101.021.

16. 28 U.S.C.A. §§ 1346(b) and 2671–2680.

17. Tivoli v. U.S., 1996 WL 1056005 (S.D.N.Y.1996); Leone v. United States, 910 F.2d 46 (2d Cir.1990).

though the master was not negligent. It is a nonfault based rule of liability. In the medical setting, most physicians are usually treated as independent contractors rather than employees; the hospital is thus relieved of any agency-based liability for their negligent acts. The mere grant of staff privileges is not sufficient control to impose vicarious liability on the hospital.[1] Traditional agency tests of the scope of employment connect the physician to the institution where the physician is a staff employee, even when the treatment steps outside the parameters of professional conduct. Interns and residents are usually employees, paid directly by the hospital and controlled by it.[2] A hospital might be liable for the acts of a physician, such as sexual relations between a physician and a patient during counseling or treatment, depending upon the time and place of the conduct, its relationship to the employee's work, or the purpose of the physician to serve his employer.[3] The test under agency law is whether the acts are within the "scope of employment", and are derived from events or conditions of employment.[4]

Hospitals continued through the sixties to be protected from most litigation for patient injuries against the treating physician, since most doctors defined their relationships with hospitals as independent contractors, and courts accepted this characterization.

a.   *The Independent Contractor Defense*

The independent contractor theory shields institutions from liability for acts of providers who are not directly employed but instead provide services as independent contractors. Since most physicians with staff privileges are independent contractors, therefore not under the hospital's control, the hospital is not responsible for their negligence. The defense is successful where the patient contracts directly with the physician for treatment and the physician then selects the hospital where the services are provided.[5]

As courts considered the range of situations in which physicians provided care in the hospital setting, they began to extend agency principles to limit the independent contractor defense. In the last four decades the courts have redefined the independent doctor's connection to the institution, using a number of doctrines to circumvent vicarious liability limitations.[6] Courts applied existing agency doctrines to the medical context, giving the plaintiff a possible defendant, where the hospital had immunity or where vicarious

---

§ 7–2

1.   Albain v. Flower Hosp., 553 N.E.2d 1038 (Ohio 1990).

2.   Shands Teaching Hosp. and Clinics, Inc. v. Pendley, 577 So.2d 632 (Fla.App.1991); Mozingo v. Pitt County Mem. Hosp., Inc., 400 S.E.2d 747 (N.C.App.1991), petition rev. denied 407 S.E.2d 537 (N.C.1991), affirmed 415 S.E.2d 341 (N.C.1992).

3.   Olson v. Connerly, 457 N.W.2d 479 (Wis. 1990) (court saw issue as whether physician who engaged in sexual relations with patient was motivated in part by a purpose to serve his employer); Doe v. Samaritan Counseling Ctr., 791 P.2d 344 (Alaska 1990) (sexual misconduct by therapist with patient; respondeat superior liability dependent on closeness of conduct to therapist's work).

4.   Lisa M. v. Henry Mayo Newhall Memorial Hospital, 907 P.2d 358 (1995)(sexual assault by ultrasound technician lacked causal nexus to employee's work); but see Roberts v. Blount Memorial Hospital, 963 S.W.2d 744 (Tenn.App. 1997)(no vicarious liability for sexual assault in hospital).

5.   Floyd v. Humana of Virginia, Inc. 787 S.W.2d 267 (Ky.App.1989)(hospital not liable for error of anesthesiologist where plaintiff admitted she had read and signed admission forms which said that physicians were independent contractors).

6.   For an overview, see Arthur F. Southwick, The Law of Hospital and Health Care Administration, Chapter XIV (2d ed. 1988).

liability would not work. Thus the "borrowed servant" rule and the "Captain of the Ship" doctrine placed the doctor in the position of responsibility in some specialized situations.

b. The Control Test

The most restrictive test for evaluating the status of the independent physician is to test whether the doctor was an employee or subject to the control of the hospital, applying a number of standard criteria for evaluating the existence of a master-servant relationship. The label given by contract to the relationship is not dispositive,[7] nor can contractual allocation of risk through indemnification clauses bind third parties. If the contract gave the hospital substantial control over the doctor's choice of patients, salary, or if the hospital furnished equipment, then an employee relationship might be found. The control test looks to the terms of the contract and the actual relationship between the hospital and the physician, particularly control over the course of treatment or medical decisions by the negligent physician.[8] A hospital's power to review appointments is not enough, since such power is aimed at maintaining professional standards.

The caselaw reflects divergent applications of the "control" test due to the breadth of the factors involved.[9] Some courts focus on the right of the hospital to control, while others look to the actual exercise of control.[10] Courts have found that radiologists and cardiologists exercise independent judgment and a hospital is not in a position to exercise control over their professional duties.[11]

Rural hospitals have been granted more leeway by the courts where several hospitals share physicians. The cases analyze issues of control over the physician's practice more conservatively; the mere provision of office staff or staff support is not considered sufficient[12] without further evidence of control.[13] The courts acknowledge that small rural hospitals lack substantial bargaining power, and therefore control, over itinerant physicians that they must share with other hospitals in the state.

c. The Ostensible Agency Test

Some courts have concluded that in some settings, such as the emergency room or the radiology labs, the hospital holds itself out as offering services to the patient through a doctor, even though the doctor who renders the service is not an employee. The ostensible agency or apparent authority test is commonly used to channel liability from the negligent physician to the health care institution. The ostensible agency or apparent authority test then looks to the patient and his or her expectations as to treatment.[14] Courts have applied agency doctrine against hospitals that permit or encourage patients to

7. Keller v. Missouri Baptist Hosp., 800 S.W.2d 35 (Mo.App.1990).

8. See e.g., Greene v. Rogers, 101 Ill.Dec. 543, 498 N.E.2d 867 (Ill.App.1986), appeal denied 106 Ill.Dec. 46, 505 N.E.2d 352 (Ill.1987).

9. See Mduba v. Benedictine Hosp., 384 N.Y.S.2d 527 (N.Y.App.Div.1976).

10. Mduba v. Benedictine, 384 N.Y.S.2d 527 (N.Y.App.Div.1976); Shepard v. Sisters of Providence, 793 P.2d 1384 (Or.App.1990), appeal after remand 793 P.2d 1384 (Or.App. 1990).

11. Kashishian v. Port, 481 N.W.2d 277 (Wis.1992).

12. Estates of Milliron v. Francke, 793 P.2d 824 (Mont.1990).

13. Gregg v. National Medical Health Care Servs., Inc., 699 P.2d 925 (Ariz.App.1985).

14. See e.g., Porter v. Sisters of St. Mary, 756 F.2d 669 (8th Cir.1985).

believe that independent contractor/physicians are, in fact, authorized agents of the hospitals. "Ostensible" or "apparent" agency or "agency by estoppel" are common terms used, although they are somewhat different. The "ostensible" or "apparent" agency theory is based on Section 429 of the Restatement (Second) of Torts (1965):

> One who employs an independent contractor to perform services for another which are accepted in the reasonable belief that the services are being rendered by the employer or by his servants, is subject to liability for physical harm caused by the negligence of the contractor in supplying such services, to the same extent as though the employer were supplying them himself or by his servants.

Two factors are relevant to a finding of ostensible agency: (1) whether the patient looks to the institution, rather than the individual physician, for care; and (2) whether the hospital "holds out" the physician as its employee. "Agency by estoppel," in contrast, is predicated on the arguably stricter standard of the Restatement (Second) of Agency § 267 (1958):

> One who represents that another is his servant or agent and thereby causes a third person justifiably to rely upon the care or skill of such apparent agent is subject to liability to the third person for harm caused by the lack of care or skill of the one appearing to be a servant or other agent as if he were such.

Under this theory, the plaintiff must actually rely upon the representations of the hospital or its agents. It imposes a heavier burden of proof on the plaintiff to show this "holding out".[15] A few decisions have even required that the plaintiff testify that he would have refused to have been treated by the physicians had he known they were independent.[16]

Most jurisdictions have allowed cases to proceed past summary judgment motions, or to go to the jury, on agency-based theories of ostensible agency or apparent authority.[17] Courts have held hospitals liable for negligent acts of independent contractors such as radiologists[18], cardiologists[19], anesthesiologists[20], neurologists, and emergency room physicians.[21] Courts hold hospitals liable for the malpractice of their independent contractor physicians where there is evidence that the hospital allowed or encouraged patients to believe that the physicians were authorized agents of the hospital.

An express representation to the patient that the treating physician is an employee of the hospital is not required. Direct testimony as to reliance by the patient is not needed, absent evidence that the patient knew or should have known that the treating physician was not a hospital employee when the

15. Baptist Memorial Hospital System v. Sampson, 969 S.W.2d 945 (Tex.1998); Grewe v. Mt. Clemens General Hosp., 273 N.W.2d 429 (Mich.1978).

16. Gasbarra v. St. James Hosp., 40 Ill.Dec. 538, 406 N.E.2d 544 (Ill.App.1979).

17. Sword v. NKC Hospitals, Inc., 714 N.E.2d 142 (Ind.1999)(and cases cited).

18. Kober v. Stewart, 417 P.2d 476 (Mont. 1966); Beeck v. Tucson Gen. Hosp., 500 P.2d 1153 (Ariz.App.1972).

19. Kashishian v. Port, 481 N.W.2d 277 (Wis.1992).

20. White v. Methodist Hosp. South, 844 S.W.2d 642 (Tenn.App.1992); Williams v. St. Claire Medical Ctr., 657 S.W.2d 590 (Ky.App. 1983); Gamble v. United States, 648 F.Supp. 438 (N.D.Ohio 1986).

21. Houghland v. Grant, 891 P.2d 563 (N.M.App.1995)(emergency room); Gilbert v. Sycamore Municipal Hospital, 622 N.E.2d 788 (Ill.1993) Strach v. St. John Hosp. Corp., 408 N.W.2d 441 (Mich.App.1987).

treatment was rendered.[22] Some courts have put it more sharply: the patient relies on the reputation of the hospital, not any particular doctor, and for that reason selects that hospital.[23] If the negligence results from emergency room care, most courts have held that a patient may justifiably rely on the physician as an agent unless the hospital explicitly disclaims an agency relationship.[24] A promotional campaign or advertising can create such reliance.[25] To avoid liability, a hospital can try to avoid patient misunderstanding by its billing procedures, the letterhead used,[26] signs[27], and other clues of the true nature of the relationship of the physician to the institution.[28] The court is likely however to cut through these devices if the reliance on reputation by the patient is strong enough.[29] A clear statement in a consent form that physicians in the hospital are independent contractors and not agents has been held to be sufficient to put a patient on notice.[30]

The second element—justifiable reliance by the patient to her detriment on the appearance of an apparent agency—has been found by many courts through the context in which health care is delivered. Hospitals are big businesses, spending millions marketing themselves through "expensive advertising campaigns."[31] They provide a range of health services, and the public expects emergency care and other functions, as a result of hospitals' self-promotion.[32] Hospitals do not actively inform the public about the various statuses of emergency room and other physicians.[33] As the role and image of the hospital have evolved, judicial willingness to stretch agency exceptions has likewise followed suit.[34] Recent decisions have declined to limit the doctrine to

22. Jackson v. Power, 743 P.2d 1376 (Alaska 1987); Hannola v. Lakewood, 426 N.E.2d 1187 (Ohio App.1980).

23. See e.g., White v. Methodist Hosp. South, 844 S.W.2d 642 (Tenn.App.1992).

24. Ballard v. Advocate Health and Hospitals Corporations, 1999 WL 498702 (N.D.Ill. 1999)

25. Clark v. Southview Hospital & Family Health Center, 628 N.E.2d 46 (Ohio 1994)(promotional and marketing campaign stressed the emergency departments); Gragg v. Calandra, 696 N.E.2d 1282 (Ill.App.1998)(unless patient is put on notice of the independent status of the professionals in a hospital, he or see will reasonably assume they are employees).

26. See Quintal v. Laurel Grove Hosp., 397 P.2d 161 (Cal.1964).

27. Cantrell v. Northeast Georgia Medical Center, 508 S.E.2d 716 (Ga.App.1998)(sign over registration desk stated that the physicians in the emergency room were independent contracts; consent form repeated this.)

28. For example, a physician with an office in the hospital, Street v. Washington Hosp. Ctr., 558 A.2d 690 (D.C.App.1989), or on the Board of Directors of the hospital, Funk v. Hancock, 498 N.E.2d 490 (Ohio App.1985). See H. Ward Classen, Hospital Liability for Independent Contractors, 40 Arkansas L.Rev. 469, 501–502 (1987).

29. Heubner v. Galesburg Cottage Hosp., 574 N.E.2d 1194 (Ill.App.1991).

30. Valdez v. Pasadena Healthcare Management, Inc., 975 S.W.2d 43 (Tex.App.1998); James v. Ingalls Memorial Hospital, 701 N.E.2d 207 (Ill.App.1998); Roberts v. Galen of Virginia, Inc., 111 F.3d 405 (6th Cir.1997), reversed 525 U.S. 249 (1999) (statement in outpatient registration and authorization for medical treatment form stated that "physicians, residents, and medical students are independent practitioners and are not employees or agents of the hospital"; even though patient had neither read nor signed this, it is the action of the hospital that governs as to ostensible agency.)

31. Kashishian v. Port, 481 N.W.2d 277 (Wis.1992) (noting the substantial sums of money spent by U.S. hospitals on advertising in 1989, and the fact the many people recall such advertising.)

32. Capan v. Divine Providence Hosp., 430 A.2d 647 (Pa.Super.1980).

33. See Arthur, 405 A.2d at 447. "This court may take judicial notice that generally people who seek medical help through the emergency room facilities of modern-day hospitals are unaware of the status of the various professionals working there." Id.

34. Kashishian v. Port, 481 N.W.2d 277 (Wis.1992); Torrence v. Kusminsky, 408 S.E.2d

just emergency room services, but rather have left it as a question of fact as to whether the patient knew the physician was an independent contractor.[35] Even the fact that a patient had contracted with a private physician as primary surgeon may not be sufficient to block the use of apparent authority doctrine.[36]

d. The Inherent Function Test

This approach, which only a few courts have applied, asks which functions of a hospital are essential to its operation. Radiology labs and emergency rooms are two such functions.[37] This notion of "inherent function" overlaps substantially with the "nondelegable duty" rule in agency law, as expressed in corporate negligence cases. Where a function is considered to be an inherent part of the functioning of the health care institution, the courts have held that the institution cannot escape liability because of the status of the physician. Vicarious liability applies in spite of a physician's independent contractor status and attempts in the service contract to characterize the physician or group as independent. The nature of the service rather than the patient's reliance or understanding as to the status of the physician determines liability. The courts applying the inherent function test have considered the expectations created by health care institutions in the public at large, through marketing and other forms of advertising to create good will[38]; the hospital's necessary reliance on specialty physicians to be successful and provide quality care; the control exercised by the hospitals over these so-called independent contractors;[39] and the lack of choice by patients as to radiologists, emergency room physicians, and other physicians encountered in the health care setting.

e. Non-delegable Duties

The non-delegable duty doctrine of agency law, like the inherent function approach, is an exception to the independent contractor doctrine. It is typically allowed where the employer has a duty to protect others and delegates performance to an independent contractor, like a common carrier.[40] The doctrine has been applied to impose obligations on hospitals to maintain responsibility for essential functions such as emergency rooms, which are imposed by statute, contract, charter or common law.[41] In *Jackson v. Power*,[42] the Alaska Supreme Court held that a hospital had a "non-delegable duty to provide non-negligent physician care in its emergency room." The court gave

684 (W.Va.1991)(general representation to the public is implied from the circumstances.)

35. Dahan v. UHS of Bethesda, Inc., 692 N.E.2d 1303 (Ill.App.1998)(physicians's contract with the hospital required him to see hospital employees free of charge; a reasonable person would conclude that he was an agent of the hospital).

36. See Kashishian v. Port, 481 N.W.2d 277, 284 (Wis.1992); Phoenix and Schlueter, supra note 23 at 879.

37. See e.g., Adamski v. Tacoma Gen. Hosp., 579 P.2d 970 (Wash.App.1978).

38. Hardy v. Brantley, 471 So.2d 358 (Miss. 1985) ("We notice a marked increase in advertisement and other forms of solicitations of patients as hospitals compete for the health-care dollar.")

39. Beeck v. Tucson General Hospital, 500 P.2d 1153 (Ariz.App.1972).

40. See Restatement (Second) Agency § 214 (failure of principal to perform non-delegable duty).

41. A non-delegable duty is an exception to the rule that an employer is not liable for the negligence of an independent contractor. W. Page Keeton et al., Prosser and Keeton on The Law of Torts, § 71 at 511–12 (5th ed. 1984). The court in Jackson observed that a non-delegable duty analysis is based upon a judicial assessment that " * * * the responsibility is so important to the community that the employer should not be permitted to transfer it to another." Id. at 512 (emphasis added). Accord, Alaska Airlines v. Sweat, 568 P.2d 916, 925–26 (Alaska 1977).

42. 743 P.2d 1376 (Alaska 1987).

a number of justifications for its analysis: the implication from the pervasive legislative regulation that the hospital is the ultimate repository of responsibility; public expectations of hospitals as responsible for the quality of care rendered by physicians, and finally the commercialization of medicine.[43] A few other decisions have used non-delegable duty analysis to impose liability on a facility for the acts of its independent contractors.[44] Other courts have resisted the extension of the non-delegable duty doctrine to the hospital emergency room, noting that emergency room services are not inherently dangerous, the usual test for the application of the doctrine.[45]

Changing judicial perceptions of the responsibility of institutions toward their providers, whether defined as employees or independent contractors, has expanded hospital vicarious liability. The hospital industry is pervasively regulated, particularly by the federal government. Health care generally is viewed as an inappropriate industry for free market principles. Most people have expectations at least as to the availability of emergency care, reinforced by hospitals over the years. The halo effect of nonprofit status, and the willingness of hospital administrators to draw on this line of credit, creates a public expectation as to emergency care, and perhaps the provision of hospital care generally.[46] Given the extent of government regulation and the special status of health care, the argument that hospitals approach the status of public utilities is a supportable position.[47] As such, it makes sense to focus liability on the hospital, whether the negligent acts are done by staff employees or independent contractor physicians. The hospital is arguably in the best position to monitor conduct within its walls, to enforce adherence to policies, and to provide a source of compensation to injured patients. Expanded liability also pushes hospitals to insure their staff and physicians on the medical staff under the same insurance carrier, to reduce their costs,[48] and to turn independent contractor physicians into employees for some hospital functions.

§ 7–3. General Negligence Liability

a. The General Duty

A health care institution, whether hospital, nursing home, or clinic, is liable to its patients for negligence in maintaining its facilities, providing and maintaining medical equipment, hiring, supervising and retaining nurses and other employees, and failing to have in place procedures to protect patients. Basic negligence principles govern hospital liability for injuries caused by

43. See also Williams v. St. Claire Medical Ctr., 657 S.W.2d 590 (Ky.App.1983).

44. See e.g., Simmons v. Tuomey Regional Medical Center, 498 S.E.2d 408 (S.C.App.998)(emergency room operation); Griffin v. Matthews, 522 N.E.2d 1100 (Ohio App.1987) (emergency room operation).

45. "The practice of emergency room medicine is not an activity that 'starts with danger and requires preventive care to make safety,' which would characterize the practice of medicine as an inherently dangerous activity; instead, the practice of emergency room medicine 'starts with safety and requires negligence to make danger.'" Kelly v. St. Luke's Hosp. of Kansas City, 826 S.W.2d 391, 396 (Mo.App. 1992).

46. Laurence D. Brown, Capture and Culture: Organizational Identity in New York Blue Cross, 16 J. Health Pol., Pol'y & Law 651, 669 (1991).

47. A.J.G. Priest, Possible Adaptation of Public Utility Concepts in the Health Care Field, 35 Law & Contemp.Prob. 839 (1970).

48. See Arthur Southwick, Hospital Liability—Two Theories Have Emerged, 4 J.Legal.Med. 1, 49 (1983).

other sources than negligent acts of the medical staff.[1] Hospitals are generally held to a national standard of care for hospitals of their size and treatment category. Where, however, a new technology of proven efficacy has been adopted by some hospitals, the standard may be used to measure the practice in all hospitals.[2]

The professional duty of a hospital is to provide a safe environment for patient diagnosis, treatment, and recovery. If an unsafe condition of the hospital's premises causes injury to a patient, as a result of the hospital's negligence, the hospital has breached its duty *qua* hospital.[3] The test is " * * * whether the negligent act occurred in the rendering of services for which the health care provider is licensed."[4] A hospital is usually not liable for intentional harms caused by its employees, absent special circumstances. If the intentional acts of its employees in assaulting or otherwise harming patients are foreseeable, however, liability will be imposed.[5]

Hospitals must have minimum facilities and support systems to treat the range of problems and side effects that accompany procedures they offer. In *Hernandez v. Smith*,[6] for example, an obstetrical clinic that lacked surgical facilities for caesarean sections was found liable for " * * * the failure to provide proper and safe instrumentalities for the treatment of ailments it undertakes to treat * * *."[7] Hospitals must provide inventories of medical equipment and make it available during medical procedures.[8] Staffing must be adequate. Short staffing has been rejected as a defense where the available staff could have been juggled to achieve closer supervision of a problem patient.[9] Failure to provide an adequate 24–hour anesthesia service may create liability.[10] The failure to provide supervision by an anesthesiologist of a certified registered nurse anesthetist, controverting the hospital's own policies, can lead to liability.[11]

Equipment must be adequate for the services offered, although it need not be the state of the art.[12] If a device such as an expensive CT scanner has come into common use, however, a smaller less affluent hospital can argue that it should be judged by the standards of similar hospitals with similar resources. This variable standard, reflecting resource differences between hospitals, would then protect a hospital in a situation where its budget does

§ 7–3

1. Lamb v. Candler General Hospital, Inc., 413 S.E.2d 720 (Ga.1992)(hospital negligent in failing to use proper replacement parts in a medical instrument).

2. Washington v. Washington Hosp. Ctr., 579 A.2d 177 (D.C.App.1990) (defendant had not yet placed end-tidal carbon dioxide monitors, allowing early detection of insufficient oxygen in time to prevent brain injury, in their operating rooms; plaintiff's injuries would have been prevented by the early detection such monitors make possible.).

3. See e.g., Pearce v. Feinstein, 754 F.Supp. 308 (W.D.N.Y.1990); Murillo v. Good Samaritan Hosp., 160 Cal.Rptr. 33 (Cal.App.1979).

4. Id. at 57.

5. Gess v. U.S., 952 F.Supp. 1529 (M.D.Ala. 1996)

6. 552 F.2d 142 (5th Cir.1977).

7. See also Valdez v. Lyman–Roberts Hosp., Inc., 638 S.W.2d 111 (Tex.App.1982).

8. See e.g., Dixon v. Taylor, 431 S.E.2d 778 (N.C.App.1993) (hospital failed to properly stock surgical cart with appropriate laryngoscope blade; whether this caused patient's death was properly a jury question).

9. Horton v. Niagara Falls Mem. Medical Ctr., 380 N.Y.S.2d 116 (N.Y.App.Div.1976).

10. Herrington v. Hiller, 883 F.2d 411 (5th Cir.1989).

11. Denton Regional Medical Center v. La-Croix, 947 S.W.2d 941(Tex.App.1997).

12. See Emory Univ. v. Porter, 120 S.E.2d 668, 670 (Ga.App.1961); Lauro v. Travelers Ins. Co., 261 So.2d 261 (La.App.1972), cert. denied 262 So.2d 787 (La.1972).

not allow purchase of some expensive devices. If an institution lacks a piece of equipment that is essential, particularly for diagnosis, it may have a duty to transfer the patient to an institution with that equipment.[13]

A hospital and its contracting physicians may be liable for damages caused by inadequate or defective systems they develop and implement, particularly where emergency care is involved. Poorly designed systems can create harm just as readily as an incompetent staff member.[14] Hospital on-call systems must work properly,[15] and systems for storing and supplying medications must function effectively.[16] Another example of such an administrative failure is when a hospital fails to properly schedule a patient consultation with a specialist, once it is required by a staff physician.[17]

b. Negligence Per Se

The usual American practice in a tort case not involving health care is to treat violation of a statute as negligence per se, giving rise to a rebuttable presumption of negligence. If the defendant fails to rebut the presumption, the trier of fact must find against him on the negligence issue. The classic statement of the rule is found in *Martin v. Herzog*[18]. Negligence per se is usually applied in cases where a statute is used to show a standard of care. In malpractice cases, however, standards are typically used to create only a permissive inference of negligence, allowing the plaintiff to get to the jury, which can then accept or reject the inference of fault.

Some states by statute have adopted corporate negligence for institutional providers. Florida, for example, has by statute incorporated "institutional liability" or "corporate negligence" in its regulation of hospitals. Hospitals and other providers will be liable for injuries caused by inadequacies in the internal programs that are mandated by the statute.[19] Once a hospital assumes a new responsibility, even if it is voluntary, it is expected to properly implement that responsibility.[20] Hospital bylaws are the source of duties by a hospital and its governing board, even though promulgated by the medical staff.[21]

Hospitals are regulated by their states. The majority are also subject generally to the standards of the Joint Commission on Accreditation of Healthcare Organizations (JCAHO). The standard of care that the courts have applied reflects a baseline mandated by JCAHO standards, including peer review through internal committee structures. This baseline has largely

---

13. See Blake v. D.C. Gen. Hosp. (discussed in Maxwell J. Mehlman, Rationing Expensive Lifesaving Medical Treatments, 1985 Wisc. L.Rev. 239).

14. Air Shields, Inc. v. Spears, 590 S.W.2d 574 (Tex.Civ.App.1979).

15. Marks v. Mandel, 477 So.2d 1036 (Fla. App.1985).

16. See Habuda v. Trustees of Rex Hospital, 164 S.E.2d 17 (N.C.App.1968), where the hospital was liable for inadequate rules for handling, storing, and administering medications; Herrington v. Hiller, 883 F.2d 411 (5th Cir.1989) (failure to provide for adequate 24–hour anesthesia service).

17. Decker v. St. Mary's Hosp., 188 Ill.Dec. 912, 619 N.E.2d 537 (Ill.App.1993).

18. 126 N.E. 814 (N.Y.App.1920).

19. West's Fla.Stat.Ann. § 768.60.

20. See e.g., Johnson v. University of Chicago Hosp., et al., 982 F.2d 230 (7th Cir.1992), on remand 1994 WL 118192 (N.D.Ill.1994) (holding that hospital that provided telemetry communications to ambulance paramedics, directing them to proper hospital in the system, could be liable for the negligent operation of the system).

21. Decker v. St. Mary's Hosp., 188 Ill.Dec. 912, 619 N.E.2d 537, 544 (Ill.App.1993).

doomed the locality rule for hospitals.[22] Courts have consistently allowed evidence of JCAHO standards, state hospital licensure laws, and the hospital's own by-laws, which the trier of fact could accept or reject, creating a permissive inference of negligence,[23] or a rebuttable presumption. Failure to properly maintain medical records, as required by state law and JCAHO regulations, can shift the burden of persuasion to the hospital, particularly where the records' absence handicaps the plaintiff's presentation of the case.[24]

Courts have proved resistant to the application of negligence per se to health care institutions, even to create an inference of negligence, unless the standard is specific and supported by expert testimony.[25] In nursing home litigation, some courts have likewise resisted the use of external standards to establish negligence.[26] In general, the more specific the standard, whether a JCAHO standard, a state regulation, or a statute, the more likely that a court will be willing to use the standard to invoke the negligence per se doctrine.

c. *Strict Liability*

The doctrine of strict liability has rarely been applied to health care services. The courts have viewed health care, whether provided by a physician or a hospital, as essentially the sale of a service in which the products are merely ancillary, and therefore inappropriate for the application of strict liability.[27] In situations where a product liability analysis might apply, such as the transfusion of infected blood, most states by statute have declared that blood is not a product.[28] Courts have also been troubled by expanding the liability of health care providers, considering (1) the experimental nature of much medical treatment; (2) factors beyond the control of the physician; and (3) lack of certainty of good results.[29] In a well-reasoned decision by the Court of Appeals of New Mexico,[30] the court recognized that hospitals are often in the chain of distribution of commercial products, but that the rationales for strict liability do not apply to them. They considered five common rationales for the application of strict liability. First, the doctrine spreads the cost of injuries on the manufacturer who can then pass the cost on to distributors, retailers and consumers. In the hospital setting, however, it is likely that the cost of liability arising from product defects will be shared by those buying any product, not just the defective one. Second, the doctrine eases the plaintiff's burden of proof of negligence. The court noted that it is easier to prove defective design than manufacturer defects, but in the hospital setting the distributor did not create the design defect. It becomes an issue of

22. See Shilkret v. Annapolis Emergency Hosp. Ass'n, 349 A.2d 245 (Md.1975). As to the JCAHO generally, see Timothy Jost, The Joint Commission on Accreditation of Hospitals: Private Regulation of Health Care and the Public Interest, 24 B.C.L.Rev. 835 (1983).

23. Decker v. St. Mary's Hospital, 188 Ill. Dec. 912, 619 N.E.2d 537 (Ill.App.1993).

24. Sweet v. Sisters of Providence in Washington, 893 P.2d 1252 (Alaska 1995).

25. Van Iperen v. Van Bramer, 392 N.W.2d 480 (Iowa 1986).

26. Makas v. Hillhaven, Inc., 589 F.Supp. 736 (M.D.N.C.1984).

27. Ayyash v. Henry Ford Health Systems, 533 N.W.2d 353(Mich.App.1995)(defective temporomandibular joint implant); Silverhart v. Mount Zion Hosp., 98 Cal.Rptr. 187 (Cal. App.1971) (defective surgical needle).

28. See Edward R. Wiest, Pricing Bad Blood: Reassessing Liability for Post–Transfusion Hepatitis, 15 Harv.J.Legis. 557 (1978).

29. Hoven v. Kelble, 256 N.W.2d 379 (Wis. 1977).

30. Parker v. St. Vincent Hospital, 919 P.2d 1104 (N.M.App.1996).

negligence selection of a product, an issue that plaintiff can prove. Third, the doctrine gives the plaintiff access to a full distribution chain for damages. This means that those in the chain of distribution put pressure on manufacturers to produce safer products. But in the health care setting incentives are complicated, since we want both advances in treatment and improved access, both of which are inhibited by high costs. If distributors only choose the high priced products to ensure indemnification, lower cost alternatives will not be developed. Fourth, fairness could be argued in enhancing compensation for plaintiffs. Both courts and legislatures however have rejected expanded liability for hospitals. Fifth, the doctrine can provide improved incentives for safety. Critics note however that hospitals might end up with incentives that force them to have their own quality control departments, which may not be cost-effective. Negligence claims may well provide adequate incentives for safety in the hospital setting.

The standard use of devices such as fetal monitors and CT scanners implicate the hospital as middleman in a stream of commerce of the sort courts discuss in products liability cases. Consider, for example, *Skelton v. Druid City Hosp. Board*,[31] where a suture needle broke off in the patient during ventral hernia repair. These needles were reused several times by the hospital, and there was no way to be sure exactly how many times. Section 2–315 of the Uniform Commercial Code, implied warranty of fitness for a particular purpose, was applied to this "hybrid" service-product transaction between hospital and patient.

Hospitals often reuse medical devices, such as pulmonary catheters, hemodialyzers, biopsy needles, electrosurgical devices, and endotracheal tubes.[32] The pressure to contain costs is one of the primary reasons for this practice. When a reused device proves defective and a patient is injured as a result, liability may fall on the manufacturer, the retailer, the hospital, and health care professionals. Strict liability and breach of warranty theories, as well as negligence, are likely to be attractive doctrines to apply, by analogy to the products liability area generally.[33] Drugs are normally prescribed by the treating physician, and are purchased by the patient from third party pharmacies. In the hospital setting, however, the patient is usually administered a variety of drugs as part of treatment and these drugs come from hospital supplies. In *Karibjanian v. Thomas Jefferson University Hospital*,[34] the plaintiff suffered injuries from the use of Thoroplast, a contract medium then in use with which he was injected during a diagnostic medical procedure called a cerebral arteriography. The hospital argued that a hospital could not be liable under § 402A when a defective surgical tool injures a patient during an operation[35], since it is in the business of supplying services, and "supplies" surgical tools only incidentally; and that the medical service could not be performed without the use of the instrument. The hospital also argued that it

31.   459 So.2d 818 (Ala.1984).

32.   Kobren et al., Medical Device Reuse: The FDA Perspective, 2 HealthSpan 6 (1985).

33.   Kahan and Gibbs, Reuse of Disposable Medical Devices: Regulatory and Liability Issues, 2 HealthSpan 12 (1985). But see Cutler v. General Electric Co., 4 UCC Rep.Serv. 300 (N.Y.Sup.1967) (defective pace-maker not cov-ered by Article 2 of the U.C.C.); Probst v. Albert Einstein Medical Ctr., 440 N.Y.S.2d 2 (N.Y.App.Div.1981) (defective spinal rod).

34.   717 F.Supp. 1081 (E.D.Pa.1989).

35.   Podrat v. Codman–Shurtleff, 558 A.2d 895 (Pa.Super.1989), appeal denied 569 A.2d 1368 (Pa.1989) (forceps).

was not in the "business of selling" Thoroplast, within the meaning of § 402A, but was rather in the business of providing services.

The federal district court concluded that "so long as a hospital *regularly* supplies contrast media to its patients, albeit as an incidental part of its service operations, it seems to fall within § 402A as explained by comment (f). The comment draws no distinction between suppliers of goods who also supply services, and those suppliers who simply supply goods." The hospital might be found by the trier of fact to be a seller of such drugs, which are held in inventory until use by patients, even though that is only incidental to the medical services provided.[36] Judge Lord noted that while such products may be termed "incidental", the product in fact makes the service possible, and the hospital has a duty to insure the safety of the equipment chosen.[37] Other courts have indicated willingness to allow a strict liability claim when the product ancillary to the service is in effect sold to the patient.[38]

Hospital administrative and mechanical services have been held to be subject potentially to strict liability[39], as have hospital operations that are not "integrally related to its primary function of providing medical services"[40]. A hospital may also be strictly liable for defective goods and materials that are not related to medical services.[41]

§ 7–4.   Corporate Negligence Doctrine

The courts' expansion of vicarious liability doctrine to hospitals made the medical personnel who used the hospital part of the "enterprise", whether they were staff employees or independent contractors. The next step was to impose corporate negligence for failures to properly select and monitor physicians. It has been defined broadly by the Pennsylvania Supreme Court, in Thompson v. Nason Hospital[1], as a doctrine imposing liability on a hospital if it fails to uphold the standard of care to "ensure the patient's safety and well-being while at the hospital. Four areas of liability are involved:

(1) A duty to use reasonable care in the maintenance of safe and adequate facilities and equipment;

(2) A duty to select and retain only competent physicians;

36. In Podrat v. Codman–Shurtleff, Inc., 558 A.2d 895 (Pa.Super.1989), appeal denied 569 A.2d 1368 (Pa.1989).

37. In footnote 5, Judge Lord offered an interesting analogy. He argued: "To offer another analogy, a restaurant patron who enjoys an exquisite souffle values the services of the chef more than the eggs with which it is made, since the eggs could be had for less than a dollar at any store. Nonetheless, if fate has it that the eggs are bad, the restaurant would be liable under § 402A as a supplier of eggs, even though the eggs were but an incidental part of what the patron paid for. And this is not to mention the services of the maitre d' who seats her, and the waiter who serves her."

38. See e.g., Mulligan v. Truman Medical Center, 950 S.W.2d 576 (Mo.Ct.App.1997)(Temporomandibular joint in-

terpositional implant; the court follows Missouri practice in allowing a strict products liability action against hospitals based on design defect and failure to warn); Mauran v. Mary Fletcher Hosp., 318 F.Supp. 297 (D.Vt.1970) (anesthetic drugs).

39. Johnson v. Sears, 355 F.Supp. 1065, 1067 (E.D.Wis.1973).

40. Silverhart v. Mount Zion Hospital, 98 Cal.Rptr. 187 (Cal.App.1971) (gift shop as example of such a nonessential function).

41. Thomas v. St. Joseph Hosp., 618 S.W.2d 791 (Tex.Civ.App.1981) (defective hospital gown that caught fire).

§ 7–4

1. 591 A.2d 703 (Pa.1991).

(3) A duty to oversee all persons who practice medicine within its walls as to patient care;

(4) A duty to formulate, adopt and enforce adequate rules and policies to ensure quality care for patients.

This articulation of the doctrine of corporate negligence by the Pennsylvania Supreme Court is broader than that of other state courts considering the issue, and the doctrine has usually been limited to the duty to select and monitor physicians and allied health care professionals. Thompson expanded the scope of the doctrine to encompass the hospital's general duties to ensure quality of care for patients. This recognizes the complexity of the modern health care institution and to need to impose a duty that is patient-centered.

a. The Duty to Supervise Medical Staff

Courts have expanded the doctrine of corporate negligence since the 1960's, recognizing the role of the modern hospital in providing care, support, and service, not just a shell for the physicians to use. A hospital is thus directly liable for the failure of administrators and staff to properly monitor and supervise the delivery of health care within the hospital. A hospital has a non-delegable duty directly to its patients and is liable for a breach of these duties. The action arises from the hospital's action or inaction regarding its policies rather than specific negligent acts of one of its employees.[2]

The case most identified with corporate negligence is *Darling v. Charleston Community Memorial Hospital.*[3] The plaintiff in *Darling* alleged that the defendant hospital was negligent in its supervision of Dr. Alexander. The hospital should have limited the kind of orthopedic work he was allowed to do; required him to review his operative procedures to bring them up to date; adequately supervised the case, especially since the treating physician, Dr. Alexander, had been placed on emergency duty by the hospital; required a consultation, particularly after complications had developed; and required its nursing staff to report developments in the case to the hospital administrator. The court relied upon several sources of standards to establish the standard of care for the hospital: JCAH Standards for Hospital Accreditation, the state licensing regulations, and the defendant's bylaws. All mandated that a hospital assume certain responsibilities for the care of the patient. The court allowed the jury to use these standards to evaluate the failures of both the nursing staff and the administrators in blowing the whistle on the defendant's handling of the case.[4]

Darling is a landmark case, recognizing the hospital's obligation to provide surveillance of the quality of patient care within the hospital. Other courts have imposed upon hospitals a duty to follow their own internal

---

2. Moser v. Heistand, 681 A.2d 1322 (Pa. 1996).

3. 211 N.E.2d 253 (Ill.1965), cert. denied 383 U.S. 946, 86 S.Ct. 1204, 16 L.Ed.2d 209 (1966). See, for a description of the Darling case by the plaintiff's lawyer, Appelman, Hospital Liability for Acts of Nonsalaried Staff Physicians, Personal Injury Annual 161 (1964); see also (describing the case), Keith E. Spero, Hospital Liability, 15 Trial 22 (July 1979).

More than twenty states have adopted the corporate negligence doctrine. See e.g., Humana Medical Corp. of Alabama v. Traffanstedt, 597 So.2d 667 (Ala.1992); Pedroza v. Bryant, 677 P.2d 166 (Wash.1984).

4. A hospital's breach of JCAHO standards are generally accepted as some evidence of negligence. See also Blanton v. Moses H. Cone Mem. Hosp., 354 S.E.2d 455 (N.C.1987).

procedures,[5] and to monitor risks to patients created by poor treatment by staff physicians.[6]

The justifications for the imposition of corporate negligence relate to the emergence of the hospital as a powerful institution.[7] First, the public perceives a hospital as a complex entity responsible for care provided, and relies on the hospital for this care. Second, the hospital is in the best position to "monitor and control physician performance", given its opportunities to observe professional practices on a daily basis, to adopt procedures to detect problems, and to use its medical staff to monitor quality. Third, tort liability creates incentives for hospitals to "insure the competency of their medical staffs".[8]

Courts have drawn some lines as to the limits of a hospital's duty to protect patients against medical errors. In *Jensen v. Archbishop Bergan Mercy Hospital*[9], the plaintiffs alleged that the nursing staff should have altered the attending physician's orders if they had reason to believe they were wrong. The court disagreed, holding that " * * * hospital staff members lack authority to alter or depart from an attending physician's order for a hospital patient and lack authority to determine what is a proper course of medical treatment for a hospitalized patient. The foregoing is recognition of the realities and practicalities inherent in the physician-hospital nurse relationship." Other courts have questioned the ability of a hospital administrator to detect medical errors. In *Albain v. Flower Hospital*[10], the Ohio Supreme Court recognized a hospital's independent duty to exercise due care in granting staff privileges and retaining competent physicians, but qualified the duty. They noted that "[m]ost hospital administrators are laypersons with no medical training at all." The limit of a hospital's duty therefore is to "remove a known incompetent," not to constantly supervise the activities of its physicians.[11] The hospital must have actual or constructive knowledge of the procedures used by the suspect physician, and the hospital's failure must have contributed to the patient's harm.[12] Maine has resisted the doctrine, finding that "there exist serious and unanswered public policy questions regarding the wisdom of requiring hospitals to control the medical judgments and actions of independent physicians practicing within their facilities. These questions implicate both quality of care and economic considerations. We will not lightly adopt a new theory of liability in an area of such significant concern for the public health."[13]

---

5. See e.g., Williams v. St. Claire Medical Center, 657 S.W.2d 590 (Ky.App.1983).

6. See e.g., Strubhart v. Perry Memorial Hospital Trust Authority, 903 P.2d 263 (Okla. 1995)(adopts doctrine of independent corporate responsibility, requiring hospitals to ensure that only competent physicians are privileged, and must take reasonable steps to ensure patient safety when it knows or should know that physicians has displayed incompetence); NKC Hospitals, Inc. v. Anthony, 849 S.W.2d 564 (Ky.App.1993).

7. Pedroza v. Bryant, 677 P.2d 166 (Wash. 1984).

8. Schoening v. Grays Harbor Community Hosp., 698 P.2d 593 (Wash.App.1985). See, Michael Nathanson, Hospital's Corporate Negligence: Enforcing the Hospital's Role of Administrator, 28 Tort and Insurance L.J. 575 (1993).

9. 459 N.W.2d 178, 183 (Neb.1990).

10. 553 N.E.2d 1038, 1046 (Ohio 1990).

11. For an older case imposing direct liability for the failure of a hospital to control the use of its facilities, see Hendrickson v. Hodkin, 11 N.E.2d 899 (N.Y.App.1937) (hospital liable for allowing a quack to treat a patient on its premises).

12. Thompson v. Nason Hosp., 535 A.2d 1177, 1182 (Pa.Super.1988), affirmed 591 A.2d 703 (Pa.1991).

13. Gafner v. Down East Community Hospital, 735 A.2d 969 (Me.1999).

Most courts have concluded that a hospital's responsibilities do not include an independent duty to get informed consent[14], or warn a patient about drug side-effects.[15] Such responsibility resides with the treating physician.[16] As one court argued, to impose upon a hospital a duty to obtain informed consent would require the hospital to intervene in the physician-patient relationship, risking its disruption.[17]

b. The Duty to Properly Select and Retain Medical Staff

Most jurisdictions have held hospitals to a duty to take reasonable steps to insure the competence of members of its medical staff.[18] A typical hospital has several categories of practicing physicians. The largest category is comprised of private physicians with staff privileges. These privileges include the right of the physicians to admit and discharge their private patients to the hospital and the right to use the hospital's facilities. Hospitals also have physicians in training, including interns, residents, and externs. Hospitals will often also have full-time salaried physicians, including teaching hospital faculty, and physicians under contract with the hospital to provide services for an agreed upon price.[19]

The organized medical staff of a hospital—private physicians with privileges—comprises the largest group of hospital-based physicians. The medical staff governs the hospital's provision of medical services. The typical medical staff operates under its own bylaws, elects its own officers, and appoints its own committees. It is not simply another administrative component of the hospital, under the authority of the governing board of the hospital. While the hospital board must approve the staff's bylaws and can approve or disapprove particular staff actions, it cannot usually discipline individual physicians without the cooperation of the medical staff or appoint administrative officers to exercise direct authority. A hospital's medical staff is therefore a powerful body within the larger organization.[20] The requirement of staff self-governance under JCAHO standards maintains and reinforces this physician authority within hospitals. The medical staff has been held independently liable in one case for its failure to supervise and regulate the activity of its members.[21]

The process by which the medical staff is selected is of crucial importance. While the medical staff is self-governing, the hospital establishes and implements procedures for staff selection and reappointment. A hospital therefore is held to have an obligation to its patients to investigate the qualifications of medical staff applicants.[22] This duty to investigate is based on a national

14. Giese v. Stice, 567 N.W.2d 156 (Neb. 1997).

15. See e.g., Goss v. Oklahoma Blood Institute, 856 P.2d 998 (Okl.App.1990).

16. See e.g., Mitchell v. Amarillo Hosp. Dist., 855 S.W.2d 857 (Tex.App.1993).

17. See Goss v. Oklahoma Blood Institute, 856 P.2d 998, 1007 (Okl.App.1990).

18. Welsh v. Bulger, 698 A.2d 581 (Pa. 1997). See generally Richard L. Griffith and Jordan M. Parker, With Malice Toward None: The Metamorphosis of Statutory and Common Law Protections for Physicians and Hospitals in Negligent Credentialing Litigation, 22 Texas Tech.L.Rev. 157 (1991).

19. H. Ward Classen, Hospital Liability for Independent Contractors: Where Do We Go From Here?, 40 Ark.L.Rev. 469, 478 (1987).

20. See generally Clark C. Havighurst, Doctors and Hospitals: An Antitrust Perspective on Traditional Relationships, 1984 Duke L.J. 1071, 1084–92.

21. Corleto v. Shore Mem. Hosp., 350 A.2d 534 (N.J.Super. Law Div.1975). This appears to be an isolated decision at present, with no other courts following suit.

22. Bell v. Sharp Cabrillo Hosp., 260 Cal. Rptr. 886 (Cal.App.1989).

standard of credentialing practice.[23] It includes solicitation and review of information from peers, current license status, malpractice claims filed, and any other relevant information.[24] Such an investigation of the background qualifications of an applicant for a staff appointment must go beyond checking basic credentials. The hospital should also investigate any limitations on privileges held by a physician at another hospital.[25] The hospital may not have to assess the truthfulness of all credentials that appear on an application for privileges renewal, particularly if a misrepresentation is unrelated to medical competence to practice.[26]

A hospital must have proper procedures developed to detect impostors.[27] Under the Health Care Quality Improvement Act of 1986 (HCQIA), hospitals must check a central registry, a national database maintained by the Unisys Corporation under contract with the Department of Health and Human Services, before a new staff appointment is made. If the hospital fails to check the registry, it is held constructively to have knowledge of any information it might have gotten from the inquiry.[28]

The monitoring and retention of hospital staff have led to expanded duties of hospitals to detect incompetence. The most extreme example of such a failure is *Gonzales v. Nork*[29], where a staff physician performed unnecessary surgery, falsified records, had a major substance abuse problem, and abused his patients. The court imposed liability on the hospital for failing to have an adequate system to detect record falsification, even though it complied with the JCAH standards of the time. The court was ahead of its time in recognizing that a properly designed utilization review process within an institution will produce data as to unnecessary procedures, high error rates, and other early warnings of problems with a staff physician. The existence of such a process will give a hospital actual notice of a problem, exposing them to liability if they fail to act to deal with the problem.[30]

A hospital should also properly restrict the clinical privileges of staff physicians who are incompetent to handle certain procedures, and detect concealment by a staff doctor of medical errors.[31] While some courts have limited this duty to only those situations where a hospital has learned of physician insufficiencies[32], others have talked of "negligent supervision" in

23. Lopez v. Central Plains Regional Hosp., 859 S.W.2d 600, 603 (Tex.App.—Amarillo 1993).

24. Johnson v. Misericordia Community Hosp., 301 N.W.2d 156 (Wis.1981).

25. Rule v. Lutheran Hosp., 835 F.2d 1250 (8th Cir.1987).

26. Taylor v. Singing River Hospital System, 704 So.2d 75 (Miss.1997)(held that hospital had no duty to discover misrepresentation in re-application for privileges, where the misrepresentation was largely irrelevant and not cause of injury; physician has misrepresented that he was board certified in cardiology when he was only board eligible).

27. Insinga v. LaBella, 543 So.2d 209 (Fla. 1989) (non-physician fraudulently obtained an appointment to the medical staff, after having

assumed the name of a deceased Italian physician).

28. Pub.L. No. 99–660, 100 Stat. 3784 (codified at 42 U.S.C.A. §§ 11101–11152) (amended by Public Health Service Amendments of 1987, Pub.L. No. 100–177, 101 Stat. 986).

29. No. 228566 (Sacramento County Super. Ct., Cal.1973), reversed on other grounds 131 Cal.Rptr. 717 (Cal.App.1976).

30. See e.g., Cronic v. Doud, 119 Ill.Dec. 708, 523 N.E.2d 176 (Ill.App.1988).

31. Cronic v. Doud, 119 Ill.Dec. 708, 523 N.E.2d 176 (Ill.App.1988), appeal denied 125 Ill.Dec. 214, 530 N.E.2d 242 (Ill.1988); Corleto v. Shore Memorial Hospital, 350 A.2d 534 (N.J.Super.Law Div.1975).

32. Albain v. Flower Hospital, 553 N.E.2d 1038 (Ohio 1990).

terms of an affirmative duty to detect problems.[33] The few cases that reject a hospital duty to monitor are increasingly outside mainstream thought on hospital responsibility.[34]

c. The Duty to Protect Non-Patients

Courts have resisted expanding a hospital's duty of care under the corporate negligence doctrine beyond hospital patients to patients treated by hospital staff members in those staff members' private office practices, where the hospital is not involved. They have worried about interfering with the doctor-patient relationship and overburdening administrators in trying to supervise physicians. Acts of malpractice committed by a staff physician outside the hospital are relevant only if the hospital has actual or constructive notice of them, and where failure to take some action as a result of such notice is negligence.[35] In *Pedroza v. Bryant*[36] the plaintiff, an obstetric patient of a physician with staff privileges, suffered injury. The plaintiff argued that it was foreseeable that the hospital's negligence in the granting or renewal of the doctor's staff privileges might result in harm to his obstetrical patients. Plaintiff argued that where the harm occurred, whether in or out of the hospital, was irrelevant. The court rejected this argument:

> The hospital holds itself out to the community as a competent provider of medical care. The hospital does *not* hold itself out as an inspector or insurer of the private office practices of its staff members. The delineation of staff privileges by the hospital can only affect the procedures used by staff members while they are inside hospital walls. The public cannot reasonably expect anything more.[37]

The *Pedroza* analysis continues to represent judicial attitudes toward non-patients.[38]

One jurisdiction has held a hospital responsible for the negligent acts of a physician outside the hospital. In *Copithorne v. Framingham Union Hospital*,[39] the plaintiff, Copithorne, a technologist at Framingham Union Hospital, was drugged and sexually assaulted by a physician with staff privileges at the hospital. She had sought the defendant physician's help, relying on his reputation as a good back specialist within the hospital where they both worked. The court assumed that the hospital was negligent in retaining him on the staff with knowledge of prior sexual assaults on hospital patients. The court limited the duty to employees who rely on a doctor's good standing within the hospital community. The court found that the facts would support a jury finding that

> the risk of injury to Copithorne was within the range of foreseeable consequences of the hospital's negligence in continuing Helfant's staff privileges. Where the hospital had received actual notice of allegations

---

33. Oehler v. Humana Inc., 775 P.2d 1271 (Nev.1989).

34. See St. Luke's Episcopal Hospital v. Agbor, 952 S.W.2d 503 (Tex.1997)(holding that Texas Medical Practice Act granted immunity from civil liability to hospital engaged in peer review, when done without malice); Hull v. North Valley Hosp., 498 P.2d 136 (Mont.1972).

35. Fridena v. Evans, 622 P.2d 463 (Ariz. 1980).

36. 677 P.2d 166 (Wash.1984).

37. Id. at 172.

38. See also Pace v. Unity House of Roman Catholic Diocese of Albany, 563 N.Y.S.2d 309 (N.Y.App.Div.1990) (patient raped in unrelated residence facility to which she was referred by hospital after discharge).

39. 520 N.E.2d 139 (Mass.1988).

that Helfant had sexually assaulted patients, both on the hospital premises and off the premises in his office and in a patient's home, and yet took only the limited measures indicated, it was not unforeseeable that Helfant would continue to act in a consistent, if not worse, manner.[40]

The relationship of the hospital to the plaintiff and the defendant makes this case special, given the plaintiff's reliance on the hospital's staff selection and retention process and an implied representation that its medical staff was trustworthy. A hospital's duty to foreseeable third parties outside the hospital setting is not hard to extend beyond the facts of Copithorne. As hospitals devote more attention to staff privileges, driven by their need to avoid liability and achieve the best possible staffs, and as physicians come to restrict their privileges to fewer hospitals, or just one, the reliance interest of the general public as well as staff also increases. Liability like that in *Copithorne* then becomes a more reasonable outcome of malpractice by a physician, even outside the hospital.

d. Duty to Monitor Informed Consent

Hospitals are generally not required to monitor the actions of non-employee staff physicians in obtaining the informed consent of patients, on the grounds that it is the treating physician's responsibility, given his or her relationship with the patient.[41] In *Petriello v. Kalman*,[42] the Connecticut Supreme Court held that a hospital had no duty to obtain a patient's consent to surgery, nor to conduct any kind of inquiry. The plaintiff had suffered a miscarriage, and the treating physician scheduled the plaintiff for a dilation and curettage to remove the fetus. A hospital nurse medicated the plaintiff before the procedure, without getting the plaintiff's signature on the consent form. While this violated a hospital policy requiring completion of such forms, the court rejected any duty on the hospital. Such a duty is resisted by the courts, on the grounds that the responsibility belongs to the attending physician: "This contention is unsound, however, because it equates the signing of the form with the actuality of informed consent, which it is the sole responsibility of the attending physician to obtain."[43]

A duty on the hospital and its staff to ensure that patient consent is properly obtained by attending physicians is emerging in the caselaw.[44] Such a duty is defensible on several grounds. First, the hospital will work harder to make sure that consent is properly obtained. Given the unwillingness of some physicians to pursue a patient's informed consent in the hospital setting, and the possibility that such consent will be overlooked because of scheduling or other conflicts, the hospital would seem to be the logical locus for insuring that a proper informed consent is obtained. Second, in other areas of the law, courts have been sympathetic to an expansion of the role of the hospital, and its corresponding obligations to supervise staff, to establish proper procedures, and to hire properly. Third, the deference to physicians that has been part of the caselaw of hospital-physician relationships is diminishing as courts recog-

40. Id. at 147.

41. See e.g., Ward v. Lutheran Hospitals & Homes Society of America, 963 P.2d 1031 (Alaska 1998); Belcher v. Charleston Area Medical Center, 422 S.E.2d 827 (W.Va.1992), reaffirming Cross v. Trapp, 294 S.E.2d 446 (W.Va.1982); Smith v. Gaynor, 591 A.2d 834 (Conn.Super.1991).

42. 576 A.2d 474 (Conn.1990).

43. Id. at 478.

44. See e.g., Doctors Mem. Hosp. v. Evans, 543 So.2d 809 (Fla.App.1989)

nize that the delivery of health care is a team operation in which support is vital to the proper care of patients in the hospital. Fourth, the impetus to complete written records in health care institutions, for reimbursement and monitoring purposes, has increased the responsibility of the institution to guarantee completeness of records. Written consent forms predominate in institutional settings, given bureaucratic pressures for a complete patient record, a desire to protect against litigation, and a sense that something is better than nothing. They are often reduced to little more than a bureaucratic formality that the institution hopes will erect a defense shield against malpractice suits. Such forms can however be improved to better facilitate doctor-patient conversation and risk disclosure, and that task should fall upon the hospital with its multiplicity of administrators. As health care reform moves toward enterprise liability and centrally managed care organizations, it is likely that health care institutions will face expanded duties to obtain patient informed consent.

§ 7–5. Conclusion

Hospitals have changed as the delivery of health services has changed. From a workshop for physicians, they have become complex institutions, less distinguishable from for-profit enterprises in the economy. As their ability to process information and manage institutional behavior has grown, so tort rules have stretched to channel liability to the hospital. The law of vicarious liability is one such example, the expansion of corporate negligence another. Health care reform that imposes some variation of enterprise liability on hospitals may well be the next logical development in hospital liability.[1]

B. TORT LIABILITY OF MANAGED CARE SYSTEMS

§ 7–6. The Theory and Practice of Managed Care

The term "managed care" is a comprehensive category that encompasses a continuum of plans—from plans that require little more than preauthorization of patient hospitalization, to staff model HMOs—that focus on utilization and price of services. The goal is reduction of health care costs, and maximization of value to both patient and payer.[1] A Managed Care Organization is a reimbursement framework combined with a health care delivery system, an approach to the delivery of health care services that contrasts with "fee-for-service" medicine. Managed care is usually distinguished from traditional indemnity plans by the existence of a single entity responsible for integrating and coordinating the financing and delivery of services that were once scattered between providers and payers.[2]

§ 7–5

1. See Kenneth S. Abraham and Paul C. Weiler, "Enterprise Liability and the Evolution of the American Health–Care System," 108 Harv.L.Rev. 381 (1994).

§ 7–6

1. See generally Peter D. Fox, Overview of Managed Care Trends, The Insider's Guide to Managed Care: A Legal and Operational Road-

map 1 National Health Lawyers Association (1990).

2. See generally Robert H. Miller and Harold S. Luft, Managed Care: Past Evidence and Potential Trends, 9 Frontiers of Health Services Management 3 (1993); Robert Shouldice, Introduction to Managed Care: Health Maintenance Organizations, Preferred Provider Organizations, and Competitive Medical Plans (1991); Jonathan P. Weiner and Gregory de Lissovoy, Razing a Tower of Babel: A Taxono-

Managed care is a growth area in health care delivery, rapidly supplanting fee-for-service medicine.[3] Such care is delivered through large managed care systems such as health maintenance organizations and preferred-provider organizations. Sixty percent of the 160 million Americans with employer-sponsored health insurance were enrolled in a managed care plan in 1987; by contrast, in 1980 only five to ten percent were enrolled in such plans.[4] HMOs and PPOs (excluding managed fee-for-service plans) enrolled over 27% of employees with group health insurance in 1987. This contrasts with 1981 figures of 4% enrollment.[5] By 1992 HMO enrollment had exceeded 40 million members, with 16% of the U.S. population enrolled in an HMO.[6]

Managed care organizations (MCOs) are most commonly represented by health maintenance organizations (HMOs), which include group models, network models, and IPAs (HMO contracts with an association of independent practitioners).[7] Other organizations include Preferred Provider Organizations (PPOs), Exclusive Provider Organizations (EPOs), utilization review organizations, and even hospitals. While a staff model HMO will have a central location for practice, other models involve physicians and dentists in their own offices, providing care to subscribers under contract to the MCO. A Health Maintenance Organization (HMO) is an entity that provides comprehensive health care services to an enrolled membership for a fixed per capita fee. HMOs are thus both insurers and providers of medical care. HMOs are usually classified into four categories based on their relationship with medical care providers: staff model HMOs directly employ physicians to provide medical care; group model HMOs contract with an independent, multi-specialty corporation or partnership of physicians to delivery care; network HMOs contract with a number of groups of physicians who also may serve patients not belonging to the HMO; and individual practice association (IPA) and HMOs contract, the IPA in turn contracts with individual physicians to provide care in their own offices. A recent study of HMOs found that 48% were IPAs, 14% networks, and 38% staff or group-model HMOs.

HMOs are governed by both state and federal law. Most states have HMO enabling acts, which address both the insurance and health care delivery aspects of HMOs. A federal statute adopted in 1973 to encourage the growth of HMOs establishes federal recognition of HMOs as well.[8] Federal policy is based upon the assumption that HMOs deliver medical care at a total annual cost per person substantially lower than non-HMO health care plans. Studies have found that HMOs cost from 10–40% less than fee for service plans,[9] admit patients to hospitals 40% less often than do fee for service plans, and

my for Managed Care and Health Insurance Plans, 18 J. Health Pol., Pol'y & Law 75 (1993).

3. See generally John K. Iglehart, The American Health Care System: Managed Care, 327 New Eng. J. Med. 742 (1992).

4. J. Gabel, et al., The Changing World of Group Health Insurance, 7 Health Affairs 48, 53 (1988).

5. Id. at 52. See also Glenn Kramon, "Managed Care" is Top Plan Now, N.Y. Times, June 14, 1988, at D2.

6. Id.

7. See Gary Scott Davis, Introduction to Managed Health Care Primer, in The Insider's Guide to Managed Care: A Legal and Operational Roadmap 1 National Health Lawyers Association (1990).

8. 42 U.S.C.A. §§ 280(c), 300(c).

9. Harold Luft, Health Maintenance Organizations: Dimensions of Performance (1981); Willard G. Manning, et al., A Controlled Trial of the Effect of a Prepaid Group Practice on the Use of Services, 310 New Eng. J. Med. 1505 (1984).

use 40% fewer hospital days.[10] Differences between utilization by HMO and non-HMO plans of discretionary surgery seem particularly large. Discretionary surgery under HMO care is less likely or frequent, therefore lowering overall costs of the program. HMOs may thus provide real cost savings, attributable primarily to the incentives created by per capita fixed fees.[11] HMOs remain an important tool for employers concerned about health care costs, in spite of some uncertainty about the cost savings over the long run.[12] HMOs vary in their structure, but different structures do not make a significant difference in utilization of health care services. IPAs for example have been found to be as effective as other model types in controlling use of services.[13]

Most managed care programs have three relevant features from a liability perspective. First, such programs select a restricted group of health care professionals who provide services to the program's participants. Second, such programs accept a fixed payment per subscriber, in exchange for provision of necessary care. This pressures managed care organizations to search for ways to minimize costs. Third, following from number two, a variety of strategies are used to ensure cost effective care.[14] Altering physician incentives is central to managed care, since physicians influence seventy percent of total health spending, while receiving only about twenty percent of each health care dollar.[15] Such plans use utilization review techniques, incentives systems, and gatekeepers to control costs.[16] Managed care organizations create a new set of relationships between payers, subscribers and providers. These new relationships create new liability risks. The subscriber typically pays a fee to the MCO rather than the provider, relinquishing control over treatment and choice of treating physician. The payor in turn shifts some of its financial risk to its approved providers, who must also accept certain controls over their practice. A physician, traditionally the patient's agent and advocate, as a quid pro quo will receive many patients from the payor.[17] Young doctors want to work in these new settings, to gain the advantages of free time and control over work load. One survey found that more than 50% of the young doctors polled preferred a guaranteed salary to traditional fee-for-service compensation, and 81% preferred a group practice or HMO, while just 11% favored solo prac-

10. Robert H. Miller, Harold S. Luft, Managed Care Plan Performance Since 1980: A Literature Analysis, 27I JAMA 1512 (1994); Manning, supra; Group Health Association of American, HMO Industry Profile: Utilization Patterns (1988).

11. See H.S. Luft and R.H. Miller, Patient Selection in a Competitive Health Care System, 7 Health Affairs 97 (1988); I. Strumwasser, et al., The Triple Option Choice: Self–Selection Bias in Traditional Coverage, HMOs and PPOs, 26 Inquiry 432 (1989).

12. J. Gabel, et al., Employer–Sponsored Health Insurance in America, 8 Health Affairs 116 (1989).

13. Randall S. Brown and Jerrold Hill, Does Model Type Play a Role in the Extent of HMO Effectiveness in Controlling the Utilization of Services? (Mathematica Policy Research, Inc., May 10, 1993).

14. J. Gabel, et al., The Changing World of Group Health Insurance, 7 Health Affairs 48, 52 (1988) (defined in study as HMOs, PPOs, or conventional plans with preadmission certification review).

15. See Alain C. Enthoven, Supply–Side Economics of Health Care and Consumer Choice Plan, in A New Approach to the Economics of Health Care 467 (Mancur Olson ed. 1981).

16. David D. Griner, Note, Paying the Piper: Third–Party Payor Liability for Medical Treatment Decisions, 25 Ga. L. Rev. 861 (1991).

17. Ernest Saward, E.K. Gallagher, "Reflections on Change in Medical Practice: The Current Trend To Large–Scale Medical Organizations," 250 JAMA 2820 (1983); Paul Starr, The Social Transformation of American Medicine, (N.Y. Basic Books ed., 1982).

tice.[18] Physicians want more time for families and personal interests. Older physicians in a solo practice or a small group may also prefer to have an organization take over the administrative burdens of billing insurers and the government, and give them access to a guaranteed pool of patients.[19]

Medical practice is thus increasingly moving toward managed care settings. These managed care organizations, such as health maintenance organizations (HMOs) and independent practice associations (IPAs), have emerged as a force in health care delivery primarily because they promise lower cost care at a time when employers and the government are worried about the escalating costs of that care.

§ 7–7. Malpractice Liability

Managed care organizations that integrate health care delivery and financing, such as HMOs, face the same vicarious and corporate liability questions as hospitals. They provide medical services through physicians, whether the physicians are salaried employees or independent contractors. These medical services can injure patients/subscribers, leading to a malpractice suit for such injuries.[1] A consideration of these principles suggests that MCOs face extensive liability risks for injuries caused by their panel physicians, dentists, and other providers.

a. Direct Institutional Liability

Managed care organizations are motivated by goals of both quality and efficiency—the objective of cost sensitive health care. The style of practice in MCOs is different from fee-for-service practice. Commentators have proposed that courts should allow MCO physicians to be judged by a different standard of care from fee-for-service physicians, in recognition of the different approach to care that MCOs have adopted to control costs.[2] Some have argued that courts should explicitly recognize these differences through standard of care jury instructions. Given the elasticity inherent in most medical practices, however, such an explicit recognition of practice differences is hardly necessary. Tort doctrines such as the "best judgment rule"[3], the "respectable minority"[4] doctrine, and the reliance on medical experts to establish the standard of care may well be sufficient to allow courts to accommodate the more conservative, cost-sensitive style of practice found in HMOs.[5] Recent decisions addressing most managed care and utilization review liability indicate judicial willingness to give providers leeway to practice a more conservative, cost-effective style.[6] The accordion-like nature of "reasonable care" allows for cost-sensitive modes of practice to be found acceptable.

18. Wall St. J., Oct. 31, 1989, at B1.

19. See George Anders, McDonald's Methods Come to Medicine as Chains Acquire Physicians' Practices, Wall St. J., Aug. 24, 1993, at B1, B6.

§ 7–7

1. See, generally, Joanne B. Stern, Malpractice in the Managed Care Industry, 24 Creighton L.Rev. 1285 (1991).

2. See Randall Bovbjerg, The Medical Malpractice Standard of Care: HMOs and Customary Practice 1975 Duke L.J. 1375 (1976).

3. See the discussion at § 6–5.

4. See discussion at § 6–5.

5. Questioning the flexibility of the negligence standard, see Maxwell J. Mehlman, The Patient–Physician Relationship in an Era of Scarce Resources: Is There a Duty to Treat?, 25 Conn. L. Rev. 349 (1993).

6. See e.g., Harrell v. Total Health Care, Inc., 781 S.W.2d 58, 61 (Mo.1989)(en banc) ("People are concerned both about the cost and the unpredictability of medical expenses. A plan such as Total offered would allow a person to fix the cost of physicians' services.").

The second institutional negligence issue concerns the standard of practice for managed care organizations generally, encompassing organization, delivery of services, and other corporate issues that facilitate the delivery of high quality care. The liability issues primarily are those of proper selection and retention of medical staff, and proper design of salary incentives, discussed below.[7] Managed care organizations may also be liable for the same types of errors as hospitals, from patient slips to medication errors.

b. *Vicarious Liability—Agency Principles*[8]

The relationship of the MCO to its member physicians is more varied that than of the hospital to its medical staff. This relationship will determine the source of liability. For example, staff model HMOs, employing physicians on a salaried basis on their own medical facilities, satisfy the master-servant requirements of agency law. A subscriber to an IPA-style managed care organization, however, may not look to it for care rather than solely to the individual physicians. In an IPA, there is no central office, staffed by salaried physicians; the subscriber instead goes to the individual offices of the primary care physicians or the specialists. The liability analysis begins with the control exercised by the plan over its physicians. Some courts have refused to extend agency principles even to staff model HMOs, the best candidates for such liability.[9] However, most courts have imposed vicarious liability on such staff model plans.

Courts look at the operation of the managed care organization, asking whether it "conducts itself in a fashion akin to a health care provider".[10] If so, it will be subject to the same liabilities, regardless of its organizational structure. In *Sloan v. The Metropolitan Health Council of Indianapolis, Inc.,*[11] the Sloans sued Metro, a health maintenance organization, alleging a negligent failure to diagnose. Metro claimed that its physicians were independent in their practice of medicine, and that Metro did not control their judgment in diagnosis or treatment decisions. It therefore invoked the "corporate practice of medicine" doctrine, which made it unlawful for a corporation to practice medicine. The defendant argued that a physician may not accept directions in diagnosing and treating ailments from a corporation, and is therefore an independent contractor.

The court rejected this defense, finding it to be a "non sequitur to conclude that because a hospital cannot practice medicine or psychiatry, it cannot be liable for the actions of its employed agents and servants who may be so licensed."[12] An HMO likewise should not be insulated from liability. The court noted that Metro's staff physicians were under the control of its medical director, a physician, and "[t]he circumstances establish an employment

---

7. See e.g., U.S. Gen. Acct. Off., Medicaid: HealthPASS: An Evaluation of a Managed Care Program for Certain Philadelphia Recipients (May 1993).

8. See discussion of vicarious liability principles in 7-2, supra . .

9. See e.g., Mitts v. H.I.P. of Greater New York, 478 N.Y.S.2d 910 (N.Y.App.Div.1984) (HMO "does not treat or render medical services or care to anyone."); Williams v. Good Health Plus, 743 S.W.2d 373 (Tex.App.1987).

10. See e.g., Decker v. Saini, 14 Employee Benefits Cas. 1556, 1991 WL 277590 (Mich.Circuit Ct., Oakland Cty., 1991)(holding an IPA model HMO to ostensible agency principles. The defendant had argued it was merely a health care insurer, not a provider; however, the advertising promised the "best care" available.).

11. 516 N.E.2d 1104 (Ind.App.1987).

12. Id. at 1108.

relationship where the employee performed acts within the scope of his employment".[13]

Some courts have pushed the boundaries even further, using agency principles to reach consulting physicians chosen by physicians employed by the HMO. In *Schleier v. Kaiser Foundation Health Plan*,[14] a staff model HMO was held vicariously liable for physician malpractice, not of its employee-physician, but of an independent consulting physician. The court found four grounds for holding the HMO vicariously liable: (1) the consultant physician had been engaged by an HMO-employed physician, (2) the HMO had the right to discharge the consultant, (3) services provided by the consultant were part of the regular business of the HMO, and (4) the HMO had some ability to control the consultant's behavior, since he answered to an HMO doctor, the plaintiff's primary care physician. This judicial willingness to impose respondeat superior liability for the negligence of a consulting, non-employee physician clearly applies to the IPA model HMOs and even PPOs.

Ostensible agency doctrine has been borrowed from the hospital setting to reach physicians who may not even be employed by the HMO. Thus, in *Boyd v. Albert Einstein Medical Center*,[15] the court asked whether the HMO through its agents created the appearance that an agency relationship existed between the HMO and the negligent physician; and whether the patient reasonably relied upon this appearance to his detriment or injury.[16]

In *Boyd*, the HMO advertised in its brochure as a "total care program", as "an entire health care system". The court seemed to rely on this advertising as a holding out, a representation from which a subscriber could conclude that the physicians of the HMOs were its employees.[17] A reliance by the subscriber on the managed care organization for their choice of physicians, and any holding out by the MCO as a provider, is sufficient. The application of vicarious liability has a powerful incentive effect on MCOs to select better physicians.

IPA-model HMOs that become "the institution", as in *Boyd*, that "hold out" the independent contractor as an employee, and that also restrict provider selection are vulnerable to ostensible agency arguments.[18] Where the HMO exercises substantial control over the independent physicians by controlling the patients they must see and by paying on a per capita basis, an agency relationship has been found.[19]

The development of complex cost and quality controls, which strengthen the supervisory role of the MCO, together with the managed care industry's preference for the capitation method of physician compensation, are likely to lead the courts to hold the IPA model HMO-physician relationship to respon-

13. Id. at 1109.

14. 876 F.2d 174 (D.C.Cir.1989).

15. 547 A.2d 1229 (Pa.Super.1988).

16. Id. at 1235.

17. See also Jones v. Chicago HMO Ltd. of Illinois, 703 N.E.2d 502(Ill.App.1998)(representations as part of "aggressive, door-to-door marketing campaign"); Petrovich v. Share Health Plan of Illinois, 696 N.E.2d 356 (Ill.App.1998)(citing Boyd with approval, and noting the aggressive marketing of the HMO);

McClellan v. Health Maintenance Organization of Pennsylvania, 604 A.2d 1053 (Pa.Super.1992) (ostensible agency based on advertisements by HMO claiming that it carefully screened in primary care physicians).

18. See e.g., McClellan v. Health Maintenance Organization of Pennsylvania, 604 A.2d 1053 (Pa.Super.1992).

19. Dunn v. Praiss, 606 A.2d 862 (N.J.Super.App.Div.1992).

deat superior liability. Even a plan-sponsored network risks exposure to ostensible agency arguments if a court can find that the plan sponsor has created an expectation on the part of patients that the plan will provide high-quality providers of care. If the plan restricts a member's choice of providers, as will be likely in most situations, the network providers look like "agents" of the sponsor. The alternative—disclaimers in a PPO directory or other subscriber material as to quality of care, reminders to patients that they are responsible for choosing their physicians—may provide a legal shield against ostensible agency arguments. Such disclaimers are, however, not very reassuring when marketing to subscribers of a network plan.

c. *Financial Disincentives to Treat, Refer, or Hospitalize Patients*

Managed care organizations aim to manage the cost of health care by reducing utilization of hospitalization, specialists and testing. The incentives that HMOs create for providers to under-utilize health care for their patients—the possibility that these incentives will "corrupt" the medical judgment of a physician—is raised frequently. The fear with managed care—and its goal of reducing expenditures by its physicians—is that some patients will be undertreated and suffer injury as a result. One example of this is provided by the case of *Bush v. Dake*.[20] The plaintiff argued that the system of incentives used by an HMO deterred the primary care physician from giving her a timely pap smear, since he was paid nothing extra for such testing. The Plan also set aside a certain amount of money each year for a "referral pool" and a "hospital/ancillary pool" for the Network physicians. The money in these pools would be depleted with each referral to a specialist or hospitalization of a patient during the year. At the end of the year, any money left over in these pools would be divided between the HMO and the individual physicians. The fewer referrals a doctor made and the fewer hospitalizations he ordered for his patients, the more money he made.

The plaintiffs contended that this system provided the physicians involved with financial disincentives to properly treat, refer, and hospitalize patients. While the court concluded that HMOs and their utilization review practices are not against public policy, the court also found "a genuine issue of material fact presented as to whether GHS's system in and of itself proximately contributed to the malpractice * * *." The delay and the effect of the HMO's incentives on the physicians was a jury question. The *Bush* case, an unpublished opinion, is one of the earliest cases raising the issue of the effect of HMO incentives on the medical care received by beneficiaries. While on appeal it was settled.[21]

The evidence that HMO incentives have a detrimental effect on patient care is equivocal at best.[22] Some form of incentive for cost-conservation in health care is desirable, and the ongoing debate is over the extent to which

20. No. 86–25767 (Saginaw County, Mich., 1989).

21. See Daniel Q. Haney & Fred Bayles, Paying a Price for Cost–Conscious HMOs, L.A. Times, Jan. 28, 1990, at A3; see also, Sweede v. Cigna Healthplan of Delaware, Inc., 1989 WL 12608 (Del.Super.) (claim that doctor withheld necessary care because of financial incentives rejected on facts of case); Pulvers v. Kaiser Foundation Health Plan, 99 Cal.App.3d 560, 160 Cal.Rptr. 392 (1979) (court held that incentives in physician plan were acceptable).

22. Robert H. Miller and Harold S. Luft, Does Managed Care Lead to Better or Worse Quality of Care? 16 *Health Affairs* 7, 18 (1997).

payment incentives can strike the right balance.[23] While incentives may create conflicts of interest, they also give physicians flexibility in their clinical decision-making. The alternative–administrative rules and review mechanisms for denying benefits–is both more inefficient and arguably more constraining of physician decision-making. This debate–incentives versus rules–is an ongoing one.[24] Plaintiffs have nonetheless argued that payment systems can cause a reduction in the quality of care delivered by physicians in managed care organizations.[25]

Managed care organizations have not been successfully sued in many cases for cost-containment failures, but their liability exposure may increase as the courts look more deeply at the structure of incentives in such organizations. In the context of ERISA preemption analysis and the duties of fiduciaries under ERISA, the nature of salary incentives has been scrutinized. The Seventh Circuit in Herdrich v. Pegram[26] considered a claim that physicians who were owners and participants in a managed care plan had breached their fiduciary duties to beneficiaries because of the salary incentive features of the plan.[27] The court noted that physicians in this dual capacity as owners and providers "simultaneously control the care of their patients and reap the profits generated by the HMO through the limited use of tests and referrals." An ERISA fiduciary analysis might find that they were not therefore acting "solely in the interest of the participants" of the Plan. The court noted that these physicians would gain financially if they limited treatments and referrals. This depletion of plan resources might operate to the detriment of patients, and this issue was for the trial court to resolve. However, the court's language suggests that the use of year-end bonus payments, a common incentive feature of many HMOs, would be prima facie evidence of a breach of fiduciary duty.

d.   Duty to Disclose Financial Incentives

Concerns about conflicting incentives on physicians in managed care settings has lead to proposals that an HMO, or its physicians, inform patients of physician risk/incentive arrangements prior to a patient's joining a plan.[28] As one physician has proposed,

> [A]ll health insurance plans should be required to provide formal disclosure statements to prospective subscribers concerning restrictions on the choice of service and capitation payments and financial incentives for reduced use. These statements should be simple and concise, and supplemented by a more complete description of the arrangement, including fees, out-of-pocket costs, and allowable benefits.[29]

23. See David Orentlicher, Paying Physicians More to Do Less: Financial Incentives to Limit Care, 30 U.Rich.L.Rev. 155 (1996).

24. See William M. Sage, Physicians As Advocates, 35 Houston L.Rev.1529, 1620 (1999) ("... the use of financial incentives in managed care preserves professional autonomy and improves efficiency even if it compromises advocacy at the margin.")

25. See the cases discussing in section 8–5, and the relationship of ERISA preemption to such claims.

26. 154 F.3d 362 (7th Cir.1998).

27. See generally ¶ 8–8 infra for a complete discussion.

28. Donald F. Levinson, Toward Full Disclosure of Referral Restrictions and Financial Incentives by Prepaid Health Plans, 317 New Eng. J. Med. 1729 (1987).

29. Id.

The idea is that patients are not aware of the cost-sensitive nature of incentives operating on physicians in MCOs, and should be made aware of them prior to joining, since physicians have a conflict of interest in such MCOs.[30] For example, many plans have salary-holdback features in which a small percentage of physician salaries in HMOs are pooled, and at the end of the budget year physicians who have too many referrals may "lose" this percentage of their salary.[31]

Disclosure is a remedy that coincides with developments in informed consent, fiduciary law, and Fraud and Abuse legislation.[32] It appears to give the patient options that she or he did not previously have.[33] Such disclosure presents several problems. First, patients may lack a choice of alternative providers, even if disclosure is made. Given the increased prevalence of managed care organizations as employee options, employees face diminishing choices between fee-for-service and managed care physicians. Second, for patients already in such MCOs or closed panel plans, they lack ready flexibility to consult physicians outside the panel who are not themselves subject to financial constraints.[34] Third, disclosure assumes that cost-sensitive care is less high quality care, when in fact fee-for-service medicine may often result in overtreatment, with its own iatrogenic costs.[35]

The earlier caselaw that discussed the disclosure issue generally rejected such claims. In *Teti v. U.S. Healthcare*,[36] the plaintiffs claimed that the

---

30. See e.g., Steven Z. Pantilat, Margaret Chesney and Bernard Lo, Effect of Incentives on the Use of Indicated Services in Managed Care, 170 West. J. Med. 137 (1999)); Alan L. Hillman, et al., How Do Financial Incentives Affect Physicians' Clinical Decisions and the Financial Performance of Health Maintenance Organizations?, 321 New Eng. J. Med. 86 (1989); Alan L. Hillman, Financial Incentives for Physicians in HMOs: Is There a Conflict of Interest?, 317 New Eng. J. Med. 1743 (1987).

31. A typical arrangement involves an HMO payment system in which the HMO pays its staff physicians by means of a "Comprehensive Referral Fund Incentive", charging the costs of referrals to specialist physicians and in-patient hospital care against that CRF. Primary physicians received a pro rata portion of any surplus remaining at year end. If, however, the primary physician's CRF is exceeded, the HMO reduces the physician's 20% holdback from the capitation grant allowed to the physician for patient care services rendered. The CRF feature of defendant's HMO plans is intended to create a financial incentive for primary physicians to minimize referrals of members. Under most HMO arrangements, subscribers are not informed of the CRF and bonus arrangements, and primary physicians are prohibited from disclosing to subscribers the existence and nature of these incentive arrangements.

32. The Stark Amendment, for example, specifically prohibits HMOs with Medicaid contracts from "knowingly making a payment, directly or indirectly, to a physician as an inducement to reduce or limit services provided

with respect to Medicare and Medicaid beneficiaries" (although its application to HMOs has been delayed after complaints by the industry). Omnibus Budget Reconciliation Act of 1986, Pub. L. No. 99–509, § 9313(c), 100 Stat. 2003, as amended by Pub. L. No. 100–203, § 4016, 101 Stat. 1330–64 and H.R. 3299, § 6207. See generally §§ 15–7 to 15–8.

33. See the discussion of disclosure of conflicts of interest in § 15–7. See also Allan S. Brett, Sounding Board: The Case Against Persuasive Advertising By Health Maintenance Organizations, 326 New Eng.J.Med. 1353 (1992).

34. Recent writing on the subject includes Paul R. Sugarman and Valerie A. Yarashus, Admissibility of Managed Care Financial Incentives in Medical Malpractice Cases, 34 Tort & Ins.L.J. 735; Stephen R. Latham, Regulation of Managed Care Incentive Payments to Physicians, 22 Am.J.L. & Med. 399 (1996); Henry T. Greely, Direct Financial Incentives in Managed Care: Unanswered Questions, 6 Health Matrix 53(1996); R.Adams Dudley et al., The Impact of Financial Incentives on Quality of Health Care, 76 The Milbank Quarterly 649 (1998); Marc A. Rodwin, Medicine, Money & Morals: Physicians' Conflicts of Interest 214–217 (1993).

35. P. Franks, et al., Sounding Board: Gatekeeping Revisited—Protecting Patients from Overtreatment, 327 New Eng. J. Med. 424, 426 (1992).

36. 1989 WL 143274 (E.D.Pa.1989), affirmed 904 F.2d 694 (3d Cir.1990).

HMO's failure to disclose the disincentives for physicians to make specialist or hospital referrals was fraud, breach of contract and RICO violations. The case was dismissed for lack of federal court jurisdiction.[37]

Judicial receptivity to such claims has increased, however, over the past few years. In Shea v. Esensten,[38] the court considered a claim that the HMO's failure to disclose its practice of giving primary-care physicians financial incentives to minimize referrals to specialists caused employee's death from heart failure. Mr. Shea's physician failed to give him a referral to a cardiologist in spite of warning signs of a cardiac condition. Mr. Shea's widow contended that if her husband had know that his doctor could earn a bonus for treating less, he would have sought out his own cardiologist. The Seventh Circuit agreed that a financial incentive system aimed at influencing a physician's referral patterns is "a material piece of information,"[39] and that a subscriber has a right to know that his physician's judgment could be "colored" by such incentives. The court rested its conclusion on the obligation of an ERISA fiduciary to speak out if it "knows that silence might be harmful."[40] The court held that information about a plan's financial incentives must be disclosed when they might lead a treating physician to deny necessary referrals for conditions covered by the plan.[41] Such a requirement of disclosure, while problematic in some aspects, is consistent with federal policy in HMO regulation and with a trend to use disclosure of information to counteract provider power in health care.[42]

The related disclosure theory is that of informed consent: a physician in an MCO should always discuss with a patient all alternative approaches, even those that are more expensive and therefore are not generally recommended by the cost-sensitive physician. Such an obligation is based upon the line of "informed refusal" cases, such as *Truman v. Thomas*.[43] *Truman* imposes on the physician a duty to disclose to a patient the risks of omitting a useful risk-free test, arguably expanding the duty to discuss more expensive diagnostic and treatment procedures that might be useful and helpful to the patient. This could expand the obligations of HMO physicians in situations where some treatments were preferred because of the cost-benefit tradeoff, but exposed patients to slightly higher risks at the same time.[44]

37. See Matthew R. Gregory, Hard Choices: Patient Autonomy in an Era of Health Care Cost Containment, 30 Jurimetrics J. 483 (1990).

38. 107 F.3d 625 (8th Cir.1997)

39. Id. at 628.

40. The court cited to Bixler v. Central Penn. Teamsters Health & Welfare Fund, 12 F.3d 1292, 1300 (3d Cir.1993) and the Restatement (Second) Of Trusts s 173 cmt. d (1959).

41. Id. at 629.

42. For an excellent discussion of these issues, see Tracy E. Miller and William M. Sage, Disclosing Physician Financial Incentives, 281 JAMA 1424 (1999); William M. Sage, Physicians as Advocates, 35 Houston L.Rev. 1529

(1999); Kim Johnston, Patient Advocates or Patient Adversaries? Using Fiduciary Law to Compel Disclosure of Managed Care Financial Incentives, 35 San Diego L.Rev. 951 (1998); Bethany J. Spielman, Managed Care Regulation and the Physician–Advocate, 47 Drake L.Rev. 713 (1999).

43. 165 Cal.Rptr. 308, 611 P.2d 902 (Cal. 1980). See also Keogan v. Holy Family Hospital, 622 P.2d 1246 (Wash.1980); Gates v. Jensen, 595 P.2d 919 (Wash.1979).

44. The court in Keogan, 622 P.2d at 1261, noted that "the cost of medical attention is escalating, seemingly at an ever-increasing rate. As this court dictates what doctors must do to protect themselves in malpractice actions, it adds to that escalation."

§ 7–8. Corporate Negligence Theories

The theory of corporate negligence holds that the health care organization, historically the hospital, has a duty to its patients to ensure the "competency of its medical staff and the quality of medical care provided through prudent selection, review and continuing evaluation of the physicians granted staff privileges."[1] Such a duty is derived from statutes in most states that hold hospitals accountable for quality care, and from the evolving conception that a hospital is an institution that arranges a total health care package for patients.[2] The duties include proper selection of medical staff[3] and a broader duty to ensure generally that patients receive good quality care.[4]

Corporate negligence doctrine has been applied to managed care organizations.[5] In Shannon v. McNulty, Shannon v. McNulty,[6] the plaintiffs claimed that HealthAmerican was liable for corporate negligence for both negligence supervision of a physician and for its lack of appropriate procedures and protocols when dispensing telephone advice to subscribers. The court applied the corporate negligence doctrine applicable to hospitals, noting that managed care organizations have become central in health care delivery.

> [W]e recognize the central role played by HMOs in the total health care of its subscribers. A great deal of today's healthcare is channeled through HMOs with the subscribers being given little or no say so in the stewardship of their care. Specifically, while these providers do not practice medicine, they do involve themselves daily in decisions affecting their subscriber's medical care. These decisions may, among others, limit the length of hospital stays, restrict the use of specialists, prohibit or limit post hospital care, restrict access to therapy, or prevent rendering of emergency room care. While all of these efforts are for the laudatory purpose of containing health care costs, when decisions are made to limit a subscriber's access to treatment, that decision must pass the test of medical reasonableness. To hold otherwise would be to deny the true effect of the provider's actions, namely, dictating and directing the subscriber's medical care.
>
> Where the HMO is providing health care services rather than merely providing money to pay for services their conduct should be subject to scrutiny. We see no reason why the duties applicable to hospitals should not be equally applied to an HMO when that HMO is performing the same or similar functions as a hospital. When a benefits provider, be it an insurer or a managed care organization, interjects itself into the rendering of medical decisions affecting a subscriber's care it must do so in a

§ 7–8

1. Elam v. College Park Hospital, 183 Cal. Rptr. 156 (Cal.App.1982).

2. See Arthur Southwick, The Hospital as an Institution—Expanding Responsibilities Change Its Relationship with the Staff Physician, 9 Cal. W.L. Rev. 429 (1973).

3. Rule v. Lutheran Hospitals & Homes Society of America, 835 F.2d 1250 (8th Cir. 1987); Johnson v. Misericordia Community Hospital, 301 N.W.2d 156 (Wis.1981). But see Pamperin v. Trinity Memorial Hospital, 423

N.W.2d 848 (Wis.1988) (hospital is not liable for acts of radiologist).

4. Thompson v. Nason Hospital, 591 A.2d 703 (Pa.1991).

5. Harrell v. Total Health Care, Inc., 781 S.W.2d 58 (Mo.1989)(duty to investigate a physician's competence); McClellan v. Health Maintenance Organization of Pa., 604 A.2d 1053 (1992). Contra, see Jones v. Chicago HMO Ltd. of Illinois, 703 N.E.2d 502(Ill.App.1998).

6. 718 A.2d 828 (Pa.Super.1998).

medically reasonable manner. Here, HealthAmerica provided a phone service for emergent care staffed by triage nurses. Hence, it was under a duty to oversee that the dispensing of advice by those nurses would be performed in a medically reasonable manner. Accordingly, we now make explicit that which was implicit in McClellan and find that HMOs may, under the right circumstances, be held corporately liable for a breach of any of the Thompson duties which causes harm to its subscribers.

a. The Duty to Properly Select Medical Staff

Courts have long acknowledged that a hospital can restrict membership to its medical staff through the staff screening process to determine providers' credentials, recognizing the importance of the selection process.[7] A hospital has been held in many jurisdictions to have an obligation to its patients to investigate the qualifications of medical staff applicants.[8] As one court noted, the hospital "is in the business of providing medical care to patients and protecting them from an unreasonable risk of harm while receiving medical treatment. [T]he competent performance of this responsibility is 'inextricably interwoven' with delivering competent quality medical care to hospital patients.'"[9] The duty of proper selection is reinforced by studies that have found a surprisingly high percentage of credential falsification among physicians applying for staff positions.[10]

The managed care organization, like the hospital, has been held to owe its subscribers a duty to properly select its panel members. In *Harrell v. Total Health Care, Inc.*[11] the court stated that an IPA model HMO owed a duty to its participants to investigate the competence of its panel members and to exclude physicians who posed a "foreseeable risk of harm." This logic also applies to PPOs, which control entry of physicians to the provider panel. While the merits of this claim were not reached, the case suggests that courts are willing to impose upon managed care organizations the duty to determine the competency of the providers on its panel.[12] In *McClellan v. HMO of Pennsylvania*,[13] the court upheld an action for negligent selection against an HMO for its selection and retention of a physician who failed to make a timely referral to a specialist, although it rejected the corporate negligence count.

The logic of a direct duty imposed on MCOs to properly select providers is even stronger for an MCO than for a hospital. In the hospital setting, the patient usually has selected the physician. He is then admitted to the hospital because his physician has admitting privileges at that hospital. By contrast, in a managed care program the patient has chosen the particular program, but

---

7. See generally Clark C. Havighurst, Doctors and Hospitals: An Antitrust Perspective on Traditional Relationships, 1984 Duke L.J. 1071, 1084–92 (1984).

8. Johnson v. Misericordia Community Hospital, 301 N.W.2d 156, 174–75 (Wis.1981).

9. Bell v. Sharp Cabrillo Hospital, 260 Cal. Rptr. 37 (1989). See also Albain v. Flower Hospital, 553 N.E.2d 1038, 1046 (Ohio 1990); Oehler v. Humana, Inc., 775 P.2d 1271 (Nev. 1989); Purcell v. Zimbelman, 500 P.2d 335 (Ariz.App.1972); Elam v. College Park Hospital, 132 Cal.App.3d 332, 183 Cal.Rptr. 156 (1982).

10. See, e.g, W.A. Schaffer, et al., Falsification of Clinical Credentials by Physicians Applying for Ambulatory–Staff Privileges, 318 New Eng. J. Med. 356 (1988) (finding that five percent of physicians applying for positions in a national ambulatory care program presented false credentials).

11. 1989 WL 153066 (Mo.App.1989), affirmed 781 S.W.2d 58 (Mo.1989).

12. See also Moshe v. Anchor Organization for Health Maintenance, 145 Ill.Dec. 681, 557 N.E.2d 451 (Ill.App.1990) (immunity in an Illinois statute).

13. 604 A.2d 1053 (Pa.Super.1992).

not the physicians who are provided. The patient must use the physicians on the panel. The patient thus explicitly relies on the MCO for its selection of health care providers. The MCO's obligations for the patient's total care are more comprehensive than in the hospital setting. A plan sponsor that establishes provider networks and channels patients to those networks is likely to be liable for negligent selection. If, however, a plan sponsor uses a PPO sponsor as an intermediary to set up PPO networks, the chance of liability is less likely, although a court may still find a duty to properly select and monitor the sponsor.

A duty of proper selection will expose a managed care organization to liability both for failing to properly screen its physicians' competence, and also for failing to evaluate physicians for other problems. If the MCO selects a panel physician or dentist who has evidenced incompetence in her practice, or has dementia from AIDS, it may risk liability.[14] This is comparable to negligently granting staff privileges to an impaired physician with alcohol or other substance abuse problems, or one with sexual pathologies that might affect patients.[15]

b. The Duty to Supervise and Control Staff

Hospitals have been held to a duty to supervise the medical care given to patients by staff physicians. Providers must detect physician incompetence or take steps to correct problems upon learning of information raising concerns of patient risk. The hospital must have proper procedures developed to detect impostors.[16] A hospital should also properly restrict the clinical privileges of staff physicians who are incompetent to handle certain procedures, or detect concealment by a staff doctor of medical errors.[17] The negligence of the institution must itself be a substantial factor in causing harm to the plaintiff.[18] A failure to implement proper procedures to detect physician problems leads to direct liability for patient injury.

Managed care organizations are likely to face similar duties to supervise. MCO liability for negligent control of its panel physicians derives from the same common law duty that underlies the negligent selection basis of liability as well as federal and state quality assurance regulations. As courts continue to characterize MCOs as health care providers, suits are likely to increase. Only PPOs with their reduced level of physician control might have an argument that liability should not be imposed for negligent supervision. However, statutes in some states require PPOs to implement quality assurance programs and others contemplate the use of such programs by PPOs.[19]

14. See generally Robert I. Simon, AIDS Dementia Complex in Healthcare Providers: Do Treating Physicians Have an Ethical and Legal Duty to Protect Endangered Patients? 2 Courts, Health Science & The Law 69 (1991).

15. K. Karker–Jennings, M.F. Berkey, Providers with HIV/AIDS—A New Dilemma, The Medical Staff Counselor 5, 39–44 (1991).

16. See e.g., Insinga v. LaBella, 543 So.2d 209 (Fla.1989) (non physician fraudulently obtained an appointment to the medical staff, after having assumed the name of a deceased Italian physician; the court applied corporate negligence, noting that at least seventeen juris-

dictions had adopted the doctrine.); Hendrickson v. Hodkin, 11 N.E.2d 899 (N.Y.App.1937) (hospital liable for allowing a quack to treat a patient on its premises).

17. See Cronic v. Doud, 119 Ill.Dec. 708, 523 N.E.2d 176 (Ill.App.1988); Corleto v. Shore Memorial Hospital, 350 A.2d 534 (N.J.Super.Law Div.1975).

18. Thompson v. Nason Hospital, 535 A.2d 1177, 1182 (Pa.Super.1988).

19. Iowa Code Ann. § 514.21; Ky. Rev. Stat. § 211.461; La. Stat. Ann.—Rev.Stat. § 22:2021; Me. Rev. Stat. Ann. tit. 24 § 2342 & tit. 24–A § 2771.

The existence of such systems, with the PPOs having the right to remove a participating physician from the panel based on information generated by the quality assurance mechanism, imposes a duty to supervise. Managed care is likely to be forced to undertake both a duty to select with care and a duty to engage in continuous supervision.

§ 7–9. Contract Theories

A breach of contract suit can be brought against an MCO on the theory of a "contract" to provide quality health care. In *Williams v. HealthAmerica*,[1] a subscriber sued an IPA model HMO, and her primary care physician, for injuries resulting from a delay in referring her to a specialist. The theory was that the physician and HMO failed to deliver quality health benefits as promised, i.e. the right to be referred to a specialist. The court upheld the breach of contract action against the primary care physician but recast the action against the HMO as a tort claim for breach of the duty to handle the plaintiff's claim in good faith.

MCO contracts and literature may also contain provisions to the effect that "quality" health care will be provided or that the organization will promote or enhance subscriber health. Where such assurances are made in master contracts of HMO-physician agreements, subscribers may be able to bring a contract action under a third party beneficiary theory. In Williams, for example, the court suggested that the subscriber could be a third-party beneficiary of the HMO-physician contract that required the physician to "promote of the rights of enrollees as patients."[2] A claim for breach of an express contract or an implied contract in fact has been allowed, based on representations by an HMO as to quality of care. This would seem to overlap with a malpractice claim to the extent it is based on a contract to provide "adequate and qualified medical care in accordance with the generally accepted standards of the community".[3] But express promises, if proven, can give rise to a separate claim.

Health care providers are not held to guarantee a cure, based on general language. "Mere puffery", as the courts view it, is not the same as a warranty of a good result, and will not create a claim.[4] However, an assurance of high quality care in marketing materials and brochures might be treated by a court or jury as a promise that standards of quality will be met, leading to warranty liability. In *Boyd v. Albert Einstein Medical Center*,[5] the plaintiff pleaded both ostensible agency and breach of warranty. The concurring opinion argued that summary judgment on the warranty count was inappropriate because there was a factual issue as to "whether the literature in which HMO 'guaranteed'

---

§ 7–9

1. 535 N.E.2d 717 (Ohio App.1987).

2. Common law fraud or state consumer fraud statutes are another possible source of recovery. Representations in contracts and marketing brochures, or omissions of material information from these documents, inducing the patient to subscribe to the MCO or submit to a certain medical treatment, might be actionable. These theories are more demanding, however, often requiring proof of intentional misrepresentation and justifiable reliance.

3. Natale v. Meia, 1998 WL 236089 (Sup. Ct.Conn., 1998)(defendant's motion to strike denied) . .

4. In Pulvers v. Kaiser Foundation Health Plan, 99 Cal.App.3d 560, 160 Cal.Rptr. 392 (1979), a breach of warranty claim was rejected on grounds that a warranty of a good result was just "generalized puffing." Id. at 566.

5. 547 A.2d 1229 (Pa.Super.1988).

and 'assured' the quality of care to its subscribers, had been distributed to * * * [the plaintiff]."[6]

MCOs also typically market themselves by describing the quality of the providers on the panel. An assertion of quality furnishes courts another reason to impose on the organization the duty to investigate the competency of participating physicians. Such assertions might even be viewed as a warranty that all panel members maintain a certain minimum competence.[7]

§ 7–10. Arbitration

Many managed care organizations, like Ross–Loos Clinic in California and Kaiser Permanente, have altered their malpractice liability by a provision in membership contracts requiring HMO members to submit malpractice claims against the HMO to binding arbitration.[1] Arbitration offers significant advantages for a managed care organization: quick processing of claims; reducing claim handling costs; non-precedential findings; and lower payouts.[2] It avoids the risks of civil litigation, limiting liability exposure and controlling the forum for dispute resolution.[3]

Several legal issues are raised by such binding contractual arbitration. The contracts are open to "adhesion contract" attacks.[4] Use of such arbitration agreements as a threshold matter upon joining a managed care organization, however, circumvents such an attack, since the patient is not ill, has other options for treatment at that point, and is generally not under any kind of duress. Courts have even allowed the group subscriber, such as employers, to elect to bind the entire group to arbitration.[5] A few states have recognized arbitration for health care disputes.[6] Such statutes may in fact create a presumption of validity for such arbitration agreements.[7] While the use of binding arbitration has been criticized as excessively pro-provider[8], it clearly has advantages to both MCO and subscriber, and is likely to be used more frequently as managed care expands.

The problem of arbitrator bias and MCO control of the arbitration process points to a less subscriber friendly, less reliable fact-finding process. A Kaiser case in California demonstrates how an MCO can affect the outcome of

---

6. Id. at 1235, 1236 (J. McEwen, concurring).

7. See generally Richard A. Hinden and Douglas L. Elden, Liability Issues for Managed Care Entities, 14 Seton Hall Legis. J. 1, 1–2 (1990).

§ 7–10

1. See David Rubsamen, The Experience of Binding Arbitration in the Ross–Loos Medical Group, Dep't. Health Educ. & Welfare, Report of the Secretary's Commission on Medical Malpractice, app. at 424 (1973).

2. See S. Henderson, Contractual Problems in the Enforcement of Agreements to Arbitrate Medical Malpractice, 58 Va. L. Rev. 947 (1972).

3. See generally U.S. Gen. Acct. Off. Medical Malpractice: No Agreement on the Problems or Solutions (GAO/HRD–86–50 1986) at 45; Arnold Rosoff, Arbitration as a Malpractice

Resolution Alternative, Business and Health (June 1986).

4. Tunkl v. Regents of the University of California, 32 Cal.Rptr. 33, 383 P.2d 441 (Cal. 1963); Wheeler v. St. Joseph Hospital, 133 Cal.Rptr. 775 (Cal.App.1976).

5. Madden v. Kaiser Foundation Hospitals, 131 Cal.Rptr. 882, 552 P.2d 1178 (Cal.1976); Dinong v. Superior Court, 102 Cal.App.3d 845, 162 Cal.Rptr. 606 (1980).

6. See George H. Friedman, Note, Medical Malpractice Arbitration: Time for a Model Act, 33 Rutgers L. Rev. 454 (1981).

7. See e.g., McKinstry v. Valley Obstetrics–Gynecology Clinic; Guertin v. Marrella, 405 N.W.2d 88 (Mich.1987).

8. See Nicholas Terry, The Technical and Conceptual Flaws of Medical Malpractice Arbitration, 30 St. Louis U. L.J. 571 (1986).

arbitration by controlling its timing. In Engalla v. The Permanente Medical Group, Inc.[9], the plaintiff attacked the arbitration program established by Kaiser for its medical malpractice claims, claiming that Kaiser had misrepresented the speed and efficiency of the program, and that its lawyers had engaged in dilatory tactics to minimize their damage exposure. The court noted that Kaiser designed and administered its program from an adversarial perspective not disclosed to plan members. The court then detailed a long series of delays after the Engallas' lawyer filed a demand for arbitration. Mr. Engallas was terminally ill, and timing was critical, but Kaiser delayed appointing the arbitrator, who then turned out not to be available. Almost 3 months later than represented in the Service Agreement, an arbitrator was appointed, but Mr. Engalla died the next day. The court described the data as to Kaiser arbitrations generally as revealing that 99 percent of all Kaiser arbitrations are delayed, that is, took longer than the sixty day period in the agreement; on average it took over 800 ays to reach a hearing.

Arbitration of iatrogenic outcomes is likely to be disadvantageous to the patient/subscriber in a large managed care organization.[10] Lawyers can drive up the costs and length of arbitration in the same way that litigation can be manipulated, but arbitration also forces the subscriber to trade off jury trials and larger awards. The "repeat player" phenomenon in labor and employment settings has meant a much higher victory rate for employers and other institutional players who regularly engage in arbitration, by contrast to one-shot players such as employees or consumers. In employment arbitration cases, one study found that the odds are 5-to-1 against the employee in a repeat-player case. Much of this imbalance may be due to the ability and incentive of repeat players to track the predisposition of arbitrators and bias the selection process in their favor.[11] The managed care organization likewise can design a system and take advantage of insider information to promote its interests to the detriment of subscribers. Given the shortage of arbitrators and the need to use the same pool repeatedly, arbitrator bias toward large managed care organizations is likely.[12] The Engalla case is only one example of how an organization can manipulate their own dispute resolution system to their advantage. All the purported advantages of arbitration evaporate if the win rate for injured patients is distinctly worse than it would be in the traditional tort system.[13] Nonetheless, the courts have generally allowed such provisions in managed care contracts.

9. 43 Cal.Rptr.2d 621 (Cal.App., First District, Division 2 1995), review granted and opinion superseded 905 P.2d 416 (1995).

10. Arbitration of benefit denials, by contrast, is a useful extension of the subscribers' ability to contest coverage disputes. While similar criticisms may be made, i.e., ability of the MCO to control the process and select arbitrators, it is at least another tool of dispute resolution to add to litigation, rather than a replacement of it.

11. See Richard C. Reuben, The Lawyer Turns Peacemaker, 82 ABA Journ. 55, 61 (August 1996). For discussion of the pros and cons of arbitration in the health care setting, see generally Amy E. Elliott, Arbitration and Managed Care: Will Consumers Suffer if the Two Are Combined? 10 Ohio St. J. on Disp. Resol.

417 (1995); Alan Bloom et al., Alternative Dispute Resolution in Health Care, 16 Whittier L.Rev. 61 (1995); Norman P. Jeddeloh, Use of Arbitration in the Health Care Industry: Non-Labor Matters, 22 J. Health & Hosp.L. 350 (1989); Thomas B. Metzloff, Alternative Dispute Resolution Strategies in Medical Malpractice, IX Alaska L.Rev. 429 (1992).

12. Edward Felsenthal, What Happens When Patients Arbitrate Rather Than Litigate, Wall Street Journal B1 (Feb. 4, 1994)(referring to belief among lawyers familiar with Kaiser arbitration that "it will be increasingly difficult to find people without ties to Kaiser").

13. Many of these problems would have been corrected under the national approach of President Clinton's Health Security Act, since

§ 7–11. Managed Care Statutory Defenses

Some jurisdictions specifically exempt Health Maintenance Organizations from civil liability, stating that they "shall not be deemed to be practicing medicine".[1] Courts interpreting such statutes have concluded that since HMOs are precluded from practicing medicine, "no HMO can direct the actions of the independent physicians with whom it contracts."[2] This means that agency law cannot be used to impute the negligence of participating physicians, who have the status of independent contractors, to the HMO.

Other states have explicitly immunized health services corporations, including HMOs, against tort liability.[3] Health maintenance organizations have been held to be Health Services Corporations under this section, which applies to Blue Cross type not-for-profit corporations that either provided health care services or made reimbursement for services provided by others.[4] Other concerns affecting HMOs addressed by state statutory requirements include fraudulent advertising, handling of patient complaints, claim settlement procedures, scope of coverage and conversion privileges.[5] The "corporate practice of medicine" doctrine, which some states still follow, can also provide a shield under some circumstances, depending on the extent of control of plan physicians[6], the structure of the HMO[7], and the particular statutes.

§ 7–12. Utilization Review Liability

a. *The Nature of Utilization Review*

The most common strategy adopted by employers and payers to control health care costs is utilization review or management. Utilization review is designed to evaluate the medical necessity and appropriateness of health services from the payer's perspective, in light of norms of acceptable practice. It is an overarching strategy of cost control, built into the very structure of HMOs but also pervasive in a range of insurance plans.[1] The term "utilization review" typically refers to external case-by-case evaluation conducted by third-party payors, purchasers, health care organizers, or utilization review contractors to evaluate the necessity and appropriateness (and sometimes the quality) of medical care. HMOs design utilization review into their structure.[2] It is a strategy that attempts to control costs by limiting demand. The

it would have created relatively equally bargaining between subscribers and managed care organizations. Unless the government steps in to the private market for MCO insurance coverage to provide such protections, the subscriber is likely to be the one disadvantaged.

§ 7–11

1. See e.g., Colorado Health Maintenance Organization Act, West's Colo. Rev. Stat.Ann. § 10–17–125(3).

2. Freedman v. Kaiser Foundation Health Plan of Colorado, 849 P.2d 811 (Colo.App. 1992).

3. See N.J. Stat. Ann. § 26:2J–25(c)–(d).

4. See Harrell v. Total Health Care, Inc., 781 S.W.2d 58, 61 (Mo.1989).

5. See generally Michaels and Rinn, Legal Trends and Developments in Alternative Delivery Systems, in Health Law Handbook 153 (A. Gosfield ed., 1989).

6. Sloan v. The Metropolitan Health Council of Indianapolis, Inc., 516 N.E.2d 1104 (Ind. App.1987).

7. Williams v. Good Health Plus, Inc., 743 S.W.2d 373 (Tex.App.1987).

§ 7–12

1. Joel L. Michaels & Sally G. Spong, Legal Concerns Related to Utilization and Quality Management in Managed Care Settings, in The Insider's Guide to Managed Care: A Legal and Operational Roadmap 105 National Health Lawyers Association (1990).

2. See e.g., U.S. Gen. Acct. Off., Utilization Review: Information on External Review Organizations (GAO/HRD–93–22FS 1992).

utilization review strategy for cost-containment is based on two assumptions: that there are wide variations in the use of many medical services; and that careful review of medical care can eliminate wasteful, unnecessary care, or harmful care.

As of 1989, 49% of employees enrolled in employment-related health benefits plans belonged to a "managed conventional" plan, which normally means a conventional insurance plan with a utilization review component. An additional 34% belonged to alternative delivery systems, most of which included a utilization review function. Only 18% belonged to a conventional plan with no utilization review. By the end of 1992, more than fifty percent of the workers employed by mid-sized and large companies were enrolled in managed care plans,[3] and the managed care industry is likely to continue its rapid growth as employers look for ways to control their costs.[4]

Modern utilization review programs stress prior or concurrent review and high-cost case management.[5] Prior review techniques include preadmission review (before elective hospital admissions); admission review (within 24 to 72 hours of emergency or urgent admissions); continued stay review (to assess length of stay and sometimes accompanied by discharge planning); preprocedure or preservice review (to review specific proposed procedures) and voluntary or mandatory second-opinions. High-cost case management addresses a small number (1–7%) of very expensive cases that may account for 30 to 60% of benefit plan costs. Case managers create individualized treatment plans for high-cost beneficiaries. Compliance with the plan is usually voluntary, but may be rewarded by the plan paying for services not otherwise covered by the insurer (such as home health or nursing home care) but less costly than covered alternatives.

Utilization review can be conducted by free-standing utilization review contractors, by payers (employers and insurers, with or without direct contracts with providers) or by providers such as HMOs. Review is usually initiated by plan beneficiaries or by physicians or hospitals, who are aware that admissions or procedures must be preapproved to secure payment. Requests for approval are usually first reviewed by nurses, who apply established criteria (often computerized) to determine appropriateness. Nurses may approve care, but if the care does not comply with applicable criteria, the case must be referred to a physician adviser for denial. Physician advisers will often contact the attending physician and negotiate an appropriate care plan, though some plans deny payment without direct contact with the attending physician. Plans usually have a formal or informal appeals process or provide other opportunity for further discussion of proposed denials.

3. Carolyn Petersen, Managed Care Enrollment Tops 50%, 2 Managed Health Care News 1 (1992).

4. Julie Johnsson, HMO Industry Expected to See Growth Spurt in 1993, American Medical News, December 28, 1992, at 14.

5. Utilization review can take several forms. The oldest form is retrospective review, under which an insurer denies payment for care already rendered, normally by judging it to be medically unnecessary, experimental, or cosmetic. Retrospective review is of limited value for containing costs, since the cost of the care has already been incurred by the time the review takes place, and thus review often leads to costly disputes between the insurer resisting payment and the provider who has already incurred the cost of the care as to whether the care was in fact necessary. Cf. Sarchett v. Blue Shield of California, 233 Cal.Rptr. 76, 729 P.2d 267 (Cal.1987); Van Vactor v. Blue Cross Association, 8 Ill.Dec. 400, 365 N.E.2d 638 (Ill.App. 1977).

Utilization review seems clearly to have reduced inpatient hospital use and inpatient costs experienced by health plans that have used it. One of the best studies found that it reduced admission of groups by 12.3%, inpatient days by 8%, and hospital expenditures by 11.9%. In particular, it reduced patient days by 34% and hospital expenditures by 30% for groups that had previously had high admission rates.[6] It is less clear that utilization review reduces total health care costs, since it often moves care from inpatient to outpatient settings (the Feldstein study found that it reduced total medical expenditures by 8.3%). Moreover, utilization review is most effective in the short run and has less effect on long-term cost increases. Nevertheless, it is one of the most acceptable cost-containment strategies to employers and employees, and thus has proved more popular than other, more drastic, strategies.[7]

b. Theories of Liability

Utilization review raises several liability issues. A review may restrict a patient's access to care that later proves to have been necessary. If the patient is harmed because of a failure to obtain necessary care, a malpractice suit is possible based on a failure to treat. Denial of payment by managed care organizations or insurers for experimental therapies such as bone-marrow transplants for the treatment of breast cancer have created a risk of substantial liability. A finding of a bad-faith denial, with the risk of punitive damages, exposes the utilization review process to substantial stress from tort damages.[8] Even a properly performed review risks a small percentage of cases where the procedure deemed unnecessary or not cost effective would have helped the patient.

1. Breaches of a UR Standard of Care and Other Claims

The process of utilization review requires a set of benchmarks, or guidelines, against which to measure the provider practice. The Utilization Review Accreditation Commission (URAC) was established in 1990 to develop review standards and to accredit review organizations.[9] The American Medical Association estimates that more than 1,300 such guidelines, parameters and protocols are now in circulation, with more being produced all the time. The

---

6. P.J. Feldstein, et al., Private Cost Containment, 318 New Eng. J. Med. 1310 (1988). See, as to managed care and cost controls, Robert H. Miller and Harold S. Luft, Managed Care: Past Evidence and Potential Trends, 9 Frontiers of Health Services Management 3 (1993).

7. On utilization review generally, see Institute of Medicine, Controlling Costs and Changing Patient Care?: The Role of Utilization Management (1989). (hereafter Controlling Costs).

8. In the case of Fox v. Health Net, a jury awarded more than $12 million in compensatory damages, and an additional $77 million in punitive damages, to the estate of a woman whose health maintenance organization refused to pay for a bone-marrow transplant to treat her breast cancer. Many other insurers have refused to pay for this experimental therapy for breast cancer. However, the jury in the

Fox case heard testimony that the HMO's decision was made to save money for the organization, over the opposition of the HMO's own physicians. See Ellen Pollock, HMO Held Liable for Refusing Coverage, The Wall St. J., Dec. 28, 1993 B5; BNA Health Care Daily, January 6, 1994.

9. Standards developed to date have included requirements that only licensed or certified and trained staff conduct utilization reviews; that written clinical criteria or protocols for appropriateness of care be established with physician involvement; that clinical review criteria be used to determine the appropriateness of care evaluation and updates; and that clinical review criteria be used by review staff when making decisions. See e.g., U.S. Gen. Acct. Off., Utilization Review: Information on External Review Organizations 10–11 (GAO/HRD–93–22FS 1992).

Agency for Health Care Policy and Research (AHCPR), a federal agency responsible for publishing government sponsored clinical practice guidelines, is beginning to develop such guidelines as are medical specialty societies and other professional groups.[10] This standard-setting process is still in its infancy, but the potential for UR negligence liability is clear—a utilization review process must base its judgments on available medical standards of care in deciding to refuse to fund patient treatments. As the standards solidify, so will the risk of liability for medical necessity determinations when they are too restrictive.

An organization that provides utilization review may also be sued for breach of contract or for bad faith breach of contract if an inappropriate denial of care results in injury.[11] If the reviewer is independent of the payer, and thus not in privity with the beneficiary, the beneficiary might sue the payer for breach of its contract with the beneficiary. Alternatively, the beneficiary might sue the reviewer, claiming third party beneficiary status to the contract between the payer and reviewer.[12] In *Hughes v. Blue Cross of Northern California*,[13] the California Court of Appeal upheld an award against Blue Cross based on a finding of a defective utilization review decision on medical necessity and found a bad faith denial of benefits for psychiatric hospitalization. It found that the Blue Cross standard of medical necessity deviated from community medical standards, and that good faith mandated that a reviewer must apply a standard of medical necessity consistent with community medical standards.[14] The physician reviewer had testified that he denied about 30% of the claims he reviewed, and that he applied a more restrictive definition of the standard of practice.[15] Such a medical necessity determination is not solely in the hands of the treating physician, however, so long as the governing policy instrument gives the insurer the authority to determine medical necessity, and it used medical experts.[16]

Failure to properly investigate a claim may result in liability in a bad faith contract action. If an insurer fails to gather all the medical facts before refusing the claim, it may be liable for bad faith, which can include a punitive damages claim.[17]

Scope of practice questions are also raised by utilization review.[18] A nurse reviewer might be considered outside of her scope of practice if she challenges the diagnosis and treatment plan of an attending physician. A physician

---

10. See generally Alice Gosfield, Utilization Management Law and Policy: Emerging Liability Trends, 9 HealthSpan 3 (1992).

11. See Hughes v. Blue Cross of Northern California, 215 Cal.App.3d 832, 263 Cal.Rptr. 850 (1989), cert. dismissed 495 U.S. 944, 110 S.Ct. 2200, 109 L.Ed.2d 527 (1990).

12. See William A. Helverstine, Legal Implications of Utilization Review in Controlling Costs supra, n. 7 at 179–181.

13. 215 Cal.App.3d 832, 263 Cal.Rptr. 850 (1989), cert. dismissed 495 U.S. 944, 110 S.Ct. 2200, 109 L.Ed.2d 527 (1990).

14. The court also found that the plan had failed to consider all relevant information, failing to obtain the complete hospital record for the patient.

15. See Slaughter v. Friedman, 185 Cal. Rptr. 244, 649 P.2d 886 (Cal.1982); Teale v. American Manufacturers Mutual Ins. Co., 687 S.W.2d 218 (Mo.App.1984), appeal after remand 797 S.W.2d 505 (Mo.App.1990).

16. See Franks v. Louisiana Health Services and Indemnity Co., 382 So.2d 1064 (La. App.1980).

17. See e.g., Taylor v. Prudential Insurance Co., 775 F.2d 1457 (11th Cir.1985).

18. John D. Blum, An Analysis of Legal Liability in Health Care Utilization Review and Case Management, 26 Houston L.Rev. 191, 221–225 (1989).

reviewer retained by a utilization review entity may arguably be engaged in the unauthorized practice of medicine if she reviews a case in a state in which she is not licensed. The acts of a utilization review entity might also violate a state's corporate practice of medicine statute.

A patient may also sue the third party payer for the reviewer's negligence. Issues of negligent selection or design, agency, or ostensible agency theories can then be argued to impose liability on the payer for the reviewer's negligence.[19]

2. Liability in the Design and Implementation of Utilization Review

The potential liability of a utilization review body may include patient harm resulting from a poorly designed and implemented system of review. This includes failure to implement existing UR standards (see § 8–6.2.1 above), faulty review processes, and inappropriate incentive systems for physicians.

The indirect uses of incentives to influence the judgment of treating physicians has been accused of corrupting physician judgment, just as HMO incentive practices have been criticized. In Varol v. Blue Cross and Blue Shield,[20] a group of psychiatrists, who had agreed to participate in a pilot program with prospective and concurrent review, objected to the incentives created by the program. They argued that the pilot program provided "powerful economic incentives for a physician to disregard his best judgment at the behest of one not licensed to render medicine and 'is in direct contradiction to the policy of this state with respect to this relationship.' "[21]The court rejected this position, noting that the program was designed to ensure that only medically necessary services are provided and paid for, a legitimate objective whether applied to a post-service reimbursement program or a concurrent review and preauthorization program. Providers have their own ethical and legal duties to counter-act any pressures from a review system. The court rejected the premise of the plaintiffs' argument—that their judgment could be easily corrupted by the pressures of incentives to be cost-effective.[22]

Wickline v. State[23] is one of the few cases to consider both utilization review liability and physician obligations to appeal utilization review limitations. The case involved a release of a patient from the hospital postoperatively in less time than the treating physician thought ideal (4 days instead of 8). The physician had applied to Medi–Cal for an extension of time for hospitalization, had been refused, and had not filed an appeal. The patient sued the State, charging that the Medi–Cal program had negligently discontinued her treatment. The jury found in her favor, but the Court of Appeals reversed, finding that the ultimate liability rested on the attending physicians. Medi–Cal was not responsible, since her physicians had signed the discharge orders and had failed to protest denial of further hospitalization.

19. See Helverstine, supra n. 7 at 188–190.

20. 708 F.Supp. 826 (E.D.Mich.1989).

21. Id. at 831.

22. "Plaintiffs are saying in effect, 'Since I am weak in my resolve to afford proper treatment, BCBSM's preauthorization program would induce me to breach my ethical and legal duties, and the Court must protect me from my own weakness.' In other words, protect me from my own misconduct. This is strange stuff indeed from which to fashion a legal argument." Id. at 833.

23. 192 Cal.App.3d 1630, 239 Cal.Rptr. 810 (1986), review granted and opinion superseded 231 Cal.Rptr. 560, 727 P.2d 753 (Cal.1986).

The court noted in dicta that third party payors may be responsible for patient injuries suffered as a result of denial of medical care:

> Third party payors can be held legally accountable when medically inappropriate decisions result from defects in the design or implementation of cost containment mechanisms as, for example, when appeals made on a patient's behalf for medical or hospital care are arbitrarily ignored or unreasonably disregarded or overridden.[24]

Such payor accountability for withholding necessary care due to defective utilization review is consistent with both insurer bad faith cases and hospital liability principles, and reinforces the value of a well-designed system of review. As industry standards develop in the utilization review and benefits determination process, it is more likely that plans that deviate from developed standards of practice will be exposed to liability for their defective processes of review.[25]

3. Provider Duties to Appeal Negative Decisions

The court in *Wickline* in dicta suggests that the court expected treating physicians to be aware of the reimbursement structure and to engage in bureaucratic infighting when necessary, exhausting procedural rights, when the utilization review process has rejected a recommendation.

> The patient who requires treatment and who is harmed when care which should have been provided is not provided should recover for the injuries suffered from all those responsible for the deprivation of such care, including, when appropriate, health care payers. [T]he physician who complies without protest with the limitations imposed by a third-party payor, when his medical judgment dictates otherwise, cannot avoid his ultimate responsibility for his patient's care. He cannot point to the health care payor as the liability scapegoat when the consequences of his own determinative medical decisions go sour.[26]

The court suggests obligations for both the utilization reviewer and the treating physician. First, a physician is expected to engage in bureaucratic infighting, exhausting his procedural rights, when the utilization review process has rejected his recommendation. If he discharges a patient against his better judgment when reimbursement was denied, he risks liability for malpractice. If further payment were available, dependent upon following an appeals procedure, and the provider was ignorant of this procedure, he might be liable for patient harm attributable to his ignorance. He has not made a good faith effort to "rescue" the patient from further bad outcomes.

Wickline was limited by Wilson v. Blue Cross of Southern California[27], which also expanded potential liability of outside reviewers. Wilson held that a physician could be jointly and severally liable with a utilization review body for a patient's bad outcome.

24. Id. at 1645, 239 Cal.Rptr. at 825.

25. See generally Joel L. Michaels & Sally G. Spong, Legal Concerns Related to Utilization and Quality Management in Managed Care Settings in The Insider's Guide to Managed Care: A Legal and Operational Roadmap 1 National Health Lawyers Association 105, 109 (1990).

26. 192 Cal.App.3d at 1645, 239 Cal.Rptr. at 825.

27. 222 Cal.App.3d 660, 271 Cal.Rptr. 876 (1990).

The relevant points of Wilson from a utilization review perspective, are that (1) the payer, utilization review bodies, HMOs, or any other managed care organization cannot pass the buck to the treating physician for discharge decision, when they have denied further payment; they may be jointly liable for a "bad" decision; (2) a doctor does not have to pursue appeal channels if they are not clearly spelled out nor well understood; the negative implication is that a doctor must appeal if the appeals process is clear.[28] Wilson thus expanded utilization review liability. Wickline seemed to provide some protection to payors and utilization review bodies by putting legal responsibility on providers, particularly attending physicians, whereas Wilson provided joint liability for providers, payers, and utilization review bodies. Wilson thus creates the possibility for providers to shift liability to reviewers when utilization review decisions alter or limit what the provider views as necessary care.[29] Both cases raise the issue of whether such utilization review is just determination of available insurance benefits, or is a medical decision in itself.

4. *Physician Duties to Help Patients Seek Funding*

Some plaintiffs injured by resource or reimbursement constraints have argued that their treating physicians, as well as their health plan, should have advised them properly as to reimbursement limits.[30] This obligation would mean that providers, including outside specialists, should know enough to refer patients to experts within a managed care organization or hospital to ascertain sources of funding for a medically necessary procedure. The bundle of services offered by the health care provider, in these times of limited resources, may include not only medically correct diagnosis and treatment that complies with the standard of care, but also information as to how to fund such care.

Wilson and Wickline address the difficult question of when a utilization review program should be held liable to a patient for the denial of medical care that ultimately turns out to have been necessary and appropriate. Such cases are analyzed under standard tort doctrine, examining the existence and breach of a duty, causation, and damages. First, the court must address the duty of the utilization reviewer to the patient. Though the reviewer is only denying payment and not the care itself, harm from an inappropriate denial is

---

28. In the subsequent jury decision in Wilson, the jury, using a clear and convincing standard, rejected liability for the utilization review body.

29. When the case was retried, the plaintiff tried to show that the insurer and the UR company had breached their good faith obligation to investigate the claim; the jury found that the defendants had not breached one of the elements of a bad faith claim, and the defendants were therefore not liable.

30. See e.g., Wilson v. Chesapeake Health Plan, Inc. This case was settled before trial, as to the health plan and the specialist named in the complaint. The plaintiff developed liver disease. He was a member of a prepaid health plan. His specialist repeatedly reassured Wilson that a liver transplant would be covered under his HMO coverage, and even made arrangements to put him on the list of donor liver recipients and to perform the transplant.

When the plaintiff arrived at the hospital, the HMO advised that they were not sure that the plan covered the transplant. His admissions was delayed, several livers were discarded, and he died before financing could be obtained. There was evidence that the state Medicaid program would have covered the transplant if the family had spent down their savings. The plaintiffs argued, among other counts, that the specialist and the HMO "knew or should have known that staff and resources existed * * * to assist the Wilsons in determining the scope of coverage provided by their HMO, other insurers, and alternative funding sources, but they failed to utilize such resources, alert plaintiffs to the existence of such resources or advise them of the need to identify a funding source." Complaint, p. 33. This count in the complaint withstood both a motion to dismiss and a motion for summary judgment.

clearly foreseeable, and the finding of a duty is appropriate. Second, there is the question of compliance with the standard of care, a question resolved in favor of the defendant in Wickline but not reached in Wilson. The reviewer's procedures and the criteria it applies must be reasonable and in compliance with the standards of the industry. And the standards of the industry must be reasonable. The third and most difficult question is that of causation. The denial of payment must cause the patient's injuries, rather than the independent actions of the treating physician.[31]

c. Defenses to Utilization Review Liability

A utilization review program may obtain some protection from tort liability by making clear in its contracts and communications with providers and patients that it is only passing judgment on its financial responsibility for care, not on the clinical advisability of the care itself.[32]

States have tried by statute to solve some of the problems posed by utilization review.[33] Louisiana for example limits liability for utilization review to "damages incurred or resulting from unreasonable delay, reduction or denial of the proposed medically necessary services or care according to the information received from the health care provider at the time of the request for a prospective evaluation or review by the duly licensed health care provider as provided in the contract".[34] The statute further defines review within two days as reasonable and delay beyond two days as potentially unreasonable, depending on the circumstances; unreasonable reduction of services as decreasing or limiting of services previously approved or of continuing services without a means of extension; and unreasonable denial as denial without review of a timely request from an insured or an insured health care provider for a service or extension of a service, or of services previously approved, or of services "deemed medically necessary according to current established medical criteria."

§ 7–13. ERISA Preemption Issues

State regulation of self-insured health care plans is governed primarily by the Employee Retirement Income Security Act of 1974 (ERISA).[1] Congress intended with ERISA to create a uniform scheme for regulating employee benefit plans. Suits against a qualified self-insured employer plan that conducts utilization review in-house or against an independent reviewer that is treated as a plan "fiduciary" under ERISA may be preempted by ERISA.[2]

31. See William A. Helverstine, Legal Implications of Utilization Review in Controlling Costs, supra n. 7, at 169, 171–179.

32. See generally Alice G. Gosfield, Utilization Management, Quality Assurance, and Practice Guidelines, Health Law Practice Guide 25–1 (1993).

33. For a complete state-by-state list of such statutes, see GHAA Utilization Review Update, in Managed Care Law Institute: Business Opportunities and Legal Issues, National Health Lawyers Association (1992).

34. La.Stat.Ann.—Rev.Stat. § 22:657.

§ 7–13

1. For a good introduction to ERISA and liability issues, see Ellin Kohn, et al., Self-Insured Employers, ERISA, ASO and Managed Care in The Insider's Guide to Managed Care: A Legal and Operational Roadmap 1 National Health Lawyers Association 123 (1990).

2. ERISA preemption is established in 29 U.S.C.A. § 1144(a), which provides in relevant part that "the provisions of this subchapter * * * shall supersede any and all state laws insofar as they may now or hereafter relate to any employee benefit plan * * *." In Pilot Life Insurance Company v. Dedeaux, 481 U.S. 41, 107 S.Ct. 1549, 95 L.Ed.2d 39 (1987), on remand 821 F.2d 277 (5th Cir.1987) the Supreme

Under such circumstances the beneficiary would be limited to the much more restricted remedies afforded by ERISA.[3] The purpose of the ERISA preemption is to protect participants from the threat of conflicting and inconsistent state and local regulations. Congress therefore established civil enforcement procedures.[4] See generally chapter 8, § 8–5, infra.

§ 7–14. Future Developments

Managed care has become a battleground in American politics, as the struggle of employers and governments to reduce health care costs clashes with provider demands for autonomy and consumer desires for choice. On the one hand, managed care appears to combine the discipline of the marketplace with the efficiencies of coordinated networks of health care delivery. As a result, several states have passed legislation that promotes managed care and managed competition.[1] Florida, for example, made integrated health care delivery a central feature of its "Health Care and Insurance Reform Act of 1993". The state requires AHPs, Accountable Health Partnerships, either health insurers or HMOs, to provide services in a network.[2] On the other hand, the clamor for limitations on ERISA preemption so that MCOs can be sued more easily reflects a discomfort with cost-conserving strategies in health care. The role of managed care will be central in the future American health care delivery system, and complex new legal arrangements are likely to spawn new liability problems for the emerging networks and super-HMOs that are created.

Court emphasized the broad sweep of the preemption clause. For a detailed analysis of ERISA, see generally Chapter 8, infra.

3. See John D. Blum, An Analysis of Legal Liability in Health Care Utilization Review and Case Management, 26 Houston L. Rev. 191, 200–212 (1989).

4. See 29 U.S.C.A. § 1132. Section 1132(a)(1)(B) provides an exclusive means for redress for a participant or beneficiary who seeks to enforce rights due under the terms of the plan.

§ 7–14

1. See generally Elaine Lu, Recent Development: The Potential Effect of Managed Competition in Health Care on Provider Liability and Patient Autonomy, 30 Harv. J. on Legis. 519 (1993).

2. 1993 Fla. Laws ch. 93–129. See generally Sandra P. Greenblatt and Michael J. Charniga, New Florida Health Reform Plan Is First Large–Scale Test of Clinton's Managed Competition Theory, 10 HealthSpan 7 (1993); Sandra P. Greenblatt and Michael J. Charniga, Florida as Health Care Bellwether: The State's New Laws Foreshadow U.S. Trends, 9 HealthSpan (1992).

Chapter 8

THE EMPLOYEE RETIREMENT INCOME SECURITY ACT OF 1974 AND HEALTH PLAN LIABILITY AND REGULATION

Research References

Am Jur 2d, Pensions and Retirement Funds §§ 1–12
ALR Index: Department of Health and Human Services; ERISA
ALR Digest: Hospitals and Other Health Care Facilities § 7
Am Jur Legal Forms 2d, Pension, Profit–Sharing, and Deferred Compensation Plans § 200:415
Am Jur Pleading and Practice Forms (Rev), Pensions and Retirement Funds § 58
43 POF3d 261, Use of Federal Estoppel Doctrine to Establish Coverage Under Group Health Insurance Policy; 2 POF3d 273, ERISA–Arbitrary Denial of Benefits under Disability Income Plan; 1 POF3d 453, Employer's Unlawful Interference with Rights Protected under ERISA

A.   ERISA: INTRODUCTION

§ 8–1.   Introduction

The Employee Retirement Income Security Act of 1974 (ERISA) is undoubtedly the most influential statute affecting the financing of health care in the United States. Remarkably, however, Congress apparently gave very

418

little thought to the effects ERISA might have on health care, and in particular how ERISA's preemption clause, added as a last minute conference committee compromise, would dramatically change the nature of health care financing regulation in the United States. ERISA was adopted in 1974 in response to highly publicized instances of fraud and mismanagement in employee pension funds, which had resulted in thousands or workers losing retirement benefits accumulated over a lifetime of work. ERISA was intended primarily as an instrument for regulating pensions, as its title suggests, and most of its substantive provisions address protection of retirement benefits.[1] ERISA also, however, applies to employee welfare benefit plans, and thus covers employer provided health insurance, the dominant vehicle for private finance of health care in the United States.

Although ERISA was adopted as a regulatory statute, its primary effect on health insurance is deregulatory. ERISA itself imposes few requirements on employee health benefits plans, and provides minimal remedies for employees who are adversely affected by health plan decisions. On the other hand, ERISA preempts a wide range of state laws and remedies intended to protect health plan beneficiaries, often leaving beneficiaries wholly stripped of legal protection from health plan abuses.

ERISA plays four primary roles with respect to employee health care benefits. First, § 514(a) of ERISA (29 U.S.C.A. § 1104(a)) provides that ERISA "supersedes" any state law that "relates to" an employee benefits plan. The reach of the term "relates to" is obviously highly elastic. Until recently, however, it was interpreted very expansively to preempt a wide range of state laws that affected employee benefit plans. Section 514(a) preemption is qualified however: § 514(b)(2)(A) saves from preemption state laws that regulate banking, investment, and insurance. This exception, however, is also limited: § 514(b)(2)(B) provides that self-insured employee benefit plans shall not be "deemed" to be insurance plans, thus exempting them from state regulation.

Second, ERISA has been interpreted to preempt not only state substantive law relating to health benefit plans, but also state jurisdiction and remedies with respect to employee benefit plans as well. Section 502(a) of ERISA (29 U.S.C.A. § 1132(a)) provides for federal court jurisdiction over specified types of claims against ERISA plans.[2] The federal courts have interpreted these provisions as indicating a Congressional intent to preempt comprehensively the "field" of judicial oversight of employee benefits plan oversight. They have, therefore, permitted defendant employee benefit plans to remove into federal court participant and beneficiary claims that were brought in state courts but could have been brought under § 502 in federal court under the "complete preemption" exception to the well-pleaded complaint rule, which rule normally only permits removal when federal claims are

§ 8–1

1. Daniel M. Fox and Daniel C. Schaffer, Health Policy and ERISA: Interest Groups and Semipreemption, 14 J. Health Pol., Pol'y & L. 239 (1989); Peter D. Jacobson & Scott D. Pomfret, Form, Function, and Managed Care Torts: Achieving Fairness and Equity in ERISA Jurisprudence, 35 Hous.L.Rev. 985 (1998).

2. In fact, § 502 provides for concurrent federal and state court jurisdiction. The courts have interpreted this provision, however, to allow the defendant to choose whether or not to litigate ERISA claims in state court, and thus to remove ERISA claims to federal court if it chooses. See McWilliams v. Metropolitan Life Ins. Co., 172 F.3d 863 at n. 1 (4th Cir. 1999) and § 8–4 infra.

explicitly raised in the plaintiff's complaint. Section 502–based field preemption further nullifies state claims and remedies that would take the place of § 502 claims. ERISA complete preemption, however, like ERISA explicit preemption, is not comprehensive. In particular, ERISA does not necessarily preempt state court malpractice cases brought against managed care plans that provide as well as pay for health care.

Third, ERISA itself permits a participant or beneficiary to sue to recover benefits "due to him under the terms of his plan, to enforce his rights under the terms of the plan, or to clarify his rights to future benefits under the terms of the plan"[3] As it has become clear that ERISA forecloses traditional state law suits against ERISA plans for benefit denials, § 502 suits have become increasingly common. A major issue in these cases, however, is the role and scope of judicial review. What standard of review, that is, should the courts apply in reviewing the decisions of benefit plan administrators?

Fourth, ERISA itself imposes substantive requirements upon employee benefit plans. First, § 404(a)(1) (29 U.S.C.A. § 1144(a)(1)) imposes upon ERISA fiduciaries the obligation to act "solely in the interest of plan participants and beneficiaries" for the exclusive purpose of providing benefits to plan participants and beneficiaries, and to act prudently in discharging this obligation. Second, § 102 (29 U.S.C.A. § 1022) requires plans to provide a "summary plan description" affording participants and beneficiaries a description of their rights. Finally, 29 U.S.C.A. § 1133. requires plans to provide participants and beneficiaries whose claims are denied with adequate notice of the denial and the specific reasons for the denial, as well as "a reasonable opportunity * * * for a full and fair review" by the fiduciary of the denial. The Secretary of Labor is authorized to issue regulations to implement this provision, and has recently proposed regulations that would significantly enhance beneficiary and participant protection under the provision.[4]

This chapter analyzes the scope of ERISA preemption under §§ 502 and 514. It will examine in particular the effect of ERISA preemption on state tort cases against ERISA managed care plans. It will then consider ERISA participant and beneficiary rights under § 502 for denial of benefits and under the substantive guarantees of ERISA. We begin first, however, with an excursus on the language of ERISA.

§ 8–2. ERISA Vocabulary and Coverage

ERISA covers generally "employee benefit plans" that are "established or maintained" by employers, employee organizations, or both.[1] ERISA specifically exempts from coverage several types of plans, including most importantly, plans maintained by federal, state, or local government entities;[2] plans maintained by churches or associations of churches;[3] and plans maintained solely to comply with state workers' compensation, unemployment compensation, or disability insurance requirements.[4]

ERISA defines the term "employee welfare benefit plan" to mean:

3. 29 U.S.C.A. § 1132(a)(1)(B).
4. 53 Fed. Reg. 48390 (Sept. 9, 1998).

§ 8–2
1. 29 U.S.C.A. § 1003(a).

2. 29 U.S.C.A. § 1002(32), 1003(b)(1).
3. 29 U.S.C.A. §§ 1002(33), 1003(b)(2).
4. 29 U.S.C.A. § 1103(b)(3).

any plan, fund, or program * * * established or maintained by an employer or by an employee organization, or by both, * * * for the purpose of providing for its participants or their beneficiaries, through the purchase of insurance or otherwise, (A) medical, surgical, or hospital care or benefits, or [other listed benefits].[5]

ERISA does not, however, define the term "benefit" as such, and its definition of the term "plan" is tautological to the extent that it defines plan to mean "plan". The courts have struggled, not wholly successfully, to delineate the scope of these terms, and much of the confusion in ERISA law is due to the fact that it is often not entirely clear whether ERISA applies at all.

Most courts apply a three part test in determining whether an arrangement is an "employee welfare benefit plan," though courts do not always apply these steps in the same order, and some courts break some of the parts into smaller units or consider additional factors as well.[6] First, the courts consider whether there is a "plan, fund, or program." A "plan, fund or program" exists under ERISA if a reasonable person can ascertain from the surrounding circumstances "the intended benefits, a class of beneficiaries, the source of financing, and procedures for receiving benefits."[7] ERISA's disclosure, reporting, and fiduciary management requirements contemplate the maintenance of a separate fund managed to finance particular benefits, in which money is often accumulated. One-time or regular fixed payments by a single employer out of its general assets, for example, do not constitute benefit plans.[8] The plan must also exist to benefit employees. A plan that only benefits a self-employed employer is not an employee plan, covered by ERISA.[9] On the other hand, if a plan in fact benefits employees, it remains an ERISA plan with respect to owners who are also covered by it.[10]

Next courts consider whether the plan is "established and maintained by an employer or employee organization." A plan is established by an employer if the employer engages in financing or arranging to fund a plan, establishes a procedure for disbursing benefits, and assures beneficiaries that a plan exists, and this activity in fact results in a plan.[11] The key issue here with respect to maintenance is whether the employer has "continuing administrative or

5. 29 U.S.C.A. § 1002(1). ERISA also defines "plan" or "employee benefit plan" to mean "employee welfare benefit plan" or an "employee pension benefit plan." 29 U.S.C.A. § 1002(3).

6. See, e.g. Slamen v. Paul Revere Life Insurance Co., 166 F.3d 1102, 1104 (11th Cir. 1999), citing Donovan v. Dillingham, 688 F.2d 1367, 1373 (11th Cir.1982).

7. Deibler v. United Food & Commercial Workers' Local Union 23, 973 F.2d 206, 209 (3d Cir.1992) (quoting Donovan v. Dillingham, 688 F.2d 1367, 1373 (11th Cir.1982)).

8. Massachusetts v. Morash, 490 U.S. 107, 109 S.Ct. 1668 (1989) (vacation pay not benefit plan); Fort Halifax Packing Co. v. Coyne, 482 U.S. 1, 107 S.Ct. 2211 (1987) (one time severance payment not plan).

9. Slamen v. Paul Revere Life Ins. Co., 166 F.3d 1102 (11th Cir.1999).

10. Englehardt v. Paul Revere Life Ins. Co., 139 F.3d 1346 (11th Cir.1998).

11. See Butero v. Royal Maccabees Life Ins. Co., 174 F.3d 1207, 1214 (11th Cir.1999). Some courts articulate a more elaborate test for "establishment" See, e.g. Kenney v. Roland Parson Contracting Co., 28 F.3d 1254 (D.C.Cir. 1994) (describing seven-factor test for establishment, including: (1) the employer's representations in internally distributed documents; (2) the employer's oral representations; (3) the employer's establishment of a fund to pay benefits; (4) actual payment of benefits; (5) the employer's deliberate failure to correct known perceptions of a plan's existence; (6) the reasonable understanding of employees; and (7) the employer's intent), citing Henglein v. Informal Plan for Plant Shutdown Benefits for Salaried Employees, 974 F.2d 391, 400 (3d Cir.1992).

financial obligations" with respect to the plan.[12] The employer must be sufficiently involved with the plan to invoke ERISA's concerns about securing employee expectations and protecting employee benefits from employer abuse.[13]

If these two requirements are met, the court must finally consider whether or not the plan fits within the regulatory safe harbor established by the Department of Labor for identifying group welfare arrangements not subject to ERISA. 29 C.F.R. § 2510.3–1(j), excepts from the definition of "employee welfare benefit plan" "group or group-type insurance program [s]" "offered by an insurer to employees." when:

> (1) No contributions are made by an employer or employee organization;
>
> (2) Participation [in] the program is completely voluntary for employees . . .;
>
> (3) The sole functions of the employer . . . with respect to the program are, without endorsing the program, to permit the insurer to publicize the program to employees or members, to collect premiums through payroll deductions or dues checkoffs and to remit them to the insurer; and
>
> (4) The employer . . . receives no consideration in the form of cash or otherwise in connection with the program. . . .

In other words, if the employee merely facilitates the employees' own efforts to secure benefits, an ERISA plan is not created—the employer itself must contribute to the funding and maintaining of the plan.

The definition of a "plan" is important in determining the scope of ERISA preemption. Thus ERISA was held not to preempt state law claims against an insurer based on a disability policy obtained under conversion rights after the termination of employment;[14] against an insurer when the employee had purchased the plan, and had merely been reimbursed by the employer for premium costs;[15] against an insurer by a dentist who wholly owned his practice and was the only person covered under a disability policy;[16] or against an insurer where the employer medical center did not pay for benefits or endorse a particular plan, but did forward payroll deductions of employees' premiums to the insurer, and allowed the insurer to make a presentation to its employees.[17]

Unlike the term "Plan," the term "benefit" is not defined in either the statute or regulations. The issue is particularly problematic with respect to managed care organizations that themselves provide services. The courts seem to assume that the services received by participants and beneficiaries are benefits,[18] but it could certainly be argued that the payments for services

---

12. Balenger v. Wyman–Gordon, 71 F.3d 451, 454 (1st Cir.1995).

13. New England Mutual Life Insurance Co. v. Baig, 166 F.3d 1 (1st Cir.1999).

14. Demars v. Cigna, 173 F.3d 443 (1st Cir.1999).

15. New England Mutual Life Ins. Co. v. Baig, 166 F.3d 1 (1st Cir.1999).

16. Slamen v. Paul Revere Life Ins. Co., 166 F.3d 1102(11th Cir.1999).

17. Bagden v. Equitable Life Assurance Society, 1999 WL 305518 (E.D.Pa.1999).

18. See Santitoro v. Evans, 935 F.Supp. 733, 736 (E.D.N.C.1996).

rather than the services themselves are benefits.[19] Understanding what precisely is the "benefit" obtained by an ERISA employee becomes important when health services are provided directly by managed care organizations, as liability suits for negligent provision of services could be preempted by ERISA if the services themselves were the benefits, but might not be if membership in an HMO was itself the benefit of the benefit plan, and not the services of the HMO itself.

Other definitions under ERISA are quite straightforward. A plan "participant" is the employee or former employee who is eligible for benefits under the plan;[20] while "beneficiaries" are persons designated by participants or employee benefits plans to benefit under the plan.[21] A participant can also be a beneficiary, but the term beneficiary often refers to dependents who are covered by a participant's plan. Some courts have recognized providers as beneficiaries where they have been assigned a claim by a participant.

A "plan sponsor" is the employer or employee organization that establishes or maintains a plan.[22] An "administrator" is the person designated under the plan to administer it, or, if no one is designated, the plan sponsor or person designated by regulation.[23] Either the employer, an insurer, or a managed care organization could be the administrator of an ERISA plan.

Fiduciaries are defined as persons who exercise discretionary authority or control over plan management, have authority to render investment advise for compensation regarding plan assets, or have discretionary authority or responsibility in plan administration.[24] Commercial insurers are plan fiduciaries if they have the discretion to approve or deny claims,[25] but merely processing of claims by itself may not be enough to confer such status.[26]

B.   ERISA PREEMPTION

§ 8–3.   ERISA Preemption

As noted at the outset, ERISA preempts state law claims through two different mechanisms. First, § 514(a) of ERISA expressly preempts any state laws that "relates to" an employee benefits plan. Second, states laws are

---

19. See Boggs v. Boggs, 520 U.S. 833, 117 S.Ct. 1754, 1770 (1997) (Breyer J. dissenting); Rice v. Panchal, 65 F.3d 637, 642 (7th Cir. 1995); Peter D. Jacobson & Scott D. Pomfret, Form, Function, and Managed Care Torts: Achieving Fairness and Equity in ERISA Jurisprudence, 35 Houston L. Rev. 985, 1019–1020 (1998).

20. 29 U.S.C.A. § 1002(7). "Employees" may include common law employees. Burrey v. Pacific Gas and Electric, 159 F.3d 388 (9th Cir.1998).

21. 29 U.S.C.A. § 1002(6).

22. 29 U.S.C.A. § 1002(16)(B).

23. 29 U.S.C.A. § 1002(16)(A).

24. 29 U.S.C.A. § 1002(21)(A). See, discussing the definition of a plan fiduciary, Jane Kheel Stanley, The Definition of a Fiduciary Under ERISA: Basic Principles, 27 Real Prop.

Prob. & Tr. J. 237 (1992); The Definition of a Fiduciary Under ERISA: Functions Covered Under Subsections 3(21)(A)(i), (ii) and (iii), 27 Real Prop. Prob. & Tr. J. 467 (1992), and The Definition of a Fiduciary Under ERISA: Particular Persons and Entities, 27 Real Prop. Prob. & Tr. J. 711 (1993).

25. See Prudential Ins. Co. of America v. Doe, 140 F.3d 785 (8th Cir.1998); McManus v. Travelers Health Network of Texas, 742 F.Supp. 377 (W.D.Tex.1990); McLaughlin v. Connecticut General Life Ins., 565 F.Supp. 434 (D.Cal.1983).

26. See e.g., Kerns v. Benefit Trust Life Ins. Co., 992 F.2d 214 (8th Cir.1993); Baker v. Big Star Division of the Grand Union Co., 893 F.2d 288 (11th Cir.1989); Munoz v. Prudential Ins., 633 F.Supp. 564 (D.Colo.1986); Cate v. Blue Cross & Blue Shield, 434 F.Supp. 1187 (E.D.Tenn.1977).

impliedly preempted by § 502(a), which provides an exclusive federal remedy for asserting claims against ERISA plans. We will discuss both theories seriatim.

Understanding the scope of ERISA preemption is crucial because the primary effect of ERISA in recent years has been to frustrate both state efforts to regulate health insurance and managed care and the attempts of insureds and members of managed care organizations to sue those entities for tort damages when they deny provision of or payment for treatment. As ERISA does not itself regulate or provide remedies against health plans except to a very limited extent, ERISA preemption generally results in a regulatory and liability vacuum, allowing health plans to behave as they choose with little accountability to their members or to the public.

a. Section 514 Express Preemption

The outline of § 514 preemption is familiar to anyone with a passing knowledge of ERISA. Section 514(a) of ERISA (29 U.S.C.A. § 1144(a)) provides that the provisions of ERISA "supersede" all state laws that "relate to" an ERISA plan. Section 514(b)(2)(A) excepts from preemption state laws that regulate insurance, banking, or securities.[1] Section 514(b)(2)(B) has been interpreted to mean that self-insured ERISA plans shall not be deemed to be insurance companies or to be engaged in the business of insurance, thus freeing them from state regulation.

The "relate to" clause reached its final form in the conference committee that reconciled the Senate and House versions of ERISA, and provides broader preemption than was contemplated by either the House or Senate version.[2] Many of the supporters of ERISA favored broad ERISA preemption—employers because it would permit uniform administration of multistate benefits plans, unions because it would permit them to establish prepaid legal clinics free of oppressive state regulation.[3] Some supporters felt uncomfortable with the sweeping breadth of the "relate to" clause, however, and the original statute called for reevaluation of the provision by the Congressional Pension Task Force.[4] Because the preemption clause has served the interests of powerful employer and insurer interests, however, Congress has never revisited it.

As of this writing in 1999, the Supreme Court has decided seventeen cases attempting to reconcile hundreds of conflicting lower court decisions attempting to define the scope of ERISA preemption.[5] The problem, of course,

§ 8–3

1. Other provisions of § 514 exempt other specific types of state law from preemption. See note 42 infra.

2. Shaw v. Delta Airlines, 463 U.S. 85, 98–100 (1983); Daniel M. Fox & Daniel C. Schaffer, Health Policy and ERISA: Interest Group and Semipreemption, 14 J. Health Pol., Pol'y & L. 239, 241–44 (1989).

3. See Fox & Schaffer, supra note 2, at 241–44.

4. See Shaw, 463 US 85 at n. 20.

5. UNUM Life Ins. Co. v. Ward, 526 U.S. 358, 119 S.Ct. 1380 (1999); Boggs. v. Boggs, 520 U.S. 833, 117 S.Ct. 1754 (1997); California

Division of Labor Standards v. Dillingham Const., 519 U.S. 316, 117 S.Ct. 832 (1997); De Buono v. NYSA–ILA Medical and Clinical Services Fund, 520 U.S. 806, 117 S.Ct. 1759 (1997); New York State Conference of Blue Cross & Blue Shield Plans v. Travelers Ins. Co., 514 U.S. 645, 115 S.Ct. 1671, 131 L.Ed.2d 695 (1995); John Hancock Mut. Life Ins. Co. v. Harris Trust and Sav. Bank, 510 U.S. 86, 114 S.Ct. 517, 126 L.Ed.2d 524 (1993); District of Columbia v. Greater Washington Bd. of Trade, 506 U.S. 125, 113 S.Ct. 580, 121 L.Ed.2d 513 (1992); Ingersoll–Rand Co. v. McClendon, 498 U.S. 133, 111 S.Ct. 478, 112 L.Ed.2d 474 (1990); FMC Corp. v. Holliday, 498 U.S. 52, 111 S.Ct. 403, 112 L.Ed.2d 356 (1990); Massa-

as the Court eventually came to understand, is that the term "relates to" is not self-limiting—everything in a sense "relates to" everything else. The Court has in recent years, therefore, struggled to articulate the degree of relationship that must be present for § 514(a) preemption to attach.[6]

The Court's first extensive consideration of § 514(a) preemption was in Shaw v. Delta Airlines,[7] an ERISA challenge to a New York law prohibiting discrimination in employee benefit plans on the basis of pregnancy. Justice Blackmun, writing for the Court in Shaw, approved a very expansive reading of the provision. Taking a textualist approach, the Court accepted a dictionary definition of "relates to" as meaning having a "connection with or reference to" a benefits plan.[8] The Court found support for this broad reading of "relates to" both in the structure of ERISA and in its legislative history. In particular, the Court recognized the intent of Congress to free employers that operate benefit plans in several states from conflicting regulatory requirements.[9] The Court rejected narrower readings of ERISA preemption that would have limited its reach to state laws that explicitly attempted to regulate ERISA plans, or that dealt with subjects explicitly addressed by ERISA.[10] The Court commented in a footnote, however, that some state actions might affect an ERISA plan in "too tenuous, remote, or peripheral a manner" to trigger preemption.[11]

For over a decade following Shaw the Court repeatedly applied the § 514(a) tests developed in Shaw in a variety of contexts, almost always finding preemption when it found an ERISA plan to exist. The "reference to" branch of the Shaw test was applied to find preemption where state laws explicitly operated on ERISA plans or where the existence of an ERISA plan was essential for the law's operation.[12] In Mackey v. Lanier Collection Agency,[13] for example, the Court held a state law that explicitly prohibited garnishment of ERISA employee welfare benefit laws to be preempted because of the explicit reference in the law to ERISA.[14] In Ingersoll Rand v. the court

chusetts v. Morash, 490 U.S. 107, 109 S.Ct. 1668, 104 L.Ed.2d 98 (1989); Mackey v. Lanier Collection Agency & Service, Inc., 486 U.S. 825, 108 S.Ct. 2182, 100 L.Ed.2d 836 (1988); Fort Halifax Packing Co. v. Coyne, 482 U.S. 1, 107 S.Ct. 2211, 96 L.Ed.2d 1 (1987); Metropolitan Life Ins. Co. v. Taylor, 481 U.S. 58, 107 S.Ct. 1542, 95 L.Ed.2d 55 (1987); Pilot Life Ins. Co. v. Dedeaux, 481 U.S. 41, 107 S.Ct. 1549, 95 L.Ed.2d 39 (1987); Metropolitan Life Ins. Co. v. Massachusetts, 471 U.S. 724, 105 S.Ct. 2380, 85 L.Ed.2d 728 (1985); Shaw v. Delta Air Lines, Inc., 463 U.S. 85, 103 S.Ct. 2890, 77 L.Ed.2d 490 (1983); and Alessi v. Raybestos–Manhattan, Inc., 451 U.S. 504, 101 S.Ct. 1895, 68 L.Ed.2d 402 (1981). See also, Howard Shapiro, Rene E. Thorne, and Edward F. Harold, ERISA Preemption: to Infinity and Beyond and Back Again? (A Historical Review of Supreme Court Jurisprudence), 58 La. L. Rev. 997 (1998)

6. Professor Karen Jordan has written several excellent articles on ERISA preemption, on which the following discussion draws in part. See Karen A. Jordan, The Shifting Preemption Paradigm: Conceptual and Interpretive Issues, 51 Vand. L. Rev. 1149 (1998) (here-

after, "The Shifting Preemption Paradigm"); Tort Liability for Managed Care: The Weakening of ERISA's Protective Shield, 25 J. Law, Med. & Ethics 160 (1997); The Complete Preemption Dilemma: A Legal Process Perspective, 31 Wake Forest L. Rev. 927 (1996); ERISA Pre–Emption: Integrating Fabe into the Savings Clause Analysis, 27 Rutgers Law J. 273 (1996) (hereafter "Integrating Fabe"); Travelers Insurance: New Support for the Argument to Restrain ERISA Preemption, 13 Yale J. on Reg. 255 (1996).

7. 463 U.S. 85 (1983).

8. Id. at 96.

9. 463 U.S. at 105, n. 25.

10. F.M.C. v. Holliday, 498 U.S. at 58–59.

11. Id at note 21.

12. Dillingham, 519 U.S. 316, at 324.

13. 486 U.S. 825, 108 S.Ct. 2182 (1988).

14. See also District of Columbia v. Greater Washington Board of Trade, 506 U.S. 125, in which the state law held to be preempted explicitly required employers that provided

held a common law claim based explicitly on the existence of an ERISA plan to be preempted.[15]

The Court has more often held State laws to be preempted under the "connection with" branch of the test, or under a simple judgment that the state laws "relate to" ERISA plans. State laws that require ERISA plans to provide specified benefits have been held to relate to ERISA plans, though in some instances they were saved from preemption under the "savings" clause, discussed below.[16] The Supreme Court has also held state laws that affect the administration of ERISA plans or the calculation of ERISA benefits to be preempted, as well as state law tort and contract claims challenging ERISA benefit determinations.[17] The Court has repeatedly expressed allegiance to the opinion that ERISA § 514(a) preemption had a "broad scope"[18] and "an extensive sweep"[19] and was "conspicuous for its breadth,"[20] and applied § 514(a) accordingly.

Attending to Supreme Court pronouncements that § 514(a) preemption was to be applied broadly, lower courts have held a wide range of state regulatory programs and common law claims that arguably "related to" the administration of an ERISA plan or imposed costs upon plans to be preempted. Thus laws regulating rates for hospitals or pharmacies,[21] that mandated health insurance coverage for employees[22], that prohibited discrimination against persons with AIDS,[23] or that limited subrogation rights,[24] have been held to be preempted by ERISA because of their impact on employee benefit plans. Courts have upheld preemption from time to time under protest, recognizing that the combined broad sweep of ERISA § 514(a) preemption and the narrow application of § 502 ERISA remedies (discussed below), often left injured ERISA participants and beneficiaries without a remedy.[25]

The Supreme Court finally recognized limits to ERISA preemption in New York State Conference of Blue Cross and Blue Shield Plans v. Travelers

ERISA health benefits to provide the same benefits for employees collecting workers' compensation.

15. Ingersoll–Rand Co. v. McLennon, 498 U.S. 133 (1990).

16. Shaw v. Delta Airlines, 463 U.S. 85; Metropolitan Life v. Massachusetts, 471 U.S. 724.

17. FMC v. Holliday, 498 U.S. 52 (law prohibiting employee benefit plans from pursuing subrogation rights); Pilot Life v. Dedeaux, 481 U.S. 41 (state court tort suit for bad faith denial of benefits.)

18. Metropolitan Life v. Taylor, 471 U.S. at 739.

19. Pilot Life v. Dedeaux, 481 U.S. at 47.

20. FMC v. Holliday, 498 U.S. at 58.

21. Travelers Ins. Co. v. Cuomo, 14 F.3d 708 (2d Cir.1993), rev'd New York State Council of Blue Cross and Blue Shield Plans v. Travelers Ins. Co., 514 U.S. 645 (1995) (hospital rate regulation); General Motors Corp. v. Caldwell, 647 F.Supp. 585 (N.D.Ga.1986) (pre-

scription rates); United Health Servs., Inc. v. Upstate Admin. Servs., Inc., 573 N.Y.S.2d 851 (N.Y.Sup.1991) (hospital rates). But see, United Wire, Metal and Machine Health and Welfare Fund v. Morristown Memorial Hospital, 995 F.2d 1179 (3d Cir.1993), cert. denied 510 U.S. 944, 114 S.Ct. 382, 126 L.Ed.2d 332 (1993) (hospital rate regulation law not preempted).

22. Standard Oil Co. v. Agsalud, 442 F.Supp. 695 (N.D.Cal.1977), affirmed 633 F.2d 760 (9th Cir.1980), affirmed mem. 454 U.S. 801, 102 S.Ct. 79, 70 L.Ed.2d 75 (1981) (striking down the Hawaii Prepaid Health Care Act, subsequently saved by an amendment to ERISA specifically protecting it, 29 U.S.C.A. § 1144(b)(5)).

23. Westhoven v. Lincoln Foodservice Products, Inc., 616 N.E.2d 778 (Ind.App.1993).

24. Provident Life & Accident Insurance Co. v. Linthicum, 930 F.2d 14 (8th Cir.1991); Baxter By and Through Baxter v. Lynn, 886 F.2d 182 (8th Cir.1989).

25. Corcoran v. United HealthCare, Inc., 965 F.2d 1321 (5th Cir.1992).

Ins. Co.[26] Travelers held that a New York law that required hospitals to charge different rates to insured, HMO, and self-insured plans was not preempted by § 514(a). The Court began its discussion of preemption by reaffirming its allegiance to a general presumption that Congress does not intend to preempt state law.[27] The Court proceeded to note that in cases involving traditional areas of state regulation, such as health care, Congressional intent to preempt state law should not to be presumed unless it is "clear and manifest."[28] Recognizing that the term "relate to" is not self-limiting, the Court turned for assistance in defining the term to the purpose of ERISA, which it determined to be freeing benefit plans from conflicting state and local regulation.[29] Preemption was intended, the Court held, to affect state laws that operated directly on the structure or administration of ERISA plans,[30] not laws that only indirectly raised the cost of various benefit options.[31] The Court did recognize, however, that possibility that state regulation of providers or insurers, downstream from ERISA plans, could be so severe as to determine in fact the choices of plan administrators, invoking preemption.[32]

The Court's four post-Travelers preemption cases suggest that the Court in fact turned a corner in Travelers. It has rejected preemption in half of these cases, though it almost never did so before Travelers. In California Division of Labor Standards Enforcement v. Dillingham,[33] the Court held state laws regulating apprentice wages to be free from preemption (ERISA identifies apprenticeship as an employee benefit). Justice Thomas, writing for the Court, interpreted Travelers to mean that "connection with" preemption should not be found where laws addressed traditional areas of state regulation, which did not impact on the key concerns of ERISA "reporting, disclosure, fiduciary responsibility, and the like," even though they created economic incentives for ERISA plans to take certain actions.[34] In another case the same term, the Court rejected preemption of a state law that imposed taxes on health care facilities, including facilities owned by ERISA plans, again finding that the indirect effects of the tax on ERISA plans were not proscribed by § 514(a).[35] In two other cases, one involving preemption of Louisiana's community property law as it applied to pensions, and another involving California's common law rule that employers functioned as agents of insurers for purposes of receiving insurance claims, the Court held state law to be preempted by ERISA. In each case, the Court focussed on the traditional importance of the area of regulation to the state and the purposes of ERISA in determining whether a legal claim or requirement was preempted by ERISA.

Post Traveler's lower court cases have on the whole continued to apply ERISA preemption broadly, generally finding that state programs aimed at regulating insurance and managed care "relate to" ERISA plan, and are

---

26. 514 U.S. 645, 115 S.Ct. 1671 (1995). The Court had hinted that it might be prepared to rethink the breadth of ERISA preemption two years earlier in John Hancock Mutual Life Ins.Co. v. Harris Trust and Savings Bank, 510 U.S. 86 (1993).

27. 514 U.S. at 654.

28. Id. at 655.

29. Id. at 656–57.

30. Id. at 657–58.

31. Id. at 658–64.

32. Id. at 668.

33. 519 U.S. 316, 117 S.Ct. 832 (1997).

34. Id. at 330–334.

35. De Buono v. NYSA–ILA Medical and Clinical Services Fund, 520 U.S. 806, 117 S.Ct. 1747, 1997.

therefore preempted. In Prudential Insurance Company of America v. National Park Medical Center,[36] for example, the Eighth Circuit concluded that the Arkansas "Patient Protection Act" related to ERISA plans because it explicitly and implicitly made reference to them. In Community Health Partners v. Kentucky,[37] the court held that Kentucky's "Any Willing Provider" law related to ERISA plans, though the court proceeded to hold that the law was saved from preemption by ERISA's savings clause. In Corporate Health Insurance v. Texas,[38] the district court held a Texas statute providing an independent review structure for adverse benefit determinations to be preempted by ERISA as having an improper connection with an ERISA plan by mandating the structure and administration of plan benefits.

A few courts, however, have attended to the more respectful approach to preemption found in the Supreme Court's post Travelers cases. In Washington Physicians Service Association v. Gregoire[39] the Ninth Circuit held that a Washington law requiring HMOs and health care service contractors to cover alternative medical treatments did not "relate to" ERISA plans because it regulated managed care organizations that sold benefits to ERISA plans rather than the plans themselves. The Ninth Circuit commented in deciding the case that "[a]fter Travelers, ERISA plans no longer have a Midas touch that allows them to deregulate every product they choose to buy as part of their employee benefit plan."[40] Similarly the court in American Drug Stores, Inc. v. Harvard Pilgrim Health Care, Inc.[41] upheld Massachusetts's any willing pharmacy provider law, concluding that the statute was merely an exercise of the state's traditional regulation of health care and insurance, and operated on insurance carriers rather than directly on ERISA plan administration.

b. *The Savings and Deemer Clauses*

A state law or claim preempted by § 514(a) because it "relates to" an ERISA benefits plan, might nonetheless be saved from preemption if it is a state law that "regulates insurance, banking, or securities"[42] Once a state law affecting health care organization or financing is found to "relate to" an employee benefits plan, the court must often proceed to determine whether the law "regulates insurance." The Court interpreted the savings clause in Metropolitan Life Insurance Company v. Massachusetts,[43] to save from preemption a Massachusetts law that mandated that health insurers cover specified minimal mental health benefits, even though the law effectively specified the substance of ERISA insurance contracts, and was not limited to regulating insurers themselves or their marketing practices. The Court held that "common sense" suggested that the law regulated insurance,[44] but that

---

36. 154 F.3d.812 (8th Cir.1998)

37. 14 F.Supp.2d 991 (W.D.Ky.1998).

38. 12 F.Supp.2d 597 (S.D.Tex.1998)

39. 147 F.3d 1039 (9th Cir.1998).

40. Id. at 1045.

41. 973 F.Supp. 60 (D.Mass.1997).

42. 29 U.S.C.A. § 1144(b)(2)(A). Section 1144 also saves from preemption a variety of other categories of state law, including state criminal laws of general application, 29 U.S.C.A. 1144(b)(4); the Hawaii Prepaid

Health Act as it existed in 1974, § 1144(b)(5); certain state laws regulating some Multiple Employee Benefit Arrangements (MEWAs), § 1144(b)(6); certain qualified state court domestic relations orders and medical child support orders, § 1144(b)(7); certain state claims based on medical support orders or recoupment rights for Medicaid payments, § 1444(b)(8); or other federal laws or state laws or regulations issued to effectuate other federal laws, § 1444(d).

43. 471 U.S. 724, 105 U.S. 2380 (1985).

44. Id. at 740.

also the law met the three part test developed in antitrust cases applying the McCarran-Ferguson Act for determining whether a law was a law regulating "the business of insurance," i.e. whether the regulation affected the transferring and spreading of policy-holder risk, whether it affected the relationship between the insurer and insured, and whether it affected only entities within the insurance industry.[45] When the Court applied this test in Pilot Life, a case involving a Mississippi common law bad faith breach of contract claim, however, it found that the law was not saved from preemption because it was not specifically "directed at" the insurance industry and did not meet the McCarran-Ferguson criteria.[46] The Court also declined to apply the savings clause in Pilot Life because it concluded that Congress had intended § 502, discussed below, to provide the exclusive remedy for ERISA beneficiaries against ERISA plans, and that the savings clause should not be interpreted to permit supplemental state remedies.[47]

ERISA's insurance savings clause has been applied to "save" from preemption a variety of state schemes directed at regulating insurers, including mandated provider laws,[48] laws banning discrimination in health insurance,[49] "any willing provider laws",[50] and coordination of benefits laws.[51] In many cases, however, courts have rejected application of the savings clause. Cases refusing to apply the savings clause have tended to do so for two main reasons. First, they have tended to reject the argument in cases that, like Pilot Life, involve the application of a state remedy rather than a substantive regulatory requirement.[52] The courts conclude in these cases that the statutes do not regulate the allocation or risk between insurers and insureds, as required by McCarran-Ferguson, but rather address remedies available to insureds or insurers, merely applying common law remedies to insurers, rather than specifically regulating insurers.[53] A second group of cases have rejected statutes that are not limited in their application to traditional insurers, but also apply to other types of health plans, such as HMOs.[54] These cases are in accord with a line of authority that holds HMOs to not be

45. Id. at 742–44.

46. Pilot Life, 481 U.S. at 50–51.

47. Id. at 51–57.

48. Washington Physicians Service Ass'n v. Gregoire, 147 F.3d 1039, 1045–47 (9th Cir. 1998) (mandate for covering alternative medicine treatments); Blue Cross and Blue Shield v. Bell, 798 F.2d 1331 (10th Cir.1986); Hayden v. Blue Cross and Blue Shield, 843 F.Supp. 1427 (M.D.Ala.1994); Blue Cross Hosp. Serv. Inc. v. Frappier, 698 S.W.2d 326 (Mo.1985).

49. PAS v. Travelers Ins. Co., 7 F.3d 349 (3d Cir. 1993).

50. Community Health Partners, Inc. v. Kentucky, 14 F.Supp.2d 991 (W.D.Ky.1998); Stuart Circle Hosp. Corp. v. Aetna Life Ins. Co., 995 F.2d 500 (4th Cir.1993); Blue Cross and Blue Shield of Va. v. St. Mary's Hosp. of Richmond, 426 S.E.2d 117 (Va. 1993).

51. Northern Group Serv's Inc. v.Auto Owners Ins. Co., 833 F.2d 85 (6th Cir.1987).

52. See, e.g. Bast v. Prudential Insurance Co. of America, 150 F.3d 1003 (9th Cir.1998)

(bad faith claim); Ramirez v. Inter–Continental Hotels, 890 F.2d 760 (5th Cir.1989) (common law and statutory claims); Kanne v. Connecticut Gen. Life Ins. Co., 867 F.2d 489 (9th Cir. 1988) (suit for breach of implied contract of good faith and fair dealing and under unfair claims practice statutes); Tingle v. Pacific Mutual Ins. Co., 996 F.2d 105 (5th Cir.1993) (law governing misrepresentations on insurance application); Brundage–Peterson v. Compcare Health Servs. Ins. Corp., 877 F.2d 509 (7th Cir.1989)(breach of contract and bad faith); Urban Health Servs., Ltd. v. Travelers Ins.Co., 703 F.Supp. 53 (N.D.Ill.1989) (suits claiming breach of insurance contract).

53. Security Life Ins. Co. of America v. Meyling, 146 F.3d 1184 (9th Cir.1998); Davies v. Centennial Life Insurance Co., 128 F.3d 934 (6th Cir.1997); McMahan v. New England Mut. Life Ins. Co., 888 F.2d 426 (6th Cir.1989).

54. Prudential Insurance Co. of America v. National Park Medical Center, Inc. 154 F.3d 812 (8th Cir.1998); Texas Pharmacy Ass'n v. Prudential Ins.Co. of America, 105 F.3d 1035 (5th Cir.1997); CIGNA Healthplan of Louisiana v. Louisiana, 82 F.3d 642 (5th Cir.1996).

insurers, and thus HMO regulation to not be protected by the savings clause.[55] These holdings turn to a large extent, however, on whether or not HMOs are considered to be insurers under state law, and a number of cases have construed HMOs to be insurers under state law, subject to the savings clause.

In recent years the Supreme Court has begun to back off the mechanical tests it set forth in Metropolitan Life and Pilot Life for determining the application of the savings clause. In United States v. Fabe,[56] the Court signaled abandonment of a wooden application of the three criteria test in applying the McCarran-Ferguson Act. In UNUM Life Insurance Company of America v. Ward,[57] the Court specifically held that the three McCarran–Ferguson criteria were merely relevant to a determination of whether the savings clause should be applied, not conclusive.[58] The Court proceeded to read two of the criteria expansively and withhold judgment on a third in upholding California's notice-prejudice rule against an ERISA challenge.[59] Perhaps most importantly, Justice Ginsberg, writing for the Court, recognized in note seven of the opinion, but did not accept or reject, the Solicitor General's argument that Pilot Life should not be applied to state laws that specifically provide remedies for beneficiaries against insurance plans [60] This note seems to open the door to later arguments that state tort or contract claims based specifically on remedial statutes governing insurance might be saved from preemption.

ERISA's § 514(b)(2)(A) savings clause is subject to its own exception, the § 514(b)(2)(B) "deemer" clause. This subsection provides that "neither an employee benefit * * * nor any trust established under such a plan, shall be deemed to be an insurance company or other insurer,* * * or to be engaged in the business of insurance * * * for purposes of any law of any State purporting to regulate insurance companies, [or] insurance contracts, * * *.[61] In FMC Corporation v. Holliday,[62] the Supreme Court interpreted this clause broadly to except self-funded ERISA plans entirely from state regulation and state law claims. It held that Congress intended, in adopting the deemer clause, to protect self-funded ERISA plans from any form of state regulation, even though insured ERISA plans were subjected to indirect state regulation to the extent that states were permitted to regulate the insurers that insured the plans.

The deemer clause does not totally shield self-insured plans from all state law claims. "Run-of-the-mill" state law claims for unpaid rent or failure to pay creditors may survive ERISA preemption, even when brought against self-insured plans.[63] State criminal laws of general applicability are also saved

---

55. See, e.g. O'Reilly v. Ceuleers, 912 F.2d 1383 (11th Cir.1990); Dearmas v. Av–Med, Inc., 814 F.Supp. 1103 (S.D.Fla.1993); Pomeroy v. Johns Hopkins Medical Services, Inc. 868 F.Supp. 110 (D.Md.1994); McManus v.Travelers Health Network, 742 F.Supp. 377 (W.D. Texas. 1990); but see American Drug Stores, Inc. v. Harvard Pilgrim Health Care, Inc., 973 F.Supp. 60 (D.Mass.1997); Cellilli v. Cellilli, 939 F.Supp. 72 (D.Mass.1996) (HMOs are insurers subject to savings clause).

56. 508 U.S. 491, 113 S.Ct. 2202 (1993), See Jordan, Integrating Fabe, supra note 6.

57. 526 U.S. 358, 119 S.Ct. 1380 (1999).

58. Id. at 1389.

59. Id. at 1389–90.

60. Id. at 1391.

61. 29 U.S.C.A. § 1144(b)(2)(B).

62. 498 U.S. 52, 111 S.Ct. 403 (1990).

63. Mackey v. Lanier Collection Agency and Service Inc., 486 U.S. 825, 833 (1988).

from preemption.[64] But the protection of self-insured plans from state regulation is well-nigh absolute.

For this reason, as well as for others,[65] self-insurance has become very common, particularly among larger employers. Self-insurance also has disadvantages—it imposes upon the employer the burden of administering the plan as well as open-ended financial exposure. To avoid these problems, self-insured employers often contract with third-party administrators to administer claims and with stop-loss insurers to limit their exposure. The courts overwhelmingly hold that employer plans remain self-insured, even though they are reinsured through stop-loss plans, and prohibit state regulation of stop loss coverage for self-insured plans.[66] Third-party administrators that administer self-insured plans also are protected from state insurance regulation.[67] Thus an employer who is willing to bear some risk can escape state regulation under the "deemer" clause, even though most of the risk of insuring the plan is borne by a stop-loss insurer and the hassle of administering the plan is assumed by a third-party administrator.

Finally, the savings clause is subject to conflict preemption. If a state law, even a law regulating insurance, directly conflicts with a federal ERISA requirement, the state law is superseded by the federal. In Parra v. John Alden Life Ins. Co.,[68] for example, the court held that an insureds claim which was completely preempted under § 502 could not be saved under the § 514(b) preemption clause.

§ 8–4. Implied and Complete Preemption: § 502

Express preemption based on § 514(a) of ERISA does not exhaust the reach of ERISA preemption. Equally important in ERISA litigation is implied preemption based on § 502(a). Section 502(a)(1), (3), and (4) of ERISA[1] afford participants and beneficiaries the right to sue to recover benefits due under an ERISA plan; to enforce rights under the plan, or clarify rights to future benefits under the plan; to enjoin or obtain other equitable relief against practices that violate ERISA; or to obtain relief for violation of specified ERISA disclosure and reporting requirements.

The Supreme Court has a developed well articulated jurisprudence for determining when a federal law or remedial scheme will be construed as

64. 29 U.S.C.A. § 1144(b)(4).

65. Including the ability of self-insured employers to design flexible plans to serve their employees better, avoid administrative costs and profits that must be paid to insurers, and control and invest reserves. See Troy Paredes, Stop–Loss Insurance, State Regulation, and ERISA: Defining the Scope of Federal Preemption, 34 Harv. J. Leg. 233 (1997).

66. See, e.g., Tri–State Machine v. Nationwide Life Ins. Co., 33 F.3d 309 (4th Cir.1994); Lincoln Mutual Casualty v. Lectron Products, Inc. 970 F.2d 206 (6th Cir.1992); Rapp v. Travelers Ins. Co., 869 F.2d 1498 (9th Cir.1989); Moore v. Provident Life & Accident Ins. Co., 786 F.2d 922 (9th Cir.1986); Thompson v. Talquin Building Products Co., 928 F.2d 649 (4th Cir.1991); United Food & Commercial Workers v. Pacyga, 801 F.2d 1157 (9th Cir.1986). but see Michigan United Food and Commercial Workers v. Baerwaldt, 767 F.2d 308 (5th Cir. 1985) (stop-loss plan is insured and thus subject to savings clause). Some courts, on the other hand, hold that state taxation or regulation of stop-loss insurers is free from preemption because these laws do not relate to ERISA plans. Bartlett v.American Medical Security, Inc. 111 F.3d 358 (4th Cir.1997); Safeco Life Ins. Company v. Musser, 65 F.3d 647 (7th Cir.1995).

67. NGS American, Inc. v. Barnes, 805 F.Supp. 462 (W.D. Texas 1992).

68. 22 F.Supp.2d 1360 (S.D.Fla.1998).

§ 8–4

1. 29 U.S.C.A. § 1132(a)(1), (3), and (4).

impliedly preempting state law in areas other than ERISA jurisprudence.[2] First, the Court will find field preemption when a federal law or regulatory scheme so pervasively or significantly dominates a field as to preclude the enforcement of state law within it.[3] Second, the Court will find conflict preemption when it finds that a federal law is in direct conflict with a state law, i.e., when "it is impossible * * * to comply with both state and federal requirements,"[4] or "where a state law stands as an obstacle to accomplishment and execution of the full purposes and objectives of Congress."[5] Though this schema has been mentioned in recent Supreme Court ERISA opinions,[6] it has not generally received much attention in either the leading Supreme Court or in lower court ERISA decisions. In fact, where ERISA decisions distinguish between field and conflict preemption, they identify conflict preemption with § 514(a) express preemption (referred to in some cases as ordinary preemption), and field preemption with § 502 remedial preemption.[7]

Section 502 preemption originates in Pilot Life v. Dedeaux, in which the Supreme Court declared that Congress had intended § 502(a) to be the exclusive means for actions by ERISA participants and beneficiaries alleging improper processing of claims.[8] The Court based this opinion on two factors: 1) the comprehensive and reticulate nature of the remedial provisions of ERISA, which suggested that Congress meant them to be exhaustive and exclusive, and 2) legislative history of ERISA which indicated that Congress modeled ERISA's remedial provisions after § 301 of the Labor Management Relations Act,[9] which had long been interpreted as preempting all state law claims in its domain.[10] Pilot Life established the principle that state tort and contract claims that are in essence claims for ERISA benefits are preempted by ERISA, which provides under § 502(a) the sole remedy for improper denial of ERISA benefits.

An equally important application of § 502(a) is to authorize removal of ERISA cases into federal court through the doctrine of "complete preemption," occasionally called "superpreemption"[11] ERISA explicitly provides for concurrent jurisdiction in the state and federal courts for beneficiary claims against ERISA plans.[12] In Metropolitan Life Ins. v. Taylor,[13] however, the

2. See Karen A. Jordan, The Shifting Preemption Paradigm: Conceptual and Interpretive Issues, 51 Vand.L.Rev. 1149 at 1165–76 (1998).

3. See English v. General Elec. Co., 496 U.S. 72, 79 (1990); Rice v. Santa Fe Elevator Corp., 331 U.S. 218, 230 (1947).

4. 496 U.S. at 79 (citing Florida Lime & Avocado Growers Inc., v. Paul, 373 U.S. 132, 142–43 (1963)).

5. Id. (citing Hines v. Davidowitz, 312 U.S. 52, 67 (1941)).

6. See John Hancock Mutual Life Ins. Co. v. Harris Trust & Savings Bank, 510 U.S. 86 (1993); California Division of Labor Standards Enforcement v. Dillingham Const. Co., 519 U.S. , 117 S.Ct. 832, 843 (Scalia, J. concurring).

7. This is clearly seen in a recent series of Fifth Circuit opinions. See, Copling v. Container Store, 174 F.3d 590 (5th Cir. 1999) (denominating field preemption as implied preemption and express preemption as conflict preemption); Giles v. NYLCare Health Plan, 172 F.3d 332 (5th Cir.1999) McClelland v. Gronwaldt, 155 F.3d 507 (5th Cir.1998).

8. 481 U.S. at 52–53.

9. 29 U.S.C.A. § 185.

10. See 481 U.S. at 52–54.

11. Butero v. Royal Maccabees Life Ins. Co., 174 F.3d 1207 (11th Cir.1999).

12. 29 U.S.C.A. § 1132(e). This provision provides for exclusive federal jurisdiction over most other ERISA claims. Under the complete preemption doctrine as described below, the defendant sued under an ERISA claim in state court essentially has the choice of either removing a case brought in state court, or effectively consenting to state court jurisdiction. See McWilliams v. Metropolitan Life Ins. Co., 172 F.3d 863 at n. 1 (4th Cir.1999).

Court, again relying on the legislative history of ERISA and parallels to Labor Management Relations Act jurisprudence, held that the intent of Congress expressed in § 502(a) was to treat ERISA cases as cases arising under federal law, subject to federal jurisdiction regardless of whether or not ERISA was invoked by the plaintiff in his or her complaint.[14] Invoking the "complete preemption" exception to the general "well pleaded complaint" rule governing federal jurisdiction, the Court held that defendants may remove any cases that could have been brought under § 502(a) into federal court, because Congress intended to completely preempt the field of claims for employee benefits.

"Complete" preemption is not truly a preemption doctrine, but is rather a principle for establishing federal removal jurisdiction. It is a powerful tool, however, for permitting defendants in cases raising state tort and contract, and even state statutory claims, to remove these cases into federal court where they can often be defeated under Pilot Life, § 502(a) implied preemption or under § 514(a) express preemption.

It is important to understand that § 502(a) and § 514(a) preemption are not coextensive—in some cases a state law claim might perhaps be preempted substantively under § 514(a) as relating to an employee benefits plan, but can not be raised in an action that can be brought under § 502(a), and thus can not be removed into federal court under the "complete preemption" doctrine.[15] In such cases the federal court lacks jurisdiction to address the question of § 514(a) preemption, and must remand a removed case to state court to deal with the issue.[16]

It is clear that not every claim in which a defendant asserts ERISA preemption is removable under the complete preemption doctrine. The reach of complete preemption, however, is far from clear. Under a test recently articulated by the Eleventh Circuit, four elements must be present before complete preemption will be found: the existence of a relevant ERISA plan, a plaintiff with standing to sue that plan (usually a participant or beneficiary), a defendant that is an ERISA entity, and a complaint that seeks compensatory relief similar to that available under § 502(b).[17] The Seventh Circuit, by contrast, has articulated three factors that are relevant to the complete preemption inquiry: 1) whether the plaintiff is eligible to bring a claim under

13.   481 U.S. 58, 107 S.Ct. 1542 (1987).

14.   Id. at 63–66.

15.   See, e.g., Franchise Tax Bd. v. Construction Laborers Vacation Trust, 463 U.S. 1, 25–27, 103 S.Ct. 2841 (1983); Toumajian v. Frailey, 135 F.3d 648, 655 (9th Cir.1998) (" . . . if the doctrine of complete preemption does not apply, even if the defendant has a defense of 'conflict preemption' within the meaning of § 1144(a) because the plaintiff's claims 'relate to' an ERISA plan, the district court, being without subject matter jurisdiction, cannot rule on the preemption issue."); Rice v. Panchal, 65 F.3d 637, 640 (7th Cir.1995) ("The difference between complete preemption under § 502(a) and conflict preemption under § 514(a) is important because complete preemption is an exception to the well-pleaded complaint rule that

has jurisdictional consequences."); Dukes v. U.S. Healthcare, Inc., 57 F.3d 350, 355 (3d Cir.1995) (emphasizing the importance of the distinction due to the jurisdictional consequences of its application); Warner v. Ford Motor Co., 46 F.3d 531, 535 (6th Cir.1995) (criticizing the failure to "keep complete preemption removal and ordinary preemption doctrine separate and distinct"). State law claims saved from preemption under the § 514 savings clause might also nonetheless be preempted under § 502, Parra v. John Alden Life Ins. Co., 22 F.Supp.2d 1360, 1364 (S.D.Fla.1998).

16.   Copling v. Container Store, 174 F.3d.590 (5th Cir. 1999); Duke v. U.S. Healthcare, Inc., 57 F.3d 350 (3d Cir. 1995).

17.   Butero v. Royal Maccabees Life Insurance Co., 174 F.3d 1207, 1212 (11th Cir.1999).

ERISA, 2) whether the plaintiff's cause of action falls within § 502(a), and 3) whether the plaintiff's state law claim cannot be resolved without an interpretation of an ERISA plan governed by federal law.[18]

It is obvious that § 502(a) preemption only applies in cases that involve ERISA plans, as defined above.[19] Section 502(a) preemption has also been denied in a number of cases involving plaintiffs that are not ERISA participants or beneficiaries or others entitled to bring an action under § 502(a).[20] For example, providers who have sued ERISA plans to collect for services provided to ERISA recipients and have claimed not as assignees of beneficiaries, but rather on their own right as victims of misrepresentations, have in some cases been able to withstand preemption and remain in state court, because they have no standing under § 502(a).[21] On the other hand, preemption has also been denied in several cases brought by ERISA participants or beneficiaries, who are proper § 502(a) plaintiffs, because the claims were brought against insurance agents who were not ERISA entities, and thus not proper § 502(a) defendants, where the defendant's liability would not affect the relationship among ERISA entities.[22]

However, where an ERISA participant or beneficiary sues an ERISA fiduciary and the suit raises issues that fall within the scope of § 502(a), the courts almost invariably find complete ERISA preemption, regardless of how the plaintiff defines the cause of action.[23] Suits that seek enforcement of an ERISA contract under state contract law, or that attempt to enforce a state law standard for evaluating performance of an ERISA contract, or that present state tort claim for improper performance of an ERISA contact are all

---

18. Speciale v. Seybold, 147 F.3d 612, 615 (7th Cir.1998) citing Jass v. Prudential Health Care Plan, Inc. 88 F.3d 1482 (7th Cir.1996). But see Mahon v. Cyganiak Planning Inc., 41 F.Supp. 910 (E.D. Wisc. 1999) (rejecting rigid application of test where not all factors met but claim nonetheless appeared to be a § 502(a) claim.)

19. This means, obviously, that a suit will not be preempted if it is brought against an benefit plan that is not covered by ERISA, but it also means that complete preemption may not attach if an ERISA policy was applied for but never issued because of fraud. Mehaffey v. Boston Mutual Life Ins. Co., 31 F.Supp. 2d 1329 (M.D.Ala.1998).

20. See, e.g. Toumajian v. Frailey, 135 F.3d 648 (9th Cir.1998) (claim of negligence by plan sponsor against person who allegedly failed to establish ERISA plan properly not preempted as plaintiff not properly plaintiff under § 502(a)); Tovey v. Prudential Ins. Co. of America, 42 F.Supp.2d 919 (W.D.Mo.1999) (action for misrepresentation and conversion brought by person who was never actually enrolled in plan was allegedly led to believe that she was); Mid West Inc. v. McDougall, 990 F.Supp. 914 (E.D.Mich.1998) (business tort suit against ERISA plan by nonparticipating firm not preempted).

21. Transitional Hospitals Corporation v. Blue Cross & Blue Shield of Texas, 164 F.3d 952, 954 (5th Cir.1999); Memorial Hospital Systems v. Northbrook Life Insurance Company, 904 F.2d 236 (5th Cir.1990). Where the provider claims as an assignee of a participant, however, the claim is completely preempted, Transitional Hospitals, 164 F.3d at 954; Hermann Hospital v. MEBA Medical & Benefits Plan, 845 F.2d 1286, 1290 (5th Cir.1988). See also Butero, 174 F.3d at 1207 (holding employer's claim against ERISA insurer not preempted, though federal court could retain jurisdiction over claim as pendant to employee's preempted claim);

22. Wilson v. Zoellner, 114 F.3d 713 (8th Cir.1997); Stetson v. PFL Insurance Co., 16 F.Supp.2d 28 (D. Maine 1998). See also Morstein v. National Insurance Services Inc., 93 F.3d 715 (11th Cir.1996) (similar holding in § 514 preemption case).

23. There is some debate whether only claims within the scope of § 502(a)(1) are preempted, or whether all claims within the scope of § 502(a) are preempted, though most courts go with the broader interpretation. Compare Joyce v. RJR Nabisco, 126 F.3d 166, 171 n. 3 (3d Cir. 1997); Anderson v. Electronic Data Systems, Corp. 11 F.3d 1311, 1315 (5th Cir.1994) and Toumajian v. Frailey, 135 F.3d 648, n. 6 (9th Cir.1998) (any § 502(a) claim) with Lupo v. Human Affairs International Inc., 28 F.3d 269 (2d. Cir.1994) (limited to 502(a)(1) claims).

essentially claims for benefits which could be brought under § 502(a)(1), and are all preempted.[24] Thus, ERISA preemption has been found in cases alleging fraud in the inducement,[25] misrepresentation,[26] bad faith,[27] negligence in denial of benefits,[28] improper processing of claims,[29] and breach of contract. Lawsuits that could be brought as claims for breach of fiduciary duty under § 502(a)(3) are also preempted, according to most courts.[30] Again, however, suits raising claims that in some way implicate an ERISA plans, but not raising issues that could be raised under § 502, however, are not preempted.[31]

Several courts of appeals have established a two-part test for complete preemption, first determining whether the state law claim is preempted by ERISA § 514, and then considering whether the claim falls within the scope of ERISA § 502.[32] This was in fact the sequence followed in Taylor, the first Supreme Court case recognizing complete preemption, but is problematic in cases where the court finds explicit conflict preemption under § 514, but then finds no complete preemption under § 502. In these cases the court must remand the case to the state court, but it has already decided the § 514 preemption issue, even though it had no jurisdiction. How the state court should deal with this essentially gratuitous opinion is problematic. For this reason, better reasoned cases consider first the complete preemption issue, and go on to consider conflict preemption only after federal jurisdiction is established.[33]

24. One remarkable outlier case is Moran v. Rush–Presbyterian HMO, 1998 WL 325204 (N.D.Ill.1998) (suit against HMO alleging wrongful determination of medical necessity because suit based on Illinois HMO Act rather than on ERISA policy).

25. Butero v. Royal Maccabees Life Ins. Co., 174 F.3d 1207 (11th Cir.1999); Hall v. Blue Cross/Blue Shield of Alabama, 134 F.3d 1063 (11th Cir.1998); Englehardt v. Paul Revere Life Insurance Company, 139 F.3d 1346 (11th Cir.1998).

26. See, e.g. Franklin v. QHG of Gadsden, Inc. 127 F.3d 1024 (11th Cir.1997) (alleged misrepresentation in benefits marketing); Smith v. Dunham–Bush, Inc., 959 F.2d 6, 10–11 (2d Cir.1992) (alleged negligent misrepresentation was promise to pay pension-related benefits); Slice v. Norway, 978 F.2d 1045 (8th Cir.1992) (misrepresentation as to amount of monthly benefits); Hermann Hosp. v. MEBA Medical & Benefits Plan, 959 F.2d 569, 578 (5th Cir.1992) ("state law claims of fraud and negligent misrepresentation are based upon the failure of MEBA to pay benefits to which Hermann was entitled"). But see Tovey v. Prudential Ins. Co. of America, 42 F.Supp.2d 919 (W.D.Mo.1999)(claim of misrepresentation of enrolled status not preempted); Hanks v. General Motors Inc., 26 F.Supp.2d 977 (E.D.Mich. 1998) (claim that misrepresentation caused her to draw pension rather than workers' compensation benefits).

27. Pilot Life Ins. Co. v. Dedeaux, 481 U.S. 41 (1987).

28. Jass v. Prudential Health Care Plan, Inc., 88 F.3d 1482 (7th Cir.1996); Corcoran v. United Healthcare, Inc. 965 F.2d 1321 (5th Cir.1992).

29. Huss v. Green Springs Health Serv's Inc., 18 F.Supp.2d 400 (D.Del.1998).

30. Joyce v. RJR Nabisco, 126 F.3d 166 (3d Cir. 1997); Romney v. Lin, 105 F.3d 806 (2d Cir.1997).

31. See, e.g. Speciale v. Seybold, 147 F.3d 612 (7th Cir.1998) (conflicting claims between ERISA plan as subrogee and other claimants to settlement fund); Aetna U.S. Healthcare Inc. v. Maltz, 1999 WL 285545 (S.D.N.Y.1999) (action under state managed care disclosure law challenging false and misleading statements made by plan about quality of care).

32. See e.g. McClelland v. Gronwaldt, 155 F.3d 507, 517 (5th Cir.1998) (" ... the first step in the complete preemption analysis is to determine whether the claim is subject to ordinary preemption under section 514(a)"); Toumajian v. Frailey, 135 F.3d 648, 654 (9th Cir. 1998); Emard v. Hughes Aircraft Co., 153 F.3d 949, 953 (9th Cir.1998); Franklin v. QHG of Gadsden, Inc., 127 F.3d 1024, 1028 (11th Cir. 1997); Franklin H. Williams Ins. Trust v. Travelers Ins. Co., 50 F.3d 144, 149 (2d Cir.1995).

33. See e.g. Joyce v. RJR Nabisco Holdings Corp., 126 F.3d 166, 172 (3d Cir.1997); Schmeling v. NORDAM, 97 F.3d 1336, 1341 (10th Cir.1996); Rice v. Panchal, 65 F.3d 637, 640 (7th Cir.1995); Tovey v. Prudential Ins. Co. of America, 42 F.Supp.2d 919 (W.D.Mo.1999).

§ 8–5. Medical Negligence Claims Under ERISA

ERISA establishes uniform national standards for employee benefit plans and broadly preempts state regulation of these plans. 29 U.S.C.A. § 1144(a) states that ERISA supersedes state laws to the extent that they "relate to any employee benefit plan" covered by ERISA. Congress passed ERISA to provide for national uniform administration of employee pension and health plans, to promote the growth of private plans by freeing them from a patchwork of state laws that complicated benefits administration.[1] ERISA plans are now the leading source of payment for health services nationwide, with more than seventy five percent of all managed care plans ERISA-qualified.

If ERISA preempts a state law claim, then the plaintiff is relegated to § 502 (a)(1)(B) of ERISA[2]. Section 502(a)(1)(B) states that a civil action may be brought "(1) by a participant or beneficiary—(B) to recover benefits due to him under the terms of his plan, to enforce his rights under the terms of the plan, or to clarify his rights to future benefits under the terms of the plan...."[3] In Massachusetts Mutual Life Insurance Co. v. Russell,[4] the Supreme Court held that an employee covered under her employer's welfare benefit plan could not recover compensatory and punitive damages for financial losses that allegedly occurred when the benefit plan mishandled the processing of the employee's claim for disability benefits. Section 409(a)'s statement that the fiduciary "shall be subject to such other equitable or remedial relief as the court may deem appropriate" precludes compensatory and punitive damages to compensate beneficiaries for personal injuries. Although a beneficiary can sue a benefit plan, a benefit plan manager, or other fiduciary, she cannot collect any personal compensatory or punitive damages under section 409(a). ERISA therefore restricts substantially the amount of recovery possible in what would otherwise be an ordinary malpractice case. ERISA allows a defendant to remove an ordinary malpractice case to federal court and invoke ERISA preemption to end the traditional lawsuit and require its reframing as a breach of ERISA. The plaintiff's potential damage award is severely curtailed as a result.[5]

ERISA was interpreted by the federal courts in the first wave of litigation as totally preempting common law tort claims.[6] It appeared from this caselaw

---

§ 8–5

1. See generally Robert L. Roth, Recent Developments Concerning the Effect of ERISA Preemption on Tort Claims Against Employers, Insurers, Health Plan Administrators, Managed Care Entities, and Utilization Review Agents, 8 The Health Lawyer 3 (Spring 1996); Larry J. Pittman, ERISA's Preemption Clause and the Health Care Industry: An Abdication of Judicial Law–Creating Authority, 46 Fla. L. Rev. 355 (1994).

2. 29 U.S.C.A. § 1132(a)(1)(B)

3. See generally Larry J. Pittman, ERISA's Preemption Clause and the Health Care Industry: An Abdication of Judicial Law–Creating Authority, 46 Fla.L.Rev. 355 (1994).

4. 473 U.S. 134 (1985)

5. In Durham v. Health Net, 108 F.3d 337 (table), 1997 WL 66558 (9th Cir. 1997)(plaintiff

sought damages under ERISA for the value of the ABMT treatment for breast cancer that she claimed was erroneously denied by her health plan. The Ninth Circuit affirmed the lower court's summary judgment, stating that ERISA § 502(a)(1)(B) "allows only for recovery of accrued benefits, and an injunction to prevent a plan administrator from wrongly refusing to pay benefits in the future ...There is no authority, found in the words of the statute, its legislative history, or the case law, which would allow a recovery for the value of withheld medical treatment under this section."

6. See, e.g., Ricci v. Gooberman, 840 F.Supp. 316 (D.N.J.1993); Butler v. Wu, 853 F.Supp. 125, 129–30 (D.N.J.1994); Nealy v. U.S. Healthcare HMO, 844 F.Supp. 966, 973 (S.D.N.Y.1994) (plaintiff's attempts to hold an HMO liable under several common law theories held preempted); Altieri v. Cigna Dental

that any managed care plan that was ERISA-qualified would receive virtually complete tort immunity. The federal courts began to split, however, as to the limits of such preemption.[7] Recent decisions have limited the preemption clause of ERISA, holding that many tort theories have little or nothing to do with the administration of pension plan or other benefits.[8] The result has been a litigation explosion against managed care as theories are imported from hospital liability caselaw, fiduciary law, and contract law to use against managed care organizations.[9]

Most managed care programs have three relevant features from a liability perspective. First, such programs select a restricted group of health care professionals who provide services to the program's participants. Second, such programs accept a fixed payment per subscriber, in exchange for provision of necessary care. This capitation model pressures managed care organizations to search for ways to minimize costs. Third, following from number two, managed care organizations use a variety of strategies to ensure cost effective care. Altering physician incentives is central to managed care, since physicians influence seventy percent of total health spending, while receiving only about twenty percent of each health care dollar.[10] Plans therefore use utilization review techniques, incentives systems, and physician gatekeepers to control costs.[11]

The watershed decision, opening up a substantial crack in preemption doctrine, was Dukes v. U.S. Healthcare, Inc.[12] In Dukes, the court found that Congress intended in passing ERISA to insure that promised benefits would be available to plan participants, and that section 502 was "intended to provide each individual participant with a remedy in the event that promises made by the plan were not kept." The court was unwilling, however, to stretch the remedies of 502 to "control the quality of the benefits received by plan participants." The court concluded that ... [q]uality control of benefits, such as the health care benefits provided here, is a field traditionally occupied by state regulation and we interpret the silence of Congress as reflecting an intent that it remain such." The court developed the distinction between benefits to care under a plan and a right to good quality care:

Health, Inc., 753 F.Supp. 61, 63–65 (D.Conn. 1990) (ERISA preempts plaintiff's negligent supervision claim against an HMO).

7. Peter D. Jacobson, Legal Challenges to Managed Care Cost Containment Programs: An Initial Assessment, 18 Health Affairs 69 (1999).

8. Prihoda v. Shpritz, DC Md, No. L–95–1392, 1/30/96 (ERISA does not preempt an action against physicians and an HMO for physicians' failure to diagnose a cancerous tumor, allowing a vicarious liability action to proceed). See also Independence HMO, Inc. v. Smith, 733 F.Supp. 983 (E.D.Pa.1990) (ERISA does not preempt medical malpractice-type claims brought against HMOs under a vicarious liability theory); Elsesser v. Hospital of the Philadelphia College of Osteopathic Medicine, 802 F.Supp. 1286 (E.D.Pa.1992) (same for a claim against an HMO for the HMO's negligence in selecting, retaining, and evaluating plaintiff's

primary-care physician); Kearney v. U.S. Healthcare, Inc., 859 F.Supp. 182 (E.D.Pa. 1994) (ERISA preempts plaintiff's direct negligence claim, but not its vicarious liability claim).

9. See generally Karen A. Jordan, Tort Liability for Managed Care: The Weakening of ERISA's Protective Shield, 25 J. Law, Med. & Ethics 160 (1997).

10. Peter D. Jacobson et al., Defining and Implementing Medical Necessity in Washington State and Oregon, 34 Inquiry 143, 148 (1997)(hidden financial incentives and provider-based review mechanisms had more influence over treatment availability than did denials of coverage by health plans based on contractual language.)

11. See generally Barry R. Furrow, Managed Care Organizations and Patient Injury: Rethinking Liability, 31 Ga.L.Rev. 419 (1997).

12. 57 F.3d 350 (3d Cir. 1995).

The plaintiffs are not attempting to define new "rights under the terms of the plan"; instead, they are attempting to assert their already-existing rights under the generally-applicable state law of agency and tort. Inherent in the phrases "rights under the terms of the plan" and "benefits due ... under the terms of [the] plan" is the notion that the plan participants and beneficiaries will receive something to which they would not be otherwise entitled. But patients enjoy the right to be free from medical malpractice regardless of whether or not their medical care is provided through an ERISA plan.

The court distinguished between the quantity of benefits due under a welfare plan and the quality of those benefits. Quality of care could be so poor that it is essentially a denial of benefits. Or the plan could describe a benefit in terms that are quality-based, such as a commitment that all x-rays will be analyzed by radiologists with a certain level of training. But absent either of these extremes, poor medical care—malpractice—is not a benefits issue under ERISA.

Theories of liability can be grouped into several categories, depending on the activity engaged in by the managed care organization. This functional organization helps determine what is preempted and what allowed under ERISA

a. *Contract Claims*

The managed care organization as insurer must recruit subscribers to its plan, typically through employment-based plans offered to employees. It must properly enroll these subscribers to ensure they are covered in exchange for their premiums. It must clearly describe any exclusions that operate under its coverage, including exclusions of coverage of certain diseases and "experimental" treatments.[13] Policies also typically impose a requirement of "medical necessity" as a prerequisite to payment for treatment. Policies may impose coverage limitations for certain treatments, such as psychiatric hospitalization. Such coverage restrictions may create a subscriber right to sue under section 502 of ERISA, but the courts have held that malpractice claims for damages for violation of this provision are preempted.[14] If a subscriber believes she is enrolled and subsequently learns she is not, after the plan has denied benefits, a claim for negligent misrepresentation and conversion has been allowed by some courts as not subject to preemption.[15]

13. See generally Mark A .Hall and Gerard F. Anderson, Health Insurers' Assessment of Medical Necessity, 140 U.Pa.L.Rev. 637(1997).

14. See, e.g., Brandon v. Aetna Services, Inc., 46 F.Supp.2d 110(D.C.Conn.1999)(claim against plan administrator for refusing to pay for in-patient and out-patient care for substance-abuse and anxiety disorder problems; held a benefits issue, preempted under ERISA); Parrino v. FHP, INC., 146 F.3d 699 (9th Cir. 1998)(patient had brain tumor removed and FHP initially refused to authorize payment for proton beam therapy prescribed by physicians as experimental and unnecessary; held that claim is completely preempted); Huss v. Green Spring Health Services, Inc., 1999 WL 225885 (E.D.Pa.1999)(failure of de-

fendant to correctly inform plaintiff of coverage under plan goes to quantity of benefits, and is preempted); Garcia v. Kaiser Foundation Hospitals, 978 P.2d 863 (1999)(plaintiff's claims that plan failed to provide him with reasonable and necessary medical treatment to which he was entitled, preempted; claims included breach of contract, tortious breach of contract, infliction of emotional distress, fraud, unfair and deceptive trade practice, loss of consortium, and punitive damages).

15. See Tovey v. Prudential Life Ins. Co. of America, 42 F.Supp.2d 919(W.D.Mo.1999); Wilson v. Zoellner, 114 F.3d 713, 717 (8th Cir. 1997); contra, see Pilot Life v. Dedeaux, 481 U.S. 41 (1987)(state claims of negligent misrep-

Common law bad faith claims are excluded under ERISA. Pilot Life Insurance Co. v. Dedeaux[16] held that actions such as bad faith sufficiently "relate to" employee benefits plans to fall within ERISA preemption. If the plan is not ERISA-qualified, courts have held that a staff model HMO acts as an insurer when it refers a subscriber to an out-of-network provider, under the contract, and then denies reimbursement for that out-of-network care without reasonable grounds. This kind of non-medical, coverage-related decision is subject to a bad faith analysis.[17]

b. *Operational Restrictions on Subscriber Choices*

Many managed care organizations restrict the choices of drugs available in their drug formularies. Hospital choices are restricted to those which whom the MCO has a contract, as is access to specialists. Use of physician gatekeepers restricts access to hospitals and specialists on the MCO's acceptable list. The courts have generally held that ERISA preempts claims based on plan strategies to discourage referrals to specialists.[18] Pre-certification and other forms of utilization review are designed to filter out demands for "unnecessary" "treatments". Such forms of review of physician medical decisions to determine their necessity and cost-effectiveness prior to treatment or hospitalization are either completely preempted under § 502(a)(1)(B)[19] or subject to an ERISA preemption defense under § 514(a)[20]. Such forms of review may affect the quantity of benefits received directly, but they have attendant effects on quality as well. Thus a failure to provide in-home visits for a subscriber, when the plan allegedly offered such a service, is a benefit issue subject to preemption under § 502.[21] Claims that fall within the administrator's core functions–determining eligibility for benefits, disbursing them to the participant, monitoring available funds and recordkeeping—are completely preempted.[22]

Denials based on "medical necessity" determinations are more complicated than the courts have generally acknowledged. They entail two determinations: first, a medical judgment that the patient's condition can be treated by available treatments of varying efficacy and cost; second, an administrative decision of whether to pay for the care, considering the cost-benefit trade-off of the treatment alternatives. The HMO decision can characterized as a medical determination, although most courts have held that refusals to pay for care that the treating physician recommends are preempted.[23] Attacks on

---

resentation preempted because of need to reference terms of the plan).

16. 481 U.S. 41 (1987).

17. McEvoy v. Group Health Cooperative of Eau Claire, 570 N.W.2d 397(Wis.1997)(allowing bad faith action against a non-ERISA HMO for a coverage denial).

18. Pell v. Shmokler, 1997 WL 83743 (E.D.Pa.1997)(refusal of treating physician to refer plaintiff to pulmonologist is a withholding of benefits, subject to complete preemption); see also Kohn v. Delaware Valley HMO, Inc. 1991 WL 275609 (E.D.Pa.1991).

19. See Jass v. Prudential Health Care Plan Inc., 88 F.3d 1482 (7th Cir. 1996)(claim against pre-certification review administrator who denied patient's request of physical therapy to rehabilitate knee after surgery held completely preempted).

20. See Kuhl v. Lincoln Nat'l Health Plan of Kansas City, Inc., 999 F.2d 298, 302 (8th Cir. 1993)(decision to delay pre-certification of heart surgery preempted); Corcoran v. United Healthcare. Inc., 965 F.2d 1321, 1332 (5th Cir. 1992).

21. Bauman v. U.S.Healthcare, Inc., 193 F.3d 151, 161 (3d Cir.1999).

22. Id.

23. Danca v. Private Health Care Sys., Inc., 185 F.3d 1 (1st Cir. 1999); Brandon v. Aetna Servs., Inc., 46 F.Supp. 2d 110(D.Conn.1999); Person v. Physicians Health Plan, Inc., 20 F.Supp.2d 918(E.D.Va.1998); Tolton v. American Biodyne, Inc., 48 F.3d 937 (6th Cir. 1995); Spain v. Aetna Life Insurance Company, 11 F.3d 129 (9th Cir. 1993); Toledo v. Kaiser Permanente Med. Group, 987 F.Supp. 1174

utilization review necessarily also attack the methods by which benefits are administered or denied.

The U.S. Supreme Court in American Manufacturers Mutual Insurance Co. v. Sullivan[24] held that in deciding whether an entity was a state actor, a distinction could be made between the payment of a Workers' Compensation (WC) claim and a utilization review decision as to the need for treatment to be paid under WC. The plaintiff had sought compensation under Pennsylvania's WC scheme for treatment for medical expenses. Only claims deemed "medically necessary" were reimbursable and WC insurers could forward claims to utilization review companies to determine medical necessity prior to payment by the insurer. In Sullivan, the Court distinguished between the insurer's payment of claims and the medical necessity determination. It ruled that payment of government benefits under WC are actions of a state actor and trigger Due Process requirements, but medical necessity determinations do not trigger those requirements and are not state action. The Court therefore found that two decisions were being made, even if by one company–a medical decision as to necessity of treatment and a payment decision based on the medical decision.

The analogy Sullivan provides to managed care is direct. The plaintiff can distinguish between benefit and medical necessity determinations, and then argue that a medical decision was made by the HMO and it is subject to a malpractice claim. This would appear to be consistent with the Dukes quality/quantity distinction and would avoid preemption under ERISA. One case to date appears to have followed this line of reasoning. In Moscovitch v. Danbury Hospital,[25] involving utilization review of the need for inpatient care for a suicidal adolescent, the District Court accepted this distinction between negligent administration of benefits and medical decision making. It held that ERISA did not preempt the claims, which were "in the nature of claims for medical negligence, not claims for the improper denial of plan benefits." The challenge was to the quality and appropriate level of care and treatment, and this is not a benefits determination. Other courts have rejected this argument and the "quality/quantity" distinction as creating an unworkable distinction.[26]

c. *Plan Design and Delivery of Health Care Services*

MCOs are businesses. They market their care to potential employers and subscribers in a competitive marketplace for health care. They recruit and organize their physicians through their networks. They design a corporate system in which health care is delivered. And they must administer this system in a safe fashion that avoids injury to subscribers caused by the negligence of plan physicians and other providers. Malpractice claims based on vicarious liability, corporate negligence, negligence per se and intentional inflection of mental distress may be allowed under current law as quality of care issues not involving ERISA claims for benefits.[27]

(N.D.Cal.1997); Schmid v. Kaiser Found. Health Plan of the Northwest, 963 F.Supp. 942 (D.Or.1997).

24. 526 U.S. 40, 119 S.Ct. 977 (1999).

25. Moscovitch v. Danbury Hospital, 25 F.Supp.2d 74 (D.Conn.1998)

26. Danca v. Private Health Care Sys., Inc., 185 F.3d 1 (1st Cir. 1999).

27. Herrera v. Lovelace Health Systems, Inc., 35 F.Supp.2d 1327 (D.N.M.1999); Hoose v. Jefferson Home Health Care, Inc., 1998 WL 114492 (E.D.Pa.1998) (claims of negligence in selection of therapists, providing post-operative care, vicarious liability, and negligence in overall supervision of care; the court noted that "this case is noting more than a medical mal-

Agency Doctrine. Under theories of agency, physicians and other professionals may be held liable and that liability imputed to the managed care organization. Such vicarious liability has been held by the majority of courts considering the question not to be preempted by ERISA[28] The Plan is irrelevant to the claim, since the claim of agency does not rise and fall with the plan[29], but is established by reference to reliance and representations, a question of fact not involving the interpretation of an ERISA plan.[30] If the underlying claim against the treating physician is a failure to treat—a denial of benefits—then it relates to the benefits plan; a vicarious liability claim would also be grounded in this benefits denial claim. The negligence claim then could not be resolved without reference to the benefits determination. In such a situation, one circuit court has held that ERISA completely preempts the agency claim.[31]

The law of vicarious liability varies substantially from state to state, and plans have argued that allowing vicarious liability claims would create a patchwork of regulations affecting ERISA plans, interfering with the administration of benefits and the need for uniformity. However, as the court noted in Prihoda,[32] while liability might vary from state to state, "[t]he liability of HMOs ... would not be subject to inconsistent administrative obligations of the type that occur when inconsistent local laws and court decisions cause benefit levels to vary from state to state."

Marketing Representations. Plan marketing in the media can give rise to claims under state fraud law for misrepresentation of the care and treatment available to enrollees. In Aetna U.S. Healthcare Inc. v. Maltz,[33] the plaintiffs sued under N.Y. General Business Law § 349, claiming that U.S. Healthcare's advertising in television commercials and press releases claimed that Aetna "provides access to the highest quality of care"; and that they misrepresented the impact of capitation. The promotional booklet given out failed to give full information on the effects of capitation on services provided to enrollees. Plaintiffs sought an injunction prohibiting Aetna from continuing the deceptive practices and from refusing to comply with the requirements of the state disclosure laws. This was held to be a claim for quality of care provided and was not preempted. Such a claim for misrepresentation could allow for damages under state consumer fraud statutes.

Treatment recommendations. When a plan or its non-physician employees get involved in treatment orders, they may be liable. In Roessert v Health Net,[34] the patient sued their HMO, medical group and treating

practice case", and refused to uphold ERISA preemption).

28. Harris v. Deaconess Health Services Corp., et al., No. 4:99–CV–701 CAS, (E.D. Mo. 1999); Herrera v. Lovelace Health Systems, Inc., 35 F.Supp.2d 1327(D.N.M. 1999); Visconti v. U.S.Healthcare, 1998 WL 968473 (E.D.Pa. 1998); Petrovich v. Share Health Plan of Illinois, Inc., 1999 WL 773524 (Ill.1999); Dykema v. King, 959 F.Supp. 736(D.S.C.1997); Prihoda v. Shpritz, 914 F.Supp. 113 (D.Maryland 1996); Pacificare of Oklahoma, Inc., v. Burrage, 59 F.3d 151 (10th Cir. 1995); Lupo v. Human Affairs Int'l, Inc., 28 F.3d 269(2d Cir.1994); Dearmas v. Av–Med, Inc., 865 F.Supp. 816 (S.D.Fla.1994); Gilbert v. Sycamore Municipal Hospital, 622 N.E.2d 788 (Ill.1993).

29. Eaccarino v. Canlas, 1998 WL 195875 (E.D.Pa.)(agency theory is a "garden variety" tort not preempted by ERISA).

30. See Rice v. Panchal, 65 F.3d 637 (7th Cir. 1995).

31. Jass v. Prudential Health Care Plan, Inc., 88 F.3d 1482 (7th Cir. 1996)

32. Supra n. 14 at 118.

33. 1999 WL 285545 (S.D.N.Y.1999).

34. 929 F.Supp. 343, 351 (N.D.Cal.1996).

physicians in part for seeking her commitment to a psychiatric facility. The court found that an action for intentional or negligent infliction of mental distress against the HMO and the medical group was not preempted by ERISA. The plan's recommendation to commit could be evaluated apart from the terms of the plan. If a plan used under-qualified employees to treat a patient and they failed to recognize the seriousness of the condition, the plan was acting as a provider, not in its administrative capacity, and the claim could proceed in state court.[35] If a plan requires that a subscriber first telephone an advisory nurse prior to seeking medical attention, this has been construed as a misdiagnosis and the giving of negligent medical advice rather than as utilization review pre-certification.[36]

Adoption of policies that discourage physicians from offering needed care. Explicit rules that discourage physicians from giving patients necessary care or hospitalization, such as keeping at-risk patients in hospitals, can be the basis for negligence claims. In Bauman v. U.S. Healthcare[37], plan participants whose newborn infant died on the day following discharge from the hospital sued. They argued that the plan policy that pressured or required that physicians discharge newborn infants and mothers within 24 hours of birth was negligent, and that a policy that discouraged readmission when health problems were identified after the original discharge was negligent. The Third Circuit held that "when the HMO acts under the ERISA plan as a health care provider, it arranges and provides medical treatment, directly or through contracts with hospitals, doctors, or nurses."[38] A 24–hour discharge policy fits within a quality of care claim, as does a hospital utilization review policy that discourages readmission. A challenge to the appropriateness of medical decisions by a plan and its agents, as to quality and level of care and treatment, have been held to fall outside § 502(a) and may be tried in state court.[39] The financial arrangement generally between the managed care organization and a hospital may arguably cause a hospital to commit malpractice, and this does not require courts to review a plan's utilization review or otherwise construe a plan's benefits. Preemption may therefore be avoided.[40]

This movement by the Third Circuit is likely to challenge the older managed care jurisprudence. By saving from preemption in Bauman the

35. Blaine v. Community Health Plan, 687 N.Y.S.2d 854 (S.C. N.Y. 1998)(claim that patient's injuries were caused by the plan's failure to provide her with a physician rather than physician's assistant, failing to provide tests, and failing to adequately supervise the physician's assistant and have written policies governing required supervision.)

36. Crum v. Health Alliance–Midwest, Inc., 47 F.Supp.2d 1013 (C.D.Ill.1999)(advisory nurse told plaintiff with chest pains that he just had gas pains, and he died that evening of acute myocardial infarction); Phommyvong v. Muniz, 1999 WL 155714 (N.D.Tex.1999). But see Jass v. Prudential Health Care Plan, Inc., 88 F.3d 1482 (7th Cir. 1996)(nurse's denial of physical therapy held to be a claim for denial of benefits).

37. 193 F.3d 151 (3d Cir. 1999).

38. 193 F.3d 151 (3d Cir. 1999).

39. Moscovitch v. Danbury Hospital, 25 F.Supp.2d 74 (D.C.Conn.1998)(suit against plan and providers for the suicide of son, on grounds that the plan failed to properly diagnose and assess the decedent's psychiatric condition, failed to monitor, care and treat him and oversee his treatment and failed to prescribe and administer the proper medications. The court held that this was a quality of care issue and the plaintiff can show on remand that the plan crossed the line form making a benefits determination to a treatment decision). See also Cyr v. Kaiser Found. Health Plan of Texas, 12 F.Supp.2d 556 (N.D.Tex. 1998)(claims for negligence, fraudulent concealment, and tortious interference with the doctor/patient relationship held not preempted.)

40. Ouellette v. The Christ Hospital, 942 F.Supp. 1160 (S.D.Ohio 1996).

plaintiff's attack on the 24–hour hospitalization limit, it subjects to tort analysis the contractual standard of care set by the managed care plan's design of their plan and benefits. State malpractice standards are thus applicable to this feature of plan benefits quite directly, under the guise of a "quality" analysis. A benefit denial then turns into a standard of medical care issue under state tort law. And the characterization of the action in the complaint, avoiding the use of benefits, has been sufficient for several federal district courts to allow complaints to proceed in state court in spite of the preemption defense.[41]

Substandard Plan Design and Administration. A claim that a managed care plan is "substandard", leading to patient injury as a result, would seem to go directly to the administration of a plan, and therefore be preempted. Claims of negligent design and administration of the delivery of health care services have been allowed in recent cases.[42] A negligence claim against a plan for providing contractual benefits in "such a dilatory fashion that the patient was injured are intertwined with the provision of safe care."[43] In the Pappas case, the issue was a delay in transporting the plaintiff to a specialty trauma unit for care. The delay was arguably caused by the utilization review process of the managed care organization, which did not allow transport to the best hospital unit in the area for spinal injuries. The case appears to involve both a system-induced delay and also a benefits question as to which hospitals were available to U.S. Healthcare providers and when a proper emergency allowed sending a subscriber outside the hospital network. Under the Dukes analysis, it is not clear in such a case where the quality-quantity distinction can be clearly drawn.

In Moreno v. Health Partners Health Plan,[44] the District Court held that there is "no relation between an action for medical malpractice and the recovery of benefits or the clarification of rights to future benefits under an ERISA plan."[45] Its analysis was based on the Ninth Circuit test for ERISA preemption.[46] In Geweke, the Ninth Circuit first asked whether the state action fell within the three areas of concern of Travelers.[47] Claims of negligent supervision of plan physicians have been allowed by courts to proceed as raising a quality issue, not preempted.[48] Likewise, a plan decision to discharge a patient from the hospital to her home rather than a skilled nursing facility is considered a "quality" issue, not suitable for preemption.[49] Where a plan is responsible for the continuum of care and it proves to be inadequate, even if

41. See, e.g., Spear v. Richard J. Caron Foundation, 1999 WL 768299 (E.D.Pa.1999) (plaintiff's complaint does not on its face allege a denial of benefits under the insurance plan and so complete preemption does not apply).

42. See McDonald v. Damian, 1999 WL 500133 (E.D.Pa.1999)(claim for inadequacies in the delivery of medical services).

43. Pappas v. Asbel, 724 A.2d 889, 893 (Pa.1998).

44. 4 F.Supp.2d 888 (D.Ariz.1998).

45. Id at 893.

46. Geweke Ford v. St. Joseph's Omni Preferred Care In., 130 F.3d 1355, 1360(9th Cir. 1997).

47. Areas of concern identified in Travelers include (1) laws that mandate employee benefits structure or their administration; (2) bind employers or plan administrators to particular choices or preclude uniform administrative practice, functioning as a result as the regulation of an ERISA plan; or (3) provide an alternative enforcement mechanisms for employees to obtain ERISA plan benefits. New York State Conference of Blue Cross & Blue Shield v. Travelers Insurance Co., 514 U.S. 645, 655 (1995)(citing to Ingersoll–Rand Co. v. McClendon, 498 U.S. 133, 142 (1990)).

48. Hoyt v. Edge, 1997 WL 356324 (E.D.Pa.1997).

49. Miller v. Riddle Memorial Hospital, 1998 WL 272167 (E.D.Pa.1998).

that means they refuse to cover a benefit at a rehabilitation hospital or other facility, courts have found this to be nothing more a complaint of substandard care, not preempted by ERISA.[50] If a plan is negligent in failing to provide appropriate screening tests and studies, this can be viewed, not as a benefits denial, but a negligent provision of benefits, not subject to ERISA.[51]

d. Physician Selection and Retention

MCOs must select physicians who have appropriate credentials and training. They must then have procedures in place for reviewing these physicians' conduct and deciding whether or not to retain physicians at the end of their contract periods. Negligence in hiring, employment and supervision of medical personnel involved in treatment is a classic example of corporate negligence, defined in the hospital setting and imported into the managed care environment.[52] As such, it is not subject to preemption, based on the Dukes rationale that such selection relates to the quality of care offered.[53]

e. Physician Payment Mechanisms

One of the primary goals of managed care is conservative, cost-efficient practice. Physician behavior in prescribing, hospitalizing and referring may be altered by designing payment systems that promote cost-sensitive practice through bonuses and penalties. Claims regarding design of and concealment of financial incentives continue to be disallowed under the complete preemption doctrine. The claim is that such incentives to undertreat cause a physician to deny benefits to a subscriber, resulting in injury. A plaintiff may claim that a physician negligently diagnosed or failed to treat, and the mere reference to the effect of an incentive system on his or her motivations will not lead to preemption.[54] When, however, the claim is that the plan is negligent in the very design of the payment system, the courts have noted that this is an attack on administrative systems designed to curb rising health care costs by rewarding physicians for not ordering tests or treatment. It is essentially a claim of a denial of benefits and as a result triggers § 502(a)(1)(B) and complete preemption.[55] If the effect of a payment incentive system is recast as having the effect, not of denying benefits, but of discouraging physicians from providing proper care, then it is viewed by some courts as a quality of care issue following the Dukes analysis and held not to be preempted.[56]

50. Snow v. Burden, 1999 WL 387196 (E.D.Pa.1999).

51. Newton v. Tavani, 962 F.Supp. 45 (D.N.J.1997).

52. See Shannon v. McNulty, 718 A.2d 828 (Sup.Ct.Pa. 1998) for the application of corporate negligence doctrine to a managed care organization. See also Santitoro v. Evans, 935 F.Supp. 733 (E.D.N.C.1996).

53. See, e.g., Giles v. NYLCare Health Plans, Inc., 172 F.3d 332 (5th Cir. 1999)(claim for negligence in selecting plan providers remanded); Visconti v. U.S.Healthcare, 1998 WL 968473 (E.D.Pa.1998).

54. Lancaster v. Kaiser Foundation Health Plan of Mid–Atlantic States, Inc., 958 F.Supp. 1137, 1145 (E.D.Va.1997)(it may be appropriate for plaintiff to show that an incentive program induced physicians to refrain from ordering tests, to rebut their claim that their decision was based on "sound medical consideration.")

55. Lancaster v. Kaiser Foundation Health Plan of Mid–Atlantic States, Inc., 958 F.Supp. 1137 (E.D.Va.1997)

56. DeLucia v. St. Luke's Hospital, 1999 WL 387211 (E.D.Pa.1999); Ouellette v. The Christ Hospital, 942 F.Supp. 1160 (S.D.Ohio 1996).

Courts are steadily eroding ERISA categorical preemption in favor of subscriber rights to sue the organization for injuries. The recasting of malpractice claims as "quality" complaints, rather than benefit denials, has been accepted by several recent federal court decisions. The courts seem inclined to narrow ERISA preemption whenever possible and are likely to continue to do so. It is now up to the Supreme Court to once again look at ERISA in the context of medical liability and decide if it wants to draw further lines that limit ERISA's reach.

C. ERISA CLAIMS AND OBLIGATIONS

§ 8-6. Benefit Claims Litigation Under ERISA

ERISA cases challenging benefit determinations are very different from typical health insurance claim denial cases. In the typical insurance case, the claimant sues for breach of contract or under a state law governing claims practices. Historically, the courts have treated insured claimants very favorably in these cases, applying the principle of contra proferentem to interpret vague or ambiguous contract terms in the insured's favor, or interpreting clauses in light of the insured's "reasonable expectations."[1] In egregious cases, the emerging law of bad faith breach of insurance contracts has given the insured the benefit of tort as well as contract law, and made possible large recoveries for consequential damages well beyond the value of the benefit denied.[2] By contrast, ERISA cases are much more like administrative review cases than like traditional contract or tort cases. ERISA plan administrators and fiduciaries make initial claim determinations, which are reviewable by the courts under ERISA's remedial provisions. The court, however, does not generally reach its own decision as to the propriety of coverage, it merely reviews the plan's own determination, almost invariably under highly deferential standards of review. This section considers first ERISA claims practices, then examines judicial review of benefit determinations

a. ERISA Claims Provisions

ERISA requires that plan fiduciaries

(1) provide adequate notice in writing to any participant or beneficiary whose claim for benefits under the plan has been denied, setting forth the specific reasons for such denial, written in a manner calculated to be understood by the participant, and

(2) afford a reasonable opportunity to any participant whose claim for benefits has been denied for a full and fair review by the appropriate named fiduciary of the decision denying the claim.[3]

Current implementing regulations mandate that ERISA plans permit the claimant or his representative to request a review, review pertinent documents, submit issues and comments in writing, and receive a written decision,

§ 8-6

1. Mark A. Hall & Gerard F. Anderson, Health Insurers' Assessment of Medical Necessity, 140 U.Pa.L.Rev. 1637, 1648–49; Richard S. Saver, Reimbursing New Technologies: Why are the Courts Judging Experimental Medicine? 44 Stan.L.Rev. 1095, 1100–03 (1992).

2. See Aetna Life Ins. Co. v. Lavoie, 505 So.2d 1050 (Ala.1987); Hughes v. Blue Cross, 263 Cal.Rptr. 850 (Cal.Ct.App.1989).

3. 29 U.S.C.A. § 1133; 29 C.F.R. § 2560.503–1.

including specific reasons for the decision and reference to specific plan provisions on which it is based, usually within 60 days.[4] In September of 1998, the Department of Labor proposed new claims regulations, that would significantly increase claimant protections under ERISA plans. Specifically, the proposed regulations would:

— prohibit plans from requiring claimants to submit claims to arbitration or to make more than one appeal before going to court;

— prohibit barriers to filing claims (such as fees) or preauthorization requirements where satisfying the requirement would jeopardize life or health;

— require prompt notification of the lack of compliance with plan requirements in filed claims;

— require expedited procedures for filing urgent claims, including provision for telephone or fax submission and communication;

— require notification of determinations on urgent claims in 72 hours or less and on other claims within 15 days, with notification including reference to specific plan provisions, including internal rules, guidelines, protocols, and criteria on which the denial was based and explanation of appeal procedures;

— require provision for appeal procedures that provide claimants the opportunity to provide written information; reasonable access to all information relevant to the claim; a review that does not give deference to the initial determination and that takes into account all information submitted by the claimant, including information submitted after the initial determination; and a decision by a person who was not involved in the initial determination, who shall consult with in independent health care professional if medical issues are involved;

— require notification of the determination on review within 72 hours for urgent claims, 30 days for others;

— provide immediate access to the courts without further exhaustion if a plan fails to establish or follow procedures consistent with the regulations;[5]

These proposals have proved very controversial, and may be modified before implementation, but as originally proposed they are remarkable both for increasing claimant protection and for strengthening the parallels between the procedures of plan fiduciaries and administrative agencies.

Because ERISA provides for administrative review of benefits, courts have uniformly required that claimants exhaust plan remedies before bringing an ERISA suit,[6] although exhaustion may be waived where requiring exhaus-

---

4. 29 C.F.R. § 2560.503–1. The regulations also state that claims procedures under a federally qualified HMO are sufficient for ERISA. 29 C.F.R. § 2560.503–1(j).

5. 63 Fed. Reg. 48390 (1998), to be codified at 29 C.F.R. § 2560.503–1.

6. See e.g., Fallick v. Nationwide Mutual Ins. Co., 162 F.3d 410, 418 at n. 4 (6th Cir. 1998) (listing decisions of ten federal circuits requiring exhaustion); Springer v. Wal–Mart Associates' Group Health Plan, 908 F.2d 897 (11th Cir.1990); Kross v. Western Elec. Co., 701 F.2d 1238 (7th Cir.1983); Makar v. Health

tion would be futile or inadequate or result in irreparable injury.[7] Plan requirements that disputes be submitted to arbitration are also generally enforced.[8]

The courts are split on the question of whether evidence can be presented on judicial review that was not presented at the time of the initial determination, with most courts refusing to accept additional evidence and limiting themselves to a review of their record considered by the plan fiduciary,[9] but some permitting the presentation of additional evidence,[10] and others rejecting additional evidence of the historical facts considered in the benefit determination, but accepting additional evidence going to the legality of the benefit determination.[11]

Courts are more willing to allow the submission of additional evidence where the plan's decision is reviewed under the de novo review standard described below, less willing if arbitrary and capricious review is applied. Also, courts may be more willing to permit the admission of additional evidence if the administrator prevented the submission of evidence in its initial decision-making process.[12] Several courts, however, have held that if the court finds that the administrator wrongfully failed to consider evidence favoring the claimant, the court must remand for further consideration by the administrator rather than substituting its own judgment.[13]

b. Claim Determination Review Actions

As noted above, a plan participant or beneficiary may bring a civil action under ERISA "to recover benefits due to him under the terms of his plan, to enforce his rights under the terms of the plan, or to clarify his rights to future benefits under the terms of the plan."[14] The Act further provides for equitable relief to enjoin acts or practices that violate ERISA or the terms of a benefits plan or to enforce the requirements of ERISA or a benefits plan.[15] Under rare

Care Corp. of Mid–Atlantic, 872 F.2d 80 (4th Cir.1989).

7. See Fallick v. Nationwide Mutual Ins. Co., 162 F.3d 410 (6th Cir.1998); Costantino v. TRW Inc. 13 F.3d 969 (6th Cir.1994); Davis v. Featherstone, 97 F.3d 734 (4th Cir.1996); Curry v. Contract Fabricators Inc. Profit Sharing Plan, 891 F.2d 842 (11th Cir.1990); and discussion in Foster v. Cordis Corp., 707 F.Supp. 517 (S.D.Fla.1989). Exhaustion may also be excused where a statutory violation rather than a violation of the terms of the plan is alleged.

8. See Bird v. Shearson Lehman/American Express Ins., 926 F.2d 116 (2d Cir. 1991); Graphic Communications Union v. GCIU–Employer Retirement Benefit Plan, 917 F.2d 1184 (9th Cir.1990) (where claim arises under the plan itself rather than under ERISA); Arnulfo P. Sulit, Inc. v. Dean Witter Reynolds, Inc., 847 F.2d 475 (8th Cir.1988).

9. Chambers v. Family HealthPlan Corporation, 100 F.3d 818 (10th Cir.1996); Lee v. Blue Cross/Blue Shield, 10 F.3d 1547, 1550 (11th Cir.1994) (requiring courts "to look only to the facts known to the administrator"); Taft v. Equitable Life Assurance Soc'y, 9 F.3d 1469, 1471–72 (9th Cir.1993); Abnathya v. Hoff-

mann–La Roche, Inc., 2 F.3d 40, 48 n. 8 (3d Cir.1993); Oldenburger v. Central States Southeast & Southwest Areas Teamster Pension Fund, 934 F.2d 171, 174 (8th Cir.1991) Perry v. Simplicity Engineering, 900 F.2d 963, 967 (6th Cir.1990). The Fourth Circuit has held that additional evidence may be considered, but only under exceptional circumstances where it is necessary to permit an adequate de novo review. Quesinberry v. Life Ins. Co. of North America, 987 F.2d 1017 (4th Cir.1993).

10. Luby v. Teamster's Health, Welfare, and Pension Trust Funds, 944 F.2d 1176 (3d Cir. 1991).

11. Wildbur v. ARCO Chemical Company, 974 F.2d 631 (5th Cir.1992)

12. Friedrich v. Intel, 1999 WL 430569 (9th Cir.1999).

13. Killian v. Healthsource Provident Administrators, Inc., 152 F.3d 514 (6th Cir.1998). But see Perry v. Simplicity Engineering, 900 F.2d 963 (6th Cir.1990) (remand not necessary if issues clear).

14. 29 U.S.C.A. § 1132(a)(1).

15. 29 U.S.C.A. § 1132(a)(3).

circumstances, where exhaustion of remedies is futile and an improper benefits determination methodology was applied to a large group of claimants, class action litigation of ERISA claims may be possible.[16] ERISA does not provide a statute of limitations, thus courts usually look to state limitation statutes, though they will also honor contractual limitations periods if they are reasonable.[17]

The Supreme Court in *Firestone Tire & Rubber Co. v. Bruch*,[18] specified that courts should exercise de novo review in reviewing benefit determinations by ERISA plan fiduciaries and administrators. The Court rejected the "arbitrary and capricious" review standard uniformly applied by courts to ERISA determinations prior to *Firestone*. The Court, however, acknowledged an exception that has in fact swallowed the rule. It stated that the deferential arbitrary and capricious standard of review should be applied where "the benefit plan gives the administrator or fiduciary discretionary authority to determine eligibility for benefits or to construe the terms of the plan."[19]

ERISA plan administrators almost invariably draft plan documents so as to bring their decisions under the "arbitrary and capricious" review standard. The courts are quite generous in reading plan documents to confer discretion. Plan clauses that specifically delegate to the administrator the power or discretion to interpret or construe the plan;[20] provisions that grant the plan administrator the power to make full, final, binding, or conclusive determinations,[21] or the ability to make "independent" determinations;[22] and clauses that state that coverage will be afforded "as determined by" the administrator,[23] have been found to confer discretionary authority. General grants of power to administer the plan are probably not enough,[24] nor is authority on the part of the insurer to "require written verification" of a claim.[25] Courts have generally interpreted the common provision that evidence offered in support of eligibility for a benefit must be "satisfactory" to the administrator to confer discretion.[26] Even a plan provision conditioned on the administrator

16. Fallick v. Nationwide Mutual Ins. Co., 162 F.3d 410 (6th Cir.1998); Forbush v. J.C. Penney Co., Inc. 994 F.2d 1101 (5th Cir.1993).

17. Northlake Regional Medical Center v. Waffle House System Employee Benefit Plan, 160 F.3d 1301 (11th Cir.1998); Duchek v. Blue Cross and Blue Shield of Nebraska, 153 F.3d 648 (8th Cir.1998); Doe v. Blue Cross and Blue Shield United of Wisconsin, 112 F.3d 869 (7th Cir.1997).

18. 489 U.S. 101, 109 S.Ct. 948, 103 L.Ed.2d 80 (1989).

19. 489 U.S. at 115, 109 S.Ct. at 956.

20. Morales v. Pan Am. Life Ins. Co., 914 F.2d 83, 87 (5th Cir.1990); Fuller v. CBT Corp., 905 F.2d 1055, 1058 (7th Cir.1990); Exbom v. Central States, Southeast and Southwest Areas Health and Welfare Fund, 900 F.2d 1138, 1141 (7th Cir.1990).

21. Jones v. Laborers Health & Welfare Trust Fund, 906 F.2d 480, 481 (9th Cir.1990); Richards v. United Mine Workers of America Health & Retirement Fund, 895 F.2d 133, 135 (4th Cir.1990); Stoetzner v. United States Steel Corp., 897 F.2d 115, 119 (3d Cir.1990).

22. Wildbur v. ARCO Chemical Co., 974 F.2d 631 (5th Cir.1992).

23. Healthcare America Plans, Inc. v. Bossemeyer, 166 F.3d 347 (10th Cir.1998).

24. Masella v. Blue Cross & Blue Shield, Inc., 936 F.2d 98 (2d Cir.1991); Cathey v. Dow Chemical Co. Medical Care Program, 907 F.2d 554 (5th Cir.1990), cert. denied 498 U.S. 1087, 111 S.Ct. 964, 112 L.Ed.2d 1051 (1991); Michael Reese Hosp. v. Solo Cup Employee Health Benefit Plan, 899 F.2d 639 (7th Cir. 1990); Guisti v. General Elec. Co., 733 F.Supp. 141 (N.D.N.Y.1990).

25. Brinks v. Blue Cross and Blue Shield of Mich., 1988 WL 278177, *4 (W.D. Mich. 1998).

26. Wilcox v. Reliance Standard Life Ins. Co., 1999 WL 170411, No. 98–1036, *2 (4th Cir. March 23, 1999); Perez v. Aetna Life Ins. Co., 150 F.3d 550 (6th Cir.1998); Ceasar v. Hartford Life & Accident Ins. Co., 947 F.Supp. 204, 206 (D.S.C.1996); Yeager v.Reliance Standard Life Ins. Co., 88 F.3d 376, 380 (6th Cir. 1996); Snow. Standard Ins. Co., 87 F.3d 327, 330 (9th Cir.1996); Donato v. Metropolitan Life Ins. Co., 19 F.3d 375, 378–80 (7th Cir.1994). A

"allowing" a claim was held by one court to be a discretionary grant.[27] Arbitrary and capricious review has in fact become the baseline standard of review in ERISA cases. Further, even applying a de novo review standard, the courts often uphold the plan's determination.[28]

Courts commonly apply a two step analysis in conducting "arbitrary and capricious" review, considering first whether the administrator has correctly interpreted to the terms of the plan (or whether the interpretation is reasonable) and second whether the administrator's interpretation of the plan is an abuse of discretion.[29] The judicial review function in ERISA cases is thus similar to the role courts assume in reviewing administrative decisions under the Chevron rule.[30] In answering the first question—whether the administrator's interpretation of the plan was legally correct—a court must consider:

(1) whether the administrator has given the plan a uniform construction,

(2) whether the interpretation is consistent with a fair reading of the plan, and

(3) whether there would be unanticipated costs resulting from different interpretations of the plan.[31]

If a court concludes that the administrator's interpretation is not technically correct, the court must then determine whether administrator abused his discretion in applying the provision to the facts of the case.

The courts apply somewhat differing interpretations of the arbitrary and capricious standard. Some see the "arbitrary and capricious" standard as requiring the court to consider whether a decision was made in good faith and supported by substantial evidence.[32] Other courts interpret it as requiring reasonable action.[33] Some courts have distinguished between arbitrary and capricious and abuse of discretion review, seeing the latter as more permissive—essentially bad faith—review.[34] Other courts reject this distinction and treat the two standards as equivalent.[35] The courts apply the arbitrary and

few cases have held that "satisfactory written proof" requirements do not confer discretion. Kearney v. Standard Ins. Co., 175 F.3d 1084, 1089–90 (9th Cir. en banc 1999). See also Bounds v. Bell Atlantic Enter., 32 F.3d 337, 339 (8th Cir.1994) ("adequate proof of loss" does not confer discretion).

27. Brown v. National City Corp., 166 F.3d 1213 (6th Cir.1998).

28. Wilczynski v. Kemper National Ins. Cos., 1999 WL 335671 (7th Cir.1999).

29. Wildbur v. ARCO Chem. Co., 974 F.2d 631, 637 (5th Cir.1992); Jordan v. Cameron Iron Works, Inc., 900 F.2d 53, 56 (5th Cir.), cert. denied, 498 U.S. 939, 111 S.Ct. 344, 112 L.Ed.2d 308 (1990). If the fiduciaries determination is legally correct, it is not necessary to decide if it is an abuse of discretion, Tolson v. Avondale Industries, Inc., 141 F.3d 604, 608 (5th Cir.1998).

30. Chevron Inc. v. Natural Resources Defense Council, Inc. 467 U.S. 837, 842 (1984).

31. Jordan v. Cameron Iron Works, 900 F.2d 53 at 56 (5th Cir.1990); Kennedy v. Elec-

tricians Pension Plan, 954 F.2d 1116, 1121 (5th cir.1992).

32. Healthcare America Plans v. Bossemeyer, 166 F.3d 347 (10th Cir.1998) ("decision arbitrary and capricious" if it is based on "lack of substantial evidence, bad faith, conflict of interest, or mistake of law.")

33. Ross v. Indiana State Teacher's Ass'n Ins. Trust, 159 F.3d 1001, 1009 (7th Cir.1998); Charter Canyon Treatment Center v. Pool Company, 153 F.3d 1132, 1135 (10th Cir.1998); Killian v. Healthsource Provident Administrators, Inc., 152 F.3d 514, 520 (6th Cir.1998).

34. See Morton v. Smith, 91 F.3d 867, 870 (7th Cir.1996)).

35. See Wildbur v. ARCO Chemical, 974 F.2d 631, 635 at n. 7 (5th Cir.1992); Gallo v. Amoco Corp., 102 F.3d 918, 921 (7th Cir.1996); Lister v. Stark, 942 F.2d 1183, 1188 (7th Cir. 1991); Chambers v. Family Health Plan Corp., 100 F.3d 818, 825 n. 1 (10th Cir.1996).

capricious review standard to the procedures applied in the decisionmaking process as well as to the decision that results form the process.[36]

Although Firestone authorized arbitrary and capricious review where a plan fiduciary is granted decisionmaking discretion, it proceeded to state: "Of course, if a benefit plan gives discretion to an administrator or fiduciary who is operating under a conflict of interest, that conflict must be weighed as a 'facto[r] in determining whether there is an abuse of discretion.' "[37]

The lower courts are sharply divided in their approaches to determining whether an administrator faces a conflict of interest in making the benefit determination, and what effect a conflict should have on the level of review if one is found.[38] At one end of the spectrum, courts hold that if the plaintiff demonstrates that the fiduciary is operating under a substantial conflict of interest, the fiduciaries decision is afforded little deference.[39] Indeed, some go so far as to hold the decision to be "presumptively void".[40] Courts applying this test tend to assume that an insurer or self-insured company faces a conflict almost by definition, since approval of any particular claim reduces its profits.[41] Under this "presumptively void" test, a decision rendered by a plan fiduciary operating under a substantial conflict of interest is presumed to be arbitrary and capricious unless the administrator can demonstrate that either (1) the result reached was nevertheless "right" if subjected to de novo review, or (2) the decision was not made to serve the administrator's conflicting interest.

Courts at the other end of the spectrum contend that conflicts of interest are rarely a problem because market competition solves the problem: i.e. denial of any one claim by a benefit plan has a negligible positive effect on the profit margins of a plan, but routine denial of claims will give a plan a bad reputation and make it less competitive.[42] Under this interpretation, arbitrary and capricious review, untempered by consideration of conflicting interests, is almost always appropriate.

Courts in the middle will only take interest conflicts into account if the plaintiff can show not only that a substantial conflict of interest exits, but also

36. Killian v. Healthsource Provident Administrators Inc., 152 F.3d 514 (6th Cir.1998) (plan arbitrary and capricious in refusing to consider information favorable to claimant).

37. 489 U.S. at 114, quoting the Restatement (Second) of Trusts § 187, Comment d (1959). Note that the existence of a conflict does not justify de novo review, but rather less deferential arbitrary and capricious review.

38. See Haavi Morreim, Benefits Decisions in ERISA Plans: Diminishing Deference to Fiduciaries and an Emerging Problem for Provider Sponsored Organizations, 65 Tenn. L. Rev. 511 (1998) (analyzing the conflict issue).

39. Killian V. Healthsource, 152 F.3d 514 (6th Cir.1998); McGraw v. Prudential Insurance Company, 137 F.3d 1253 (10th Cir.1998); Doe v. Group Hospitalization and Medical Serv's, 3 F.3d 80 (3d Cir. 1993).

40. See Armstrong v. Aetna Life Ins. Co., 128 F.3d 1263 (8th Cir.1997); Brown v. Blue Cross & Blue Shield, 898 F.2d 1556, 1566–67 (11th Cir.1990).

41. Killian v. Healthsource Provident Administrators, 152 F.3d 514, 521 (6th Cir.1998); Peruzzi v. Summa Med. Plan, 137 F.3d 431, 433 (6th Cir.1998); Edmonds v. Hughes Aircraft Company, 145 F.3d 1324 (4th Cir.1998).

42. See Mers v. Marriott International Group Accidental Death & Dismemberment Plan, 144 F.3d 1014 (7th Cir.1998); Farley v. Arkansas Blue Cross and Blue Shield, 147 F.3d 774 (8th Cir.1998). This argument was accepted in Doe v. Travelers Ins. Co., 167 F.3d 53 (1st Cir.1999), but the court nevertheless held the administrator's decision to be unreasonable, illustrating that the court's resolution of the conflict issue does not always resolve the underlying issue of the legality of the determination. See also, Cozzie v. Metropolitan Life Ins.Co., 140 F.3d 1104 (7th Cir.1998) (no conflict where insurer obligated to comply with terms of collective bargaining agreement).

that the conflict in fact caused a breach of the fiduciary's duty and motivated an improper decision.[43] Courts considering this approach might view the failure of a plan to consult independent reviewers in processing a claim,[44] or to follow internal plan procedures,[45] as evidence of improper decisionmaking. On the other hand, decisions made through the use of independent consultants or by salaried employees who do not face direct incentives to approve or deny claims, or through the application of fair procedures, support noninterference.[46] Other courts apply a "sliding scale" approach, using an abuse of discretion review standard, but exercising greater scrutiny where a greater conflict is found.[47]

Most courts have held that the finding of a conflict of interest does not result in the abandonment of the arbitrary and capricious standard, but rather in giving it "more bite,"[48] but a few courts apply de novo review when a conflict is found.[49]

The general and increasing willingness of the courts to defer to the decisions of ERISA plan administrators regarding benefit claims is based on judicial recognition that plan fiduciaries have not only responsibilities to the individual claimant, but also to all beneficiaries of the benefit plan.[50] Improperly paying out a claim for one beneficiary reduces the pot available to other beneficiaries. While traditional insurance regulation and litigation, that is, seems to be based on protecting and expanding the rights of individual beneficiaries, ERISA litigation recognizes that funds for benefits are limited, and must be shared responsibly. Thus, contra proferentem is rejected in "arbitrary and capricious" review ERISA cases in favor of deference to the plan administrator's interpretation of ambiguous clauses, because contra proferentem is unduly favorable to the individual claimant and unfavorable to other plan beneficiaries.[51]

---

43. See Friedrich v. Intel Corp., 1999 WL 430569 (9th Cir.1999); Barnhart v.UNUM Life Ins. Co., 179 F.3d 583, 588 (8th Cir.1999); Atwood v. Newmont Gold,Inc. 45 F.3d 1317, 1322 (9th Cir.1995); Ellsworth v. Consolidate Edison Co., 10 F.Supp.2d 427 (S.D.N.Y.1998); Sullivan v. LTV Aerospace and Defense Co., 82 F.3d 1251 (2d Cir.1996).

44. Woo v. Deluxe Corp., 144 F.3d 1157 (8th Cir.1998); McGraw v. Prudential Ins. Co. of America, 137 F.3d 1253 (10th Cir.1998).

45. Friedrich v. Intel Corp. 1999 WL 430569 (9th Cir.1999).

46. See Hendrix v. Standard Ins. Co., 1999 WL 369877 (9th Cir.1999); Jones v. Kodak Medical Assistance Plan, 169 F.3d 1287 (10th Cir.1999); Hightshue v. AIG Life Ins. Co., 135 F.3d 1144 (7th Cir.1998).

47. See Chambers v. Family Health Corp., 100 F.3d 818, 825 (10th Cir.1996); Sullivan v. LTV Aerospace & Defense Co., 82 F.3d 1251, 1255 (2d Cir.1996); Taft v. Equitable Life Assurance Soc'y, 9 F.3d 1469, 1474 (9th Cir. 1993); Doe v. Group Hospitalization & Medical Servs., 3 F.3d 80, 87 (4th Cir.1993); Van Boxel v. Journal Co. Employees' Pension Trust, 836 F.2d 1048, 1052–53 (7th Cir.1987). See also

Healthcare America Plans, Inc. v. Bossemeyer, 166 F.3d 347, 1999 WL 869627 (10th Cir. 1998) (Henry, J. concurring, commenting on the difficulty of applying this standard).

48. Doyle v. Paul Revere Ins. Co., 144 F.3d 181 (1st Cir.1998). This is the effective result of the sliding scale approach, See Woo v. Deluxe Corp., 144 F.3d 1157 (8th Cir.1998) (where court required "substantial evidence bordering on a preponderance" to support decision).

49. Armstrong v. Aetna Life Ins. Co., 128 F.3d 1263 (8th Cir.1997). The "presumptively void" standard has the same effect, in that the court normally applies de novo review after it determines that the administrator's decision was arbitrary and capricious. See Brown v. Blue Cross & Blue Shield, 898 F.2d 1556, 1162 (11th Cir.1990).

50. Barnhart v. UNUM Life Ins. Co., 179 F.3d 583, 589 (8th Cir.1999).

51. Morton v. Smith, 91 F.3d 867, 871 n. 1 (7th Cir.1996), but see IV Services of America, Inc. v. Trustees of the American Consulting Engineers Council Ins. Trust Fund, 136 F.3d 114 (2d Cir. 1998) (accepting contra proferentem as federal common law.)

In deciding ERISA cases, courts apply federal common law.[52] In creating federal common law, the courts take into account a number of sources, including state law and general contract law if it is consistent with ERISA.[53] Thus, for example, courts have looked to state law for interpreting the effects of intoxication on qualification for accidental death benefits.[54] Though there is limited authority for applying federal common law of estoppel in some ERISA cases,[55] estoppel is rarely applied because ERISA requires plans and plan modifications to be in writing.[56] Common law restitution may also sometimes be available in ERISA cases, as when fiduciaries pursue payments wrongfully made to beneficiaries.[57] Courts are reluctant, however, to use federal common law as a tool of expanding the rights Congress has afforded beneficiaries.[58]

It is quite clear that punitive or other extracontractual damages are not available in ERISA actions. The Supreme Court in *Massachusetts Mutual Life Insurance v. Russell*[59] determined that a beneficiary could not sue a plan fiduciary for extracontractual or punitive damages under 29 U.S.C.A. § 1109(a) (which provides for liability of plan fiduciaries) or under an implied private right of action not expressly authorized by ERISA, but left open the question of whether other extracontractual relief might be available under 42 U.S.C.A. § 1132.[60] The lower courts, however, with very few exceptions held that extra-contractual relief and punitive damages were not available under ERISA.[61] Moreover, the Supreme Court in *Mertens v. Hewitt Associates*[62] seems to settle this controversy decisively by rejecting the possibility of extracontractual damages.

The vast majority of federal courts have held that juries are not available in ERISA cases.[63] Prevailing claimants may be awarded to the prevailing party

52. Firestone Tire & Rubber Co. v. Bruch, 489 U.S. 101, 110, 109 S.Ct. 948 (1989); Babikian v. Paul Revere Life Ins. Co., 63 F.3d 837, 839–40 (9th Cir.1995). See Jeffrey A. Brauch, the Federal Common Law of ERISA, 21 Harv. J. L. & Pub. Pol'y 541 (1998)

53. Perez v. Aetna Life Ins. Co., 150 F.3d 550 (6th Cir.1998); Baker v. Provident Life & Accident Ins. Co., 171 F.3d 939 (4th Cir.1999); Deegan v. Continental Casualty Co., 167 F.3d 502 (9th Cir.1999); Wickman v. Northwestern Nat'l Ins. Co., 908 F.2d 1077 (1st Cir.1990).

54. See Cozzie v. Metropolitan Life Ins. Co., 140 F.3d 1104, 1110 (7th Cir.1998).

55. Black v. TIC Investment Corp., 900 F.2d 112 (7th Cir.1990).

56. See Coker v. Trans World Airlines, 165 F.3d 579 (7th Cir.1999); Miller v. Coastal Corp., 978 F.2d 622 (10th Cir.1992). See Kimberly A. Kralowec, Estoppel Claims Against ERISA Employee Benefit Plans, 25 U.C.Davis L. Rev. 487 (1992).

57. Heller v. Fortis Benefits Ins. Co., 142 F.3d 487 (D.C.Cir.1998).

58. Silcott v. Wal–Mart Stores, Inc. Assoc. Health & Welfare Plan, 1998 WL 422032, *2 (E.D.Pa.1998).

59. 473 U.S. 134, 105 S.Ct. 3085, 87 L.Ed.2d 96 (1985).

60. See 473 U.S. 134, 139 n. 5, 105 S.Ct. 3085, 3088 n. 5, 87 L.Ed.2d 96 (1985). See also 473 U.S. 134, 157–58, 105 S.Ct. 3085, 3094–95, 87 L.Ed.2d 96 (1985) (Brennen, J. dissenting).

61. Bast v. Prudential Insurance Co. of America, 150 F.3d 1003 (9th Cir.1998).; McRae v. Seafarers' Welfare Plan, 920 F.2d 819 (11th Cir.1991); Drinkwater v. Metropolitan Life Ins. Co., 846 F.2d 821 (1st Cir.1988), cert. denied 488 U.S. 909, 109 S.Ct. 261, 102 L.Ed.2d 249 (1988). But see, James A. Dooley Assoc. Employees Retirement Plan v. Reynolds, 654 F.Supp. 457 (E.D.Mo.1987); Gilliken v. Hughes, 609 F.Supp. 178 (D.Del.1985), recognizing extracontractual damages.

62. 508 U.S. 248, 113 S.Ct. 2063, 124 L.Ed.2d 161 (1993).

63. Tischmann v. ITT/Sheraton Corp., 145 F.3d 561 (2d Cir.1998); Sprague v. General Motors Corp., 133 F.3d 388 (6th Cir.1998); Wardle v. Central States, S.E. & S.W. Areas Pension Fund, 627 F.2d 820 (7th Cir.1980), cert. denied, 449 U.S. 1112, 101 S.Ct. 922, 66 L.Ed.2d 841 (1981); Borst v. Chevron Corp., 36 F.3d 1308 (5th Cir.1994), cert. denied, 519 U.S. 1066, 115 S.Ct. 1699, 131 L.Ed.2d 561 (1995); Cox v. Keystone Carbon Co., 894 F.2d 647 (3d Cir.), cert. denied, 498 U.S. 811, 111 S.Ct. 47, 112 L.Ed.2d 23 (1990); Howard v. Parisian, Inc., 807 F.2d 1560 (11th Cir.1987); Berry v.

in ERISA cases.[64] Attorney's fees are not routinely granted, however, but are only available where the losing party's position was not substantially justified and taken in good faith.[65]

ERISA does not by its terms permit providers to sue plans.[66] Courts have generally rejected the argument that providers are "beneficiaries" under ERISA plans.[67] Providers have enjoyed, however, some success in asserting their rights as assignees of participants and beneficiaries,[68] though a few courts have held that assignees have no standing to sue as they are not mentioned as protected parties within the statute.[69] Courts have generally upheld anti-assignment clauses in plan contracts.[70]

Some courts have also permitted providers to recover from insurers when the insurer leads the provider to believe that the insured or the service is covered, and then subsequently refuses payment and claims ERISA protection. Several courts, including the Fifth and Tenth Circuits have held that ERISA is intended to control relationships between employers and employees and should not preempt common law or statutory misrepresentation claims brought by providers.[71] Other courts, including the Sixth Circuit, have held that misrepresentation claims are claims for benefits that are preempted by ERISA.[72] Finally, several courts have allowed a provider to sue an ERISA plan on a breach of contract claim, stating that the claim was not preempted by ERISA because the provider had no standing to sue under ERISA.[73]

Ciba–Geigy Corp., 761 F.2d 1003 (4th Cir. 1985). But see Stamps v. Teamsters Joint Council, 431 F.Supp. 745 (E.D.Mich.1977) (holding that a jury trial was appropriate in an ERISA case).

64. Doe v. Travelers Insurance Company, 167 F.3d 53 (1st Cir.1999) (plaintiff); Tomczk v. Blue Cross and Blue Shield United, 951 F.2d 771 (7th Cir.1991) (defendant).

65. Molasky v. Principal Mutual Life Ins. Co., 149 F.3d 881 (8th Cir.1998); Quinn v. Blue Cross & Blue Shield Ass'n, 161 F.3d 472 (7th Cir.1998).

66. See generally, David P. Kallus, ERISA: Do Health Care Providers Have Standing to Bring a Civil Enforcement Action Under Section 1132(a)? 30 Santa Clara L. Rev. 173 (1990).

67. Pritt v. Blue Cross & Blue Shield, Inc., 699 F.Supp. 81 (S.D.W.Va.1988); Cameron Manor, Inc. v. United Mine Workers, 575 F.Supp. 1243 (W.D.Pa.1983).

68. City of Hope National Medical Center v. Healthplus, Inc., 156 F.3d 223 (1st Cir. 1998); Cagle v. Bruner, 112 F.3d 1510 (11th Cir.1997); Hermann Hosp. v. MEBA Medical & Benefits Plan, 845 F.2d 1286 (5th Cir.1988), appeal after remand 959 F.2d 569 (1992); Misic v. Building Serv. Employees Health and Welfare Trust, 789 F.2d 1374 (9th Cir.1986).

69. See e.g., Northeast Dep't ILGWU Health and Welfare Fund v. Teamsters Local Union No. 229 Welfare Fund, 764 F.2d 147, 154 n. 6 (3d Cir. 1985); Health Scan Ltd. v. Travelers Ins. Co., 725 F.Supp. 268 (E.D.Pa. 1989). See also Rallis v. Trans World Music

Corp., 1994 WL 52753 (E.D.Pa.1994) (Hospital has no right to intervene in beneficiary's suit against insurer or to sue itself under ERISA).

70. City of Hope National Medical Center v. Healthplus, Inc. 156 F.3d 223 (1st Cir.1998); Davidowitz v. Delta Dental Plan, Inc., 946 F.2d 1476 (9th Cir.1991); Parkside Lutheran Hospital v. R.J. Zeltner & Associates, Inc. ERISA Plan, 788 F.Supp. 1002 (N.D.Ill.1992); Washington Hosp. Ctr. Corp. v. Group Hospitalization and Medical Servs., Inc., 758 F.Supp. 750 (D.D.C.1991).

71. Transitional Hospitals Corp. v. Blue Cross & Blue Shield of Texas, 164 F.3d 952 (5th Cir.1999); In Home Health Inc. v. The Prudential Ins. Co., 101 F.3d 600 (8th Cir., 1996); Hospice of Metro Denver, Inc. v. Group Health Ins. of Okla., Inc., 944 F.2d 752 (10th Cir.1991); Memorial Hosp. Sys. v. Northbrook Life Ins. Co., 904 F.2d 236 (5th Cir.1990). See Jeffrey A. Brauch, Health Care Providers Meet ERISA: Are Provider Claims for Misrepresentation of Coverage Preempted? 20 Pepp. L. Rev. 496, 516–522 (1993).

72. Cromwell v. Equicor–Equitable HCA Corp., 944 F.2d 1272 (6th Cir.1991), cert. denied 505 U.S. 1233, 113 S.Ct. 2, 120 L.Ed.2d 931 (1992); Barnes Hospital v. Sanus Passport/Preferred Services, Inc., 809 F.Supp. 725 (E.D.Mo.1992). See Brauch, supra note 71 at 511–516.

73. Faith Hosp. Ass'n v. Blue Cross & Blue Shield of Missouri, 857 S.W.2d 352 (Mo.App. 1993); Lifetime Medical Nursing Serv., Inc. v. New England Health Care Employees Welfare Fund, 730 F.Supp. 1192 (D.R.I.1990).

§ 8–7. ERISA's Fiduciary Obligations Provisions

In addition to its claims processing requirements, ERISA also imposes limited fiduciary obligations and substantive requirements on health benefit plans. Section 404(a) of ERISA (29 U.S.C.A. § 1104) provides

> (1) * * * [A] fiduciary shall discharge his duties with respect to a plan solely in the interest of the participants and beneficiaries and—
>
> > (A) for the exclusive purpose of:
> >
> > > (i) providing benefits to participants and their beneficiaries; and
> > >
> > > (ii) defraying reasonable expenses of administering the plan;
> >
> > (B) with the care, skill, prudence, and diligence under the circumstances then prevailing that a prudent man acting in a like capacity and familiar with such matters would use in the conduct of an enterprise of a like character and with like aims;
>
> * * *
>
> and
>
> > (D) in accordance with the documents and instruments governing the plan insofar as such documents and instruments are consistent with the provisions of [ERISA].

Though these provisions would seem to give sweeping rights to beneficiaries with respect to plan fiduciaries, in fact they turn out to provide little protection at all in the health benefit plan context. First, the remedial provisions of ERISA permit participants and beneficiaries to sue only for equitable relief when these fiduciary obligations are violated. The Supreme Court has limited this provision to traditional equitable remedies, such as injunction and restitution,[1] and has specifically held that it excludes legal damages in general and extracontractual damages in particular.[2] Compensation for denied benefits, therefore, is only available under Section 1132(a), discussed above, not under breach of fiduciary duty theories.[3] Moreover, the Court has held that § 1132(a)(2), which permits recoveries under § 1109 for breach of fiduciary duty, only provides for recoveries on behalf of a benefits plan, not on behalf of its individual members.[4] The only remedy available to beneficiaries is a suit for traditional equitable relief, such as an injunction, and even that may not always be available.

Second, the notion of fiduciary obligations takes on an unconventional meaning in ERISA plans. As noted above, plan fiduciaries owe obligations not

---

§ 8–7

1. Constructive Trust may also be an available remedy in some situations. See FMC Medical Plan v. Owens, 122 F.3d 1258, 1261–62 (9th Cir.1997); Waller v. Blue Cross, 32 F.3d 1337 (9th Cir.1994).

2. Mertens v. Hewitt Assoc., 508 U.S. 248, 113 S.Ct. 2063 (1993); Massachusetts Mutual Life Ins. Co. v. Russell, 473 U.S. 134, 105 S.Ct. 3085 (1985).

3. Weiner v. Aetna Health Plans of Ohio, 149 F.3d 1185, 1998 WL 381642 (6th Cir.1998);

Tolson v. Avondale Ind. Inc. 141 F.3d 604 (5th Cir.1998). Specifically, claims for unjust enrichment cannot be used as a means of collecting benefits. Weiner, supra.

4. Russell, 473 U.S. 134. Under this provision, for example, a third party administrator may be liable to a plan for failing to inform the plan about a stop-loss insurers refusal to cover a particular treatment before obligation for the treatment was incurred. Harold Ives Trucking Co., v. Spradley & Coker, 1999 WL 308571 (8th Cir.1999).

just to a particular individual participant or beneficiary claiming benefits from the plan, but also to all other beneficiaries as well. Paying out questionable benefits to one beneficiary depletes the plan of resources that might be needed to fund benefits for other beneficiaries.[5] Moreover, the plan administrator has responsibilities to the employer, who often funds the plan, as well as to the plan's participants and beneficiaries. Courts are quite sensitive to the multiple obligations of ERISA fiduciaries, and thus the notion of fiduciary obligation rarely dictates a result urged by an individual claimant in a particular case.

Third, the general ERISA provisions dealing with fiduciary obligations are generally interpreted to yield to more specific ERISA provisions dealing with particular issues. Thus courts have interpreted § 404, for example, as not imposing greater obligations on fiduciaries for reporting and disclosure than those imposed by more specific ERISA provisions addressing these issues.[6]

Finally, fiduciary obligations only extend to issues of plan administration, not to questions of plan scope and design. An employer is not obligated under ERISA to provide any particular coverage.[7] Thus, for example, the Fifth Circuit in *McGann v. H & H Music Co.*,[8] upheld an employer's dramatic reduction of non-vested coverage for AIDS after an employee contracted the disease and the Supreme Court denied certiorari.[9] At least one court has gone further, holding that utilization review guidelines and criteria are completely discretionary and not subject to judicial review.[10]

ERISA's fiduciary obligations do have some content, however. An ERISA fiduciary, for example is obligated to process a claim submitted by a beneficiary.[11] It may even be liable for paying out a claim for a person not entitled to beneficiary status.[12] Finally, under separate provisions of ERISA, an employer may not fire an employee to avoid obligations for the cost of health insurance benefits.[13]

§ 8–8.   Information and Disclosure Requirements Under ERISA

ERISA plans must provide their participants with a Summary Plan Description. The language of this document prevails when there is a conflict between the summary and the plan itself.[1] ERISA intended the SPD to be the

5. IT Corporation v. General American Life Ins. Co., 107 F.3d 1415 (9th Cir.1997).

6. Sprague v. General Motors Corp., 133 F.3d 388 (6th Cir.1998).

7. Shaw v. Delta Airlines, 463 U.S. 85, 103 S.Ct. 2890 (1983); Nazay v. Miller, 949 F.2d 1323 (3d Cir.1991).

8. 946 F.2d 401 (5th Cir.1991), cert. denied 981 U.S. 506, 113 S.Ct. 482, 121 L.Ed.2d 387 (1992). The action in McGann took place prior to the effective date of the Americans with Disabilities Act, which may require a different result. See § 9–5.

9. This case evoked considerable controversy, both because the employer's conduct seemed egregiously unfair and because it seemed to penalize the employee for claiming insurance benefits, seemingly in violation of 29 U.S.C.A. § 1140. See Note, Carl A. Greci, Use it and Lose it: The Employer's Absolute Right Under ERISA Section 510 to Engage in Post–Claim Modifications of Employee Welfare Benefit Plans, 68 Ind. L. J. 177 (1992).

10. Jones v. Kodak Medical Assistance Plan, 169 F.3d 1287 (10th Cir.1999).

11. Krohn v. Huron Mem. Hosp., 173 F.3d 542 (6th Cir.1999).

12. IT Corporation v. General American Life Ins. Co., 107 F.3d 1415 (9th Cir.1997).

13. ERISA § 510; Seaman v. Arvida Realty Sales, 985 F.2d 543 (11th Cir.1993).

§ 8–8

1. Semtner v. Group Health Serv. Of Oklahoma, Inc. 129 F.3d 1390 (10th Cir.1997).

employee's primary source of plan information, thus employees are entitled to rely on its language.[2] If, however, the SPD is silent on an issue or there is no direct conflict between the SPD and master plan, the language of the master plan prevails.[3] Moreover, because Congress intended that SPDs be in fact summaries rather than exhaustive descriptions of coverage, courts are more tolerant of ambiguity and silence than they are in normal insurance cases, where silence and ambiguity in an insurance contract usually redound to the favor of beneficiaries.[4]

ERISA also imposes duties on plan fiduciaries to provide correct information to plan participants about their rights and status,[5] which may include informing participants that coverage has been terminated because of the employer's non-payment of the premium,[6] or that payment for further services is being denied under the plan's utilization review provisions.[7] ERISA fiduciaries are specifically obligated to respond completely and accurately to information requests from beneficiaries.[8] They may not, however, be liable for allegedly incorrect oral advice provided to plan beneficiaries by plan employees.[9] ERISA's disclosure obligations are also limited in scope. For example, an HMO's failure to disclose its right to assert subrogation claims and its provision of information that it was claiming amounts actually paid rather than the reasonable value of services rendered was held not to violate ERISA disclosure obligations.[10]

Managed care plans typically use a variety of financial incentives to reduce plan utilization. These devices include bonus and withhold, pools that set aside a percentage of a physician's salary, in order to provide incentives to reduce hospitalization and referrals to specialists. Pure capitation systems tie income directly a pool of money available each year for subscriber care. And bonuses can be tied to reductions in utilization. These incentives have been controversial, with critics contending that physicians are forced into a conflict of interest between their own income needs and the needs of their patients.[11] The evidence however has been equivocal at best, with no clear findings that managed care offers poor quality care in the aggregate.[12] The federal courts

2. Moriarity v. United Tech. Corp. Represented Employees Retirement Plan, 158 F.3d 157, 160 (2d Cir.1998).

3. Charter Canyon v. Pool Co., 153 F.3d 1132 (10th Cir.1998); Mers v. Marriot International Group Accidental Death and Dismemberment Plan, 144 F.3d 1014 (7th Cir.1998); Sprague v. General Motors Corp., 133 F.3d 388 (6th Cir.1998). If, however, the SPD is not sufficiently comprehensive to "reasonably apprise plan participants of their rights and obligations," 29 U.S.C.A. § 1022, silence in the SPD might not be excusable. See Mers, supra 144 F.3d at 1021.

4. Walker v. Wal–Mart Stores, 159 F.3d 938, 940 (5th Cir.1998).

5. See e.g., Eddy v. Colonial Life Ins. Co., 919 F.2d 747 (D.C.Cir.1990).

6. See e.g., Willett v. Blue Cross & Blue Shield, 953 F.2d 1335 (11th Cir.1992).

7. See e.g., Newell v. Prudential Ins. Co., 904 F.2d 644 (11th Cir.1990).

8. Krohn v. Huron Memorial Hosp., 173 F.3d 542 (6th Cir.1999); Anweiler v. American Elec. Power Service Corp., 3 F.3d 986 (7th Cir.1993); Eddy v. Colonial Life Ins. Co., 919 F.3d 747 (D.C. Cir. 1990).

9. Frahm v. Equitable Life Assurance Society, 137 F.3d 955 (7th Cir.1998).

10. Ince v. Aetna Health Management, Inc. 173 F.3d 672 (8th Cir.1999).

11. Marsha Angell, The Doctor As Double Agent, 3 Kennedy Inst. Ethics J. 279 (1993); Mark A. Rodwin, Conflicts in Managed Care, 332 N.Eng.J.Med. 604 (1995).

12. See generally R. Miller and Harold S. Luft, Does Managed Care Lead to Better or Worse Quality of Care? 16 Health Affairs 7 (1997); see also Barry R. Furrow, Managed Care Organizations and Patient Injury: Rethinking Liability, 31 Ga. L. Rev. 419 (1997) for a summary of the health services research comparing the quality of care in managed care versus fee-for-service medicine.

have generally held that the details of HMO incentives need not be specifically explained to participants in ERISA plans, nor have they challenged the underlying legality of such incentive systems.[13]

Two federal decisions have expanded the meaning of "fiduciary" in an ERISA-qualified health plan, imposing in one case a duty to disclose physician incentive plans or and in a second allowing a challenge to the underlying validity of such plans as a possible breach of an ERISA fiduciary's responsibility to plan subscribers. In Shea v. Esensten,[14] the court considered a claim that the HMO's failure to disclose its practice of giving primary-care physicians financial incentives to minimize referrals to specialists caused an bemployee's death from heart failure. Mr. Shea's physician failed to give him a referral to a cardiologist in spite of warning signs of a cardiac condition. Mr. Shea's widow contended that if her husband had known that his doctor could earn a bonus for treating less, he would have sought out his own cardiologist. The Eighth Circuit agreed that a financial incentive system aimed at influencing a physician's referral patterns is "a material piece of information,."[15] and that a subscriber has a right to know that his physician's judgment could be "colored" by such incentives. The court rested its conclusion on the obligation of an ERISA fiduciary to speak out if it "knows that silence might be harmful."[16] The court held that information about a plan's financial incentives must be disclosed when they might lead a treating physician to deny necessary referrals for conditions covered by the plan.[17]

Such a requirement of disclosure, on the one hand, is consistent with federal policy in HMO regulation and with use of information disclosure to counteract provider power in health care.[18] On the other hand, such a disclosure requirement is problematic. First, it assumes that plan subscribers are ignorant of managed care's purpose—to offer cost-effective care. Second, disclosure fails to address all of the devices used by plans to reduce utilization, such as utilization review, drug formularies, discounts with hospitals, and so on. The sole focus of physician incentives fails to achieve what the Shea court wanted.

The Seventh Circuit in Herdrich v. Pegram[19] considered a claim that physicians who were owners and participants in a managed care plan had breached their fiduciary duties to beneficiaries because of the salary incentive features of the plan. The defendant-physicians managed the Plan, including the doctor referral process, the nature and duration of patient treatment, and the extent to which participants were required to use Carle-owned facilities. The board of directors consisted exclusively of the Plan physicians who were thus in control of each and every aspect of the HMO's governance, including

13. Anderson v. Humana, Inc., 24 F.3d 889 (7th Cir.1994).

14. 107 F.3d 625 (8th Cir. 1997)

15. Id at 628.

16. The court cited to Bixler v. Central Penn. Teamsters Health & Welfare Fund, 12 F.3d 1292, 1300 (3d Cir.1993) and the Restatement (Second) Of Trusts § 173 cmt. d (1959).

17. Id at 629.

18. For an excellent discussion of these issues, see Tracy E. Miller and William M. Sage, Disclosing Physician Financial Incentives, 281 JAMA 1424 (1999); William M. Sage, Physicians as Advocates, 35 Houston L.Rev. 1529 (1999); Kim Johnston, Patient Advocates or Patient Adversaries? Using Fiduciary Law to Compel Disclosure of Managed Care Financial Incentives, 35 San Diego L.Rev. 951 (1998); Bethany J. Spielman, Managed Care Regulation and the Physician–Advocate, 47 Drake L.Rev. 713 (1999).

19. 154 F.3d 362 (7th Cir. 1998)(Cert. granted September 1999, No. 98–1949.)

their own year-end bonuses. The plaintiff contended that the defendant physicians had the exclusive right to decide all disputed and non-routine claims, and the court found that this level of control was sufficient to satisfy ERISA's requirement that a fiduciary maintain "discretionary control and authority."

The court noted with approval the plaintiff's description of the "intricacies of the defendants' incentive structure." The plan administrators were physicians who had a dual role: deciding whether claims would be paid and the extent of care to be given; and receiving year-end bonuses from any cost-savings realized by their decisions. The bonuses were based on the difference between total plans costs in providing medical services and revenues, and they therefore had an incentive to limit treatment and costs. In their words, "[w]ith a jaundiced eye focused firmly on year-end bonuses, it is not unrealistic to assume that the doctors rendering care under the Plan were swayed to be most frugal when exercising their discretionary authority to the detriment of their membership."

The court noted that physicians in this dual capacity as owners and providers "simultaneously control the care of their patients and reap the profits generated by the HMO through the limited use of tests and referrals." An ERISA fiduciary analysis might find that they were not therefore acting "solely in the interest of the participants" of the Plan. The court noted that these physicians would gain financially if they limited treatments and referrals. This depletion of plan resources might operate to the detriment of patients, and this issue was for the trial court to resolve. However, the court's language suggests that the use of year-end bonus payments, a common incentive feature of many HMOs, would be prima facie evidence of a breach of fiduciary duty. On motion for rehearing, Judge Easterbrook J., dissenting,[20] noted that the panel decision looked like a blanket condemnation of managed care generally, in favor of fee-for-service medicine. Even though the panel had tried to distinguish this case by its physician ownership and control, the use of bonuses and salary holdbacks by any managed care plan could be similarly criticized.

A sweeping condemnation of incentive systems would prevent MCOs from using payment incentives to reduce utilization, the very purpose for which MCOs were designed and created.[21] Federal law governing Medicare and Medicaid HMOs requires limited disclosure of physician incentive systems for plans of 25,000 subscribers or smaller, while otherwise accepting capitation and other incentive devices as legitimate in HMOs.[22] Incentive payment systems can create patient risk, but a properly designed system can also constrain health care costs by reducing expenditures on treatments are not cost-effective. Regulation might well be valuable, to control abuses. But the holding of the Seventh Circuit in Herdrich is a backlash against managed care, ignoring past precedent, the policies reflected in federal HMO law, and

---

20. Herdrich v. Pegram, 170 F.3d 683 (7th Cir 1999)(motion for rehearing on banc denied)

21. Ezekiel J. Emanuel and Lee Goldman, Protecting Patient Welfare in Managed Care: Six Safeguards, 23 J.Health Pol.Pol'y & L. 635, 646 (1998)(noting that financial incentives cannot be prohibited and should instead be regu-

lated in light of seriousness of harm caused by them).

22. 42 CFR § 417.479, Requirements for Physician Incentive Plans, imposes reporting requirements and other constraints on HMO incentive plans, but does not prohibit such incentive plans.

the empirical evidence. The U.S. Supreme Court will have to resolve this tension between a national policy favoring managed care and the hostility of the Herdrich court, among others, toward essential features of such plans.[23]

ERISA provides a $100 a day penalty against plans that fail to provide required information within 30 days of a request,[24] but this provision only covers information covered by ERISA's disclosure requirements. It has been held, for example, that the penalty provisions do not cover nondisclosure of specific utilization review guidelines.[25] As noted above, when a plan denies a claim, it must give specific reasons in writing for the denial, as well as information on how to perfect the claim.[26]

§ 8–9. ERISA Coverage Requirements

ERISA has been amended in recent years to require plan coverage of several specific benefits. The "COBRA coverage" requirements of ERISA with respect to continuation of insurance coverage, the only requirement that antedates this period, are discussed above at section 9–6. Several statutes enacted in 1997, including the Health Insurance Accountability and Affordability Act of 1977, impose additional requirements, discussed at section 9–7. 29 U.S.C.A. § 1181 limits ERISA plan preexisting condition exclusions. 29 U.S.C.A. § 1182 prohibits discrimination in eligibility or premiums for group health insurance based on the health status of the insured or the insured's dependents.[1] 29 U.S.C.A. § 1185 requires ERISA plans to offer 48 hours of coverage for mothers and newborns undergoing a normal vaginal delivery, and 96 hours where a Cesarean section is involved. 29 U.S.C.A. § 1185a prohibits plans that offer both medical and surgical and mental health benefits from imposing more restrictive lifetime or annual limits on mental health coverage than they impose on medical and surgical benefits, subject to several exceptions. 29 U.S.C.A. § 1185b requires that health plans that cover mastectomies must also cover breast reconstruction, surgery on the other breast as necessary to maintain symmetry, prostheses and treatment of the physical complications of mastectomy, including lymphedemas.

Under 1993 amendments to ERISA, group health plans are required to acknowledge and effectuate "qualified medical child support orders" creating or recognizing in a child the right to receive under the group health plan of the child's parent benefits otherwise provided under the plan.[2] The amendments also require that ERISA plans provide coverage of adopted children under the same terms and conditions as natural children and prohibits enforcement of pre-existing conditions clauses against adopted children with

---

23. The U.S. Supreme Court granted certiorari in Herdrich in September, 1999.

24. 29 U.S.C.A. § 1132(c).

25. Doe v. Travelers Ins. Co., 167 F.3d 53 (1st Cir.1999).

26. Bellanger v. Health Plan of Nevada, Inc., 814 F.Supp. 918 (D.Nev.1993).

§ 8–9

1. This provision does not require insurers to cover particular conditions and permits them to impose restrictions on the amount, level, extent and nature of benefits. 29 U.S.C.A. § 1182(a)(2). Plans may also provide premium discounts or rebates for compliance with disease prevention programs. § 1182(b)(2).

2. 42 U.S.C.A. § 1169. Faye M. Martin, New ERISA Provision Expands Group Health Coverage for Children, 11 HealthSpan, Jan. 1994 at 11. This law supplements Medicaid law provisions that obligate insurers to cover children under certain circumstances. See 42 U.S.C.A. § 1396g and § 14–8 below.

respect to conditions existing at the time of adoption.[3] Finally, the amendments forbid ERISA plans that covered pediatric vaccines as of May 1, 1993 from reducing their coverage below that offered on that date.[4]

3. 29 U.S.C.A. § 1169(c).   **4.** 29 U.S.C.A. § 1169(d).

Chapter 9

REGULATION OF PRIVATE HEALTH CARE FINANCING

Table of Sections

A. REGULATION OF PRIVATE INSURANCE

§ 9–1. Introduction

In 1997, 188.5 million Americans were covered by some form of private health insurance, including Blue Cross–Blue Shield plans, commercial insurance, self-funded employer plans, or prepaid plans such as HMOs.[1] In that same year private health insurance paid out $348 billion for health care, accounting for about 32% of national health expenditures. Private insurance accounted for over 30% of national expenditures on hospital care and over 50% of expenditures on physician services. In 1997, 165.1 million Americans were covered under employment-related health insurance, and 23.4 million by other forms of private health insurance. 62.0 million persons were covered by self-insured employer plans (in 1996), though the proportion of employees covered by self-insured plans seems to be dropping. Seventy-eight percent of employees had health insurance coverage in 1997, but many employers, particularly small employers, do not offer health insurance as a benefit, and many employees who are offered employment-related coverage decline coverage because of the cost or because they are covered by a spouse's policy.[2]

Health insurance in the United States is a product of the Depression of the 1930s and World War II. Prior to the Great Depression, most health care costs were paid out of pocket. During the Depression, however, many persons found themselves unable to afford health care, while physicians and hospitals increasingly had difficulty remaining solvent because of the lack of paying patients. Out of this context emerged the Blue Cross and Blue Shield plans, nonprofit plans initiated by hospitals and doctors as a means of financing health care costs.[3] These plans were given federal and state tax exemption and otherwise treated favorably by regulators in exchange for their willingness to make insurance widely available throughout the community and to provide insurance at relatively low cost to low and moderate income persons. During the 1930s commercial insurance plans also became common. These plans usually provided "indemnity" coverage, under which they would indemnify their insureds amounts specified in the policy for particular services, in contrast to the Blue Cross "service benefits" plans, which paid providers directly and fully for services rendered.[4]

§ 9–1

1. This figure probably overcounts the number whose insurance is paid for by private employers. See Olveen Carrasquillo, et al., A Reappraisal of Private Employers' Role in Providing Health Insurance, 340 New Eng. J. Med. 109 (1999).

2. The data in this paragraph are from the Health Insurance Association of America, Source Book of Health Insurance Data, 1999 and 2000. See also Paul B. Ginsburg, Jon R. Gabel, and Kelly A. Hunt, Tracking Small–Firm Coverage, 1989–1996, Health Aff. Jan./

Feb. 1998 at 167; Kenneth E. Thorpe and Curtis S. Florence, Why are Workers Uninsured? Employer–Sponsored Health Insurance in 1997, Health Aff. March/June 1999 at 213.

3. See Charles D. Weller, "Free Choice" as a Restraint of Trade in American Health Care Delivery and Insurance, 69 Iowa L. Rev. 1351 (1984).

4. Much of the material in the preceding paragraph is drawn from Congressional Research Service, Health Insurance and the Uninsured: Background Data and Analysis (1988).

Health insurance coverage as an employment benefit expanded rapidly during World War II as wartime wage-caps encouraged augmentation of benefits. During the 1950s employment-related health insurance continued to expand rapidly, and by the middle of the decade 122.5 million Americans had health insurance, ten times the number who were insured in 1940. Health insurance coverage continued to expand more slowly throughout the 1960s and 1970s.

In recent years, however, coverage has declined rather dramatically. The percentage of nonelderly employees who receive health insurance through their jobs declined sharply form 69.2% in 1987 to 63.5% in 1993, rising slightly to 64.2% by 1997.[5] This decline is not primarily attributable to a decrease in the number of employers offering insurance—in fact this number has increased slightly in recent years—but rather to a significant decline in the number of employees who elect employer-offered coverage, from 88.3% in 1987 to 80.1% in 1996.[6] Though many of these employees refused coverage because they were covered through other family members, many also did so because they could not afford employer-offered coverage. In recent years fewer employers have paid the full cost of employee health insurance, the premium share paid by employees and other employee cost-sharing obligations have increased, and health insurance has become increasingly less accessible to lower income employees.[7]

Not only has coverage declined in recent years, the nature of health insurance has continued to change. First, the Blues (Blue Cross and Blue Shield), which dominated health insurance in the early years, now cover only about 66 million insureds. The Blues have also come to look more and more like commercial insurers as they have been forced to compete with them for business. Thus Blue Cross plans have widely abandoned "community" rating (under which all insureds in a particular class pay the same rates regardless of health care claims experience, thus averaging and spreading risks among insureds) in favor of "experience" rating (under which rates are based on the claims of a particular group). Other Blue plans have begun to offer indemnity as well as service benefit plans. Finally, domination of the Blues by hospitals and physicians has ended, in part because of antitrust suits and FTC enforcement (see Chapter 14).

A second major change has been the growth (and recent decline) of employer self-insurance. Many large employers have effectively become their own insurers, carrying themselves the risk of their employees' medical expenses. To accomplish this, fully self-insured employers often enter into administrative-services-only (ASO) contracts with conventional insurers or with third party administrators (TPAs) to process claims, which are ultimately paid by the employer. Some employers also contract with insurers to partially self-insure through a Minimum Premium Plan (MPP), under which the employer carries the risk up to a specified level while the insurer both handles claims administration and insures against extraordinary large claims exceeding a set level, or through simply purchasing stop loss coverage. In

5. Robert Kuttner, The American Health Care System: Employer–Sponsored Health Coverage, 340 New Eng.J.Med. 248 (1999).

6. Philip F. Cooper & Barbara Scheinberg Schone, More Offers, Fewer Takers for Em-

ployment–Based Health Insurance: 1987 and 1997. 16 Health Aff, Nov./Dec. 1997 at 142.

7. Kutner, supra note 5.

1996, $42.1 billion were paid by fully insured group health plans, $49. billion by ASO contracts, and $5.5 billion by MPPs.[8]

Self-insurance has become widespread for two reasons. First, it allows large companies to maintain control over insurance reserves until they are actually needed to pay claims. Second, self-insured plans escape state insurance premium taxes and regulatory mandates, as the Employee Retirement Income Security Act of 1974 (ERISA) (described in chapter 8) prohibits the states from regulating self-insured benefit plans.

The prevalence of self-insurance has always varied by firm size—a recent survey of self-insurance in seven states found that 55% of firms with 500 or more employees self-insured, while only 3% of firms with fewer than 100 employees did so.[9] In the recent past, moreover, the prevalence of self-insurance seems to be declining with respect to all firms. The same survey found that the percentage of employees in self-insured plans had diminished from 40% in 1993 to 33% in 1997.

The third and most important change in private health insurance in recent years (and the most important explanatory factor in the decline of self-insurance just noted) has been the growth of managed care. The general rubric of "managed care" encompasses a variety of private approaches to health care cost containment, ranging from health maintenance organizations, preferred provider organizations, and point-of-service plans to simple utilization review. In 1998, 34% of enrollees in employer-sponsored group health plans were insured through PPOs, 30% through HMOs, 22% through Point of Service plans, 14% through fee-for-service plans with utilization management.[10]

Health insurance is written on both a group and an individual basis. Groups are commonly employment-based. Individual coverage tends to be much more costly than group coverage because marketing and administrative costs are higher and because risks are harder to predict. For the same reasons insurance for small groups costs more than insurance for larger groups, a factor that partially explains the fact that many small businesses do not offer health insurance as a fringe benefit. Health insurance can be made more affordable for small business through the use of Multiple Employer Welfare Associations (MEWAs) or other arrangements by which employers combine to pool risks and purchase insurance.

Health insurance is usually subject to some form of cost-sharing, under which the insured pays some share of medical costs. Cost-sharing is primarily intended to diminish the incidence of "moral hazard"—the excessive use of services because the service is paid for by the insurer rather than the insured—but it also reduces the cost of insurance directly by shifting some of the cost of services to the insured. Employees commonly pay some part of the premium for employment-related health insurance. Insurance is also often subject to a deductible (e.g. the first $500 of covered expenses) that the insured must pay each year before expenses begin to be covered. After the

8. Health Insurance Association of America, Source Book on Health Insurance Data, 1999–2000, 41 (1998).

9. H. Susan Marquis and Stephen H. Long, Recent Trends in Self–Insured Employer Health Plans, Health Aff. May/June 1999 at 161.

10. HIAA, supra note 8, at 23.

deductible is met, most insurance plans impose either a percentage coinsurance (e.g. 20% of covered expenses) or a flat per-service copayment (e.g. $10 per doctor visit) on the insured. Cost-sharing obligations are commonly subject to an annual out-of-pocket maximum obligation of the insured (usually $1000 to $2000), but the insurer is also often limited to a maximum obligation over the lifetime of the insured (commonly $1 million or more). In recent years employee cost-sharing has tended to increase, though maximum lifetime benefits have increased as well.

Health insurance coverage is based in the first instance on a contract between the insurer and the insured individual or group. Initially, therefore, questions of insurance coverage depend on contract interpretation (see § 9–2). An insurer's denial of benefit in breach of the insurance contract may also under some circumstances results in a suit in tort (see § 9–3).

Health insurers are extensively subject to regulation by the states, in part due to a vestigial survival of the former notion that insurance was not commerce and thus not subject to federal regulation under the Commerce Clause.[11] This notion was enshrined in the McCarran–Ferguson Act, which reaffirmed state supremacy over insurance regulation and largely excepted insurers from antitrust scrutiny.[12] States regulate commercial insurers to assure their solvency and commonly review insurance policies to assure that they are not unfair or deceptive. States also regulate Blue Cross and Blue Shield plans, and frequently review their rates as well as their solvency. In the last quarter century states have also increasingly mandated the terms of insurance contracts, in particular requiring that insurance contracts cover certain benefits (mandated benefits laws), providers (mandated provider laws), or insureds (mandated coverage laws). States have taken an active role in regulating HMOs, PPOs and utilization review (see §§ 9–9—9–12 below). The National Organization of Insurance Commissioners (NAIC), an association of state insurance regulators, has been very effective in coordinating state regulation through drafting and disseminating model statutes and regulations addressing a wide variety of regulatory issues.

The federal government has also in recent years taken an increasingly active role in regulating health insurance. This trend began with the 1983 federal HMO act (substantially modified in 1988) which regulates federally-qualified HMOs (see § 9–10). It continued with the Consolidated Omnibus Budget Reconciliation Act of 1986 (COBRA), which mandated a continuing opportunity for coverage for certain persons who otherwise would have been terminated from coverage under group health insurance plans (see § 9–6). The Pregnancy Discrimination Act prohibits discrimination in health benefits against pregnancy or childbirth related conditions (see § 9–5), while § 105 of the Internal Revenue Code limits the excludability from taxable income of benefits of self-insured plans provided discriminatorily to highly compensated individuals (see § 9–5). The Americans with Disabilities Act limits the ability of employers to subject the disabled to discriminatory treatment in the provision of insurance (see § 9–5). Perhaps most significantly, the Health Insurance Portability and Accountability Act of 1996 limits the use of preex-

---

11. See United States v. South–Eastern Underwriters Association, 322 U.S. 533, 64 S.Ct. 1162, 88 L.Ed. 1440 (1944), in which the Supreme Court belatedly abandoned this position.

12. 15 U.S.C.A. §§ 1011–1015.

isting conditions clauses, facilitates the ability of small groups to get health insurance, increases access by individuals who leave employment to individual insurance, and proscribes discrimination within insured groups in terms of access to insurance or premiums on the basis of health status (See § 9–7).

The most significant federal law affecting health insurance is, however, fundamentally deregulatory rather than regulatory. The Employee Retirement Income Security Act (ERISA) preempts state regulation of self-insured benefits plans, including health insurance plans. It has pervasively frustrated state efforts to regulate health insurance comprehensively. While ERISA does impose some obligations on insurers, its primary effect is to free self-insured group plans from state regulation. ERISA has become such an important factor in health care financing that it is given its own chapter in this second edition (Chapter 8).

This chapter does not pretend to present an exhaustive treatment of the law of health insurance. Several treatises that do this are available.[13] Rather, we touch on the major insurance issues encountered by health care providers and insured individuals, focusing on issues of regulation and only minimally discussing issues of contract interpretation.

§ 9–2. The Health Insurance Contract

a. Interpretation

In the first instance the obligations of the insurer to the insured are governed by the insurance contract. Though many provisions of this contract are dictated by state or federal law or regulations, it remains fundamentally a private agreement and is treated as such by the courts, though this may becoming less true in the context of employment-related group plans governed by ERISA.

Individual insurance contracts are adhesion contracts. They are based on forms issued by the insurance company and are not subject to negotiation. As such they are generally construed by the courts against the insurer under the principle of contra proferentem and to protect the reasonable expectations of the insured.[1] It is less clear that group policies are adhesion contracts, as the bargaining power of the employer or other group policy holder is more equal to that of the insurer. Nevertheless, cases have generally held that group contracts are also interpreted against the insurer.[2]

In accordance with these principles, the reasonable expectations of a policy holder will usually be supported by the courts, often through the doctrines of waiver or estoppel, even though the technical language of the

---

13. See e.g., Bertram Harnett and Irving I. Lesnick, The Law of Life and Health Insurance.

§ 9–2

1. Robert H. Jerry III, Understanding Insurance Law, §§ 25A—25D (2d Ed., 1996); Robert E. Keeton & Alan I. Widiss, Insurance Law, §§ 2.8(c), 6.3 (1988).

2. See e.g., Beynon v. Garden Grove Medical Group, 161 Cal.Rptr. 146 (Cal.App.1980).

See also McLaughlin v. Connecticut Gen. Life Ins. Co., 565 F.Supp. 434 (N.D.Cal.1983) (holding any ambiguity or uncertainty to be construed against insurer even if insurance contract not contract of adhesion). But see Robin v. Blue Cross Hosp. Serv., Inc., 637 S.W.2d 695 (Mo.1982) (group policy based on negotiation between equally strong insurer and employer not adhesion contract.)

policy could be interpreted to free the insurer from obligation.[3] Where policy language is clear, however, it will be enforced as written, even where enforcement disadvantages the insured.

The group health insurance policy consists of the group policy, the application of the group policy holder, and any applications of insured individual members. Group members have traditionally been issued a certificate, which describes the group policy and its benefits in summary form. The Employment Retirement Income Security Act of 1974 (ERISA) (discussed at chapter 8) imposes a federal requirement that beneficiaries of employee group benefit plans be issued a "Summary Plan Description," that effectively serves the same purpose.[4] It has been held under state law that the group insurance certificate is not part of the group contract.[5] Where the language of the certificate contradicts or is inconsistent with the language of the master policy to the advantage of the insured, however (e.g. where the master policy contains an exclusion from coverage not noted on the certificate), courts have frequently held the insurer to the terms of the certificate, often relying on estoppel.[6] It has also been held under federal law that where the ERISA summary plan description contradicts the master insurance policy, the terms of the summary plan description take precedence.[7] The insurer may also be estopped from denying coverage promised by advertisements or pamphlets issued for solicitation purposes where the terms of the master policy are less generous than those advertised.[8] Where an insurer makes a payment to a medical provider for services rendered to a beneficiary and subsequently determines that the service was not covered and that the payment was made by "mistake", the insurer will not ordinarily be able to recover the payment unless the provider procured the payment by fraud.[9] Finally, an insured may have a claim against an employer or other group policyholder based on contract or estoppel where the policyholder fails to obtain or maintain insurance promised to the group member or misadvises a group member as to coverage.[10]

3. See e.g., Cain v. Aetna Life Ins. Co., 659 P.2d 1334 (Ariz.App.1983); Sarchett v. Blue Shield, 233 Cal.Rptr. 76, 729 P.2d 267 (Cal. 1987); Providence Hosp. v. Morrell, 427 N.W.2d 531 (Mich.1988); Brown v. Blue Cross and Blue Shield of Mississippi , Inc., 427 So.2d 139 (Miss.1983); Little v. Blue Cross, 424 N.Y.S.2d 553 (N.Y.App.Div.1980).

4. 29 U.S.C.A. § 1022(b). See also 29 C.F.R. § 2520.102–3 (describing the content of the SPD).

5. Boseman v. Connecticut General Life Ins. Co., 301 U.S. 196, 57 S.Ct. 686, 81 L.Ed. 1036 (1937); Morrison Assur. Co. v. Armstrong, 264 S.E.2d 320 (Ga.App.1980); Straub v. Crown Life Ins. Co., 496 S.W.2d 42 (Mo.App. 1973). Other cases have found, however, the certificate to be part of the contract, Fryer v. Kaiser Foundation Health Plan, Inc., 34 Cal. Rptr. 688 (Cal.App.1963).

6. See e.g., Van Vactor v. Blue Cross Ass'n, 8 Ill.Dec. 400, 365 N.E.2d 638 (Ill.App.1977); Blue Cross and Blue Shield, Inc. v. Chestnut Lodge, Inc., 567 A.2d 147 (Md.App.1989), cert. denied 570 A.2d 864 (Md.1990); Davey v. Loui-

siana Health Serv. & Indem. Co., 357 So.2d 1170 (La.App.1978), cert. denied 359 So.2d 194 (La.1978); Beck v. Southern Oregon Health Serv., Inc., 469 P.2d 622 (Or.1970); Republic Nat'l Life Ins. v. Blann, 400 S.W.2d 31 (Tex. Civ.App.1966). David M. Zupanec, Annotation, Group Insurance: Binding Effects of Limitations on or Exclusions of Coverage Contained in Master Group Policy but not in Literature Given Insureds, 6 A.L.R.4th 835 (1981 & Supp. 1998).

7. McKnight v. Southern Life & Health Ins. Co., 758 F.2d 1566 (11th Cir.1985).

8. See Robin Cheryl Miller, Annotation, Waiver or Estoppel of Insurer on Basis of Statements or Omissions in Promotional, Illustrative, or Explanatory Materials Given to Insureds, 63 A.L.R.5th 427 (1998).

9. City of Hope National Medical Center v. Superior Court of Los Angeles County, 10 Cal. Rptr.2d 465 (Cal.App.1992).

10. See e.g., Boucher v. Valus, 298 A.2d 238 (Conn.Cir.Ct.1972); Dawes Mining Co. v. Callahan, 267 S.E.2d 830 (Ga.App.1980); Peyton v. United States Steel Co., 84 A.2d 192 (Pa.1951).

b. Eligibility and Coverage of Insureds

Much of the caselaw in the area of health insurance concerns the question of whether a particular individual is insured with respect to a particular condition. With respect to individual policies, disputes often turn on whether the policy was void at the outset because of fraudulent misrepresentation by the insured, for example with respect to insured status. These disputes in turn frequently raise questions as to the applicability of incontestability clauses, which limit the ability of the insurance company to claim that the insurance policy was void after a specified, usually fairly short, period of time. Insurance coverage has also often been denied for specific conditions under "preexisting conditions" clauses, though these clauses are increasingly regulated under state and federal law.

Disputes have arisen with fair frequency as to the scope of benefits provided by health insurance policies. These disputes often turn on interpretation of the provisions of the contract that define coverage. More commonly, disputes involve interpretation of exclusion rather than coverage clauses.

Among the most common sources of litigation between insurers and insureds or providers in recent years have been exclusions involving "unnecessary" or "experimental" services. A major factor in causing recent dramatic increase in health care costs has been the proliferation of expensive and often unvalidated medical technology. Another has been the widespread use of diagnostic and treatment services that may not be indicated in a particular situation. Insurers have responded to both by including in their policies blanket exclusions for "experimental" or "medically unnecessary" services, and by establishing utilization review programs to evaluate on a case-by-case basis the necessity of particular services.[11]

Attempts by insurers to limit their liability for "unnecessary" or "experimental" treatment have been successful only at the margin. Professor Hall found that the patient won in 61% of reported medical necessity cases when the determination was made under state contract law in state court.[12] Courts have been willing to construe policies against the insurer to override denials of payment for services even though the treatment is not universally accepted by the scientific community.[13] Where courts are limited to "arbitrary and capricious standard" review of ERISA plans that are granted discretionary

---

11. See generally, Annotation, What Services, Equipment, or Supplies or "Medically Necessary" for Purposes of Coverage Under Medical Insurance, 75 A.L.R.4th 763 (1990 & Supp. 1998). For a comprehensive overview of the problem of determining medical necessity, with an ultimate recommendation that processes for resolving disputes be established by contract, see Mark A. Hall & Gerard F. Anderson, Health Insurers' Assessment of Medical Necessity, 140 U. Pa. L. Rev. 1637 (1992). Professor Hall followed up this article with an empirical study of coverage determinations in Mark A. Hall, Judicial Protection of Managed Care Consumers: An Empirical Study of Insurance Coverage Disputes, 26 Seton Hall L. Rev. 1055 (1996). This study is discussed in William M. Sage, Judicial Opinions Involving Health Insurance Coverage: Trompe L. 'Oeil or Window on the World, 31 Indiana L. Rev. 49 (1998). For an international comparative perspective on this issue, see Timothy Stoltzfus Jost, Health Care Rationing in the Courts: A Comparative Study, 21 Hastings Int. and Comp. L. Rev. 639 (1998).

12. Hall, "Judicial Protection" supra note 11, at 1062.

13. See, e.g., DiDomenico v. Employers Coop. Ind. Trust, 676 F.Supp. 903 (N.D.Ind. 1987) (liver transplant for biliary cirrhosis). See also Stringfield v. Prudential Ins. Co., 732 F.Supp. 69 (E.D.Tenn.1989) (issue of fact existed precluding summary judgment for insurance company on whether radial keratotomy was "experimental" or "investigational").

authority (see below), insurers have considerable scope for denying experimental treatment.[14]

The most hotly contested experimental treatment issue in the recent past has been coverage of high dose chemotherapy with autologous bone marrow transplant (HDCT–ABMT) for various cancers, most notably breast cancer.[15] HDCT–ABMT is a very expensive, still not fully validated, treatment for a widespread and potentially fatal condition. The courts are split on this issue, with some upholding an insurers' denial of HDCT–ABMT as experimental or as not medically necessary,[16] others holding that HDCT–ABMT is a scientifically accepted treatment, and thus not experimental within the meaning of exclusion clauses.[17]

Cases challenging denials based on exclusions of medically unnecessary care have also had mixed results. Some courts, interpreting ambiguous medical necessity clauses against the insurer and attempting to fulfil the insured's reasonable expectations, permit the insured's physician the final say as to whether a procedure is necessary.[18] More commonly courts defer to insurer denials based on medical necessity where the insurer has in place a reasonable procedure for determining necessity.[19] Issues of experimental treatment and necessary care also arise in the Medicaid and Medicare programs. See §§ 11-7 and 12-6 for a discussion of these issues in the Medicare and Medicaid context.

One of the most controversial coverage issues in this area has been denial of benefits for treatment of infertility. Several courts have denied treatment for infertility, finding in one case that the inability to conceive a child due to previous voluntary sterilization was not a "sickness,"[20] and in others that in vitro fertilization or reversal of sterilization procedures were not "medically necessary."[21] On the other hand, several recent cases have recognized infertili-

---

14. See chapter 8.

15. See, listing many of these cases, Whitney v. Empire Blue Cross & Blue Shield, 920 F.Supp. 477, 482, n. 5 (S.D.N.Y.1996), vacated and remanded, 106 F.2d 475 (2d Cir. 1997). See also, Richard S. Saver, Note: Reimbursing New Technologies: Why are the Courts Judging Experimental Medicine? 44 Stan. L. Rev. 1095 (1992) (discussing court decisions evaluating experimental treatment in general and the ABMT cases in particular). See, discussing the various approaches that insurers have taken to paying for this technology, William P. Peters & Mark C. Rogers, Variation in Approval by Insurance Companies for Autologous Bone Marrow Transplantation for Breast Cancer, 330 N.Eng.J.Med. 473 (1994).

16. Fuja v. Benefit Trust Life Ins. Co., 18 F.3d 1405 (7th Cir.1994); Farley v. Benefit Trust Life Ins. Co., 979 F.2d 653 (8th Cir. 1992); Healthcare America Plans v. Bossemeyer, 953 F.Supp. 1176 (D.Kansas 1996); Sweeney v. Gerber Prod. Co. Medical Benefits Plan, 728 F.Supp. 594 (D.Neb.1989); Thomas v. Gulf Health Plan, Inc., 688 F.Supp. 590 (S.D.Ala. 1988). The latest medical research indicates that the efficacy of HDCT–ABMT is far from

established. See Karen Antman, et al. High Dose Chemotherapy for Breast Cancer, 282 JAMA 1701 (1999).

17. See e.g. Velez v. Prudential Health Plan of New York, Inc., 943 F.Supp. 332 (S.D.N.Y.1996); Adams v. Blue Cross/Blue Shield, Inc., 757 F.Supp. 661 (D.Md.1991); Pirozzi v. Blue Cross–Blue Shield, 741 F.Supp. 586 (E.D.Va.1990). See Frank P. James, The Experimental Treatment Exclusion Clause: A Tool For Silent Rationing of Health Care? 12 J. Legal Med. 359 (1991).

18. E.g., Van Vactor v. Blue Cross Assoc., 8 Ill.Dec. 400, 365 N.E.2d 638 (Ill.App.1977).

19. E.g., Stock v. SHARE, 18 F.3d 1419 (8th Cir.1994). See also Siegal v. Health Care Serv. Corp., 36 Ill.Dec. 899, 401 N.E.2d 1037 (Ill.App.1980) (medical necessity is jury question).

20. E.g., Marsh v. Reserve Life Ins. Co., 516 So.2d 1311 (La.App.1987).

21. Reuss v. Time Ins. Co., 340 S.E.2d 625 (Ga.App.1986) (reversal of vasectomy); Kinzie v. Physician's Liability Insurance Company, 750 P.2d 1140 (Okl. App.1987) (in vitro fertilization); Connecticut Gen. Life Ins. Co. v. Shelton, 611 S.W.2d 928 (Tex.Civ.App.1981) (reversal of tubal ligation).

ty as an "illness" within the meaning of the governing insurance plans, and thus covered by insurance.[22]

Resolution of coverage disputes is often influenced by statutory law, discussed more fully below. First, states often respond to coverage disputes by adopting mandated benefits laws, discussed further at § 9–4(b) below. As of 1989, for example, seven states required that insurers provide or offer coverage for in vitro fertilization.[23] Twenty-eight states required mental health coverage and 37 required coverage of alcoholism treatment.[24] In recent years, moreover, states have also adopted laws addressing the decision-making process itself, particularly when prospective review by managed care firms is at issue. These laws are discussed in sections 9–9—9–12 below. Cutting the other way is the federal Employee Retirement Income Security Act (ERISA), discussed in the previous chapter. ERISA frees self-insured benefit plans from regulation by the states, including state mandates. Though the general de novo review standard applied in ERISA cases permits courts freedom to review benefit denials, ERISA plans can also, if they choose to do so and make their election clear, retain considerable discretion over benefits, and be subject only to review for "arbitrary and capricious" decisions. (See chapter 8)

In sum, insurers that rely on broad and vague terms such as "medical necessity" or "experimental treatment" will often not prevail where an insured seeks payment for treatment judged necessary by the insured's physician, even though the treatment is not fully validated scientifically. The court is likely to construe ambiguities in the policy against the insurer and protect the insured's reasonable expectations, particularly if the insured suffers from a life threatening condition. On the other hand, if a plan clearly and explicitly sets out excluded treatments or its method for determining medical necessity, denials of benefits are likely to be upheld. An ERISA plan that retains discretion is also more easily defended than a plan not protected by ERISA when it denies coverage for medical treatment.

c. *Coordination of Benefits*

Because of the multiple sources of insurance in American society, it is quite common for insured individuals to have multiple sources of coverage. In a family, for example, where both spouses are employed, each may be the primary insured under his or her own employer's policy and a dependent under the other spouse's coverage. Children may also be covered as dependents under both policies. Children of persons who are divorced and remarried may be covered by the insurance policies of both of their parents and also of both of their stepparents. Individuals with two jobs may be covered by

22. Egert v. Connecticut Gen. Life Ins. Co., 900 F.2d 1032 (7th Cir.1990); Witcraft v. Sundstrand Health & Disability Group Benefit Plan, 420 N.W.2d 785 (Iowa 1988). See also, Northrup v. Blue Cross and Blue Shield of Utica–Watertown, Inc., 652 N.Y.S.2d 902 (App. Div. 1997) (Gamete Interfallopian Transfer not excluded by artificial insemination exclusion); See, Edward L. Raymond, Jr., Annotation, Coverage of Artificial Insemination Procedures or Other Infertility Treatments by Health, Sickness, or Hospitalization Insurance, 80 A.L.R.4th 1059 (1990 and Supp. 1998); Pamela J. Prager, Infertility: The Unrecognized Illness in the Health Insurance Industry, 39 Drake L.

Rev. 617 (1989–90). A related issue is whether denial of coverage for infertility violates the Americans with Disabilities Act or Pregnancy Discrimination Act. The limited authority on this question is negative. Krauel v. Iowa Methodist Medical Ctr., 95 F.3d 674 (8th Cir.1996).

23. Jack B. Helitzer, State Developments in Employee Benefits: States Mandating Coverage of In Vitro Fertilization, 2 Benefits L. J. 529 (1989/90).

24. HIAA Research Bulletin, The Price of Mandated Benefits, 4 (1989).

insurance under two policies, as may persons working in one job and retired from another. Finally, private health insurance may also cover medical bills that are covered by Medicare, Medicaid, worker's compensation, no-fault auto insurance, or other sources of payment for medical coverage. Where an insured must pay for all or part of the health insurance benefits, the insured is likely to attempt to minimize duplicate coverage, though the complexity of insurance contracts may make this difficult. Where insurance is provided with no or minimal cost to the insured, however, duplicate coverage is likely. Indeed, where indemnity policies are involved, duplicate payments for services are also quite possible.

Whenever duplicate coverage is present, it is tempting for each insurer to deny coverage, attempting to impose responsibility for any particular expense on the other insurer or insurers. Insurance policies commonly have clauses attempting to make their coverage secondary to that of another insurer. "Coordination of benefits," (COB) is thus necessary to assure that the insured is covered by at least one insurer and to avoid endless disputes among insurers as to who is primary. Coordination issues are often addressed by state or federal law.

Where COB is not provided by statute, courts have attempted to reconcile competing coverage provisions either by attempting to discern the intent of the parties or by prorating liability.[25] Approximately 45 states have now adopted COB statutes or regulations, about 40 of which are based on the NAIC (National Association of Insurance Commissioners) Model Guidelines. One common approach is the "birthday rule," under which primary coverage responsibility is placed on the insurer of the party whose birthday comes earliest in the year.[26]

Federal law makes Medicare and Medicaid secondary payers to private insurance to conserve the resources of the federal government.[27] State legislation often attempts to make no-fault policies secondary to group health insurance to reduce the cost of no-fault insurance.[28] Liability under worker's compensation statutes tends to be primary to health insurance obligations.[29]

The federal Employee Retirement Income Security Act (ERISA) (discussed in chapter 8) preempts state COB statutes and common law when applied to self-insured benefit plans.[30] COB conflicts involving self-insured ERISA plans are determined by federal common law.[31]

25. Compare William C. Brown Co. v. General Am. Life Ins. Co., 450 N.W.2d 867 (Iowa 1990); Blue Cross & Blue Shield v. Riverside Hosp., 703 P.2d 1384 (Kan.1985); and Jones v. Medox, Inc., 430 A.2d 488 (D.C.App.1981) (reconciling contract provisions) with Lamb–Weston, Inc. v. Oregon Auto. Ins. Co., 341 P.2d 110 (Or.1959) (coverage prorated). See, discussing the state of the law, Andrea G. Nadel, Annotation: Priority and Apportionment of Liability Between Medical and Hospital Expense Insurers, 25 A.L.R.4th 1022 (1983 and Supp. 1998).

26. See PM Group Life Insurance Co. v. Western Growers Assurance Trust, 953 F.2d 543 (9th Cir.1992).

27. See 42 U.S.C.A. §§ 1395y(b), 1396a(a)(25)(A), 1396b(o); 42 C.F.R. §§ 411.20–411.75, 433.138; and §§ 13–33 and 14–8.

28. See e.g., Frankenmuth Mut. Ins. Co. v. Meijer, Inc., 440 N.W.2d 7 (Mich.App.1989), cert. dismissed 493 U.S. 1065, 110 S.Ct. 1104, 107 L.Ed.2d 1012 (1990) (applying such a state law and finding it not preempted by ERISA). See also, Brown v. Snohomish County Physicians Corporation, 845 P.2d 334 (Wash.1993) (insurance policy excluding benefits to the extent they were available from uninsured motorist coverage invalidated).

29. E.g., Kennedy v. Cochran, 475 So.2d 872 (Ala.Civ.App.1985); Stetson v. Blue Cross, 261 N.W.2d 894 (N.D.1978).

30. FMC Corp. v. Holliday, 498 U.S. 52, 111 S.Ct. 403, 112 L.Ed.2d 356 (1990).

§ 9–3. Extra–Contractual Liability of Insurers

The responsibilities of a health insurer to the insured are determined in the first instance by the insurance contract. When an insurer egregiously fails to honor these commitments, however, it may in some states be subject to liability in excess of that established by the policy. If the liability of an insurer could never under any circumstances exceed the amounts it owed under its policies, an incentive would exist for insurers to avoid their responsibilities, paying only in close cases when sued. Some courts have for this reason recognized liability claims against insurers for extra-contractual compensatory or punitive damages in tort based on fraud,[1] intentional infliction of emotional distress,[2] or bad faith breach of the insurance obligation.[3] Other courts have imposed punitive damages in contract where an insurance company's conduct has been egregious.[4]

The law of bad faith breach of insurance obligations arose first in the context of liability insurance, where the insurer finds itself in a natural conflict of interest with its insured when a third party claim arises in excess of the policy limit. Under these circumstances the insurer may find it in its interest to defend a claim even though the insured wishes to settle the claim for the policy limit to avoid potential personal liability. In instances where the insurer refuses to settle unreasonably and the insured ends up liable to the third party claimant for amounts in excess of the policy limit, courts have held the insurer liable to the insured on a bad faith theory.[5] The relationship between the insured and a first-party insurer (like a health insurer) is much more like a typical contractual arrangement, with a less clear cut conflict of interest between the parties. For this reason the law developed in the liability insurance context fits poorly in the context of first-party insurance and plaintiffs seeking to impose liability under this theory are often denied relief.[6]

---

31. Lincoln Mut. Cas. Co. v. Lectron Products, Inc., 970 F.2d 206 (6th Cir.1992); Auto Club Ins. Ass'n v. Health and Welfare Plans, Inc., 961 F.2d 588 (6th Cir.1992). But see Inter Valley Health Plan v. Blue Cross/Blue Shield of Conn., 19 Cal.Rptr.2d 782 (Cal.App.1993) (Since ERISA has no coordination of benefits rule, coordination of benefits should be determined by law of forum state, here California).

§ 9–3

1. E.g., Blue Cross/Blue Shield v. Weiner, 543 So.2d 794 (Fla.App.1989), cert. denied 494 U.S. 1028, 110 S.Ct. 1475, 108 L.Ed.2d 612 (1990).

2. See Morgan v. American Family Life Assurance Co. of Columbus, 559 F.Supp. 477 (W.D.Va.1983) (motion to dismiss and summary judgment against claim denied).

3. See e.g., Berry v. United of Omaha, 719 F.2d 1127 (11th Cir.1983); McEvoy by Finn v. Group Health Cooperative by Eau Clare, 570 N.W.2d 397 (Wisc. 1997); Rederscheid v.

Comprecare, Inc., 667 P.2d 766 (Colo.App. 1983); von Hagel v. Blue Cross and Blue Shield, 370 S.E.2d 695 (N.C.App.1988) (claim upheld against motion to dismiss or summary judgment).

4. Linscott v. Rainier Nat'l Life Ins. Co., 606 P.2d 958 (Idaho 1980) (punitives limited to attorney's fees and other costs of bringing action); Fox v. Health Net of Calif., 3 BNA Health Law Rptr. 18 (Cal.Super.Ct. Dec. 23, 1993) (Jury awards $12.3 million in compensatory damages and $77 million in punitive damages to estate of patient denied coverage of bone marrow transplant by HMO).

5. See e.g., Crisci v. Security Ins. Co. of New Haven Conn., 58 Cal.Rptr. 13, 426 P.2d 173 (Cal.1967).

6. Mary Elizabeth Phelan, The First Party Dilemma: Bad Faith or Bad Business? 34 Drake L. Rev. 1031 (1984–85) (discussing difficulties of applying bad faith doctrine developed in liability insurance situation to first party insurance).

Many more cases have denied liability where the insurer denied benefits in good faith[7] or where bad faith conduct was that of an agent acting outside of his authority.[8]

However, where a health insurer has acted egregiously in wrongfully refusing to cover one of its insureds[9] or in refusing to pay or wrongfully delaying payment of a claim,[10] a number of courts have imposed compensatory damages in excess of policy obligations or punitive damages. Some have done so on the basis of "unreasonable" conduct,[11] others have required additional proof of malice or an evil state of mind.[12] Because liability is based on breach of a fiduciary relationship with the insured, however, liability for punitive damages probably does not extend to third parties affected by a claims denial, such as providers denied reimbursement.[13]

Here, as elsewhere, ERISA has had a significant impact. In *Pilot Life Insurance Co. v. Dedeaux*,[14] the Supreme Court held that suits alleging bad faith claims processing against employer sponsored group health insurance plans are a form of state interference with the operation of such plans and are thus preempted by ERISA. As they are not state regulation of insurance, they are not saved from preemption by the ERISA "savings" clause (see Chapter 8 above).[15] It also seems clear at this point that no cause of action is possible under ERISA for punitive damages where an insurer engages in egregious conduct.

7. See e.g., Guy v. Commonwealth Life Ins. Co., 894 F.2d 1407 (5th Cir.1990); Higgins v. Blue Cross, 319 N.W.2d 232 (Iowa 1982).

8. See International Sec. Life Ins. Co. v. Finck, 496 S.W.2d 544 (Tex.1973). But see Underwriters Life Ins. Co. v. Cobb, 746 S.W.2d 810 (Tex.App.1988) (insurance company liable for wrongdoing of agents where insurer had previous knowledge of misdealings by agents).

9. Southern Life & Health Ins. Co. v. Smith, 518 So.2d 77 (Ala.1987) (insurer that refused to cover pregnancy despite agent's representations at sale of policy that pregnancy was covered held liable for compensatory and punitive damages); Employers Equitable Life Ins. Co. v. Williams, 665 S.W.2d 873 (Ark.1984) (cancellation of insurance based on late payments when payments in fact timely made but computer records altered to reflect late payments). See also Pacific Mutual Life Ins. Co. v. Haslip, 499 U.S. 1, 111 S.Ct. 1032, 113 L.Ed.2d 1 (1991) (punitive damages award against insurer upheld as not unconstitutional where insureds defrauded by agent of insurer).

10. Blue Cross & Blue Shield v. Maas, 516 So.2d 495 (Miss.1987) (improper denial of claim); Sparks v. Republic Nat'l Life Ins. Co., 647 P.2d 1127 (Ariz.1982), cert. denied 459 U.S. 1070, 103 S.Ct. 490, 74 L.Ed.2d 632 (1982) (improper termination of coverage); Hughes v. Blue Cross of Northern California, 263 Cal.Rptr. 850 (Cal.App.1989), cert. dismissed 495 U.S. 944, 110 S.Ct. 2200, 109 L.Ed.2d 527 (1990) (improper determination that care not medically necessary); Poling v.

Wisconsin Physicians Serv., 357 N.W.2d 293 (Wis.App.1984) (improper denial of skilled nursing care as custodial).

11. Sparks v. Republic Nat'l Life Ins. Co., 647 P.2d 1127, 1136 (Ariz.1982), cert. denied 459 U.S. 1070, 103 S.Ct. 490, 74 L.Ed.2d 632 (1982).

12. See e.g., Eichenseer v. Reserve Life Ins. Co., 682 F.Supp. 1355, 1363 (N.D.Miss.1988), affirmed 881 F.2d 1355 (5th Cir.1989), rehearing denied 894 F.2d 1414 (1990), judgment vacated on other grds. 499 U.S. 914 (1991) (must show willful or malicious wrong or gross or reckless disregard for the rights of others).

13. See St. Joseph's Hosp. & Medical Ctr. v. Reserve Life Ins. Co., 742 P.2d 804 (Ariz. App.1986), reversed on other grounds 742 P.2d 808 (Ariz.1987).

14. 481 U.S. 41, 107 S.Ct. 1549, 95 L.Ed.2d 39 (1987) (see chapter 8 supra).

15. ERISA may not preempt litigation for fraud external to the plan. See e.g. HealthAmerica v. Menton, 551 So.2d 235 (Ala.1989), cert. denied 493 U.S. 1093, 110 S.Ct. 1166, 107 L.Ed.2d 1069, and rehearing denied 494 U.S. 1052, 110 S.Ct. 1520, 108 L.Ed.2d 758 (1990) (state common law action against insurer that fraudulently induced cancellation of existing policy not preempted by ERISA). See also Theresa A. DiPaola, Wrongful Denial of Health Insurance Benefits, 26 Trial. Mar. 1990 at 74 (discussing the scope of ERISA preemption in wrongful denial cases).

§ 9-4. State Regulation of Insurance

a. Generally

In 1869 the Supreme Court decided in *Paul v. Virginia*[1] that "[i]ssuing a policy of insurance is not a transaction in commerce." As the business of insurance was, therefore, not interstate commerce subject to federal control, insurance regulation was left to the states. By 1944 when the Supreme Court reversed this position in *United States v. South-Eastern Underwriters Association*,[2] state regulation of insurance was firmly established. The following year, therefore, Congress adopted the McCarran-Ferguson Act, expressing its intention that the regulation of insurance be left to the states,[3] subject to limited applicability of the antitrust laws.

State regulation of private insurance is at this point pervasive.[4] States charter insurance companies and license insurance agents. All states tax the premiums of commercial insurers and about half of the states tax Blue Cross/Blue Shield plan premiums. States oversee the financial solvency of insurers both by imposing minimal requirements for financial reserves and for allowable investments, and through requiring annual statements and conducting periodic examinations of insurers (usually on a triennial basis). State law in most states requires that policy forms be filed and approved before they are used, though some states allow a policy form to be used once it has been filed with the insurance commissioner (if it is not disapproved), while others require explicit approval of the policy form before it can be used.[5] States also regulate insurance marketing and claims practices, including coordination of benefits.[6] State insurance commissioners investigate consumer complaints and place insolvent companies into receivership. The National Association of Insurance Commissioners (NAIC) has issued model codes and regulations on many of these subjects, the wide adoption of which has brought about some uniformity among the states.

b. State Insurance Mandates

As of 1999, by one count, state governments had imposed 1,260 mandates on health plans and insurers.[7] Among the most common are mandates that insurers pay for services provided by specified practitioners if they would pay for the same services if provided by a medical doctor (mandated provider laws); mandates that insurers cover certain benefits, (mandated benefit laws); and mandates that insurers cover certain insureds, including laws requiring

---

§ 9-4

1. 75 U.S. (8 Wall.) 168, 183, 19 L.Ed. 357 (1868).

2. 322 U.S. 533, 64 S.Ct. 1162, 88 L.Ed. 1440 (1944), rehearing denied 323 U.S. 811, 65 S.Ct. 26, 89 L.Ed. 646 (1944).

3. 15 U.S.C.A. §§ 1011–1015. The Constitutionality of the McCarran Act was upheld in Prudential Ins. Co. v. Benjamin, 328 U.S. 408, 66 S.Ct. 1142, 90 L.Ed. 1342 (1946). For discussion of the McCarran-Ferguson Act, see § 10–2.

4. See Kathleen Heald Ettlinger, Karen L. Hamilton, & Gregory Krohm, State Insurance Regulation (1995).

5. Where approval of a policy is required before issuance, an unapproved policy is not void insofar as enforcement of the policy would benefit the insured, but it should be reformed so as to conform to the law.

6. See § 9–2 above.

7. See, More Mandates on their Minds, 17 Business and Health 20 (1999). See also, Gail A. Jensen and Michael Morrisey, Mandated Benefit Laws and Employer-Sponsored Health Insurance (1999). See, for earlier counts, Jon R. Gabel & Gail A. Jensen, Health Insurance Association of America Research Bulletin: The Price of Mandated Benefits, 3 (1989); also found at 26 Inquiry 419 (1989).

guaranteed issue and renewal of policies or limiting waiting periods or preexisting condition exclusions (mandated coverage laws). Additional state laws do not require insurers to pay for a service as such, but rather require insurers to offer the service to purchasers as an option (mandated option laws).

As of 1996 thirty-seven jurisdictions had mandates for coverage of optometrists, forty-one of chiropractors, thirty-four of dentists, and forty-one of psychologists.[8] Less common are mandates for providing equal coverage for a variety of other professions including acupuncturists, audiologists, dieticians, lay midwives, mechanotherapists, naturopaths, nutritionists, occupational therapists, pharmacists, physical therapists, physician assistants, radiology technicians, recreational therapists, respiratory care therapists, social workers, and speech pathologists. Twenty-nine states have recently adopted laws aimed at plans with gatekeeper requirements requiring direct access to obstetricians and gynecologists, without referral by a primary-care gatekeeper.[9]

Mandated benefit laws tend to be more effective in expanding coverage, but also have a more significant impact on the cost of insurance. Common mandated benefits include alcoholism treatment (forty-three states in 1996), mental health coverage (thirty-two states), mammography screening (forty-six states) and maternity length-of-stay (thirty-four states).[10] Nineteen states have recently adopted laws requiring payment for emergency room services in situations deemed by state law to be an "emergency".[11] Other mandated benefits include home health or hospice care and infertility treatment. Where inclusion of a benefit is mandated and insurance policies do not cover mandated services, the policy will be reformed to reflect the coverage.[12]

Mandated coverage laws attempt to expand the coverage of group health insurance policies, requiring that dependent coverage extend to newborns from the point of birth (thirty-eight states in 1989), continue to cover mentally or physically handicapped children beyond the health insurance contract's normal limiting age (thirty-four states in 1996), or to cover adopted children (eighteen states in 1989).[13] In the late 1980s and early 1990s, states also adopted laws attempting to improve insurance availability, particularly to employees of small businesses, by requiring guaranteed renewal and portability of coverage, limitations on pre-existing conditions clauses, and restricting premium rating. By 1995, forty-five states had adopted some of these restrictions, and thirty-six states had adopted all of them.[14]

States vary dramatically in the prevalence of mandates, with some states having as few as six mandates, others as many as thirty-three.[15] The number of mandates has grown steadily in recent years, particularly as concerns about restrictions on coverage under managed care have become politically salient.

8. Jensen & Morrisey, supra note 7, at 1. For an excellent earlier fifty state survey of mandated provider laws, see Helitzer, State Developments in Employee Benefits, 4 Benefits L.J. 253 (1991).

9. Jensen & Morrisey, supra note 7, at 5.

10. Id.

11. Id. at 2.

12. See e.g., DiPascal v. New York Life Ins. Co., 749 F.2d 255 (5th Cir.1985); Rudloff v. Louisiana Health Serv. & Indem. Co., 385 So.2d 767 (La.1979).

13. Jensen & Morrisey, supra note 7, at 1; Gabel & Jensen, supra note 7, at 6.

14. Jensen & Morrisey, supra note 7, at 2.

15. Id. at 3.

Insurers argue stridently, however, that mandates are usually counterproductive, leading to increased insurance cost and thus to decreased insurance coverage.

Closely related to coverage mandates are laws prohibiting insurers from discrimination. Several states currently have laws prohibiting discrimination on the basis of handicaps or disabilities[16] or sex.[17] Attempts by insurance companies to avoid insuring persons with AIDS or who are HIV seropositive have led to a variety of antidiscrimination statutes and regulations. NAIC guidelines, adopted in several states, prohibit discrimination on the basis of sexual orientation or living arrangements.[18] A few states attempted to ban the use of HIV tests for determining insurability, though the regulations of New York and Massachusetts banning such tests were nullified by the courts.[19] More common are state laws requiring informed consent for AIDS testing, imposing strict confidentiality requirements on test results, or specifying which tests are permissible or testing procedures that must be followed. Several states that permit AIDS testing prohibit by statute or regulation inquiry concerning previous AIDS tests.

c. *State Small Group and Individual Market Reforms*

The number of uninsured in America has grown steadily over the past decade, and at this writing nearly 44 million, one in six Americans, were uninsured and the number was climbing every month. Most of the uninsured are either employed or the dependents of employed persons. A major reason why so many employed persons are uninsured is that persons who are self-employed or who are employed by small employers are far less likely to be insured, or even to have insurance available through their place of employment, than are employees of large businesses. Only about half of employers with fewer than 200 employees offer health insurance benefits, while nearly all employers with more than 200 do.[20] Although the increase in the number of the uninsured is attributable to an increase in the number of employees declining insurance offered by their employers as well as a decrease in the number of employers offering insurance, employees of small firms still purchase insurance at high rates when it is offered, encouraging the hope that an increase in the number of small employers offering health insurance as an option might decrease the number of the uninsured.[21]

16. See West's Ann.Cal. Ins. Code § 10144; Ohio Rev. Code § 3999.16. Distinctions based on sound actuarial principles or prior experience are permitted.

17. See e.g., Ark. Code Ann. § 23–66–206(7)(G).

18. See NAIC, Medical/Lifestyle Questions and Underwriting Guidelines, Proposed Bulletin (1989).

19. See Life Ins. Ass'n of Mass. v. Commissioner of Ins., 530 N.E.2d 168 (Mass.1988); Health Ins. Ass'n v. Corcoran, 551 N.Y.S.2d 615 (N.Y.App.Div.1990). One of the few remaining provisions limiting the use of HIV tests for determining insurability is West's Ann.Cal. Health & Safety Code, § 120980(f). See also, Henry T. Greeley, AIDS and the American Health Care Financing System, 51 U. Pitt. L. R. 73, 96–97 (1989); Benjamin Schatz, The AIDS Insurance Crisis: Underwriting or Overreaching? 100 Harv. L. Rev. 1782 (1987); Karen A. Clifford & Russell P. Iuculano, AIDS and Insurance: The Rationale for AIDS–Related Testing, 100 Harv. L. Rev. 1806 (1987); and Joyce Nixon Hoffman & Elizabeth Zieser Kincaid, AIDS: The Challenge to Life and Health Insurers' Freedom of Contract, 35 Drake L. Rev 709 (1986–87).

20. See Paul B. Ginsburg, Jon R. Gabel & Kelly A. Hunt, Tracking Small-firm Coverage, 1989–1996, Health Aff., Jan/Feb. 1998 at 167.

21. See Ibid.; Jon Gabel, et al., Health Benefits of Small Employers in 1998, 5–7 (1999).

To make health insurance more available to small employers, and more affordable by both small employers and their employees, virtually every state has adopted small-group and individual market reforms during the past decade.[22] These reforms were to some extent encouraged by the Health Insurance Portability and Accountability Act of 1996 (see § 9–7 below), which mandated the enactment of certain small group and individual reforms. Many of the reforms required by HIPAA, however, were already in place in many of the states, thus HIPAA's incremental effects have been marginal.

Indeed, it appears that the effect of small group and individual market reforms in aggregate on the incidence of uninsurance has been marginal, though the reforms have certainly helped some individuals and firms that might otherwise not have been able to secure insurance.[23] On the other hand, the disastrous effects that some predicted the reforms might have on insurers have not materialized either.[24] Insurers have remained in business even in states that have adopted rigorous reforms, and markets have remained competitive. To a considerable degree, however, the effects that small group reforms might have had on insurers or insureds have been masked by a dramatic growth in the prevalence of managed care in small group markets, holding down increases in premiums that reforms might otherwise have caused.

All states currently require insurers that sell in small group markets to offer coverage to any small group and to guarantee renewal to any small group that requests it, regardless of the health status or claims experience of the groups members.[25] Thirty-eight states had guaranteed issue and forty-three guaranteed renewal requirements before HIPAA, but HIPAA made these requirements universal.[26] HIPAA also required restrictions on preexisting conditions clauses, which had existed in 45 of the states before HIPAA.[27] A number of states go beyond HIPAA in limiting preexisting conditions clauses, however, including three states that outlaw them altogether in small group markets and ten additional states that impose stricter limits than HIPAA.[28]

Though HIPAA does not address insurance premiums, many states do. Twenty-seven states limit premiums charged to small groups to a band range of 2:1 for experience, health status, or duration of coverage, as recommended by the National Association of Insurance Commissioners.[29] Four states impose tighter rating bands, and fifteen states require adjusted community rating insofar as they prohibit rating based on experience, health status or duration of coverage.[30] New York, the most restrictive of the states, even limits variance of premiums based on age. Ten states have also adopted mandatory reinsurance pools and twenty voluntary reinsurance pools, assuring that small

22. Gail A. Jensen & Michael A. Morrisey, Small Group Reforms and Insurance Provision by Small Firms, 1989–1995, 36 Inquiry 176 (1999).

23. See Leigh Page, Insurance Reform Effect: Coverage Drop, 41 Am.Med. News, Sept. 21, 1998 at 5; Jensen & Morrisey, supra note 22.

24. Mark Hall, The Competitive Impact of Small Group Health Insurance Reform Laws, Mich.J.L.Rev. (forthcoming.)

25. Blue Cross/Blue Shield, State Legislative Health Care and Insurance Issues, 1998 Survey of Plans (1999).

26. Gail A. Jensen and Michael A. Morrisey, Mandated Benefit Laws and Employer–Sponsored Health Insurance (1999).

27. Ibid.

28. Blue Cross/ Blue Shield, supra note 25.

29. Id.

30. Id.

group plans that end up carrying high risk groups can spread some of their risks to small group insurers with more favorable risk experience.[31]

The most common individual market reform is guaranteed renewal, required by HIPAA but adopted by twenty-one states before HIPAA.[32] Thirty one states have adopted restrictions on preexisting conditions limitations covering persons beyond those who must be covered under HIPAA. Among other individual market reforms adopted by the states are 1) restrictions on the use of experience, health status or duration for setting premiums (8 states); 2) prohibitions against the use of experience, health status or duration of coverage in underwriting (6 states); provision for voluntary or mandatory participation in reinsurance pools (9 states); and designation of minimum loss ratios (percentage of premiums that must be paid out in claims) (9 states).[33]

HIPAA includes a requirement that health plans offer coverage to any individual regardless of health status or claims experience if the individual has had at least eighteen months of prior continuous group coverage without a lapse of 63 or more days since the most recent coverage.[34] States may opt out of imposing this requirement, however, by providing an acceptable alternative mechanism. In fact, as of December 1998, only a thirteen states were complying with the HIPAA guaranteed issue alternative, while the remaining states relied on an alternative. Twenty-one states provided coverage through a high risk insurance pools, with most funded through an assessment on insurers. Only two states have more than 10,000 current enrollees in their high risk pools, and most states have a 1500 or fewer enrollees.

Finally, about twenty-one states have laws authorizing the formation of small group purchaser pools, to facilitate small groups banding together to achieve economies in purchasing insurance. Though approximately a third of establishments with fewer than 10 employees and 28% of firms with 10–49 employees purchase health insurance through pooled arrangements, pools seem to have had little impact on the affordability or availability of insurance.[35]

In the end, regulatory approaches seem to have had only limited impact for good or for ill on insurance availability in small group and individual markets. In part this seems to be due to the endless creativity of insurers in evading regulation and limiting their risk. By manipulation of coverage, cost-sharing, and marketing efforts insurers can still often control the risk to which they are exposed, allowing them on the one hand to remain prosperous, but on the other hand, permitting continued limitations on coverage.

d. Genetic Discrimination

One particular concern of state insurance regulators in the past decade has been discrimination on the basis of genetic characteristics.[36] The genetic

---

31. Id.

32. Id.

33. Id.

34. See § 9–7 infra.

35. See Stephen H. Long and H. Susan Marquis, Pooled Purchasing: Who Are the Players? Health Aff. July/Aug. 1999 at 105.

36. See, among the many excellent articles discussing this topic, Barbara Berry, The Hu-

man Genome Project and the End of Insurance, 7 U.Fla.J.L. & Pub. Pol'y 205 (1996); Richard A. Epstein, The Legal Regulation of Genetic Discrimination: Old Responses to New Technology, 74 B.U.L. Rev. 1 (1994); Mark Hall, Insurers' Use of Genetic Information, 37 Jurimetrics J. 13 (1996); Eric Mills Holmes, Solving the Insurance/Genetic Fair/Unfair Discrimination Dilemma in Light of the Human Genome Project, 85 Ky.L.J. 503 (1997) (the

makeup of individuals plays a very influential role in determining their susceptibility to various diseases. Individuals possessing some kinds of genetic abnormalities are almost certain to develop particular conditions; those possessing others 04 face an enhanced likelihood of contracting other conditions, depending on environmental factors and on chance. Currently available techniques of genetic testing permit quite accurate identification of genetic factors affecting a variety of conditions. The Human Genome Project, which is attempting to map the entire human genome by the 2005 (and will probably be done earlier), will greatly enhance our ability to read genes to predict future health problems.

Life and disability insurers can obviously benefit from access to genetic information respecting applicants for insurance. Insurers in the individual market for health insurance (about 15% of health insurance contracts) are also interested in this information, as may be insurers that insure small groups with respect to individuals who make up those small groups. Most Americans, however, obtain private health insurance through larger employment groups, where insurers would have much less reason to be interested in the genetics of particular individuals. This is particularly true since the Health Insurance Portability and Accountability Act (discussed below) outlawed setting premiums or determining eligibility on an individual basis within groups.

Risk underwriting is by its very nature discriminatory—persons who are at greater risk pay higher premiums for insurance because they are more likely to use it, and as risk approaches certainty insurers may simply deny coverage. Insurers already consider many factors in setting premiums. Some of these factors, like age and sex, are similar to genetic information in being beyond the control of the applicant. Insurers argue that they should also be able to take into accounts the results of genetic testing.

For insurers not to consider genetic predictors, some argue, is unfair to insureds with favorable genetic characteristics, who are forced to pay unjustifiably high rates to subsidize those with poor genes. In fact, the laws of many states would seem to mandate consideration of reliable predictors like some genetic tests insofar as those laws require that insurance rates discriminate fairly between insureds so that each pays according to the quality of his or her risk. Genetic information is not very different from other medical information, such as cholesterol levels of blood pressure that insurers already routinely consider in risk underwriting. Indeed distinguishing between "genetic" information and other health status information poses both definitional problems (since most diseases contain a genetic component) and practical problems (since medical records often contain both types of information

review of pro and con arguments that follows is largely drawn from Holmes' thorough overview of the problem); John V. Jacobi, The Ends of Health Insurance, 30 U.C. Davis L. Rev. 311 (1997); Karen H. Rothenberg, Genetic Information and Health Insurance: State Legislative Approaches, 23 J.L.Med. & Ethics 312 (1995). Mark A. Rothstein and Sharona Hoffman, Genetic Testing, Genetic Medicine, and Managed Care, 34 Wake Forest L. Rev. 849 (1999); Deb-

orah A. Stone, The Implications of the Human Genome Project for Access to Health Insurance, in The Human Genome Project and the Future of Health Care, 133 (Thomas H. Murray, Mark A. Rothstein and Robert F. Murray Jr., 1996). See also, Task Force on Genetic Information and Insurance, NIH–DOE Working Group on Ethical, Legal and Social Implications of Human Genome Research, Genetic Information and Health Insurance (1993).

inseparably entwined, thus insurers would have to be denied access to medical records generally to fully protect genetic information).[37]

Finally, and most importantly, if individuals can gain access to information about their genetic makeup, but insurers are forbidden from doing so, insurers are at great risk of adverse selection. Adverse selection, in turn, places insurance markets at risk as rates rise to cover the needs of high risk insureds while low risk insureds self-insure rather than pay the higher rates.

Consumer and disability advocacy groups, and many ethicists, argue, on the other hand, that insurers should be denied access to genetic information. First, they argue that it is unfair for insurers to penalize persons for their genetic makeup, which they did not choose and cannot change. These persons already suffer the risk of disease or even an early death because of their genetic makeup—should they have to endure higher insurance rates, or insurance denial, as well? The problem of unfair discrimination is compounded because insurers may well misunderstand and misuse genetic information, in particular viewing genetic tests and characteristics as being far better predictors of future disease than is in fact warranted. Moreover, if individuals with poor genetic predictors are denied private insurance, they will often become dependent on public programs, increasing the tax burden placed on society.

At stake here is the proper vision of insurance. Insurers argue that it is their task to segment their insureds through underwriting so that each insured pays his own way and that none is forced unfairly to subsidize others. Those who would proscribe the use of genetic information in insurance underwriting have a different vision of insurance (or at least of health insurance) as a manifestation of social solidarity in which the more fortunate ought to bear the less fortunate along. Historically, our insurance industry in the United States has chosen the former individualistic model, but state insurance regulation often seems to based on a more communitarian vision of insurance.

The argument against insurer use of genetic testing results in insurance underwriting is based not only on a particular understanding of fairness, however, it is also based on a concern about privacy. Genetic knowledge may lead to severe psychological distress in the individual and to serious social stigmatization should the information become public. Genetic knowledge may not only affect the individual, moreover, but also relatives of that individual. If genetic information is based on faulty testing, the distress and stigma can be completely unwarranted. Many individuals, therefore, might prefer to remain in a state of genetic ignorance. If insurers require genetic testing, however, individuals lose this option if they want insurance.

There is a real concern about the ability of insurers to maintain the confidentiality of genetic information. If this information reaches employers (as is very likely if the employer is self-insured for health benefits), or if it is published more broadly, severe consequences may ensue. Moreover, if there is a general belief that genetic information cannot be kept private, individuals will be less likely to voluntarily undergo genetic testing, and thus lose the

---

37. See Mark A. Rothstein, Why Treating Genetic Information Separately is a Bad Idea, 1 Tex. Rev. of L. Pol. 33 (1999).

advantages that genetic information can provide for making life choices and for medical diagnosis and treatment.[38]

Because of these considerations of privacy and equity, the vast majority of the states, forty-four at last count, have adopted statutes limiting access to and use of genetic information by insurers.[39] All of these laws address the use of genetic information in health insurance underwriting, but some extend also to life, disability, or other forms of insurance. These laws take various forms.

First, the earliest genetic information statutes simply prohibited discrimination based on specific genetic traits, such as the sickle-cell trait, the hemoglobin C trait, or the Tay–Sachs trait.[40] Since some of these conditions are predominantly found in certain racial or ethnic groups, these statutes reflected to a degree long-standing prohibitions against underwriting based on racial or ethnic characteristics.

Second, the statutes of some states prohibit underwriting based on genetic information that is not justified on the basis of actuarial data.[41] These statutes can also be viewed as simply specific applications of more general state law requirements of fair and nondiscriminatory underwriting.

Third, as concern about genetic discrimination increased, state laws were adopted to prohibit insurers from requiring applicants or insureds to submit to genetic tests.[42] At the present time these laws impose minimal obligations on insurers, as genetic tests are still expensive and not wholly reliable, and thus to date are not commonly required by insurers.[43] To the extent, moreover, that these laws leave the door open for insurers to request insureds to supply information they have already obtained from genetic tests the insireds have voluntarily undergone, these laws do not leave insurers unprotected from adverse selection.

This protection is not afforded insurers by a fourth type of laws that completely exclude insurers from 12 access to genetic information.[44] These laws provide greater protection for the privacy and confidentiality of genetic information, and from underwriting based on genetic information. They also, however, pose difficult problems in terms of defining genetic information and separating it from other forms of health information.[45]

A fifth group of laws simply limits the ability of insurers to consider genetic information in underwriting.[46] These laws could have much broader effects than those simply prohibiting genetic testing, as they potentially bar consideration of genetic information gained through health records or questionnaires and not simply from tests. Similar laws prohibit the denial of insurance on the basis of genetic traits, but permit the adjusting of premiums or benefits to reflect genetic information; or permit denial, but not refusal of

38. See Rothstein and Hoffman, supra note 36 at 866.

39. The most recently available survey of state laws affecting genetic discrimination as of this writing is William F. Mulholland, II and Ami S. Jaeger, Genetic Privacy and Discrimination: A Survey of State Legislation, 39 Jurimetrics 317 (1999) (as of January 15, 1999).

40. See, eg. N.C. Gen Stat. § 58–65–70 (1975); Fla. Stat. Ann. § 626.9707 (1978); Md. Code Ann., Ins., § 223 (1986).

41. See Ariz. Rev. Stat. Ann. § 20–448; Mont. Code Ann. § 33–18–206.

42. See, e.g. Ala. Code § 27–53–2.

43. See Holmes, supra note 36, at 555.

44. See, E.g. Colo. Rev. Stat. Ann. 10–3–1104.7; Ga. Rev. Code Tit. 33, ch. 54.

45. See, Rothenberg, supra note 36 at 313.

46. See e.g. Cal. Ins. Code § 10123.3(d); Tex. Rev. Civ. Stat. art. 21.402; N.J. Stat. Ann. § 10:5–12.

renewal, based on genetic traits.[47] Still other statutes prohibit the treatment of genetic traits as preexisting conditions.

Finally, a sixth group of statutes, not specifically directed to genetic information, require guaranteed issue and community rating generally, thus totally eliminating genetic information, as well as many other factors, from underwriting consideration.[48] Some states combine one or more of these approaches.

Though our consideration is here focused on state insurance regulation, four federal laws also affect, at least potentially, insurer's use of genetic information. First, ERISA, discussed in chapter 8, preempts any state attempts to limit underwriting based on genetic information by self-insured employee health benefit plans, though state genetic discrimination and privacy statutes would otherwise be saved from preemption as the state regulation of insurance. Second, the Health Insurance Portability and Accountability Act prohibits consideration of genetic information as a preexisting condition (in the absence of a diagnosis of a related condition) in preexisting condition exclusions in group health policies or individual policies afforded persons who lose group coverage under the statute.[49] HIPAA also prohibits discrimination against individuals within covered groups in determining eligibility to enroll of premiums on the basis of genetic information.[50] Third, the Americans with Disabilities Act arguably limits discrimination by insurers based on genetic information. The limited impact of the ADA on insurance underwriting is discussed in section 9–5 below. An additional consideration here is whether a genetic abnormality would be considered to be a "disability" under the ADA, a difficult problem to say the least.[51] Finally, recently proposed regulations promulgated by the Department of Health and Human Services to govern privacy of medical information would permit the release of medical information, including presumably genetic information, to insurers regarding their insureds without a release from the insured, but would deny this information to insurers considering applications unless the applicant specifically authorizing release of the information.[52]

B. FEDERAL INSURANCE REGULATION

§ 9–5. Federal Insurance Regulation: Antidiscrimination Provisions

a. The Americans with Disabilities Act

When the Americans with Disabilities Act (ADA)[1] was adopted in 1990, it was widely believed that the Act would cabin the ability of employers and

47. See, e.g. Alaska Stat. § 21.54.100; Conn. Gen. Stat. § 38a–816; Mont. Code Ann. § 33–18–206; Wis. Stat. Ann. § 631.89.

48. Consol. L. New York Ann., Ins. L. § 3231.

49. 29 U.S.C.A. § 1181(b)(1)(B); 42 U.S.C.A. §§ 300gg(b)(1); 300gg–41.

50. 29 U.S.C.A. § 1182(a)(1)(F).

51. The EEOC has issued interpretive guidelines under which employers who discriminate against individuals on the basis of genetic traits are "regarding" those individuals as disabled, in contravention of the ADA, 3 EEOC Compliance Manual 902–45 (March 1995), but its interpretations are not binding on the courts, which have shown little regard for "regarded as" arguments.

52. Proposed Rules, DHHS, Standards for Privacy of Individually Identifiable Health Information, 64 Fed. Reg. 59,918, 60,052, 600,-055, 600,056, to be codified at 45 C.F.R. §§ 165.504, 165.506(a)(1)(i); 165.508(a)(2)(ii)(D).

insurers to vary the terms and conditions of coverage by medical condition.[2] A spate of recent cases, however, indicate that the impact of the ADA on health care financing will be very limited. The ADA raises many complex issues—what is a "disability" or who is a "qualified individual with a disability", for example, that are well beyond the scope of this section. Rather this section will be limited to issues peculiar to ADA coverage in the health insurance setting.

Title I of the ADA prohibits discrimination "against a qualified individual with a disability because of the disability of such individual in regard to * * * [the] terms, conditions, and privileges of employment."[3] Under the statute and regulations, proscribed discrimination extends to "fringe benefits."[4] Title II similarly prohibits discrimination by public entities.[5] Title III proscribes discrimination "on the basis of disability in the full and equal enjoyment of the goods, services, facilities, privileges, advantages, or accommodations of any place of public accommodation * * *."[6] "Public accommodation" is specifically defined to include an "insurance office."[7] Finally, Title V of the Act contains a specific "safe harbor" providing that the ADA is not to be construed to restrict insurers, HMOs, employers, plan or administrators from "underwriting risks, classifying risks, or administering such risks that are based on or not inconsistent with State law," as long as the entity does not use this provision "as a subterfuge to evade the purposes" of the ADA.[8]

The ADA would seem to prohibit insurers and employers administering benefit plans from imposing coverage terms and conditions that discriminate against persons with particular disabilities. Cases have been brought under the ADA, therefore, challenging policies that provided less coverage for treatment of mental than for treatment of physical conditions,[9] that capped coverage for AIDS but not for other conditions,[10] or that excluded coverage for particular services, like heart transplants[11] or infertility.[12]

---

§ 9–5

1. 42 U.S.C.A. §§ 12101–12113. The ADA applies to employers who employ 15 or more employees in each of 20 or more weeks a year. 42 U.S.C.A. § 12111(5)(A).

2. See, early commentary on the ADA and insurance issues, Michael A. Dowell, The Americans With Disabilities Act: The Responsibilities of Health Care Providers, Insurers and Managed Care Organizations, 25 J. Health & Hosp. L. 289 (1992); Ronald S. Cooper, The Treatment of Employee Benefit Programs Under the Americans with Disabilities Act of 1990, 17 J. Pension Plan. & Compliance 37 (1991); Lawrence O. Gostin, The Americans With Disabilities Act and the U.S. Health System, 11 Health Aff., Fall 1992 at 248, 253–254.

3. 42 U.S.C.A. § 12112.

4. 42 U.S.C.A. § 12112(b)(4); 29 C.F.R. § 1630.4(f).

5. 42 U.S.C.A. § 12132.

6. 42 U.S.C.A. § 12182.

7. 42 U.S.C.A. § 12181(7)(F).

8. 42 U.S.C.A. § 12201(c). See 29 C.F.R. §§ 1630.16(f) & App. to Pt. 1630, at § 1630.16(f).

9. Rogers v. Dept.of Health and Environmental Control, 174 F.3d 431 (4th Cir.1999); Ford v. Schering–Plough Corp., 145 F.3d 601 (3d Cir. 1998); EEOC v. CNA Ins. Cos., 96 F.3d 1039 (7th Cir.1996).

10. Doe v. Mutual of Omaha, 179 F.3d 557 (7th Cir.1999)

11. Lenox v. Healthwise of Ky. Ltd., 149 F.3d 453 (6th Cir.1998).

12. Krauel v. Iowa Methodist Medical Center, 95 F.3d 674 (8th Cir.1996). See D'Andra Millsap, Sex, Lies and Health Insurance: Employer–Provided Health Insurance Coverage of Abortion and Infertility Services and the ADA, 22 Am.J. Law & Med. 51 (1996).

Though some of these cases have succeeded, they have increasingly run into serious difficulties. First, several courts have held that the ADA does not require employers or insurers to offer any particular form of coverage, but merely prohibits them from offering different terms and conditions of coverage to disabled persons than those offered to nondisabled persons.[13] The ADA does not demand that all disabilities be treated similarly, but only that disabled persons be not disfavored in comparison to nondisabled persons.[14] Discrimination against coverage of particular conditions in insurance, moreover, is not even necessarily discrimination against persons with a disability unless the condition itself is a disability or unless discrimination in coverage of a particular condition disproportionately affects disabled persons. An employer or insurer who offers limited coverage for mental illness and unlimited for physical conditions is in compliance, as long as it offers the same terms and conditions of coverage to all of its employees, regardless of disability.[15] In the specific context of differential coverage of mental and physical conditions, courts have relied further on the limited scope of the mental health parity act of 1997 to support their position that Congress did not intend in the ADA to achieve sweeping parity in treatment for all conditions.[16]

Second, there is considerable debate as to when and whether the ADA applies to insurers. Though Title III clearly covers insurers, a number of courts that have addressed the issue have held that it only requires physical accessibility to insurance offices and does not extend to the terms and conditions of the products the insurers offer,[17] though the EEOC Guidelines and a number of courts have recognized that Title III might extend to the contents of insurance policies as well.[18] Of course, if insurance is offered through an employer, discrimination is prohibited under Title I even if the insurer's practices are not covered by Title III.

Third, several courts have read Title V's insurance "safe harbor" broadly to protect insurer practices that are not intentional stratagems to effectuate discrimination beyond the particular benefit at issue, following Supreme Court precedent in interpreting the term "subterfuge" in other areas.[19] Other courts, however, have required actuarial support for treating different condi-

---

13. Doe v. Mutual of Omaha Ins. Co., 179 F.3d 557 (7th Cir.1999); Ford v. Schering–Plough Corp., 145 F.3d 601 (3d Cir. 1998).

14. Lenox v. Healthwise of Ky., Ltd., 149 F.3d 453 (6th Cir.1998); Parker v. Metropolitan Life Ins. Co., 121 F.3d 1006 (6th Cir.1997) (en banc); EEOC v. CNA Insurance Co., 96 F.3d 1039 (7th Cir.1996).

15. Rogers v. Dept.of Health and Environmental Control, 174 F.3d 431 (4th cir.1999).

16. Lewis v. Kmart Corp., 174 F.3d 431, 436 (4th Cir.1999); Parker v. Metropolitan Life Ins. Co., 121 F.3d 1006, 1017–18 (6th Cir.1997) (en banc).

17. Lenox v. Healthwise of Ky., Ltd., 149 F.3d 453 (6th Cir.1998); Parker v. Metropolitan Life Ins. Co., 121 F.3d 1006 (6th Cir., 1997) (en banc). See also Pappas v. Bethesda Hosp. Assn., 861 F.Supp. 616 (S.D.Ohio 1994).

18. See, Pallozzi v. Allstate Life Ins. Co., 198 F.2d 28 (2d Cir. 1999); Carparts Distribution Ctr., Inc. v. Automotive Wholesaler's Ass'n of New England, 37 F.3d 12 (1st Cir. 1994); Winslow v. IDS Life Ins. Co., 29 F.Supp.2d 557 (D.Minn.1998); Doukas v. Metropolitan Life Ins., Co., 950 F.Supp. 422 (D.N.H.1996); Cloutier v. Prudential Ins. Co., 964 F.Supp. 299 (N.D.Cal.1997); Kotev v. First Colony Life Ins., Co., 927 F.Supp. 1316 (C.D.Cal.1996); Chabner v. United of Omaha Life Ins. Co., 994 F.Supp. 1185 (N.D.Cal.1998).

19. Ford v. Schering–Plough Corp., 145 F.3d 601 (3d Cir. 1998) and Krauel v. Iowa Methodist Medical Center, 95 F.3d 674, 678–9 (8th Cir.1996); relying on Public Employees Retirement System of Ohio v. Betts, 492 U.S. 158, 175 (1989).

tions differently, particularly when the insurance practice is also suspect under state law.[20]

Finally, the McCarran–Ferguson Act, discussed earlier, is emerging as a brooding presence in ADA insurance litigation. Some courts are reluctant to find that Congress meant to turn the job of regulating insurance underwriting practices over from the states to the federal courts in the absence of excruciating clear Congressional intent to accomplish this result—intent that is lacking in the ADA setting.[21] Again, however, the courts are not uniform in taking this position, and the force of McCarran–Ferguson is diminished where state laws parallel rather than are preempted by the ADA.[22]

The ADA is far from dead as a means of challenging egregious insurance practices. The absolute refusal of an employer or insurer to provide health insurance on the basis of disability, for example, would violate the Act.[23] Moreover, the EEOC continues to press for a broader reading of the Act to combat unjustifiable discriminatory treatment of disabling conditions. But the ADA is increasingly proving a disappointment for advocates who had hoped that it would lead to more equitable and rational insurance coverage.

b. *Other Antidiscrimination Laws*

A number of other federal laws prohibit discrimination in health insurance on other bases, though their impact is relatively modest. First, an employer covered by Title VII of the Civil Rights Act[24] cannot treat medical costs associated with pregnancy or childbirth different than other medical costs covered by its health insurance plan. Title VII of the Civil Rights Act of 1964, as amended, provides that it is unlawful for an employer to discriminate against any individual with respect to "compensation, terms, conditions, or privileges of employment," on the basis of (among other characteristics) sex.[25] The Pregnancy Discrimination Act of 1978 (PDA) defines sex discrimination to include treating pregnancy, childbirth, or related medical conditions differently from other medical conditions under fringe benefit programs.[26] If an employer offers a choice of several health insurance plans, maternity-related benefits must be offered under all plans to avoid forcing an employee to purchase a more expensive policy to obtain maternity-related coverage.[27] Maternity-related medical conditions must, therefore, be treated the same as other medical conditions under group health insurance with respect to terms of reimbursement (including payment maximums); deductibles, copayments,

---

20. Winslow v. IDS Life Ins. Co., 29 F.Supp.2d 557 (D.Minn.1998); Morgenthal v. American Telephone and Telegraph Co., 1999 WL 187055 (S.D.N.Y.1999); Chabner v. United of Omaha Life Ins. Co., 994 F.Supp. 1185 (N.D.Cal.1998); Piquard v. City of East Peoria, 887 F.Supp. 1106 (N.D.Ill.1995). The EEOC's interpretive guidelines also support the position that an employer cannot discriminate in the terms under which insurance is offered on the basis of disability unless the disparate treatment is attributable to legitimate risk classification and underwriting. EEOC, Interim Enforcement Guidelines, 12 (June 8, 1993).

21. Doe v. Mutual of Omaha Ins. Co., 179 F.3d 557 (7th Cir.1999); Ford v. Schering–Plough Corp., 145 F.3d 601 (3d Cir. 1998).

22. Winslow v. IDS Life Ins. Co., 29 F.Supp.2d 557 (D.Minn.1998).

23. Winslow v. IDS Life Ins.Co., 29 F.Supp.2d 557 (D.Minn.1998).

24. That is, an employer who employs 15 or more employees for each working day of 20 or more weeks in the current or preceding calendar year. 42 U.S.C.A. § 2000e(b).

25. 42 U.S.C.A. § 2000e–2(a)(1).

26. 42 U.S.C.A. § 2000e(k). See also, implementing EEOC Guidelines, 29 C.F.R. § 1604.10 and Appendix to Pt. 1604. This subsection does not require employers to pay for health insurance benefits for abortions, except where carrying the fetus to term would endanger the life of the mother or where medical complications have arisen from an abortion, but it does not preclude an employer from offering abortion-related benefits.

27. See 29 C.F.R. App. to Pt. 1604, Question 24.

coinsurance, and out-of-pocket maximums; preexisting condition limitations; extension of benefits following termination of employment; and limitations on freedom of choice.[28] The Supreme Court held in *Newport News Shipbuilding & Dry Dock v. EEOC*,[29] that Title VII requires employers to extend the same benefits to male employees as female. Because, therefore, the PDA requires employers that offer group health insurance to cover the maternity related expenses of female employees, group health insurance plans that insure the dependent spouses of employees must also cover the maternity-related expenses of the wives of male employees. It does not, however, extend to coverage of fertility services.[30]

Second, the Age Discrimination in Employment Act (ADEA)[31] limits the ability of employers to discriminate among employees with respect to the provision of health insurance benefits. The Older Workers Benefit Protection Act of 1990 amended the ADEA to clarify that discrimination in the provision of benefits, including health insurance benefits is prohibited.[32] The Act and implementing regulations, however, do permit employers offering bona fide benefit plans to offer older workers fewer benefits or to charge older workers more for benefits in voluntary contributory plans (as long as the proportion of total premium charged does not change with age), if the distinctions are justified by cost data and the employer does not pay less than it does for benefit plans for younger workers.[33]

Third, Section 105 of the Internal Revenue Code limits the ability of self-insured employer health plans to discriminate in favor of highly-compensated individuals.[34]

§ 9–6. Federal COBRA Continuation Coverage

One of the earliest and still most significant federal mandates with respect to insurance is found in the provisions of the Consolidated Omnibus Budget Reconciliation Act of 1985 amending ERISA to provide for the continuation of group insurance coverage for specified periods of time for certain employees and their dependents who would otherwise lose their group insurance coverage.[1] Group insurance generally costs much less than individu-

28. See 29 C.F.R. App. to Pt. 1604, Questions 25–29.

29. 462 U.S. 669, 103 S.Ct. 2622, 77 L.Ed.2d 89 (1983). See Harriet Beth Robbins-Ost, Note, The Family Unit Protected from Pregnancy Discrimination, 33 DePaul L. Rev. 545 (1984).

30. Krauel v. Iowa Methodist Medical Ctr., 95 F.3d 674 (8th Cir.1996).

31. 29 U.S.C.A. §§ 621–630. The ADEA covers employers who employ 20 or more employees in each of 20 or more weeks a year. 29 U.S.C.A. § 630(b).

32. 29 U.S.C.A. § 630(l). The Supreme Court in Public Employees Retirement System v. Betts, 492 U.S. 158, 109 S.Ct. 2854 , 106 L.Ed.2d 134(1989) had held that the ADEA did not generally prohibit discrimination in the provision of benefits. The Older Workers Bene-

fit Protection Act was adopted to overrule this case.

33. 29 U.S.C.A. § 623(f)(2)(B)(1); 29 C.F.R. § 1625.10.

34. 26 U.S.C.A. § 105(h), 26 C.F.R. §§ 1–105–5–1–105–11(c). Between 1986 and 1989 Section 89 of the Tax Reform Act of 1986 imposed broader nondiscrimination prohibitions on employment related benefit plans, including health insurance. That provision was repealed in 1989. See discussing Section 105 in greater detail, Allen R. Norris, Discrimination Rules Affecting Health Benefits and Group Term Life Insurance After the Repeal of Section 89, 16 J. Pension Planning & Compliance 147, 148–52 (1990).

§ 9–6

1. 29 U.S.C.A. §§ 1161–1168. Basically identical provisions affecting private employers

al insurance because of savings in marketing costs and because risks can be predicted with greater confidence when large groups are involved. It makes sense, therefore, to permit individuals who lose their insured status because they are laid off or because they are no longer insured dependents an opportunity to obtain continuing insurance coverage at a rate approximating the group rate for a transitional period until they can find employment and regain insured status. The administrative costs, and, in some instances the increased medical costs, incurred by employers because of continuation coverage have led to complaints, however, that COBRA unfairly imposes on employers a burden that should be borne by society generally.[2]

COBRA applies to private employers and state and local government entities that employ 20 or more employees on a typical business day and that sponsor a group health plan.[3] It applies to all group health plans, including self-insured plans, plans that offer care through managed care organizations, and dental and vision plans. COBRA protects "qualified beneficiaries" whose group insurance is terminated because of a "qualifying event." Qualified beneficiaries include covered employees and their spouses and dependent children who were plan beneficiaries on the day before the qualifying event, and children who are born or adopted during the period of continuation coverage.[4] Qualifying events entitling active employees to continuation coverage are loss of coverage because of termination from employment (other than termination because of the employee's gross misconduct) or reduction of hours.[5] Qualifying events entitling the spouses and dependent children of employees to continuation coverage include loss of coverage due to the death of the covered employee, termination of the employee's employment or reduction in hours, divorce or legal separation of the covered employee from the employee's spouse, eligibility of the employee for Medicare, or the cessation of dependent child status under the health plan.[6] Filing of bankruptcy proceedings by an employer is a qualifying event with respect to a retired employee and the employee's spouse, dependent child, or surviving spouse, where the employer substantially eliminates coverage with respect to the covered employee within one year before or after the bankruptcy filing and the employee retired before the elimination of coverage.[7]

are found in the Internal Revenue Code at 26 U.S.C.A. § 4980B. These provisions are not cited here if they are identical to those found in 29 U.S.C.A. Provisions covering state and local government employees are found at 42 U.S.C.A. §§ 300bb–1 to 300bb–8. Regulations implementing COBRA were promulgated by the IRS in 1999 and are found at 26 C.F.R. Part 54.

2. See Thomas H. Somers, COBRA: An Incremental Approach to National Health Insurance, 5 J. of Contemp. Health Law & Policy 141 (1989). See also, on COBRA generally, Oddi Jaffe & Edmund Spacapan, COBRA: Continuation of Health Benefits for Employees; Snake–in–Grass to Employers, 14 J. of Pension Planning & Compliance 197 (1988).

3. 29 U.S.C.A. § 1161; 42 U.S.C.A. § 300bb–1.

4. 29 U.S.C.A. § 1167(3), 42 U.S.C.A. § 300bb–8(3). To be eligible for continuation coverage an employee must actually have been covered as of the qualifying event, not merely eligible for insurance. Thus an employee who has elected not to be covered by a group health plan is not eligible for continuation coverage upon the occurrence of a qualifying event.

5. 29 U.S.C.A. § 1163(2); 42 U.S.C.A. § 300bb–3(2).

6. 29 U.S.C.A. § 1163; 42 U.S.C.A. § 300bb–3.

7. 29 U.S.C.A. §§ 1163(6), 1167(3)(C). Retirees are also given special protection under the bankruptcy code, including a right to the continued timely payment of benefits while the employer is in bankruptcy. 11 U.S.C.A. § 1114.

Qualified beneficiaries are entitled upon the occurrence of a qualifying event to purchase continuation coverage. Continuation coverage lasts for 18 months where the qualifying event is termination of work or reduction in hours; until the death of the retiree or qualified beneficiary (or 36 months after the death of the retiree for the retiree's surviving spouse and dependents) where the qualifying event is a bankruptcy filing; for 29 months if the employee or covered dependent is determined to be disabled within 60 days of the original qualifying event, or for 36 months for all other qualifying events.[8] If a second qualifying event occurs during the 18 months following a termination or reduction of hours, the period may be extended up to 36 months from the original qualifying event.[9] If continuation coverage is required by state law, it runs concurrently with the COBRA required coverage. The right to continuation coverage terminates before the end of the coverage period if the employer ceases to provide group health insurance to any employee; the qualified beneficiary fails to make a timely payment of the plan premium; the qualified beneficiary becomes covered under another group health plan which does not exclude or limit coverage for a preexisting condition; or the qualified beneficiary becomes eligible for Medicare (except for retirees and their spouses and dependents who qualify because of the employer's bankruptcy).[10] COBRA continuation coverage cannot be denied because the beneficiary is already covered as a dependent under another group plan.[11] At the conclusion of the coverage period, the plan must offer the beneficiary the option of enrolling in any conversion health plan generally available under the plan for 180 days prior to the termination of continuation coverage.[12] Continuation coverage cannot be based upon or limited because of lack of evidence of insurability.[13]

Benefits under continuation coverage must be identical to the coverage provided to plan beneficiaries who continue under the plan.[14] If coverage under the plan for current beneficiaries is modified, coverage for qualified beneficiaries may be modified correspondingly.[15]

The premium paid by the qualified beneficiary for continuation coverage may not exceed 102% of the total cost of the plan for similarly situated beneficiaries who continued to be covered.[16] Where the employer is self-insured, the employer may either make a reasonable estimate of plan cost for similarly situated beneficiaries on an actuarial basis or base the premium on the costs of the preceding determination period adjusted for inflation.[17] The premium is set for a period of 12 months and must be established before the

8. 29 U.S.C.A. § 1162(2); 42 U.S.C.A. § 300bb–2(2).

9. 29 U.S.C.A. § 1162(2)(A)(ii); 42 U.S.C.A. § 300bb–2(2)(A)(ii).

10. 29 U.S.C.A. § 1162(2)(B), (C), (D); 42 U.S.C.A. § 300bb–2(2)(B), (C), (D).

11. Geissal v. Moore Medical Corp., 524 U.S. 74, 118 S.Ct. 1869 (1998).

12. 29 U.S.C.A. § 1162(5); 42 U.S.C.A. § 300bb–2(5).

13. 29 U.S.C.A. § 1162(4); 42 U.S.C.A. § 300bb–2(4).

14. 29 U.S.C.A. § 1162(1); 42 U.S.C.A. § 300bb–2(1).

15. Id.

16. 29 U.S.C.A. §§ 1162(3), 1164; 42 U.S.C.A. §§ 300bb–2(3), 300bb–4. Where coverage is extended from 18 to 29 months because of the disability of the beneficiary, the premium increases to 150% of the cost of insurance for covered employees after the 18th month. Id.

17. 29 U.S.C.A. § 1164(2); 42 U.S.C.A. § 300bb–4(2).

beginning of an insured period, may not be made payable prior to 45 days after the election of coverage, and may be paid in monthly installments.[18]

§ 9–7. The Health Insurance Portability and Accountability Act

The Health Insurance Portability and Accountability Act of 1996 (HIPAA) also known as the Kennedy–Kassebaum law after its two principal Senate sponsors, Edward Kennedy and Nancy Kassebaum, amended ERISA, the Public Health Services Act, and the Internal Revenue Code, to, among other things, improve the portability and continuity of health insurance coverage in the group and individual market.[1]. The statute was born out of the least controversial remnants of the much more ambitious 1993 Clinton health reform plan.

In addition to dealing with health care plan access, portability, and renewability, HIPAA also expanded fraud and abuse prohibitions and penalties; addressed administrative simplification; and established more favorable tax treatment for medical savings accounts, long term care insurance, viatical settlements and accelerated death benefits, and state high-risk insurance pools.

Title I amends the Employment Retirement Income Security Act, the Public Health Services Act, and the Internal Revenue Code to:

1) limit the extent to which health plans may impose preexisting conditions limitations;

2) prohibit discrimination by health plans against individual participants and beneficiaries based on health status;

3) require insurers who market insurance in the small group market (to employers with 2–50 employees) to guarantee coverage and renewability to small employers who seek coverage; and

4) require insurers who sell individual insurance policies to make them available to certain individuals who had previously been covered by group policies.

Preexisting conditions clauses are commonly used by insurers to limit adverse selection—the tendency of persons who are already ill to seek out insurance. HIPAA provides that group health insurers can only impose a preexisting condition exclusion if the exclusion relates to a physical or mental condition for which medical advice, diagnosis, care, or treatment was recommended or received within the six-month period ending on the enrollment date.[2] A preexisting condition exclusion may only last for a maximum period of twelve months (or eighteen months in the case of a person who enrolls in a plan later than the time the plan is initially available to that person unless the delay was based on the fact that the enrollee was covered under COBRA

18. 29 U.S.C.A. §§ 1162(3), 1164(3); 42 U.S.C.A. §§ 300bb–2(3), 300bb–4(3).

§ 9–7

1. 29 U.S.C.A. §§ 1181–1182; 42 U.S.C.A. § 300gg–41. See Jack A. Rovner, Federal Regulation Comes to Private Health Care Financing: The Group Health Insurance Provisions of the Health Insurance Portability and Accountability Act of 1996, 7 Ann.Health L. 183 (1998); Coleen E. Medill, HIPAA and its Related Legislation: A New Role for ERISA in the Regulation of Private Health Plans, 65 Tenn. L.Rev. 485 (1998).

2. 29 U.S.C.A. §§ 1181(a)(1); 300gg(a)(1).

continuation coverage or as a dependent of another).[3] Moreover, the period of any such preexisting condition exclusion must be reduced by the aggregate of the periods of time that the beneficiary had previously been enrolled under another private or public health plan, providing that it has not been more than sixty-three days since coverage under the other policy ended.[4] In other words, if a person who has been insured under a group health plan at one job for twelve months or more moves directly into another job, covered by a different plan, without being uninsured for more than two months between jobs, the new plan cannot impose a preexisting condition exclusion.[5] Preexisting condition clauses, moreover, cannot be imposed on the basis of a genetic predisposition to a particular condition. They also cannot ordinarily be imposed with respect to newborns, adopted children, or pregnant women.[6]

Second, HIPAA prohibits insurers from discriminating against individuals in determining eligibility to enroll in a group health plan or in setting premiums for individuals within group health plans on the basis of health status-related characteristics of the insured individual or a dependent of the insured individual, including health status, medical condition (including both physical and mental illnesses), claims experience, receipt of health care, medical history, genetic information, evidence of insurability (including conditions arising out of acts of domestic violence), or disability.[7] The statute places no limits, however, on the premiums that insurers may charge the employer sponsors of groups that include disabled persons. It also, significantly, does not require plans to provide any particular benefits or any minimal level of benefits.[8]

Third, the statute stipulates that insurers that offer coverage in the small employer group market (with small employer defined as an employer with 2–50 employees) must accept every small employer in the state that applies for such coverage.[9] This rule does not apply to managed care plans with limited geographic coverage and to plans whose financial limitations require them to limit the number of persons whom they covered, as long as those plans comply with certain requirements intended to assure equitable treatment. The statute also guarantees that an insurer who agrees to provide coverage to a small group must continue to do so as long as the group sponsor meets certain requirements, including paying premiums and avoiding fraud.[10]

Fourth, HIPAA provides that each health insurance issuer that offers health insurance coverage in the individual market in a State may not refuse to offer insurance coverage to, or deny enrollment of, an individual who desires insurance, has been previously insured for at least eighteen months under a group policy, and meets other requirements.[11] The insurer must offer at least two different plans that meet certain requirements.[12] The statute does not apply in states that provide an acceptable alternative for assuring insurance coverage to individuals who lose group insurance coverage.[13] Many States

3. 29 U.S.C.A. §§ 1181(a)(2), (f)(1); 300gg(a)(2), (f)(1).

4. 29 U.S.C.A. §§ 1181(a)(3); 300gg(a)(3).

5. 29 U.S.C.A. §§ 1181(a)(3), (c); 300gg(a)(3), (c).

6. 29 U.S.C.A. §§ 1181(d); 300gg(d).

7. 29 U.S.C.A § 1182(a) & (b).

8. 29 U.S.C.A. § 1182(a)(2).

9. 42 U.S.C.A. § 300gg–11(a).

10. 42 U.S.C.A. §§ 300gg–12(a) & (b).

11. 42 U.S.C.A. §§ 300gg–41(a) & (b).

12. 42 U.S.C.A. § 300gg–41(c).

13. 42 U.S.C.A. § 300gg–44.

have done so (see 9–4 above). Plans must also guarantee reissue to individuals who purchase this insurance.[14] Again, there are no limits to the rates insurers may charge individuals.

These insurance portability statutes generally do not preempt state laws more protective of insureds. The requirements imposed by the Act are to be enforced by the states or by the federal government where the states fail to enforce the Act effectively.

HIPAA was accompanied by two smaller federal mandates. The first, required group health plans to cover at least 48 hours of hospital care in connection with a normal childbirth for the mother and newborn, and at least 96 hours of hospitalization for a Cesarean section.[15] Plans may also not impose penalties or offer incentives to limit stays, but mothers may, of course, leave the hospital before the time limits are reached, or even avoid the hospital altogether.[16] The second law forbids health plans from imposing annual or lifetime limits on mental health benefits more restrictive than those imposed on physical health benefits.[17] The law does not apply to substance abuse and chemical dependency treatment, restrict other limitations placed on mental health coverage, or even require it to be offered at all, and it expires on September 30, 2001.[18] It also permits employers to be excluded from the prohibition if they can demonstrate that complying with it would raise their costs more than one per cent.

Though HIPAA was passed with considerable fanfare, it has in fact had little impact on expanding or protecting employment-related coverage. More than one third of the states had laws on their books before HIPAA providing for guaranteed issue or renewal in small group markets and a number limited preexisting conditions clauses in group insurance contracts. While the individual coverage mandate of HIPAA goes beyond the laws of many states, at least thirty-four states have opted out of HIPAA requirements, (usually by establishing a high risk pool as an alternative)and only nine have explicitly chosen to adopt the HIPAA alternative. Even in these states, there is evidence that HIPAA is being largely circumvented by insurers, who are charging very high prices for HIPAA coverage, refusing to pay brokers commissions for selling it, delaying processing of applications to cause a break in coverage in excess of the sixty-three days permitted by the statute, or suspending issuance of individual policies during the HIPAA implementation period.[19] While only a handful of employers have sought express exemption from the mental health parity requirement that accompanied HIPAA, many offered parity before the requirement went into effect, and others have easily evaded the requirement through the use of limitations other than maximum coverage caps, such as maximum number of treatment or days of hospitalization limits.

Most importantly, however, HIPAA does nothing to require employers to provide coverage, to limit the cost of insurance premiums charged to individu-

14.   42 U.S.C.A. §§ 300gg–42(a) & (b).

15.   29 U.S.C.A. § 1185(a)

16.   29 U.S.C.A. § 1185(b).

17.   29 U.S.C.A. § 1185a(a). A third mandate, adopted later requires breast reconstruction, prosthesis and treatment of complications following mastectomies, 29 U.S.C.A. 1185b.

18.   29 U.S.C.A. §§ 1185a(b), (c)(2), (e)(4), (f),

19.   See U.S.General Accounting Office, Health Insurance Standards: New Federal Law Creates Challenges for Consumers, Insurers, Regulators, GAO/HEHS–98–67 (Feb. 1998).

als or groups, or to assure that insurance coverage that is offered is adequate in scope. In the end the Act insures continued coverage for some persons already covered by insurance, but does little to extend coverage to those who do not currently enjoy this privilege.[20]

C. REGULATION OF MANAGED CARE

§ 9–8. Regulation of Managed Care: Introduction

During the 1990s, "managed care" replaced fee-for-service insurance as the predominant mode of health care financing in the United States.[1] For much of the last decade, moreover, more restrictive forms of managed care—plans that control enrollee access to specialists, hospitals, and even emergency care through gatekeeper programs or prospective utilization review or that encourage providers to ration care through the use of capitation, withholds and bonuses—have also became prevalent (though this trend may have reversed somewhat at the end of the decade). The dramatic growth of managed care had an equally dramatic effect on restraining the growth of health care costs in the mid 1990s, though at the end of the 1990s, with most of the population moved into managed care and increasing resistance against the most restrictive forms of managed care, costs were again on the increase.[2] At the same time, however, insured Americans, not used to health care rationing, have become increasingly uncomfortable with the restrictions that managed care imposes on their access to care. This discomfort has been fed by a continual diet of media coverage of managed care disasters—instances where denial or delay of care has resulted in death or serious injury. At the close of the 1990s, therefore, managed care regulation was at the top of the health care political agenda at both the federal and state level, with managed care legislation considered by Congress and by every state in 1999.[3] The 1997 BBA, which expanded Medicare and Medicaid managed care options, also imposed new regulatory restrictions on these plans. The federal government is also proceeding with regulatory implementation of the consumer protection recommendations of the 1998 Report of the President's Advisory Commission on Consumer Protection and Quality in the Health Care Industry.[4] The issue of managed care regulation, moreover, has provoked a torrent of commentary in law reviews and political science journals.

20. See Robert Kuttner, The American Health Care System: Health Insurance Coverage, 340 New Eng.J.Med. 163 (1999); Robert Kuttner, The Kassebaum–Kennedy Bill—The Limits of Incrementalism, 337 New Eng.J. Med. 64 (1997).

§ 9–8

1. The term "managed care," as well as the terms commonly used to refer to various forms of managed care, such as "health maintenance organization" or "point of service plan" are notoriously difficult to define precisely, in large part because the arrangements they describe vary significantly from jurisdiction to jurisdiction, and indeed from plan to plan. See, e.g. James C. Robinson, The Future of Managed

Care Organizations, 18 Health Aff. March/Apr. 1999 at 7. One of the best managed care taxonomies is still Jonathan Weiner, et al., Razing a Tower of Babel: A Taxonomy for Managed Care and Health Insurance Plans, J. Health Pol., Pol'y & L 75 (1993), though it is somewhat dated at this point.

2. See Shelia Smith, et al., The Next Decade of Health Spending: A New Outlook, Health Aff. July/Aug. 1999 at 86.

3. See Managed Care Bills Top State Agendas in 1999; Legislation Pending in Every State, BNA Health Care Daily, Dec. 11, 1998.

4. Quality First: Better Health Care for All Americans (1998).

Managed care regulatory laws and proposed laws reflect a variety of regulatory concerns and political agendas.[5] At the most superficial level, they often are often knee-jerk quick-fix responses to highly publicized anecdotes and media issues de jour. The classic example of this was the response to "gag clause," managed care contracts provisions that supposedly prohibited plan physicians from discussing potentially beneficial but uncovered care with patients. After the issue of gag clauses surfaced in 1995, gag clause prohibitions were adopted by forty-seven of the states, as well as by Congress with respect to the Medicare and Medicaid managed care.[6] A 1997 GAO Report, however, was unable to find pure gag clauses in any of the 1150 contracts from 529 HMOs that it examined, though it did find confidentiality, anti-disparagement, and non-solicitation clauses, which could chill frank physician/patient discussions of possible treatments.[7] The legislative fix, however, addressed poorly the broader underlying problem.

"Body part" managed care coverage mandates, popular in the late 1990s, including legislation responding to "drive through" deliveries and mastectomies, also represents an immediate response to public outrage at particularly severe forms of managed care rationing. Other managed care mandates may reflect more traditional lobbying by providers or special interest groups, such as mandates requiring coverage of diabetic equipment, cancer screening, or off-label drug use.

Much more significant in their impact on real world managed care practice are proposals to increase the accountability of managed care coverage determination and utilization review processes.[8] Among the most important of these are proposals to subject managed care decisions to external review; to require MCOs to follow certain procedures and comply with designated time frames in internal coverage and utilization review determinations; to compel MCOs to utilize in internal review processes decisionmakers possessing certain characteristics, such as non-involvement in earlier decisions or professional licensure; to require plans to describe clearly their decisions and to disclose their basis; or even to subject plans to civil liability for the injurious consequences of their bad decisions.[9] Proposals to permit physicians to determine the "necessity" of medical care also are aimed at limiting the discretion of MCOs. These proposals have been vigorously resisted by MCOs, as they require changes in practice[10] and additional expenses for many plans, but they have been adopted in a fair number of jurisdictions.

---

5. See Donald W. Moran, Federal Regulation of Managed Care: An Impulse in Search of a Theory? Health Aff., Nov./Dec.1997 at 7.

6. See Tracy E. Miller, Managed Care Regulation: In the Laboratory of the States, 278 J.Am.Med.Assoc. 1102 (1997).

7. See GAO, Managed Care: Explicit Gag Clauses Not Found in HMO Contracts, But Physician Concerns Remain, GAO/HEHS–97–115(1997). See generally, David A. Hyman, Consumer Protection and Managed Care: With Friends Like These . . ., in Alice G. Gosfield, Health Law Handbook, 1998 Edition, 283 (1998), discussing the gag clause issue.

8. See Eleanor D. Kinney, Procedural Protections for Patients in Capitated Plans, 22

Am.J.L. & Med. 301 (1996), surveying the range of laws addressing procedural protections.

9. See, discussing this legislation, Douglas A. Hastings, Patient Rights Meet Managed Care: Understanding the Underlying Conflicts, 31 J. Health Care 241 (1998); Tracy E. Miller, Center Stage on the Patient Protection Agenda: Grievance and Appeal Rights, 26 J.L.Med. & Ethics 89 (1998).

10. A recent GAO study found many of these features missing in existing HMOs. U.S. General Accounting Office, HMO Complaints and Appeals: Most Key Procedures in Place, but Others Valued by Consumers Largely Absent, GAO/HEHS–98–119 (198)

Another group of proposals, and a great deal of academic commentary, focuses on professional accountability within health plans[11]. Managed care arrangements are increasingly altering the incentives faced by physicians, raising the specter of a breakdown of physician loyalty to the patient or of patient trust of the physician.[12] Statutory and regulatory restrictions on the use of physician incentive programs or requirements that incentive arrangements be disclosed to patients attempt to address these issues.[13]

Still other legislative proposals combat restrictions on patient "choice", that is on patient access to certain professionals or items (or on the access of professionals to patients).[14] Among the most widely adopted statutes here are provisions that prohibit plans from imposing primary care gatekeeper arrangements on women that restrict direct access to gynecologists or obstetricians. A number of states also require direct access to dermatologists or chiropractors. Also common are statutes that mandate coverage of emergency care, often requiring plans to cover emergency room care in situations where a "prudent layperson" would have believed that an emergency existed.[15] "Any willing provider" laws, usually limited to particular kinds of providers, have been common for over a decade. More recent statutes require employers of over a certain size (e.g. fifty employees) to offer point of service options if they offer closed panel HMO options. Another group of "continuity of care" statutes permit health plan enrollees to continue receiving services from providers terminated from the plan for a period of time, e.g. 90 days after termination. Many states have adopted laws placing limits on the use of restrictive drug formularies and several have prohibited health plans from requiring their enrollees to use mail order pharmacies. Finally, some states have adopted statutes providing procedural protections for providers terminated from plan participation or some form of "any willing provider legislation," again arguably to promote enrollee choice and continuity of care.[16] It is perhaps not necessary to point out that many of these provisions benefit providers at least as much as consumers, and provider organizations mount aggressive lobbying campaigns for their adoption.[17]

---

11. See, e.g., discussing these issues, M. Gregg Bloche, Clinical Loyalties and the Social Purpose of Medicine, 281 JAMA 268 (1999); Martin Gunderson, Eliminating Conflicts of Interest in Managed Care Organizations Through Disclosure and Consent, 25 J.L.Med. & Ethics, 192 (1997); Mark A. Hall, The Ethics of Managed Care: A Dose of Realism, 28 Cumberland L. Rev. 287 (1997–98); Steven D. Pearson, James E. Sabin & Ezekiel J. Emanuel, Ethical Guidelines for Physician Compensation Based on Capitation, 339 New Eng. J. Med. 689 (1998); William A. Sage, Physicians as Advocates, 35 Houston L. Rev. 1529 (1999); William M. Sullivan, What is Left of Professionalism after Managed Care, 29 29 Hastings Ctr. Rpt., March/April 1999 at 7.

12. See, describing these arrangements, Thomas Bodenheimer, The American Health Care System: Physicians and the Changing Medical Marketplace, 340 New Eng.J. Med. 584 (1999); Kevin Grumbach, et al., Primary Care Physicians' Experience of Financial In-

centives in Managed–Care Systems, 339 New Eng.J.Med. 1516 (1998).

13. See, Tracy E. Miller & William M. Sage, Disclosing Physician Financial Incentives, 281 JAMA 1424 (1999).

14. See U.S. General Accounting Office, Managed Care: State Approaches on Selected Patient Protections, GAO/T–HEHS–99–85 (1999).

15. See, critiquing these statutes, David A. Hyman, Consumer Protection in a Managed Care World: Should Consumers Call 911? 43 Vill.L.Rev. 409 (1998).

16. See John D. Blum, The Evolution of Physician Credentialing into Managed Care Selective Contracting, 22 Am.J.L.Med. 173 (1996); Mark A. Kadzielski, Provider Deselection and Decapitation in a Changing Healthcare Environment, 41 St. Louis U.L.J. 891 (1997).

17. See, e.g. E. Clarke Ross, Regulating Managed Care: Interest Group Competition for

While most legislative proposals affecting managed care take a traditional command-and-control approach, there is also considerable political support and scholarly interest in approaches that attempt to facilitate the operation of markets rather than to rely on direct regulation to address managed care abuses.[18] A number of proposals, therefore, would require plans to disclose plan characteristics (such as drug formularies) or quality audit information. The hope is that consumers will use comparative information to choose MCOs that best meet their needs, and that abusive MCOs will be driven from the market. The extent to which disclosure alone can correct for managed care abuses, particularly in markets where choice is constrained in many ways, is contested, but most consumer advocates welcome disclosure at least as an adjunct to regulation.

Another alternative approach to regulation with some support is reliance on accreditation.[19] Several accrediting agencies, including the National Council on Quality Assurance (NCQA), the Utilization Review Accreditation Council (URAC) the Joint Commission on Accreditation of Healthcare Organizations (JCAHO), and the Medical Quality Commission (TMQC) accredit some forms of MCOs.[20] Because accrediting agencies in managed care tend to include purchaser representatives, MCO accreditation is less simply self-regulation than is true in other areas of health care. Several states look to accreditation as evidence of compliance with some regulatory requirements.

Disclosure and accreditation strategies are often attempts to address the issue of quality of care in managed care. Though quality of care is much discussed in the scholarly literature,[21] it is very difficult to address through traditional regulatory approaches, except insofar as accountability might also improve quality. Several states have adopted statutes requiring health plans to have quality improvement programs or to collect and disclose quality data. Requirements that plans have internal or external grievance procedures are another attempt to provide some oversight of quality problems.

Regulators continue to worry about the most traditional insurance regulatory concern of plan solvency, an issue that periodically troubles providers and consumers when things go radically wrong with a plan. Because managed care plans are often service providers as well as a risk bearers, they cannot be treated simply like traditional insurers. This is most obviously true with provider-sponsored organizations, where professionals and providers themselves agree to deliver care to enrollees for a set capitated fee.[22] Requiring

Control and Behavioral Health Care, 24 J. Health Pol., Pol'y & L. 599 (1999).

18. See, e.g. Clark C. Havighurst, Health Care Choices: Private Contracts as Instruments of Health Reform (1995); William M. Sage, Regulating through Information: Disclosure Laws and American Health Care, 99 Column. L.Rev. 1701 (1999); Marc A. Rodwin, Consumer Protection and Managed Care: Issues, Reform Proposals, and Trade–Offs, 32 Houston L. Rev. 1319 (1996).

19. See Barry R. Furrow, Regulating the Managed Care Revolution: Private Accreditation and a New System Ethos, 43 Vill.L.Rev. 361 (1998); Robert Kuttner, Must Good HMOs

Go Bad? The Search for Checks and Balances, 338 New Eng.J.Med. 1635 (1998).

20. See Alice G. Gosfield, II Guide to Key Legal Issues in Managed Care Quality (1996).

21. See, e.g. Symposium, Quality in a Changing System, 16 Health Aff., May/June 1997 at 7ff., esp. Alice G. Gosfield, Who is Holding Whom Accountable for Quality, 16 Health Aff., May/June 1997 at 26; and Achieving Quality in Managed Care: The Role of Law (John D. Blum, ed., 1997).

22. See Allison Overbay & Mark Hall, Insurance Regulation of Providers that Bear Risk, 22 Am.J.L. & Med. 361 (1996); Linda Lamel, Significance of Risk in Direct Contracts

such organizations to maintain the same level of reserves as traditional insurers makes no sense—their continuing existence guarantees the continuing direct provision of care to enrollees—but some level of reserves may be needed to assure that continuing existence, as well as to cover carve-out services or out-of-plan care.

Finally, patients rights that have traditionally been recognized in the patient-provider relationship become regulatory issues for MCOs where the plan is involved in care delivery or oversight. Particularly troublesome here are issues of privacy and confidentiality, which are severely threatened when patient information gets out of the physician's file cabinet and into the MCO's electronic database.[23] Traditional notions of informed consent also take on a new meaning when the MCO joins the physician and patient in the treatment decisionmaking process.

State legislation is far from uniform in its classification of managed care entities for the purpose of litigation. A few states have adopted comprehensive legislation applying to all organizations that undertake health care financing functions, such as Ohio's law governing "Health Insuring Corporations."[24] More common is legislation, particularly patient's rights legislation, addressed globally to "managed care", usually defined in terms of the use of financial incentives to limit access to care.[25] A number of states have also adopted the term "health plan" from the federal HIPAA as a term for defining regulatory scope, particularly in the context of state legislation implementing HIPAA. However, state regulatory schemes still predominantly address more or less separately the three classic forms of managed care—health maintenance organizations (including point of service option plans); preferred provider arrangements; and utilization review entities. A number of states have also recently supplemented this legislation with statutes regulating providers sponsored organizations or networks (PSOs or PSNs).[26] We will, therefore, address these regulatory schemes separately.

§ 9–9. Regulation of Utilization Review

The earliest managed care cost control strategy to achieve widespread acceptance was utilization review or management. As early as 1991, 38% of employees enrolled in employment-related health benefits plans belonged to a fee-for-service insurance plan with a utilization review component, while another 54% belonged to managed care organizations, which at that time often depended on utilization review as a primary strategy for controlling the services provided by their network members. Only 8% belonged to a conventional plan with no utilization review.[1] By the end of the 1990s utilization review had been supplemented by a variety of incentive arrangements that

with Health Providers, in Achieving Quality, supra note 21; Douglas J. Witten, Regulation of "Downstream": and Direct Risk Contracting by Health Care Providers: The Quest for Consumer Protection and a Level Playing Field, 23 Am.J.L. & Med. 449 (1997).

23. See, e.g. David M. Studdert, Direct Contracts, Data Sharing and Employee Risk Selection: New Stakes for Patient Privacy in Tomorrow's Health Insurance Markets, 25 Am. J.L. & Med. 233 (1999).

24. Ohio Rev. Code §§ 1751.01—1751.71.

25. See, e.g. Ark.Code Ann. § 23–99–403(6); Id. Stat. 41–3903(15); Nev. Rev. Stat. § 695G.040.

26. See section 9–12 infra.

§ 9–9

1. Cynthia Sullivan, et al., Employer–Sponsored Health Insurance in 1991, 11 Health Aff., Winter 1992 at 176.

moved rationing responsibilities from the health plan to the health provider, but most insureds still belonged to PPO or conventional plans that relied predominantly on utilization review for controlling the volume of services consumed, while fee-for-service indemnity plans without utilization review had essentially disappeared.

Utilization review usually refers to external case by case evaluation to determine the necessity and appropriateness (and sometimes the quality) of medical care. It is a strategy that attempts to control costs by limiting demand. The utilization review strategy for cost-containment is based on the knowledge that there are wide variations in the use of many medical services, and the belief that careful review of the use of medical care can eliminate wasteful and unnecessary care, and might eliminate some care that is actually harmful.

Utilization review can take several forms, including prior review, concurrent review and high cost case management. Prior and concurrent review techniques include preadmission review (before elective hospital admissions); admission review (within 24 to 72 hours of emergency or urgent admissions); continued stay review (to assess length of stay in health care institutions and sometimes accompanied by discharge planning); preprocedure or preservice review (to review specific proposed procedures); and voluntary or mandatory second-opinions. High-cost case management addresses a small number (1%–7%) of very expensive cases that may account for 30% to 60% of benefit plan costs. Under these programs, case managers create individualized treatment plans for high-cost beneficiaries. Compliance with the plan is usually voluntary, but may be rewarded by the plan paying for services not otherwise covered by the plan (such as home health or nursing home care) but less costly than covered alternatives. The traditional concern of utilization review has been to assure that care is provided in the least expensive appropriate setting and that hospitalization is not unnecessarily prolonged. More recently, utilization review has also considered the necessity or appropriateness of particular procedures.

Utilization review can be conducted by free-standing utilization review contractors, by payers (employers and insurers, with or without direct contracts with providers) or by providers. Review is usually initiated by plan beneficiaries, or by physicians or hospitals who are aware that admissions or procedures must be preapproved to secure payment. Requests for approval are usually first reviewed by nurses or other reviewers who apply established criteria (often computerized) to determine appropriateness. The reviewers may approve care, but if the care does not comply with applicable criteria, the case must usually be referred to a physician adviser for denial. Physician advisers will often contact the treating physician and negotiate an appropriate care plan, though some plans deny payment without direct contact with the treating physician. Plans usually have a formal or informal appeals process or provide other opportunity for further discussion of proposed denials.[2]

2. See generally Institute of Medicine, Controlling Costs and Changing Patient Care? The Role of Utilization Management (1989).

Health plans that have employed utilization review have experienced reduced inpatient hospital use and inpatient care expenditures.[3] It is less clear that utilization review reduces total health care costs, since it often moves care from inpatient to outpatient settings. Moreover, utilization review is most effective in the short run and has less effect on long-term cost increases. Nevertheless, it is one of the most acceptable cost-containment strategies to employers and employees, and thus has proved more popular than other, more drastic, strategies.

Though utilization review has proved popular with employers, it has proved decidedly unpopular with others. Doctors have objected to utilization review decisions that second-guess their treatment decisions, especially when the utilization review decision is made by a physician not qualified in their specialty (or, even worse, by a nonphysician), and when the decision is communicated to their patients. They are also upset by the paperwork that utilization review imposes upon them. Mental health care professionals and providers in particular, have seen their caseloads decline precipitously under utilization review controls. Patients have experienced seemingly arbitrary denials of payment by their insurers, occasionally with disastrous results.

State legislatures responded quickly to these concerns. Maryland adopted the first law regulating utilization review in 1988. By the fall of 1998, 36 states had adopted statutes regulating at least some aspects of utilization review.[4]

Many of the provisions of utilization review legislation are fairly uniform and noncontroversial. Statutes usually require that utilization review information be kept confidential.[5] Statutes commonly require that firms provide information about their procedures to providers and health plan enrollees[6] and disclose to the state the qualifications of their employees and contractors.[7] Statutes also commonly impose time limits on utilization review determinations,[8] and in particular require expedited decisions or automatic coverage in emergencies.[9]

Thirty-two statutes require an appeal process,[10] and some an expedited appeal process in emergencies.[11] Eight require additional external appeals.[12] Some also authorize judicial review of utilization review decisions.[13]

3. One of the best studies found that it reduced admission of patients by 12.3%, inpatient days by 8%, and hospital expenditures by 11.9%. In particular, it reduced patient days by 34% and hospital expenditures by 30% for groups that had previously had high admission rates. Paul J. Feldstein, et al., Private Cost Containment: The effects of Utilization Review Programs on Health Care Use and Expenditures, 318 New Eng. J. Med. 1310, 1310 (1988).

4. See American Accreditation Healthcare Commission/Utilization Review Accreditation Commission, Survey of State Utilization Review Laws and Regulations (1998) (hereafter "AAHC/URAC").

5. E.g., Ark. Code Ann. § 20–9–909(4): Md. Code, Health–Gen. § 19–1305(a)(4); Miss. Code §§ 41–83–9(1)(d), 41–83–17.

6. E.g., Ark. Code Ann. § 20–9–909(5); Official Code of Ga.Ann. § 33–46–5(b)(3).

7. Ark. Code Ann. § 20–9–909(2): Miss. Code § 41–83–9(1)(b).

8. West's Ann.Ind. Code § 27–8–17–11 (2 days to respond to phone calls, two days to make determination once information received); S.C. Code § 38–70–20(c)(1) (5 business days).

9. Official Code of Ga.Ann. § 33–46–4(2) (immediate admission in emergencies if medical necessity is subsequently documented); West's Ann.Ind. Code § 27–8–17–11(9) (enrollee has 48 hours to contact reviewer in emergency), Ind. Code Ann. § 27–8–17–12(c) (appeals in emergency cases must be decided within 48 hours); Vernon's Ann.Mo.Stat. § 374.510.1(3),(7) (utilization reviewer must allow 48 hours for patient to notify the reviewer, must make decision in 2 days, and must permit immediate admission where a physician determines the situation to be life-threatening).

10. AAHC/URAC, supra note 4; See, e.g., Miss. Code § 41–83–9(1)(a).

One of the most controversial issues in the regulation of utilization review has been the role of physicians in the utilization review process. Those who support direct and intimate involvement of physicians in the utilization review process argue that only physicians are qualified to understand and comment on the treatment decisions of other physicians. Some go even further, and would require that reviewing physicians be specialty matched to those whose decisions they review. The AMA supports review performed by or under the close supervision of physicians and based on criteria developed by physicians. The utilization review industry, on the other hand, argues that proposals that physicians be involved continuously throughout the review process reflect physician arrogance and add unnecessary expense to the review process. As long as physician review is available at some point in the process, they argue, physicians need not be involved at every step.

Statutes vary in their response to this controversy, though they generally take a moderate approach. Quite common are requirements that initial decisions be made by a physician or appropriate licensed professional or in accordance with standards approved by a physician or professional.[14] Also common are requirements that physicians review all denials,[15] or be involved in decisions involving particular kinds of care. Twenty-six states mandate that only physicians (or their clinical peers) may render adverse decisions.[16] At least one state court has held that a physician making utilization review decisions involving medical treatment is engaged in the practice of medicine and subject to regulatory oversight by the medical licensure board.[17] Seven states require that health care professionals involved in utilization review be licensed in the state in which they are conducting review activities.[18]

A second major controversy has involved the accessibility of the standards and criteria utilization reviewers apply in making decisions. Physicians believe that access to this information is essential for understanding and contesting utilization review decisions. The AMA supports mandatory disclosure of utilization review criteria to physicians. Utilization review companies, on the other hand, resist disclosure of this information, both because they regard it as proprietary and because they fear that its disclosure will lead to gaming the system. Statutes span the spectrum from requiring full disclosure to the public or to providers;[19] to requiring disclosure of information to the regulatory agency, which will protect the information from further disclosure;[20] to requiring that in any particular utilization review encounter the physician be given sufficient information to allow a challenge to the decision.[21]

11. E.g., La.Stat.Ann.—Rev.Stat. § 40:2727(D)(3); Minn. Stat. Ann. § 62M.06.2; Tenn. Code Ann. § 56–6–705(a)(4)(C).

12. AAHC/URAC, supra note 4, at 14. Additional states may require external appeals through other managed care laws. Id.

13. E.g., Miss. Code § 41–83–23.

14. E.g., La.Stat.Ann.—Rev.Stat. § 40:2727[B]; Vernon's Ann.Mo.Stat. § 376.1361[2].

15. E.g., Vernon's Ann.Mo.Stat. § 376.1361[2].

16. AAHC/URAC, supra note 4, at 13.

17. Murphy v. Board of Medical Examiners, 1997 WL 393091 (Ariz.App. Div. 1997).

18. AAHC/URAC, supra note 4, at 14.

19. See, e.g., Official Code of Ga.Ann. § 33–46–4(1).

20. E.g., Ark. Code Ann. §§ 20–9–906(a)(2); V.A.T.S., Ins. Code art. 21.58A, § 4(i).

21. E.g., V.A.T.S., Ins. Code art. 21.58A § 5(1c).

Twenty-five states establish requirements for the clinical review criteria on which utilization review decisions are based, including several states also provide that standards and criteria should be based on input from practicing physicians.[22]

Eleven states require utilization review organizations to have quality assurance programs.[23] Nineteen states have laws prohibiting utilization review organizations form offering their reviewers financial incentives based on the number or rate of adverse determinations.[24]

Twenty-eight states require licensure, registration or certification for entities conducting utilization review.[25] The utilization review industry has formed an accrediting agency, the Utilization Review Accreditation Commission, and has sought a role for it in utilization review equivalent to the role of the Joint Commission for Accreditation of Health Care Organizations in hospital regulation.[26] To date, fourteen states provide waivers or exemptions from licensure or registration requirements for utilization review firms accredited by URAC or other recognized accreditors.[27]

Common law tort liability of utilization review organizations is discussed in Chapter 7. Several of the regulatory statutes address the issue of liability of utilization reviewers, a few directly, others more obliquely. Statutes in Texas, California and Georgia provide that managed care organizations can be held liable for injuries caused by adverse utilization review decisions. The Arkansas and Louisiana statutes, for example, provide that they are not intended to reduce or expand the liability for utilization review activities.[28] The Virginia statute states that it is not intended to create a private right of action against utilization reviewers.[29]

An organization that conducts utilization review may also be sued for breach of contract or for bad faith breach of contract if an inappropriate denial of care results in injury. If the reviewer is independent of the payer and thus not in privity with the beneficiary, the beneficiary might sue the payer for breach of its contract with the beneficiary. Alternatively, the beneficiary might sue the reviewer, claiming third party beneficiary status to the contract between the payer and reviewer.[30] Physicians whose care has been determined to be "unnecessary" or "inappropriate" by an insurer have also in some cases been permitted to sue the reviewer for defamation or interference with a contractual relationship.[31] ERISA preemption, of course, bars suits against ERISA benefit plan administrators and sponsors.

22. AAHC/URAC, supra note 4 at 13. See, e.g., V.A.T.S., Ins. Code art. 21.58A § 4(i).

23. AAHC/URAC, supra note 4, at 7.

24. Id.

25. AAHC/URAC, supra note 4, at 13.

26. See id. at 8–11, describing the formation and history of URAC.

27. Id. at 14. See e.g., Conn. Gen. Stat.Ann. § 38a–226d; West's Ann.Ind. Code § 27–8–17–14; Neb. Rev. Stat. § 44–5420; N.D.Cent. Code § 26.1–26.4–04; R.I. Gen. Laws § 23–17.12–8; Tenn. Code Ann. § 56–6–705(a).

28. Ark. Code Ann. § 20–9–914; La.Stat. Ann.—Rev.Stat. § 40:2733.

29. Va. Code § 32.1–138.14.

30. See Helverstine, Legal Implications of Utilization Review in Institute of Medicine, supra note 2 at 179–181.

31. See Slaughter v. Friedman, 185 Cal. Rptr. 244, 649 P.2d 886 (Cal.1982); Teale v. American Mfrs. Mutual Ins. Co., 687 S.W.2d 218 (Mo.App.1984).

§ 9–10.   Regulation of Health Maintenance Organizations

a.   Federal Regulation of HMOs

A Health Maintenance Organization (HMO) is an entity that provides comprehensive health care services to an enrolled membership for a fixed, per capita, fee. HMOs are thus both insurers and providers of medical care. HMOs are traditionally classified into four categories based on their relationship with medical care providers: staff model HMOs directly employ physicians to provide medical care; group model HMOs contract with an independent, multi-specialty corporation or partnership of physicians to deliver care; network HMOs contract with a number of groups of physicians who also may serve patients not belonging to the HMO; and individual practice association (IPA) HMOs contract with an IPA, which in turn contracts with individual physicians to provide care in their own offices. A 1990 study found that 8.8% of HMO enrollees were in staff model HMOs, 21.6 in group and network models, and 67.1% in IPAs.[1]

HMOs are governed by both state and federal law. Most states have HMO enabling acts, which address both the insurance and health care delivery aspects of HMOs. A federal statute adopted in 1973 to encourage the growth of HMOs, establishes federal recognition of HMOs as well.[2]

The federal law imposes substantial burdens on federally qualified plans. To qualify under the federal law, HMOs must offer comprehensive benefits. At least 90% of physician services provided by the plan (other than unusual or emergency services) must be provided by physicians associated with the plan.[3] A federally qualified HMO must make health services available and accessible with reasonable promptness, and when medically necessary, 24 hours a day and 7 days a week, and reimburse members for emergency services obtained elsewhere.[4] Services must be provided for a fixed premium, except for nominal cost-sharing amounts, deductibles for services received out of plan, and amounts collected from liability insurance or workers compensation.[5] Equivalent premiums must be charged for individuals and families of the same composition within groups, but rates from groups can be experience rated prospectively subject to some limitations.[6]

Organizationally, federally qualified HMOs must be fiscally sound and make adequate provision against insolvency; assume financial risk for the provision of services to their members (subject to specified provisions for reinsurance); enroll persons who are demographically representative of the service area (with not more than 75% of the members being medically undeserved individuals) and accept Medicaid beneficiaries; not expel or refuse to re-enroll members because of health status or needs; provide grievance procedures; establish outcome based quality assurance measures; make speci-

§ 9–10

1.   Elizabeth W. Hoy, et al., 10 Health Aff., Winter 1991 at 18, 22–23.

2.   42 U.S.C.A. §§ 300e to 300e–17. See also 42 C.F.R. §§ 417.100–417.166. On federal policy regarding HMOs, see Lawrence D. Brown, Politics and Health Care Organizations: HMOs as Federal Policy (1983).

3.   42 U.S.C.A. § 300e(b)(3).

4.   42 U.S.C.A. § 300e(b)(4).

5.   42 U.S.C.A. § 300e(b)(1).

6.   42 U.S.C.A. §§ 300e(b)(1), (2), 300e–1(8). Full-time college students are excepted from the community rating requirement. 42 U.S.C.A. § 300e(b)(1)(C).

fied arrangements for protecting members if the organization becomes insolvent; and develop, evaluate, and report performance statistics.[7]

b. State Regulation of HMOs

As HMOs began to emerge as a significant force in health care in the early 1970s, they faced significant barriers in state laws. HMOs resembled insurers, yet the reserve and liquidity requirements commonly imposed on health insurers by state law posed a substantial obstacle to the creation of HMOs. State corporate practice or medicine doctrines called into question some HMO arrangements while certificate of need laws were used to impede the growth of other HMOs.[8] The need became apparent for state enabling acts crafted specifically to regulate, and facilitate, HMOs.

Legislation authorizing and defining HMOs currently exists in virtually every state.[9] This legislation varies dramatically in length and complexity, consisting of a few brief sections in smaller states with minimal HMO penetration, but running on for page after page in states like California and Florida, which have large HMO industries and have encountered serious problems at times with regulating HMOs.[10] The term "HMO" tends to be used in regulatory statutes, as in the popular press, to broadly include a wide range of arrangements through which care is provided comprehensively on a prepaid basis, directly or contractually through a network of affiliated providers.[11] HMOs are commonly regulated by both the Department of Insurance and the Department of Health, which respectively oversee the insurer and provider functions of HMOs. The legislation of most of the states is patterned after model legislation drafted by the NAIC, first proposed in 1972. The NAIC, working together with the National Association of HMO Regulators (NAHMOR), has been quite influential in the area of HMO regulation.

The NAIC Model Act addresses many of the same concerns addressed by the federal legislation. Under the Model Act, an HMO must have a certificate of authority to do business in the state.[12] The application for the certificate must be accompanied by a variety of information, including copies of provider contracts, financial statements and feasibility plans, a description of the HMO's grievance procedures and quality assurance plan, and a list of all providers with whom the HMO contracts.[13] HMOs must establish on-going internal quality assurance programs, including procedures for problem identification, corrective action, and interpretation and analysis of patterns of care rendered to individual patients by individual providers.[14] HMO contracts must disclose information on a variety of topics including emergency care benefits, out of area benefits, copayments and deductibles, limitations and exclusions,

---

7. 42 U.S.C.A. § 300e; 42 C.F.R. § 417.106.

8. See Institute of Medicine, Health Maintenance Organizations: Toward a Fair Market Test (1974).

9. An excellent description of this legislation is found in Mark S. Joffe, Current Developments in State and Federal Regulation of Managed Care Organizations, in National Health Lawyers Association, The Insider's Guide to Managed Care, 37, 42–52 (1990).

10. See on the Florida legislation, Jack F. Monahan & Michael Willis, Special Legal Status for HMOs: Cost Containment Catalyst or

Marketplace Impediment? 18 Stetson L. Rev. 353 (1989); Ahern, The Evolution and Impact of State HMO Regulation: A Case Study, 10 J. Ins. Reg. 110 (Fall 1991).

11. See, e.g. Col.Stat.Ann. § 10–16–102(23); Fla.Stat.Ann. § 641.19(13); Ann.Ind. Code § 27–13–1–19.

12. NAIC, Health Maintenance Organization Act of 1990, § 3.A.

13. Id. at § 3.C.

14. Id. at § 7.

grievance procedures, and conversion and extension of benefits provisions, and not be misleading or deceptive.[15] HMOs must provide grievance procedures for their enrollees, and maintain records of complaints for review by the state.[16] The Act requires the protection of confidentiality of patient records and creates an HMO peer review evidentiary privilege and liability immunity.[17]

Whether or not state HMO laws are expressly based on the NAIC Model Act, they generally contain provisions similar to those found in it. The most significant deviation from the Model Act is found in increasingly frequent mandates requiring HMOs to cover various types of treatment or of treatment by various providers, discussed in the previous section. Most of the managed care consumer and provider protection statutes discussed above also apply to HMOs.

A particular concern of regulatory agencies is the financial solvency of HMOs. Several states have established HMO guaranty funds to supplement other insolvency protections.[18] Another concern is advertising and marketing practices, which some state laws regulate more specifically than the Model Act.[19]

Tort litigation against HMOs is discussed in Chapter 7.

§ 9–11. Regulation of Preferred Provider Arrangements

A preferred provider arrangement (PPA) (also known as a preferred provider organization or PPO) is an organized system of health care providers who agree to provide services on a negotiated basis to subscribers. PPA subscribers are not limited to using professionals and institutions with plan contracts (as they would be in a traditional HMO) but face financial disincentives, such as deductibles or larger copayments, if they choose non-preferred providers. PPAs usually pay providers on a fee-for-service basis, in contrast to HMOs which more commonly pay on a capitation basis. PPAs usually have utilization review and sometimes quality assurance, requirements. PPAs may be sponsored by hospitals, physician groups, commercial insurers, Blue–Cross/Blue Shield plans, investors, union trusts, or others.

PPAs offer employers potential cost controls through negotiated rate discounts and utilization review. Some PPAs further enhance their ability to control costs by attempting to select providers on the basis of cost-consciousness or by using primary care gate-keepers to control access to specialists. At the same time, PPAs offer employees a wider choice of providers than do HMOs, and access to any provider if the employee is willing to assume the additional costs imposed for out-of-plan providers. PPAs often also offer employees greater coverage of preventive care than do conventional plans. They are more acceptable to many physicians than are HMOs—since they pay on a fee-for-service basis—and more attractive than conventional plans because they offer preferred access to the beneficiary pool and more efficient

15. Id. at § 8.
16. Id. at § 11.
17. Id. at § 28.
18. See West's Fla. Stat. Ann. §§ 641.227, 641.228; 215 ILCS 125/4–7.

19. West's Ann.Cal. Health & Safety Code §§ 1359–1966; West's Fla. Stat. Ann. § 641.3901, 641.3903; Mich. Comp. Laws Ann. § 333.21054s, 333.21054t.

claims processing than that offered by conventional plans. They are also very attractive to hospitals, which see them as an opportunity to increase occupancy by securing patient and preferred physician allegiance. PPAs grew rapidly in the late 1980s and have continued to grow into the late 1990s. They now cover 35% of insured employees.[1]

A preferred provider arrangement, in contrast to an HMO, is not so much an entity as a manner of organizing and paying for health care services. As was noted earlier, most PPAs are not free-standing, but are rather offered as managed care products by existing entities, such as insurers, Blue Cross/Blue Shield plans, or employers. Thus, while legislation is necessary to permit the organization of HMOs, it is not strictly necessary to authorize the creation of a PPA. Nevertheless, 35 states have some level of PPO regulation, and 13 have reasonably comprehensive legislation.[2]

PPA authorization statutes exist for two reasons. First, without them PPAs might have historically violated existing law in many states.[3] "Freedom of choice" or "any willing provider" statutes, found in many states, prohibited insurers from requiring that services be provided by a particular hospital or person.[4] These laws potentially barred insurer-sponsored PPAs from encouraging their members to choose preferred providers.[5] The insurance antidiscrimination laws of some states also prohibited insurers from unfairly discriminating among covered individuals in the level of premiums, fees, or benefits.[6] These laws could be used to challenge the ability of PPAs to limit benefits based on choice of preferred or nonpreferred providers. Finally, the statutes of several states prohibited insurers from paying different rates to different providers, or hospitals from charging different rates to different insurers, unless the differentials are cost-justified.[7] Such laws would make the preferential provider contracting on which PPAs are based questionable.

Second, states have adopted PPA authorization legislation to protect consumers, and often providers, from perceived abuses of PPAs. In authorizing PPAs, therefore, these laws also place limits, often severe, on the ability of PPAs to choose among providers and on the incentives and disincentives

§ 9–11

1. Employee Benefits: Health Costs Rose Nearly Twice as Fast as Medical CPI in 1998, Mercer Survey Finds, BNA Health Care Daily, Jan. 26, 1999).

2. American Healthcare Accreditation Commission/URAC, The PPO Guide, 27 (Garry Carneal, ed., 1999) (hereafter AAHC/URAC). A serious problem in locating and classifying these laws is that there is no universally understood definition of Preferred Provider Arrangement or Organization, and a number of states use other terms to denominate PPAs, such as "health plan," "managed care plan," "network plan carrier" or "prudent purchaser contract." Id. at 29–30.

3. See, I and II, Elizabeth S. Rolph, et al., State Laws and Regulations Governing Preferred Provider Organizations (1986); Elden & Hinden, Legal Issues in Creating PPOs, 1 J. L. & Health, 1, 23–25 (1985–86); Thomas Greaney, Competitive Reform in Health Care: The Vulnerable Revolution, 5 Yale J. Reg. 179, 185–189 (1988); Elizabeth Rolph, et al., The Regulation of Preferred Provider Arrangements, Health Aff., Fall 1987 at 32; Comment, Cost v. Quality in the Regulation of Preferred Provider Arrangements: A "Green Light to the Gold Rush?" 41 Southwestern L. J. 1155 (1988).

4. See e.g., Official Code of Ga.Ann. § 33–18–17; Ky.Rev. Stat. § 304.18–040; Or. Rev. Stat. § 743.531(2)(b).

5. The Federal Trade Commission has taken the position that such laws deny consumers potential cost-savings. See FTC Staff Encourages Sunset of State's "Any Willing Provider" Section of PPO Law, 2 BNA Health L. Rep. 196 (2/18/93).

6. See e.g., Elizabeth S. Rolph, et al., State Laws and Regulations Governing Preferred Provider Organizations, Executive Summary, 10 (1986).

7. Rolph, supra note 6, at 10.

PPAs can include to encourage use of preferred providers and discourage use of others. PPA statutes also commonly require disclosure of contract terms, require quality assurance, and regulate utilization review to protect members from abuses that the incentives PPAs could cause. Finally, state laws are particularly concerned with the regulation of PPAs that bear risk, and thus resemble insurers or risk-bearing managed care organizations.[8]

Fourteen states require PPOs to be licensed or certified.[9] This license is usually obtained from the Commissioner of Insurance. Eight of the states requiring licensure impose solvency requirements as a condition of licensure.[10] Some states that do not require licensure impose registration requirements instead.[11]

PPA authorization statutes often impose some limitations on the ability of PPAs to limit providers with which they contract. Some statutes require PPAs to permit "any willing provider," who will accept the terms offered by the plan to participate.[12] Some go further, requiring PPAs to give notice to providers in the PPA's coverage area of the opportunity to participate, to give reasons for denial of preferred status, or to offer appeal procedures to rejected providers.[13] Others require plans to consider, though not necessarily accept, the application of all providers.[14]

More common are statutes permitting PPAs to choose among providers as long as the choice is based on reasonable criteria, such as economic, quality, and accessibility criteria.[15] Some of these statutes specify that price differences can be based on negotiated rates or market conditions.[16] The most liberal statutes simply require that PPAs not discriminate among providers on prohibited grounds, such as religion, race, sex, national origin, or marital status.[17] The statutes of a number of states further prohibit plans from discriminating on the basis of type of provider, offering nonphysicians the same privileges as physicians.[18] Finally, a few states also prohibit PPAs from limiting participating providers from also participating in other PPAs.[19] Many believe that laws that limit the ability of PPAs to contract selectively with providers serve little purpose except to preserve the interests of the providers, and limit the use of competitive contracting to control costs.[20]

---

8. See AAHC/URAC, supra note 2, at 30–31.

9. AAHC/URAC, supra note 2, at 31. Where PPOs are administered by insurers, of course, all states require the insurer to be licensed.

10. Id.

11. Id.

12. See e.g., West's Ann. Ind. Code § 27–8–11–3(c); Neb. Rev. Stat. § 44–4111; Wyo. Stat. § 26–22–503.

13. See N.C. Gen. Stat. § 58–50–55 (notice and reason for denial); Tex.Admin. Code tit. 28, § 3.3703(1) (notice and appeal procedures); Utah Code Ann. § 31A–22–618 (hearing by commissioner). The Maine statute requires a public hearing before a PPA can be established if the Superintendent of Insurance decides to hold one or if one is requested by an interested party. Me. Rev. Stat. Ann. tit. 24A § 2675.

14. See e.g., West's Ann. Cal. Ins. Code § 10180; Tex. Admin. Code tit. 28 § 3.3703(1) (health care providers "may apply for and shall be afforded a fair, reasonable, and equivalent opportunity to become preferred providers.")

15. Mass. Gen. Laws Ann. ch. 176I, § 4 (cost, availability and quality). Some statutes prohibit a plan from requiring that a provider have staff privileges as a criteria for selection. Mont. Code Ann. § 33–22–1705(2).

16. 215 ILCS 5/370h; West's Ann. Ind. Code § 27–8–11–3(b).

17. N.H. Rev. Stat. Ann. § 420–C:5.

18. Neb. Rev. Stat. § 44–4112; Va. Code § 38.2–3407.

19. Wis. Stat. Ann. § 628.36.2(b)[2]. The Texas regulations also prohibit PPAs from contracting with hospitals that require PPA membership as a condition of staff privileges. Tex. Admin. Code tit. 28 § 3.3703(2).

Some PPA statutes also limit the ability of PPAs to encourage their members to use the services of preferred providers. Statutes generally require PPAs to cover emergency care at preferred provider payment levels, whether or not it is provided by a preferred provider.[21] Some also require plans to pay for medically necessary care provided by an out-of-plan provider at the preferred rate if it is not available from a preferred provider or to assure continuity of care for treatment underway at the time a participant enrolls in a plan.[22] Most statutes also place limits on financial incentives and disincentives. These either limit deductible and coinsurance amounts imposed for utilization of non-preferred providers or limit differences in payment between preferred and non-preferred providers, usually in terms of percentage differences.[23] Several states expressly prohibit exclusive provider arrangements, which provide no coverage for out of plan providers.[24]

PPA statutes commonly require that plans make medical services reasonably accessible to their members.[25] In rural states access requirements are sometimes defined in terms of distances that must be traveled or travel times necessary to get to providers.[26] Some states expressly outlaw gatekeeper arrangements, whereby access to specialists is contingent on referral by a participating primary care physician.[27] Several states also attempt to regulate utilization review practices[28] or payment arrangements (such as payment by capitation[29] or systems that put a gatekeeper at risk for the cost of specialist services[30]) intended to limit unreasonable restraints on access to care.

Most state PPA statutes require that the plans provide their members with lists of preferred providers and information on the costs of choosing out-of-plan providers.[31] PPA laws also frequently require reporting of information to the state insurance commissioner.[32] Twenty-six states have laws requiring

20. See, discussing these statutes, Thomas L. Greaney, Competitive Reform in Health Care: The Vulnerable Revolution, 5 Yale J. Reg. 179, 185–189 (1988).

21. Official Code of Ga. Ann. § 33–30–24; Mass. Gen. Laws Ann. ch. 176I, § 3(b); N.D. Cent. Code § 26.1–47–03.

22. Nev. Rev. Stat. § 689B.061[7]; N.D. Cent. Code § 26.1–47–03[1][b]; Wis. Stat. Ann. § 609.20(2).

23. Official Code of Ga. Ann. § 33–30–23(b)(3), (4) (only 30% difference in cost-sharing permitted between preferred and non-preferred providers, subject to a maximum cost-sharing of 40% for non-preferred providers); Mass. Gen. Laws Ann. ch. 176I, § 3(a) (benefit levels for nonpreferred providers shall be at least 80% of levels for preferred providers).

24. Ga. Regs. § 120–2–44–.05(3); Tex. Admin. Code tit. 28, § 3.3703. Michigan permits EPO plans only if an alternative non PPA plan is available for groups of 25 or more members, Mich. Comp. Laws Ann. §§ 500.3405, 500.3631.

25. Twenty-nine states impose such requirements, AAHP/URAC, supra note 2, at 32. See, e.g., Off. Code Ga. Ann. 33–30–23(b)(5); West's Ann. Ind. Code § 28–9–11–4. The Mich-

igan law requires preferred providers to conspicuously post a list of PPA panels of which the provider is a member. Mich. Comp. Laws Ann. § 550.55.

26. See e.g., Me. Rev. Stat. Ann. tit. 24–A § 2673[2]; N.D. Cent. Code § 26.1–47–03; Wis. Stat. Ann. § 609.20(1).

27. Tex. Admin. Code tit. 28 § 3.3703(3); Wyo. Stat. § 26–22–503(b). Pennsylvania has separate regulations for gate-keeper arrangements. Pa. Admin. Code §§ 152.102–152.105.

28. Mass. Regs. Code tit. 211 § 51.07(8); Wisconsin Admin. Code § 3.3705. Some states also require utilization review. N.D. Cent. Code § 26.1–47–02.

29. The Massachusetts regulations permit capitation, but require that the plan regularly assess the financial condition of risk-bearing providers. Mass. Code Regs. tit. 211 § 51.07(7)(j).

30. Tex. Admin. Code tit. 28 § 3.3703.

31. See e.g., 215 ILCS 5/370m; Me. Rev. Stat. Ann. tit. 24A § 2675; Mass. Code Regs. tit. 211 § 51.04(h).

32. See e.g., Mass. Gen. Laws Ann. ch. 176I, § 2; Mich. Comp. Laws Ann. § 550.56.

complaint or grievance procedures.[33] Twenty-three states have laws protecting the confidentiality of member information.[34] Eighteen states have laws requiring PPAs to credential health care practitioners to assure their competence, though these laws vary significantly in their comprehensiveness.[35] Finally, the statutes of twenty-three states require quality management programs, sometimes requiring that these be physician led.[36]

There has been a substantial amount of litigation in recent years challenging PPAs that have failed to pass negotiated discounts on to members in the form of reduced copayments. In these situations, members who were obligated to pay a 20% copayment, for example, were required to pay the copayment based on the provider's actual charge rather than on the negotiated discount rate, thus obligating the member to pay a rate substantially in excess of 20% of the amount the provider was actually paid. The discount rate, in these situations, was not disclosed to the members. In a number of cases courts have permitted suits under breach of ERISA fiduciary duty or breach of contract in these situations.[37] The Supreme Court has recently permitted a RICO suit to prevail challenging this practice, holding that the suit was not blocked by McCarran–Ferguson.[38]

§ 9–13. Regulation of Provider Sponsored Networks

As managed care entities that both bore risk and provided care became increasingly common in the late 1980s and early 1990s, the idea became popular among providers of cutting out the middleman insurer and contracting directly with purchasers such as employers. Thus the concept of the provider sponsored network (also called, provider sponsored organizations, risk-bearing provider groups, integrated delivery systems, or physician hospital organizations), was born. Provider-sponsored networks (PSNs) are organized by health care institutions or by physician groups. They contract directly with employers or other purchasers on a per-enrollee capitated basis to provide a range of services.[1]

The problem that PSNs immediately posed was whether they should be subjected to insurance solvency and reserve requirements.[2] From one perspective, these entities do not offering an insurance product, but rather contract to provide themselves a particular set of services for a fixed price, much like a

---

33. AAHC/URAC, supra note 2, at 35. See e.g., Wis. Stat. Ann. § 609.15.

34. AAHC/URAC, supra note 2, at 35.

35. Id. at 33–34.

36. See Id. at 34–35. See, e.g., Mass. Code Regs. ch. 211 § 51.07(9); 31 Pa. Admin. Code § 152.4; Utah Code Ann. § 31A–22–617(4).

37. See, e.g. McConocha v. Blue Cross & Blue Shield, 898 F.Supp. 545 (N.D.Ohio 1995); See also Ellen M. Doyle & George G. Mahfood, The 80/20 Percent Solution: Enforcing Medical Coverage Promises, Trial, Oct. 1996 at 34.

38. Humana v. Forsyth, 525 U.S. 299, 119 S.Ct. 710 (1999).

§ 9–13

1. See Edward B. Hirschfeld, Provider Sponsored Organizations and Provider Service Networks—Rationale and Regulation, 22 Am. J.L. & Med. 263 (1996).

2. See, discussing regulatory issues, Hirschfeld, supra note 1; Allison Overbay & Mark Hall, Insurance Regulation of Providers that Bear Risk, 22 Am.J.L. & Med. 361 (1996); Douglas J. Witten, Regulation of "Downstream" and Direct Risk Contracting by Health Care Providers: The Quest for Consumer Protection and a Level Playing Field, 23 Am.J.L. & Med. 449 (1997); Ericka L. Rutenberg, Managed Care and the Business of Insurance: When is a Provider Group Considered to be at Risk? 1 DePaul J. Health Care L., 267 (1996).

maintenance contract.[3] PSNs, moreover, are rarely in a position to raise the capital necessary to meet traditional insurance reserve requirements, thus treating them as insurers would severely limit their growth. On the other hand, PSNs that overextend themselves might put their enrollees at risk, much like HMOs. Further, to the extent the networks assume responsibility for the cost of carve out services or services provided by out-of-network providers (as in emergencies), they have risk-bearing responsibilities much like traditional insurers. Moreover, traditional insurers objected vigorously to the emergence of competitors that did not have to meet the same regulatory restrictions they did. Finally, PSNs were opposed by providers who were either not in a position to or did not want to organize PSNs, but also did not want to be excluded from treating insureds by PSNs.

A number of states have adopted special laws regulating PSNs to meet these concerns. These statutes usually adopt some modified level of reserve requirements, reflecting the reduced risk born by PSNs.[4] The NAIC has recommended regulating risk-bearing PSNs as insurers.[5] The federal Balanced Budget Act of 1997 also established its own reserve requirements for Medicare PSNs through a negotiated rulemaking process, and excused Medicare PSNs from state licensure on a temporary basis in states that imposed undue restrictions on PSNs.[6] PSNs growth has remained, however, slow and uneven, with few successes and many failures.

3. Overbay & Hall, supra note 2, at 370–371.

4. See Ohio Rev. Code § 1751.28.

5. See Whitten, supra note 2, at 475–79; Risk–Bearing Entities Working Group, National Association of Ins. Comm'rs, The Regulation of Health Risk–Bearing Entities (1996).

6. 42 U.S.C.A. §§ 1395w–25, 1395w–26; 42 C.F.R. § 422, Subpart H.

Chapter 10

OBLIGATIONS TO PROVIDE MEDICAL CARE

Table of Sections

509

Research References

Am Jur 2d, Physicians, Surgeons, and Other Healers §§ 234–244

ALR Index: Medical Care and Treatment; Medical Care Recovery Act

ALR Digest: Physicians and Surgeons § 18

47 POF2d 1, Malpractice by Emergency Department Physician; 46 POF2d 373, Existence of Physician and Patient Relationship

§ 10–1. Introduction

The U.S. Constitution does not guarantee a right to health care. There is no duty under the United States Constitution on the part of the federal government to provide health care,[1] though there are constitutional restrictions on the administration of benefit programs that the government does provide,[2] and state constitutions may provide an affirmative right to health care.[3]

One approach to filling the gaps in private insurance and government programs and to meeting the health care needs of the population is to place the obligation to satisfy those needs upon health care providers themselves. These obligations come in a variety of forms. Often they are linked to government-financed health care programs. For example, state and federal statutes may impose an obligation of nondiscrimination based on source of payment or may limit providers in charging fees in excess of those provided under a government payment program.[4] States increasingly have looked to health care providers as sources of revenue for the support of government health care programs.[5]

The relative positions of the individual physician and the health care facility have differed in relation to legal obligations to provide health care. Clearly, the starting point for individual physicians in modern times has been that there is no legal or professional ethical obligation to provide care. Obligations on the part of individual doctors have developed as exceptions to this premise. For example, physicians have a duty not to abandon a patient once a physician-patient relationship has begun. This duty not to abandon patients has been an important doctrine in litigation challenging decisionmaking within the strictures of cost-containment programs.[6] Except as prohibited under recent antidiscrimination legislation[7] or as required by hospital policy

§ 10–1

1. See e.g., Harris v. McRae, 448 U.S. 297, 100 S.Ct. 2671, 65 L.Ed.2d 784 (1980), rehearing denied 448 U.S. 917, 101 S.Ct. 39, 65 L.Ed.2d 1180 (1980). But see, Wendy E. Parmet, Health Care and the Constitution: Public Health and the Role of the State in the Framing Era, 20 Hastings Constitutional Law Quarterly 267 (1993); Roy G. Spece, Jr., AIDS: Due Process, Equal Protection and the Right to Treatment, 4 Issues in Law & Medicine 283 (1988).

2. See e.g., Goldberg v. Kelly, 397 U.S. 254, 90 S.Ct. 1011, 25 L.Ed.2d 287 (1970).

3. For example, the New Jersey constitution provides that all persons enjoy certain rights including "pursuing and obtaining safety and happiness." N.J.S.A. Const. Art. I

(1947). This provision was used to support a right to publicly funded abortion. Right to Choose v. Byrne, 450 A.2d 925 (N.J.1982); Moe v. Secretary of Administration and Finance, 417 N.E.2d 387 (Mass.1981); Committee to Defend Reproductive Rights v. Myers, 172 Cal. Rptr. 866, 625 P.2d 779 (Cal.1981).

4. See §§ 13–26 and 14–8 and Massachusetts Medical Society v. Dukakis, 815 F.2d 790 (1st Cir.1987), cert. denied 484 U.S. 896, 108 S.Ct. 229, 98 L.Ed.2d 188 (1987).

5. See e.g., Daily Tax Report, State Developments: Oklahoma (BNA) 104 D–23 (1992); Daily Tax Report, State Developments: Nevada (BNA) 40 HB4 (1992).

6. See Chapter 7.

7. See e.g., McKinney's—N.Y.Educ.Law § 6509(6).

applicable to doctors through medical staff bylaws or contract,[8] doctors may refuse to enter a physician-patient relationship for any reason. Some legislative initiatives have attempted to encourage doctors to treat certain patients by relieving them of liability claims by those patients.[9]

Regulatory standards creating an obligation to provide medical care have been more prevalent in the regulation of health care facilities, particularly hospitals, than in the regulation of physicians. For this reason, this chapter focuses on legal obligations of institutions to provide care, although these obligations often necessarily create obligations upon physicians and some of the more recent statutes apply to doctors and health care facilities alike.

A variety of regulatory standards require hospitals and other health care facilities to provide care. For example, standards for tax-exempt status under § 501(c)(3) of the Internal Revenue Code require that any health care provider holding this status, including hospitals, nursing homes and health maintenance organizations, must provide some level of access to health care for indigent persons.[10] State tax systems often have similar requirements for exemption from state taxation.[11] Restrictions under Medicare and Medicaid on the ability of nursing homes to transfer or discharge patients, even though discharge for nonpayment is allowed, create an obligation to provide care.[12] States may condition approval for new facilities on provision of care to underserved populations.[13] Most of the federal requirements concerning obligations to provide health care services have relied upon the federal financing authority and so have been enacted as part of federal funding programs such as the Hill–Burton Act and the Medicare and Medicaid programs.[14] In addition, federal antidiscrimination statutes, such as the Rehabilitation Act and Title VI of the Civil Rights Act of 1964, apply only to providers that receive federal funds. Most recently, however, the Americans with Disabilities Act has created obligations to provide care and is not limited to providers receiving federal funds.

This section first reviews obligations under the federal Emergency Medical Treatment and Labor Act, as well as related state requirements, and the Hill–Burton program, both of which focus on uncompensated care. Lack of access to adequate health care is not entirely explained by financial limitations, however.[15] This chapter also includes a discussion of the federal antidiscrimination statutes that address some of the nonfinancial barriers to access.

8. See e.g., Hiser v. Randolph, 617 P.2d 774 (Ariz.App.1980). See also §§ 4–9 and 4–10.

9. See § 6–5.

10. See § 2–3,§§ 2–12 through 2–15.

11. See § 2–3.

12. See § 1–13.

13. See e.g., N.Y. State Health Facilities Association v. Axelrod, 568 N.Y.S.2d 1, 569 N.E.2d 860 (N.Y.1991), upholding requirement that new nursing home facilities admit a "reasonable percentage of Medicaid patients," defined as a rate equivalent to 75% of the nursing home Medicaid population in the relevant county.

14. See e.g., §§ 10–2 through 10–17.

15. Recent empirical research reveals significant racially-based disparities in medical treatment decisions by physicians. See e.g., Council on Ethical and Judicial Affairs, American Medical Association. Black–White Disparities in Health Care, 263 J.A.M.A. 2344 (1990); Mark B. Wemaker and Arnold M. Epstein, Racial Inequalities in the Use of Procedures for Patients with Ischemic Heart Disease in Massachusetts, 261 J.A.M.A. 253 (1989). Mistaken notions of health status and prognosis may also affect whether care is received. See e.g., Pediatric AIDS, AIDS Policy and Law, (6/27/90), reporting on research revealing medical treatment decisions based on inaccurate perceptions of rate of HIV infection of infants born to HIV positive mothers.

These acts include Title VI, the Rehabilitation Act and the Americans with Disabilities Act. Reference is made to related state statutes where appropriate.

A. EMERGENCY MEDICAL TREATMENT AND LABOR ACT

§ 10–2. Major Provisions

The Emergency Medical Treatment and Labor Act applies to hospitals that participate in the federal Medicare program[1] and have emergency departments. The Act requires covered hospitals to provide a medical screening examination[2] to any patient coming to the emergency department[3] of the hospital. If an emergency medical condition[4] is present, the hospital must provide treatment to stabilize[5] the patient's medical condition unless the patient requests transfer in writing knowing of the hospital's obligation under the Act or a physician certifies that the benefits to the patient of transfer in an unstabilized condition outweigh the risks.[6] If the hospital transfers the patient,[7] the transport support provided must meet the statutory standards for adequacy of equipment and personnel; the receiving facility must agree to accept transfer; and the transferring hospital must provide all medical records to the receiving facility.[8] Patients may refuse treatment; may refuse to consent to transfer; and may request transfer.[9]

The statute also applies to women in labor.[10] For a "pregnant woman who is having contractions," an emergency medical condition exists if there is inadequate time for transfer prior to delivery or if the transfer presents a threat to the health of the woman or the unborn child.[11] Similarly, the statutory definition of appropriate transfer of a woman in labor includes

§ 10–2

1. 42 U.S.C.A. § 1395dd(e)(2); Interim Final Rule with Comment Period, 59 Fed.Reg. 32086 (1994).

2. The statute provides that "the hospital must provide for an appropriate medical screening examination within the capability of the hospital's emergency department, including ancillary services routinely available to the emergency department, to determine whether or not an emergency medical condition . . . exists." 42 U.S.C.A. § 1395dd(a).

3. 42 U.S.C.A. § 1395dd(a).

4. The statute defines this term as "a medical condition manifesting itself by acute symptoms of sufficient severity (including severe pain) such that the absence of immediate medical attention could reasonably be expected to result in (i) placing the health of the individual (or, with respect to a pregnant woman, the health of the woman or her unborn child) in serious jeopardy, (ii) serious impairment to bodily functions, or (iii) serious dysfunction of any bodily organ or part." 42 U.S.C.A. § 1395dd(e)(1).

5. The statute defines the terms "to stabilize" and "stabilized" with reference to the

potential for material deterioration in the patient's condition, i.e., "no material deterioration of the condition is likely, within reasonable medical probability" resulting from or occurring during transfer. 42 U.S.C.A. § 1395dd(e)(3)(A) and (B).

6. 42 U.S.C.A. § 1395dd(c)(1).

7. The statute includes discharge of the patient within the definition of "transfer." 42 U.S.C.A. § 1395dd(e)(4).

8. 42 U.S.C.A. § 1395dd(c)(2).

9. 42 U.S.C.A. § 1395dd(b)(2) and (3) and (c)(1)(A)(i). But see 64 Fed. Reg. 61353 (No. 10, 1999) for a special advisory from HCFA that warns hospitals to monitor why patients leave the waiting room, even if "voluntarily," without receiving a medical exam. Hospitals are also required to inform patients who are leaving that treatment will be offered and to explain the benefits of treatment and risks of non-treatment.

10. The Act originally applied to women in "active labor," but was amended in 1989 to apply to "women in labor." Pub.L.No. 101–239, § 6211(h)(2)(A).

11. 42 U.S.C.A. § 1395dd(e)(1)(B).

reference to the medical condition of the unborn child as well as the woman.[12] Stabilization of an emergency medical condition for a woman having contractions is defined as delivery.[13]

The Act provides for a private cause of action for violation of the statute. Any individual suffering harm as a "direct result" of a hospital's violation of the statute has a cause of action against the hospital.[14] The Act has stimulated a significant amount of litigation. In addition, any medical facility that suffers a financial loss as a result of a violation may recover damages from the hospital.[15] The statute also provides for civil monetary penalties against the hospital and against the "responsible" physician for violations of the Act.[16]

§ 10–3. Defendants to Civil Suits by Patients

The Emergency Medical Treatment and Labor Act specifically provides for a private right of action for damages[1] or equitable relief by "any individual who suffers personal harm as a direct result of a participating hospital's violation" of the Act.[2] Patients have attempted to sue individual physicians under the Act. The specific language of the quoted section supports the courts' nearly uniform rejection of private civil suits under the Act against individual physicians and physician groups[3] and against payers.[4]

In addition to the private right of action provided to patients, the statute provides that "any medical facility that suffers a financial loss as a direct result of a participating hospital's violation of a requirement of [the Act]"[5] may file suit against the participating hospital for damages for that financial loss as well as for equitable relief. The remainder of this section is devoted to actions by patients.[6]

§ 10–4. Medical Malpractice and the Act

Although claims under EMTALA are to be distinguished from claims for medical malpractice, the two are often associated in litigation, with plaintiffs usually claiming both a violation of EMTALA and medical malpractice. Proof of malpractice is not required for an EMTALA claim to succeed.[1]

12. 42 U.S.C.A. § 1395dd(c)(1)(A)(ii), (2)(A).

13. 42 U.S.C.A. § 1395dd(e)(3)(A) and (B).

14. 42 U.S.C.A. § 1395dd(d)(2)(A).

15. 42 U.S.C.A. § 1395dd(d)(2)(B).

16. 42 U.S.C.A. § 1395dd(d)(1)(A) and (B).

§ 10–3

1. See discussion of government enforcement in § 10–12.

2. 42 U.S.C.A. § 1395dd(d)(2)(A).

3. See e.g., Baber v. Hospital Corporation of America, 977 F.2d 872 (4th Cir.1992); Delaney v. Cade, 986 F.2d 387 (10th Cir.1993); Hutchinson v. Greater Southeast Community Hospital, 1993 WL 30902 (D.C.Cir.1993). See also Ballachino v. Anders, 811 F.Supp. 121 (W.D.N.Y.1993); Jones v. Wake County Hosp. System, Inc., 786 F.Supp. 538 (E.D.N.C.1991); Holcomb v. Monahan, 807 F.Supp. 1526 (M.D.Ala.1992); Richardson v. Southwest Mississippi Regional Medical Center, 794 F.Supp.

198 (S.D.Miss.1992); Urban v. King, 783 F.Supp. 560 (D.Kan.1992); Helton v. Phelps County Regional Medical Center, 817 F.Supp. 789 (E.D.Mo.1993). See also, McDougal v. LaFourche Hospital Service District, 1993 WL 185647 (E.D.La.1993), concerning third party claim by hospital against physician. But see, Sorrells v. Babcock, 733 F.Supp. 1189 (N.D.Ill. 1990).

4. Dearmas v. Av–Med, Inc., 814 F.Supp. 1103 (S.D.Fla.1993).

5. § 1395dd(d)(2)(B).

6. For an overview of the requirements of EMTALA litigation, see Barry R. Furrow, An Overview and Analysis of the Impact of the Emergency Medical Treatment Act, 16 J. Leg. Med. 325 (1995).

§ 10–4

1. See e.g., Kilcop v. Adventist Health Care, Inc., 57 F.Supp.2d 925 (N.D.Cal.1999). See also discussion in § 10–7.

A few courts have considered the applicability of state statutes requiring some form of prelitigation procedure to claims under EMTALA. Of course, the scope of the state statute will determine whether the EMTALA claim falls within the actions for which prelitigation procedures are required. It is likely that statutes that require prelitigation procedures only for medical malpractice claims will not govern claims under the federal Act,[2] while statutes with a broader scope may apply.[3] State statutes that do capture EMTALA claims within their scope may be preempted under the Act if any requirement under the statute "directly conflicts with a requirement" of the federal Act.[4] Courts have varied on the question of whether procedural requirements if they do apply, are preempted by the Act.[5]

§ 10–5.   Location of Treatment

The Act provides that "if any individual . . . comes to the emergency department,"[1] it is the hospital's duty to assess whether the patient presents an emergency medical condition.[2] The Fourth Circuit has held that "the hospital's duty . . . arises only if the patient seeks treatment from the emergency department," and concluded in *Baber v. Hospital Corporation of America*, that plaintiff did not state a claim against a hospital for failure to provide an appropriate medical screening where the patient was admitted directly to the hospital's psychiatric ward upon transfer from another hospital's emergency room.[3]

A claim of transfer in an unstable condition does not require that the patient enter the hospital through the emergency room.[4] Patients who enter the hospital through the emergency room[5] but who are discharged from another department of the hospital can state a claim under the Act. The concern in such a situation is that a hospital will circumvent the Act simply by admitting the patient to the hospital and then discharging the patient. The

---

2. See e.g., Hewett v. Inland Hospital, 39 F.Supp.2d 84 (D. Maine 1999); Brooks v. Maryland General Hospital, 996 F.2d 708 (4th Cir. 1993); Holcomb v. Monahan, 807 F.Supp. 1526 (M.D.Ala.1992), holding that state statute requiring enhanced specificity in complaints claiming medical malpractice does not apply to EMTALA. See also, discussion of the applicability of medical malpractice damage caps. See discussion in § 10–11.

3. See e.g., Hardy v. New York City Health and Hospitals Corp., 164 F.3d 789 (2d Cir. 1999); Draper v. Chiapuzio, 9 F.3d 1391 (9th Cir.1993).

4. 42 U.S.C.A. § 1395dd(f).

5. See e.g., Hardy v. New York City Health & Hospitals Corp., 164 F.3d 789 (2d Cir.1999) and Draper v. Chiapuzio, 9 F.3d 1391 (9th Cir.1993) state procedure not preempted. But see, Smith v. Richmond Memorial Hospital, 416 S.E.2d 689 (Va.1992), cert. denied 506 U.S. 967, 113 S.Ct. 442, 121 L.Ed.2d 361 (1992); HCA Health Services v. Gregory, 596 N.E.2d 974 (Ind.App.1992); Reid v. Indianapolis Osteopathic Medical Hospital, 709 F.Supp. 853

(S.D.Ind.1989). Statutory damage caps are discussed in § 10–11.

§ 10–5

1. The statutory language requires that the patient request examination or treatment, but the request for treatment from a patient in the emergency room has not generally been the subject of dispute. However, see Stevison v. Enid Health Systems, 920 F.2d 710 (10th Cir. 1990).

2. 42 U.S.C.A. § 1395dd(a).

3. 977 F.2d 872 (4th Cir.1992). See also Daniels v. Wills Eye Hospital, 1992 WL 103009 (E.D.Pa.1992). But see, Helton v. Phelps County Regional Medical Center, 794 F.Supp. 332 (E.D.Mo.1992).

4. Lopez-Soto v. Hawayek,175 F.3d 170 (1st Cir.1999); McIntyre v. Schick, 795 F.Supp. 777 (E.D.Va.1992).

5. See Loss v. Song, 1990 WL 159612 (N.D.Ill.1990); Smith v. Richmond Memorial Hospital, 416 S.E.2d 689 (Va.1992), cert. denied 506 U.S. 967, 113 S.Ct. 442, 121 L.Ed.2d 361 (1992).

focus in these cases properly is upon the medical condition of the patient rather than the location of the patient upon discharge.[6]

Johnson v. University of Chicago Hospitals[7] is the most notable case on the question of the location of care. In *Johnson*, plaintiff sued the University of Chicago Hospitals (UCH) for actions taken as part of its service as resource hospital for a mobile intensive care system and as the operator of telemetry communications with paramedics providing emergency services. The patient in *Johnson* was an infant whose mother had called 911 when the infant stopped breathing. The paramedics informed UCH that the infant was in full cardiac arrest and that they were five blocks from UCH. Rather than directing the paramedics to bring the baby to UCH, UCH instructed them to take the child to another hospital. The reason given for diverting the child from UCH was that UCH had declared a "partial bypass" at the time due to the lack of available pediatric intensive care beds; however, the hospital to which UCH directed the paramedics had no pediatric intensive care unit, and the infant later was transferred from that hospital to Cook County Hospital. The child died after the second transfer. The District Court dismissed plaintiff's claim under the Emergency Medical Treatment and Labor Act for failure to allege that the patient came to the UCH emergency room. The Seventh Circuit first reversed the dismissal, but later vacated its opinion and issued a new opinion upholding the District Court's dismissal of the EMTALA claim.[8] In its second opinion, however, the Court of Appeals held open the possibility that the Act might be violated if there were persuasive proof that a hospital "used a telemetry system in a scheme to dump patients."[9] The appellate court also specifically noted that the ambulance workers had contacted the telemetry system and not the UCH emergency department itself, implying that the two situations could be distinguished, although this difference would appear to be insubstantial.[10]

This holding is consistent with later 1997 federal regulations which define "comes to the emergency department" to mean that "the individual is on the hospital property."[11] "Hospital property" includes ambulances owned and operated by the hospital, regardless of the location of the ambulance. A person in a non-hospital-owned ambulance is not considered to be on hospital property unless the ambulance is located on hospital grounds. This rule applies even if a member of the ambulance staff contacts the hospital by telephone or telemetry communications and informs the hospital that they want to transport the individual to the hospital for examination and treatment.[12]

6. See e.g., Thornton v. Southwest Detroit Hospital, 895 F.2d 1131 (6th Cir.1990).

7. 982 F.2d 230 (7th Cir.1992). See also Miller v. Medical Center of Southwest Louisiana, 22 F.3d 626 (5th Cir.1994).

8. Johnson v. University of Chicago Hospitals, 982 F.2d 230, (7th Cir.1992); 982 F.2d 230 (7th Cir.1992). The court also changed its opinion on the plaintiff's common law negligence claims, first upholding the District Court's dismissal of these claims and then reversing the dismissal. See also, Arrington v. Wong, 19 F.Supp.2d 1151 (D.Hawaii 1998).

9. See discussion of motive in § 10–4.

10. See 42 C.F.R. § 489.24 for regulation allowing refusal by telephone or telemetry if hospital is in "diversionary status." See also, Davis v. Johns Hopkins Hospital, 585 A.2d 841 (Md.App.1991), addressing common law claims.

11. 42 C.F.R. § 498.24(b). See, Hernandez v. Starr County Hospital District, 30 F.Supp.2d 970 (S.D.Tex.1999).

12. 42 C.F.R. § 498.24(b)

§ 10–4.   Motive for Transfer or Discharge

An early conflict in litigation under the Act involved whether the Act provided a cause of action to persons who were not indigent. Three early cases dismissed the claims of persons who were not indigent or who provided no evidence that their economic condition influenced the medical treatment provided to them.[1] After these early cases, the courts almost uniformly have concluded that proof of indigency is not required for a claim under EMTALA.[2]

Although proof of indigency is not a required element for a claim under the Act, there has been a significant amount of litigation considering whether or not proof of the hospital's or the physician's improper motive is required to establish a violation of the Act. In 1999, the Supreme Court held, in the case of *Roberts v. Galen of Virginia*,[3] that it is not necessary to establish improper motive to prove that the Act's stabilization requirement was violated.

Although the *Roberts* decision resolved the question of the relevance of motive in claims that the patient was not stabilized before transfer, it left open the question of whether proof of improper motive is required to establish a violation for failure to provide an "appropriate medical screening."[4] The *Roberts* Court noted that only the Sixth Circuit requires proof of improper motive to establish a violation of the "appropriate medical screening examination" requirement,[5] but expressed no opinion as that issue was not before it. It is likely that the Supreme Court will decide this issue soon, although it is not clear what the Court will decide. The *Roberts* opinion does not necessarily predict whether improper motive would be required in the case of failure to screen as the statutory standard of care for the screening requirement differs from that of the stabilization requirement.[6]

§ 10–7.   Standard of Care: Appropriate Medical Examination

Under the Act, a hospital must provide the patient "an *appropriate* medical screening examination within the capability of the hospital's emergency department" to determine whether the patient is in an emergency medical condition.[1] The Sixth Circuit, in considering the meaning of this

§ 10–6

1. See Evitt v. University Heights Hospital, 727 F.Supp. 495 (S.D.Ind.1989); Nichols v. Estabrook, 741 F.Supp. 325 (D.N.H.1989); Stewart v. Myrick, 731 F.Supp. 433 (D.Kan.1990).

2. See e.g., Cleland v. Bronson Health Care Group, 917 F.2d 266 (6th Cir.1990); Brooker v. Desert Hospital Corp., 947 F.2d 412 (9th Cir. 1991); Collins v. DePaul Hospital, 963 F.2d 303 (10th Cir.1992); Gatewood v. Washington Healthcare Corp., 933 F.2d 1037 (D.C.Cir. 1991); Deberry v. Sherman Hospital Association, 769 F.Supp. 1030 (N.D.Ill.1991). But see, DiGicomo v. St. Joseph's Hospital, 582 N.Y.S.2d 887 (N.Y.App.Div.1992).

3. 525 U.S. 249, 119 S.Ct. 685, 142 L.Ed.2d 648 (1999).

4. See Lancaster v. Loyola University Medical Center, 1992 WL 318618 (N.D.Ill.1992), holding that utilization review records of a health maintenance organization, though irrelevant to plaintiff's wrongful death claim

against the hospital were relevant to plaintiff's claim against the hospital under the federal statute and allowing discovery of those records. See also Cleland v. Bronson Health Care Group, 917 F.2d 266 (6th Cir. 1990).

5. Roberts, 119 S.Ct., at 687. Compare Cleland v. Bronson Health Care Group, 197 F.2d 266 (6th Cir. 1990) (requiring proof of improper motive) with Summers v. Baptist Med. Ctr. Arkadelphia, 91 F.3d 1132, 1137–38 (8th Cir. 1996) (en banc), Correa v. Hospital San Francisco, 69 F.3d 1184, 1193–94 (1st Cir.1995); Repp v. Anadarko Mun. Hosp., 43 F.3d 519, 522 (10th Cir.1994); Power v. Arlington Hospital Association, 42 F.3d 851, 857 (4th Cir. 1994); Gatewood v. Washington Healthcare Corp., 933 F.2d 1037, 1041 (D.C.Cir.1991) (not requiring proof of improper motive).

6. See §§ 10–7 and 10–8.

§ 10–7

1. 42 U.S.C.A. § 1395dd(a). Emphasis added.

statutory language, declared the word appropriate "one of the most wonderful weasel words in the dictionary, and a great aid to the resolution of disputed issues in the drafting of legislation."[2] While it may be a great aid to legislative compromise, the indeterminacy of the requirement of an appropriate medical screening examination has vexed plaintiffs claiming under the Act.

The issue of the standard to be used in deciding whether a medical screening examination satisfies the requirements of the Act arises most frequently in cases involving misdiagnosis of the patient's condition. An instinctive interpretation of the standard of appropriateness in relation to medical services is that those services should meet the standards of the profession. One thing is clear in litigation under EMTALA, however; the courts consistently have declared that the Act does not create a federal malpractice claim and proof of violation of the statute requires something other than proof of malpractice.[3]

The statute itself includes language that indicates a departure from ordinary malpractice standards. The Act provides that the hospital is to provide a medical screening "within [its] capabilities."[4] The Sixth Circuit relied in part upon this language to conclude that the statute "precludes resort to a malpractice or other objective standard of care."[5] Still, the statute's reference to the institution's capabilities could be viewed as limited to questions of institutional resources alone. While a malpractice or negligence claim based on misdiagnosis in the emergency room might include a claim that the emergency room did not meet the industry's standards for adequate equipment, for example, a suit under EMTALA, at least under this language, would not include such a claim.

Rejecting professional standards for the appropriate medical screening examination required by the Act, the courts generally have adopted a standard of differential treatment. For example, some Circuits have adopted positions similar to that used by the Sixth Circuit in *Cleland v. Bronson Health Care Group* :[6] " 'appropriate' must ... be interpreted to refer to the motives with which the hospital acts. If it acts in the same manner as it would have for the usual paying patient, then the screening provided is 'appropriate' ...".[7] The courts appear to be eliminating from EMTALA only those claims that are based on alleged deficiency in *medical* judgment concerning whether certain tests or treatments are required for patients in particular medical situations.

The rejection of professional standards for determining whether a medical examination is appropriate under the statute obviously influences the evidence required of plaintiff to avoid dismissal or summary judgment. In *Baber*

---

2. Cleland v. Bronson Health Care Group, 917 F.2d 266 (6th Cir.1990).

3. See e.g., Collins v. DePaul Hospital, 963 F.2d 303 (10th Cir.1992); Gatewood v. Washington Healthcare Corporation, 933 F.2d 1037 (D.C.Cir.1991); Coleman v. McCurtain Mem. Medical Management, 771 F.Supp. 343 (E.D.Okl.1991); Evitt v. University Heights Hospital, 727 F.Supp. 495 (S.D.Ind.1989).

4. 42 U.S.C.A. § 1395dd(a).

5. Cleland v. Bronson Health Care Group, 917 F.2d 266 (6th Cir.1990). See also Baber v.

Hospital Corporation of America, 977 F.2d 872 (4th Cir.1992); Deberry v. Sherman Hospital Association, 769 F.Supp. 1030 (N.D.Ill.1991).

6. 917 F.2d 266 (6th Cir.1990).

7. See also Baber v. Hospital Corporation of America, 977 F.2d 872 (4th Cir.1992); Gatewood v. Washington Healthcare Corporation, 933 F.2d 1037 (D.C.Cir.1991); Gardner v. Elmore Community Hospital, 64 F.Supp.2d 1195 (M.D.Ala.1999).

v. Hospital Corporation of America,[8] the court upheld summary judgment for defendant. The appellate court rejected the affidavit of plaintiff's expert witness, which stated that professional standards required a more complete neurological examination, holding that the affidavit did not create "a material question of fact as to whether [the doctor] examined Ms. Baber differently from any other patient with a similar history, signs, and symptoms." The court indicates, instead, that plaintiff's expert should have stated whether "his requirements for good and appropriate medical care corresponded with or deviated from [the hospital's] standard medical screening examination" and that plaintiff's expert did not address "the essential issue of whether Ms. Baber received disparate treatment."

Plaintiff must discover the hospital's standard practice in regard to the particular condition or prove that its policy is to conform with professional standards. To the extent that the hospital has established written guidelines or has followed consistent practices in emergency medical examinations, it is, of course, essential for plaintiff to prove their content.[9] But if, as is more likely, the hospital has not developed written guidelines or clearly established practices or has developed only the most barebones policies,[10] plaintiff will have to reach for other evidence of the hospital's departure from its norm. Documents such as contracts with emergency room physicians may reveal a standard adopted by the hospital. Records for patients presenting with similar conditions may also be probative of a departure from the hospital's customary examination standards.

Because the analysis of disparate treatment is at the core of the standard that these courts have adopted and because some courts have adopted a deferential stance toward the judgment of the treating physician,[11] plaintiff may need to focus on proving motive,[12] as part of the proof that the medical examination provided the patient departed from the quality of care ordinarily available in that hospital, even if the jurisdiction does not require proof of improper motive and an independent element of the Act.[13] Obviously, the most

---

8. 977 F.2d 872 (4th Cir.1992).

9. But see, Collins v. DePaul Hospital, 963 F.2d 303 (10th Cir.1992), in which the court "accept[ed] as true counsel's assertion that ordinarily" such a patient would have had a certain diagnostic procedure and that the hospital staff had thought the procedure had been done even though in fact it had not and in which the court upheld summary judgment for defendant because the statute does not "require a hospital to determine * * * all of the emergency medical conditions from which a particular individual may be suffering." The applicability of this statement should be limited to the facts of *Collins*: the patient was transported to the emergency room with multiple injuries, including a fractured skull, and he stayed at the hospital for nearly a month recovering from his injuries. A fractured hip was not detected.

10. See e.g., Hutchinson v. Greater Southeast Community Hospital, 793 F.Supp. 6 (D.D.C.1992), affirmed 1993 WL 30902 (D.C.Cir.1993); Griffith v. Mt. Carmel Medical Center, 831 F.Supp. 1532 (D.Kan.1993).

11. Baber v. Hospital Corporation of America, 977 F.2d 872 (4th Cir.1992).

12. See e.g., Helton v. Phelps County Regional Medical Center, 817 F.Supp. 789 (E.D.Mo.1993), holding that hospital policy stating that "patients with inadequate financial coverage will be discharged and referred to other sources" created issue of fact and required denial of summary judgment for defendant.

13. The court in *Cleland v. Bronson Health Care Group* identifies a list of impermissible motives, including discrimination based on race, sex, ethnic group, medical condition (specifically AIDS), personal dislike, and political opinions. The court states that disparate treatment for any of these reasons would "fall squarely" within the Act. The court also states, however, that a hospital that provides inadequate medical examination "for any reason" may be liable under the Act. 917 F.2d 266 (6th Cir.1990). See also Burditt v. United States, 934 F.2d 1362 (5th Cir.1991), proof of violation in civil fine action made by "evidence that

persuasive of such evidence is testimony from other hospital staff or other witnesses as to comments made by the treating physicians, which apparently has been available in some cases.[14] Although motive may be relevant for proving a departure from the hospital's standard practices, the motive need not be related to ability to pay. Plaintiff is not required to prove financial motive in order to succeed under the Act. The question of whether plaintiff is required to prove improper motive, not limited to ability to pay, has not been resolved as to the screening requirement.[15]

Each of the cases that have relied on the defendant hospitals themselves as the source of the standard for appropriateness has allowed that there might be cases in which the examination provided was so cursory or inadequate as to amount to no examination at all. Several courts have stated that the Act could be violated in these hypothetical cases.[16]

Finally, under a recent advisory bulletin from HCFA, hospitals are not allowed to seek prior authorization from an insurer until after the medical screening examination and necessary stabilizing treatment is begun.[17] The hospital can contact the health plan at that point.

§ 10–8. Standard of Care: Stabilization and Transfer

A hospital violates the Act if it fails to provide an "appropriate medical screening examination" to the patient presenting in the emergency room. If the hospital provides an appropriate examination that detects an emergency condition or if the patient's emergency condition is otherwise known to the hospital, the hospital is liable under the Act if it transfers or discharges the patient in an unstable medical condition.

Courts have required plaintiff to prove that the hospital actually knew of the plaintiff's emergency condition in order to trigger the duty to stabilize prior to transfer or discharge.[1] Where the hospital lacks actual knowledge of the patient's emergency condition as a result of a statutorily inadequate medical screening examination, the hospital would be liable at least for violating the examination requirement of the Act.[2] Whether the hospital actually knew of the patient's emergency condition is a question of fact for the jury, and testimony by the treating physician concerning lack of actual knowledge need not be determinative.[3]

something other than the present or projected medical needs of [the hospital's] patients determined the treatment provided." But see, Gatewood v. Washington Healthcare Corporation, 933 F.2d 1037 (D.C.Cir.1991), stating that the statute does not refer to the motive for departing from the hospital's "normal screening procedure."

14. See e.g., Burditt v. United States, 934 F.2d 1362 (5th Cir.1991); Griffith v. Mt. Carmel Medical Center, 831 F.Supp. 1532 (D.Kan. 1993).

15. See § 10–6.

16. See e.g., Baber v. Hospital Corporation of America, 977 F.2d 872 (4th Cir.1992); Cleland v. Bronson Health Care Group, 917 F.2d 266 (6th Cir.1990).

17. 64 Fed. Reg. 61353 (Nov. 10, 1999).

§ 10–8

1. See e.g., Cleland v. Bronson Health Care Group, 917 F.2d 266 (6th Cir.1990); Baber v. Hospital Corporation of America, 977 F.2d 872 (4th Cir.1992); Gardner v. Elmore Community Hosp., 64 F.Supp.2d 1195 (M.D.Ala.1999); Urban v. King, 834 F.Supp. 1328 (D.Kan.1993).

2. See Abercrombie v. Osteopathic Hospital Founders Ass'n, 950 F.2d 676 (10th Cir.1991), for jury instructions on liability for violation of each of the requirements of the Act.

3. See e.g., Griffith v. Mt. Carmel Medical Center, 831 F.Supp. 1532 (D.Kan.1993).

Several factors enter the courts' analysis of whether the patient was stable before transfer or discharge. First, the courts appear less likely to allow plaintiffs to reach the jury if the hospital actually admitted and treated the patient for a significant amount of time.[4] As with the question of whether the examination was appropriate, some courts have deferred to the medical judgment of the treating physician.[5] Cases where deterioration actually has occurred in patients known to present an emergency medical condition but who were transferred to another facility may result in a shift in the burden of proof to defendant hospital.[6]

In comparison with the question of the appropriateness of the examination, the Act leaves no doubt that the question of whether the patient's medical condition was stabilized should be judged from the perspective of professional standards rather than standards established by each hospital.[7] The Act explicitly defines "stabilized" as a condition in which "no material deterioration of the condition is likely, *within reasonable medical probability*, to result from or occur during the transfer."[8] It is not clear whether avoidable pain is to be considered a material deterioration of the patient's condition. The control of avoidable physical pain is a significant goal and duty of medical treatment, however, and physical pain that would have been avoided with appropriate medical care should be considered a material deterioration of the patient's condition.[9]

The Act allows transfer of the patient in an unstable medical condition if the physician certifies that "the medical benefits reasonably expected from the provision of appropriate medical treatment at another medical facility outweigh the increased risks to the individual, or if the patient requests the transfer in writing, knowing of the hospital's duties under the Act."[10] Few cases have interpreted this section. In two such cases, the courts concluded that the physician's testimony as to his weighing of the benefits and risks of transfer was credible. In both cases, there was evidence that the physician's motive in transferring the patient was other than the potential benefits to the patient.[11]

§ 10–9. Standard of Care: Effecting an Appropriate Transfer

An "appropriate transfer" under the Act requires that the transferring facility minimize risks to the patient and provide all medical records to the receiving facility; that the receiving facility have adequate space and personnel and has agreed to accept transfer; and that the transfer is "effected

---

4. See e.g., Collins v. DePaul Hospital, 963 F.2d 303 (10th Cir.1992); Thornton v. Southwest Detroit Hospital, 895 F.2d 1131 (6th Cir. 1990).

5. See e.g., Thornton v. Southwest Detroit Hospital, 895 F.2d 1131 (6th Cir.1990); Brooker v. Desert Hospital Corp., 947 F.2d 412 (9th Cir.1991).

6. See e.g., Delaney v. Cade, 986 F.2d 387 (10th Cir.1993); Lee v. Alleghany Regional Hospital, 778 F.Supp. 900 (W.D.Va.1991).

7. See e.g., Burditt v. United States, 934 F.2d 1362 (5th Cir.1991); Delaney v. Cade, 986 F.2d 387 (10th Cir.1993); Green v. Touro Infirmary, 992 F.2d 537 (5th Cir.1993).

8. 42 U.S.C.A. § 1395(e)(3)(A). Emphasis added.

9. But see, Wey v. Evangelical Community Hospital, 833 F.Supp. 453 (M.D.Pa.1993).

10. 42 U.S.C.A. § 1395dd(c)(1). See Urban v. King, 834 F.Supp. 1328 (D.Kan.1993), holding under earlier version of the statute that patient had consented to the transfer.

11. See e.g., Owens v. Nacogdoches County Hospital District, 741 F.Supp. 1269 (E.D.Tex. 1990); Burditt v. United States, 934 F.2d 1362 (5th Cir.1991).

through qualified personnel and transportation equipment."[1] Few cases have had occasion to review this requirement of the Act.

The court in *Owens v. Nacogdoches County Hospital District*,[2] held that a direction to go to another hospital was a transfer and that a 1976 Ford Pinto, the patient's car, did not meet the Act's requirements for adequate transportation. In *Burditt v. United States*,[3] a woman in labor with extremely high blood pressure and no prenatal care was transferred to a hospital three hours away. Because neither the medical personnel nor the equipment in the ambulance were adequate to perform a cesarean section, which may have been necessary in the patient's condition, the court held this violated the appropriate transfer requirement of EMTALA. The court in *Wey v. Evangelical Community Hospital*,[4] however, held that transfer by personal car was allowable, even though the patient was not able to comply with directions to keep the injured limb elevated and suffered pain for some time as the pain medication administered at the transferring hospital wore off. Plaintiff had provided no expert testimony that such transport was medically inappropriate.

§ 10–10. Stabilization and Treatment of Women in Labor

As originally enacted, the statute applied to women in "active labor."[1] In 1989, Congress amended the statute to apply to "women in labor."[2] The statute currently defines "emergency medical condition" with respect to a pregnant woman having contractions as a situation in which "there is inadequate time to effect a safe transfer to another hospital before delivery" or where the "transfer may pose a threat to the health or safety of the woman or the unborn child."[3] The statute also defines stabilization of this emergency medical condition as delivery.[4]

Cases involving transfer or delay in treatment of women in labor seem to be more successful than most, perhaps because the difficulties involved in judging whether the medical screening examination was appropriate and whether the patient's condition was stable are not present under the definitions of those terms relative to women in labor. Even under the earlier version of the Act, where the term "active labor" presented a point of dispute, several cases held defendant liable or held that plaintiff successfully stated a claim against the hospital.[5]

§ 10–11. Damages Under EMTALA

The statute provides that civil damages[1] for a hospital's violation of the Act shall be "those damages available for personal injury under the law of the

§ 10–9

1. 42 U.S.C.A. § 1395dd(c)(2).
2. 741 F.Supp. 1269 (E.D.Tex.1990).
3. 934 F.2d 1362 (5th Cir.1991).
4. 833 F.Supp. 453 (M.D.Pa.1993).

§ 10–10

1. See Burditt v. United States, 934 F.2d 1362 (5th Cir.1991), for a discussion of the active labor requirement.
2. Pub. L. No. 101–239, § 6211(h)(2)(A).
3. 42 U.S.C.A. § dd(e)(1)(B).

4. 42 U.S.C.A. § 1395dd(e)(3).

5. See e.g., Owens v. Nacogdoches County Hospital District, 741 F.Supp. 1269 (E.D.Tex. 1990); Thompson v. St. Anne's Hospital, 716 F.Supp. 8 (N.D.Ill.1989); Loss v. Song, 1990 WL 159612 (N.D.Ill.1990); McIntyre v. Schick, 795 F.Supp. 777 (E.D.Va.1992).

§ 10–11

1. The statute provides that a plaintiff in a civil action under the Act may receive "such equitable relief as is appropriate." Few reported cases thus far have issued equitable relief,

State in which the hospital is located."[2] This limitation in the statute has generated two legal issues. The first is whether state statutory limitations on damages for medical malpractice actions limit the damages available to a plaintiff under EMTALA; and the second is the broader question of whether the damages claimed by plaintiff are recognized under state law.

The courts have been somewhat diverse in their treatment of the applicability or preemption of state statutory damage caps.[3] The absolute bar of damages under state law concerning charitable immunity or Good Samaritan immunity ordinarily would be preempted under preemption doctrine. Immunity under state law for emergency services would be in direct conflict with the federal statute.[4] Sovereign immunity for a public hospital may still apply, however, under the Eleventh Amendment.[5]

The second question raised is whether the particular type of damages claimed by plaintiff are available under state law. Few cases have directly addressed this question.[6]

The meaning of the statutory language concerning damages is ambiguous as it is not always clear whether a particular state tort doctrine is a doctrine of duty, a doctrine of causation or a doctrine of damages. For example, tort doctrine concerning claims based on a theory of emotional distress variably views such claims as raising an issue of whether the defendant owed a duty toward the injured party or as raising an issue of whether such damages are available.[7]

The significance of the question is apparent in these two illustrations. If state law recognizes claims for emotional distress only when accompanied by physical injury and this doctrine is viewed as a question of available damages, plaintiff claiming damages under EMTALA in the absence of physical injury would fail to recover. If the same state law is viewed as a question of duty rather than available damages, plaintiff would recover as defendant's duty is established by EMTALA itself. Similarly, if loss of chance is viewed as a question of available damages, plaintiff claiming that his or her chances for recovery or survival were decreased due to the acts committed in violation of the Act would receive no damages. In contrast, if loss of chance is viewed as a question of causation, plaintiff would be bound by the Act's requirement of causation,[8] rather than the state law, and could recover for loss of chance.

but see, Owens v. Nacogdoches County Hospital District, 741 F.Supp. 1269 (E.D.Tex.1990).

2. 42 U.S.C.A. § 1395dd(d)(2)(A).

3. See e.g., Feighery v. York Hospital, 38 F.Supp.2d 142 (D. Maine 1999); Lee v. Allegheny Regional Hospital, 778 F.Supp. 900 (W.D.Va.1991); Power v. Arlington Hospital, 800 F.Supp. 1384 (E.D.Va.1992); also, Reid v. Indianapolis Osteopathic Med. Hosp., 709 F.Supp. 853 (S.D.Ind.1989).

4. See e.g., Helton v. Phelps County Regional Medical Center, 817 F.Supp. 789 (E.D.Mo.1993).

5. Ward v. Presbyterian Healthcare Services, 72 F.Supp.2d 1285 (D.N.M. 1999).

6. Owens v. Nacogdoches County Hospital District, 741 F.Supp. 1269 (E.D.Tex.1990); Huckaby v. East Alabama Medical Center, 830 F.Supp. 1399 (M.D.Ala.1993).

7. See e.g., Kilcup v. Adventist Health, Inc., 57 F.Supp.2d 925 (N.D.Cal.1999); Owens v. Nacogdoches County Hospital District, 741 F.Supp. 1269 (E.D.Tex.1990). See also Griffith v. Mt. Carmel Medical Center, 842 F.Supp. 1359 (D.Kan.1994), holding that Kansas law on comparative fault not applicable to EMTALA claim.

8. The statute specifies that the harm suffered must be a "direct result" of the hospital's violation of the Act. 42 U.S.C.A. § 1395dd(d)(2)(A).

Clearly, Congress intended EMTALA to address the specific problem of "patient dumping;" that is, the inappropriate transfer or treatment of persons with emergency medical conditions. The types of "personal harm"[9] caused by delay in treatment and transfer are often among those, such as emotional distress and loss of chance, that are either unrecognized or treated gingerly under state law. The remedial purposes of the private cause of action under EMTALA arguably would be better served by a broader scope of recognizable injury.

§ 10–12. Enforcement by Government Action

The Act provides for "civil money penalties" for violation of the Act by hospitals and by physicians.[1] A hospital is subject to a fine when it negligently violates a requirement of the Act.[2] A physician[3] is subject to civil penalties if the physician negligently violates the statute, specifically including signing a certification for transfer stating that the transfer is required for the benefit of the patient[4] when the "physician knew or should have known that the benefits did not outweigh the risks" of transfer or misrepresents "an individual's condition or other information, including a hospital's obligation" under the statute.[5] A responsible physician is also subject to exclusion from Medicare and "state health care programs" if "the violation is gross and flagrant or is repeated."[6] These penalties are to be levied by the Secretary of the Department of Health and Human Services and do not support a claim for private enforcement.[7] A hospital that believes it has received a patient transferred from another hospital in violation of EMTALA is required to report the incident to the Health Care Financing Administration (HCFA) or a state survey agency.[8] The Office of Inspector General of the Department of Health and Human Services has reported that they are aggressively pursuing violators and that fines and settlements have substantially increased in the last two years.[9]

B. OBLIGATIONS TO PROVIDE EMERGENCY CARE UNDER STATE LAW

§ 10–13. Compared to EMTALA

Because the federal Emergency Medical Treatment and Labor Act applies to any hospital that is a Medicare provider, it reaches nearly every hospital that operates an emergency department. State law regarding the duty to

---

9. 42 U.S.C.A. § 1395dd(d)(2)(A).

§ 10–12

1. 42 U.S.C.A. § 1395dd(d)(1). See Cherukuri v. Shalala, 175 F.3d 446 (6th Cir.1999) overturning penalty against physicians on the merits; Burditt v. U.S. Department of Health and Human Services, 934 F.2d 1362 (5th Cir. 1991).

2. 42 U.S.C.A. § 1395dd(d)(1)(A).

3. Civil fines apply to "any physician who is responsible for the examination, treatment, or transfer of an individual in a participating hospital, including a physician on call for the

care of such an individual." 42 U.S.C.A. § 1395dd(d)(1)(B).

4. 42 U.S.C.A. § 1395dd(c)(1)(A)(ii),(iii).

5. 42 U.S.C.A. § 1395dd(d)(1)(B).

6. 42 U.S.C.A. § 395dd(d)(1)(B).

7. See e.g., Baber v. Hospital Corporation of America, 977 F.2d 872 (4th Cir.1992); Deberry v. Sherman Hospital Association, 769 F.Supp. 1030 (N.D.Ill.1991).

8. 42 C.F.R. § 489.20.

9. Emergency Care: HHS Broadly Interprets EMTALA, BNA Health Care Daily Report, June 30, 1999.

provide emergency treatment[1] is perhaps less important now than the federal statute, but state law still retains vitality. State statutes governing the transfer of indigent patients may have a wider scope than the federal statute. For example, the state statute may prohibit economically-motivated transfers even when the patient is not in an emergency condition.[2] The state may provide for different enforcement sanctions as well.[3]

Some states have created specific statutory obligations on the part of hospitals to provide emergency treatment as a condition of licensure. These statutes may require that a hospital provide emergency services, while EMTA-LA applies only to hospitals that accept Medicare and operate emergency departments.[4] In others, courts have construed licensure as implicitly requiring some degree of emergency care for indigent patients who present at the hospital's emergency room.[5]

§ 10–14. Common Law Duties

In several states, courts have held hospitals liable for failure to provide emergency care under a variety of common law theories.[1] *Wilmington General Hospital v. Manlove*,[2] is a foundational case in establishing a duty to provide emergency care even though the court remanded the case for expert testimony on whether the emergency room nurse should have detected the urgent nature of the patient's condition. In *Manlove*, the Delaware Supreme Court based the hospital's potential liability specifically upon a theory of "negligent termination of gratuitous services," although it focused on the detrimental reliance a seriously injured patient may place on the availability of emergency treatment in a hospital emergency room. Other courts have based liability on an abandonment theory,[3] reasoning that while there may be no duty to provide treatment, once treatment is begun, the hospital must exercise reasonable care in continuing or terminating treatment.[4]

The basis for the duty to provide emergency care, whether under licensure standards or under common law theories, may result in differences in the scope of the duty. For example, the reliance premise adopted in *Manlove* creates a duty, at least to the extent of evaluating the patient's condition, that arises when a seriously injured person presents at the emergency room. A theory that bases liability on the initiation of a "hospital-patient" relationship

---

§ 10–13

1. For an excellent analysis of the duty to provide emergency treatment under state law, see Karen Rothenberg, Who Cares? The Evolution of the Legal Duty to Provide Emergency Care, 26 Hous. L. Rev. 21 (1989).

2. See e.g., N.Y. McKinney's, Pub. Health Law 2805–b(1); Pa. Stat. tit. 35, 449.8(a).

3. See e.g., N.Y. McKinney's, Pub. Health Law 2805–b(2), providing for criminal prosecution and fine.

4. See e.g., Pa. Stat. tit. 35, 449.8(a); N.Y. McKinney's, Pub. Health Law 2805–b(2)(a), governing cities with over 1 million population.

5. See e.g., Guerrero v. Copper Queen, 537 P.2d 1329 (Ariz.1975); Thompson v. Sun City Community Hospital, Inc., 688 P.2d 605 (Ariz. 1984).

§ 10–14

1. As with EMTALA claims, claims of denial of emergency care under state law raise malpractice issues of the standard of care required in a particular case. See e.g., Pogge v. Hale, 192 Ill.Dec. 637, 625 N.E.2d 792 (Ill.App. 1993), holding that expert testimony was required to interpret and apply the hospital's emergency medical screening policies and by-laws to the plaintiff's particular situation.

2. 174 A.2d 135 (Del.1961).

3. See Chapter 6.

4. See e.g., New Biloxi Hospital, Inc. v. Frazier, 146 So.2d 882 (Miss.1962). See also, Davis v. Johns Hopkins Hospital, 585 A.2d 841 (Md.App.1991), affirmed 622 A.2d 128 (Md. 1993).

may delay the point at which the duty arises and may provide the hospital with more flexibility in limiting its duty to provide care. Neither theory supports a duty to operate an emergency room or provide other uncompensated care.

C. OBLIGATIONS UNDER THE HILL–BURTON ACT

§ 10–15. Statutory Requirements

First enacted in 1945 in response to post-World War II and Depression needs for hospital construction, the Hill–Burton Act[1] provided federal financing for the construction and expansion of health care facilities. The statute requires that the state provide adequate hospitals for all persons in the state, furnishing necessary services for those unable to pay. It also authorizes the federal agency administering the program to require assurances from applicants for federal financing that they would make the federally financed facility "available to all persons residing in the territorial area of the applicant" and would provide in the financed facility "a reasonable volume of services to persons unable to pay therefor [unless] such a requirement is not feasible from a financial viewpoint."[2] The duty to make the financed facilities available to all persons residing in the territorial area of the facility is known as the "community service obligation," requiring nondiscrimination in the provision of services, and continues indefinitely.[3] The duty to provide a reasonable volume of services to indigent persons is known as the "uncompensated care obligation."

§ 10–16. Litigation Over Regulations

After years of conflict over the implementation of the Hill–Burton uncompensated care obligation, the Secretary of the Department of Health and Human Services issued regulations that established quantified standards for uncompensated care. These regulations specified that care provided to Medicare or Medicaid patients was not to be included in meeting the standard for uncompensated care[1] and that any amount unmet because of financial infeasibility would be carried over to subsequent years. The American Hospital Association challenged the regulations as beyond the scope of the Secretary's statutory authority under the Act and as arbitrary and capricious.[2] The Seventh Circuit Court of Appeals rejected both arguments, holding that specific language in the statute requiring uncompensated care and the failure of hospitals to voluntarily comply with the requirement justified the Secretary's more restrictive regulations. The court also rejected the Association's contractual argument that facilities that had accepted funds years earlier

§ 10–15

1. 42 U.S.C.A. § 291.

2. 42 U.S.C.A. § 291c(e)(2).

3. See e.g., Metropolitan Medical Center v. Harris, 693 F.2d 775 (8th Cir.1982); Lugo v. Simon, 426 F.Supp. 28 (N.D.Ohio 1976).

§ 10–16

1. Other litigated disputes concerning what counts as uncompensated care include Lile v. University of Iowa Hospitals and Clinics, 886 F.2d 157 (8th Cir.1989), holding that care provided under state indigent care program could count.

2. American Hospital Association v. Schweiker, 721 F.2d 170 (7th Cir.1983), cert. denied 466 U.S. 958, 104 S.Ct. 2169, 80 L.Ed.2d 553 (1984).

were being held to new and increased obligations. The court noted that the federal government exercised "its authority under the spending power to bring about certain public policy goals" and relied upon statutory construction rather than contractual standards to measure the validity of the Secretary's regulations.[3]

This decision has been praised and criticized, with its supporters claiming that the decision is fully consistent with the statute[4] and its detractors claiming that the decision conflicts with the original intent and the subsequent practice relating to the obligation to provide uncompensated care and community service.[5] Undoubtedly critical to the result in the Seventh Circuit was the victory at the administrative level for advocates of more aggressive enforcement of the obligation, as the challengers then bore a substantial burden in persuading the court that the regulations were beyond the scope of statutory authority or were arbitrary and capricious.

Enforcement of the uncompensated care obligation under the new regulations was not altogether satisfactory to persons representing indigent patients.[6] The 1979 regulations and litigation also did not end the administrative controversy over the enforcement of the requirements of Hill–Burton. In 1987, the Secretary promulgated regulations that retained much of the 1979 regulations, but did allow credit toward the obligation despite failure to comply with the regulations in particular situations.[7] In 1988, the Secretary promulgated a regulation that adjusted compliance in a way that resulted in substantial credits for hospitals nationwide toward the obligation.[8] The 1987 and 1988 regulations were challenged, under a claim that their promulgation violated the Administrative Procedures Act, but the Ninth Circuit rejected this claim on the ground that the regulations were interpretive rather than substantive.[9] The Court of Appeals also upheld the 1987 and 1988 rules as reasonable, stating that "it is not unreasonable for an agency to adopt an enforcement strategy that focuses on compliance with the spirit and not simply the letter of the law."[10]

§ 10–17. Private Litigation

In addition to federal enforcement of the Hill–Burton obligation, the Act has played a limited role in private litigation regarding access to care.[1] For example, regulations under the Act require that recipients of Hill–Burton funds notify patients of the hospital's Hill–Burton obligation. A hospital's

---

3. See also Wyoming Hospital Ass'n v. Harris, 727 F.2d 936 (10th Cir.1984), holding that changes did not unconstitutionally impair contractual rights or violate due process.

4. See e.g., Kenneth Wing, The Community Service Obligation of Hill–Burton Health Facilities, 23 B.C.L.Rev. 577 (1982).

5. See e.g., James Blumstein, Court Action, Agency Reaction: The Hill–Burton Act as a Case Study, 69 Iowa L.Rev. 1227 (1984).

6. See e.g., Michael A. Dowell and Armin Freifeld, Hill–Burton Uncompensated Care: HHS Administrative Decisions and Remedies, 19 Clearinghouse Rev. 133 (1985).

7. 52 Fed.Reg. 46022–039 (1987).

8. 53 Fed.Reg. 44954 and 44955 (1988). Result of alteration in policy described in Flagstaff Medical Center v. Sullivan, 962 F.2d 879 (9th Cir.1992).

9. Flagstaff Medical Center v. Sullivan, 962 F.2d 879 (9th Cir.1992).

10. Id. at 887.

§ 10–17

1. Karen H. Rothenberg, Who Cares? The Evolution of the Legal Duty to Provide Emergency Care, 26 Hous. L. Rev. 21 (1989), for criticisms of Hill–Burton approach to access.

failure to comply with the notice requirement has provided indigent patients with an affirmative defense to nonpayment.[2]

Individual patients do not have a private right of action for medical treatment but do have a right to seek enforcement of the Act.[3] This limited private action for enforcement cannot be filed against the Department,[4] but may be filed against the hospital.[5]

In *Flagstaff Medical Center v. Sullivan*,[6] the Ninth Circuit Court of Appeals considered the case of a hospital that had unilaterally suspended its compliance with its Hill–Burton obligations for several years. The hospital later settled an enforcement action by the Department of Health and Human Services by liquidating its Hill–Burton obligation over several months through providing a total of over $1 million in free care.[7] The Court of Appeals allowed suit by private plaintiffs, however, and upheld a district court order that provided a remedy directly to persons who had been denied care during the time the hospital had suspended its obligation.[8]

In *Yale New Haven Hospital v. Mitchell*, the hospital brought an action against two former patients seeking payment for medical services rendered.[9] The former patients maintained that they had a right to refuse payment of a hospital bill because of the alleged failure of the hospital to comply with its Hill–Burton obligations. The Superior Court of Connecticut held that the former patients had a private right of action under the Hill–Burton Act, so that the hospital's alleged failure to comply with the notice requirements of the Act's regulations was a valid defense to the suit on the unpaid hospital bill.

D. NONDISCRIMINATION OBLIGATIONS UNDER TITLE VI

§ 10–18. Scope

Congress passed Title VI of the 1964 Civil Rights Act to prevent discrimination against minorities in federally-funded programs. The statute provides: "No person in the United States shall, on the ground of race, color, or national origin, be excluded from participation in, be denied the benefits of, or

2. See e.g., Hospital Center at Orange v. Cook, 426 A.2d 526 (N.J.Super.App.Div. 1981); Dark v. Prince George's County, 430 A.2d 629 (Md.App.1981).

3. 42 U.S.C.A. § 300s–6. Wey v. Evangelical Community Hospital, 833 F.Supp. 453 (M.D.Pa.1993).

4. See e.g., Gillis v. U.S. Department of Health and Human Services, 759 F.2d 565 (6th Cir.1985); Davis v. Ball Memorial Hospital, 640 F.2d 30 (7th Cir.1980).

5. White v. Moses Taylor Hospital, 763 F.Supp. 776 (M.D.Pa.1991).

6. 962 F.2d 879 (9th Cir.1992).

7. See also United States v. St. James Parish, 792 F.Supp. 1419 (E.D.La.1992); National Medical Enterprises v. United States, 28 Fed. Cl. 540 (1993); Crawford County v. Heckler,

629 F.Supp. 328 (W.D.Ark.1986). These cases interpret the statutory right of the government to recover Hill–Burton funds when a facility that has received Hill–Burton financing within twenty years prior to the transfer, is transferred to a for profit entity or ceases to be a public or nonprofit facility. 42 U.S.C.A. § 291i.

8. The district court had ordered refunds to all named plaintiffs and other eligible persons for payments made to the hospital during that time period and publication of notices inviting certain groups of persons to apply for benefits. Flagstaff Medical Center v. Sullivan, 773 F.Supp. 1325 (D.Ariz.1991). Contra, White v. Moses Taylor Hospital, 763 F.Supp. 776 (M.D.Pa.1991), holding that the private remedy available under the Act was much more restrictive.

9. 683 A.2d 1362 (Conn. Super. Ct. 1995).

be subjected to discrimination under any program or activity receiving Federal financial assistance."[1] Increasing evidence of racial discrimination in health care supports the continued viability of the Title VI prohibition.[2]

The Civil Rights Restoration Act broadly defined "program and activity."[3] If a corporation provides health care services and receives federal financial assistance, the entire corporation is covered by the provisions of Title VI, not just the division receiving federal funds. Most hospitals, nursing homes and other health-related institutions are the recipients of federal financial assistance through the Hill–Burton Act or the Medicare/Medicaid programs, and thus are required to comply with the antidiscrimination provisions of Title VI.[4]

§ 10–19. Litigation Under Title VI

Title VI specifically provides only for administrative enforcement.[1] However, the Supreme Court has implied a private right of action under Title VI.[2] Private litigants who are the victims of racial discrimination cannot seek termination of federal assistance, but can recover damages and equitable relief.[3]

Private plaintiffs have used Title VI to contest hospital closings which would diminish access to health care for minorities.[4] Title VI has also been used to halt Medicaid payment limitation policies which were facially race-neutral, but disproportionately impacted minority Medicaid recipients.[5]

A critical question in Title VI cases, as with most civil rights statutes, is whether the plaintiff may succeed by proving that the defendant's action had a disparate adverse impact on the protected group or whether the plaintiff must prove that the defendant intended to discriminate against the protected group.[6] The Supreme Court has addressed this question under Title VI.[7] In *Lau v. Nichols*, the Court held that Title VI prohibits both intentional and

§ 10–18

1. 42 U.S.C.A. § 2000d (1982).

2. See, e.g., Vernellia R. Randall, Racist Health Care Reforming An Unjust Health Care System to Meet the Needs of African–Americans, 3 Health Matrix 127 (1993).

3. The Civil Rights Restoration Act of 1987, Pub. L. No. 100–259, 102 Stat. 28 (1988); United States v. Harris Methodist Fort Worth, 970 F.2d 94, 97 n. 1 (5th Cir.1992). See Sidney D. Watson, Reinvigorating Title VI: Defending Health Care Discrimination—It Shouldn't Be So Easy, 58 Fordham Law Review 939, 945 n.2 (1990).

4. United States v. Baylor Univ. Medical Center, 736 F.2d 1039, 1046 (5th Cir.1984), cert. denied 469 U.S. 1189, 105 S.Ct. 958, 83 L.Ed.2d 964 (1985); Vakharia v. Swedish Covenant Hosp., 824 F.Supp. 769 (N.D.Ill.1993); NAACP v. Medical Center, 657 F.2d 1322 (3d Cir.1981); Doe v. St. Joseph's Hosp., 788 F.2d 411, 418 (7th Cir.1986).

§ 10–19

1. 42 U.S.C.A. § 2000d–1, 2 (1982).

2. Guardians Ass'n v. Civil Service Comm'n, 463 U.S. 582, 594, 103 S.Ct. 3221, 3228, 77 L.Ed.2d 866 (1983).

3. Franklin v. Gwinnett County Public Schools, 503 U.S. 60, 112 S.Ct. 1028, 1035, 117 L.Ed.2d 208 (1992), on remand 969 F.2d 1022 (11th Cir.1992), holding that damages are available for intentional violations of Title VI.

4. Bryan v. Koch, 627 F.2d 612 (2d Cir. 1980); NAACP v. Medical Center, 657 F.2d 1322 (3d Cir.1981).

5. Linton v. Commissioner of Health and Environment, 779 F.Supp. 925 (M.D.Tenn. 1990), affirmed 65 F.3d 508 (6th Cir.1995).

6. Alexander v. Choate, 469 U.S. 287, 292–293, 105 S.Ct. 712, 715–716, 83 L.Ed.2d 661 (1985); NAACP v. Medical Center, 657 F.2d 1322, 1329 (3d Cir.1981). See e.g., Mitchell A. Horwich, Title VI of the 1964 Civil Rights Act and the Closing of a Public Hospital, 1981 Duke L.J. 1033 (1981).

7. Sidney D. Watson, Reinvigorating Title VI: Defending Health Care Discrimination—It Shouldn't Be So Easy, 58 Fordham Law Review 939, 949 (1990).

disproportionate adverse impact discrimination.[8] The Court later in *Alexander v. Choate* concluded that Title VI itself prohibits only intentional discrimination,[9] but that the regulations enacted to interpret Title VI could be used as a basis for a disproportionate adverse impact claim.[10] Based on this case, it now appears that "plaintiffs can prevail upon a showing of disproportionate adverse impact without proof of intent to discriminate as long as they are careful to allege a violation of the Title VI regulations."[11]

Courts deciding Title VI disproportionate adverse impact cases tend to adopt standards developed in Title VII employment discrimination cases. Under this analysis, a Title VI plaintiff must demonstrate that the defendant used a specific practice that causes a disproportionate adverse impact. The burden then shifts to the defendant to show that the challenged practice is "demonstrably necessary to meet an important . . . [business] goal."[12] If this is shown, then the plaintiff can still prevail by showing that a less discriminatory alternative exists.[13]

However, two early Title VI cases involving hospital decisions to relocate out of primarily African American neighborhoods applied a less stringent standard of justification when a plaintiff proves a disproportionate adverse racial or ethnic impact.[14] The Second and Third Circuits have held that the defendant hospitals met their burden of justification by putting forward a legitimate nondiscriminatory reason for their decision. Basically, the courts found that because the decisions to relocate were rationally related to a legitimate hospital need, Title VI was not violated.[15] The two hospital relocation cases appear to be aberrations. Their evidentiary standards have not been followed in more recent Title VI decisions.[16]

Private activity under Title VI has recently increased but with limited success thus far. The most successful of these claims was a challenge to Tennessee's Medicaid plan in *Linton v. Tennessee Commissioner of Health and Environment*.[17] In this litigation, the district court judge found that the state Medicaid plan allowing nursing homes to limit the number of "beds" certified for Medicaid reimbursement within the facility violated Title VI. The district court adopted the State's plan to address the Title VI violations. The

8. 414 U.S. 563, 568, 94 S.Ct. 786, 789, 39 L.Ed.2d 1 (1974).

9. 469 U.S. 287, 293, 105 S.Ct. 712, 716, 83 L.Ed.2d 661 (1985).

10. 45 CFR § 80.3(b)(2).

11. Sidney D. Watson, Reinvigorating Title VI: Defending Health Care DiscriminationCIt Shouldn't Be So Easy, 58 Fordham Law Review 939, 953 (1990). See also, Linton v. Commissioner of Health and Environment, 779 F.Supp. 925, 935 (M.D.Tenn.1990), holding that a Tennessee policy which limited the number of nursing home beds available for Medicaid patients "had a disparate impact on racial minorities in Tennessee," and thus violated Title VI.

12. See e.g., Elston v. Talladega County Bd. of Educ., 997 F.2d 1394 (11th Cir.1993) (Title VI education case).

13. Id.

14. Bryan v. Koch, 627 F.2d 612 (2d Cir. 1980); NAACP v. Medical Center, Inc., 657 F.2d 1322 (1981). Daniel K. Hampton, Title VI Challenges by Private Parties to the Location of Health Care Facilities: Toward a Just and Effective Action, 37 B.C.L.Rev. 517 (1996).

15. See Sidney D. Watson, Reinvigorating Title VI: Defending Health Care Discrimination B It Shouldn't Be So Easy, 58 Fordham L. Rev. 939 (1990).

16. For a discussion of burden shifting, see Theodore Y. Blumoff & Harold S. Lewis, Jr., The Reagan Court and Title VII: A Common–Law Outlook on a Statutory Task, 69 N.C.L. Rev. 1 (1990).

17. 779 F.Supp. 925 (M.D.Tenn.1990); affirmed 65 F.3d 508 (6th Cir.1995). See also, Latimore v. County of contra Costa, 77 F.3d 489 (9th Cir.1996), opinion at 1996 WL 68196. But see, Madison–Hughes v. Shalala, 80 F.3d 1121 (6th Cir.1996).

Sixth Circuit affirmed the district court's acceptance of the plan over the objections of nursing home providers.

Scholars reviewing the implementation of Title VI by the government or in private litigation generally have concluded that its effectiveness has been limited by ineffective federal enforcement and by burdens of proof that are disadvantageous to plaintiffs in pursuing disparate impact claims. Some scholars have gone so far as to propose new civil rights legislation for the health care setting.[18]

E. DISCRIMINATION AGAINST PERSONS BASED ON MEDICAL CONDITION

§ 10–20.　Federal Statutes

Two federal statutes, Section 504 of the Rehabilitation Act of 1973[1] and the Americans with Disabilities Act,[2] prohibit discrimination against persons who are handicapped or disabled. While the Rehabilitation Act applies only to facilities receiving federal funds,[3] the Americans with Disabilities Act applies to public accommodations operated by private entities.[4] Both Acts provide a private right of action.[5] In addition, the Department of Health and Human Services enforces § 504 of the Rehabilitation Act.[6] The Department of Justice enforces the public accommodations provisions of the Americans with Disabilities Act.[7]

§ 10–21.　§ 504 of the Rehabilitation Act of 1973

The most well-known litigation under § 504 is the dispute over the "Baby Doe" regulations issued by the Department of Health and Human Services and eventually reviewed by the U.S. Supreme Court.[1] Although most claims under § 504 allege discrimination in the denial of treatment, at least two cases have attempted to claim, unsuccessfully, that § 504 is violated by aggressive medical treatment.[2]

In order to succeed in a claim for health care services under § 504, plaintiffs must prove, not only that they are handicapped within the definition of the Act, but that they are "otherwise qualified" for the program, at least with "reasonable accommodations"[3] for their handicap, and that the discrimi-

18. See, Sidney D. Watson, Minority Access and Health Reform: A Civil Right to Health Care, 22 J. of Law, Med. & Ethics 127 (1994).

§ 10–20

1. 29 U.S.C.A. § 794.

2. 42 U.S.C.A. §§ 12101–12213.

3. 29 U.S.C.A. § 702(b). See Dorer v. Quest Diagnostics, Inc., 20 F.Supp.2d 898 (D.Md. 1998), holding that any entity receiving Medicaid payment (including payment for lab services alone) is covered by the Act; U.S. v. Baylor University Medical Center, 736 F.2d 1039 (5th Cir.1984), cert. denied 469 U.S. 1189, 105 S.Ct. 958, 83 L.Ed.2d 964 (1985), holding that hospital that received Medicare funds fell within the reach of the Act.

4. 42 U.S.C.A. § 12182(a).

5. 29 U.S.C.A. § 794(a), referring to remedies available under Title VI of the Civil Rights Act of 1964, 42 U.S.C.A. § 2000d et seq.; 42 U.S.C.A. § 12117(a).

6. 29 U.S.C.A. § 721(b).

7. 42 U.S.C.A. § 12188(b).

§ 10–21

1. Bowen v. American Hospital Association, 476 U.S. 610, 106 S.Ct. 2101, 90 L.Ed.2d 584 (1986). See Chapter 16.

2. Gerben v. Holsclaw, 692 F.Supp. 557 (E.D.Pa.1988); Ross v. Hilltop Rehabilitation Hospital, 676 F.Supp. 1528 (D.Colo.1987).

3. See e.g., Nichols v. St. Luke Center of Hyde Park, 800 F.Supp. 1564 (S.D.Ohio 1992), holding that nursing home patient's violent

nation was based "solely" on their handicap. Allegations of multiple motives for refusal of treatment may defeat the § 504 claim. For example, the Tenth Circuit Court of Appeals has held that that allegation of discrimination based on socioeconomic status defeated the claim that discrimination was based solely on handicap.[4] This holding, though literally accurate, would eliminate a wide range of cases in which the discriminatory action arises from mixed motivation.

Although § 504 may be useful in challenging outright refusals to treat or to admit for treatment,[5] challenging specific medical decisions for individual patients presents special difficulties. The courts, for example, have tended to defer to medical judgment that the particular treatment is not warranted in light of the patient's medical condition, and so the patient is not "otherwise qualified" for the treatment. Two significant Circuit Court decisions have commented that proof of illegal discrimination in relation to an individual medical treatment decision under § 504 is nearly impossible.[6] The Tenth Circuit in *Johnson v. Thompson*,[7] stated that

> the 'otherwise qualified' language, when considered in conjunction with the 'solely' language . . ., poses a formidable obstacle for anyone alleging discrimination in violation of section 504. . . . Such a plaintiff must prove that he or she was discriminatorily denied medical treatment because of the birth defect and at the same time, must prove that, in spite of the birth defect, he or she was "otherwise qualified' to receive the denied medical treatment."[8]

In *United States v. University Hospital*,[9] the Second Circuit held that the condition that the plaintiff be "otherwise qualified" for the treatment "cannot be applied in the comparatively fluid context of medical treatment decisions without distorting its plain meaning."[10]

The courts have allowed closer review of refusals to provide treatment to persons with AIDS or HIV infection where it appears that the refusal was based on other than a medical judgment of effectiveness of the treatment. The Rehabilitation Act has been central to suits alleging discrimination by health care facilities against persons with AIDS.[11]

behavior was a result of a handicap but could not be reasonably accommodated.

4. Johnson v. Thompson, 971 F.2d 1487 (10th Cir.1992), cert. denied 507 U.S. 910, 113 S.Ct. 1255, 122 L.Ed.2d 654 (1993).

5. See generally Lawrence O. Gostin, The AIDS Litigation Project: A National Review of Court and Human Rights Commission Decisions, Part II: Discrimination, 263 J.A.M.A. 2086 (April 18, 1990), reporting on Office of Civil Rights investigation of nursing home refusals to admit HIV patients and noting that even in cases of outright refusal to treat, rights may be ineffective if hearings are prolonged.

6. See also Bowen v. American Hospital Association, 476 U.S. 610, 106 S.Ct. 2101, 90

L.Ed.2d 584 (1986), stating that the Court would not resolve the issue of whether the Act applies to "individual medical treatment decisions involving handicapped infants."

7. 971 F.2d 1487 (10th Cir.1992), cert. denied 507 U.S. 910, 113 S.Ct. 1255, 122 L.Ed.2d 654 (1993).

8. Id. at 1493.

9. 729 F.2d 144 (2d Cir.1984).

10. 729 F.2d 144, 156 (2d Cir.1984). But see, In the Matter of Baby K, 832 F.Supp. 1022 (E.D.Va.1993), affirmed on other grounds 16 F.3d 590 (4th Cir.1994).

11. Doe v. Centinela Hospital, 1988 WL 81776 (C.D.Cal.1988). See also, Glanz v. Vernick, 750 F.Supp. 39 (D.Mass.1990).

§ 10–22. Americans With Disabilities Act

The Americans with Disabilities Act, in comparison with § 504, expands the right to treatment considerably in some ways. Most notably, the ADA public accommodation requirements extend to private parties who do not receive federal funds.[1] The statute also does not require that plaintiff prove that denial of access was based "solely" on disability.[2]

The statute specifically provides that the "professional office of a health care provider" and a "hospital" are public accommodations.[3] The regulations provide that a public accommodation may not deny services and may not offer unequal services or unnecessarily segregated services to persons with disabilities.[4] The regulations also define specific duties for public accommodations. An illustration of such specific duties, provided in the regulations, refers to health care providers and states that such providers may refer disabled persons to other providers if the person requires treatment outside of the provider's medical specialty and if the referring provider would make a similar referral for any other individual.[5]

The Act also includes, as does § 504, an exception to the duty to provide services if the disabled person presents a "direct threat" to the health and safety of others.[6] The regulations define direct threat as "a significant risk to the health or safety of others that cannot be eliminated by a modification of policies, practices or procedures, or by the provision of auxiliary aids or services." The regulations require that the determination of whether the individual poses a direct threat must be the result of an "individualized assessment, based on reasonable judgment that relies on current medical knowledge or on the best available objective evidence." The assessment is to ascertain the nature, duration, and severity of the risk; the probability that the potential injury will actually occur; and whether reasonable modifications will mitigate the risk.[7]

Although the ADA more explicitly addresses persons with HIV or AIDS and imposes more specific duties upon providers, the suspension of the duty to provide services when there is a direct threat to the health or safety of others, including the practitioner one assumes, may limit its effectiveness. While there is certainly a risk of transmission of HIV from patients to health care workers in certain treatment circumstances, the risk of transmission does not exist at all in a great many medical interventions.[8] The statute does not require zero-risk; it allows a suspension of duties under the Act only where the risk is significant and unavoidable.[9]

§ 10–22

1. 42 U.S.C.A. § 12181(6).

2. 42 U.S.C.A. § 12188(a)(1).

3. 42 U.S.C.A. § 12181(7)(H)(L); 28 C.F.R. § 36.104.

4. 42 U.S.C.A. § 12182(b)(1)(A)(ii); 28 C.F.R. § 36.202.

5. 28 C.F.R. § 36.302.

6. 42 U.S.C.A. § 12182(b)(3).

7. 28 C.F.R. § 36.208. These standards have been applied in litigation claiming employment discrimination based on HIV infection. See § 4–23.

8. See generally Lawrence O. Gostin, Hospitals, Health Care Professionals and AIDS: The Right to Know the Health Status of Professionals and Patients, 48 Maryland L. Rev. 12 (1989).

9. See § 4022. See also, Joel Neugarten, The Americans with Disabilities Act: Magic Bullet or Band–Aid for Patients and Health Care Workers Infected with the Human Immunodeficiency Virus?, 57 Brooklyn L. Rev. 1277 (1992).

In 1998 the Supreme Court decided the landmark case of *Bragdon v. Abbott*.[10] In *Bragdon*, a patient infected with HIV brought suit against a dentist who refused to fill a cavity in her tooth in his dental office, but offered to perform the procedure at a hospital, if she paid the additional expenses. The patient asserted that she had a disability under the ADA and was illegally discriminated against by the dentist.

The first issue before the Court was whether or not Abbott had a disability under the ADA. The statute defines disability as "a physical or mental impairment that substantially limits one or more of the major life activities of such individual."[11] The majority, consisting of Justices Kennedy, Stevens, Souter, Ginsburg and Breyer, first determined that Abbott's condition constituted a physical impairment from the moment of infection "in light of the immediacy with which the virus begins to damage the infected person's white blood cells and the severity of the disease."[12] The majority then determined that the impairment affected a major life activity, reproduction, and that the limitation on that major life activity was substantial. The majority, therefore, held that HIV (both symptomatic and asymptomatic) constitutes a disability under the ADA. Justice Ginsburg wrote a concurring opinion in which she stated that HIV infection affects many life activities, not just reproduction.

Justice Rehnquist, joined by Justices Scalia and Thomas, wrote a dissenting opinion. They argued that reproduction is not a "major life activity" as contemplated in the statute and even if it were, Abbott had not proven that she suffered from a substantial limitation of that activity. Justice O'Connor also dissented, indicating that reproduction is not a major life activity; and, therefore, it was not necessary to proceed with the analysis to determine if Abbott suffered a substantial limitation. Rehnquist equated reproduction decisions with decisions regarding whether and whom to marry and what to do for a living. He argues that the "major life activities" contemplated by the statute are those which are "repetitively performed and essential to the day-to-day existence of a normally functioning individual."[13]

Risk assessment was the second issue before the Court.[14] As to this issue, the core of agreement is very narrow. All of the Justices agree that "the existence or nonexistence, of a significant risk must be determined from the standpoint of the person who refuses the treatment or accommodation, and the risk assessment must be based on medical or other objective evidence."[15] All of the Justices also agree that the subjective belief of the treating physician that a significant risk exists, even if maintained in good faith, will not justify a refusal to treat a patient. However, the Justices disagree on what sort of evidence should be given deference by the Court.

10. 524 U.S. 624, 118 S.Ct. 2196 (1998).

11. 42 U.S.C.A. § 12102(2). See further discussion of disability in § 4–23.

12. *Bragdon* at 2204.

13. Id. at 2215. See also Sarah Lynn Oquist, Reproduction Constitutes a "Major Life Activity" Under the ADA: Implications of the Supreme Court's Decision in Bragdon v. Abbott, 32 Creighton L. Rev. 1357 (1999) and Christiana M. Ajalat, Is HIV Really A "Disability"?: The Scope of the Americans With Disabilities Act After Bragdon v. Abbott, 22 Harv. J.L. & Pub. Pol'y 751 (1999).

14. See § 4–23.

15. Bragdon at 2210, citing School Board of Nassau County v. Arline, 480 U.S. 273 at 288 (1987).

Justices Kennedy, Souter, Stevens, Breyer and Ginsburg (the majority) stated that "[i]n assessing the reasonableness of [the dentist's] evidence, the views of public health authorities, such as the U.S. Public Health Service, CDC, and the National Institutes of Health, are of special weight and authority."[16] However, they believed that such views are not conclusive and can be refuted with other credible evidence. The lower court had relied on the 1993 CDC Dentistry Guidelines and the 1991 American Dental Association Policy on HIV in determining that the dentist's refusal to treat was improper.

The case was remanded to the lower court to determine if the Supreme Court's analysis of the CDC Guidelines and American Dental Association Policy would change its conclusion that the dentist's refusal to treat Abbott had violated the ADA. In a concurring opinion, Justice Stevens, joined by Justice Breyer, stated that the lower court carefully and extensively studied the evidence, and he would prefer to affirm the lower court's decision, but joined Justice Kennedy's opinion for the sake of obtaining a majority.

Justices Kennedy, Souter, and Ginsburg in contrast, believe that it was improper to rely on the CDC Guidelines because, in the view of the Justices, these guidelines do not assess the level of risk. With regard to the American Dental Association Policy (ADA), these Justices stated:

> We note, however, that the Association is a professional organization, which, although a respected source of information on the dental profession, is not a public health authority. It is not clear the extent to which the Policy was based on the Association's assessment of dentists' ethical and professional duties in addition to its scientific assessment of the risk to which the ADA refers. Efforts to clarify dentists' ethical obligations and to encourage dentists to treat patients with HIV infection with compassion may be commendable, but the question under the statute is one of statistical likelihood, not professional responsibility.[17]

In dissenting opinions, Justices Rehnquist, Scalia, Thomas and O=Connor indicated that they did not agree that the views of public health authorities should be given special deference. These Justices believe that "official" and "private" medical judgment should be given the same level of respect.[18] Additionally, these Justices believe that the dentist had brought evidence sufficient to withstand summary judgment and create a triable issue of fact. The opinions expressed *in Bragdon* with regard to the CDC Guidelines and ADA Policy are a significant departure from previous opinions.

Several states have enacted legislation or have administrative regulations specifically making refusal to treat persons with AIDS illegal.[19] In addition, state statutes prohibiting discrimination against disabled persons may create an obligation to provide care to HIV positive persons.[20] Beyond any legal

---

16. Id. at 2211.

17. Id. at 2212.

18. Id. at 2217.

19. See e.g., Wis. Stat. Ann. § 146.024(2)(a) and (4).

20. See e.g., Hurwitz v. New York City Commission on Human Rights, 553 N.Y.S.2d

323 (N.Y.App.Div.1990). See Lawrence O. Gostin, The AIDS Litigation Project: A National Review of Court and Human Rights Commission Decisions, Part II: Discrimination, 263 J.A.M.A. 2086 (April 18, 1990), for a discussion of both reported and unreported cases litigating refusals to treat persons with HIV.

duties to provide care, physicians have an ethical obligation to treat persons with AIDS.[21]

The ADA also may increase access to health care through its prohibition against discrimination in employment.[22] The Act has been interpreted by the Equal Employment Opportunity Commission, which enforces the employment coverage of the ADA, to prohibit discrimination by employers in health insurance coverage.[23]

F. CONCLUSION

§ 10–23. Conclusion

Current law compelling health care providers to furnish health care service consists of a patchwork of requirements, each with a narrow focus. Legal mandates to provide care may depend on the type of care at issue; for example, only emergency medical services are required for every patient who comes to a facility offering such services. Beyond the requirements for emergency care, statutory mandates for health care address certain categories of discrimination, including discrimination based on race and discrimination based on handicap or disability. This current approach of narrow unfunded mandates and anti-discrimination laws is limited in its capacity for addressing unmet needs for necessary health care services.

21. Council Report on Ethical Issues, 259 J.A.M.A. 1360 (1988); Bernard Lo, Obligations to Care for Persons with Human Immunodeficiency Virus, 4 Issues in Law & Medicine 367 (1988); Gregory P. Gramelspacher and Mark Siegler, Do Physicians Have a Professional Duty to Care for Patients With HIV Disease?, 4 Issues in Law & Medicine 383 (1988); A. Jonsen, "The Duty to Treat Patients with AIDS and HIV Infection" in AIDS and the Health Care System, (Gostin, ed. 1990) Yale University Press pp. 155–170.

22. 42 U.S.C.A. § 12111.

23. See § 11–5.

Chapter 11

MEDICARE

Table of Sections

Research References

Am Jur 2d, Social Security and Medicare §§ 1 et seq.
ALR Index: Medicare
ALR Digest: Social Security §§ 21–23
Am Jur Legal Forms 2d, Social Security and Medicare §§ 235:131–235:136, 235:221–235:223
Am Jur Pleading and Practice Forms (Rev), Social Security and Medicare §§ 1 et seq.

§ 11–1. Introduction and Overview

Unlike virtually every other industrialized nation, the United States has not, as of this writing, developed a program for making health care comprehensively available to its citizens. Rather, it has depended for financing health care largely on employment-related group health insurance, supplemented by individual insurance policies for those who can afford them and a variety of federal, state and local programs aimed at special populations. Despite the absence of any comprehensive program, government sponsorship of health care has a long history in the United States. The first federal medical program was established in 1798 to provide care for sick seamen in the coastal trade. State hospitals for the mentally ill and local public hospitals were well established by the mid-nineteenth century. Today government at all levels finances a plethora of health care institutions and programs. In 1997, government accounted for 44% of personal health care expenditures. Health care expenditures constitute 20.7% of federal expenditures and 24.5% of state and local expenditures. By far the largest single government health care program is the Medicare program, which accounts for almost 22% of the nation's health care spending.

Medicare is the product of a series of complex and evolving political compromises.[1] Though the idea of a comprehensive federal health insurance

§ 11–1   **1.** See Judith Feder, Medicare: the Politics

program has been debated for much of this century, what emerged from President Johnson's Great Society in 1965 was a program that covered only persons over sixty-five, and for this group only hospital care, physician's services, and a limited set of related services. The Medicare program was enacted at Title XVIII of the Social Security Act and began operation on January 1, 1966. Medicare has expanded somewhat since its enactment, and now covers the long-term disabled and those who require renal dialysis. The list of services it covers has also expanded, though an attempt to dramatically increase coverage under the Medicare Catastrophic Care Act in 1988 was quickly repealed because of the additional costs it would have imposed on Medicare beneficiaries. Though Medicare remains a program limited in eligibility and scope, it pays for a significant share of health care in the United States because it covers the part of the population most in need of medical care and the most expensive types of care required by this population.

The Medicare Program is really three programs, Parts A, B and C. Part A, the Hospital Insurance program, covers inpatient hospital, skilled nursing, home health, and hospice services.[2] Part A is funded (much like the social insurance programs of central European nations) by payroll taxes assessed against employers, employees, and the self-employed[3] and by interest income on this trust fund. General revenues may not be used to fund the Part A program, though Part A may borrow from other federal social insurance trust funds.

Part B (Supplemental Medical Insurance) benefits help pay for physician's services, outpatient hospital services, renal dialysis, speech and physical therapy, ambulatory surgery, home health services, durable medical equipment, rural health clinic services, comprehensive outpatient rehabilitation facility services, and some diagnostic tests.[4] Part B is a voluntary program. Only eligible persons who pay the Part B premium may receive its benefits.[5]

Part B was originally designed as a premium-financed insurance program to address the concern of doctors that they not become part of a system of "socialized medicine." In fact, however, the Part B trust fund has increasingly been financed by general revenue funds, which now cover about 75% of the costs of the Part B program.[6] Because state Medicaid programs pay Part B premiums for persons eligible for both Medicare and Medicaid, a significant share of Part B premium revenues also come from state revenues.[7]

Part C, the Medicare + Choice managed care program, was established by the Balanced Budget Act of 1997. Under the Medicare + Choice program, Medicare contracts with a wide variety of prepaid health plans on a risk basis to provide care to its beneficiaries. Medicare Part C managed care plans are required to cover all of the basic benefits offered by Parts A and B, and plans may offer additional supplemental benefits as well. Medicare Part C is funded

Marmor, The Politics of Medicare (2d Ed. 1999); Herman Miles Somers and Anne Ramsey Somers, Medicare and the Hospitals: Issues and Prospects (1967).

2. 42 U.S.C.A. § 1395d.

3. 42 U.S.C.A. § 1395i, 26 U.S.C.A. §§ 1401(b), 3101(b), and 3111(b).

4. 42 U.S.C.A. § 1395k; 42 C.F.R. § 410.3.

5. 42 U.S.C.A. § 1395j.

6. 42 U.S.C.A. § 1395r(a) sets the amount of the Part B premium. For 1999 it is $45.50.

7. 42 U.S.C.A. §§ 1396a(a)(10)(E), 1396d(p).

out of the Part A and Part B trust funds. Currently about 17% of Medicare beneficiaries are covered through managed care plans.

A. AUTHORITY AND ADMINISTRATION

§ 11–2. Authority

The Medicare program is established and governed by Title XVIII of the Social Security Act, codified at 42 U.S.C.A. §§ 1395–1395ggg. Medicare provisions are often referred to by their Social Security Act section numbers rather than their codified section number, and the numbers bear little relationship one to another. For example, § 1801 of the Social Security Act is 42 U.S.C.A. § 1395; § 1818 is § 1395i–2. This book uses U.S. Code references only to avoid confusion. Medicare regulations are codified at 42 C.F.R. Parts 405–424, and 482–498. The Medicare program is also governed through a variety of manuals and instructions. The most important of the manuals, which contain procedures and interpretive material, are the Provider Reimbursement Manual (HIM–15), the Intermediary Manual, the Carriers Manual, and the Coverage Issues Manual.[1] The Health Care Financing Administration also issues a steady stream of program memoranda, Administrator rulings, and miscellaneous letters and statements. The most comprehensive and current source of material on the Medicare program is the CCH Medicare and Medicaid Guide, which is supplemented weekly. Another valuable source of information on the program is the American Health Lawyers Association Institute on Medicare and Medicaid Payment Issues, which offers each spring a comprehensive overview of recent Medicare developments.

§ 11–3. Administration

The Medicare program is administered by the Health Care Financing Administration (HCFA) of the Department of Health and Human Services (HHS). The headquarters of HCFA is located in Washington, D.C., but many of the agency's functions are centered in Woodlawn, Maryland. HCFA also has ten regional offices, each headed by a Regional Administrator.

A number of other public and quasi-public entities play key roles in the Medicare program. The Office of Inspector General (O.I.G.) of HHS is responsible for enforcing the Medicare fraud and abuse proscriptions.[1] The Medicare Utilization and Quality Control Peer Review Organization (PRO) program oversees the utilization and quality of Medicare-financed services.[2] The Medicare Payment Advisory Commission (MEDPAC) advises Congress and HCFA on Medicare payment issues.[3] MEDPAC (like the Prospective Payment Assessment Commission and Physician Payment Review Commission which preceded it prior to 1997) publishes annual reports to Congress that provide highly

---

§ 11–2

1. Most manuals are available at http://www.hcfa.gov/pubforms/progman.htm.

§ 11–3

1. See below at Chapter 14.

2. See §§ 3–26 to 3–35.

3. MEDPAC was established by the Balanced Budget Act of 1997, combining the preexisting Prospective Payment Assessment Commission (ProPAC) and Physician Payment Review Commission (PPRC) which addressed hospital and physician payment issues respectively.

informative and up-to-date overviews of major issues facing the Medicare program.

Non-government entities also play a key role in the Medicare program. The bulk of the responsibility for processing and paying Medicare claims, handling the day-to-day administration of the program, and determining many coverage issues is assigned to Part A fiscal intermediaries and Part B carriers. These are private entities, often Blue Cross or Blue Shield Associations, under contract with the Secretary of HHS.[4] Each carrier serves a particular geographic area, though more than one intermediary may serve providers in the same area.[5] Private entities were relied on to administer the program in an effort to make the program more palatable to providers and professionals at the outset, but their presence in the program increases its administrative complexity and leads in some instances to lack of uniformity.

B. ELIGIBILITY

§ 11–4. Eligibility

Medicare eligibility is generally linked to eligibility for Social Security, the other major social insurance program of the United States. Persons eligible for retirement benefits under Social Security are automatically eligible for Medicare Part A benefits upon reaching age sixty-five.[1] If a person eligible for Social Security decides to continue working beyond age sixty-five, he or she may still begin receiving Medicare at sixty-five, though Medicare only covers expenses not otherwise covered under employment-related health insurance coverage.[2] Spouses or former spouses who qualify for Social Security as dependents may also begin receiving Medicare Part A benefits at sixty-five, as may former federal employees eligible for Civil Service Retirement and Railroad Retirement beneficiaries.[3] State and local government employees who were hired before April 1, 1986, and whose employer has not elected to participate in Medicare, are not qualified for Medicare.[4]

Disabled persons who are eligible for Social Security or Railroad Retirement benefits (or who would be eligible except for their earnings)[5] may receive Medicare Part A, but only after they have been eligible for cash benefits for at least two years.[6] Medicare Part A benefits are also available to persons with end-stage renal (kidney) disease after a three-month waiting period.[7] Finally, United States residents not otherwise eligible for Medicare, but over sixty-five years of age and citizens of the United States or lawful permanent residents for at least five years, may voluntarily enroll in Part A, but must pay a

4. The responsibilities of intermediaries and carriers, and the processes under which they are chosen, are found at 42 U.S.C.A. § 1395h (intermediaries) and 42 U.S.C.A. § 1395u(a), (b)(1) & (2); (c), (d), (e), (f) (carriers).

5. Special regulations require DME suppliers to deal with regional carriers. 42 U.S.C.A. § 1325m(a)(12).

§ 11–4

1. 42 U.S.C.A. §§ 426, 1395c.

2. See § 11–28, infra.

3. 42 U.S.C.A. §§ 426, 1395c.

4. 42 U.S.C.A. §§ 410(p)(3), 418(n), 426(a).

5. 42 U.S.C.A. § 1395i–2a (this coverage is only available on payment of premiums).

6. 42 U.S.C.A. § 426(b).

7. 42 U.S.C.A. § 426–1.

premium.[8]

Persons who are eligible for Medicare Part A or over sixty-five and either a citizen or a lawfully admitted permanent resident alien (who has resided in the United States for at least five years) are eligible for Part B benefits.[9] Part B enrollment is voluntary and contingent on continued payment of the Part B premium, set at $45.50 per month for 1999. Persons eligible for Part A, however, are automatically enrolled in Part B unless they choose to disenroll.[10] State Medicaid plans must pay Part B premiums and Medicare deductible and coinsurance amounts (discussed below) for persons entitled to Medicare Part A eligibility whose income does not exceed 100% of federal poverty guidelines and whose resources do not exceed twice the Supplemental Security Income resource eligibility level.[11]

C. COVERED AND EXCLUDED SERVICES

§ 11–5. Part A Covered Services

Part A covers inpatient hospital care for up to ninety days for any "spell of illness," plus up to sixty "life time reserve days" available on a one time basis.[1] A "spell of illness" is defined as a period of time beginning with the day a beneficiary is hospitalized or admitted to a nursing home and ending after the beneficiary has been out of the hospital or nursing home for sixty days.[2] For hospital patients, Medicare part A covers semiprivate accommodations;[3] ordinary nursing services; use of hospital facilities and social services; drugs, biologicals, supplies, appliances and equipment ordinarily furnished in the hospital for hospital care; and other diagnostic or therapeutic items or services ordinarily furnished by the hospital to inpatients.[4] Though Part A does not cover physician's services, it does cover services hospital patients receive from interns or residents and from attending physicians in teaching hospitals when the physicians do not otherwise bill for their services under Part B.[5]

Part A also covers up to 100 days per spell of illness of post-hospital extended care services in a skilled nursing facility (SNF).[6] Services are normally considered post-hospital if they begin within thirty days of a hospital stay and last at least for three days.[7] Beneficiaries rarely can take advantage of the entire 100 days of nursing home services, however, because restrictive interpretation of the skilled nursing requirement and the statutory exclusion of "custodial care"[8] has eliminated from Medicare Part A coverage much of

---

8. 42 U.S.C.A. § 1395i–2.

9. 42 U.S.C.A. § 1395o.

10. 42 U.S.C.A. § 1395p.

11. 42 U.S.C.A. § 1396d(p). See Patricia B. Nemore & Jeanne Finberg, MCCA Updates: Qualified Medicare Beneficiaries and Restrictive Medicaid Rules, Clearinghouse Rev., Oct. 1992 at 601.

§ 11.5

1. 42 U.S.C.A. § 1395d(a).

2. 42 U.S.C.A. § 1395x(a).

3. Unless semiprivate accommodations are not available or private accommodations are

necessary because of the patient's condition. 42 C.F.R. § 409.11.

4. 42 U.S.C.A. § 1935x(b); 42 C.F.R. §§ 409.10–409.19.

5. 42 U.S.C.A. § 1395x(b)(6) & (7); 42 C.F.R. § 409.15.

6. 42 U.S.C.A. §§ 1395d(a)(2), (f); 1395x(i). Medicare also covers non-post hospital extended care services under certain circumstances. 42 U.S.C.A. § 1395d(f).

7. 42 U.S.C.A. § 1395x(i).

8. 42 U.S.C.A. § 1395y(a)(9).

the care that is commonly provided in nursing homes.[9] Part A also covers hospice care, under certain circumstances and subject to limitations.[10]

Home health services are covered under both Part A and Part B. Historically most home health services were covered by Part A. The 1997 Balanced Budget Act, however limited Part A home health care to the first hundred home health visits initiated within fourteen days of a three-day hospital stay or a SNF stay, thus shifting much of the costs of the home health program to Part B.[11] Home health services include part-time or intermittent nursing or home health aide care; physical, occupational, and speech therapy; medical social services; and medical supplies and durable medical equipment.[12] The part-time or intermittent requirement is imposed to assure that home health care is not used for patients who in fact need full time skilled nursing care. The courts interpreted intermittent care to normally mean six or fewer days a week and part time to mean less than eight hours a day.[13] In the BBA, however, Congress defined the terms to mean less than 8 hours per day and 28 hours per week, or in particular cases less than 8 hours per day and 35 hours per week.[14] Drugs and biologicals (except for covered osteoporosis drugs), housekeeping services, and transportation services are not included.[15]

For each spell of illness the beneficiary is responsible for an inpatient hospital deductible,[16] set at $768 for 1999. For the sixtieth through the ninetieth day of inpatient hospital services the beneficiary must also pay a co-insurance amount equal to one quarter of the deductible, and for the ninety-first through the 150th lifetime reserve days, a co-insurance amount equal to half the deductible.[17] For the twentieth through the 100th day of SNF care, the beneficiary is responsible for a co-payment equal to one eighth of the deductible.[18] A beneficiary must also pay co-insurance for drugs and biologicals and respite care received in a hospice[19] and pay for the first three pints of whole blood received in a calendar year while a patient in a hospital or SNF.[20] The deductible and co-insurance obligations of Medicare recipients eligible for Medicaid are covered by Medicaid.[21]

§ 11–6. Part B Covered Services

Part B benefits include indemnification payments to the beneficiary, or direct payments to the practitioner or provider on the beneficiary's behalf, for medical and health services,[1] including:

9. See 42 C.F.R. §§ 409.30–409.36. To qualify for this benefit the beneficiary must need skilled technical or professional services ordered by a physician that are required on a daily basis and must as a practical matter be provided in a SNF or hospital.

10. 42 U.S.C.A. §§ 1395d(a)(4), (d), 1395x(dd); 42 C.F.R. §§ 418.200–204.

11. 42 U.S.C.A. § 1395d(a)(3).

12. 42 U.S.C.A. § 1395x(m); 42 C.F.R. §§ 409.40–409.50.

13. Duggan v. Bowen, 691 F.Supp. 1487 (D.D.C.1988).

14. 42 U.S.C.A.§ 1395x(m).

15. 42 U.S.C.A. § 1395x(m); 42 C.F.R. § 409.49.

16. 42 U.S.C.A. § 1395e(a)(1).

17. 42 U.S.C.A. § 1395e(a)(1).

18. 42 U.S.C.A. § 1395e(a)(3).

19. 42 U.S.C.A. § 1395e(a)(4).

20. 42 U.S.C.A. § 1395e(a)(2).

21. 42 U.S.C.A. §§ 1396a(a)(10)(E), 1396d(p)(3).

§ 11–6

1. 42 U.S.C.A. § 1395k.

1) physicians services (including the services of medical doctors, osteopaths, dentists, podiatrists, chiropractors, and optometrists);[2]

2) services and supplies commonly administered in a physician's office and covered by the physician's bill, including drugs and biologicals that cannot be self-administered;[3]

3) outpatient and partial hospital services incident to physician services;[4]

4) outpatient diagnostic services;[5]

5) outpatient physical and occupational therapy and speech pathology services;[6]

6) rural health clinic services, federally qualified health clinic services and telehealth services;[7]

7) home dialysis supplies and equipment, self-care home dialysis support services, and institutional dialysis services and supplies;[8]

8) antigens prepared by a physician for administration to a particular patient;[9]

9) services provided in a Medicare HMO or Competitive Medical Plan by a physician's assistant; nurse practitioner, clinical psychologist, or clinical social worker;[10]

10) blood clotting factors for self-administration by hemophiliacs;[11]

11) immunosuppressive drugs provided organ transplant recipients within a period of three years following the transplantation;[12]

12) physician's services performed legally by physician's assistants, nurse practitioner or clinical nurse specialist in collaboration with a physician where the services are not otherwise covered by provider payments under Part A;[13]

13) certified nurse-midwife services;[14]

14) qualified clinical psychologist services;[15]

15) clinical social worker services;[16]

2. 42 U.S.C.A. § 1395x(q), (r), (s)(1); 42 C.F.R. §§ 410.20, 410.22, 410.23, 410.24, 410.25.

3. 42 U.S.C.A. § 1395x(s)(2)(A); 42 C.F.R. § 410.26.

4. 42 U.S.C.A. § 1395x(s)(2), (ff); 42 C.F.R. § 410.27.

5. 42 U.S.C.A. § 1395x(s)(2)C); 42 C.F.R. § 410.28.

6. 42 U.S.C.A. § 1395x(g), (p), (s)(2)(D), (ll); 42 C.F.R. §§ 410.60, 410.62.

7. 42 U.S.C.A. § 1395x(s)(2)(E), (aa); 42 C.F.R. § 410.45. Section 4207 of the Balanced Budget Act of 1997 also established a demonstration project for informatics and telemedicine and electronic education.

8. 42 U.S.C.A. § 1395x(s)(2)(F), (O); 42 C.F.R. §§ 410.50, 410.52.

9. 42 U.S.C.A. § 1395x(s)(2)(G); 42 C.F.R. § 410.68.

10. 42 U.S.C.A. §§ 1395mm, 1395x(s)(2)(H), (aa)(5), (hh).

11. 42 U.S.C.A. § 1395x(s)(2)(I); 42 C.F.R. § 410.63.

12. 42 U.S.C.A. § 1395x(s)(2)(J).

13. 42 U.S.C.A. § 1395x(s)(2)(K), (aa)(5); 42 C.F.R. §§ 410.74 & 419.75.

14. 42 U.S.C.A. § 1395x(s)(2)(L), 1395x(gg); 42 C.F.R. § 410.77.

15. 42 U.S.C.A. § 1395x(s)(2)(M), (ii); 42 C.F.R. § 410.71.

16. 42 U.S.C.A. §§ 1395x(s)(2)(N), (hh); 42 C.F.R. § 410.73.

16) erythropoietin for dialysis patients;[17]

17) prostate cancer screening tests once a year,[18] colorectal cancer screening tests once a year,[19] screening mammography once a year,[20] screening pap smears and pelvic examinations every three years,[21] and bone mass measurement;[22]

18) oral anticancer chemotherapeutic drugs and antiemetic drugs for anticancer chemotherapeutic regimens.[23]

19) diabetes outpatient self-management training services;[24]

20) diagnostic X-ray tests, laboratory tests, and other diagnostic tests;[25]

21) X-ray, radium, and radioactive isotope therapy;[26]

22) surgical dressings, splints and casts;[27]

23) durable medical equipment;[28]

24) ambulance services where necessary;[29]

25) prosthetic devices, including colostomy bags and one pair of eyeglasses or contact lenses furnished subsequent to a cataract surgery with insertion of an intraocular lens;[30]

26) leg, arm, back and neck braces and artificial arms, legs and eyes;[31]

27) pneumonia, influenza, and, where appropriate, hepatitis B vaccines;[32]

28) services of a certified registered nurse anesthetist;[33] and

29) under limited circumstances, orthopedic shoes;[34]

Payment may also be made on behalf of the beneficiary for home health services;[35] and some Part B services provided by or under arrangement by a Part A provider;[36] outpatient physical and occupational therapy services;[37] rural health clinic services and federally qualified health center services.[38]

17. 42 U.S.C.A. § 1395x(s)(2)(O).

18. 42 U.S.C.A.§ 1395x(s)(2)(P), 1395x(oo).

19. 42 U.S.C.A. § 1395x(s)(2)(R), 1395x(pp).

20. 42 U.S.C.A. § 1395x(s)(13), 1395x(jj); 42 C.F.R. § 410.34.

21. 42 U.S.C.A. § 1395x(s)(14), (nn). Certain high risk women can receive this service every year.

22. 42 U.S.C.A. §§ 1395x(s)(15), 1395x(rr).

23. 42 U.S.C.A. § 1395x(s)(2)(Q) & (T).

24. 42 U.S.C.A. § 1395x(s)(2)(S), (qq).

25. 42 U.S.C.A. § 1395x(s)(3); 42 C.F.R. § 410.32.

26. 42 U.S.C.A. § 1395x(s)(4); 42 C.F.R. § 410.35.

27. 42 U.S.C.A. § 1395x(s)(5); 42 C.F.R. § 410.36(a)(1).

28. 42 U.S.C.A. § 1395x(n), (s)(6); 42 C.F.R. § 410.38.

29. 42 U.S.C.A. § 1395x(s)(7); 42 C.F.R. § 410.40.

30. 42 U.S.C.A. § 1395x(s)(8); 42 C.F.R. § 410.36(a)(2).

31. 42 U.S.C.A. § 1395x(s)(9); 42 C.F.R. § 410.36(a)(3).

32. 42 U.S.C.A. § 1395x(s)(10); 42 C.F.R. §§ 410.57, 410.63.

33. 42 U.S.C.A. §§ 1395x(s)(11), (bb); 42 C.F.R. § 410.69.

34. 42 U.S.C.A. § 1395x(s)(12).

35. 42 U.S.C.A. §§ 1395k(a)(2)(A), 1395x(m); 42 C.F.R. §§ 409.40–.50, 410.80.

36. 42 U.S.C.A. § 1395k(a)(2)(B).

37. 42 U.S.C.A. § 1395k(c)(2)(C).

38. 42 U.S.C.A. §§ 1395k(a)(2)(D), 1395x(aa); 42 C.F.R. § 410.45.

comprehensive outpatient rehabilitation facility (CORF) services;[39] ambulatory surgical facility services;[40] outpatient critical access hospital services;[41] prosthetic devices, orthotics, prosthetics and durable medical equipment furnished by Part A providers,[42]and partial hospitalization services provided by a community mental health center.[43]

In addition to the monthly premium charged Part B beneficiaries, each beneficiary must meet an annual $100 deductible before most Part B benefits become available.[44] Thereafter Part B generally pays 80% of reasonable cost or charge, the beneficiary must pay the remaining 20% plus whatever additional the provider or practitioner may legally charge.[45] There is no Part B beneficiary deductible or coinsurance obligation, however, for specified services, including clinical diagnostic laboratory tests paid under assignment and on the basis of a fee schedule or negotiated rate,[46] home health services,[47] pneumococcal and influenza vaccine,[48] and kidney donation.[49] Additionally, there is no coinsurance obligation for ambulatory surgical center services or outpatient surgery,[50] and outpatient critical access hospital services;[51] and no deductible for federally qualified health center services,[52] screening mammographies,[53] or pap or pelvic examinations.[54] The beneficiary is also responsible (as under Part A) for the cost of the first three pints of blood used in a calendar year.[55]

§ 11–7. Exclusions and Coverage Determinations

The Medicare statute and regulations explicitly identify a number of services that Medicare will not pay for. These fall into three broad categories, with a few additional miscellaneous exclusions. First there are a number of services that fall outside of the hospital/physician focus of the Medicare program, even though they are medical in nature. Most dental, optical, and outpatient pharmaceutical items and services, for example, are not covered by Medicare.[1]

The second category of exclusions denies payment for services for which the beneficiary is not financially liable or which are covered by another source of payment. Medicare will not pay, for example, for services covered by employee benefits plans or workers compensation.[2]

39. 42 U.S.C.A. §§ 1395k(a)(2)(E), 1395x(cc); 42 C.F.R. §§ 410.100–410.105.

40. 42 U.S.C.A. § 1395k(a)(2)(F); 42 C.F.R. §§ 416.1–416.150.

41. 42 U.S.C.A. §§ 1395k(a)(2)(H), 1395x(mm)(3).

42. 42 U.S.C.A.§§ 1395k(a)(2)(G) & (I).

43. 42 U.S.C.A. §§ 1395k(a)(2)(J), 1395x(ff). 42 C.F.R. §§ 410.43, 410.110, 410.172.

44. 42 U.S.C.A. § 1395l(b); 42 C.F.R. § 410.160.

45. 42 U.S.C.A. § 1395l(a). For screening sigmoidoscopies and colonoscopies the coinsurance amount is 25% for facility charges, based on a fee schedule. 42 U.S.C.A. §§ 1395m(d)(2)(C)(ii) & 1395m(d)(3)(C)(ii).

46. 42 U.S.C.A. § 1395l(a)(1)(D), (2)(D), (b)(3), (h)(6).

47. 42 U.S.C.A. § 1395l(a)(2)(A), (b)(2).

48. 42 U.S.C.A. § 1395l(a)(1)(B), (b)(1).

49. 42 C.F.R. § 410.163.

50. 42 U.S.C.A. § 1395l(a)(4).

51. 42 U.S.C.A. § 1395l(a)(6).

52. 42 U.S.C.A. § 1395l(b)(4).

53. 42 U.S.C.A.§ 1395l(b)(5).

54. 42 U.S.C.A. § 1395l(b)(6).

55. 42 U.S.C.A. § 1395l(b).

§ 11–7

1. As this book goes to press, there is considerable interest in the creation of a Medicare outpatient prescription drug benefit. See Lynn Etheredge, Purchasing Medicare Prescription Drug Benefits: A New Proposal, Health Aff. July/Aug. 1999 at 7.

2. See Section 11–28, infra.

Third, Medicare excludes items and services that are of questionable medical value. A broad general exclusion excludes payment for services "not reasonably necessary for the diagnosis or treatment of illness or injury or to improve the functioning of a malformed body part."[3]

The requirement that Medicare services be reasonable and necessary compels intermediaries and carriers constantly to make decisions as to whether particular services will be covered under particular circumstances. The key coverage decision as to major procedures at the national level is the assignment of a ICD–9–CM or HCPCS procedure code so that the procedure can be billed. But coverage decisions must often also be made on an individual basis at the carrier or intermediary level. HCFA has determined that no conclusive presumption should be given to a treating physician's medical opinion in making decisions regarding the necessity of hospital or SNF care, but that the opinion should be considered together with other pertinent medical information.[4]

Periodically, however, the development of new technologies or of new applications of existing technologies necessitates decisions on coverage that are national in scope.[5] HCFA published proposed rules for making such decisions in the late 1980s, but these rules faced strong opposition, and were never implemented.[6] Instead, HCFA proceeded informally, publishing in its Coverage Issues Manual its coverage determinations.[7] In 1995 HCFA also published regulations permitting payment, under some circumstances, for investigational devices categorized as non-experimental (Category B) by the FDA.[8]

In late 1998 HCFA created a Medicare Coverage Advisory Committee (MCAC), consisting of 120 health care experts to assist it in developing Medicare coverage policy.[9] In May of 1999, HCFA published a notice describing the procedures it intends to use for making national coverage decisions using the MCAC.[10] HCFA intends to use this panel, together with review by its own staff and independent research and extramural assessment to develop coverage policy. It will review technologies either at its own instance or in response to formal requests. It intends to respond to formal requests within 90 days. It will rely heavily on the use of its internet home page to air coverage issues. Despite the creation of a more formal national coverage policy decisionmaking process, the vast majority of individual coverage decisions continue, as always, to be made by carriers and intermediaries.

3. 42 U.S.C.A. § 1395y(a)(1).

4. HCFA Ruling No. 93–1, Medicare & Medicaid Guide (CCH) ¶ 41,444 (May 18, 1993).

5. See David M. Frankford, Food Allergy and the Health Care Financing Administration: A Story of Rage, 1 Widener L. Symp. J. 160 (1996) ; Gordon B. Schatz, Medical Technology Coverage and Coding, in 1990 Health Law Handbook, 413 (Alice G. Gosfield ed., 1990); Louis B. Hays, Medicare Coverage, 262 JAMA 2794 (1989) (describing the coverage determination process). Eleanor Kinney, Setting Limits: A Realistic Assignment for the Medicare Program, 33 St. Louis LJ 631 (1989),

Eleanor Kinney, National Coverage Policy Under the Medicare Program: Problems and Proposals for Change, 32 St. Louis LJ 869 (1988).

6. 54 Fed. Reg. 4,302 (1989) (to be codified at 42 C.F.R. Pts. 400 and 405) (proposed Jan. 30, 1989).

7. General Notice, 54 Fed. Reg. 34,555 (1989).

8. 60 Fed.Reg. 48417, codified at 42 C.F.R. §§ 405,201–.215.

9. 63 Fed. Reg. 68780 (1998).

10. 64 Fed. Reg. 22619 (1999).

A person adversely affected by a coverage decision may seek reconsideration of the decision, but decisions are only subject to limited review. They may not be reviewed by an administrative law judge or held unlawful for noncompliance with the Administrative Procedures Act.[11] If a court decides that a decision was based on an incomplete record or inadequate information, it must remand for supplementation of the record, and cannot determine that the item is covered except on review of the supplemented record.[12]

The medical necessity determination that has probably caused the most disputes is the exclusion of "custodial" care.[13] Custodial care includes services that assist in activities of daily living (such as bathing, using the toilet, getting in and out of bed or administration of medications that are normally self-administered) but that do not require skilled medical personnel.[14] Custodial care thus includes the services provided in hospitals to patients held for observation or because a community placement is not available[15] and much of the care provided in nursing facilities.[16] In determining whether care is merely "custodial" or not, the patient's total condition must be considered,[17] and the attending physician's opinion as to the care required should be a key factor.[18]

Where a patient receives services that are not "reasonable and necessary" or that constitute custodial care, Medicare may nonetheless pay for the services if the services were provided by a provider or by a practitioner or supplier that accepted assignment and neither the beneficiary nor the person who provided the service "knew, or could reasonably have been expected to know, that the services were excluded from coverage."[19] If the provider, practitioner or supplier knew or should have known that the service was not covered, but the beneficiary did not know and could not reasonably have been expected to know this, Medicare will not pay for the service. If the beneficiary paid for the service and requests indemnification, Medicare will indemnify the beneficiary and recover from the provider, practitioner and supplier.[20] If a physician furnishes service not paid for on an assignment basis[21] and the service is subsequently determined to not have been reasonable and necessary, the physician must refund any payments collected from the beneficiary.[22]

D.   PROVIDER PARTICIPATION

§ 11–8.   Participation Agreements

For health care institutions or entities to receive payment from Medicare they must meet the Medicare conditions of participation (for Part A services)

11. 42 U.S.C.A. § 1395ff(b)(3)(A) & (B).

12. 42 U.S.C.A. § 1395ff(b)(3)(C). See, Wilkins v. Secretary of HHS, 1989 WL 265473 (D.Ill.1989).

13. 42 U.S.C.A. § 1395y(a)(9); 42 C.F.R. § 411.15(g) (custodial care may be available in the context of otherwise covered hospice care).

14. See Hayner v. Weinberger, 382 F.Supp. 762 (E.D.N.Y.1974).

15. Monmouth Medical Ctr. v. Harris, 646 F.2d 74 (3d Cir.1981).

16. Sokoloff v. Richardson, 383 F.Supp. 234, 238 (E.D.N.Y.1973).

17. Landa v. Shalala, 900 F.Supp. 628 (E.D.N.Y.1995); Ridgely v. Secretary of HEW, 475 F.2d 1222 (4th Cir.1973); Whitman v. Weinberger, 382 F.Supp. 256 (E.D.Va.1974).

18. Ridgely v. Secretary of HEW, 475 F.2d 1222 (4th Cir.1973); Breeden v. Weinberger, 377 F.Supp. 734 (M.D.La.1974).

19. 42 U.S.C.A. § 1395cc(a)(1)(B); 42 C.F.R. § 411.400(a)(2).

20. 42 C.F.R. § 411.402(a).

21. See below at § 13–26.

22. 42 C.F.R. § 411.408.

or conditions of coverage (for Part B services).[1] Part A providers must also enter into a contract with Medicare called a provider agreement, and some Part B suppliers must meet requirements similar to those found in provider agreements. Professionals who provide services under Part B are not required to enter into special agreements with Medicare (other than "participating physicians" described at below). Conditions of participation and coverage are specific to the type of provider or supplier and are described in the next section. Provider agreement provisions are discussed here.

The term "provider of services" includes hospitals, critical access hospitals, skilled nursing facilities (SNFs), comprehensive outpatient rehabilitation facilities (CORFs), home health agencies (HHAs), and hospice programs.[2] Providers seeking to enter into provider agreements must comply with HHS regulations implementing title VI of the Civil Rights Act of 1964[3] and with federal ownership and control disclosure requirements.[4] Certain providers, including home health agencies, DME suppliers, comprehensive outpatient rehabilitation facilities, and physical therapy agencies must post a surety bond of at least $50,000 before they can become Medicare providers.[5] HCFA may refuse to enter into an agreement with a provider that has been convicted under the fraud and abuse laws or that is bankrupt or insolvent.

The basic terms of the provider agreement are set out at 42 U.S.C.A. § 1395cc. These include promises:

1) not to charge beneficiaries or other persons for items or services covered by Medicare (or for excluded services received without fault of the beneficiary, services for which payment is denied by a PRO, or services for which payment would have been made but for the hospital's failure to comply with procedural requirements) except for charges for permitted deductibles, coinsurance, and copayments or for items and services that the beneficiary requests that are more expensive than those covered by Medicare (such as a private room);[6]

2) to refund any money incorrectly collected from beneficiaries or other persons;[7]

3) to disclose the hiring of any person who was employed in the previous year in a responsible position by a carrier or intermediary;[8]

4) to maintain an agreement with a PRO to perform required utilization and quality review;[9]

§ 11–8

1. 42 U.S.C.A. § 1395cc., Payment can be made to non-participating hospitals for emergency services if the hospital complies with specified requirements, and if the hospital is more accessible than the nearest participating hospital that can provide the needed services. 42 U.S.C.A. § 1395f(d); 42 C.F.R. §§ 424.100–424.109.

2. 42 U.S.C.A. § 1395x(u).

3. See 42 C.F.R. § 489.10(b); 45 C.F.R. Pts. 80, 84, 90.

4. 42 U.S.C.A. §§ 1320a–3, 1320a–5. Disclosure requirements also apply to Part B agencies. 42 U.S.C.A. § 1320a–3a.

5. 42 U.S.C.A. §§ 1395m(a)(16); 1395x(o)(7); 1395x(p)(4)(A)(v)l; 1395x(cc)(2)(I); 42 C.F.R. §§ 489.60–.73.

6. 42 U.S.C.A. §§ 1395cc(a)(1)(A), (B), (G) & (K); 42 C.F.R. §§ 489.20(a), 489.21, 489.30–35.

7. 42 U.S.C.A. § 1395cc(a)(1)(C); 42 C.F.R. §§ 489.20(b), 489.40–489.42.

8. 42 U.S.C.A. § 1395cc(a)(1)(D); 42 C.F.R. §§ 489.20(c); 420.203.

9. 42 U.S.C.A. § 1395cc(a)(1)(F); 42 C.F.R. § 489.20(e).

5) to furnish, in the case of hospitals or critical access hospitals, directly or by arrangement, all items and services for which the beneficiary is entitled to have payment made by Medicare, except for professional services otherwise covered by Medicare;[10]

6) to comply, in the case of hospitals or critical access hospitals, with the EMTALA emergency treatment (anti-dumping) requirements of 42 U.S.C.A. § 1395dd (described in chapter 10), and to maintain documentation of compliance;[11]

7) to participate, in the case of hospitals, in the CHAMPUS, CHAMPVA, and Veterans' Administration Programs;[12]

8) to provide beneficiaries, in the case of hospitals, at or about the time of admission, with the Important Message From Medicare, informing them of their rights as Medicare patients;[13]

9) to make available to patients, in the case of hospitals and critical access hospitals, the Medicare directory of participating physicians for the area; to identify appropriate participating physicians as alternatives when a referral is made to a nonparticipating physician; and to post conspicuously a notice as to whether or not the hospital participates in Medicaid;[14]

10) to accept as payment in full payments made by Medicare + Choice organizations for their members;[15]

11) to supply, in the case of HHAs, ostomy care supplies to beneficiaries who require them;[16]

12) to comply with the advanced directives requirements of OBRA 1990, described at chapter 15;[17]

13) to comply with the requirements of the Medicare as Secondary Payer program, including identifying and billing primary insurers and refunding funds collected from primary payers to Medicare;[18]

14) to not condition admission on prepayment of charges for services, and not evict or threaten to evict a patient for non-payment of copayments or deductibles.[19]

15) to maintain and disclose to HCFA information regarding referrals to entities that have a specified financial relationship with the provider,[20]

HCFA may refuse to enter into a provider agreement with a provider whose principals have been convicted of Medicare fraud or that otherwise does not meet the requirements set out above.[21]

10. 42 U.S.C.A. § 1395cc(a)(1)(H); 42 C.F.R. § 489.20(d).

11. 42 U.S.C.A. § 1395cc(a)(1)(I); 42 C.F.R. §§ 489.20(m),(q), & (r).

12. 42 U.S.C.A. § 1395cc(a)(1)(J); 42 C.F.R. § 489.25 & .26.

13. 42 U.S.C.A. § 1395cc(a)(1)(M), 42 C.F.R. § 489.27.

14. 42 U.S.C.A. § 1395cc(a)(1)(N).

15. 42 U.S.C.A. § 1395cc(a)(1)(O).

16. 42 U.S.C.A. § 1395cc(a)(1)(P); 42 C.F.R. § 489.20(K).

17. 42 U.S.C.A. § 1395cc(a)(1)(Q), (f)(1); 42 C.F.R. §§ 489.100—.104.

18. 42 C.F.R. § 489.20(f)-(j). See § 11–28 below.

19. 42 C.F.R. § 489.22. The hospital may require prepayment for clearly non-covered services.

20. 42 U.S.C.A. § 1395cc(a)(1)(S).

21. 42 U.S.C.A. § 1395cc(b)(2); 42 C.F.R. §§ 489.10, 489.12.

HCFA may terminate the provider agreement of a provider that fails to comply substantially with the requirements of the Medicare Act or regulations or to comply substantially with relevant conditions of participation, or that has been excluded from participation from the program for Medicare fraud.[22] HCFA must give the provider and the public at least fifteen days notice prior to termination of a provider agreement. It may, however, terminate a SNF on two days notice where deficiencies immediately jeopardize the health and safety of patients.[23] A terminated provider may appeal under the appeal provisions of 42 C.F.R. Part 498, discussed below at § 11–26.

§ 11–9.   Conditions of Participation

Part A providers must, in addition to entering into Provider Agreements, also meet specified "Conditions of Participation." Some Part B suppliers must also meet "Conditions for Coverage." These conditions are found in the definitions of the various institutions or services found in the Medicare statute and in elaborations on these definitions found in the Medicare regulations.

Compliance of providers with conditions of participation is determined by state health agencies, which inspect facilities under agreement with HHS.[1] State survey and certification requirements, including long term care survey forms, are found in Part 488 of 42 C.F.R. The state survey agency must survey the facility and make a recommendation to HCFA prior to initial certification.[2] Thereafter the state survey agency must periodically review compliance, normally on an annual basis.[3] If the state survey agency finds that a facility is out of compliance and that the noncompliance substantially limits the facility's capacity to provide adequate care or adversely affects the health and safety of patients, the survey agency must report this to HCFA, which can then determine that the facility does not qualify for participation in Medicare.[4] If deficiencies do not rise to this level, the facility can be recertified subject to a correction plan.[5] Special requirements apply to nursing facilities with deficiencies, which are discussed in Chapter 1.[6] The findings of certification surveys must be made available by HCFA in a readily accessible form and place.[7]

In order to participate under the Medicare program a hospital must conform to the definition of 42 U.S.C.A. § 1395x(e) and the conditions of participation found in 42 C.F.R. Part 482. Psychiatric hospitals must meet the requirements of 42 U.S.C.A. § 1395x(f) and 42 C.F.R. §§ 482.60–482.62.

22. 42 U.S.C.A. § 1395cc(b)(2). 42 C.F.R. § 489.53 also permits termination of providers that, inter alia, place restrictions on Medicare beneficiaries not applied uniformly to all other patients; fail to furnish HCFA with information necessary to determine whether payments are due; refuse to allow HCFA access to their books and records to verify payment information; fail to disclose correctly ownership information required by 42 C.F.R. §§ 420.204, 420.205 or 420.206; or violate the civil rights laws, fail to comply with EMTALA, fail to furnish a notice of discharge rights, or fail to accept Medicare payment as payment in full.

23. 42 C.F.R. § 489.53 (see Chapter 1 for further discussion of Medicare sanctions applicable to SNFs.)

§ 11–9
1. 42 U.S.C.A. § 1395aa(c).
2. 42 C.F.R. §§ 488.11, 488.12.
3. 42 C.F.R. § 488.20.
4. 42 C.F.R. § 488.24. The facility can appeal this determination under 42 C.F.R. Part 498.
5. 42 C.F.R. § 488.28.
6. 42 C.F.R. §§ 488.400–.456.
7. 42 U.S.C.A. § 1395aa(a).

Alternatively, a hospital accredited by the Joint Commission on Accreditation of Healthcare Organizations or the American Osteopathic Association is deemed to meet the hospital conditions of participation if the institution authorizes the accreditation agency to release to HCFA its accreditation report and HCFA has not otherwise found significant deficiencies in the hospital.[8]

To participate in Medicare, skilled nursing facilities must meet the requirements set out in 42 U.S.C.A. § 1395i–3(a)—(d) and regulations found at 42 C.F.R. §§ 483.1–483.75. Nursing facility conditions of participation are explored further in Chapter 1. HCFA regulations also permit deemed status for other types of providers where the accrediting agency is recognized by HHS.[9]

E. MEDICARE PROSPECTIVE PAYMENT UNDER DIAGNOSIS–RELATED GROUPS

§ 11–10. Basic Principles

When Medicare was established in the mid–1960s, it borrowed from the Blue Cross programs a system of paying hospitals based on their reported allowable costs. The inflationary possibilities that could have been predicted from such a system in fact materialized: between 1967 and 1983 Medicare hospital expenditures (which then constituted two-thirds of program expenditures) increased elevenfold from $3 billion to $33 billion. In 1982 Congress, impressed by the success of state rate regulation systems in controlling costs, mandated the implementation of a prospective payment system that would pay hospitals based on a predetermined rate instead of one determined retrospectively based on reported costs. One of the models that Congress looked to was that of New Jersey, where diagnosis-related groups (DRG) prospective payment, implemented through an all-payer reimbursement system, had dramatically reduced hospital costs. Between 1980 and 1982, New Jersey experienced the second lowest hospital per diem cost increase in the country and dropped from 18th to 32nd in health care costs. Congress sought to emulate this success.

On October 1, 1983 Medicare began implementing a DRG-based prospective payment system.[1] DRG-based payment considers hospitals as entities that coordinate services to produce particular products—i.e. the diagnosis and treatment of specific conditions such as heart attacks, ulcers, and tumors. Medicare pays hospitals, therefore, a predetermined rate specific to the

---

8. 42 U.S.C.A. § 1395bb; 42 C.F.R. § 488.5 HCFA may require validation surveys on a random basis in response to substantial allegations of significant deficiencies to validate JCAHO or AOA accreditation. 42 C.F.R. § 488.7. HCFA may not disclose the information received from the Joint Commission or AOA (other than home health agency surveys) except as necessary in enforcement proceedings. 42 U.S.C.A. § 1395bb(c).

9. 42 C.F.R. § 488.6.

1. 42 U.S.C.A.§ 1395ww(d). David Frankford has written two excellent articles exploring the complexity of and critiquing the DRG reimbursement system: The Complexity of Medicare's Hospital Reimbursement System: The Paradoxes of Averaging, 78 Iowa L. Rev. 517 (1993); The Medicare DRGs: Efficiency and Organizational Rationality, 10 Yale J. on Reg. 273 (1993). See also, describing the politics of the adoption of DRG, Paying for Medicare: The Politics of Reform (1992).

condition at issue, assuming that each patient with the same diagnosis requires roughly the same consumption of medical resources.

The initial prospective payment system (PPS) legislation mandated the development by 1986 of a methodology for prospectively reimbursing capital costs by 1986. Though this deadline was delayed by successive budget reconciliation acts, final rules implementing a capital costs PPS were published by HCFA on August 30, 1991.[2] Capital cost prospective payment has been gradually phased in over a ten-year transition period.

Because the DRG–PPS system was basically designed to pay for short-term hospitalizations, it did not apply to hospitals that treat patients on a long term basis. Institutions excluded from PPS include psychiatric hospitals, rehabilitation hospitals, children's hospitals, long-term care hospitals, cancer hospitals, hospitals located in U.S. territories outside of the continental United States,[3] and distinct part psychiatric or rehabilitation units in acute care hospitals.[4] These PPS-exempt facilities continued to be reimbursed on a cost basis after the implementation of PPS[5] (See § 11–17 below), though HHS was directed by Congress to develop prospective payment methodologies for non-PPS hospitals by 1992.[6] The Balanced Budget Act of 1997 required the development of a prospective payment system for rehabilitation hospitals, which will serve as a model for developing PPS for other specialized hospitals.[7]

The fundamental idea behind DRG–PPS payment is that all hospitals ought to be paid for inpatient hospital care on a flat-rate per-case basis so that efficient hospitals will be rewarded for their efficiency and inefficient hospitals will have an incentive to become more efficient. The key variable for determining payment under the DRG system is the diagnosis of the patient being treated because it was believed that this variable explained most of the legitimate variation in the level of resources needed to care for different patients. Though rates are now largely determined on a national basis, the formula for determining payment recognizes that labor costs (which constitute about 3/4 of hospital costs) vary dramatically throughout the country, and that other costs also differ between urban and rural areas. Rates are also adjusted significantly to accomplish various public policy goals, such as supporting medical education, preserving isolated rural hospitals, or underwriting otherwise uncompensated care.

To arrive at a basic PPS per patient payment amount, each Medicare patient discharged by a PPS hospital is first assigned to a diagnosis-related group (DRG), and thus a DRG weight. This weight is then multiplied by a "standardized amount", the cost in dollars of treating the average Medicare patient discharged during the year. This standardized amount is the sum of two components, the labor portion (adjusted by the wage-index to account for labor cost variations between areas of the country) and the non-labor portion

2. Prospective Payment System for Inpatient Hospital Capital–Related Costs, 56 Fed. Reg. 43,358 (August 30, 1991) (to be codified at 42 C.F.R. Pts. 412 and 413).

3. 42 U.S.C.A. § 1395ww(d)(1)(B); 42 C.F.R. § 412.23.

4. 42. C.F.R. §§ 412.25, 412.27, 412.29, 412.30.

5. 42 C.F.R. § 412.22(b).

6. Omnibus Budget Reconciliation Act of 1990, Pub. L. No. 101–508, § 4005(b), 104 Stat. 1388 (1990).

7. 42 U.S.C.A. §§ 139522(b)(3)(B)(i); (d)(3)(A), (j).

(which varies depending on whether the hospital is located in a "large-urban" or other areas). The standardized amount, and thus DRG reimbursement, in increased each year by a percentage established by Congress, which allows Congress to control program cost growth.[8]

Thus, for example, to determine the basic standardized operating cost payment a hospital located in Columbus, Ohio would receive for a patient treated for a coronary bypass with cardiac catheterization in the year following October 1, 1999, one would multiply the weight of DRG 107, coronary bypass with cardiac catheterization, (5.4891) times the sum of the non-labor related large urban standardized amount ($1,128.44) and product of the labor-related large urban standardized amount ($2,776.21) and the Columbus, Ohio wage index (.9929) as follows:

$$5.4891 \quad X \ (\$1,128.44 + (\$2,776.21 \ X \ .9929) = \$21,324.82$$

This amount is then adjusted depending on the specific type of hospital involved and added to capital costs and non-PPS costs (such as direct medical education costs) to reach a final payment amount for the particular patient.

§ 11-11. Calculation of PPS Rates

PPS rates cover most routine operating costs attributable to patient care, including room and board, routine nursing services, ancillary services such as radiology or laboratory services, special care unit operating costs, and malpractice insurance costs.[1] All services provided to a patient in a hospital, except physician's services, must be furnished by the hospital directly or through arrangements with another and be paid for under the PPS payment. "Unbundling"—billing for services provided a hospitalized patient separately under Part B—is prohibited.[2] Effective as of 1991, the PPS payment also covers all diagnostic services and other services related to admission that are delivered by a hospital or its wholly owned subsidiary in the three days prior to admission.[3] In recent years, HHS has aggressively pursued hospitals suspected of unbundling under the Medicare fraud laws.[4]

PPS rates explicitly do not cover direct medical education costs, compensation of physicians in teaching hospitals paid under Part B, outpatient services, the cost of qualified nonphysician anesthetists' services, services covered by Part B, bad debts attributable to Medicare beneficiaries, the costs of photocopying and mailing medical records requested by a PRO, the costs of blood clotting factors, and organ acquisition costs incurred by transplantation centers, all of which are either reimbursed on a cost or fee schedule basis.[5]

The target adjustment of the standardized amount has varied since the establishment of PPS depending on whether the hospital was rural, urban, or large urban, giving Congress some power to distribute its largess from year to year among its varied constituents. Initially, the standardized amounts favored urban hospitals over rural. This differentiation was based on the

8. 42 U.S.C.A.§ 1395ww(b).

§ 11-11

1. 42 C.F.R. § 412.2(b), (c).

2. 42 U.S.C.A. §§ 1395y(a)(14), 1395cc(a)(1)(H); 42 C.F.R. § 489.20(d).

3. 42 U.S.C.A. § 1395ww(a)(4), 42 C.F.R. §§ 412.2(c)(5), 413.40(c)(2).

4. See GAO, Medicare: Application of the False Claims Act to Hospital Billing Practices, HEHS–98–195 (1998).

5. 42 C.F.R. §§ 412.2(e), 412.115.

assumption that rural hospitals faced lower costs and generally treated less sick patients less intensively than urban hospitals. The disparity led, however, to charges that rural hospitals have been treated unfairly, in particular those that are on the fringes of urban areas and must compete with urban hospitals in the same labor pool.

In 1988, Congress accommodated the problems of individual hospitals by permitting rural hospitals to be treated as if they were located in adjacent urban areas under some circumstances.[6] It also created the Medicare Geographic Classification Review Board (MGCRB) to permit hospitals located in one geographic classification to argue that they ought to be reclassified to another, neighboring, geographic area whose wage index or standardized amount more accurately reflected their real wage expenses.[7] For example, a hospital located in a rural area immediately adjacent to an urban MSA could argue that it had to compete with hospitals in the urban area for medical personnel by paying equivalent wages, and thus was being underpaid by PPS payments based on the state's rural wage index and the rural standardized amount. Beginning in 1994, Congress eliminated the differential between rural areas and urban area standardized rates, though classification still remains important because of the wage index. It retained a distinction between urban and large urban area hospitals.

The labor portion of the standardized amount is multiplied by a wage index to take account of the fact that wage levels vary dramatically across the country.[8] A separate wage index has been calculated for each metropolitan statistical area in the country and for the rural areas of each state that has counties outside of MSAs. For FY 1999 the wage index varied from 1.5644 for Barnstable–Yarmouth, Mass. to .4521 for San Juan–Bayamon, Puerto Rico.

§ 11–12. Hospital and Case Specific Adjustments to PPS Rates

After a per-case payment is arrived at by multiplying the DRG weight times the wage-level-adjusted standardized amount, further modifications are made to account for hospital—or case-specific considerations. First, additional payments are made for "outliers," extraordinarily costly patient stays.[1]

Second, indirect education cost adjustments are made to increase reimbursement for teaching hospitals. The direct medical costs of running a medical education program are reimbursed by Medicare on a cost basis, as described below at § 11–17. Medical education programs also, however, impose indirect costs reflecting the increased number of tests and procedures ordered by interns and residents, the need of teaching hospitals to maintain more detailed records, and the sicker patients attracted to teaching hospitals.

6. 42 U.S.C.A. § 1395ww(d)(8). See Cullman Regional Med. Ctr. v. Shalala, 945 F.Supp. 287 (D.D.C.1996); Universal Health Services of McAllen, Inc. v. Sullivan, 770 F.Supp. 704 (D.D.C.1991), affirmed 978 F.2d 745 (D.C.Cir. 1992) (upholding HHS guidelines on reclassification).

7. 42 U.S.C.A. § 1395ww(d)(10). See 42 C.F.R. §§ 412.230–412.234 for the criteria applied by the MGCRB in considering reclassification, and 42 C.F.R. §§ 412.246–412.280

governing its composition and procedures. Hospitals can also be reclassified for disproportionate share payment adjustments.

8. 42 U.S.C.A. § 1395ww(d)(3)(E).

§ 11–12

1. 42 U.S.C.A. § 1395ww(d)(5)(A); 42 C.F.R. §§ 412.80, .84. Prior to 1997, extra payments were also made for extraordinary lengthy stays, "day outliers".

Congress has, therefore, authorized upward adjustment of PPS payments to hospitals to reflect these increased costs.[2] Since teaching hospitals tend to be located in inner-city areas and thus to attract indigent patients, this adjustment has resulted in a subsidy not only for medical education but also for the poor uninsured.

Specific types of hospitals also receive favored treatment under DRG–PPS reimbursement. First, some hospitals are categorized as disproportionate share hospitals (DSHs), hospitals that serve a high proportion of low income patients. Such hospitals are singled out for special treatment because of the belief that low income patients tend to be in poorer health and require additional services, but the extra payments also help to keep open hospitals that provide a disproportionate amount of uncompensated care. Initially, Congress simply requested HCFA to develop a methodology for identifying and compensating DSHs, but when the Reagan–era HCFA balked at this request, Congress itself adopted a formula for identifying and reimbursing DSHs.[3]

Several categories of rural hospitals that Congress has chosen to subsidize through the Medicare program, and thus to preserve, are also entitled to enhanced reimbursement. First, "sole community hospitals" are isolated rural hospitals that are either located more than thirty-five miles from the nearest neighboring hospital or are otherwise the only hospital readily available to patients in the area because of factors such as travel time, weather conditions, or topography receive enhanced payments under a special formula.[4] "Medicare-dependent small rural hospitals," (rural hospitals of less than 100 beds, 60% of whose inpatient days and discharges are attributable to Medicare patients) are reimbursed under a special complicated formula.[5] "Rural referral centers" are large rural hospitals that resemble large urban hospitals in their operating characteristics.[6] Referral hospitals have their reimbursement based on the urban rather than the rural standardized amounts.

DRG payments are attributable to discharged patients. Where a hospital transfers a patient to another hospital rather than discharging the patient, the transferring hospital is paid on a per diem basis for the time the patient remained in the hospital. Because hospitals are "discharging" patients earlier and earlier into post-acute settings, Congress in the 1997 BBA provided that for ten DRGs (such as stroke or hip and joint replacement) discharges would be paid under the transfer rate or a blended rate.[7]

§ 11–13. PPS Capital Cost Reimbursement

When PPS was initially adopted in 1983, it was clear that implementing a prospective payment system for paying for hospital capital costs would be even more difficult than implementing prospective payment for operating costs. Hospitals vary substantially, not only with respect to the cost of their land and buildings, but also with respect to how recently major capital

2. 42 U.S.C.A. § 1395ww(d)(5)(B); 42 C.F.R. § 412.105.

3. 42 U.S.C.A. § 1395ww(d)(5)(F); 42 C.F.R. § 412.106(c).

4. 42 U.S.C.A. § 1395ww(d)(5)(D); 42 C.F.R. § 412.92.

5. 42 U.S.C.A. § 1395ww(d)(5)(G); 42 C.F.R. § 412.108.

6. 42 U.S.C.A. § 1395ww(d)(5)(C); 42 C.F.R. § 412.96.

7. 42 U.S.C.A. § 1395ww(d)(5)(I) & (J).

investments were made, what proportion of the hospital's total capital is debt financed, and what interest rates are being paid on debt. These variations made the design of an equitable prospective payment system a daunting task.

The system HHS ultimately designed addresses the conundrum of widely varied capital costs by phasing in full PPS reimbursement over a long period of time (ten years) and by making generous provision for the consideration of the capital costs of individual hospitals during the phase-in period.[1] It is based on a uniform national capital cost rate, adjusted for DRG weight, and by factors adjusting for geographic location and disproportionate share status, indirect medical education provision, and outliers cases.[2]

§ 11–14. Litigation Under PPS

In contrast to cost-related reimbursement, which has generated endless litigation between providers and HHS, PPS raises remarkably few justiciable issues. Issues raised by PPS are by and large either political questions—such as what the standardized amount update level should be for any particular year—or technical questions—such as how a particular DRG should be weighted or which DRG should be assigned by a hospital to a particular admission. Congress has made it clear that it does not want the courts getting involved in these determinations and has barred judicial review of updates of the standardized amounts, the definition of DRGs, the methodology for classifying discharges into DRGs, and DRG weight determinations.[1] Congress has established a tri-partite colloquy among itself, HHS, and an independent body which was initially called the Prospective Payment Assessment Commission, and which is now merged into the Medicare Payment Advisory Commission, to determine these questions and has left little room for the courts.[2] The complexities of this discussion are discussed thoroughly in David Frankford's article, The Complexity of Medicare's Hospital Reimbursement System.[3] Its aggregate result has been to give Congress a great deal of power to increase or, as has been more often the case, to decrease payment amounts in response to budgetary considerations.[4]

Most reported cases brought during the early years of PPS involved the cost-based hospital specific portion of the blended rate that applied during the first several years of transition from cost reimbursement to PPS. They were thus, in fact, cost reimbursement cases. Most involved the question of what notice HHS had to give a hospital before the hospital could appeal the hospital specific portion of its rate.[5]

§ 11.13

1. Prospective Payment System for Inpatient Hospital Capital–Related Costs, 56 Fed. Reg. 43,358 (August 30, 1991) to be codified at 42 C.F.R. §§ P 412.308–.352.

2. 42 C.F.R. § 412.312.

§ 11–14

1. 42 U.S.C.A. § 1395ww(d)(7); 42 C.F.R. § 405.1804.

2. See Eleanor D. Kinney, Making Hard Choices Under the Medicare Prospective Payment System: One Administrative Model for Allocating Resources Under a Government Health Insurance Program, 19 Ind. L. Rev.

1151 (1986); David G. Smith, Paying for Medicare: The Politics of Reform (1992).

3. 78 Iowa L. Rev. 517 (1993).

4. See Timothy Stoltzfus Jost, Governing Medicare, 51 Admin. L. Rev. 39, 65–82 (1999).

5. See Sunshine Health Systems v. Bowen, 809 F.2d 1390 (9th Cir.1987); Georgetown Univ. Hosp. v. Bowen, 862 F.2d 323 (D.C.Cir. 1988); Washington Hosp. Center v. Bowen, 795 F.2d 139 (D.C.Cir.1986), appeal after remand 698 F.Supp. 290 (D.D.C.1987), affirmed 862 F.2d 323 (D.C.Cir.1988).

Medicare provider payment litigation continues to consist primarily of fact-intensive disputes entailing particular providers. Cases raise the question of whether a particular hospital qualifies for special treatment under PPS as a disproportionate share hospital,[6] sole community hospital,[7] urban hospital,[8] rehabilitation hospital,[9] "new" hospital entitled to reimbursement under the "federal" rate,[10] or rural referral center.[11] Only a few cases have successfully challenged HHS PPS payment policy on a more general basis.[12]

Several cases have involved retroactive application of wage-index adjustments. The Supreme Court in *Good Samaritan Hospital v. Shalala*,[13] upheld the refusal of HHS to apply retroactively to the years 1980 to 1984 changes made in 1986 to the wage-index to account for distortions in rates due to use of a disproportionate number of part time employees by six rural Nebraska hospitals. Another case, *Methodist Hospital of Sacramento v. Shalala*,[14] upheld the HHS policy of making corrections in the hospital wage index only on a prospective basis.

To the extent that some costs, for example, graduate medical education costs or bad debts attributable to Medicare cost-sharing, are still passed through under PPS, the opportunity exists for raising traditional accounting-type questions.[15] Regions Hospital v. Shalala,[16] for example, challenged regulations authorizing the reaudit of GME costs that hospitals had reported for 1984 for use as a baseline for calculating future GME payments, while Thomas Jefferson University v. Shalala,[17] concerned the allocation of educational expenses between a teaching hospital and a medical school. The persistence of cost-related capital cost reimbursement throughout the phase-in period of capital cost PPS has also sustained continued litigation in this complex area.[18] Case-specific decisions are also subject to administrative review: a hospital may request an intermediary to reconsider a DRG assignment[19] or the provider reimbursement review board to review reimbursement issues not precluded from review by statute.[20] Finally, there is also still the possibility of a Constitutional challenge to the whole edifice, though such a challenge will almost certainly be rejected based on rational basis analysis.[21]

6. North Broward Hosp. Dist. v. Shalala, 172 F.3d 90 (D.C.Cir.1999); Rye Psychiatric Hosp. Ctr. v. Shalala, 52 F.3d 1163 (2d Cir. 1995); Samaritan Health Ctr. v. Heckler, 636 F.Supp. 503 (D.D.C.1985).

7. Bradford Hosp. v. Shalala, 954 F.Supp. 1031 (W.D.Pa.1996).

8. Medical Center Hosp. v. Bowen, 1989 WL 234524 (M.D.Fla.1989).

9. Delaware Co. Mem. Hosp. v. Bowen, 871 F.2d 10 (3d Cir.1989).

10. Sunshine Health Sys. v. Bowen, 809 F.2d 1390 (9th Cir.1987); Community Hosp. v. Sullivan, 963 F.2d 1206 (9th Cir.1992).

11. Board of Trustees of Knox Co. Hosp. v. Shalala, 135 F.3d 493 (7th Cir.1998); Providence Hosp. v. Bowen, 1986 WL 15606 (N.D.Ohio 1986).

12. See e.g. Alvarado Community Hosp. v. Shalala, 155 F.3d 1115 (9th Cir.1998), amended 166 F.3d 950 (9th Cir. 1999) (requiring HHS to recalculate day outlier payments for FY 1985).

13. 508 U.S. 402, 113 S.Ct. 2151, 124 L.Ed.2d 368 (1993).

14. 38 F.3d 1225 (D.C.Cir.1994).

15. See, e.g. University Health Servs., Inc. v. HHS, 120 F.3d 1145 (11th Cir.1997) (disallowance of bad debts claim upheld).

16. 522 U.S. 448, 118 S.Ct. 909 (1998).

17. 512 U.S. 504, 114 S.Ct. 2381 (1994).

18. See, e.g. Shalala v. Guernsey Memorial Hospital, 514 U.S. 87, 115 S.Ct. 1232 (1995) (involving the treatment of amortization of defeasance losses on advanced refunding of bonded debt).

19. 42 C.F.R. § 405.1811.

20. 42 C.F.R. § 405.1835.

21. See Good Samaritan Medical Ctr. v. Heckler, 605 F.Supp. 19 (S.D.Ohio 1984)(challenging urban-rural distinction).

§ 11–15. Evaluation

Any evaluation of DRG–PPS must certainly be mixed. PPS has succeeded at its principal goal, limiting the escalation of Medicare expenditures for inpatient care: during the six years preceding PPS Medicare inpatient hospital payments grew at a real rate of 9.1% per year, during the six years following the implementation of PPS they grew at a real rate of 2.5% per year.[1] It has also succeeded in doing this without a substantial decline in the quality of care received by Medicare beneficiaries.[2] It did not, however, succeed in stemming the growth of hospital costs generally, resulting for a time in a disparity between what hospitals care cost and what Medicare paid, requiring increasing cost-shifting of the cost of caring for Medicare patients to the private sector. PPS has also resulted in (or at least been accompanied by) a massive shift of care from the hospital to other settings. Surgery that used to be done on an inpatient basis is now done outpatient, patients who used to remain in the hospital are now discharged to nursing homes.[3] This has, in turn, increased the cost of other parts of the Medicare program, though the overall effect of PPS has probably been to lower the annual increase in Medicare expenditures. DRG–PPS does not seem to have brought about a hoped for rationalization of the health care industry: hospitals do not seem to have tailored their production to specialize in delivering services they can produce most efficiently to maximize profits under DRG reimbursement.[4] Finally, DRG–PPS has grown increasingly complex over time as it attempts to respond to a wide variety of policy concerns, straying ever further from its goal of simplifying hospital reimbursement.[5]

§ 11–16. Prospective Payment for Providers Other Than Acute Care Hospitals

The Balanced Budget Act of 1997 mandated expansion of prospective payment to cover nursing homes and rehabilitation hospitals under Part A, outpatient hospital services and outpatient rehabilitation services under Part B, and home health providers under Parts A and B. Rehabilitation hospital PPS payment rates will be weighted reflecting facility resource use based on patient case-mix groups, classified with respect to factors such as impairment, age, related prior hospitalization, comorbidities and functional capacity, outpatient hospital services, and rehabilitation hospitals.[1] Payments will be adjusted for area wage rates and provision made for outlier cases.

The BBA also required the establishment of a skilled nursing facility PPS, to be transitioned in over a four year period. The rate will combine operating, capital, and most ancillary and therapy services into a single per

§ 11–15

1. See Prospective Payment Assessment Commission, Report and Recommendations to Congress (1993).

2. See Katherine L. Kahn, et al., Comparing Outcomes of Care Before and After Implementation of DRG-based Prospective Payment System, 254 JAMA 1984 (1990); William H. Rogers, et al., Quality of Care Before and After Implementation of the DRG–Based Prospective Payment System, 264 JAMA 1989 (1990).

3. See summarizing these developments and evaluating PPS generally, David Frankford, Efficiency and Organizational Rationality, 10 Yale J. Reg. 273 (1993).

4. Id. at 314–28.

5. David Frankford, The Complexity of Medicare's Hospital Reimbursement System: The Paradoxes of Averaging, 78 Iowa L. Rev. 517 (1993).

§ 11–16

1. 42 U.S.C.A. § 1395ww(j).

diem rate, which will be adjusted for a relative resource utilization based on case mix using the Resource Utilization Groups (RUGs) system.[2] Payment rates for a 15 categories of patients were substantially increased under the 1999 BBA Refinement Bill because of a concern that SNF rates were being cut too drastically under prospective payment.

The BBA further mandated the creation of a prospective payment system for outpatient hospital services, which are funded under Part B.[3] Outpatient costs grew dramatically during the 90s as it become technically possible to perform more procedures on an outpatient basis, and inpatient PPS made outpatient provision more attractive financially. The new system requires a classification of outpatient services based on clinical comparability and comparable resource use and for payment rates based on these groups, with adjustments based on geographic wage differences, outliers, and certain classes of hospitals, and controls over unnecessary volume increases. In 1998, HCFA published regulations to implement this system, based on a Ambulatory Patient Classification (APC) system it developed.[4]

Payments for outpatient therapy services and comprehensive outpatient rehabilitation are to transition under the BBA to a prospective fee schedule.[5] Payment for physical therapy (including speech therapy) and for occupational therapy services under the BBA were limited to $1500 per beneficiary per year by the BBA.[6] These limitations have affected a significant number of Medicare beneficiaries, and in particular residents of SNFs not covered by SNF benefits.

Finally, the BBA also mandates a transition to prospective payment for home health. Again, payments will be based on a standard amount, adjusted for case mix, geographical wage variation, and outliers.[7] The BBA also redistributed much of the burden of the costs of home health from Part A to Part B, and required providers to send beneficiaries copies of all bills submitted on their behalf, to compensate to some extent for the lack of beneficiary monitoring under the home health program due to the absence of coinsurance obligations. Reductions in home health payments required under the BBA were delayed under the 1999 BBA Refinement bill, out of a concern that the BBA had gone too far in cutting rates.

F.   COST–BASED REIMBURSEMENT

§ 11–17.   Generally

Though Medicare now pays for inpatient hospital services on a DRG-based prospective payment basis, cost-based reimbursement continues to play an important role in Medicare. Hospitals and units of hospitals that care for patients on a long term basis were excluded from PPS because of the difficulty of correlating length of stay, and thus costs, with diagnosis. These excluded institutions include psychiatric hospitals, hospitals, children's hospitals, long-

---

2. 42 U.S.C.A. § 1395yy(e); 42 C.F.R. §§ 413.330-.348

3. 42 U.S.C.A. § 1395l(t).

4. 63 Fed. Reg. 47,552 (1998).

5. 42 U.S.C.A.§ 1395m(k). Certain small hospitals were exempted from this transition under the 1999 BBA Refinement Bill.

6. 42 U.S.C.A. § 1395l(g)(1).

7. 42 U.S.C.A. § 1395fff.

term care hospitals, cancer hospitals, critical access hospitals, and until recently rehabilitation hospitals;[1] and psychiatric and rehabilitation distinct part units of hospitals.[2] Cost reimbursement principals also were also until recently for non-hospital Part A providers, including outpatient hospital services, SNFs and home health agencies; and for PPS-pass through costs, including, for example, bad debts, direct medical education costs, and organ acquisition costs.

The Medicare statute defines reasonable cost as "the cost actually incurred [by providers], excluding therefrom any part of incurred costs found to be unnecessary in the efficient delivery of needed health services, [which] shall be determined in accordance with regulations establishing the method or methods to be used."[3] The Act further requires that Medicare regulations take into account both direct and indirect costs of providers to assure that Medicare will bear the necessary costs of caring for its recipients, but will not pay for the costs of caring for non-recipients.[4] Finally, cost reimbursement for PPS-excluded hospitals are subject to limits first established by the Tax Equity and Fiscal Responsibility Act of 1982 (TEFRA), commonly referred to as the TEFRA limits and periodically adjusted in subsequent legislation.[5]

To determine appropriate payment levels for cost-based reimbursement, therefore, Medicare must first identify a provider's allowable costs, then appropriately apportion those costs among Medicare beneficiaries and other patients, and finally trim reimbursed costs to statutorily defined limits. Because cost-based reimbursement is based on the individualized determination of discrete costs claimed by particular institutions (as opposed to broad-based determinations based in policy) it has proved an extraordinarily fertile source of litigation. Even at this point, when most hospitals have shifted to PPS reimbursement, cost-based reimbursement continues to account for a large proportion of Part A litigation.

G. MEDICARE PART B PAYMENT

§ 11–18. Medicare Part B Payment

Medicare Part B payment for most services was based traditionally, at least in theory, on reimbursement of actual charges (minus deductibles and co-insurance). Over time, however, actual charges have become subject to increasingly numerous and restrictive screens that have rendered the relationship between actual charges and actual payments ever more tenuous. Beginning in the early 1990s, moreover, Congress moved away from any pretense of charge reimbursement toward payment systems based on administered fees, most notably the resource based relative value scale (RBRVS) for physicians, but also fee schedule payments for clinical laboratory services, durable medical equipment, and ambulatory surgical centers.

§ 11–19. Charge–Based Reimbursement

Though Medicare Part B has always paid for some services on a cost basis and increasingly pays on a fee schedule basis, Part B historically paid for most

§ 11–17
1. 42 C.F.R. § 412.23(a), (b), (d), (e), (f).
2. 42 U.S.C.A. § 1395ww(d)(1)(B); 42 C.F.R. §§ 412.25, 412.27, 412.29, 412.30.
3. 42 U.S.C.A. § 1395x(v)(1)(A).
4. Id.
5. 42 U.S.C.A. § 1395ww(b)(1).

services, and still pays for some, based on charges. Where Medicare pays on a charge basis, it pays the appropriate percentage (usually 80% as the beneficiary pays the 20% coinsurance rate) of "reasonable" charges.

Reasonable charges are defined by Medicare as the lesser of:

(a) the actual charge to the Medicare beneficiary by the physician or supplier;

(b) the "customary" charge by the physician or supplier for similar services;

(c) the "prevailing" charge in the locality for similar services;

(d) the carrier's usual payment rate for comparable services to its own policyholder's or subscribers under comparable circumstances;[1]

(e) the inherently reasonable charge for the service determined by HCFA or the carrier where application of the other screens would result in "grossly deficient or excessive charges," though application of inherently reasonableness screens should not in most cases decrease or increase payments for a particular item or service by more than 15% in a single year.[2]

Further limitations are placed on the charges of specific professionals or suppliers.[3]

Because reasonable charges for physicians were limited by the prevailing charge, which in turn was limited to charges prevailing in 1973 plus small annual inflation increases, the prevailing charge limit effectively became a Congressionally-determined fee schedule for physicians. Because that fee schedule was based on updated historic charges rather than on a policy or science-based judgments, it resulted often in arbitrary and irrational results. Moreover, fee constraints often resulted in upcoding or volume increases, which have in turn resulted in steady increases in part B spending. Congress, therefore, ultimately abandoned the reasonable charge approach to setting physician's fees in favor of a more explicit and rationally administered fee approach, the RBRVS reimbursement approach, described below.

§ 11–20. RBRVS Fee Schedule Payment for Physicians

a. Introduction

The restrictions imposed on charge reimbursement in the 1980s ultimately failed to stem the tide of increases in physician payments under Part B, which grew nearly three times faster than expenditures for Part A between 1985 and 1989 and nearly doubled between 1983 and 1988. Even during years in which physician fees were frozen, expenditures for physician services continued to grow rapidly because of increases in the volume and intensity of the services physicians provided.

§ 11–19

1. Where the carrier only partially reimburses claims for its own policyholders or subscribers, this screen does not limit Medicare payments to these partial payment amounts. 42 C.F.R. § 405.508(a).

2. 42 U.S.C.A. § 1395u(b)(3), (8), (9); 42 C.F.R. § 405.502(a), (g), (h).

3. Under 42 U.S.C.A. § 1395u(s)(1) HHS may also establish statewide or areawide fee schedules for enumerated items such as medical supplies and home dialysis supplies otherwise reimbursed on a reasonable charge basis.

Concern about beneficiary access to affordable services also increased during the 1980s. In the early 1980s, there was concern that many physicians were not accepting Medicare beneficiaries on an assignment basis. The participating physician incentive program (see below) had some effect—by 1989, 41% of physicians billing Medicare were participating physicians and over 80% of claims were billed on an assigned basis. Several states also enacted laws prohibiting physicians from "balance-billing" (billing beneficiaries for charges above the Medicare payment amount), thus effectively requiring physicians to take assignment for all or for low-income Medicare beneficiaries[1] Yet participation rates remained low in some specialties, and balance billing continued to stretch the resources of some Medicare beneficiaries.

Awareness also increased in the late 1980s of the inequities inherent in reasonable charge reimbursement. Reasonable charge reimbursement merely accepted the charge structure existing in the market for physician services without questioning the rationality of that structure. Were the market competitive and free from distortions, this might be acceptable. Given the severe distortions found in the market for physician services, however, this structure had become increasingly irrational and politically unacceptable. In particular, the disparity between the generous reimbursement offered by Medicare for technical procedures and its parsimonious payments for cognitive services has become impossible to rationalize.

Finally, policy-makers also became increasingly concerned that Medicare physician reimbursement did not do enough to encourage the quality and appropriateness of care provided beneficiaries. In 1989 a political consensus came together around a package of reforms designed to address these problems, which were enacted by the Omnibus Budget Reconciliation Act of 1989 and codified at 42 U.S.C.A. §§ 1395w–4(a) to (j).[2]

b. The Physician Fee Schedule

At the heart of the payment reform was the creation of a physician fee schedule. As with Part A DRG prospective payment, fees are determined by multiplying a weighted value (in this case representing a medical procedure rather than a diagnosis) by a conversion factor, adjusted to consider geographic variations in cost. Medicare then pays 80% of this fee, the beneficiary the other 20%. The conversion factor was calibrated initially to assure budget neutrality during the transition and has been updated annually thereafter to account for inflation. The inflation update is also to be adjusted, however, to compensate for unwarranted increases in volume or intensity of services that would otherwise increase the cost of physician care. Finally, provisions in the reform limit the ability of physicians to bill in excess of the fee schedule, thus protecting Medicare beneficiaries from unreasonable increases in physician fees.

§ 11–20

1. See Massachusetts Medical Soc'y v. Dukakis, 815 F.2d 790 (1st Cir.1987), cert. denied 484 U.S. 896, 108 S.Ct. 229, 98 L.Ed.2d 188 (1987) (upholding legislation prohibiting balance-billing in Massachusetts).

2. Physician Payment Review Commission (PPRC), Annual Report to Congress, 19–21, 24–32 (1990). See discussing RB–RVS, David Smith, Paying for Medicare: The Politics of Reform (1992); David Bluementhal & Arnold M. Epstein, Physician–Payment Reform—Unfinished Business, 326 New Eng. J. Med. 1330 (1992); William C. Hsiao, et al., Assessing the Implementation of Physician–Payment Reform, 328 New Eng. J. Med. 928 (1993); John K. Iglehart, The New Law on Medicare's Payments to Physicians, 322 New Eng. J. Med. 1247 (1990).

Relative value units (RVUs) are assigned to procedures based on the HCFA Common Procedure Coding System (HCPCS) and AMA Common Procedural Terminology (CPT) codes.[3] These codes do not vary by specialty.[4] The Relative Value Scale consists of three components: a physician work component, a practice expense component, and a malpractice component.[5] Thus, for example, for CPT 66983, "remove cataract, insert lens," the work RVU is 8.99, the practice expense RVU for facility-based practice for 1999 is 9.47, the malpractice RVU is .74, and the total RVU is 19.20. The relative weighing for the three components of each RVU is determined by multiplying the relative weight of each component for each specialty that performs the service by the relative frequency the service is performed by each such specialty.[6]

The physician work component is based on estimates prepared by William Hsiao and his colleagues at Harvard of the relative time and intensity of physician work in delivering specified services.[7] With respect to major surgeries, physician work is defined globally to include pre-operative evaluation and consultation (inpatient or outpatient) beginning with the day before surgery and post-operative care for a normal recovery from surgery for the ninety days following the surgery.[8] The physician work component accounts for slightly more than half of the total relative value scale.

The practice expense component accounts for physician overhead, including, for example, rent and office expenses.[9] Practice expenses specifically include office medical supplies commonly considered part of a physician's office expenses.[10] The practice expense component is currently moving from a historical charge-based to a resource use-based measure. Different practice expense RVUs are applied depending on whether the services are furnished in a facility (hospital, SNF or ASC) or in a physicians office or site. Malpractice expenses for a particular service are separated out from other practice expenses, and as of the year 2000 are based on the malpractice expense involved in furnishing the service.[11]

A RVU is adjusted by a geographic adjustment factor (GAF)[12] before it is multiplied by the conversion factor to reach a final fee payment amount (of which Medicare pays 80%). The GAF recognizes that the various costs included in the RVUs differ in different parts of the country. Three different GAFs are calculated, corresponding respectively to regional differences in 1) practice expenses and 2) malpractice expenses, and to 3) one quarter of differences in the value of physician work. These are then multiplied by corresponding components of the RVU before the conversion factor is applied.[13]

3. 42 U.S.C.A. § 1395w–4(c); 42 C.F.R. §§ 414.22 & .24.

4. 42 U.S.C.A. § 1395w–4(c)(6).

5. 42 U.S.C.A. § 1395w–4(c); 42 C.F.R. § 414.22.

6. 42 U.S.C.A. § 1395w–4(c)(3).

7. Hsiao, W.C., P. Braun & E. Becker, et al., Harv. Sch. of Pub. Health, A National Study of Resource–Based Relative Value Scales for Physician Services: Final Report (1988).

8. Medicare Program; Fee Schedule for Physicians' Services, 56 Fed. Reg. 59,502, 59,-513 (1991) (to be codified at 42 C.F.R. Pts. 405, 413, and 414).

9. 42 U.S.C.A. § 1395w–4(c)(1)(B); 42 C.F.R. § 414.22(b).

10. 42 C.F.R. § 414.34.

11. 42 U.S.C.A. § 1395w–4(c)(2)(C)(iii); 42 C.F.R. § 414.22(c).

12. 42 U.S.C.A. § 1395w–4(e).

13. 42 U.S.C.A. § 1395w–4(e); 42 C.F.R. § 414.26.

c. The Conversion Factor and Volume Performance Standard

HCFA established the conversion factor (CF) for 1992 to assure budget neutrality, that is, to assure that total payments for physician services would not exceed the amount paid in 1991 plus an inflation update amount of 1.9%. The CF for 1992 was established at $31.001. For later years the CF was, according to the original plan, to be established by Congress, based on a recommendation by HCFA to be published by April 15 of each year for the following year.[14] In default of Congressional action on this recommendation, the update for most services was to equal the MEI adjusted to take account of the extent to which the actual expenditures for the second previous fiscal year were greater or less than the Medicare Volume Performance Standard (MVPS) for that year.[15] The conversion factor for 1999 was $34.7315

The MVPS represented a Congressional attempt to create a global budget for physician expenditures. Previous attempts to hold down physician expenditures by capping fees often resulted in volume and intensity increases that in turn resulted in continued escalation in total Medicare payment for physician services. The MVPS set a target rate for growth in intensity and volume. If this rate was exceeded in a year, the CF of the second following year was adjusted downward, so that total expenditures would continue to grow at a target rate.

The volume performance adjustment in RBRVS failed to achieve its goal, and Congress repeatedly intervened directly to change the conversion factor. Finally in the 1997 Balanced Budget Act, Congress abandoned the MVPS in favor of a "sustainable" growth rate based on growth in the real gross domestic product and increases in Medicare population and coverage.[16] This rate will allow physician payment growth in line with growth in the larger economy, but is unlikely to keep pace with growth in physician income outside of Medicare.

§ 11–21. Special Payment Rules for Particular Professionals

In addition to the general charge-based reimbursement rules set out above, Medicare Part B also has special rules for reimbursing physicians who practice in an educational setting as teaching physicians or as interns or residents; for provider-based radiologists, anesthesiologists, and pathologists; and for non-physician health professionals including clinical nurse specialists and physician assistants.[1] In each instance, the professionals are reimbursed by Medicare at 80% of the allowed rate, with the beneficiary paying the other 20% as coinsurance.

§ 11–22. Payment for Durable Medical Equipment

Durable medical equipment (DME) is equipment, like oxygen tents, hospital beds, or wheelchairs, that can withstand repeated use, is primarily and customarily used for a medical purpose, is not generally useful in the

14. 42 U.S.C.A. § 1395w–4(d)(2) (repealed effective 1998).

15. 42 U.S.C.A. § 1395w–4(d)(3) (repealed effective 1998).

16. 42 U.S.C.A. § 1395w–4(f).

§ 11–21

1. See, e.g. 42 C.F.R. §§ 414.52–.62, 414.202.

absence of an illness or injury, and is appropriate for home use.[1] It does not include items that are primarily and customarily used for nonmedical purposes, such as air conditioners or elevators, even though they may be of value to persons with certain medical conditions.[2] The equipment must be used in the patient's home, which may include an institution in which the patient lives other than a hospital or skilled nursing facility.[3] DME must be medically necessary, as determined usually by a physician's prescription.[4] Its use must also be reasonable, considering the relationship between the expense of the item and its therapeutic benefit and the availability of alternatives, including equipment already available to the beneficiary.[5] Certain items thought to be subject to overutilization, including transcutaneous electrical nerve simulators and motorized scooters, must be approved by the carrier in advance.[6] DME claims must be submitted, under recent rules, to one of four regional carriers depending on the region where the beneficiary resides.[7]

DME purchase and rental has been reimbursed by Medicare since 1989 on a fee schedule basis, with reimbursement limited to 80% of the lesser of the actual charge for the item or the fee schedule amount.[8]

H. BILLING AND CLAIMS

§ 11–23. Billing—Assignment and Participating Physician Status

Payments under Part B can be made either to the beneficiary or directly to the physician or supplier (on an "assigned basis") on behalf of the patient.[1] Payments may be made on an assigned basis only to a physician or supplier who agrees to accept the reasonable charge allowed by Medicare as payment in full for an item or service.[2] A physician or supplier that accepts assignment can only bill the beneficiary for allowable deductible and coinsurance amounts. Physicians must take assignment for claims for services provided by their own office laboratories and for services provided to Medicaid beneficiaries or to other Medicare beneficiaries qualified for payment of their coinsurance and deductibles by Medicaid.[3] Several states also prohibit licensed physicians from "balance billing" Medicare beneficiaries, in effect requiring them to take assignment.[4] Otherwise physicians are not required to take assignment.

§ 11–22

1. 42 U.S.C.A. § 1395x(n), 42 C.F.R. § 405.514.

2. U.S. Dep't of Health & Human Services, Health Care Fin. Admin., HIM–19, Medicare Carrier's Manual (hereafter MCM), Part 3, at § 2100.1.

3. 42 U.S.C.A. § 1395x(n); 42 C.F.R. § 410.38(a).

4. MCM Part 3, supra note 2, at § 2100.2.

5. Id.

6. 42 U.S.C.A. § 1395m(a)(15).

7. 42 C.F.R. § 421.210.

8. 42 U.S.C.A. § 1395m(a); 42 C.F.R. § 414.210(a).

§ 11–23

1. 42 U.S.C.A. § 1395u(b)(3); 42 C.F.R. §§ 424.53, 424.55.

2. 42 U.S.C.A. § 1395u(b)(3)(B)(ii); 42 C.F.R. § 424.55(b).

3. 42 U.S.C.A. §§ 1395l(h)(5)(C), 1395w–4(g)(3).

4. See Massachusetts Medical Soc'y v. Dukakis, 637 F.Supp. 684 (D.Mass.1986), affirmed, 815 F.2d 790 (1st Cir.1987), cert. denied 484 U.S. 896, 108 S.Ct. 229, 98 L.Ed.2d 188 (1987); Pennsylvania Medical Soc'y v. Marconis, 942 F.2d 842 (3d Cir.1991); Medical Soc'y of N.Y. v. Cuomo, 976 F.2d 812 (2d Cir.1992); Medical Soc'y of N.Y. v. New York Dept. of Health, 611 N.Y.S.2d 114, 633 N.E.2d

For the first two decades of the Medicare program, physicians who chose not to accept assignment were free to bill patients at any rate they thought they could collect. By the mid–1980s, however, it became clear that a large proportion of physicians were not accepting assignment and that Medicare beneficiaries were paying for an ever larger proportion of their medical expenditures out-of-pocket. On July 1, 1984, therefore, Congress froze both the amount Medicare paid physicians and the amount that physicians who did not accept assignment could bill to Medicare patients.[5] The fee freeze, initially imposed through September 30, 1985, was extended through December 31, 1986. Congress then imposed the Maximum Allowable Actual Charge (MAAC) limitation, which strictly limited annual increases in the fees that physicians who did not agree to accept assignment in all of their Medicare cases could charge beneficiaries.[6] Finally, the Omnibus Budget Reconciliation Act of 1989 imposed a "limiting charge" restriction that after 1992 restricts physicians who do not accept assignment for all of their cases to 115% of the recognized payment amount for non-participating physicians, which equals 109.25% of the amount paid participating physicians (who agree to accept the Medicare reasonable charge as payment in full).[7] Physicians who do not accept assignment are also not entitled to appeal HHS determinations regarding their payments.[8] The Second Circuit in *Garelick v. Sullivan,* held that the limiting charge statute did not violate the takings clause of the Fifth Amendment since physicians participate voluntarily in the Medicare program.[9]

A physician who performs an elective surgery on a non-assigned basis for which the charge will be more than $500 must also either disclose in writing and in advance the cost of the procedure, the estimated Medicare payment, and the difference between the two, or refund any payment collected above the Medicare reasonable charge.[10] Physicians who violate these limits are subject to civil charges and exclusion from Medicare.[11] HCFA must monitor physician charges and changes in the utilization of and access to services for Medicare beneficiaries and report to Congress any problems that develop under the fee schedule.[12]

468 (N.Y.App.1994) (upholding legislation limiting or forbidding balance billing of Medicare beneficiaries).

5. Deficit Reduction Act of 1984, Pub. L. No. 98–369, § 2306, 98 Stat. 494, 1070–1073 (1984) (prior to 1986 amendment). The fee freeze was upheld against both substantive due process and takings claims in Whitney v. Heckler, 780 F.2d 963 (11th Cir.1986), cert. denied 479 U.S. 813, 107 S.Ct. 65, 93 L.Ed.2d 23 (1986); and equal protection claims in A.M.A. v. Heckler, 606 F.Supp. 1422 (S.D.Ind.1985).

6. Omnibus Budget Reconciliation Act of 1986, Pub.L. No. 99–509, § 9331, 100 Stat. 1874, 2018–2022. A challenge to this provision failed on procedural grounds in A.M.A. v. Bowen, 857 F.2d 267 (5th Cir.1988).

7. 42 U.S.C.A. § 1395w–4(g). This provision was upheld against substantive due process and takings claims in Garelick v. Sullivan, 987 F.2d 913 (2d Cir.1993), cert. denied 510 U.S. 821, 114 S.Ct. 78, 126 L.Ed.2d 47 (1993).

8. But see Furlong v. Shalala, 156 F.3d 384 (2d Cir.1998) (rejecting equal protection challenge to this nonreviewability, but recognizing property interest and remanding for consideration of due process claim).

9. 987 F.2d 913 (2d Cir.1993), cert. denied 510 U.S. 821, 114 S.Ct. 78, 126 L.Ed.2d 47 (1993). See discussing the limiting charge and other pro-beneficiary participating physician provisions, Bess M. Brewer & Alfred J. Chiplin, Jr., Cutting Costs: Medicare Part B Advocacy Tools, Clearinghouse Rev., Oct., 1992 at 629.

10. 42 U.S.C.A. § 1395u(m). See Bess M. Brewer & Alfred J. Chiplin, Jr., Cutting Costs: Medicare Part B Advocacy Tools, Clearinghouse Rev., Oct., 1992, at 629, 631–632 discussing these provisions.

11. 42 U.S.C.A. §§ 1395u(j)(1), 1395w–4(g)(1).

12. 42 U.S.C.A. § 1395w–4(g)(6) & (7).

Physicians who serve Medicare beneficiaries have historically not been able to deal with the beneficiaries strictly on a private basis, without the possibility of Medicare reimbursement. As controls on balance-billing have become stricter, this has become more of an issue. The Balanced Budget Act of 1997, in response to physician complaints, made provision for private contracting for services for which no Medicare claim was submitted or payment received.[13] To protect beneficiaries, however, private provision of services is only permitted pursuant to a written, signed contract, entered into when the beneficiary is not facing an emergency or urgent health situation, and only when the physician agrees not to submit any claims to Medicare for the following two years.[14] These provisions set off a storm of controversy provoked by those who saw it as a tightening, rather than a loosening, of private contract rights, but a lawsuit to enjoin implementation of the provision failed[15] and Congress has to date not amended the provision.

Congress has also provided carrots as well as sticks to encourage physicians and suppliers to accept assignment. Physicians and suppliers are encouraged to sign annual "participation" agreements, by which they agree to accept assignment for all services provided to Medicare beneficiaries during that year.[16] Participation agreements must be signed before the year in which they become effective and may not be dropped during that year.[17] Once a participation agreement is signed, it is renewed from year to year unless cancelled. A physician or supplier that chooses not to become a participating physician may still accept assignment on a case by case basis.

Each year HHS must publish local directories of participating physicians and suppliers and make these available to beneficiaries at Social Security and carrier offices, the offices of senior citizen organizations, and hospitals.[18] Carriers must also mail this directory without charge to a beneficiary who requests it.[19] Carriers must provide toll-free telephone lines through which beneficiaries can obtain the names, addresses, telephone numbers and specialties of participating physicians.[20] Hospital personnel (including emergency room and outpatient personnel) who refer Medicare beneficiaries to non-participating physicians must inform the beneficiary of this fact and whenever practicable identify at least one qualified participating physician who could also supply the service.[21] Beneficiaries are to be reminded about the participating physician/supplier program (including information about the toll-free number and directory) annually and each time they receive an explanation of benefits form concerning non-assigned claims.[22] Participating physicians and suppliers may file claims electronically to receive faster payment and be paid higher prevailing charge rates (nonparticipating physicians receive only 95% of the rate paid participating physicians.)[23]

13. 42 U.S.C.A. § 1395a(b)(1).

14. 42 U.S.C.A. § 1395a(b); 42 C.F.R. §§ 405.400—.455. If the service is not covered by Medicare because it is not medically necessary, a physician can provide the beneficiary with an ABN (advanced beneficiary notice) of this fact, and, with the beneficiaries consent, provide the service without regard to otherwise applicable private contracting requirements. 63 Fed. Reg. at 58851 (1998).

15. United Seniors Ass'n v. Shalala, 2 F.Supp.2d 39 (D.D.C.1998).

16. 42 U.S.C.A. § 1395u(h), (i).

17. 42 U.S.C.A. § 1395u(h)(1).

18. 42 U.S.C.A. § 1395u(h)(5), (6).

19. 42 U.S.C.A. § 1395u(h)(2).

20. 42 U.S.C.A. § 1395u(h)(2).

21. 42 U.S.C.A. § 1395cc(a)(1)(N).

22. 42 U.S.C.A. § 1395u(h)(5), (7).

23. 42 U.S.C.A. § 13952–4(a)(3).

Though Medicare encourages assignment of claims, it prohibits reassignment. Early in the history of the Medicare program some physicians and suppliers "factored" their claims, selling them at discount to third parties to receive immediate cash. This resulted in incorrect and fraudulent claims, as well as increased charges to compensate for the discount. Because of these problems, Congress prohibited reassignment of claims by physicians and suppliers and assignment by patients other than to physicians and suppliers.[24] There are several exceptions to this basic prohibition against reassignment, including reassignment to billing agents who recover payment only on behalf of physicians or suppliers and whose compensation is not related to the amount billed or collected.[25] Reassignment in violation of these prohibitions can result in revocation of the right of the physician or supplier to receive Medicare benefits.[26]

Physicians who supervise residents in teaching hospitals may themselves bill for a service provided in part by a resident only when the teaching physician was present for "key" portions of the procedure, or, in the case of surgery or a complex procedure, during all of the procedure or its "critical" portions, and this presence is documented in the patient's chart.[27] HCFA has actively pursued under the fraud and abuse statutes teaching hospitals where physicians have billed for services without complying with this requirement.[28]

§ 11–24. Overpayments

Providers that collect payments from beneficiaries incorrectly must refund the payments within sixty days.[1] If a provider fails to refund incorrectly collected amounts, HCFA may offset the amount not refunded against moneys due to the provider and pay directly the beneficiary who has not received a refund.[2]

In a program the size of the Medicare program, incorrect overpayments are inevitably made. These are debts owed the federal government, which HCFA must attempt to collect. Overpayments to a beneficiary or to a provider, physician or supplier on the beneficiary's behalf are ultimately the responsibility of the beneficiary if the beneficiary has benefited from the payment.[3] Where overpayments are made because of an error on the part of a carrier or intermediary, or because of a dispute regarding a payment, it is often not fair to hold the beneficiary liable. A provider, physician, or supplier that receives an overpayment is liable for repayment unless the intermediary or carrier determines that it was "without fault" in collecting the overpayment.[4] If the provider is without fault, the beneficiary must pay unless the intermediary or carrier determines that the beneficiary was "without fault"[5]

24. 42 U.S.C.A. § 1395u(b)(6); 42 C.F.R. §§ 424.70—420.90.

25. These are set out at 42 U.S.C.A. § 1395u(b)(6); 42 C.F.R. §§ 424.73 & 424.80.

26. 42 C.F.R. § 424.82.

27. 42 C.F.R. § 415.172.

28. GAO, Medicare: Concerns with Physicians at Teaching Hospitals, HEHS 98–174 (1998).

§ 11–24
1. 42 U.S.C.A. § 1395cc(a)(1)(C), 42 C.F.R. §§ 489.20(b), 489.41.

2. 42 C.F.R. § 489.42.

3. 42 U.S.C.A. § 1395gg(a); 42 C.F.R. §§ 405.350, 405.351.

4. 42 C.F.R. § 405.355; 20 C.F.R. § 404.509—.512.

5. This is only relevant in cases of overpayments for medically unnecessary services or custodial care.

or decides to waive liability. Liability will be waived if the beneficiary was without fault or if recovery would defeat the purpose of the Social Security Act or be "against equity and good conscience."[6] HCFA also does not attempt to recover overpayments where a determination that the payment was incorrect is made more than three years after a notice of the payment was sent to the beneficiary or provider absent fraud or similar fault.[7]

HCFA may also decide to pay for services not technically eligible for Medicare coverage—effectively waiving beneficiary liability for such care—where the claim was disallowed because the care was not reasonable or necessary, was custodial care, or was home health services for a person not confined to his home or not requiring intermittent skilled care if certain conditions are met.[8] If the beneficiary had knowledge of the noncoverage of the service, the ultimate liability rests on the beneficiary for payment. Unless the beneficiary had written notice that the claim would not be covered, however, it is presumed that the beneficiary did not have knowledge of noncoverage.[9] If neither the beneficiary nor the provider knew or could reasonably have been expected to have known that the service would not be covered, Medicare will pay for the noncovered service (beyond coinsurance and deductibles). If the beneficiary has paid for noncovered services covered by waiver of liability, the beneficiary will be indemnified by Medicare.[10] There is also a presumption that physicians or suppliers did not know a service would not be covered absent evidence to the contrary. Hospitals, SNFs and HHAs are not presently favored by a presumption of nonknowledge, however, and waiver of liability cases involving them are resolved on a case by case basis.[11]

I. MEDICARE PART C: MEDICARE MANAGED CARE

§ 11–25. Medicare + Choice Organizations

Though Medicare began as a fee-for-service program, and continues to operate predominantly in a fee-for-service mode, it has contracted with prepaid health care organizations to offer services to beneficiaries since the early 1980s. Medicare initially offered services through federally qualified HMOs and through competitive medical plans (prepaid health care providers that were not federally-qualified), and paid for HMO services on both a cost and risk basis.[1] Medicare managed care grew slowly, though steadily, through the mid–1990s, and then began to grow much more rapidly, doubling in membership from 3 million to 6 million between 1995 and 1998. Currently about 17 percent of Medicare recipients receive services through MCOs.

Section 4001 of the Balanced Budget Act of 1997 dramatically transformed Medicare Managed Care through the creation of Medicare + Choice (M + C), Medicare Part C.[2] Medicare + Choice expands the menu of managed

6. 42 C.F.R. § 405.355.

7. 42 C.F.R. §§ 405.350(c).

8. 42 U.S.C.A. § 1395pp; 42 C.F.R. § 411.400.

9. 42 C.F.R. § 411.404. See Malvasi v. Harris, [1980 Transfer Binder] Medicare & Medicaid Guide (CCH) ¶ 30,629 (N.D.N.Y. July 30, 1980).

10. 42 U.S.C.A. § 1395pp(b); 42 C.F.R. § 411.402.

11. 42 C.F.R. § 411.406.

§ 11–25

1. Medicare also contracted with Health Care Prepayment plans for the delivery of Part B services on a prepaid basis.

2. Lynn Etheredge, The Medicare Reforms of 1997: Headlines you Didn't Read, 23 J. Health Pol., Pol'y & L. 573 (1998).

care options available to beneficiaries to include virtually all options available in the private sector. Under M + C, beneficiaries can choose among traditional health maintenance organizations (HMOs), HMOs with a point of service option, preferred-provider organizations (PPOs), provider-sponsored organizations (PSOs), private-fee-for-service plans, and medical savings accounts (MSAs). Although the BBA initially kept in place traditional liberal Medicare provisions for managed care enrollment and disenrollment at will, by 2003 it will only permit beneficiary enrollment and disenrollment during a three month open enrollment period every year. The BBA also abolished the fifty percent rule, which had required HMOs to limit their Medicare population to half their total members to assure that the plan was in fact acceptable in commercial markets, but put in place in its place meaningful consumer protections and quality oversight requirements. It also significantly changed Medicare's approach to paying for managed care. Historically Medicare had paid managed care plans 95% of its fee-for-service payments for the County with minor risk adjustment. This payment scheme had allowed HMOs, which tended to attract healthier recipients, to do quite well, and also led to wide payment disparities across the U.S., with rural areas experiencing very low rates and few HMOs. The BBA makes payments more equitable, but this led in the first year to a mass exodus of HMOs from some areas.

HCFA issued an interim final rule, 42 C.F.R. Part 422, in June of 1998 to govern the M + C program.[3] Though the rules generally track the BBA's requirements, they do go beyond the BBA in some areas, particularly in adopting consumer protections recommended by the President's Commission on Consumer Rights, as urged by the President's Executive Order of February 1998. In early 1999 HCFA amended its regulations in some respects to give managed care organizations more flexibility.[4]

Three basic types of M + C plans are recognized under the Balanced Budget Act—coordinated care plans, MSA plans, and private-for-service plans.[5] Coordinated care plans may be offered by HMOs (with or without POS options), PPOs, and PSOs.[6] Managed care organizations that contracted with Medicare prior to the BBA will be transitioned to risk-based M + C options by 2002, by which time all cost-based Medicare managed care will be eliminated.

M + C organizations must be organized and licensed under state law—federal qualification under the old federal HMO act is no longer required.[7] State laws that are inconsistent with federal laws are preempted, however,[8] as are state laws mandating benefit coverage, relating to the inclusion or treatment of providers, or providing coverage determination grievance and appeal procedures.[9] The statute also permits provision of Medicare services through provider-sponsored organizations (PSOs) under a federal waiver without state licensure (for up to three years) where the state delays processing a licensure application unduly, applies discriminatory standards or conditions to the PSO, or applies solvency standards different than those imposed by Medicare, though waivered organizations are still subject to nondiscrimina-

3. 63 Fed. Reg. 34968 (1998).
4. 64 Fed. Reg. 7968 (1999).
5. 42 U.S.C.A. § 1395w–21(a)(2).
6. 42 U.S.C.A. § 1395w–21(a)(2)(A).
7. 42 U.S.C.A. § 1395w–25(a)(1).
8. 42 C.F.R. § 422.402(a).
9. 42 C.F.R. § 422.402(b).

tory state consumer protection and quality standards.[10] PSOs are entities organized and operated by health care providers or groups of affiliated health care providers that provide a substantial proportion of health care items and services themselves, whose providers are at substantial financial risk with respect to such items and services, and whose providers have a majority financial interest in the entity.[11] PSO solvency regulations promulgated by HCFA through a negotiated rulemaking process require an initial minimum capitalization of $1.5 million and an ongoing minimum net worth of the greater of $1 million, 2% of annual premium revenues (up to $150 million), 3 months of uncovered health care expenditures, or a designated percentage of expenditures paid to non-affiliated providers.[12] M + C organizations must have at least 5000 members in urban areas, 1500 in rural areas, with smaller numbers for PSOs.[13]

The BBA recognized MSAs on an experimental basis, permitting only up to 390,000 participants. MSA plan beneficiaries are covered by a catastrophic insurance plan with a deductible of up to $6000. MSA plan beneficiaries receive from Medicare the difference between the premium of the high deductible plan and the amount that Medicare would pay for other M + C plans to be deposited in a tax free MSA from which medical expenses can be paid, and from which money can eventually be withdrawn for other purposes.[14] Private FFS plans are not limited as to the premiums they can charge, and are permitted to allow providers to charge higher balanced billing rates. The private FFS option seems to have been established to allow elite providers to charge higher rates to wealthy beneficiaries. As of 1999, no insurers were offering M + C MSA or private fee-for-service plans.

Medicare beneficiaries who are entitled to Part A and enrolled in Part B, who do not have end stage renal disease, and who reside in a plan service area may elect M + C coverage. Beneficiaries can enroll in a M + C plan upon first becoming entitled to benefits and, after a transition period through 2002, each year during a three month open enrollment period, or during special enrollment periods available, for example, if a beneficiary moves or the organization to which a beneficiary belongs terminates its contract or seriously violates its obligations.[15] HCFA is responsible for providing comparative information to beneficiaries to assist the exercise of this choice.[16] M + C organizations must accept any beneficiary who applies as long as they have the capacity to accept additional members.[17] M + C organization must submit marketing material to HCFA for review 45 days before use, and may not offer cash or rebates as inducements for beneficiaries to enroll, discriminate in marketing, solicit beneficiaries door to door, or engage in misleading or confusing marketing activities.[18]

M + C plans must offer at least the basic benefits that are covered by Parts A and B of Medicare, either directly, through arrangement, or by

10. 42 U.S.C.A. § 1395w–25(a)(2).

11. 42 U.S.C.A. § 1395w–25(d), 42 C.F.R. § 422.350(b).

12. 42 C.F.R. § 422.382.

13. 42 U.S.C.A. § 1395w–27(b).

14. 42 U.S.C.A. §§ 1395w–21(d)(3) & (4); 1395w–23(e), 1395w–28(b)(3).

15. 42 U.S.C.A. § 1395w–21(e).

16. 42 U.S.C.A. § 1395w–21(d).

17. 42 U.S.C.A. § 1395w–21(g) (1) & (2).

18. 42 U.S.C.A. § 1395w–21(h).

payment.[19] They must also cover supplemental benefits (or provide reduced premiums or cost-sharing or both) to the extent that their M + C payment exceeds their costs.[20] Coordinated care plans must pay out-of-plan providers for emergency services, urgently needed services and renal dialysis for beneficiaries temporarily out of the service area, and post-stabilization care services that were either pre-approved or not disapproved within an hour of an approval request for their plan members.[21] Plans may also offer optional supplemental benefits for an additional premium to their members (with HHS approval if the benefits are mandatory, without if they are optional).[22] Historically Medicare managed care organizations have offered a much richer menu of benefits than fee-for-service Medicare, in particular being more likely to cover drug benefits. M + C organizations, at least initially, are offering fewer supplemental benefits.

M + C organizations are responsible for providing their members with detailed descriptions of plan provisions, including disclosure of any coverage limitations or regulations.[23] M + C coordinated care plans must provide access to providers 24 hour a day, 7 day a week; must ensure services are "culturally competent", ensure that hours of operation of providers are convenient and non-discriminatory, provide adequate and coordinated specialist treatment for persons with complex or serious medical conditions, and allow women enrollees direct access to women's health specialists.[24] Plans must have written standards for assuring timeliness of access to care and written policies and procedures for determining medical necessity and for assuring provider consideration of beneficiary input into treatment plans.[25] M + C organizations must establish procedures to safeguard the privacy of enrollee information, maintain medical records in an accurate and timely manner, and provide timely access of enrollees to their records.[26]

M + C plans must have an ongoing quality assurance and performance improvement program.[27] The must have in place mechanisms to detect both under- and over-utilization. Most types of plans must make provision for independent quality review. Organizations accredited by approved national accreditation agencies can be deemed to meet quality requirements.[28]

M + C organizations may not discriminate against professionals on the basis of their licensure or certification, and must provide notice and hearing to physicians whose participation rights are terminated.[29] Organizations may not interfere with provider advice to enrollees regarding care and treatment.[30] The statute also regulates and requires disclosure of plans that might provide physicians with incentives to reduce care.[31] Medicare + choice organizations are required to make prompt payments to providers and suppliers. If they fail

19. 42 U.S.C.A. § 1395w–22(a)(1).

20. 42 U.S.C.A. § 1395w–24(f)(1)(A).

21. 42 C.F.R. § 422.100(b).

22. 42 U.S.C.A. § 1395w–22(a)(3).

23. 42 U.S.C.A. § 1395w–22(c); 42 C.F.R. § 422.111.

24. 42 U.S.C.A. § 1395w–22(d), 42 C.F.R. § 422.112.

25. 42 C.F.R. § 422.112(a)(7).

26. 42 U.S.C.A. § 1395w–22(h); 42 C.F.R. § 422.18.

27. 42 U.S.C.A. § 1395w–22(e), 42 C.F.R. §§ 422.152–.154.

28. 42 U.S.C.A. § 1395w–22(e)(4); 42 C.F.R. §§ 422.156–158.

29. 42 C.F.R. § 422.204(b) & (c).

30. 42 U.S.C.A. § 1395w–22(j)(3); 42 C.F.R. § 422.206.

31. 42 U.S.C.A. § 1395w–22(j)(4), 42 C.F.R. § 422.208, 210.

to do so, HCFA may, after notice and hearing, pay itself and deduct the payment, plus its costs, from the M + C organization's payment.[32]

For most types of plans and enrollees Medicare pays M + C organizations on a monthly basis based on an annual capitation rate. The rate is risk adjusted for age, disability status, sex and institutional status, and after 2000, for health status.[33] The annual capitation rate is the larger of the minimum rate ($4404 for 1998), adjusted by a minimum percentage increase, or a blended area-specific and national rate.[34] Gradually the national rate will become more important in this formula, leading to more uniform national rates for managed care organizations. In the initial implementation phase, managed care organizations covering about 7% of Medicare managed care beneficiaries withdrew from the program, in part because of unfavorable payment rates.[35] The BBA also established a small-scale competitive pricing demonstration project to explore the possibility of price and quality competition among M + C organizations[36] and another competitive bidding project for the acquisition of Part B services.[37] Competitive bidding has proved intensely unpopular among providers, and HHS has had a difficult time getting the projects underway. As of 1999, one competitive bidding project involving DME was being implemented in Polk County, Florida, but only after HHS prevailed in a lawsuit challenging the project.

M + C plans must charge the same premiums and cost-sharing for all plan members in the service area.[38] M + C HMOs, PPOs, and PSOs may not charge enrollees more for premiums, deductibles, copayments and coinsurance for basic benefits than the actuarial value of beneficiary cost-sharing for traditional Medicare and cannot charge more for supplemental benefits than they charge their commercial populations.[39]

HCFA makes a new determination each year as to whether a M + C organization may continue in the program. Terminated or non-renewed programs are entitled to due process.[40] Plans that fail substantially to provide medically necessary services where the failure adversely affects (or is substantially likely adversely to affect) health, impose unpermitted premiums, wrongly expels or refuses to reenroll a beneficiary, provide false information, interfere with practitioner's advice to enrollees, or commit other specified wrongful acts, may be subject to civil money penalties of not more than $25,000 and plans that deny or discourage enrollment of persons on the basis of medical condition or provide false information to HCFA are subject to fines of up to $100,000.[41] HCFA may also impose civil penalties of $25,000 for

32. 42 C.F.R. §§ 422.502(c), 442.520.

33. 42 C.F.R. § 422.250.

34. 42 U.S.C.A. § 1395w–23(c).

35. United States General Accounting Office, Medicare Managed Care Plans: Many Factors Contribute to Recent Withdrawals; Plan Interest Continues, GAO/HEHS–99–91 (1999).

36. Section 4011. Implementation of this program was delayed by the BBA Refinement bill in 1999 until at least 2002 because of strong opposition. Section 4015 of the BBA also provided for payment to the Department of Defense for treatment of Medicare-eligible military retirees and dependents in a DOD managed care plan using military treatment facilities at 95% of M + C rates under the Medicare subvention demonstration project for three years. Other sections of the BBA established a variety of other demonstration projects.

37. 42 U.S.C.A. § 1395w–3.

38. 42 U.S.C.A. § 1395w–24(c).

39. 42 U.S.C.A. § 1395w–24(e).

40. 42 U.S.C.A. § 1395w–27(h); 42 C.F.R. §§ 422.641–422.698.

41. 42 U.S.C.A. 1395w–27(g)(2); 42 C.F.R. §§ 422.750, .752.

deficiencies that directly affect or have a substantial likelihood of adversely affecting enrollees, plus $10,000 a week if the deficiency remains uncorrected.[42] HCFA takes the position that the False Claims Act applies to statements and certifications made by and to M + C organizations.[43] It also requires MCOs to have fraud and abuse compliance plans in place, the only Medicare providers required to do so.[44]

J. ADMINISTRATIVE APPEALS AND JUDICIAL REVIEW OF MEDICARE DETERMINATIONS

§ 11–26. Administrative Appeals

a. *Generally*

Most, though not all, decisions affecting Medicare beneficiaries, providers, physicians or suppliers are subject to administrative review, and many are subject to judicial review. Different routes of review are provided, however, for different categories of decisions, with more thorough processes available on the whole for decisions involving larger sums of money. Most processes are quite time consuming, and those who seek review are generally discouraged from skipping steps in the process. An excellent discussion of the role of judicial review in the Medicare program is found in Eleanor D. Kinney, The Role of Judicial Review Regarding Medicare and Medicaid Program Policy: Past Experience and Future Expectations.[1]

Decisions regarding the entitlement of beneficiaries for Part A or Part B benefits are made by the Social Security Administration, subject to reconsideration, review by a Social Security Administrative Law Judge, the Appeals Council, and, ultimately judicial review.[2]

The initial decision as to whether a provider or supplier qualifies under conditions of participation to participate in the Medicare program is made by HCFA.[3] HCFA may also terminate provider agreements under some circumstances.[4] The Department's Office of Inspector General (OIG) may also terminate, suspend, or exclude practitioners, suppliers or providers.[5] Prospective providers and suppliers dissatisfied with HCFA's determination may request a reconsideration.[6] Prospective providers and suppliers dissatisfied with a reconsidered determination, and terminated or suspended providers, suppliers or practitioners may appeal to an administrative law judge (ALJ), and then to the Appeals Council.[7] Excluded providers and suppliers or providers or suppliers subject to civil money penalties may appeal to an ALJ and to the Departmental Appeals Board.[8] Medicare + Choice organizations that are denied contracts, terminated or not renewed may appeal to an ALJ,

42. 42 U.S.C.A. § 1395w–27(g)(2); 42 C.F.R. § 722, 758.

43. 42 C.F.R. § 422.502(h)(2).

44. 42 C.F.R. § 422.501(b)(vi).

§ 11–26

1. 35 St. Louis U. L.J. 759 (1991). See also Eleanor D. Kinney, The Medicare Appeals System for Coverage and Payment Disputes: Achieving Fairness in a Time of Constraint, I Ad.L.J. 1 (1987).

2. 42 U.S.C.A. § 1395ff; 20 C.F.R. §§ 404.900–404.999(d).

3. 42 C.F.R. § 498.3(b).

4. See e.g. 42 C.F.R. §§ 489.53, 498.3(b).

5. 42 U.S.C.A. § 1320a–7; 42 C.F.R. §§ 489.54, 498.3(c), 1001.1–1001.1701.

6. 42 C.F.R. § 498.5(a).

7. 42 C.F.R. § 498.5.

8. 42 C.F.R. §§ 1005.2, 1005.21.

and M + C organizations that are terminated or not renewed may further appeal to the administrator.[9]

b. Part A Appeals

A beneficiary denied Part A benefits in whole or in part will receive a total or partial denial or disallowance notice. Where Medicare Part A pays for a service, it will send a Medicare Benefit Notice, which may reflect limitations on payment due to deductibles, coinsurance, limits on inpatient, SNF, or lifetime reserve days, or other matters affecting beneficiary liability. The intermediary may also make a decision adverse to the beneficiary or to a provider on the issue of waiver of liability where services are not covered because the intermediary determines that they are not reasonable and necessary or are custodial care. All of these decisions are initial determinations subject to review.[10]

An individual dissatisfied with an initial decision regarding Part A services may request a reconsideration by HCFA within sixty days regardless of the amount in controversy, usually submitting additional documentation with the request.[11] A provider may also request a reconsideration, but only if the beneficiary states in writing that he does not intend to request reconsideration or if the intermediary has waived beneficiary liability.[12] If the person who requested reconsideration is dissatisfied with the result, he may, within sixty days, request a hearing before an ALJ if the amount in controversy is $100 or more.[13] A person dissatisfied with an ALJ determination may request review by the Departmental Appeals Board (DAB).[14] Alternatively, where all parties to a reconsidered decision, including the Secretary, concur that the only issue precluding a favorable determination is a statutory provision which the individual requesting review alleges to be unconstitutional or a regulation, HCFA ruling, or national coverage determination that the individual alleges to be invalid, the administrative hearing and DAB review can be bypassed so that the individual can appeal directly to court, since there is little point in exhausting administrative remedies before tribunals that are bound by the statute or regulation in any event.[15]

c. Part B Appeals

With respect to Part B services, the carrier makes an initial determination on issues such as whether the services are covered under Part B, whether the deductible has been met, whether the receipted bill or other evidence of payment is acceptable, whether charges are reasonable, and whether waiver of liability conditions are met.[16] Notice of an initial determination is contained in an Explanation of Medical Benefits form sent to the beneficiary and also to the physician or supplier if benefits were assigned. A beneficiary or assignee dissatisfied with an initial decision may request review by the carrier within six months.[17]

9. 42 C.F.R. §§ 422.641–422.696.

10. 42 C.F.R. § 405.704.

11. 42 C.F.R. § 405.710(a).

12. 42 C.F.R. § 405.710(b).

13. 42 U.S.C.A. § 1395ff(2)(a); 42 C.F.R. §§ 405.720, 405.722.

14. 42 C.F.R. § 405.724. The DAB follows the procedures of the Social Security Appeals Council. Appeals Council procedures are set out in 20 C.F.R. §§ 404.967–404.982.

15. 42 C.F.R. §§ 405.718.

16. 42 C.F.R. § 405.803.

17. 42 C.F.R. § 405.807.

If the amount in controversy is $100 or more, a party dissatisfied with a review decision may request a fair hearing before a hearing officer appointed by the carrier within six months.[18] The hearing may be conducted by telephone if the claimant elects to proceed in this manner and a telephone hearing is otherwise appropriate.[19] The hearing officer may also, if requested, render an "on the record" (OTR) decision without taking oral testimony.[20] A preliminary OTR decision may be provided even though an oral evidentiary hearing has been requested.[21] If the party who requested the hearing is dissatisfied with the OTR review, he may proceed to an oral hearing before a different hearing officer or, if $500 or more is at issue, proceed directly to an ALJ hearing.[22] A party dissatisfied with a final carrier hearing decision may, in any case where $500 or more is involved, seek administrative review before an ALJ and further review before the Appeals Council as described above with respect to Part A benefits.[23]

Final administrative decisions involving both Part A and Part B can be reviewed in the federal courts if $1000 or more is at issue.[24] Claims involving the delivery of similar or related services to the same individual or involving common issues of law and fact arising from services furnished to two or more individuals can be aggregated to reach the jurisdictional amount.[25]

d. Medicare + Choice Appeals

M + C organizations must provide meaningful grievance resolution mechanisms.[26] They must explain their adverse coverage determinations in writing and must make initial determinations within 30 days for payment decisions, 14 days for health care services requests, and 72 hours for requests for services where lack of the service could seriously jeopardize life or health.[27] If a reconsideration is requested, it must be completed in 60 days if payment or 30 days if a health service is requested, and, if the adverse determination was based on medical necessity, a physician of the appropriate specialty other than the physician who made the initial determination must participate in the reconsideration.[28] Where an expedited determination is requested by an enrollee or physician because of a serious threat to life, health, or functioning, a determination must be made within 72 hours.[29] If an M + C organization determines that further hospitalization is no longer needed for a hospitalized

18. 42 C.F.R. §§ 405.815, .821. See, regarding Part B appeals, Nancy M. Kelley (Note), Dollars and Sense: An Introduction to Medicare Part B Appeals, 25 New Eng. L. Rev. 617 (1990).

19. U.S. Dep't of Health & Human Serv's, Health Care Fin. Admin., HIM–19, Medicare Carrier's Manual (hereafter MCM), Part 3, at § 12017.

20. MCM, Part 3, supra note 19 at § 12021.

21. Id.

22. Id.

23. The requirement that a claimant pursue a hearing before a carrier before receiving an ALJ hearing was upheld in Isaacs v. Bowen, 865 F.2d 468 (2d Cir.1989).

24. 42 U.S.C.A. § 1395ff(b)(2).

25. Id. 42 C.F.R. § 405.817.

26. 42 U.S.C.A. § 1395w–22(f), 42 C.F.R. § 422.564. This process applies to beneficiary complaints that do not involve an organizational determination, as defined in 42 C.F.R. § 422.565, .564(b).

27. 42 U.S.C.A. § 1395w–22(g); 42 C.F.R. §§ 422.568, .570, .572. For a thorough examination of M + C appeal procedures, see Jennifer E. Gladieux, Medicare + Choice Appeal Procedures: Reconciling Due Process Rights and Cost Containment, 25 Am.J.L. & Med. 61 (1999). See also, U.S. GAO, Medicare Managed Care: Greater Oversight Needed to Protect Beneficiary Rights, GAO/HEHS–99–68.

28. 42 U.S.C.A. § 1395w–22(g)(2); 42 C.F.R. §§ 422.578—.590.

29. 42 U.S.C.A. § 1395w–22(h); 42 C.F.R. § 422.590(d).

beneficiary, the beneficiary may request review by a PRO, which must proceed immediately with the review.[30] Coverage reconsiderations may be appealed to an independent review organization under contract with HCFA, and may ultimately be appealed to an administrative law judge if $100 or more is at stake, and to court if the amount in controversy is $1000 or more.[31]

In Grijalva v. Shalala,[32] the Ninth Circuit held that notice and appeal provisions then in effect for Medicare managed care organizations violated the requirements of the Due Process Clause. The court held that the HMOs were making decisions for the Medicare program, and were thus "government actors" rather than private entities and thus covered by the Constitution. The Supreme Court vacated and remanded the Ninth Circuit appeal for further consideration in light of the new managed care appeal procedures imposed by the BBA and implementing regulations.[33] Significantly, however, the Court also required further consideration in light of its decision in American Manufacturers Mutual Insurance Co. v. Sullivan,[34] which had held that the decisions of utilization review organizations participating in a workers compensation program were not state actors. Should the Court ultimately hold that Medicare managed care organizations are private actors not subject to constitutional constraints, the federal government would be effectively permitted to contract out its responsibilities under the Medicare program beyond constitutional control, though it would probably still have to provide some government means of review for managed care decisions.

e. The Provider Reimbursement Review Board

For review of decisions involving payment of hospitals and other institutional providers the Medicare statute affords a special tribunal, the Provider Reimbursement Review Board (PRRB).[35] The Board is appointed by the Secretary of HHS and is composed of five members, including two provider representatives and at least one CPA.[36] A provider dissatisfied with an intermediary's "final determination" of total amount of payment due (the "notice of amount of program reimbursement" or NPR) under either cost reimbursement or prospective payment, may request PRRB review within 180 days.[37] Where the intermediary informs a PPS hospital prospectively of its PPS rates, a majority of circuits have held that the hospital may appeal immediately and need not await a final NPR at the close of the year.[38] PRRB review is only available if the amount in controversy is $10,000 or more,

30. 42 C.F.R. §§ 422.620, .622.

31. 42 U.S.C.A. § 1395w–22(g)(4) & (5); 42 C.F.R. §§ 422.592—.616. See, e.g. Rogers v. Shalala, 1998 WL 325248 (N.D.Ill.1998); Kelly v. Bowen, 1987 WL 120016 (W.D.Wash.1987) (reviewing HMO coverage determination).

32. 152 F.3d 1115 (9th Cir.1998), certiorari granted and judgment vacated and case remanded, ___ U.S. ___, 119 S.Ct. 1573 (1999).

33. ___ U.S. ___, 119 S.Ct. 1573 (Mem. 1999).

34. 526 U.S. 40, 119 S.Ct. 977 (1999).

35. 42 U.S.C.A. § 1395oo. See Phyllis E. Bernard, Empowering the Provider: A Better Way to Resolve Medicare Hospital Payment Disputes, 49 Admin.L.Rev. 269 (1997); Phyllis E. Bernard, Social Security and Medicare Adjudications at HHS: Two Approaches to Adminis-

tration of Justice in an Ever-expanding Bureaucracy, 3 Health Matrix 339 (1993).

36. 42 U.S.C.A. § 1395oo(h).

37. 42 U.S.C.A. § 1395oo(a); 42 C.F.R. §§ 405.1835–405.1841.

38. See Doctors Hosp. v. Bowen, 811 F.2d 1448 (11th Cir.1987); Sunshine Health Systems v. Bowen, 809 F.2d 1390 (9th Cir.1987); St. Francis Hosp. v. Bowen, 802 F.2d 697 (4th Cir.1986). But see Springdale Memorial Hosp. Ass'n, Inc. v. Bowen, 818 F.2d 1377, rehearing denied 828 F.2d 491 (8th Cir.1987)(en banc) (holding that Secretary's conclusion that notice of prospective reimbursement was a prerequisite to administrative review was entitled to substantial deference).

though groups of providers may aggregate claims involving less than $10,000 individually if in aggregate they total $50,000 or more and involve common issues of fact or interpretation of law.[39] Providers under common ownership and control must file a group appeal with respect to matters involving common issues and more than $50,000.[40]

The Board is bound by HCFA rulings and regulations, as well as by the statute, and must afford great weight to HCFA interpretive rules, general statements of policy, and rules of agency organization, procedure and practice.[41] The Board's decision must be on the record and supported by substantial evidence.[42] Though HCFA has taken the position that the PRRB cannot consider appeals involving "self-disallowed" costs, i.e. costs not claimed originally by the provider on a cost report, the Supreme Court has rejected this position where the provider failed to claim costs because it followed HHS regulations in completing the cost report.[43] A Court of Appeals has extended this holding to the situation where a provider fails to claim costs in compliance with a manual provision.[44]

Decisions of the PRRB are reviewable by the Administrator (who delegates the responsibility to the Deputy Administrator) of HCFA at his or her discretion.[45] The provider may then seek judicial review of the PRRB or administrator's decision within sixty days, in the court for the district in which the provider is located or in the District of Columbia.[46]

Provider reimbursement disputes involving more than $1000 but less than $10,000 are heard by a hearing officer or panel designated by the intermediary.[47] The intermediary hearing decision can be reviewed by the Administrator, either at his discretion or at the request of the affected provider, for consistency with the statute, regulations, HCFA rulings and general instructions.[48] There is no judicial review of intermediary hearing decisions.

Decisions of intermediaries, carriers, hearing officers, ALJs, and the Appeals Council, are subject to reopening within twelve months (or within four years for good cause shown). PRRB decisions and decisions of the Administrator are subject to reopening for up to three years.[49] While these provisions may provide the only means of relief available to providers when time limits have otherwise run, they also deprive decisions favorable to providers of finality. The authority of the Appeals Council to reopen ALJ decisions favorable to claimants has been questioned but generally upheld.[50]

39. 42 U.S.C.A. § 1395oo(b); 42 C.F.R. §§ 405.1837, 405.1839.

40. 42 C.F.R. § 405.1837.

41. 42 C.F.R. § 405.1867.

42. 42 U.S.C.A. § 1395oo(d); 42 C.F.R. § 405.1871.

43. Bethesda Hosp. Ass'n v. Bowen, 485 U.S. 399, 108 S.Ct. 1255, 99 L.Ed.2d 460 (1988).

44. Adams House Health Care v. Bowen, 862 F.2d 1371 (9th Cir.1988).

45. 42 U.S.C.A. § 1395oo(f)(1); 42 C.F.R. § 405.1875.

46. 42 U.S.C.A. § 1395oo(f)(1); 42 C.F.R. § 405.1877.

47. 42 C.F.R. §§ 405.1809–405.1833.

48. U.S. Dep't of Health & Hum. Services, Health Care Fin. Admin., Health Ins. for the Aged, HIM–15, Provider Reimbursement Manual, PRM, Part I, at § 2917.

49. 42 C.F.R. §§ 405.750, 405.841, 405.1885(a). Decisions procured by fraud can be reopened at any time. 42 C.F.R. § 405.1885(d).

50. Compare McCuin v. Secretary of HHS, 817 F.2d 161 (1st Cir.1987); Butterworth v. Bowen, 796 F.2d 1379 (11th Cir.1986) (cases may be reopened after the expiration of the 60–day period only upon motion of the claimant); with Fox v. Bowen, 835 F.2d 1159 (6th

The Supreme Court has held that an intermediary's refusal of a provider's request to reopen is not reviewable by the PRRB and the courts.[51]

§ 11–27. Judicial Review

Review is available in federal court for specified final administrative decisions involving Medicare, including decisions of the Appeals Council (or of an ALJ which the Appeals Council refused to review) regarding eligibility or involving benefits worth $1000 or more under Part A or Part B[1] and of the PRRB or Administrator involving claims to provider reimbursement valued at $10,000 or more.[2] Judicial review is subject to a variety of limits, however.

First, judicial review is usually available only after the exhaustion of lengthy administrative processes involving multiple levels of review. Section 205(h) of the Social Security Act,[3] incorporated into the Medicare law,[4] has been interpreted by the Supreme Court to include a nonwaivable requirement that a claim be presented to the government and a waivable requirement that all available administrative remedies be exhausted by the claimant.[5] The Court has further held that reviewing courts can, where appropriate, determine that the government has unreasonably refused to waive exhaustion, thus permitting direct judicial relief.[6]

Expedited review procedures provided with respect to some Medicare administrative procedure permit some levels of administrative review to be bypassed. Where expedited review is not permitted or is not an adequate remedy, however, court decisions are not clear as to what must be shown to avoid exhaustion. In a Social Security case the Supreme Court indicated that exhaustion could be waived if the issue in the case was "collateral" to the substantive claim to benefits,[7] but in a subsequent Medicare case the Court held that even if purely procedural claims are raised, they must still be presented through administrative processes, at least where there is any possibility that an award of benefits would remedy the problem.[8]

The lower courts have in most instances rejected attempts to avoid exhaustion of administrative remedies and seek direct judicial relief of unfavorable Medicare decisions.[9] Some courts have even refused to permit direct challenges to statutes defensively in fraud and abuse enforcement actions.[10]

Cir.1987); Cieutat v. Bowen, 824 F.2d 348 (5th Cir.1987); Munsinger v. Schweiker, 709 F.2d 1212 (8th Cir.1983) (cases may be reopened after the expiration of the 60–day period for good cause by both the Appeals Council and the claimant).

51. In Your Home Visiting Nurse Servs., Inc. v. Shalala, 525 U.S. 449, 119 S.Ct. 930 (1999).

§ 11–27

1. 42 U.S.C.A. § 1395ff(b)(1), (2).

2. 42 U.S.C.A. § 1395oo(f).

3. 42 U.S.C.A. § 405(h).

4. 42 U.S.C.A. § 1395ii.

5. Mathews v. Eldridge, 424 U.S. 319, 96 S.Ct. 893, 47 L.Ed.2d 18 (1976).

6. Id.

7. 424 U.S. at 330, 96 S.Ct. at 900.

8. Heckler v. Ringer, 466 U.S. 602, 104 S.Ct. 2013, 80 L.Ed.2d 622 (1984).

9. See e.g., Ancillary Affiliated Health Serv. Inc. v. Shalala, 165 F.3d 1069 (7th Cir.1998); Abbey v. Sullivan, 978 F.2d 37 (2d Cir.1992); Rodabaugh v. Sullivan, 943 F.2d 855 (8th Cir. 1991); Association of Am. Medical Colleges v. Califano, 569 F.2d 101 (D.C.Cir.1977).

10. United States v. Royal Geropsychiatric Serv. Inc., 8 F.Supp.2d 690 (N.D.Oh.1998). Courts have also in general not permitted direct challenges to the validity of standards applied in national fraud and abuse enforcement audits. Assoc. of Am. Medical Colleges v. U.S., 34 F.Supp.2d 1187 (C.D.Cal.1998) but see Ohio Hosp. Ass'n v. Shalala, 201 F.3d 418 (6th Cir. 1998).

Courts have also demanded exhaustion of administrative remedies in the Medicare managed care program.[11] Several cases have accepted direct review, however, where administrative remedies are clearly inadequate,[12] or where payment methodology as opposed to payment amount is at issue in a Part B case.[13] Several recent cases have excused exhaustion in provider challenges to HCFA enforcement actions,[14] but the Supreme Court rejected this position in a recent decision.[15] Attempts to sue intermediaries or carriers directly in tort as an alternative to pursuing administrative remedies have generally been rejected.[16] Attempts to file third-party complaints against HHS in hospital collection efforts, claiming Medicare's liability for the bill, have also failed.[17] Some courts have permitted state tort claims against Medicare HMOs for medical negligence, however.[18]

Second, judicial review of certain issues is specifically precluded by the Medicare statute. These include issues involving the establishment of DRGs, the methodology for classifying discharges within the DRGs, and the weightings assigned DRGs;[19] the determinations of the historical payment basis, relative values and relative value units, conversion factors, geographic adjustment factors, and coding systems for RBRVS;[20] and regulations or instructions relating to the method of determining the amount of payment under Part B issued prior to 1981.[21] Provisions of the Balanced Budget Act of 1997 creating prospective payment systems for other services also preclude judicial review for many services.[22] Prior to 1986 the Medicare statute did not permit judicial review of disputes involving the amount of Part B reimbursement. This

11. Roen v. Sullivan, 764 F.Supp. 555 (D.Minn.1991).

12. See Tataranowicz v. Sullivan, 959 F.2d 268 (D.C.Cir.1992), cert. denied 506 U.S. 1048, 113 S.Ct. 963, 122 L.Ed.2d 120 (1993) (exhaustion futile where Secretary unlikely to change position in appeals process); Beverly Hosp. v. Bowen, 872 F.2d 483 (D.C.Cir.1989) (available procedures could not redress problem); Mt. Sinai Medical Ctr. of Greater Miami v. Sullivan, [1992–1 Transfer Binder] Medicare and Medicaid Guide (CCH) ¶ 39,516 (Ct. Cl., Aug. 9, 1991) (PRRB review not available because facts not known in time for timely appeal).

13. Downtown Medical Ctr. v. Bowen, 944 F.2d 756 (10th Cir.1991); Outpatient Ophthalmic Surgery Soc'y, Inc. v. Sullivan, 1990 WL 236113 (D.D.C.1990); Ioptex Research Inc. v. Sullivan, 1990 WL 284512 (C.D.Cal.1990), interpreting Bowen v. Michigan Academy of Family Physicians, 476 U.S. 667, 106 S.Ct. 2133, 90 L.Ed.2d 623 (1986) to waive exhaustion where challenges to methodology are involved in Part B cases. See, however, Shalala v. Illinois Council on Long Term Care, 120 S.Ct. 1084 (2000). (limiting Michigan Academy to situations where administrative review was 05 expressly precluded.)

14. Illinois Council of Long Term Care, Inc. v. Shalala, 143 F.3d 1072 (7th Cir.1998), rev'd Shalala v. Illinois Council on Long Term Care, 120 S.Ct. 1084 (2000); Northern Health Facilities, Inc., 39 F.Supp.2d 563 (D.Md.1998); Mul-

tiplex of Mass., Inc. v. Shalala, 39 F.Supp.2d 88 (D.Mass.1999); Libbie Rehab. Ctr. v. Shalala, 26 F.Supp.2d 128 (D.D.C.1998). But see Affiliated Prof. Home Health Care Agency v. Shalala, 164 F.3d 282 (5th Cir.1999); Core Care Health Servs., Inc. v. Shalala, 1999 WL 124419 (E.D.Pa.1999); Sunrise Healthcare Corp. v. Shalala, 50 F.Supp.2d 830 (S.D.Ill.1999).

15. Shalala v. Illinois Council on Long Term Care, Inc., 120 S.Ct. 1084 (2000).

16. See e.g., Pani v. Empire Blue Cross & Blue Shield, 152 F.3d 67 (2d Cir., 1998); Bodimetric Health Servs. v. Aetna Life & Casualty, 903 F.2d 480 (7th Cir.1990), cert. denied 498 U.S. 1012, 111 S.Ct. 579, 112 L.Ed.2d 584 (1990). See also Gerardi v. Travelers Ins. Co., 961 F.Supp. 28 (D.C.Conn.1996) (no punitive damages against carrier for wrongful decision).

17. See e.g., Washington Hosp. Ctr. v. Beaner, 1993 WL 152423 (D.D.C.1993).

18. See, e.g. Ardary v. Aetna Health Plans of California, 98 F.3d 496 (9th Cir.1996); Wartenberg v. Aetna U.S. Healthcare, 2 F.Supp.2d 273 (E.D.N.Y.1998).

19. 42 U.S.C.A. § 1395ww(d)(7).

20. 42 U.S.C.A. § 1395w–4(i)(1).

21. 42 U.S.C.A. § 1395ff(b)(4).

22. 42 U.S.C.A.§ 1395ww(j)(7) (rehabilitation services); 42 U.S.C.A. § 1395yy(e)(8) (skilled nursing facility services); 42 U.S.C.A.

preclusion was upheld by the Supreme Court in *United States v. Erika, Inc.*[23] It was subsequently undermined, however, by *Bowen v. Michigan Academy of Family Physicians*,[24] which held that judicial review was available to review the method by which payment was determined, though not the actual amount of payment. Congress subsequently amended the statute to permit review of Part B decisions involving more than $1000,[25] largely mooting the impact of *Michigan Academy*.[26]

Third, judicial review is precluded either by law or as a practical matter with respect to some categories of cases. There is, for example, no judicial review available for Part A and B claims involving less than $1000. Some vendors of health care goods or services also have no standing to appeal Medicare determinations that affect payments for their products.[27] In a situation where a provider refuses to deliver services that HCFA has specified are not covered by Medicare, the Supreme Court in *Heckler v. Ringer*,[28] refused a direct attack on the policy, even though the beneficiary is precluded from filing a claim and thus from exhausting administrative remedies. In other cases, judicial review, though technically available, is as a practical matter of limited benefit since it is afforded only after implementation of an administrative decision such as suspension from the Medicare program.[29]

Fourth, remedies available to courts reviewing certain decisions are limited by statute. For example, national coverage determinations, which decide whether a particular class of items or services is covered under Medicare, cannot be held unlawful or set aside for lack of compliance with the Administrative Procedure Act (APA) rulemaking provisions.[30] Moreover, where a court determines that the record is incomplete or otherwise lacks adequate information to support the validity of a national coverage determination, it must remand the matter to the Secretary for additional proceedings to supplement the record and may not determine that the item or service is covered except upon review of the supplemented record.[31]

Attempts to obtain judicial review where it is not available by statute and precluded by 42 U.S.C.A. 405(h) have generally been rejected by the Supreme Court, despite repeated attempts by the lower courts to find some jurisdictional toehold. Successive Supreme Court cases rejected arguments for review under 28 U.S.C.A. § 1331,[32] through the Administrative Procedures Act,[33] or in the Court of Claims.[34] In *Heckler v. Ringer*,[35] the Court rejected a challenge

§ 1395l(t)(9) (outpatient hospital services); 42 U.S.C.A. § 1395fff(d) (home health benefits).

23. 456 U.S. 201, 102 S.Ct. 1650, 72 L.Ed.2d 12 (1982).

24. 476 U.S. 667, 106 S.Ct. 2133, 90 L.Ed.2d 623 (1986).

25. 42 U.S.C.A. § 1395ff(b)(2)(B).

26. See cases cited at note 38, infra.

27. TAP Pharmaceuticals v. HHS, 163 F.3d 199 (4th Cir.1998) (drug manufacturers whose anticancer drugs were covered by Part B.)

28. 466 U.S. 602, 104 S.Ct. 2013, 80 L.Ed.2d 622 (1984).

29. Rodabaugh v. Sullivan, 943 F.2d 855 (8th Cir.1991).

30. 42 U.S.C.A. § 1395ff(b)(3)(B). See also Friedrich v. Secretary of HHS, 894 F.2d 829 (6th Cir.1990), cert. denied 498 U.S. 817, 111 S.Ct. 59, 112 L.Ed.2d 34 (1990) (holding national coverage determinations to be interpretive rules not subject to APA rulemaking requirements).

31. 42 U.S.C.A. § 1395ff(b)(3)(C).

32. Weinberger v. Salfi, 422 U.S. 749, 95 S.Ct. 2457, 45 L.Ed.2d 522 (1975).

33. Califano v. Sanders, 430 U.S. 99, 97 S.Ct. 980, 51 L.Ed.2d 192 (1977).

34. United States v. Erika, Inc., 456 U.S. 201, 102 S.Ct. 1650, 72 L.Ed.2d 12 (1982). See also, St. Vincent's Medical Center v. United States, 32 F.3d 548 (Fed.Cir.1994); Bloomington Hosp. v. United States, 29 Fed.Cl. 286

to a Part A policy even though the challenge was cast as a procedural challenge (rather than a challenge to the denial of the claim itself) and though one of the claimants, who had not yet received a treatment for which coverage was denied, had no other practical means of review. Though the Supreme Court held in *Bowen v. Michigan Academy of Family Physicians*,[36] that courts could hear challenges to the "method by which Part B awards are computed (as opposed to the computation)* * *.",[37] post Michigan Academy cases have tended to limit the scope of this exception[38] and the Supreme Court has recently limited Michigan Academy to cases where administrative review was totally precluded.[39]

The federal courts in recent years have been remarkably deferential to HHS in its administration of Medicare, and the level of deference becomes greater the higher the court. The Secretary has won each of the six Supreme Court cases she has litigated in the 1990s.[40] During two recent years surveyed in a recent article,[41] HHS prevailed in 88% of the cases it litigated at the court of appeals level and 70% of the cases it litigated at the district court level.[42] The courts have rigorously applied in Medicare cases, the Chevron doctrine, under which they must defer to an administrative agency in its interpretation of a statute that it administers if the interpretation is not clearly contrary to the plain meaning of a statute, and if the agency's interpretation of the rule is reasonable.[43] The courts also defer to HHS in its interpretations of its own rules, which, under Thomas Jefferson v. Shalala,[44] the courts may not ignore unless the interpretation is "plainly erroneous or inconsistent with the regulation."[45] The courts show little interest in taking control of this complex and technical program from HHS, and rarely intervene except where HHS seems clearly to be overreaching.

K.   THE MEDICARE AS SECONDARY PAYER PROGRAM

§ 11–28.   The Medicare as Secondary Payer Program

In an effort to control the cost of the Medicare program and to avoid double recoveries by beneficiaries, Congress has attempted with increasingly

(Fed.Cl.1993) (recent cases denying Court of Claims jurisdiction over Medicare disputes).

35. 466 U.S. 602, 104 S.Ct. 2013, 80 L.Ed.2d 622 (1984).

36. 476 U.S. 667, 106 S.Ct. 2133, 90 L.Ed.2d 623 (1986).

37. 476 U.S. at 676, 106 S.Ct. at 2139.

38. Compare American Academy of Dermatology v. DHHS, 118 F.3d 1495 (11th Cir. 1997); Martin v. Shalala, 63 F.3d 497, 503 (7th Cir.1995); Michigan Ass'n of Indep. Clinical Labs. v. Shalala, 52 F.3d 1340 (6th Cir.1994); Farkas v. Blue Cross & Blue Shield of Mich., 24 F.3d 853 (6th Cir.1994); National Kidney Patients Association v. Sullivan, 958 F.2d 1127 (D.C.Cir.1992), cert. denied 506 U.S. 1049, 113 S.Ct. 966, 122 L.Ed.2d 122 (1993); Abbey v. Sullivan, 978 F.2d 37 (2d Cir.1992) (refusing judicial review); with Karnak Educ. Trust v. Bowen, 821 F.2d 1517 (11th Cir.1987); Linoz v. Heckler, 800 F.2d 871 (9th Cir.1986) (permitting review).

39. Shalala v. Illinois Council on Long Term Care, 120 S.Ct. 1084 (2000).

40. In Your Home Visiting Nurse Servs., Inc. v. Shalala, 525 U.S. 449, 119 S.Ct. 930 (1999); Regions Hospital v. Shalala, 522 U.S. 448, 118 S.Ct. 909 (1998); Shalala v. Guernsey Mem. Hosp., 514 U.S. 87 (1995); Thomas Jefferson Univ. v. Shalala, 512 U.S. 504 (1994); and Good Samaritan Hosp. v. Shalala, 508 U.S. 402 (1993).

41. 1995 and the second half of 1997 and the first half of 1998

42. Timothy Stoltzfus Jost, Governing Medicare, 51 Admin.L.Rev. 39,56 (1999).

43. Chevron v. Natural Resources Defense Council, Inc., 467 U.S. 837, 842 (1984). See, applying Chevron, Good Samaritan Hosp. v. Shalala, 508 U.S. 402(1993) and Regions Hospital v. Shalala, 522 U.S. 448, 118 S.Ct. 909, 911 (1998).

44. 512 U.S. 504 (1994).

45. 512 U.S. at 512.

greater vigor since 1980 to make the obligation of Medicare to finance medical care for its beneficiaries secondary to the obligations of other potential sources of funding.[1] The payers currently covered by the program include automobile or liability insurers, no fault insurance plans, workers' compensation plans, and employer group health plans under certain circumstances.[2] As a practical matter, a provider or professional must first look to these sources of payment, and may only bill Medicare to the extent that the primary payer does not cover the reasonable cost or reasonable charge for the service.[3]

§ 11–28

1. 42 U.S.C.A. § 1395y(b); 42 C.F.R. §§ 411.20–411.175. Excellent discussions of the Secondary Payor Program are found in Edward F. Shay, Medicare Secondary Payor Program, in 1990 Health Law Handbook, 367 (Alice G. Gosfield, ed. 1990) and James C. Dechene, Medicare Secondary Payer Program, Implications for Providers and Third Party Payers, in 1991 Health Law Handbook, 397 (Alice G. Gosfield, ed., 1991).

2. 42 U.S.C.A. § 1395y(b)(2).

3. 42 U.S.C.A. § 1395y(b)(4). See Appalachian Regional Healthcare, Inc. v. Shalala, 131 F.3d 1050 (D.C.Cir.1997) (limiting total Medicare payments to hospital for secondary payer claims to amount Medicare would have paid for service minus secondary payer payments); Zinman v. Shalala, 67 F.3d 841 (9th Cir.1995) (Medicare entitled to receive full refund of payment made for service subsequently paid for by primary payer, even when payment made at discounted rate).

Chapter 12

MEDICAID

Table of Sections

A. INTRODUCTION

Research References

Am Jur 2d, Social Security and Medicare §§ 1 et seq.
ALR Index: Medicaid
ALR Digest: Public Assistance §§ 14–16
24 Am Jur Trials 699, Social Security Hearings and Appeals in Disability Cases
Am Jur Pleading and Practice Forms (Rev), Welfare Laws §§ 15, 24

A. INTRODUCTION

§ 12–1. Generally

Medicaid is a cooperative federal and state program (or rather fifty-six separate state and territorial programs) that finances health care for the poor.[1] The program is established by title XIX of the Social Security Act.[2] The Medicaid program has come to serve at least three different functions. First, Medicaid began as, and still remains to a considerable extent, a program to finance health care for the "worthy poor" who receive cash assistance through the federal Supplemental Security Income Program or who would have been eligible to receive the federally assisted Aid to Families with Dependent Children program before it was abolished in 1996.[3] Persons who have minimal income and assets and are aged, blind, disabled or dependent children and their parents fall into this category. The link between Medicaid and cash assistance has grown steadily more tenuous in recent years, as Medicaid has moved on to other purposes.[4] Second, Medicaid is a catastrophic insurance program for those whose otherwise adequate income and assets have been or would be wholly consumed by extraordinary medical bills, particularly bills for care in nursing facilities or facilities that care for the mentally retarded. This category includes a small but vexatious group of middle income elderly persons who have been divested of their assets to render them eligible for Medicaid payment for nursing facility care, though a string of federal statutes has attempted to eliminate this strategy.[5] Third, Medicaid has in the recent past been expanded to cover low income children and pregnant women, regardless of eligibility for cash assistance. Nationwide, about 44% of non-elderly persons with income levels below the federal poverty limit are covered by Medicaid, but coverage varies dramatically from state to state, ranging from 32% in Florida and Texas to 68% in New England.

The federal government contributes from 50% to 83% of Medicaid program costs (depending on the per capita income of the state) with the state

§ 12–1

1. An excellent brief description of the program, from which many of the statistics in this introduction are taken, is found in John K. Iglehart, The American Health Care System: Medicaid, 340 New Eng. J. Med. 430 (1999).

2. The provisions of title XIX are often referred to by their Social Security Act section numbers, § 1901 et seq. For ease of reference, we will cite statutes in this text by their parallel U.S. Code citations. Section 1396a is generally regarded to be the longest sentence in the English language, coming to over 10,800 words.

3. For a history of the Medicaid program and its antecedents, see Rosemary Stevens and Robert Stevens, Welfare Medicine in America (1974).

4. See Sandra Tanenbaum, Medicaid Eligibility Policy in the 1980s: Medical Utilitarianism and the "Deserving" Poor, 20 J. Health Pol., Pol'y & L. 933 (1995).

5. See infra, § 12–4(c).

covering the rest. This contribution is referred to as federal financial participation (FFP) and accounts for 40% of all federal funds received by the states. Federal statutes and regulations establish basic requirements for eligibility, benefits, payment, and administration, but significant differences exist among the states in virtually all aspects of the Medicaid program. Moreover, the "New Federalism" philosophy represented by the Balanced Budget Act of 1997 has worked a substantial change in the balance of power over the Medicaid program, devolving much greater power to the states to design and govern their Medicaid programs. This devolution has been accomplished in part through waiver programs, which antedated the BBA but were substantially broadened under that legislation. As of the summer of 1999, seventeen state programs were operating wholly or in part under Section 1115 waivers, the broadest of the waiver programs, and several other waiver applications were approved but not implemented or were under consideration.[6] With increasing reliance on federal waivers in recent years, differences among the states seem to be increasing.

Medicaid coverage tends to expand and contract depending on the economic health and political philosophy of the nation and of particular states. Thus the program contracted dramatically in the early 1980s, grew dramatically in the late 1980s and early 1990s, and seems to be contracting again in the late 1990s.

Medicare is generally perceived to be a social insurance program like Social Security and the national health insurance programs of central European countries. Part A is funded by payroll taxes paid by employed persons and Part B by general revenue funds and by premiums paid by beneficiaries. Eligibility is not means tested. No stigma is attached to receiving benefits, which are considered to be an earned entitlement. Medicare is entirely a federal program and receives broad-based political support. Medicaid, by contrast, is clearly a welfare program. Though the original goal of Medicaid was to provide mainstream medical care for the poor, payment rates for professionals and providers have been held to such low levels for so many years in most states that Medicaid recipients in many places now receive most of their health care through a distinct system of "welfare medicine." Eligibility for Medicaid is means-tested, and recipients are subject to all of the stigma that attaches in our society to being a welfare recipient. The program is wholly funded by general revenue funds. The Medicaid program is one of the largest items in the budgets of most states, and is always politically controversial and vulnerable.

This chapter first considers eligibility for Medicaid, then Medicaid benefits, next Medicaid reimbursement, then administration, and finally appeals and judicial review. It concludes with a description of the State Children's Health Insurance Program (SCHIP) created by the 1997 BBA as a supplement to Medicaid. As Medicaid varies significantly from state to state, coverage in this chapter will be limited by and large to the federal law governing the program supplemented with occasional mention of representative state law. The chapter will further focus on the federal law affecting the fifty states, largely omitting provisions uniquely affecting the territories.[7] Fuller discus-

6. see   http://www.hcfa.gov/medicaid/org-demo.htm.

7. Parallel authority affecting territorial programs is generally not cited. Where the law

sion of state law is found in the CCH Medicare and Medicaid Guide, Medicaid State Charts, ¶¶ 15,501–15,660. Ultimately, however, the attorney concerned with issues unique to individual state Medicaid programs must refer to relevant state statutes, regulations, and manual provisions.

B. ELIGIBILITY

§ 12–2. Groups Covered by Medicaid

To be eligible for Medicaid, a person must be both poor and deserving, that is one must both fit into a designated eligibility classification and meet financial need requirements. Groups of persons who can be included within state Medicaid programs are designated by federal law. Some of these groups are mandatory, i.e. a state that participates in the Medicaid program must cover these individuals. Other groups are optional, a state may choose to cover or not to cover these individuals, but may receive federal matching funds (federal financial participation or FFP) if it does cover them. Finally, states may cover any additional groups they choose to cover under their state medical assistance programs but may not claim federal matching funds for these groups. Ultimately many persons who are poor, including most non-elderly childless persons, fit into none of these categories and thus do not receive Medicaid benefits. Historically Medicaid recipients were classified into two classifications—the categorically and medically needy, the first consisting of persons who received or were eligible for cash assistance (or who would be were it not for an eligibility requirement that does not apply to Medicaid) and the second consisting of those who were not eligible for cash assistance because of their income, but who were nonetheless impoverished because of their medical expenses.[1] This distinction survives in the federal regulations governing Medicaid eligibility, 42 C.F.R. Part 435, but has become detached from its original meaning as Medicaid has become delinked from cash assistance. This section will delineate the groups eligible for Medicaid, and then proceed to describe the non-financial and financial eligibility requirements that apply to all groups.

a. Groups That Must Be Covered

Under the Medicaid statute, states that participate in Medicaid must cover certain groups. Historically this included recipients of the two major federal cash assistance programs, Aid to the Aged, Blind, and Disabled (which became the Supplemental Security Income (SSI) program in 1972) and Aid to Families with Dependent Children. Though the AFDC program was abolished by the Personal Responsibility and Work Opportunity Reconciliation Act of 1996 (P.L. 104–193) (PRWORA), states must continue to cover under their Medicaid program families who would have been eligible for the state's AFDC program as in effect on July 16, 1996.[2] A state may, however, lower its income

and regulations affecting territorial programs are different from those affecting the states, differences are not generally explored. These differences have to do principally with eligibility (see 42 C.F.R. Part 436 affecting eligibility in Guam, Puerto Rico, and the Virgin Islands) and the extent of federal financial participation in territorial programs (see 42 U.S.C.A. §§ 1308(f), 1396b(d)).

§ 12–2

1. See Massachusetts Ass'n of Older Americans v. Sharp, 700 F.2d 749, 750 (1st Cir.1983).

2. 42 U.S.C.A. §§ 1396a(a)(10)(A)(i)(I); 1396u–1(a).

standards for determining eligibility to a level as low as those in effect on May 1, 1988, may increases its income or resource standards above those in effect in 1996 in accordance with increases in the CPI, or may use income or resource methodologies less restrictive than it used in 1996.[3] Though states are not permitted to terminate Medicaid coverage for persons simply because they lose eligibility for Temporary Assistance for Needy Families (TANF) program, which replaced AFDC, states may terminate coverage for individuals (but not their minor children) who are terminated from TANF because of refusal to work and who are not otherwise eligible for Medicaid.[4] Families covered because of former AFDC eligibility (who were eligible during 3 or the preceding 6 months) are eligible for six months of additional coverage, and may be eligible for up to six months beyond that with the payment of a premium.[5]

Though Congress intended that Medicaid coverage for needy families survive the end of cash assistance effected by PRWORA, it appears that in fact PRWORA has led to a dramatic decline in Medicaid coverage.[6] Under the TANF program, states are entitled to discourage or divert applicants from receiving cash assistance, but most states continue to use the same form for TANF and Medicaid applications, and many appear to not process Medicaid applications when TANF applications are denied or withdrawn.[7] Moreover, many families who would previously have applied for cash assistance, and incidentally received Medicaid, now do not apply for Medicaid until they end up in a hospital or emergency room in a medical emergency.

States must also cover families not in fact receiving dependent child payments but deemed to be AFDC recipients for Medicaid purposes,[8] individuals who would have been denied AFDC because of AFDC rules that do not apply to Medicaid requiring the deeming of income of relatives,[9] and families not eligible for the former AFDC program because of technicalities inapplicable under Medicaid.[10]

States participating in the Medicaid program must also cover aged, blind and disabled persons who are either eligible for the federal Supplemental Security Income (SSI) program, or, at the state's election, eligible under standards more restrictive than those applied by the SSI program but not more restrictive than those in effect in the state for its assistance to the aged, blind, and disabled program on January 1, 1972 (the "209(b)" option).[11]

3. 42 U.S.C.A. § 1396u–1(b)(2).

4. 42 U.S.C.A. § 1396u–1(b)(3).

5. 42 U.S.C.A. §§ 608a(11)(A), 1396r–6(a) & (b). Families who become ineligible because of the collection of child or spousal support may also be eligible under certain circumstances. 42 U.S.C.A. § 608a(11)(B).

6. See Families USA, Losing Health Insurance: The Unintended Consequences of Welfare Reform (1999); Mark Greenberg, Kaiser Commission on Medicaid and the Uninsured: Participation in Welfare and Medicaid Enrollment (1998); Robert Pear, Poor Workers Lose Medicaid Coverage Despite Eligibility, New York Times, Ap. 12, 1999 at A1.

7. See Reynolds v. Giuliani, 35 F.Supp.2d 331 (S.D.N.Y. 1999), modified in part 43 F. Supp.2d 492 (S.D.N.Y. 1999) (enjoining City of

New York to accept and process Medicaid applications); See also, DHHS, Letter to TANF Administrators, State Medicaid Directors, and CHIP Directors, March 22, 1999 (http://www.hcfa.gov/medicaid/wrdl3229.htm) and accompanying Administrators Supporting Families in Transition: A guide to Expanding Health Coverage in the Post–Welfare World, http://www.hcfa.gov/medicaid/welfare.htm (explaining state's obligation to accept and process promptly applications).

8. 42 C.F.R. §§ 435.115; 436.114.

9. 42 C.F.R. § 435.113.

10. 42 C.F.R. §§ 435.112, 436.111.

11. 42 U.S.C.A. § 1396a(a)(10)(A)(i)(II), (f); 42 C.F.R. §§ 435.120, 435.121.

Fourteen states have elected to determine eligibility under the 209(b) option. The 209(b) option was originally authorized to permit states to avoid the burden they faced with the influx of new beneficiaries into the state Medicaid programs in the early 1970s when the federal SSI program replaced earlier state aid to the aged, blind, and disabled (AABD) programs, which had often had much more restrictive financial eligibility requirements. States must also cover disabled children who lost SSI eligibility under PRWORA;[12] "Qualified severely impaired individuals," who lose SSI eligibility because of employment but need Medicaid coverage to continue employment;[13] aged, blind and disabled persons who receive mandatory state supplements;[14] and a variety of aged, blind and disabled persons who are not eligible for SSI because of various technicalities or because of increases in Social Security benefits under various laws.[15]

Mandatory Medicaid coverage has been expanded over the years to cover a number of categories of persons who are not recipients of cash assistance. First, Medicaid must cover a pregnant woman who would be eligible for AFDC (as it stood in 1996) if her child was born[16] and pregnant women and infants under the age of one in families with income not exceeding 133% of the poverty level.[17] Medicaid must also be provided to children under the age of nineteen and born after September 30, 1983, whose families would be eligible for AFDC if it still existed;[18] children under age five in families with income not exceeding 133% of the federal poverty line;[19] children age six through eighteen, born after September 30, 1983, and with income not exceeding 100% of the federal poverty line;[20] and children for whom foster care or adoption maintenance payments are being made.[21] Finally, pediatric immunizations must be provided to all Medicaid eligible, uninsured, or Indian children.[22]

State Medicaid programs must also cover Medicare premiums, coinsurance and deductible costs for certain dually-eligible individuals. First, states must cover Medicare cost-sharing obligations for "qualified Medicare beneficiaries" (QMBs), Medicare eligible persons whose family income does not exceed 100% of the federal poverty limit and whose resources do not exceed twice the SSI eligibility limit.[23] States must also pay Part A premiums for "qualified disabled and working individuals" (Medicare eligible persons whose family income does not exceed 200% of the federal poverty level;[24] and Part B premiums for persons who would be QMBs except that their income exceeds

---

12. 42 U.S.C.A. § 1396a(a)(10)(i)(II). About 300,000 children were eliminated from SSI under PRWORA.

13. 42 U.S.C.A. §§ 1396a(a)(10)(A)(i)(II); 1396d(q).

14. 42 C.F.R. § 435.130.

15. 42 C.F.R. §§ 435.122, .131, .132, .133, .134, .135, .137, & .138.

16. 42 U.S.C.A. § 1396a(a)(10)(A)(i)(III); 1396d(n)(1).

17. 42 U.S.C.A. § 1396a(a)(10)(A)(i)(IV), (l)(1)(A), (B), (2)(A)(ii)(II).

18. 42 U.S.C.A. §§ 1396a(a)(10)(A)(i)(III); 1396d(n)(2).

19. 42 U.S.C.A. § 1396a(a)(10)(A)(i)(VI), (l)(1)(C), (l)(2)(B).

20. 42 U.S.C.A. § 1396a(a)(10)(A)(i)(VII), (l)(1)(D), (l)(2)(C).

21. 42 C.F.R. § 435.145.

22. 42 U.S.C.A. § 1396s.

23. 42 U.S.C.A. §§ 1396a(a)(10E); 1396d(p). The extent of the states obligation to cover coinsurance amounts where the amount Medicare pays plus the coinsurance exceeds the amount Medicaid would pay for the service has proved a very controversial question, which is discussed below at § 12–9.

24. 42 U.S.C.A. §§ 1395a(a)(10)(E)(ii); 1396d(s).

1005 of the poverty level, but is less than 120% of the poverty level.[25] Finally, states must, for the years 1998 to 2002, cover Part B premiums for "qualifying individuals" whose family income is at least 120 percent, but not more than 135% of the poverty level, but payments for these individuals is capped, and allocated on a first come-first served basis.[26]

b. Groups That the States May Cover at Their Option

The federal law also permits the states to cover at their option a number of groups for whom coverage is not required under federal law. States that elect to cover such groups may not impose eligibility requirements prohibited by Title XIX or more restrictive than their former AFDC, SSI or 209(b) requirements, and must use reasonable group classifications that do not result in arbitrary or inequitable treatment.[27]

First, state Medicaid programs may include a variety of groups of persons who would be eligible for AFDC (if AFDC still existed), SSI or optional state supplements but for certain factors.

Medicaid coverage may be provided, at the option of the state, to individuals who would be eligible for AFDC, except for the fact that:

1) the state AFDC program was not as broad as that permitted by federal law;[28]

2) their work-related child care costs are covered by the state rather than out of their income;[29]

3) they are not "dependent children" because they are above the age of eighteen but under the age of twenty-one (the "Ribicoff children");[30] or

4) they are being placed for adoptions, but cannot be placed unless special needs for medical or rehabilitative care are covered.[31]

States may extend coverage to pregnant or postpartum women and infants under the age of one and who earn less than 185% of the federal poverty limit, and may charge a premium for such coverage to persons with an income exceeding 150% of the poverty limit.[32] States may also cover "targeted low income" children, in conjunction with the SCHIP program, whose family income does not exceed 200% of the poverty level or 150% of the state's Medicaid eligibility limit.[33]

States may provide, at their election, Medicaid coverage for aged, blind, and disabled persons who receive, because of their income, only state supplements and not SSI, if the payment is need-based, equal to the difference

25. 42 U.S.C.A. §§ 1396a(a)(10)(E)(iii).

26. 42 U.S.C.A. §§ 1396a(a)(10)(E)(iv), 1396u–3.

27. 42 C.F.R. § 435.401. Optional categories that may be covered by 209(b) states are described in 42 C.F.R. § 435.230.

28. 42 U.S.C.A. § 1396a(a)(10)(A)(ii)(III); 42 C.F.R. § 435.223.

29. 42 U.S.C.A. § 1396a(a)(10)(A)(ii)(II); 42 C.F.R. §§ 435.220, 436.220.

30. 42 U.S.C.A. §§ 1396a(a)(10)(A)(ii), 1396d(a)(i); 42 C.F.R. §§ 435.222. The state may decide to cover children under the age of 21, 20, 19, or 18, and may also decide to cover only particular categories of such children, such as those who are in foster care, subsidized adoptions, intermediate care facilities for the mentally retarded or psychiatric institutions. Id.

31. 42 U.S.C.A. § 1396a(a)(10)(A)(ii)(VIII); 42 C.F.R. §§ 435.227.

32. 42 U.S.C.A. §§ 1396a(a)(10)(A)(ii)(IX), (l)(1) & (2)(A)(i).

33. 42 U.S.C.A. §§ 1396a(a)(10)(ii)(A)(XIV), 1396d(u)(2)(C), 1397jj(B).

between countable income and the state supplement eligibility level, and available statewide;[34] and persons whose families earn less than 250% of the poverty level subject to payment of premiums and cost-sharing.[35] They may also cover persons who are in medical institutions for at least thirty days and meet welfare resource eligibility levels and whose income does not exceed 300% of SSI levels;[36] and persons receiving home and community based care and hospice care who would be eligible for Medicaid if they were institutionalized.[37] States may also provide Medicaid for TB infected individuals for defined TB-related services if the person would be eligible for Medicaid if disabled.[38] States may provide Medicaid coverage to aged or disabled persons whose income does not exceed levels established by the state up to 100% of the federal poverty limit and whose resources do not exceed SSI or more restrictive state limits.[39] A state may also pay premiums for persons entitled to COBRA continuation coverage (see § 9–6) under group health plans, whose income does not exceed 100% of the federal poverty limit and whose resources do not exceed 200% of the SSI resource limit, if the state determines that COBRA premiums are likely to cost less than Medicaid would cost.[40] States may provide all-inclusive care for the elderly (PACE) services persons over 55 who require nursing facility level care and are otherwise eligible.[41] Finally, under legislation adopted late in 1999, states may at their option, extend Medicaid to workers with disabilities, and, through demonstration projects, to persons with potentially disabling diseases such as HIV.

The most important optional category is the "medically needy."[42] The medically needy are persons who fit into the "worthy poor" categories, i.e. they are aged, blind, or disabled persons or families of dependent children, but who are not eligible for cash assistance because their income or assets exceed state eligibility levels for cash assistance. States have considerable flexibility in designing their medically needy programs. A state that offers a medically needy program must cover pregnant women and children under the age of eighteen who would be eligible as categorically needy but for their income and resources, and children born to the medically needy women for up to one year or so long as the woman remains eligible and the child remains in her household.[43] States must also cover persons who were covered under the state's medically needy program as aged, blind, and disabled persons in December of 1973 as long as they continue to be eligible by 1973 standards for disability or blindness and otherwise eligible under both 1973 and current standards.[44] Otherwise, the state may cover under its medically needy program children under the age of twenty-one, twenty, nineteen, or eighteen or any reasonable category of such children,[45] caretaker relatives of such chil-

34. 42 U.S.C.A. § 1396a(a)(10)(A)(ii)(XI); 42 C.F.R. §§ 435.232, 435.234, 435.1006.

35. 42 U.C.S.A. § 1396a(a)(10)(A)(XIII).

36. 42 U.S.C.A. §§ 1396a(a)(10)(A)(ii)(V), 1396b(f)(4)(C); 42 C.F.R. §§ 435.236, 435.1005. See further discussion of the 300% income cap below at § 12–4(b).

37. 42 U.S.C.A. §§ 1396a(a)(10)(VI) & (VII), 42 C.F.R. § 435.217.

38. 42 U.S.C.A. §§ 1396a(a)(10)(A)(ii)(XII); 1396a(z).

39. 42 U.S.C.A. § 1396a(a)(10)(A)(ii)(X), (m).

40. 42 U.S.C.A. § 1396a(a)(10)(F); 1396a(u).

41. 42 U.S.C.A. § 1396u–4.

42. 42 U.S.C.A. §§ 1396a(a)(10)(C), 1396d(a); 42 C.F.R. §§ 435.300–350; 435.4.

43. 42 U.S.C.A. § 1396a(a)(10)(C)(ii), (e)(4); 42 C.F.R. § 435.301(b).

44. 42 C.F.R. § 435.340.

45. 42 C.F.R. §§ 435.308.

dren,[46] persons over age sixty-five,[47] the blind,[48] the disabled,[49] presumptively eligible pregnant women,[50] or individuals enrolled in Medicaid HMOs who lose their eligibility.[51] 209(b) states may cover medically needy individuals applying 209(b) eligibility standards.[52] Thirty-four states currently cover both the categorically and medically needy, while sixteen states and territories currently limit coverage to the categorically needy only.

The long-term trend has been towards greater and greater complexity in the definition of groups eligible for Medicaid coverage either on a mandatory or optional basis. First, there has been a tendency to extend the list of groups covered to capture sub-groups of persons who would fit into one of the standard large cash-assistance categories but for some technicality, such as institutionalized status or excessive income because of increased social security benefits. Second, as has already been noted, federal law has begun in the past decade to break totally the historic link between Medicaid and cash-assistance programs, by including groups such as pregnant women or children between the ages of eighteen and twenty-one, with eligibility linked to relationship between income and the federal poverty level, and by continuing AFDC-related eligibility after the end of AFDC.

On the other hand, this growing complexity may be undergoing a reversal in favor of simplicity and flexibility. Almost twenty states are currently operating their Medicaid programs under Section 1115 waiver programs, which effectively means that eligibility is defined through negotiations between the state and DHHS. A number of these programs broadly cover low-income uninsureds without regard to traditional categories that have defined Medicaid eligibility. While Medicaid still remains, by and large, a program for the "worthy poor" as traditionally defined, the discontinuities that are beginning to become apparent between cash assistance eligibility and Medicaid eligibility raises the possibility of Medicaid becoming a general health insurance program for the poor.

§ 12–3. Non-financial Conditions of Eligibility

A state may not impose as a condition of Medicaid eligibility any residence requirement that excludes any person who is otherwise eligible and intends to remain permanently or indefinitely in the state, regardless of how long the person has actually been in the state, whether or not residence is maintained permanently at a fixed address, or whether or not the person was a resident of the state before entering an institution in the state.[1] Indeed, states must affirmatively make Medicaid available to eligible homeless persons.[2] States must also make provision for providing medical assistance to persons temporarily absent from the state, including persons placed by the state in out-of-state institutions.[3]

46. 42 C.F.R. §§ 435.310.

47. 42 C.F.R. §§ 435.320, 435.330.

48. 42 C.F.R. §§ 435.322, 435.330.

49. 42 C.F.R. §§ 435.324, 435.330.

50. 42 U.S.C.A. §§ 1396a(a)(47), 1396r–1.

51. 42 C.F.R. § 435.326.

52. 42 C.F.R. § 435.330.

§ 12–3

1. 42 U.S.C.A. § 1396a(b); 42 C.F.R. §§ 435.403.

2. 42 U.S.C.A. § 1396a(a)(48).

3. 42 U.S.C.A. § 1396a(a)(16); 42 C.F.R. §§ 435.403(e), (j)(3).

Medicaid programs must cover citizens of the United States and until 1996 covered legal permanent resident aliens who were otherwise eligible.[4] The PRWORA dramatically restricted Medicaid (and later SCHIP) coverage for many legal immigrants who had formerly been eligible. Statutes adopted in 1997 and 1998 reversed some of these restrictions, but aliens entering the United States after August 22, 1996 and those with temporary alien status are still generally barred from Medicaid coverage.[5] Medicaid does, however, covers emergency medical treatment for otherwise eligible aliens regardless of these restrictions (though not including organ transplantation services).[6]

States may not impose an age requirement of more than sixty-five years for Medicaid eligibility.[7] States must either use the Supplemental Security Income program's definition of disability or blindness or their own more restrictive definitions, though more restrictive definitions may not be more restrictive than that in the state plan in force in January of 1972.[8]

Federal financial participation (FFP) is not available for coverage of services for inmates in public institutions (other than medical institutions).[9] FFP is also not available for care or services for patients in mental institutions for persons under the age of sixty-five[10] or for inpatient psychiatric hospital services for persons above the age of twenty-one.[11] These provisions were adopted to assure that states would continue their traditional role of financing psychiatric hospitals, but have led to vigorous disputes as to whether or not nursing or intermediate care facilities are mental institutions.[12]

Eligibility determinations must be made within ninety days for disabled applicants and within forty-five days for all other applicants.[13] States must make Medicaid eligibility effective no later than the third month preceding the month of application if the applicant received Medicaid covered services during the three month period and would have been eligible at the time had he or she applied.[14] Medicaid eligibility continues until the recipient is found ineligible, but may continue for a longer period of time if the recipient is

---

4. 42 U.S.C.A. §§ 1396a(a), (b), 1396b(v)(1); 42 C.F.R. §§ 435.406.

5. 8 U.S.C.A. §§ 1611, 1612, 1613.

6. 42 U.S.C.A. § 1396b(v)(2), (3); 42 C.F.R. §§ 435.350, 436.330, 440.255(c). See Greenery Rehabilitation Group v. Hammon, 150 F.3d 226 (2d Cir.1998) (does not cover ongoing care of chronic condition following initial stabilization); Norwood Hosp. v. Commissioner of Public Welfare, 627 N.E.2d 914 (Mass.1994)(holding treatment rendered undocumented alien did not qualify for emergency exception). But see Aliessa v. Whalen, 694 N.Y.S.2d 308 (N.Y.Sup.1999) (finding that provisions of New York law barring lawful aliens from Medicaid coverage violated federal and state constitutions).

7. 42 U.S.C.A. § 1396a(b)(1); 42 C.F.R. §§ 435.520. Rules for determination of age are set out in 42 C.F.R. §§ 435.522, 436.522.

8. 42 C.F.R. §§ 435.121, 435.530, 435.540.

9. 42 U.S.C.A. § 1396d(a)(27)(A); 42 C.F.R. §§ 435.1008.

10. 42 U.S.C.A. § 1396d(a)(27)(B); 42 C.F.R. §§ 435.1008. See, 42 U.S.C.A. § 1396d(i) (defining "institution for mental diseases").

11. 42 U.S.C.A. § 1396d(a)(16), (h); 42 C.F.R. §§ 435.1008.

12. See e.g., Connecticut Dep't of Income Maintenance v. Heckler, 471 U.S. 524, 105 S.Ct. 2210, 85 L.Ed.2d 577 (1985).

13. 42 U.S.C.A. § 1396a(a)(8); 42 C.F.R. § 435.911. States that operate a joint application process for TANF and Medicaid may not fail to process Medicaid applications if they attempt to discourage or defer TANF application.

14. 42 U.S.C.A. § 1396a(a)(34); 42 C.F.R. § 435.914. Where an applicant has paid for medical care provided during the three month period of retroactive coverage, the provider must refund the payment and collect instead from Medicaid. Cohen v. Quern, 608 F.Supp. 1324 (N.D.Ill.1984).

terminated from SSI;[15] loses dependent child-related assistance because of employment;[16] is a child covered by a state extension of benefits option;[17] is overcoming a condition of eligibility (such as disability, blindness or incapacity) but is still eligible for cash assistance;[18] is enrolled in a managed care plan;[19] or requests a hearing to protest the termination or the action that has resulted in termination.[20] Medicaid programs must continue to pay for care provided persons determined to be eligible until they are subsequently determined to be ineligible.[21]

§ 12–4. Financial Eligibility Criteria

a. For the Categorically and Medically Needy

Medicaid is a welfare program and is only available to persons whose income and resources fall below specified levels. Categorically needy persons must be eligible for cash assistance, either under the standards applied under the former 14 AFDC program or as SSI or state supplement recipients under the federal SSI or the state supplement program.[1] In 1998 the income threshold level for eligibility for a family of three ranged from $3,036 in Alabama to $37,538 in Minnesota.[2] The SSI income eligibility level for an individual was $500 per month, $752 for a couple. If a state chooses under the 209(b) option to apply financial eligibility standards to the aged, blind, and disabled that are more restrictive than those applied by SSI, the state must, before applying its eligibility income standards, allow specified deductions. These include deductions for incurred medical expenses (in Medicaid parlance, the applicant "spends down" by incurring such expenses); any SSI benefits or optional state supplements the applicant receives, and certain Social Security cost of living increases.[3]

If a state Medicaid plan covers the medically needy, it must apply a single resource and income standard to all groups, which must not be more restrictive than the standard applied by the cash assistance programs to which categorical eligibility is linked.[4] Generally income eligibility levels may not exceed 133 1/3% of the former AFDC cash payment level for a family of the same size as the medically needy unit.[5] In determining the eligibility of the medically needy, the state must disregard income not counted in establishing eligibility for the categorically needy, and must allow the applicant to "spend

---

15. For the recipient terminated from SSI, eligibility continues through the end of the month if the state is notified by the tenth of the month, through the end of the following month if the state is notified after the tenth. 42 C.F.R. § 435.1003.

16. See § 14–2(a).

17. 42 U.S.C.A. § 1396a(e)(12) (for up to 12 months from eligibility).

18. 42 C.F.R. § 435.1004.

19. 42 U.S.C.A. § 1396a(e)(2) (six month guaranteed eligibility).

20. In which case, benefits continue until a decision is issued, but the state may recover payments made if the decision is adverse to the claimant. 42 C.F.R. §§ 431.230, 435.1003(a)(3).

21. 42 C.F.R. § 435.930.

§ 12–4

1. 42 C.F.R. § 435.4. General rules for application of financial eligibility methodologies are found at 42 C.F.R. § 435.601. FFP is only available for persons receiving state supplements but not SSI if their income before deductions does not exceed 300% of the SSI benefit amount. 42 C.F.R. § 435.1006.

2. Families USA, Losing Health Insurance: The Unintended Consequences of Welfare Reform, 1999.

3. 42 C.F.R. §§ 435.121, 435.631.

4. 42 U.S.C.A. § 1396a(a)(10)(C); 42 C.F.R. § 435.811. Medically needy resource standards are discussed at 42 C.F.R. §§ 435.840, 435.843, and 435.845.

5. 42 U.S.C.A. § 1396b(f)(1)(B); 42 C.F.R. §§ 435.811, 435.1007.

down" to the eligibility level by incurring medical expenses, including the cost of health insurance premiums.[6] States may compute eligibility by considering income and expenses over a period of up to six months.[7] The longer the time period applied by the state in computing eligibility, the less likely it is that medical expenses incurred during one episode of illness or injury will render the applicant eligible under the spend down provisions. Resource standards applied to the medically needy must also be at least as high as those applied to the categorically needy.[8]

From the outset, Medicaid was based on a public policy of accepting public responsibility for health care costs for indigent individuals and relieving members of the extended families of such individuals from any responsibility they had taken for such costs previously. Thus, in determining Medicaid eligibility, states may only consider the income and resources of the applicant and of the applicant's spouse or, if the applicant is under twenty-one, the applicant's parents.[9] Courts have generally rejected attempts by the states to consider income of other relatives living with a Medicaid applicant, such as siblings or nonparental caretakers (such as grandparents) to be available to the applicant, even though such deeming was permitted in determining AFDC eligibility.[10]

b. *Eligibility of Institutionalized Persons*

The most complex and controversial issues involving Medicaid eligibility have arisen with respect to eligibility for the institutionalized elderly and disabled. The average cost per year is about $51,000, but ranges from $33,000 a year in Louisiana to more than $73,000 a year in Connecticut.[11] At these rates, many elderly persons with significant income and assets are rapidly impoverished once they are admitted to a nursing facility. As elderly persons face a significant chance of requiring nursing home care[12] and long-term care insurance for the elderly is very costly, many elderly persons end up on Medicaid, our country's catastrophic insurance program of last resort. In 1997, 26% of Medicaid funds were spent on nursing facility care, and 48% of nursing facility care was financed by Medicaid,[13] even though less than 7% of Medicaid recipients use nursing facility services.[14]

6. 42 C.F.R. §§ 435.831, 436.831. States also are permitted, but not required, to allow spending down of resources to establish eligibility. Allen v. Utah Dept. of Health, 850 P.2d 1267 (Utah 1993).

7. 42 C.F.R. § 435.831(a). Hogan v. Heckler, 769 F.2d 886 (1st Cir.1985), cert. denied 478 U.S. 1007, 106 S.Ct. 3301, 92 L.Ed.2d 715 (1986); DeJesus v. Perales, 770 F.2d 316 (2d Cir.1985), cert. denied 478 U.S. 1007, 106 S.Ct. 3301, 92 L.Ed.2d 715 (1986). See Atkins v. Rivera, 477 U.S. 154, 106 S.Ct. 2456, 91 L.Ed.2d 131 (1986) (upholding the six month period).

8. 42 C.F.R. §§ 435.840. 209(b) states, however, may apply lower resource standards for the medically needy aged, blind, and disabled as long as the standard is not lower than the 1972 AABD resource standard. 42 C.F.R. § 435.840(c).

9. 42 U.S.C.A. § 1396a(a)(17)(D); 42 C.F.R. §§ 435.602.

10. See e.g., Addis v. Whitburn, 153 F.3d 836 (7th Cir.1998); Malloy v. Eichler, 860 F.2d 1179 (3d Cir.1988); Mitchell v. Lipscomb, 851 F.2d 734 (4th Cir.1988); Georgia Dep't of Medical Assistance v. Bowen, 846 F.2d 708 (11th Cir.1988); Childress v. Bowen, 833 F.2d 231 (10th Cir.1987); Olson v. Norman, 830 F.2d 811 (8th Cir.1987); Reed v. Blinzinger, 816 F.2d 296 (7th Cir.1987).

11. Mary Beth Franklin, Insuring Against Life's Frailties, 53 Kiplinger's Personal Finance Magazine, July 1, 1999.

12. 43% of those who turned 65 in 1990 will use nursing home care at some time during their remaining lifetime. Peter Kemper & Christopher M. Murtaugh, Lifetime Use of Nursing Home Care, 324 New Eng. J. Med. 595 (1991).

13. Bradley R. Braden, et al., National Health Expenditures, 1997, Table 12, 20 Health Care Financing Review, Fall 1998 at 83, 124. By contrast, only about 5% of nursing home care was paid for by private insurance.

Because Medicaid is a welfare program, its rules have historically required an institutionalized applicant to spend virtually all income and resources on medical care to establish eligibility. It also until the late 1980s strictly limited the ability of an institutionalized recipient to contribute income or resources to the support of a non-institutionalized (community) spouse.[15] These limitations have stimulated considerable creativity on the part of lawyers attempting to protect the income or resources of applicants and their spouses. In 1988, as part of the Medicare Catastrophic Care Act, Congress dramatically extended the protection afforded community spouses while also defining more clearly the circumstances under which voluntary impoverishment to create Medicaid eligibility would not be permitted.[16] While these amendments alleviated the situation of the community spouse, creative "Medicaid estate planning" efforts (discussed below) continued to secure Medicaid eligibility while protecting the assets (effectively the children's inheritance) of middle-income persons who required nursing facility care. The 1993 budget bill severely limited the possibilities of such planning, but skirmishing between Congress and Medicaid estate planners has continued in subsequent years.

The same income and resource levels are used to determine eligibility for institutionalized Medicaid applicants as for non-institutionalized applicants, except that states may set higher income limits for aged, blind, and disabled applicants, up to 300% of the SSI level (currently $500 per month).[17] States that have medically needy programs that include nursing facility care may cover any individual, as long as that individual's income is not sufficient to pay for nursing home costs after subtraction of permissible allowances and deductions.[18] In the approximately twenty states that do not have medically needy programs covering nursing facility care, the 300% limit renders persons ineligible for Medicaid whose income exceeds three times the SSI level, even though such persons do not have enough income to finance their nursing home care.[19] This quandary cannot normally be avoided by refusing or diverting the income, which usually comes from sources like Social Security or pensions that cannot be diverted. It has been averted, however, through the use of judicially-created trusts, under which the income is paid into the trust, with only an amount slightly less than the 300% limit distributed to the beneficiary.[20] These trusts have been authorized under 1993 amendments to the Medicaid law.[21]

14. Dept. Health & Human Serv. Medicare and Medicaid Data Book, 1990 at 83 (1990).

15. The institutionalized spouse could only contribute from his income to the non-institutionalized (community) spouse income equivalent to the level permitted for SSI recipients or the medically needy. 209(b) states were also permitted to deem the income of the community spouse to be available to the institutionalized spouse. Schweiker v. Gray Panthers, 453 U.S. 34, 101 S.Ct. 2633, 69 L.Ed.2d 460 (1981).

16. An excellent discussion of the issues raised under the 1988 legislation is found in Finberg & Nemore, Medicaid and the Elderly Poor—A Second Look at the Medicare Catastrophic Coverage Act: Transfer of Assets and Spousal Impoverishment, 25 Clearinghouse Rev. 1316 (1992).

17. 42 C.F.R. § 435.1005.

18. 42 C.F.R. §§ 435.831, 435.1007.

19. This predicament is referred to as the "Utah Gap." Haines and Combs, Income Caps in Medicaid Eligibility, 3 The ElderLaw Report 1(5) (Dec. 1991). See, Jill Quadagno, et al., Falling Into the Medicaid Gap: The Hidden Long–Term Care Dilemma, 31 The Gerontologist 521 (1991) (discussing what happens to persons who are affected by these caps.)

20. See Miller v. Ibarra, 746 F.Supp. 19 (D.Colo.1990).

When one spouse of a couple is institutionalized, Medicaid deems as available to the institutionalized spouse all of the income that is paid solely in his or her name, and half of the income that is paid jointly to the recipient and his or her spouse.[22] An institutionalized person determined eligible for Medicaid may retain from his or her income a reasonable personal needs allowance of not less that $30 per month,[23] and deduct a maintenance allowance for his or her community spouse and family living at home (discussed below). The applicant may also deduct for purposes of determining Medicaid eligibility amounts that are owed for Medicare premiums, deductibles, or coinsurance charges; amounts owed for incurred expenses for medical and remedial care recognized under state law but not paid for by Medicaid, German reparation payments, and certain Veterans pension payments.[24] All remaining income must be applied monthly to payment of the costs of care in the institution, to be supplemented as necessary by Medicaid to reach the level of reimbursement Medicaid permits for the institution.

In determining eligibility, Medicaid exempts from consideration resources that are not considered in determining eligibility for SSI, including most notably a home (regardless of its value), household goods, personal effects and an automobile.[25] One strategy for establishing Medicaid eligibility, therefore, is to transfer as much wealth as possible into exempt resources, as by paying down a mortgage on or repairing and improving an existing home, or even purchasing a larger home.[26] A state may place a lien on the property of a Medicaid recipient in a nursing home who is not likely to return home or recover payments it has received from the estate of a recipient over age sixty-five. It may not, however, place a lien on or recover against a recipient's home if it is occupied by the individual's spouse, dependent child, or a sibling who has an equity interest in the home and occupied it for at least one year prior to the institutionalization of the individual.[27] A Medicaid recipient may also transfer his or her home to the individuals just listed, or to a child who lived in the home for two years prior to the institutionalization taking care of the recipient, thus avoiding completely the imposition of a lien.[28]

Prior to 1993, states had the option of recovering from the estates of deceased nursing home residents or recipients over the age of sixty-five. Under the 1993 amendments states must attempt to recover the cost of Medicaid from the estates of deceased nursing facility residents or of persons who received Medicaid when they were over 55 for nursing facility services,

21. 42 U.S.C.A. § 1396p(d)(4). Medicaid liens must be satisfied, however, before funds may be placed in supplemental needs trusts. Norwest Bank North Dakota v. Doth, 159 F.3d 328 (8th Cir.1998).

22. 42 U.S.C.A. § 1396r–5(b).

23. 42 U.S.C.A. § 1396a(a)(50), (q).

24. 42 U.S.C.A. §§ 1396r–5(d)(1), 1396a(r); 42 C.F.R. §§ 435.725, 435.733, 435.832. The state may also permit deduction of the cost of maintaining a home in the community for up to six months if a physician certifies that the institutionalized individual is likely to return to the home. 42 C.F.R. § 435.733(d).

25. 42 U.S.C.A. §§ 1382b(a), (d). In some states the house remains an exempt resource for only six months unless it is occupied by the institutionalized individual's spouse or family or unless the resident intends to or is likely to return to it.

26. John J. Bowe and Ann I. Weber, The Home in Medicaid Planning: Eight Options, The ElderLaw Report, March 1994 at 1.

27. 42 U.S.C.A. § 1396p(a)(1), (2); 42 C.F.R. § 433.36.

28. 42 U.S.C.A. § 1396p(c)(2).

home and community services, related hospital and prescription drug services, or, at the states' option, any other services.[29] The statute requires the states to claim against real and personal property included in the estate under state law, but also permits them, at their option, to reach assets conveyed through joint tenancies, life estates, living trusts, or other forms of conveyance that would not normally be considered part of the estate.[30]

c. Asset Transfers and Trusts

One strategy for establishing Medicaid resource eligibility is to give away assets, becoming impoverished voluntarily. An even more attractive strategy has been to place the assets in trust, retaining a beneficial interest, but rendering the assets immune from consideration for establishing eligibility. Congress has made a number of attempts to limit such asset transfers, the most recent of which was adopted in 1993. Under that law (which only applies to assets transferred after October 1, 1993), an institutionalized individual who (or whose spouse) during a 36 month period preceding the date of institutionalization or (if later) the date the person applied for Medicaid, transferred an asset for less than fair market value, is ineligible for Medicaid coverage for nursing facility or waiver-based home or community-based services for the number of months determined by dividing the total, cumulative uncompensated value of the resources transferred by the average cost of private nursing facility services in the state or community.[31] If a state chooses, it may extend this disqualification to cover noninstitutionalized applicants for home or community-based health care or other forms of personal care.[32] If the assets were transferred to a trust, the look-back date is in most instances sixty months.[33] The disqualification does not apply if the assets were transferred to the applicant's spouse, to another for the sole benefit of the spouse, from the applicant' spouse to another for the sole benefit of the spouse, to a dependent child or to a trust for the benefit of a dependent child; (or, if a home, to a sibling with an equity interest in the home and living in it for one year prior to the institutionalization or to an adult child who lived with and cared for the individual for two years prior to institutionalization); if the assets were transferred for a purpose other than qualifying for Medicaid; or if denial of eligibility would work an undue hardship.[34]

If assets are held in joint tenancy or tenancy in common, they are considered transferred to the extent an action taken reduces or eliminates the applicant's ownership or control of the assets.[35] Where an applicant, his or her spouse, or another on the applicant's behalf has transferred assets to a trust, attempting to make the assets unavailable to the applicant, during the sixty months prior to determination of eligibility, the transferor is ineligible for Medicaid coverage for nursing or home or community-based services for the number of months determined by dividing the total, cumulative uncompensated value of the resources transferred by the average cost of private nursing

29. 42 U.S.C.A. § 1396p(b)(1). This requirement does not apply where undue hardship would result or where the state had an approved plan as of May 14, 1993 to disregard assets or resources related to a long-term care insurance policy.

30. 42 U.S.C.A. § 1396p(b)(4).

31. 42 U.S.C.A. § 1396p(c)(1)(A).

32. 42 U.S.C.A. § 1396p(c)(1)(C)(ii).

33. 42 U.S.C.A. § 1396p(c)(1)(B).

34. 42 U.S.C.A. § 1396p(c)(2).

35. 42 U.S.C.A. § 1396p(c)(3).

facility services in the state or community.[36] The sixty month "look back" period dates from the point in time when the trust was established, or, if later, the date on which payment to the applicant was foreclosed. Thus, in the case of "trigger trusts", which go into effect when the individual enters a nursing home or applies for Medicaid, the disqualification dates from the time of the triggering event. Additionally, if a trust is revocable, or if it is irrevocable and there are any circumstances under which payment could be made for the benefit of the applicant, the corpus and income continue to be considered available to the applicant.[37] If only the income, and not the corpus, of a self-created irrevocable trust is available to the applicant under the terms of the trust, however, only the income and not the corpus will be considered available for determining eligibility purposes.[38] The statute recognizes certain exceptions to the trust provisions for trusts containing the assets of disabled individuals under sixty-five, for income trusts in certain states where income eligibility requirements might otherwise disqualify applicants from Medicaid, for "pooled" trusts for disabled individuals, or where the state determines that an undue hardship would result from their application.[39]

The 1993 amendments made it more difficult to transfer assets to create eligibility, but did not bar all possibilities. It remains possible, for example, to transfer half one's assets and then to spend down the other half until they are consumed. More exotic possibilities using installment sales and private annuities are also possible.[40] To discourage Medicaid estate planning, Congress in the Health Insurance Portability and Accountability Act of 1997 made it a felony to "knowing and willfully dispose of assets" to establish Medicaid eligibility.[41] This provision, known as the "Granny Goes to Jail" law, raised a storm of protest and was repealed a year later. In its place was put a provision making it a felony to knowingly and willfully counsel or assist a person in disposing of assets to establish eligibility for a fee.[42] Enforcement of this provision has been enjoined, and the Attorney General has announced that she does not intend to defend the law as it is unconstitutional.[43]

d. Financial Responsibility of and for the Community Spouse

A final financial eligibility issue, already alluded to several times, is the financial relationship between the institutionalized and the community spouse. Prior to 1988 Medicaid eligibility requirements often created severe hardships for community spouses of institutionalized Medicaid recipients. If community spouses did not have income of their own, they could only be supported by an institutionalized spouse at welfare levels. Further, resources of the institutionalized spouse and joint resources had to be almost wholly consumed before the institutionalized spouse would become Medicaid eligible.

36. 42 U.S.C.A. § 1396p(d). See Harry S. Margolis, More on OBRA–93, The ElderLaw Report, October 1993 at 1, 2, discussing drafting problems and unclear provisions of this statute.

37. 42 U.S.C.A. § 1396p(d)(3).

38. See Harry S. Margolis, Income-only Trusts Resuscitated under HCFA Interpretation of OBRA–93. The ElderLaw Report, Feb. 1994 at 1, quoting letter to this effect by Sally K. Richardson, Director, Medicaid Bureau, dated Dec. 23, 1993.

39. 42 U.S.C.A. § 1396p(d)(4) & (5).

40. Davie Correira, Using Private Annuities and Installment Notes in Estate Planning, 25 Est. Plan. 381 (1998).

41. Pub. L. 104–191 § 204.

42. 42 U.S.C.A. § 1320a–7b(a)(6).

43. New York State Bar Association v. Reno, 999 F.Supp. 710 (N.D.N.Y.1998).

On the other hand, if the community spouse had resources of her own, these were not available to the institutionalized spouse, as they are under the present, post–1988 law. Thus, community spouses are on the whole better off under the new law, but in some cases they may be dramatically worse off.[44]

Under current law, instituted by 1988 amendments, income is allocated between the community and institutionalized spouses based on to whom it is paid. Income received in the name of the community spouse is not deemed available to the institutionalized spouse.[45] On the other hand, the community spouse is permitted an allowance from the income of the institutionalized spouse to the extent that the "minimum monthly maintenance needs allowance" (MMMNA), determined according to a statutory formula, exceeds income otherwise available to the community spouse.[46] The MMMNA is set by the state, but must be at least 150% of one twelfth of the annual federal poverty limit for a family of two plus an excess shelter allowance equal to the amount by which the sum of the spouse's expenses for rent, mortgage payments (including principal and interest), taxes, insurance, and required condominium maintenance charges for the spouse's principal residence plus the state's standard utility allowance (or the spouse's actual utility allowance if the state does not use such an allowance) exceed 30% of the 150% figure.[47] The MMMNA established by the state may not exceed $1500, adjusted for inflation since 1988 ($2,049 in 1999).[48] A community spouse may seek a greater amount by proving in administrative proceedings exceptional circumstances causing financial duress,[49] or by seeking court ordered support for a greater amount.[50] A monthly allowance is also permitted for other dependent family members of the institutionalized spouse equal to at least the difference between one third of one twelfth of the annual federal poverty limit for a family of two and the income of the family member.[51]

Although the income of a community spouse is not deemed to be available to the institutionalized spouse for eligibility purposes, the resources of the community spouse are considered to be fully available, regardless of state marital property law. At the time a person is institutionalized who may during the period of institutionalization become eligible for Medicaid, the joint resources of the institutionalized and community spouses may be assessed at

44. See Cherry v. Sullivan, 30 F.3d 73 (7th Cir.1994) (upholding the constitutionality of this distinction).

45. 42 U.S.C.A. § 1396r–5(b)(1).

46. 42 U.S.C.A. § 1396r–5(d)(2). Community property states may, moreover, apply community property law in allocating income between spouses. New Mexico Dept. of Human Services v. Department of HHS, 4 F.3d 882 (10th Cir.1993). The courts are divided as to whether states are permitted to transfer the income of a recipient to the community beneficiary to meet the MMMNA before transferring resources, thus maximizing the resources available to an institutionalized person to meet medical needs (the "income-first" policy). Compare Cleary v. Waldman 167 F.3d 801 (3d Cir. 1999); Chambers v. Ohio Dept. of Human Serv., 145 F.3d 793 (6th Cir.1998) (yes) with Gruber v. Ohio Dept. of Human Services, 647

N.E.2d 861 (Ohio App.1994), and Golf v.New York State Dept of Social Services, 697 N.E.2d 555 (N.Y.App.1998) (no). See Omar N. Ahmad, Medicaid Eligibility Rules for the Elderly Long–Term Care Applicant, 20 J. Leg. Med. 251 (1999).

47. 42 U.S.C.A. § 1396r–5(d)(3). If the condominium or cooperative maintenance charge includes utility charges, utility expenses are not considered separately in computing the excess shelter allowance.

48. 42 U.S.C.A. § 1396r–5(d)(3)(C).

49. 42 U.S.C.A. § 1396r–5(e)(2)(B).

50. 42 U.S.C.A. § 1396r–5(d)(5). See Jenkins v. Fields, 1996 WL 221614 (S.D.N.Y.1996); and Gomprecht v. Sabol, 652 N.E.2d 936 (N.Y.App.1995) (applying these provisions).

51. 42 U.S.C.A. § 1396r–5(d)(1)(C).

the request of either the institutionalized or community spouse.[52] For this purpose the total resources of the community and institutionalized spouses are combined.[53] Only non-exempt resources are considered, however, excluding from consideration the exempt resources discussed above (the family home, automobile, burial plot, household goods, personal effects, etc.).[54] All included resources belonging to either spouse are then attributed to the institutionalized spouse, except for those the community spouse is permitted to retain.[55] The statute permits the community spouse to keep a "community spouse resource allowance" (CSRA) equal to the greatest of $12,000 adjusted for inflation ($16,392 in 1999) or one half of the couple's resources up to $60,000 adjusted for inflation ($81,960 in 1999).[56] The state may also simply permit the community spouse to retain resources up to the inflation adjusted $60,000 figure.[57] Alternatively, by court order, or by the decision of an administrative judge, where additional resources are necessary to produce income to support the community spouse, the community spouse may be permitted to keep a greater amount.[58] Where resources held in the name of the community spouse are less than the CSRA, the institutionalized spouse may transfer to the community spouse sufficient resources to make up the difference between the two amounts.[59] Any resources obtained by the community spouse after the institutionalized spouse is determined eligible for benefits are not considered as available to the institutionalized spouse.[60]

Any non-exempt resources remaining available to the institutionalized applicant after the allocation of resources to the community spouse must be spent down to the Medicaid eligibility level (the SSI level, currently $2000 for an individual, or a permissible, more restrictive standard in 209(b) states) before the applicant becomes eligible. The institutionalized person can be found eligible even if these conditions are not met, however, if the community spouse refuses to contribute available resources and the institutionalized spouse assigns support rights to the state, or if the institutionalized spouse lacks the capacity to assign support rights but the state has the right to bring a support action without an assignment, or if denial of eligibility would work undue hardship.[61]

C. BENEFITS

§ 12–5. Covered Services

Although eligibility under the Medicaid programs of most states tends to be tightly restricted, benefits are on the whole quite generous compared to other insurance programs, reflecting the fact that Medicaid recipients cannot otherwise afford any medical or remedial care. The federal statute[1] and regulations[2] provide that federal financial participation is available to state Medicaid programs to help pay for:

52. 42 U.S.C.A. § 1396r–5(c)(1)(B).
53. 42 U.S.C.A. § 1396r–5(c)(1)(A).
54. 42 U.S.C.A. § 1396r–5(c)(5).
55. 42 U.S.C.A. § 1396r–5(c)(2)(A), (B).
56. 42 U.S.C.A. § 1396r–5(f)(2)(A)(i).
57. 42 U.S.C.A. § 1396r–5(f)(2)(A)(i).
58. 42 U.S.C.A. § 1396r–5(f)(3), (e)(2)(C).

59. 42 U.S.C.A. § 1396r–5(f)(1).
60. 42 U.S.C.A. § 1396r–5(c)(4).
61. 42 U.S.C.A. § 1396r–5(c)(3).

§ 12–5

1. 42 U.S.C.A. § 1396d(a).
2. 42 C.F.R. §§ 440.1–440.186.

1) inpatient hospital services;[3]

2) outpatient hospital services, rural health clinic services, and federally-qualified health clinic services;[4]

3) other laboratory or X-ray services;[5]

4) (a) nursing facility services (other than services in an institution for mental diseases) for individuals twenty-one years old or older;[6]

(b) early and periodic screening, diagnostic, and treatment services (EPSDT);[7]

(c) family planning services and supplies;[8]

5) physician's services and medical and surgical services legally furnished by a dentist;[9]

6) medical care or other remedial care furnished by other licensed practitioners within their scope of practice (including podiatrists, chiropractors, and optometrists);[10]

7) home health services;[11]

8) private duty nursing services;[12]

9) clinic services furnished by or under the direction of a physician, including nurse midwife services;[13]

10) dental services;[14]

11) physical therapy and related services;[15]

12) prescribed drugs, dentures, prosthetic devices, and eyeglasses;[16]

13) other diagnostic, screening, preventive, and rehabilitative services;[17]

14) inpatient hospital and nursing facility services for persons sixty-five years of age or older in an institution for mental diseases;[18]

3. 42 U.S.C.A. § 1396d(a)(1); 42 C.F.R. § 440.10.

4. 42 U.S.C.A. § 1396d(a)(2); 42 C.F.R. § 440.20. Until October 1, 2003, payments for the latter two services must be based on a specified and declining proportion of reasonable cost. 42 U.S.C.A. § 1395a(a)(13)(C).

5. 42 U.S.C.A. § 1396d(a)(3); 42 C.F.R. § 440.30.

6. 42 U.S.C.A. § 1396d(a)(4)(A); 42 C.F.R. § 440.40(a).

7. 42 U.S.C.A. § 1396d(a)(4)(B); 42 C.F.R. 441.50, .62.

8. 42 U.S.C.A. § 1396d(a)(4)(C); 42 C.F.R. 441.20.

9. 42 U.S.C.A. § 1396d(a)(5); 42 C.F.R. § 440.50.

10. 42 U.S.C.A. § 1396d(a)(6); 42 C.F.R. § 440.60.

11. 42 U.S.C.A. § 1396d(a)(7); 42 C.F.R. §§ 440.70, 441.15.

12. 42 U.S.C.A. § 1396d(a)(8); 42 C.F.R. § 440.80.

13. 42 U.S.C.A. § 1396d(a)(9); 42 C.F.R. § 440.90.

14. 42 U.S.C.A. § 1396d(a)(10); 42 C.F.R. § 440.100.

15. 42 U.S.C.A. § 1396d(a)(11); 42 C.F.R. § 440.110.

16. 42 U.S.C.A. § 1396d(a)(12); 42 C.F.R. § 440.120. Medicaid programs may not pay for drugs for which Medicare payment is prohibited because they are less than effective. 42 U.S.C.A. § 1396b(i)(5). Outpatient drugs also may not be paid for unless the manufacturer complies with the drug rebate program required under 42 U.S.C.A. § 1396r–8. Occasionally litigation has been brought concerning the exclusion of particular drugs. See, Weaver v. Reagen, 886 F.2d 194 (8th Cir.1989) (prohibiting the exclusion from coverage of AZT as a drug treatment for AIDS).

17. 42 U.S.C.A. § 1396d(a)(13); 42 C.F.R. § 440.130.

18. 42 U.S.C.A. § 1396d(a)(13); 42 C.F.R. §§ 440.140, 441.100–441.106.

15) services in an intermediate care facility for the mentally retarded (ICF–MR);[19]

16) inpatient psychiatric hospital services for individuals under age twenty-one;[20]

17) legally authorized nurse-midwife services;[21]

18) hospice care;[22]

19) case-management services and TB-related services;[23]

20) respiratory care services;[24]

21) legally authorized pediatric or family nurse practitioner services;[25]

22) home and community care for functionally disabled elderly individuals;[26]

23) community supported living arrangement services;[27]

24) personal care services prescribed by a physician in accordance with a plan of treatment, provided by a qualified person not a member of the recipient's family, supervised by a registered nurse, and furnished in the recipient's home or another non-institutional location);[28]

25) primary care case management services;[29]

26) program for all-inclusive care for the elderly (PACE) services;[30]

27) any other medical care or remedial care recognized under state law and approved by the Secretary (including care in Christian Science sanatoria);[31] and

28) payment of private group health care plan premiums, and cost-sharing for Medicaid eligible individuals where enrollment in the group plan would be cost-effective.[32]

A state Medicaid program must provide to the categorically needy at least the services enumerated at one through five, seventeen, and twenty-one above and home health care to persons over twenty-one.[33] If a state plan covers the medically needy, it must at least provide them with ambulatory services for

---

19. 42 U.S.C.A. § 1396d(a)(15); 42 C.F.R. § 440.150.

20. 42 U.S.C.A. § 1396d(a)(16), (i); 42 C.F.R. §§ 440.160, 441.150–441.182.

21. 42 U.S.C.A. § 1396d(a)(17); 42 C.F.R. §§ 440.165, 441.21.

22. 42 U.S.C.A. § 1396d(a)(18); 42 U.S.C.A. § 1396*o*).

23. 42 U.S.C.A. § 1396d(a)(19), as defined in 42 U.S.C.A. §§ 1396n(g)(2) and 1396a(z)(2)(F).

24. 42 U.S.C.A. § 1396d(a)(20), as defined in 42 U.S.C.A. § 1396a(e)(9)(C); 42 C.F.R. § 440.185.

25. 42 U.S.C.A. § 1396d(a)(21); 42 C.F.R. § 441.22.

26. 42 U.S.C.A. § 1396d(a)(22), as defined in 42 U.S.C.A. § 1396t; 42 C.F.R. §§ 440.180—.181, 441–.300—.365.

27. 42 U.S.C.A. § 1396d(a)(23), as defined in 42 U.S.C.A. § 1396u(a); 42 C.F.R. § 440.167.

28. 42 U.S.C.A. § 1396d(a)(24).

29. 42 U.S.C.A. §§ 1396d(a)(25); 1396d(t). Primary case managers, including physicians, nurse practitioners, certified nurse-midwives, or physician assistants for locating, coordinating and managing primary care services for enrolled individuals, subject to specified conditions.

30. 42 U.S.C.A. §§ 1396d(a)(26); 1396u–4.

31. 42 U.S.C.A. § 1396d(a)(27). 42 C.F.R. § 440.170.

32. 42 U.S.C.A. § 1396e(a).

33. 42 U.S.C.A. § 1396a(a)(10)(A); 42 C.F.R. § 440.210.

persons under eighteen or persons entitled to institutional services and prenatal care and delivery services for pregnant women.[34] If a medically needy program covers ICF–MR services or services for persons in institutions for mental diseases, it must cover the services listed in one through five and seventeen above, or any seven of the services listed in paragraphs one through twenty-one above. This provision limits the ability of states to simply shift responsibility for their mental hospitals to Medicaid without offering mental patients additional medical services. State plans may make home health services available to any person who is eligible under the state plan for nursing facility services.[35] Medicaid must also cover medical transportation for all recipients.[36]

State plans must also make available medical assistance to cover Medicare premiums, deductibles, coinsurance and copayments for qualified Medicare beneficiaries (QMBs).[37] Medicaid must pay Part A premiums for qualified disabled and working individuals and Part B premiums for specified low-income Medicare beneficiaries.[38]

§ 12–6. Extent of Covered Services: Amount, Duration, and Scope

States must provide covered services "with reasonable promptness."[1] A state's Medicaid plan must specify the amount, duration, and scope of each service that it provides for the categorically needy and each group of the medically needy.[2] Each service must be of sufficient amount, duration, and scope reasonable to achieve its purpose.[3] A state Medicaid regulation limiting reimbursable physician visits to three per month, except in emergencies, was upheld under this regulation,[4] but an excessively restrictive drug formulary was not.[5] The Medicaid agency may not arbitrarily deny or reduce the amount, duration, or scope of a required service solely because of the diagnosis, type of illness, or condition.[6] Thus a state provision covering eyeglasses for individuals suffering from eye disease, but not for individuals with refractive error, was invalidated,[7] as was a $50,000 cap on payment for hospital services which precluded coverage of $200,000 liver transplants,[8] and a refusal to cover

34. 42 U.S.C.A. § 1396a(a)(10)(C)(iii).

35. 42 U.S.C.A. § 1396a(a)(10)(D); 42 C.F.R. § 441.15.

36. 42 C.F.R. § 431.53.

37. 42 U.S.C.A. §§ 1396a(10)(E)(i); 1396d(p). See section 12–9 below discussing the extent of the obligation of state plans to cover cost-sharing where provider charges exceed Medicaid payment limits.

38. 42 U.S.C.A. § 1396a(a)(10)(E)(ii), (iii); 1396d(p).

§ 12–6

1. 42 U.S.C.A. § 1396a(a)(8). See Doe v. Chiles, 136 F.3d 709 (11th Cir.1998) (finding that disabled individuals placed on a waiting list for ICF services were not provided services with "reasonable promptness").

2. 42 C.F.R. § 440.230(a).

3. 42 C.F.R. § 440.230(b).

4. Curtis v. Taylor, 625 F.2d 645 (5th Cir. 1980), rehearing denied, opinion modified 648 F.2d 946 (1980).

5. Dodson v. Parham, 427 F.Supp. 97 (N.D.Ga.1977).

6. 42 C.F.R. § 440.230(c).

7. White v. Beal, 555 F.2d 1146 (3d Cir. 1977).

8. Montoya v. Johnston, 654 F.Supp. 511 (W.D.Tex.1987). See also Miller v. Whitburn, 10 F.3d 1315 (7th Cir.1993) (agency's decision that bowel-liver transplant was experimental is reviewable); Meusberger v. Palmer, 900 F.2d 1280 (8th Cir.1990) (rejecting a state's refusal to pay for a pancreas transplant as experimental); Todd v. Sorrell, 841 F.2d 87 (4th Cir.1988) (rejecting a state's refusal to fund a liver transplant based on diagnosis); Allen v. Mansour, 681 F.Supp. 1232 (E.D.Mich.1986) (invalidating a state's requirement of two year's absti-

sex reassignment surgery.[9] A state may, however, place appropriate limits on a service based on medical necessity or utilization control criteria.[10] The concept of medical necessity, found also in private insurance policies (see § 9–2) and in Medicare (see § 11–7) may become increasingly important as health reform efforts attempt to squeeze Medicaid expenditures.

The Rehabilitation Act and Americans with Disabilities Act also impose limits on state Medicaid plans. In Alexander v. Choate,[11] the Supreme Court held that a 14 day limit on inpatient hospital stays did not violate the Rehabilitation Act because it afforded disabled recipients the same access as nondisabled and did not deny them meaningful access. In Olmstead v. L.C.,[12] on the other hand, the Court held that Georgia's policy of denying the mentally disabled community placements potentially violated the ADA, noting Medicaid coverage of community care.[13] The impact of these acts on Medicaid coverage raises complex issues well beyond the scope of this treatise, but must be noted by those who litigate Medicaid issues.[14]

State plans must have in effect methods and procedures to safeguard against unnecessary utilization of care and services.[15] The state Medicaid plan must also provide that services available to the categorically needy are not less in amount, duration and scope than those available to the medically needy, and that services provided to the categorically needy, and to any group of the medically needy, are generally comparable in amount, duration, and scope.[16] The general requirement of comparability is subject to a long, and growing, list of exceptions, however, by which particular groups have been targeted for particular benefits or specifically limited to particular benefits.[17] A state Medicaid plan must generally operate uniformly throughout the state, though several exceptions are permitted in the regulations for particular services or payment arrangements.[18]

One group particularly targeted for favorable treatment is children eligible for the EPSDT program. The EPSDT program requires the states to provide necessary medical treatment services to children, including presumably organ transplantation services where necessary.[19] 42 U.S.C.A. § 1396b(i)(1), on the other hand, requires the states, as a condition of federal funding, to promulgate written standards respecting coverage of organ transplantation that treat similarly situated individuals alike and that provide that restrictions on facilities and practitioners which may provide organ transplantation are "consistent with the accessibility of high quality care to individuals

nence from alcohol as a condition for a liver transplant).

9. Smith v. Palmer, 24 F.Supp. 2d 955 (D.Iowa 1998).

10. 42 C.F.R. § 440.230(d). See e.g., Medical Soc'y of N.Y. v. Toia, 560 F.2d 535 (2d Cir.1977); Cowan v. Myers, 232 Cal.Rptr. 299 (Cal.App.1986), cert. denied 484 U.S. 846, 108 S.Ct. 140, 98 L.Ed.2d 97 (1987).

11. 469 U.S. 287, 105 S.Ct. 712 (1985).

12. 527 U.S. 581, 119 S.Ct. 2176 (1999).

13. Id. at 2179 . See also Anderson v. Pennsylvania Dept. of Pub. Welfare, 1 F.Supp.2d 456 (E.D.Pa.1998) (MMC organization must provide accessible providers.)

14. See Alexander Abbe, "Meaningful Access" to Health Care and the Remedies Available to Medicaid Managed Care Recipients Under the ADA and the Rehabilitation Act, 147 U.Penn.L.Rev. 1161 (1999); Mary Crossley, Medicaid Managed Care and Disability Discrimination Issues, 65 Tenn. L. Rev. 419 (1998).

15. 42 U.S.C.A. § 1396a(a)(30).

16. 42 U.S.C.A. § 1396a(a)(10)(B); 42 C.F.R. § 440.240.

17. 42 C.F.R. § 440.250.

18. 42 U.S.C.A. §§ 1396a(a)(1), 1396n(a); 42 C.F.R. §§ 431.50, 431.54.

19. 42 U.S.C.A. § 1396d(a)(4)(B).

eligible for the procedures under the State plan." Several federal courts have interpreted these provisions as giving the states discretion over the extent to which their Medicaid programs will cover organ transplantation.[20] Other courts, however, have read these provisions as subordinate to the general requirement that Medicaid cover necessary organ transplants to children under EPSTD, and have ordered transplants not available under state law.[21] Still others have interpreted state standards as covering,[22] or potentially covering,[23] organ transplants in situations where the state had denied coverage.

Federal Medicaid coverage of abortions is limited to situations where the life of the mother would be endangered if the fetus were carried to term or where the pregnancy results from rape and incest.[24] Federal regulations have also been promulgated to assure that Medicaid will only finance sterilizations and hysterectomies where the recipient gives informed consent.[25] State plans covering organ transplantation must assure equitable coverage and high quality services.[26]

Consistent with the general philosophy of the Medicaid program that recipients are to receive "mainstream" medical care, state plans have historically been required to permit recipients the right to choose freely among qualified and participating providers.[27] States may, however, "lock-in" recipi-

---

20. Dexter v. Kirschner, 984 F.2d 979 (9th Cir.1992); Ellis v. Patterson, 859 F.2d 52 (8th Cir.1988). See Lisa Deutsch, Medicaid Payment for Organ Transplants: The Extent of Mandated Coverage, 30 Col. J.L. & Soc. Prob. 185 (1997); C. David Flower, State Discretion in Funding Organ Transplants under the Medicaid program: Interpretive Guidelines in Determining the Scope of Mandated Coverage, 79 Minn. L. Rev. 1233 (1995); David L. Weigert, Tragic Choices: State Discretion over Organ Transplant Funding for Medicaid Recipients, 89 Nw. L. Rev. 268 (1994).

21. Pittman v. Fla. Dept. Health & Rehab. Serv's, 998 F.2d 887 (11th Cir.1993); Pereira v. Kozlowski, 996 F.2d 723 (4th Cir.1993).

22. Meusberger v. Palmer, 900 F.2d 1280 (8th Cir.1990).

23. Miller v. Whitburn, 10 F.3d 1315 (7th Cir.1993) (remand to determine if liver-bowel transplant properly characterized as "experimental".)

24. 42 C.F.R. §§ 441.200–441.203. These provisions implement the "Hyde Amendment", Pub. L. 97–12, § 402, 95 Stat. 14, 95–96 and subsequent amendments to appropriations bills, which were upheld against federal constitutional challenges in Harris v. McRae, 448 U.S. 297, 100 S.Ct. 2671, 65 L.Ed.2d 784 (1980). The Hyde Amendment has been recently amended to require states to cover abortions in the instance of rape or incest. P.L. 103–112 § 509, 107 Stat. 1082, 1113. Several states resisted this requirement, resulting in litigation. See Hern v. Beye, 57 F.3d 906 (10th Cir.1995); Hope Medical Group v. Edwards, 63 F.3d 418 (5th Cir.1995); Planned Parenthood

v. Engler, 73 F.3d 634 (6th Cir.1996) (state must cover abortions for rape or incest caused conceptions). State limitations on the funding of abortions under Medicaid programs were also upheld in Williams v. Zbaraz, 448 U.S. 358, 100 S.Ct. 2694, 65 L.Ed.2d 831 (1980); Maher v. Roe, 432 U.S. 464, 97 S.Ct. 2376, 53 L.Ed.2d 484 (1977); and Beal v. Doe, 432 U.S. 438, 97 S.Ct. 2366, 53 L.Ed.2d 464 (1977). Seven state courts have found, however, a state constitutional obligation to fund abortions under state Medicaid programs at the state's expense. See New Mexico Right to Choose v. Johnson, 975 P.2d 841 (N.M.1998); Right to Choose v. Byrne, 450 A.2d 925 (N.J.1982); Moe v. Secretary of Admin. and Finance, 417 N.E.2d 387 (Mass.1981); Doe v. Maher, 515 A.2d 134 (Conn.Super.1986); Women of Minn. v. Gomez, 542 N.W.2d 17 (Minn. 1995); Women's Health Ctr. of W.Va., Inc. v. Panepinto, 446 S.E.2d 658 (W.Va.1993); Committee to Defend Reproductive Rights v. Myers, 172 Cal. Rptr. 866, 625 P.2d 779 (Cal.1981). But see, Saxon v. Director of the Michigan Dep't of Social Serv., 479 N.W.2d 352 (Mich.1991); Hope v. Perales, 611 N.Y.S.2d 811 (N.Y.App. 1994); Rosie J. v. North Carolina Dep't of Human Resources, 491 S.E.2d 535 (N.C.1997); Fischer v. Dept. of Pub. Welfare, 502 A.2d 114 (Pa.1985)(rejecting state constitutional claims).

25. 42 C.F.R. §§ 441.250–441.259.

26. 42 U.S.C.A. § 1396b(i)(1). This provision has been interpreted as giving states discretion in determining whether or not to cover organ transplantation.

27. 42 U.S.C.A. § 1396a(a)(23); 42 C.F.R. § 431.51.

ents to a single provider for a reasonable period of time when the recipient has been found, after notice and an opportunity for hearing, to have used items or services in an amount greater than medically necessary.[28] States may also obtain waivers to limit free choice through primary care case-management, competitive bidding, and other contract-based cost-containment strategies.[29] Finally, states may, under the provisions of the Balanced Budget Act of 1997 and under Section 1115 waivers limit recipient choice in managed care settings. In fact, however, participation of some providers, particularly physicians, has historically been so low in some states that choice of providers that choice has never been truly free.[30]

States Medicaid plans must include a description of the methods and standards to be used to assure that care and services provided to recipients are of high quality.[31] Plans are also to contain safeguards to assure that care and services are provided in a manner consistent with simplicity of administration and the best interests of recipients.[32] States may not require a recipient to undergo care to which the patient (or his or her parent or guardian if the recipient is a minor) objects on religious grounds.[33]

§ 12–7. Waivers

The foregoing requirements are not, however, absolute. The federal Medicaid statute includes a number of specific provisions permitting waiver of general statutory requirements to implement specific programs or demonstration projects.[1] Freedom of choice waivers were mentioned above. Waivers can also be granted from comparability, statewideness, and certain eligibility requirements for home and community based care as an alternative to nursing home care for certain individuals, including the elderly and certain children under five who have tested positively for HIV or were drug dependent at birth.[2]

Most importantly, general waivers of the requirements of 42 U.S.C.A. § 1396a and of the funding limitations imposed by 42 U.S.C.A. § 1396b to implement experimental, pilot or demonstration projects are permitted under 42 U.S.C.A. § 1315 ("Section 1115 waivers"). Section 1115 waivers were grudgingly granted prior to 1992, but have been much more liberally awarded thereafter. The 1997 BBA provides for extensions of such projects for up to 3 years at the request of a state governor, and such requests are deemed to be

---

28. 42 U.S.C.A. § 1396n(a)(2); 42 C.F.R. § 431.54(e).

29. 42 U.S.C.A. § 1396n(b) ("§ 1915b"); 42 C.F.R. § 431.55.

30. See W. Pete Welch & Mark E. Miller, Mandatory HMO Enrollment in Medicaid: The Issue of Freedom of Choice, 66 Milbank Q. 618 (1988).

31. 42 U.S.C.A. § 1396a(a)(22); 42 C.F.R. § 440.260.

32. 42 U.S.C.A. § 1396a(a)(19).

33. 42 U.S.C.A. § 1396f; 42 C.F.R. § 440.270.

§ 12–7

1. See, discussing Medicaid waivers, Allen Dobson, Donald Moran, and Gary Young, Role

of Federal Waivers in the Health Policy Process, Health Aff. Winter 1992 at 72.

2. 42 U.S.C.A. § 1396n, (c), (d), (e); 42 C.F.R. §§ 431.50(c)(2); 435.217, 435.726, 435.735, 440.180, 440.250(k), 441.300–441.310. See Frances J. v. Bradley, 1992 WL 390875 (N.D.Ill.1992) (upholding the determination of need evaluation of the Illinois home and community-based care waiver program under federal requirements). See discussing home and community-based care waivers, Nancy A. Miller, Medicaid 2176 Home and Community-Based Care Waivers: The First Ten Years, Health Aff. Winter 1992 at 162.

granted unless HCFA turns them down within six months.[3] As noted above, over one third of the states now operate all or part of their Medicaid programs under § 1115 waivers. The practical effect of this is that much that is said in this chapter about Medicaid may not apply, or applies only partially, in those states.

The most publicized Medicaid waiver request to date is the request submitted by Oregon to expand and refocus its Medicaid program. Oregon proposed to expand its Medicaid program to cover all persons under the poverty line, increasing by 120,000 the 243,000 persons currently on Medicaid. It proposed to do this by ranking 688 health services and denying coverage for low ranked procedures. The Bush Administration denied the Oregon waiver request on Aug. 3, 1992 because of concerns that the proposed Oregon program would violate the Americans with Disabilities Act by denying coverage for some services to persons with certain disabilities. For example, the rationing program originally proposed by Oregon would have denied liver transplants for alcoholic cirrhosis or for extremely low-birth-weight babies under twenty-three weeks gestation. The Clinton Administration approved a revised waiver request on March 19, 1993 for the period from January 1, 1994 to January 1, 1998. The waiver was approved conditional upon Oregon meeting certain requirements that would lessen the impact of considerations of disability on prioritizing treatments. The Oregon plan provoked extensive commentary.[4] The waiver was extended in 1998, however, and the project is generally regarded to have been successful as an experiment in extending Medicaid coverage. Many of the services that fell below the ranking cut off are in fact being provided, and those services not provided have turned out to generally be inessential. On the other hand, the rationing of services seems to have made the program more palatable politically, and the program now enjoys widespread political support.[5]

The Tennessee TennCare waiver program, approved late in 1993, forms an alternative model for Medicaid reform.[6] Under this plan, uninsured Tennessee residents with incomes below 200% of the federal poverty level could receive benefits through managed care plans, with premiums and cost-sharing based on income. Tennessee currently has more its population covered by Medicaid and a smaller proportion uninsured than any other state, and generally high levels of beneficiary satisfaction with the program, though providers are much less happy with it.[7]

---

3. 42 U.S.C.A. § 1315(e).

4. A symposium on health care rationing, including several articles discussing the Oregon proposal, appeared at 140 U. Pa. L.Rev. 1505–1998 (1992). Another is found in 1 Health Matrix, 135–273 (1992). Articles discussing the Oregon plan include, Sara Rosenbaum, Mothers and Children Last, 18 Am. J. L. & Med. 97 (1992) Robert L. Schwartz, Medicaid Reform Through Setting Health Care Priorities, 35 St. Louis U. L.J. 837 (1991); and W. John Thomas, The Oregon Medicaid Proposal: Ethical Paralysis, Tragic Democracy and the Fate of a Utilitarian Health Care Program, 72 Or. L. Rev. 49 (1993).

5. Howard Leichter, Oregon's Bold Experiment: Whatever Happened to Rationing? 24 J.

Health Pol., Pol'y & L. 147 (1999); Lawrence Jacobs, Theodore Marmor, & Jonathan Oberlander, The Oregon Health Plan and the Political Paradox of Rationing: What Advocates and Critics Have Claimed and What Oregon Did, 24 J. Health Pol., Pol'y & L. 161 (1999).

6. See TennCare Demonstration Fact Sheet and Special Terms and Conditions for Medicaid Waiver, Medicare & Medicaid Guide (CCH) ¶ 41,908 (HHS News Release, Fact Sheet, and HCFA Special Terms and Conditions, Nov. 18, 1993).

7. James Blumstein and Frank Sloan, Healthcare Through Medicaid Managed Care: Tennessee (TennCare) as a Case Study and Paradigm, (1999).

D. MEDICAID PAYMENT FOR SERVICES

§ 12–8. General Considerations

The rates that Medicaid pays for services are set by the states, subject in most instances only to broad federal guidelines. Because state budgetary constraints commonly result in payment rates set far below private pay rates and significantly below Medicare rates, litigation involving Medicaid rates is quite frequent. Federal Medicaid law requires generally that payment rates be "consistent with efficiency, economy, and quality of care and * * * sufficient to enlist enough providers so that care and services are available under the plan at least to the extent that such care and services are available to the general population in the geographic area."[1] It is not clear to what extent this provision, however, provides substantive or procedural rights to providers or beneficiaries.

In Orthopaedic Hospital v. Belshe,[2] the Ninth Circuit held that the provision requires states to set rates that bear a reasonable relationship to the costs of efficient and economical hospitals.[3] In Florida Pharmacy Ass'n v. Cook,[4] the court held that the statute did not create a judicially enforceable right to rates consistent with efficiency, economy and quality, and that the access provision imposes only minimal requirements. Several other courts have also recognized an enforceable right under the access provisions of the statute.[5] In Minnesota HomeCare Ass'n, Inc. v Gomez,[6] and Rite Aid of Pennsylvania v. Houstoun,[7] moreover, the court held that the provision does not compel the state to follow any particular methodology in rate-setting.

The regulations further require that state agencies specify in the state plan the policy and methods to be used for setting payment rates for each type of service the state program covers;[8] audit records appropriately if rates are based on costs;[9] maintain documentation of payment rates;[10] and provide public notice of significant proposed changes in the methods and standards of setting payment rates for services.[11]

Medicaid payments must normally be made directly to a provider rather than the recipient, in contrast to non-assigned Medicare Part B claims or to the situation that exists with respect to many private insurance programs that operate on an indemnity basis.[12]

§ 12–8

1. 42 U.S.C.A. § 1396a(a)(30); 42 C.F.R. §§ 447.200, 447.204.

2. 103 F.3d 1491 (9th Cir.1997) cert. denied 522 U.S. 1044, 118 S.Ct. 684 (1998).

3. Accord Arkansas Med. Soc'y , Inc. v. Reynolds, 6 F.3d 519 ((8th Cir. 1993); Ohio Hosp. v. Ohio Dept. of Human Servs., 579 N.E.2d 695 (Ohio 1991)

4. 17 F.Supp.2d 1293 (N.D.Fla.1998).

5. Arkansas Medical Soc'y v. Reynolds, 6 F.3d 519 (8th Cir.1993); Visiting Nurse Ass'n of N. Shore, Inc. v. Bullen, 93 F.3d 997 (1st Cir.1996). But see Methodist Hosp., Inc. v. Sullivan, 91 F.3d 1026 (7th Cir.1996) (state not obligated to conduct access analysis).

6. 108 F.3d 917 (8th Cir.1997)

7. 171 F.3d 842 (3d. Cir. 1999).

8. 42 C.F.R. § 447.201.

9. 42 U.S.C.A. § 1396a(a)(42); 42 C.F.R. § 447.202.

10. Including an estimate of the percentile of the range of customary charges to which revised payment structures for payment of individual practitioners equates. 42 C.F.R. § 447.203.

11. 42 C.F.R. § 447.205. See Illinois v. Shalala, 4 F.3d 514 (7th Cir.1993)(even legislatively mandated changes in methods and standards must be published so as to give public notice).

Providers must accept Medicaid payment rates as payment in full for their services, except for permitted cost-sharing or spend down amounts.[13] Indeed, charging money or consideration in excess of Medicaid rates is a felony.[14] Nominal deductibles (up to $2.00 per family per month) and cost-sharing (coinsurance of up to 5% or copayments of up to $3.00) are permitted under the Medicaid statute and regulations, but may not be imposed on certain categories of recipients (including children, pregnant women or institutionalized individuals) or for certain services (such as emergency or family planning services).[15] States may also charge premiums based on income to some of the medically needy.[16] A provider may not deny a recipient services, however, on the basis of the recipient's inability to pay deductibles or cost-sharing charges, though the recipient remains liable for the charge.[17]

Medicaid, like Medicare, is secondary in its responsibility to pay for care to other third-party payers, such as health or liability insurers (including ERISA plans) or responsible absent parents. States must prohibit insurers from taking into account Medicaid eligibility status in enrolling or making benefit payments with respect to an individual.[18] States must also require insurers or employers who provide family coverage insurance to cover the child of an insured or employed parent who is responsible under court or administrative order to provide health coverage for the child or when the employed parent, the state Medicaid agency, or the other parent requests coverage.[19] The insurer may not refuse coverage because the child was born out of wedlock, is not claimed by the insured as a dependent for tax purposes, or does not reside with the insured parent.[20] The employer may withhold from the employee's compensation any premiums required to pay for this coverage.[21]

§ 12–9. Payment of Hospitals and Nursing Homes

About 38% of Medicaid funds are spent on hospital care and another 26% on nursing home care. Nationally, Medicaid accounts for 16% of hospital and 48% of nursing home expenditures.[1] Attempts by the states to limit these hospital and nursing home payments stimulated a considerable volume of litigation throughout the 1970s, 1980s and early 1990s under the 1976 "Boren Amendment," which required the states to pay for hospital, skilled nursing facility and intermediate care facilities on a "reasonable cost related basis, as determined in accordance with methods and standards * * * developed * * * on the basis of cost-finding methods approved and verified" by HHS.[2] This litigation gained momentum after The Supreme Court's 1990 decision in

12. 42 U.S.C.A. § 1396a(a)(32); 42 C.F.R. § 447.10.

13. 42 C.F.R. § 447.15.

14. 42 U.S.C.A. § 1320a–7b(d).

15. 42 U.S.C.A. §§ 1396a(a)(14), 1396o(a); 42 C.F.R. §§ 447.50–447.59.

16. 42 U.S.C.A. § 1396o(b)(1); 42 C.F.R. §§ 447.51(b), (c), 447.52.

17. 42 U.S.C.A. § 1396o(e); 42 C.F.R. § 447.15.

18. 42 U.S.C.A. § 1396a(a)(25)(H).

19. 42 U.S.C.A. § 1396g–1(a)(2), (3).

20. 42 U.S.C.A. § 1396g–1(a)(1).

21. 42 U.S.C.A. § 1396g(3)(D).

§ 12–9

1. Bradley R. Braden, et al., National Health Expenditures, 1997, 20 Health Care Fin. Rev., Fall 1991, Table 12, at 83, 124.

2. former 42 U.S.C.A. § 1396a(a)(13)(E).

Wilder v. Virginia Hospital Association,[3] affirming that providers had a right of action under 42 U.S.C.A. § 1983 to challenge Medicaid reimbursement rates under the Boren Amendment in federal court.[4]

Though Boren amendment litigation was always a risky enterprise for providers, usually resulting at best in a temporary reprieve from budget cuts while the state redid its rate-setting following proper procedures, it was a major source of annoyance to the states. In the 1997 BBA, therefore, Congress abolished the Boren Amendment, putting in its place a much less burdensome process, requiring the states to publish proposed rates, including the methodologies underlying them and the justifications supporting them; afford providers, beneficiaries, and others a reasonable opportunity to comment on them; and to publish final rates, their methodologies and justifications.[5] A subsequent court decision has held that the intent of Congress in repealing the Boren amendment was to preclude future litigation in federal court involving state provider ratesetting.[6]

Another major source of litigation in the early 1990s concerned the question of whether the state's statutory obligation to pay Medicare cost-sharing for qualified Medicare beneficiaries (QMBs) meant that the states were obligated to pay coinsurance and deducible amounts to providers where the payment would result in compensation in excess of the rate the state would pay the provider for a non QMB Medicaid recipient's care. Several Courts of Appeals had held for the providers on this issue,[7] though lower courts had held for the states. Congress in § 4714 of the 1997 BBA took the side of the states, limiting their QMB obligation to the extent of Medicaid payment for the care of non-QMBs. Subsequent cases split on the retroactive effect of the amendment.[8]

§ 12–10. Payment for Other Services

No specific federal constraints limit state discretion in setting physician fees other than the broad requirement that payment rates must be sufficient to enlist enough providers so that services are available to Medicaid beneficiaries to the same extent that they are available to the general public.[1]

3. 496 U.S. 498, 110 S.Ct. 2510, 110 L.Ed.2d 455 (1990).

4. 2 Michael MacDonald, et al., Treatise on Health Law, § 8.26 (1991); Joel M. Hamme, Medicaid Reimbursement Litigation by Hospitals and Nursing Homes, in 1991 Health Law Handbook, 301 (Alice G. Gosfield, ed. 1991); Joel Hamme, Long–Term Care Reimbursement, in 1990 Health Law Handbook, 345 (Alice G. Gosfield, ed. 1990); Robert A. Ringer, Boren Amendment Litigation: An Analysis, J. Health & Hosp.Law, March 1994 at 65. Academic consideration of Boren amendment litigation is found in Gerard F. Anderson & Mark A. Hall, The Adequacy of Hospital Reimbursement Under Medicaid's Boren Amendment, 13 J. Legal Med. 205 (1992); Rand E. Rosenblatt, Statutory Interpretation and Distributive Justice: Medicaid Hospital Reimbursement and the Debate over Public Choice, 35 St. Louis U. L. J. 793 (1991).

5. 42 U.S.C.A. § 1396a(a)(13)(A).

6. HCMF Corp. v. Gilmore, 26 F.Supp.2d 873 (W.D.Va.1998). Repeal of the Boren Amendment, however, was not retroactive, thus pre–1997 Boren Amendment litigation continues. Exeter Memorial Hospital Assn. v. Belshe, 145 F.3d 1106 (9th Cir.1998).

7. See e.g. New York City Health & Hosp. Corp. v. Perales, 954 F.2d 854 (2d Cir.1992); Rehabilitation Ass'n of Virginia v. Kozlowski, 42 F.3d 1444 (4th Cir.1994); Haynes Ambulance Serv. Inc. v. Alabama, 36 F.3d 1074 (11th Cir.1994).

8. Compare Beverly Community Hospital Assn. v. Belsche, 132 F.3d 1259 (9th Cir.1997) with Paramount Health Systems v. Wright, 138 F.3d 706 (7th Cir.1998).

§ 12–10

1. See 42 U.S.C.A. 1396a(a)(30)(A); Fulkerson v. Commissioner, 802 F.Supp. 529 (D.Me. 1992) (recognizing a claim based on this provision for recipients challenging imposition of per-service, per-day copayment charges).

However, the general requirement that payments must be consistent with "efficiency, economy, quality of care, and equal access" prohibits rate-setting based solely on budgetary considerations.[2] In general, Medicaid physician fees tend to be very low compared to fees paid by other insurers, but they vary considerably from state to state.[3]

As of 1989, forty-two states paid physicians using fee schedules (including fifteen that used relative value schedules) and eight paid physicians reasonable charges.[4] Considerable interest has been expressed by the states in resource based/relative value schedules, though few have implemented them as of this point. Physician payments vary greatly among the states, with fees for a comprehensive office visit for a new patient varying in 1989 from $10 to $104, a vaginal delivery from $200 to $901.[5] Nationally, Medicaid fees average about 64% of Medicare allowed charges,[6] and about 75% of physicians accept some Medicaid patients, with participation varying by specialty and by region.[7]

E. MEDICAID MANAGED CARE

§ 12–11. Medicaid Managed Care

The vision that motivated Medicaid at its origins was that recipients would receive "mainstream" medical care. In the 1960s this meant fee-for-service care, and from the outset the Medicaid statute guaranteed recipients free choice of provider.[1] From the beginning, however, some states were attracted to managed care as an approach to delivering health care services to poor people. In the late 1960s and early 1970s, California's Medi–Cal program, under the leadership of then Governor Ronald Reagan, launched an aggressive campaign to move Medicaid beneficiaries into prepaid health care. The result is generally adjudged to have been a disaster, with extensive fraud, substandard care, and corruption.[2]

In response to these problems, Congress adopted legislation in 1976 that significantly restricted the ability of states to develop Medicaid managed care (MMC) plans.[3] In particular, states were only permitted to contract with plans that could attract at least 50% of their members from the commercial sector, and recipients were permitted the right to disenroll voluntarily at any time.[4] These constraints, combined with the low payment rates the states offered managed care plans, and the difficulties plans faced in dealing with state

2. 42 U.S.C.A. § 1396a(a)(30)(A).

3. David C. Colby, Medicaid Physician Fees, 1993, 13 Health Aff. 255, Spring II 1994 at 255.

4. Physician Payment Review Commission, Physician Payment Under Medicaid, Report to Congress, July 1, 1991, at 18–19 (Arizona used negotiated capitation rates).

5. Id. at 27.

6. Id. at 34.

7. Id. at 21–26.

§ 12–11

1. 42 U.S.C.A. § 1396a(a)(23).

2. See Michael Sparer, Medicaid Managed Care and the Health Reform Debate: Lessons from New York and California, 21 J. Health Pol., Pol'y & L 433 (1996); David Chavkin and Anne Treseder, California's Prepaid Health Program: Can the Patient be Saved? 28 Hastings L. J. 685 (1977); Andreas Schneider & Joanne Stern, Health Maintenance Organizations and the Poor: Problems and Prospects, 70 Nw.U.L.Rev. 99 (1975).

3. Pub.L. No. 94–460, § 202(a), codified at 42 U.S.C.A. § 1396b(m).

4. In 1981 Congress amended 1396b(m) to permit managed care plans to enroll up to 75% Medicaid recipients.

bureaucracies and with continual and rapid changes in Medicaid recipient eligibility, generally discouraged the growth of MMC.

In 1981, however, Congress amended the Medicaid statute to permit states to mandate MMC enrollment under "freedom of choice" or 1915(b) waivers.[5] In 1982, moreover, Arizona, which until that point had been the sole remaining state without a Medicaid program, obtained an 1115(a) research and demonstration project to operate a state-wide MMC program. During the 1980s MMC grew slowly from 300,000 recipient enrollees in 1983 to 2.7 million in 1991, through by 1991 fewer than 10% of Medicaid beneficiaries were in managed care plans.

In the 1990s, however, the Medicaid environment became much more hospitable to managed care. At the federal level, President Clinton, a former state governor, was much more hospitable to granting states flexibility in administering their Medicaid programs through federal waivers than previous administrations had been. The Republican Congress, elected in 1994, wanted to drive "new federalism" even further, attempting in 1995 to block grant Medicaid, thus giving the states almost total freedom in administering the program. Though President Clinton vetoed the 1995 legislation, two years later Congress in the 1997 Balanced Budget Act (BBA), enacted provisions opening the door widely to state MMC programs.

At the same time, interest at the state level in MMC increased dramatically. The cost of state Medicaid programs grew rapidly in the early 1990s with eligibility expansions, expansion of federal eligibility mandates and general health care cost inflation. Managed care was showing some success in holding down costs in the private sector, and the states wanted to emulate this success. There was also hope, however, that managed care might increase access of Medicaid beneficiaries to providers.[6] Though Medicaid had permitted recipients free choice of provider, it had also permitted providers free choice of participation, and the extent of provider participation and of recipient choice in many parts of the country was often inadequate. Some advocates of MMC hoped that Medicaid recipients might obtain access through managed care to providers who were unwilling to participate directly in Medicaid. States also hoped that through managed care they might get better control over abusive overuse of services by recipients, particularly of emergency room care. Finally, as "mainstream" medicine became managed care in the 1980s and 1990s, state policy-makers came to believe that moving Medicaid recipients into managed care simply meant treating them like everyone else.[7]

For all of these reasons MMC grew rapidly in the 1990s: by 1996 13.3 million (40% of all recipients) were in managed care. By the end of 1998, that figure had swollen to 16.8 million, over 54% of all recipients. In twenty-one states, moreover, more than 70% of Medicaid recipients were in MMC plans by the end of 1998. Although most states began by moving families and children to MMC, by the end of 1998, 1.6 million disabled Medicaid recipients

5. 42 U.S.C.A. § 1396n(b).

6. See John Holahan, et al., Medicaid Managed Care in Thirteen States, Health Aff., May/June 1998 at 43; Colleen M. Grogan, The Medicaid Managed Care Policy Consensus for Welfare Recipients: A Reflection of Traditional Welfare Concerns, 22 J. Health Pol., Pol'y & L. 815 (1997); Diane Rowland, et al., Medicaid and Managed Care: Lessons from the Literature (1995).

7. Grogran, supra note 6.

were enrolled in MMC, 12% of the total MMC enrollment and a quarter of all disabled enrollees.[8]

The Medicaid statute, as amended by the 1997 BBA, permits states to require recipients to enroll with a MMC organizations or primary care case manager.[9] States are not permitted, however, to require Medicare beneficiaries, Native Americans, or certain special need children to enroll in MMCs.[10] States must generally permit recipients a choice of two or more MMC plans, but this requirement is loosened for rural areas.[11] Medicaid recipients who do not exercise their choice may be assigned by the State through a default enrollment process, and states may establish enrollment priorities for plans that are oversubscribed.[12] Recipients may terminate (or change) enrollment in an MMC for cause at any time, but may only do so without cause during the 90 day period following enrollment and once a year thereafter.[13] MMC plans are not permitted to discriminate on the basis of health status or requirements for health service in enrollment, reenrollment, or disenrollment of recipients.[14]

MMC plans are required to make available to enrollees and potential enrollees information regarding the identity, location, qualifications and availability of participating providers, enrollee rights and responsibilities, grievance and appeal procedures, and covered items and services.[15] States are required to provide recipients annually and upon request comparative information regarding benefits, cost-sharing, service area, and quality and performance.[16] States are also required to inform beneficiaries how to access carve out services not covered by an MMC plan.[17]

The federal law establishes a number of protections for MMC beneficiaries. Beneficiaries must be afforded access to services to evaluate and stabilize emergency medical conditions (as identified by a prudent lay person) without prior authorization requirements or provider participation limitations.[18] The statute prohibits MMC organizations from interfering with health care professional communications with beneficiaries, and requires plans to have in place grievance procedures.[19] MMC plans are required to offer an appropriate range of services and a sufficient number, mix, and geographic distribution of

---

8. See Mary Crossley, Medicaid Managed Care and Disability Discrimination Issues, 65 Tenn.L.Rev. 419 (1998) (describing these programs).

9. 42 U.S.C.A. § 1396u–2. Medicaid managed care organizations must comply with definitional requirements found in § 1396b(m). Section 1396d(t) defines primary care case manager. Current regulations governing Medicaid managed care are found at 42 C.F.R. Part 434. Proposed regulations to implement the Medicaid managed care sections of the BBA were published on September 28, 1998 at 63 Fed. Reg. 52022 et seq. It should be noted that many states operate their MMC programs under federal waivers, which permit considerable flexibility in variances from federal requirements.

10. 42 U.S.C.A. § 1396u–2(a)(2).

11. 42 U.S.C.A. § 1396u–2(a)(3). See Rebecca T. Slifkin, et al., Medicaid Managed Care

Programs in Rural Areas: A Fifty State Overview, Health Aff., Nov./Dec. 1998 at 217 for a report on the development of rural MMC.

12. 42 U.S.C.A. § 1396u–2(a)(4)(C) & (D).

13. 42 U.S.C.A. § 1396u–2(a)(4)(A). The MMC plan must inform the beneficiary of this right. 42 U.S.C.A. § 1396b(m)(2)(A)(vi).

14. 42 U.S.C.A. § 1396b(m)(2)(A)(v). This requirement may also apply under the Americans with Disabilities Act. See Crossley, supra, note 8.

15. 42 U.S.C.A. § 1396u–2(a)(5).

16. 42 U.S.C.A. § 1396u–2(a)(5)(C).

17. 42 U.S.C.A. § 1396u–2(a)(5)(D).

18. 42 U.S.C.A. §§ 1396b(m)(2)(A)(vii); 1396u–2(b)(2);.

19. 42 U.S.C.A. § 1396u–2(b)(3) & (4).

providers, and may not discriminate against providers on the basis of the provider's license or certification.[20] MMCs must also make timely payments to providers.[21]

States that operate MMC plans are required to develop and implement a quality improvement strategy that complies with standards developed by HCFA and addresses concerns of timely access to care, continuity of care, quality and appropriateness of care and services.[22] MMC organizations must also have contracts providing for an annual (as appropriate) external independent review of quality outcomes and of timely access to items and services, the results of which shall be available to providers, enrollees and potential enrollees.[23] State quality oversight is optional for Medicare + Choice organizations, and external review activities are not to duplicate accreditation reviews for accredited managed care organizations.[24]

A variety of fraud and abuse prohibitions apply to MMC organizations. They may not be owned or managed by, or employ or consult with an individual who is or is affiliated with a person debarred, suspended or excluded form federal programs.[25] MMC organizations must have their marketing material approved by the state, may not include false or materially misleading information in the materials, must distribute the material through their entire service area, may not seek to influence an individual's enrollment in conjunction with other sale of insurance, and may not conduct door-to-door, telephonic, or other "cold call" marketing.[26]

States must have available "intermediate sanctions" for dealing with MMC organizations that fail substantially to provide medically necessary items; impose unpermitted premiums or cost-sharing; discriminate among enrollees on the basis of health status or requirements for health services or engage in practices that would reasonably be expected to deny or discourage enrollment by persons "whose medical condition or history indicates a need for substantial future medical services;" misrepresent or present false information to HCFA or to enrollees, potential enrollees, or providers; or operate prohibited physician incentive plans.[27] Intermediate sanctions include civil penalties of up to $25,000 ($100,000 for discrimination and false statements); the appointment of temporary management for continued egregious behavior that poses a substantial risk to the health of enrollees; permitting disenrollment of enrollees without cause; suspension of enrollment; suspension of payment, and, with notice and hearing, contract termination.[28]

Primary care case management is an alternative to risk based MMC. PCCM programs use primary care providers as gatekeepers to managed primary care and to control access to other items and services.[29] The intent of PCCM is to expand provider participation in Medicaid by offering case management fees, and to better manage the care of recipients.[30] Because

20. 42 U.S.C.A. § 1396u–2(b)(5) & (7).
21. 42 U.S.C.A. § 1396u–2(f).
22. 42 U.S.C.A. § 1396u–2(c)(1).
23. 42 U.S.C.A. § 1396u–2(c)(2).
24. 42 U.S.C.A. § 1396u–2(c)(2)(B) & (C).
25. 42 U.S.C.A. § 1396u–2(d)(1).
26. 42 U.S.C.A. § 1396u–2(d)(2).
27. 42 U.S.C.A. § 1396u–2(e)(1).

28. 42 U.S.C.A. § 1396u–2(e)(2), (3), and (4); 1396b(m)(5). See MEDCARE HMO v. Bradley, 788 F.Supp. 1460 (N.D.Ill.1992) (providing a Medicaid HMO with a pretermination hearing).

29. 42 U.S.C.A. § 1396d(t).

30. See Colleen M. Grogan, The Medicaid Managed Care Policy Consensus for Welfare Recipients: A Reflection of Traditional Welfare

PCCM largely leaves fee-for-service Medicaid in place, and does not deal with health care costs as aggressively as do managed care organizations, states seem to be moving to risk-based MMC plans where they are available or can be created.

F. ADMINISTRATION

§ 12–12. The "State Plan" and State Administration

States must provide Medicaid under a "State Plan" that complies with numerous federal requirements.[1] State plans and plan amendments must be presented to the state's Governor or his designee for review, and then must be submitted to HCFA for review and approval.[2] All material changes in state law or of the organization, policy or operation of the state Medicaid program must be submitted as plan amendments,[3] as must all changes in hospital and nursing facility reimbursement.[4] A state plan or amendment is approved unless HCFA disapproves it within ninety days.[5] An approved plan amendment for reimbursement of inpatient services is effective on the first day of the calendar quarter in which it is submitted to HCFA; any other plan amendment on any date requested by the state and approved by HCFA.[6] If HCFA disapproves of a state plan or amendment as being in "nonconformity" with federal requirements, the state may seek a hearing, and if it is dissatisfied with the results of the hearing, judicial review in the federal court of appeals.[7]

HHS may withhold FFP (federal financial participation) if it determines (after notice and hearing) that a state plan or its administration does not comply with the requirements of the Medicaid Act.[8] Alternatively, HCFA may "disallow" FFP for expenditures made in violation of the Medicaid law.[9] Disallowances are appealable to the Departmental Appeals Board,[10] and reviewable in federal district court under the Administrative Procedures Act.[11] HHS prefers to act against states through the disallowance rather than the conformity procedures, as disallowance permits HHS to refuse FFP for service already delivered, while a finding of nonconformity only allows prospective withholding if the position of HHS is ultimately upheld after lengthy appellate proceedings.

Concerns, 22 J. Health Pol., Pol'y & L. 815 (1997)

§ 12–12

1. See e.g., 42 U.S.C.A. § 1396a(a)(1)-(58); 42 C.F.R. § 430.12.

2. 42 U.S.C.A. § 1316; 42 C.F.R. §§ 430.12–430.15.

3. 42 C.F.R. § 430.12(c). Compare, interpreting materiality requirement, Wisconsin Hosp. Ass'n v. Reivitz, 733 F.2d 1226, 1235 (7th Cir.1984) (3 month freeze may be significant) with Mississippi Hosp. Ass'n v. Heckler, 701 F.2d 511, 522–23 (5th Cir.1983) (change of single component of rate not material where overall change not significant).

4. 42 C.F.R. § 447.253(b).

5. 42 U.S.C.A. § 1316; 42 C.F.R. § 430.16.

6. 42 C.F.R. §§ 430.20(b)(2), (3), 447.256(c).

7. 42 U.S.C.A. § 1316(a).

8. 42 U.S.C.A. § 1396c; 42 C.F.R. § 430.35. HCFA will not normally proceed to hearing on such actions unless a reasonable effort has been made to resolve the dispute informally. 42 C.F.R. § 430.35(a).

9. 42 U.S.C.A. § 1316(d); 42 C.F.R. § 430.42.

10. 42 U.S.C.A. § 1316(d); 42 C.F.R. § 430.42(b).

11. Bowen v. Massachusetts, 487 U.S. 879, 108 S.Ct. 2722, 101 L.Ed.2d 749 (1988).

States must publish public notice of significant changes in the methods and standards for setting payment rates for services.[12] Failure to give notice of a change may invalidate the change,[13] though some courts have refused to invalidate an amendment where those challenging the change received actual notice of it.[14] Providers, recipients, and others adversely affected by a plan amendment may present their objections to HCFA during its consideration of the plan amendment, and may seek to intervene or participate as amicus curiae in conformity hearings if a plan amendment is rejected.[15]

G. FEDERAL AND STATE MEDICAID FUNDING

§ 12–13. Federal Financial Participation

As was stated at the outset, the federal government pays a fixed share of the costs of the Medicaid program, the now familiar FFP (federal financial participation).[1] The figure applied for service expenditures, which may not fall below 50% and may not exceed 80%, is determined by a formula set out in the Act based on the relationship of average per capita income in the state and in the nation as a whole.[2] A 90% match is available, however, for family planning services.[3] Additional federal funds are also available to some states for providing emergency health services to undocumented aliens.[4]

The federal government pays 50% of the cost of most administrative expenditures.[5] Higher percentages, however, are paid as an incentive to encourage the states in certain endeavors.

H. MEDICAID APPEALS AND JUDICIAL REVIEW

§ 12–14. Medicaid Appeals

A state Medicaid plan must provide an opportunity for a hearing to any individual whose claim for medical assistance is denied or not acted on with reasonable promptness.[1] When a state agency takes any action affecting an individual's claim to Medicaid, it must state the action it intends to take, set out its reasons for taking the action and the regulations or law that requires it, and explain the individual's right to a hearing (if one is available) and the circumstances under which assistance will be continued if a hearing is requested.[2] Notice must ordinarily be given ten days before the proposed

12. 42 C.F.R. § 447.205.

13. Wisconsin Hosp. Ass'n v. Reivitz, 733 F.2d 1226, 1234 (7th Cir.1984); Independent Nursing Home v. Simmons, 732 F.Supp. 684, 690 (S.D.Miss.1990); Senn Park Nursing Ctr. v. Miller, 74 Ill.Dec. 123, 455 N.E.2d 153 (Ill. App.1983), affirmed 83 Ill.Dec. 609, 470 N.E.2d 1029 (Ill.1984).

14. California Ass'n of Bioanalysts v. Rank, 577 F.Supp. 1342, 1350 (C.D.Cal.1983).

15. 42 C.F.R. § 430.76(b), (c).

§ 12–13

1. 42 U.S.C.A. § 1396b(a); 42 C.F.R. § 433.10.

2. 42 U.S.C.A. §§ 1301(a)(8), 1396d(b). Special rules apply for the territories and for Indian Health Services facilities.

3. 42 U.S.C.A. § 1396b(a)(5).

4. 8 U.S.C.A. § 1611 note.

5. 42 U.S.C.A. § 1396b(a)(7).

§ 12–14

1. 42 U.S.C.A. § 1396a(a)(3); 42 C.F.R. §§ 431.200–431.250.

2. 42 C.F.R. § 431.210. Individual notice is necessary even though the change in benefits is one of general applicability. Mitchell v. Johnston, 701 F.2d 337, 343–44, n. 9 (5th Cir.1983); Kimble v. Solomon, 599 F.2d 599, 604 (4th

action.[3] A hearing must be afforded if it is timely requested unless the sole issue involved is one of federal or state law requiring an automatic change affecting some or all recipients.[4] The state may also consolidate individual requests for hearings and hold a group hearing where the sole issue is one of state or federal law.[5]

Hearings must be conducted after reasonable notice at a reasonable time, date and place by an impartial person or persons who was or were not involved in the initial determination.[6] The applicant or recipient, or his representative, must be given an opportunity to examine the applicant's or recipient's case file and all documents or records relied on by the state, bring witnesses and present evidence, present argument, and cross examine adverse witnesses.[7] The applicant or recipient must receive a written notice of the decision and of any rights to judicial review.[8] The state must continue Medical assistance during the pendency of a hearing unless it is determined at the hearing that the issue is solely one of state or federal law or policy and the agency promptly informs the recipient in writing that services are to be terminated or reduced pending the hearing decision.[9] The state may, however, recoup payments made during the pendency of the hearing if it ultimately prevails. The state must also make corrective payments when an unfavorable decision is reversed and the recipient or applicant has incurred expenses because of the decision.[10]

Current regulations under the pre-BBA–1997 law require MMC organizations to have "grievance procedures" that can be used to resolve coverage disputes.[11] Proposed regulations implementing the BBA would require timely written notice of a MMC organization's intent to "deny, limit, reduce, delay, or terminate a service," explaining the action, its reasons, laws and regulation that support it, the beneficiary's right to file a complaint with the MMC organization or a fair hearing with the state, and other relevant beneficiary rights.[12] They would further require the MMC organization to hear the grievance using an "impartial" individual not involved in the earlier decision, and to use a physician with appropriate expertise to review medical necessity denials.[13] Standard grievances must be resolved within 30 days, and expedited grievances involving serious jeopardy to life, health, or ability to regain maximum function must be resolved within 24 hours.[14] Benefits must be continued while a grievance or state fair hearing request is pending and a service must be provided within 30 days if a denial is reversed.[15] States may not substitute the MMC grievance process for the state fair hearing, but may, according to the preamble of the proposed regulation, require exhaustion of MMC organization remedies if the process can be completed within 90 days.[16]

Cir.1979), cert. denied 444 U.S. 950, 100 S.Ct. 422, 62 L.Ed.2d 320 (1979).

3. 42 C.F.R. § 431.211.

4. 42 C.F.R. §§ 431.220, 431.221.

5. 42 C.F.R. § 431.222.

6. 42 C.F.R. § 431.240.

7. 42 C.F.R. § 431.242.

8. 42 C.F.R. § 431.245.

9. 42 C.F.R. § 431.230.

10. 42 C.F.R. § 431.246.

11. 42 C.F.R. § 434.32.

12. 63 Fed.Reg. 52086, to be codified at 42 C.F.R. § 438.404.

13. 63 Fed. Reg. at 52087, to be codified at 42 C.F.R. §§ 438.406(c) & (d).

14. 63 Fed Reg. at 52087, to be codified at 42 C.F.R. §§ 438.408 & .410.

15. 63 Fed. Reg. at 52088, to be codified at 42 C.F.R. §§ 438.420, .421.

16. 63 Fed. Reg. 52055, 42 C.F.R. § 438.402(d).

Whether MMCs owe beneficiaries procedural rights other than those specified in federal regulations depends on whether they are "state actors" and thus bound by the Constitution. If they are not, of course, a state could avoid its obligation to provide Medicaid recipients constitutional due process simply by contracting out its administrative obligations to private MMC organizations. The lower courts have held that MMC organizations are state actors[17] These decisions were made, however, prior to the Supreme Court's recent decision in American Mfrs. Mutual Ins. Co. v. Sullivan,[18] holding the decisions of a private utilization review agency in a state workers' compensation program not to constitute state action, which may call them in question, at least in situations where the MMC organization is not granted final decisionmaking authority.[19] If MMC organizations are proper defendants in civil rights suits under 42 U.S.C.A. § 1983, they are probably not protected by the Eleventh Amendment or by 1983 qualified governmental immunity, though they may be able to raise an affirmative defense based on good faith.[20]

The federal statute and regulations provide much more limited administrative relief for providers. The only requirement is that Medicaid agencies must provide an appeal or exception procedure for individual providers with respect to such issues as the agency deems appropriate regarding payment rates for hospitals and long term care facilities.[21] Many states, however, assure providers broader relief under their Medicaid statute or administrative procedures act.

§ 12–15. Judicial Review

Judicial review of state appeal procedures may be available under state law to recipients, providers, or both. Relief may also be available in state court by way of a direct challenge to state regulations in a suit for injunctive and declaratory relief.[1] State claims may be based on state constitutions, statutes, or regulations, or on federal law. Depending on the facts of the case and the administrative law of the particular state, recipients and providers are usually required to exhaust administrative law remedies before obtaining judicial review in state court.[2]

Alternatively, recipients and providers may sue the state in federal court under federal law. The Supreme Court has long recognized the right of recipients to sue under 42 U.S.C.A. § 1983 in federal court for violations of

17. J.K. v. Dillenberg, 836 F.Supp. 694 (D.Ariz.1993); Perry v. Chen, 985 F.Supp. 1197 (D.Ariz., 1996); Daniels v. Wadley, 926 F.Supp. 1305 (M.D.Tenn.1996) vacated on other grds., Daniels v. Manke, 145 F.3d 1330 (6th Cir. 1998). See also Catanzano v. Dowling, 60 F.3d 113 (2d. Cir.1995) (holding determinations by private home health agencies of medical necessity for Medicaid to be state action.)

18. 526 U.S. 40, 119 S.Ct. 977 (1999).

19. See James Blumstein and Frank Sloan, Healthcare Through Medicaid Managed Care: Tennessee (Tenncare) as a Case Study and Paradigm, (1999).

20. See Richardson v. McKnight,521 U.S. 399, 413 (1997), Wyatt v. Cole, 504 U.S. 158, 169 (1992). Blumstein & Sloan.

21. 42 C.F.R. § 447.253(c).

§ 12–15

1. See e.g., Doe v. Maher, 515 A.2d 134 (Conn.Super.1986) (challenge to abortion law); Crespin v. Kizer, 276 Cal.Rptr. 571 (Cal.App. 1990) (coverage of aliens).

2. See e.g., Provincial House, Inc. v. Department of Social Servs., 422 N.W.2d 241, 244 (Mich.App.1988) (review of issue denied where exhaustion waived). But see, Anthony L. Jordan Health Corp. v. Axelrod, 532 N.Y.S.2d 480 (N.Y.Sup.1988) (exhaustion not required where no factual issues to resolve; Cowan v. Myers, 232 Cal.Rptr. 299, 303 (Cal.App.1986), cert. denied 484 U.S. 846, 108 S.Ct. 140, 98 L.Ed.2d 97 (1987) (exhaustion not required where direct challenge to state law).

the provisions of the federal Social Security laws,[3] and has recently recognized the rights of providers to bring § 1983 suits as well.[4] At this point, however, the Supreme Court seems eager to cut back on federal court jurisdiction over benefit program disputes,[5] and the latest Supreme Court precedents are clearly intended to undermine direct access to the courts by beneficiaries of federal programs.[6] A recent federal statute, although it is very poorly drafted, seems to support congressional intent to keep the federal courts open to recipients,[7] and attempts in the 1995 federal budget bill to eliminate federal jurisdiction in Medicaid disputes failed to become law.[8] The lower courts have tended to continue to accept beneficiary suits under § 1983,[9] but some have interpreted recent Supreme Court precedents as barring private suits to enforce Medicaid regulations.[10] One court has held also that a state may not be sued under § 1983 for violation of its state plan.[11]

Prevailing parties in § 1983 actions are entitled to attorneys fees under 42 U.S.C.A. § 1988.[12] Class actions have frequently been certified in Medicaid cases,[13] and associations have been permitted to represent both providers and recipients.[14]

Federal courts generally do not require exhaustion of state administrative or judicial remedies prior to the initiation of a § 1983 action,[15] though they

3. Maine v. Thiboutot, 448 U.S. 1, 100 S.Ct. 2502, 65 L.Ed.2d 555 (1980).

4. Wilder v. Virginia Hosp. Ass'n, 496 U.S. 498, 110 S.Ct. 2510, 110 L.Ed.2d 455 (1990). A provider, however, has no right to be a Medicaid provider if the state chooses to limit its provider contracts. Macombs Pharmacy v. Wing, 1998 WL 696008 (S.D.N.Y. Oct. 5, 1998).

5. See Rand Rosenblatt, The Courts, Health Care Reform, and the Reconstruction of American Social Legislation, 18 J. Health Pol., Pol'y & L. 439, 456–468 (1993).

6. See Blessing v. Freestone, 520 U.S. 329, 117 S.Ct. 1353 (1997); Suter v. Artist M., 503 U.S. 347, 112 S.Ct. 1360 (1992).

7. 42 U.S.C.A. § 1320a–2; See Cherry v. Thompson, [1995–2 Transfer Binder], Medicare and Medicaid Guide (CCH) 43,485 (S.D. Ohio. 1995)(interpreting statute in Medicaid claim context). See also Brian D. Ledahl, Congress Overruling the Courts: Legislative Changes to the Scope of Section 1983, 29 Col. J.L. & Soc. Prob. 411 (1996).

8. See the Balanced Budget Act of 1995, H.R. 2491, § 2154(e)(1) (prohibiting judicial review of state Medicaid plans under federal law except by the Secretary of HHS.) A recent court of appeals decision, however, holds that federal regulations requiring the states to provide particular Medicaid services not required by statute are not enforceable under § 1983. Harris v. James, 127 F.3d 993 (11th Cir.1997).

9. See, e.g. Doe v. Chiles, 136 F.3d 709 (11th Cir.1998); Boatman v. Hammons, 164 F.3d 286 (6th Cir.1998); Visiting Nurse Ass'n v. Bullen, 93 F.3d 997 (1st Cir.1996); Wood v. Tompkins, 33 F.3d 600 (6th Cir.1994); Rodri-

guez v. DeBuono, 44 F.Supp.2d 601 (S.D.N.Y. 1999), reversed on other grounds 197 F.3d 611 (2d Cir.1999); Wellington v. District of Columbia, 851 F.Supp. 1 (D.D.C.1994).

10. Harris v. James, 127 F.3d 993 (11th Cir.1997); Graus v. Kaladjian, 2 F.Supp. 2d 540 (S.D.N.Y.1998).

11. Concourse Rehabilitation & Nursing Center v. Wing, 150 F.3d 185 (2d Cir.1998).

12. Maine v. Thiboutot, 448 U.S. 1, 100 S.Ct. 2502, 65 L.Ed.2d 555 (1980).

13. See e.g., Lynch v. Dawson, 820 F.2d 1014, 1016 (9th Cir.1987) (class action permitted despite fact that named representative suffered no immediate injury where class contained some members who would suffer injury); Mitchell v. Johnston, 701 F.2d 337 (5th Cir.1983) (class of all persons under 21 receiving Medicaid certified).

14. Virginia Hosp. Ass'n v. Baliles, 868 F.2d 653, 656–58 (4th Cir.1989), affirmed on other grounds, sub nom. Wilder v. Virginia Hosp. Ass'n, 496 U.S. 498, 110 S.Ct. 2510, 110 L.Ed.2d 455 (1990) (hospital association); Schweiker v. Gray Panthers, 453 U.S. 34, 40 n. 8, 101 S.Ct. 2633, 2638 n. 8, 69 L.Ed.2d 460 (1981) (advocacy organization for elderly).

15. See Wilder v. Virginia Hosp. Ass'n, 496 U.S. 498, 523–25, 110 S.Ct. 2510, 110 L.Ed.2d 455 (1990); Skubel v. Fuoroli, 113 F.3d 330 (2d Cir.1997); Alacare, Inc.-North v. Baggiano, 785 F.2d 963, 965–970 (11th Cir.1986), cert. denied 479 U.S. 829, 107 S.Ct. 111, 93 L.Ed.2d 59 (1986). But see, New York City Health & Hosps. Corp. v. Heckler, 593 F.Supp. 226 (S.D.N.Y.1984) (federal challenge to state law

may abstain to permit resolution of an issue of state law.[16] As federal administrative remedies are not generally available for review of state Medicaid policies, exhaustion of federal administrative remedies is not an issue.[17] Attempts by the states to join federal officials as necessary parties have also generally been rejected.[18]

The plaintiff, of course, bears the burden of proof in Medicaid appeals.[19] Federal courts commonly state that they accord substantial deference to the states in administering their Medicaid programs.[20] State Medicaid regulations or decisions will be invalidated only if shown to be arbitrary and capricious or in violation of federal law.[21] Federal courts are not reluctant to make this finding, however, where the state is sufficiently unreasonable.[22] Federal approval of a state plan, on the other hand, is commonly provided little deference by the courts, which recognize the cursory nature of federal review.[23]

The Eleventh Amendment significantly limits the relief that is available to prevailing plaintiffs in Medicaid cases. A suit may not be brought against a state unless the state consents, and a state does not consent to suit simply by participating in the Medicaid program.[24] Suit may be brought against officials that administer a state Medicaid program, but only for prospective relief.[25] Retroactive relief that affects the state treasury is prohibited. Even injunctive or declaratory relief may be unavailable if the state alters its regulations or practices before relief is obtained.[26] This makes preliminary injunctive relief

not ripe for adjudication pending resolution of factual issues in the state administrative process).

16. Heartland Hosp. v. Stangler, 792 F.Supp. 670 (W.D.Mo.1992) (abstention appropriate where state administrative remedy and federal intervention would disrupt state efforts to establish a coherent policy); St. Michael Hosp. v. Thompson, 725 F.Supp. 1038, 1045 (W.D.Wis.1989) (issues under review predominantly local issues appropriate to resolution in state appeal); St. Joseph Hosp. v. Electronic Data Systems Corp., 573 F.Supp. 443, 451–52 (S.D.Tex.1983) (abstention appropriate where complex state administrative framework available to address important state issues).

17. But see Greenery Rehab. Group v. Sabol, 841 F.Supp. 58 (N.D.N.Y.1993) (exhaustion of federal remedies not required where state sues federal government in third party claim).

18. Jones v. Blinziner, 536 F.Supp. 1181, 1194–95 (N.D.Ind.1982); Degregorio v. O'Bannon, 86 F.R.D. 109, 120 (E.D.Pa.1980). See Jane Perkins, Dispensing with the Dispensable: Rule 19 Motions in Medicaid Cases, 22 Clearinghouse Rev. 488 (1988). See also Johnson v. Rank, 110 F.R.D. 99, 101–102 (N.D.Cal. 1986) (rejecting attempt to implead federal official as third-party defendant.)

19. See e.g., Colorado Health Care Ass'n v. Colorado Dep't of Social Servs., 842 F.2d 1158, 1164–65 (10th Cir.1988); Wisconsin Hosp.

Ass'n v. Reivitz, 733 F.2d 1226, 1236 (7th Cir.1984).

20. See e.g., Unicare Health Facilities v. Miller, 481 F.Supp. 496, 498 (N.D.Ill.1979).

21. Colorado Health Care Ass'n v. Colorado Dep't of Social Services, 842 F.2d 1158, 1164 (10th Cir.1988); Mississippi Hosp. Ass'n v. Heckler, 701 F.2d 511, 516 (5th Cir.1983).

22. See e.g., Temple Univ. v. White, 729 F.Supp. 1093 (E.D.Pa.1990), affirmed 941 F.2d 201 (3d Cir.1991).

23. Alabama Hosp. Ass'n v. Beasley, 702 F.2d 955, 961–62 (11th Cir.1983).

24. Florida Dep't of Health and Rehab. Servs. v. Florida Nursing Home Ass'n, 450 U.S. 147, 101 S.Ct. 1032, 67 L.Ed.2d 132 (1981).

25. See Edelman v. Jordan, 415 U.S. 651, 662–64, 94 S.Ct. 1347, 1355–56, 39 L.Ed.2d 662 (1974); Doe v. Chiles, 136 F.3d 709 (11th Cir. 1998); Amisub (PSL), Inc. v. Colorado Dep't of Social Services, 879 F.2d 789, 792–93, n. 7 (10th Cir.1989), cert. denied 496 U.S. 935, 110 S.Ct. 3212, 110 L.Ed.2d 660 (1990).

26. Green v. Mansour, 474 U.S. 64, 68–74, 106 S.Ct. 423, 425–29, 88 L.Ed.2d 371 (1985). A state may also be ordered to issue notices informing recipients of damages or other retroactive relief that may be available under state law in state courts or administrative actions if the notice is ancillary to some other permissible form of relief. Quern v. Jordan, 440 U.S.

essential in Medicaid cases.[27] Where state officials are sued in their individual, as opposed to representative capacity, they will usually be able to claim absolute or qualified immunity.[28]

Medicaid litigators generally prefer to bring litigation involving federal challenges to state Medicaid law in federal court, where judges are usually somewhat more detached from state budgetary and political concerns, exhaustion is less likely to be required, and § 1988 attorney's fees are available. Where federal issues are not involved, however, or on issues where the state court bench may be more sympathetic than the federal court (state constitutional requirements to fund abortions, for example), litigation in state court is necessary.

Excellent discussions of the procedural issues and strategic considerations encountered in Medicaid litigation are found in Jeanne Finberg, Federal Practice Tips: Litigating Medicaid Class Actions;[29] Ann B. Lever and Herbert A. Eastman, "Shake it up in a Bag": Strategies for Representing Beneficiaries in Medicaid Litigation;[30] and Matthew M. Strickler, Practical Issues in Representing Providers in Legal Actions Under the Boren Amendment.[31]

I. THE STATE CHILDREN'S HEALTH INSURANCE PROGRAM (SCHIP)

§ 12–16. The State Children's Health Insurance Program (SCHIP)

Though one of the primary functions of Medicaid in recent years has been to provide health insurance for children, many children remain uninsured. Under Medicaid eligibility expansions adopted by Congress in the late 1980s and early 1990s, the number of low income children enrolled in Medicaid grew from less than 10 million in 1986 to more than 17 million in 1995. Nevertheless, over 10 million children, many of them in low-income families, remained uninsured.[1]

In response to this continuing problem, Congress created, as part of the 1997 BBA the State Children's Health Insurance Program (SCHIP), title XXI of the Social Security Act.[2] The SCHIP program, however, was created in a very different political climate than the Medicaid program, and was thus not established as an entitlement for recipients, but rather as a grant-in-aid program to the states, established for ten years with a budget of $20.3 between the fiscal years of 1998 and 2002, which affords the states considerable flexibility in program administration within broad federal guidelines.[3] The

---

332, 346–49, 99 S.Ct. 1139, 1147–49, 59 L.Ed.2d 358 (1979).

27. See e.g., Kansas Health Care Ass'n v. Kansas Dept. of Social & Rehabilitation Servs., 822 F.Supp. 687 (D.Kan.1993) (where court ordered state to revise its nursing home rates using a designated nursing home inflation index pending revision of the rate to comply with federal law).

28. See AGI–Bluff Manor, Inc. v. Reagen, 713 F.Supp. 1535, 1542–43 (W.D.Mo.1989).

29. Clearinghouse Rev. April 1993 at 1592.

30. 35 St. Louis U. L. J. 863 (1991).

31. 35 St. Louis U. L. J. 893 (1991).

§ 12–16

1. See GAO, Health Insurance for Children: Many Remain Uninsured Despite Medicaid Expansions, GAO/HEHS–95–175 (1995).

2. 42 U.S.C.A. §§ 1397aa—1397jj.

3. See Sara Rosenbaum, et al., The Children's Hour: the State Children's Health Insurance Program, Health Aff., Jan./Feb. 1998 at 75.

SCHIP program was intended to insure 2.8 million previously uninsured children, and to expand Medicaid coverage to another 660,000 children identified through SCHIP outreach programs. By early 1999, SCHIP covered over 800,000 children.

States that wish to participate in the SCHIP program must submit a plan to DHHS.[4] States may either use SCHIP funds to expand Medicaid coverage for children or to establish a new SCHIP program to cover children who are neither eligible for Medicaid nor covered by private health insurance or use a combination of these approaches.[5] As of the Spring of 1999, 50 states and territories had SCHIP plans in place, with about half expanding Medicaid and half establishing new programs or combining new programs with Medicaid expansions.

SCHIP programs are supposed to target children in families with incomes of at or below 200% of the federal poverty level and 50% above the state's Medicaid applicable income level.[6] States may set eligibility standards that take into account geographic location, age, income and resources, residency, disability status, access to coverage under other health coverage, and duration of eligibility, but cannot discriminate on the basis of diagnosis or exclude children on the basis of preexisting condition.[7] SCHIP clearly and explicitly does not create an entitlement for any particular child to receive coverage.[8] Children who are eligible for Medicaid coverage, however, must be enrolled under Medicaid, and SCHIP coverage is not to substitute for coverage under group health plans.[9] States are also not supposed to cover children with higher family incomes unless children from poorer families are covered) nor may they cover children in state institutions or children eligible for insurance as dependents of state employees.[10] States are to establish outreach programs to identify children eligible for SCHIP coverage or other public programs, including Medicaid.[11]

States that choose to establish separately administered SCHIP programs must provide health care benefit packages equivalent to coverage provided by one of several benchmark benefit plans (including the standard Blue Cross/ Blue Shield FEHBP package, state employee coverage, and the state's largest HMO); or that include certain basic services and have an aggregate actuarial value equal to a benchmark plan; or that are approved by HHS.[12] States may, if granted waivers, provide coverage through contracts with community-based health delivery services or by purchase of family coverage under group health plans, if doing so would not substitute for coverage otherwise available.[13]

States may impose cost-sharing obligations on SCHIP beneficiaries, but may not do so with respect to well-baby and well-child care, and may not impose cost-sharing obligations in excess of those permitted under Medicaid on children whose family income is less than 150% of the poverty level or on

4. 42 U.S.C.A. §§ 1397aa, 1397ff. Plan amendments must also be submitted to HHS. 42 U.S.C.A. § 1397ff(b). If plans or plan amendments are not disapproved within 90 days, they are deemed to be approved. 42 U.S.C.A. § 1397ff(c).

5. 42 U.S.C.A. § 1397aa(a).

6. 42 U.S.C.A. §§ 1397bb(b)(1); 1397jj(b), (c)(4)

7. 42 U.S.C.A. § 1397bb(b)(1).

8. 42 U.S.C.A. § 1396bb(b)(4).

9. 42 U.S.C.A. § 1397bb(b)(3).

10. 42 U.S.C.A. § 1397bb(b)(1)(B)(i), 1397ii(b)(2).

11. 42 U.S.C.A. § 1397bb(c).

12. 42 U.S.C.A. § 1397cc(a)-(c).

13. 42 U.S.C.A. § 1397cc(c)(2)(B) & (3).

other children in excess of 5% of family income.[14] Children covered through Medicaid expansion are subject to Medicaid limits on cost-sharing.[15]

States that participate in CHIP must match federal funds in accordance with a formula that generally provides more generous federal participation than is afforded under Medicaid.[16] Federal funds are allotted according to a formula that takes into account the number of low income children in the states and geographic variations in health care costs.[17] States must use CHIP funds to supplement, not substitute for, state Medicaid expenditures. They may not spend more than 10% of their CHIP allotments on administrative costs.[18]

In summary, CHIP is a remarkably different program than Medicaid, evidencing a very different philosophy of federal responsibility for health care financing. It creates no entitlements in its beneficiaries enforceable in the courts; indeed it imposes minimal accountability of any kind on the states.[19] It affords maximum flexibility to the states, apparently in the hope that they will generously and responsibly provide for poor children if given an incentive to do so. It remains to be seen if this dream will be realized.

14. 42 U.S.C.A. § 1397ee(e).

15. 42 U.S.C.A. § 1397cc(e)(4).

16. 42 U.S.C.A. § 1397ee(b).

17. 42 U.S.C.A. § 1397dd.

18. 42 U.S.C.A. § 1997ee(c).

19. States are supposed to involve the public in plan development and implementation and give the public notice of plan proposals and amendments, 42 U.S.C.A. § 1397ff(b)(3)(B)(i), 1397gg((c).

Chapter 13

MEDICARE AND MEDICAID
FRAUD AND ABUSE

Table of Sections

A. INTRODUCTION

Research References

 Am Jur 2d, False Pretenses § 25.5; Physicians, Surgeons, and Other Healers § 396; Social Security and Medicare §§ 1531–1536

 ALR Index: Department of Health and Human Services; Fraud and Deceit; Malpractice By Medical or Health Professions

 ALR Digest: Public Assistance §§ 30–35

 Am Jur Pleading and Practice Forms (Rev), Welfare Laws §§ 60, 61

 66 Am Jur Trials 1, Use of Surveillance Videotape to Prove Workers' Compensation Fraud

A. INTRODUCTION

A. INTRODUCTION

§ 13–1. Generally

A large and continually growing body of federal law forbids—under the threat of criminal or civil penalties or exclusion from federal health care programs—participants in the health care industry from engaging in a wide variety of activities. These laws are often accompanied by parallel state laws. This body of law is generically referred to as Medicare and Medicaid fraud and abuse law, though much of it has little to do with common law fraud and only constitutes abuse as that term is broadly defined.[1] Some of these prohibitions address conduct easily recognizable as lying and stealing: e.g. filing false claims for payment or misrepresenting one's qualifications for participating in a federal health care program. Others police Medicare cost-control initiatives—punishing overservice or improper coding by providers paid on a fee-for-service or cost basis or underservice by providers paid through risk-sharing contracts. A few cases have been brought against providers who have violated their obligations to Medicare or Medicaid by providing poor quality items or services. A complex and confusing body of law prohibits under the rubric "bribes and kickbacks" a variety of rebates, discounts, and profit-

§ 13–1

1. The Medicare Carrier's Manual (MCM) defines abuse as: "Incidents or practices, which, although not considered fraudulent acts, may directly or indirectly cause financial losses to the Medicare/Medicaid programs or to beneficiaries/ recipients. Abuse is those practices wherein providers, physicians, or other suppliers of health care goods or services oper- ate in a manner inconsistent with accepted sound fiscal, business or medical practices in such a way that these practices result in an unnecessary financial loss to the Medicare or Medicaid programs and are not within the concept of reasonable and necessary services as defined in the Medicare or Medicaid laws." MCM § 11,012.

sharing arrangements that in other industries might pass as a permissible division of the proceeds of collective activity. The parallel Stark legislation prohibits self-referrals. Finally, a long list of specific prohibitions promote various federal policies, including improving the quality of nursing home care, assuring emergency treatment regardless of ability to pay, and protecting persons who purchase Medicare supplement insurance.

This body of law has had a profound impact on the health care industry and on relationships among providers. Aggressive enforcement of the false claims prohibitions in recent years is considered to have played a role in dramatically reducing Medicare cost increases, which had been driven in part in the past by "creative" billing practices. The bribe and kickback prohibition and accompanying legislation limiting self-referrals discourage doctors from acquiring interests in other health care providers while encouraging them to form group practices, to become employees of health care entities, or to become part of risk-sharing organizations or arrangements, thus supporting greater concentration in the health care industry.[2] This may have the ultimate effect of creating a better organized, more competitive health care industry. These laws are also intended to discourage provider-induced demand, though they might in many instances simply make it more profitable for a physician to provide a service himself or within his group rather than to refer a patient to a more specialized practitioner, since the referrer cannot receive a referral fee.[3] Though these laws are aimed at limiting the situations where the interests of physicians comes in conflict with the interests of their patients by prohibiting physicians from obtaining payment for the referral of patients, such conflicts are ubiquitous and perhaps unavoidable.[4] Fraud and abuse law has, in any event, proved a gold-mine for health lawyers, who must be at the side of their health care clients continually to steer them through the treacherous narrows of these federal and state prohibitions, violation of which can result in imprisonment or impoverishment.

Authority for investigating fraud and abuse violations and for enforcing most fraud and abuse administrative penalties and program exclusions is delegated to the Office of Inspector General (OIG) of HHS.[5] In recent years the OIG has aggressively enforced the fraud and abuse laws with strong congressional support. The Department of Justice (DOJ) has authority to enforce the criminal fraud and abuse laws and the civil False Claims Act, violations of which are investigated by the Federal Bureau of Investigations (FBI). Funding for the fraud and abuse enforcement efforts of the OIG, DOJ, FBI, and Health Care Financing Administration (HCFA) was dramatically increased by the Health Insurance Portability and Accountability Act of 1996 (HIPAA), which established a generously funded Health Care Fraud and Abuse Control Account.[6] HIPAA also established a "Medicare Integrity Pro-

2. See David M. Frankford, Creating and Dividing the Fruits of Collective Economic Activity: Referrals Among Health Care Providers, 89 Colum. L. Rev. 1861 (1989); James G. Wiehl, "Physician Integration"; The Legal Pressures for Consolidation of Health Care Services, 34 St. Louis U. L. J. 917 (1990).

3. Mark A. Hall, Making Sense of Referral Fee Statutes, 13 J. Health, Pol., Pol'y & L., 623 (1988).

4. See Generally Marc A. Rodwin, Medicine, Money & Morals (1992).

5. See Statement of Organizations, Functions and Delegations of Authority: Office of Inspector General, 50 Fed. Reg. 45,488 (1985).

6. 42 U.S.C. § 1395i(k). See Ted Acosta & Howard J. Young, The Health Insurance Portability and Accountability Act of 1996 and the Evolution of the Government's Anti–Fraud and

gram" under which HCFA can enter into contracts with private entities to conduct medical, utilization, fraud and audit reviews to identify fraud in the Medicare program,[7] and a national data bank to collect information on persons sanctioned for fraud and abuse.[8] Encouraged by federal funding of 75% to 90%,[9] most states have established Medicaid fraud control units (often within the Attorney General's office) and passed laws prohibiting Medicaid fraud.[10] As of 1993 such units are mandatory for most states.[11]

Because Medicare and Medicaid criminal and civil sanctions affect virtually the entire range of health care law, coverage of these sanctions is not limited to this chapter. In particular, sanctions policing the quality of nursing home care are covered in chapter 1, sanctions assuring compliance with emergency treatment requirements are addressed in chapter 10, sanctions that can be imposed on managed care organizations are discussed in chapters 11 and 12, and sanctions imposed by Medicare Peer Review Organizations are explored in chapter 3. Other sanctioning authorities are noted in passing throughout the Medicare and Medicaid chapters, but are reviewed again here.

B. FALSE CLAIMS AND STATEMENTS

§ 13–2. False Claims and Statements, Introduction

Though, "Medicare and Medicaid fraud" covers a wide variety of conduct, the clear majority of criminal prosecutions, civil recoveries, and administrative penalty and sanction cases brought against Medicare and Medicaid providers (including suppliers and professionals) involve false claims.[1] The Medicare and Medicaid systems spend enormous amounts of money, and attract both sophisticated criminal enterprises and petty thieves. Some of the crimes of these providers are quite bizarre, including an Illinois psychiatrist who billed Medicaid for 4800 hours in one year, a physician who in 48 separate instances billed Medicaid for performing two abortions within a month on the same patient, or another who billed Medicaid for treating a 22–year old college football player for diaper rash.[2] Recent fraud alerts identify various fraudulent claims practices such as billing Medicare for weight-loss programs as "psychiatric care," double billing of the VA and Medicare for nursing home care; and billing Medicare for hospital beds supplied to adult

Abuse Agenda, 30 J.Health & Hosp. L. 37 (1997).

7. 42 U.S.C.A. § 1395ddd.

8. 42 U.S.C.A. § 1320a–7e.

9. 90% funding during the first three years of funding, 75% thereafter. 42 U.S.C.A. § 1396b(a)(6) & (q).

10. See e.g., West's Ann. Cal. Penal Code §§ 72; West's Ann. Cal. Welf. & Inst. Code, §§ 14107–14107.4; La. Stat. Ann.–Rev. Stat. § 14:70.1; Mass. Gen. Laws Ann. ch. 118E, §§ 21A–21G, 39–46A; Va. Code §§ 32.1–310–321.

11. 42 U.S.C.A. § 1396a(a)(61).

§ 13–2

1. Year after year the semi-annual reports of the Office of Inspector General identify false

claims as the most common kind of criminal fraud, as well as the most common ground for recovery under the civil monetary penalty act. Insofar as false claims result in criminal convictions, they also generally lead to exclusion from program participation. See, www.dhhs.gov/progorg/oig/semann/index.htm. Two excellent symposia on fraud and abuse were published while this text was in print, one in the Journal of Health Law, vol. 32, No. 4 (1999). The other in the Alabama Law Review, vol. 51 No. 1 (1999).

2. See Paul Jesilow, et al., Fraud by Physicians Against Medicaid, 266 JAMA 3318, 3319 (1991).

care homes for residents who do not require medical treatment.[3] The low reimbursement rates paid by Medicaid in many states, the ease with which claims can be inflated through coding manipulation, and the perception that cheating Medicare or Medicaid is a "victimless crime," combine to make fraudulent billing quite common, accounting for, by some estimates, 10% of program cost.[4]

False claims are not limited to obviously criminal conduct, however. They also include an assortment of other attempts to manipulate the Medicare and Medicaid payment systems to receive payment to which a provider is not entitled, including cost report fraud, upcoding, unbundling, or billing for unnecessary services. In fact, a primary purpose of the law of false claims is to police the boundaries of the Medicare and Medicaid payment systems, assuring that providers code, claim, and report costs in accordance with program regulations and directives. The diverse payment systems used by Medicare and Medicaid establish various incentives. False claims law polices responses to these incentives that are so aggressive as to imperil other program goals. Thus, in *United States v. Larm*,[5] the Court of Appeals upheld the conviction of an allergist on seventeen counts of Medicaid Fraud for using CPT Code 90040, "brief examination, evaluation and/or treatment same or new illness," rather than CPT Code 90030, "minimal service: injections, minimal dressings, etc. not necessarily requiring the presence of a physician," for nurse administered allergy shots.[6] The false claims prohibitions, moreover, protect the health of patients to the extent that false claims prosecutions deter providers from overprovision of unnecessary or underprovision of necessary medical care. They have even been used to prosecute nursing homes and psychiatric hospitals that failed to provide their residents with quality care meeting Medicare and Medicaid certification standards.

In the late 1990s, false claims enforcement actions began to focus more on "legitimate" mainstream providers, and not just on criminals of a more traditional sort. Civil false claims actions were brought or threatened under national enforcement initiatives against hospitals for billing for the services of attending physicians who did not supervise residents in accordance with Medicare standards,[7] for filing claims for unnecessary laboratory tests, for billing for services provided in the 72 hours prior to admission for surgery in violation of Medicare payment requirements, for improper upcoding of certain conditions, and for charging for investigational devices that were not covered by Medicare.[8] These enforcement actions, aggressively pressed against prestigious hospitals, proved intensely controversial and provoked legislative proposals to rein in enforcement.[9] Congress backed off this legislation in 1998, when the DOJ and OIG issued guidelines to constrain their enforcement initiatives. Aggressive enforcement, however, plays an important role in a

3. See IG Fraud Alerts Warn Contractors of Current Schemes to Defraud Medicare, 2 Health L. Rep (BNA) 674 (1993).

4. Jesilow, supra note 2.

5. 824 F.2d 780 (9th Cir.1987), cert. denied 484 U.S. 1078, 108 S.Ct. 1057, 98 L.Ed.2d 1019 (1988).

6. Id. at 782–83.

7. See U.S. General Accounting Office, Medicare: Concerns with Physicians at Teach-

ing Hospitals (PATH) Audits, GAO/HEHS–98–174 (1998).

8. See U.S. General Accounting Office, Medicare: Application of the False Claims Act to Hospital Billing Practices, GAO/HEHS–98–195 (July 1998).

9. See Timothy Stoltzfus Jost & Sharon L. Davies, The Empire Strikes Back, 51 Ala. L. Rev. 239 (2000).

system where the utilization review and claims auditing systems found in private health insurance are largely absent.[10]

§ 13–3.   False Claims and Statements: Criminal Sanctions

The federal and state governments have available a host of tools for dealing with false claims.[1] First, It is a felony, punishable by up to five years imprisonment and a fine of up to $25,000, to knowingly and willfully make or cause to be made a false statement or representation of a material fact in a claim for a benefit or payment under a plan or program funded by the United States or a state health care program.[2] It is also a felony to conceal or to fail to disclose knowledge of the occurrence of an event affecting an individual's right to a benefit or payment with the intent to secure fraudulently the benefit or payment; to convert a Medicare benefit or payment intended for the use of another; or to bill for a physician's service knowing that the individual that provided the service was not a physician.[3] It is a misdemeanor, punishable by a fine of up to $10,000 and up to one year's imprisonment, for a person other than one who furnishes medical items or services (e.g. a secretary or billing clerk) to commit one of these offenses.[4] Recently adopted legislation more broadly makes it a federal crime to knowingly and willfully execute, or attempt to execute, a scheme or artifice to defraud any health care benefit program; steal or embezzle money from a health care program; make a materially false statement to or conceal material information from a health benefit program; obstruct the criminal investigation of health care offenses; or launder money in connection with federal health care offenses.[5] This statute federalizes fraud committed against private health plans, but the federal government is still leaving private health care fraud enforcement largely to the states.

Despite the existence of this body of specific health care fraud law, most federal criminal prosecutions for health care fraud are in fact brought under more general federal criminal statutes such as the federal criminal false claims act and the mail and wire fraud acts. The general federal false claims act makes it a crime knowingly to 1) present a claim to the United States; 2) that is "false, fictitious, or fraudulent" where 3) the defendant knows that the claim was false, fictitious or fraudulent.[6] "Conscious avoidance" of knowledge of the truth or reckless disregard for the truth can form the basis of a finding of "knowledge" of falsity, though mere negligence is not sufficient.[7] Knowingly and willfully making of material false or fraudulent statements or representations to the federal government is also a crime.[8] Use of the mails for the purposes of obtaining money or property by fraud constitutes the federal

---

10. Id.

§ 13–3

1. See Pamela H. Bucy, Crimes by Health Care Providers, 1996 U.Ill.L.Rev. 589 (1996).

2. 42 U.S.C.A. § 1320a–7b(a). See, surveying criminal laws dealing with health care provider crimes, Pamela Bucy, Crimes by Health Care Providers, 1996 U.Ill.L.Rev. 589 (1996).

3. Id.

4. Id.

5. 18 U.S.C.A. §§ 1347, 669, 1035, 1518, 1956(c)(7)(F).

6. See Tedd J. Kochman & Garen Megueri-an, False Claims, 31 Am. Crim. L. Rev. 525, 528 (1994).

7. United States v. Nazon, 940 F.2d 255, 258–60 (7th Cir.1991); United States v. Precision Medical Labs., Inc., 593 F.2d 434, 442–446 (2d Cir.1978).

8. 18 U.S.C.A. § 1001.

crime of mail fraud,[9] and use of electronic communications to defraud is wire fraud.[10] The mail and wire fraud provisions apply to fraud against private as well as public programs. Submission of false claims on two or more occasions in association with an "enterprise" engaged in interstate commerce may constitute a violation of RICO, the Racketeer Influenced and Corrupt Organizations statute.[11] Assisting another in creating or presenting a false claim is aiding and abetting,[12] while conspiracy to submit a false claim is also a separate offense.[13] Prosecutors and federal judges are familiar with these statutes from other contexts, and tend to rely on them in pursuing health care fraud claims in lieu of more specific statutory provisions.

Although providers often characterize fraud cases as ordinary billing disputes that have resulted in brutal prosecutorial overreactions, only a tiny proportion of cases that involve questionable billing end up being investigated, and even fewer end up in prosecution. Physicians, supply companies, or diagnostic laboratories have only a 3 in 1000 chance of having their billing practices audited by Medicare in a given year.[14] Most cases in which problems are identified are settled with the provider agreeing to make restitution.[15] Often penalties are not pursued because the provider declares bankruptcy or otherwise hides its assets after the fraud is detected, making the pursuit of a recovery futile.[16] In sum, though federal and state prosecutors and agencies possess a considerable armamentarium for dealing with false claims, most questionable claims seem to go unpunished.

§ 13–4. False Claims and Statements, Civil Offenses

a. Under the Federal Civil False Claims Act

Though there are a variety of civil penalty statutes that cover the Medicare and Medicaid programs, false claims civil actions are brought almost invariably under the general federal Civil False Claims Act (FCA). The FCA, 31 U.S.C.A. § 3729, like its companion criminal law provision, 18 U.S.C.A. § 287, was adopted during the civil war to address the problem of rampant war contractor fraud.[1] It has become one of the most frequently used tools in the war against health care fraud. It is attractive to the government because its remedial provisions permit recoveries of three times the amount of

9. 18 U.S.C.A. § 1341.

10. 18 U.S.C.A. § 1343.

11. 18 U.S.C.A. § 1961. See Humana Inc. v. Forsyth, 525 U.S. 299, 119 S.Ct. 710 (1999); United States v. Hale, 106 F.2d 402, No. 95–5915, 1997 WL 34697 (6th Cir. Jan.28, 1997), cert. denied, 522 U.S. 860, 118 S.Ct. 161 (1997); RICO Charges Place Health Fraud in Realm of Organized Crime, BNA's Health Care Fraud Report, Feb. 26, 1997 at 128 (reporting successful use of RICO against five persons who defrauded Medicare of $25 million marketing DME to nursing homes).

12. 18 U.S.C.A. § 2.

13. 18 U.S.C.A. § 286.

14. GAO, Medicare, Reducing Fraud and Abuse Can Save Millions, 7 (GAO/T–HEHS–95–157, May 16, 1995). See also, Timothy S.

Jost & Sharon L. Davies, The Empire Strikes Back, 51 Ala. L. Rev. 239 (2000).

15. GAO, Medicare, Modern Management Strategies Needed to Curb Program Exploitation, 7–8 (GAO/T–HEHS–95–183, June 15, 1995).

16. GAO, Medicare, Adapting Private Sector Techniques Could Curb Losses to Fraud and Abuse, 9–10 (GAO/T–HEHS–95–211, July 19, 1995).

§ 13–4

1. Adam G. Snyder, The False Claims Act Applied to Health Care Institutions: Gearing Up for Corporate Compliance, 1 DePaul J. of Health Care L. 1, 6 (1996). See generally, Pamela H. Bucy, Civil Prosecution of Health Care Fraud, 30 Wake Forest L. Rev. 693 (1995).

damages sustained by the government, plus penalties of $5000 to $10,000 per claim. The FCA also offers the government prosecutor advantages not available under alternative criminal statutes. First, the government need only meet the civil, preponderance of the evidence, standard of proof.[2] Second, as amended in 1986, the statute permits recoveries without proof of specific intent to defraud. The statute is also popular with private litigants, who can recover a portion of the damages to which the government is entitled under the statute's qui tam provisions.[3]

Section 3729 provides that a person who knowingly presents a false or fraudulent claim or uses a false record or statement to secure payment of a false claim is liable for a civil penalty of $5000 to $10,000 plus treble damages.[4] The statute defines the terms "knowing" and "knowingly" to mean that a person has actual knowledge of information; acts in deliberate ignorance of the truth or falsity of information; or acts in reckless disregard of the truth or falsity of the information; and no proof of specific intent to defraud is required.[5] Upcoded claims or claims for medically unnecessary services can be false claims.[6]

The FCA has become the government's primary weapon in combatting fraud and abuse by genuine providers (as opposed to traditional criminals). Because the fines that can be imposed by the FCA are so substantial, considering the huge numbers of claims filed by health care providers, FCA cases rarely go to trial, and almost invariably settle. Settlements in the millions of dollars are common, including recent settlements of $325 million with Smith–Kline, $255 million with First American Health Care, and $379 million with National Medical Enterprises.[7]

One of the most controversial elements of the FCA is its qui tam provisions. Qui tam is an abbreviated version of "qui tam pro domino rege quam pro se ipso in hac parte sequitur"—he who litigates for himself as well as for the king.[8] When the federal FCA was adopted in 1863 to combat defense contractor fraud during the civil war, it included qui tam provisions.

Qui tam actions are seen as a tremendous threat by providers. Only the government can initiate criminal prosecutions and administrative sanctions, and the limited resources of federal and state prosecutors compel them to focus their efforts on a relatively small number of usually egregious cases. Under 31 U.S.C.A. § 3730(b)(1), however, any private person who has direct and independent knowledge of wrongdoing (not based on publicly disclosed information) can bring a qui tam action on behalf of the government to enforce the Civil FCA. The potential for recovery of bounties of up to 25–30% of the false claim recovery creates a significant incentive for private litigants to bring such cases, and the potential for statutory attorney's fees (plus

2.   31 U.S.C.A. § 3731(c).

3.   The Civil False Claims Act and its qui tam provisions are treated exhaustively in an excellent treatise by John Boese, Civil False Claims and Qui Tam Actions (1995).

4.   31 U.S.C.A. § 3729(a).

5.   See, e.g., United States v. Krizek, 111 F.3d 934 (D.C.Cir.1997).

6.   See United States v. McKean, 31 F.Supp.2d 1308 (W.D.Okla.1998); United States v. Lorenzo, 768 F.Supp. 1127 (E.D.Pa. 1991).

7.   See M.D. Krohn, Comment: False Claims Act and Managed Care: Blowing the Whistle on Underutilization, 28 Cumb.L.Rev. 443, 461 (1998).

8.   See David Ryan, The False Claims Act: An Old Weapon with New Firepower Is Aimed at Health Care Fraud, 4 Annals of Health L. 127, 150 (1995).

possible contingency fees) makes these cases very attractive to attorneys as well. Qui tam actions are often brought by disgruntled current or former employees, (a fact that employers should be acutely aware of) but can also be brought by competitors, beneficiaries, or even corporate officers, directors, compliance officers, or attorneys. Qui tam filings are increasing exponentially in the health care area, and every health care provider should be attentive to this threat.

A qui tam action is filed in camera under seal, and is not served on the defendant until the court so orders.[9] The complaint remains sealed for 60 days while the government considers whether or not to intervene.[10] The seal provision allows the government to investigate the allegations confidentially, prevents wrongdoers from being tipped off before such an investigation can be completed, and protects the defendant's reputation while the government is reviewing the merits of the case.[11] The government can move for an extension of the time that the case remains sealed.[12] Though the government must substantiate the reason why it seeks an extension,[13] cases often remain under seal for months after they are filed. The government only intervenes in about one fifth of qui tam cases, but as of late 1998, cases in which the government had intervened had resulted in judgments and settlements of over $2.25 billion since the 1986 amendments went into effect, cases declined by the government had only amounted to $60 million, thus the decision is very important for qui tam relators.[14]

A successful qui tam relator is entitled to 15% to 25% of the recovery if the government intervenes, 25% to 30% where the government declines intervention.[15] Qui tam relators may recover costs and attorney's fees if they prevail,[16] but a prevailing defendant may also recover attorney's fees in an action where the government declines intervention if the plaintiff's case was frivolous, vexatious, or brought for harassment.[17] The FCA provides protections for relators who are discharged, demoted, suspended, threatened, harassed, or discriminated against in their employment, including double back wages and attorney's fees, where appropriate.[18]

Although the FCA has been used predominantly to pursue fraudulent billing schemes, it has also been used creatively in recent years to address other issues. Several cases have been brought against nursing homes that have claimed Medicare or Medicaid payment for services while not complying with federal quality certification requirements. A number of these cases have ended in consent decrees requiring the facilities to comply with specified quality requirements.[19] Cases are also being brought against managed care

---

9.   31 U.S.C.A. § 3730(b)(2).

10.   Id.

11.   Erickson ex rel. United States v. American Institute for Biological Sciences, 716 F.Supp. 908, 912 (E.D.Va.1989), citing S. Rep. No. 345, 99th Cong., 2d Sess. 24, reprinted in 1986 U.S.C.C.A.N. 5266, 5289.

12.   31 U.S.C.A. § 3730(b)(3).

13.   United States ex rel. McCoy v. California Medical Review, Inc., 715 F.Supp. 967, 968–69 (N.D.Cal.1989).

14.   See Fraud and Abuse: Some $2.2 Billion Recovered Since 1986 Under False Claims

Act, Justice Announces, BNA Health Care Daily, Oct. 26, 1998.

15.   31 U.S.C.A. § 3730(d).

16.   31 U.S.C.A. § 3730(d).

17.   31 U.S.C.A. § 3730(d)(4).

18.   31 U.S.C.A. § 3730(h).

19.   See David R. Hoffman, The Role of the Federal Government in Ensuring Quality of Care in Long–Term Care Facilities, 6 Annals of Health L. 147 (1997); John R. Munich & Elizabeth W. Lane, When Neglect Becomes Fraud: Quality of Care and False Claims, 43 St. Louis L. Rev. 27 (1999).

organizations that bill Medicare or Medicaid, falsely claiming to have met program requirements that they have in fact violated.[20]

The government has in several cases pursued civil money penalties in cases where there has been a criminal conviction. In *United States v. Halper*,[21] a case involving the False Claims Act, the Supreme Court held that, although civil penalties are not criminal and thus do not ordinarily give rise to double jeopardy problems, a penalty grossly disproportionate to the government's damages could constitute criminal punishment raising a problem under the double jeopardy prohibition of the Constitution.[22] In Hudson v. United States,[23] the Court overruled Halper, holding that the controlling question was not the size of the fine but rather whether the sanction was a criminal punishment. The FCA is quite clearly intended to be a civil rather than criminal sanction. Sanctions imposed under the FCA may still, however, run afoul of other constitutional constraints, such as the excessive fines prohibition, if they are grossly disproportionate to the offense. In fact, the Department of Justice is usually quite cautious in its actual charging of offenses to avoid this issue. In one case in which the DOJ became overly aggressive, the court eventually limited it to recovery for days in which a doctor, guilty of egregious upcoding, claimed for more than 24 hours of treatment in a single day.[24] The government ultimately, therefore, recovered a few thousand dollars rather than the $80 million it had sought.

Constitutional issues are also raised in FCA cases brought against the states by qui tam relators. States operate large hospitals and teaching and research institutions and administer sizable federal programs. When states defend FCA actions, however, two significant issues, one statutory and one constitutional, must be addressed.[25] First, are states "persons" within the meaning of section 3729(a), which provides for FCA liability against "persons" who commit certain acts. Second, if the FCA suit is brought by a qui tam relator, and the federal government chooses not to intervene, is the suit barred by the Eleventh Amendment, which prohibits damage suits in federal court by private persons against a state.[26]

The federal courts of appeal are divided on these issues. The D.C. Circuit has held that states are not "persons" who can be sued under the FCA,[27]

20. See Fraud and Abuse: Health Care Enforcement Efforts Moving in New Direction, Sheehan Says, BNA Health Care Daily, July 1, 1998; Sharon L. Davies and Timothy Stoltzfus Jost, Managed Care: Placebo or Wonder Drug for Health Care Fraud and Abuse, 31 Ga. LO. Rev. 373 (1997).

21. 490 U.S. 435, 109 S.Ct. 1892, 104 L.Ed.2d 487 (1989).

22. 490 U.S. at 449–51, 109 S.Ct. at 1902–03.

23. 522 U.S. 93, 118 S.Ct. 448 (1997)

24. United States v. Krizek, 7 F.Supp.2d 56 (D.D.C.1998) The Court of Appeals subsequently reversed the district court on the severe limitations it placed with respect to claims over the 24 hours limit, though it did not set aside the 24 hour baseline. United States v. Krizek, 192 F.2d 1024 (D.C.Cir.1999).

25. One recent federal case has also rejected a third argument based on the 10th Amendment. United States ex rel Garibaldi v. Orleans Parish School Board, 46 F.Supp.2d 546 (E.D.La.1999). The Court held that since the FCA merely protects the expenditure of federal funds, and can be avoided by declining federal funding, it does not impose a burden on the states that would violate the 10th Amendment. If. at 558.

26. In addition, some cases raise the issue of whether states are liable to qui tam plaintiffs under the whistleblower protection provisions of the FCA (31 U.S.C.A. § 3730(h)) if they take retaliatory action against them, See United States v. Texas Tech University, 171 F.3d 279, 295 (5th Cir.1999)

27. United States ex rel. Long v. SCS Business & Technical Institute, 173 F.3d 870 (D.C.Cir.1999), supp. opinion 173 F.3d 890 (D.C.Cir.1999).

while the Fifth Circuit has held that the Eleventh Amendment bars suits against the states in qui tam suits in which the federal government declines intervention.[28] On the other hand, the Second[29] and Eighth[30] circuits have held both that states are persons who can be sued under the FCA and that the Eleventh Amendment does not bar qui tam cases, while the Fourth[31] and Ninth Circuit,[32] without explicitly addressing the "person" issue, have decided that the Eleventh Amendment does not bar qui tam suits against the states. The Supreme Court has taken certiorari on the Second Circuit case, and these issues will, it is hoped, soon be resolved.

b. Administrative Penalties Under the Federal Civil Money Penalties Act

In addition to the general civil FCA, there are also administrative false claims civil money penalty (CMP) provisions that apply to false claims in federal and state health care financing programs. Civil penalties in the amount of up to $10,000 per item or service, plus assessments equalling three the amount claimed, may be imposed administratively for false claims under this statute.[33] A person is liable for civil penalties if that person "knows or should know," that the claim is false or that the service was "not provided as claimed." The meaning of the "should know" is defined in the statute, after 1996 amendments, to include deliberate ignorance or reckless disregard, the civil FCA standard of knowledge.[34] The "not provided as claimed" standard, again, permits imposition of penalties for miscoding as well as for fictitious claims. In *Anesthesiologists Affiliated v. Sullivan*,[35] for example the court upheld a $258,000 penalty assessment despite arguments that the physicians had merely described services rendered "unartfully," with the court stating, "The standard of care imposed by this requirement is an exacting one, and an 'unartful' description of medical services in a Medicare claim *is* a description of services that were not provided as claimed."[36] Specific civil money authorities also provide for penalties for a pattern and practice of upcoding or providing medically unnecessary services.[37]

28. United States v. Texas Tech University, 171 F.3d 279 (5th Cir. 1999). The two circuits split as to which issue should be resolved first, as a decision either way defeats the cause of action. The 5th Circuit addressed the Eleventh Amendment issue first, considering it to be jurisdictional, but the D.C. Circuit opined in a supplemental opinion that the Eleventh Amendment was "quasi jurisdictional" rather than "jurisdictional," the two issues were closely related, and that courts should first decide whether the statute provides "jurisdiction to determine jurisdiction." Long v. SCS, 173 F.3d 890.

29. United States ex rel. Stevens v. State of Vermont Agency of Natural Resources, 162 F.3d 195 (2d. Cir.1998).

30. United States ex rel Zissler, 154 F.3d 870 (8th Cir.1998); United States ex rel Rodgers v. Arkansas, 154 F.3d 865 (8th Cir.1998).

31. United States ex rel Berge v. University of Alabama, 104 F.3d 1453 (4th Cir.1997);

United States ex rel Milam v. University of Texas, 961 F.2d 46 (4th Cir.1992).

32. United States ex rel. Fine v. Chevron, U.S.A., Inc., 39 F.3d 957 (9th Cir.1994), rev'd and remanded en banc on other grounds 72 F.3d 740 (9th Cir. 1995).

33. 42 U.S.C.A. § 1320a–7a(a)(1)(A), (B). The terms "claim," "items or services" and "request for payment" are defined in the statute and regulations. See 42 U.S.C.A. § 1320a–7a(i)(2),(3); 42 C.F.R. § 1003.101.

34. 42 U.S.C.A. 1320a–7a(i)(7).

35. 941 F.2d 678 (8th Cir.1991).

36. Id. at 681. An excellent article on this subject is Alice G. Gosfield, Unintentional Part B False Claims: Pitfalls for the Unwary, in 1993 Health Law Handbook, 205 (Alice G. Gosfield, ed., 1993).

37. 42 U.S.C.A. § 1320a–7(a)(1)(A) & (E).

The CMP statute permits the OIG considerable discretion in determining the amount of penalty to be assessed. The statute and regulations regarding the determination of penalties and assessments list as mitigating or aggravating factors the nature and circumstances of the claim (including the amount and number of claims), the degree of culpability of the person submitting the claim, any history of prior offenses, the financial condition of the person submitting the claim, and other matters as justice may require.[38] The OIG will also consider other wrongful conduct, whether or not it has resulted in a conviction, penalty, or exclusion, and whether or not the statute of limitations for civil money penalties has run with respect to such conduct.[39] Because the OIG must normally refer a case to the DOJ for prosecution before proceeding with the case itself, and because the DOJ prefers to proceed under the FCA, relatively few civil penalty cases are pursued under this more specific statute.

In addition to the civil penalties that can be imposed under 42 U.S.C.A. § 1320a–7(a), civil penalties of $5000 per claim plus assessments of double the amount of the false claim can also be imposed administratively for false claims under the general federal Program Fraud and Civil Remedies Act.[40] This statute is rarely used in health care fraud cases as its penalties are less than those available under other statutes

c. *Program Exclusion for False Claims and Statements*

One of the most serious consequences of conviction of a criminal offense relating to the delivery of an item or service reimbursed under Medicare, Medicaid, or a state health care program funded under Title V or XX is mandatory exclusion from participation in those programs for at least five years.[41] Commission of an offense in violation of the civil money penalties or criminal provisions of the federal health care program fraud statute can also result in an exclusion.[42] An exclusion can be imposed on a physician based on a criminal plea even though the plea purported to settle all civil and criminal claims, as a Medicare exclusion is not a civil or criminal claim.[43] For a doctor dependent on Medicare or Medicaid funding, a five year exclusion can weigh more heavily than a substantial civil penalty, or even a criminal conviction.

The Medicare and Medicaid statutes also include a variety of other provisions authorizing civil sanctions or exclusions for improper billing practices.[44]

38. 42 U.S.C.A. § 1320a–7a(d); 42 C.F.R. § 1003.106. See Sanford V. Teplitzky, et al., Medicare and Medicaid Fraud and Abuse, in 1989 Health Law Handbook, 507, 516–518 (Alice G. Gosfield, ed., 1989), discussing ALJ decisions applying these factors.

39. 42 C.F.R. § 1003.106(b)(4).

40. 31 U.S.C.A. §§ 3801–3812.

41. 42 U.S.C.A. § 1320a–7(a)(1). Conviction is defined broadly to include nolo contendere pleas or entrance into diversion programs. 42 U.S.C.A. § 1320a–7(i). It even includes Alford pleas, in which the defendant pleads not guilty but accepts the conviction to avoid a trial. Hein v. Inspector General, Medicare &

Medicaid Guide (CCH) ¶ 41,366 (Feb. 26, 1993).

42. 42 U.S.C.A. § 1320a–7(b)(7).

43. United States v. Potrocky, 989 F.2d 496, 1993 WL 69537 (4th Cir.1993). See, discussing settlement issues generally, James M. Becker, et al., Avoiding Multiple Sanctions and Collateral Consequences When Settling Fraud and Abuse Cases, in 1993 Health Law Handbook, 187 (Alice G. Gosfield, ed., 1993).

44. See Timothy S. Jost & Sharon L. Davies, Medicare and Medicaid Fraud and Abuse § 2–5 (1998)(listing these sanction authorities).

C. BRIBES, KICKBACKS, AND MUCH ELSE

§ 13–5. The Statute and Its Scope

Although most fraud and abuse enforcement activity has involved false claims, far more controversy has surrounded the bribes and kickbacks provisions of the fraud and abuse statute. 42 U.S.C.A. § 1320a–7b(b) provides that it is a felony for a person to knowingly and willfully solicit or receive, or to offer or pay, any remuneration (including any kickback, bribe or rebate) directly or indirectly, overtly or covertly, in cash or in kind, in return for referral of a patient for or for purchasing, leasing, ordering, arranging for or recommending items or services paid for under a federally funded or state health care program.[1] The OIG can also exclude from program participation and impose a civil penalty of $50,000 plus three times the total amount of remuneration involved against an individual or entity that engages in a prohibited remuneration scheme.[2]

This provision, which has been in force since 1972, addresses broadly the situation in which one provider of federally financed health care services refers a patient to another provider in return for receiving something of value, rather than because of an independent judgment based solely on the best interests of the patient that the second provider is the most appropriate source of items or services needed by the patient. The law is justified by several considerations.[3] First, it is based on the belief that permitting referral fees would result in overutilization of services, subjecting beneficiaries to unnecessary testing and procedures. A second consideration is that of cost, both because the unnecessary tests generated by bribes and kickbacks will be billed to government health care programs, and because the referral fee itself may become an item ultimately billed to government health care programs.[4] Third is the belief that if kickbacks are permitted, referrals will be based primarily on what is most lucrative for the provider, not on what is the most appropriate or most convenient source of services for the beneficiary. This position is not universally accepted; indeed some commentators suggest that fee-splitting is necessary to override the incentives created by fee-for-service reimbursement for physicians to treat patients themselves even though a referral would be in the patient's best interests.[5] A fourth consideration is that referral fees interfere with such free market competition as might exist in health care because they impede the possibility of purchasing decisions being made on the basis of cost or quality. Whatever free choice patient's currently have in choosing Medicare providers will be further constrained if

---

§ 13–5

1. It is important to note that the statute only applies to federally funded services. As long as a health care provider or professional does not receive bribes or kickbacks for referring federally funded patients, the statute does not reach conduct involving other patients. This conduct may be governed, however, by state prohibitions. See infra, § 13–15.

2. 42 U.S.C.A. §§ 1320a–7a(a)(7), 1320a–7b(b)(7).

3. See Briefing by OIG, Safe Harbor Regulations (Aug. 6, 1991). But see, David A. Hyman & Joel V. Williamson, Fraud and Abuse, Regulatory Alternatives in a "Competitive"

Health Care Era, 19 Loyola U. Chicago L. J. 1133, 1156–1166 (1988) (criticizing justifications of the legislation).

4. See James F. Blumstein, The Fraud and Abuse Statute in an Evolving Health Care Marketplace: Life in the Health Care Speakeasy, 22 Am.J.L. & Med. 205 (1996) (contending that cost concerns are the primary justification of the statute).

5. Mark Hall, Institutional Control of Physician Behavior: Legal Barriers to Health Care Cost Containment, 137 U.Pa.L.Rev. 431 (1988); Mark Pauly, The Ethics and Economics of Kickbacks and Fee Splitting, 10 Bell J. Econ. 344 (1979).

provider remuneration becomes a key consideration in directing referrals. Finally, trafficking in Medicare and Medicaid beneficiaries for profit is simply unseemly.

Medical ethics, supplemented in some instances by state law,[6] has traditionally condemned fee-splitting when physicians referred patients to specialists.[7] The rapid development in recent years of diagnostic technology, which makes ordering of testing or imaging or referrals for review by subspecialists ever more frequent; the massive and ongoing reorganization of the health care industry, which results continually in new business relationships among physicians, health care institutions and suppliers; and the constant search by physicians for new revenue sources as traditional opportunities for earning become more constrained, have created new temptations and opportunities for abuse that go well beyond traditional fee-splitting.

The referral fee prohibition, designed to cover this extensive assortment of improper conduct, also potentially sweeps in a wide variety of harmless, or even beneficial business relationships. Physicians employed by hospitals, for example, who order tests for their patients from the hospital laboratory, might arguably receive some share of their salary in consideration for the business they generate for the hospital. Group purchasing agents, who receive a fee from suppliers based on the purchases made by their clients, seem clearly to receive a fee for inducing a purchase, in violation of the statute. Physicians who hold stock in a large, publicly traded national laboratory, arguably receive slightly larger dividends when they refer more business to the laboratory. Physicians who do not collect deductibles or coinsurance from beneficiaries are arguably paying the beneficiaries for their business. The bribe and kickback general prohibition contains both statutory and regulatory limitations and exceptions to define and protect beneficial conduct otherwise prohibited by the statute, a factor that has greatly complicated the statutory scheme.

Moreover, the referral fee statute is accompanied by a separate statute addressing much of the same conduct, the Stark self-referral prohibition of 1989,[8] which prohibits doctors from referring Medicare patients to entities in which the doctor has an ownership interest or from which the doctor receives compensation. This legislation (which was extended significantly in scope in 1993) supplements the general prohibition of referrals to others for remuneration has been supplemented by a more specific prohibition of self-referrals for remuneration.

The potential sweep of these prohibitions has generated a great deal of anxiety among providers, physicians, and suppliers, augmented no doubt by an aggressive HHS Inspector General who interpreted the prohibition broadly and by lawyers who have been very creative in imagining potential dangers presented by the statute. This concern has been exacerbated by an IRS General Counsel's Memorandum indicating that hospitals that enter into joint ventures that violate the fraud and abuse laws may risk losing their tax-exempt status.[9]

6. E.g., Mich. Comp. Laws Ann. § 750.428; Minn. Stat. Ann. § 147.091, subd. 1(p), N.M. Stat. Ann. § 61–6–15(D)(16).

7. See Marc A. Rodwin, Medicine, Money & Morals 19–52 (1993).

8. 42 U.S.C.A. § 1395nn.

9. Internal Revenue Service Gen. Couns. Mem., 39,862 (Nov. 22, 1991).

The OIG has in fact interpreted the terms of the bribe and kickback statute very broadly.[10] Referral is defined broadly to include not only referrals by physicians as traditionally understood, but also any actions of hospitals or other health care providers that influence patient decisions in the use of health care services, such as a hospital contracting with a radiologist to perform all radiology services in the hospital or a discharge planner encouraging a patient to use a particular home health agency upon discharge.[11] Remuneration is defined broadly to include any economic benefit, including the opportunity to generate a fee or relief from a cost that would otherwise have to be incurred.

Perhaps the most important issue, however, is the mens rea that must exist when a referral that flows in one direction and remuneration in the other for the law to be violated. Early cases read the statute restrictively. In *United States v. Porter*,[12] the Fifth Circuit Court of Appeals held that physicians who had received a "handling fee" from a laboratory to which they had sent blood samples had not received a bribe or kickback, because the payment was not "corrupt" and did not defraud the government.[13] In the landmark case of *United States v. Greber*,[14] however, the Third Circuit Court of Appeals held that physicians who had referred patients for Holter monitor services and were paid "interpretation fees" or "consultation fees" had violated the statute, because one apparent purpose of the fees was to induce referrals, "even if the payments were also intended to compensate for professional services."[15] This interpretation of the statute was subsequently adopted by the Ninth and First Circuits.[16] The OIG also adopted this position in its exclusion regulations, which provide that an individual or entity can be excluded for soliciting, receiving, offering or paying remuneration for a referral, "irrespective of whether the individual or entity may be able to prove that the remuneration was also intended for some other purpose."[17]

In the much heralded *Hanlester Network* case, however, the Ninth Circuit held that the statute's "knowing and willful" language requires the government not only to prove that the defendant intentionally engaged in prohibited conduct, but did so with knowledge that his conduct violated the law.[18] Thus in Hanlester, the government failed to obtain exclusions against several individuals who had formed a joint venture alleged to be in violation of the

10. See Sanford V. Teplitzky, et al., Medicare and Medicaid Fraud and Abuse, in 1989 Health Law Handbook, 507, 532–35 (Alice G. Gosfield, ed., 1989).

11. See 3 Medicare Compliance Alert Newsletter, April 29, 1991 at 4; 3 Medicare Compliance Alert Newsletter, April 1, 1991, at 4.

12. 591 F.2d 1048 (5th Cir.1979).

13. 591 F.2d at 1054, 1055. See also United States v. Zacher, 586 F.2d 912 (2d Cir.1978) (holding that a required payment of $4 per day to supplement Medicaid payments did not constitute bribery absent a showing that the term "bribe" in the statute was intended to encompass more than it had at the common law.) These cases were decided before 1977 amendments to the statute, which broadened its coverage.

14. 760 F.2d 68 (3d Cir.1985), cert. denied 474 U.S. 988, 106 S.Ct. 396, 88 L.Ed.2d 348 (1985).

15. 760 F.2d at 72.

16. See United States v. Kats, 871 F.2d 105 (9th Cir.1989); United States v. Bay State Ambulance and Hosp. Rental Serv., Inc., 874 F.2d 20 (1st Cir.1989) (Bay State affirmed a felony conviction based on an instruction that the unlawful purpose must be the "primary" purpose, though the court indicated it would apply the broader Greber "one purpose" test in the appropriate case.) See also Michael W. Peregrine & Thaddeus J. Nodzenski, Expanded Enforcement of the Fraud and Abuse Laws, 23 J. Health & Hosp. L. 10 (1990).

17. 42 C.F.R. § 1001.951(a)(2)(i).

18. Hanlester Network v. Shalala, 51 F.3d 1390 (9th Cir.1995).

statute because it failed to prove that the individuals knew that the arrangement violated the terms of the anti-kickback laws and specifically intended to violate the law.[19]

The Ninth Circuit in Hanlester relied on Ratzlaf v. United States, a Supreme Court case involving a financial reporting statute.[20] Subsequent to Hanlester the Supreme Court in Bryan v. United States,[21] limited Ratzlaf, deciding that at least in cases not involving "highly technical statutes," the government needed only to prove that the defendant possessed an "evil meaning mind", i.e. "acted with the knowledge that his conduct was unlawful."[22] Subsequently, the Eleventh Circuit in United States v. Starks held that the bribe and kickback legislation was not "highly technical" and that jury instructions that permitted conviction on the basis of "a bad purpose, either to disregard or disobey the law" were appropriate.[23]

§ 13–6. Limitations on the Scope of the Referral Fee Prohibitions: Statutory Exceptions

While efforts by physicians and providers to narrow the scope of the statute through judicial interpretation have by and large proved unsuccessful, Congress has not been wholly unresponsive. The statute itself contains several explicit exceptions. First, discounts or reductions in price obtained by providers of services, literally proscribed by the language of the statute, are permitted if properly disclosed and appropriately reflected in the claimed costs or charges of the provider.[1] It is obviously not in the interest of the federal government to discourage providers from receiving volume or other discounts as long as these savings are passed along to federal programs. Second, amounts paid by employers to bona fide employees are exempted.[2] While this provision recognizes the difficulty of disentangling licit and illicit remuneration in the employment setting, it contributes to the general tendency of the fraud and abuse laws to encourage further integration of health care enterprises.[3] A third exception permits group purchasing organizations to be compensated by obtaining rebates from vendors where the purchasing agent has a contract with the individuals or entities for whom the purchases are made specifying the fixed amount or fixed percentage of value to be paid to the agent, and, if purchases are made for a Medicare provider, the agent discloses to the provider, and to HHS on request, the amount of rebates received.[4] Fourth, federally qualified health centers may waive Medicare Part B coinsurance obligations for persons who qualify for subsidized services

---

19. 51 F.3d 1390.

20. 510 U.S. 135, 138 ,114 S.Ct. 655, 657 (1994).

21. 118 S.Ct. 1939 (1998).

22. 118 S.Ct. at 1946. See Sharon L. Davies, Guidance on the Meaning of "Willfulness" Looming? How Bryan might Affect the Hanlester Debate, 4 Health Law. 14 (1998).

23. 157 F.3d 833, 838 (11th Cir.1998). Accord, United States v. Davis, 132 F.3d 1092, 1094 (5th Cir.1998). See also United States v. Jain, 93 F.3d 436, 441 (8th Cir.1996) (sufficient for Government to prove defendant knew that his conduct was "wrongful", without hav-

ing to show that defendant violated a "known legal duty".)

§ 13–6

1. 42 U.S.C.A. § 1320a–7b(b)(3)(A). Procedures for reporting discounts are discussed further in the safe harbor regulations, see infra, § 13.6(a).

2. 42 U.S.C.A. § 1320a–7b(b)(3)(B).

3. See David M. Frankford, Creating and Dividing the Fruits of Collective Economic Activity: Referrals Among Health Care Providers, 89 Colum. L. Rev. 1861 (1989).

4. 42 U.S.C.A. § 1320a–7b(b)(3)(C).

under the Public Health Service Act.[5] Finally, the Health Insurance Portability and Accountability Act added additional exceptions for risk-sharing arrangements, specifically excepting 1) remuneration between a Medicare or Medicaid Managed Care Organization and an entity or individual providing items and services pursuant to a written agreement with the MCO (including arrangements between upstream individuals and entities and their downstream subcontractors), or 2) risk sharing arrangements pursuant to written agreements which place an individual or entity at substantial financial risk for the cost or utilization of the items or services paid for on a fee-for-service basis by Medicare or Medicaid.[6]

§ 13–7. Limitations on the Scope of the Referral Fee Prohibitions: Practices Safely Harbored

These explicit exceptions, however, do not begin to cover all of the situations in which innocent or desirable conduct may be deterred by the anti-kickback statute. In the late 1970s the Office of Program Integrity of HCFA issued opinion letters offering its view as to the legality of various proposed arrangements, but in 1981 it ceased doing so, determining that it was inappropriate for an administrative agency to offer advisory opinions as to violation of the criminal law. Attempts by the OIG to get the Department of Justice to commit itself not to prosecute certain activities also did not succeed.[1] In the Medicare and Medicaid Patient and Program Protection Act of 1987, however, Congress authorized HHS to issue "safe harbor" regulations, delineating conduct that HHS determined should not be subject to prosecution or exclusion under the anti-kickback statute. The Health Insurance Portability and Accountability Act of 1996 further required HHS to annually solicit additional safe harbors or modifications of existing safe harbors, as well as advisory opinions and special fraud alerts.[2]

The safe harbor regulations do not purport to identify all conduct that either does not violate the statute or that violates the statute in a sufficiently trivial way as not to justify civil penalties or criminal prosecution. They also do not immunize conduct from prosecution under state laws, which may vary from the federal law. They do, however, describe conduct that is safe from sanction under the bribe and kickback laws. They are supplemented by OIG Fraud Alerts, which attempt to describe conduct particularly vulnerable to prosecution. Where an arrangement involves conduct falling under more than one safe harbor, it must independently comply with each.

a. Safe Harbors Elaborating on Statutory Exceptions

Three of the safe harbors elaborate on three of the statutory exceptions. "Employee" is defined as in the Internal Revenue Code.[3] Discounts are defined to include price reductions related to "arms length" transactions, including rebate checks, credits or coupons, and, for cost-report buyers, end of the year discounts; but not including cash payments, bundled purchase

5. 42 U.S.C.A. § 1320a–7b(b)(3)(D).

6. 42 U.S.C. § 1320a–7b(b)(3)(F).

§ 13–7

1. See Sanford V. Teplitzky, et al., Medicare and Medicaid Fraud and Abuse, in 1989 Health Law Handbook, 507, 537–38 (Alice G.

Gosfield, ed., 1989) (recounting OIG efforts to obtain commitment from the Department of Justice not to prosecute hospitals that waived Part A deductibles and coinsurance).

2. 42 U.S.C.A.§ 1320a–7d(a).

3. 42 C.F.R. § 1001.952(i).

arrangements (under which one product is provided free upon the purchase of another product), reductions in price not available to Medicare or Medicaid, routine reductions or waivers of coinsurance or deductible amounts owed by beneficiaries, warranties, or services provided in accordance with personnel services or management contracts.[4]

The Group Purchasing Organization (GPO) safe harbor describes qualified GPOs and provides that the written agreement between the GPO and the entities for which it purchases must specify the exact amount or rate, or if not known, the maximum amount, of the GPO fee if it exceeds 3%.[5]

Regulations implementing the statutory risk-sharing exception are discussed in the managed care subsection below.

b. Investment Interest Safe Harbors

The most complex safe harbor deals with investment interests. This safe harbor should be read in tandem with the OIG's Special Fraud Alert on Joint Venture Arrangements. This fraud alert identified suspect joint ventures as those which investors chosen were potential referral sources; the investment shares of physician investors were proportionate to the volume of referrals; physicians were encouraged to refer to the entity or to divest their interest if referrals fell below an "acceptable level" or if the physicians became unable to refer; investment interests were nontransferable; the joint venture was structured as a "shell," existing primarily to channel business to another entity and profits to its investors; or the amount of the investments were disproportionately small (or even borrowed from the entity) and returns disproportionately large.[6] Joint ventures with these characteristics are viewed by the OIG as transparent attempts to purchase referrals.

The investment interest safe harbor describes, by way of contrast, joint ventures and other investment interests that are permitted. Investment interest is defined to include both equity and debt interests in corporations, partnerships, or trusts, whether held directly, or indirectly through family members or other indirect ownership vehicles.[7] Investments in large, publicly-traded entities that are registered with the SEC and have $50 million or more in undepreciated net tangible assets related to the provision of health care items and services are safe if the investment interest is obtained on terms equally available to the public when trading on a registered national securities exchange, the entity markets items and services in the same way to investors and non-investors, funds are not directly or indirectly loaned or guaranteed by the entity to the investor to obtain the investment interest, and dividends are proportionate to the size of the investment.[8] There is little risk that physicians who hold a few shares of a major national laboratory will change their referring practices based on that fact.

Investment in small entities is also permitted if certain stringent conditions are met to assure that the entity is not merely a channel for kickbacks. These conditions are different for active investors (investors who are either

4. 42 C.F.R. § 1001.952(h)(5).

5. 42 C.F.R. § 1001.952(j).

6. April 1989, described in Sanford V. Teplitzky & S. Craig Holden, 1989 Developments in Medicare and Medicaid Fraud and Abuse, in

1990 Health Law Handbook, 433, 454–56 (Alice G. Gosfield, ed. 1990).

7. 42 C.F.R. § 1001.952(a).

8. 42 C.F.R. § 1001.952(a)(1).

responsible for the day to day management of the entity and general partners under the Uniform Partnership Act or who have agreed in writing to undertake liability for the entity's agents) and passive (all other) investors.[9] After the 1993 expansion of Stark, this safe harbor is less important, as many investment interests in small joint ventures are prohibited by Stark.

Separate safe harbors protect investments in particular kinds of entities. A recently promulgated safe harbor protects investments in certified Ambulatory Surgical Centers (ASCs) if referred patients are informed of the investment interest, the terms of the investment are not related to the volume or value of referrals, payment to an investor is directly proportional to the amount of capital invested, the entity does not loan the investor funds for the investment, the entity and its investors do not discriminate against Medicare or Medicaid patients, and other requirements specific to different categories of ASCs are met.[10] Another protects investments in group practices what conform with the Stark group practice definition and in solo practice professional corporations if certain requirements are met.[11]

c. Rental, Personal Services, and Management Contracts

Three safe harbors for space and equipment rentals and for personal services and management contracts have very similar standards. These arrangements have in the past served on occasion as thinly disguised kickbacks—e.g. when a laboratory paid a physician rental payments for a closet in the physician's office that equaled the rent on the entire office suite. Leases for space or equipment must be in writing and signed by the parties; identify the space or equipment covered; specify when and for how long space or equipment will be used and the precise rental charge for each use if the lease is not for full time use; be for at least one year; cover all the space or equipment leased between the parties; and not be for an amount of space or equipment in excess of that necessary to accomplish the commercially reasonable business purposes of the rental.[12] Per use rental agreements will receive particularly close scrutiny. The amount of rent must be set in advance, must not take into account the volume and value of any referrals or business generated, and, most importantly, must reflect the fair market value of the space or equipment.[13] Fair market value is defined as the value of the property for "general commercial purposes," or "the value of the equipment when obtained from a manufacturer or professional distributor," and cannot take into account the proximity or convenience of the equipment or space to the referral source.[14] Thus hospitals that rent offices to staff physicians for less than fair market value are not protected by this safe harbor. Below market leases entered into to induce referrals may also be unenforceable as illegal contracts.[15]

The requirements for personal services or management contracts are nearly identical to the rental provisions, with an additional requirement that the services performed under the agreement may not involve counseling or

9. 42 C.F.R. § 1001.952(a)(2).
10. 42 C.F.R. § 1001.952(r).
11. 42 C.F.R. § 1000.652(p).
12. 42 C.F.R. § 1001.952(b), (c).
13. Id.
14. Id.

15. Vana v. Vista Hospital Systems Inc., No. 233623 (Calif. Super. Ct. Oct. 25, 1993), noted at 2 BNA Health Law Rep. 1475 (1993). See Michael v. Peregrine, et al. Hospital/Physician Contracting and the Illegality Defense, 27 J. Health & Hosp.L. 129 (1994).

promotion of a business arrangement or other activity that violates any state or federal law.[16]

d. Sales of Practices

A limited safe harbor exists to protect sales of practices by retiring physicians. The sale must be normally be completed within one year from the date of the agreement, after which the selling practitioner must no longer be in a professional position to refer Medicare or Medicaid patients or otherwise generate business for the purchasing practitioner.[17] Sale options are not permitted unless they are completely performed within a year. If the sale is within a health professional shortage area, however, the sale can take up to three years if the purchasing entity undertakes diligent and good faith efforts to recruit a physician to fill the practice.[18]

The practice of hospitals purchasing the practices of physicians who thereafter are retained on staff, which became common in the 1990s, is explicitly not protected by this rule, though a separate safe harbor for physician recruitment currently under consideration may protect some of these activities, and buying out a physician for a flat payment and then later employing the physician may be permissible.[19] Sale of an individual practitioner's practice to another practitioner or to a group, where there is an ongoing relationship between the seller and buyer (as where an ophthalmologist purchases the practice of an optometrist, who thereafter becomes a "partner") is viewed as suspect and not protected.

e. Referral Service Safe Harbor

Payments to services that refer patients are protected if the referral service:

1) does not exclude any individual or entity who meets its participation requirements;

2) assesses payments equally from all participants based on the cost of operating the service and not on the volume or value of referrals;

3) does not impose any requirement on the professionals to which it refers patients as to how they provide their services except that they charge referred patients the rate that they charge other persons not referred by the service or provide services free or at a reduced charge; and

4) discloses the manner in which it selects its participants, whether the participant pays a fee, how it selects a particular participant for a particular referred person, the relationship between the referral service and the group of persons to whom it refers, and the basis on which it would exclude an individual or entity from continuing as a participant, with the disclosure evidenced by a signed writing.[20]

f. Warranty Safe Harbor

Though warranties have not been a major area of abuse, they are clearly a benefit provided by a manufacturer to induce the purchase of a product, and

---

16.   42 C.F.R. § 1001.952(d).

17.   42 C.F.R. § 1001.952(e).

18.   42 C.F.R. § 1001.952(e)(2).

19.   Concern regarding the legality of such practice acquisitions was expressed in a letter from the Office of Inspector General to the IRS reported at 1993 Medicare and Medicaid Guide (CCH) ¶ 41,099.

20.   42 C.F.R. § 1001.952(f).

thus facially violate the statute. Certain warranties are, therefore, protected under a safe-harbor regulation. A warranty is defined by the safe harbor regulation as either an agreement that complies with the requirements of the Federal Trade Commission or an agreement by a manufacturer or supplier to replace another manufacturer's or supplier's defective item on terms equal to those found in the warranty on the item replaced.[21]

g. Beneficiary Cost–Sharing and Incentives Safe Harbors

The regulations recognize a limited safe harbor for waivers of beneficiary coinsurance and deductible amounts in two situations. First, a hospital may waive coinsurance and deductibles for services paid under PPS where the waiver is offered without regard to the beneficiary's reason for admission, length of stay or diagnosis; the amount waived is not later claimed as a bad debt or otherwise shifted to another payer; and the waiver is not part of a price reduction agreement between the hospital and a third party payer that would otherwise be responsible for the beneficiary cost-sharing obligation (other than a Medicare SELECT Medigap policy).[22] Second, certain federally funded health care facilities may waive the Part B or Medicaid deductible or coinsurance obligations of persons who qualify for subsidized services under specific federal programs.[23] While local government health care providers that waive coinsurance or deductibles in exchange for reduced payment at the time of service for the extreme indigent population they serve are not explicitly protected by the safe harbor, the OIG has expressed its lack of concern with this practice.

The OIG is quite concerned that routine waiver of cost-sharing by providers and practitioners may result in increased utilization and other abuses. The coinsurance and deductible waiver safe harbor is very narrow in scope, therefore, and does not protect providers other than hospitals or charge-reimbursed physicians and suppliers. It must be read in tandem with the fraud alert on waiver of the Part B deductible and coinsurance issued in January of 1991. That fraud alert identified as suspect practices advertisements that stated "Medicare accepted as payment in full" or that promised discounts to Medicare beneficiaries, routine use of "financial hardship" forms, collection of coinsurance and deductibles only where the beneficiary has Medigap insurance, charges to Medicare beneficiaries that are higher than those made to others for similar services or items, failure to collect deductibles or coinsurance for reasons unrelated to indigency, or "insurance programs" that cover coinsurance or deductible amounts only for items or services provided by the entity offering the insurance. Increasing Medicare charges to cover waived coinsurance and deductible amounts may constitute a false claim as well as a violation of the kickback statute.

h. Managed Care Safe Harbors

A number of critics have pointed out that the bribe and kickback prohibition makes little sense, and are indeed pernicious, in the managed care context, where financial incentives encourage underutilization rather than overutiliza-

21. 42 C.F.R. § 1001.952(g).
22. 42 C.F.R. § 1001.952(k)(1). See generally on the waiver of cost-sharing obligations, Mark S. Lachs, et al., The Forgiveness of Coinsurance, Charity or Cheating? 322 New Eng. J. Med. 1599 (1990).
23. 42 C.F.R. § 1001.952(k)(2).

tion.[24] Safe harbors adopted in the early 1990s provided limited protection to Medicare and Medicaid managed care arrangements. One allowed Medicare and Medicaid managed care organizations to offer incentives to their enrollees, including increased benefits and waivers of deductible and coinsurance amounts.[25] To qualify for this safe harbor, risk-based plans (see § 11–25) must offer the same incentives to all enrollees.[26] This requirement is intended to assure that the plan does not engage in favorable selection or use incentives to encourage improperly the use of certain services. Managed care plans paid on a reasonable cost or other basis may also offer incentives to their enrollees if they offer the same incentives to all enrollees and if they do not claim the cost of the incentives as bad debts or otherwise shift the cost of these incentives.[27] Also permitted are price reductions offered to Medicare and Medicaid managed health care plans by contract health providers under a written agreement for the purpose of furnishing enrollees with items or services covered by the health plan, Medicare, or Medicaid, as long as specific requirements are met that vary depending on the type of provider.[28] The purpose of this safe harbor was to permit managed care organizations to negotiate discounts with specific providers, but its limited scope renders its protection of limited value.

As described above, the risk-sharing exception enacted by HIPAA dramatically expands the protection provided to Medicare + Choice organizations and Medicaid Managed Care Organizations. Regulations implementing this section were drafted through the use of a negotiated rulemaking panel, as required by HIPAA.[29] The rules, in accordance with the statute, provide two separate safe harbors, one for price reductions offered to eligible managed care organizations (including HMOs and CMPs with risk or cost-based contracts, Medicare + Choice plans, Medicaid managed care organizations and other Medicaid plans paid on a risk-based contract, PACE programs, and federally qualified HMOs)[30] and another for price reductions offered by contractors with substantial financial risk to managed care organizations.[31] Because the first safe harbor covers such a broad range of organizations, the second is likely to have very limited application, applying primarily to employer-sponsored health plans that cover retirees who are also eligible for Medicare.

The regulations protect "first-tier" providers that contract directly with managed care organizations, and, under some circumstances, "downstream" providers who subcontract directly or indirectly with first tier providers. Contracts must be in writing, specify covered items or services, and last at

---

24. James Blumstein, Rationalizing the Fraud and Abuse Statute, 15 Health Aff. 118 (Winter 1996); James F. Blumstein, The Fraud and Abuse Statute in an Evolving Health Care Marketplace: Life in the Health Care Speakeasy, 22 Am.J. L. & Med. 205 (1996). But see Timothy Stoltzfus Jost & Sharon Davies, The Fraud and Abuse Statute: Rationalizing or Rationalization? 15 Health Aff., Winter 1996 at 129 (contending that bribes and kickbacks are still a concern in a managed care environment.)

25. 42 C.F.R. 1001.952(*l*)(i). See discussing this safe harbor, Gabriel L. Imperato, 1992–1993 Developments in Health Care Fraud and

Abuse, in 1993 Health Law Handbook, 147, 168–79 (Alice G. Gosfield, ed., 1993).

26. Id. HCFA or a state Medicaid program can authorize exceptions to this rule.

27. 42 C.F.R. § 1001.952(*l*)(ii).

28. 42 C.F.R. 1001.952(m). See discussing this safe harbor, Imperato, supra note 25 at 169–171.

29. See DHHS OIG, Interim Final Regulations, Statutory Exception to the Anti–Kickback Statute for Shared Risk Arrangements, 64 Fed. Reg. 63504 (1999).

30. See 42 C.F.R. § 1001–952(t).

31. 42 C.F.R. § 1000.952(u).

least a year.[32] The regulations do not generally protect situations where the managed care plan or its contractors or subcontractors receive additional fee-for-service or cost-based payments under federal health care programs or participate in "trading" or "swapping" arrangements in which discounts are offered for managed care business in order induce referrals of patients for whom payment is made by a federal health program on a fee-for-service or cost basis.[33] For purposes of the second safe harbor, the regulations define "substantial financial risk" to includes situations where the provider is paid through capitation, percentage of premium, federal DRGs, or bonus or withhold arrangements that meet certain requirements.[34]

i. Safe Harbors for Improving Services in Underserved Areas

In late 1999, the OIG promulgated a series of safe harbors intended to encourage the provision of services in medically underserved areas.[35] First, investments in entities in underserved areas that do not meet the small entity investment safe harbor may nonetheless be protected if they meet certain specified requirements.[36] Second, a new safe harbor protects practitioner recruitment for health professional shortage areas.[37] The recruitment agreement must be in writing for a term of no more than 3 years and not require that the practitioner make referrals to the recruiting entity or limit the recruited practitioner from having staff privileges or referring patients to other entities. The recruited practitioner must agree to treat Medicare and Medicaid patients in a nondiscriminatory manner, and receive at least 75% of his or her revenues from patients residing in the medically underserved area.[38] A third safe harbor would protect hospitals or other entities that pay all or part of the malpractice premiums of practitioners who provide obstetric services in primary health care professional shortage areas if certain requirements are met.[39]. A fourth safe harbor for sales of physician practices in health professional shortage areas is described above.

j. Other Safe Harbors

Finally, the most recent safe harbor regulations include two miscellaneous safe harbors relating to relationships among physicians and providers. One protects arrangements where one individual or entity refers a patient to another for specialty services with an understanding that the patient will be referred back at a certain time or under certain circumstances, if specific safeguards are met.[40] The other protects referrals and payments between, on

---

32. 42 C.F.R. §§ 1001.952(t)(1)(i)(A); 1001.952(u)(1)(i)(A).

33. 42 C.F.R. §§ 1001.952(1)(i)(B) & (C).

34. 42 C.F.R. § 1001.952(u)(1)(i)(C). See also, Douglas A. Blair, The New Proposed Safe Harbors for Certain Managed Care Plans and Risk–Sharing Arrangements: A History, Analysis, and Comparison with Existing Safe Harbors and Federal Regulations, 9 Health Matrix 37 (1999).

35. As defined by the Health Resources and Services Administration.

36. 42 C.F.R. § 1000.952(3).

37. 42 C.F.R. § 1001.952(n).

38. Recruitment arrangements outside of healthcare practitioner shortage areas are not protected by the safe harbor. This does not mean that other arrangements are illegal, but they are certainly at risk. An illegal physician recruitment contract may have private as well as public law consequences. In *Polk County, Texas v. Peters*, 800 F.Supp. 1451 (E.D.Tex. 1992), a federal court refused to permit a hospital to recover from a physician more than $30,000 advanced under a recruitment contract that explicitly required patient referrals, holding that the contract violated the fraud and abuse laws and was thus void and unenforceable.

39. 42 C.F.R. § 1000.952(*o*).

40. 42 C.F.R. § 952.1001(s).

the one hand, cooperative hospital service organizations, formed by two or more tax exempt "patron" hospitals to provide specific services for the benefit of patron hospitals, and, on the other, the patron hospitals where certain conditions are met.[41]

In the final analysis, the safe harbor regulations only cover a small proportion of business arrangements potentially subject to the fraud and abuse laws, and tend to cover those arrangements quite narrowly. In the absence of safe harbor regulations, arrangements that serve a valid business purpose other than encouraging referrals, that do not discriminate among participants and beneficiaries on the basis of referrals, and that reward contributions such as capital or services rather than patient referrals are likely not to result in sanctions, while arrangements that are likely to increase the cost of federal health care programs or to lead to overutilization of services; that restrict patient's freedom of choice; or that link participation or profit to past, present, or future referrals of beneficiaries of federally financed health care programs, are suspect.

k. Advisory Opinions

Because of continuing provider uncertainty as to the reach of the bribe and kickback prohibition, even with the assistance of regulatory safe harbors, Congress in the Health Insurance Portability and Accountability Act of 1996 required HHS, in coordination with DOJ, to issue advisory opinions on request as to whether arrangements or proposed arrangements comply with the bribe and kickback prohibition.[42] Advisory opinions are binding on the party requesting the opinion and on HHS.[43] Advisory opinions may not address the questions of whether fair market value has been paid in a transaction or whether an individual is a bona fide employee.[44] HHS must issue an advisory opinion within sixty days of receiving a request, and must charge a fee equalling the cost of processing the request.[45] HHS has published regulations implementing the advisory opinion process.[46] It published six advisory opinions in the first year of operation, 1997; eighteen in 1998, the second year; and thirteen in 1999. Though providers were initially skeptical of the process, an ever increasing number of opinions are being sought. Though opinions are only available to actual parties proposing genuine transactions, it is widely believed that some opinions are sought for strategic reasons by providers seeking to forestall arrangements of their competitors.

D. SELF–REFERRALS

§ 13–8. The Problem

The bribe and kickback prohibitions address the situation in which one practitioner or provider remunerates another to induce a referral. In the late 1980s and early 1990s, the attention of Congress and of several state legislatures focused on a closely related concern, physician referrals to facilities in which they themselves have an ownership interest or from which they receive compensation (self-referrals). Self-referral prohibitions are in general con-

---

41. 42 C.F.R. § 952.1001(q).

42. 42 U.S.C.A. § 1320a–7d(b).

43. 42 U.S.C.A. § 1320a–7d(b)(4)(A).

44. 42 U.S.C.A. § 1320a–7d (b)(3)(A).

45. 42 U.S.C.A. § 1320a–7d(5).

46. 42 C.F.R. § 1008.1—.59.

cerned with the same sort of conduct as is proscribed by the antikickback legislation, though the focus of the concern is different. The antikickback legislation is primarily directed at financial relationships among providers and practitioners who refer to each other, the self-referral legislation focuses solely on the financial incentives of the referrer.

There was considerable evidence in the late 1980s and early 1990s that "self-referrals" had become quite common, and quite costly. An OIG study issued in 1989 found that of 2690 physicians who responded to its study, 12% had ownership interests and 8% had compensation arrangements with businesses to which they referred patients. It further determined that nationally 25% of independent clinical laboratories (ICLs), 27% of independent physiological laboratories, and 8% of durable medical equipment suppliers were owned at least in part by referring physicians. Beneficiaries treated by physicians who owned or invested in ICLs received 45% more clinical laboratory services and 34% more services directly from ICLs than beneficiaries in general, resulting in $28 million in additional costs to the Medicare program.[1] This study was followed by several others, finding self-referral abuses with respect to other services. It should also be noted that the studies finding high rates of self-referral do not necessarily establish that the additional services provided were unnecessary, only that they were in excess of services provided in the absence of self-referrals.

While medical ethics authorities at first refused to condemn self-referrals,[2] the AMA Council of Ethical and Judicial Affairs in December of 1991, issued ethical guidelines that found it generally unethical for physicians to refer a patient to health care facilities outside of their office practice at which they do not directly provide care or services but in which they have an investment interest.[3] Under these guidelines, physicians may invest in facilities to which they refer only if they themselves provide care or services to the patient in the facility or if the facility is needed in the community and alternative sources of capital are not available and then must disclose their investment interest to referred patients. The AMA also suggested compliance with the OIG's investment safe harbors.[4] The AMA House of Delegates initially rejected this position in June of 1992, voting that self-referral was ethical if disclosed to the patient, but subsequently voted in December of 1992 to adopt the Council's position.[5] An excellent discussion of the entire history of the ethical position of organized medicine on the issue of self-referrals is found in Marc A. Rodwin, Medicine, Money & Morals (1993).[6]

§ 13–8

1. Office of Inspector General, Financial Arrangements Between Physicians and Health Care Businesses: Report to Congress (1989) described in John K. Iglehart, The Debate over Physician Ownership of Health Care Facilities, 321 New Eng. J. Med. 198, 202 (1989).

2. American Medical Association, Council on Ethical and Judicial Affairs, Report of the Council on Ethical and Judicial Affairs: Conflicts of Interest (1986).

3. Report of the American Medical Association Council on Ethical and Judicial Affairs; Report C (1–91), Dec. 11, 1991, with clarifications published in Council on Ethical and Judi-

cial Affairs, American Medical Association, Conflicts of Interest: Physician Ownership of Medical Facilities, 267 JAMA 2366–2369 (1992).

4. See Thomas S. Crane, The Problem of Physician Self-referral Under the Medicare and Medicaid Antikickback Statute, 268 JAMA 85, 89–90 (1992); Council on Ethical and Judicial Affairs, American Medical Association, Conflicts of Interest: Physician Ownership of Medical Facilities, 267 JAMA 2366 (1992).

5. See Arnold Relman, Self–Referral— What's at Stake, 327 New Eng. J. Med. 1522 (1992).

Though, as noted above, most conduct violating the bribe and kickback law also violate the self-referral law, the coverage of the laws is not identical. The self-referral laws only covers items and services financed by Medicare and Medicaid,[7] while the bribe and kickback laws cover items covered by other federally financed state health care programs.[8] Some conduct within the reach of the bribe and kickback prohibition, such as waiver of deductibles and co-insurance, would not be covered by the self-referral laws as it does not involve a physician referral. Each law has both broader and narrower exceptions than are found under the other law. The employment exception of the bribe and kickback law,[9] for example, is more absolute than that found in the self-referral law,[10] while the group practice exception to the self-referral law[11] is broader than any of the statutory or regulatory exceptions to the bribe and kickback law. The sanctions attached to the laws also differ: violations of the self-referral law can only result in denial of payment and civil penalties,[12] while violation of the bribe and kickback prohibition can result in criminal or civil sanctions.[13] In general, the bribe and kickback prohibition is broader and vaguer, and subject to more limited exceptions, the self-referral law is more focused and subject to more generous but very detailed exceptions.

§ 13–9.   The Stark Bill and OBRA 1993 Amendments

a.   The Prohibition

Congress took the first step towards banning self-referrals with adoption of the Stark I bill, also referred to as the Ethics in Patient Referrals Act, as part of the Omnibus Budget Reconciliation Act of 1989.[1] The legislation was extensively amended by the 1993 budget bill) often referred to as Stark II. Rules implementing Stark I were published in August of 1995.[2] Regulations to implement Stark II were published in January of 1998, but were not finalized as of this writing.[3] The reach of the Stark legislation was severely limited by the budget bill that passed Congress in 1995, but this bill was vetoed by President Clinton. The Stark laws remain a great source of dissatisfaction among health care providers and always vulnerable to repeal or substantial amendment.

As enacted in 1989, the Stark Bill prohibited only referrals to clinical laboratories, and contained a number of exceptions. It did not prohibit physician ownership of laboratories, but rather banned referrals of Medicare patients to such laboratories. The 1993 amendments extended its reach to cover physical therapy services; occupational therapy services; radiology and other diagnostic services; radiation therapy services; durable medical equip-

6. See also Marc A. Rodwin, The Organized American Medical Profession's Response to Financial Conflicts of Interest, 1890–1992, 70 Milbank Q. 703 (1992).

7. 42 U.S.C.A. §§ 1395nn(a)(1)(A), 1396b(s).

8. 42 U.S.C.A. § 1320a–7(h).

9. 42 U.S.C.A. § 1320a–7b(b)(3)(B).

10. 42 U.S.C.A. § 1395nn(e)(2).

11. 42 U.S.C.A. § 1320nn(b)(1) & (2).

12. 42 U.S.C.A. § 1395nn(g).

13. 42 U.S.C.A. §§ 1320a–7(b)(7), 1320a–7b(b).

§ 13–9

1. 42 U.S.C.A. § 1395nn.

2. 60 Fed. Reg. 41914 (1993) (codified at 42 C.F.R. §§ 411.350—.361.

3. See 63 Fed. Reg. 1659 (1998) (to be codified at 42 C.F.R. pt. 411, 424, 434, and 455.)

ment; parenteral and enteral nutrients, equipment and supplies; prosthetics, orthotics and prosthetic devices; home health services; outpatient prescription drugs; and inpatient and outpatient hospital services as of January 1, 1995.[4] It also extended coverage of the law to Medicaid financed services.[5] About two thirds of the states also place some restrictions on self-referrals, though many of the statutes were quite limited in their reach.[6]

The legislation generally prohibits a physician from referring a Medicare or Medicaid patient to an entity for the furnishing of the specified services if the physician (or an immediate family member) has a financial relationship with the entity.[7] An entity to which a prohibited referral is made may not present a Medicare or Medicaid claim, or bill any individual, third party payer or other entity for any service provided pursuant to such a referral.[8] An entity that does so will be denied payment and must refund any amounts collected.[9] Violators of these provisions are also liable for civil penalties of up to $15,000 for each service billed or refund not made where it knew or should have known of the violation.[10] In addition, physicians or entities that enter into schemes to circumvent the self-referral prohibitions (such as cross-referral schemes, in which two physicians each agree to refer their patients to laboratories owned by the other) are liable for civil money penalties of up to $100,000.[11] HHS must issue on request advisory opinions as to whether referrals (other than for clinical laboratory services) are prohibited by these provisions.[12] HHS has, as of this writing, issued two such two such opinions.

A referral is defined as the request by a physician for an item or service. This may include a request for a consultation with another physician and any test or procedure ordered by or to be performed by or under the supervision of that other physician. It may also include the request or establishment of a plan of care by a physician when the plan includes furnishing of the designated services.[13]

Financial relationships are defined broadly to include both ownership or investment interests (including equity, debt, or other interests and interests in holding companies that hold interests in designated entities) and compensation arrangements between a physician (or an immediate family member) and the designated entity.[14] Compensation arrangements are defined by

---

4. 42 U.S.C.A. § 1395nn(h)(6).

5. 42 U.S.C.A. § 1396b(s).

6. See Timothy S. Jost and Sharon L. Davies, Medicare and Medicaid Fraud and Abuse § 4–9 (1998), and, e.g., West's Fla. Stat. Ann. §§ 458.327(2)(c), 458.331(1)(gg); Official Code of Ga. Ann. § 43–1B–1—43–1B–8; Md. Code, Health Occ. § 1–301—1–306; Minn. Stat. Ann. § 147.091, subd. 1(p)(3); Vernon's Ann. Mo. Stat. § 334.253; N.J. Stat. Ann. § 45:9–22.5; N.Y., McKinney's Pub. Health L. § 238–a; Nev. Rev. Stat. §§ 630.305(3), (4). See generally Effectiveness of State Efforts to Restrict Referrals is Questioned, 2 Health L. Rep. (BNA) 494 (1993).

7. 42 U.S.C.A. § 1395nn(a)(1)(A).

8. 42 U.S.C.A. § 1395nn(a)(1)(B).

9. 42 U.S.C.A. § 1395nn(g)(1) & (2).

10. 42 U.S.C.A. § 1395nn(g)(3).

11. 42 U.S.C.A. § 1395nn(g)(4).

12. 42 U.S.C.A. § 1395nn(g)(6).

13. 42 U.S.C.A. 1395nn(h)(5). Under this definition if a physician refers a patient to another physician for consultation, and the consulting physician refers the patient to a clinical laboratory with which the initial physician has a financial relationship, the statute has been violated, even though the consulting physician has no financial relationship with the laboratory. It is prudent, therefore, that physicians notify physicians to whom they refer patients for consultation of any entities with which they have financial relationships.

14. 42 U.S.C.A. §§ 1395nn(a)(2), (h)(1). Under the proposed Stark II regulations financial relationships would include any indirect ownership or investment interest, "no matter how many levels removed from direct owner-

regulations to include all forms of remuneration.[15] Remuneration, however, does not include forgiveness of amounts owed for inaccurate or mistakenly performed tests and procedures; the correction of minor billing errors; the provision of items, devices, or supplies used to collect, transport, process, or store specimens or to order or communicate the results of tests or procedures; or the payment by an insurer or self-insured entity on a fee-for-service basis for services provided to an insured.[16]

b. Exceptions

The general prohibition of the statute is subject to an number of exceptions, some of which closely resemble the safe-harbor regulations promulgated under the anti-kickback law and some of which are more general. The overall tendency of these exceptions is to exclude from the prohibition financial arrangements that exist for reasons independent of referrals, integrated practices where the designated services are done within the practice, and situations where designated services may not be available in the absence of physician investment. Here, as elsewhere in fraud and abuse law, the exceptions encourage integration of practice, even though it is not demonstrably clear that the abuses of overutilization are any less of a threat where tests are done within a practice rather than referred outside to an entity owned by the practice.

The statute first recognizes three general exceptions to both the ownership and compensation arrangement prohibitions. The first exception covers physician's services provided personally by (or under the personal supervision of) another physician in the same group practice as the referring physician.[17] Second, the statute provides exceptions for "in-office" ancillary services furnished personally by the referring physician, by another physician in the same group practice as the referring physician, or by an individual who is directly supervised by the referring physician or another in the group.[18] The service must be provided in a building (under the proposed rules, a single building—not connected by walkways or tunnels) in which the referring physician or another group member furnishes services unrelated to the designated services or in another building used by the group practice for clinical laboratory services or for the centralized provision of other services.[19] Services must be billed by the physician performing or supervising the service, the group practice, or another entity wholly owned by the referring physician or group practice.[20] This exception does not apply to durable medical equipment (except infusion pumps) or to parenteral and enteral nutrients, equipment or supplies.[21] A third exception covers services furnished by HMOs,

ship." Proposed Stark II regulations, 63 Fed. Reg. at 1686.

15. 42 C.F.R. § 411.351) (defining "compensation arrangement" and "remuneration"). Compensation arrangements can include payments by, as well as to, the referrer. They can also include transfers and cross-subsidies among co-owners or participants in integrated delivery systems. Such arrangements must, therefore, be carefully scrutinized for self-referral violations. See Leonard C. Homer, Impact of Physician Self–Referral Prohibitions, 11 Health Span, April 1994 at 21.

16. 42 U.S.C.A. § 1395nn(h)(1).

17. 42 U.S.C.A. § 1395nn(b)(1).

18. 42 U.S.C.A. § 1395nn(b)(2)(A)(i). Under proposed Stark II regulations, direct supervision requires a physicians' presence in the office suite and immediate availability during the time the service is being performed to provide assistance and direction. 63 Fed. Reg. at 1684–85.

19. 42 U.S.C.A. § 1395nn(b)(2)(A)(ii).

20. 42 U.S.C.A. § 1395nn(b)(2)(B).

21. 42 U.S.C.A. § 1395nn(b)(2).

CMPs, and certain other prepaid plans.[22]

The Secretary is authorized to make additional exceptions for relationships that do not pose a risk of program or patient abuse. HHS has proposed three such exceptions under the Stark II proposed regulations. First, HHS has proposed a general exception for written compensation arrangements for a specified period based on fair market value and not reflecting the volume and value of referrals.[23] Second, HHS has proposed an exception for discounts based on the volume of referrals as long as the discount is passed on in full to patients or Medicare, and does not inure to the benefit of the referrer.[24] Third, HHS would recognize a de minimis exception for non cash compensation available to providers without regard to the volume and value of referrals, which is limited to $50 per gift or $300 per year in aggregate.[25] The fair market value exception in particular could easily swallow up much of the compensation prohibition.

For the first and second exceptions, a group practice is defined as a partnership, professional corporation, faculty practice plan, or other association in which:

    1) each physician group member provides substantially all physician's services through the joint use of shared office space, facilities, equipment or personnel;

    2) substantially all services of group members are provided through the group and are billed in the name of the group and amounts received are treated as receipts of the group;

    3) overhead expenses and income are distributed in accordance with methods previously determined by the group;

    4) no physician receives compensation related to the volume or value of referrals (though profit-sharing arrangements and productivity bonuses unrelated to referrals are permitted); and

    5) at least 75% of the patient encounters of the group are conducted by group physicians.[26]

Under the proposed Stark II regulations, independent contractor physicians would not qualify as group members.[27]

Note that the group practice exception does not extend to "shared laboratories," in which two or more physicians practicing independently share a suite containing a laboratory, which they use to service their patients, and which is owned by the independent physicians as a partnership or through some other form of ownership. Provisions for protection of shared laboratories were included in the 1993 House Energy and Commerce Committee bill, but were not included in the final budget legislation.

Specific exceptions also exist separately for ownership arrangements and compensation arrangements. First, an exception is recognized for ownership interests in publicly traded corporations or regulated investment companies with total assets exceeding $75 million which were purchased on terms

22. 42 U.S.C.A. § 1395nn(b)(3).

23. 63 Fed. Reg. at 1699.

24. Id. at 1694.

25. Id. at 1699.

26. 42 U.S.C.A. § 1395nn(h)(4).

27. 63 Fed. Reg. at 1689.

generally available to the public.[28] Second, ownership interests in rural hospitals are excepted, though under the Stark I regulations the exception only applies to tests done by the rural laboratory itself on its premises (if tests are referred out, they must be billed by the laboratory that does them) and to rural laboratories that furnish at least 75% of their tests to individuals who reside in rural areas and hospitals in Puerto Rico.[29] Finally, physicians who have a general ownership interest in hospitals in which they are authorized to perform services, may refer to that hospital.[30]

Several specific exceptions are also recognized solely for compensation arrangements. The first permits payment of rental for office space or for equipment under conditions nearly identical to the bribe and kickback rental safe harbor.[31]

A second exception permits physicians to refer to entities with which they have "bona fide" employment or service arrangements if the arrangement is for an identifiable service and the remuneration is consistent with fair market value and not related to the volume or value of referrals.[32]

A third exception permits remuneration for specific personal services where:

> 1) there is a written agreement signed by the parties that specifies the services covered and is for a term of at least one year;

> 2) periodic payments are provided that are set in advance, are consistent with fair market value, do not vary based on volume of referral, and are commercially reasonable; and

> 3) the arrangement covers all services provided by the physician.[33]

This exception includes physician incentive plans designed to limit directly or indirectly the provision of services with respect to individuals enrolled in the entity, as long as payments are not targeted at reducing services to specific individuals and the requirements of 42 U.S.C.A. § 1395mm(i)(8)(A)(ii) relating to HMOs are met if the plan places a physician or physician group at substantial risk.[34]

A fourth exception permits payment by hospitals to physicians where the remuneration is not related to provision of the designated services.[35] Physicians may also be compensated under a fifth exception, which permits physician recruitment arrangements to induce geographic relocation of physicians to become a member of the medical staff of a hospital, where there are

28. 42 U.S.C.A. § 1395nn(c)(1).

29. 42 U.S.C.A. § 1395nn(d)(1) & (2).

30. 42 U.S.C.A. § 1395nn(d)(3).

31. 42 U.S.C.A. § 1395nn(e)(1). Equipment rental under the proposed regulations may be on a "per click" basis, as long as payments do not reflect per click payments for patients referred by a physician-lessor. 63 Fed. Reg. at 1714.

32. 42 U.S.C.A. § 1395nn(e)(2). The 1993 amendments permit payment of productivity bonuses based on services personally per-

formed, but the proposed regulations would not permit productivity bonuses directly related to the volume or value of the physician's own referrals to herself for designated health services. 63 Fed.Reg. at 1700.

33. 42 U.S.C.A. § 1395nn(e)(3). The proposed regulations do not include any exceptions for administrative services.

34. 42 U.S.C.A. § 1395nn(e)(3)(B). See § 13–29.

35. 42 U.S.C.A. § 1395nn(e)(4).

no referral requirements and the physician remuneration takes no consideration of the volume and value of referrals.[36]

The sixth exception permits compensation for isolated transactions, such as the one time sale of property.[37] A seventh exception covers health services provided by a group practice and billed in the name of a hospital if the arrangement began prior to December 19, 1989 and specified requirements are met.[38] A final exception permits physicians to pay laboratories or other service providers for services where the price paid is consistent with fair market value.[39]

c. Liability for Bribes and Kickbacks and for Self–Referrals under the Civil False Claims Act and in Qui Tam Litigation.

Though administrative penalties are available for knowing violation of the self-referrals prohibition and have recently become available under the bribe and kickback statute as well, the self-referral prohibition has been largely self-enforcing and the bribe and kickback laws have been enforced through criminal prosecutions. There has been considerable interest in enforcing these laws, however, through the general federal Civil False Claims Act, particularly on the part of potential qui tam relators. The civil FCA, and its qui tam provisions, does not explicitly apply to bribes and kickbacks and self-referrals, and it can certainly be argued that Congress could have specifically extended FCA penalties to these offenses had it meant to.[40] On the other hand, claims submitted pursuant to certifications that the claimant has complied with all federal laws are arguably false if the claimant in fact has violated the bribe and kickback and self-referral prohibitions.

Though the issue is far from settled, the leading case to address the issue so far held that an FCA case can be brought for anti-kickback and self-referral violations if the violator has certified its own compliance with statutory or regulatory requirements and if such certifications was a prerequisite to obtaining a government benefit.[41] Though the Fifth Circuit remanded this case to determine if such a certification was in fact a prerequisite, the district court on remand held that HCFA did in fact rely on such certifications in making payment, and that claims submitted in violation of Stark were in fact false claims.[42] The Department of Justice has entered into a number of sizeable settlements of civil false claims act cases based on bribes and kick backs.

36. 42 U.S.C.A. § 1395nn(e)(5).

37. 42 U.S.C.A. § 1395nn(e)(6).

38. 42 U.S.C.A. § 1395nn(e)(7).

39. 42 U.S.C.A. § 1395nn(e)(8).

40. See U.S. Ex rel Joslin v. Community Home Health of Maryland, Inc., 984 F.Supp. 374 (D.Md.1997) (false certification of CON compliance not FCA violation). See also Robert Salcido, Mixing Oil and Water: The Government's Mistaken Use of the Medicare Anti-Kickback Statute in False Claims Prosecutions, 6 Ann. Health L. 105 (1997), Lisa Michelle Phelps, Calling off the Bounty Hunters: Dis-

crediting the Use of Alleged Anti–Kickback Violations to Support False Claims Actions, 51 Vand.L.Rev. 1003 (1998).

41. United States ex rel Thompson v. Columbia/HCA Health Corp., 125 F.3d 899 (5th cir.1997). See also United States ex rel Pogue v. American Healthcorp, 914 F.Supp. 1507 (M.D.Tenn.1996).

42. United States ex rel Thompson v. Columbia/HCA Healthcare Corp., 20 F.Supp.2d 1017 (S.D.Tex.1998).

E. CIVIL PENALTIES AND EXCLUSIONS

§ 13–10. Introduction

Extensive reference has already been made to Medicare and Medicaid civil penalties and program exclusions in the false claims section above. The original Medicare and Medicaid fraud and abuse statute adopted in 1972 provided only for criminal penalties. Criminal penalties required, of course, proof beyond a reasonable doubt. Prosecution of criminal cases also required a substantial commitment of resources from the Department of Justice to mastering the complexities of Medicare and Medicaid law and to understanding practices that violate that law. Given other demands on their resources, prosecutions were relatively infrequent in the early years of the law. In 1981, therefore, Congress amended the statute to permit the OIG authority to impose civil money penalties for violation of the Medicaid fraud laws. Authority was also added for the OIG to exclude from program participation persons who violated various program obligations. Both the civil money penalty and exclusion authorities were substantially expanded by the Medicare and Medicaid Patient and Program Protection Act of 1987 (MMPPPA), and additional grounds for OIG civil sanctions have been added with each annual budget reconciliation act. The Health Insurance Portability and Accountability Act of 1996 (HIPAA) made particularly important modifications in the program.[1]

The basic provisions for fraud and abuse civil money penalties are found at 42 U.S.C.A. § 1320a–7a, and the basic provisions for exclusions at 42 U.S.C.A. § 1320a–7. Additional provisions for exclusions and civil money penalties are found, however, throughout the Social Security Act. Regulations implementing the civil money penalty authority are found at 42 C.F.R. Pt. 1003, Medicare exclusions at 42 C.F.R. Pt. 1001, and Medicaid exclusions at 42 C.F.R. Pt. 1002.[2]

§ 13–11. Exclusions, Denials, and Terminations

a. *Generally*

If an entity or individual is "excluded," neither Medicare nor a state health care program may pay for services rendered by the excluded person or entity or for services rendered by the order of, or under the supervision of, an excluded person, regardless of whether the claim in question is assigned or non-assigned.[1] Thus, a hospital that renders services to a beneficiary admitted by an "excluded" physician could not receive Medicare payment for the stay unless it could show that it did not know or have reason to know of the exclusion.[2] A person who submits a claim for which payment cannot be made because of an exclusion is also liable for a civil penalty, as is an excluded person who retains an interest in or manages an entity participating in Medicare or a state health program, or an entity that knowingly contracts with an excluded entity.[3]

---

§ 13–10

1. These were implemented by regulations published at 63 Fed.Reg. 46676 (1998), codified at 42 C.F.R. Parts 1000, 1001, 1002, and 1005.

2. Final regulations implementing the MMPPPA were adopted on January 29, 1992, and appear at 57 Fed. Reg. 3298 (1992).

1. 42 U.S.C.A. §§ 1320a07(a) & (b), 1395u(j)(2), 1395y(e), 1396b(i)(2); 42 C.F.R. § 1001.2.

2. 42 U.S.C.A. § 1395y(e)(1)(B).

3. 42 U.S.C.A. § 1320a–7a(a)(1)(D), (a)(4) & (a)(6).

While civil money penalties and exclusion are often available for the same conduct, the focus of the two sanctions is different. Civil money penalties are imposed to make the wrongdoer pay the government for the misconduct and to deter future misconduct, in particular where the motivation for the misconduct is primarily financial. Exclusion, on the other hand, is designed to remove the sanctioned individual or entity from the program, and is particularly appropriate when the continued participation of an individual or entity poses a risk to the program or its beneficiaries. If, however, a person successfully defends against imposition of a civil penalty, the OIG will not subsequently institute exclusion proceedings for the same offense.

While the key issue in determining whether or not to exclude a provider or practitioner who commits an offense warranting exclusion is "trustworthiness," the Departmental Appeals Board decided in the *Hanlester* case, discussed above, that exclusion may be appropriate even though the OIG does not prove that the respondent is likely to engage in unlawful or harmful conduct in the future.[4] In *Hanlester*, the ALJ had decided that although three of the respondents had violated the law, exclusion would serve no purpose because of the lack of evidence that they would violate it again in the future.[5] The DAB reversed. Though it did not endorse the OIG's position that exclusion should be automatic whenever an excludable offense is found, it did hold that the respondent bears the burden of proof of establishing trustworthiness once a violation if found, a burden not met in the *Hanlester* case.[6] It further noted that, although the primary purpose of exclusion was remedial, incidental deterrent or punitive effects did not invalidate a remedial sanction.[7] The DAB also held that "willingness to flirt" with a violation was enough to ground the sanction, even though the exact reach of the law was unclear before the decision in the case.[8] The *Hanlester* decision was reversed in part on appeal. The Court of Appeals concluded that all but one of the individual defendant's had not violated the bribe and kickback statute because they lacked sufficient mens rea. It upheld the exclusion of one individual, and the vicarious liability of the corporations that employed her. It reversed the corporate exclusions, however, finding that the guilt of the corporations was strictly derivative, and with the exclusion of the guilty individual, no remedial purpose was served by excluding her employers.[9] Hanlester, therefore, places a heavy burden on the Government pursuing exclusions to show that the party against the exclusion is sought is itself guilty of an excludable defense, requiring a remedial sanction.

Exclusion is a particularly harsh sanction because some practitioners are almost totally dependent on Medicare and Medicaid for their business. Some have argued, therefore, that mandatory exclusion is a cruel and unusual punishment, violative of the Eighth Amendment. The cruel and unusual punishment prohibition of the Eighth Amendment, however, applies only to criminal punishments and not to civil sanctions.[10] Civil sanctions disqualifying

4. [1992–2 Transfer Binder] Medicare & Medicaid Guide (CCH), ¶ 40,406B (July 24, 1992), rev'd in part, 51 F.3d 1390 (9th Cir. 1995).

5. [1992–2 Transfer Binder] Medicare & Medicaid Guide (CCH), ¶ 40,064 (Mar. 10, 1992).

6. Hanlester, supra note 4 at 31,799–31,-801.

7. Id. at 31,801.

8. Id. at 31,803.

9. 51 F.3d 1390, 1402 (9th Cir. 1995).

10. See e.g., Powell v. Texas, 392 U.S. 514, 531–32, 88 S.Ct. 2145, 2153–54, 20 L.Ed.2d

individuals from receiving certain benefits based on prior convictions do not violate the Eighth Amendment, even when they apply automatically to all offenders without regard to the circumstances of the offense,[11] and at least one ALJ has held that Medicare exclusions do not.[12] The statute has also been upheld against due process objections.[13]

b. Mandatory Exclusions

Exclusion from program participation for at least five years is mandatory under four circumstances. The first is conviction of a criminal offense related to the delivery of an item or service reimbursed under Medicare or a state health care program.[14] This provision has already been discussed above.[15] The second is conviction of a crime relating to neglect or abuse of patients in connection with the delivery of health care.[16] The third is conviction of a felony in connection with the delivery of a health care item or service or of a felony relating to financial misconduct in a health care program financed by federal, state, or local government.[17] The fourth is conviction of a felony relating to controlled substances.[18] Mandatory exclusions can be for a period in excess of five years where there are aggravating circumstances. A person convicted of three or more criminal offenses involving Medicare or a state health care program must be permanently excluded.[19]

c. Discretionary Exclusions

The basic exclusion statute also authorizes discretionary exclusions under a variety of circumstances. In determining the length of these exclusions, the aggravating and mitigating factors considered in determining the length of mandatory exclusions, if appropriate, are generally considered. In addition the availability of alternative sources of health care in the community and other circumstances specifically applicable to the particular violation are considered. Five of these permissive exclusion authorities are derivative—they are based on the actions of another. These include exclusions for:

　　　1) conviction of misdemeanors relating to fraud, theft, embezzlement, breach of fiduciary duty or other financial misconduct in the delivery of health care in general or in a government health care program or of financial misconduct in other government programs;[20]

　　　2) conviction of obstruction or interference with a criminal investigation related to Medicare or state health care program fraud, patient neglect or abuse, or fraud in the delivery of health care or in a governmental program;[21]

1254 (1968); Stamp v. Commissioner of Internal Revenue, 579 F.Supp. 168, 171 (N.D.Ill. 1984); Popow v. City of Margate, 476 F.Supp. 1237, 1242 n. 2 (1979).

11. See Blount v. Smith, 440 F.Supp. 528, 533 (M.D.Pa.1977).

12. In re Strausbaugh [1992 Transfer Binder] Medicare & Medicaid Guide (CCH), ¶ 40,-244 at 30,702 (Sept. 16, 1991).

13. Erickson v. U.S.D.H.H.S. 67 F.3d 858 (9th Cir.1995).

14. 42 U.S.C.A. § 1320a–7(a)(1). Though these exclusions are mandatory, they may be waived at the request of a state where the excluded individual or entity is a sole community physician or the sole source of essential specialized services in a community. 42 U.S.C.A. § 1320a–7(c)(3)(B); 42 C.F.R. § 1001.1801(b).

15. See supra at § 13.4(c).

16. 42 U.S.C.A. § 1320a–7(a)(2).

17. 42 U.S.C.A. § 1320a–7(a)(3).

18. 42 U.S.C.A. § 1320a–7(a)(4).

19. 42 U.S.C.A. § 1320a–7(c)(3)(G).

20. 42 U.S.C.A. § 1320a–7(b)(1).

21. 42 U.S.C.A. § 1320a–7(b)(2).

3) conviction of crimes relating to the unlawful manufacture, distribution, prescribing or dispensing of a controlled substance;[22]

4) revocation or suspension of a license to provide health care, or surrender of such a license while a disciplinary proceeding was pending, for reasons bearing on professional competence or performance or financial integrity;[23] and

5) exclusion from participation in another federal health care program, including Veteran's Administration programs or CHAMPUS, or a state health care program.[24]

Exclusions under the first three authorities are normally for three years, and under the last two for the period of time that the revocation, suspension, or exclusion persists.[25]

The statute also authorizes a number of "nonderivative" grounds for exclusions, including:

1) filing of claims to Medicare or a state health care program including charges or costs substantially in excess of usual claims or costs;[26]

2) furnishing health care to any patient (whether or not eligible for services under Medicare or a state health care program) substantially in excess of the needs of such patients or of a quality that fails to meet professionally recognized standards;[27]

3) in the case of a Medicaid HMO, a primary care case-management system, a specialty physician services arrangement, or Medicare HMO or CMP, failing substantially to provide medically necessary services, where the failure adversely affects a plan member or is substantially likely to do so;[28]

4) committing an act which is a criminal offense under the criminal provisions of the fraud and abuse laws,[29] including false claims and kickbacks,[30] or for which a fraud and abuse civil penalty can be imposed;[31]

5) being owned or managed by a person, or having a person as an officer, director, agent, or managing employee, who has been convicted criminally of Medicare or Medicaid fraud and abuse or been subjected to a fraud and abuse exclusion or civil penalty or being owned or managed by a family member or household member of a sanctioned individual to which an entity was transferred to avoid exclusion;[32]

6) failing to make disclosures required by law[33] concerning the identity of individuals with an ownership or control interest in the entity or

22. 42 U.S.C.A. § 1320a–7(b)(3).

23. 42 U.S.C.A. § 1320a–7(b)(4).

24. 42 U.S.C.A. § 1320a–7(b)(5).

25. 42 U.S.C.A. § 1320a–7(c)(3)(D) & (E).

26. 42 U.S.C.A. § 1320a–7(b)(6)(A). HHS has declined to define "usual charges" or "substantially in excess," stating that it will analyze billing patterns on a case-by-case basis.

27. 42 U.S.C.A. § 1320a–7(b)(6)(B). These exclusions must last at least a year. This provision overlaps the authority of the OIG to exclude providers, practitioners or suppliers upon the recommendation of a Medicare Peer Review Organization for utilization or quality related problems;

28. 42 U.S.C.A. § 1320a–7(b)(6)(C), (D).

29. 42 U.S.C.A. § 1320a–7b.

30. 42 C.F.R. §§ 1001.901, 1001.951.

31. Under 42 U.S.C.A. § 1320a–7a. 42 U.S.C.A. § 1320a–7(b)(7).

32. 42 U.S.C.A. § 1320a–7(b)(8).

33. 42 U.S.C.A. §§ 1320a–3, 1320a–5.

who act as officers, directors, agents or managing employees of the entity;[34]

7) failing to make on request statutorily required disclosures[35] regarding the ownership of subcontractors with whom the entity has had business transactions within the preceding twelve months in excess of $25,000 or significant business transactions between the entity and any subcontractor or wholly owned supplier within the preceding five years;[36]

8) failing to supply upon request information (such as medical records or x-rays) necessary to determine whether Medicare or Medicaid payments are due or their amount, or to permit examination of records to verify the information;[37]

9) failing to grant immediate (on the spot) access for HHS or appropriate state agencies to certain facilities for the purposes of performing reviews or surveys or determining compliance with conditions of participation, or, access for the OIG or for state Medicaid control units upon twenty-four hours notice to records and documents;[38]

10) in the case of a hospital, failing to comply substantially with a corrective action plan required under 42 U.S.C.A. § 1395ww(f)(2) to correct actions taken by the hospital to circumvent DRG-prospective payment, such as inappropriate or multiple admissions or improper practice patterns;[39]

11) defaulting on a health education loan or scholarship obligation where all reasonable steps have been taken to secure repayment;[40] or

12) having a direct or indirect controlling interest in a sanctioned entity where the owner knows or should know of the action on which the sanction is based, or being an officer or managing employee of a sanctioned entity.[41]

The OIG may also exclude a practitioner, provider or supplier on the recommendation of a PRO for certain violations. This authority is explored in chapter 3. Exclusions may also be based on certain improper charges or billing practices, noted above in § 13–3.

34. 42 U.S.C.A. § 1320a–7(b)(9). As to this and the next two authorities dealing with failure to provide required information, exclusions will not be imposed for isolated or unintentional violations unless they have a significant impact on the program or its beneficiaries.

35. 42 U.S.C.A. § 1320a–3.

36. 42 U.S.C.A. § 1320a–7(b)(10).

37. 42 U.S.C.A. § 1320a–7(b)(11).

38. 42 U.S.C.A. § 1320a–7(b)(12); 42 C.F.R. § 1001.1301(a)(3). If there is reason to believe that records are about to be altered or destroyed, the OIG or MCUs can insist on immediate access. On the other hand, entities can be granted more than twenty-four hours to comply where unusual situations require a longer period of time.

39. 42 U.S.C.A. § 1320a–7(b)(13). In review of these exclusions, only information regarding compliance with the corrective action plan would be considered.

40. 42 U.S.C.A. § 1320a–7(b)(14). This exclusion is not to be imposed if the physician is a sole community physician or sole source of essential specialized services in a community and the state requests that the physician not be excluded. The Secretary must also take into account the impact that an exclusion will have on access to services under Medicare and Medicaid. The OIG will rely on the Public Health Service to take the required reasonable actions to collect, but will find that all reasonable steps have been taken if the PHS offers a Medicare offset agreement.

41. 42 U.S.C.A. § 1320a–7(b)(15)

d. Consequences of Exclusion

If the OIG excludes an individual or entity from Medicare program participation, state Medicaid agencies must also exclude that individual or entity from participation in Medicaid for the same period of time.[42] States may, however, request that exclusion from state health programs be waived.[43] States may also at their own initiative exclude an individual or entity from participation in Medicaid for any of the reasons that the individual or entity could have been excluded from participation under Medicare under 42 U.S.C.A. §§ 1320a–7, 1320a–7a, or 1395cc(b)(2), or may impose exclusions for longer periods of time than those imposed by the OIG.[44] States must also exclude from their Medicaid programs Medicaid managed care organizations that are owned or managed by or that have substantial contractual relationships with individuals who have been convicted of certain crimes or sanctioned by Medicare, or who employ or contract with individuals excluded from Medicare participation.[45] Under Executive Orders 12549 and 12689, Medicare exclusions are also given government-wide effect to bar participation in any other federal program.[46]

The OIG must notify appropriate state or local licensing or certification agencies of exclusion, request that an appropriate investigation be made and sanctions invoked, and request that the agency inform the OIG of any action it takes in response to the request.[47] The OIG also gives notice of the program exclusion to the public; entities where the person excluded is employed or serves in some capacity; state Medicaid fraud control units; PROs; hospitals, skilled nursing facilities, home health agencies and health maintenance organizations; medical societies and other professional organizations; contractors, health care prepayment plans, private insurance companies and other affected agencies and organizations; state and area agencies on aging; the National Practitioner Data Bank; other departmental operating divisions, federal agencies, and other agencies or organizations, as appropriate; and to the Attorney General in the case of an mandatory exclusion for a program-related crime to which 21 U.S.C.A. 824(a)(5) (involving controlled substances) applies.[48]

In addition to the authorities the exclusion statute provides for excluding providers and practitioners entirely from program participation, various authorities exist elsewhere in the Medicare and Medicaid statutes for denying payment for particular services or for terminating providers from eligibility to receive Medicare or Medicaid payments.

e. Terminating or Refusing to Renew Provider Agreements

General authority for refusing to enter into or to renew, or for terminating, provider agreements that fail to meet the requirements of provider status is found in 42 U.S.C.A. § 1395cc. Special provisions also exist authorizing termination of other entities, including hospital providers of extended care services,[49] Medicare + Choice organizations,[50] end stage renal disease facilities or providers, and end stage renal disease network administrative organiza-

42. 42 U.S.C.A. §§ 1320a–7(d), 1396a(a)(39).

43. 42 U.S.C.A. § 1320a–7(d)(3)(B).

44. 42 U.S.C.A. §§ 1320a–7(d)(3)(B)(ii); 1396a(p)(1).

45. 42 U.S.C.A. § 1396a(p)(2).

46. 42 C.F.R. § 1001.1901.

47. 42 U.S.C.A. § 1320a–7(e).

48. 42 C.F.R. § 1003.129.

49. 42 U.S.C.A. § 1395tt(c).

50. 42 U.S.C.A. § 1395w–7(c)(2), (g), & (h).

tions.[51] Hospitals are also subject to termination or suspension of their provider agreements for violation of the Emergency Medical Treatment Act.[52] The Medicaid statute or regulations provide for termination of intermediate care facilities for the mentally retarded,[53] psychiatric facilities,[54] nursing facilities,[55] rural health clinics,[56] and drug manufacturers and wholesalers who do not comply with drug rebate requirements.[57] In addition, exclusion of a provider may result in termination of the provider agreement.[58]

§ 13–12. Civil Money Penalty Authorities

Provisions authorizing civil money penalties and assessments for false claims, other improper billing practices, and bribes and kickbacks have been discussed above. There are a number of other civil money penalty authorities found in the Medicare and Medicaid statutes.[1]

The basic civil money penalty statute, 42 U.S.C.A. § 1320a–7a, also authorizes civil money penalties of up to $15,000 for giving any person information that the person giving the information knows or should know to be false or misleading that could reasonably be expected to influence a decision as to when to discharge the person who was given the information or another person from the hospital.[2]

Another provision of the basic civil money penalty statute, adopted in 1986, authorizes civil money penalties of up to $2000 per patient against hospitals or rural primary care hospitals that knowingly make a payment, directly or indirectly, to a physician to reduce or limit services to a Medicare or Medicaid patient under the care of the physician or against physicians who accept such payments.[3] This provision addresses the reverse situation from that addressed by the antikickback and self-referral provisions, which are aimed at overprovision of care. The OIG has recently interpreted this "underprovision" prohibition to exclude "gainsharing" arrangements, under which a hospital shares a portion of cost-savings achieved by the hospital with its physicians in exchange for efforts by the physicians to reduce costs, usually by sharing a predetermined share of a sum or money.[4]

Until 1990 this provision also extended to HMOs and CMPs with risk contacts, which face similar incentives for underservice. The HMO situation was more difficult, however, since managed care is based on the notion of controlling utilization and financial relationships between HMOs and their physicians are much more complex. For this reason, Congress first delayed implementation of this provision with respect to HMOs and then repealed it. In its place Congress adopted provisions prohibiting HMOs and CMPs (now

---

51. 42 U.S.C.A. § 1395rr(c)(1)(A)(ii)(II), (c)(3).

52. 42 U.S.C.A. § 1395dd(d).

53. 42 U.S.C.A. §§ 1396r–3(e)(2), 1396a(i)(1).

54. 42 U.S.C.A. § 1396a(y).

55. 42 U.S.C.A. § 1396r(h)(1).

56. 42 U.S.C.A. § 1396i(9); 42 C.F.R. § 405.2404(b).

57. 42 U.S.C.A. § 1396r–8(b)(4)(B).

58. 42 U.S.C.A. § 1395cc(b)(2)(C).

1. See 42 C.F.R. § 1003.102 for a further partial listing of Medicare and Medicaid civil penalty authorities. See also Timothy S. Jost & Sharon L. Davies, Medicare and Medicaid Fraud and Abuse, § 5–4 (1998).

2. 42 U.S.C.A. § 1320a–7a(a)(3).

3. 42 U.S.C.A. § 1320a–7a(b)(1), (2).

4. 64 Fed. Reg. 491617 (1999). See HHS IG prohibits Gainsharing, Says CMP Law Bans Incentives to Curb Care, 8 BNA Health Law Rptr. 1133 (1999).

Medicare + Choice organizations) from making specific payments to induce physicians to withhold or limit services from particular enrollees and requiring Medicare + Choice organizations to provide "adequate and appropriate" stop-loss insurance for physicians or physician groups who are at "substantial" financial risk for services they provide.[5] They must also periodically survey their membership to determine their participants degree of access to services and satisfaction with quality and provide HHS with descriptive information about their incentive plans.[6] Plans are liable for civil fines of up to $25,000 per violation and suspension of enrollments or plan payments for violations of these provisions.[7]

Other civil money penalty provisions are found throughout the Medicare and Medicaid statutes and address a wide variety of concerns. Medicare + Choice and Medicaid managed care organizations are subject to intermediate sanctions, including civil penalties, for a variety of violations, described in chapters 11 and 12.

Civil money penalties that may be imposed against Medicare and Medicaid nursing facilities, home health care agencies and clinical laboratories are discussed elsewhere in this hornbook (chapter 1). Separate chapters also discuss civil money penalties that may be imposed by the OIG upon the recommendation of PROs (chapter 3), and sanctions under the emergency medical treatment act (chapter 10).

The civil money authorities generally grant the OIG considerable discretion in determining the proper amount of a civil money penalty or assessment to impose. Factors considered in imposing civil money penalties for false claims were discussed above. The regulations also list factors considered in imposing other penalties and assessments.[8] Generally, where there are substantial aggravating factors the amount should be set sufficiently close to the maximum amount to reflect this fact, and where there are substantial mitigating factors the penalty or assessment must be correspondingly reduced.[9] Absent extraordinary mitigating factors, however, the amount should never be less than twice the amount of damages and costs incurred by the United States or any state, including costs attributable to the investigation, prosecution and administrative review of the case.[10] Doubling this amount assures that less tangible costs, such as the diversion of scarce resources from and the erosion of public confidence in the integrity of federal and state health care programs, are also considered.[11] An ALJ imposing a civil sanction must also independently consider whether, however, the sanction imposed results in an unconstitutionally excessive sanction.[12]

§ 13–13. Investigations

5. 42 U.S.C.A. § 1395w–22(j)(4).
6. Id.
7. 42 U.S.C.A. § 1395w–27(g).
8. 42 C.F.R. § 1003.106.
9. 42 C.F.R. § 1003.106(c)(1), (2).
10. 42 C.F.R. § 1003.106(c)(3).

11. See Chapman v. U.S., Department of Health and Human Servs., 821 F.2d 523, 528 (10th Cir.1987); Mayers v. United States Dep't of Health and Human Servs., 806 F.2d 995, 999 (11th Cir.1986).

12. 42 C.F.R. § 1003.106(e)(1).

F. INVESTIGATIONS BY THE OFFICE OF INSPECTOR GENERAL AND COMPLIANCE PLANS

The OIG has wide-ranging investigative powers. As the consequences of discovery of improper practices by the OIG can be very serious, OIG investigations must be taken very seriously. Several excellent articles are available discussing OIG audits and investigations.[1] Fraud and abuse investigations are also conducted by state Medicaid fraud control units (discussed below), by the FBI, and by the Comptroller General.[2]

§ 13–14. Compliance Plans

Because violations of the fraud and abuse laws are commonly criminal offenses, the federal sentencing guidelines are an important consideration for potential violators. With respect to organizational violators, a central consideration is the organization's attempts prior to the offense to assure corporate compliance.[1] An organization that has an operational compliance program in place faces much less severe sanctions if its employees do nonetheless commit fraud. It is also, of course, less likely that an organization's employees will violate the fraud and abuse laws if a compliance program is functioning. For these reasons, health care organizations that contract with the government have gone to a great deal of effort in recent years to devise and implement corporate compliance plans. The OIG of HHS has encouraged this trend by publishing model compliance plans for various types of providers. It also routinely insists on "corporate integrity agreements" implementing compliance plans when it settles fraud cases. Finally, providers also hope that by adopting corporate compliance plans they will make qui tam cases less likely and more defensible.[2]

HHS has as of the middle of 1999 issued compliance program guides for hospitals, home health agencies, clinical laboratories, and third-party medical billing companies, and durable medical equipment, orthotics and prosthetic companies, and is working on guidelines for Medicare + Choice organizations and hospices. Compliance guides provide generally for seven components:

- written compliance policies and procedures, including standards of conduct;

- designation of a compliance officer responsible for operating and monitoring the compliance program (preferably an officer who reports to high level leadership, for example, directly to the board of directors);

- training of employees in compliance standards and procedures

- a reporting mechanism to receive anonymous complaints;

- corrective action polices and procedures, including disciplinary policies;

- monitoring and auditing systems in place and operation;

§ 13–13

1. James G. Sheehan, Fraud Investigations and Prosecutions: A Perspective, in 1992 Health Law Handbook (Alice G. Gosfield, ed. 1992); Eugene Tillman and Carol Colborn, Fraud and Abuse Audits and Investigations: Practical Guidelines, in 1991 Health Law Handbook (Alice G. Gosfield, ed. 1991); Robert A. Griffith, Techniques for Defending Health Care Fraud and Abuse Cases, 4 Medical Staff Counsellor, Spring 1990 at 61.

2. 42 U.S.C.A. § 1320a–4.

§ 13–14

1. Timothy S. Jost & Sharon L. Davies, Medicare and Medicaid Fraud and Abuse, §§ 8–8—8–21 (1998).

2. But see, Ankur J. Goel, Compliance and the Risks of Whistleblower Lawsuits and Disclosures to the Government, in 1999 Health Law Handbook, 367 (Alice G. Gosfield, ed., 1999).

• investigations and correction of problems, including, where appropriate, removing of sanctioned individuals.[3]

The OIG also encourages self-reporting of violations that are uncovered, which may be required under a corporate integrity agreement.[4] Self-reporting may reduce fines and penalties, and diminish the risk of qui tam suits, but does not guaranty leniency on the part of the government, and thus is accompanied by some risk.

G. STATE MEDICAID FRAUD AND ABUSE LAWS

§ 13–15. State Medicaid Fraud and Abuse Laws

Though the federal fraud and abuse laws have garnered much more attention in recent years, the states have also been very active in prosecuting Medicaid fraud and abuse. Most states have statutes specifically prohibiting Medicaid fraud, though some rely on more general statutes prohibiting fraud or theft by deception or false statements to public officials.[1] Statutes prohibiting false claims or obtaining payments through misrepresentation are most common,[2] though many states also prohibit bribes and kickbacks.[3] Some statutes closely track the federal law, or some earlier version of it.[4] Only a few include the provisions added by the MMPPPA dealing with exceptions to the bribe and kickback prohibition, however.[5] Several states have additional prohibitions supplementing the federal law.[6] Thus a number of states have

3. See, e.g. U.S. General Accounting Office, Medicare: Early Evidence of Compliance Program Effectiveness is Inconclusive, GAO/HEHS–99–59 (1999); Sanford V.Teplitzky & S. Craig Holden, 1997 Developments in Health Care Fraud and Abuse, in Health Law Handbook, 1998, 85 (Alice G. Gosfield, ed., 1998).

4. See, Office of the Inspector General, Publication of OIG's Provider Self–Disclosure Protocol, 63 Fed. Reg. 58399 (1998).

§ 13–15

1. See Pamela Bucy, Health Care Fraud (1996); Timothy S. Jost & Sharon L. Davies, Medicare and Medicaid Fraud and Abuse, § 2–6 (1998); Pamela H Bucy, Fraud by Fright: White Collar Crime by Health Care Providers, N.C.L.Rev. 855 (1989). See e.g., Me. Rev. Stat. Ann. tit. 17–A § 354; McKinney's—N.Y. Penal Law § 175.35. See also, listing state Medicaid fraud statutes, Gregory P. Miller, Recent Developments in the Enforcement and Interpretation of Medicare/Medicaid Anti–Fraud and Abuse Statutes, in Medicare Fraud and Abuse: Understanding the Law, 32, 36–39 (Jeanie M. Johnson & Janet Seifert, eds., 1986); Mary J. Cavins, Annotation, Criminal Prosecution or Disciplinary Action Against Medical Practitioner for Fraud in Connection with Claims under Medicaid, Medicare, or Similar Welfare Program for Providing Medical Services, 50 A.L.R.3d 549 (1973). The North Carolina Medicaid Investigations Unit has compiled a comprehensive digest of published federal and state appellate court decisions involving Medicare and Medicaid cases.

2. See Conn. Gen. Stat. Ann. § 17B–99, 53A–290—53A–296; West's Fla. Stat. Ann. § 409.920; Hawaii. Rev. Stat. § 346–43.5; La. Stat. Ann.–Rev. Stat. § 14:70.1; Mich. Comp. Laws Ann. 400.607; Miss. Code §§ 43–13–13, 43–13–129, 43–13–205, 43–13–213, 43–13–217; N.H. Rev. Stat. Ann. § 167:17–b; N.M. Stat. Ann. §§ 30–44–1—30–44–8; Ohio Rev. Code. Ann. § 2913.40.

3. West's Fla. Stat. Ann. § 409.920; Md. Code art. 27, § 230B(5); Miss. Code § 43–13–207; N.M. Stat. Ann. § 30–44–7. See, as an example of a state case involving a kickback issue, People v. Bynum, 145 Ill.Dec. 468, 557 N.E.2d 238 (Ill.App.1990) (holding that kickback includes referring laboratory work to laboratory that pays salary of doctor's receptionist).

4. E.g., Ark. Code Ann. § 5–55–111(6); 305 ILCS 5/8A–3; N.J. Stat. Ann. § 30:4D–17(c).

5. See e.g., 305 ILCS 5/8A–3; N.J. Stat. Ann. § 30:4D–17(c); R.I.Gen. Laws. § 40–8.2–3. Other states create their own exceptions.

6. See e.g., N.M. Stat. Ann. 30–44–5 (crime to fail to retain records documenting Medicaid claims for 5 years); R.I.Gen. Laws § 40–8.2–3(a)(3) (submitting claim for which provider has already received or claimed reimbursement from another source).

prohibitions against the provision of unnecessary care[7] or care of inadequate quality.[8] Several prohibit providers and practitioners from charging Medicaid a fee higher than they charge members of the general public.[9] State Medicaid fraud statutes are routinely upheld against constitutional challenges based on vagueness.[10]

Statutes authorizing civil penalties[11] or restitution[12] and suspension or termination from program participation of those who commit Medicaid fraud are also frequent.[13] Penalties based on double or triple the amount fraudulently obtained are common.[14] Other states provide for forfeiture of profits or property attributable to the offense.[15] Several states have provision for return of improperly obtained payments with interest, but without additional penalties, where no intention to defraud is shown.[16] A number of states also provide for assessments for the cost of the investigation in addition to any other penalties.[17] Finally, several states have qui tam or "whistleblower" statutes, allowing persons whose complaints result in civil recoveries for the state to share in the recovery.[18] Under most state statutes authorizing civil penalties, the penalties must be imposed through judicial proceedings.[19] Such penalties are generally held to be civil in nature and thus not to impose double jeopardy where there is also a criminal conviction.[20]

The state of mind that must be shown to establish liability is one of the most frequently litigated issues under the state Medicaid fraud statutes. Most statutes establish a standard of knowingly committing an offense. Though some state courts impose strict requirements for showing intent to defraud,[21]

7. Conn. Gen. Stat. Ann. § 53a–290(3) & (4) (performing of services not needed or without prior authorization, where required); West's Fla. Stat.Ann. § 409.913 (furnishing care that is not medically necessary.)

8. West's Fla. Stat. Ann. § 409.913(1)(A)(failure to meet professionally recognized standards of care); 305 ILCS 5/8–7.1 (termination for care that is harmful or of "grossly inferior quality").

9. E.g. Pa. Stat. tit. 62, § 1407(a)(8).

10. People v. Bynum, 145 Ill.Dec. 468, 557 N.E.2d 238 (Ill.App.1990); State v. Dorn, 496 A.2d 451 (Vt.1985).

11. Ark. Code Ann. § 5–55–108; West's Fla. Stat. Ann. § 409.913(15); Miss. Code § 43–13–225. See also Francis M. Dougherty, Annotation, Imposition of Civil Penalties, Under State Statute, Upon Medical Practitioners for Fraud in Connection with Claims Under Medicaid, Medicare, or Similar Welfare Programs for Providing Medical Services, 32 A.L.R. 4th 671 (1984).

12. See Ark. Code Ann. § 5–55–107.

13. Ark. Code Ann. § 5–55–110; Conn. Gen. Stat. Ann. § 17B–99.

14. See e.g., Ark. Code Ann. § 5–55–108 (double amount fraudulently received plus up to $2000 for each claim judicially found to be fraudulently claimed); 305 ILCS 5/8–A–7(b) (triple damages plus $2000 per violation).

15. See e.g., 305 ILCS 5/8–7(b).

16. See e.g., N.J. St. Ann. § 30:4D–17(f); Ohio Rev. Code. § 5111.03(D).

17. See e.g., N.M. Stat. Ann. § 30–44–8(C); Ohio. Rev. Code § 5111.03(B)(4); Okla. Stat. Ann. tit. 56, § 1007(A)(3).

18. See, John T. Boese & Shannon L. Haralson, Private Enforcement of State Fraud Laws: A Comparative Analysis of State Qui Tam Provisions, 31 J. Health & Hosp. L. 34 (1998).

19. See Ark. Code Ann. § 5–55–108; 305 ILCS 5/8A–7(c); N.H. Rev.Stat. Ann. ch. 167, § 61. But see West's Fla. Stat. Ann. § 409.913(15) (authorizing administrative imposition of sanctions).

20. People ex rel. Dep't of Pub. Aid v. Bell, 77 Ill.Dec. 422, 460 N.E.2d 478 (Ill.App.1984); State Dep't of Public Aid v. Greenlee, 19 Ill. Dec. 78, 378 N.E.2d 579 (Ill.App.1978); In re Garay, 444 A.2d 1107 (N.J.1982); Harvey–Cook v. Miroff, 515 N.Y.S.2d 551 (N.Y.App.Div.), appeal denied 526 N.Y.S.2d 436, 521 N.E.2d 443 (N.Y.1988).

21. People v. Lee, 351 N.W.2d 294, 300 (Mich.App.1984) (statistical evidence of improbability of treatment not enough); Commonwealth v. Lurie, 569 A.2d 329 (Pa.1990) (Medicaid fraud requires proof of knowing or intentional conduct, mere recklessness or negligence do not suffice).

others are more open to circumstantial evidence.[22] The Florida statute goes
the furthest in imposing liability by creating an inference that one who signs
a false claim knows it to be false.[23]

Another issue that has been litigated in several cases is the applicability
of evidentiary privileges in resisting subpoenas for patient records or other
documents. Fifth Amendment privileges are routinely rejected either because
the records are required to be kept by law[24] or because the records are
corporate records (if the records are owned by a clinic or professional
corporation).[25] Though doctor-patient privilege claims have prevailed in a few
cases,[26] privilege or privacy claims are generally rejected either on the grounds
that the federal law overrides state privileges,[27] that state interest in prosecuting Medicaid claims has generally been held to take precedence over privileges,[28] or that Medicaid recipients have waived the privilege in submitting
claims.[29]

The federal statute authorizes federal funding for state Medicaid fraud
control units (MFCUs).[30] All states must have such units unless they can
demonstrate that the unit would not be cost-effective because minimal Medicaid fraud exists in the state and beneficiaries are adequately protected from
neglect and abuse without a MFCU.[31]

22. See e.g., State v. Romero, 574 So.2d 330
(La.1990) (instructions to bill for comprehensive visits regardless of services rendered constitute fraud); State v. McDermitt, 406 So.2d
195 (La.1981); People v. American Medical
Centers of Mich., 324 N.W.2d 782 (Mich.App.
1982), cert. denied 464 U.S. 1009, 104 S.Ct.
529, 78 L.Ed.2d 711 (1983) (constructive
knowledge sufficient to convict clinic and physician of Medicaid fraud).

23. West's Fla. Stat. Ann. § 409.920(5).

24. Grand Jury v. Kuriansky, 513 N.Y.S.2d
359, 505 N.E.2d 925 (N.Y.1987), cert. denied
482 U.S. 928, 107 S.Ct. 3211, 96 L.Ed.2d 698
(1987).

25. In re Special Investigation No. 281, 473
A.2d 1 (Md.1984); Matter of Progressive Labs,
505 N.Y.S.2d 787 (N.Y.1986).

26. E.g., Hawaii Psychiatric Soc'y v. Ari-
yoshi, 481 F.Supp. 1028 (D.C.Hawai'i 1979)
(patient psychiatric records cannot be seized
under administrative warrant where state's
interest supporting seizure does not outweigh
privacy interests). See also Commonwealth v.

Kobrin, 479 N.E.2d 674 (Mass.1985) (portions
of records dealing with appointments, fees, diagnoses, treatment plans and recommendations and somatic therapies must be disclosed
to grand jury; portions of records that reflected patient's thoughts and feelings and
psychotherapeutic dialogue were privileged).

27. People v. Ekong, 164 Ill.Dec. 25, 582
N.E.2d 233 (Ill.App.1991).

28. McKirdy v. Superior Court, 188 Cal.
Rptr. 143 (Cal.App.1982) (psychotherapist patient files); In re A Special Investigation No.
202, 452 A.2d 458 (Md.App.1982) (accoun-
tant/client privilege not applicable); In re
Grand Jury Investigation, 441 A.2d 525 (R.I.
1982) (federal Medicaid fraud law preempts
state privileges).

29. In re Search Warrant, 709 P.2d 597
(Colo.App.1985).

30. 42 U.S.C.A. § 1396b(a)(6). After the
initial 12 calendar quarters of operation the
funding decreases to 75%.

31. 42 U.S.C.A. § 1396a(a)(61).

Chapter 14

ANTITRUST LAW

Table of Sections

A. STATUTES AND INTERPRETATIVE PRINCIPLES

Research References

Am Jur 2d, Monopolies, Restraints of Trade, and Unfair Trade Practices §§ 426, 427

ALR Index: Antitrust Laws; Restraints of Trade and Monopolies

ALR Digest: Restraints of Trade and Monopolies §§ 24–26

A.   STATUTES AND INTERPRETATIVE PRINCIPLES

§ 14–1.   Introduction and Overview

Following the Supreme Court's decision in *Goldfarb v. Virginia State Bar*[1] in 1975, antitrust law emerged as a powerful overseer of institutional and professional arrangements in the health care sector. The erosion of a series of legal impediments to applying antitrust to the health care industry resulted in extensive litigation challenging a host of private restraints that had for years insulated providers from market discipline. By protecting professional discretion, eliminating interference by third parties and establishing the industry's control over important economic variables such as the division of labor, reimbursement methods and entry, these restraints had made competition among providers almost unimaginable.

Not only did antitrust litigation bring about significant changes in institutions in the health care industry, but it also helped shift public attitudes and shape public policy. Perhaps more than any legislative action, these cases served to challenge what Clark Havighurst has called the "professional paradigm"—the assumption that decisions regarding medical care were essentially scientific ones, best entrusted exclusively to professionals whose autonomy and authority needed to be protected.[2] In its place emerged a more widespread acceptance of the idea that medical providers and insurers might become responsive to consumer preferences and more likely to economize on costs if they engaged in direct competition and bargaining. As competition became the norm in the health care industry, antitrust law enforcement began to assume a more regulatory role, influencing significantly the behavior and organizational forms of health care organizations.

§ 14–1

1. 421 U.S. 773, 95 S.Ct. 2004, 44 L.Ed.2d 572 (1975).

2. Clark C. Havighurst, The Professional Paradigm of Medical Care: Obstacles to Decentralization, 30 Jurimetrics J. 415 (1990); see

also, James Blumstein, The Application of Antitrust Doctrine to the Healthcare Industry: The Interweaving of Empirical and Nomative Issues, 31 Ind. L. Rev. 91 (1998); Paul Starr, The Social Transformation of American Medicine (1982).

Applying antitrust law to health care markets entails some special problems. Although the Supreme Court has left no doubt that antitrust is fully applicable to the health industry and has left very little room for consideration of factors other than competitive effect, the peculiarities and distortions of health care markets often necessitate more sophisticated analyses in order to reach economically sound results in antitrust cases. Moreover, widespread regulatory interventions by state and federal governments frequently call for difficult judgements about when conduct is truly private and hence within antitrust's purview. Finally, antitrust law has sometimes been used by private plaintiffs for strategic purposes to accomplish selfish economic objectives that actually thwart the competitive process. This section sets out the statutory and doctrinal framework that guides antitrust analysis and discusses the unique issues posed by the economics of health care insurance and delivery. Subsequent sections examine the application of antitrust principles in five contexts: issues pertaining to the concept of "professionalism"; relationships between physicians and hospitals; health financing arrangements; and relationships among hospitals and other health facilities.

§ 14–2. The Statutory Framework

The principal antitrust statutes are notable for their highly generalized proscriptions. Rather than specify activities that it deemed harmful to competition, Congress vested the federal courts with the power to create a common law of antitrust. Behind the spare language of these acts, however, one finds clear legislative concerns about excessive economic power and a strong preference for competitive markets free of private restraints.

a. The Sherman Act

1. Collective Restraints (Sherman Act, Section 1)

Section 1 of the Sherman Act prohibits "every contract, combination * * * or conspiracy in restraint of trade."[1] This broad proscription establishes two substantive elements for finding a violation: an agreement and conduct that restrains trade. The concept of an agreement—the conventional shorthand for Section 1's "contract, combination or conspiracy" language[2]—limits the Act's reach to *concerted* activities, i.e., those that are the result of a "meeting of the minds" of two or more independent persons or entities. Nothing more than a "conscious commitment to a common scheme"[3] is required, however. Thus tacit understandings, informal gentlemen's agreements,[4] unspoken agreements,[5] and even those resulting from coercion of one party[6] satisfy the requirement. By contrast, unilateral actions—those motivat-

§ 14–2

1. 15 U.S.C.A. § 1.

2. Section 3 of the Clayton Act similarly prohibits certain exclusive contracts entered into "on the condition, agreement or understanding" that a party will not deal in the goods of a competitor of the other party. 15 U.S.C.A. § 14.

3. Monsanto Co. v. Spray–Rite Serv. Corp., 465 U.S. 752, 764, 104 S.Ct. 1464, 1470, 79 L.Ed.2d 775 (1984).

4. United States v. Socony–Vacuum Oil Co., 310 U.S. 150, 179, 60 S.Ct. 811, 824, 84 L.Ed. 1129 (1940).

5. United States v. Foley, 598 F.2d 1323, 1331 (4th Cir.1979).

6. Albrecht v. Herald Co., 390 U.S. 145, 149–50, 88 S.Ct. 869, 871–72, 19 L.Ed.2d 998 (1968).

ed by independent business interests and which lack other indicia of interdependence—are beyond the reach of § 1.

The second requirement of Section 1, that the agreement restrains trade, has generated extensive analysis by the courts. Recognizing that all agreements restrain trade, the Supreme Court has narrowed the inquiry to condemn only "unreasonable restraints" and has developed presumptive rules to simplify judicial inquiries. Although it is customary to classify conduct in categories of restraints e.g. "price fixing" or "group boycott," contemporary antitrust doctrine engages in a more subtle process before attaching labels or condemning restraints as "unreasonable." In section 14–4(b) below, we review the process by which courts evaluate the likely effects of such conduct.

2. *Monopolization Offenses (Sherman Act, Section 2)*

Section 2 prohibits monopolization, attempted monopolization and conspiracies to monopolize.[7] Unlike Section 1, it is directed primarily at unilateral conduct. The elements of monopolization are: (1) the possession of monopoly power, defined as "the power to control market prices or exclude competition;"[8] and (2) the willful acquisition or maintenance of that power "as distinguished from growth or development as a consequence of a superior product, business acumen or historic accident."[9] Notably, the latter requirement suggests that a monopoly, honestly acquired, is not subject to challenge.

Attempted monopolization requires (1) proof of defendant's specific intent to monopolize; (2) predatory conduct or a per se violation of § 1 in furtherance of that intent; and (3) a dangerous probability that, if left unchecked, the conduct will result in actual monopolization. A claim of conspiracy to monopolize requires proof of an agreement and an overt act in furtherance of the agreement. The conspiracy claim is similar to attempted monopolization in that it requires specific intent, but differs in that a plaintiff need not show a dangerous probability of success.

The essential facilities doctrine is a subspecies of monopolization claims under Section 2. It is invoked in situations in which the defendant has monopoly power and controls a facility or resource which is essential for effective competition, which rivals cannot practicably duplicate and to which access can be granted without interference with defendant's use.[10] The remedy under this doctrine is that defendant must provide access to the facility on fair and nondiscriminatory terms. Finally, another cause of action under Section 2 is what is sometimes called "monopoly leveraging." Under this doctrine, a firm with lawful market power in one market may violate § 2 by using that power to gain an unwarranted competitive advantage in a second market. Where the advantage flows from the defendant's use of market power in the monopolized market, some courts have found a violation even though there is no attempt to gain market power in the second market.[11]

---

7. 15 U.S.C.A. § 2.

8. United States v. E.I. du Pont de Nemours & Co., 351 U.S. 377, 391, 76 S.Ct. 994, 1005, 100 L.Ed. 1264 (1956).

9. United States v. Grinnell Corp., 384 U.S. 563, 570–71, 86 S.Ct. 1698, 1703–04, 16 L.Ed.2d 778 (1966).

10. MCI Communications Corp. v. American Telephone & Telegraph Co., 708 F.2d 1081 (7th Cir.1983).

11. See Kerasotes Michigan Theatres, Inc. v. National Amusements, Inc., 854 F.2d 135 (6th Cir.1988), cert. dismissed 490 U.S. 1087, 109 S.Ct. 2461, 104 L.Ed.2d 982 (1989); Berkey Photo, Inc. v. Eastman Kodak Co., 603 F.2d 263 (2d Cir.1979).

b. The Clayton Act

The Clayton Act condemns several kinds of restrictive practices which are discussed below. The impact of its prohibition of specific practices is limited, however, because the Act condemns those practices only to the extent that their effect "may be substantially to lessen competition" or "tend to create a monopoly in any line of commerce." At the same time, this language condemns anticompetitive conduct in its incipiency, encompassing a broader range of conduct than the Sherman Act.[12]

1. Price Discrimination and Related Robinson–Patman Act Provisions (Clayton Act, Section 2)

Section 2 of the Clayton Act, as amended by the Robinson–Patman Act of 1936, prohibits price discrimination between purchasers of goods of like grade and quality. This complex and widely-criticized statute contains a number of qualifications and exceptions that limit its application.[13] A variety of other provisions make certain brokerage payments illegal,[14] outlaw commercial bribery,[15] and prohibit discriminatory payments of certain promotions and advertising expenses and provision of facilities to customers.[16]

2. Tying and Exclusive Dealing Arrangements (Clayton Act, Section 3)

Section 3 of the Clayton Act prohibits requirements contracts, tying arrangements and exclusive dealing arrangements.[17] Although these restraints may be condemned under either the Clayton or the Sherman Acts, Section 3 has a somewhat broader scope, except that it is limited to restraints involving commodities, not services. A claim under the Clayton Act is made by showing either that "the seller enjoys a monopolistic position in * * * the 'tying' product [market], or [that] a substantial volume of * * * the 'tied' product is restrained."[18] In order to show that the challenged conduct is an unreasonable restraint of trade under the Sherman Act, the plaintiff must prove both prongs.

3. Mergers, Acquisitions & Joint Ventures (Clayton Act, Section 7)

Section 7 prohibits mergers, acquisitions and certain joint ventures that may substantially lessen competition or tend to create a monopoly.[19] The original provision was a response to Congressional alarm about the harmful effects of mergers and reflects strong populist sentiments about the risks, political and economic, of large corporate organizations swallowing locally owned businesses.[20] These concerns were even more prevalent in 1950 when Congress strengthened the Clayton Act with amendments passed as part of the Cellar–Kefauver Act.[21]

12. See, e.g., Brunswick Corp. v. Pueblo Bowl–O–Mat, Inc., 429 U.S. 477, 485, 97 S.Ct. 690, 696, 50 L.Ed.2d 701 (1977); F.T.C. v. Procter & Gamble Co., 386 U.S. 568, 577, 87 S.Ct. 1224, 1230, 18 L.Ed.2d 303 (1967); Brown Shoe Co. v. United States, 370 U.S. 294, 82 S.Ct. 1502, 8 L.Ed.2d 510 (1962).

13. See Herbert Hovenkamp, Federal Antitrust Policy: The Law of Competition and Its Practice § 14 (1999).

14. 15 U.S.C.A. § 13(c).

15. Id.

16. Id. at § 13(d) and (e).

17. 15 U.S.C.A. § 14.

18. Times–Picayune Publishing Co. v. United States, 345 U.S. 594, 608–09, 73 S.Ct. 872, 880–81, 97 L.Ed. 1277 (1953).

19. 15 U.S.C.A. § 18.

20. See Robert H. Lande, Wealth Transfers as the Original and Primary Concern of Antitrust: The "Efficiency" Interpretation Challenged, 34 Hastings L.J. 67 (1982).

21. Id. at 131, quoting Brown Shoe Co. v. United States, 370 U.S. 294, 82 S.Ct. 1502, 8 L.Ed.2d 510 (1962) (primary purpose of the Clayton Act is to limit economic concentration,

4. *Interlocking Directorates (Clayton Act, Section 8)*

Section 8 prohibits "interlocking directorates," that is, competing companies sharing common board members or officers.[22] The bar applies where the two companies are competitors—defined to mean entities between which any agreement eliminating competition would violate the antitrust laws. In addition, Section 8's prohibitions apply where the two companies have "capital, surplus and undivided profits in excess of $10 million" and do not meet the requirements for certain de minimis exceptions.[23] The prohibitions of Section 8 probably extend to not-for-profit corporations. However, it should not preclude intra-corporate interlocks between parents and wholly-owned subsidiaries or between sibling corporations.[24]

c. *The Federal Trade Commission Act*

The Federal Trade Commission Act of 1914 created a federal administrative agency to enforce both the antitrust laws and the specific provisions of the FTC Act. The FTC Act grants the Commission power to issue prospective decrees, but not to enforce criminal sanctions. Section 11 gives the Commission concurrent authority with the Department of Justice to enforce certain sections of that Act.[25] Recent case law has interpreted this power broadly, finding the FTC has authority to obtain temporary and permanent injunctions and disgorgement of profits in district court.[26] Section 5, the substantive provision of the FTC Act, empowers the Commission to bring enforcement actions against "unfair methods of competition in or affecting commerce and unfair or deceptive acts or practices in or affecting commerce."[27] Courts have interpreted Section 5's condemnation of "unfair methods of competition" to include Sherman Act offenses.[28] Thus, the reach of the FTC Act is largely co-extensive with the Sherman and Clayton Acts, subject to certain qualifications. For example, the substantive reach of Section 5 extends beyond that of the Sherman Act to prohibit in some circumstances unilateral restraints of trade.[29] The FTC lacks criminal enforcement powers and is subject to restrictions regarding not-for-profit organizations.

The FTC Act also authorizes the Commission to promulgate industry-wide trade regulation rules defining unlawful acts and practices.[30] Although the FTC has largely confined its administrative rulemakings to consumer

to retain "local control" over industry, and to provide protection for small businesses).

22. 15 U.S.C.A. § 19. Amendments to § 8 passed in 1990 extended the ban on interlocking directorates to include officers of competing firms as well, a change precipitated by the Supreme Court's holding in Bankamerica Corp. v. United States, 462 U.S. 122, 103 S.Ct. 2266, 76 L.Ed.2d 456 (1983) that officers were not covered by the Act.

23. See 15 U.S.C.A. §§ 19(a)(1)-(2).

24. See Kennecott Copper Corp. v. Curtiss–Wright Corp., 584 F.2d 1195 (2d Cir.1978).

25. Section 13(b) of the Act, added in 1973, permits the Commission to proceed directly to district court (i.e., without conducting an administrative proceeding) to seek permanent injunctive relief "in proper cases where it has reason to believe an entity is violating or is about to violate" any provision of law enforced by the FTC. 15 U.S.C.A. § 13(b). § 11 of the Clayton Act empowers the Commission to enforce §§ 2, 3, 7 and 8 of that Act.

26. FTC v. Mylan Laboratories, Inc., 62 F.Supp.2d 25 (D.D.C.1999).

27. 15 U.S.C.A. § 45(a)(2).

28. FTC v. Cement Inst., 333 U.S. 683, 68 S.Ct. 793, 92 L.Ed. 1010 (1948).

29. See In re Quality Trailer Products Corp., No. C–3403, 1992 WL 696531 (Nov. 5, 1992)(FTC Complaint). See generally Deborah K. Owen, Commissioner, Federal Trade Commission, New Trends in FTC Antitrust Enforcement, Remarks Before the Dallas Bar Ass'n (Sept. 29, 1992).

30. § 6(g) of the FTC Act. See also 16 C.F.R. §§ 1.7 & 1.22 (1975).

protection issues, there is no explicit limitation upon the FTC's rule-making authority on antitrust issues.[31]

1. FTC Jurisdiction Over Not–for–Profit Organizations

Although the Federal Trade Commission Act provides for Commission jurisdiction over "corporations,"[32] the Act defines corporations as entities "organized to carry on business for its own profit or that of its members."[33] A not-for-profit corporation that does not issue shares of stock, is organized and engaged in business for charitable purposes, and does not derive profits for itself or its members is beyond the Commission's jurisdiction.[34] Trade associations operating under not-for-profit organizational structures are nevertheless subject to the jurisdiction of the FTC when they engage in activities that confer economic benefits on their members, such as providing advantageous insurance and financing for members, or that engage in lobbying, litigation, marketing and public relations for their benefit.[35] Finally, most courts have found FTC jurisdiction over mergers of not-for-profit institutions.

d. Defenses

Several common law and statutory defenses limit the applicability of the antitrust laws. Those of particular importance to the health care sector are discussed below.

1. The McCarran–Ferguson Act Exemption

This statutory exemption provides that the Sherman, Clayton and FTC Acts are only "applicable to the business of insurance to the extent that such business is not regulated by State law."[36] Thus as long as an activity that would otherwise violate the antitrust laws (e.g. price fixing) is part of the "business of insurance" and authorized and regulated by the state, it is immune from attack. The Supreme Court has interpreted the "business of insurance" requirement strictly, holding that insurers' provider contracts that did not involve "spreading and underwriting of a policyholder's risk" were not exempt.[37] The exemption does not apply to acts of "boycott, coercion, or intimidation."[38]

2. The State Action Doctrine

Because antitrust is aimed at private conduct and not regulatory decisions of state and local governments, this doctrine exempts restraints authorized or compelled by governmental action. Originally enunciated in *Parker v.*

---

31. See National Petroleum Refiners Ass'n v. FTC, 482 F.2d 672 (D.C.Cir.1973).

32. 15 U.S.C.A. § 45.

33. 15 U.S.C.A. § 44.

34. Community Blood Bank v. FTC, 405 F.2d 1011, 1019–20 (8th Cir.1969).

35. California Dental Ass'n v. F.T.C., 526 U.S. 756, 119 S.Ct. 1604 (1999); American Med. Ass'n v. FTC, 638 F.2d 443 (2d Cir.1980), affirmed per curiam by an equally divided court 455 U.S. 676, 102 S.Ct. 1744, 71 L.Ed.2d 546 (1982).

36. 15 U.S.C.A. § 1011.

37. Group Life & Health Ins. Co. v. Royal Drug Co., 440 U.S. 205, 211, 99 S.Ct. 1067,

1073, 59 L.Ed.2d 261 (1979). For criticism of this analysis see Herbert Hovenkamp, Federal Antitrust Policy: The Law of Competition and Its Practice § 19.7(c) (1999); see also UNUM Life Insurance Co. v. Ward, 526 U.S. 358, 119 S.Ct. 1380 (1999) (interpreting "business of insurance" broadly in ERISA context).

38. See St. Paul Fire & Marine Ins. Co. v. Barry, 438 U.S. 531, 98 S.Ct. 2923, 57 L.Ed.2d 932 (1978)(insurers' collective agreement to insure medical malpractice only if it occurred during the policy period constitutes "boycott" and hence not exempt).

Brown,[39] the doctrine exempts anticompetitive conduct engaged in by the government acting as sovereign, although cities and other governmental subdivisions are not themselves sovereign.[40] States may not confer immunity on private conduct merely by authorizing antitrust violations. Under the two-prong test developed by the Supreme Court, the conduct must be (1) undertaken pursuant to a "clearly articulated and affirmatively expressed * * * state policy" and (2) "actively supervised" by the state.[41]

3. *The Organized Labor Exemption*

There is both a statutory and non-statutory exemption for certain activities involving organized labor. The statutory exemption provides that the antitrust laws should not be construed to forbid the existence and operation of labor unions or members from carrying out their "legitimate objects,"[42] but does not apply to union agreements with nonlabor groups. The nonstatutory exemption protects employer-labor agreements, provided the union is acting in its self-interest, the agreement affects primarily only the bargaining parties, and certain other requirements are met.[43]

Courts and the FTC have rejected physician "unions" claiming protection under the exemption for collective agreements in connection with bargaining with third party payors. These cases have emphasized that independent physicians are independent contractors, not employees, and that negotiations concerning reimbursement terms are not the equivalent of labor negotiations over terms of employment.[44] Physicians employed by HMOs present a closer case, however, depending on the extent to which the physician might be regarded as an employee and his payment considered a wage.[45]

4. *The Noerr–Pennington Doctrine*

Competitors do not violate the antitrust laws when they act solely to elicit legislative, judicial or administrative agency action. In *Eastern R.R. Presidents Conference v. Noerr Motor Freight, Inc.*,[46] the Supreme Court interpreted the Sherman Act not to reach actions connected with petitioning the government even where those seeking the action do so with the intent of suppressing competition. This limitation on actions alleging illegal conspiracies, monopolization, attempted monopolization and other actions is extremely important given the pervasive role played by governmental activity in health care and the tendency of such actions to create monopolies or restrain trade. The

---

39. 317 U.S. 341, 63 S.Ct. 307, 87 L.Ed. 315 (1943).

40. Community Communications Co. v. City of Boulder, 455 U.S. 40, 102 S.Ct. 835, 70 L.Ed.2d 810 (1982).

41. California Retail Liquor Dealers Ass'n v. Midcal Aluminum, Inc., 445 U.S. 97, 105, 100 S.Ct. 937, 943, 63 L.Ed.2d 233 (1980).

42. 15 U.S.C.A. § 17; see also 15 U.S.C.A. § 20.

43. See Connell Constr. Co. v. Plumbers & Steamfitters Local Union No. 100, 421 U.S. 616, 95 S.Ct. 1830, 44 L.Ed.2d 418 (1975); Mackey v. National Football League, 543 F.2d 606 (8th Cir.1976), cert. dismissed 434 U.S. 801, 98 S.Ct. 28, 54 L.Ed.2d 59 (1977).

44. See Indiana Federation of Dentists, 101 F.T.C. 57 (1983), vacated 745 F.2d 1124 (7th Cir.1984), reversed 476 U.S. 447, 106 S.Ct. 2009, 90 L.Ed.2d 445 (1986); see also Colorado v. Colorado Union of Physicians & Surgeons, 1990 WL 56176 (D.Colo.1990) (consent decree) (purported physicians' union not an exempt "labor organization" and physicians not "employees" as defined by labor law).

45. See discussion of physician unions, infra § 14–28; see also American Med. Ass'n v. United States, 317 U.S. 519, 63 S.Ct. 326, 87 L.Ed. 434 (1943).

46. 365 U.S. 127, 81 S.Ct. 523, 5 L.Ed.2d 464 (1961). The Court elaborated on the doctrine several years later in UMW v. Pennington, 381 U.S. 657, 85 S.Ct. 1585, 14 L.Ed.2d 626 (1965).

doctrine has many important qualifications. The doctrine does not protect "sham petitioning";[47] actions in which the restraint is imposed directly by a boycott or price fixing, albeit with an ultimate legislative objective in mind;[48] or private standard-setting actions aimed at influencing governmental action where the "context and nature" of the activity suggest that safeguards against abuses from private collective action are lacking and the standard will have an effect in the marketplace.[49] The doctrine has been involved in a number of contexts such as challenges to anticompetitive practices associated with certificate of need regulation.[50]

e. State Antitrust Laws and State Exemptions for Health Care Providers

Every state except Arkansas, Vermont and Pennsylvania has adopted antitrust statutes of general application. Most contain provisions identical to or similar to Section 1 of the Sherman Act and many have provisions paralleling Section 2. Many states have adopted "baby Sherman Acts" or "little FTC Acts" that are identical to federal law[51] or that specifically provide that the law shall be interpreted in a manner consistent with interpretations of federal antitrust law,[52] or have been interpreted by courts to be co-extensive with federal antitrust law.[53] A number of state statutes, however, differ from federal law in substantive scope,[54] in limiting recovery to actual damages,[55] and in other respects. State laws parallelling the merger provisions of the Clayton Act are common; but many state laws permit merger challenges under their Section 1 analogues.[56] To the extent that state antitrust law extends beyond federal law, federal law does not pre-empt the field and state law may condemn conduct that is lawful under the Sherman Act[57] and the Clayton Act.[58]

A number of state statutes specifically exempt certain activities involving health care from their antitrust laws or restrict the application of those statutes. Hospital mergers, joint ventures, peer review, HMOs and certain cost-saving cooperative ventures have been singled out in certain instances for

---

47. See California Motor Transport Co. v. Trucking Unlimited, 404 U.S. 508, 92 S.Ct. 609, 30 L.Ed.2d 642 (1972); Professional Real Estate Investors, Inc. v. Columbia Pictures Industries, Inc., 508 U.S. 49, 113 S.Ct. 1920, 123 L.Ed.2d 611 (1993).

48. FTC v. Superior Court Trial Lawyers Ass'n, 493 U.S. 411, 110 S.Ct. 768, 107 L.Ed.2d 851 (1990).

49. Allied Tube & Conduit Corp. v. Indian Head, Inc., 486 U.S. 492, 108 S.Ct. 1931, 100 L.Ed.2d 497 (1988).

50. See § 14–38.

51. See, e.g., Ariz. Rev. Stat. § 44–1402; Idaho Code §§ 48–101, 48–102; Minn. Stat. Ann. § 325D.53; West's Ann. Cal. Bus. & Prof. Code §§ 16720, 16726.

52. See, e.g., Or. Rev. Stat. § 646.715(2).

53. See U.S. Healthcare, Inc. v. Healthsource, Inc., 986 F.2d 589 (1st Cir.1993).

54. The California, District of Columbia and New York statutes contain certain provi-

sions that are broader than federal antitrust laws. See, e.g., West's Ann. Cal. Bus. & Prof. Code § 16750(a) ("Cartwright Act"); D.C. Code § 28–4509(a); McKinney's—N.Y. Gen. Bus. Law § 340 ("Donnelly Act").

55. See, e.g., Ala. Code § 6–5–60(a).

56. See, e.g., People v. Milk Exchange, Ltd., 39 N.E. 1062 (N.Y.App.1895); Morehead City Sea Food Co. v. Way, 86 S.E. 603 (N.C.1915); but see California ex rel. Van de Kamp v. Texaco, Inc., 252 Cal.Rptr. 221, 762 P.2d 385 (Cal.1988).

57. See, e.g., New Motor Vehicle Bd. v. Orrin W. Fox Co., 439 U.S. 96, 99 S.Ct. 403, 58 L.Ed.2d 361 (1978). See generally Herbert Hovenkamp, State Antitrust in the Federal Scheme, 58 Ind. L.J. 375 (1983).

58. See California ex rel. Van de Kamp v. Texaco, Inc., 252 Cal.Rptr. 221, 762 P.2d 385 (Cal.1988).

protection.[59] A number of states have broadened the role of their health care planning boards by empowering them to issue "certificates of public advantage."[60] Some have attempted to design these regulations to meet the requirements of the state action doctrine and thus exempt certain conduct from federal antitrust law. These regulatory schemes entail approval and supervision of hospital mergers, joint ventures and other collaborative activities.[61] Whether this enhanced involvement by state regulators will be sufficient to invoke the protection of the state action doctrine to shield competitor collaboration from challenge under the federal antitrust laws remains to be seen. After the Supreme Court's decision in *Ticor*, the answer would seem to depend on the degree to which a state's regulatory regime engages in meaningful pre-and post-approval supervision of the venture's competitive impact.[62]

f. Government Advisory Opinions and Other Sources of Information

Important sources of information on antitrust law enforcement policies are the public statements and advisory opinions of the Federal and State enforcement agencies. The FTC's "advisory opinion" procedure[63] and the Department of Justice's "business review" procedure[64] provide prospective statements of each agency's enforcement intentions regarding proposed conduct. Neither immunizes conduct: both agencies reserve the right to commence law enforcement proceedings at any time. The agencies have indicated that they will expedite certain requests for advisory opinions on certain health care issues and, in most cases, will respond within ninety days after all necessary information is submitted.[65] Many state attorneys general offer advisory opinions under similar conditions. State and Federal enforcement agencies have also been particularly active in issuing general guidelines for specific areas such as mergers[66] and joint ventures[67] and most recently in health care.[68] Finally, speeches, testimony and other public statements by law enforcement officials frequently shed light on the agencies' views on particu-

---

59. See, e.g. Colo. Rev. Stat. 12.3605–101 et seq. (exemption for peer review; review by committee on anticompetitive conduct). See generally, David Marx, Jr. & James Sneed, Antitrust & Health Care: Meeting the Challenge 23–4 (1998); Kevin E. Grady, A Framework for Antitrust Analysis of Health Care Joint Ventures, 61 Antitrust L.J. 765 (1993).

60. For example, Maine's Hospital Cooperation Act of 1992 authorizes the State to issue "certificates of public advantage" to hospitals entering into voluntary cooperative agreements for sharing services or facilities, allocating patients and other cooperative undertakings. Applicants must demonstrate by clear and convincing evidence that the benefits resulting from cooperation outweighs competitive harms. Me. Rev. Stat. Ann. tit. 22, §§ 1881, 1883(4); see also, Minn. Stat. Ann. § 62J.09 (West); 1991 Wis. Act 250; Ohio Rev. Code § 3727.21 (Baldwin); 1992 Vt. Laws 160, § 9409.

61. See generally, Sara S. Vance, Immunity for State–Sanctioned Provider Collaboration after *Ticor*, 62 Antitrust L.J. 409 (1993).

62. See FTC v. Ticor Title Ins. Co., 504 U.S. 621, 112 S.Ct. 2169, 119 L.Ed.2d 410 (1992). See generally, Sarah S. Vance, Immunity for State–Sanctioned Provider Collaboration after *Ticor*, 62 Antitrust L.J. 409 (1993); see infra § 14–45.

63. See 16 C.F.R. § 1.3 (1988).

64. See 16 C.F.R. § 50.6 (1987).

65. See U.S. Department of Justice and Federal Trade Commission, Statements of Antitrust Enforcement Policy in Health Care (1996), reprinted in 4 Trade Reg. Rep. (CCH) ¶ 13,153. (promising to respond within 90 days for all matters except mergers and within 120 days concerning multiprovider networks).

66. See § 14–48 infra.

67. See §§ 14–39—14–32.

68. U.S. Department of Justice and Federal Trade Commission, Statements of Antitrust Enforcement Policy in Health Care (1996), reprinted in 4 Trade Reg. Rep. (CCH) ¶ 13,153.

lar practices. Over 80 speeches have been given on health care and antitrust since 1981.[69]

§ 14–3. Private Antitrust Litigation: Standing and Other Prerequisites

Antitrust violations frequently have wide-reaching "ripple" effects, as the impact of anticompetitive activity may be felt by a large number of private parties. For example, a restraint of trade directed at a nurse-midwife may affect not only her business, but that of her landlord, her equipment suppliers, and third party payers, in addition to having an important impact on her patients. Courts have developed a number of doctrines limiting the class of persons who may bring private treble damages actions, focusing principally on the directness of the injury to the plaintiff and the link between the injury and the substantive antitrust harm involved. Private plaintiffs must satisfy all of the following requirements.

a. Injury-in-Fact and Causation

Plaintiff must establish that she indeed suffered injury from defendants' acts. Injuries that do not harm the plaintiff (as is the case in some suits brought by competitors charging cartel activities by the rivals)[1] do not establish a private cause of action under the federal antitrust laws. Moreover, the harm must be caused in substantial part by defendant, not by another party[2] or by plaintiff's own doing.

b. The "Business or Property" Requirement

Section 4 of the Clayton Act authorizes private treble damages actions only for injuries to a person's "business or property."[3] Injunctive relief under § 16 of the Clayton Act, however, has not been similarly limited.[4] The Supreme Court has interpreted the phrase "business or property" broadly, holding that consumers can maintain treble damages actions if they suffer monetary injury as a result of a restraint of trade.[5] In *Ancar v. Sara Plasma, Inc.*,[6] the Fifth Circuit held that a homeless person who depended on the sale of plasma for his livelihood and alleged pecuniary losses caused by an illegal conspiracy among plasma centers met the "business or property" requirement. The requisite injury to "business or property" has been found where commercial enterprises suffer lost profits[7] or injuries to property or property rights occur.[8] In addition, courts have recognized injury to potential business opportunities where plaintiff shows loss of opportunity to work[9] or sufficient

69. See 4 John J. Miles, Health Care & Antitrust Law (1992).

§ 14–3

1. Matsushita Elec. Indus. Co. v. Zenith Radio Corp., 475 U.S. 574, 106 S.Ct. 1348, 89 L.Ed.2d 538 (1986).

2. Brown v. Presbyterian Healthcare Serv., 101 F.3d 1324 (10th Cir.1996); Federal Prescription Serv. Inc. v. American Pharm. Ass'n, 663 F.2d 253 (D.C.Cir.1981).

3. 15 U.S.C.A. § 15.

4. See Mid–West Paper Products Co. v. Continental Group, Inc., 596 F.2d 573 (3d Cir.

1979) (protecting non-commercial interests in an injunctive proceeding).

5. Reiter v. Sonotone Corp., 442 U.S. 330, 99 S.Ct. 2326, 60 L.Ed.2d 931 (1979).

6. 964 F.2d 465 (5th Cir.1992).

7. Osborn v. Sinclair Refining Co., 324 F.2d 566 (4th Cir.1963).

8. See, e.g., Fontana Aviation, Inc. v. Beech Aircraft Corp., 432 F.2d 1080 (7th Cir.1970).

9. Quinonez v. National Ass'n of Securities Dealers, 540 F.2d 824 (5th Cir.1976).

evidence of "intention and preparedness" to go into business.[10]

c. Antitrust Injury

Private plaintiffs in antitrust cases must show more than a causal connection between an alleged violation and a plaintiff's injury. The Supreme Court succinctly summarized this requirement in its *Brunswick* decision:

> Plaintiffs must prove *antitrust* injury, which is to say injury of the type the antitrust laws were intended to prevent and that flows from that which makes defendants' acts unlawful.[11]

Although this limitation was clearly compelled by the language of § 4 of the Clayton Act governing private antitrust damages actions,[12] the principle also applies to private equity suits despite the differing language of § 16.[13]

The antitrust injury doctrine has become an increasingly important device for securing summary judgment in health care cases. The doctrine has been successfully asserted by defendants in cases involving staff privileges disputes,[14] monopsony power by insurance companies,[15] and others.[16] Where they interpret plaintiff's claim to call for sharing in defendant's monopoly profits or avoiding competition, courts find no antitrust injury.[17] For example, courts sometimes presume that "less efficient" providers seeking access to monopolized markets are seeking to join a cartel rather than compete with it.[18] The doctrine is also applied where the plaintiff's injury would have occurred regardless of defendant's actions[19] or no cognizable antitrust claim is raised.[20]

d. Standing

Antitrust standing requirements for private plaintiffs go beyond the "case or controversy" requirements of constitutional standing. Courts closely evaluate a variety of prudential factors with an eye to assuring that only proper or "efficient" plaintiffs enforce the antitrust laws.

The Supreme Court's interpretation of standing for private parties under § 4 of the Clayton Act has sharply limited the class of persons able to file antitrust treble damages actions. The first significant case in this regard was

---

10. See, e.g, Solinger v. A & M Records, Inc., 586 F.2d 1304 (9th Cir.1978).

11. Brunswick Corp. v. Pueblo Bowl–O–Mat, Inc., 429 U.S. 477, 489, 97 S.Ct. 690, 698, 50 L.Ed.2d 701 (1977) (emphasis in original).

12. "[A]ny person who shall be injured in his business or property by reason of anything forbidden in the antitrust laws may sue therefore in any district court of the United States. * * * and shall recover three fold the damages by him sustained, and the cost of the suit, including a reasonable attorney's fee." 15 U.S.C.A. § 15.

13. Cargill, Inc. v. Monfort of Colorado, Inc., 479 U.S. 104, 107 S.Ct. 484, 93 L.Ed.2d 427 (1986).

14. Todorov v. DCH Healthcare Auth., 921 F.2d 1438 (11th Cir.1991).

15. Kartell v. Blue Shield of Massachusetts, Inc., 749 F.2d 922 (1st Cir.1984).

16. Klamath–Lake Pharm. Ass'n v. Klamath Med. Serv. Bureau, 701 F.2d 1276 (9th Cir.1983).

17. Doctor's Hosp. of Jefferson v. Southeast Med. Alliance, 123 F.3d 301 (5th Cir. 1997); Levine v. Central Fla. Med. Affiliates, 864 F.Supp. 1175 (M.D.Fla.1994), aff'd 72 F.3d 1538 (11th Cir.1996).

18. Todorov v. DCH Healthcare Auth., 921 F.2d 1438 (11th Cir.1991); but cf. Ertag v. Naples Community Hosp., 121 F.3d 721, 1997–2 Trade Cas. (CCH) ¶ 71,996 (11th Cir.1997) (upholding standing where complaint alleged damages from inability to compete).

19. Brunswick Corp. v. Pueblo Bowl–O–Mat, Inc., 429 U.S. 477 (1977).

20. Patel v. Scotland Mem'l Hosp., 91 F.3d 132 (4th Cir.1996).

Blue Shield of Virginia v. McCready,[21] in which the Court considered whether a subscriber, covered by a Blue Shield health insurance policy that did not provide for reimbursement of payments to clinical psychologists, had standing to sue Blue Shield, which plaintiff alleged, had engaged in a concerted refusal to deal with psychologists. The Court found that the plaintiff had standing to sue because the boycott of patients was the means by which the defendant achieved its anticompetitive ends; hence, plaintiff's injury "was inextricably intertwined with the injury the conspirators sought to inflict on psychologists and the psychotherapy market."[22] The following year, however, in *Associated General Contractors*,[23] the Supreme Court enunciated a laundry list of factors that it deemed relevant to the standing inquiry and appreciably narrowed the range of appropriate plaintiffs. These factors included the directness of plaintiff's injury; whether damages are speculative; the risk of duplicative recovery and problems of apportioning damages; and defendant's intent. Perhaps most important, however, was the Court's emphasis on the fact that the plaintiff union was neither a "consumer or competitor" in the market in which trade was restrained.[24]

Courts applying the *Associated General Contractors* formula have tended to construe its requirements narrowly, and have generally denied standing for persons who are not consumers or competitors.[25] For example, the Ninth Circuit required the plaintiff, a nurse anesthetist claiming anticompetitive exclusion from practice at a hospital, to demonstrate that he was a "participant in the same market as the alleged malefactor," a physician anesthesiologist allegedly excluding the former from practice.[26] In health care markets, however, identifying the most "efficient" plaintiff may not be a simple matter. One court found in a staff privileges dispute that, although patients will suffer the resulting competitive harm, collective action problems and lack of sufficient information undermined the normal presumption that they should be regarded as preferred plaintiffs.[27]

e. The Direct Purchaser Requirement

In cases involving illegal overcharges due to price fixing agreements, only plaintiffs who purchase directly from co-conspirators have standing to sue. In *Illinois Brick Co. v. Illinois*,[28] the Supreme Court held that "indirect purchasers" lack standing even though the overcharge may have been passed on to consumers who buy from the first purchaser. Thus consumers may not recover damages for price fixing by pharmaceutical companies where the direct purchaser is a pharmacy, wholesaler or provider,[29] and patients may not be able to bring antitrust price fixing claims against providers where the insurer is the direct purchaser.[30] There are several important exceptions to

21. 457 U.S. 465, 102 S.Ct. 2540, 73 L.Ed.2d 149 (1982).

22. Id. at 484, 102 S.Ct. at 2551.

23. Associated Gen. Contractors of California, Inc. v. California State Council of Carpenters, 459 U.S. 519, 103 S.Ct. 897, 74 L.Ed.2d 723 (1983).

24. Id. at 539, 103 S.Ct. at 909.

25. See Note, Private Antitrust Standing: A Survey and Analysis of the Law After Associated General, 61 Wash. U. L.Q. 1069 (1984).

26. Bhan v. NME Hosps., Inc., 772 F.2d 1467 (9th Cir.1985), affirmed 929 F.2d 1404 (9th Cir.1991).

27. Leak v. Grant Med. Center, 893 F.Supp. 757 (S.D.Ohio 1995).

28. 431 U.S. 720, 97 S.Ct. 2061, 52 L.Ed.2d 707 (1977).

29. In re Brand Name Prescription Drugs Antitrust Litigation, 123 F.3d 599 (7th Cir. 1997).

30. Blue Cross & Blue Shield v. Marshfield Clinic, 65 F.3d 1406 (7th Cir.1995).

the direct purchaser rule. It does not apply to cases in which the direct purchaser and the indirect purchaser have a pre-existing, fixed quantity, cost-plus contract that passes on the overcharge to the indirect buyer. Second, where the first purchaser is controlled or owned by the price-fixer, a person buying from the first purchaser may bring the claim.[31] In addition, *Illinois Brick* does not apply to vertical price fixing conspiracies because in such circumstances plaintiff actually purchases from a co-conspirator. Finally, although not specifically addressed in *Illinois Brick*, injunctive actions do not appear to be barred because the risks associated with indirect purchaser suits (e.g., speculative damages, duplicative recovery, multiple litigation) are not present.

§ 14–4. Interpretative Principles

The "reasonableness" of conduct generally guides courts in assessing legality under the antitrust laws. Reasonable agreements between competitors or vertically-related firms do not offend Section 1 of the Sherman Act; reasonable actions by monopolists do not violate Section 2; mergers, tying and exclusive dealing arrangements are analyzed under the Clayton Act applying standards which, at least in practice, rely on essentially the same principles that inform reasonableness analyses under the Sherman Act.[1] Care must be taken, however, to distinguish reasonableness as used in antitrust from the "reasonable man" standard familiar in tort law and other contexts. The antitrust "reasonableness" standard is tightly constrained by the purposes of that body of law: hence, conduct is judged by its reasonable propensity to promote competition.

Early in antitrust's history, however, Congress and the judiciary realized that by itself "reasonableness" was too vague a concept to limit judicial discretion or effectively proscribe inappropriate conduct. Hence, the law has developed presumptions and interpretive principles to guide applications of the concept. Unfortunately, the courts have been less than successful in articulating economic or other bases for these interpretive rules and uncertainty in this area has sometimes been a source of confusion and cynicism.

a. The Law's Exclusive Focus on Competitive Concerns

One constant in the shifting jurisprudence of antitrust law has been its exclusive focus on the competitive consequences of business conduct. There has long been widespread agreement that the law should assess competitive effects and should not take into account purported noneconomic benefits, such as advancing various social policies or norms or even protecting public safety. This self-imposed boundary is based on judicial skepticism about its competence to balance disparate social policies and the normative judgment that such concerns are more appropriately addressed to the legislature. Thus, under Section 1 of the Sherman Act, courts will not consider justifications other than those asserting that a practice on balance promotes competition. Monopolization claims under Section 2 may be refuted by business justifications tending to show that the conduct of the dominant firm advances

---

31. Illinois Brick Co. v. Illinois, 431 U.S. 720, 736 n. 16, 97 S.Ct. 2061, 2070 n. 16, 52 L.Ed.2d 707 (1977).

1. See 7 Philip E. Areeda, Antitrust Law ¶ 1500, at 361 (1986).

competitive goals and is not designed to thwart rivalry. Merger analyses under Section 7 reject out of hand justifications based on non-competition factors or procompetitive benefits occurring in markets other than those of the merging firms. Only in Robinson–Patman cases, where the legislation directs courts away from competition-based concerns, does one find antitrust law sometimes receptive to non-competitive concerns.

b. Per Se Rules and the Rule of Reason

Historically, judicial analyses of conduct under Section 1 of the Sherman Act identified two classes of agreements: those that, because of their pernicious effect on competition and lack of any redeeming virtue are deemed "per se" illegal and those warranting further inquiry into context, purpose and ultimate effect, are examined under the so-called "rule of reason."[2] The classic formulation of the rule of reason, enunciated by Justice Brandeis, contemplates a broad and complex analysis addressing a variety of issues but affords no particular guidance as to the relative weight or significance of the various factors.[3] In practice, the classification process seemed to subsume analysis of competitive effect: generally plaintiffs have prevailed in cases in which courts applied the per se rule while defendants have prevailed whenever the rule of reason has been employed. More significant, however, has been the increasing concern that the per se rule has prohibited arrangements that offered significant efficiency benefits.[4]

A series of Supreme Court decisions has shifted antitrust analyses away from a rigid per se/rule of reason dichotomy, treating the approaches as "complementary" and essentially establishing a continuum of levels of scrutiny. The modern approach allows courts to undertake threshold examinations of competitive effect before characterizing conduct as governed by the per se rule. Likewise, it permits "quick look" scrutiny under the rule of reason which obviates the need for prolonged factual examinations when truncated review reveals that purported efficiency benefits are lacking or anticompetitive effect is obvious.[5] Thus, the analytic approach (and hence the strength of the presumption) now depends on the severity of the restraint and the plausibility of efficiency justifications. There is, however, no clear formula as to which analytic approach will be used. The Supreme Court has recently stated that courts should apply "an enquiry meet for the case, looking to the circumstances, details, and logic of a restraint" in order to determine the level

2. The rationale for the per se rule is set forth in Northern Pac. Ry. Co. v. United States, 356 U.S. 1, 78 S.Ct. 514, 2 L.Ed.2d 545 (1958); the rule of reason is elaborated and justified in Chicago Bd. of Trade v. United States, 246 U.S. 231, 38 S.Ct. 242, 62 L.Ed. 683 (1918).

3. In *Chicago Board of Trade*, Justice Brandeis described the rule of reason as follows:

The true test of legality is whether the restraint imposed is such as merely regulates and perhaps thereby promotes competition or whether it is such as may suppress or even destroy competition. To determine that question the court must ordinarily consider the facts peculiar to the business to which

the restraint is applied; its condition before and after the restraint was imposed; the nature of the restraint and its effect, actual or probable. The history of the restraint, the evil believed to exist, the reason for adopting the particular remedy, the purpose or end sought to be attained, are all relevant facts.

Id. at 238, 39 S.Ct. at 244.

4. See Robert Bork, The Antitrust Paradox: A Policy at War with Itself (1978); Oliver E. Williamson, Antitrust Economics (1986).

5. National Collegiate Athletic Ass'n v. Board of Regents, 468 U.S. 85, 104 S.Ct. 2948, 82 L.Ed.2d 70 (1984); FTC v. Indiana Fed'n of Dentists, 476 U.S. 447, 106 S.Ct. 2009, 90 L.Ed.2d 445 (1986).

of scrutiny it merits.[6] Contrary to some expectations, however, these developments have not led to the abandonment of per se analysis. In several recent pronouncements, the Supreme Court has freely employed the per se rule[7] and has noted its linkage to substantive law but at the same time has been reluctant to apply an abbreviated analysis where the professional context of the restraint or market imperfections make it more difficult to reach a confident conclusion about competitive effects.[8]

c. Economics and Antitrust: The Rise of the Chicago School and Its Challengers

Whether or not other factors have some role to play, there is substantial agreement that economic efficiency should be the dominant goal of antitrust analyses. "Competition" is generally understood to entail the process that promotes efficiency by forcing sellers to sell their goods or services at the marginal cost of production. Under this view, when price equals cost, resources are allocated efficiently in the sense that consumer desires are satisfied and social output is maximized. The goal of antitrust law is thus to assure that market structure and conduct do not interfere with market forces which, it is assumed, would achieve those ends.

A competing view, a "post–Chicago" school of economic analysis, rejects some cherished tenets and assumptions of the Chicago school and places greater emphasis on game-theoretic and strategic behavior models.[9] This literature emphasizes that in real world markets, products are often highly differentiated, information is imperfect and other conditions depart from neoclassical economic assumptions.[10] Moreover, competitors may pursue strategies that can create entry barriers, raise rivals' costs, or engage in nonprice predation so as to increase their profits and harm consumers.[11] Critics of "post-Chicago" scholarship have questioned the frequency of such strategic behavior and the capacity of courts to apply the complex analysis it requires.[12] Notably, the Supreme Court's decision in *Eastman Kodak Co. v. Image Technical Services, Inc.*[13] may represent an important milestone for Post–Chicago economic analysis. The Court held in that case that Kodak could have

---

6. California Dental Ass'n. v. FTC, 526 U.S. 756, 119 S.Ct. 1604 (1999).

7. Palmer v. BRG of Georgia, Inc., 498 U.S. 46, 111 S.Ct. 401, 112 L.Ed.2d 349 (1990)(market allocation); Arizona v. Maricopa County Med. Soc'y, 457 U.S. 332, 102 S.Ct. 2466, 73 L.Ed.2d 48 (1982) (price fixing); Jefferson Parish Hosp. Dist. No. 2 v. Hyde, 466 U.S. 2, 104 S.Ct. 1551, 80 L.Ed.2d 2 (1984)(tying).

8. California Dental Ass'n. v. FTC, 526 U.S. 756, 119 S.Ct. 1604 (1999); FTC v. Superior Court Trial Lawyers Ass'n, 493 U.S. 411, 433–35, 110 S.Ct. 768, 780–82, 107 L.Ed.2d 851 (1990).

9. A leading critique of Chicago analysis and its assumptions is Herbert Hovenkamp, Antitrust Policy After Chicago, 84 Mich. L. Rev. 213 (1985).

10. See, e.g., Thomas J. Campbell, Predation and Competition in Antitrust: The Case of Nonfungible Goods, 87 Colum. L. Rev. 1625

(1987); Louis Kaplow, The Accuracy of Traditional Market Power Analysis and a Direct Adjustment Alternative, 95 Harv. L. Rev. 1817, 1828 (1982); Richard Schmalensee, Another Look at Market Power, 95 Harv. L. Rev. 1789, 1800 (1982).

11. See, e.g., Thomas G. Krattenmaker & Steven C. Salop, Anticompetitive Exclusion: Raising Rivals' Costs to Achieve Power Over Price, 96 Yale L.J. 209 (1986); Steven C. Salop & David T. Scheffman, Raising Rivals' Costs, 73 Am. Econ. Rev. 267 (1983). See generally Nonprice Predation Under Section 2 of the Sherman Act, ABA Section on Antitrust Law: Monograph No. 18 (1991).

12. See, e.g., Timothy J. Brennan, Understanding "Raising Rivals' Costs," 33 Antitrust Bull. 95 (1988); Frank H. Easterbrook, Workable Antitrust Policy, 84 Mich. L. Rev. 1696 (1986).

13. 504 U.S. 451, 112 S.Ct. 2072, 119 L.Ed.2d 265 (1992).

market power in the market for its own replacement parts because consumers may be "locked-in" and may lack adequate information to take steps to avoid exploitation. Among the most important implications of *Kodak* for health care markets is that imperfect information may require more narrowly-drawn markets because it limits consumers' ability to choose substitutes. Further, information inadequacies may override market share and other structural proof to establish market power.[14]

d. The Peculiar Economics of the Health Care Industry

In health care a variety of circumstances are at variance with the neoclassical economic model of a perfectly competitive market. First, consumers and sellers alike lack good information, and the information that is available is asymmetrically distributed. Because of the technical nature of medical information and the complexity of diagnoses and treatment alternatives, patients and third party payers find it difficult to evaluate the cost and quality of health services. Indeed, the considerable uncertainty that attends medical treatments makes judgments on causation (and hence on the costs and benefits of the treatment) difficult.[15] Further, the fact that information is asymmetrically distributed among providers, patients and payers may permit physicians to induce demand for their services; at a minimum it makes information costly for buyers to acquire.

Perhaps the most significant manifestation of market imperfections associated with information problems occurs in health insurance. Two phenomena, moral hazard and biased selection, have a significant effect on the allocative efficiency of insurance markets. Biased selection occurs in two ways. Adverse selection describes the tendency of persons who expect to need health services to purchase insurance and to seek coverage for the specific coverage they need. At the same time, insurers make efforts to attract healthy consumers who will have less costly claims, a phenomenon called "favorable selection." These biases in the selection process tend to cause competition to unravel, decrease the social benefits of insurance and ultimately undermine the risk-spreading function of insurance.[16] Moral hazard refers to the tendency of insurance to reduce the insured's incentives to arrest the hazard. In the case of health insurance, some claim that moral hazard interferes to some extent with efficient resource allocation by reducing incentives to avoid illness. Far more important, however, is the effect of lessening the insured's incentives to economize on the cost of care.[17] That is, given full insurance, insureds and their doctors have relatively little reason to choose cost-effective treatments or providers.

14. See Robert H. Lande, Chicago Takes it on the Chin: Imperfect Information Could Play a Crucial Role in the Post-*Kodak* World, 62 Antitrust L.J. 193 (1993).

15. The seminal analysis of the effects of market failure caused by information problems, uncertainty and transaction costs is Kenneth J. Arrow, Uncertainty and the Welfare Economics of Medical Care, 53 Am. Econ. Rev. 941 (1963). Arrow's assessment of the health industry's structure has been sharply criticized for its failure to appreciate the medical profession's role in shaping the way market institutions are organized. Paul Starr, The Social

Transformation of American Medicine 227–30 (1982). See also Mark V. Pauly, Is Medical Care Different?, in Competition in the Health Care Sector: Past, Present and Future 28–40 (Warren Greenberg ed., 1978).

16. See Wilensky & Rossiter, Patient Self Selection in HMOs Health Affairs 66 (1986).

17. For an excellent analysis of moral hazard in health insurance and the capacities of government regulation to control it, see Paul L. Joskow, Controlling Hospital Costs: The Role of Government Regulation (1981).

Another difference between health care markets and neoclassical assumptions is the fact that services are highly heterogeneous. Quality may vary considerably, depending upon the providers' talents, training, personal attributes (e.g. "caring," and interpersonal skills) and other factors. Other variables such as geographic location and variations between outcomes among providers underscore the heterogeneity of health care services markets. As is increasingly recognized, the existence of product differentiation may significantly affect evaluations of market power and potential anticompetitive conduct. Next, in contrast to the neoclassical assumption that barriers to entry do not exist, potential sellers of health services are subject to impediments to entry and mobility especially in the form of governmental and private licensure and practice requirements.

Finally, perfect competition assumes that large numbers of buyers and sellers operate in a market free of cartels or other private agreements to curtail rivalry. The health care market, by contrast, has a long history of private "self-regulation"[18] and government-sponsored arrangements that restricted free competition. Many of these activities entailed actions that exacerbated other market imperfections. For example, collective provider agreements that deny quality-related information to third party payors perpetuated inadequate production of information in the market. This exposes the bootstrap nature of many justifications for self-regulation: the market "imperfections" relied upon to rationalize private regulation are often caused in part by private collective action in the first place.

The presence of these market imperfections in the availability of information and other departures from optimal market conditions give rise to two important questions. First, given these differences, will application of competition principles improve consumer welfare at all? We will dodge this legitimate and central policy question except to note that if it is to be decided at all, that decision will probably be left to the political arena. It should be noted, however, that a sizeable and growing economic literature tends to show that conventional economic principles such as high concentration of sellers resulting in higher prices obtain in health care markets.[19]

Secondly, can the legal system fashion antitrust principles that are sensitive to the unique market conditions of the health care industry? As noted above, the Supreme Court's decision in *Kodak* seems to suggest that courts will be charged with appreciating the special economic circumstances of the cases before them, and its *California Dental Association* opinion instructs courts to be sensitive to peculiarities of health industry markets. The remainder of this chapter will attempt to set forth the numerous areas in which antitrust disputes arise and offer some assistance in meeting that obligation.

18. See, e.g., Paul Starr, The Social Transformation of American Medicine (1982); Charles D. Weller, "Free Choice" as a Restraint of Trade in American Health Care Delivery and Insurance, 69 Iowa L. Rev. 1351 (1984).

19. See infra § 14–25; § 14–44; see generally Martin Gaynor & William B. Vogt, Antitrust and Competition in Health Care Markets, in Handbook of Health Economics (A. Culyer & J. Newhouse, Eds. 1999).

B. PROFESSIONALISM AND COMPETITION

§ 14–5. Introduction: The Tension Between Professional Values and Competitive Systems

A central feature of health care organization and delivery is the dominant role played by health care professionals. The impact of professional influence on the American health care system has been vigorously debated by a wide spectrum of authorities.[1] As public policy and legal doctrine have shifted toward favoring markets and decentralized decision-making in health care, certain aspects of "professionalism" have come into conflict with market-oriented public policies. In particular, the medical profession's insistence on professional discretion, freedom from lay interference and self-regulation have engendered practices that run afoul of antitrust principles.

On the other hand, professionals operate in markets that differ from many consumer goods and their ethical norms may provide important protection from abuse. In addition, professional societies may adopt standards and certification arrangements that promote competition by signalling quality and improving information in the marketplace. As Justice O'Connor has noted, "heightened ethical demands" may be required of professionals "because market forces, and the ordinary legal prohibitions against force and fraud, are simply insufficient to protect the consumers of their necessary services from the peculiar power of the specialized knowledge that these professionals possess."[2]

Explicit deference in antitrust law to the professional status of providers has been sharply curtailed. A number of doctrines, defenses and interpretative norms that once shielded professionals from antitrust scrutiny have been discarded or narrowed considerably. Nevertheless, many of the unique features of market transactions in health care that underlie notions of "professionalism" are still very much in evidence in antitrust case law. Calls to "level the playing field" between professionals and managed care organizations may increase the attention paid to these issues in the future. Coping with the difficult issues presented by accommodating legitimate professional concerns in a competitive market ranks among antitrust's most difficult tasks.

§ 14–6. The Learned Professions Defense

In its landmark decision in *Goldfarb v. Virginia State Bar*,[1] the Supreme Court rejected the notion that the "learned professions" were not engaged in "trade or commerce" and hence should be exempt from § 1 of the Sherman Act. The Court's holding that "the public service aspect of professional practice" could not justify a total exemption for the sale of legal services[2] (along with its holding that professional services met the interstate commerce

---

§ 14–5

1. See, e.g., Kenneth J. Arrow, Uncertainty and the Welfare Economics of Medical Care, 53 Am. Econ. Rev. 941 (1963); Paul Starr, The Social Transformation of American Medicine (1982); Eliot Freidson, The Centrality of Professionalism to Health Care, 30 Jurimetrics 431 (1990); Clark C. Havighurst, The Changing Locus of Decision Making in the Health Care Sector, 11 J. Health Pol., Pol'y & Law 697 (1986); Philip C. Kissam, Government Policy Towards Medical Accreditation and Certification: The Antitrust Laws and Other Procompetitive Strategies, 1983 Wis. L. Rev. 1.

2. Shapero v. Kentucky Bar Ass'n, 486 U.S. 466, 490, 108 S.Ct. 1916, 1930, 100 L.Ed.2d 475 (1988) (O'Connor, J., dissenting).

§ 14–6

1. 421 U.S. 773, 95 S.Ct. 2004, 44 L.Ed.2d 572 (1975).

2. Id. at 787, 95 S.Ct. at 2013.

requirements of the Sherman Act) opened the door for successful antitrust challenges to a wide range of practices in the medical profession.

The *Goldfarb* opinion, however, did not on its face preclude special treatment of the professions under the antitrust laws. In a suggestive footnote, the Court qualified its holding:

> "The fact that a restraint operates upon a profession as distinguished from a business is, of course, relevant in determining whether that particular restraint violates the Sherman Act. It would be unrealistic to view the practice of professions as interchangeable with other business activities, and automatically to apply to the professions antitrust concepts which originated in other areas. The public service aspect, and other features of the professions, may require that a particular practice, which could properly be viewed as a violation of the Sherman Act in another context, be treated differently. We intimate no view on any other situation than the one with which we are confronted today."[3]

Initially, Footnote 17 was interpreted as foreshadowing a flexible antitrust standard that would give the professions some additional "elbowroom" for "professional ordering" or otherwise sanction trade-restricting activities undertaken on ethical grounds.[4] While the Court has spoken in terms that seem to repudiate the notion of favored treatment,[5] it has recently cited the footnote in explaining why the disparities in information between health professionals and patients are cause for closer scrutiny of a dental association's restrictions on advertising.[6]

The Supreme Court's disinclination to apply Footnote 17 expansively is well-justified. First, to the extent that the passage is read to suggest that "public service" and other social goals should somehow be weighed against anticompetitive effects, it runs squarely into the teaching of *Professional Engineers*.[7] The inquiry would be fundamentally a legislative one, posing difficult questions such as how much and what kind of "public service" should trump anticompetitive harm. Serious doubt also exists as to whether elastic concepts such as "quality of care" and other social benefits can be meaningfully measured and balanced against economic harms.[8] Ultimately, *Professional Engineers* can be read to suggest that the only deference to be accorded to professional services is the recognition that "the nature of competition in such services may vary"[9] and hence evaluations of competitive effects must take into account the peculiarities of those professional markets.

Courts interpreting state statutes modeled on federal antitrust laws have generally followed *Goldfarb* and have found restraints by professionals within

---

3. Id. at 788–89 n.17.

4. National Soc'y of Professional Eng'rs v. United States, 435 U.S. 679, 699, 98 S.Ct. 1355, 1369, 55 L.Ed.2d 637 (1978)(Blackmun, J., concurring).

5. See Jefferson Parish Hosp. District No. 2 v. Hyde, 466 U.S. 2, 25 n. 41, 104 S.Ct. 1551, 1565 n. 41, 80 L.Ed.2d 2 (1984).

6. California Dental Ass'n. v. FTC, 526 U.S. 756, 119 S.Ct. 1604 (1999). See infra §§ 14–7, 14–10.

7. National Soc'y of Professional Eng'rs v. United States, 435 U.S. 679 (1978).

8. See Thomas L. Greaney, Quality of Care and Market Failure Defenses in Antitrust Health Care Litigation, 21 Conn. L. Rev. 605, 616–618 (1989); Thomas E. Kauper, The Role of Quality of Health Care Considerations in Antitrust Analysis, 51 Law & Contemp. Probs. 273, 281–92 (1988).

9. National Society of Professional Engineers v. United States, 435 U.S. 679, 696, 98 S.Ct. 1355, 1368, 55 L.Ed.2d 637 (1978).

their reach.[10] However, several state antitrust laws do not extend to the activities of licensed professionals when they relate to the provision of professional services.[11]

§ 14–7. Weighing the Effects of Professional Activities on Quality of Care

Despite the Supreme Court's categorical rejection of defenses premised on non-economic justifications, concerns about quality of care have surfaced repeatedly in health care cases. As discussed earlier, the Supreme Court has stressed that in antitrust, the "inquiry is confined to a consideration of impact on competitive conditions,"[1] and has steadfastly resisted defenses premised on worthy purposes, public safety, quality enhancements, social norms and non-economic social benefits.[2] As a matter of doctrine, courts make no assessment of the magnitude of purported non-economic benefits because they simply do not count.

The Court's clearest expression of this principle is found in its decision in the *National Society of Professional Engineers* case in 1978.[3] The engineers' national trade association had adopted an ethical norm that discouraged competitive bidding. Defendants' justification was that some engineers would reduce quality in order to submit the lowest bid and consequently defective structures would be built thus threatening public safety. The Supreme Court characterized this as an appeal to public interest considerations that was more properly addressed to Congress. The antitrust laws, it stated, reflected Congress' judgement that "ultimately competition will not only produce lower prices, but also better goods and services."[4]

The Court's next rejection of quality-based justifications applied and amplified these principles in the health care context. In *FTC v. Indiana Federation of Dentists,*[5] a group of dentists had formed an ad hoc association to continue earlier efforts to curb utilization review practices of third party payers. In essence, the dentists agreed among themselves not to provide x-rays of their patients to insurance companies requesting them. Upholding the practice, the Ninth Circuit had repeatedly emphasized that a "legal, moral and ethical policy of quality [of] care" underlay defendants' refusal to provide x-rays.[6] Citing *Professional Engineers*, the Supreme Court found the quality defense "flawed both legally and factually."[7] While reaffirming the principle

---

10. See, e.g., Adkins v. Sarah Bush Lincoln Health Ctr., 110 Ill.Dec. 947, 511 N.E.2d 1267 (Ill.App.1987), affirmed 136 Ill.Dec. 47, 544 N.E.2d 733 (Ill.1989); Katz v. Ohio State Bd. of Psychology, 433 N.E.2d 624 (Ohio 1979).

11. People v. Roth, 438 N.Y.S.2d 737, 420 N.E.2d 929 (N.Y.App.1981); Frahm v. Urkovich, 69 Ill.Dec. 572, 447 N.E.2d 1007 (Ill.App. 1983).

§ 14–7

1. National Soc'y of Professional Eng'rs v. United States, 435 U.S. 679, 688, 98 S.Ct. 1355, 1363, 55 L.Ed.2d 637 (1978).

2. Id.; FTC v. Superior Court Trial Lawyers Ass'n, 493 U.S. 411, 110 S.Ct. 768, 107 L.Ed.2d 851 (1990); FTC v. Indiana Fed'n of Dentists, 476 U.S. 447, 106 S.Ct. 2009, 90 L.Ed.2d 445

(1986); Jefferson Parish Hosp. District No. 2 v. Hyde, 466 U.S. 2, 25 n. 41, 104 S.Ct. 1551, 1565 n. 41, 80 L.Ed.2d 2 (1984).

3. National Soc'y of Professional Eng'rs v. United States, 435 U.S. 679, 98 S.Ct. 1355, 55 L.Ed.2d 637 (1978).

4. Id. at 695, 98 S.Ct. at 1367.

5. 476 U.S. 447, 106 S.Ct. 2009, 90 L.Ed.2d 445 (1986).

6. Indiana Fed'n of Dentists v. FTC, 745 F.2d 1124, 1135 (7th Cir.1984), reversed on other grounds 476 U.S. 447, 106 S.Ct. 2009, 90 L.Ed.2d 445 (1986).

7. 476 U.S. at 462, 106 S.Ct. at 2020.

that benefits other than improving competitive conditions will not save anticompetitive restraints, the Court briefly examined the factual support for those impermissible justifications. Notably, however, it did not even allude to its suggestion in *Goldfarb* that professional concerns might alter the framework for analysis and expressed skepticism that professional judgment can be automatically equated with patient welfare.[8] On the other hand, the Court's willingness to accept rather facile invocations of professional and quality-based concerns to require a fuller inquiry in *California Dental* may signal a changing standard in this area.[9]

The teachings of *Professional Engineers and Indiana Federation of Dentists* have been applied rigorously in cases involving challenges to profession-sponsored activities under Section 1 of the Sherman Act. Lower courts and the FTC have shown little tolerance for self-policing activities by medical associations when they impair competitive conditions.[10] The rule has also led courts to limit the admissibility of evidence of quality of care benefits or motivations.[11] Moreover, antitrust's refusal to consider non-economic justifications applies with equal force to both "naked" restraints of trade and to those having economic justifications that are evaluated under the rule of reason.[12] Nevertheless, a number of courts have found indirect means to bring quality of care issues into Section 1 inquiries. For example, quality issues may be highly relevant in evaluating motive under the rule of reason or determining whether a party was pursuing independent self-interests rather than conspiring with another.[13] One conspicuous attempt to inject quality of care issues into the evaluation of restraints under the rule of reason is the patient care defense announced by the Seventh Circuit in *Wilk v. American Medical Association*.[14] The court's four-part test affords defendant the opportunity to demonstrate a dominant, "objectively reasonable" concern for issues going to the "scientific method" underlying the care given to patients but requires that less restrictive means of policing quality were not available. This approach, which had not been followed by other circuits, actually reformulates the rule of reason, and, by blending subjective and objective standards, invites an open-ended inquiry into scientific issues and motives that may confuse both judges and juries.[15]

§ 14–8. The Rule of Reason Standard in Professional Restraints of Trade Cases

The courts' most important concession to professional discretion has been the tendency to review alleged restraints of trade under the rule of reason

---

8. 476 U.S. at 464 n. 4, 106 S.Ct. at 2021 n. 4.

9. See § 14–10.

10. See, e.g., Michigan State Med. Soc'y, 101 F.T.C. 191 (1983); In re American Med. Ass'n, 94 F.T.C. 701 (1979), modified and enforced, American Med. Ass'n v. FTC, 638 F.2d 443 (2d Cir.1980), affirmed by an equally divided court 455 U.S. 676, 102 S.Ct. 1744, 71 L.Ed.2d 546 (1982).

11. See Koefoot v. American College of Surgeons, 652 F.Supp. 882 (N.D.Ill.1986)(excluding quality of care evidence from trial); but see Wilk v. American Med. Ass'n, 719 F.2d 207,

227 (7th Cir.1983) (proposing limited role for quality of care concerns).

12. National Soc'y of Professional Eng'rs v. United States, 435 U.S. 679, 98 S.Ct. 1355, 55 L.Ed.2d 637 (1978).

13. See Charity Scott, Medical Peer Review, Antitrust and the Effect of Statutory Reform, 50 Md. L. Rev. 316 (1991).

14. 719 F.2d 207 (7th Cir.1983). See discussion infra § 14–12(b)2.

15. See Thomas L. Greaney, Quality of Care and Market Failure Defenses in Antitrust Health Care Litigation, 21 Conn. L. Rev. 605 (1989).

rather than the *per se* rule. When defendants assert that their actions are based on professional concerns, courts have generally examined the alleged restraint under the rule of reason.[1] However, following the Supreme Court's admonition that the rule of reason should not be applied simply because a restraint is entered into by professionals,[2] several courts have suggested that justifications premised upon professional concerns must satisfy some threshold level of plausibility before the rule will be invoked.[3]

§ 14–9. Restrictions on Price Competition or Contracting

"Ethical" restrictions imposed by professional associations upon the pricing or contracting practices of their members were among the first norms to be challenged under the antitrust laws. Justifications offered for these practices included arguments that professionals should be regarded as engaged in something other than a traditional commercial enterprise;[1] that professional control over pricing was necessary to avoid degradation in quality;[2] that desirable cross-subsidies to low income individuals resulted from these practices;[3] that contractual links to lay organizations would undermine professional judgements;[4] and that consumers were ill-equipped to evaluate professional services.[5] As discussed above, the Supreme Court's decisions in *Goldfarb* and *National Society of Professional Engineers* left little room for accepting such justifications. Although the *California Dental Association* decision can be read to signal somewhat greater receptiveness to such justifications, where restraints directly affect the pricing mechanism and do not plausibly enhance efficiency under ancillary restraints analysis, courts are likely to continue to condemn them under per se or highly truncated rule of reason modes of analysis.

The earliest challenge to medical ethical proscriptions involving attempts to obstruct price-cutting by physicians was the Justice Department's criminal prosecution of the AMA in the 1940's.[6] Courts and the FTC have subsequently struck down many other collective efforts to deny cooperation necessary to compete to innovative, cost-reducing payment plans.[7]

§ 14–8

1. California Dental Ass'n. v. FTC, 526 U.S. 756, 119 S.Ct. 1604 (1999); FTC v. Indiana Fed'n of Dentists, 476 U.S. 447, 458, 106 S.Ct. 2009, 2018, 90 L.Ed.2d 445 (1986); See also Kreuzer v. American Academy of Periodontology, 735 F.2d 1479 (D.C.Cir.1984).

2. Arizona v. Maricopa County Med. Soc'y, 457 U.S. 332, 102 S.Ct. 2466, 73 L.Ed.2d 48 (1982); see also Wilk v. American Med. Ass'n, 719 F.2d 207, 222 (7th Cir.1983) ("an agreement to fix prices will not escape per se treatment simply because it is entered into by professionals and accompanied by ethical protestations.").

3. See, e.g., Kreuzer v. American Academy of Periodontology, 735 F.2d 1479, 1492 (D.C.Cir.1984).

§ 14–9

1. Goldfarb v. Virginia State Bar, 421 U.S. 773, 95 S.Ct. 2004, 44 L.Ed.2d 572 (1975); American Med. Ass'n v. FTC, 638 F.2d 443 (2d Cir.1980), affirmed 455 U.S. 676, 102 S.Ct. 1744, 71 L.Ed.2d 546 (1982).

2. National Soc'y of Professional Eng'rs v. United States, 435 U.S. 679, 98 S.Ct. 1355, 55 L.Ed.2d 637 (1978).

3. American Med. Ass'n v. United States, 317 U.S. 519, 63 S.Ct. 326, 87 L.Ed. 434 (1943); see generally Reuben A. Kessel, Price Discrimination in Medicine, 1 J.L. Econ. 20 (1958).

4. American Med. Ass'n, 94 F.T.C. 701 (1979) (consent order).

5. FTC v. Indiana Fed'n of Dentists, 476 U.S. 447, 106 S.Ct. 2009, 90 L.Ed.2d 445 (1986).

6. American Med. Ass'n v. United States, 130 F.2d 233 (D.C.Cir.1942), affirmed 317 U.S. 519, 63 S.Ct. 326, 87 L.Ed. 434 (1943).

7. See, e.g., Group Health Co–op. of Puget Sound v. King County Med. Soc'y, 237 P.2d 737 (Wash.1951); United States v. Halifax Hosp. Med. Ctr., 1981–1 Trade Cas. (CCH)

Professional norms directly interfering with the price mechanism have also been condemned. Most obviously, professional societies setting maximum or minimum prices through fee schedules constitutes illegal price fixing.[8] While the Supreme Court has intimated that the promulgation of "purely advisory" fee schedules may not be illegal,[9] this caveat is probably best understood to require evidence of an agreement rather than to impose any additional substantive burden under the rule of reason. Other, less direct restraints on price rivalry have been found to violate the antitrust laws. Perhaps the most important such case was the FTC's challenge to the AMA's restrictions on "contract practice." These ethical standards opposed physicians agreeing to provide medical services for a specified price or on a salaried basis; companion norms prohibited physicians from accepting "inadequate" compensation or from "underbidding" other physicians.[10]

At the same time, not all price-related ethical restrictions merit summary condemnation; in some cases plausible efficiency justifications may be advanced. For example, ethical bans on acceptance of contingent fees and referral fees by professionals present much closer questions.[11] Referral fees, like advertising, may attract customers and reduce search costs and hence have plausible pro-competitive justifications. On the other hand, such referral arrangements also involve conflicts of interest and lack of disclosure in markets in which information is highly imperfect. Economic analysis does not provide clear guidance as to whether these practices consistently impair or promote competition.[12] Thus, close scrutiny of particular facts under the rule of reason is required to assess whether the prohibition is on balance pro-or anticompetitive.

§ 14–10. Professional Restrictions on Advertising, Solicitation and Related Activities

Restraints on professional advertising and other forms of solicitation imposed by professional groups and by state agencies require somewhat more refined analysis than do direct price restraints. Typically, these restrictions carry at least colorable claims of improving market performance and their anticompetitive effects are not always facially apparent.

¶ 64,151, 1981 WL 2101 (M.D.Fla.1981)(consent decree); Forbes Health Sys. Med. Staff, 94 F.T.C. 1042 (1979)(consent order). See §§ 14–24—14–28, infra.

8. Goldfarb v. Virginia State Bar, 421 U.S. 773, 95 S.Ct. 2004, 44 L.Ed.2d 572 (1975); Arizona v. Maricopa County Med. Soc'y, 457 U.S. 332, 102 S.Ct. 2466, 73 L.Ed.2d 48 (1982).

9. Goldfarb v. Virginia State Bar, 421 U.S. 773, 781, 95 S.Ct. 2004, 2010, 44 L.Ed.2d 572 (1975).

10. American Med. Ass'n, 94 F.T.C. 701, 1011–12 (1979), affirmed as modified on other grounds, 638 F.2d 443 (2d Cir.1980), affirmed on an equally divided court, 452 U.S. 960, 101 S.Ct. 3107, 69 L.Ed.2d 970 (1981). See also American Soc'y of Anesthesiologists, 93 F.T.C. 101 (1979) (consent order) (medical society rule restricting members from rendering services other than on a fee-for-service basis).

11. The FTC has accepted consent decrees prohibiting the American Institute of Certified Public Accountants from barring contingent and referral fees. In re American Institute of Certified Public Accountants, Dkt. No. C–3297, 55 Fed.Reg. 40944 (October 5, 1990).

12. Compare Mark V. Pauly, The Ethics and Economics of Kickbacks and Fee Splitting, 10 Bell J. Econ. 344 (1979) (demonstrating the efficiency-enhancing potential of paid referrals in some circumstances) with Deborah Owen, The Federal Trade Commission's Health Care Program, in Antitrust Health Care Enforcement and Analysis 163–64 (M. Elizabeth Gee ed. 1992) (citing information-improving effects of banning referral fees in limiting physician conflicts of interest and promoting public confidence in professional services).

Restrictions on advertising and solicitation have been successfully challenged as horizontal restraints of trade under the Sherman Act,[1] as unfair methods of competition[2] and unfair acts or practices[3] under the Federal Trade Commission Act and, where state action is present, as unconstitutional abridgements of First Amendment rights.[4] The FTC has brought a number of antitrust cases against private associations that have adopted ethical codes or other restrictions barring or restricting advertising and solicitation.[5] Some of these cases have involved more narrowly-tailored ethical restrictions such as prohibitions on advertisements that: mention price or discounts; contain specific information about the practitioner, his qualifications or unique services; and contain matter deemed undignified or "unprofessional."[6] In addition, the FTC and Justice Department have challenged restrictions on advertising imposed by state boards regulating professions when those boards are dominated by members of the profession they regulate.[7] Restraints of trade imposed by such boards are shielded by the state action doctrine only when "clearly articulated and affirmatively expressed as state policy."[8]

The issue of the appropriate legal standard for evaluating advertising restrictions was before the Supreme Court in *California Dental Association v. FTC*.[9] In its administrative hearings, the FTC found that the CDA's Code of Ethics restricted two types of truthful, nondeceptive advertising: price advertising and advertising relating to the quality of dental services. It concluded that the restrictions on price advertising amounted to a "naked attempt to eliminate price competition" and hence warranted per se condemnation;[10] it also struck down the nonprice advertising rules under a somewhat abbreviated analysis.[11] In affirming the Commission, the Ninth Circuit examined the conduct using a "quick look" rule of reason analysis, and found the evidence adequate to support the FTC's conclusions about likely adverse competitive

§ 14–10

1. See, e.g., United States v. Texas State Bd. of Public Accountancy, 464 F.Supp. 400 (W.D.Tex.1978), affirmed and modified 592 F.2d 919 (5th Cir.1979); American Med. Ass'n, 94 F.T.C. 701 (1979) (consent order).

2. See, e.g., American Med. Ass'n, 94 F.T.C. 701 (1979); Massachusetts Bd. of Registration in Optometry, 110 F.T.C. 549 (1988).

3. American Med. Ass'n, 94 F.T.C. 701 (1979).

4. See, e.g., Peel v. Attorney Registration & Disciplinary Comm'n of Illinois, 496 U.S. 91, 110 S.Ct. 2281, 110 L.Ed.2d 83 (1990); Zauderer v. Office of Disciplinary Counsel, 471 U.S. 626, 105 S.Ct. 2265, 85 L.Ed.2d 652 (1985); but cf. Friedman v. Rogers, 440 U.S. 1, 99 S.Ct. 887, 59 L.Ed.2d 100 (1979).

5. See, e.g., Michigan Optometric Ass'n, 106 F.T.C. 342 (1985) (consent order); Oklahoma Optometric Ass'n, 106 F.T.C. 556 (1985) (consent order); American Academy of Optometry, Inc., 108 F.T.C. 25 (1986) (consent order); Tarrant County Med. Soc'y, 110 F.T.C. 119 (1987) (consent order).

6. See, e.g., Connecticut Chiropractic Ass'n, 56 Fed. Reg. 23586 (1991) (consent order) (restrictions on sensational advertising, use of coupons, advertising of expertise or free services); Broward County Med. Ass'n, 99 F.T.C. 622 (1982) (consent order) (prohibitions of advertising concerning fees, acceptance of Medicare or credit cards, knowledge of foreign languages, hours and office locations, professional training and experience).

7. See, e.g., Massachusetts Bd. of Registration in Optometry, 110 F.T.C. 549 (1988); Texas Bd. of Chiropractic Examiners, 57 Fed. Reg. 20,279 (1992).

8. California Retail Liquor Dealers Ass'n v. Midcal Aluminum, Inc., 445 U.S. 97, 105, 100 S.Ct. 937, 943, 63 L.Ed.2d 233 (1980).

9. 526 U.S. 756, 119 S.Ct. 1604 (1999).

10. In Re California Dental Association, 121 F.T.C. 190, 300 (1996), aff'd 128 F.3d 720, vacated, 526 U.S. 756, 119 S.Ct. 1604 (1999)(concluding that CDA's restrictions on price advertising "effectively preclude its members from making low fee or across-the-board discount claims regardless of their truthfulness").

11. These rules precluded members from making subjective or ambiguous claims such as "gentle dentistry in a caring environment" or "the finest dental care." Id. at 318.

effects of the restrictions.[12] In a 5–4 decision, the Supreme Court vacated and remanded the judgement to the court of appeals for a fuller inquiry into whether the CDA's activities constituted a violation of the antitrust laws. The Court stated that the restrictions and the proffered justifications (which were based on professional context in which they operated and the desirability of preventing confusion and deceptive practices in a market beset with information imperfections) merited a "less quick look" than given by the Ninth Circuit. A vigorous dissent argued that the record was replete with evidence sufficient to support condemnation under the rule of reason; indeed, the majority seemed to concede that a more searching explication of the evidence by the Ninth Circuit might have sufficed.[13]

The Court's resolution of the California Dental Association case raises more questions than it answers. First, the opinion sheds no light on the proper methodology for conducting abbreviated inquiries into advertising restrictions or other restraints of trade that have obvious antitcompetitive tendencies but that may be justified in some cases. The preferred approach, which finds support in the case law and the analytic scheme set forth in Justice Breyer's dissent, would be to require the FTC to establish the restriction's anticompetitive "tendencies," and if a "nearly naked" restraint is shown, shift the burden to defendants to establish a procompetitive justification.[14] Absent such proof, quick or per se condemnation is warranted; if defendants present evidence of justification, a full rule of reason inquiry (which would require proof of effect or market power) would be necessary. The majority opinion is opaque as to its methodology for examining the restrictions and seems to accept the barest of allegations from defendant to require a "less quick" examination. Second, the decision gives significant weight to the "professional context" in which the restraint operates and the information asymmetries which affect consumers' understanding of treatments and advertising. While consideration of the economic realities of health care markets is undoubtedly appropriate, it would be a mistake to adopt rules that presumptively treat those markets differently than others. This conclusion is based on the difficulties inherent in distinguishing the effects of information in imperfect markets and the argument that the absence of state legislation condoning such professional restrictions should counsel caution before selectively adjusting antitrust rules for specific industries.[15] It may also be noted that the Court relied upon rather abstract generalizations about market imperfections to justify shifting onto defendants a significant burden of proving anticompetitive effects. This represents something of a sea change in antitrust jurisprudence involving health professionals, which had long let lay dormant footnote 17 of Goldfarb v. Virginia State Bar[16] (which alluded to

12. 128 F.3d 720 (9th Cir.1997).

13. Id. at 1617 ("[h]ad the Court of Appeals engaged in a painstaking discussion in a league with Justice Breyer's ... and had it confronted the comparability of these restricitions to bars on clearly verifiable advertising, its reasoning might have sufficed to justify its conclusion.")

14. Philip E. Areeda & Herbert Hovenkamp, Antitrust Law ¶ 1901.1b5 (1999 Supp.).

15. Philip E. Areeda & Herbert Hovenkamp, Antitrust Law ¶ 1901.1b5 (1999

Supp.)(Noting the absence of legislation allowing health professionals to engage in self regulation and concluding, "[w]e would not treat horizontal restrictions on advertising in the learned professions in a significantly different manner than such restrictions are treated in the general run of markets, subject to the qualification that we would ordinarily classify them as 'nearly naked' rather than absolutely naked restraints.")

16. 421 U.S. 773, 778 n. 17 (1975).

the possibility of greater elbowroom for professionals), and which had been loathe to allow facile incantations of market imperfections to disturb conventional antitrust analysis.[17] One would have expected the Court to justify this metamorphosis with record evidence or scholarship indicating that conventional competition principles needed to be adjusted.

The FTC's remedies in its advertising cases reveal some of the tensions inherent in applying antitrust principles in markets with imperfect information and in circumstances that raise First Amendment issues. The FTC's original order in the *AMA* case contained a blanket prohibition against restrictions on "the advertising of services, facilities, or prices," but permitted the AMA to disseminate "reasonable ethical guidelines governing the conduct of its members with respect to representations, including unsubstantiated representations that would be false or deceptive within the meaning of Section 5 of the Federal Trade Commission Act."[18] On appeal, the Second Circuit extended the AMA's mandate for self-regulation even further, modifying the Commission's order to make it clear that the AMA would be permitted to police any conduct that it "reasonably believes" to be false and deceptive within the meaning of the FTC Act.[19] Although delegating authority to regulate to a trade association found to have abused is regulatory authority may be surprising, it can be justified as correcting market failure. False and deceptive advertising might taint all provider-supplied information; hence its removal promotes competition, as discussed in the following section.

§ 14–11. Professional Standard–Setting and Certification Activities

An important function of trade and professional associations is setting quality and performance standards for the goods and services their members provide. Profession-sponsored health care standards may take a variety of forms. They may establish norms governing who can perform certain procedures, the circumstances under which those procedures may be performed, or what degree of skill, training or experience is required. The context in which

---

17. See e.g. Jefferson Parish Hosp. Dist. No. 2 v. Hyde, 466 U.S. 2 (1984); Wilk v. American Med. Ass'n 895 F.2d 352 (7th Cir. 1990); Koefoot v. American College of Surgeons, 652 F.Supp. 882 (N.D.Ill.1986).

18. In *Chicago Board of Trade*, Justice Brandeis described the rule of reason as follows:

The true test of legality is whether the restraint imposed is such as merely regulates and perhaps thereby promotes competition or whether it is such as may suppress or even destroy competition. To determine that question the court must ordinarily consider the facts peculiar to the business to which the restraint is applied; its condition before and after the restraint was imposed; the nature of the restraint and its effect, actual or probable. The history of the restraint, the evil believed to exist, the reason for adopting the particular remedy, the purpose or end sought to be attained, are all relevant facts. Id. at 238, 39 S.Ct. at 244.

19. American Med. Ass'n v. F.T.C., 638 F.2d 443, 452 (2d Cir.1980), affirmed 455 U.S. 676, 102 S.Ct. 1744, 71 L.Ed.2d 546 (1982). The court did not explain the basis for its modification, noting only the AMA's claims of overbreadth and vagueness and the Commission's acknowledgement of the " 'special role' of organized medicine * * * [that] necessarily confers on AMA a measure of discretion to develop 'principles of conduct.' "Id. quoting Bates v. State Bar of Arizona, 433 U.S. 350, 384, 97 S.Ct. 2691, 2709, 53 L.Ed.2d 810 (1977). The FTC has included substantially identical provisos permitting policing of deceptive advertising in orders involving state regulatory boards charged with conspiring to restrain trade by various kinds of advertising and related conduct. See, e.g., Massachusetts Bd. of Registration in Optometry, 110 F.T.C. 549 (1988); Rhode Island Bd. of Accountancy, 107 F.T.C. 293 (1986). See also American Academy of Ophthalmology, 101 F.T.C. 1018 (1983) (advisory opinion).

these standards are set also varies considerably. It may include norms or rules of professional groups; conditions for membership in the group; advisory or hortatory statements communicated to members and third parties; or information supplied without specific requirements. In many instances the association's conduct amounts to nothing more than supplying information or expressing a collective opinion. Typically this is done either by dispensing information directly to consumers or members or by "certification"—certifying achievement of the group's standard by granting seals of approval, membership in an organization, or other indicia. In other instances—far more problematic from an antitrust perspective—the collective activity of the association goes further and entails compulsory standard-setting. This conduct entails agreements to abide by a standard or not to deal with those who fail to meet the standard or with third parties dealing with nonapproved providers.

Standardization and certification programs can pose a variety of competitive risks. They may act as a facilitating device or a cover for a cartel that fixes prices, allocates markets, limits output, limits competition as to inputs, members' efforts or other competitive variables. In addition, standardization carries the risk of anticompetitive exclusion either in the traditional sense of coordinating collective refusals to deal, or raising rivals' costs. These activities may also eliminate quality competition in more subtle ways. Professional standards may reduce innovation by ossifying technology, excluding competitors or raising their costs, or facilitating oligopolistic pricing by reducing monitoring and enforcement costs.[1] In addition, economic analysis suggests that professional self-regulation imposing minimum levels of quality is apt to set inefficiently high standards.[2]

At the same time it is clear that these arrangements usually offer important efficiency benefits principally by improving the flow of information in health care markets. Standardization programs in health care tend to improve market performance by reducing high transaction costs that consumers would have to incur if they attempted to overcome the information deficiencies of the market. To give one example, the cost of negotiating and specifying all preferred modes of treatments in health insurance contracts is obviously prohibitive for individual consumers and probably for most health plans. However, when a medical society promulgates practice guidelines it establishes a less costly and more convenient mechanism which buyers and sellers can use to negotiate the kinds and quality of services they wish to exchange.

Because they are "public goods" (i.e., individual buyers and sellers cannot recapture the costs of producing them), standards and certification are underproduced in the market. Hence, from an economic standpoint, policies encouraging their development tends to improve the efficiency of market

§ 14–11

1. See Kenneth G. Elzinga, The Compass of Competition for Professional Services, in Regulating the Professions (Roger D. Blair & Stephen Rubin eds., 1980); 7 Philip E. Areeda, Antitrust Law ¶ 1503a (1986); 16A Julian O. von Kalinowski, Business Organizations: Antitrust Laws and Trade Regulation § 61.03 (1989).

2. Hayne E. Leland, Quacks, Lemons and Licensing: A Theory of Minimum Quality Standards, 87 J. Pol. Econ. 1328 (1979). Frederic M. Scherer, Industrial Market Structure and Economic Performance 1013 (2d ed. 1980) (self regulation may retard growth of low-cost firms).

transactions.[3] Such activities may also eliminate "free riding" by low-quality providers who enjoy the benefits of the reputation of their colleagues. Identifying "bad apples" enables and encourages providers to maintain quality at efficient levels.[4]

§ 14–12. Professional Society Membership and Practice Restrictions

A large part of the *raison d'etre* of professional societies is the exchange of scientific information and opinion both among members and with buyers and others who lack expertise. Professional societies also confer a variety of important benefits on their members. In some cases, membership in the organization itself carries with it prestige or recognition that the member supplies services of high quality or has superior training or experience. However, membership may also signal conformance with certain restrictions on the way members compete and hence raise issues of anticompetitive exclusion or standardization.

a. *Exclusions From Membership*

Those who are denied membership in a professional society that confers reputational or other benefits on its members sometimes allege that their exclusion constitutes a boycott by competitors. Courts have rejected such claims where there is no evidence that the exclusion carried with it collateral agreements to standardize practice or otherwise limit members' competitive behavior. This is the case even where doubts exist as to the professional basis for exclusion. As one court aptly put it, "It is axiomatic that trade standards must exclude some things as substandard and it is unsurprising that standard-setting bodies sometimes err. A single such error does not amount to a conspiracy."[1]

Marrese v. American Academy of Orthopaedic Surgeons[2] is instructive in this regard. The court's decision rested on plaintiff's failure to prove his assertion that denial of membership in a professional academy caused a restraint of trade. Noting that membership was not necessary to practice medicine, obtain a staff appointment or receive referrals, the court found no restriction of output in any market. Moreover, it rejected the claim that withholding membership, which plaintiff analogized to a "seal of approval," stigmatized Dr. Marrese. Besides questioning whether such a stigma was significant (because plaintiff continued to receive referrals), the court stated that the loss of referrals would not be sufficient absent evidence that the academy had prevented others from dealing with the doctor.[3] Although the

---

3. See Clark C. Havighurst, Practice Guidelines for Medical Care: The Policy Rationale, 34 St. Louis U. L.J. 777, 792–800 (1990).

4. George A. Akerlof, The Market for "Lemons": Quality Uncertainty and the Market Mechanism, 84 Q.J. Econ. 488 (1970). See generally Timothy S. Jost, The Joint Commission on Accreditation of Hospitals: Private Regulation of Health Care and the Public Interest, 24 B.C. L. Rev. 835 (1983); Robert H. Heidt, Industry Self–Regulation and the Useless Concept "Group Boycott", 39 Vand. L. Rev. 1507 (1986).

§ 14–12

1. Consolidated Metal Products v. American Petroleum Inst., 846 F.2d 284, 294 (5th Cir.1988) (citations omitted).

2. 977 F.2d 585 (7th Cir.1992) (unpublished opinion).

3. Id. (citing Schachar v. American Academy of Ophthalmology, Inc., 870 F.2d 397 (7th Cir.1989). See infra § 14–13.

Seventh Circuit's narrow reading of the boycott doctrine is open to question, the *Marrese* decision makes it clear that plaintiffs challenging membership denials face heavy burdens and must closely link the denial to effects on competition.

In addition, plaintiffs must show that the denial of certification or membership caused them to suffer "antitrust injury."[4] In *Sanjuan v. American Board of Psychiatry and Neurology, Inc.*,[5] in which plaintiffs challenged their denial of certification by defendant board, the court held that plaintiffs lacked standing because they had alleged only that the denial had prevented them from receiving higher fees. Plaintiffs were able to practice psychiatry without board certification, but were unable to charge fees comparable to board-certified psychiatrists. This, the court held, was not the kind of injury antitrust law was designed to protect and dismissed their claim. This analysis illustrates the hazard of too narrowly defining the class of appropriate plaintiffs under the antitrust injury doctrine. The court ignored the possibility that the market for psychiatric services may have been segmented: greater competition in the "credentialled" portion of the market might drive down those prices, something that plaintiffs might not have been able to without obtaining certification.[6]

b. *Practice Restrictions Associated With Professional Society Membership*

Instances in which members of a professional society collectively agree to practice in a certain manner or restrict other competitive dimensions of their practice pose more obvious antitrust issues. We first discuss the category of restrictions that generally lack justification and merit summary treatment and then turn to three cases that illustrate the complexity of balancing the competitive harms and benefits of practice rules when some procompetitive justifications are proffered.

1. *Practice Restraints Lacking Justifications*

Many of the trade association restraints discussed above, obviously directed at restraining trade, bore little relationship to professional aspects of their members' practices and were analyzed under the per se rule or highly truncated rule of reason.[7] The FTC has challenged a host of restrictions that on brief examination lack plausible justification. Although their competitive impact is less obvious than naked restraints such as price fixing, these activities have generally been viewed as inherently suspect and not warranting extensive scrutiny under the rule of reason. An important question raised by the Supreme Court's California Dental decision is whether abbreviated analysis will still apply to these restraints.[8] In addition to its cases overturning advertising and related restrictions discussed above, the FTC has challenged anticompetitive restraints involving trade association rules restricting operations of franchises or branch offices,[9] prohibiting providers from selling

4. See supra § 14–3c.

5. 40 F.3d 247 (7th Cir.1994).

6. See Philip E. Areeda & Herbert Hovenkamp, Antitrust Law ¶ 362 (1999 Supp.).

7. E.g., FTC v. Indiana Fed'n of Dentists, 476 U.S. 447, 106 S.Ct. 2009, 90 L.Ed.2d 445 (1986); see supra § 14–9.

8. See § 14–10 supra

9. See, e.g., Oklahoma Optometric Ass'n, 106 F.T.C. 556 (1985).

products related to their services,[10] prohibiting affiliations with other categories of providers[11] and limiting the number of office locations.[12] Although the immediate competitive effect of such restraints is not always obvious, economic analysis suggests that they enable parties to strategically raise their own costs and reap higher profits. Thus, factfinders may dispense with requiring extensive proof of market effects, market power and other issues as required under a full blown rule of reason analysis.[13]

2. Restrictions With Plausible Justifications

Wilk v. AMA

Ethical prohibitions against physician referrals and other forms of cooperation with chiropractors were at issue in *Wilk v. American Medical Association*.[14] The AMA's conduct illustrates how certain practice standards that obviously restrain competition can also present non-frivolous justifications based on preserving quality of care.

In applying the Seventh Circuit's "special" rule of reason on remand,[15] the trial court undertook a "moderately truncated" inquiry into the effects of defendant's practices.[16] First, it concluded that defendant AMA had market power based on the fact that a majority of all medical physicians are AMA members and the high proportion of all medical fees paid to AMA members. Notably, the court did not require proof of impact on price and output. Instead, it inferred anticompetitive effect from several reliable proxies: the AMA's market power and specific intent to destroy chiropractic, economic evidence that denying access to facilities and equipment imposed higher costs upon chiropractors, and the presence of barriers to entry for new chiropractors.[17] Given the nature of the restraints at issue, the court was able to satisfy itself as to effect without more exacting proof.

In assessing benefits under the rule of reason, the trial court rejected as speculative the AMA's claim that procompetitive informational benefits flowed from the boycott (which the AMA characterized as "nonverbal communication" about differences in quality of care provided by chiropractors).[18] Essentially, the defendants argued that rules prohibiting cooperation signalled important facts and professional judgments about chiropractic, and thus improved medical doctors' competitiveness by allowing them to act on the basis of better information. In principle, certain collective actions by professional associations may improve competition by overcoming market imperfections in information about providers and the quality of care they supply. However, the court was entirely correct in rejecting this alleged benefit on the record before it. Given that the AMA's absolute boycott was designed to destroy chiropractic practice, a far more compelling showing of the nature and

10. See, e.g., Michigan Optometric Ass'n, 106 F.T.C. 342 (1985).

11. Iowa Chapter of the American Physical Therapy Ass'n, No. C–3242 (1988)(consent order).

12. See, e.g., American Academy of Ophthalmologists, 108 F.T.C. 25 (1986).

13. See In re Detroit Auto Dealers Ass'n, 955 F.2d 457 (6th Cir.) (upholding FTC's truncated analysis of agreement among automobile dealers to restrict hours of business), 506 U.S.

973, 113 S.Ct. 461, 121 L.Ed.2d 369 (1992); cf. California Dental Ass'n v. FTC, 526 U.S. 756, 119 S.Ct. 1604 (1999) (discussed supra, § 14–10).

14. 895 F.2d 352 (7th Cir.1990).

15. See supra § 14–7.

16. Wilk v. American Med. Ass'n, 671 F.Supp. 1465 (N.D.Ill.1987).

17. Id. at 1478–79.

18. Id.

magnitude of these benefits and the absence of less restrictive alternatives should be required to overcome such restraints.[19]

Kreuzer

Where the proffered benefits of a medical society's rule are clearer and the harms more ambiguous, courts face a difficult task under the rule of reason. In *Kreuzer v. American Academy of Periodontology*,[20] a licensed dentist who had practiced periodontics and had received advanced training in a subfield of periodontology was denied "active" membership in the American Academy of Periodontology (AAP) because he failed to meet the Academy's requirement that all active members confine their practice to periodontics. Dr. Kreuzer had practiced periodontal prothesis, a subfield not within the American Dental Association's definition of periodontics.

Reversing summary judgment, the district court rejected defendant's patient care defense, holding that the absence of anticompetitive intent could not absolve the Academy under the rule of reason. The court went on to suggest that the AAP's limited practice requirement may harm competition in several ways.[21] The facts in the record were far from complete and the AAP had not set forth an economically coherent defense of its conduct.[22] However the court's intuition was probably correct given the market in which the restraint operated. AAP members likely possessed "market power or exclusive access to an element essential to effective competition," and the rule may have permitted dentists to limit competition by allocating markets among themselves and perhaps deterred entry by raising their rivals' costs.[23]

On the other side, there were undeniable benefits associated with the AAP directory. Plainly, it improved information for patients and their agents (referring dentists and third party payors). By certifying that members devote their practice exclusively to periodontology, AAP signalled a quality-related fact by differentiating practitioners who are willing to specialize. In so doing, the AAP's activities not only reduced transactions costs to buyers and their agents in obtaining information, but also provided appropriate incentives to specialize.

19. See Thomas L. Greaney, Quality of Care and Market Failure Defenses in Antitrust Health Care Litigation, 21 Conn. L. Rev. 605 (1989).

20. 735 F.2d 1479 (D.C.Cir.1984); cf. Machovec v. Council for Nat'l Register of Health Serv. Providers in Psychology, Inc., 616 F.Supp. 258 (E.D.Va.1985).

21. The potential anticompetitive effects of the limited practice rule cited by the court were: preventing periodontists desiring active AAP status from competing with dentists; preventing periodontists who decide to compete with general dentists from competing with other periodontists by denying them referrals; artificially limiting the number of periodontists competing; and imposing costs and inefficiencies on consumers who are denied "one stop dental service." Id. at 1493–94.

22. In focusing on a patient care motives, the AAP arguably neglected its best possible defense: it should have acknowledged self-interested basis for promulgating the directory and stressed the procompetitive benefits of providing such useful information to consumers. See Clark C. Havighurst, et al., Health Care Law and Policy: Readings, Notes, and Questions 886 (2d ed. 1998). See generally, Machovoc v. Council for the Nat'l Register of Health Serv. Providers in Psychology, 616 F.Supp. 258 (E.D.Va.1985) (selective directory providing access to information did not constitute an illegal boycott).

23. See Thomas L. Greaney, Quality of Care and Market Failure Defenses in Antitrust Health Care Litigation, 21 Conn. L. Rev. 605, 656–57 (1989); Brief of the United States Department of Justice as Amicus Curiae, Kreuzer v. American Academy of Periodontology, 735 F.2d 1479 (D.C.Cir.1984).

The Circuit Court's opinion in *Kreuzer* sets forth a doctrinally sound approach for weighing the pro-and anticompetitive aspects of the directory under the rule of reason. First, it emphasizes that the trial court must examine the conflict of interest of the self-regulator proffering quality justifications.[24] Second, it states that even if evidence of a procompetitive effect was present, defendant must show that the means chosen are the least restrictive available.[25] This approach at least suggests that the inquiry should focus on the procompetitive virtues of enhanced information and whether the membership rule and the directory listing policy were narrowly tailored to accomplish such ends without unduly limiting rivalry among members. If, for example, the membership rules and directory fostered consumer search and patient referrals without impeding entry or impairing market structure, the practice should be upheld.

Koefoot

Another difficult case, *Koefoot v. American College of Surgeons*, illustrates circumstances in which information benefits might not necessarily justify a practice restriction.[26] *Koefoot* involved an antitrust challenge to a bylaw of the American College of Surgeons (ACS) that proscribed "itinerant surgery." Under this rule, ACS surgeons were prohibited from delegating post-operative care of their patients to physicians other than surgeons. Plaintiffs contended that the promulgation and enforcement of the bylaw by ACS constituted an illegal market allocation by ACS surgeons enabling them to block entry into their markets; that it constituted a boycott of Dr. Koefoot and other visiting surgeons and a boycott of general physicians providing post-operative care; and that the arrangement constituted an illegal tie-in of two separate services.[27] Despite the trial court's rulings holding the *Wilk* "patient care motive" defense inapplicable[28] and limiting the role of "harm" evidence at trial,[29] plaintiffs were unable to persuade the jury that defendants' conduct constituted an unreasonable restraint of trade.[30]

It is certainly possible that the itinerant surgery rule reduced competition in rural markets. In markets in which there were no local surgeons, patients had to travel to more densely populated areas for surgery, hence reducing a form of competition among surgeons who might have otherwise incurred greater costs by themselves traveling to rural hospitals. Where a few surgeons were present in rural markets, the rule inhibited competition because it empowered those surgeons to foreclose entry to outsiders by denying cooperation in the form of post-surgical care for visiting surgeons' patients.[31] Given

---

24. Kreuzer v. American Academy of Periodontology, 735 F.2d 1479, 1494 (D.C.Cir.1984) ("When the economic self-interest of the boycotting group and its proffered justifications merge the rule of reason will seldom be satisfied.").

25. Id. at 1494–95.

26. 610 F.Supp. 1298 (N.D.Ill.1985) (hereinafter "Koefoot I"); Koefoot v. American College of Surgeons, 652 F.Supp. 882 (N.D.Ill. 1986) (hereinafter "Koefoot II").

27. Koefoot II, 652 F.Supp. 882, 885 (N.D.Ill.1986).

28. Koefoot I, 610 F.Supp. 1298, 1306 (N.D.Ill.1985).

29. Koefoot II, 652 F.Supp. 882, 898 (N.D.Ill.1986).

30. See Koefoot v. American College of Surgeons, 1987–1 Trade Cas. (CCH) ¶ 67,510, 1987 WL 7292 (N.D.Ill.1987) (denying plaintiffs' motion for new trial).

31. Defendants evidently recognized this potential, as an ACS internal document revealed the society's concern that itinerant surgery would "freez[e] out young men who might wish to come into a community to practice." Koefoot I, 610 F.Supp. at 1603.

the possibility that ACS membership conferred market power[32] or that circumstances allowed them to raise rivals' costs, the itinerant surgery rule may thus have restrained competition.

The inquiry therefore should move to whether the itinerant surgery rule offered procompetitive benefits that outweighed its possible harms. Here, a careful assessment of information imperfections and the rule's ameliorating effects is crucial. In this vein, the ACS label provided a signal to consumers regarding the nature of post-operative care they would receive if they chose a Fellow to perform their surgery. As such, the rule arguably mitigated market imperfections by succinctly conveying information, reducing transactions costs and removing uncertainty in the purchase of surgical services. However, these informational benefits should not necessarily save the itinerant surgery rule because it exacerbated conflicts of interests by empowering members to restrict competition. Assuming the market position of ACS surgeons conferred market power on members, there is reason to believe that the rule operated in rural markets to inhibit entry and entrench oligopolistic power of local surgeons. Moreover, less restrictive alternatives for achieving competitive benefits may have been available. Information deficits addressed by the itinerant surgery rule could have been dealt with by requiring that patients be informed and given a choice of their post-surgical care provider. These options would preserve competition and alleviate information gaps without requiring ACS members to coordinate their behavior or empowering them to exclude rivals.

§ 14–13. Practice Guidelines

The need for sound scientific guidance as to appropriate methods of practice has caused many private organizations such as medical specialty societies, payers, institutional providers, utilization review groups and quality assurance agencies promulgate "practice guidelines."[1] The term remains somewhat ill-defined, but generally embraces a wide range of research and opinion setting forth standards of practice or recommended strategies for patient management.[2]

Because guidelines often entail close collaboration among competing physicians and are designed to achieve some degree of standardization of practice, antitrust issues may be raised. There are two principle kinds of anticompetitive conduct that can flow from promulgation of practice guide-

---

32. Although only 60% of all Board certified surgeons were members of ACS, the organization's rules commanded widespread adherence and many practitioners attached considerable importance to membership. See Thomas L. Greaney, Quality of Care and Market Failure Defenses in Health Care Antitrust Litigation, 21 Conn. L. Rev. 605 (1989); see also Koefoot I v. American College of Surgeons, 610 F.Supp. 1298 (N.D.Ill.1985).

§ 14–13

1. See U.S Gen Accounting Office, Practice Guidelines: The Experience of Medical Specialty Societies (1991) (interviews and review of information from 27 medical specialty societies and AMA and Council of Medical Specialties

finding wide diversity of approaches, motivations and views about guidelines). In addition to practice guidelines a number of other forms of evaluative review of medical practice exist. For example, many private entities engage in "technology assessment," see Martin Rose & Robert F. Leibenluft, Antitrust Implications of Medical Technology Assessment, 314 New Eng. J. Med. 1490 (1986), and other entities perform review of the need for medical facilities and equipment through state certificate of need laws.

2. See American Medical Association, Legal Implications of Practice Parameters 2–4 (1990).

lines by competing physicians: (1) where interested groups do no more than supply information or opinion, but do so in a manner that lessens competition such as by promulgating inaccurate, biased or misleading guidelines in order to raise their incomes, deny entry, or raise rivals' costs; and (2) where those promulgating prescriptive guidelines take steps beyond dispensing information, for example, agreeing to conform to the edicts of the guidelines or to abstain from dealing with non-compliers.

A number of antitrust doctrines limit the risk of promulgating guidelines. First, under Section 1 of the Sherman Act, the "restraint" flowing from the guidelines must be the produce of an agreement. However, promulgation of informational guidelines, even if accepted by powerful payers, is unlikely to constitute a vertical agreement absent evidence that the payer acted against its own self interest.[3] Claims that promulgating such guidelines constitutes a horizontal conspiracy are more likely to escape summary dismissal because of antitrust precedent treating most activities of trade associations as conspiracies. However, such claims should not face close scrutiny if defendants can establish that the guidelines are nothing more than an expression of a collective judgment without an implicit agreement to conform their behavior to a promulgator's edict.[4] Second, the use of guidelines to influence governmental actions or even to influence private entities (if legitimately designed to influence some governmental ultimate action) may also enjoy *Noerr* protection.[5] Where, however, guidelines are employed in such a manner as to coerce the government (e.g., a threatened boycott of the Medicaid program unless the guidelines are adopted), the exemption will not apply.[6] Further, where an economically interested party manipulates the process so as to exercise decision-making power in standard-setting by a private body,[7] *Noerr* has been held not to apply. However, where the harm to the plaintiff flows directly from governmental action and not from the stigma of the private actions, defendants' conduct will be immunized.[8]

Assuming plaintiff is able to overcome the foregoing obstacles, the guidelines would be evaluated under the rule of reason. Case law assisting in this murky evaluation is scarce, but a few general observations are possible. First, there is no obligation arising under antitrust law to provide reasonable procedures or due process in formulating or promulgating guidelines.[9] However, abusive procedures, misleading or fraudulent statements, or unfair practices by guideline promulgators may be evidence of anticompetitive intent and effect.[10]

3. Monsanto Co. v. Spray–Rite Serv. Corp., 465 U.S. 752, 104 S.Ct. 1464, 79 L.Ed.2d 775 (1984); see supra § 14–11.

4. See, e.g., Consolidated Metal Products, Inc. v. American Petroleum Inst., 846 F.2d 284 (5th Cir.1988).

5. See Allied Tube & Conduit Corp. v. Indian Head, Inc., 486 U.S. 492 108 S.Ct. 1931, 100 L.Ed.2d 497 (1988); see supra § 14–2(d)4.

6. See FTC v. Superior Court Trial Lawyers Ass'n, 493 U.S. 411, 110 S.Ct. 768, 107 L.Ed.2d 851 (1990); Michigan State Med. Soc'y., 101 F.T.C. 191, 303 (1983).

7. Allied Tube & Conduit Corp. v. Indian Head, Inc., 486 U.S. 492, 510–511 n. 13, 108

S.Ct. 1931, 1942–43 n. 13, 100 L.Ed.2d 497 (1988) (court must distinguish between an "activity involving the exercise of decision-making authority and market power," which is not protected, and one that attempts to persuade decision-makers which is protected).

8. Sessions Tank Liners v. Joor Mfg., Inc., 17 F.3d 295 (9th Cir.1994).

9. Northwest Wholesale Stationers, Inc. v. Pacific Stationery & Printing Co., 472 U.S. 284, 293, 105 S.Ct. 2613, 2619, 86 L.Ed.2d 202 (1985).

10. See Sessions Tank Liners, Inc. v. Joor Mfg., Inc., 786 F.Supp. 1518 (C.D.Cal.1991) reversed on other grounds 17 F.3d 295 (9th

The case that is most directly analogous to practice guideline promulgation by a medical society is *Schachar v. American Academy of Ophthalmology*.[11] *Schachar* involved statements issued by the American Academy of Ophthalmology (AAO) labeling a new surgical procedure, radial keratotomy, "experimental" and urging that it be approached "with caution" until additional research was completed. A group of ophthalmologists claimed that the AAO's actions constituted an unreasonable restraint of trade in that it induced medical societies to declare a moratorium on the practice and influenced third party payers not to reimburse providers for performing the procedure. Upholding a jury verdict, the Seventh Circuit concluded the AAO's conduct could not constitute a restraint of trade because the society had merely provided information and had not constrained others to follow its recommendations. The holding of the case stands for the proposition that purely information-generating conduct by an influential medical society, even if false or misleading was beyond the reach of antitrust law unless it enlisted others or policed compliance among members.

Judge Easterbrook's opinion suggests in dictum a somewhat extreme form of deference to standard-setting. Emphasizing the lack of enforcement mechanisms and the fact that AAO had not "prevented [anyone] from doing what he wished" or imposed sanctions,[12] the opinion suggests that trade associations violate Section 1 of the Sherman Act only when they take affirmative steps to assure compliance with their views. This approach may be questioned on several counts. It sweeps aside the possibility that members of a professional society might agree among themselves to abide by the society's pronouncements and do so tacitly without adopting explicit coercive mechanisms.[13] Moreover, Judge Easterbrook's interpretation of the case law as requiring explicit coercion is debatable; courts have often struck down professional agreements that are voluntary or enforced by others.[14] The court did not explain its refusal to entertain the possibility that abuse of information dissemination could lead to appreciable market power in the hands of standard setters. Collusive manipulation of demand through intentionally inaccurate or misleading statements may cause marketplace distortions. This is particularly likely in the professional context where an open marketplace of

Cir.1994); (economically interested party knowingly made false statements, prevented rivals from presenting views, failed to notify rivals when a vote would be taken); see also Allied Tube & Conduit Corp. v. Indian Head, Inc., 486 U.S. 492, 108 S.Ct. 1931, 100 L.Ed.2d 497 (1988).

11. 870 F.2d 397 (7th Cir.1989).

12. Schachar v. American Academy of Ophthalmology, Inc., 870 F.2d 397, 399 (7th Cir.1989).

13. The court noted that plaintiff had been able to perform racial keratotomy procedures notwithstanding the AAO's actions. It is questionable whether proof that some procedures were being performed refuted the contention that competition had been restrained, i.e., whether the impact of the society's position lowered market-wide output. See Herbert Hovenkamp, Antitrust Policy After Chicago, 84 Mich. L. Rev. 213 (1985) (criticizing Chicago School analysis for propensity to commit "static market fallacy").

14. See, e.g., Goldfarb v. Virginia State Bar, 421 U.S. 773, 95 S.Ct. 2004, 44 L.Ed.2d 572 (1975) (only threatened, not actual discipline; impact of voluntary compliance noted by Court); Wilk v. American Med. Ass'n., 719 F.2d 207, 230 (7th Cir.1983), 467 U.S. 1210, 104 S.Ct. 2398, 81 L.Ed.2d 355 (1984) ("even without coercive enforcement a court may find members of as association promulgating guidelines sanctioning conduct" violate § 1); see also, American Soc'y of Mechanical Eng'rs, Inc. v. Hydrolevel Corp., 456 U.S. 556, 559, 102 S.Ct. 1935, 1939, 72 L.Ed.2d 330 (1982) (treating codes as "advisory" and noting they can "have a powerful influence").

ideas is hampered by information imperfections.[15]

§ 14–14. Credentialing and Accreditation

The American health care system relies extensively on private credentialing bodies to certify and approve practitioners and organizations. These bodies are particularly powerful because their decisions strongly influence the actions of private institutions such as third party payors and hospitals in setting minimum standards for providing care. In addition, private credentialing is frequently relied upon by governmental agencies that accept their standards for purposes of licensure, funding and regulation.

Credentialing and accrediting bodies not controlled by interested groups raise no serious antitrust problems. For the most part, profession-controlled credentialing bodies in health care such as medical specialty boards do not agree to limit the output of other, non-certified practitioners and hence are not engaged in exclusionary activity. Moreover, to the extent that they only issue "seals of approval" and do not constrain their members to act in a specified manner, they are probably subject to the same limited scrutiny applied to medical society memberships discussed above.

Courts have uniformly upheld professional credentialing and educational certification programs as procompetitive cooperative activity, although they have been less than clear in their analysis of effects.[1] However, a competitor-sponsored program imposing limitations on the scope of practice as a condition of certification may well constitute an illegal market division agreement while limitations placed on dealing with others may be a boycott. Antitrust pressures played an important role in influencing JCAH to amend its accreditation standards to permit hospitals to extend staff privileges to allied health professionals such as psychologists and nurse midwives.[2] A challenge by the state of Ohio, subsequently mooted, charged that JCAH accrediting standards forced hospitals to limit the admitting privileges of psychologists.

In addressing challenges to certification, courts may identify a relevant market in credentialling or information. For example, in *American Council of Certified Podiatric Physicians and Surgeons v. American Board of Podiatric Surgery, Inc.*,[3] the Sixth Circuit defined a relevant market that consisted of annual podiatrist certifications, rejecting the district court's view that the market definition must reflect recognition within the health care community. While ease of entry might seem to dilute potential market power, the Sixth Circuit found that significant price differentials between the defendant and its rivals coupled with the importance of reputation constituted sufficient evi-

15. See Mark R. Patterson, Antitrust Liability for Collective Speech: Medical Society Practice Standards, 27 Indiana L. Rev. 51 (1993); John E. Lopatka, Antitrust and Professional Rules: A Framework for Analysis, 28 San Diego L. Rev. 301, 333–35 (1991) (acknowledging possibility of demand distortions through misleading professional society statements but questioning whether courts could effectively assess such problems).

§ 14–14

1. See Veizaga v. National Bd. for Respiratory Therapy, 1979–1 Trade Cas. (CCH) ¶ 62,-496, 1979 WL 1591 (N.D.Ill.1979); Zavaletta v. American Bar Ass'n, 721 F.Supp. 96 (E.D.Va. 1989); cf. Bogus v. American Speech & Hearing Ass'n, 582 F.2d 277 (3d Cir.1978).

2. Note, Denying Hospital Privileges to Non–Physicians: Does Quality of Care Justify a Potential Restraint on Trade?, 19 Ind. L. Rev. 1219 (1986); Clark C. Havighurst & Nancy M.P. King, Private Credentialing of Health Care Personnel: An Antitrust Perspective (Part Two) 9 Am. J. L. & Med. 263, 314–25 (1983).

3. 185 F.3d 606 (6th Cir.1999).

dence to avoid summary judgment on the issue.[4] Entry issues may also play an important role in determining whether a practice restrains trade. Professors Havighurst and King have argued that the practice of "grandfathering"—raising certification standards for new applicants without requiring incumbents to meet the new, elevated standards—may violate the antitrust laws. Assuming the absence of other good sources of information, grandfathering arguably enables incumbents to exploit market imperfections by distorting information available to consumers.[5] This in turn raises entry barriers (or imposes higher costs on rivals) and ultimately limits output. Commentators have also suggested that extensive professional control over accreditation of medical schools and graduate medical education may violate the antitrust laws.[6]

C. PHYSICIAN–HOSPITAL RELATIONSHIPS

§ 14–15. An Introduction to Staff Privileges and Peer Review

Staff privileges refers to the conditional grant of permission from a hospital board enabling a provider to practice his or her profession in the hospital. The extension of privileges is a principal means by which hospitals exercise some measure of control over the quantity and quality of care delivered in the hospital. Antitrust challenges to hospital actions denying, revoking or placing limitations on staff privileges comprise the single largest number of antitrust cases involving the health care industry. The privileges in question may entail membership on the medical staff, authority to admit patients or the right to render specific services in the hospital. Challenges to adverse decisions arise in a variety of contexts: e.g., initial applications for privileges,[1] reappointment to the medical staff,[2] suspension or revocation of privileges,[3] or qualifications or limitations placed upon privileges.[4]

Antitrust litigation concerning staff privileges arises principally in three contexts. The first and most prevalent factual pattern involves adverse actions that occur as a result of medical staff peer review, a process by which physicians recommend action or otherwise participate in decisions affecting the privileges of other providers. The second category concerns exclusive contracts or agreements between hospitals and physicians or physician groups; such agreements are common in such specialties as anesthesiology, radiology and pathology. Because these agreements preclude other providers from rendering certain services at the hospital, they are often challenged for their exclusionary effects in the marketplace. The third category involves

---

4. Id.

5. Clark C. Havighurst & Nancy M.P. King, Private Credentialing of Health Care Personnel: An Antitrust Perspective (Part Two), 9 Am. J. L. & Med. 263 (1983).

6. Philip C. Kissam, Government Policy Toward Medical Accreditation and Certification: The Antitrust Laws and Other Procompetitive Strategies, 1983 Wis. L. Rev. 1; Note, Restrictive Practices in Accreditation of Medical Schools: An Antitrust Analysis, 51 S. Cal. L. Rev. 657 (1978).

§ 14–15

1. See, e.g., Weiss v. York Hosp., 745 F.2d 786 (3d Cir.1984), 470 U.S. 1060, 105 S.Ct. 1777, 84 L.Ed.2d 836 (1985).

2. See, e.g., Pontius v. Children's Hosp., 552 F.Supp. 1352 (W.D.Pa.1982).

3. See, e.g., Goss v. Mem. Hosp. Sys., 789 F.2d 353 (5th Cir.1986) (privileges suspended); Robles v. Humana Hosp. Cartersville, 785 F.Supp. 989 (N.D.Ga.1992).

4. See, e.g., Hayden v. Bracy, 744 F.2d 1338 (8th Cir.1984).

allegations that medical staff members conspired outside of the privileges process to exclude a provider from the staff through coercive actions such as threatened boycotts or retaliation against the hospital or other physicians should privileges be granted.

Remarkably few plaintiffs have prevailed in staff privileges cases,[5] although hundreds have been litigated under antitrust theories.[6] Indeed, a review of the facts in the reported antitrust staff privileges decisions reveals a wide range of human foibles and shortcomings underlying most denials of privileges: disruptive behavior, incompetence, racial or ethnic antagonisms, uncooperative behavior and professional jealousy, to name a few. While these factors may or may not reflect on a practitioner's qualifications, they do not shed much light on the competitive effects of a staff privileges determination.

In any event, an array of legitimate business and professional concerns affecting both hospital and staff interests justify the vast majority of privileges determinations. Credentialing criteria commonly used by hospitals include such factors as the practitioner's malpractice history; malpractice insurance coverage; attendance at required hospital meetings; maintenance of appropriate medical records; service on hospital committees; participation in continuing medical education programs; and, increasingly in recent years, adherence to hospitals' parameters on utilization of services.[7] In addition, most staff privileges disputes arise in the context of medical peer review in which medical staff participation is mandated under state and private accreditation standards. Thus, most peer reviews center on medical credentials, clinical competence and past performance, areas in which neither hospital boards or courts have competence to second-guess professional judgments.[8]

Yet one should not be too quick to dismiss the possibility that the process occasionally may be subverted to serve the anticompetitive ends of rival physicians. As the Ninth Circuit observed, "The peer review process allows doctors to agree to eliminate a competitor from the market because they believe his or her product is substandard. An analogous scheme would allow General Motors, Chrysler and Ford to review the safety of Toyotas to determine if the public should be allowed to drive them. Clearly such an arrangement would raise antitrust concerns."[9] Given the structure of hospital administration and the high degree of physician autonomy in that setting, it is apparent that the hospitals, at least historically, have not exercised a strong countervailing influence in the privileges process that would counteract the self-interestedness and economic motivations of physicians. These risks appear to have been recognized by both the Supreme Court, which has on

---

5. Brown v. Presbyterian Healthcare Servs., 101 F.3d 1324 (10th Cir.1996); Weiss v. York Hosp., 745 F.2d 786 (3d Cir.1984); Boczar v. Manatee Hosps. & Health Sys., Inc., 993 F.2d 1514 (11th Cir.1993); Oltz v. St. Peter's Community Hosp., 861 F.2d 1440 (9th Cir. 1988); see also Patrick v. Burget, 486 U.S. 94, 108 S.Ct. 1658, 100 L.Ed.2d 83 (1988); Medical Staff of Memorial Medical Ctr., 110 F.T.C. 541 (1988) (nurse-midwife consent order); Health Care Mgt. Corp., 107 F.T.C. 285 (1986) (podiatrist consent order).

6. For compilation and analysis of the numerous cases involving staff privileges cases

brought under the antitrust laws, see 2 John J. Miles, Health Care & Antitrust Law § 10:1 (1992).

7. See John D. Blum, Economic Credentialing: A New Twist in Hospital Appraisal Processes, 12 J. Legal Med. 427, 441 (1991).

8. Patel v. Scotland Mem. Hosp., 91 F.3d 132 (4th Cir.1996) (characterizing staff privileges issue as a "staffing decision" that "the court is not in a position to second-guess").

9. Patrick v. Burget, 800 F.2d 1498, 1506 (9th Cir.1986), reversed on other grounds 486 U.S. 94, 108 S.Ct. 1658, 100 L.Ed.2d 83 (1988).

several occasions declined to extend protection to peer reviewers in staff privileges cases,[10] and by Congress, which enacted extremely narrow immunity legislation for peer reviewers while explicitly acknowledging anticompetitive dangers.[11]

§ 14–16. Jurisdiction and Immunities

a. Interstate Commerce

Prior to the Supreme Court's recent decision in *Summit Health Ltd. v. Pinhas*,[1] staff privileges cases were about the only instance in which plaintiffs had difficulty satisfying the interstate commerce requirements of the Sherman Act. The Supreme Court had previously stated that the proper test was whether the defendant's "activities which allegedly have been infected by a price-fixing conspiracy be shown * * * to have a not insubstantial effect on the interstate commerce involved."[2] A majority of the circuits had interpreted this passage restrictively, requiring plaintiffs to establish that the particular activity allegedly "infected" by unlawful conduct had a substantial effect on interstate commerce.[3] Under this view the defendant's activities which are challenged as a restraint of trade—in this context, medical staff peer review— must have a nexus with interstate commerce. Other courts read the requirement even more narrowly, requiring that the very restraint itself (e.g., the denial of privileges to a particular physician) must demonstrate the requisite nexus.[4] A minority of the circuits construe Supreme Court precedent broadly and literally, requiring only that defendant's "general business activities" affect interstate commerce. Under this approach, evidence that any part of the full range of a hospital's business, such as its receipt of payments in interstate commerce, purchases of equipment, drugs and supplies, treatment of patients from out of state, were in or affecting commerce would suffice to met the test.[5]

Rather than choosing one of these competing interpretations of the interstate commerce requirement, the Supreme Court enunciated a surprisingly different approach in *Summit Health*. Although it is a test that plaintiffs should rarely have difficulty satisfying, the majority's opinion is not without ambiguity and attracted a vigorous dissent from four Justices. It is thus entirely possible that limits will be placed on *Summit Health's* reach in the future.

10. Summit Health, Ltd. v. Pinhas, 500 U.S. 322, 111 S.Ct. 1842, 114 L.Ed.2d 366 (1991); Patrick v. Burget, 486 U.S. 94, 108 S.Ct. 1658, 100 L.Ed.2d 83 (1988); Jefferson Parish Hosp. Dist. No. 2 v. Hyde, 466 U.S. 2, 104 S.Ct. 1551, 80 L.Ed.2d 2 (1984).

11. See infra § 14–22 discussing Health Care Quality Improvement Act of 1986, 42 U.S.C.A. §§ 11101–11152.

§ 14–16

1. 500 U.S. 322, 111 S.Ct. 1842, 114 L.Ed.2d 366 (1991).

2. McLain v. Real Estate Bd. of New Orleans, Inc., 444 U.S. 232, 246, 100 S.Ct. 502, 511, 62 L.Ed.2d 441(1980); See also, Fuentes v. South Hills Cardiology, 946 F.2d 196 (3d Cir. 1991).

3. Furlong v. Long Island College Hosp., 710 F.2d 922 (2d Cir.1983); Crane v. Inter- mountain Health Care, Inc., 637 F.2d 715 (10th Cir.1980) (en banc); Seglin v. Esau, 769 F.2d 1274 (7th Cir.1985); Anesthesia Advantage, Inc. v. Metz Group, 912 F.2d 397 (10th Cir.1990); Stone v. William Beaumont Hosp., 782 F.2d 609 (6th Cir.1986) (Opinion of Krupansky, J.); Cordova & Simonpietri Ins. Agency Inc. v. Chase Manhattan Bank N.A., 649 F.2d 36 (1st Cir.1981).

4. Stone v. William Beaumont Hosp., 782 F.2d 609 (6th Cir.1986); Furlong v. Long Island College Hosp., 710 F.2d 922 (2d Cir.1983).

5. El Shahawy v. Harrison, 778 F.2d 636 (11th Cir.1985); Western Waste Serv. Sys. v. Universal Waste Control, 616 F.2d 1094, 1097 (9th Cir.); Sweeney v. Athens Regional Med. Ctr., 709 F.Supp. 1563 (M.D.Ga.1989).

The thrust of *Summit Health* seems to be directed at establishing an entirely different approach to interstate commerce issues, at least with regard to those arising in boycott cases. The principal issue for the Court was the effect on commerce of the activity from which plaintiff has been excluded.[6] It required plaintiff to show the restraint's impact "on participants and potential participants in the market from which [plaintiff] has been excluded."[7] This requirement was readily satisfied given the Court's discussion of the nature of the antitrust issues in the case, wherein it emphasized that the "essence of any violation of § 1 is the illegal agreement itself rather than the overt acts performed in furtherance of it."[8] Although the boycott in question did not have any obvious impact on a market in the same way price fixing and territorial divisions do, the Court noted that boycotts run the risk that conspirators might destroy rivals one at a time and ultimately affect interstate commerce. This would suggest that a broader effect may be assigned to boycotts than that of the limited impact on a given competitor and accordingly one must look to the intended harm of the restraint. However, a narrower interpretation of *Summit Health* is also possible. The Court may have seen the practice as part of a market-wide featherbedding scheme which was effectuated through the boycott.[9]

A sharp dissent authored by Justice Scalia faulted the majority for suggesting that the effect of the exclusion of a single physician was to be tested by the entire market, i.e., Los Angeles, in which ophthalmological services were provided. The dissenters also stressed that even within that market, exclusion of Dr. Pinhas could, as a matter of practical economics have no effect.[10] Remarkably, the dissent would have denied interstate commerce jurisdiction even if featherbedding practice were treated as a price fixing scheme. It argued that the fact that other hospitals had abolished the practice established the local nature of the conspiracy and its intrastate character. The dissent's implicit approach would radically alter inquiries under the interstate commerce requirement. It would import analysis of competitive effects into the interstate commerce inquiry, a shift that would be especially significant if the commerce requirement is treated as jurisdictional and would undermine significantly the power of per se rules.[11]

Not surprisingly, staff privileges cases since *Summit Health* have uniformly found the interstate commerce requirement satisfied. For example, allegations that a denial of privileges affected a physician's practice that had generated a national reputation and attracted out of state patients for a hospital has been held to satisfy interstate commerce requirements.[12] Also

---

6. Id. at 1850. The Court's approach is in substantial accord with the "class of activities" test advocated by the Solicitor General in his amicus brief to the Court. Brief for The United States as Amicus Curiae Supporting Respondent, id.

7. Summit Health, Ltd. v. Pinhas, 500 U.S. 322, 111 S.Ct. 1842, 1848, 114 L.Ed.2d 366 (1991).

8. Id. at 1844 (1991).

9. Id. at 1059. See Summit Health, Ltd. v. Pinhas, 500 U.S. 322, 332, 111 S.Ct. 1842, 1848, 114 L.Ed.2d 366 (1991) (requiring "a general evaluation of the impact of the re-

straint on other participants and potential participants in the market from which he has been excluded.").

10. Summit Health, Ltd. v. Pinhas, 500 U.S. 322, 337, 111 S.Ct. 1842, 1851, 114 L.Ed.2d 366 (1991).

11. See Stephen Caulkins, The 1990–91 Supreme Court Term and Antitrust: Toward Greater Certainty, 60 Antitrust L.J. 603, 630, 635 (1992).

12. Brader v. Alleghany Gen. Hosp., 64 F.3d 869 (3d. Cir. 1995); Fuentes v. South Hills Cardiology, 946 F.2d 196 (3d Cir.1991).

deemed sufficient were general allegations regarding a restraint's effects on out-of-state purchases of supplies, insurance payments and treatment of out-of-state patients.[13] Likewise, alleged effects on plaintiff physician's ability to get hospital privileges elsewhere and general allegations, coupled with a court's inference that a privilege denial would affect the entire hospital staff, were found adequate under the *Summit Health* standard.[14] The inquiry, however, is distinct from the question of whether the conduct at issue satisfies the substantive requirements of the Sherman Act: plaintiffs must still allege and prove that the conduct restrains trade.[15]

b. The State Action Doctrine

A defense frequently invoked in staff privileges cases is the state action doctrine. Under this doctrine, sometimes loosely referred to as an exemption, a two-pronged analysis applies. First, the action must be "one clearly articulated and affirmatively expressed as state policy;" second, the policy must be "actively supervised by the state."[16] In the case of political subdivisions such as municipalities or other local governmental entities, the latter requirement need not be met.[17] In addition, relying on state enabling legislation, courts have held that hospitals owned by health care authorities, special hospital districts and other similar government-controlled entities should be treated as municipalities and hence need only show that their activities are undertaken pursuant to a clearly articulated and affirmatively expressed state policy.[18] Although public hospitals have sometimes claimed they should qualify for automatic immunity (obviating the need to satisfy the first prong of the test) because they are "subordinate state agencies,"[19] such arguments have been rejected.[20]

1. The Requirement of a "Clearly Articulated" State Policy

Whether a government-controlled hospital will meet the clear articulation requirement under state action analysis turns on the interpretation of the statute authorizing operation of the hospital by a public entity. Courts must inquire first whether the statute authorized the conduct in question, and second whether the anticompetitive effects were contemplated by the legislature or were reasonably foreseeable.[21] A number of cases have found articulation sufficient to constitute state policy in statutes authorizing municipalities to operate and maintain hospitals and to determine which physicians may practice in them[22] or make decisions based on the "appropriate utilization of hospital facilities."[23] However, courts have found that a state's general grant of authority do not contemplate or foresee certain anticompetitive conspira-

13. Oksanen v. Page Mem. Hosp., 945 F.2d 696 (4th Cir.1991).

14. Brown v. Our Lady of Lourdes Med. Ctr., 767 F.Supp. 618 (D.N.J.1991), affirmed 961 F.2d 207 (3d Cir.1992); Pudlo v. Adamski, 789 F.Supp. 247 (N.D.Ill.1992).

15. Patel v. Scotland Mem. Hosp., 91 F.3d 132 (4th Cir.1996).

16. City of Lafayette v. Louisiana Power & Light Co., 435 U.S. 389, 98 S.Ct. 1123, 55 L.Ed.2d 364 (1978). See supra § 10–2d.

17. Hallie v. Eau Claire, 471 U.S. 34, 46, 105 S.Ct. 1713, 1720, 85 L.Ed.2d 24 (1985).

18. Bolt v. Halifax Hosp. Med. Ctr., 891 F.2d 810, 824–25 (11th Cir.1990); Cohn v. Bond, 953 F.2d 154 (4th Cir.1991).

19. See Hoover v. Ronwin, 466 U.S. 558, 104 S.Ct. 1989, 80 L.Ed.2d 590 (1984).

20. Bolt v. Halifax Hosp. Med. Ctr., 891 F.2d 810, 825 (11th Cir.1990).

21. Hallie v. Eau Claire, 471 U.S. 34, 105 S.Ct. 1713, 85 L.Ed.2d 24 (1985).

22. See, e.g., Cohn v. Bond, 953 F.2d 154, 158 (4th Cir.1991).

23. Crosby v. Hosp. Auth., 93 F.3d 1515 (11th Cir.1996).

cies, especially when the hospital's actions go beyond merely relying on staff peer reviewers' recommendations.[24] Moreover, where a state has contemplated that special governmental hospital districts will operate in a competitive environment and has taken other steps to *enhance* competition rather than replace it, a broad grant of authority will not satisfy the clear articulation requirement.[25] This analysis has been interpreted to shield the individual members of the peer review committee even in jurisdictions that do not recognize hospitals and their staffs as a single entity for purposes of intra-enterprise conspiracy analysis.[26]

Cases involving peer review in private hospitals have met with mixed results under the first prong of the state action doctrine. As a preliminary matter, courts will apply the doctrine where the facts suggest routine performance of peer review,[27] but not where the complaint alleges extra-official proceedings.[28] In attempting to establish clear articulation, defendants have invoked various state regulatory schemes including those governing medical licensing, hospital accreditation, peer review as well as the state judicial system. Where statutory schemes require medical staffs to perform peer review or where the scheme closely regulates peer review courts have found the clear articulation prong satisfied.[29]

2. The "Active Supervision" Requirement

The second prong of the state action doctrine, applicable only to private hospitals, requires that the state must engage in active supervision of peer reviewers' actions. The Supreme Court has made clear that this requirement is designed to assure that the states consciously and knowingly undertake the actions that displace federal antitrust law. In *Ticor*, it held that the existence of a staffed and funded regulatory program is by itself insufficient to constitute active state supervision.[30] Likewise, "negative option" regulation was deemed inadequate to satisfy the test in the absence of evidence that the "state officials have undertaken the necessary steps to determine the specifics" of the challenged conduct.[31] However, the Court did suggest, somewhat cryptically, that the stringent standard for judging the adequacy of state supervision might be modified in cases involving offenses less "pernicious"

---

24. Bolt v. Halifax Hosp. Med. Ctr., 891 F.2d 810, 825 (11th Cir.1990);Quinn v. Kent Gen. Hosp., Inc., 617 F.Supp. 1226 (D.Del. 1985); see also Wicker v. Union County Gen. Hosp., 673 F.Supp. 177 (N.D.Miss.1987).

25. Lancaster Community Hosp. v. Antelope Valley Hosp. Dist., 940 F.2d 397 (9th Cir.1991).

26. Crosby v. Hosp. Auth., 93 F.3d 1515 (11th Cir.1996).

27. See, e.g., Marrese v. Interqual, Inc., 748 F.2d 373 (7th Cir.1984), 472 U.S. 1027, 105 S.Ct. 3501, 87 L.Ed.2d 632 (1985).

28. See, e.g., Posner v. Lankenau Hosp., 645 F.Supp. 1102 (E.D.Pa.1986); Quinn v. Kent Gen. Hosp., Inc., 617 F.Supp. 1226 (D.Del.1985).

29. See, e.g., Bolt v. Halifax Hosp. Med. Ctr., 891 F.2d 810, 825 (11th Cir.1990); Mar-

rese v. Interqual, Inc., 748 F.2d 373 (7th Cir. 1984).

30. FTC v. Ticor Title Ins. Co., 504 U.S. 621, 112 S.Ct. 2169, 2171, 119 L.Ed.2d 410 (1992) ("[T]he purpose of the active supervision inquiry * * * is to determine whether the State has exercised sufficient independent judgment and control so that the details of the rates or prices have been established as a product of deliberate state intervention, not simply by agreement among private parties * * * The question is not how well state regulation works but whether the anticompetitive scheme is the State's own").

31. 112 S.Ct. at 2179 (disapproving regulatory scheme in which prices were set initially by private parties "subject only to a veto if the State chooses to exercise it").

than price fixing.[32] Arguably, then, quality-based peer review activities, which are invariably judged under the rule of reason, might qualify for more lenient treatment.

The Supreme Court addressed the quantum of supervision required in staff privileges cases in *Patrick v. Burget.*[33] The Court made it clear that supervision by State officials must include the authority to review decisions and reverse them where necessary.[34] It went on to hold that Oregon's judiciary did not supply active supervision because there was no statute permitting review and, in practice, judicial review had been confined to ensuring that reasonable procedures were afforded. The Court noted the absence of judicial review on the merits of peer decisions and questioned whether state courts can adequately supervise peer review decisions for purposes of the state action doctrine.[35]

Lower courts addressing the active supervision requirement since *Patrick* have usually found state regulatory reviews inadequate. In these cases the state agencies' failure to exercise ultimate control[36] or the fact that despite complex statutory regulation, no agency reviewed the merits of individual decisions has been decisive.[37]

c. *Primary Jurisdiction*

Another doctrine implicating governmental regulation is the primary jurisdiction doctrine. Primary jurisdiction "requires judicial abstention where protection of the integrity of a regulatory scheme dictates preliminary resort to the agency which administers the scheme."[38] In essence, the doctrine allows a court to stay an action to allow an agency to make findings of fact within its special area of expertise that may prove helpful to the court in resolving difficult factual issues.[39] Although the doctrine has been almost uniformly invoked to defer to federal administrative agencies, the Second Circuit has applied it in the staff privileges context to require a plaintiff to comply with New York law mandating that physicians whose staff privileges are terminated must first seek redress before a state administrative tribunal.[40] The Court of Appeals rejected, however, the district court's application of the doctrine of exhaustion of remedies, which applies only where a claim is cognizable in the first instance by an administrative agency alone. Given that federal courts have exclusive jurisdiction over the Sherman Act, the court concluded the exhaustion doctrine was inapplicable.[41] Further, no exhaustion requirement

---

32. "Our decision should be read in light of the gravity of the antitrust offense, the involvement of private actors throughout, and the clear absence of state supervision." 112 S.Ct. at 2180.

33. 486 U.S. 94, 108 S.Ct. 1658, 100 L.Ed.2d 83 (1988).

34. Id. at 101, 108 S.Ct. at 1663.

35. Id. at 103, 108 S.Ct. at 1664.

36. See, e.g., Miller v. Indiana Hosp., 930 F.2d 334 (3d Cir.1991); Jiricko v. Coffeyville Memorial Hosp. Med. Ctr., 700 F.Supp. 1559 (D.Kan.1988).

37. See, e.g., Shahawy v. Harrison, 875 F.2d 1529 (11th Cir.1989); Pinhas v. Summit

Health, Ltd., 880 F.2d 1108 (9th Cir.1989), reversed on other grounds 894 F.2d 1024 (9th Cir.1989) (en banc), affirmed 500 U.S. 322, 111 S.Ct. 1842, 114 L.Ed.2d 366 (1991).

38. United States v. Philadelphia Nat'l Bank, 374 U.S. 321, 353, 83 S.Ct. 1715, 1736, 10 L.Ed.2d 915 (1963).

39. See United States v. Western Pac. R.R. Co., 352 U.S. 59, 77 S.Ct. 161, 1 L.Ed.2d 126 (1956).

40. Johnson v. Nyack Hosp., 964 F.2d 116 (2d Cir.1992).

41. Id.

applies to the procedural remedies afforded by the hospital.[42]

d. Standing and Antitrust Injury

Of increasing importance in private antitrust cases are the standing and antitrust injury doctrines. These devices are frequently employed to dismiss causes of action prior to trial, obviating the need for an extensive factual inquiry that a full-blown rule of reason analysis requires.[43] Although standing is routinely assumed in cases alleging that the denial of staff privileges amounted to a boycott, courts have on several occasions denied standing to doctors claiming that their exclusion from a medical staff was part of a price fixing scheme by hospitals and their medical staffs. These cases appear to rest on plaintiffs' failure to claim any market impact from the conspiracy and the proposition that other potential plaintiffs such as patients, insurers or the government, are more efficient enforcers of the antitrust laws.[44] Similarly, courts have found no standing or antitrust injury in exclusive dealing cases where the essence of plaintiff's claim is not lessened competition in the market, but a personal lost opportunity to compete.[45]

§ 14–17. The Conspiracy Requirement

The requirement under Section 1 of the Sherman Act that plaintiffs establish a "contract, combination, or conspiracy" has given rise to two distinct issues. First, because Section 1 does not reach unilateral conduct, plaintiffs must prove that the action was undertaken by a plurality of actors. Considerable case law has developed under the so-called "intraenterprise conspiracy doctrine" as to when, as a matter of law, a corporation possesses the legal capacity to conspire with its subsidiaries, employees, or agents. The second requirement is that plaintiffs must show that the two entities actually engaged in concerted action. Prompted by recent Supreme Court precedent, courts now readily grant directed verdicts or summary judgment for defendants where the evidence of conspiracy is merely consistent with the existence of a conspiracy. As discussed below, both prongs of the conspiracy requirement have provided important weapons for defendants in seeking to short-circuit staff privileges litigation through summary procedures.

a. Legal Capacity to Conspire

Most antitrust staff privileges cases include charges that the hospital has conspired with its medical staff, credentialing committee or certain physicians on staff. The question of when a corporation may be deemed a separate entity from its subsidiaries, employees or agents for purposes of section 1 has been controversial. However, in *Copperweld Corp. v. Independence Tube Corp.*,[1] the Supreme Court brought some measure of order to the intraenterprise conspiracy doctrine. In that case, the Court held that as a matter of law a parent corporation lacked capacity to conspire with its wholly-owned subsidiary. It

42. Kaczanowski v. Medcial Ctr. Hosp., 612 F.Supp. 688 (D.Vt.1985).

43. See supra § 14–3.

44. See, e.g., Drs. Steuer & Latham v. National Med. Enter., Inc., 672 F.Supp. 1489 (D.S.C.1987); Todorov v. DCH Healthcare Authority, 921 F.2d 1438, 1454 (11th Cir.1991); Robles v. Humana Hosp. Cartersville, 785 F.Supp. 989, 999 (N.D.Ga.1992).

45. See, e.g., Drs. Steuer & Latham v. National Med. Enter., Inc., 672 F.Supp. 1489 (D.S.C.1987), affirmed 846 F.2d 70 (4th Cir. 1988).

§ 14–17

1. 467 U.S. 752, 104 S.Ct. 2731, 81 L.Ed.2d 628 (1984).

reasoned that the internal decision-making process of the corporate entity did not "raise the antitrust dangers that § 1 was designed to police."[2] This is so because intraenterprise "agreements" such as those between a parent and its wholly-owned subsidiary do not involve parties with separate or disparate interests. Inasmuch as both parties pursue the ends of the same entity (i.e., those of the parent), parent and subsidiary have a "complete unity of interest."[3] In addition, the Court noted the totality of the parent's control over its subsidiary and its ability to reverse promptly any decision not in accord with its own interests. *Copperweld* also made it clear that the same logic extends to the actions of corporate officers and employees, but explicitly left open the issue of whether a parent corporation could conspire with its partially-owned subsidiary.[4] In addition, it noted without comment that some lower courts had declined to apply the intraenterprise conspiracy doctrine where corporate officers act out of an independent economic motive.[5]

1. Hospital–Employee Relationships

In certain circumstances, application of the intraenterprise conspiracy doctrine to disputes over hospital staff privileges is relatively straightforward. Physicians, officers, staff and other agents who are full-time employees of a hospital fall within *Copperweld's* dictum that "officers or employees of the same firm" should not be regarded as providing the plurality of actors necessary for Section 1 purposes. In these cases the underlying rationale of *Copperweld* is comfortably satisfied: there is both a "complete unity of interest" and the parent hospital may exert control over its employee if he takes actions inconsistent with the hospital's interest. Accordingly, courts have held that employees on the medical staff[6] and a hospital's attorney[7] lacked the capacity to conspire with an employer hospital. Similar reasoning should guide analyses of HMO-owned hospitals staffed by physician-employees and academic medical centers with full-time faculty employees on staff.[8]

Somewhat more ambiguous is the case of physician groups operating pursuant to an exclusive contract but lacking a "complete unity of interest" with the hospital. Although such groups might be considered agents or employees of the hospital for some purposes, the better view in these circumstances is they are independent contractors pursing their own economic interest when they seek to eliminate a rival as a competitor.[9] Thus, anesthesi-

2. Id. at 769, 104 S.Ct. at 2741.

3. Id. at 771, 104 S.Ct. at 2741.

4. Lower courts have divided on this issue. See Novatel Communications, Inc. v. Cellular Telephone Supply, Inc., 1986–2 Trade Cas. ¶ 67,412, 1986 WL 15507 (N.D.Ga.1986) (parent incapable of conspiring with 51%-owned subsidiary); Aspen Title & Escrow, Inc. v. Jeld–Wen, Inc., 677 F.Supp. 1477 (D.Or.1987) (conspiracy found where parent owned 75% of subsidiary). See also, American Vision Centers. v. Cohen, 711 F.Supp. 721 (E.D.N.Y.1989) (conspiracy possible where some individuals owned 100% of one firm and 54% of the other).

5. Copperweld Corp. v. Independence Tube Corp., 467 U.S. 752, 104 S.Ct. 2731, n. 15, 81 L.Ed.2d 628 (1984).

6. Patel v. Scotland Me. Hosp., 91 F.3d 132 (4th Cir.1996); McMorris v. Williamsport Hosp., 597 F.Supp. 899 (M.D.Pa.1984).

7. Potters Med. Ctr. v. City Hosp. Ass'n, 800 F.2d 568 (6th Cir.1986).

8. See James F. Blumstein & Frank A. Sloan, Antitrust and Hospital Peer Review, 51 Law & Contemp. Probs. 7 (1988). Likewise, a university employing physicians to work at a hospital that it owns lacks the capacity to conspire with those physicians. See Advanced Health–Care Servs., Inc. v. Radford Community Hosp., 910 F.2d 139 (4th Cir.1990), on remand 846 F.Supp. 488 (W.D.Va.1994).

9. See Oltz v. St. Peter's Community Hosp., 861 F.2d 1440 (9th Cir.1988); see also Vakharia v. Little Co. of Mary Hosp., 917

ologists operating under a contract with a hospital have been held capable of conspiring with the hospital when they pressured it to terminate a rival's privileges because the collaboration between the group and hospital "coalesced economic power previously directed at disparate goals."[10]

It would be erroneous, however, to treat non-employee physicians on the hospital staff performing peer review or credentialing functions as "employees or officers" for purposes of *Copperweld* analysis. Most physicians are plainly not in an employer-employee relationship with the hospitals at which they have staff privileges. While some cases have rather loosely analogized the role of the medical staff to that of corporate employees or officers,[11] there are important functional dissimilarities that go to the heart of the *Copperweld* rationale. Hospitals simply do not share a complete unity of interest with medical staff members and lack the ability to assert full control over the staff's actions. Staff-hospital relations cannot be made to fit under the "employee or officer" branch of the intraenterprise doctrine and, as discussed below, should be functionally analyzed in light of the doctrine's underlying purpose.

2. The Independent Personal Stake Exception

An important exception exists when applying the intraenterprise conspiracy doctrine to employees or other agents acting on behalf of the corporation. Where an employee or officer is acting in his own economic interest rather than that of his employer, some courts have recognized an "independent personal stake" exception which removes the *Copperweld* rule of conspiratorial incapacity and requires the factfinder to determine whether such an agreement did in fact occur.[12] Following the analytic path of *Copperweld*, the justification for this exception rests upon an appraisal of the "economic realities" underlying the relations of the parties. An employee of a corporation who is not acting exclusively on behalf of her corporation must be acting in her own interests or those of another employer. Lacking complete unity of interest and control by the corporation, the employee should therefore be regarded as a separate economic actor and hence legally capable of conspiring with the corporation.

The independent personal stake exception has been criticized[13] and one circuit has explicitly declined to adopt it.[14] For the most part, these criticisms have focused on ambiguities surrounding the contours of the rule and its proof requirements. Concerns have been expressed about what kind of "independent interest" should trigger the exception; the requisite magnitude of the independent interest; and the need for proof that the disloyal employee caused

---

F.Supp. 1282 (N.D.Ill.1996) (hospital had capacity to conspire with corporation controlled by medical staff members, but not capacity to conspire with staff).

10. Id. at 1450.

11. See, e.g., Oksanen v. Page Mem'l Hosp. 945 F.2d 696, 703 (4th Cir.1991); Weiss v. York Hosp., 745 F.2d 786, 817 (3d Cir.1984).

12. For cases applying the independent personal stake exception in the staff privileges context and holding defendant legally capable of conspiring, See, e.g., Robinson v. Magovern, 521 F.Supp. 842 (W.D.Pa.1981), affirmed per

curiam 688 F.2d 824 (3d Cir.1982); Williams v. Kleaveland, 534 F.Supp. 912 (W.D.Mich.1981).

13. See 7 Philip E. Areeda, Antitrust Law ¶ 1471 (1986); Note, "Conspiring Entities" Under Section 1 of the Sherman Act, 95 Harv. L. Rev. 661 (1982); Smith v. Northern Michigan Hosps., Inc., 703 F.2d 942, 950 n. 15 (6th Cir.1983).

14. Nurse Midwifery Assocs. v. Hibbett, 689 F.Supp. 799, 804 (M.D.Tenn.1988), affirmed in relevant part 918 F.2d 605 (6th Cir. 1990); Potters Med. Center v. City Hosp. Ass'n, 800 F.2d 568 (6th Cir.1986).

the restraint of trade.[15] Without doubt these concerns have some validity. Nevertheless, it is unnecessary and unwise to rely on these concerns as a basis for disavowing altogether the independent personal stake exception. As discussed in the next section, the requirement that a plaintiff prove "conspiracy-in-fact" provides an effective filter against cases in which defendant's participation in the peer review process does not amount to an agreement notwithstanding his independent economic motivations. Further, where selfish interests are mooted by economic realities such as an inability to cause the restraint or the de minimis economic significance of his independent interest, no conspiracy should be found.

3. Conspiracies Between Hospitals and Their Staffs

Several appellate courts have applied the intraenterprise conspiracy doctrine to hold that hospitals are legally incapable of conspiring with their medical staffs (or committees thereof).[16] These cases hold that hospitals delegating to their medical staffs some responsibility for credentialing while retaining ultimate control over the final decision on privileges are acting as a single entity with their staffs and, as a matter of law, cannot conspire with them. Two circuits have rejected this analysis,[17] arguing that the legally distinct character of the medical staff distinguishes the situation from *Copperweld*. As will be seen, resolution of this issue requires an understanding of the peer review and credentialing processes in hospitals.

In the leading case of *Weiss v. York Hospital*,[18] a medical staff comprised of allopathic physicians was found to have applied discriminatorily stringent standards in reviewing the credentials of osteopathic physicians applying for privileges at York Hospital. Noting that the "medical staff was empowered to make staff privilege decisions on behalf of the hospital,"[19] the Third Circuit reasoned that the staff, as an entity, was acting on behalf of its hospital much like an officer would act on behalf of a corporation. As such, the staff lacked any economic interest "in competition with the hospital" and therefore was legally incapable of conspiring with it.[20] (A second conspiracy holding in *Weiss*—that the actions of the medical staff should be viewed as a conspiracy among the individual doctors who make it up—is discussed in the next section).

There are several justifications for applying the intraenterprise conspiracy doctrine to hospital-staff actions regarding staff privileges. Courts have emphasized the similarity between the role of the medical staff and that of an officer of a corporation. Functionally viewed, a medical staff passing on physician qualifications for privileges may be seen as "a natural component of the hospital's management structure."[21] Moreover, the staff is said to have a

15. 7 Philip E. Areeda, Antitrust Law ¶ 1471c-g (1986); see Barbara K. Miller, Defending the System: application of the Intraenterprise Immunity Doctrine in Physician Peer Review Antitrust Cases, 75 Tex. L. Rev. 409 (1996).

16. Weiss v. York Hosp., 745 F.2d 786, 817 (3d Cir.1984); Oksanen v. Page Mem'l Hosp., 945 F.2d 696, 703 (4th Cir.1991); Nurse Midwifery Assoc. v. Hibbett, 918 F.2d 605 (6th Cir.1990).

17. Bolt v. Halifax Hosp. Med. Ctr., 891 F.2d 810 (11th Cir.1990); Oltz v. St. Peter's Community Hosp., 861 F.2d 1440 (9th Cir. 1988).

18. 745 F.2d 786 (3d Cir.1984).

19. Id. at 817.

20. Id.

21. Oksanen v. Page Mem'l Hosp., 945 F.2d 696, 703 (4th Cir.1991).

unity of interest with the hospital in upgrading the quality of patient care.[22] To the extent that the hospital board retains power to control the staff and retains final decisionmaking responsibility, that unity of interest is assured.[23] Finally, courts have emphasized the efficiency benefits flowing from allowing hospitals to delegate responsibilities as they see fit.[24]

Courts have applied the holding in *Weiss* in circumstances in which the medical staff had only an advisory role and in which the hospital had ultimate control over a peer review decision[25] and where committees of the medical staff were delegated responsibility for making recommendations on privileges.[26] An issue left open by *Weiss,* whether a hospital may conspire with individual members of the medical staff, has not been resolved.[27]

Two circuits[28] and persuasive commentary[29] have rejected the *Weiss* holding that a hospital is legally incapable of conspiring with its staff. In *Bolt v. Halifax Hospital Medical Center,*[30] the Eleventh Circuit concluded that the analogy between hospital-staff relationships and corporation-employee relationships was "faulty." The Court stated:

> The rule for corporations is based on considerations unique to the corporate context. Theoretically, a "conspiracy" involving a corporation and one of its agents would occur every time an agent performed some act in the course of his agency, for such an act would be deemed an act of the corporation. Thus, the rule that a corporation is incapable of conspiring with its agents is necessary to prevent erosion of the principle that section 1 does not reach unilateral acts. A hospital and the members of its medical staff, in contrast, are legally separate entities, and consequently no similar danger exists that what is in fact unilateral activity will be bootstrapped into a "conspiracy."[31]

The holding in *Weiss* may also be faulted for being internally inconsistent. On the one hand, the Third Circuit held that because each member of a medical staff practices medicine independently and is a separate economic entity, staff physicians are capable of engaging in a horizontal conspiracy with each other.[32] At the same time the Court rejected the possibility of a vertical conspiracy between hospital and staff based upon the complete unity of interest that existed between the parties. There is no obvious reason to disregard entirely those economic factors in the vertical context. Indeed, it should be apparent that, just as members of the staff have competitive interests that diverge from each other, they also have a multitude of interests

---

22. Oksanen v. Page Memorial Hosp., 945 F.2d 696, 703 (4th Cir.1991).

23. Id. at 704.

24. Id. at 703–704.

25. Oksanen v. Page Mem'l Hosp., 945 F.2d 696 (4th Cir.1991).

26. Nanavati v. Burdette Tomlin Mem'l Hosp., 857 F.2d 96 (3d Cir.1988).

27. Id. (noting that the issue had been left open by Weiss and finding the evidence of such a conspiracy lacking).

28. Bolt v. Halifax Hosp. Med. Ctr., 891 F.2d 810 (11th Cir.1990); Oltz v. St. Peter's Community Hosp., 861 F.2d 1440 (9th Cir. 1988).

29. See James F. Blumstein & Frank A. Sloan, Antitrust and Hospital Peer Review, 51 Law & Contemp. Probs. 7, 39–53 (1988); Mark A. Hall & Ira Mark Ellman, Health Care Law and Ethics 1991 (1990).

30. 891 F.2d 810 (11th Cir.1990).

31. Id. at 819.

32. Weiss v. York Hosp., 745 F.2d 786, 814 (3d Cir.1984); see infra for discussion of conspiracies among members of medical staffs.

that diverge from those of the hospital.[33] Moreover, the approach of *Weiss* and subsequent cases overlooks the realities of organizational structure and decisionmaking at most hospitals. Commentary suggests that the not-for-profit organizational form and strong physician influence over the internal decisions of those institutions (reinforced by the JCAHO regulations) distinguish the hospital-staff relationship from the corporation-employee relationship.[34]

4. *Conspiracies Among the Medical Staff*

Less controversial than its holding that the medical staff was incapable of conspiring with its hospital was the *Weiss* court's disposition of the alleged conspiracy among the allopathic physicians on the York Hospital staff. The court concluded that:

> as a matter of law, the medical staff is a combination of individual doctors and therefore that any action taken by the staff satisfies the "contract, combination, or conspiracy" requirement of section 1 * * * The York medical staff is a group of doctors, all of whom practice medicine in their individual capacities, and each of whom is an independent economic entity in competition with other doctors in the York medical community. Each staff member, therefore, has an economic interest separate from and in many cases in competition with the interests of other medical staff members.[35]

Subsequent cases have extended *Weiss* to hold that the actions of committees of the medical staff can be a combination for purposes of Section 1 of the Sherman Act.[36]

This holding rests on firm ground to the extent that it establishes that the intraenterprise doctrine poses no barrier to establishing a conspiracy among medical staff members in proper circumstances. Courts have uniformly accepted the principle that staff members may conspire among themselves to restrain trade through use (or abuse) of the peer review/credentialing process.[37] This conclusion is consistent with a long line of Supreme Court precedent to the effect that the actions of trade associations will be treated as concerted activity unless those associations were "joint ventures" or integrated enterprises sharing risk.[38] Note, however, that under this analysis a truly integrated joint venture of physicians (such as a group practice providing

---

33. See James F. Blumstein & Frank A. Sloan, Antitrust and Hospital Peer Review, 51 Law & Contemp. Probs. 7, 51 n.322 (1988) (listing physicians' interests in ordering more services, extending patient stays and citing constraints on hospitals such as fixed payments and corporate practice of medicine laws); See also Philip C. Kissam et al., Antitrust and Hospital Privileges: Testing the Conventional Wisdom, 70 Cal. L. Rev. 595, 639–40 (1982) (physicians as "outside agents" and "independent entrepreneurs" capable of conspiring with hospital).

34. See, e.g., Robert Charles Clark, Does the Nonprofit Form Fit the Hospital Industry?, 93 Harv.L. Rev. 1416 (1980); Paul J. Feldstein, Health Care Economics 231–36 (3d ed. 1988); Mark V. Pauly & Michael A. Redisch, The Not-for–Profit Hospital as a Physician's Cooperative, 63 Am. Econ. Rev. 87 (1973).

35. Weiss v. York Hosp., 745 F.2d 786, 815 (3d Cir.1984).

36. Nanavati v. Burdette Tomlin Mem'l Hosp., 857 F.2d 96 (3d Cir.1988).

37. See, e.g., Pinhas v. Summit Health, Ltd., 894 F.2d 1024 (9th Cir.1989) (en banc), affirmed 500 U.S. 322, 111 S.Ct. 1842, 114 L.Ed.2d 366 (1991); Oksanen v. Page Mem'l Hosp., 945 F.2d 696, 706 (4th Cir.1991).

38. See, e.g., Arizona v. Maricopa County Med. Soc'y, 457 U.S. 332, 102 S.Ct. 2466, 73 L.Ed.2d 48 (1982); National Soc'y of Professional Eng'rs v. United States, 435 U.S. 679, 98 S.Ct. 1355, 55 L.Ed.2d 637 (1978); United States v. Topco Assocs., Inc., 405 U.S. 596, 92 S.Ct. 1126, 31 L.Ed.2d 515 (1972).

anesthesia services and sharing risk under contract with a hospital) should be found incapable of conspiring among themselves.[39] Finally, further support for the conclusion that medical staff members participating in the peer review process might constitute a conspiracy is found in Congress' adoption of the Health Care Quality Improvement Act,[40] which seems to have been premised upon an assumption that such activities could be actionable under Section 1.[41]

Some commentators have expressed concern that the *Weiss* decision regarding staff conspiracies would lead to the result that any action undertaken by a medical staff would be deemed to constitute a conspiracy even though participating doctors were not competitors of the excluded physician or had set their independent interests aside in performing their peer review function.[42] In apparent reaction to these concerns some courts have gone so far as to require plaintiffs to show that medical staff members had a direct, personal economic interest in conflict with the applicant for privileges.[43] A more balanced approach is found in the Sixth Circuit's *Nurse Midwifery* opinion rejecting the *Weiss* holding that the staff can *never* be considered a single entity and suggesting that the intraenterprise doctrine should shield physician staff members when they are acting solely as agents of the hospital.[44]

b. *Proving a Conspiracy*

That members of a medical staff are legally capable of conspiring does not establish that the conspiracy requirement of section one has been satisfied. Rather, plaintiffs' burden is to prove "a conscious commitment to a common scheme designed to achieve an unlawful objective."[45] A "meeting of minds in an unlawful arrangement" is the essence of the requirement.[46] The fact that one party is unwilling or coerced, however, does not negate the existence of a conspiracy.[47]

Because direct evidence is rarely available, most conspiracies are proved by inferences drawn from the behavior of co-conspirators. However, the

39. See James F. Blumstein & Frank A. Sloan, Antitrust and Hospital Peer Review, 51 Law & Contemp. Probs. 7, 45 (1988) (conduct of doctor group conducting peer review should be deemed unilateral and not conspiracy among member physicians to the extent group exhibits characteristics of joint venture). Likewise peer review conducted by physicians who are employees of a group under contract with a hospital should not be regarded as a conspiracy among member physicians.

40. 42 U.S.C.A. §§ 11101–11152. See infra § 10–22.

41. See James F. Blumstein & Frank A. Sloan, Antitrust and Hospital Peer Review, 51 Law & Contemp. Probs. 7, 45 n.273 (1988).

42. Mark A. Hall, Health Care Law and Ethics 189 (1990).

43. Friedman v. Delaware County Mem'l Hosp., 672 F.Supp. 171 (E.D.Pa.1987), affirmed 849 F.2d 600 (3d Cir.1988) (requiring plaintiff to show defendants acted out of personal economic interests and granting summary judgment for defendant physicians who performed some of the same procedures as plaintiff but did not seek to compete with him in perform-

ing the specific procedure that was the subject of peer investigation). See also Kaczanowski v. Med. Ctr. Hosp., 612 F.Supp. 688, 695 (D.Vt. 1985) (no conspiracy among medical staff without proof that members were acting to further their individual practices to the detriment of the profession or the hospital).

44. Nurse Midwifery Assocs. v. Hibbett, 918 F.2d 605, 614 (6th Cir.1990). Nurse Midwifery Assocs. v. Hendersonville Community Hosp., 502 U.S. 952, 112 S.Ct. 406, 116 L.Ed.2d 355 (1991).

45. Monsanto Co. v. Spray–Rite Serv. Corp., 465 U.S. 752, 768, 104 S.Ct. 1464, 1472, 79 L.Ed.2d 775 (1984) (summarizing standard for plaintiff to survive motion for summary judgment).

46. American Tobacco Co. v. United States, 328 U.S. 781, 810, 66 S.Ct. 1125, 1139, 90 L.Ed. 1575 (1946).

47. Perma Life Mufflers, Inc. v. International Parts Corp., 392 U.S. 134, 88 S.Ct. 1981, 20 L.Ed.2d 982 (1968); Albrecht v. Herald Co., 390 U.S. 145, 88 S.Ct. 869, 19 L.Ed.2d 998 (1968); Oltz v. St. Peter's Community Hosp., 861 F.2d 1440 (9th Cir.1988).

Supreme Court has limited the range of permissible inferences in antitrust cases based on circumstantial evidence. Plaintiff must adduce evidence that reasonably "tends to exclude the possibility of independent action,"[48] while conduct equally consistent with permissible activities as with illegal conspiracy will not by itself support an inference of conspiracy.[49]

At the same time, courts have elaborated upon the kinds of proof that will permit an inference as to the existence of a conspiracy. "Conscious parallelism"—antitrust shorthand for uniform conduct by rivals that is probative of conspiracy between them—will establish a conspiracy under section 1 under some conditions. Not only must competitors consciously engage in parallel business behavior, but one or more "plus factors" must be identified to support the inference. The Supreme Court has set forth the following examples of "plus factors":

- where defendant's activity marked a radical departure from prior practice;

- where defendant was aware of the conduct of co-defendants and that they had been invited to engage in similar conduct;

- where defendant had a profit motive to engage in uniform conduct; and

- where defendant's conduct was truly "interdependent," i.e., he would not benefit economically unless all the other defendants also complied.[50]

Even if one or more of these "plus factors" are present, however, parallel conduct only establishes a rebuttable presumption of conspiracy which defendant may overcome. Thus, if defendant comes forward with plausible evidence of profit-maximizing business justifications that makes independent conduct rational, conspiracy based on conscious parallelism will not be found.[51]

§ 14–18. Unreasonable Restraints Involving Use of Coercion, Collective Action or Threats of Boycott to Induce Staff Privilege Denials

The most problematic joint activity involving staff privileges occurs when providers act collectively outside of the peer review process to deny staff privileges to rivals. In these cases, the collective agreement typically involves threats of retaliation against a hospital if it does not comply or coercion against other physicians who may be in a position to influence the decision on privileges. These cases are often classic boycotts because they entail coercive agreements directed at horizontal rivals and there is no justification based on integrative cooperation between hospital and staff.

Perhaps the paradigmatic example is the government's criminal prosecution in *American Medical Association v. United States*.[1] The facts showed that the AMA tried to suppress group health medical plans (forerunners of HMOs)

48. Monsanto Co. v. Spray–Rite Serv. Corp., 465 U.S. 752, 104 S.Ct. 1464, 79 L.Ed.2d 775 (1984).

49. Matsushita Elec. Indus. Co. v. Zenith Radio Corp., 475 U.S. 574, 588, 106 S.Ct. 1348, 1356, 89 L.Ed.2d 538 (1986).

50. Interstate Circuit v. United States, 306 U.S. 208, 59 S.Ct. 467, 83 L.Ed. 610 (1939).

51. Theatre Enters., Inc. v. Paramount Film Distrib. Corp., 346 U.S. 537, 74 S.Ct. 257, 98 L.Ed. 273 (1954).

§ 14–18

1. 317 U.S. 519, 63 S.Ct. 326, 87 L.Ed. 434 (1943).

by orchestrating denials of hospital privileges to doctors in the District of Columbia who participated in such plans and by taking coercive actions against physicians who cooperated with other physicians who were affiliated with the plans. The Circuit Court distinguished the AMA's attempt to enforce its beliefs from legitimate efforts to persuade the medical community of the risks associated with alternative practice arrangements.

The FTC has successfully challenged coercive actions by physicians such as threatened walkouts and other economic reprisals directed at hospitals in connection with extensions of staff privileges.[2] For example, in *Sherman Hope*, the Commission alleged a boycott among physicians threatening to discontinue emergency room coverage in order to force a hospital to stop plans to recruit a new physician under financial terms the physicians opposed.[3] Similarly, it has asserted that coercive boycotts directed at physicians and designed to obstruct other providers' access to hospitals violate the FTC Act.[4] In essence, these actions amount to an agreement among physicians not to deal with the hospital except on collectively-determined terms and lack procompetitive justification. In the view of the FTC, joint coercion is unreasonable even if denial or restriction of staff privileges might otherwise be justifiable; it would apply a truncated analysis with no detailed evaluation or weighing of procompetitive benefits and anticompetitive effects.[5]

One case in which such coercion was present is *Oltz v. St. Peter's Community Hospital*,[6] in which staff anesthesiologists collusively threatened to leave the hospital if nurse anesthetists retained staff privileges. In that case, the Ninth Circuit upheld a jury verdict condemning the restraint and stressed the coercive character of defendants' joint efforts to remove a competitive threat to their practice. However, the court also expressly relied on evidence of actual detrimental effects on competition among providers of anesthesia services in the market to support its holding.[7]

§ 14–19. Staff Privileges in the Peer Review Context

a. The Relevant Legal Standard Under Section 1 of the Sherman Act

Cases involving staff privileges determinations undertaken through a hospital's peer review process usually involve § 1 Sherman Act claims that a group boycott was directed at the excluded provider. In *Northwest Wholesale*

2. See, e.g., Medical Staff of Broward Gen. Medical Ctr., 56 Fed. Reg. ¶ 49,184 (1991) (consent order); Robert Fojo, M.D., 57 Fed. Reg. 9258–01 (1992) (consent order); Medical Staff of Doctors' Hosp. of Prince George's County, 110 F.T.C. 476 (1988) (consent order).

3. In re Sherman A. Hope, M.D., 98 F.T.C. 58 (1981).

4. See, e.g., In re Health Care Management Corp., 107 F.T.C. 385 (1987)(consent order)(physicians pressuring other doctors not to co-admit patients with podiatrists and placing unreasonable non-quality-based conditions on access to hospital); In re Physicians of Meadville, 109 F.T.C. 61 (1987)(threatened denial of referrals and withholding hospital admissions directed at physician group opening satellite office); In re Eugene M. Addison, M.D., 111 F.T.C. 339 (1988) (denial of privileges to physicians associated with HMOs); Certain Sioux Falls Obstetricians, 16 C.F.R. Pt. 13 (1988) (consent order).

5. Mark J. Horoschak, Medical Staff Privileges and The Antitrust Law: A View From the Federal Trade Commission, 6 Medical Staff Counselor 17, 19 (Spring 1992)(joint coercion is always unreasonable).

6. 861 F.2d 1440 (9th Cir.1988).

7. Id. at 1448 (anesthesiologists' annual earnings increased by 40 to 50 per cent after termination of nurse anesthetists).

Stationers,[1] the Supreme Court reviewed the criteria for applying the *per se* rule to a concerted refusal to deal. It suggested that plaintiffs need to show "market power or exclusive access to an element essential to effective competition" and the absence of any plausible contention that the conduct would "enhance overall efficiency and make markets more competitive."[2]

Cases applying the *per se* rule in the peer review context are virtually non-existent. The sole exception is *Weiss v. York Hospital*[3] in which the Third Circuit characterized defendants' denial of privileges to osteopathic physicians as a naked restraint and hence *per se* illegal. The court's invocation of the *per se* rule may be harmonized with *Northwest Wholesale Stationers* by observing the unusual facts before the court. First, defendant hospital occupied a dominant position in the relevant market (80% of the relevant market in acute care services market and dominance in tertiary care). Second, defendants had not contended that osteopaths were unqualified to practice, proffered any procompetitive strategy as justification, or offered any other legitimate explanation for discriminating in the award of privileges.[4] Thus, in the absence of any legitimate procompetitive justification, hospitals with market power could at least in theory face per se scrutiny.[5]

In cases decided since *Northwest Wholesale Stationers*, however, defendants have had no trouble avoiding the *per se* rule, invoking, for example, defendants' lack of market power[6] or a large assortment of procompetitive justifications such as enforcing quality standards or promoting other administrative objectives.[7] Courts have properly noted that where the privileges action occurs in the context of peer review or is based on factors relevant to the hospital's competitive standing, the rule of reason is appropriate because it is impossible to conclude that the challenged activity is one that would almost always tend to be anticompetitive.[8]

b. Applying the Rule of Reason

To amend Justice Stewart's remark about antitrust merger law in the 1960s,[9] analysis under the rule of reason in staff privileges cases demonstrates

§ 14–19

1. Northwest Wholesale Stationers, Inc. v. Pacific Stationery & Printing Co., 472 U.S. 284, 105 S.Ct. 2613, 86 L.Ed.2d 202 (1985).

2. Id. at 294–5, 296; on the ambiguities in this formulation, see Philip E. Areeda & Herbert Hovenkamp, Antitrust Law ¶ 1510c (1991 Supp.).

3. 745 F.2d 786 (3d Cir.1984). Although decided before Northwest Wholesale Stationers, the Supreme Court denied certiorari in Weiss the same year as its decision in Northwest. See also Sweeney v. Athens Regional Med. Ctr., 709 F.Supp. 1563, 1573 (M.D.Ga. 1989) (allowing staff privileges case to proceed to trial under per se test).

4. The Third Circuit expressly noted that it did not doubt that "a hospital could exclude an applicant from staff privileges either because he is not medically qualified or because of unprofessional conduct, so long as the hospital applies the same standard to all applicants."

Weiss v. York Hospital, 745 F.2d 786, 820–21 (3d Cir.1984). See Flegel v. Christian Hosp. Northeast–Northwest, 4 F.3d 682 (8th Cir. 1993); Bhan v. NME Hosps. Inc., 929 F.2d 1404 (9th Cir.1991).

5. See James F. Blumstein & Frank A. Sloan, Antitrust and Hospital Peer Review, 51 Law & Contemp. Probs. 7, 73 (1988).

6. See, e.g., Goss v. Memorial Hosp. Sys., 789 F.2d 353 (5th Cir.1986).

7. See, e.g., Bhan v. NME Hosps., Inc., 929 F.2d 1404 (9th Cir.1991); Mathews v. Lancaster Gen. Hosp., 87 F.3d 624 (3d Cir.1996).

8. Id.; Tarabishi v. McAlester Regional Hosp., 951 F.2d 1558 (10th Cir.1991); Miller v. Indiana Hosp., 843 F.2d 139, 144 n. 6 (3d Cir.1988).

9. United States v. Von's Grocery Co., 384 U.S. 270, 301, 86 S.Ct. 1478, 1495, 16 L.Ed.2d 555 (1966) (Stewart, J., dissenting)("The sole consistency that I can find is that in litigation under § 7, the government always wins.").

little consistency except that defendant always wins. Admittedly, judges face a daunting task in assessing the net competitive effect of an alleged restraint under the rule of reason. They are called upon to evaluate and weigh the harms and benefits associated with the restraint, giving due consideration to the existence of less restrictive alternatives and the intentions of the parties.[10] Nevertheless, the cases do not paint a very clear picture of the nature of the competitive harm flowing from privilege denials or how procompetitive factors can offset those harms.

1. Market Power

Understandably, courts have devised shortcuts to aid in this task. Most prominently, where defendant's market share is not large enough to imply a significant threat to competition, courts freely grant summary judgement, holding plaintiff has not carried his burden of establishing prima facie unreasonableness. Defendant is not obliged in these circumstances to establish the strength of his justification or the reasonable necessity of the restraint.[11] Plaintiffs, however, may circumvent the market power "screen" by demonstrating actual anticompetitive effects such as a reduction in output.[12]

Where market power is sufficient to suggest some risk to competition, courts must evaluate and weigh procompetitive justifications and anticompetitive effects. In these circumstances, courts commonly look to evidence of an anticompetitive intent[13] and less anticompetitive alternatives to accomplish the purported justifications as signposts for anticompetitive harm.[14]

In cases in which the plaintiffs have failed to produce sufficient evidence to define a relevant market, courts usually dismiss for failure to meet their the burden of proof.[15] Although the issue of market definition is a question of fact, courts have frequently rejected proposed markets as a matter of law when an excessively narrow geographic market,[16] such as one comprised of a single hospital, is advanced. Finally, where the relevant market includes a number of comparable alternative hospitals, the cases generally conclude that a denial of privileges is unlikely to have anticompetitive effects because the doctor may continue to practice elsewhere.[17]

10. Commentators have decried the futility of efforts to quantify, evaluate and balance such incommensurable factors. See, e.g., 7 Philip E. Areeda, Antitrust Law ¶ 1501–1511 (1986). For perhaps the sharpest criticism of the balancing test mandated under the rule of reason, see Frank H. Easterbrook, The Limits of Antitrust, 63 Tex. L. Rev. 1 (1984) (characterizing formulations of the rule of reason as "empty" and arguing that neither courts nor economists are capable of conducting a full economic inquiry into the costs and benefits of a particular business practice).

11. 7 Philip E. Areeda, Antitrust Law ¶ 1507 (1986).

12. See Oltz v. St. Peter's Community Hosp., 861 F.2d 1440 (9th Cir.1988).

13. See Chicago Board of Trade v. United States, 246 U.S. 231, 38 S.Ct. 242, 62 L.Ed. 683 (1918) (benign purpose will not save anticompetitive conduct but anticompetitive intent will shed light on probable consequences of conduct).

14. See National Collegiate Athletic Ass'n v. Board of Regents, 468 U.S. 85, 104 S.Ct. 2948, 82 L.Ed.2d 70 (1984).

15. See, e.g., Flegel v. Christian Hosp. Northeast–Northwest, 4 F.3d 682 (8th Cir. 1993) (failure to produce sufficient evidence of product market consisting of referrals for osteopathic physicians or geographic market limited to local environs of hospital); Brown v. Our Lady of Lourdes Med. Ctr., 767 F.Supp. 618 (D.N.J.1991), affirmed 961 F.2d 207 (3d Cir. 1992) (summary judgment granted, plaintiff failed to produce evidence supporting market and court took judicial notice of presence of nearby hospitals).

16. Brader v. Allegheny Gen. Hosp., 64 F.3d 869 (3d Cir.1995); Oksanen v. Page Mem'l Hosp., 945 F.2d 696 (4th Cir.1991).

17. See, e.g., Robinson v. Magovern, 521 F.Supp. 842 (W.D.Pa.1981), affirmed 688 F.2d 824 (3d Cir.1982); Miller v. Indiana Hosp., 814 F.Supp. 1254 (W.D.Pa.1992), affirmed 975 F.2d 1550 (3d Cir.1992); Drs. Steuer & Latham v.

2. *Assessing Competitive Effects*

If plaintiff fails to demonstrate market power, she must produce evidence that the privileges determination will have an anticompetitive effect. Because of the number of economic variables and difficulties in proving causation, direct proof of lowered output or higher prices will rarely be available even where such effects are present.[18] Nevertheless, many courts have granted summary judgment based in part upon plaintiff's failure to present evidence raising triable issues on the issue of the competitive effect of the staff privileges determination. These cases emphasize that plaintiff must adduce evidence probative of harm to competition, not merely adverse effects upon her own practice.[19] Some courts have insisted that this proof be more than anecdotal and demonstrate that the restraint's effect was "substantially adverse."[20] For example, one court has suggested that plaintiffs in staff privileges cases must show: (1) a rise in the price of medical services above the competitive level; (2) a decrease in the supply of doctors in the relevant market; or (3) a decrease in the quality of medical services provided.[21] However, another recent case, citing *Summit Health v. Pinhas*, has questioned whether plaintiffs alleging group boycotts should be held to such onerous proof requirements.[22] Courts have discounted the possibility of anticompetitive effects where the staff privileges determination was only a "partial" restraint of trade, such as a temporary limitation on privileges or some other form of intermediate sanction short of revocation.[23] Several cases emphasize the abundance of competing physicians in plaintiff's area of practice, suggesting that exclusion of one physician can have no market-wide impact on competition, while others stress the availability of other hospitals in the market at which plaintiff might practice.[24]

Many courts give decisive weight to the presence of procompetitive factors that presumably outweigh any harms resulting from the privileges action. Of particular import are facts indicating that the hospital's competitive stature would be enhanced by the challenged action. For example, a hospital's desire to improve quality, rid itself of incompetent or disruptive practitioners, or otherwise promote the hospital's competitive strategy frequently has been stressed.[25] Today, economic factors such as the physician's utilization practices

---

National Med. Enters., Inc., 672 F.Supp. 1489 (D.S.C.1987), affirmed 846 F.2d 70 (4th Cir. 1988).

18. One notable exception is Oltz v. St. Peter's Community Hosp., 861 F.2d 1440 (9th Cir.1988), in which the court found the exclusion of a nurse anesthetist in a single-hospital community resulted in increases of 40 to 50 per cent in the revenues of anesthesiologists.

19. Baglio v. Baska, 116 F.3d 467 (3d Cir. 1997); Todorov v. DCH Healthcare Auth., 921 F.2d 1438 (11th Cir.1991).

20. Miller v. Indiana Hosp., 814 F.Supp. 1254, 1265 (W.D.Pa.1992), affirmed 975 F.2d 1550 (3d Cir.1992) (quoting United States v. Arnold, Schwinn & Co., 388 U.S. 365, 375, 87 S.Ct. 1856, 1863, 18 L.Ed.2d 1249 (1967)); see also Drs. Steuer & Latham v. National Med. Enters., Inc., 672 F.Supp. 1489 (D.S.C.1987), affirmed 846 F.2d 70 (4th Cir.1988).

21. Miller v. Indiana Hosp., 814 F.Supp. 1254 (W.D.Pa.1992), affirmed 975 F.2d 1550 (3d Cir.1992); see also Oksanen v. Page Mem'l Hosp., 945 F.2d 696 (4th Cir.1991).

22. Shafi v. St. Francis Hosp., 937 F.2d 603 (4th Cir.1991).

23. See, e.g., McElhinney v. Med., Protective Co., 549 F.Supp. 121 (E.D.Ky.1982).

24. See Drs. Steuer & Latham v. National Med. Enters., Inc., 672 F.Supp. 1489 (D.S.C. 1987), affirmed 846 F.2d 70 (4th Cir.1988); Farr v. Healtheast, Inc., 1993–1 Trade Cas. (CCH) ¶ 70,294, 1993 WL 220680 (E.D.Pa. 1993).

25. See, e.g., Oksanen v. Page Mem'l Hosp., 945 F.2d 696 (4th Cir.1991) (complaints that plaintiff was disrupting patient care warranted disciplinary action); Robinson v. Magovern, 521 F.Supp. 842 (W.D.Pa.1981), affirmed

and the financial significance of his practice to the hospital are becoming of increasing importance to the competitive posture of most hospitals. Although no reported cases explicitly turn on economic justifications of this sort, such concerns are likely to count as a significant procompetitive factor in the future as health care reform forces closer alliances between physicians and hospitals.[26]

While the various procompetitive benefits just discussed undoubtedly reflect important considerations under the rule of reason and can effectively refute allegations of anticompetitive purposes, the analytical approach of the cases is often quite confused. Courts frequently fail to match the nature of the benefits with the conspiratorial allegations advanced by plaintiff. Thus, it is sometimes the case that competitive objectives of a hospital are used to justify an adverse privileges determination when the gravamen of the plaintiffs' allegation is that a physician cartel dominated the hospital's decision-making process.

§ 14–20. Section 2 Analyses of Privileges Cases

a. Monopolization, Attempted Monopolization and Conspiracies to Monopolize

Excluded practitioners frequently contend that an adverse staff privilege decision constitutes monopolization, attempted monopolization and/or conspiracy to monopolize in violation of § 2 of the Sherman Act. Often filed as an afterthought to § 1 claims and half-heartedly litigated, these claims have been uniformly unsuccessful.

Plaintiffs litigating under a monopolization theory must first define a relevant market in which defendant possesses monopoly power. As with cases brought under Section 1, absence of proof of market power has been the principle basis for disposing of these claims. Courts have dismissed a large number of cases for failure to identify any relevant market at all or reliance upon a market in hospital services in which courts have found physicians do not compete.[1] If plaintiffs succeed in establishing a relevant market, market share statistics will make out a prima facie case that defendants possess market power, absent contrary evidence such as ease of entry or highly elastic demand. Case law under Section 2 suggests that as a matter of law market shares below 30% cannot constitute market power and market shares less than 50–60% often fail as well.[2] In staff privileges cases, courts have dismissed

---

688 F.2d 824 (3d Cir.1982) (denial of privileges to competent physician justified based on hospital marketing plan emphasizing teaching and research) ; Stone v. William Beaumont Hosp., 1983–2 Trade Cas. (CCH) ¶ 65,681, 1983 WL 1890 (E.D.Mich.1983), affirmed in relevant part 782 F.2d 609 (6th Cir.1986) (denial justified on basis of proximity to hospital and physician profile designed by hospital to avoid overburdening cardiac catheterization facilities).

26. See John D. Blum, Economic Credentialing: A New Twist in Hospital Appraisal Processes, 12 J. Legal Med. 427 (1991); see also supra §§ 10–16, 10–18.

§ 14–20

1. See, e.g., Tarabishi v. McAlester Reg'l Hosp., 951 F.2d 1558 (10th Cir.1991); White v. Rockingham Radiologists, Ltd., 820 F.2d 98 (4th Cir.1987).

2. Verducci v. Sonoma Valley Hosp. Dist., 87 F.3d 1325 (9th Cir.1996); United States v. Aluminum Co. of America, 148 F.2d 416 (2d Cir.1945) (90% market share constituted monopoly; 64% market share "doubtful"; 33% insufficient); United States v. Grinnell Corp., 384 U.S. 563, 86 S.Ct. 1698, 16 L.Ed.2d 778 (1966). See also Dimmitt Agri Indus., Inc. v. CPC Int'l Inc., 679 F.2d 516 (5th Cir.1982)

monopolization claims for failure to prove market power where market shares did not exceed 30%.[3] An additional element of proof of monopoly power imposed by some courts is the requirement that defendants possess the power to control price.[4]

Plaintiffs also have had no success in establishing the second prong of their monopolization claims: willful acquisition or maintenance of monopoly power. To satisfy this requirement, the excluded provider must show that a jury could find no valid business reason or efficiency justification for the hospital's denial of staff privileges.[5] As discussed above, the litany of concerns that a hospital might advance to rebut plaintiffs' case is substantial: quality of care, administrative convenience, and reputation of the hospital, to name a few. Because these justifications are usually present and almost always asserted in staff privilege disputes, this requirement poses an almost insuperable barrier to most plaintiffs. Finally, a claim that an adverse privileges determination constitutes a conspiracy to monopolize or attempted monopolization under Section 2 of the Sherman Act also requires proof of unlawful intent. The justifications just discussed tend to preclude a finding of the requisite intent; that is, legitimate, procompetitive reasons for excluding a physician offer an alternative motive for the action.

b. *Essential Facilities Claims*

Attempts to treat hospitals as "essential facilities" and require access for excluded providers under § 2 of the Sherman Act have likewise been unsuccessful. Under the essential facilities doctrine plaintiff must establish the following elements: (1) the decision-making process of the essential facility hospital is controlled by competitors of the excluded practitioner; (2) the essential facility hospital is controlled by a monopolist or, in and of itself, constitutes a relevant market; (3) no reasonably adequate substitutes exists in the area for the excluded provider to use; (4) the excluding entity lacks business justifications for its actions; and (5) granting access is feasible.[6]

Plaintiffs asserting essential facilities claims have foundered on several of these elements. For example, a putative essential facility hospital is not a monopoly or unique resource where other area hospitals compete for its patients and staff physicians and offer alternatives in which plaintiff may practice.[7] In addition, courts have refused to apply the doctrine on the grounds that the facility cannot practicably grant access or it has ample business justifications for the denial because the hospital has common law and regulatory responsibilities to screen the qualifications of physicians who practice in it. Indeed, some courts have gone so far as to hold that for "public

---

(market shares in the range of 15–25% absent other structural evidence insufficient as a matter of law to support monopolization claim).

3. Minnesota Ass'n. of Nurse Anesthetists v. Unity Hosp., 5 F.Supp. 2d 694 (D.Minn. 1998).

4. See, e.g., Tarabishi v. McAlester Reg'l Hosp., 951 F.2d 1558, 1568 (10th Cir.1991).

5. LeBaud v. Frische, 156 F.3d 1243, (10th Cir.1998).

6. Willman v. Heartland Hosp., 34 F.3d 605 (8th Cir.1994); McKenzie v. Mercy Hosp., 854 F.2d 365 (10th Cir.1988); see generally MCI Communications Corp. v. American Telephone & Telegraph Co., 708 F.2d 1081 (7th Cir.1983); 4 Philip E. Areeda & Herbert Hovenkamp, Antitrust Law ¶ 772–774 (1998).

7. McKenzie v. Mercy Hosp., 854 F.2d 365 (10th Cir.1988) (hospital obstetrical care unit not essential for physician performing some services in his own office).

policy reasons" the essential facilities cause of action is inapplicable to hospital staff privileges decisions.[8]

§ 14–21. Exclusive Contracting and Staff Privileges

Another kind of staff privileges dispute that has generated extensive antitrust litigation is exclusive contracting by hospitals with physician groups. Typically these arrangements entail contractual commitments by a hospital to make a single physician (or group of physicians) the only provider able to perform certain services at the hospital. Exclusive contracts are common in "hospital based" services such as anesthesiology, radiology, pathology and emergency room services and also occur in others such as cardiology.

a. *Exclusive Dealing Analysis*

Analytically, the most plausible antitrust theory under which contractual exclusivity is challenged is as illegal exclusive dealing under § 1 of the Sherman Act.[1] Under this theory, plaintiff must prove first, the existence of an exclusive agreement, and second that the agreement unreasonably restrained trade.

Because most exclusive dealing arrangements involve explicit agreements between hospitals and physicians, the "contract, combination or conspiracy" requirement is usually satisfied. However, courts have found no plurality of actors where the contracting physician is an employee of the hospital.[2] In addition, factual questions as to whether the agreement between the hospital and physician was truly "exclusive" have sometimes precluded application of the doctrine.[3] Moreover, no conspiracy exists among members of a multispecialty professional corporation that has an exclusive contract when its members agree to refer to each other because the group is considered to be a single entity.[4]

Exclusive dealing arrangements are analyzed under the rule of reason because, despite certain anticompetitive propensities, they may also have important procompetitive effects. Prominent among these are lower transaction costs for buyers and sellers, reduced uncertainty, and amelioration of free riding problems.[5] The principal anticompetitive concerns raised by exclusive contracting are: first, "foreclosure," i.e., a lessening of competition because rivals will not be able to find outlets to sell their goods and services; and second, raising barriers to entry or increasing rivals' costs, as potential

---

8. Willman v. Heartland Hosp., 34 F.3d 605 (8th Cir.1994); Tarabishi v. McAlester Reg'l Hosp., 951 F.2d 1558, 1568 (10th Cir.1991); McKenzie v. Mercy Hosp., 854 F.2d 365, 371 n. 12 (10th Cir.1988); Pontius v. Children's Hosp., 552 F.Supp. 1352, 1370 (W.D.Pa.1982); Robles v. Humana Hospital Cartersville, 785 F.Supp. 989 (N.D.Ga.1992).

§ 14–21

1. Section 3 of the Clayton Act also forbids exclusive dealing and tying arrangements but is usually not applicable here because it applies only to "sale or contract for sale of good, wares, merchandise, machinery supplies, or other commodities." 15 U.S.C.A. § 14.

2. See, e.g., McMorris v. Williamsport Hosp., 597 F.Supp. 899 (M.D.Pa.1984).

3. Anesthesia Advantage, Inc. v. Metz Group, 759 F.Supp. 638 (D.Colo.1991).

4. Smith v. Northern Michigan Hosps., Inc., 703 F.2d 942 (6th Cir.1983).

5. See Richard M. Steuer, Exclusive Dealing After Jefferson Parish, 54 Antitrust L.J. 1229 (1986); Roger D. Blair & David L. Kaserman, Antitrust Economics 409 (1985); Howard P. Marvel, Exclusive Dealing, 25 J.L. & Econ. 1 (1982).

competitors will have to vertically integrate (or contract exclusively), thus increasing the cost of entry.

In applying the rule of reason to analyze exclusive dealing, the Supreme Court has stopped short of requiring that plaintiffs show actual anticompetitive effects. A substantial amount of foreclosure in a properly defined relevant market is sufficient to support a showing of illegality.[6] However the requisite amount of foreclosure remains unsettled.[7] In addition, the case law suggests that unreasonableness will turn on several factors besides statistical evidence of foreclosure. Courts have taken into account, for example, the duration of the exclusive contract, the extent of foreclosure based on the existence of other exclusive contracts in the market, and whether procompetitive benefits outweigh harms.[8]

Exclusive dealing cases involving hospital contracting reflect some of the analytic uncertainty discussed above, but courts have uniformly upheld such arrangements. As a preliminary matter, some courts have found that plaintiffs lack standing or have not adequately alleged antitrust injury under exclusive dealing theories.[9] Most decided cases, however, have found plaintiff's proof of foreclosure wanting.

A major source of confusion in the case law has been the delineation of the relevant geographic and products market within which the effects of exclusive hospital contracts are to be measured, an issue the Supreme Court did not resolve in *Jefferson Parish Hosp. Dist. No. 2 v. Hyde*.[10] On one view, the relevant geographic market should be the area in which anesthesiologists compete for the business of *patients*, usually a relatively localized region.[11] Under this approach, the germane effect is that felt by consumers (patients and their agents) whose demand is limited in geographic scope. The alternative view holds that the proper focus for antitrust should be much broader, as exclusive contracting involves negotiations between hospitals and physicians in a regional or national geographic market. The argument is buttressed by the fact that patients do not seek out or negotiate separately for certain hospital-based services, like pathology. Thus, the hospital in reality shops for and contracts for physicians' services on behalf of buyers; this bargaining, for

6. See Standard Oil Co. v. United States, 337 U.S. 293, 69 S.Ct. 1051, 93 L.Ed. 1371 (1949); Tampa Elec. Co. v. Nashville Coal Co., 365 U.S. 320, 81 S.Ct. 623, 5 L.Ed.2d 580 (1961); see also Jefferson Parish Hosp. Dist. No. 2 v. Hyde, 466 U.S. 2, 45, 104 S.Ct. 1551, 1575, 80 L.Ed.2d 2 (1984) (O'Connor, J., concurring) ("Exclusive dealing is an unreasonable restraint on trade only when a significant fraction of buyers or sellers are frozen out of a market by the exclusive deal").

7. See Standard Oil Co. v. United States, 337 U.S. 293, 69 S.Ct. 1051, 93 L.Ed. 1371 (1949) (40% foreclosure warranted condemnation under Clayton Act § 3); Tampa Elec. Co. v. Nashville Coal Co., 365 U.S. 320, 81 S.Ct. 623, 5 L.Ed.2d 580 (1961) (foreclosure of less than 1% of market involving long term requirements contract did not violate § 3 of the Clayton Act); see also Jefferson Parish Hosp. Dist. No. 2 v. Hyde, 466 U.S. 2, 33, 104 S.Ct.

1551, 1569, 80 L.Ed.2d 2 (1984) (O'Connor, J., concurring) (30% insufficient); In re Beltone Elecs. Corp., 100 F.T.C. 68 (1982) (20% insufficient).

8. See Roland Mach. Co. v. Dresser Indus., Inc., 749 F.2d 380 (7th Cir.1984); Joyce Beverages, Inc. v. Royal Crown Cola Co., 555 F.Supp. 271 (S.D.N.Y.1983).

9. Drs. Steuer & Latham v. National Med. Enterprises, 672 F.Supp. 1489 (D.S.C.1987), affirmed 846 F.2d 70 (4th Cir.1988).

10. 466 U.S. 2, 104 S.Ct. 1551, 80 L.Ed.2d 2 (1984) (suggesting that the market for anesthesiologists could be local or regional).

11. Courts have rejected the view that the relevant market should consist of a single hospital. See Drs. Steuer & Latham v. National Med. Enters., Inc., 672 F.Supp. 1489 (D.S.C. 1987), affirmed 846 F.2d 70 (4th Cir.1988).

the most part, occurs in regional or national markets.[12] A third line of cases holds that courts should look at the effect of competition in both markets and determine whether competition is lessened in either one. Thus, an exclusive contract that restrained competition either among physicians marketing their services to hospitals or among physicians selling services to patients and insurers would violate the antitrust laws.[13]

The point at which the several relevant factors (magnitude of foreclosure, duration of the agreement and other contractual terms) cause an exclusive contract to cross the line to become an unreasonable restraint remains unclear. Several courts have pronounced challenged contracts not unreasonable based on their short duration[14] or because low market shares were foreclosed.[15] Other cases stress specific circumstances that reduce the likelihood that competition will be lessened by an exclusive contract. For example, there is said to be less competitive risk where the exclusive contract is awarded through competitive bidding and where it may be terminated at the discretion of the hospital.[16]

In addition, most cases also find procompetitive benefits sufficient to offset any anticompetitive effects. Often cited are improved administrative and monitoring functions by the hospital, standardization of procedures, greater teamwork, round-the-clock coverage for staff physicians in certain specialties, and avoidance of excessive demand by physicians for specific services.[17]

b. Boycott Analysis

Several cases have examined challenges to exclusive contracts as boycotts under Section 1. Because procompetitive justifications are almost always available, the arrangement is scrutinized under the rule of reason and the analysis in large part tracks that of the exclusive dealing cases. On the requirement of a "contract, combination or conspiracy," courts have found no concerted action where the contract did not completely foreclose plaintiffs from rendering services or where the evidence did not support an inference that the decision was other than the hospital's independent judgment.[18]

c. Tying Doctrine Analysis

A "tie-in" or tying arrangement is a vertical agreement pursuant to which a seller sells one good or service (the "tying product") to a buyer only on the condition that the buyer purchase a second good or service (the "tied product") from the seller. In the context of hospital exclusive contracting with physicians, the claim is usually that a hospital has conditioned the sale of its

12. See, e.g., Collins v. Associated Pathologists, Ltd., 844 F.2d 473 (7th Cir.1988).

13. See Burnham Hosp., 101 F.T.C. 991 (1983) (advisory opinion); Oltz v. St. Peter's Community Hosp., 861 F.2d 1440 (9th Cir. 1988).

14. See Konik v. Champlain Valley Physicians Hosp. Med. Ctr., 733 F.2d 1007 (2d Cir. 1984).

15. Collins v. Associated Pathologists, Ltd., 844 F.2d 473, 479 (7th Cir.1988) (de minimis foreclosure where market for pathologists was national).

16. See White v. Rockingham Radiologists, Ltd., 820 F.2d 98 (4th Cir.1987).

17. See, e.g., Burnham Hospital, 101 F.T.C. 991 (1983) (advisory opinion). See also Jefferson Parish Hosp. Dist. No. 2 v. Hyde, 466 U.S. 2, 33, 104 S.Ct. 1551, 1569, 80 L.Ed.2d 2 (1984) (O'Connor, J., concurring).

18. See, e.g., McMorris v. Williamsport Hosp., 597 F.Supp. 899 (M.D.Pa.1984); Konik v. Champlain Valley Physicians Hosp. Med. Ctr., 733 F.2d 1007 (2d Cir.1984).

general acute care services (use of operating rooms, inpatient services, 24–hour nursing care, etc.) on the purchase of certain professional services (e.g., anesthesiology or pathology) from the physician or group with which the hospital has an exclusive contract.

As a threshold matter, it would seem that in order to state a cause of action, plaintiff must allege that the seller of the tying product receives an economic benefit from the sale of the tied product. Absent some financial interest in the tied product, it is difficult to see how a monopolist benefits from steering or forcing business to another party other than through achieving efficiencies through the contract. Most courts have recognized the requirement that the seller receive some direct economic benefit from the sale of the tied product,[19] but a few have not.[20]

The basic requirements of the cause of action under a tying theory are as follows: (1) the sale of two separate products; (2) a significant amount of interstate commerce in the tied product;[21] (3) the conditioned or "forced" sale of the tying product on the purchase of the tied product; (4) market power or sale of a unique service in the tying product; and (5) an adverse effect on competition.

The Supreme Court continues to recognize a per se rule, albeit one of limited strength in tying cases. The chief benefit of per se treatment for plaintiffs is that they may dispense with proving actual effects on competition once the other elements of the cause of action are established.[22] Widespread skepticism concerning the economic basis for tying law is reflected in the continuing expansion of plaintiff's burden under the per se rule and strict interpretation of those requirements by the courts.[23]

The Supreme Court's most definitive, although sharply divided, exposition of antitrust tying doctrine is found in *Jefferson Parish Hospital District No. 2 v. Hyde*,[24] a case involving a challenge to an exclusive contract between a large acute care hospital and a group providing anesthesiology services. Plaintiff, an excluded anesthesiologist, complained that the hospital had tied its acute care hospital services to the provision of anesthesiology services through a specified group (the Roux group), thereby preventing him from obtaining privileges at the hospital. Although the Court was unanimous in

19. See, e.g., Beard v. Parkview Hosp., 912 F.2d 138 (6th Cir.1990); White v. Rockingham Radiologists, Ltd., 820 F.2d 98, 103–104 (4th Cir.1987).

20. See, e.g., Gonzalez v. St. Margaret's House Housing Dev. Fund Corp., 880 F.2d 1514 (2d Cir.1989).

21. This requirement has been satisfied with as little as $10,000 in commerce; it is rarely examined closely by the courts.

22. Jefferson Parish Hosp. Dist. No. 2 v. Hyde, 466 U.S. 2, 104 S.Ct. 1551, 80 L.Ed.2d 2 (1984).

23. In a widely-noted concurrence Justice O'Connor joined by three other members of the Court, urged abandonment of the per se rule for tying cases. Id. at 32. Her arguments in large part reflect the extensive scholarly criticism of the doctrine that emphasizes the many circumstances in which tying arrangements may have benign or procompetitive consequences and questions the adverse effects often attributed to such arrangements. See generally Herbert Hovenkamp, Economics and Federal Antitrust Law 222–40 (1985); Ward S. Bowman, Jr., Tying Arrangements and the Leverage Problem, 67 Yale L.J. 19 (1957). Recent scholarship has challenged the assumptions of the critics, pointing out the possibility that market power may sometimes be extended through leverage. See, e.g., Louis Kaplow, Extension of Monopoly Power Through Leverage, 85 Colum. L. Rev. 515 (1985); cf. Note, An Economic Analysis of Tie–In Sales: Re-examining the Leverage Theory, 39 Stan. L. Rev. 737 (1987).

24. 466 U.S. 2, 104 S.Ct. 1551, 80 L.Ed.2d 2 (1984).

upholding the arrangement, it divided sharply on the reasoning and analytic methodology. The courts found that anesthiological and hospital services constituted separate products and concluded that the hospital's thirty per cent market share did not constitute sufficient proof of market power to sustain a per se tying claim. Four concurring Justices sharply questioned the risks often attributed to tying arrangements and argued that rule of reason should apply in all cases.[25]

Challenges to hospital exclusive arrangements are likely to founder on the requirement that the hospital have an economic interest in the sale of the tied product because most hospitals lack a direct financial interest in their exclusive contracts.[26] In addition, courts since *Jefferson Parish* have relied on the full arsenal of other issues to reject virtually all tying claims asserted in staff privileges disputes. For example, despite the Supreme Court's holding that anesthesiology and acute care hospital services constituted separate products, that analysis does not necessarily imply that other hospital services will be treated the same. Thus, professional pathology services, for which there is no distinct demand (as evidenced by the absence of consumer requests for specific pathologists), have been found not to constitute a product separate and distinct from hospital services.[27]

Courts have also rejected tying claims based on failures of proof of market power in the tying product[28] and in various circumstances in which a hospital's joint sale of two products did not constitute "conditioning."[29] An issue reopened by *Kodak*, however, is whether courts will be more sympathetic to claims of market power where plaintiffs can demonstrate substantial information gaps and switching costs.[30] Taking their cue from the concurrence in *Jefferson Parish*, a number of lower courts have also weighed offsetting procompetitive benefits in tying cases.[31] Finally, for the few plaintiffs who persist, the rule of reason would pose an almost insuperable obstacle, requiring proof of actual effects such as a lessening of output caused by the tie-in sale.

§ 14–22. The Health Care Quality Improvement Act of 1986

The Health Care Quality Improvement Act of 1986 (HCQIA)[1] is a Congressional response to several problems associated with peer review. It seeks

25. Jefferson Parish Hosp. Dist. No. 2 v. Hyde, 466 U.S. 2, 32, 104 S.Ct. 1551, 1568, 80 L.Ed.2d 2 (1984) (O'Connor, J., concurring).

26. See, e.g., Beard v. Parkview Hosp., 912 F.2d 138 (6th Cir.1990); White v. Rockingham Radiologists, Ltd., 820 F.2d 98 (4th Cir.1987); Drs. Steuer & Latham v. National Med. Enters., Inc., 672 F.Supp. 1489 (D.S.C.1987), affirmed 846 F.2d 70 (4th Cir.1988).

27. Collins v. Associated Pathologists, Ltd., 844 F.2d 473 (7th Cir.1988).

28. See, e.g., Drs. Steuer & Latham v. National Med. Enters., Inc., 672 F.Supp. 1489 (D.S.C.1987), affirmed 846 F.2d 70 (4th Cir. 1988) (market share of less than 15% inadequate market power); Burnham Hosp., 101 F.T.C. 991 (1983) (advisory opinion) (hospital with 11% market share lacks sufficient market power); but cf. McMorris v. Williamsport Hosp., 597 F.Supp. 899 (M.D.Pa.1984) (market share of 55–60% and evidence that some procedures were not provided elsewhere posed genuine issue of fact).

29. See, e.g., White v. Rockingham Radiologists, Ltd., 820 F.2d 98 (4th Cir.1987); Konik v. Champlain Valley Physicians Hosp. Med. Ctr., 733 F.2d 1007, 1017 (2d Cir.1984). See also McMorris v. Williamsport Hosp., 597 F.Supp. 899 (M.D.Pa.1984).

30. See supra § 14–4(c).

31. Jefferson Parish Hosp. Dist. No. 2 v. Hyde, 466 U.S. 2, 43, 104 S.Ct. 1551, 1574 , 80 L.Ed.2d 2 (1984) (O'Connor, J., concurring); see also IBM Corp. v. United States, 298 U.S. 131, 56 S.Ct. 701, 80 L.Ed. 1085 (1936).

§ 14–22

1. 42 U.S.C.A. §§ 11101–11152.

to address the malpractice problem by encouraging professional reviews of the quality of care in hospitals and other settings; it attempts to reverse the medical community's growing reluctance to participate in professional peer review by granting immunity from private antitrust actions and other federal and state laws; and it seeks to improve the flow of information about quality of care by requiring reporting of disciplinary actions to state medical boards and by establishing a National Practitioner Data Bank.

The legislative intent of the Act is something of a mixed bag.[2] Congress' primary concern was that the threat of antitrust enforcement "unreasonably discourage[d] physicians from participating in effective professional peer review."[3] At the same time, the Act implicitly recognizes the anticompetitive risks associated with peer review by rival practitioners in that it retains significant antitrust enforcement authority and grants only limited immunity in specified circumstances. As discussed below, the HCQIA provides weak disincentives to litigation and arguably immunizes only conduct that would not have violated the antitrust laws prior to its enactment.

a. The Scope of Immunity Under the HCQIA

The HCQIA immunizes "professional review bodies" and individuals participating in "professional review actions" from damages under federal law (except civil rights laws) and state law. It also immunizes individuals providing information to these bodies as long as the information is not knowingly false.[4] While support for HCQIA was undoubtedly driven by desires to promote peer review and deter frivolous litigation, its practical usefulness is open to question in view of the many limitations on its scope of coverage. The HCQIA affords only limited immunity and does not apply at all to certain categories of conduct. First, it only provides protection from actions for monetary damages, thus not precluding criminal prosecutions or suits for injunctive or declaratory judgment relief. Second, it does not reach litigation by the federal government or state attorneys general.[5] Third, peer review of non-physicians is not covered by the Act.[6] Fourth, the Act applies to broadly-defined "professional review actions" which include peer reviews undertaken not only in the hospital context but by other entities such as professional

2. See 42 U.S.C.A. § 11101 (Congressional Findings to the Health Care Quality Improvement Act) stating:

(1) The increasing occurrence of medical malpractice and the need to improve the quality of medical care have become nationwide problems that warrant greater efforts than those that can be undertaken by any individual State.

(2) There is a national need to restrict that ability of incompetent physicians to move from State to State without disclosure or discovery of the physician's previous damaging or incompetent performance.

(3) This nationwide problem can be remedied through effective professional peer review.

(4) The threat of private money damage liability under Federal laws, including treble damage liability under Federal antitrust law, unreasonably discourages physicians from participating in effective professional peer review.

(5) There is an overriding national need to provide incentive and protection for physicians engaging in effective professional peer review.

3. 42 U.S.C.A. § 11101(4). See also id. at 11101(5) (citing an "overriding national need to provide incentive and protection for physicians engaging in effective professional peer review"); see generally Bernard D. Reams, The Health Care Quality Improvement Act of 1986: A Legislative History of Pub. L. 99–660 (1990).

4. 42 U.S.C.A. § 11111(a)(2).

5. 42 U.S.C.A. § 11111(a)(1).

6. 42 U.S.C.A. § 11111.

groups meeting the statutory definition of a "peer review body."[7] However, these covered activities are limited to actions or recommendations concerning "conduct of a professional review activity, which is based on the competence or professional conduct of an individual physician which conduct affects (or would affect) the health or welfare of a patient or patients * * *."[8] Thus, HCQIA immunity does not reach actions not based on professional competence, such as exclusive contracts, economic credentialing, personality issues or personal disputes not affecting competence or professional conduct.[9]

In addition, in order to qualify for immunity a professional review action must meet four reasonableness standards set forth in the act.[10] The Act establishes a rebuttable presumption that actions falling within the definition of "peer review actions" meet these tests; the presumption may be rebutted by "a preponderance of the evidence."[11] Additionally, it specifies detailed procedural steps that will satisfy the notice and hearing requirements of section (3) above,[12] but allows for implementation of less cumbersome but unspecified "other procedures."[13]

b. Litigation Disincentives

The HCQIA supplies three disincentives to litigation. First, it imposes sanctions in order to deter abusive litigation;[14] second, it establishes a presumption of non-liability in favor of peer review participants; and third, it identifies a four-part test for limited immunity.

Sanctions under the HCQIA provide for the payment of costs (including attorney's fees) if the suit was "frivolous, unreasonable, without foundation, or [brought] in bad faith."[15] Commentators have pointed out that sanctions available under Rule 11 and other rules which dealing with litigation abuses[16] provide at least as much protection against abusive litigation as do the

---

7. The Act defines "peer review body" as:

a health care entity and the governing body or any committee of a health care entity which conducts professional review activity, and includes any committee of the medical staff of such an entity when assisting the governing body in a professional review activity.

42 U.S.C.A. § 11151(11).

8. Id. at 11151(9).

9. The Act sets forth several examples of reasons for peer review actions deemed not to be based upon the competence or professional conduct of a physician: viz., association membership, fee arrangements other than fee-for-service, advertising, or practicing in association with non-physicians. 42 U.S.C.A. § 11151(9).

10. 42 U.S.C.A. § 11112(a).

11. 42 U.S.C.A. § 11112.

12. The recommended procedures include notice of the action informing the physician of his right to a hearing and notice of the time and place of the hearing and a list of witnesses. §§ 11112(b)(1–2). The procedures also provide that the hearing be before either an arbitrator mutually acceptable to both parties or a hearing officer or panel selected by the health care

entity and made up of physicians not in competition with the physician involved. § 11112(b)(3)(A). The Act further specifies that the physician should have the right to:

1. representation by an attorney;

2. a formal record;

3. examine and cross-examine witnesses;

4. present evidence; and

5. receive a written recommendation and or decision including a basis for that recommendation or decision.

§§ 11112(b)(3)(C–D).

13. § 11112(b).

14. 42 U.S.C.A. § 11113.

15. 42 U.S.C.A. § 11113.

16. Rule 11 of the Federal Rules of Civil Procedure provides for cost shifting for unreasonable claims, Fed. R. Civ. P. 11. Likewise, Rules 16, 26, and 37 also contain provisions aimed at deterring litigation abuse, Fed. R. Civ. P. 16(f), 26(g) and 37. See Charity Scott, Medical Peer Review, Antitrust, and the Effect of Statutory Reform, 50 Md. L. Rev. 316, 337–41 (1991).

HCQIA sanctions.[17] On the other hand, as one court has noted, the award of attorneys' fees under the HCQIA is mandatory whereas it is discretionary under Rule 11; moreover, the underlying purpose of the HCQIA's penalties—shifting the costs of litigation—may imply a different standard than Rule 11, which is directed at penalizing and deterring abusive litigation.[18]

Of greater possible significance than the sanctions, however, is the rebuttable presumption of limited immunity from peer review liability provided by § 11111. In essence, the Act creates a presumption of nonliability and places a "preponderance of the evidence" burden on plaintiffs seeking to rebut that presumption. Though the Act creates a presumption in defendants' favor, where the court finds that a reasonable jury could conclude by a preponderance of the evidence that one of the Acts prerequisites was not satisfied no immunity will be granted.[19] Whether this presumption of nonliability creates any significant new disincentives to litigation has been questioned. Arguably, in *Monsanto* and *Matsushita* the Supreme Court established a standard for summary judgment governing commercial conduct analogous to peer review that in effect created a rebuttable presumption of legality.[20]

Finally, the immunity provisions themselves are quite narrow and carve out little that would not otherwise escape antitrust sanction. Professor Charity Scott has argued that the conduct actually immunized by the Act—reasonable peer review actions of individual physicians based on incompetence or misconduct and subject to due process protections—are amply protected by existing case law from antitrust challenges.[21] Hence, she concludes that the litigation-deterring effects of HCQIA are minimal.

c. The Effects of the HCQIA on Staff Privileges Litigation

Despite its limited scope, the HCQIA does make an important adjustment to the substantive issue presented to courts in staff privileges issues. It does so by explicitly approving good faith quality-oriented peer reviews, thus condoning reliance on the purpose of the reviewers and other non-competition centered factors. This shift has been somewhat obscured by the fact that many courts have introduced purpose and quality issues *sub rasa* into their analyses under the rule of reason. Nevertheless, the Act may play an important role in certain circumstances. It would, for example, immunize good faith peer reviews by professional review bodies in hospitals possessing market power or controlling unique facilities that might qualify for per se analysis. At the same time, in non-immunized cases the Act may encourage courts to focus

17. See Charity Scott, Medical Peer Review, Antitrust, and the Effect of Statutory Reform, 50 Md. L. Rev. 316, 340 (1991) ("it is difficult to imagine a case where a sanction would be appropriate under the Act, but not available under Rule 11").

18. Wei v. Bodner, 1992 WL 165860 (D.N.J. 1992), affirmed per curiam 970 F.2d 901 (3d Cir.1992). The district court in Wei awarded defendant over $450,000 in attorneys fees under both Rule 11 and the HCQIA, finding that "the complaint was without factual basis from the start and Dr. Wei did not consider whether his claims had any merit whatsoever prior to filing his lawsuit." Id. at 12. See also Johnson v. Nyack Hosp., 773 F.Supp. 625 (S.D.N.Y. 1991), affirmed 964 F.2d 116 (2d Cir.1992)

(finding complaint not "frivolous or without foundation" and refusing to award attorneys fees under HCQIA).

19. Brown v. Presbyterian Healthcare Servs., 101 F.3d 1324 (10th Cir.1996).

20. See Charity Scott, Medical Peer Review, Antitrust, and the Effect of Statutory Reform, 50 Md. L. Rev. 316, 342 (1991) ("a judicial rule that prevents the factfinder from inferring illegality * * * is tantamount to a Congressional [presumption of] non-liability.").

21. Charity Scott, Medical Peer Review, Antitrust, and the Effect of Statutory Reform, 50 Md. L. Rev. 316, 352–57 (1991).

attention exclusively on competitive effects rather than purpose or noncompetitive values.[22]

Although courts applying the HCQIA have not uniformly granted immunity, the cases suggest that it may be of some use to defendants in the future. Courts now frequently grant motions for summary judgment, concluding it was improper to permit plaintiffs to go to the jury on the issue of whether the prerequisites of the HCQIA were met[23] and citing Congress' intention that the HCQIA provide immunity at an early stage of litigation.[24] An important procedural issue concerns the timing of permissible appeals of orders denying defendant's immunity. The Fourth Circuit has held that because the HCQIA establishes immunity from liability only, not from suit,[25] defendants may not immediately appeal motions to dismiss under the HCQIA and thus must face pretrial and trial litigation costs.

In weighing the evidence on motions for summary judgment, courts have emphasized that the Act's "reasonable belief" provision sets an objective standard that does not require proof of the state of mind of the peer reviewers.[26] Further, in finding compliance with the four reasonableness requirements, judicial inquiries have focused on the presence of good faith peer review, while disclaiming any responsibility to pass on the "correctness" of defendants' acts.[27] Thus, interpretations of the Act confirm that courts will not upset "good faith mistakes" in judgment that arguably might give rise to liability under antitrust doctrine.[28] While holding that each "peer review action" taken requires separate examination under the Act, courts have resisted attempts to fragment the inquiry into judicial approvals of every step in the process or to require that the entire course of investigative conduct meet the Act's requirements.[29] Finally, immunity has been denied where a hospital failed to comply with the Act's reporting requirements,[30] where defendant was able to adduce evidence raising triable issues of fact about whether the action was based on quality of care concerns and in good faith,[31] and where issues were raised about whether peer reviewers acted after a reasonable effort to obtain the facts of the matter.[32]

22. For contrasting views on the advisability of explicitly weighing quality factors in antitrust litigation compare Charity Scott, Medical Peer Review, Antitrust, and the Effect of Statutory Reform, 50 Md. L. Rev. 316, 370–71 (1991) with Thomas L. Greaney, Quality of Care and Market Failure Defenses in Antitrust Health Care Litigation, 21 Conn. L. Rev. 605, 627–49 (1989). See supra Section 10–7.

23. Bryan v. James E. Holmes Regional Med. Center, 33 F.3d 1318, 1333 (11th Cir. 1994) (HCQIA requires "plaintiff bear the burden of proving that peer review was *not* reasonable; Egan v. Athol Mem. Hosp., 971 F.Supp. 37 (D.Mass.1997); Austin v. McNamara, 731 F.Supp. 934 (C.D.Cal.1990), affirmed 979 F.2d 728 (9th Cir.1992); Fobbs v. Holy Cross Health Sys. Corp., 789 F.Supp. 1054 (E.D.Cal.1992), affirmed 29 F.3d 1439 (9th Cir.1994).

24. Fobbs v. Holy Cross Health Sys. Corp., 789 F.Supp. 1054, 1063 (E.D.Cal.1992), affirmed 29 F.3d 1439 (9th Cir.1994).

25. Decker v. IHC Hosps., Inc., 982 F.2d 433 (10th Cir.1992).

26. Brader v. Allegheny General Hosp., 167 F.3d 832 (3d Cir.1999); Austin v. McNamara, 979 F.2d 728 (9th Cir.1992) (bad faith immaterial).

27. See Fobbs v. Holy Cross Health Sys. Corp., 789 F.Supp. 1054 (E.D.Cal.1992), affirmed 29 F.3d 1439 (9th Cir.1994).

28. See M. Elizabeth Gee, Health Care Quality Improvement Act Immunity: An Antitrust Help or Hinderance?, in American Bar Association, Antitrust and Health Care: Cutting Edge Issues (Oct. 15–16, 1992).

29. Fobbs v. Holy Cross Health Sys. Corp., 789 F.Supp. 1054 (E.D.Cal.1992), affirmed 29 F.3d 1439 (9th Cir.1994).

30. Manion v. Evans, 1991 WL 575715 (N.D.Ohio 1991).

31. Id.

D. HEALTH CARE FINANCING: RELATIONSHIPS BETWEEN PROVIDERS AND PAYERS

§ 14–23. Introduction

The hundreds of antitrust challenges involving disputes between providers and third-party payers span the full gamut of causes of action under Sections 1 and 2 of the Sherman Act. The claims range from naked restraints of trade, such as price fixing and efforts to thwart the growth of competitive payment systems; to loose forms of cooperation that restrict rivalry to some degree but have the potential to improve competitive conditions; to full or partial integration of providers creating new payment systems; and finally, to alleged abuses by payers in obtaining or exercising market power.

1. CONCERTED PROVIDER ACTIONS LACKING JUSTIFICATION

Courts have examined a variety of horizontal agreements among competing providers designed to lessen competition by interfering with payment systems. Perhaps as a result of mixed signals sent by the Supreme Court,[1] the federal courts and the FTC have been slow to invoke the *per se* rule, even though in most instances these provider activities constitute "naked" restraints of trade.[2] That is, the concerted action in these cases typically lacks plausible procompetitive justification and is not undertaken ancillary to a legitimate joint venture. Courts are increasingly applying "quick look" analysis, examining purported justifications and condemning such restraints without elaborate inquiry into market power, purpose or effect where the justifications are found wanting.

§ 14–24. Price Fixing, Fee Schedules and Boycotts in Support Thereof

The leading case striking down provider price agreements through jointly-set fee schedules is *Arizona v. Maricopa County Medical Society*.[1] In that case, the Court held that two physician-controlled foundations for medical care which collectively set the maximum fees for foundation-approved insurance plans engaged in illegal price fixing. A slender four-Justice plurality invoked the *per se* rule, ostensibly relying on the nature of the agreement (price fixing) without regard to the foundation's market power or efficiency justifications for the agreement. Notably, the Court distinguished the foundations from physician-controlled HMOs, observing that the element of risk sharing entitled the latter to expanded scrutiny under the rule of reason and

---

32. Brown v. Presbyterian Healthcare Servs., 101 F.3d 1324 (10th Cir.1996).

§ 14–23

1. Compare Arizona v. Maricopa County Med. Society, 457 U.S. 332, 102 S.Ct. 2466, 73 L.Ed.2d 48 (1982) with FTC v. Indiana Fed'n of Dentists, 476 U.S. 447, 106 S.Ct. 2009, 90 L.Ed.2d 445(1986). See generally Thomas A. Piraino, Jr., Beyond Per Se, Rule of Reason or

Merger Analysis: A New Antitrust Standard for Joint Ventures, 76 Minn. L. Rev. 1 (1991).

2. See, e.g., Michigan State Med. Society, 101 F.T.C. 191 (1983).

§ 14–24

1. 457 U.S. 332, 102 S.Ct. 2466, 73 L.Ed.2d 48 (1982).

that such joint ventures are more appropriately regarded as "a single firm competing with other sellers in the market."[2]

Although criticized for its wooden application of the *per se* rule, Justice Stevens' opinion in *Maricopa* took pains to examine, albeit briefly, justifications premised on purported pro-competitive benefits of the fee schedule. The Court went on to apply a less restrictive alternative analysis noting "[e]ven if a fee schedule is * * * desirable, it is not necessary that doctors do the price fixing."[3]

A criticism raised by the dissenting Justices was that it was at least possible that efficiency benefits might accrue to consumers from providers setting a maximum level of fees and hence closer scrutiny under the rule of reason was appropriate.[4] For example, the fee schedule might help overcome information inadequacies by signalling the availability of lower priced physicians. Yet, while closer scrutiny was perhaps desirable, it is unlikely that net benefits would flow from a maximum fee schedule in the factual context of *Maricopa*. As Justice Stevens noted, there was good reason to believe that the lower price offered by the physician cartel was designed to discourage entry by more efficient systems such as HMOs. Hence, the likely end result would be to continue supra-competitive pricing, albeit at a lower level than existed before the foundation's activities.[5]

For the most part, lower courts have followed *Maricopa* by applying *per se* or "quick look" analysis to condemn provider-initiated fee schedules and other horizontal price-setting activities that lack pro-competitive justifications. For example, in *Michigan State Medical Society*,[6] the FTC struck down an agreement among physicians to coerce payors into increasing fee-for-service payment levels through threats of "departicipation." Likewise, the Ninth Circuit upheld per se jury instructions in a criminal price fixing case involving a conspiracy among dentists to fix the copayment amounts they would receive and to force payers to accept these agreed-upon terms.[7]

The government has successfully challenged the use of collectively-set fee schedules by physicians engaged in joint negotiations with HMOs;[8] collective agreements by pharmacies to eliminate discounts on co-payments of prescription drugs;[9] agreements optometrists to raise prices for eye exams through the activities of their professional society;[10] use of PHOs and physician associations to raise fees and discourage discounting;[11] and hospitals' joint refusal to

---

2. Id. at 346.

3. Id. at 352.

4. See Frank H. Easterbrook, Maximum Price Fixing, 48 U. Chi. L. Rev. 886 (1981); Peter M. Gerhart, The Supreme Court and Antitrust Analysis: The (Near) Triumph of the Chicago School, 1982 Sup. Ct. Rev. 319.

5. For a fuller economic analysis of the likely competitive effects of the Maricopa fee schedule, see Keith B. Leffler, Arizona v. Maricopa County Med. Soc'y: Maximum–Price Agreements in Markets With Insured Buyers, 2 Sup. Ct. Econ. Rev. 187 (1983).

6. 101 F.T.C. 191 (1983).

7. United States v. Alston, 974 F.2d 1206 (9th Cir.1992) (jury need only find that defen-

dants knowingly participated in an agreement to raise co-payment fees).

8. United States v. Massachusetts Allergy Soc'y, Inc., 1992–1 Trade Cas. (CCH) ¶ 69,846, 1992 WL 178713 (D.Mass.1992) (consent decree).

9. Maryland ex rel. Curran v. Prescription Network of Maryland Inc., No. JH–90–2425 (D. Md., Filed Sept. 17, 1990).

10. U.S. v. Lake County Optometric Soc'y., 6 Trade Reg. Rep. (CCH) ¶ 45,095 at 4781 (W.D. Tex. Dec. 15, 1995).

11. Montana Associated Physicians, Inc., 62 Fed. Reg. 11201 (March 11, 1997) (consent order).

extend discounts in bidding for contracts.[12] In addition, a number of courts have held or implied that certain provider-controlled prepayment plans will be treated as *per se* illegal price fixing agreements. These cases, which are discussed below, turn on the absence of sufficient integration among providers in the plans and generally apply the *per se* rule where provider control is clear.[13]

Voluntary agreements among providers to control costs by setting price caps will also fall under per se scrutiny when they restrict individual competitors' pricing freedom. The Department of Justice has rejected a proposal by the Pharmaceutical Manufacturers' Association to agree to limit their members' price increases so as not to exceed the increase in the Consumer Price Index in any year.[14] The Department's business review letter noted that maximum price agreements have been treated as per se offenses because of their tendency to become agreements on actual prices. It rejected justifications that the agreement was necessary to avoid the greater evil of mandatory governmental price controls because adoption of such controls is not certain and in any event would not supply an excuse for private collective action.

§ 14–25. Collective Negotiations by Providers With Third Party Payers

Closely related to overt price fixing schemes are agreements among providers to negotiate collectively with third party payers. *Per se* analysis is appropriate where collective negotiations are not undertaken by an integrated joint venture among providers and where the joint negotiation is coercive, i.e., it is coupled with a threat of departicipation or a refusal to act independently. A good example (albeit one in which the FTC did *not* apply *per se* analysis) is the *Michigan State Medical Society* case.[1] There a physician association linked its bargaining demands with threats of boycotting Medicaid and Blue Shield patients and gathered departicipation proxies from its members in order to force payers to raise fee schedules. Boycotts in aid of price fixing and enforced by coercive threats or actions are universally recognized as meriting summary treatment under Section 1 of the Sherman Act,[2] so the FTC was perhaps overly cautious in applying even a truncated rule of reason analysis. Indeed, the recent Department of Justice/FTC Policy Statements on Health Care seems to adopt the view that per se analysis is appropriate in such circumstances.[3] The Ninth Circuit, however, has expressed the view in dicta that because of departures from normal competitive markets, providers should be allowed to band together to negotiate aspects of reimbursement with third

---

12. United States v. North Dakota Hosp. Ass'n, 640 F.Supp. 1028 (D.N.D.1986).

13. See, e.g., Hahn v. Oregon Physicians' Serv., 868 F.2d 1022 (9th Cir.1988); Glen Eden Hosp., Inc. v. Blue Cross & Blue Shield of Michigan, Inc., 740 F.2d 423 (6th Cir.1984). See infra § 14–32.

14. Letter from Anne K. Bingaman, Assistant Attorney General, Antitrust Division, U.S. Department of Justice to John R. Ferguson, Esq. (October 1, 1992).

§ 14–25

1. 101 F.T.C. 191 (1983).

2. FTC v. Superior Court Trial Lawyers Ass'n, 493 U.S. 411, 436 n. 19, 110 S.Ct. 768, 782 n. 19, 107 L.Ed.2d 851 (1990) (boycott that aids price fixing agreement "consistently analyzed as per se violation for many decades").

3. U.S. Department of Justice and Federal Trade Commission, Statements of Antitrust Enforcement Policy in Health Care, Statements 8 & 9 (1996), reprinted in 4 Trade Reg. Rep. (CCH) ¶ 13,152.

party plans without coming under per se analysis.[4] There is little, if any, doctrinal support for altering Section 1 inquiries to account for powerful buyers, and, in any event, the opinion's assumptions about the economics of health care markets are highly questionable. For example, there is strong empirical evidence in the economic literature for the proposition that competition among payers elicits more competitive payment rates from providers.[5] If anything, collective negotiations will exacerbate market imperfections by hindering payers' efforts to deal with the problems through innovation.

Likewise, the superficially appealing argument that providers should be allowed to bargain collectively in order to "level the playing field" against powerful managed care buyers finds little support in law or economics.[6] Antitrust law does not recognize as a defense to concerted action under Section 1 of the Sherman Act the fact that sellers face large buyers in the market. As a matter of economics, consumers are generally not better off under conditions of "bilateral monopoly" than when firms in a competitive market at one level of distribution deal with firms having market power at another.[7]

State and federal governments have prosecuted a number of provider boycotts of Medicaid and other government payment programs. These cases have included concerted activity by physicians,[8] pharmacists,[9] nursing homes,[10] and optometrists[11] aimed at exerting collective pressure to achieve higher reimbursement. Although frequently advanced, the Noerr–Pennington doctrine has not protected defendants from liability for concerted price fixing or boycott activities aimed at governmental payers. Noerr shields collective action by provider associations to secure anticompetitive legislation or other governmental actions favorable to their members; however it does not afford protection in boycott cases involving coercive refusals to deal with Medicaid and other governmental entities. The Supreme Court has made this point clear, holding that the doctrine has no applicability where conduct crosses the line from "mere solicitation" of government action and becomes a collective

---

4. United States v. Alston, 974 F.2d 1206, 1214 (9th Cir.1992) (collective negotiations by providers concerning payment procedures, types of documentation they must provide, methods of referring patients and the mechanism for adjusting disputes should be permissible absent explicit or implicit threats of mass withdrawals from plans).

5. D. Gaskin & J. Hadley, The Impact of HMO Penetration on the Rate of Hospital Cost Inflation, 34 Inquiry 205 (1997); Joan C. Robinson, Decline in Hospital Utilization and Cost Inflation under Managed Care in California, 276 JAMA 1060 (1996).

6. Roger D. Blair & Jeffrey Harrison, Monopsony (1993).

7. See also remarks of Robert Pitofsky, Chairman, Federal Trade Commission, "Thoughts on Leveling the Playing Field," Nat'l. Assn. Of Health Lawyers Program on Antitrust in the Healthcare Field (Feb. 13, 1997).

8. College of Physician–Surgeons of Puerto Rico, Civ. No. 2466–HL (D. Puerto Rico) (Octo-

ber 2, 1997) (boycott through "strike" against indigent care program); see Maine v. Alliance for Healthcare, Inc., 1991–1 Trade Cas. (CCH) ¶ 69, 339, 1991 WL 290818 (Me.Super.1991) (consent decree).

9. See New York v. Empire City Pharmaceutical Soc'y, Inc., 1978–2 Trade Cas. (CCH) ¶ 62,383, 1978 WL 15573 (N.Y.Sup.1978) (consent decree) (boycott of Medicaid program).

10. See United States v. Montana Nursing Home Ass'n, Inc., 1982–2 Trade Cas. (CCH) ¶ 64,852, 1982 WL 1867 (D.Mont.1982) (consent decree enjoining boycott of state Medicaid program).

11. See New York v. New York State Soc'y of Ophthalmic Dispensers, Inc., 1980–1 Trade Cas. ¶ 63,074 , 1979 WL 3914 (N.Y.Sup.1979), (consent decree) (boycott of state Medicaid program); Iowa v. Iowa Optometric Ass'n, 1983–2 Trade Cas. (CCH) ¶ 65,483, 1983 WL 14928 (D.Iowa 1983) (consent decree).

boycott designed to evoke change in governmental policy.[12] As a practical matter, however, this is a boundary that is not clearly marked and it is sometimes necessary to walk a fine line in order to observe the legitimate petitioning right of associations. For example, although the FTC has resisted arguments that Medicaid boycotts constitute legitimate political lobbying protected by *Noerr*,[13] it has been careful to preserve defendants' First Amendment rights to petition the government on reimbursement policies in consent decrees and judgments entered in these cases.[14]

§ 14-26. Concerted Efforts to Thwart Cost Control or Entry by Alternative Delivery Systems

Collusive agreements that obstruct cost control efforts of third party payers are also treated as naked restraints or summarily struck down under "quick look" analysis. For example, in the *Indiana Federation of Dentists* case, the Supreme Court classified defendant dentists' collective refusal to provide patients' x-rays to third party payers as conduct directly interfering with market mechanisms and thus not requiring close examination into effect or purpose. Rejecting defendants' objections that the information might not be competitively significant because no proof had been offered that denying the x-rays to insurers had raised the cost of dental care, the Court stated:

> "A concerted and effective effort to withhold (or make more costly) information desired by consumers for the purpose of determining whether a particular purchase is cost justified is likely enough to disrupt the proper functioning of the price-setting mechanism of the market that it may be condemned even absent proof that it resulted in higher prices or, as here, the purchase of higher priced services, than would occur in its absence."[1]

As we have seen, summary condemnation is common where conduct palpably interferes with the market such as the Indiana dentists' collusive efforts to thwart buyers seeking lower prices. Less widely appreciated by the courts and commentary is that such actions pose pronounced risks of harm to consumers because they reinforce market imperfections in health care. Applying conventional cartel theory, such cartels are probably less susceptible to breaking down because they afford greater certainty and higher rewards to their participants. Therefore, where payers seek to overcome problems of moral hazard and imperfect information (as was the case in the *Indiana Federation* case), their efforts merit utmost protection because they are likely to yield significant benefits in reducing large efficiency losses associated with those market imperfections.

12. FTC v. Superior Court Trial Lawyers Ass'n, 493 U.S. 411, 110 S.Ct. 768, 107 L.Ed.2d 851 (1990) (no *Noerr* or First Amendment protection for boycott by lawyers protesting government-set fees for representation of indigent clients).

13. Michigan State Med. Soc'y, 101 F.T.C. 191, 278–79 (1983).

14. In enjoining certain anticompetitive practices of a pharmacy association, the FTC specifically allowed defendants to "suggest arguments to present to legislatures in criticizing a government sponsored third party prescription plan in order to encourage pharmacy firms to lobby for changes in the terms of the plan, so long as it did not do so as a sham to encourage the pharmacy firms to boycott the third party prescription plan." Chain Pharmacy Ass'n, 56 Fed. Reg. 12534, 12540 (1991) (consent order).

§ 14-26

1. FTC v. Indiana Fed'n of Dentists, 476 U.S. 447, 461, 106 S.Ct. 2009, 2019, 90 L.Ed.2d 445 (1986).

Another form of interference with cost control involves concerted actions by providers to block entry or otherwise hinder HMOs through boycotts or other means. Early efforts to discourage association by physicians with HMOs were undertaken by medical societies which expelled doctors from membership and coerced and harassed physicians cooperating with new delivery systems.[2] By far the largest number of cases, however, have concerned concerted actions by physicians jointly refusing to cooperate with providers or facilities associated with HMOs and other alternative delivery systems.[3]

§ 14–27.   "Sham" PPOs and IPAs

The final category of activities appropriately treated under per se or "quick look" analysis involves provider collusion through establishment of "sham" PPOs or IPAs. These organizations lack any meaningful integration of activities and sometimes do not even function as an organized entity. Unlike legitimate PPOs and IPAs, sham arrangements undertake few cooperative business activities such as marketing, adoption of utilization controls or the like. Instead, they serve almost exclusively as mechanisms by which members collectively agree on price and engage in joint bargaining with third parties. Following the teaching of *Maricopa*, the FTC and the Department of Justice have treated these organizations essentially as price fixing schemes because, absent any meaningful integration of activities or risk sharing, procompetitive justifications are lacking.[1] Likewise, the government has challenged a hospital "network" that refused to grant discounts or limited the amount of price concessions given to payers.[2]

§ 14–28.   Physician Unions

Physicians have begun to seek legal authority to collectively bargain through unions. However, for the large majority of the nation's physicians who are not employees of HMOs, hospitals or other entities, antitrust law imposes a substantial barrier to engaging in the principal activities associated with unions: collective bargaining over compensation and working conditions. The critical issue facing physicians attempting to collectively bargain through unions is whether they qualify for the labor exemption under the antitrust laws. This exemption has two parts: (1) statutory exemptions, found in sections 6 and 20 of the Clayton Act[1] and section 4 of the Norris LaGuardia Act,[2] which together combine to protect unions and their members carrying out their legitimate objectives and permit strikes and boycotts in the course of disputes "concerning terms and conditions of employment"; and (2) a non-

2. American Med. Ass'n v. United States, 130 F.2d 233 (D.C.Cir.1942), affirmed 317 U.S. 519, 63 S.Ct. 326, 87 L.Ed. 434 (1943); Health Corp. of America, Inc. v. New Jersey Dental Ass'n, 424 F.Supp. 931 (D.N.J.1977). See generally Clark C. Havighurst, Professional Restraints on Innovation in Health Care Financing, 1978 Duke L.J. 303. See supra § 14–9.

3. See supra §§ 14–9, 14–18. See, e.g., American Med. Ass'n v. United States, 130 F.2d 233 (D.C.Cir.1942), affirmed 317 U.S. 519, 63 S.Ct. 326, 87 L.Ed. 434 (1943); Group Health Co–op. of Puget Sound v. King County Med. Soc'y, 237 P.2d 737 (Wash.1951).

§ 14–27

1. Southbank IPA, Inc., 57 Fed. Reg. 2913 (1990) (consent decree). See § 14–24 supra.

2. United States v. Classic Care Network, Inc., 1995–1 Trade Cas. (CCH) ¶ 70,997, 1995 WL 367908 (E.D.N.Y.1995) (consent decree).

§ 14–28

1. 15 U.S.C.A.§ 17 (1999).

2. 29 U.S.C.A.§ 101 (1999).

statutory exemption that harmonizes antitrust policy with the National Labor Relations Act of 1935 (NLRA) and that extends antitrust immunity to certain concerted actions involving unions and employers. Both the statutory and non-statutory exemptions require the activity to arise out of a "labor dispute." That is, it must involve a bona fide labor organization comprised only of employees, not independent contractors, and must involve the promotion of legitimate labor interests as opposed to entrepreneurial or nonlabor interests unrelated to the employer-employee relationship.[3]

A key issue for physicians under contract with managed care plans is whether they can or will be regarded as de facto "employees" of such organizations because the plans exercise extensive control over their practices and have strong economic leverage over them.[4] However, courts have interpreted the labor exemption not to apply to physicians in independent practice.[5] The government has challenged several attempts to organize physician unions that did not meet the standard for an exemption under the antitrust law.[6] To improve their prospects of being treated as employees for antitrust exemption purposes, some physicians in independent practice have sought certification by the National Labor Relations Board. In an important decision, the Board rejected such a petition, finding that the managed care company with which the physicians contracted did not have substantial control "with respect to the physical conduct in the performance of the services" the doctors provide and that the doctors had "wide entrepreneurial discretion that affects the profitability of their practices."[7]

Faced with this obstacle to collective bargaining, it appears that physicians will seek legislative relief. For example, federal legislation has been

3. Section 2(3) of the NLRA gives the right to bargain collectively only to "employees" and the Taft–Hartley amendments to the act provided that the term "employee" does not include "any individual having the status of an independent contractor." 29 U.S.C.A.§ 152 (3). The House Report accompanying the amendment stated:

> "Employees" work for wages or salaries under direct supervision. "Independent contractors" undertake to do a job for a price, decide how the work will be done, usually hire others to do the work, and depend for their income not upon wages, but upon the difference between what they pay for goods, materials, and labor and what they receive for the end result, that is, upon profits.

H.R. Rep. No. 245, 80th Cong., 18 (1947).

4. See Edward B. Hirshfeld, Physicians, Unions and Antitrust, 32 J. Health L. 39 (1999). An additional qualification is that employees holding managerial or supervisory positions are not authorized to bargain collectively through labor organizations under the NRLA. NLRB v. Yeshiva University, 444 U.S. 672 (1980).

5. See American Med. Ass'n v. United States, 317 U.S. 519 (1943); FTC v. Indiana Federation of Dentists, 101 F.T.C. 57 (1983), rev'd on other grounds, 745 F.2d 1124 (7th Cir.1984), *rev'd*, 476 U.S. 447 (1986).

6. FTC v. College of Physicians–Surgeons, 5 Trade Reg. Rep. (CCH) ¶ 24,335 (D.P.R. Oct. 2, 1997); United States v. Federation of Physicians and Dentists, Inc., No. CIV.A. 98–475 (D. Del. Aug. 12, 1998)(complaint charging a physician union, consisting of nearly all orthopedic surgeons in Delaware, with organizing a boycott and jointly terminating contracts in order to resist a fee reduction).

7. Employee Status: Regional Director Finds HMO Physicians in New Jersey are Independent Contractors, Health Law Rep. (BNA) No. 8 at 864 (May 27, 1999). The regional director of the NLRB found that while AmeriHealth had control over which health services the physicians could supply, "factors of the common law agency test weigh heavily in favor of independent contractor status for the petitioned-for physicians." Her findings emphasize that physicians exert substantial control over how they perform those services, retain their own economic separateness from AmeriHealth, practice and advertise in their own names, perform their work at their own facilities without supervision from AmeriHealth, and have wide entrepreneurial discretion that affects the profitability of their practices. AmeriHealth Inc./AmeriHealth HMO and United Food & Commercial Workers Union, Case–4–RC–19260 (NLRB 4th Region, May 24, 1999).

introduced that would grant healthcare professionals "the same treatment under the antitrust laws" as that afforded to bargaining unions under the NLRA.[8] In addition, organized medicine has moved to endorse the concept of physician unionization as the House of Delegates of the American Medical Association (AMA) voted in June to abandon previous opposition to such affiliations.[9] Further, Texas has enacted legislation that gives physicians a limited exemption to state antitrust laws by allowing collective bargaining with health plans over fee-related issues where (1) the health plan has "substantial market power and those terms and conditions have already affected or threatened to adversely affect the quality and availability of patient care" and (2) the physicians represent not more than ten percent of the physician in the plan's geographic service area.[10] The Texas statute requires that physicians seeking this exemption must first file a report with and obtain the approval of the state Attorney General. The significance of the Texas law will hinge on two issues: whether it is too administratively complex and limited in scope to provide the kind of relief physicians desire and its impact on federal antitrust enforcement. The key question on the latter issue will be whether the statute provides for sufficient oversight and control by the state so as to afford state action immunity from federal antitrust laws immunity to the conduct.[11]

2. CONCERTED PROVIDER ACTIONS WITH PURPORTED JUSTIFICATIONS

§ 14–29. Price Surveys and Other Exchanges of Information Among Providers

Information sharing among competitors runs afoul of Section 1 of the Sherman Act when the circumstances surrounding the exchange of information demonstrate that competitors have conspired with the purpose or effect of increasing price or otherwise restraining competition. Recognizing that reduced uncertainty and transaction costs can help both buyers and sellers respond to competitive opportunities, courts uniformly examine such arrangements under the rule of reason.[1] Where, however, the evidence demonstrates that information sharing is part of an agreement to fix prices or reduce output, or where it "spills over" into price fixing arrangements in other markets in which the participants compete, per se analysis is appropriate.[2]

Although a wide variety of circumstances and market conditions are pertinent to evaluating the likelihood that an information exchange will restrain competition, several factors figure prominently in the cases. Courts have looked favorably on the following kinds of arrangements:

8. The Quality Health–Care Coalition Act of 1999, H.R. 1304, 106th Cong. (1999).

9. Unionized Medicine, New York Times, June 25, 1999, at A22.

10. Tex. Ins Code §§ 29.06(a) & 29.09(b).

11. See §§ 14–2(d)(2), 14–16(b).

§ 14–29

1. See United States v. Container Corp. of America, 393 U.S. 333, 338–39, 89 S.Ct. 510, 513–14, 21 L.Ed.2d 526 (1969) (Fortas, J., concurring); Maple Flooring Mfrs. Ass'n v. United States, 268 U.S. 563, 45 S.Ct. 578, 69 L.Ed.

1093 (1925); see also United States v. United States Gypsum Co., 438 U.S. 422, 98 S.Ct. 2864, 57 L.Ed.2d 854 (1978). Richard A. Posner, Information and Antitrust: Reflections on the Gypsum and Engineers Decisions, 67 Geo. L.J. 1187 (1979).

2. See U.S. Department of Justice and Federal Trade Commission, Statements of Antitrust Enforcement Policy in Health Care, Statement 5 (1996), reprinted in 4 Trade Reg. Rep. (CCH) ¶ 13,152; Norman R. Prance, Price Data Dissemination as a Per Se Violation of the Sherman Act, 45 U. Pitt. L. Rev. 55 (1983).

- exchanges that do not involve price, output or other sensitive information;

- those involving historical rather than present or future prices;

- those in which the information appears in summary or aggregate form and does not identify individual customers;

- agreements lacking enforcement mechanisms or coercion to pressure individual sellers;

- exchanges in which the information is made available to nonmembers and customers; and

- exchanges affecting markets that are not highly concentrated or predisposed to collusive stabilization of prices.[3]

United States v. Burgstiner,[4] a case involving price exchanges among competing physicians, illustrates the risks of price information exchanges in the managed care contracting context. In that case, which was settled by civil consent decrees, the government alleged that twenty-two obstetrician/gynecologists in Savannah, Georgia had exchanged information regarding their fees in a series of meetings after local businesses had announced their intention to form a PPO. The government's complaint alleged that as a result of these activities defendants were able to increase their fees for normal deliveries and caesarean sections by an average of approximately $500. The link between the information exchange and defendants' pricing practices and the absence of plausible justifications made it unlikely that this arrangement would survive analysis under the rule of reason.

In a case illustrating the ambiguous borderline between voluntary exchanges of information and illegal collective action, a number of independent allergists in Massachusetts formed a committee to deal with fees paid by an HMO.[5] The committee met with the HMO's representative and proposed a fee schedule. The HMO's representative responded to the HMO's proposals and indicated that while the allergists did not exert pressure on him, the HMO ultimately raised its fees but not to the levels proposed by the committee. While initially examining the conduct as a possible criminal violation of Section 1, the Department of Justice ultimately settled for a civil consent decree. Apparently, the absence of explicit coercion and the willing participation of the HMO in the discussions made the case unsuitable for criminal prosecution. Whether the conduct at issue would even make out a civil case is unclear. The collective submission of a fee schedule unaccompanied by any express or implicit coercion would likely fall short of the Sherman Act's agreement requirement and the cooperation of the buyer may raise legitimate questions as to whether the conduct restrained trade.[6]

Concern about this kind of conduct appears to have been on the mind of the FTC and Department of Justice when they established a "safety zone" for

3. United States v. Container Corp. of America, 393 U.S. 333, 89 S.Ct. 510, 21 L.Ed.2d 526 (1969).

4. 1991–1 Trade Cas. (CCH) ¶ 69,422, 1991 WL 90885(S.D.Ga.1991) (consent decree).

5. United States v. Massachusetts Allergy Soc'y., 1992–1 Trade Cas. (CCH) ¶ 69,846, 1992 WL 178713 (D.Mass.1992) (consent decree).

See generally, 2 J. Miles Health Care & Antitrust Law § 15:5 at 15–22.

6. See Schachar v. American Academy of Ophthalmology, Inc., 870 F.2d 397 (7th Cir. 1989); see also United States v. Alston, 974 F.2d 1206 (9th Cir.1992).

collective provision of information by physicians to purchasers. The statements provide only limited leeway in this area, announcing that the agencies will not challenge, "absent extraordinary circumstances," physicians' collective provision of underlying medical data concerning the mode, quality or efficiency of treatment, outcome data and practice parameters. Specifically excluded from the safety zone was physicians' collective provision of fee-related information and attempts through threats of boycott to coerce payers to follow joint recommendations.[7]

Where information sharing among health care providers is likely to produce pro-competitive benefits and adequate safeguards have been undertaken to protect against cartel practices or spillover collusion, government enforcement agencies have repeatedly approved arrangements. For example, little risk to competition is presented by information exchanges among providers when organized by third party payers or where the information is freely shared with them. Thus, the FTC found no competitive harm in a physician-organized peer review program conducted for third party payers in which the physicians gathered information and engaged in nonbinding peer review of hospital admissions, discharges and other matters.[8] Government advisory opinions have also approved a large number of arrangements pursuant to which third party payers or coalitions of employers have gathered price information from providers.[9]

Although price information exchanges among provider groups or their representatives[10] are more problematic, government advisory opinions have uniformly approved provider proposals to collect and distribute price information.[11] While the facts and circumstances surrounding these programs vary, frequently cited in support of the government's decision not to challenge the program are: an unconcentrated market structure in which the providers compete; the absence of anticompetitive purposes; the presence of legitimate procompetitive benefits arising out of the exchange; distribution of information to consumers and third party payers as well as providers; voluntary participation by providers; collection of historical rather than current or future price information; and aggregate information not identifying specific prices of providers or identifying customers. Similar issues are raised by "benchmarking" programs which enable providers to share information about competitors' practices, clinical effectiveness, procedures and outcomes. The government has approved sharing such information where safeguards are similar to those required for exchanges of price information.[12]

7. U.S. Department of Justice and Federal Trade Commission, Statements of Antitrust Enforcement Policy in the Health Care, Statement 5 (1996), reprinted in 4 Trade Reg. Rep. (CCH) ¶ 13,153. On the risks of medical societies using practice guideline promulgation or other information-supplying activities to restrain trade, see supra, §§ 14–13 & 14–14.

8. Rhode Island Professional Standards Review Organization, 101 F.T.C. 1010 (1983). See discussion of peer review of fees infra § 14–30.

9. See, e.g., Antitrust Division, Department of Justice, Business Review Letter to St. Louis Area Business Health Coalition (Mar. 24, 1988); Department of Justice, Business Review Letter to Lexecon Health Service (June 20, 1986).

10. The mere fact that a third party or trade association is gathering the information does not by itself relieve the providers of antitrust risk. See Department of Justice, Business Review Letter to Hyatt, Imler, Ott & Blount, P.C. (June 12, 1992).

11. The Department of Justice has cleared eleven requests and the FTC has cleared seven requests concerning proposed exchanges of information. See http:/www.usdoj.gov/atr/busreview; http:/www.ftc.gov.bc/adop/index.

12. Letter from Anne K. Bingaman, Assistant Attorney General, Antitrust Division, to David Johnson (June 20, 1994).

Antitrust law treats collusion on input prices such as wages under the same strict standard applicable to price fixing on output. Similarly, information exchanges among providers or the prices they pay, such as for salaries, will run afoul of the Sherman Act where the circumstances indicate a likely restraining effect on competition. In *United States v. Utah Soc. for Healthcare Human Resources Admin.*,[13] the Justice Department charged that an agreement among hospitals to exchange prospective information about the wages paid to their nursing staffs violated the Sherman Act; ultimately the parties agreed to a consent decree allowing the hospitals to undertake wage surveys which complied with the standards set forth subsequently in its Policy Statements. The"safety zone" regarding information exchanges among hospitals contained in those statements goes somewhat further than previous advisory statements and creates some ambiguities in the process. The agencies state that they will not challenge, "absent extraordinary circumstances," hospital participation in written surveys about hospital prices and wages, salaries or benefits of hospital personnel if three conditions are satisfied.[14] First, the survey must be managed by a third party. Second, the information must be based on data that is at least three months old. Third, there must be at least five reporting hospitals, with no hospital representing more than 25 percent of the data and all data disseminated must be sufficiently aggregated so that the data of individual hospitals cannot be identified. Notably, this safety zone would appear to permit exchanges of information regarding prices submitted for competitive bidding to third parties and does not seem to require proof that shared information was desired by third parties. The agencies do not explain how such exchanges could promote competitive ends.

§ 14–30. Provider Peer Review of Fees

The practice of allowing competing providers to review or make recommendations about their rivals' fees raises obvious competitive concerns. Traditionally, peer review of fees has entailed providers scrutinizing specific charges of other providers which have been flagged as excessive. In recent years more comprehensive reviews of provider pricing has become common, and providers have been called upon to review and interpret others' overall pricing practices. Obviously, having competitors pass on the reasonableness of rivals' prices raises risks that explicit or implicit collusion may occur. Without safeguards, the process can encourage providers to gravitate toward standardized prices. Because few benchmarks are available other than "customary" or prevailing rates, peer review of fees invites price stabilization by reenforcing agreed-upon norms affecting prices. At the same time, there can be plausible, competition-enhancing justifications for peer review of fees. Physicians may be able to supply valuable expertise to payers concerning the appropriateness of a given fee based on their medical expertise, especially where medical diagnosis, treatment alternatives and other scientific factors are at issue. Second, peer review of fees may address interrelated issues of professional ethics such as fraud, provision of unnecessary services or taking advantage of an impaired patient.

13. 1994–2 Trade Cas. (CCH) ¶ 70,795, 1994 WL 729931 (D.Utah 1994).

14. U.S. Department of Justice and Federal Trade Commission, Statements of Antitrust Enforcement Policy in the Health Care, Statement 6 (1996), reprinted in 4 Trade Reg. Rep. (CCH) ¶ 13,152.

Antitrust doctrine shields such peer review activities where third party payers employ or contract with professionals to give advice on the reasonableness of fees. Courts have recognized that in the absence of a horizontal agreement among payers, an insurer's use of such consultants is simply a means by which it arrives at a reasonable price to pay for services.[1] Moreover, no Sherman Act Section 1 case should lie against the peer reviewers themselves where they merely provide advice to the payer because in such circumstances the element of the horizontal conspiracy is lacking.

Where rival providers control the peer review process and exert coercion over payors or act to sanction other providers, a horizontal price fixing conspiracy may be established. For example, a professional association desiring to punish "fee gougers" as part of its monitoring of ethical norms has all the earmarks of a conspiracy to fix or stabilize prices. The good intentions (e.g., preventing fraud) of the reviewers are unlikely to save such arrangements. Where peer reviewers lack coercive power, however, it is likely the arrangement will be characterized as primarily an information-sharing scheme.[2]

The advice of the federal enforcement agencies suggests certain features of physician fee peer review programs that may give rise to an antitrust challenge. In one such opinion, the staff of the FTC refused to give clearance because of the mandatory nature of the proposed program. Under the rules of a county medical association, physicians were required to participate in the review of fees and were bound to abide by its decisions.[3] The risk in this case, as the FTC saw it, was that physicians would be compelled to accept a committee-approved "fee schedule" or that a review program would facilitate an anticompetitive boycott. Other advisory opinions have approved peer review of fees where such mandatory features were not present.[4]

In response to a request by the American Medical Association, the FTC has issued an advisory opinion allowing professional groups more freedom to engage in peer review of fees.[5] The AMA had argued that the requirements set forth above make it almost impossible for professional societies to exercise their appropriate function of assisting in the disciplining of "fee gougers." The FTC advisory opinion stated that the medical societies could require participation in nonbinding, advisory peer review of fees. The Commission noted the potential of such grievance committees to benefit consumers as long as the disciplinary aspects of the program was limited to "abusive conduct" that involves fraud, deception, undue influence or the provision of unneces-

§ 14–30

1. Zinser v. Rose, 868 F.2d 938 (7th Cir. 1989) (rejecting claim of a vertical price fixing conspiracy arising out of a payer's use of two chiropractors to provide information regarding reasonableness of prices); Bartholomew v. Virginia Chiropractors Ass'n, Inc., 612 F.2d 812 (4th Cir.1979), Even payers with market power face no significant antitrust obstacles to employing peer reviewers to provide advice on fees as courts have held that monopolists have the right to bargain for the best possible price. See Kartell v. Blue Shield of Massachusetts, Inc., 749 F.2d 922 (1st Cir.1984); see § 14–36 infra.

2. See, e.g., Ratino v. Medical Service of the District of Columbia (Blue Shield), 718 F.2d 1260 (4th Cir.1983).

3. FTC Staff Advisory Opinion Letter to Passaic County Medical Soc'y (January 3, 1986).

4. See, e.g., Iowa Dental Ass'n, 99 F.T.C. 648 (1982); FTC Staff Letter to National Capital Soc'y of Plastic and Reconstructive Surgeons (Apr. 23, 1991).

5. Letter to Kirk B. Johnson, and John M. Peterson from Donald S. Clark, Secretary, Federal Trade Commission, February 14, 1994 (advisory opinion).

sary services. Although the FTC took pains to confine its approval to advisory reviews of abusive practices, one may question whether there are sound economic grounds for granting further latitude in this area. First, there is no obvious reason why payers and others cannot adequately detect and police such practices, employing the expertise of professionals on a consultancy basis. Second, although the AMA relies on the latitude afforded it for self-regulation of advertising,[6] the economics of fee review are not closely analogous. Unlike advertising, there is no obvious market failure or imperfection in the fee-setting process. Buyers and sellers face no special obstacles to bargaining because a few unscrupulous doctors do not have the power to ruin the market for all. Thus, self-regulation of fees cannot be justified on the ground that removing the fee gouger improves competition in the marketplace at large.

3. Providers With Market Power

§ 14–31. Misuse of Joint Ventures and Tying Arrangements to Increase Reimbursement

Antitrust analysis has focused considerable attention on a variety of contractual arrangements among physicians that may enhance their market power vis-a-vis third party payers. For example, physicians in increasing numbers have formed joint ventures to provide services or goods in markets functionally related to their professional practice. Studies suggest that resulting financial incentives from such ownership interests may cause physicians to overprescribe services of the entity in which they have a financial interest or to "self-refer" where an objective appraisal of price and quality would dictate the choice of a competitor.[1]

Several antitrust theories are available to challenge these practices. Where competing physicians with market power combine to form a joint venture with power to raise price (or reduce quality or output), a Sherman Act monopolization claim may be made out. Illegality under Section 2 analysis would turn on whether formation of the joint venture and channeling patients were viewed as exclusionary conduct or constituted "competition on the merits."[2] A Section 1 claim might prevail if an agreement among joint venturers to refer to the commonly-owned facility was proven, and anticompetitive effects of the captive referrals outweighed any procompetitive efficiency justifications.[3] Finally, a monopoly leveraging theory analogous to that employed to challenge hospital downstream integration might also be advanced under § 2 of the Sherman Act.[4]

Whether the self-referral is challenged under Section 1 or Section 2, market power will be a central issue. Applying conventional neoclassical

6. See § 14–10 supra.

§ 14–31

1. See Jean M. Mitchell & Elton Scott, Evidence of Complex Structures of Physician Joint Ventures, 9 Yale J. on Reg. 489 (1992) (discussing the Florida Health Care Cost Containment Board Survey). See generally Marc A. Rodwin, Medicine, Money and Morals: Physicians Conflicts of Interest (1993). See generally § Chapter 13 infra.

2. See 3 Philip E. Areeda & Donald Turner, Antitrust Law, 626a (1978); United States v. Grinnell Corp., 384 U.S. 563, 570–71, 86 S.Ct. 1698, 1703–04, 16 L.Ed.2d 778 (1966).

3. See Kevin J. Arquit, Director, FTC Bureau of Competition, Remarks Before the National Health Lawyers Ass'n, 7 Trade Reg. Rep. (CCH) ¶ 50,073 (Jan. 30, 1992).

4. See infra § 14–43.

economic analysis to this issue, courts might be tempted to rely on market shares as the sole gauge of the referring physicians' market power. However, the Supreme Court's recent decision in *Eastman Kodak* suggests that careful analysis of the effects of information gaps and switching costs on market power is required before equating low market shares with the absence of market power.[5] Arguably, the physician-patient relationship is beset with more severe market imperfections than the markets under investigation in *Kodak*.[6] The influence of physicians over patients in the choice of ancillary services is considerable owing to significant information asymmetries between these groups and patients' "locked-in" status once they have undergone initial treatment or consultation. It has been questioned, however, whether the consumer harm resulting from inappropriate self-referrals alone is actionable under the antitrust laws.[7]

The FTC has examined physician joint ventures that create or enhance market power in markets for ancillary goods or services and result in higher prices and lower quality to consumers.[8] For example, it settled by consent orders charges that pulmonologists constituting approximately 60% of the market engaged in unfair competition when they participated in a joint venture to provide home oxygen systems to patients.[9] However, the cases did not condemn outright physician self-referrals, charging that ownership interests by a large proportion of the market's pulmonologists enabled them to acquire and maintain market power and created barriers to entry in the market for home oxygen systems. The Commission's analysis of the case did go so far as to suggest that the market power of the joint ventures was in part attributable to the doctors' ability to influence their patients' choice of medical equipment supplier.[10]

Providers with market power may also run afoul of antitrust law when they try to increase profits by employing tying arrangements. For example, in one case settled by consent order, the FTC charged a dialysis provider with illegal tying of inpatient and outpatient services.[11] In addition, in the first multi-state case brought by a group of state attorneys general, the states charged a pharmaceutical company with illegally tying the sale of Clozaril, a medication for the treatment of schizophrenia, to a package of commonly available blood monitoring and lab testing services.[12] Although the economic

5. Eastman Kodak Co. v. Image Technical Servs., Inc., 504 U.S. 451, 112 S.Ct. 2072, 119 L.Ed.2d 265 (1992). See § 14–4(c) supra.

6. For analyses of hospitals' influence over patients in choosing equipment, see Advanced Health–Care Servs., Inc. v. Radford Community Hosp., 910 F.2d 139 (4th Cir.1990), on remand 846 F.Supp. 488 (W.D.Va.1994); M & M Med. Supplies & Serv. v. Pleasant Valley Hosp., 981 F.2d 160 (4th Cir.1992).

7. See Home Oxygen & Medical Equipment Co., 59 Fed.Reg. 54,460–02 (Oct. 31, 1992) (consent order) (Commissioner Starek dissenting).

8. Mark J. Horoschak, Antitrust Perspectives on Joint Ventures Among Health Care providers, 6 Antitrust Health Care Chronicle 2 (1992).

9. See Home Oxygen & Medical Equipment Co., 59 Fed.Reg. 54,460–02 (Oct.31, 1992) (consent order).

10. Id. (Analysis of Proposed Consent Order to Aid Public Comment).

11. In re Friedman, 55 Fed. Reg. 27,686 (1990) (consent order) (physician prohibited from conditioning use of out-patient dialysis facilities on use of his in-patient dialysis services or in any way impairing another physician's staff privileges at out-patient facility based on latter's use of rival's dialysis service).

12. In re Clozapine Antitrust Litigation, MDL docket No. 874 (N.D.Ill.). The case was settled in 1992 by a consent decree applicable to all 50 States. See generally Note, Bundling Patented Drugs and Medical Services: An Antitrust Analysis, 91 Colum. L. Rev. 1188 (1991)(criticizing application of tying law to the Clozapine tie-in).

underpinnings of the tying doctrine are controversial, cases such as these are particularly well justified from an economic standpoint because the arrangement enables a defendant to avoid rate regulation by using the tie-in to obtain excess profits from the nonregulated market. There is no serious dispute about the adverse welfare effects of such arrangements.

§ 14–32. Provider Control of Payment Systems

Distinguishing anticompetitive collusion from efficiency-enhancing cooperation among competitors has proved to be one of the most vexing and politically-charged issues in modern antitrust law. The problems posed by provider-controlled payment systems require both careful economic analysis and an appreciation of the changing nature of health care financing in America.

The origins of physician and hospital control of payment systems can be traced back to the development of Blue Shield and Blue Cross plans in the 1930s. The rapid growth of those plans helped assure providers an adequate and reliable source of payment for their services while at the same time insulating them from "lay" interference and cost controls by third parties.[1] Although application of antitrust principles has largely eliminated direct provider control of Blue Cross and Blue Shield plans, physician control of HMOs, IPAs, PPOs, PHOs and other financing and delivery plans has become commonplace.[2]

Provider participation in and cooperation with these plans is of central importance to lessening the problems of moral hazard and other market imperfections in the payment system. At the same time, provider control of these payment systems poses the risk of anticompetitive collusion on fees that would negate the procompetitive benefits of such plans. Although traditional antitrust principles are employed to assess competitive harms and justifications, it is essential to bear in mind when making such appraisals the somewhat subtle distinctions among the economic arrangements of the plans.[3]

a. Provider Control of Blue Cross and Blue Shield Plans

A number of courts have held that physician control over Blue Shield plans and hospital control over Blue Cross plans amounted to price fixing under the analysis set forth in the Supreme Court's *Maricopa* decision.[4]

---

§ 14–32

1. See Paul Starr, The Social Transformation of American Medicine (1982).

2. For purposes of this discussion, HMOs may be defined as entities combining both the insurance (or "financing") and service delivery functions in a single entity and usually entailing integration of physicians' practices. IPAs are organizations comprised of physicians in independent practice who contract through the IPA with an HMO. IPA physicians share risk to some extent by virtue of their reimbursement arrangements with the HMO but do not perform the insurance function and do not integrate their practices. PPOs typically do not perform any insurance function or integrate their practices and physicians are paid on a fee-for-service basis and rarely assume risk. Both IPA and PPO physicians continue to com-

pete for patients who are enrolled in insurance plans not served by their IPA or PPO. See generally § xxx infra.

3. Although it is customary to group HMOs by their organizational form ("group model," "staff model," and IPA), economic analysis suggests that more useful distinctions may be drawn based on the incentives, cost containing performance and structure of the payment systems. See W. Pete Welch et al., Toward New Typologies For HMOs, 68 Milbank Q. 221 (1990). Of particular relevance is empirical research showing that the payment methods within HMOs affect the success of those systems in containing costs.

4. See, e.g., Barry v. Blue Cross of California, 805 F.2d 866 (9th Cir.1986); Hahn v. Oregon Physicians' Serv., 868 F.2d 1022 (9th Cir.

Where providers control the plan, an agreement respecting all matters including price is presumed; consequently, courts have characterized the arrangement as price fixing under Section 1 of the Sherman Act. These cases have inferred "control" of the payment plan from the power of the providers to choose a majority of the entity's board of directors and have held that such control satisfies the "contract, combination or conspiracy" requirements of Section 1. Although commentators have suggested that sufficient control might be proven in the absence of a provider-selected majority on the board, no court has found this to be true as yet.[5] On the other hand, where a fully integrated entity such as a hospital chain establishes a PPO and sets price, no conspiracy is present.[6] Likewise, staff model HMOs are treated as single entities and cannot constitute a conspiracy among their controlling providers.[7]

b. Provider–Controlled IPAs, PPOs and Physician Network Plans

1. Assessing the Degree of Integration

Under *Maricopa* and the ancillary restraints doctrine, a provider-controlled plan will not be treated as a price fixing agreement and can avoid per se condemnation where the providers "sufficiently" integrate their practices and where the price agreement is necessary to the success of the arrangement. The question of "how much integration is enough" has provoked considerable controversy and confusion. At one extreme, "sham" PPOs or IPAs or management services organizations which act as bargaining agents over prices are treated as naked restraints because of the total absence of integration.[8]

At the other end of the spectrum are provider-controlled HMOs and IPAs to which physicians make capital contributions and assume a degree of risk through capitation payments or financial incentives such as substantial fee withholds contingent on achieving utilization goals. These plans are deemed sufficiently integrated, both because they share the risk of the enterprise and because their integration creates a new product. Such arrangements clearly fit the paradigm of ancillary restraints. Where physicians are at financial risk, the group as a whole has an incentive to economize and hence the product is one that no individual physician could offer individually. Moreover, an agreement on fees is "reasonably necessary" for the HMO or IPA to operate because some mechanism is required for allocating payments among participating providers from the premiums or other payments received for rendering services. The case law[9] and federal enforcement agency Policy Statements[10]

1988). See also Virginia Academy of Clinical Psychologists v. Blue Shield of Virginia, 624 F.2d 476 (4th Cir.1980) (physician majority on board of plan constitutes evidence of control). See § 14–24 supra.

5. See Gary M. Smith, Note, Provider Control of Health Insurers: Are Doctors Still Calling the Shots? 34 St. Louis U. L. J. 1079 (1990).

6. Antitrust Division, Department of Justice, Business Review Letter to Hospital Corp. of America (Sept. 21, 1983).

7. Hassan v. Independent Practice Assocs., 698 F.Supp. 679 (E.D.Mich.1988).

8. See Southbank IPA, Inc., 5 Trade Reg. Rep. (CCH) ¶ 23065 (1991) (consent decree); see also supra §§ 14–25 and 14–27.

9. See Hassan v. Independent Practice Assocs., 698 F.Supp. 679 (E.D.Mich.1988) (acceptance of capitation payments by IPA sufficient integration to avoid per se treatment where providers share risks of loss).

10. U.S. Department of Justice and Federal Trade Commission, Statements of Antitrust Enforcement Policy in Health Care, Statement 8 & 9 (1996), reprinted in 4 Trade Reg. Rep. (CCH) ¶ 13,153.

and opinions[11] have concluded that acceptance of capitation payments constitutes sufficient integration to avoid per se treatment.

The federal agencies have given detailed guidance about the kinds of financial integration that a network venture needs to avoid per se classification. The Policy Statements identify the following arrangements that may entail sharing financial risk so as to fall within "safe harbor" provisions: capitation payments; fee for service payments with substantial withholds penalties or bonuses; and payment methodologies based on percentages of premiums or revenues, global fees or all-inclusive case rates.[12] Before one assumes that adoption of one of these payment arrangements will suffice (even for the limited purposes of passing muster with the government), a number of caveats must be considered. It is important to bear in mind that financial risk sharing allows physicians to avoid per se price fixing charges because it assures that each physician has a meaningful incentive to ensure that the joint ventures' goals (i.e., greater efficiency or cost containment) are met and because an agreement on price is necessary to that end. Hence, the agencies have made it clear that these financial arrangements must shift risk to the entire group and not just to individual doctors; that is, where risk *sharing* is absent, the arrangement does not alter incentives so as to warrant treating the arrangement as a legitimate joint venture.[13] Likewise, where the magnitude of the risk shifted by these financial arrangements is not substantial, per se analysis may still be warranted. For example, the FTC examined the financial arrangements of a PPO comprised of approximately half of the physicians in its state proposing to pay physicians at the eighty-eighth percentile of physicians usual and customary fees with a 15 per cent risk withhold.[14] The FTC staff noted that these arrangements would allow most physicians to receive their normal fees even if they did not recover the risk withhold. Further, with so many physicians participating, each physician would have relatively few PPO patients. Under these circumstances, the financial risk sharing was inadequate to provide assurance that the members would act to restrain costs and promote the joint ventures objectives; hence the FTC refused to find sufficient integration to justify joint price setting. A final caveat is that the withhold must revert to the payer or some disinterested entity (e.g., a provider of indigent care) in the event the network physicians fail to meet the utilization or other performance standard.[15]

Between the polar cases of sham PPOs and financially integrated HMOs fall the organizational arrangements of a large number of provider-controlled

11. See, e.g., FTC Staff Advisory Opinion Letter from Arthur N. Lerner, Assistant Director, FTC Bureau of Competition to Gilbert M. Friment (Mar. 22, 1984).

12. U.S. Department of Justice and Federal Trade Commission, Statements of Antitrust Enforcement Policy in Health Care, Statement 8 (1996), reprinted in 4 Trade Reg. Rep. (CCH) ¶ 13,152.

13. See Letter from Mark J. Horoschak, Assistant Director, Bureau of Competition, Federal Trade Commission, to Stephen P. Nash, Esq. (September 21, 1995) (Staff Advisory Opinion).

14. Letter from Mark J. Horoschak, Assistant Director, Bureau of Competition, Federal Trade Commission, to Paul M. McVay (July 5, 1994). Cf. Letter from Mark J. Horoschak, Assistant Director, Bureau of Competition, Federal Trade Commission, to Wise, Carter & Carraway (July 5, 1994) (finding a fee schedule set at the sixtieth percentile with a 15 per cent withhold and a limited provider panel was sufficient risk sharing). Notably the 1996 Policy Statements removed an example in the previous edition of the Statements that had deemed a 20 per cent fee withhold sufficient.

15. FTC Staff Advisory to Stephen P. Nash (September 21, 1995).

PPOs and other managed care organizations. The least integrated of these arrangements are so-called "direct contracting" organizations. Under these plans, physicians combine to offer a package of services to employers and managed care plans at a specified price without integrating operations at all. Although direct contracting undoubtedly offers some transactional savings such as reducing search costs, it falls short of the kind of integration envisioned by the Supreme Court in *Maricopa*[16] and is inconsistent with ancillary restraints principles. Likewise, many physician-hospital organizations[17] entail relatively little integration and are formed for no other purpose than setting prices in managed care contracting. Elevating the existence of some costs savings (which are also realized by most cartels) to the status of the integration necessary to create a new product in the market is entirely unwarranted. Such savings are probably of questionable magnitude and, in any event, are not required for the product to be offered. PPOs offer a greater array of integrative benefits. Typically, such plans conduct utilization review, engage in administrative and billing services, enlist or poll physicians about pricing, utilization and other matters of importance to third party payers, and assemble panels suitable for their needs.

After much soul-searching and under the threat of Congressional action,[18] the federal antitrust enforcement agencies reversed their position in 1996. They revised their Policy Statements to provide that certain network joint ventures that do *not* involve sharing of substantial financial risk could nevertheless involve sufficient integration so as to avoid per se treatment. The Statements identify instances of "substantial clinical integration" in which networks have significant on-going programs to select (and deselect) physicians and monitor their performance in a manner that assures a significant degree of independence. These programs may include: (1) establishing mechanisms to monitor and control utilization to as to control costs and promote quality of care; (2) selectively choosing physicians who are likely to further these objectives; and (3) a significant investment of both monetary and human capital in the infrastructure necessary to realize the network sufficiencies.[19] Recognition of clinical integration is consistent with the principles underlying joint venture analysis, although the agency's approach may appear to be in conflict with the square holding of *Maricopa*. In any event, a rationale for the agency's approach would be that it is necessary to assure that the network take steps to effectively bond providers in a common enterprise in order to assure that the arrangement truly has the potential to create efficiencies, which after all, is the basis for allowing coordination. However, it is far from clear how much integration will be required and, given the somewhat amorphous nature of these kinds of efficiencies, it is likely to be a point of contention and debate in the coming years.

16. See supra § 14–24.

17. For a description of these organizations, see § 5–49 supra.

18. In March of 1996, the House Judiciary Committee reported out the "Antitrust Health Care Advancement Act of 1996." HR 2925,- 104TH Cong. (1996). The Act would have required that courts examine provider controlled networks under the Rule of Reason even when the network was not characterized by any significant clinical or financial integration.

19. U.S. Department of Justice and Federal Trade Commission, Statements of Antitrust Enforcement Policy in Health Care, Statement 8 (1996), reprinted in 4 Trade Reg. Rep. (CCH) ¶ 13,153. In a series of illustrative examples and discussion contained in the text, the agencies emphasize the importance of case management, utilization review, information gathering and setting of practice parameters as indicia of interdependence. Id. at Statements 8 & 9.

Part of the problem may be the tendency, fostered by a rigid dichotomization between the rule of reason and per se methodologies, to engage in an "all or nothing" determination of whether the PPO possesses "sufficient" integration to escape per se classification. A preferable approach might be to allow all PPOs engaged in some plausibly integrative endeavors like utilization review to avoid per se treatment, but to factor in the absence of significant efficiency benefits under the rule of reason analysis explicitly. Hence, minimal integration and weak efficiency justifications should not overcome presumptive risks based on market power under the rule of reason. By the same token, plans with greater integration and strong efficiency justifications might merit some relaxation of concentration thresholds.[20]

2. Analysis of Competitive Effects Under the Rule of Reason

Following the ancillary restraint model, a provider-sponsored plan sufficiently integrated to be examined under the rule of reason must still clear several hurdles. First, membership in the plan must not be "overinclusive". The problem of overinclusiveness, as opposed to the exclusion of particular individuals, has been identified as the principal anticompetitive risk arising from joint ventures.[21] Second, restraints (such as agreements on prices, exclusion of rival providers and sharing information) must be ancillary to the plan and reasonably necessary to achieving its integrative benefits.[22] Finally, the agreement must avoid spillover collusion, i.e., illegal collusion among participating providers outside of the joint venture.

Market Definition. The general principles used in merger and joint venture analyses to define markets and assess concentration can be employed in analyzing PPOs and other partially integrated networks, albeit with some refinements. Thus market definition should generally follow the principles outlined in the Federal Horizontal Merger Guidelines.[23] Services provided by a recognized medical specialty may delineate a separate product market if there are no reasonably interchangeable alternatives for the specialty.[24] However, in instances in which significant overlap of services provided by different physician specialties justifies inclusion of more than one specialty, the market may be so defined. Thus, in one Business Review Letter, the Department of Justice concluded that general surgeons were substitutable with colon and rectal surgeons for certain surgical services and hence had to be included in the same market.[25] On the other hand, in certain instances where substitution is possible across specialties, the market will not necessarily be broadly defined if strong buyer preferences indicate that consumers would not freely substitute in the event of a small but significant increase in price. Thus, in a

20. See Thomas L. Greaney & Jody L. Sindelar, Physician Sponsored Joint Ventures: An Antitrust Analysis of Preferred Provider Organizations, 18 Rutgers L.J. 513, 580–81, 586–89 (1987).

21. See Antitrust Guidelines for International Operations, 53 Fed. Reg. 21584 (1988); William F. Baxter, Assistant Attorney General, Antitrust Division, Remarks Before the National Ass'n of Manufacturers (May 10, 1983).

22. See Broadcast Music, Inc. v. Columbia Broadcasting Sys., 441 U.S. 1, 19, 99 S.Ct. 1551, 1562, 60 L.Ed.2d 1 (1979).

23. See infra § 14–49.

24. See U.S. Department of Justice and Federal Trade Commission, Statements of Antitrust Enforcement Policy in Health Care, Statement 8 (1996), reprinted in 4 Trade Reg. Rep. (CCH) ¶ 13,153. (services provided by each specialty ordinarily will be considered separate markets, but overlapping demand for services provided by different specialties may justify including physicians from more than one specialty in the same market).

25. Letter from Anne K. Bingaman, Assistant Attorney General, Antitrust Division to Randall S. Yavitz (July 1, 1996).

Business Review Letter involving a PPO comprised of pediatricians, the Antitrust Division declined to extend the relevant product market beyond pediatrics.[26] In defining PPO physician services markets, the opinions of buyers, particularly managed care plans and employers, are likely to weigh heavily in the delineation of the product market, the key factual question being whether they would likely substitute across specialty lines when contracting for services for their subscribers. Geographic market definition requires estimation of the geographic area in which buyers (here, third party payers) would turn for alternatives.[27] As a practical matter, the preferences and bargaining practices of third party payers should provide highly probative evidence about the dimensions of the relevant markets.

Calculating and Assessing Concentration. Calculating concentration data poses a number of complications. The "market share" of a PPO's physicians (usually the ratio of physicians controlling the PPO to all physicians in the market) gives only a very crude estimate of the PPO's competitive significance even if one were to take into account entry barriers and other relevant factors identified in the Merger Guidelines.[28] Where physicians in the provider-controlled PPO also join other plans, the measure will overstate the PPO's actual market power. On the other hand, where a PPO captures a large share of all physicians practicing in a competitively-important specialty, the measure may understate the market power of the plan.

Another complication is posed by the existence of exclusivity clauses. Where, for example, a provider-controlled PPO requires that its members not join any alternative plan, this may exacerbate an otherwise threatening level of concentration. On the other hand, exclusivity may provide procompetitive benefits by assuring physicians' loyalty and commitment to a plan; hence, where the market shares of the plan are not excessive, exclusivity clauses may improve a PPO's competitiveness and service to subscribers.

The Department of Justice/FTC Statements of Enforcement Policies set forth a "safety zone" for plans with less than 20 per cent of the market's physicians in each physician and 30 per cent for "non-exclusive" network plans.[29] For "exclusive" network plans not falling within the safety zone, the Statements describe the required analysis under the rule of reason, setting forth a number of factors designed to address the competitive effects of the network, specifically whether the network would be able to raise prices above competitive levels and whether the network would inhibit the development of competing networks. The Statements set forth a variety of relevant factors,

26. Letter from Anne K. Bingaman, Assistant Attorney General, Antitrust Division, to Steven J. Kern (March 1, 1996). See also Letter from Anne K. Bingaman, Assistant Attorney General Antitrust Division, to Milissa J. Fie (December 5, 1995) (separate product market for dermatologists because other physicians providing same services were not substitutable in the eyes of managed care plan).

27. See U.S. Department of Justice and Federal Trade Commission Statements of Antitrust Enforcement Policy in Health Care, Statement 8 (1996), reprinted in 4 Trade Reg. Rep. (CCH) ¶ 13,153.

28. See § 14–51—14–52 infra (discussing the significance of concentration measures under the Merger Guidelines).

29. U.S. Department of Justice and Federal Trade Commission, Statements of Antitrust Enforcement Policy in Health Care, Statement 8 (1996), reprinted in 4 Trade Reg. Rep. (CCH) ¶ 13,153 (plans within statistical thresholds will not be challenged absent "extraordinary circumstances"). Whether a plan is exclusive or not is determined by whether network physicians "are restricted in their ability to, or do not in practice, individually contract or affiliate with other "networks or plans." Id.

including the network's market share, based on participation percentage of physicians, the incentives that network physicians face, the number of competing networks in the relevant market and the availability of physicians to form competing networks.[30] The agencies have issued a number of advisory opinions clearing physician networks that exceed (often by a large amount) the safety zone thresholds.[31] In general, the agencies have seemed particularly willing to approve networks where there were no apparent actual or implicit barriers to physicians joining other networks and where managed care entities did not need a large number of providers of a particular specialty to cover their needs.[32]

In a controversial decision, the Eleventh Circuit approved an arrangement under which twelve hospitals formed a PPO arrangement pursuant to which they solicited bids from providers of nursing services.[33] The hospitals agreed to fill their nursing needs from providers submitting the lowest bids; however, once the chosen providers were no longer able to meet the needs of the hospitals, the latter were free to turn to others for services. Finding no per se price fixing or boycott, the Court of Appeals stressed that no nursing organization was precluded from competing to become a preferred agency and remain free to provide services should the need not be met by the preferred agencies. It went on to state "although the PPP may stabilize prices to some degree, it is not the kind of 'stabilization' that can be viewed as price fixing, especially when the escape clauses in the contracts are taken into account. These escape clauses allow the market and not the [hospital association] to be the ultimate decision maker for each hospital and each agency on the issues of price, demand, supply, and terms of dealing."[34] Although the court cited problems associated with in the nursing care market (e.g., "phantom booking," where a hospital requests a specific nurse and is sent a different one, and fraudulent billing), it is far from clear why these abuses required collective action or whether they were of such magnitude to override the risks associated with joint buying decisions. Likewise, the court's casual assertion that no boycott was present because the hospitals were not "refusing to deal" (in the sense that every agency was free to bid) is hardly satisfactory. The collective decision to deal conditioned on a mutually agreed upon price would seem too close to the classic or naked boycott agreement to allow it to escape stricter scrutiny.

Finally, the Policy Statements emphasize the need to assess efficiencies offered by the plans.[35] Of particular importance should be the determination

---

30. U.S. Department of Justice and Federal Trade Commission, Statements of Antitrust Enforcement Policy in Health Care, Statement 8 (1996), reprinted in 4 Trade Reg. Rep. (CCH) ¶ 13,153.

31. See, e.g., FTC Staff Advisory Opinion to Southeast Managed Care, Inc. and Jackson Medical Cooperative, Inc. (July 5, 1995) (clearing physician network with 45% of obstetricians and 50% of pediatricians in relevant market where other networks already existed.) Letter from Anne K. Bingaman, Assistant Attorney General, Antitrust Division, to Mark Peterzell (November 3, 1995) (approving network with 43.4% of physicians in relevant market).

32. See, e.g., Letter from Anne K. Bingaman, Assistant Attorney General, Antitrust Division, to Dee Hertzog (Oct. 27, 1994) (approving network consisting of up to 50 percent of chiropractors in market where managed care plans could fulfill their needs for chiropractic services with a small number of chiropractors).

33. All Care Nursing Service v. High Tech Staffing Services, 135 F.3d 740 (11th Cir.1998).

34. Id. at 746.

35. U.S. Department of Justice and Federal Trade Commission, Statements of Antitrust Enforcement Policy in Health Care, Statement 8 (1996), reprinted in 4 Trade Reg. Rep. (CCH) ¶ 13,153.

of the minimum efficient scale at which a physician network can operate. Where the relevant market is small, only a few plans may be feasible, and even then the percentages of member physicians may surpass concentration thresholds. Hence, it will be necessary to develop benchmarks as to the minimum number of doctors required to assure adequate physician coverage for each other and patient choice.[36] As to other claimed efficiencies that must somehow be weighed against anticompetitive risks,[37] the Statements' standardless approach is subject to the criticism that it cedes open-ended discretion to the factfinder. Problems of measurement and the likelihood that subjective judgements will predominate in the balancing process probably outweigh the potential usefulness of the exercise.

3. Means of Avoiding Liability: "Messenger Models" and Subcontracting Options

Networks have at their disposal several means to avoid claims of price fixing and that may enable them to assemble networks consisting of a large percentage of the relevant provider market. Under the so-called "messenger model," the network uses an agent or third party to convey to purchasers information obtained individually from providers about prices or other terms that the providers are willing to accept. Where the network messenger acts simply as a conduit and in no way facilitates collusion among providers, this arrangement obviates all problems associated with price fixing because there is no agreement among competitors over prices.[38] Hence, the message model may permit the network to include all of the physicians in a market. For the arrangement to avoid liability under the antitrust laws, it is essential that the messenger not convey information to the payer which would put the messenger in the position of acting as a representative of the providers, e.g., indicating which fees would be "acceptable" to members or identifying those for which he could secure acceptance. At the same time, a messenger may provide objective or empirical information about the terms of an offer to help providers understand the contract and may, in certain circumstances, obtain pre-commitments from providers ("standing offers") which they will accept from various payers. A second method which the antitrust enforcement agencies have endorsed that allows inclusion of greater numbers of providers is the subcontracting model. Under this arrangement, providers controlling

36. The agencies' Policy Statements provide two examples of plans that would not be challenged including a venture in a small community in which minimum scale considerations overcome large market shares. U.S. Department of Justice and Federal Trade Commission, Statements of Antitrust Enforcement Policy in Health Care, Statement 8 (1996), reprinted in 4 Trade Reg. Rep. (CCH) ¶ 13,153.

37. The Agencies' Statements announce that they are "most likely to recognize" efficiencies associated with cost savings resulting from assumption of financial risk by physicians but will also consider other efficiencies such as reduced administrative costs, improved utilization review, improved case management, quality assurance and economies of scale. Id. See generally, Thomas L. Greaney, Regulating for Efficiency in Health Care Under the Antitrust Laws, 1995 Utah L. Rev. 465.

38. See Policy Statements Statement 9; letter from Mark J. Horoschak, Assistant Director, Bureau of Competition, Federal Trade Commission, to John D. Dunn (September 28, 1995). For misunderstanding the concept, see Levine v. Central Florida Med. Affiliates, Inc., 72 F.3d 1538 (11th Cir.1996) (incorrectly assuming that physician board consisting of representatives of physicians could constitute a messenger arrangement). For a detailed discussion of messenger model variations and arrangements, see United States v. Women's Hospital Foundation, 1996–2 Trad. Cas. (CCH)¶ 71, 561 at 77,980, 1996 WL 634211 (M.D.La.1996) (consent decree); David Marks & James H. Sneed, Antitrust & Health Care: Meeting the Challenge, 139–43 (1998).

the network ("owner providers") subcontract with other providers, and, as long as the other providers have a "adverse economic interest" to that of the owner-providers, the latter's participation in the network would not be considered when applying participation percentage limitations contained in the Statements.[39] An adverse interest is defined generally as having the economic incentive to obtain the lowest possible price from a subcontracting provider. Thus, a provider-controlled network might accept capitation and subcontract with other physicians on a fee for service basis thereby giving owner-physicians the economic incentive adverse to that of the contracting physicians, i.e., the incentive to pay them a low price. Such arrangements could conceivably allow physician networks to form with a large percentage of area physicians participating as long as the percentage of owner-physicians remains within appropriate concentration thresholds.

4. Ancillary Restraints and Exclusion of Providers

Apart from overinclusion, other risks associated with provider-sponsored PPOs must also be considered. One such risk is that information shared among providers in connection with the PPO plan could spill over into collusive arrangements outside of the plan. Information about price, utilization and other factors shared within the PPO might facilitate collusion among PPO physicians on prices they would charge patients outside the plan. If it did, the conduct would be regarded as unnecessary to the plan's operation and probably illegal per se.[40] Many managed care plans today make efforts to involve third parties or mask information disclosures to avoid such risks.

A frequently-raised claim is that exclusion of providers who want to join a plan constitutes an illegal restraint of trade. If a provider-controlled PPO passes muster under the foregoing tests, exclusion of individual providers should not generally provide a separate cause for concern. This is so because the competitive benefits of such plans lie precisely in their ability to be *selective*. To secure provider participation, PPOs must promise greater numbers of patients, and to attract the business of insurers and employers they must offer a panel of providers meeting their needs in terms of quality, geography and other variables. Thus, exclusion of certain providers is a necessary, and indeed, desirable aspect of PPOs. As such, exclusion can be justified as an ancillary restraint: it is both reasonable and necessary for the integrative benefits to be realized and the venture to succeed.

Courts have adopted this view, holding that exclusion of particular providers from a plan, differential reimbursement to participating versus non-participating providers and other forms of "discrimination" are not per se illegal.[41] Absent market power in the provider-controlled plan,[42] exclusion of

39. See United States v. HealthCare Partners, Inc., 1996–1 Trad. Cas. (CCH) ¶ 71,337, 1996 WL 193753 (D.Conn.1996) (consent decree); United States Women's Hospital Foundation (1996–2 Trad. Cas. (CCH) (¶ 71,561 at 77,980, 1996 WL 634211 (M.D.La.1996) (consent decree).

40. U.S. Department of Justice and Federal Trade Commission, Statements of Antitrust Enforcement Policy in Health Care, Statement 8 (1996), reprinted in 4 Trade Reg. Rep. (CCH) ¶ 13,153.

41. See, e.g., Hahn v. Oregon Physicians' Serv., 868 F.2d 1022 (9th Cir.1988); Northwest Med. Labs. v. Blue Cross & Blue Shield of Oregon, Inc., 775 P.2d 863 (Or.App.1989), affirmed 794 P.2d 428 (Or.1990).

42. Levine v. Central Florida Med. Affiliates, 72 F.3d 1538 (11th Cir.1996). The exceptional case would involve markets with only one plan, constitute an essential facility under Sherman Act § 2 case law. See MCI Communications Corp. v. American Telephone & Telegraph Co., 708 F.2d 1081 (7th Cir.1983), How-

nonparticipating providers is properly treated as a justifiable ancillary restraint, reasonably necessary to achieve the benefits of the venture.[43] For the same reasons, payment plans that lack market power and contract only with selected providers should not face serious challenge as exclusive dealing arrangements.[44] However, the Ninth Circuit has found a violation of Section 1 of the Sherman Act where an exclusion of an entire class of practitioners lacked plausible justification.[45]

4. INSURERS WITH MARKET POWER

§ 14–33. Introduction

This section analyzes cases in which providers have cried "foul" against insurers and other third party payers. A large number of these cases involve allegations that payers have entered into anticompetitive vertical or horizontal agreements that exclude providers, fix prices, or otherwise restrain competition. These claims almost uniformly have been rejected by the courts. Appropriately so, because they are often opportunistic attempts to subvert competition by hindering payers' cost containment efforts. More troublesome antitrust allegations, however, have been lodged under § 2 of the Sherman Act against third party payers with market power. Although courts have been slow to recognize the potential anticompetitive harm flowing from the exercise of such market power, these cases may gain increasing prominence in the future especially where integrated delivery systems acquire power in insurance or service delivery markets.

As a preliminary matter, however, an anticompetitive agreement or exercise of market power by a payer might be exempt from antitrust scrutiny under the McCarran–Ferguson Act.[1] The narrow construction given to the exemption by the courts[2] has resulted in a large number of payer practices *not* falling within its protection. In general, insurer services that do not directly involve the function of risk-spreading such as providing administrative services for a self-insured plan or offering an HMO product (which combines delivery of health services with the insurance function) are not exempt.[3] Thus, provider agreements,[4] peer review[5] and exclusion of non-physician providers[6]

ever, mere exclusion is not sufficient to trigger mandatory access under the essential facilities doctrine. Among other requirements, the facility need only grant access on the same terms applicable to others and need not do so at all, if access is not feasible. See discussion of applying the essential facilities doctrine in staff privileges cases, supra § 14–20b.

43. Hassan v. Independent Practice Assocs., 698 F.Supp. 679 (E.D.Mich.1988); Capital Imaging Assocs. v. Mohawk Valley Med. Assocs., 996 F.2d 537 (2d Cir.1993).

44. Capital Imaging Assocs. v. Mohawk Valley Med. Assocs., 996 F.2d 537 (2d Cir. 1993). See generally discussion of exclusive dealing claims in staff privileges disputes, § 14–21 supra.

45. Hahn v. Oregon Physicians' Serv., 868 F.2d 1022 (9th Cir.1988).

§ 14–33

1. 15 U.S.C.A. §§ 1011–1015. See § 14–2d supra.

2. The Supreme Court has defined the "business of insurance" to require that the activity involve (1) spreading or transferring risk and (2) the relationship between insurer and insured and not parties outside the insurance industry. Although state regulation must be present, this requirement has been broadly construed so that a general regulatory scheme is covering the unfair or anticompetitive practices is sufficient. See supra, § 14–2d.

3. Reazin v. Blue Cross & Blue Shield of Kansas, 663 F.Supp. 1360 (D.Kan.1987), affirmed and remanded, 899 F.2d 951 (10th Cir. 1990).

4. Group Life & Health Insurance Co. v. Royal Drug Co., 440 U.S. 205, 99 S.Ct. 1067, 59 L.Ed.2d 261 (1979).

5. Union Labor Life Insurance Co. v. Pireno, 458 U.S. 119, 102 S.Ct. 3002, 73 L.Ed.2d 647 (1982).

are not within the protection of the Act. In addition, by its terms McCarran–Ferguson does not reach actions constituting an "act of boycott, coercion, or intimidation."[7] On the other hand, providers offering group insurance policies that included prescription drug benefits,[8] insurers offering service benefit plans and HMO-like risk-spreading plans,[9] insurers' decisions as to the kind of policies they will sell,[10] and horizontal agreements among insurers on risk assessment or rates[11] are immune.

§ 14–34.　Vertical Price Fixing and Boycott Claims

A number of antitrust cases brought by providers have attacked payers' contractual agreements with providers. For example, agreements that payers will reimburse only the providers' "usual, customary and reasonable" (UCR) price; that participating providers will not bill patients for the balance left when charges exceed UCR payment; and that parties agree to fixed co-payment and deductibles have all been challenged, usually as vertical or horizontal price fixing under § 1 of the Sherman Act.[1] Second, providers unable or unwilling to meet insurers' selective contracting requirements often claim that insurer contracts with compliant providers amounted to anticompetitive "group boycotts."[2] These cases have foundered on several grounds. First, courts have refused to find an agreement under § 1 of the Sherman Act where the insurer is truly independent (i.e., not controlled by providers) and there is no evidence that the insurer had not acted independently and in its own interest.[3] Moreover, the cases repeatedly reject attempts to analogize provider contracting by insurers to vertical price fixing, instead likening insurers to buyers seeking the lowest possible price in the marketplace.[4]

In *U.S. Healthcare v. Healthsource*,[5] the claim was that a dominant HMO restrained trade and monopolized the market for HMO services by entering into quasi-exclusive contracts with its physicians. The HMO's contracts provided that participating doctors would receive greater capitation payments (amounting to about 14% more than otherwise paid) if they agreed not to serve any other HMO. A large proportion of defendants' physicians agreed to

---

6. Hartford Fire Ins. Co. v. California, 509 U.S. 764, 113 S.Ct. 2891, 125 L.Ed.2d 612 (1993) (boycott occurs where, in order to coerce a target into certain terms on a transaction, parties refuse to engage in other unrelated transactions with the target); Ocean State Physicians Health Plan v. Blue Cross & Blue Shield of Rhode Island, 883 F.2d 1101 (1st Cir.1989).

7. 15 U.S.C.A. § 1013(b).

8. Klamath–Lake Pharmaceutical Ass'n v. Klamath Med. Serv. Bureau, 701 F.2d 1276 (9th Cir.1983) (operation of pharmacy by insurer is business of insurance).

9. Ocean State Physicians Health Plan v. Blue Cross & Blue Shield of Rhode Island, 883 F.2d 1101 (1st Cir.1989).

10. Anglin v. Blue Shield, 693 F.2d 315 (4th Cir.1982).

11. See Group Life & Health Insurance Co. v. Royal Drug Co., 440 U.S. 205, 221, 99 S.Ct. 1067, 1078, 59 L.Ed.2d 261 (1979). In re Workers' Compensation Ins., 867 F.2d 1552 (8th Cir.1989) (1989). See also, Virginia Academy of Clinical Psychologists v. Blue Shield, 624 F.2d 476, 484 (4th Cir.1980) (refusal to underwrite risk might constitute business or insurance).

§ 14–34

1. See, e.g., Kartell v. Blue Shield of Massachusetts, Inc., 749 F.2d 922 (1st Cir.1984) (balance billing).

2. See, e.g., Royal Drug Co. v. Group Life and Health Ins. Co., 737 F.2d 1433 (5th Cir. 1984).

3. Barry v. Blue Cross of California, 805 F.2d 866 (9th Cir.1986) (finding Blue Cross had acted independently in rejecting claims that physician's adherence to the plan constituted "conscious parallelism").

4. National Benefit Adm'rs v. Blue Cross and Blue Shield of Ala., 1989–2 Trade Cas. (CCH) ¶ 68,831, 1989 WL 146413 (M.D.Ala. 1989), aff'd 907 F.2d 1143 (11th Cir.1990).

5. 986 F.2d 589 (1st Cir.1993).

this exclusivity arrangement and plaintiff charged that it inhibited it and other HMOs from entering the market. In a well-reasoned opinion, the First Circuit upheld the plan, finding that the contracts violated neither Section 1 or 2 of the Sherman Act.[6] Likening the arrangement to a joint venture which some but not all were allowed to join, the court found the activities did not constitute a per se boycott or concerted refusal to deal.[7] On the claim that the contracts constituted illegal exclusive dealing, the court noted three flaws in the plaintiff's proof.[8] First, it failed to show that the price differential had operated "economically to restrict doctors." Second, in view of the duration of the exclusivity arrangement, plaintiff was obliged to introduce facts proving the restraint was not de minimis. Third, plaintiff failed to establish that significant quantitative foreclosure had occurred, as only 25 per cent of all primary care physicians in the market signed the exclusivity agreements.

One instance in which vertical agreements were found to have adverse effects is *Reazin v. Blue Cross & Blue Shield of Kansas, Inc.*[9] Upholding jury findings that defendant had conspired with two hospitals to terminate plaintiff hospital's status as a participating provider in return for the conspiring hospitals' lowering their prices to the Blues, the Tenth Circuit found an unreasonable restraint of trade. The market for health care financing was adversely affected, the court found, because the decision to terminate the hospital was an outgrowth of defendants' concerns about plaintiff's vertical integration. Plaintiff was part of a hospital chain offering a successful rival HMO and defendant was also concerned about potential competition from other alternative delivery systems. The court concluded that the threat of termination and reduction of hospital payments, and the coercion of other hospitals to refuse to do business with the Blues' competitors constituted willful maintenance of monopoly power in violation of Section 2 of the Sherman Act.[10] Although not identified by the court as such, the underlying problem fits the raising rival's cost model of anticompetitive exclusion.[11]

§ 14–35. Horizontal Restraints

Horizontal agreements between competing payers are far more likely to violate Section 1 of the Sherman Act. Where the antitrust laws are found to apply, an agreement between insurers to boycott a certain class of provider

---

6. The court's analysis of the monopolization claims are discussed infra, § 14–36a.

7. 986 F.2d at 594 (citing Northwest Wholesale Stationers v. Pacific Stationery & Printing Co., 472 U.S. 284, 294–98 (1985). The court also rejected plaintiff's attempt to characterize the arrangement as a horizontal conspiracy among the stockholder-physicians who allegedly predominated on the Healthsource board of directors. The court credited proof tending to show that defendant's chief operating officer devised the exclusivity arrangement primarily to assure loyalty of participating physicians. Id. at 594. The opinion inexplicably did not analyze the alleged boycott under the rule of reason; however, given its findings on market power, discussed infra § 14–36a, plaintiff's claim could not succeed under this mode of analysis.

8. Id. at 595–97.

9. 899 F.2d 951 (10th Cir.1990).

10. Id. at 966–68. The court found that defendant's market share (nearly 60%) coupled with market power deriving from its use of a most-favored-nations clause established market power in the relevant market. Id. at 973. See discussion of most-favored-nations clauses in § 2 cases, § 14–36b, infra.

11. See Jonathan B. Baker, Vertical Restrictions Among Hospitals, Physicians and Health Insurance that Raise Rivals' Costs, 14 Am. J.L. & Med. 147 (1988); see also Steven C. Salop, Exclusionary Vertical Restraint Law: Has Economics Mattered?, 83 Am. Econ. Rev. 168 (1993).

may violate the Sherman Act.[1] An agreement among independent Blue Shield plans to divide markets on a territorial basis also may violate Section 1.[2] Joint negotiations by independent third party payers or employer groups regarding provider contracts might raise questions of illegal price fixing under § 1. If undertaken without any meaningful integration, buyer price fixing may be characterized as "naked" and can be illegal per se.[3] However, where buyer cooperatives can demonstrate that efficiencies flow from the joint buying venture, the rule of reason will apply.[4] Inasmuch as many cooperative arrangements between independent insurers may lack justifications based on tangible cost savings, the legality of such undertakings remains an open question.[5]

§ 14–36. Exercise of Monopoly and Monopsony Power by Payers

A number of cases have been brought in recent years claiming monopolization or attempted monopolization by third party payers under Section 2 of the Sherman Act. These cases typically rest on contentions that a dominant third party payer has exercised or obtained "monopsony" power in the health care financing market by its practices in contracting for services from providers. Although few antitrust cases have dealt with the use of buyer power ("monopsonization") under Section 2, in principle the same requirements must be met to make out as in a monopolization or attempted monopolization case.[1] As an economic matter, the exercise of monopsony power enables powerful buyers to distort markets by reducing prices for goods or services below competitive levels. This results in wealth transfers from sellers to monopsonists, misallocations of resources and higher consumer prices.[2]

Provider challenges to the exercise of monopsony power by insurers have met with little success. In *Kartell v. Blue Shield of Massachusetts, Inc.*,[3] physicians claimed that defendant's policy of prohibiting participating physicians from "balance billing" (i.e., surcharging patients for the amount above defendant's fixed reimbursement to physicians) constituted monopolization

§ 14–35

1. See Virginia Academy of Clinical Psychologists v. Blue Shield of Virginia, 624 F.2d 476 (4th Cir.1980). See Clark C. Havighurst, Doctors and Hospitals: An Antitrust Perspective on Traditional Relationships, 1984 Duke L.J. 1071 (reading the court's ambiguous opinion in the *Virginia Academy* case as resting on an illegal agreement between unaffiliated Blue Shield plans to boycott clinical psychologists).

2. See Garot Anderson Agencies v. Blue Cross & Blue Shield United of Wisconsin, 1993–1 Trade Cas. (CCH) ¶ 70,235, 1993 WL 78756 (N.D.Ill.1993) (agreement by Blue Cross with another insurer to cancel its plans in latter's territory could constitute per se market allocation).

3. See, e.g., Mandeville Island Farms v. American Crystal Sugar Co., 334 U.S. 219, 68 S.Ct. 996, 92 L.Ed. 1328 (1948); Vogel v. American Soc'y of Appraisers, 744 F.2d 598, 601 (7th Cir.1984).

4. See Northwest Wholesale Stationers, Inc. v. Pacific Stationery & Printing Co., 472 U.S. 284, 105 S.Ct. 2613, 86 L.Ed.2d 202 (1985).

5. See Robert E. Youle & Paul C. Daw, Preferred Provider Organizations: An Antitrust Perspective, 29 Antitrust Bull. 301, 327 (1984). Cf. FTC Staff Advisory Opinion Letter to Michael L. Denger, Esq. (Sept. 24, 1985) (approving PPO formed by several insurance companies).

§ 14–36

1. See Vogel v. American Society of Appraisers, 744 F.2d 598 (7th Cir.1984); see infra § 14–41.

2. Roger D. Blair & Jeffrey L. Harrison, Antitrust Policy and Monopsony, 76 Cornell L. Rev. 297 (1991). For a case involving allegations of monopsony power created through a merger, see discussion of the Aetna Prudential merger infra § 14–48.

3. 749 F.2d 922 (1st Cir.1984).

and attempted monopolization. The First Circuit held that the balance billing ban did not constitute monopolization or an attempt to monopolize under Section 2. The court relied heavily on its characterization of Blue Shield as a "buyer" of medical services on behalf of its insureds. Repeating the familiar principle that even entities with market power are free to exploit that power when bargaining with sellers, it concluded that Blue Shield was legitimately aggregating the purchasing power of its subscribers.[4]

a. Market Definition and Market Power

Section 2's requirement of proof of market power poses another obstacle to providers claiming exploitation at the hands of monopsonistic insurers. In *Ball Memorial Hospital, Inc. v. Mutual Hospital Insurance, Inc.*, the Seventh Circuit rejected plaintiff's claim of monopolization against a Blue Cross/Blue Shield organization commanding a large but unspecified percentage of the private health insurance market. Market share data was insufficient, the court held, because the absence of entry barriers in the health insurance field refuted the possibility that the Blues possessed market power.[5] Relying on the large number of licensed insurers in the market and the absence of significant regulatory barriers and capitalization requirements, the court concluded there were "no barriers to entry."[6] Commentators have questioned whether the Seventh Circuit's sweeping conclusions about entry conditions are justified given the economics of health insurance markets. In particular, they emphasize the importance of brand loyalty, reputational factors and transactions costs as factors inhibiting consumers from switching insurers.[7] Moreover, the Blues' tax advantages and longstanding direct relationships with providers and insureds are seen as important factors buttressing market share evidence of market power. By contrast, the court in *Reazin* found evidence of Blue Cross' high market share and use of most-favored-nations clauses sufficient to establish market power and refute claims of ease of entry into the market.[8] Finally, one court has rejected the argument that an HMO had market power because its members were "locked in and had high switching costs."[9] The court was willing to assume that HMO subscribers or their employees could switch readily in response to a price increase.

The First Circuit's analysis in *U.S. Healthcare v. Healthsource*,[10] discussed above, also offers a sound approach to market definition and market power issues involving an allegedly dominant insurer. Plaintiff's claim was that the exclusive contracts with participating physicians allowed it to exclude

4. See id. at 931 (acknowledging court's reluctance to "condemn too speedily ... an arrangement that ... appears to bring low price benefits to the consumer").

5. 784 F.2d 1325 (7th Cir.1986).

6. Id. at 1335.

7. See Mark V. Pauly, Competition in Health Insurance Markets, 51 Law & Contemp. Probs. 237, 267–68 (1988); Frances H. Miller, Vertical Restraints and Powerful Health Insurers: Exclusionary Conduct Masquerading as Managed Care?, 51 Law & Contemp. Probs. 195, 227 (1988). See also Clark C. Havighurst, Health Care Law and Policy: Readings, Notes, and Questions, 1185 (1988) (difficult to sell an efficient, competitive insur-

ance product without extensive integration of financing and delivery). In any event, plaintiff's underlying claim in Ball Memorial was highly questionable. Plaintiff hospitals were resisting the Blues' attempt to impose cost controls through a PPO that engaged in competitive contracting. Following *Kartell*, it is unlikely such hard bargaining would constitute a violation of Section 2 of the Sherman Act.

8. Reazin v. Blue Cross & Blue Shield of Kansas, Inc., 899 F.2d 951 (10th Cir.1990).

9. Brokerage Concepts v. U.S. Healthcare, 140 F.3d 494 (3d Cir.1998).

10. 986 F.2d 589 (1st Cir.1993). See supra § 14–34.

rivals and maintain market power in the HMO services market. The court upheld the lower court's finding that the proper relevant market consisted of all health care financing but acknowledged the possibility that a separate HMO market could exist assuming differences in price and quality between HMOs and other financing systems. The court properly framed the question as whether a sole supplier of HMO services could profitably raise price over costs, observing that facts such as usage patterns, customer surveys, features of the plans, actual profit levels would assist the factfinder in answering the question.[11]

b. *Most Favored Nations Clauses and Other Forms of Strategic Behavior*

Monopolization cases against dominant insurers by other payers illustrate that assessing the exclusionary effects of a monopsonist's practices requires an appreciation of strategic behavior. In the first case examining the practices of a dominant insurer, *Travelers Insurance Company v. Blue Cross of Western Pennsylvania*,[12] a commercial insurance company asserted that a Blue Cross plan's standard contract with area hospitals enabled defendants to pay some 15% less for hospital services than was paid by or on behalf of non-Blue Cross patients. The effect of the lower hospital prices was to assure Blue Cross correspondingly lower rates than those of private insurance companies. After finding the McCarran–Ferguson Act immunized the practice, the Third Circuit went on to observe that Travelers Insurance was not disabled from seeking similar price reductions. Blue Cross, it suggested in dicta, could withstand scrutiny under Section 1 and 2 because it was doing "no more than conduct[ing] its business as every rational enterprise does, i.e., get the best deal possible."[13] A number of other courts have dismissed analogous claims.[14]

A more sophisticated analysis of the underlying relationships in *Travelers* might have produced a different result. Close examination of the Blue Cross plan's ability to extract sizeable price concessions from the hospitals suggests it was engaged in strategic behavior that rings a strikingly anticompetitive note. The explanation for the arrangement apparently lays in the mutual appreciation by hospitals and the Blues that by granting the largest insurer a standard discount, the hospitals could reduce pressures to grant any other discounts because there would be no other formidable buyers in the market. The absence of competition at the payer level was neatly assured because no rival could match the lower hospital costs of the Blue Cross plan.[15] These facts

---

11. Id. at 597. The Department of Justice appears to have followed this analysis closely in its challenge to a merger of insurers selling HMO products. See infra § 14–49a.

12. 481 F.2d 80 (3d Cir.1973).

13. Id.

14. For cases rejecting arguments that cost shifting made possible by Blue Cross provider contracts constituted a Section 2 violation, see Austin v. Blue Cross & Blue Shield of Alabama, 903 F.2d 1385 (11th Cir.1990) (patients lack standing); Laughlin v. Evanston Hosp., 140 Ill.Dec. 861, 550 N.E.2d 986 (Ill.1990) (state antitrust law does not reach claims of discrimination); see also National Benefit Administrators, Inc. v. Blue Cross, 1989–2 Trade Cas. (CCH) ¶ 68,831, 1989 WL 146413 (M.D.Ala.1989), affirmed without opinion 907 F.2d 1143 (11th Cir.1990) (easy entry into already competitive insurance market negates predatory pricing claim).

15. See Clark C. Havighurst, The Questionable Cost–Containment Record of Commercial Health Insurers, Health Care in America: The Political Economy of Hospitals & Health Insurance, 221, 252 (H. E. Frech, ed., 1988).

fit models of exclusionary use of vertical contracting set forth in the economic literature on raising rivals' costs.[16]

An even more striking example of the use of strategic behavior by a dominant insurer is *Ocean State Physicians Health Plan, Inc. v. Blue Cross & Blue Shield of Rhode Island,*[17] a case involving a challenge to a "most favored nations" (MFN) clause in the provider contracts of Blue Cross/Blue Shield, which controlled 80% of the Rhode Island private health insurance market. When Ocean State, a new HMO, began to make significant inroads, the Blues responded by imposing a requirement that participating physicians grant the Blues the same discount they granted to Ocean State. The First Circuit affirmed a judgment notwithstanding the verdict, finding that the "most favored nations" clause was a legitimate competitive strategy to assure that the Blues could get the lowest price for services rather than an attempt to monopolize the health insurance market. As such, it held the conduct was not "exclusionary" as a matter of law and did not violate Section 2.[18]

The First Circuit's analysis in *Ocean State* may be faulted on several grounds. First, it adopts a static view of markets, ignoring the fact that MFN clauses eliminate the market's dynamic process that ratchets down prices.[19] Second, it overlooks the beneficial effects of differential (discriminatory) pricing in expanding output, an economic fact long relied upon by critics of bans on price discrimination.[20] Third, the opinion gives no credence to the strategic effects that targeting a rival is likely to have.[21] Notably the court also downplayed strong corroborative evidence that Blue Cross undertook the MFN program in order to "crush" the upstart HMO.[22] The *Ocean State* analysis may be contrasted with *Reazin* in which the Tenth Circuit adopted a less sanguine view of MFN agreements, finding the practice contributed to the market power of a dominant insurer.[23]

Although several courts have expressed the view that MFNs are procompetitive,[24] others have not been willing to categorically approve such arrangements.[25] A Rhode Island district court refused to dismiss the government's

16. See, e.g., Steven C. Salop, Exclusionary Vertical Restraint Law: Has Economics Mattered, 83 Am. Econ. Rev. 168 (1993); See § 10–4c supra.

17. 883 F.2d 1101 (1st Cir.1989).

18. Id. at 1110.

19. See Arnold Celnicker, A Competitive Analysis of Most Favored Nations Clauses in Contracts Between Health Care Providers and Insurers, 69 N.C. L. Rev. 863 (1991).

20. Id.

21. See Jonathan B. Baker, Vertical Restraints with Horizontal Consequences: Competitive Effects of "Most Favored Nations Clauses," 64 Antitrust L.J. 517 (1996); see also, Steven Salop & Gary Roberts, Economic Analysis of the Effects on Competition of Blue Cross and Blue Shield of Western Pennsylvania's Most Favored Nation's Clause (Aug. 16, 1993).

22. Id. at 1113; accord Ball Mem'l Hosp., Inc. v. Mutual Hosp. Ins., Inc., 784 F.2d 1325

(7th Cir.1986) (limited value of intent evidence).

23. Reazin v. Blue Cross & Blue Shield of Kansas, Inc., 899 F.2d 951 (10th Cir.1990), 497 U.S. 1005, 110 S.Ct. 3241, 111 L.Ed.2d 752 (1990).

24. See, e.g., Blue Cross & Blue Shield v. Michigan Ass'n of Psychotherapy Clinics, 1980–2 Trade Cas. (CCH) ¶63351 (E.D.Mich.). The Seventh Circuit initially offered the view that MFNs are "standard devices" to minimize costs and constitute the "sort of conduct that the antitrust laws seek to encourage," but later amended this statement to make it clear that it was not ruling out the possibility the MFNs may lessen competition under some circumstances. Blue Cross & Blue Shield v. Marshfield Clinic, 65 F.3d 1406 (7th Cir.1995). Willamette Dental Group v. Oregon Dental Serv., 882 P.2d 637 (Ore. App. 1994).

25. Blue Cross and Blue Shield v. Bingaman, 1996–2 Trade Cas. (CCH) ¶71600, 1996 WL 677094 (N.D. Ohio 1996) (refusing to

Section 1 challenge to a dental insurer's MFN clause, distinguishing *Ocean State* on the ground that the government's claim was that the MFN enabled Delta to raise, not lower prices.[26] Although Delta Dental had only a 35–45 per cent share of the market for dental insurance, the Justice Department contended that its contracts with over 90 per cent of Rhode Island dentists gave it power to foreclose competition by rivals.

E. RELATIONSHIPS AMONG HOSPITALS AND OTHER HEALTH FACILITIES

1. HORIZONTAL COLLUSION AMONG HOSPITALS

§ 14–37. Naked Restraints

Price fixing among competing health care facilities may take two forms. The first involves collusion concerning their prices, usually the billed charges or other terms they will accept from third party payors. It would seem that such agreements, which are plainly "naked" restraints of trade, should be governed by *per se* analysis. Although one district court declined to apply the *per se* rule to such an agreement among acute care hospitals, it did condemn the arrangement under a truncated rule of reason analysis.[1] Similarly, "Medicaid boycotts" by nursing homes and other providers seeking higher reimbursement from state agencies have been successfully challenged by the government. These collective actions typically coupled demands for increased payment with threats of de-participation from the Medicaid program and sometimes entailed actual boycotts in aid of the common price objective.[2] A second kind of price fixing involves horizontal collusion by hospitals to set the price they pay for goods or services. Collusion of this sort, to exercise buyer (monopsony) power, is treated as a *per se* restraint of trade just as seller price fixing is.[3] Thus, the FTC has challenged concerted action by nursing homes to boycott a nursing registry which had announced a significant price increase.[4] Such a boycott in aid of a price fixing agreement with no integration or procompetitive justification fits comfortably within the category of agreements meriting summary condemnation. Finally, information exchanges and collective refusals to deal which are really a cover for horizontal price fixing should be *per se* illegal, and perhaps warrant criminal prosecution.[5]

Another restraint of trade involves market allocations among competing hospitals. Conspiracies among competitors to divide markets, whether along

quash a governmental demand for information pursuant to civil investigative demand and rejecting argument that MFN cannot restrain trade as a matter of law).

26. United States v. Delta Dental, 943 F.Supp. 172 (D.R.I.1996). The case was subsequently settled by consent decree, 1997–2 Trade Cas. (CCH) ¶ 71,860 (D.R.I. 1997).

§ 14–37

1. United States v. North Dakota Hosp. Ass'n, 640 F.Supp. 1028 (D.N.D.1986).

2. See, e.g., United States v. Montana Nursing Home Ass'n, 1982–2 Trade Cas.

(CCH) ¶ 64,852, 1982 WL 1867 (D.Mont.1982) (consent decree); United States v. South Carolina Health Care Ass'n, 1980–2 Trade Cas. (CCH) ¶ 63,316, 1980 WL 1831 (D.S.C.1980) (consent decree).

3. Mandeville Island Farms v. American Crystal Sugar Co., 334 U.S. 219, 68 S.Ct. 996, 92 L.Ed. 1328 (1948).

4. In re Debes Corp., 57 Fed. Reg. 39205 (1992) (consent order).

5. See United States v. Hospital Ass'n of Greater Des Moines, 57 Fed. Reg. 45401–02 (1992). See infra, § 14–40.

geographic, customer, or product lines, are *per se* illegal.[6] Several state and federal advisory opinions have made it clear that the government believes that agreements among competing hospitals to allocate services among themselves would likewise constitute *per se* violations.[7] These advisory opinions are careful to point out, however, that *per se* analysis would not apply to market divisions that are part of an integrated, cost-saving joint effort to purchase equipment or build facilities that could not be undertaken by individual hospitals at minimum unit cost.

§ 14–38. Joint Action to Influence Health Care Regulation

In the past, state and federal regulation encouraged hospitals to undertake cooperative "planning" activities and even agreements allocating markets. However, laws establishing such regulations have not immunized cooperative actions from application of the federal antitrust laws.[1] Although federal planning legislation has been repealed, many states retain certificate of need (CON) approvals for hospital capital expenditures[2] and some states have adopted health care reforms that explicitly encourage hospital cooperation to avoid duplication of services.[3]

Hospital involvement in CON proceedings may raise antitrust questions in several circumstances. First, hospitals' actions may constitute an illegal product market division when they effectively decide among themselves which services each will apply for and agree not to contest each other's applications. Another anticompetitive tactic entails use of CON proceedings to obstruct entry by competitors. For example, filing frivolous objections to a rival's application for a CON, unnecessarily delaying the process, or submitting false information may constitute an actionable abuse of the regulatory process to restrain competition.[4] Such theories of liability are consistent with cases finding that misuse of governmental processes to deter entry or hinder competition constitutes a restraint of trade under Section 1 or an act of monopolization or attempted monopolization under Section 2 of the Sherman Act.[5] In addition, abuse of the regulatory process fits squarely within models

6. See Palmer v. B.R.G. of Georgia, Inc., 498 U.S. 46, 111 S.Ct. 401, 112 L.Ed.2d 349 (1990).

7. See, e.g., FTC Staff Advisory Opinion to Wichita, Kansas, Chamber of Commerce (May 22, 1991) ("[I]f two competing hospitals were to agree that one would exclusively offer radiation oncology service while the other would exclusively offer cardiac surgery services, such an agreement, without more, would be per se illegal, even though the hospitals might have sincerely believed that the elimination of their rivalry served the public good"); see also Op. Att'y Gen. Utah No. 85–002 (Oct. 21, 1985), in 1985–2 Trade Cas. (CCH) ¶ 66,882; Op. Att'y Gen. Iowa, (Jan. 9, 1984), in 1984–1 Trade Cas. (CCH) ¶ 65,813.

§ 14–38

1. See National Gerimedical Hosp. & Gerontology Ctr. v. Blue Cross, 452 U.S. 378, 101 S.Ct. 2415, 69 L.Ed.2d 89 (1981). Cf. Antitrust Division, Department of Justice, Business Re-

view Letter to Central Virginia Health Systems Agency (May 6, 1980).

2. See James B. Simpson, Full Circle: The Return of Certificate of Need Regulation of Health Facilities to State Control, 19 Ind. L.J. Rev. 1025 (1986).

3. See § 10–2e supra.

4. See, e.g., St. Joseph's Hosp., Inc. v. Hospital Corp. of America, 795 F.2d 948 (11th Cir.1986); Potters Med. Ctr. v. City Hosp. Ass'n, 800 F.2d 568 (6th Cir.1986).

5. See, e.g., Otter Tail Power Co. v. United States, 410 U.S. 366, 93 S.Ct. 1022, 35 L.Ed.2d 359 (1973) (lawsuits to delay establishment of rival power systems); Handgards, Inc. v. Ethicon, Inc., 601 F.2d 986 (9th Cir.1979), 444 U.S. 1025, 100 S.Ct. 688, 62 L.Ed.2d 659 (1980) (bad faith patent infringement suits); see generally James D. Hurwitz, Abuse of Governmental Processes, the First Amendment, and the Boundaries of Noerr, 74 Geo. L.J. 65 (1985).

of "non-price predation" and strategic behavior designed to "raise rivals' costs."[6]

Two important defenses may apply to allegations that hospitals undertook cost-raising strategies directed at competitors. First, many such claims will fall within the Noerr–Pennington doctrine, which protects collective activity soliciting governmental action even if undertaken for an anticompetitive purpose and with anticompetitive effects.[7] Although an exception applies in the case of "sham" petitioning (i.e., actions directed at governmental bodies designed specifically to harm rivals and not to advance petitioning interests), the Supreme Court has construed this exception narrowly.[8] An interesting–and perhaps overbroad–application of the sham exception is *Armstrong Surgical Center Inc. v. Armstrong County Memorial Hospital*[9] in which the court considered alleged concerted activity by opponents to block plaintiff's proposed ambulatory surgery center. The Third Circuit held that the sham exception protected both a rival hospital's submission of false and misleading statements to the CON authority and defendant physicians' threat of boycott, relying on the fact that the decision to deny the CON was made by a disinterested board. The court's opinion also appeared to question whether the misrepresentation exception survived the Supreme Court's decision in *City of Columbia v. Omni Advertising*. However, it is doubtful that the Supreme Court meant to permit material misrepresentations in an adjudicatory context that "infected the core" of the defendants' statements to the CON authority.[10] Even less likely is the majority's view the central concern of the Noerr doctrine–petitioning the government–protects activities that are themselves illegal such as threats of boycotts.[11] Other circuits have been unwilling to adopt the Third Circuit's approach,[12] perhaps because it would invite misrepresentations in adjudicatory fora which depend on the reliability of participants' assertions.

Participation in the certificate of need process or cooperative actions undertaken pursuant to state approval may also be protected under the state action doctrine upon a finding that the conduct is clearly articulated and expressed as a policy of the state and is actively supervised.[13] Where state CON legislation clearly evidences an intent to substitute regulation by a bona fide administrative process for competition and the effects of that process on competition are foreseeable, courts have found sufficiently clear articulation

---

6. See Thomas G. Krattenmaker & Steven C. Salop, Anticompetitive Exclusion: Raising Rivals' Costs to Achieve Power Over Price, 96 Yale L.J. 209 (1986); see generally ABA Antitrust Section, Monograph No. 18, Non–Price Predation Under Section 2 of the Sherman Act (1991).

7. See supra § 14–2d(4).

8. See Professional Real Estate Investors, Inc. v. Columbia Pictures Industries, Inc., 508 U.S. 49, 113 S.Ct. 1920, 123 L.Ed.2d 611 (1993) (to qualify for sham exception, litigation must be objectively baseless and conceal an attempt to interfere with business relationships of a competitor using government process as an anticompetitive device).

9. 185 F.3d 154 (3d Cir.1999).

10. Id. (Schwartz, dissenting).

11. See California Motor Transp., 404 U.S. at 513 ("other forms of illegal and reprehensible practice ... may corrupt the judicial or administrative process and ... may result in antitrust violations").

12. See, e.g., Kottle v. Northwest Kidney Centers, 146 F.3rd 1056 (9th Cir.1998); St. Joseph's Hosp., Inc. v. Hospital Corp. of America, 795 F.2d 948 (11th Cir.1986); Potters Med. Ctr. v. City Hosp. Ass'n, 800 F.2d 568 (6th Cir.1986).

13. See supra § 14–2d(2) and infra § 14–45.

to satisfy the first prong of the doctrine.[14] However, the Supreme Court's recent decisions in this area also require close, active and ongoing supervision.[15] It seems unlikely that regulatory approvals of hospital trade restraints will be protected under the state action doctrine unless the state carefully reviews the hospital's conduct and continues to scrutinize the effects of the conduct after initial approval.

2. HOSPITAL JOINT VENTURES AND OTHER AGREEMENTS WITH PROCOMPETITIVE JUSTIFICATIONS

§ 14–39. General Standards

The vast majority of cooperative activities undertaken by hospitals raise no competitive concerns. A wide variety of collaborative arrangements have received antitrust clearance based on plausible procompetitive justifications and integrative benefits flowing from cooperation. Indeed, not a single joint venture among hospitals has ever been challenged by government enforcement agencies. These arrangements are properly analyzed under the ancillary restraints doctrine, focussing on the three questions suggested by Judge Taft's *Addyston Pipe* decision: (1) are the possible restraints subordinate and collateral to a separate, legitimate undertaking?; (2) are they necessary to the success of that joint undertaking?; and (3) are they no more restrictive of competition than necessary to accomplish the procompetitive ends?[1]

§ 14–40. Sharing of Information

As analyzed previously in § 14–29, information exchanges among competitors are judged under the rule of reason unless the circumstances indicate that the exchange is a cover for a price fixing cartel or other restraint of trade. A large number of government advisory opinions have approved information exchanges collecting and disseminating data about hospital prices and costs. However, most of these exchanges were designed with an abundance of caution and are not controversial. For example, many were sponsored by buyer coalitions, third party payors or independent entities.[1] The Department of Justice/ FTC Policy Statements establish a "safety zone" for surveys and other among competing hospitals regarding prices and salaries.[2] However, the

---

14. See Armstrong Surgical Ctr. v. Armstrong County Mem'l Hosp., 185 F.3d 154 (3d Cir.1999); General Hosps. of Humana v. Baptist Med. Sys., 1986–1 Trade Cas. (CCH) ¶ 66,-996, 1986 WL 935 (E.D.Ark.1986); Trident Neuro–Imaging Lab. v. Blue Cross and Blue Shield, 568 F.Supp. 1474 (D.S.C.1983).

15. FTC v. Ticor Title Ins. Co., 504 U.S. 621, 112 S.Ct. 2169, 119 L.Ed.2d 410 (1992); Patrick v. Burget, 486 U.S. 94, 108 S.Ct. 1658, 100 L.Ed.2d 83 (1988).

§ 14–39

1. United States v. Addyston Pipe & Steel Co. 85 Fed. 271 (C.C.A.6 1898), affirmed and modified 175 U.S. 211, 20 S.Ct. 96, 44 L.Ed. 136 (1899). See generally See Federal Trade Commission & U.S. Dep't of Justice, Antitrust Guidelines for Collaborations Among Competitors (Draft, Oct. 1, 1999), available at www.usdoj.gov/atr/public/guidelines/jointindex.htm.

§ 14–40

1. See, e.g., Letter from Charles F. Rule, Assistant Attorney General, Antitrust Division, Department of Justice, to James C. Stutz, Executive Director, St. Louis Area Business Coalition (Mar. 24, 1988); Antitrust Division, Department of Justice, Business Review Letters to: Lexecon Health Service Inc. (June 20, 1986).

2. U.S. Department of Justice and Federal Trade Commission, Statements of Antitrust Enforcement Policy in Health Care, Statement 6 (1996), reprinted in 4 Trade Reg. Rep. (CCH) ¶ 13,153, analyzed supra § 14–29. See also Letter from Anne K. Bingaman, Assistant Attorney General, Antitrust Division, U.S. Department of Justice to Brian M. Foley, Esq., (Feb. 18, 1994) (approving wage survey in general compliance with Policy Statements' safety zone standard).

government has alleged a Section 1 conspiracy where hospitals acting through their hospital association have crossed the line by exchanging of information about current and prospective wages in circumstances that had the effect of stabilizing or lowering those salaries.[3]

§ 14–41. Group Purchasing Organizations

Virtually all hospitals today are engaged in group purchasing through one or more cooperative buying ventures, usually with other hospitals. These organizations purchase a variety of goods and services including pharmaceuticals, medical equipment and other supplies. No group purchasing arrangement involving the health care industry has ever been struck down under an antitrust challenge[1] and the enforcement agencies have been sympathetic to the procompetitive objectives of these practices.[2] The analysis that follows confirms that such arrangements rarely pose significant competitive threats.

There are three basic risks associated with buyer coalitions. First, the coalition may, in fact, be a cover for a cartel that fixes prices to input suppliers. Where such an anticompetitive purpose and effect can be shown, *per se* analysis is appropriate.[3] The second risk is that a large group of buyers may exercise monopsony power to drive prices below the competitive level. In these circumstances, monopsony is regarded as the "mirror image of monopoly," and poses risks of allocative inefficiency resulting from distortions on the supply side.[4] Exercise of monopsony power is less likely to occur than monopoly power, however, because it usually requires high levels of buyer concentration and specialized capital or other inputs that do not have a wide variety of uses.[5] Finally, monopsony power may result in collusion in the "output" market (i.e. hospitals selling their services to third parties). For this risk to be realized, however, the monopsonized input must constitute a significant proportion of the cost of the output service.

The Justice Department has fashioned a "safety zone" for group purchasing arrangements that reflects these considerations. Under its so-called "35/20 Rule," established in a number of advisory opinions outside the health care area,[6] the Department will not challenge buyer cooperatives, absent extraordinary circumstances, as long as (1) members collectively account for less than 35% of the total sales of the purchased product or service in the relevant market and (2) the cost of the jointly purchased input represents less

---

3. United States v. Utah Society for Healthcare Human Resources Admin., 1994–2 Trade Cas. (CCH) ¶ 70,795, 1994 WL 729931 (D. Utah 1994).

§ 14–41

1. For a decision closely analyzing the relevant markets and competitive effects of a hospital group purchasing organization, see White and White, Inc. v. American Hosp. Supply Corp., 723 F.2d 495 (6th Cir.1983).

2. U.S. Department of Justice and Federal Trade Commission, Statements of Antitrust Enforcement Policy in Health Care, Statement 7 (1996), reprinted in 4 Trade Reg. Rep. (CCH) ¶ 13,153; Antitrust Division, Department of Justice, Business Review Letter to Ohio Hosp. Ass'n (June 9, 1982).

3. See Mandeville Island Farms v. American Crystal Sugar Co., 334 U.S. 219, 68 S.Ct. 996, 92 L.Ed. 1328 (1948); see supra § 14–36.

4. See Vogel v. American Soc'y of Appraisers, 744 F.2d 598 (7th Cir.1984).

5. Roger D. Blair & Jeffrey L. Harrison, Monopsony (1993); Philip E. Areeda & Donald F. Turner, Antitrust Law ¶ 964 (1978) (monopsony power exercised where marginal costs are increasing; industries with constant marginal costs would not result in lower prices). See supra § 14–36.

6. See, e.g., Antitrust Division, Department of Justice, Business Review Letters to FRA Shippers' Ass'n (June 17, 1988) and to National Telecommunications Network (June 17, 1986).

than 20% of the total revenue from all products or services sold by each participating member. The second requirement applies only when participants are direct competitors.[7] When either threshold is exceeded, the Department more closely examines market structure and other factors to determine whether the cooperative is likely to restrain trade.

The logic of this analysis rests on the fact that unless a group purchasing organization (GPO) represents a significant proportion of the buyers in the market for a good, it probably cannot exercise monopsony power to drive prices of purchased goods or services below competitive levels. Thus, any lower prices negotiated likely reflect efficiency benefits such as economies of scale. In addition, as noted above, the risk that participation in a GPO will facilitate collusion is present primarily where the input constitutes a large share of the members' output prices. Where the cooperative buying arrangement pertains to a limited number of inputs, or a limited percentage of total costs, as is usually the case in hospital GPOs, there is relatively little risk of collusion. However, the second prong of this safety zone may give a distorted picture of the effect of group purchasing arrangements in some circumstances. Instead of calculating the proportion the shared input represents of the costs of the specific services in which the input is used, it simply uses the total revenues for all hospital services as the denominator in its calculation. This approach, which was adopted for administrative convenience, will tend to underestimate the effect of joint purchasing arrangements in some cases because the inputs may be used in a relatively small subset of all hospital services.

§ 14–42. Hospital Shared Services Organizations and High Technology Joint Ventures

Other kinds of cooperative joint ventures among competing hospitals have become commonplace. Typical shared service arrangements entail common ownership or operation of laundry services, transportation services, expensive equipment such as magnetic resonance imagers and ancillary medical facilities such as laboratories and free standing outpatient care centers. Although some concern has been expressed that antitrust law has chilled the development of such ventures,[1] the FTC has pointed out that not a single such venture has ever been challenged by the federal antitrust enforcement agencies.[2]

Antitrust law governing horizontal joint ventures again supplies the framework for analyzing these cooperative arrangements. Where integrative benefits are absent, such as when the joint venture label is used as a cover for a cartel, price-fixing and other naked restraints, the arrangements are con-

7. U.S. Department of Justice and Federal Trade Commission, Statements of Antitrust Enforcement Policy in Health Care, Statement 7 (1996), reprinted in 4 Trade Reg. Rep. (CCH) ¶ 13,153.

§ 14–42

1. See American Hospital Association, Hospital Collaboration: The Need for an Appropriate Antitrust Policy (1992).

2. Kevin J. Arquit, Director, FTC Bureau of Competition, Remarks Before American Bar Association, Antitrust Law Section, Health Care Committee (Apr. 2, 1992). But cf. FTC Staff Advisory Opinion to Wichita, Kansas, Chamber of Commerce (May 22, 1991).

demned per se offenses.[3] The essential inquiry under the rule of reason is into the efficiencies and harms of the venture. As a general matter, most joint venture analyses posit that the primary antitrust concern is the risk of overinclusive membership. That is, will the combination create or facilitate the exercise of market power through enhanced risks of collusion or unilateral exercise of market power?[4] This harm may occur in either the market in which the joint venture will operate or in "spillover markets," i.e., those in which joint venture members are actual or potential competitors outside the joint venture. The second, and less emphasized, risk is exclusion.

Where a legitimate joint venture is found, analysis of potential competitive harm proceeds along several dimensions. Courts must take into account, first, the nature of the venture. Distinctions may be drawn among ventures that entail only limited aspects of the production process (e.g. R & D); ventures that entail joint production of a product or service; and those that involve joint decisionmaking on marketing or output-related factors. These examples, broadly speaking, represent progressively greater potential for reducing output and less opportunity for enhancing efficiency.[5]

A second dimension is the competitive relationship among the co-venturers. Factors such as whether they are direct competitors, the proximity of their products, and their market power are elements of this inquiry. As often noted, market power can be an effective screen in analysis under the rule of reason, for without it there can be no risk of harm.[6] Third, where restraints are identified, courts assess whether they are reasonably necessary to achieve the benefits of the venture. Finally, where competitive harm is established, courts must undertake some evaluation of efficiencies, attempting to assess whether net savings will offset the identified harms.[7] The complexity and ambiguity of the foregoing balancing scheme renders it highly uninviting to courts. While some presumptive approaches have been suggested,[8] it appears that most joint venture analyses rely heavily on market power screens to shortcut the process and that weighing of harms, benefits and less restrictive alternatives is rarely undertaken.

The Department of Justice and FTC have outlined their approach to analyzing joint ventures involving "high technology or other expensive health

---

3. See, e.g., Timken Roller Bearing Co. v. United States, 341 U.S. 593, 71 S.Ct. 971, 95 L.Ed. 1199 (1951); Virginia Excelsior Mills, Inc. v. FTC, 256 F.2d 538 (4th Cir.1958).

4. See Joseph F. Brodley, Joint Ventures and Antitrust Policy, 95 Harv. L. Rev. 1521, 1540–56 (1982).

5. See E. Thomas Sullivan & Jeffrey Harrison, Understanding Antitrust and its Economic Implications 150 (1998).

6. See, e.g., Polk Bros., Inc. v. Forest City Enters., Inc., 776 F.2d 185, 191 (7th Cir.1985). Proof of actual anticompetitive effects, however, obviates the need for proof of market power. National Collegiate Athletic Ass'n v. Board of Regents, 468 U.S. 85, 104 S.Ct. 2948, 82 L.Ed.2d 70 (1984).

7. See Robert Pitofsky, A Framework for Antitrust Analysis of Joint Ventures, 54 Antitrust L.J. 893 (1985); for the view that this balancing is beyond judicial capabilities, see

Rothery Storage & Van Co. v. Atlas Van Lines, Inc., 792 F.2d 210, 229 n. 11, (D.C.Cir.1986), 479 U.S. 1033, 107 S.Ct. 880, 93 L.Ed.2d 834 (1987). The debate over weighing efficiencies in merger litigation is discussed infra at 14–54.

8. See Joseph F. Brodley, Joint Ventures and Antitrust Policy, 95 Harv. L. Rev. 1521 (1982); Robert Pitofsky, A Framework for Antitrust Analysis of Joint Ventures, 54 Antitrust St. L.J. 893 (1985); Thomas L. Greaney, Regulating for Efficiency Through the Antitrust Laws, 1995 Utah L.Rev. 465. The federal enforcement agencies have recently undertaken to develop joint venture guidelines. See Federal Trade Commission & U.S. Dep't of Justice, Antitrust Guidelines for Collaborations Among Competitors (Draft, Oct. 1, 1999), available at www.usdoj.gov/atr/public/guidelines/jointindex.htm.

care equipment"[9] and "specialized clinical or other expensive health care services."[10] The analysis generally follows the principles described above. The Statement on high technology equipment first establishes a "safety zone," which provides that the agencies would not challenge a venture to purchase, operate, and market such services "if the joint venture includes only the number of hospitals whose participation is needed to support the equipment, absent extraordinary circumstances."[11] Thus, where a group of hospitals can demonstrate that each was unable to recover the costs of such equipment, their joint venture generally would not be challenged.

For ventures falling outside the safety zone, the Statements sketch the rule of reason analysis that would be employed. Initially, the joint venture's relevant market must be determined and should include any other providers that could offer a service that patients or physicians would consider a good substitute. Competitive effects are evaluated first under a structural screen that would find little prospect for competitive harm if "there are many providers that would compete with the joint venture."[12] Where structural analysis suggests risks, it is necessary to evaluate the extent of potential anticompetitive effects. This entails an evaluation of the number of competing providers and factors making collusive or unilateral exercise of market power unlikely.[13] Still further balancing is then required, as the agency must assess the procompetitive efficiencies that may flow from the venture and weigh them against identified harms. Finally, in all cases, even where market structure analysis reveals little risk, the inquiry must assure that there are no ancillary agreements or conditions that unreasonably restrict competition. For example, an agreement among joint venture participants purchasing a mobile lithotripter setting the daily room charge each would assess for lithotripsy would be viewed as unnecessary to the venture and would likely be challenged.[14] Although the Statements provide no safety zone for joint ventures involving specialized clinical or other expensive services, the analytic approach is similar. In an advisory opinion applying the Statement to a proposal of two hospitals to open a new hospital providing specialized services, the FTC closely examined the likelihood of entry by the parties absent the joint

---

9. U.S. Department of Justice and Federal Trade Commission, Statements of Antitrust Enforcement Policy in Health Care, Statement 2 (1996), reprinted in 4 Trade Reg. Rep. (CCH) ¶ 13,153.

10. U.S. Department of Justice and Federal Trade Commission, Statements of Antitrust Enforcement Policy in Health Care, Statement 3 (1996), reprinted in 4 Trade Reg. Rep. (CCH) ¶ 13,153.

11. U.S. Department of Justice and Federal Trade Commission, Statements of Antitrust Enforcement Policy in Health Care, Statement 2 (1996), reprinted in 4 Trade Reg. Rep. (CCH) ¶ 13,153. In order to determine whether a hospital or group of hospitals could be expected to recover costs over the useful life of the equipment, the Statements commend the following information: the cost of the equipment, its expected useful life, the minimum number of procedures needed to break even, the expected

number of procedures to be demanded and the expected price to be charged. Additional hospitals may also be included if they could not support the equipment on their own or through the formation of a competing joint venture. Id.

12. Id.

13. The Statements identify three factors that could restrain supracompetitive pricing: regulatory restraints on price; market characteristics making anticompetitive agreements unlikely; and likely entry by others. Id.

14. See Urological Stone Surgeons, Inc., FTC No. C–3791 (consent order issued April 10, 1998) (settling charges that three companies and two doctors providing lithotripsy services illegally fixed prices for professional urologist services for lithotripsy procedures).

venture and risks that the venture might "spill over" to adversely affect competition in a market in which the venturers are competitors.[15]

§ 14–43. Hospital Diversification Through Vertical Integration

In response to changing financing arrangements and economic pressures and in order to serve patients who do not need inpatient care, hospitals often vertically integrate to provide a variety of services. Many hospitals have established subsidiaries to own or participate in joint ventures offering various ancillary, subacute, or continue-on services such as durable medical equipment (DME), nursing home care, free standing outpatient care and diagnostic services. In several cases, competing service providers have challenged hospital diversification alleging monopolization, attempted monopolization, leveraging, and restraint of trade, usually claiming that the hospital used its market power and advantageous access to its patients to "steer" them to its own company. Although plaintiffs have enjoyed occasional success in litigating these claims, there is no definitive precedent as yet and the relevant legal principles in this area are still unsettled.[1]

Under a monopolization or attempted monopolization theory, plaintiff must show substantial market power. In most cases, courts have relied upon the large market shares of defendant hospitals to conclude that the market power requirement was satisfied.[2] Although this evidence does not necessarily prove the existence of market power in the market allegedly being monopolized (DME services), such power might be inferred from the hospital's ability to steer its patients to its own suppliers.[3] As to the second requirement of monopolization claims, that defendant must prove a willful acquisition of that power through conduct that may be characterized as exclusionary, predatory, or anticompetitive, courts may find a predatory refusal to deal with rival DME companies. For example, in *Venice Hospital* the monopolist hospital was found to have made " 'an important change in a pattern of distribution that had

---

15. Letter from Mark J. Horoschak, Assistant Director, Bureau of Competition, Federal Trade Commission, to Carlos C. Smith (May 31, 1995).

§ 14–43

1. In Key Enterprises of Delaware, Inc. v. Venice Hospital, the leading hospital diversification case, the Eleventh Circuit vacated a panel decision reinstating a jury verdict of $2.3 million in favor of an independent DME supplier. The appeal was subsequently dismissed as moot. Key Enters. of Delaware, Inc. v. Venice Hosp., 919 F.2d 1550 (11th Cir.1990), rehearing granted and opinion vacated 979 F.2d 806 (11th Cir.1992), appeal dismissed 9 F.3d 893 (11th Cir.1993), 511 U.S. 1126, 114 S.Ct. 2132, 128 L.Ed.2d 863 (1994). See also M & M Med. Supplies & Serv., Inc. v. Pleasant Valley Hosp., Inc., 981 F.2d 160 (4th Cir.1992), 508 U.S. 972, 113 S.Ct. 2962, 125 L.Ed.2d 662 (1993) (vacating summary judgment for hospital on monopolization, attempted monopolization and leveraging claims); Advanced Health–Care Servs., Inc. v. Radford Community Hosp., 910 F.2d 139 (4th Cir.1990), on remand 846 F.Supp. 488 (W.D.Va.1994) (denying hospitals' motion to dismiss on Section 2 claims). Several other cases involving similar claims have been settled prior to trial.

2. Key Enters. Of Delaware, Inc. v. Venice Hosp., 919 F.2d 1550 (11th Cir.1990), rehearing granted and opinion vacated 979 F.2d 806 (11th Cir.1992), appeal dismissed 9 F.3d 893 (11th Cir.1993); M & M Medical Supplies & Serv., Inc. v. Pleasant Valley Hosp., Inc., 981 F.2d 160 (4th Cir.1992); Advanced Health–Care Servs., Inc. v. Radford Community Hosp., 910 F.2d 139 (4th Cir.1990), on remand 846 F.Supp. 488 (W.D.Va.1994). Although this evidence does not necessarily prove the existence of market power in the market allegedly being monopolized (DME services), such power might be inferred from the hospital's ability to steer its patients to its own supplier.

3. Eastman Kodak v. Image Technical Services, Inc., 504 U.S. 451, 112 S.Ct. 2072, 119 L.Ed.2d 265 (1992) ("in some instances, one brand can constitute a single product.")

originated in a competitive market and had persisted for several years.' "[4] In addition, courts have stressed that the absence of efficiency justifications for the exclusionary action, especially where the vertically integrated hospital's ancillary service was of inferior quality or more expensive, may give rise to an inference that the practice was "not motivated by efficiency concerns and that it was willing to sacrifice short-run benefits and consumer good will in exchange for a perceived long-run impact on its smaller rival."[5]

Under the controversial and rarely-invoked monopoly leveraging doctrine, a firm using its monopoly power in one market to obtain a competitive advantage in a second market violates Section 2 of the Sherman Act.[6] Courts deciding hospital diversification cases appear to have accepted in principal that monopoly leveraging may apply where a hospital steers its patients to its own DME provider.[7] A difficult question left unanswered by these cases is the extent to which plaintiff must prove that defendant hospital's "advantage" in the DME market was the product of its power in the first market and not synergies or efficiencies resulting from its having a presence in both markets. While it is clear that there must be some connection between the market power of the hospital and its success in the leveraged market,[8] the plaintiff's burden of proof regarding the extent of that effect remains unclear.

Finally, steering or channeling patients by vertically integrated hospitals may also be challenged as a restraint of trade. Where an independent party (such as a home health care nurse) is a participant in the alleged conspiracy or where the referral is to an entity not owned by the hospital, the requisite plurality of actors will be present.[9] In *Venice Hospital*, a panel of the Eleventh Circuit upheld plaintiff's theory of Section 1 liability based on "coercive reciprocity."[10] Under this claim the hospital had agreed with home health

4. Key Enters. Of Delaware, Inc. v. Venice Hosp., 919 F.2d 1550 (11th Cir.1990), rehearing granted and opinion vacated 979 F.2d 806 (11th Cir.1992), appeal dismissed 9 F.3d 893 (11th Cir.1993) (quoting Aspen Skiing Co. v. Aspen Highlands Skiing Corp., 472 U.S. 585, 105 S.Ct. 2847, 86 L.Ed.2d 467 (1985)). See also Advanced Health–Care Servs., Inc. v. Radford Community Hosp., 910 F.2d 139, 149 (4th Cir.1990), on remand 846 F.Supp. 488 (W.D.Va.1994).

5. Aspen Skiing Co. v. Aspen Highlands Skiing, Corp., 472 U.S. 585, 610–611, 105 S.Ct. 2847, 2861–2862, 86 L.Ed.2d 467 (1985). See Key Enters. Of Delaware, Inc. v. Venice Hosp., 919 F.2d 1550, 1558 (11th Cir.1990), rehearing granted and opinion vacated 979 F.2d 806 (11th Cir.1992), appeal dismissed 9 F.3d 893 (11th Cir.1993).

6. Berkey Photo, Inc. v. Eastman Kodak Co., 603 F.2d 263 (2d Cir.1979), cert. denied 444 U.S. 1093, 100 S.Ct. 1061, 62 L.Ed.2d 783 (1980). Kerasotes Michigan Theatres, Inc. v. National Amusements, Inc., 854 F.2d 135 (6th Cir.1988). Contrast Alaska Airlines, Inc. v. United Airlines, Inc., 948 F.2d 536 (9th Cir. 1991). See also Spectrum Sports v. McQuillan, 506 U.S. 447, 113 S.Ct. 884 (1993).

7. M & M Medical Supplies & Serv., Inc. v. Pleasant Valley Hosp., 981 F.2d 160, 168 (4th

Cir.1992) (assuming for purposes of remand that monopoly leveraging is separate cause of action); Key Enters. or Delaware, Inc. v. Venice Hosp., 919 F.2d 1550, 1567, 1568 (11th Cir. 1990), rehearing granted and opinion vacated 979 F.2d 806 (11th Cir.1992), appeal dismissed 9 F.3d 893 (11th Cir.1993); Advanced Health–Care Servs., Inc. v. Radford Community Hosp., 910 F.2d 139, 149 (4th Cir.1990), on remand 846 F.Supp. 488 (W.D.Va.1994) (same).

8. As the Second Circuit noted in Berkey Photo, "an integrated business [does not] offend the Sherman Act whenever one of its departments benefits from association with a division possessing a monopoly in its own market." 603 F.2d 263, 276 (2d Cir.1979).

9. See Advanced Health–Care Servs., Inc. v. Radford Community Hosp., 910 F.2d 139, 144 (4th Cir.1990), on remand 846 F.Supp. 488 (W.D.Va.1994) (hospitals conspiring with independent DME provider). Following *Copperweld*, however, a conspiracy will not be found between a hospital and its wholly-owned subsidiary or between two wholly-owned subsidiaries of the same percent.

10. Key Enters. Of Delaware, Inc. v. Venice Hosp., 919 F.2d 1550, 1562 (11th Cir.1990), rehearing granted and opinion vacated 979 F.2d 806 (11th Cir.1992), appeal dismissed 9 F.3d 893 (11th Cir.1993).

agencies that the latter's nurses would continue to have access to patients in defendant's hospital in exchange for the nurses preferentially referring their patients to the hospital's DME company. The arrangement was deemed coercive because the agencies acceded to the agreement as a result of the hospital's market power and threatened denial of access to patients.

3. Mergers of Health Care Providers and Payors

§ 14–44. Introduction

Close antitrust scrutiny of mergers of health care institutions, particularly acute care hospitals, began in the mid–1980's. The Federal Trade Commission took the lead, successfully challenging two horizontal mergers involving acute care hospitals.[1] Subsequently, the Department of Justice, the FTC, and State Attorneys General have closely monitored hospital acquisitions and have sought injunctions in many cases.[2] Antitrust enforcement has also focused on mergers in many other sectors including physicians,[3] nursing homes,[4] prescription drug wholesalers,[5] pharmacies,[6] and managed care companies.[7]

Antitrust issues arise whenever a merger between competitors either (1) produces a single entity with sufficient market power to increase price or reduce output unilaterally or (2) reduces the number of firms and increases concentration so as to increase the likelihood that the remaining firms will coordinate their behavior and exercise market power. Courts and the FTC have treated mergers among hospitals or among physicians much like mergers in any other industry. This seems entirely appropriate in the context of the changing economic incentives facing providers. The degree to which pressures from payers seeking to negotiate favorable rates will drive down costs depends upon competitive market structures.[8] Indeed, one can hardly expect the cost-

§ 14–44

1. American Med. Int'l, Inc., 104 F.T.C. 1 (1984); Hospital Corp. of America, 106 F.T.C. 361 (1985), affirmed 807 F.2d 1381 (7th Cir. 1986).

2. See, e.g., United States v. Rockford Mem'l Corp., 898 F.2d 1278 (7th Cir.1990), 498 U.S. 920, 111 S.Ct. 295, 112 L.Ed.2d 249 (1990) (granting preliminary injunction); FTC v. Butterworth Health Corp., 121 F.3d 706 (6th Cir. 1997) (denying preliminary injunction); U.S. v. Mercy Health Servs., 107 F.3d 632 (8th Cir.1997), 902 F.Supp. 968 (N.D.Iowa 1995), vacated as moot, FTC v. University Health, Inc., 938 F.2d 1206 (11th Cir.1991); Pennsylvania v. Capital Health Sys. Serv., 1995–2 Trade Cas. (CCH) ¶ 71,205, 1995 WL 787534 (M.D.Pa.1995) (consent decree).

3. See, e.g., HTI Health Services v. Quorum Health Group, 960 F.Supp. 1104 (S.D.Miss.1997); Maine v. Maine Heart Surgical Associates, P.A., 1996–2 Trade Cas. (CCH) ¶ 71,653, 1996 WL 773330 (Me.Super.Ct.1996) (consent decree); Letter from Joel Klein, Assistant Attorney General, Antitrust Division, U.S. Department of Justice to Donald H. Lipson (July 7, 1997) (Business Review Letter); Letter from Joel Klein, Assistant Attorney General, Antitrust Division, U.S. Department of Justice

to Bob D. Tucker (April 16, 1997) (Business Review Letter).

4. United States v. Beverly Enterprises, 1984–1 Trade Cas. (CCH) ¶ 66,052, 1984 WL 2958 (M.D.Ga.1984) (consent decree).

5. FTC v. Cardinal Health, Inc., 12 F.Supp.2d 34 (D.D.C.1998).

6. Rite Aid Abandons Proposed Acquisition of Revco after FTC Sought to Block Transaction, FTC News (April 24, 1996).

7. United States v. Aetna, No. Civ. A. 3–99CV1398–, 1999-2 Trade Cas. (CCH) ¶ 72,730 (N.D.Tex.1999), 64 Fed. Reg. 44, 946 (Aug. 18, 1999) (consent decree and competitive impact statement).

8. A number of economic analyses show a positive correlation between hospital market structure and price or profits. See, e.g., David Dranove & R. Ludwick, Competition and Pricing by Non Profit Hospitals: A Reassessment of Lynk's Analysis, 18 Journal of Health Economics 87 (1999); E.B. Keeler, et al., The Changing Effects of Competition on Non Profit and For Profit Hospital Pricing Behavior, 18 Journal of Health Economics 69 (1999); R.A. Conner, et al., The Effects of Market Concentration in Horizontal Mergers on Hospital Costs and Prices, 5 International Journal of Economics of

saving benefits of selective contracting and managed care to be realized if physicians or hospitals can unilaterally or collectively resist competitive pressures to lower price or control utilization. At the same time, however, several recent cases have questioned whether nonprofit entities in the health care market fit the antitrust paradigm, and suggest more leniency for mergers in that sector. Moreover, it is likely that some procompetitive benefits will be associated with many mergers. For example, a merger between competing hospitals may help hospitals achieve economies of scale and other efficiencies, thus lowering unit costs and, absent the exercise of market power, result in lower prices. This phenomenon may be particularly apparent in hospital markets undergoing rationalization. As discussed below, addressing such possible trade-offs between competitive harms and benefits is a controversial and complex task for merger analyses.

§ 14–45. Jurisdiction and the Effect of State Regulation

Section 7 of the Clayton Act as amended in 1980 requires that both parties to a merger be either "engaged in" interstate commerce or "in any activity affecting" interstate commerce. Given the fact that most health care institutions receive significant payments from out-of-state payers, purchase equipment and supplies from interstate sources and treat out-of-state patients, the "affecting commerce test" easily can be met.[1] Where the question has been raised, courts have found that hospitals meet the "in commerce" test as well.[2] In addition, given the Supreme Court's expansive approach to the "affecting commerce" test under Section 1 of the Sherman Act, it is likely that the jurisdictional requirements will be readily satisfied in cases brought under that act as well.[3]

An issue of increasing importance is whether state regulation limits the scope of antitrust review of hospital mergers by the FTC and the federal courts.[4] Over twenty states have enacted laws that establish procedures for granting regulatory approvals to health care providers (usually hospitals)

Business 159 (1998). On the possibility that hospital competition encourages inefficient technology expenditures, see J.C. Robinson and H.S. Luft, The Impact of Hospital Market Structure on Patient Volume, Average Length of Stay, and the Cost of Care, 4 J. of Health Economics 315 (1985); David Dranove, Mark Shanley and Carol Simon, Is Hospital Competition Wasteful?, 23 Rand J. of Econ. 247 (1992).

§ 14–45

1. United States v. Hospital Affiliates Int'l, Inc., 1980–81 Trade Cas. (CCH) ¶ 63,721, 77,-853, 1980 WL 1983, (E.D.La.1980). (unpublished opinion); American Med. Int'l, 104 F.T.C. 1, 14 (1991) (initial decision); Hospital Corp. of America, 106 F.T.C. 361, 385 (1985) (initial decision).

2. American Med. Int'l, Inc., 104 F.T.C. 1, 220 (1984).

3. See Summit Health, Ltd. v. Pinhas, 500 U.S. 322, 111 S.Ct. 1842, 114 L.Ed.2d 366 (1991).

4. Originally, the question was one of implied repeal, as it was argued that federal health planning scheme impliedly repealed antitrust laws applicable to hospital mergers. The Supreme Court held that these laws did not work any blanket repeal as to the health care industry, but it left open the possibility that in some specific circumstances implied repeal might be necessary for the Planning Act to work. National Gerimedical Hosp. & Gerontology Ctr. v. Blue Cross of Kansas City, 452 U.S. 378, 101 S.Ct. 2415, 69 L.Ed.2d 89 (1981). North Carolina ex rel. Edmisten v. P.I.A. Asheville, Inc., 740 F.2d 274, 279–85 (4th Cir.1984) (no repeal of federal antitrust merger law in North Carolina's certificate of need scheme.) Thus, while it is conceivable that implied repeal of federal merger law might have been found in an appropriate regulatory context, the issue became moot with the repeal of health planning laws.

contemplating mergers and other forms of consolidation or cooperation.[5] Entities meeting specified criteria (which typically include cost reduction, improved quality of care or access and reduced duplication of services) receive exemption from state antitrust laws. Although many of these statutes are also designed to afford immunity from federal antitrust laws under the State Action Doctrine, the statutes must satisfy two doctrinal requirements before immunity will be found. First, in order to satisfy the clear articulation requirement, the state's regulatory review must evidence an intent to interfere with competition as a matter of state policy or suggest that such was the foreseeable result of the regulation.[6] More problematic for defendants seeking to invoke the state action doctrine to immunize hospital mergers is the active state supervision prong. In *Ticor*, the Supreme Court rejected passive, "negative option" regulation and stressed the need to closely monitor competitive performance. This would seem to require plenary regulatory review of hospital competitive practices, including, perhaps, price regulation.[7]

Mergers between governmental or "public" hospitals may also qualify for immunity under the state action doctrine. Where the acquiring hospital or other entity is operated by a municipality or other political subdivision, the transaction will be immune if the hospital is acting as an "instrumentality" of the state[8] and pursuant to a "clearly articulated state policy." That policy, however, need not be explicit; courts frequently infer legislative intent from broad mandates to engage in practices that have the foreseeable result of displacing competition.[9] Some courts have interpreted the "foreseeability" standard quite broadly, finding it satisfied by a broad grant of powers to local hospital boards where legislative intent was found to implicitly support such powers.[10] These courts appear to have improperly inferred a state policy to displace competition from authorizations of conduct that may only injure competitors, not competition, and that do not substitute regulation for competition.[11]

5. E.g., Me. Rev. Stat. Ann. Tit. 22 § 1883, sub. Ch. IV; Ohio Rev. Code Ann. 3727.21–3727.24 (1996); Fla. Stat. Ann. § 381.04065; Tex. Health & Safety Code Ann. §§ 314.001–314.008 (1993).

6. FTC v. Ticor Title Ins. Co., 504 U.S. 621, 627, 112 S.Ct. 2169, 2176, 119 L.Ed.2d 410 (1992). See Askew v. DCH Reg'l Health Care Auth., 995 F.2d 1033, 1035 (11th Cir.1993).

7. Illustrative of this strict reading of the doctrine is the Fourth Circuit's holding that the North Carolina CON program failed to meet the state supervision requirement because the State failed to regulate hospital prices, monitor provider behavior or impose penalties for non-compliance with regulation. North Carolina ex rel. Edmisten v. P.I.A. Asheville, 740 F.2d 274, 278 (4th Cir.1984); cf. General Hosps. of Humana, Inc. v. Baptist Med. Sys., Inc., 1986–1 Trade Cas. (CCH) ¶ 66,-996, 62,116–17, 1986 WL 935 (E.D.Ark.1986) (unpublished opinion) (active supervision requirement satisfied where cost overruns must be approved by regulatory process and other detailed supervision present).

8. Whether the hospital is "public" or the equivalent of a government subdivision will depend on whether it possesses governmental powers or recognition by statute or other government entity. See Askew v. DCH Reg'l Health Care Authority, 995 F.2d 1033 (11th Cir.1993).

9. Town of Hallie v. City of Eau Claire, 471 U.S. 34, 105 S.Ct. 1713, 85 L.Ed.2d 24 (1985); City of Columbia v. Omni Outdoor Advertising, Inc., 499 U.S. 365, 372–73, 111 S.Ct. 1344, 113 L.Ed.2d 382 (1991).

10. FTC v. Hosp. Bd. of Directors of Lee County, 38 F.3d 1184 (11th Cir.1994). For a critique of this decision, see Dean M. Harris, State Action Immunity from Antitrust Laws for Public Hospitals: The Hidden Time Bomb for Health Care Reform, 44 U. Kan. L.Rev. 459 (1996).

11. See Peter C. Ward, State Antitrust Immunity for Public Hospitals: It Depends on What You Mean by "Forseeable," 33 J. Health L. 1 (2000).

§ 14–46. Standing for Private Parties

The dearth of private suits challenging mergers of health institutions is explained by the economic incentives facing plaintiffs and the formidable legal obstacles that stand in the way of private suits. As a practical matter, competitor challenges to mergers may be unattractive because of the absence of treble damage remedies under § 7 and the uncertainties inherent in proving prospective damages. More importantly, however, formidable legal obstacles bar many potential private suits. First, competitor plaintiffs can rarely satisfy the requirement of showing "antitrust injury." Unless a competitor alleges that the merger is likely to result in predatory activity, the competitor would actually be in a position to *benefit* from increased market concentration resulting from the merger. In such circumstances, "antitrust injury" is absent because the competitor-plaintiff is not harmed and indeed may profit from the anticompetitive consequences of the merger.[1] Where a plaintiff hospital's claim is that it would suffer injury from potential predation by the merged entity, standing is appropriate. However, the Supreme Court has expressed skepticism about such claims and has encouraged lower courts to reject them at preliminary stages of litigation.[2]

Other parties, such as employees, physicians and consumers may assert standing based on potential loss of income or higher prices resulting from market power caused by the merger. Courts interpreting antitrust standing requirements have been sympathetic to consumer suits,[3] but have often been reluctant to find standing for target companies challenging takeovers,[4] employees or vendors.[5] Given the Supreme Court's stated preference for customers or consumers as proper plaintiffs,[6] it seems likely that a judiciary unsympathetic to expanding private standing will reject suits brought by others.

§ 14–47. "Virtual Mergers" and Commonly–Controlled Entities

Many hospitals have entered into agreements with other hospitals to substantially integrate their operations and governance without undertaking a full-blown acquisition or merger. They do this through various contractual arrangements, including strategic alliances and joint operating agreements, pursuant to which control of the hospitals is typically ceded to a single board or other entity. These affiliations often involve a nonprofit or religiously affiliated hospital that is reluctant to give up its own identity or autonomy in a merger. A critical issue in these arrangements is whether the hospitals will be treated as a single entity for antitrust purposes. If it is not, the affiliated hospitals are viewed as separate firms and their joint actions on pricing and

---

§ 14–46

1. Brunswick Corp. v. Pueblo Bowl–O–Mat, Inc., 429 U.S. 477, 97 S.Ct. 690, 50 L.Ed.2d 701 (1977).

2. See Cargill, Inc. v. Monfort of Colorado, Inc., 479 U.S. 104, 107 S.Ct. 484, 93 L.Ed.2d 427(1986); cf. Eastman Kodak Co. v. Image Technical Servs., Inc., 504 U.S. 451, 112 S.Ct. 2072, 119 L.Ed.2d 265 (1992).

3. See Nelson v. Monroe Reg'l Med. Ctr., 925 F.2d 1555 (7th Cir.1991).

4. See, e.g., Central Nat'l Bank v. Rainbolt, 720 F.2d 1183 (10th Cir.1983); Carter Hawley

Hale Stores, Inc. v. The Limited, Inc., 587 F.Supp. 246 (C.D.Cal.1984); see Frank H. Easterbrook & Daniel R. Fischel, Antitrust Suits by Targets of Tender Offers, 80 Mich. L. Rev. 1155 (1982).

5. Reibert v. Atlantic Richfield Co., 471 F.2d 727 (10th Cir.1973).

6. Associated Gen. Contractors of California, Inc. v. California State Council of Carpenters, 459 U.S. 519, 103 S.Ct. 897, 74 L.Ed.2d 723 (1983).

other competitive variables may constitute per se violations of section 1 of the Sherman Act. If, on the other hand, the affiliation is deemed to create a single entity, traditional merger analysis under Section 7 of the Clayton Act is applied.

The most pertinent case law involves arrangements between parent and subsidiary corporations in which the courts have questioned whether single entity status is appropriate. In the leading case, *Copperweld Corp. v. Independence Tube Corp.*,[1] the Supreme Court held that a parent corporation and its wholly-owned subsidiary constituted a single entity. Therefore the parent and subsidiary were incapable, as a matter of law, of conspiring under the Sherman Act. The Court emphasized that the parent-subsidiary relationship is distinguished by a complete unity of the entity's purposes and interests and also by the ability of the parent corporation to exercise its control to assure that the aligned interests are pursued. Application of these principles in the case of virtual mergers between hospitals entails a close factual examination of purposes of the undertaking and of the specific control arrangements among the affiliated hospitals.[2] Key indicia would include whether one hospital retains veto power over significant transactions, the role of each hospital's board in choosing or replacing board members, the entity's individual control over strategic decisionmaking, budgets and contracting, and the parties' rights of termination.[3]

Another question is whether two affiliates with a common parent will be immune from challenge under the Sherman or Clayton Acts. *Copperweld*[4] would preclude a challenge to a merger between sister subsidiaries wholly-owned by a common parent under Section 1 because of the absence of a conspiracy. The logic of *Copperweld* would also seem to exempt such mergers from a Section 7 challenge: essentially, courts should view wholly-owned subsidiaries as one and the same with their parent corporation.[5] A more complex and intriguing question is raised by consolidation of two affiliates of a nonprofit entity, such as a religious organization. A strong argument can be made that in contrast to subsidiaries of for-profit enterprises, entities affiliated with not-for-profit organizations may have distinct and competing interests from those of their parent or sibling entities.[6] By this analysis, however, it is important to remember that market shares of affiliated nonprofit hospitals would not be combined for purposes of computing concentration data.

§ 14–47

1. 467 U.S. 752 (1984).

2. The Attorney General of the State of New York has claimed that the joint activities of an affiliation of competing hospitals constitute a price fixing and market allocation scheme. In support of its contention that the Copperweld doctrine would not apply, the State's complaint emphasized the lack of financial integration between the hospitals and other indicia of separateness. Toby G. Singer, Challenge in Poughkeepsie is First To "Virtual Mergers" in Health, 7 Health L. Rep. (BNA) 525, Mar. 26, 1998.

3. See generally Roxanne C. Busey, Antitrust Aspects of "Virtual Mergers" and Affiliations, Remarks before the American Health Lawyers Association Annual Meeting (July 1, 1998); Mark J. Botti, Virtual Mergers of Hospitals: When Does the Per Se Rule Apply? in Antitrust and Health Care: Insights into Analysis and Enforcement (Douglas Ross, ed. 1999).

4. Copperweld Corp. v. Independence Tube Corp., 467 U.S. 752, 104 S.Ct. 2731, 81 L.Ed.2d 628 (1984).

5. See Jonathan B. Baker, The Antitrust Analysis Hospital Mergers and the Transformation of the Hospital Industry, 51 Law & Contemp. Probs. 93, 110–11 (1988).

6. See id. Thus where a not-for-profit affiliate is independently controlled, has independent interests and makes independent operational judgments, it is appropriate to treat the entities as distinct for merger analysis under Section 1 or Section 7; but cf. Proctor v. General Conference of Seventh–Day Adventists, 651 F.Supp. 1505, 1524 (N.D.Ill.1986).

§ 14–48.   The Analytic Framework Under § 7 and The Merger Guidelines

Perhaps the most significant development in merger analysis under the Clayton Act has been the promulgation of Merger Guidelines by the Department of Justice and the FTC.[1] Although these guidelines do not have the force of law and purport to reflect only the government's enforcement policies, they have been highly influential in shaping judicial analyses of mergers. Despite some significant disagreements about certain aspects of the federal guidelines, they nevertheless reflect a broad consensus of economic, legal and judicial opinion concerning the proper approach to analyzing mergers.

The Merger Guidelines explain that the principal objective of merger law has been to block those mergers that create or enhance market power[2] or facilitate its exercise. There are two important ways by which a merger may create or enhance these risks: (1) it may create a single firm with the capacity to unilaterally exercise market power; or (2) it can enhance the ability of firms in the market to exercise market power collectively, either by explicit collusion or tacit coordination of their behavior.

To assess these risks, merger analysis proceeds in four steps. First, a factfinder must define the product and geographic markets (the "relevant markets") in which the merging firms compete. Second, he must identify other firms competing in those markets and calculate the market shares of the firms and the concentration level of the markets. Third, if the foregoing market share concentration data and other factors give rise to a presumption that the merger will lessen competition, the antitrust tribunal must determine whether the presumption has been rebutted. In this phase, it will consider a number of market conditions including ease of entry and facts peculiar to competition in the specific market tending to prove that unilateral effects or coordinated behavior is more or less likely. Finally, if the merger is found likely to substantially lessen competition, the factfinder may consider certain defenses—whether the merger will produce significant efficiencies or involves a failing company—that would permit the merger to go forward notwithstanding its demonstrated anticompetitive harms. We examine each step in turn.

§ 14–49.   Market Definition

An essential first step in merger analysis is the identification of economically meaningful markets. Because the dimensions of the product and geo-

§ 14–48

1. There have been several sets of merger guidelines issued by federal government enforcement agencies. The most recent iteration is the United States Dep't of Justice & Federal Trade Commission, Horizontal Merger Guidelines, 57 Fed. Reg. 41, 552 (1992), as revised, 4 Trade Reg. Rep. (CCH) ¶ 13,104 (1997) (hereinafter, "Merger Guidelines"). An alternative and less influential set of guidelines has been promulgated by the state attorneys general. Horizontal Merger Guidelines of the National Ass'n of Attorneys General, 64 Antitrust & Trade Reg. Rep. (BNA) No. 1608 (Special Supp. April 1, 1993).

2. The definition of "market power" utilized in the Guidelines is "the ability profitably to maintain price above competitive levels for a significant period of time." Merger Guidelines § 0.1. Accord Jefferson Parish Hosp. District No. 2 v. Hyde, 466 U.S. 2, 27 n. 46, 104 S.Ct. 1551, 1566 n. 46, 80 L.Ed.2d 2 (1984) ("Market power exists whenever prices can be raised above the levels that would be charged in a competitive market.").

graphic markets delimit the universe within which the merging parties compete and thus affect the magnitude of their market shares, the issue is of central importance in most merger litigation. Needless to say, it is also usually hotly-contested.

The generally-accepted paradigm for market definition in contemporary merger analyses is set forth in the Merger Guidelines. This approach defines markets in terms of the ultimate anticompetitive harm threatened by mergers. Thus, markets are those geographic areas and products groups within which firms could effectively exercise market power if they were monopolists or were able to perfectly coordinate their actions. The Guidelines frame the underlying test as follows:

> A market is defined as a product or group of products and a geographic area in which it is produced or sold such that a hypothetical profit-maximizing firm, not subject to price regulation, that was the only present and future producer or seller of those products in that area likely would impose at least a small but significant and non-transitory increase in price, assuming the terms of sale of all other products are held constant.[1]

This somewhat convoluted and hypothetical articulation of the concept of a market is probably best understood as an expression of the essential principles that must guide factual determinations rather than a precise analytic tool to be used for that process. The Guidelines' approach has achieved general (albeit not unanimous) acceptance in the courts and the academic commentary.[2]

a. Product Market Definition

In determining the relevant product market in merger cases, antitrust tribunals attempt to identify those products or services which, from the perspective of consumers, have no attractive substitutes in a competitive market. Put another way, the inquiry is whether a hypothetical cartel of producers of the good or service might successfully increase price without losing so many customers as to decrease their profits. Thus, a product market must include all effective substitutes to which buyers could turn should a cartel reduce output and increase price. The Merger Guidelines supplement this rather conceptual inquiry by identifying evidence that is particularly suggestive in defining product markets: e.g., evidence that buyers have shifted or considered shifting purchases between products; proof that sellers base business decisions on the prospect of buyer substitution; the influence of downstream competition; and the timing and cost of switching products.[3]

Hospital Services. Strict application of these principles in the acute care hospital context might suggest a large number of distinct product and service markets: e.g., intensive care services, neo-natal services, general surgery, vascular surgery, emergency room care, x-ray and other diagnostic services,

---

1. Merger Guidelines § 1.0. Although a large number of relevant markets might satisfy this test, antitrust analysis focuses on the smallest market satisfying market definition requirements.

2. For criticism, see, e.g, Robert G. Harris & Thomas M. Jorde, Antitrust Market Defini-

tion: An Integrated Approach, 72 Cal. L. Rev. 1 (1984); for alternative approaches, see, e.g., NAAG Merger Guidelines, 52 Antitrust & Trade Reg. Rep. (BNA) No. 1306 (Special Supp. Mar. 12, 1987).

3. Merger Guidelines § 1.11.

and so forth. However, patients (acting through their agents such as purchasing alliances, HMOs, or other managed care entities) typically purchase a *group* of interrelated services from a hospital. A patient admitted for surgery would need laboratory and diagnostic services, 24–hour nursing care, use of surgical facilities, and other services. Hence, to the extent that many hospital services are functionally interrelated and in practice are purchased as a package, it is obviously more realistic to group or "cluster" products for product market definition purposes.[4] Moreover, hospital services are bought in packages by third part payers because it is convenient and less costly to select facilities and negotiate with them for a broad array of services and products.

Several important caveats must be added regarding cluster analysis. First, the justifications described above will not rationalize cluster markets for antitrust analysis when hospitals do not share a common "core" of in-patient services which buyers view as substitutes. Under such circumstances, market shares of hospitals based on aggregated services will reflect essentially different products. Moreover, entry conditions will likely vary for each grouping. By the same token, however, it may be entirely appropriate in some circumstances to identify individual services within the cluster as separate product markets for antitrust purposes. Thus, the government has challenged a merger involving competition between an acute care hospital and a stand-alone facility in the provision of outpatient surgical services.[5]

Courts and the FTC have almost uniformly adopted the cluster market approach for defining hospital markets. The decided cases have generally grouped acute care in-patient services together as the appropriate product market within which to analyze mergers among acute care hospitals.[6] In several recent cases, courts have limited the cluster market to exclude tertiary services[7] or have identified separate markets for in-patient primary care services and general acute care in-patient services.[8] Excluding tertiary services or care requiring sophisticated treatment is supported by the tendency of buyers to "carve out" certain services and negotiate separately for them. The same reasoning has led courts to exclude from the in-patient acute care market specialty facilities providing a limited range of in-patient services such as psychiatric hospitals and rehabilitation facilities. Such facilities are unlikely to provide any constraint on acute care hospital pricing especially with

4. See United States v. Rockford Mem'l Corp., 898 F.2d 1278 (7th Cir.1990). See generally, Jonathan B. Baker, The Antitrust Analysis of Hospital Mergers and the Transformation of the Hospital Industry, 51 Law & Contemp. Probs. 93, 119–48 (1988).

5. In re Columbia/HCA Acquisition of Medical Care America, FTC docket No. C–3544, 60 Fed. Reg. 464 (Jan. 4, 1995) (defining market to include facilities providing services used by doctors to perform surgical procedures on patients not confined for more than twenty-three hours in an acute care hospital or other facility for recovery after surgery); see also, Santa Cruz Medical Clinic v. Dominican Santa Cruz Hosp., 1995–2 Trade Cas. (CCH) ¶ 71,254, 1995 WL 853037 (N.D.Cal.1995).

6. United States v. Rockford Mem'l Corp., 717 F.Supp. 1251, 1260–61 (N.D.Ill.1989), aff'd

898 F.2d 1278 (7th Cir.1990); FTC v. University Health, Inc., 1991–1 Trade Cas. (CCH) ¶ 69,-444, 1991 WL 117432 (S.D.Ga.1991), vacated 938 F.2d 1206 (11th Cir.1991); but see United States v. Carilion Health Sys., 707 F.Supp. 840, 844 (W.D.Va.1989), aff'd 892 F.2d 1042 (4th Cir.1989) (unpublished opinion) (seeming to group large range of services provided at clinics, doctors offices and other settings with hospital services provided by hospitals).

7. FTC v. Butterworth Health Corp., 946 F.Supp. 1285 (W.D.Mich.1996), aff'd 121 F.3d 708 (6th Cir.1997).

8. U.S. v. Long Island Jewish Med. Ctr., 983 F.Supp. 121 (E.D.N.Y.1997); FTC v. Tenet Healthcare Corp., 17 F.Supp. 2d 937 (E.D.Mo. 1998) rev'd on other grounds, 186 F.3d 1085, (8th Cir.1999).

regard to managed care contracting. Again, however, because these entities compete with acute care hospitals for the provision of certain in-patient services (e.g., psychiatric care), the product market for analyzing mergers between specialty hospitals (or an acquisition of a specialty hospital by an acute care hospital) should include acute care hospitals to the extent they provide the relevant service unless there is evidence that they are not viewed as substitutes.[9]

In one notable case, *United States v. Long Island Jewish Medical Center*,[10] the Department of Justice proposed a market consisting of services provided by "anchor hospitals"–those hospitals having special importance to managed care buyers because of their reputation, sophisticated services and high quality medical staff. In cases involving highly differentiated products, like hospital services, it is undoubtedly important to recognize that such factors may affect the dimensions of product market and that in some cases anchor hospitals can exercise market power even where they face competition from numerous community hospitals. However, the district court in the *Long Island Jewish Medical Center* case found the government's proof on this issue wanting, concluding that anchor facilities compete with most acute care hospitals in the provision of other services.[11]

Physician Services. Mergers or the formation of partnerships, professional corporations or other profit-share entities by physicians or physician groups that compete in providing services are categorized as horizontal mergers. Determining whether the merging physicians compete in the same product market follows the same methodology as that described for hospital mergers. That is, factfinders must ascertain what services are deemed close substitutes by consumers, and, where appropriate, may group those services in economically-meaningful clusters.

In the only reported case analyzing a physician merger, *HTI Health Services, Inc. v. Quorum Health Group, Inc.*,[12] the district court held that plaintiff had properly alleged four distinct physician service markets: primary care, general surgery, urology, and otolaryngology; in addition, it accepted a primary care submarket for pediatrics. At the same time, it rejected plaintiff's argument that a distinct market for physician services provided to managed care purchasers could be established based on buyers' discounting practices. Likewise, federal and state advisory opinions and investigations of proposed mergers of physician groups have identified narrow markets for physician services. For example, in reviewing a proposed merger between a group comprised of cardiovascular thoracic surgeons and a group of vascular surgeons, the Justice Department analyzed the specific vascular procedures that the two groups performed and defined the relevant product markets based on sixty or more overlapping procedures performed by these specialists.[13] By

9. Cf. United States v. Hospital Affiliates Int'l, Inc., 1980–81 Trade Cases ¶ 63,721, 1980 WL 1983 (E.D.La.1980) (relevant product market defined as in-patient psychiatric hospitals and non-government general acute care hospitals).

10. 983 F.Supp. 121 (E.D.N.Y.1997).

11. See discussion of unilateral effects analysis, infra § 14–52(d).

12. 960 F.Supp. 1104 (S.D.Miss., 1997). As discussed infra, the court refused to enjoin a merger of the two largest physician clinics in Vicksburg, Mississippi based on its analysis of entry conditions and likely competitive effects.

13. Letter from Joel I. Klein, Assistant Attorney General, Antitrust Division, U.S. Department of Justice to Bob D. Tucker (Re: CVT

contrast, in another business review letter, it concluded that although there was some overlap in the procedures performed by gastroenterologists and other physician specialties, gastroenterologists could probably collectively raise prices because managed care organizations viewed having gastroenterologists on their panels as a "critical selling point."[14] The Department also concluded that the service market was highly localized because many patients had "psychological barriers" to traveling even a small distance for treatment. Finding the two merging groups held between 63 and 86 per cent of the market for gastroenterological services, the Justice Department indicated that there was a substantial likelihood that it would challenge the proposed merger.[15]

Managed Care. In *United States v. Aetna and Prudential Insurance Co.*, the Department of Justice for the first time challenged an acquisition involving competing health insurance firms.[16] The government's complaint alleged that the merger would lessen competition in two product markets. First, it contended that the proposed merger would have made Aetna the dominant seller of health maintenance organization and HMO-based point of service (HMO–POS) plans in Houston and Dallas, with sixty-three and forty-two percent of enrollees, respectively, in those areas. The case was settled by consent decree but had it gone to trial, this market definition would have been sharply contested. Virtually every court that has considered the question has rejected the argument that managed care should be treated as a separate product market, choosing instead to include all forms of third-party healthcare financing.[17] However, these decisions have relied on broad economic principles of demand and supply substitution, rather than a close examination of evidence concerning the dynamics of competitive conditions in the markets at issue. In the most analytically sound approach to the issue, the First Circuit has outlined the appropriate methodology and evidentiary standard for dealing with the question. While ultimately rejecting the existence of a separate HMO product market on the facts before it,[18] the court observed that differences in price and quality between HMOs and other financing systems could establish a legally sufficient market. The court went on to frame the question of whether a sole supplier of HMO services could profitably raise price over costs, thereby suggesting that facts such as usage patterns, custom-

Surgical Center and Vascular Surgery Associated) (Apr. 16, 1997).

14. Letter from Joel I. Klein, Assistant Attorney General, Antitrust Division, U.S. Department of Justice to Donald H. Lipson (Gastroenterology Associates Limited, et al.) (July 7, 1997).

15. Id. See also Letter from Charles F. Rule, Assistant Attorney General, Antitrust Division, to William L. Trombetta (Aug. 18, 1987) (objecting to merger of two physician groups providing general surgery services); Maine v. Cardiovascular & Thoracic Assocs., P.A., 1992–2 Trade Cas. (CCH) ¶ 69,985, 1992 WL 503594 (Me.Super.Ct.1992) (consent decree).

16. 64 Fed. Reg. 44,946 (Aug. 18, 1999).

17. *See, e.g.*, Blue Cross & Blue Shield United v. Marshfield Clinic, 65 F.3d 1406, 1410–11 (7th Cir.1995) (demand and supply substitution considerations militate finding that HMOs do not constitute separate product market); Ball Mem'l Hosp., Inc. v. Mutual Hosp. Ins., Inc., 784 F.2d 1325, 1331 (7th Cir. 1986) ("Employers and individual prospective patients easily may switch from one financing package to another; nothing binds an employer or patient to one plan."); Hassan v. Independent Practice Assocs., 698 F.Supp. 679 (E.D.Mich.1988); Kartell v. Blue Shield, 582 F.Supp. 734 (D.Mass.), aff'd in relevant part, 749 F.2d 922 (1st Cir.1984). See also U.S. Healthcare v. Healthsource, 986 F.2d 589 (1st Cir.1993).

18. Plaintiffs had alleged that defendants had monopolized a distinct product market, narrowly defined as healthcare financing through IPA model HMO plans. U.S. Healthcare v. Healthsource, 986 F.2d 589, 597–98 (1st Cir.1993). See supra § 14–36b.

er surveys, features of the plans, actual profit levels, and similar data would assist the factfinder in answering the question.[19] In Aetna/Prudential, the government apparently planned to satisfy its burden by stressing demand side preferences for HMO and HMO–POS plans and the unique characteristics of those products. According to its complaint, evidence of "benefit design differences, pricing differentials and other factors" supported its contention that PPOs and indemnity plans are not reasonable substitutes for HMO and HMO–POS plans.[20] Moreover, the government noted the fact that "[n]either employers nor employees view HMOs and PPOs as the same product, and enrollees who leave an HMO disproportionately select another HMO, rather than a PPO, for their next plan."[21]

Also controversial was the product market contained in the government's alternative theory of harm. That claim was based on a monopsony theory: the merger would enable Aetna, as a buyer, to exercise market power in the market for physician services.[22] The government's market allegations asserted that there are no purchasers to whom physicians can sell their services other than "individual patients or the commercial and government health insurers who purchase physician services."[23] Therefore, the relevant product market consisting of sales of physician services to those purchasers exists on the seller's side.

Nursing Homes and Subacute Care Facilities. Mergers of nursing homes or subacute care facilities raise complex market definition issues. In its cases challenging nursing home mergers, the government has distinguished among facilities by the level of care provided.[24] Thus, skilled nursing care services may constitute a distinct market from intermediate care services because consumers would not readily substitute one for the other given the differing needs and capacities of individuals needing such care. However, the possibility that home care may substitute for the lower-service care provided by intermediate care (or subacute care) facilities may require inclusion in that relevant market. A final complexity is introduced when one considers the geographic dimensions of these product markets. Is the "origin" of the resident his or her former home? Or is it that of the closest relative? Answering this question may require knowing whether the true decision-maker in choosing the home is the resident or the family member.

Pharmaceuticals and Innovation Product Markets. Recognizing the significance of innovation in the competitive process, the government has on occasion sought to define the product market in merger cases in terms of effects on research and intellectual property. In challenging the merger of two large pharmaceutical firms, Ciba–Geigy and Sandoz, the Federal Trade Commission applied this controversial concept, analyzing the merger's effect on "innovation markets." Based on its conclusion that the combining companies'

19. *Id.* at 599.

20. *See* Complaint at ¶ 17, United States v. Aetna, No. CIV. A.3–99CV1398–H, 1999-2 Trade Cas. (CCH) ¶ 72,730 (N.D.Tex.1999) <http://www.us-doj.gov/atr/cases/12500/2571.htm>.

21. Id.

22. Id. at ¶ 33 ("the proposed acquisition will give Aetna the ability to depress physi-

cians' reimbursement rates in Houston and Dallas, likely leading to a reduction in quantity or degradation in quality of physicians' services.").

23. Id. at ¶ 17.

24. See United States v. Beverly Enterprises, Inc., 1984–1 Trade Cas. (CCH) ¶ 66,052, 1984 WL 2958 (M.D.Ga.1984)(consent decree).

competing gene therapy technologies would reduce "innovation competition" and create a monopoly in basic research in gene therapy techniques, the FTC required, as a condition of merger approval, that the firms share with competitors their "unmatched portfolio of intellectual property assets ... necessary to commercialize gene therapy markets."[25]

b. Geographic Market Definition

As with product market definition, delineating geographic markets requires an inquiry into substitution responses. Accordingly, the Guidelines mandate a determination of market responses to a hypothetical monopolist imposing a "small but significant and non-transitory" increase in price.[26] The process entails identifying the location of each merging firm and asking what would happen in the event of such a price increase. If the hypothetical price increase would not be profitable, the factfinder then adds locations which are the next best substitutes. The process is repeated until a geographic area is identified in which the participants could collectively raise price without suffering so extensive a loss of customers as to make the price increase unprofitable. In the hospital context, the question can be framed as determining the area in which patients can practicably turn and within which acute care hospitals compete for sales. However, in practice, markets are by no means capable of precise definition and judgments and accommodations are sometimes necessary in drawing boundaries. In litigation, practical indicia such as customer purchasing patterns (particularly in response to price changes), sellers' marketing and other business practices, and the costs of switching suppliers are of critical importance in evaluating substitution responses.[27] Market definitions in health care need to be particularly sensitive to local characteristics and preferences of consumers and to the imperfect market in which sellers operate.[28]

Acute Care Hospital Services. Antitrust tribunals defining markets in hospital merger cases initially tended to place heavy reliance on past usage patterns, relying particularly on data showing the geographic migration of patients. Typically, the factfinder collects data on the number of patients coming into or going out of an area for hospital services. This data, which consists of the zip code of each patient in each hospital, is used to derive an approximation of the actual sales practices or "service area" of the merging firms.[29] Although such patient flow statistics may have great intuitive and

25. Ciba–Geigy Limited, Proposed Consent Agreement, 62 Fed. Reg. 409, 411 (Jan. 3, 1997). On the concept of innovation markets, see Richard J. Gilbert & Steven C. Sunshine, Incorporating Dynamic Efficiency Concerns in Merger Analysis: The Use of Innovation Markets, 63 Antitrust L.J. 569 (1995); Robert J. Hoerner Innovation Markets: New Wine in Old Bottles? 64 Antitrust L. J. 49 (1995).

26. Merger Guidelines § 1.2.

27. Id. at § 1.21.

28. See, e.g., Delaware Health Care v. MCD Holding Co., 957 F.Supp. 535 (D.Del.1997), aff'd 141 F.3d 1153 (3d Cir.1998) (limited geographic market for home health care services

provided to post-release hospital patients who were not mobile and chose providers on non-price basis; home infusion therapy services required larger market because providers delivering services in the home could travel greater distance).

29. See Kenneth G. Elzinga & Thomas F. Hogarty, The Problem of Geographic Market Delineation in Antitrust Suits, 18 Antitrust Bull. 45 (1973) (suggesting somewhat lower thresholds, e.g., 70%, constitute "weak" evidence of a market while levels, e.g., 90%, constitute "strong evidence"); see also United States v. Rockford Mem'l Corp., 717 F.Supp. 1251, 1272 (N.D.Ill.1989), affirmed 898 F.2d 1278 (7th Cir.1990).

pragmatic appeal, a number of difficulties have been identified with exclusive reliance on such approaches.[30] This criticism, echoed by a number of courts,[31] argues that patient flow data paints a "static" picture that does not address the critical "dynamic" question of where patients would turn in the event of the exercise of market power.

Recognizing the shortcomings of patient flow statistics, the Merger Guidelines and most courts have required proof of likely patient and competitor responses to supracompetitive pricing in putative hospital markets. Although evidence derived from hypothetical questions to patients, insurers, physicians and others are occasionally used, a number of more reliable evidentiary proxies are available.[32] For example, courts look to the actual behavior of buyers and sellers such as bargaining and shopping by third party payers and employers; physician referral and staff privileges patterns; internal planning documents; and advertising and promotion by hospitals.[33]

Courts attempting to apply this standard in hospital merger cases have reached rather startlingly different conclusions about the dimensions of the geographic market. Several have concluded that hospitals compete in highly localized markets, such as one or two counties, finding that patients prefer to stay close to family and friends when hospitalized and that evidence of physician preferences and employer responses to possible price increases pointed in the same direction.[34] A number of more recent cases have drawn much wider geographic boundaries (in one case finding that a market extended 70–100 miles[35]), emphasizing the possibility that a "critical loss" of patients, induced to choose more distant hospitals if prices were raised significantly after the merger, warranted expanding the size of the relevant market.[36] Obviously, the determination of the geographic market is a highly fact-sensitive process and markets can be expected to vary significantly based on local demographics, commuting and business conditions and the availability of comparable alternative acute care hospitals. However, the cases have produced a confusing jurisprudence on how factfinders should approach answering the "dynamic" question of where patients would turn in the event of a small but significant price increase. Several courts have been inexplicably reluctant to credit the opinions of employers and insurers about their likely response and have seemed to place on plaintiffs the burden of demonstrating

---

30. See Gregory J. Werden, Market Delineation and the Justice Department's Merger Guidelines, 1983 Duke L.J. 514; The Limited Relevance of Patient Migration in Market Delineation for Hospital Merger Analyses, 8 J. Health Econ. 479 (1989); Jonathan B. Baker, The Antitrust Analysis of Hospital Mergers and the Transformation of the Hospital Industry, 51 Law & Contemp. Probs. 93, 144–45 (1988).

31. See, e.g., FTC v. Freeman Hosp., 69 F.3d 260 (8th Cir.1995).

32. An important change in the 1992 Guidelines is the emphasis on behavioral evidence rather than opinions as evidence of buyer responses to changes in price. See Paul T. Denis, An Insider's Look at the New Horizontal Merger Guidelines, 6 Antitrust, Vol. 36 (Summer 1992).

33. See, e.g., United States v. Rockford Mem'l Corp., 717 F.Supp. 1251, 1265–77

(N.D.Ill.1989), affirmed 898 F.2d 1278 (7th Cir. 1990).

34. FTC v. University Health, Inc., 938 F.2d 1206 (11th Cir.1991); United States v. Rockford Mem'l Corp., 717 F.Supp. 1251 (N.D.Ill.1989), aff'd. 898 F.2d 1278 (7th Cir. 1990).

35. United States v. Mercy Health Services, 902 F.Supp. 968 (N.D.Iowa 1995), vacated 107 F.3d 632 (8th Cir.1997).

36. See, e.g., FTC v. Tenet Health Care Corp., 186 F.3d 1045 (8th Cir.1999); FTC v. Freeman Hospital, 69 F.3d 260 (8th Cir.1995). See generally, Barry C. Harris & Joseph C. Simons, Focusing Market Definition: How Much Substitution is Necessary?, Res. In L. & Econ. 207 (1989) (economic model of critical loss analysis).

with particularity why consumers would not choose alternatives outside the market.[37] Given the somewhat speculative and uncertain nature of the inquiry, it would seem entirely appropriate for courts to give greater credence to the opinions of those who will either bear the costs of price increases (employers and employees) or those who will attempt to market health plans with incentives to travel greater distances for hospital plans (insurers). Indeed, an economically sound approach would recognize that hospital markets are subject to competition at two stages: competition of plans to enlist hospitals in their networks and competition among hospitals to attract patients, whether in their network or not.[38] In addressing the dynamic issue, courts also should not entirely ignore historical patient flow patterns which provide at least inferential proof of the strength of patient preferences.[39]

Physician Services. Defining the geographic market for physician services requires a methodology similar to that employed in the hospital merger cases. The factfinder will need to assess the geographic area from which each physician or physician group receives its patients and then determine the likely response in the face of a small but significant increase in price. Hospital data will be of obvious use for hospital-based physician practices, but because similar data is generally not available for office-based practices, less objective evidence may be required to establish current usage patterns.[40] As to the "dynamic" issue of where patients will turn, the testimony of third party payers should be given considerable weight. For example, in an advisory opinion the government suggested that where payers believed that they could steer patients needing anesthesia services to hospitals outside the local service area of merging anesthesiologists, the physician services market should be broadened to include anesthesiologists practicing at those more distant locations.[41]

§ 14–50. Identifying Market Participants

Having defined product and geographic markets, it is next necessary to determine which entities should be included when calculating market shares. The identification of market participants begins with all present sellers of the relevant product market within the relevant geographic market. It is usually appropriate to treat all hospitals in a market, which are commonly-controlled, as a single entity. Courts have also aggregated market shares for hospitals *managed* by the same firm on the theory that pricing decisions made by a single entity will be coordinated.[1] On the other hand, affiliation by two or

37. FTC v. Tenet Health Care Corp.,186 F.3d 1045 (8th Cir.1999)(implying testimony of market participant is not reliable); FTC v. Freeman Hospital, 69 F.3d 260, 270 (8th Cir.1995)(payer testimony must "specifically address the practicable choices available to consumers").

38. See Gregory S. Vistnes, Defining Geographic Markets for Hospital Mergers, 13 Antitrust 28 (Spring 1998); David Dranove & William White, Emerging Issues in the Antitrust Definition of Healthcare Markets, 1 Electronic Health Economics Letters 10 (Nov. 1997).

39. Thomas L. Greaney, Night Landings on an Aircraft Carrier: Hospital Mergers and Antitrust Law, 23 Am J. L. & Med. 191 (1997).

40. See HTI Health Services, Inc. v. Quorum Health Group, Inc., 960 F.Supp. 1104 (S.D.Miss.1997)(finding localized markets for several primary and secondary care physician specialties based on patient migration patterns and preferences for local physicians).

41. Letter from Anne K. Bingaman, Assistant Attorney General, Antitrust Division, to Terence L. Smith (Oct. 17, 1996).

§ 14–50

1. Hospital Corp. of America, 106 F.T.C. 361 (1985), affirmed 807 F.2d 1381 (7th Cir.

more hospitals with a common religious order should not invoke treatment as a single entity for merger analysis if they lack common control and are not functionally linked to a single operating unit.[2]

Under the Merger Guidelines, "market participants" includes all present sellers as well as "uncommitted entrants," i.e., those sellers who would likely enter the market within one year without the expenditure of significant sunk costs of entry in response to a price increase.[3] Thus, firms that have the capability to enter are considered to be current participants if they are likely to achieve acceptance in the market within a short period of time. Given the costs and delay facing any de novo entrant into a hospital market, it is unlikely that an entity would be considered an "uncommitted entrant" under these standards. In the case of physician mergers, however, where physicians could readily begin to perform services practiced by the merging physicians, the former should be included in the product market.[4]

§ 14–51. Market Share and Concentration Data and Their Significance

The next step is to calculate the market shares of each market participant and then determine market concentration levels. In merger analysis, the appropriate measure of concentration depends on the nature of the product market involved. In hospital markets the number of patient beds is the best available measure of capacity while patient revenues (or to a lesser extent, the number of patient days) provide a proxy for hospital output. In practice, however, the decided cases have calculated market shares and concentration levels using all available data, usually noting that no variation in outcome would be caused by considering any one of the measures.[1]

Following the lead of the 1982 Merger Guidelines, most contemporary cases employ the Herfindahl–Hirschmann Index (HHI) to measure market concentration. In contrast to measures of concentration used by the courts prior to the 1980s, the HHI is sensitive to the number, size and disparity in size of market participants. To calculate the HHI the factfinder need merely sum the squares of the market shares of each firm. The change in HHI resulting from a merger is the difference between the pre-merger HHI (with the merging firms treated as separate entities) and the post-merger HHI (combining the market share of the merged firms).[2]

1986), 481 U.S. 1038, 107 S.Ct. 1975, 95 L.Ed.2d 815 (1987).

2. See supra § 14–47.

3. Merger Guidelines § 1.3. (defining such costs as those "which would not be recouped within one year of the commencement of the supply response," assuming a "small but significant and nontransitory" price increase in the relevant market).

4. See Letter from Anne K. Bingaman, Assistant Attorney General, Antitrust Division, to James M. Parket (Oct. 31, 1994) (concluding that many physicians who are not pulmonologists can provide pulmonology services); see generally. Blue Cross & Blue Shield United of Wisconsin v. Marshfield Clinic, 65 F.3d 1406 (7th Cir.1995).

§ 14–51

1. See, e.g., United States v. Rockford Mem'l Corp., 717 F.Supp. 1251 (N.D.Ill.1989), affirmed 898 F.2d 1278 (7th Cir.1990).

2. As an example, a market consisting of four firms with market shares of 30%, 30%, 20% and 20% has a pre-merger HHI of 2600. Should the two firms with 20% shares merge, the post-merger HHI would be 3400, an increase of 800.

The Merger Guidelines provide for three levels of scrutiny based on the post-merger HHI and the change caused by the merger.[3] For mergers in markets with post-merger HHIs below 1,000, the Guidelines create a "safe harbor": it states that such mergers are unlikely to have adverse competitive effects and ordinarily require no further analysis.[4] With respect to post-merger HHIs between 1,000 and 1,800, the Guidelines state that mergers producing increases of less than 100 points are unlikely to have adverse competitive consequences while those causing increases greater than 100 points "potentially raise significant competitive concerns depending on the [other factors set forth in the Guidelines]".[5] Finally, with respect to post-merger HHIs above 1,800 (highly concentrated markets), the Guidelines state that increases of less than 50 points are unlikely to have adverse competitive consequences. Increases between 50 and 100 points "potentially raise significant concerns depending on" the other factors discussed below. Where the HHI increase is greater than 100 points, the Guidelines state "it will be presumed" such mergers "are likely to create or enhance market power or facilitate its exercise."[6] This presumption may be overcome by evidence concerning other factors elaborated in the Guidelines. This considerably watered-down presumption for highly concentrated markets marks a significant change from earlier revisions of the guidelines—and arguably from the rule announced in *Philadelphia National Bank*.[7]

The Merger Guidelines establish a separate level of scrutiny for mergers creating firms that may be able to diminish competition through unilateral behavior. Although ambiguously worded, where the combined share of the merging firms exceeds 35%,[8] the Guidelines appear to attach a somewhat stronger presumption of competitive harm than that applicable to other highly concentrative mergers. Two theories of unilateral harm are set forth. The first involves markets with differentiated products in which the merging entities are viewed as particularly close substitutes for one another.[9] The anticompetitive effects of such mergers do not require cooperation of rivals and are imposed primarily upon consumers who had viewed the services of the merging firms as their first and second choices. The second theory involves mergers in which the services sold are relatively undifferentiated and in which the merged firm possesses a substantial market share (greater than 35%) in an industry that is producing near capacity and in which expanding capacity is difficult.[10] In such circumstances, unilateral price increases or other harms are possible depending on a variety of factual issues.

The Department of Justice/FTC Policy Statements announce a "safety zone" for mergers of general acute care hospitals. Absent extraordinary

---

3. Merger Guidelines § 1.51.

4. Merger Guidelines § 1.51(a).

5. Id. § 1.51(b). These factors are discussed below in § 14–52.

6. Merger Guidelines § 1.51(c).

7. See infra § 14–52. The 1984 Guidelines had provided that "only in extraordinary cases will [other] factors establish that the merger is not likely substantially to lessen competition" in highly concentrated markets with increase of over 100 points in the HHI. 1984 Merger Guidelines § 2.0.

8. See Merger Guidelines § 2.211(under some circumstances in markets with differentiated products "market share data may be relied upon" to demonstrate that a significant number of consumers "would be adversely affected by the merger"); id. at § 2.22 (for undifferentiated product markets with firms with different capacities, "merged firms may find it profitable" to unilaterally raise price and reduce output).

9. Id. at § 2.21.

10. Id. at § 2.22.

circumstances, the agencies will not challenge mergers where one of the hospitals has fewer than 100 beds and an average daily inpatient census of fewer than 40 patients provided the hospital is at least five years old.[11] For mergers not falling within the "safety zone," the Statements indicate that Merger Guidelines principles apply and observe that the agencies have elected not to challenge hospital mergers in the past based on showings of substantial cost savings created by the merger, the unlikelihood of collusion, significant differentiation between hospitals and failing company considerations.[12]

§ 14–52.   Factors Affecting the Significance of Market Shares and Concentration Data

a.   *The Legal Standard for Rebutting the Presumption*

The rule established by the Supreme Court in *United States v. Philadelphia National Bank* provides that when market concentration and market share statistics exceed the level of presumptive illegality, the merger "must be enjoined in the absence of evidence clearly showing that the merger is not likely to have such anticompetitive effects."[1] However, the 1992 Merger Guidelines indicate, without explanation, that the Department of Justice and the FTC adopt a considerably weaker presumption: for example, in highly concentrated markets and in which the merger causes a significant increase in concentration, the Guidelines state that "the presumption may be overcome by a showing" that factors set forth in the Guidelines "make it unlikely that the merger will create or enhance market power or facilitate its exercise, in light of market concentration and market shares."[2] For moderately concentrated markets with significant increases in the HHI, the presumption all but disappears.[3]

A close examination of the *General Dynamics* case,[4] however, does not support the theory that it implicitly eviscerated the presumptive rule of *Philadelphia National Bank*. What the Supreme Court made clear was that the rule of presumptive illegality was only as strong as the data that underlie conclusions about concentration and market share. Thus, to avoid the *Philadelphia National Bank* presumption based on market share and concentration, defendants must produce evidence showing that the plaintiff's statistics give an inaccurate account of the acquisition's probable effects on competition.[5] Short of proof of the unreliability of statistical measures as a prediction of future performance, the presumptive rule should be given effect. That is, the force of the concentration-performance relationship should not be sum-

---

11. U.S. Department of Justice and Federal Trade Commission, Statements of Antitrust Enforcement Policy in Health Care, Statement 1 (1996), reprinted in 4 Trade Reg. Rep. (CCH) ¶ 13,153.

12. Id.

§ 14–52

1. United States v. Philadelphia Nat'l Bank, 374 U.S. 321, 363, 83 S.Ct. 1715, 1741, 10 L.Ed.2d 915 (1963).

2. Merger Guidelines § 1.51. See Philip E. Areeda, Antitrust Law ¶ 913.2f (1991 Supp.) (describing 1984 Guideline thresholds as "far

more hospitable to horizontal mergers than the general run of merger decisions.").

3. See Merger Guidelines at § 1.51 (such mergers "potentially raise significant competitive concerns depending on the factors set forth in §§ 2–5 of the Guidelines").

4. United States v. General Dynamics Corp., 415 U.S. 486, 94 S.Ct. 1186, 39 L.Ed.2d 530 (1974).

5. United States v. Citizens & Southern Nat'l Bank, 422 U.S. 86, 120, 95 S.Ct. 2099, 2118, 45 L.Ed.2d 41 (1975); United States v. General Dynamics Corp., 415 U.S. 486, 94 S.Ct. 1186, 39 L.Ed.2d 530 (1974).

marily dismissed any time defendants can raise some possible impediments to post-merger coordinated action. Instead, the language and holding of *Philadelphia National Bank* and the legislative history of § 7 of the Clayton Act would seem to require that a prima facie showing can be rebutted only where the evidence effectively establishes that interdependent pricing was unlikely to occur and collusive behavior would be thwarted by market conditions.[6]

Moreover, interpretation of market share data should be a two-way street. For example, inferences to be drawn from market statistics depend upon the degree of product differentiation or geographic distance between firms in the market and substitutes outside the market. Thus, as the Merger Guidelines suggest, where there is a wide gap between firms in the market and substitutes exist "at the edge of the product in geographic market," *more* market power may be present than would otherwise be inferred from market share statistics.[7]

b. *Entry Conditions*

In many recent merger cases outside the health care industry, the absence of entry barriers has been the determinative factor condoning mergers despite significant market shares and enormous levels of concentration.[8] These decisions have found as factual matter that entry by rivals was "easy" or not impeded by obstacles not already overcome by incumbents and have applied that finding to "trump" all risk to competition that might otherwise be inferred from concentration data and other evidence. The cases, however, have been criticized for failing to consider a variety of factors that must precede the determination that entry factors will mitigate anticompetitive effects. In particular, courts have often failed to make the probabilistic assessment of the likelihood of entry occurring, or consider the time frame within which that entry is likely to occur and the magnitude of entry are all highly relevant factors in the inquiry.[9]

Entry analysis has been critical in evaluating the effects of physician mergers. In *HTI Health Services, Inc. v. Quorum Health Group, Inc.*, the district court relied on the lack of entry barriers into the market and the past history of a local hospital successfully recruiting physicians to overcome presumptions of illegality resulting from market shares ranging from 67 to 100 percent in primary care, surgery and other specialty service product markets.[10] In contrast, in objecting to certain physician mergers, the Justice

---

6. See Horizontal Merger Guidelines of the National Ass'n of Attorneys General, 64 Antitrust Trade Reg. Rep. (BNA) No. 1608 (Spec. Supp. April, 1993).

7. Merger Guidelines § 1.522.

8. See, e.g., United States v. Baker Hughes, Inc., 908 F.2d 981 (D.C.Cir.1990); United States v. Syufy Enters., 712 F.Supp. 1386 (N.D.Cal.1989), affirmed 903 F.2d 659 (9th Cir. 1990). Echlin Mfg. Co., 105 F.T.C. 410 (1985); United States v. Waste Management, Inc., 743 F.2d 976 (2d Cir.1984); United States v. Country Lake Foods, Inc., 754 F.Supp. 669 (D.Minn. 1990).

9. See Merger Guidelines § 3. Perhaps not surprisingly in view of the government's suc-

cession of defeats based on entry analysis (and the propensity of some judges to note seeming inconsistencies between the arguments made by the government in litigation and in its 1984 Merger Guidelines), the revised Guidelines devote extensive attention to these factors. See generally, Jonathan B. Baker, The Problem With Baker Hughes and Syufy: On the Role of Entry in Merger Analysis, 65 Antitrust L.J. 353 (1997).

10. 960 F.Supp. 1104 (S.D.Miss.1997). See also Letter from Anne K. Bingaman, Assistant Attorney General, Antitrust Division, to Terence L. Smith (Oct. 17, 1996)(likely entry by anesthesiologists not practicing in the relevant geographic market reduced likelihood that merger would lessen competition).

Department has found that various factors, such as impediments to acquiring staff privileges[11] or the effects of physician oversupply and obstacles to establishing a new practice,[12] constituted entry barriers in the market under review.

Hospital merger cases have not posed difficult entry barrier issues principally because state regulatory requirements, economies of scale and overbedding in the market usually constitute major deterrents to entry. State CON laws requiring prior approval for building a hospital or expanding existing facilities typically impose substantial costs and administrative delay upon new entrants.[13] Likewise, potential entrants face significant practical delays in obtaining building permits, securing medical staff, and planning and constructing (or rehabilitating) a physical facility.[14]

c. *Nonprofit Status and Hospital Governance Structure*

Nonprofit hospitals have long argued that antitrust merger analysis should take into account their nonprofit status when assessing the likely competitive effects of mergers. Lacking the incentive to maximize profit, nonprofits may be less likely to increase prices or exercise market power and hence conventional assumptions regarding the relationship between market structure and performance should not apply. A number of courts have specifically rejected this contention, some flatly finding that there is nothing inherent in the structure of nonprofit entities that would operate to deter anticompetitive behavior[15] and others suggesting that there is insufficient empirical support for the proposition and rejecting a priori economic reasoning.[16]

Other courts, however, have based their conclusions that mergers are unlikely to lessen competition at least in part on the nonprofit status of the merging hospitals.[17] In the *Butterworth Hospital* case, for example, the district court examined the economic literature and expert testimony regarding the behavior of nonprofit hospitals both in Michigan and elsewhere to find that, contrary to the economic theory, nonprofits tend to charge lower prices in more concentrated markets.[18] The economic studies[19] relied upon for conclud-

---

11. Letter from Charles F. Rule, Assistant Attorney General, Antitrust Division to William L. Trombetta (Aug. 28, 1987).

12. Letter from Joel I. Klein, Assistant Attorney General, Antitrust Division, to donald H. Lipson (July 7, 1997).

13. "Entry" here includes entities opening de novo facilities, expansion by existing hospitals and new offerings of hospital services by existing providers switching to provide acute care services. As discussed above, see § 14–50, entities that can make such changes quickly and without substantial sunk cost are treated as current market participants under the Guidelines. 1992 Merger Guidelines § 1.32.

14. See, e.g., FTC v. University Health, Inc., 938 F.2d 1206, 1219 (11th Cir.1991); Hospital Corp. of America v. FTC, 807 F.2d 1381, 1387 (7th Cir.1986).

15. U.S. v. Mercy Health Services, 902 F.Supp. 968 at 989 (N.D.Iowa 1995); FTC v. University Health, Inc., 938 F.2d 1206 (11th Cir.1991).

16. United States v. Rockford Mem'l Corp., 898 F.2d 1278 (7th Cir.1990).

17. United States v. Carilion, Health Sys., 707 F.Supp. 840 (W.D.Va.1989), aff'd 892 F.2d 1042 (4th Cir.1989); FTC v. Freeman Hosp., 911 F.Supp. 1213 (W.D.Mo.1995), aff'd 69 F.3d 260 (8th Cir.1995) . See also, FTC v. Butterworth Health Corp., 946 F.Supp. 1285 at 1297 (W.D.Mich.1996) (nonprofit status "not a dispositive consideration, but ... material" given expert's empirical findings about pricing patterns of nonprofits).

18. FTC v. Butterworth Health Corp., 946 F.Supp. 1285 at 1296–97 (W.D.Mich.1996),, aff'd 121 F.3d 708 (6th Cir. 1997).

19. E.g., William J. Lynk, Nonprofit Hospital Mergers and the Exercise of Market Power, 38 J. Law & Econ. 437 (1995).

ing that nonprofit entities may not exercise market power have been questioned[20] and do not appear at this time to justify upsetting the normal presumption that market structure is a reliable indicator of the future exercise of market power. Moreover, as discussed earlier, nonprofit hospitals have in fact engaged in direct collusion, and evidence of past collusion has often been uncovered in hospital merger cases.[21] Finally, the cases have noted studies suggesting that administrators of nonprofits may tend to maximize personal benefits and perquisites and that nonprofits are motivated to maximize returns because of their need to cover sizable unreimbursed costs of care for indigent patients.[22]

The second implication the district court drew from the merged hospital's nonprofit status in *Butterworth* was that, despite its market power, the hospital would operate benignly because of its governance structure.[23] Noting that the merged hospital would be "comprised of community business leaders who have a direct stake in maintaining high quality, low cost hospital services,"[24] the court apparently concluded that these individuals would help check any price-elevating tendencies attributable to the hospitals' dominant market position. While the reliability of inferences drawn from market concentration and market share data certainly presents a cognizable issue, it is far from certain that such a result should be presumed given the roles that board members play in most corporations. First, outside members of boards of sizable business enterprises rarely involve themselves in day-to-day business decisions like pricing policies and discounting practices.[25] Second, even where a sufficient number of outside directors undertake such supervision, it is well established that they must act in the interests of the corporation on whose board they serve. Corporate law imposes fiduciary duties of loyalty, care and obedience on boards of nonprofit and for-profit corporations, and these duties preclude conflicts of interest, negligent mismanagement and failure to assure fulfillment of the entity's charitable purposes.[26] In the case of a nonprofit hospital with a charitable mission, an outside director insisting on low consumer prices may in some circumstances be in conflict with one or more of these duties.

d. Unilateral Effects Analysis

Unilateral effects exist when merging firms "find it profitable to alter their behavior unilaterally following the acquisition by elevating price and

20. E.B. Keeler et al., The Changing Effects of Competition on Non–Profit Hospital Pricing Behavior, 18 J. Health Economics 69 (1999); David Dranove & R. Ludwig, Competition and Pricing by Nonprofit Hospitals: A Reassessment of Lynk's Analysis 18 J. Health Econ. (1999).

21. See, e.g., Hospital Corp. of America, 106 F.T.C. 361 (1985), affirmed 807 F.2d 1381 (7th Cir.1986).

22. Hospital Corp. of America, 106 F.T.C. 361 (1985), affirmed 807 F.2d 1381 (7th Cir. 1986).

23. See FTC v. Butterworth Health Corp., 946 F.Supp. 1285 at 1297 (W.D.Mich.1996), aff'd 121 F.3d 708 (6th Cir.1997).

24. See id. at 1296.

25. See Robert W. Hamilton, Reliance and Liability Standards For Outside Directors, 24 Wake Forest L. Rev. 5, 9 (1989) (observing that "[m]odern boards of directors have practically nothing to do with the day-to-day business of the corporation"); see also supra at § 5–2 (describing for-profit corporations); Daniel L. Kurtz, Board Liability: Guide for Nonprofit Directors 6 (1988) (describing distinctive features of nonprofit boards).

26. See supra §§ 5–5 & 5–15—5–18.

suppressing output."[27] Government enforcement agencies have come to view unilateral effects as the primary danger in mergers involving firms supplying products or services that are differentiated. Markets particularly prone to the exercise of unilateral market power are (1) those in which products or suppliers are differentiated and (2) those in which the firms are distinguishable by the degree to which they are capacity constrained.[28] Unilateral effects are most likely to occur when the merger involves differentiated products which are the first and second choice substitutes of consumers; in these circumstances, the merged firm may be able to raise the price of one product and capture any resulting lost sales when buyers switch to the second choice product also sold by the merged firm following the merger.[29] Although in theory unilateral effects analysis can obviate the need for defining markets and calculating market shares, structural analyses remain an important aspect of assessing the likely effects of such mergers.[30]

Recent challenges to hospital mergers illustrate the potential application of unilateral effects analysis. In *FTC and State of Missouri v. Tenet Health*, the district court found that the merger would create a hospital with a dominant share (84%) of a local geographic market and would eliminate the substantial competition between the two hospitals that had existed prior to the merger, evidenced by testimony of local employers that they had played one merging hospital off against the other to secure favorable pricing. The district court found few viable substitutes, based on the quality and reputation of competing hospitals in the geographic market and that there was little opportunity for expansion or new entry.[31] In the *Long Island Jewish Medical* case, the government's theory rested on the claim that managed care buyers regarded anchor hospitals as distinct from other acute care hospitals and a "must buy" for their networks in order to satisfy their insureds' demand for a high quality, prestigious option when special needs arose.[32] It is perhaps instructive that the government was unsuccessful in both cases, as the district court in the *Long Island Jewish Medical* and the Eighth Circuit in Tenet found the government's market definitions wanting. Unilateral effects analysis has yet to establish a firm foothold in the case law and the necessity of conforming proof in such cases to long-established precedent on issues such as market definition may limit the applicability of the theory in litigation.[33]

27. Merger Guidelines § 2.2.

28. Merger Guidelines § 2.21.

29. See Jonathan B. Baker, Mergers Among Sellers of Differentiated Products, 11 Antitrust 23, (Spring 1997); Carl Shapiro, Mergers with Differentiated Products, 10 Antitrust 23 (Spring 1996). See also, FTC v. Staples, Inc., 970 F.Supp. 1066, 1088–90 (D.D.C. 1997).

30. The Merger Guidelines explain that a danger of a unilateral price increase exists where there is "a significant share of sales in the market accounted for by consumers who regard the products of the merging firms as their first and second choices, and that repositioning of the non-parties' product lines to replace the localized competition lost through the merger is unlikely." Where the merging firms' post-merger market share is at least 35%, the Guidelines appear to assume that a significant number of customers regard the merging firms' products as their first and second choices. Merger Guidelines § 2.211. See generally, Note, Analyzing Differentiated–Product Mergers: the Relevance of Structural Analysis, 111 Harv. L. Rev. 2420 (1998).

31. FTC v. Tenet Healthcare Corp., 17 F. Supp. 2d 937, 948 (E.D.Mo.1998), rev'd on other grounds, 186 F.3d 1085 (8th Cir.1999).

32. United States v. Long Island Jewish Med. Ctr., 983 F.Supp. 121 (E.D.N.Y.1997).

33. The government also pursued a unilateral effects theory in a merger involving two large pharmacy chains, contending that it would effectively force managed care companies offering pharmacy benefits to deal with the merged firm owing to the number, quality and geographic distribution of its pharmacies.

e. Factors Relevant to Anticompetitive Effects Through Coordinated Interaction

Although the enforcement agencies now emphasize unilateral effects in health sector mergers, many of the decided cases are based on oligopoly theory and hence the case law focuses on conditions that tend to impede coordination among firms. As noted above, these factors have taken on considerable importance with the erosion of the presumptive force of market share evidence. The 1992 Guidelines attempt to incorporate the insights of collusion theory[34] into merger analysis, identifying three general requirements for successful coordinated interaction: reaching terms of coordination that are profitable to the firms involved, the ability to detect deviation from those terms, and the ability to punish such deviations.[35] Using the analytic approach suggested by the Guidelines, we next discuss the factors relevant to possible collusion among hospitals.

1. Differences Among Firms

Coordination among sellers is particularly difficult where the products or services they sell are differentiated or each seller has different costs. In such circumstances, successful collusion requires agreements upon a host of factors and cheating by cartel members tends to be more likely. Hospitals sell highly differentiated services that vary along many dimensions: mix of services, amenities, reputation, geographic location, staff and quality of care, to mention a few. This suggests that colluding hospital administrators would have difficulties achieving a consensus on an appropriate collusive price because of differences in the services they offer and their costs.

Although the cases have recognized that heterogeneity and cost differences among hospitals make coordination more difficult, they have not given overriding significance to this fact.[36] Courts have instead been impressed with the fact that hospitals have overcome obstacles and colluded in the past.[37] With third party payers increasingly purchasing services through competitive bidding or negotiation and using global or per diem pricing, the number of salient variables has been reduced, thus making collusion at the bidding level less difficult despite differences among hospitals.[38] In any event, coordination may be possible with respect to limited groups of buyers or concerning limited parts of the cluster of services.

2. Demand Conditions

Collusion theory suggests that firms are less likely to successfully coordinate their activities when there are large, sophisticated buyers. So-called

---

The merging parties ultimately abandoned their plans when the FTC indicated its intention to file suit. See Jonathan B. Baker, Mergers Among Sellers of Differentiated Products, 11 Antitrust 23 (Spring 1997)(analyzing FTC's investigation of the Rite Aid/Revco merger).

34. See George J. Stigler & Robert A. Sherwin, The Extent of the Market, 28 J.L. & Econ. 555 (1985).

35. Merger Guidelines §§ 2.0–2.2.

36. American Med. Int'l, Inc., 104 F.T.C. 1, 200 (1984); Hospital Corp. of America, 106 F.T.C. 361 (1985), affirmed 807 F.2d 1381, 1390 (7th Cir.1986). Cf. United States v. Cari-

lion Health Sys., 707 F.Supp. 840 (W.D.Va. 1989), affirmed 892 F.2d 1042 (4th Cir.1989) (unpublished opinion).

37. Hospital Corp. of America v. FTC, 807 F.2d 1381 (7th Cir.1986).

38. See Hospital Corp. of America v. FTC, 807 F.2d 1381, 1390 (7th Cir.1986) (heterogeneity makes collusion more difficult, but "there is no established threshold of complexity beyond which it is infeasible."); United States v. Rockford Mem'l Corp., 898 F.2d 1278 (7th Cir.1990).

"power buyers" are likely to detect collusion among sellers and by virtue of having a large share of the seller's market, may be more able to resist anticompetitive pricing. Although this defense has been accepted in some recent non-health care cases,[39] it has been rejected on the facts presented in hospital merger cases.[40] The FTC, for example, found in one case that coordinated pricing was not readily detectable by Blue Cross despite its large market share where a charge-based system rather than competitive bidding was used.[41] Moreover, even if detected, the FTC observed that provisions in subscriber contracts and the difficulty of sending insureds to out-of-area hospitals would make it difficult to resist collusion despite the insurers' large presence in the market. On the other hand, in analyzing physician mergers[42] and hospital mergers,[43] courts and the agencies increasingly rely on the opinions of employers and managed care companies as to whether the merged entity would be able to raise price. These opinions, which are usually highly conclusory, may reflect underlying views on buyer power or the likelihood of coordinated action.

A second demand-side factor concerns the magnitude and frequency of sales by the seller. Where, for example, hospitals sign only a few, large contracts with employers, insurers and other third party purchasers, there are greater incentives to cheat on collusive arrangements. This factor has not been significant in hospital merger cases decided to date, as few health markets are dominated by a relatively small number of buyers making large purchases.[44] Moreover, even large buyers may lack good information, and even well-informed buyers may be unable to protect themselves if good alternatives are not available.

The nature of the demand for hospital services may be considered in weighing the likelihood of collusion. Courts have noted that the price elasticity of demand for hospital services is low, meaning that price increases do not lead to sharp decreases in the demand for those services.[45] In such circumstances, collusion not only is more likely, but earns higher monopoly profits, as monopoly rents resulting from reduced output are higher than in less price-elastic markets. Another demand-side factor suggesting that anticompetitive behavior is likely arises from the fact that consumers cannot arbitrage or resell services (as is often possible with commodities). Hence, colluding sellers may be able to discriminate against specific groups of buyers. In the hospital

39. See e.g., United States v. Baker Hughes, Inc., 908 F.2d 981 (D.C.Cir.1990). See generally Barbara Ann White, Countervailing Power—Different Rules for Different Markets?, Conduct and Context in Antitrust Law and Economics, 41 Duke L.J. 1045 (1992); cf. Mary Lou Steptoe, The Power Buyer Defense in Merger Cases, 61 Antitrust L. J. 493 (1993).

40. FTC v. University Health, Inc., 938 F.2d 1206, 1213 (11th Cir.1991); Hospital Corp. of America v. FTC, 807 F.2d 1381 (7th Cir.1986) (stating that "concentration of the buying side does tend to inhibit collusion.").

41. Hospital Corp. of America, 106 F.T.C. 361 (1985), affirmed 807 F.2d 1381 (7th Cir. 1986).

42. See e.g., Letter from Anne K. Bingaman, Assistant Attorney General, Antitrust Division, to Terence L. Smith (Oct. 17, 1996).

43. See, e.g., FTC v. Tenet Healthcare Corp., 17 F. Supp. 2d 937, 948 (E.D.Mo.1998), rev'd on other grounds, 186 F.3d 1085 (8th Cir.1999).

44. In recognition of the importance of the characteristics of the demand side, however, the views of group purchasers, HMOs and third party payers are given weight in close cases by enforcement authorities in making enforcement decisions. Charles F. Rule, Assistant Attorney General, Antitrust Division, Department of Justice, Remarks Before the National Health Lawyers Ass'n (Jan. 21, 1988). See also Adventist Health Sys./West, FTC No. 9234 (April 1, 1994) (noting absence of opposition to the merger from third party payers).

45. See Hospital Corp. of America v. FTC, 807 F.2d 1381, 1388 (7th Cir.1986).

context, therefore, a cartel can focus its pricing scheme on a particular insurance company, Medicaid program, HMO or other seller without the necessity of involving other groups.[46]

3. Attributes of the Merging Parties

As discussed above, courts occasionally credited arguments that the nonprofit status or governance structure of hospitals lessen the risk that they will exercise market power.[47] A number of other firm-specific considerations may also reduce the likelihood that firms will collude. For example, some courts have given weight to the financial health of the merging firms. Defendants have argued that existing and likely future financial weaknesses of one or both of the merging parties render their market shares an inaccurate measure of their future competitive significance. Relying on *General Dynamics*, some courts have held that a firm's weakened and deteriorating financial condition undermines the government's prima facie showing based on statistical concentration and market share data.[48] Federal antitrust enforcement agencies have relied upon this kind of evidence in electing not to challenge mergers far in excess of standards of presumptive illegality,[49] and the concept has been accepted in principle by at least one court evaluating a hospital merger.[50] A central difficulty is the intractability of assessing the magnitude and likely duration of financial weakness and the availability of means other than merger to rectify the problem.

One somewhat counterintuitive gauge of potential anti-competitive effects suggested by the Seventh Circuit, holds that complaints from rival hospitals concerning contemplated mergers should indicate the *absence* of competitive harm.[51] The logic of this argument rests on the observation that competing hospitals would have cause to complain about a merger that increased efficiency but would remain silent about or support anticompetitive mergers from which they would stand to benefit because of increasingly oligopolistic market structures and the potential for cartelization.[52] This factor is of questionable utility in litigation, however, and should not be afforded much weight. Rival firms will often lack information or sophistication about the kinds of potential harms the antitrust laws are designed to prevent, and their complaints may just as easily reflect personal jealousies or animosities. Moreover, if such a rule were adopted in antitrust litigation, it would likely invite strategic behavior by firms that could easily adapt their response to prospective mergers.

46. Hospital Corp. of America, 106 F.T.C. 361 (1985), affirmed 807 F.2d 1381 (7th Cir. 1986).

47. See supra § 14–52c.

48. United States v. Baker Hughes Inc., 908 F.2d 981 (D.C.Cir.1990); United States v. International Harvester Co., 564 F.2d 769 (7th Cir.1977).

49. See Charles F. Rule, Assistant Attorney General, Antitrust Division, Department of Justice, Remarks Before the National Health Lawyers Ass'n (Jan. 21, 1988).

50. See FTC v. University Health, Inc., 938 F.2d 1206, 1221 (11th Cir.1991) (weakness of acquired firm may be relevant evidence if it undermines predictive value of government's market share statistics, a defense that will be credited "only in rare cases"); but see FTC v. Tenet Healthcare Corp., 17 F.Supp. 2d 937 (E.D.Mo.1998); rev'd on other grounds, 186 F.3d 1085 (8th Cir.1999) (defense rejected where firm is profitable and viable); United States v. Rockford Mem'l Corp., 717 F.Supp. 1251, 1289 (N.D.Ill.1989), affirmed 898 F.2d 1278 (7th Cir.1990).

51. Hospital Corp. of America v. FTC, 807 F.2d 1381, 1391 (7th Cir.1986) (citing competitor complaints as defendant's "most telling point"); see, Frank H. Easterbrook, The Limits of Antitrust, 63 Tex. L. Rev. 1 (1984).

52. See Frank H. Easterbrook, The Limits of Antitrust, 63 Tex.L.Rev. 1 (1984).

Finally, a factor considered in a number of hospital merger cases has been the existence of a past history of collusion or anticompetitive behavior in the marketplace. Such evidence constitutes highly persuasive proof that the parties have overcome obstacles to collusion and therefore significant impediments to future collusive activity are unlikely.[53] While reliance on this factor is entirely appropriate, it should not obscure the importance of the other evidence that should suffice when no evidence of past collusion is present.

§ 14–53. The Failing Firm Defense

The failing firm defense is a judicially-created doctrine which, when successfully invoked, legitimizes a merger regardless of the magnitude of the parties' market shares, market concentration or other evidence. Its rationale rests on the idea that the failure of a firm causes its assets to exit the market. Therefore, the post-merger performance of the market would probably be no worse if the least anticompetitive horizontal merger were permitted than if the merger had been blocked and the firm's assets were lost to the market entirely. In addition, the defense seeks to protect the interests of creditors, employees and stockholders who would incur substantial losses absent the merger. The failing firm defense has three requirements: imminent failure, inability of the firm to reorganize in bankruptcy, and the absence of alternative purchasers.[1]

By its terms, the defense places an onerous factual burden on defendants. Financial failure must be imminent and there must be no possibility of reorganization under the bankruptcy laws. The mere fact that a firm is losing money is not sufficient. Moreover, there must be unsuccessful good faith efforts to elicit reasonable alternative offers from entities not already in the market or posing a less severe danger to competition. The Merger Guidelines define a "reasonable" offer as any offer to purchase the assets of the failing firm for a price above the liquidation value of those assets—"the highest valued use outside of the relevant market or equivalent offer to purchase the stock of the failing firm."[2] The Guidelines also recognize that "divisions" of companies may also qualify for the same treatment applicable to failing firms. However, stringent proof requirements are imposed concerning intra-corporate cost allocations and other matters.[3]

§ 14–54. The Efficiencies Defense

The issue of whether courts should weigh significant efficiencies generated by a merger against anticompetitive effects has been the subject of

53. FTC v. Cardinal Health Inc., 12 F.Supp.2d 34 (D.D.C.1998); Hospital Corp. of America, 106 F.T.C. 361, 500 (1985), affirmed 807 F.2d 1381 (7th Cir.1986); United States v. Rockford Mem'l Corp., 717 F.Supp. 1251, 1276 (N.D.Ill.1989), affirmed 898 F.2d 1278 (7th Cir. 1990).

§ 14–53

1. See Citizen Publishing Co. v. United States, 394 U.S. 131, 89 S.Ct. 927, 22 L.Ed.2d 148 (1969); Merger Guidelines § 5.1. The Guidelines add the further requirement that defendants demonstrate that "absent the ac-

quisition, the assets of the failing firm would exit the relevant market." See generally Thomas J. Campbell, The Efficiency of the Failing Company Defense, 63 Tex.L.Rev. 251 (1984).

2. Merger Guidelines § 5.1 n.36. The unexplained deletion from earlier Guidelines of the caveat that the defense should be "strictly construed" was criticized by a dissenting FTC Commissioner. See Dissenting Statement of Mary L. Azcuenaga (April 12, 1992).

3. Merger Guidelines § 5.2.

considerable dispute. The Supreme Court's somewhat ambiguous statements on the subject seem to reject such a defense.[1] While some courts interpret these statements as barring reliance on efficiencies altogether,[2] others argue that the court was only restricting use of speculative evidence purporting to demonstrate efficiencies.[3] In any event courts and the government agencies now routinely evaluate and weigh efficiencies. Though the claim of efficiencies is usually characterized as a "defense" to an otherwise illegal merger, courts have never approved a merger with strong anticompetitive tendencies based on potential cost savings.[4] Instead courts are increasingly evaluating efficiencies as one of several factors that may reduce the likelihood or magnitude of harm to consumers suggested by concentration and market share data.[5]

In the hospital merger context, savings resulting from consolidation of facilities such as laundries and specialized equipment, administrative savings and elimination of duplicative equipment and services have been considered.[6] In addition, though the government's Merger Guidelines caution otherwise, courts are increasingly willingly to credit more inchoate efficiencies such as those accruing from larger size and sophistication.[7] The law places stringent burdens on defendants asserting an efficiency defense. Notably, most authorities agree that only net efficiencies should be considered and that purported efficiencies should not be credited if comparable savings can reasonably be achieved by means other than merger.[8] The cases have adopted "clear and convincing evidence" or substantial evidence tests[9] and the burden of proof rests with the proponents of the merger.

Perhaps most difficult of all, defendants must demonstrate that the net efficiencies are greater than the potential competitive harms. Courts and

§ 14–54

1. See F.T.C. v. Procter & Gamble Co., 386 U.S. 568, 579, 87 S.Ct. 1224, 1230, 18 L.Ed.2d 303 (1967) ("[p]ossible economies cannot be used as a defense to illegality" in § 7 cases); United States v. Philadelphia Nat'l Bank, 374 U.S. 321, 371, 83 S.Ct. 1715, 1746, 10 L.Ed.2d 915 (1963) (merger that lessens competition "is not saved because on some ultimate reckoning of social or economic debits and credits it may be deemed beneficial.").

2. See RSR Corp. v. FTC, 602 F.2d 1317 (9th Cir.1979); Alan A. Fisher & Robert H. Lande, Efficiency Considerations in Merger Enforcement, 71 Cal. L. Rev. 1580, 1595 (1983).

3. See FTC v. University Health, Inc., 938 F.2d 1206, 1222 (11th Cir.1991) (presence of significant efficiency in a merger is an important consideration in predicting whether acquisition will substantially lessen competition, but will not insulate a merger that will substantially lessen competition). See also Philip E. Areeda & Donald F. Turner, Antitrust Law ¶ 941b (1991 Supp.); Timothy J. Muris, The Efficiency Defense Under Section 7 of the Clayton Act, 30 Case W. Res. L. Rev. 381, 412–13 (1980); Oliver Williamson, Economies as an Antitrust Defense Revisited, 125 U. Pa. L. Rev. 699 (1977).

4. See Merger Guidelines § 4 ("efficiencies almost never justify a merger to monopoly or near monopoly").

5. FTC v. Tenet Health Care Corp., 186 F.3d 1045 (8th Cir.1999) (although district court properly rejected efficiencies defense, "it should have considered evidence of enhanced efficiency in the context of the competitive effects of the merger").

6. See FTC v. University Health, Inc., 938 F.2d 1206, (11th Cir.1991); United States v. Rockford Mem'l Corp., 717 F.Supp. 1251, 1288 (N.D.Ill.1989), affirmed 898 F.2d 1278 (7th Cir. 1990); American Med. Int'l, Inc., 104 F.T.C. 1 (1984).

7. FTC v. Tenet Health Care Corp., 186 F.3d 1045 (8th Cir.1999) (merged hospital could provide better medical care and attract more highly qualified physicians and specialists and offer integrated delivery and some tertiary care). Cf. Merger Guidelines, § 4 (rejecting vague and speculative efficiencies, favoring those "subject to verification").

8. Merger Guidelines § 4.

9. See, e.g., United States v. Rockford Mem'l Corp., 717 F.Supp. 1251, 1289 (N.D.Ill. 1989), affirmed 898 F.2d 1278 (7th Cir.1990), 498 U.S. 920, 111 S.Ct. 295, 112 L.Ed.2d 249 (1990); American Med. Int'l, Inc., 104 F.T.C. 1, 218 (1984).

administrative law judges evaluating efficiencies in hospital merger cases have attempted to quantify the magnitude of net savings. To do so, however, involves the rather intractable task of calculating cost savings from elimination of duplicative operations (e.g., spreading fixed costs, achieving economies of scale, etc.) and subtracting from those costs the expenses of the consolidation itself. This figure must then be compared to the dollar amount representing the expected harm to competition—by most accounts a virtually impossible figure to calculate.[10] Not surprisingly, factfinders have relied on eyeball judgments that efficiencies did not seem large or that defendants had failed to show that they would be passed on to consumers.[11]

10. Alan A. Fisher & Robert H. Lande, Efficiency Considerations in Merger Enforcement, 71 Cal. L. Rev. 1580 (1983).

11. See United States v. Rockford Mem'l Corp., 717 F.Supp. 1251, 1288 (N.D.Ill.1989), affirmed 898 F.2d 1278 (7th Cir.1990) (benefits to consumers and area economy deemed irrelevant in light of preservation of competition); American Med. Int'l, Inc., 104 F.T.C. 1, 88–104 (1984).

Chapter 15

DEFINITIONS OF DEATH

Table of Sections

Research References

Am Jur 2d, Death §§ 543–569
ALR Index: Death and Death Actions; Instantaneous Death; Simultaneous Death; Uniform Simultaneous Death Act
ALR Digest: Death §§ 2–11.5; Insurance § 940
19 POF2d 377, Circumstances Warranting Inference of Death; 16 POF2d 87, Time of Death: Medicolegal Considerations

§ 15–1. Introduction

There are several discrete legal consequences of death. These include the creation and distribution of an estate,[1] the distribution of life insurance proceeds, the distribution of government and privately funded benefits, the termination of certain kinds of legal actions, the termination of contractual interests such as health insurance coverage,[2] the termination of the right to hold office or vote,[3] and, of course, the obligation to provide for the burial or other disposition of the body. Until recently, there was no difficulty in determining when death had occurred, and no suggestion that death might be defined differently for any of these purposes, or for the purposes of medicine, theology or any other discipline. Until the 1960s, at least, there was virtually no disagreement about the indicia of death, even if its noncorporeal consequences were the subject of intense speculation and disagreement. When all of the major organ systems of the body (including the heart, the lungs, and the

---

§ 15–1

1. See generally Lawrence W. Waggoner et al., Family Property Law (1991).

2. Health insurance policies generally cover only "necessary" medical care, and, by definition, care provided after death cannot be "necessary" to serve any of the interests of medicine. Thus, health insurance companies appropriately refuse to provide payment or indemnity for services supplied after an insured's death.

3. In most counties.

brain) ceased functioning, death had occurred. There was little reason to distinguish the cessation of the various body functions; when one ceased, the others already had ceased as well, or they would very soon. It is only with the advent of the ability to keep some of those processes (like heart and lung function) going after others (like brain stem function) cease that we have had to decide which of these functions is so fundamentally related to human life that its absence constitutes death.

Although scientists and philosophers have long recognized that death may be best analyzed as a process rather than an event occurring at a discrete moment in time,[4] and while the arguments for considering the breakdown of the human body as the process of death are powerful ones, the law and legal institutions need a certainty in time of death that may not be necessary for theologians, psychologists, and sociologists. Thus, while it is still sensible for theologians, grief counsellors, social workers and others to speak about the process of death, and to insist that our social institutions treat it as a process, the law does not have that luxury. Doctors may find it appropriate to delay declaring death until relatives have come to take a last look at the deceased, or until a proper support mechanism is in place for the survivors; there is nothing wrong with such a manipulation of the time of death, and it may be required by principles of ethically sound medicine. On the other hand, the law does need some definite time of death, even if there is an element of arbitrariness in the determination of that time.

§ 15–2.   Distinction Between Death and Dying

It is important to distinguish between the issue of the definition of death, where we have reached a legal and social consensus, and the question of the "right to die," where we remain far from a legal or social consensus. Discussions about the "right to die"[1] and the dying process are not discussions about the definition of death. There is no question that Karen Quinlan[2] and Nancy Cruzan,[3] for example, were alive when their highly publicized litigation was brought before the courts; the question in both cases was whether the subject of the litigation should be kept alive. The question is not whether terminally ill patients are dead but, rather, whether they should be allowed to die.

The decision to allow a dying person to discontinue life sustaining treatment is not the decision to define that person as "dead." While some people—perhaps the terminally ill, those in intractable pain, or those who simply do not wish to live any longer—may possess a right to forgo medical treatment and thus end their lives, they (or their surrogates) also maintain a correlative right to choose medical treatment that will maintain their lives. Those who are dead possess no such right. The next of kin or the estate of a

---

4. For an account of this debate and a list of the justifications for calling death either a process or an event, see the excellent debate between Robert Morrison, Death: Process or Event, 173 Science 694 (1971) and Leon Kass, Death as an Event, A Commentary on Robert Morrison, 173 Science 698 (1971).

2. In re Quinlan, 355 A.2d 647 (N.J.1976), cert. denied 429 U.S. 922, 97 S.Ct. 319, 50 L.Ed.2d 289 (1976).

3. Cruzan v. Director, Missouri Department of Health, 497 U.S. 261, 110 S.Ct. 2841, 111 L.Ed.2d 224 (1990).

§ 15–2

1. See Chapter 16.

dead person may have a right to have the body treated with appropriate respect, but that is far different from possessing a right to further medical treatment.

§ 15–3. The Traditional Heart–Lung Definition of Death

For centuries, death has been evidenced by the contemporaneous cessation of heart and lung function. What is more, these two functions have been inextricably related, so that the cessation of breathing will lead almost immediately to the cessation of heart function, and the cessation of cardiac activity will lead almost immediately to the cessation of breathing.[1] Further, the cessation of these functions was accompanied, or immediately followed, by cessation of all cognitive activity, all other brain function, and all responsiveness generally.[2]

Of these various indicia of death, the disappearance of any heart beat and the cessation of breathing were the simplest to identify, and they occurred earlier than some of the more obvious attributes of death, like putrefaction. The development of the stethoscope made the use of heart function an even easier test of life (and, given its technological base, a more apparently scientific one). The use of heart and lung function as the test of death became so well accepted, and it proved so consistent with popular expectations about death, that the irreversible cessation of all heart and lung function came to be perceived not only as evidence of death, but as the very definition of death itself. Today all states accept this "heart-lung" definition of death as at least an alternative definition; when a person's heart and lung functions have irreversibly ceased, that person is dead. Today most deaths in the United States are determined by application of the traditional heart-lung definition of death.[3]

§ 15–4. The Development of the Brain Death Definition

Two developments rendered the "heart-lung" definition inadequate. The first was the use of equipment, such as sophisticated ventilators and heart-lung machines, that allowed the heart to keep beating and the lungs operating even in the absence of any other indicia of life. Until this technological advance, the heart and lungs could be controlled only by the brain stem, and it would have been impossible for the heart and lungs to work in the absence of a functioning brain stem. After the development of this new technology, the heart and lungs could continue to function even in the absence of a functioning brain stem.

The second development that rendered the heart-lung definition inadequate was the advent of successful organ transplant techniques. While irreversible damage to the brain stem would eventually lead to the cessation of the function of the heart and lungs, that would take some time—time during which potentially transplantable organs might not be sufficiently oxygenated. Rather than delay the certain declaration of death and destroy the possibility of the transplant of healthy organs, many began suggesting that death be

§ 15–3

1. Paul Ramsey, On Updating Death, in Updating Life and Death 31 (Donald R. Cutler, ed., 1969).

2. Id. at 32.

3. Arthur E. Walker, Cerebral Death 15 (3d. ed. 1985).

declared early enough so that the organs would be available for transplantation. Ultimately, the result of these two developments was the acceptance of alternative criteria for death—the traditional heart-lung criterion in most cases, and the newer "brain death" criterion in cases where the use of life support systems, or the potential for the use of the decedent's organs for transplantation, made the traditional criteria impossible or inefficient.

In 1968, the Ad Hoc Committee of the Harvard Medical School to Examine the Definition of Brain Death proposed a new criterion for death that would meet the needs created by the two developments. This study became the first authoritative statement of the medical profession recognizing the "brain death" criterion.[1] The Ad Hoc Committee called the new criterion "irreversible coma," and it included the following characteristics: unreceptivity and unresponsivity, no movements or breathing, no reflexes, and a flat electro-encephalogram. The Ad Hoc Committee also recommended some procedures for the declaration of death: the ventilator should be removed after death is declared; the physician (and not the family) should make the decision to declare death; the physician could choose to consult with others (although the physician could choose not to do so) before declaring death; and the declaration should not be made by one with an interest in the subsequent use of the tissue of the patient.

The Ad Hoc Committee's recommendations are still considered sensible by the medical community, and they continue to be recognized today. The Committee's use of the term "irreversible coma," however, has brought about substantial misunderstanding. The "irreversible coma" defined by the Committee is not really a "coma" at all; rather, it is the complete and irreversible cessation of all brain (including brain stem) activity. The term "irreversible coma" is now sometimes used to describe a persistent vegetative state,[2] a medical condition in which all higher brain function is lost. This is different from the meaning given to the term by the Committee, which required full brain (not just higher brain) death, and there has never been any question that the "brain death" definition of death requires the complete and irreversible cessation of every part of the brain, including the brain stem.

In 1970, Kansas became the first state to adopt a statute recognizing the brain death definition of death.[3] The Kansas statute identified both the traditional heart-lung definition of death and the Ad Hoc Committee's "brain death" definition as alternative definitions, providing that "[t]hese alternative definitions are to be utilized for all purposes in this state, including the trials of civil and criminal cases, any laws to the contrary notwithstanding."[4]

The Kansas statute was the subject of a great deal of commentary and criticism, and some commentators were concerned that it might lead some to think that a person could be alive under one of the alternative statutory definitions of death and dead under the other.[5] Of course, the statute was

§ 15–4

1. See Report of the Ad Hoc Committee of the Harvard Medical School to Examine the Definition of Brain Death, 205 JAMA 85 (1968).

2. See Chapter 16 for a full description of persistent vegetative state.

3. Kan. Stat. Ann. 77–205 (originally enacted as Law of 1970, ch. 378, § 1, Kan. Stat. Ann. § 77–202 (1970)).

4. Id.

5. For a superb discussion of this debate, see Alexander Capron and Leon Kass, A Statutory Definition of the Standards for Determin-

designed to provide for alternative forms of evidence that death had occurred, not to provide for true alternative definitions of death. We do not speak of direct proof of negligence and res ipsa loquitur as being alternative torts; they are merely alternative ways of proving negligence. Physicians may use a host of different techniques to diagnose the same condition; a different combination of personal history, blood tests, physical examinations, and other alternative diagnostic tools may be used to diagnose the same cancer in different patients. Similarly, the "heart-lung" and "brain death" definitions of death are not different kinds of death; they are alternative ways of diagnosing (or proving) the same condition—death. Because the condition of death is generally perceived to be a medical one, physicians are generally called upon to determine which of these alternative methods of proof will be used to determine death in any particular case. As a general matter, physicians use the "heart-lung" definition except when the person to be declared dead is maintained on an apparatus that keeps the heart and lungs functioning; in that case, physicians use the "brain death" definition.

The response to the Kansas statute was a flurry of model acts, most designed to meet the intent of the Ad Hoc Committee. The American Bar Association, the American Medical Association, and several other organizations pressed their own versions of an appropriate statute until the National Conference of Commissioners on Uniform State Laws promulgated the Uniform Brain Death Act in 1978. This was superseded by the Uniform Determination of Death Act in 1980. The most enduring of these, the Uniform Determination of Death Act, which has been adopted in 26 states and provides the basis for the statutes adopted in several other states, says:

> An individual who has sustained either (1) irreversible cessation of circulatory and respiratory functions, or (2) irreversible cessation of all functions of the entire brain, including the brain stem, is dead. A determination of death must be made in accordance with accepted medical standards.[6]

Where no statute defining death has been promulgated, courts have been willing to accept the brain death definition in the unusual case where that is at issue, although many would seem to prefer the decision be made by legislative action.[7]

§ 15–5. Higher Brain Death

Some scholars have suggested that the permanent and irreversible cessation of all higher brain, or neocortical, functions ought to be enough to constitute death for all purposes.[1] Those who take this position argue that it is the neocortex that provides the integrative function that turns a mass of

ing Human Death: An Appraisal and a Proposal, 121 U. Pa. L. Rev. 87 (1972).

6. Unif. Determination of Death Act, § 1, 12A U.L.A. 593 (1996).

7. See e.g., People v. Eulo, 482 N.Y.S.2d 436, 472 N.E.2d 286 (N.Y.1984); Strachan v. John F. Kennedy Memorial Hosp., 538 A.2d 346 (N.J.1988); State v. Velarde, 734 P.2d 449 (Utah 1986).

§ 15–5

1. For the best account of this position, see George Smith, Legal Recognition of Neocortical Death, 71 Cornell L. Rev. 850 (1986). For another interesting approach to this issue, see Roger Magnusson, The Sanctity of Life and the Right to Die: Social and Jurisprudential Aspects of the Euthanasia Debate in Australia and the United States, 6 Pac. Rim L. & Pol'y 1 (1997).

human tissue into a human being, and that it thus makes sense to declare the death of the human being when all hope of this integrative function has ceased. This "higher brain death" or "neocortical brain death" is different from the currently well accepted form of brain death in that it would, contrary to the Uniform Determination of Death Act and all alternative statutory brain death schemes, allow for the declaration of death even when the brain stem is functioning.

It seems extremely unlikely that "higher brain death" will develop any legal significance for several reasons. First, there is no objective medical test for the complete cessation of higher brain function. While there is virtually no uncertainty in the medical diagnosis of whole brain death, there is substantial uncertainty in how much brain dysfunction is necessary for a neocortex to lose its integrative function. Second, there is a worry that accepting "higher brain death" is inappropriately allowing an act of definition to substitute for an act of policy making—most commonly, policy making regarding when someone without higher brain function should be allowed to die. Third, there is a risk that allowing for the expansion of categories of death whenever public policy appears to require it will place us on a slippery slope which will eventually tumble us into a pit where all people with cognitive impairments— and perhaps all social undesirables—can be defined away as dead. Finally, there are substantial practical problems with accepting "higher brain death." For example, it would require that we bury (or otherwise dispose of) bodies that are still breathing, and that still possess beating hearts—a macabre prospect for most people in our society.

No jurisdiction has accepted the "higher brain death" definition by statute or judicial opinion, although Virginia amended its brain death statute to remove its reference to the brain stem and, thus, has created an ambiguity about whether "higher brain death" might be accepted in that state.[2]

§ 15–6. Anencephalic Infants

Arguments in favor of "higher brain death" are somewhat more convincing in situations involving anencephalic infants.[1] Anencephaly is the most common severe birth defect in the United States.[2] An anencephalic infant is born without substantial portions of the skull and brain, including certain cerebral hemispheres and the cerebral cortex. However, these infants often have partially functioning brain stems which regulate heart and lung activity. Because anencephalic infants are permanently unconscious (due to the absence of the cerebral cortex), anencephaly has been compared to a persistent vegetative state.[3] It is invariably fatal, and, until the last few years, survival beyond a few days was extremely rare.[4] In part, this may be because little effort was made to maintain the life of those born with anencephaly. When

2. Va. Code 1950, § 54.1–2972.

§ 15–6

1. For an excellent brief bibliography on the application of the brain death standard to anencephalic newborns, see the bibliography to Council on Ethical and Judicial Affairs, American Medical Association, The Use of Anencephalic Neonates as Organ Donors, 273 JAMA 1614 (1995). For a good account of the arguments against such a practice, see Lisa Hanger,

The Ethical. Legal and Medical Objections to Procuring Organs from Anencephalic Infants, 5 Health Matrix 347 (1995).

2. In re T.A.C.P., 609 So.2d 588, 590 (Fla. 1992).

3. *Id.*

4. David A. Stumpf et al., The Infant with Anencephaly, 322 New Engl.J.Med. 669, 671 (1990) (stating that two months was the longest documented survival).

the full panoply of medical interventions is applied to such children, they may live for months, or even years. In one case, the mother of an anencephalic infant litigated a highly publicized action to assure her anencephalic daughter continuing emergency treatment under the Emergency Medial Treatment and Active Labor Act.[5] She was ultimately successful in the Fourth Circuit, and the child, who was provided all available treatment on her regular emergency admissions to the hospital, lived for more than two years.

Since anencephalic infants have at least a partially functioning brain stem, their condition would not fulfill the criterion of whole brain death under either the Uniform Determination of Death Act or alternative statutory schemes.[6] Nonetheless, there have been suggestions that whole brain death be expanded to specifically include anencephaly or, alternatively, that a new definition of death be created based on this condition. Currently there is a great need for transplantable organs among small children, and it is estimated that up to half of these children die before an appropriate organ becomes available.[7] Because at birth an anencephalic infant may have some healthy organs, such as a heart, a liver, or kidneys, the infant is a potentially good candidate for organ donation. However, these organs are no longer suitable for transplantation by the time whole brain death occurs.[8] As a result, any transplantation would have to occur within the few days between birth and whole brain death. Although some states may allow parents to terminate life-sustaining treatment for an anencephalic infant, the existence of a functioning brain stem would require some affirmative act, not sanctioned by the law, to end the infant's life. Thus, unless these infants are declared dead under some alternative standard, they would not be eligible to donate any organs.[9]

In one case, parents of an anencephalic infant petitioned the Florida courts to allow their child to be declared dead so that the infant's organs could be used for transplantation.[10] After deciding that state and federal constitutional provisions and the state statute did not resolve the case,[11] the court discussed whether the common law definition of death should be expanded to include anencephaly. The Court found no consensus that either public necessity or any interest in preserving fundamental rights would be served by including anencephaly in the common law definition of death. The

---

5. In the Matter of Baby K, 16 F.3d 590 (4th Cir. 1994). See chapter 10 for a discussion of the Act.

6. In fact, the Task Force on the Determination of Brain Death in Children of the American Academy of Pediatrics has determined that the "brain death" criterion should not be used in children under 7 in any case, and thus anencephalic infants are not candidates for a declaration of "brain death" even if they otherwise meet the requirements. See Task Force on the Determination of Brain Death in Children, Guidelines for the Determination of Brain Death in Children, 80 Pediatrics 298 (1987).

7. Jeffrey R. Botkin, Anencephalic Infants as Organ Donors, 82 Paediatrics 250 (1988); see also Joyce L. Peabody et al., Experience With Anencephalic Infants as a Source for Pediatric Organ Transplants, 90 Colum. L. Rev. 917 (1990); Kathleen L. Paliokas, Note, Anencephalic Newborns as Organ Donors: An As-

sessment of "Death" and Legislative Policy, 31 Wm. & Mary L. Rev. 197 (1989). For an excellent analysis of this issue, see American Academy of Pediatrics Committee on Bioethics, Report on Infants With Anencephaly as Organ Sources: Ethical Considerations, 89 Pediatrics 1116 (1992).

8. Stephen Ashwal et al., Anencephaly: Clinical Determination of Brain Death and Neuropathologic Studies, 6 Pediatric Neurology 233, 239 (1990).

9. In re T.A.C.P., 609 So.2d 588, 593 n. 9 (Fla.1992).

10. *Id.* at 589 ("[P]arents both testified in court that they wanted to use this opportunity to give life to others.").

11. *Id.* at 593 n.9. The Court pointed out that Roe v. Wade did not attempt to "resolve the difficult question of when life begins." 410 U.S. 113, 159, 93 S.Ct. 705, 730, 35 L.Ed.2d 147 (1973).

incidence of anencephaly is decreasing yearly as a result of better prenatal care and, possibly, increasing antenatal screening.[12] In addition, transplantation procedures using organs of anencephalic infants have been questioned by the medical community.[13] Further, the Court recognized the concern among some scholars that defining these infants as dead for purposes of transplantation could lead to further extensions of the definition of death in other areas to meet various societal needs.[14] Finally, the Court recognized that individuals and organizations in both the legal and medical communities have not reached a consensus on whether this condition should be included in the definition of death.[15] Thus, the Court refused to extend the common law definition of death to include anencephaly.

In 1995 the Council on Ethical and Judicial Affairs of the American Medical Association reversed its 1988 determination that organs could be harvested from anencephalic infants only after their death and it announced that "it is ethically acceptable to transplant the organs of anencephalic neonates even before the neonates die, as long as there is parental consent and other safeguards are followed."[16] The Council detailed the shortage of organs available for transplant in infants and young children and the utilitarian benefits of permitting such transplants, and pointed out that such transplants would be permitted only when "(1) the diagnosis of anencephaly is certain and is confirmed by two physicians *with special expertise* who are not part of the organ transplant team; (2) the parents of the neonate *initiate any discussions about organ retrieval* and indicate their desire for retrieval in writing, and (3) there is compliance with the Council's Guidelines for Transplantation of Organs."[17] This opinion proved to be highly controversial among physicians across the country, and it was withdrawn almost immediately after its release, although the original 1988 opinion prohibiting the harvesting of organs from anencephalics before death. was never reinstated. The issue has remained under study since that time, and it is not the subject of any current AMA Council opinion.

Since the incidence of anencephaly appears to be decreasing, as the Florida Supreme Court recognized, and other ways of providing transplants for neonates and children are being developed, this controversial issue is likely to become increasingly less important. It seems likely that future state legislative debates on this issue will parallel that of the Florida court.

§ 15–7. Allowing Individuals to Choose Their Own Personal Definitions of Death

Some scholars have suggested that individuals should be able to choose the definition of death that best fits their own values and interests. One

---

12. Shlomo Shinnar et al., Ethical Issues in the Use of Anencephalic Infants as Organ Donors, 7 Ethical Issues in Neurologic Practice 729, 741 (1989).

13. D. Alan Shewmon et al., The Use of Anencephalic Infants as Organ Sources, 261 JAMA 1773, 1774–1775 (1989).

14. Debra H. Berger, The Infant With Anencephaly: Moral & Legal Dilemmas, 5 Issues in L. & Med. 67, 84–85 (1989); see also Arthur Caplan, Should Fetuses or Infants be

Utilized as Organ Donors?, 1 Bioethics 119 (1987).

15. In re T.A.C.P., 609 So.2d 588, 594 (Fla. 1992).

16. See Council on Ethical and Judicial Affairs, American Medical Association, The Use of Anencephalic Neonates as Organ Donors, 273 JAMA 1614 (1995).

17. Current Opinion 2.162, Anencephalic Neonates as Organ Donors [subsequently withdrawn], *id.*

leading bioethicist, John Fletcher, has executed a living will asking that his organs be made available for transplantation if he is in a persistent vegetative state (i.e., if all of the cognitive portions of his brain permanently and irreversibly cease functioning).[1] While he may prefer to think of this as a method for choosing his own definition of death, it might also be viewed as a request that he be killed when life has lost all value to him and when his death can improve the quality of life for others. Whether he should be able to make such a choice might better be discussed as a question of whether one ought to be able to terminate one's own life for the benefit of others, rather than as a question of whether one ought to be able to declare one's own death or set the criteria for someone else to do so.

Generally, states do not recognize a statutory right for individuals to choose the definition of death that will apply to their own demise. However, one state—New Jersey—has given formal authority to a family to effectively overrule an attempt to declare a relative dead using brain death criteria if the family's rejection of the concept of brain death is based on religious beliefs.[2] In such a case, the individual would not be declared dead until the criteria for heart-lung death could be established.[3]

The New Jersey family veto of the whole brain definition of death and the Fletcher attempt to permit individual choice in the definition of death reflect a misunderstanding of the way law and medicine have perceived death, as well as a continuing confusion over the difference between finding that a person is dead and allowing that person to die. The definition of death is a factual and medical landmark evaluated by scientifically verifiable criteria in accordance with accepted medical standards; the decision that someone should be allowed to die is a value laden decision. Death is a medical matter; allowing one to die is a matter infused with policy. Just as we do not allow individuals to decide to choose their age by counting from either the moment of birth or the moment of conception, whichever is most consistent with their own religious views, we ought not allow them to choose the time of their death based on the application of alternative definitions of death.

§ 15–8. Definition of Death and Homicide

In several cases, defendants in homicide actions have argued that they cannot be guilty of homicide because the victims of their violent acts did not exhibit the complete cessation of heart and lung function until those victims were removed from life support systems. Thus, it is argued, the death that ensued was caused by the physician's act of removing the patient from necessary medical care and not by the defendant's act. The defendant cannot, therefore, be guilty of anything more than causing some form of grievous bodily harm; the actus reus for homicide simply is not present even if the mens rea could be established. In addition, under the common law and the criminal laws of some states, a person cannot be prosecuted for a homicide if the death did not occur within a year and a day of the act; the theory was that causation would be too tenuous if the death followed the act by so much time.

§ 15–7

1. Gina Kolata, Ethicists Debate New Definitions of Death, New York Times, April 29, 1992, p. C–13.

2. N.J. Stat. Ann. 26:6A–5.

3. Id.

Thus, the defendant may also argue that a victim kept alive for a year and a day by the use of life support should not provide the corpus delecti for the homicide.

Defendants have also argued that the physician's motivation in terminating the life support systems is to harvest the organs for transplantation. This doctor-as-intervening-cause defense has never been successful in a homicide prosecution.[1] Whether the case is one in which the victim is allowed to die while on a ventilator or other life support or one in which the victim is simply declared brain dead while on such support, the courts have found that the act which necessitated the life support is the legal cause of the death. One court has pointed out that even if the announcement of death were made prematurely "due to a doctor's negligence," the subsequent removal of life support systems "would not constitute a superseding cause of death relieving defendants of liability."[2] In order for the doctor's act to be a superseding cause it must either be grossly negligent, intentional, or "a grave deviation from accepted medical practices or [constitute a] disregard for legally cognizable criteria for determining death."[3] As a matter of general course, courts have been willing to accept brain death in homicide cases even if their state legislature has not adopted a statute explicitly recognizing it, although some courts have limited their acceptance of brain death to homicide cases under such circumstances.[4] Finally, one court has suggested that the question of what definition of death ought to be applied to the victim in a homicide case is itself a question for the jury.[5]

§ 15–9. The Process for the Declaration of Death

Because the declaration of death is a scientific medical matter, it is governed by medical standards, not legal ones. The Uniform Determination of Death Act[1] provides that the determination of death is to be made "in accordance with accepted medical standards." Because the medical standards will change over time and because those standards may depend on the various diagnostic tools available at different times and in different places, it is sensible for the law to provide for the basic definition, but for good medical practice to determine what counts as good evidence that the definitional requirement has been met.

Currently, for a physician declaring death based upon brain death criterion, good medical practice requires the confirmation of the absence of any response to stimulus and the absence of any spontaneous respiration and cardiac activity.[2] In addition, the Ad Hoc Committee's advice that life support systems not be removed before the declaration of death is made and the recommendation that any physician involved in the subsequent transplant of

§ 15–8

1. See e.g., Commonwealth v. Golston, 366 N.E.2d 744 (Mass.1977).

2. People v. Eulo, 482 N.Y.S.2d 436, 447, 472 N.E.2d 286, 297 (N.Y.1984).

3. Id.

4. Commonwealth v. Golston, 366 N.E.2d 744 (Mass.1977); State v. Meints, 322 N.W.2d 809 (Neb.1982).

5. People v. Lai, 516 N.Y.S.2d 300 (N.Y.App.Div.1987).

§ 15–9

1. Unif. Determination of Death Act, § 1, 12A U.L.A. 593 (1996). For the text of the act, see § 16–4.

2. See generally Arthur Walker, Cerebral Death (3d ed. 1985).

organs from a cadaver not be involved in the declaration of death[3] remain good advice, although they are not required by law. Generally, a physician declaring a patient dead by the application of either the heart-lung criterion or the brain death criterion has a certain amount of leeway at the time the declaration of death is made. While it would be inappropriate to manipulate the time of death for financial advantage (so that the hospital could bill for one more day of service, for example), it is well accepted medical practice for the physician to act with a concern and sensitivity to family members and others affected by the death. It would not be inappropriate to allow a few hours for the arrival of distant relatives, who could thus see their family member "alive" once more, before declaring the patient dead.

3. See Report of the Ad Hoc Committee of the Harvard Medical School to Examine the Definition of Brain Death, 205 JAMA 85 (1968).

Chapter 16

Making Decisions About Death and Dying

Table of Sections

Research References

Am Jur 2d, Guardian and Ward §§ 101, 129

ALR Index: Guardian and Ward; Health Care; Life Support; Power of Attorney

ALR Digest: Guardian and Ward §§ 31.3–37

Am Jur Legal Forms 2d, Agency §§ 14:176–14:179

Am Jur Pleading and Practice Forms (Rev), Incompetent Persons § 453

19 POF3d 335, AIDS Dementia–Incapacity to Execute Will; 18 POF3d 185, Alzheimer's and Multi–Infarct Dementia–Proceedings to Appoint Guardian Based on Incapacity; 17 POF3d 219, Alzheimer's and Multi–Infarct Dementia–Incapacity to Execute Will

63 Am Jur Trials 1, Decisionmaking at the End of Life

A. INTRODUCTION—THE RIGHT TO FORGO LIFE SUSTAINING TREATMENT

§ 16–1. Decisions to Forgo Life Sustaining Treatment

Our interests in death are necessarily as important as our interests in life; death is the only inevitable attribute of life (for those with good tax counsel, in any case). The personal freedom and integrity that are implicated in choices regarding death are, thus, part of the personal freedom and integrity important to leading a good life; as Justice Stevens has pointed out, "death is not life's simple opposite, or its necessary terminus, but rather its completion. Our ethical tradition has long regarded an appreciation of mortality as essential to understanding life's significance."[1] Given the mystery of death, the value laden nature of inquiries surrounding death, and the variety of ethical and religious approaches to this issue, it would be surprising if there were any social consensus on the conditions under which death is "appropriate". Because individuals' attitudes on death are built, in the greatest part, upon their belief about what makes life meaningful, it is hard to imagine a question upon which there are more diverse individual attitudes than issues involving death.

Whether a person should choose death over continuing life in any particular instance is, of course, a far different question than whether a person should have the opportunity to make the choice. The law has intervened to define rare circumstances in which a person should (indeed, must) choose continuing life, while also generally accepting the principle that the choice can be made by the individual in most circumstances.

The principled conflict in this area arises out of two different streams of well accepted ethical analysis, each of which is reflected in a well established principle of law. On the one hand, the law has traditionally acted to preserve life and, formally, to respect the sanctity of life. Most states have laws against aiding and abetting suicide, and all societies have laws against murder. Further, the defense of consent, available in other assault cases, is never available in cases of homicide. On the other hand, one's control over one's own body, and the right to determine what kind of medical care one will receive, is equally well respected and historically grounded. It is a violation of tort law, at the very least, to provide medical care without the consent of the patient. What, then, is the position of the law when a person chooses a course

§ 16–1

1. Cruzan v. Director, Missouri Dept. of Health, 497 U.S. 261, 343, 110 S.Ct. 2841, 2885, 111 L.Ed.2d 224 (1990) (Stevens, J., dissenting).

of action that will result in that person's death—i.e., when a person claims a "right to die"?

The answer is often uncertain, and it depends upon a host of factors that take on different levels of significance in different jurisdictions. Where the individual making the choice concerning medical treatment is competent, the issue is likely to be treated differently than when that person is incompetent. When the incompetent person whose life is at stake has articulated a clear and certain choice before the ensuing incompetence, the issue is likely to be treated differently than when that person has never articulated the choice, or has articulated the choice in an uncertain or unreliable manner, or has never been sufficiently competent to make the choice. When the person making the choice is terminally ill, or in severe pain, that choice may have a different legal status than a choice made by a healthy person. Not surprisingly, adults are given a much greater range of choice than children. A request to withhold or withdraw treatment will be granted more easily than a request to have a physician affirmatively cause death. In some jurisdictions the choice to forgo medical care designed to provide nutrition and hydration is treated differently from the choice to forgo medical care designed to sustain other life processes.

The development of varying substantive law in different states also reflects different procedural mechanisms that have brought these issues before the courts and the different parties considered appropriate in these cases. Some cases have come before the courts as guardianship or declaratory judgment actions, some as other wardship proceedings under states' probate codes, some as civil rights actions, some as declaratory judgment actions commenced by health care providers to protect themselves from liability, some as habeas corpus or other extraordinary writ actions, some as actions for damages, and some in unspecified form under general jurisdictional requirements. In addition, they have been argued on a host of different substantive legal bases, including the due process and equal protection clauses of the United States Constitution, the equivalent provisions of state constitutions, state constitutional and statutory rights of privacy, and the common law, including the common law of negligence manifested in the law of informed consent.

Finally, rights recognized in the substantive law may become meaningless as a result of the procedural requirements imposed by some state courts. State courts requiring clear and convincing evidence of a patient's actual statements that treatment be discontinued place such a procedural burden on those seeking the termination of treatment that the substantive law is virtually irrelevant.[2] Whatever the law in those states, it will be impossible for those seeking termination of treatment to adduce evidence sufficient to meet the burden of proof.

"Right to die" law is only beginning to mature. State statutory law varies a great deal, and while Oregon goes so far as to permit physician assisted suicide in some cases, most commonly state law is limited to the legal form and enforceability of advance directives. The uniform laws promulgated in this area have not been well received in the states.[3] State common law is

---

2. See Cruzan v. Harmon, 760 S.W.2d 408 (Mo.1988); In re Westchester County Medical Center on behalf of O'Connor, 534 N.Y.S.2d 886, 531 N.E.2d 607 (N.Y.1988).

3. See Unif. Rights of the Terminally Ill Act, § 10, 9B U.L.A. 93 (1989); see also Mar-

equally diverse and inconsistent. Finally, except for Congressional efforts to limit the availability of prescription drugs for use in physician assisted death, there has been no serious attempt to make this law consistent nationally. The United States Supreme Court has announced that the United States Constitution supplies few limitations on what states can do in this area.[4] An understanding of this area of law, then, requires an understanding of the loose United States Constitutional framework as well as the state constitutional and statutory law, and principles of the common law that have been applied to resolve these questions.[5]

§ 16–2. The Federal Constitutional Foundation

The United States Supreme Court has addressed directly the right to forgo life sustaining treatment in only one case.[1] Unfortunately, the ambiguous holding in this case has created more uncertainty about the Constitutional status of any right to forgo life sustaining treatment than it has resolved, and it has left those who favor both broad and narrow interpretations of this right looking to state legislatures and state courts for support. The five justice majority was itself fractured by two concurring opinions, one by Justice O'Connor[2] and one by Justice Scalia[3], that seem inconsistent with the opinion of the Court by the Chief Justice. Indeed, Justice O'Connor seemed far more comfortable with the reasoning of the dissenters,[4] Justice Brennan[5] and Justice Stevens.[6] Justice Scalia rejected most of the fundamental principles adopted by the other eight Justices.[7] While the Supreme Court revisited some aspects of this "right to die" case several years later in two companion cases seeking to establish a right to a physician assisted death[8], the uncertainty created by the original case has been dissipated more by the practical medical acceptance of decisions to terminate life sustaining treatment than by any subsequent judicial decision.

Nancy Cruzan was injured in a one-car automobile accident on a late January night in 1983. She was probably without oxygen for twelve to fourteen minutes, and she suffered what soon proved to be profound and irreversible brain damage. Doctors aggressively treated Ms. Cruzan when she arrived at the hospital because they were uncertain about her condition. Despite this treatment, Ms. Cruzan remained in a coma for three weeks

querite Ann Chapman, "The Uniform Rights of the Terminally Ill Act: Too Little, Too Late?" 42 Ark. L. Rev. 319, (1989).

4. Cruzan v. Director, Missouri Dept. of Health, 497 U.S. 261, 278–84, 110 S.Ct. 2841, 2851–55, 111 L.Ed.2d 224 (1990).

5. The best general reference on the right to die, and one that could be cited in virtually every section of this chapter, is Alan Meisel, The Right to Die (1989 and 1994 cum.supp.).

§ 16–2

1. Cruzan v. Director, Missouri Dept. of Health, 497 U.S. 261, 110 S.Ct. 2841, 111 L.Ed.2d 224 (1990); see generally Thomas W. Mayo, "Constitutionalizing the 'Right to Die,'" 49 Md.L.Rev. 103 (1990).

2. Cruzan, 497 U.S. at 287, 110 S.Ct. at 2856 (O'Connor, J., concurring).

3. See id. at 292, 110 S.Ct. at 2858 (Scalia, J., concurring).

4. See id. at 292, 110 S.Ct. at 2858 (O'Connor, J., concurring).

5. Id. at 301, 110 S.Ct. at 2863 (Brennan, J., dissenting) (joined by Justices Marshall and Blackmun).

6. Id. at 330, 110 S.Ct. at 2878 (Stevens, J., dissenting).

7. Id. at 293, 110 S.Ct. at 2859 (Scalia, J., concurring).

8. Washington v. Glucksberg 521 U.S. 702, 117 S.Ct. 2258 (1997); Vacco v. Quill 521 U.S. 793, 117 S.Ct. 2293 (1997). For a discussion of these cases, see section 16–72 below.

before she was able to take any nutrition by mouth. Eventually, doctors surgically inserted a gastrostomy and hydration tube (a flexible tube designed to allow nutrition to be put directly in the stomach). In addition, various health care workers commenced a host of different therapies aimed at returning any potential function Ms. Cruzan might be able to attain. The treatments proved unsuccessful and Ms. Cruzan was diagnosed as being in a persistent vegetative state—a state which the Supreme Court defined as "a condition in which a person exhibits motor reflexes but evinces no indications of significant cognitive function."[9] Ms. Cruzan did not need ventilator support because she could breathe on her own. While there was no chance that Ms. Cruzan would regain any cognitive function, she could remain alive for years—indeed, for decades—if she were to receive proper nutrition. The cost of Ms. Cruzan's treatment was paid by the state of Missouri.

Six years after the accident, Ms. Cruzan's parents asked the state hospital where she was being maintained to discontinue her nutrition and hydration and allow her to die. Either because the administration and staff thought that this was an ethically and medically inappropriate action, or because they were concerned about their potential liability, they refused to allow for the removal of the nutrition and hydration without a judicial order supporting such action. Ms. Cruzan's parents, who were also her legal guardians, received a court order from the state probate court allowing the discontinuation. The court based its decision on Ms. Cruzan's general assertion to a friend that she "would not wish to continue her life unless she could live at least halfway normally"[10] as well as on her own best interests and her family's wishes.

Against strong dissents, the Supreme Court of Missouri reversed the probate court in a 4–3 decision that established a new and extremely rigorous procedure for the termination of life sustaining treatment in the case of an incompetent patient.[11] The Missouri Supreme Court determined that life sustaining treatment could be removed in such cases only upon the presentation of evidence of statements by the patient herself that prove, by clear and convincing evidence, that the patient would want the particular treatment in question removed under the circumstances then faced by that patient. Ultimately, the Missouri decision was significant because it required 1) evidence in the form of the words of the patient herself, and 2) that this evidence clearly and convincingly show that the patient would discontinue the treatment at issue under these circumstances. In addition, the court appeared to require the patient to have considered the precise kind of treatment she was receiving, under the precise conditions in which she was now receiving it. A petitioner could rarely—if ever—meet these standards without manipulating evidence to take the required form. In other words, the Missouri Supreme Court allowed for the termination of treatment as a substantive matter, but effectively prohibited it as a matter of process.

Ms. Cruzan's family sought review in the United States Supreme Court, which affirmed the decision of the Missouri Supreme Court and suggested that the issue was one more likely to be resolved at the state, rather than federal, level. As Chief Justice Rehnquist pointed out in the prologue to his

9. Cruzan v. Director, Missouri Dept. of Health, 497 U.S. 261, 266, 110 S.Ct. 2841, 2845, 111 L.Ed.2d 224 (1990).

10. Id. at 268, 110 S.Ct. at 2846.

11. Cruzan v. Harmon, 760 S.W.2d 408 (Mo.1988).

legal analysis of this question, "[s]tate courts have available to them for decision a number of sources—state constitutions, statutes, and common law—which are not available to us. In this Court, the question is simply and starkly whether the United States Constitution prohibits Missouri from choosing the rule of decision which it did."[12] The Supreme Court found that the Missouri requirement that there be "clear and convincing evidence" that the patient would want nutrition and hydration discontinued before allowing for termination was not a violation of the due process clause of the United States Constitution. This procedure—like virtually any other a state might impose before permitting the withdrawal of treatment on an incompetent person—was within the discretion of the state. While such a procedure is not Constitutionally required, it is not forbidden, either.

One of the few issues thus resolved by the Cruzan case is the breadth permitted to state law by the United States Constitution: virtually any procedure developed by a state to implement that state's substantively defined rights will be consistent with the United States Constitutional requirements. However, the Court did set some outside limits on the states' manipulation of these rights. First, the Court accepted the principle, at least "for the purposes of this case,"[13] that a competent person's right to forgo medical treatment—including nutrition and hydration—is a protected liberty interest under the Fourteenth Amendment of the United States Constitution. The fact that the four dissenters and Justice O'Connor all explicitly recognize that there is such a protected Constitutional interest has led some to say that the Cruzan case was the first to find a Constitutional right to die[14]. Second, the Court explicitly announced that the Constitutional inquiry would focus on the general "liberty interest," and not on the right of privacy that had given the Court so much difficulty in abortion related cases.[15] Third, the Court recognized that states may assert an "unqualified interest in the preservation of human life."[16] The state does not have to consider the quality of that life when deciding how to balance the preservation of life against the liberty interest of the individual; the Court thus suggested that statutory restrictions on assisting suicide are constitutional. Fourth, the majority held that the state could distribute the risk of erroneous decisionmaking as it saw fit, leaving the state the power to impose any procedural burden it wished in cases involving the right to forgo

---

12. Cruzan, 497 U.S. at 277, 110 S.Ct. at 2850.

13. Id. at 279, 110 S.Ct. at 2852.

14. Subsequently in Washington v. Glucksberg 521 U.S. at 725, 117 S.Ct. at 2270, the Chief Justice restated that this was merely an "assumption" for the purposes of the Cruzan case. On the other hand, in her concurring opinion in that case Justice O'Connor (for herself, Justice Ginsburg and Justice Breyer) argued:

"Cruzan makes it clear that some individuals who no longer have the option of deciding whether to live or to die because they are on the threshold of death have a constitutionally protected interest that may outweigh the state's interest in preserving life at all costs."

Id. at 745, 117 S.Ct. at 2307. These justices also agree that Cruzan gave patients a right to avoid suffering at the end of life, "even when doing so would hasten their deaths." Id. at 738, 117 S.Ct. at 2303.

15. Cruzan v. Director, Missouri Dept. of Health, 497 U.S. 261, 279 n. 7, 110 S.Ct. 2841, 2852 n. 7, 111 L.Ed.2d 224 (1990) (stating that although many state courts had analyzed this issue in terms of privacy, the liberty interest under the Fourteenth Amendment provides the proper framework, citing Bowers v. Hardwick, 478 U.S. 186, 106 S.Ct. 2841, 92 L.Ed.2d 140 (1986)).

16. Id. at 282, 110 S.Ct. at 2853.

life sustaining treatment.[17] Finally, the opinion of the Court announced that states need not permit any surrogate decision making; they may choose to defer only to the wishes of the patient.[18]

This last point was strictly qualified. The Chief Justice pointed out that the opinion did not address the question of whether a state would be required to carry out the wishes of a surrogate appointed by the patient while the patient was still competent.[19] Indeed, Justice O'Connor's concurring opinion points out that recognizing a patient appointed surrogate's decision "may well be constitutionally required to protect the patient's liberty interest in refusing medical treatment."[20] This is a point on which she seems to agree with the four dissenting Justices.

The four dissenting Justices and Justice O'Connor agreed on two other significant issues left open in the majority opinion—they agreed that a competent patient has a liberty interest in avoiding unwanted medical treatment and that the provision of artificial nutrition and hydration by medical devices is a form of medical care to be treated no differently than any other form of medical treatment. It is hard to know the jurisprudential value of these agreements; they concern principles not addressed by the Court in its majority opinion, but adopted independently by a majority of the Justices sitting on the Court in 1990.

The dissenting opinions vividly articulate the arguments rejected by the Court. The most significant of these is the argument that the state can have no interest in the continuation of mere biological life. Despite Justice Brennan's dissenting argument that "the state has no * * * interest in someone's life, completely abstracted from the interest of the person living that life, that could outweigh the person's choice to avoid medical treatment,"[21] the majority was willing to find that a state could decide that mere biological existence could be accorded recognition as the primary legal attribute of human life. Further, even though "Missouri is virtually the only [state] to have fashioned a rule that lessens the likelihood of accurate determinations,"[22] the majority rejected the argument that the procedures developed by a state for removing life sustaining treatment must be designed to increase the accuracy of those determinations. The majority seems to find an inaccurate result tolerable so long as it is justified by some public policy. In this situation, the majority found that the inaccuracy reduces one kind of error (the inappropriate removal of treatment) even if it increases another (the inappropriate continuation of treatment), and the direction of error is a matter of substantive state policy.[23]

Ultimately, the most important differences between the majority and the dissent are the amount of significance given to the liberty interest at stake and the degree of deference given to any state in developing procedural law arguably inconsistent with the effective exercise of a person's Constitutional

17. Id. at 282–83, 110 S.Ct. at 2854.

18. Id. at 286–87, 110 S.Ct. at 2855–56.

19. Id. at 287 n. 12, 110 S.Ct. at 2856 n. 12.

20. Cruzan v. Director, Missouri Dept. of Health, 497 U.S. 261, 289, 110 S.Ct. 2841, 2857, 111 L.Ed.2d 224 (1990) (O'Connor, J., concurring).

21. Id. at 313, 110 S.Ct. at 2869 (Brennan, J., dissenting).

22. Id. at 326, 110 S.Ct. at 2876 (Brennan, J., dissenting).

23. Cruzan v. Director, Missouri Dept. of Health, 497 U.S. 261, 283, 110 S.Ct. 2841, 2854, 111 L.Ed.2d 224 (1990).

right to forgo life sustaining treatment. Justice Brennan points out that the majority's "express[ion] [of] great deference to the policy choice made by the state legislature" reflects a position that incompetent people have virtually no liberty interest because they are unable to exercise decisionmaking functions.[24] Justice Stevens adds that such a position is both "patently unconstitutional" and "dangerous" because it would allow states to prefer death for the incompetent in the same way that Missouri prefers life.[25] Justice Brennan suggests that the Court allows states too much deference by not asking the constitutionally relevant question—i.e., whether the state's act burdens a fundamental right; "[i]f a requirement imposed by a State significantly interferes with the exercise of a fundamental right, it cannot be upheld unless it is supported by sufficiently important state interests and is closely tailored to effectuate only those interests."[26] Effectively, the majority defers to state law as a default position, even if that law significantly burdens the exercise of a fundamental right. For the majority, that default position can be overcome only if the state cannot articulate any reason for its policy. The dissent sets as a default position the vindication of that right, even though that gives less deference to state law. For the dissent, that default position should be overcome only if the state law does not burden the exercise of the right or if it serves a compelling state interest.

The *Cruzan* case fails to resolve a number of questions. It does not directly address whether the Constitution recognizes a competent person's right to terminate medical treatment and how such a right would be consistent with laws punishing suicide or the aiding and abetting of suicide. Although the Court forecloses further argument based on a right of privacy in this context, it does not explain if there is anything left to the right, which formed the basis for the Court's abortion opinions and was also the basis of many state court analyses of the Constitutional issue in "right to die" cases. Even though Justice O'Connor and the dissenters apparently would recognize a Constitutional status of a surrogate appointed by the patient, the majority decision does not address this issue.

In addition, the opinion of the Court does not address whether cost is a relevant consideration. The decision does not explain whether the person paying for the care (in this case, the state of Missouri) has any special status in determining what treatment should be provided. As a consequence, it does not determine whether a patient's family might be required to pay for extremely costly care believed to be entirely repugnant, but which the state requires as a matter of state law. In addition, the *Cruzan* decision does not determine whether a state may discontinue treatment of some patients, or choose not to commence it initially, because the state wishes not to pay for that treatment.

The *Cruzan* case requires that the law in this area be developed on a state by state basis, and this has given rise to a wide variety of state laws. The evidence required to remove life sustaining treatment in one state may be insufficient to serve that purpose in the next. The *Cruzan* case does not

24. Id. at 313, 110 S.Ct. at 2870 (Stevens, J., dissenting).

25. Id.

26. Cruzan v. Director, Missouri Dept. of Health, 497 U.S. 261, 303, 110 S.Ct. 2841, 2864, 111 L.Ed.2d 224 (1990) (Brennan, J., dissenting) (citing Zablocki v. Redhail, 434 U.S. 374, 388, 98 S.Ct. 673, 682, 54 L.Ed.2d 618 (1978)).

address whether it would be permissible for a family or guardian to move a person from one state to another to take advantage of the second state's law governing the termination of life sustaining treatment. For example, a family might want to move a patient from Missouri, with its very conservative law on the removal of treatment, to Minnesota, which is much more willing to allow that discontinuation.[27] Alternatively, a guardian may choose to move a patient from Minnesota to Missouri as a result of a fear that Minnesota doctors would be too quick to discontinue treatment in support of the patient's liberty interest. The *Cruzan* case gives no guidance on whether such moves might be Constitutionally permissible.

Finally, the most cynical analysts of the *Cruzan* case have argued that it merely provides a different required form for testimony in cases involving discontinuation of life sustaining treatment in Missouri. The extreme consequences of failure to provide testimony of the unambiguous statements of the patient requesting the discontinuation of precisely the kind of treatment currently being provided may result in the miraculous recall of highly specific articulations that meet the evidentiary requirements. At worst, this could lead to the kind of pleading practice and fabrication of evidence that was so common in fault divorce proceedings, where the law generally tolerated statements which were made under oath, but which all parties knew to be false, because of the inadequate operation of the law without this fraudulent practice. Indeed, following the United State Supreme Court opinion in *Cruzan* several of Ms. Cruzan's friends recalled specific statements by her that proved, by clear and convincing evidence, that she would want this type of treatment to be discontinued. The Attorney General of Missouri, who fought this case with vigor at every stage of the proceedings, did not object to the introduction of this new evidence and did not appeal the decision permitting the discontinuation of treatment.

When the first physician assisted death cases came before the Supreme Court in 1997[28], the Court gave slight consideration to its earlier decision in the Cruzan case. The Court did distinguish the issue of the discontinuation of life sustaining treatment that was addressed in Cruzan from the issue of physician assisted death, and clarified one issue:

> Our assumption of a right to refuse treatment was grounded not . . . on the proposition that patients have a general and abstract "right to hasten death," [ ] but on well established, traditional rights to bodily integrity and freedom from unwanted touching.[29]

§ 16–3. The Common Law Basis

As Justice Rehnquist pointed out in the opinion of the Court in *Cruzan*, state courts are not limited to federal Constitutional law when analyzing the

---

27. This is exactly what happened with Christine Busalacchi, whose father was attempting, presumably, to take advantage of Minnesota's more liberal laws in this area. See Pete Busalacchi, How Can They? 20 Hastings Center Rep. 6 (1990). The case was ultimately decided by the Missouri Court of Appeals. In re Busalacchi, 1993 WL 288532(Mo.1993) (holding that the father would breach his duty as guardian to attempt to move her solely to avoid

the operation of Missouri law and that the Missouri courts would not allow forum shopping in a life and death matter).

28. Washington v. Glucksberg 521 U.S. 702, 117 S.Ct. 2258 (1997); Vacco v. Quill 521 U.S. 793, 117 S.Ct. 2293 (1997). For a discussion of these cases, see section 16–72 below.

29. Vacco v. Quill 521 U.S. at 807, 117 S.Ct. at 2301.

legal status of decisions to forgo life sustaining treatment.[1] Virtually every court that has addressed the issue has evaluated the common law status of such decisions. Whether these courts find a right to forgo life sustaining treatment based in the United States Constitution or some other federal source, they find a strong common law basis for the variably defined and variably limited right.[2] Courts have found that the common law provides the most flexible and the most easily reviewed source of law because it allows courts the power to construct the right as they deem appropriate, without concerns over the specifics of constitutional and statutory provisions, while still allowing the legislature or judges to change the law whenever appropriate. Because of the flexibility inherent in basing such a right on the common law as well as the controversial nature of the federal constitutional right to privacy, state courts have increasingly looked to the common law as one basis—often, the sole basis upon which they may decide cases implicating the right to terminate life sustaining treatment.

a. The Right to Forgo Life Sustaining Treatment as a Part of the Right to Give Informed Consent

Generally, the common law right to forgo life sustaining treatment is viewed as a subspecies of the law of informed consent. While this area of the law is itself based in the principle of autonomy,[3] which asserts that each person has the right to control his or her own destiny and determine his or her own fate, it is most commonly founded on the law of battery and negligence. Justice Cardozo's famous admonition that "[e]very human being of adult years and sound mind has a right to determine what shall be done with his own body * * *" has been oft-cited in this context, where it is probably more apposite than in negligence-based informed consent cases where it is endlessly repeated.[4] Indeed, just as early informed consent cases were viewed as actions in battery, one court has recognized that providing unwanted treatment to prolong life, at least in the case of a competent adult, constitutes a battery.[5] Further, in *Bouvia v. Superior Court*[6] the California Court of Appeal announced that the principles of informed consent actions also extend to a common law "right to die."

As Chief Justice Rehnquist recognized when rejecting a Constitutional right to die in *Cruzan*, "[t]he informed consent doctrine has become firmly entrenched in American tort law * * * [and] [t]he logical corollary of the doctrine of informed consent is that the patient generally possesses the right not to consent, that is, to refuse treatment."[7] The logical extension from the

---

§ 16–3

1. Cruzan v. Director, Missouri Dept. of Health, 497 U.S. 261, 277, 110 S.Ct. 2841, 2850, 111 L.Ed.2d 224 (1990).

2. Id. at 269–70, 110 S.Ct. at 2846–47; see also Union Pacific R. Co. v. Botsford, 141 U.S. 250, 251, 11 S.Ct. 1000, 1001, 35 L.Ed. 734 (1891) ("No right is held more sacred, or is more carefully guarded, by the common law, than the right of every individual to the possession and control of his own person, free from all restraint or interference of others, unless by clear and unquestionable authority of law.").

3. See Barry Furrow et al., Bioethics: Health Care Law & Ethics 207–210 (2d ed. 1991).

4. Schloendorff v. Society of New York Hospital, 105 N.E. 92, 93 (N.Y.1914).

5. See Bartling v. Superior Court, 209 Cal. Rptr. 220, 224 (Cal.App.1984) (quoting Barber v. Superior Court, 195 Cal.Rptr. 484 (Cal.App. 1983), "where a doctor performs treatment in the absence of informed consent, there is an actionable battery.").

6. 225 Cal.Rptr. 297 (Cal.App.1986).

7. Cruzan v. Director, Missouri Dept. of Health, 497 U.S. 261, 270, 110 S.Ct. 2841,

common law right to informed consent to a right to forgo life sustaining treatment has been recognized so often that courts are able to infer that the latter is as long and widely recognized a right as the former.

b. Medical Recognition of the Right to Forgo Life Sustaining Treatment

The fundamental nature of the patient's right to choose to forgo treatment is also recognized outside of case law. It was recognized clearly, even if its form was not fully developed, by the President's Commission for the Study of Ethical Problems in Medicine and Biomedical and Behavioral Research, which concluded in 1983 that:

> The voluntary choice of a competent and informed patient should determine whether or not life sustaining therapy will be undertaken, just as such choices provide the basis for other decisions about medical treatment. * * * Health care professionals serve patients best by maintaining a presumption in favor of sustaining life, while recognizing that competent patients are entitled to choose to forgo any treatments, including those that sustain life.[8]

Similar positions have been adopted by the American Medical Association and the American Hospital Association and by virtually every other professional organization whose members may participate in decisions to terminate life sustaining treatment. While outside professional recognition is hardly necessary for the courts to assert that this is the common law position, it adds support to the argument that the right to make health care decisions—even those that will result in death—is deeply embedded in the principles that govern health care in America.

c. Continued State by State Development of the Common Law Right to Forgo Life Sustaining Treatment

If the current common law right to discontinue treatment is so well established and respected in the medical community, why are courts asked to confirm this right with such frequency? Many of the judicial actions that have raised these common law questions have been instigated because physicians or other health care professionals are concerned about the risk of malpractice liability or criminal prosecution if they accede to patient's requests that their treatment be discontinued.[9] While these cases are most often formally commenced by patients or their families when the health provider refuses to grant their wishes,[10] the underlying purpose of the litigation is often to reassure potential malpractice (and, frequently, informed consent) defendants that the common law will not hold them liable for carrying out the patient's wishes. As the common law right to discontinue life sustaining treatment is recognized in the courts and in medical communities across the country, the potential for liability of a medical staff which grants a patient's request to discontinue

2847, 111 L.Ed.2d 224 (1990). Once a court finds a common law right, it is not necessary to determine whether the right is also conferred by either the federal or state constitutions or by statute.

8. President's Commission for the Study of Ethical Problems in Medicine and Biomedical and Behavioral Research, Deciding to Forgo Life Sustaining Treatment 23 (1983).

9. See Bartling v. Superior Court, 209 Cal. Rptr. 220, 226 (Cal.App.1984).

10. See David H. Bamberger, Comment, Mercy Hospital, Inc. v. Jackson: A Recurring Dilemma for Health Care Providers in the Treatment of Jehovah's Witnesses, 46 Md. L. Rev. 514, 530 (1987).

medical treatment is diminished. Medical professionals as well as individuals who work outside the medical profession should begin to lose the fear that they will be the subject of malpractice actions for properly treating (or refraining from treating) their patients by honoring those patients' right to forgo life sustaining treatment.

The fact that virtually all courts recognize some kind of common law right to refuse medical treatment does not say very much about the content of that right. The common law has been interpreted very narrowly in some states (like Missouri[11] and New York[12]) and much more broadly in others (like California[13] and New Jersey[14]). Thus, despite the fact that state common law rules are drawn from similar principles of autonomy and privacy and founded upon similar legal foundations, they have developed in different ways. For example, the fact that a state recognizes a common law right to discontinue "treatment" does not answer the question of whether the provision of nutrition and hydration constitutes "treatment" for common law purposes (see § 17–77, below), or whether that right may be exercised by families, surrogates or only by patients themselves (see § 17–23, below).

Thus, while one issue is well resolved in state courts—recognition of a common law right to choose one's own form of medical treatment—the dimensions, attributes and qualifications of this right are not fully developed. This variability is evident in the continuing litigation in states trying to define the parameters of the right to refuse life sustaining medical treatment.

§ 16–4. The Development of State Statutory and Constitutional Law

The Supreme Court's very restricted application of the United States Constitution to the right decisions to forgo life sustaining treatment in the *Cruzan* case has left state courts to search for other legal sources for such a right. Some state courts remain wary of depending upon a common law right, preferring to look for state statutory and constitutional bases for these decisions. Some state legislatures have chosen to address the issue by enacting statutes. Other states have seen the creation of populist movements which have been successful in amending the state constitution—often an easy process—in ways that affect the rights of citizens to terminate medical treatment.

a. State Statutes

While a few states have adopted statutes, like the Uniform Health Care Decisions Act[1], which explicitly provide for a right to forgo life sustaining medical treatment, most state statutes that directly address this right have

---

11. Cruzan v. Harmon, 760 S.W.2d 408 (Mo.1988).

12. In re Westchester County Medical Center on Behalf of O'Connor, 534 N.Y.S.2d 886, 531 N.E.2d 607 (N.Y.1988); In re Storar, 438 N.Y.S.2d 266, 420 N.E.2d 64 (N.Y.), cert. denied 454 U.S. 858, 102 S.Ct. 309, 70 L.Ed.2d 153 (1981).

13. See Bouvia v. Superior Court, 225 Cal. Rptr. 297 (Cal.App.1986); Bartling v. Superior Court, 209 Cal.Rptr. 220 (Cal.App.1984).

14. In re Quinlan, 355 A.2d 647 (N.J.), cert. denied sub nom. Garger v. New Jersey, 429 U.S. 922, 97 S.Ct. 319, 50 L.Ed.2d 289 (1976).

§ 16–4

1. Uniform Health Care Decisions Act (1993) § 4, Part 2. See e.g., Delaware—16 Del.C. §§ 2501 to 2517, Maine—18–A M.R.S.A §§ 5–801 to 5–817, Mississippi—Code 1972 §§ 41–41–201 to 41–41–229, New Mexico—NMSA 1978 §§ 24–7a–1 to 24–7a–18.

been written to provide for "living wills," durable powers of attorney, or, alternatively, for the formal recognition of the rights of families or other surrogates to make health care decisions for incompetent patients. A few state legislatures have added more limited or ambiguous provisions to other statutes, such as probate, guardianship or conservator statutes,[2] that may affect the opportunity of patients to choose to forgo life sustaining treatment. By deciding a case on the basis of a state statute, the state court is able to put the responsibility for its decision on the legislature, which may change the legislation if it believes that the case was wrongly decided. Courts that depend upon state statutory law to find some form of a right to forgo life sustaining treatment often also depend upon state common law, which itself is interpreted in light of the values and interests that are expressed in state legislation. Thus, a very conservative statute could be used as evidence of relatively narrow state common law in Missouri,[3] while the more expansive statute in Connecticut,[4] for example, gave courts substantially greater support in finding a more expansive state common law.

b. State Constitutions

Applicable state constitutional provisions take various forms. In many states, constitutions are comparatively easy to amend, and provisions that might affect the right to forgo life sustaining treatment have been swept into those constitutions either because of the public attention given to the issue or because of the similarity between the principles that underlie both this issue and abortion. As the Supreme Court has granted states more latitude to fashion their own abortion laws (see Chapter 18 below), both pro-choice and pro-life groups continue to fight to amend state constitutions to incorporate each side's particular interests. As this battle continues, provisions addressing the right to privacy and liberty are likely to be added to more state constitutions so that there will be a larger number of relevant, albeit ambiguous, provisions that apply in right to die cases. Further, even though state constitutions are generally more difficult to change than either statutes or the common law, state constitutional grounds may be the strongest legal basis for decisions available to a state court as such grounds are not generally reviewable by the United States Supreme Court (absent the improbable position, given the holding in *Cruzan*, that the state constitution itself is in violation of the United States Constitution).

State constitutional provisions that are designed to free citizens from excessive intrusions by their state governments have already become the bases of some "right to die" decisions. For example, the privacy right that is enshrined in the California constitution was one basis of the *Bouvia* decision,[5] and the Florida constitutional provision that "[e]very natural person has the right to be left alone and free from governmental intrusion into his private life except as otherwise provided herein"[6] has been cited in several cases involving the decision to forgo life sustaining treatment in that state.[7] Ari-

---

2. See e.g., Idaho Code § 39–4502.

3. Cruzan v. Harmon, 760 S.W.2d 408, 419–20 (Mo.1988) (interpreting Mo. Rev. Stat. § 459.010 as embodying a policy strongly favoring the preservation of life).

4. See McConnell v. Beverly Enterprises–Connecticut, 553 A.2d 596, 601–602 (Conn. 1989).

5. Bouvia v. Superior Court, 225 Cal.Rptr. 297 (Cal.App.1986).

6. West's Fla.S.A. Const., Art. 1, § 23.

7. See e.g., Corbett v. D'Alessandro, 487 So.2d 368 (Fla.App.1986).

zona's constitution, which provides that "[n]o person shall be disturbed in his private affairs or his home invaded, without authority of law,"[8] has also been cited in the seminal Arizona case dealing with the right to refuse life sustaining treatment.[9] Although these state constitutional provisions, generally designed to limit the degree of state interference, will hardly be dispositive of right to die cases, they will certainly affect courts' approach in the discussion of those issues.[10]

B. SIGNIFICANT STATE INTERESTS THAT LIMIT THE JUDICIALLY RECOGNIZED RIGHT TO FORGO LIFE SUSTAINING TREATMENT

§ 16–5. Significant Interests That Limit the Judicially Recognized Right to Forgo Life Sustaining Treatment: Introduction

Wherever the right to forgo life sustaining treatment is based—the United States Constitution, state constitutions, statutes, or state common law—the right is not absolute. The right to die may be narrowed, limited, defined, and, in the rare case, outweighed absolutely by independent interests of the state. Courts have consistently invoked four interests as potential limitations upon the right of patients to forgo life sustaining treatment. These four state interests, first recognized in a case involving the decision to forgo life sustaining treatment by the Massachusetts Supreme Judicial Court, are:

(1) the preservation of life;

(2) the protection of innocent third parties;

(3) the prevention of suicide; and

(4) the maintenance of the ethical integrity of the medical profession and allied health care workers.[1]

§ 16–6. The State Interest in the Preservation of Life

The most frequently cited state interest that may outweigh a patient's interest in having the choice to forgo life sustaining treatment is the state's interest in the preservation of life. This is the only interest mentioned by the majority in the *Cruzan* case.[1] As a result, there is United States Supreme Court authority formally recognizing the state interest in the preservation of life *simpliciter*. In *Glucksberg* the majority explicitly determined that Washington's ban on physician assisted death served the state's "unqualified interest in the preservation of human life."[2] The Glucksberg Court recognized

---

8. Ariz. Const., Art. 2, § 8.

9. Rasmussen v. Fleming, 741 P.2d 674 (Ariz.1987).

10. See, for example, In the Matter of Tavel, 661 A.2d 1061 (Del.1995), where the Court found that the common law right was bolstered by both the United States Constitution and Article I, section 7 of the Delaware Constitution.

§ 16–5

1. Superintendent of Belchertown State School v. Saikewicz, 370 N.E.2d 417, 425 (Mass.1977).

§ 16–6

1. Cruzan v. Director, Missouri Dept. of Health, 497 U.S. 261, 282, 110 S.Ct. 2841, 2853, 111 L.Ed.2d 224 (1990).

2. Washington v. Glucksberg 521 U.S. at 728, 117 S.Ct. at 2272.

that Washington had rejected a "sliding scale" approach to the value of life and appropriately sought to preserve all human life, "from beginning to end, regardless of physical or mental condition."[3] On the other hand, very few judges (outside of those on the Missouri Supreme Court in *Cruzan v. Harmon*) have given this principle substantial weight when confronted with the facts of an actual case. For example, the Massachusetts Supreme Court stated that:

> [w]hen we balance the State's interest in prolonging a patient's life against the rights of the patient to reject such prolongation, we must recognize that the State's interest in life encompasses a broader interest than mere corporeal existence. In certain, thankfully rare, circumstances the burden of maintaining the corporeal existence degrades the very humanity it was meant to serve.[4]

The dissenting Justices in *Cruzan* were especially critical of the notion that the state possessed some interest in the preservation of the corporeal existence of a person who, in all likelihood, would not desire that continued existence herself. The problem with finding that the "preservation of life" is a state interest that can outweigh the individual interest in choosing to undergo or forgo treatment is, in the words of Justice Stevens, that "[l]ives do not exist in abstraction from persons, and to pretend otherwise is not to honor but to desecrate the State's responsibility for protecting life."[5]

While courts have described the preservation of life as an interest countervailing to the interest of patients to make their own health care decisions, those same courts have tended to discount this state interest in a number of relevant instances. For example, courts have considered the preservation of life to be less significant under any of the following circumstances: (1) where the life to be preserved would be short anyway; (2) where the disease to be treated is terminal in any case; and (3) where continued life would be painful, undignified or burdensome to the patient.

§ 16–7. The State Interest in the Protection of the Interests of Innocent Third Parties

Much like the preservation of life, this countervailing state interest does not withstand much scrutiny. It is not clear who counts as a party who is both "innocent" and "third" to the patient, and why the patient's significant interests should be weighed against someone else's interests. This countervailing interest has been applied in cases in which a parent of young children or a pregnant woman wishes to forgo medical treatment (most commonly, a blood transfusion) for religious reasons. In some early cases, judges who tended to be unsympathetic to the parent's religious views searched for some way to deny that parent the right to make what the judge thought to be an unreasonable decision. They looked to child abuse and neglect laws and the principles behind child support laws to find that parents could not allow themselves to die if one consequence were that their children would be inadequately fed, dressed, sheltered, or, most broadly, required to bear an unnecessary emotional burden.[1]

3. Id. at 729, 117 S.Ct. at 2272

4. Brophy v. New England Sinai Hospital, Inc., 497 N.E.2d 626, 635 (Mass.1986).

5. Cruzan, 497 U.S. at 356–57, 110 S.Ct. at 2892 (Stevens, J., dissenting).

§ 16–7

1. See In re President and Directors of Georgetown College, Inc., 331 F.2d 1000, 1008 (D.C.Cir.1964) cert. denied 377 U.S. 978, 84 S.Ct. 1883, 12 L.Ed.2d 746 (1964) (blood trans-

The use of this countervailing interest places the court on a slippery slope. What other dangerous activities could be denied parents because an accident could make their children orphans? Would parents be required to maintain high paying jobs to assure the financial security of their children? Would they be required to stop smoking or drinking or bronco riding? One doesn't shed rights when one has children, and it is strange for courts to require that parents act inconsistently with their deepest religious and ethical beliefs to remain within the law. As a consequence, this countervailing interest, while always mentioned in the litany of potential interests that could outweigh a patient's right to forgo life sustaining treatment, is rarely given any significance today.

§ 16-8.   The State Interest in the Prevention of Suicide

Traditionally, American law has recognized state power to try to prevent suicide, and the propriety of the exercise of this power was confirmed, against a Constitutional challenge, in *Washington v. Glucksberg*.[1] This power has included the authority to try to prevent "suicide by refusing to take appropriate measures necessary to preserve one's life."[2] The state interest in preventing suicide seems inapposite in "right to die" cases.[3] First, suicide requires an intent to cause one's own death. Most people who choose to forgo life sustaining treatment do so to ameliorate physical pain and suffering, not to cause death.[4] Second, when someone dies following the denial of life sustaining treatment, it is the underlying disease process that is the cause of death, not the "act" of denying treatment.[5] In any case, most states have now removed their criminal sanctions for suicide[6] and attempted suicide.[7] In most

fusion ordered to save the life of a mother, despite her religious beliefs to the contrary, given the state interest in preventing the abandonment of her child and the mother's "responsibility to the community to care for her infant."). For a more modern approach to this same issue, see Stamford v. Vega, 674 A.2d 821 (Conn.1996). See also Cruzan v. Director, Missouri Dept. of Health, 497 U.S. 261, 313, 110 S.Ct. 2841, 2869, 111 L.Ed.2d 224 (1990) (Brennan, J., dissenting).

If Missouri were correct that its interests outweigh Nancy's interest in avoiding medical procedures as long as she is free of pain and physical discomfort * * * it is not apparent why a State could not choose to remove one of her kidneys without consent on the ground that society would be better off if the recipient of that kidney were saved from renal poisoning * * * Patches of her skin could also be removed to provide grafts for burn victims, and scrapings of bone marrow to provide grafts for someone with leukemia * * * Indeed, why could the State not perform medical experiments on her body, experiments that might save countless lives, and would cause her no greater burden than she already bears by being fed through the gastrostomy tube? This would be too brave a new world for me and, I submit, for our Constitution.

Id. at 313 n.13, 110 S.Ct. at 2869 n.13.

§ 16-8

1. 521 U.S. 702, 117 S.Ct. 2258 (1997).

2. Cruzan v. Director, Missouri Dept. of Health, 497 U.S. 261, 293, 110 S.Ct. 2841, 2859, 111 L.Ed.2d 224 (1990) (Scalia, J., concurring).

3. See Philip Peters, "The State's Interest in the Preservation of Life: From Quinlan to Cruzan," 50 Ohio St. L.J. 891, 962–70 (1989).

4. However, at common law, suicide in order to relieve pain did not excuse one from liability. Cruzan, 497 U.S. at 295, 110 S.Ct. at 2860 (Scalia, J., concurring).

5. See In re Conroy, 486 A.2d 1209, 1224 (N.J.1985) ("Refusing medical intervention merely allows the disease to take its natural course; if death were eventually to occur, it would be the result, primarily, of the underlying disease, and not the result of a self-inflicted injury,"); but see Cruzan, 497 U.S. at 296–298, 110 S.Ct. at 2861–62 (Scalia, J., concurring) (stating that other methods of suicide through "inaction" are not constitutionally protected).

6. But see Cruzan v. Director, Missouri Dept. of Health, 497 U.S. 261, 294, 110 S.Ct. 2841, 2860, 111 L.Ed.2d 224 (1990) (Scalia, J., concurring) (stating that criminal penalties were abolished to spare the "innocent family," not to legitimize suicide).

jurisdictions, penalties remain only for aiding and abetting suicide. In addition, as the *Saikewicz* court pointed out when it first listed the prevention of suicide as one of the four countervailing state interests, "the underlying State interest in this area lies in the prevention of irrational self destruction."[8] The fact that there can be a right to forgo life sustaining treatment implies that this can be a rational choice, not an act of irrational self destruction. In short, the recognition of the prevention of suicide as a countervailing state interest is an anachronism based on religious views and social policy that are now largely irrelevant to questions related to decisions to forgo life sustaining treatment.

§ 16–9.   The State Interest in the Maintenance of the Ethical Integrity of the Medical Profession

In Glucksberg the Supreme Court accepted the proposition that the state has "an interest in protecting the integrity and ethics of the medical profession."[1] However, there is no reason to believe that the maintenance of ethical integrity of the medical profession, under current standards, requires the health care system to ignore a patient's desires to terminate life sustaining treatment. The American Medical Association, the American Hospital Association, and virtually all other professional organizations recognize that there will be situations when good ethics and good medicine require the discontinuation of life sustaining treatment,[2] and there are few physicians who would demand their patients accept all forms of useful treatment when those patients don't want it. As early as 1977, the *Saikewicz* court pointed out that "[p]revailing medical ethical practice does not, without exception, demand that all efforts toward life prolongation be made in all circumstances. Rather, "* * * the prevailing ethical practice seems to be to recognize that the dying are more often in need of comfort than treatment."[3] Thus, the court was able to conclude that, "[i]t is not necessary to deny a right of self determination to a patient in order to recognize the interest of doctors, hospitals, and medical personnel in attendance on the patient."[4]

§ 16–10.   When the Countervailing State Interests in Requiring Treatment Outweigh the Patient's Interest in Forgoing Treatment

Given the weaknesses of the four countervailing state interests, it is not surprising that courts commonly have found that these interests do not

---

7. Many courts have held that refusing life sustaining medical treatment does not constitute suicide. See e.g., Foody v. Manchester Memorial Hosp., 482 A.2d 713, 720 (Conn.Super.1984); Superintendent of Belchertown State School v. Saikewicz, 370 N.E.2d 417, 426 n. 11 (Mass.1977); In re Conroy, 486 A.2d at 1224; Matter of Welfare of Colyer, 660 P.2d 738, 743 (Wash.1983).

8. Saikewicz, 370 N.E.2d at 426 n.11. At least one court has found a fourteenth amendment constitutional right to commit "rational suicide." People v. Kevorkian, 1993 WL 603212 (Wayne Co., Mich., 1993). See also the District Court opinion in Compassion in Dying v. Washington, 850 F.Supp. 1454 (W.D.Wash. 1994), reversed 49 F.3d 586 (9th Cir.1995).

reversed *sub nom.* Washington v. Glucksburg, 521 U.S. 702, 117 S.Ct. 2258 (1997).

§ 16–9

1. Glucksberg, 521 U.S. at 730, 117 S.Ct. at 2273.

2. See President's Commission for the Study of Ethical Problems in Medical and Biomedical and Behavioral Research, Deciding to Forego Life–Sustaining Treatment, 126–36 (1983).

3. Superintendent of Belchertown State School v. Saikewicz, 370 N.E.2d 417, 426 (Mass.1977).

4. Id. at 427.

outweigh a patient's decision to forgo life sustaining treatment. The only exceptions have been in cases where (1) the patient was incompetent and there was insufficient evidence that the patient would choose to forgo life sustaining treatment (such as Cruzan), (2) the refusal of treatment was based on religious grounds and the patient had parental obligations recognized by law, (3) the patient was a child, or (4) the patient had some special status that made the initial right to refuse treatment weaker than it would be in other cases (for example, where the patient was prisoner seeking to disrupt the prison system[1]), or where there was another special countervailing state interest that applies.

C. DETERMINING DECISIONAL CAPACITY OR COMPE-TENCY OF PATIENTS FOR WHOM LIFE SUSTAIN-ING MEDICAL TREATMENT IS APPROPRIATE

§ 16–11. Competency, Decisional Capacity, and The Notion of Variable Capacity

Whether a patient has the right to forgo life sustaining treatment, and the method by which that right can be exercised, depend fundamentally on whether that patient is competent to make the decision. Despite the significance of this issue, though, courts have been reluctant to give formal definitions of competency, and few courts have proposed tests for determining the competency of patients in particular cases. The use of the term "competency" to describe the state of mind of one who is able to make such decisions has caused some courts to resort to analysis based in the traditional law of guardianship and conservatorship. These courts sometimes assume that every person must be either legally "competent" or legally "incompetent" at any moment; i.e., that a person is either competent for all legal and medical purposes or incompetent for such purposes.[1]

In part as a reaction against this logically nonsensical all-or-nothing approach to competency, over the last several years courts have been prodded by legislatures to replace their analysis of competency with an analysis of "decisional capacity," which, often as a statutory matter, formally recognizes that many individuals—perhaps most for whom this is an issue—possess "variable capacity." These individuals may have the capacity to make some kinds of decisions but not others (and thus have a capacity that varies by nature of the decision), or they may have the capacity to make particular decisions at some times, but not at others (and thus have a capacity that varies by time).[2] It would not be surprising to find that a person had the

---

§ 16–10

1. For example, see Polk v. Iowa, 594 N.W.2d 421 (Iowa 1999) and Laurie v. Senecal, 666 A.2d 806 (R.I.1995).

§ 16–11

1. See Elyn R. Saks, Competency to Refuse Treatment, 69 N.C. L. Rev. 945, 994 n.200 (1991). For a good general discussion of the history of evaluating patient capacity for health care decisionmaking, see Wendy Margolis, Comment, The Doctor Knows Best?: Patient

Capacity for Health Care Decisionmaking, 71 Or.L.Rev. 909 (1992).

2. See Kevin R. Wolff, Note, Determining Patient Competency in Treatment Refusal Cases, 24 Ga. L. Rev. 733 (1990); Benjamin Freedman, Competence, Marginal and Otherwise: Concepts and Ethics, 4 Int.J. of L. & Psychiatry 53, 56 (1981) ("The test for competency varies from one context to another").

attributes of competence necessary to make decisions about routine blood tests or payment of the electric bill, but lacked those attributes as to whether she should undergo chemotherapy or invest her life savings in a Mexican gold mine.

§ 16–12. The Presumption of Competency

The now disapproved all-or-nothing approach to competency was accompanied by one other traditional legal presumption that has never been given much credence by the courts: the presumption that a person was competent unless a court had made an alternative finding.[1] While some state statutes have reinforced and codified this presumption,[2] it makes little sense to treat a comatose patient as a competent patient just because a court has not had an opportunity to make a formal finding about the status of the patient. Likewise, it makes little sense to convene an emergency hearing to determine whether the comatose patient being wheeled into the emergency room is decisionally incapacitated. In fact, while the presumption of competence has value in reminding courts of the gravity and importance of making a finding of incompetency (or decisional incapacity), strict adherence to this legal principle would make medical care for the incompetent impossibly burdensome because it would so substantially increase the caseload of the courts. There are, of course, genuine cases of arguable competency that require judicial determination,[3] but they do not represent the majority of cases involving patients making decisions regarding life sustaining treatment.

§ 16–13. Judicial Considerations of Questions of Competency

Most cases questioning the decisional capacity of patients have arisen when patients have disagreed with the physicians' proposed course of treatment. Studies show that where physicians view the utility of treatment as high and the risks as low, there is a very high threshold for competency, i.,e, physicians assume their patients incompetent if they disagree with the medical recommendation and choose to forgo that treatment. In addition, judges seem to have the same presumption as do physicians. This arbitrariness in the way that the law of competency is applied in individual cases may be exacerbated by the fact that other attributes irrelevant to a determination of competency—age, social class and gender, for example—appear also to affect the decisions that physicians (and others, including judges) make in determining decisional capacity.[1]

§ 16–14. Legal Tests of Competency

Even those courts that directly address the competency of patients to make decisions to forgo life sustaining treatment are not likely to articulate

§ 16–12

1. See Kevin R. Wolff, Note, Determining Patient Competency in Treatment Refusal Cases, 24 Ga. L. Rev. 733, 743 (1990).

2. See V.T.C.A., Health & Safety Code § 576.002; Mass. Gen. Laws, Ann. c.201D, § 2; D.C. Code 1981, § 6–1921.

3. For a review of cases deciding patients' competency to make treatment decisions, see Elyn R. Saks, Competency to Refuse Treatment, 69 N.C. L. Rev. 945, at 978–84 (1991).

§ 16–13

1. See In re Quackenbush, 383 A.2d 785 (N.J.1978); see also Steven H. Miles and Allison August, "Courts, Gender, and The Right To Die," 18 Law, Med., & Health Care 85 (1990) (suggesting that gender may be an important factor in determining competency by showing that courts tend to manifest respect and deference to men's wishes while discounting those of women).

the formal test they are applying in making the decision. One group of scholars has suggested that the range of tests generally applied fits into five categories—(1) patient's demonstration of a choice; (2) reasonableness of the outcome of the choice; (3) rational bases for the choice; (4) patient's ability to understand the relevant risks, benefits and alternatives to treatment; and (5) patient's actual understanding of the relevant risks, benefits and alternatives.[1] As the authors of that study point out,

> " * * * within limits, and when the patient's competency is not absolutely clear cut, a test of competency that will achieve the desired medical or social end despite the actual condition of the patient may be selected. We do not imply that this is done maliciously either by physicians or the court; rather we believe that it occurs as a consequence of the strong societal bias in favor of treating treatable patients * * *."[2]

In 1980, the President's Commission for the Study of Ethical Problems in Medicine and Biomedical and Behavioral Research attempted to create a test to determine competency.[3] This test remains the most acceptable offered to date, despite the difficulty in applying it to particular cases. The President's Commission found that such capacity requires, "to a greater or lesser degree," each of the following:

(1) possession of a set of values and goals;

(2) the ability to communicate and to understand information; and,

(3) the ability to reason and to deliberate about one's choice.[4]

The first of these elements is the most problematic; it is very difficult to determine whether a person possesses a set of values and goals. Logically, of course, the President's Commission is correct in requiring that the values and goals be sufficiently consistent to allow the patient's choice to be stable, at least over short periods of time—or, as the Commission suggested, "at least long enough for the course of therapy to be initiated with some prospect of being completed."[5] No reported opinion has directly addressed this element of competency, however, and the few courts that have looked at this issue seem to focus almost exclusively on the second and third elements.

The second and third elements are easier for courts to evaluate, but there is no clear point at which a patient can be said to fall below the standards prescribed. While it is certainly important for a patient to "communicate and understand" information, no patient will have a perfect understanding of any medical procedure. Something less than full and perfect understanding—how much less remains unclear—is all that is required to fulfill the requirement of this element. What is more, as the President's Commission pointed out,

> "[t]hese abilities can be evaluated only as they relate to the task at hand and are not solely cognitive, as they ordinarily include emotive elements. To use them, a person also needs sufficient life experience to appreciate the meaning of potential alternatives: what it would probably be like to

§ 16–14

1. Loren H. Roth et al., Tests of Competency to Consent to Treatment, 134 Am. J. Psychiatry 279 (1977).

2. Id. at 281.

3. President's Commission for the Study of Ethical Problems in Medicine and Biomedical and Behavioral Research, 1 Making Health Care Decisions, 57–60 (1982).

4. Id. at 57.

5. Id. at 58.

undergo various medical procedures, for example, or to live in a new way required by a medical condition or intervention."[6]

The third element—the ability to act rationally and deliberately—is also reasonably subject to judicial evaluation. Note that the President's Commission would only require the *ability* to act rationally, not rational action itself. The latter standard would give the courts too much leeway to overcome individual decisions of patients. Again, perfect rationality is not required, and the patient does not have to be able to draw the syllogism that shows how she derived the treatment choice from her values and the information she was provided in order to be determined to be competent. How much deviation from perfect rationality is acceptable remains unclear. In both the second and third elements of the President's Commission's test—the elements that courts actually do consider—expert testimony of physicians or psychologists may be relevant, although given the value-laden nature of those elements, it is difficult to understand how that testimony could be dispositive.

D.   THE RIGHT TO FORGO LIFE SUSTAINING TREATMENT AND COMPETENT ADULTS

§ 16–15.   The Right to Forgo Life Sustaining Treatment and Competent Adults

It is now well established law that competent adults have the right to choose to forgo life sustaining treatment, just as they have the right to choose to undergo (or forgo) any other form of treatment.[1] While ancillary issues, such as the competence of the patient, may be given special consideration when the treatment under question will be life sustaining, the substantive right to refuse life sustaining treatment is identical to the substantive right to deny any other form of proposed medical intervention.[2] Currently there is no court which fails to recognize this right, even though the constitutional, statutory and common law bases of the right may vary from jurisdiction to jurisdiction.[3] In fact, it is remarkable that it took until 1984, in *Bartling v. Superior Court*,[4] for a court to formally articulate the principle that competent patients have a right to forgo life sustaining treatment.

In concluding that competent patients have the right to forgo life-sustaining treatment, courts have left many unanswered questions about the nature of that right. Patients rarely have available to them an unambiguous

6. President's Commission for the Study of Ethical Problems in Medicine and Biomedical and Behavioral Research, 1 Making Health Care Decisions 58 (1982). This is reflected in the definition of "capacity" that appears in the Uniform Health Care Decisions Act: "capacity" means an individual's ability to understand the significant benefits, risks, and alternatives to proposed health care, and to make and communicate a health-care decision. Uniform Health Care Decisions Act, § 1(3).

§ 16–15

1. See Cruzan v. Director, Missouri Dept. of Health, 497 U.S. 261, 269B77, 110 S.Ct. 2841,

2846B51, 111 L.Ed.2d 224 (1990). The Court adverts to this right, without formally confirming it, in Washington v. Glucksberg, 521 U.S. 702 (1997). The statutory right of every competent adult to make all health care decisions is explicitly provided in the Uniform Health Care Decisions Act.

2. See id. at 270, 110 S.Ct. at 2847.

3. See Section 16–4.

4. 209 Cal.Rptr. 220 (Cal.App.1984). See also, Thor v. Superior Court, 21 Cal.Rptr.2d 357, 855 P.2d 375 (Cal.1993) (extending the right to a competent adult prisoner serving a life sentence).

choice between a full, long-lasting healthy life and an immediate painless death. Rather, the choice is essentially between chances and percentages—a chance to return to a better quality life and the possibility of resuming some of life's pleasures, or a hope that forgoing treatment will lead to recovery (or to a quick, relatively painless death). Further, the line between palliative care and therapeutic intervention often is not a clear one, and the line between allowing a patient to forgo treatment and helping him end his life is not always a bright one.[5] The law has yet to deal with many of the subtle issues raised by these complexities.

First, the law has not yet resolved whether the competent patient may choose medically unaccepted alternatives to life-sustaining treatment. The law generally recognizes that patients can choose among medically reasonable alternative forms of treatment, but patients do not have the right to choose an alternative treatment that is medically unreasonable. For a discussion of the right to demand futile treatment, see 16–77 below.

Second, the law has not addressed the question of whether competent patients must be told of alternative ways that they might choose to die. Must a description of the risks, benefits and alternatives of treatment include a description of the risks and benefits of dying in different ways under different treatment regimens?[6]

Third, the law has not resolved the question of whether there is an obligation on health care professionals, or on the health care system as a whole, to help competent patients who have chosen to forgo life sustaining medical treatment, and thus to die. Must competent patients who have decided to forgo life sustaining treatment be offered appropriate palliative care, even if the health care providers believe that the patient's decision is inconsistent with sound medicine or sound ethics?[7]

Fourth, the courts have had little opportunity to address the consequences of a competent patient's choice of death upon criminal liability and tort liability. Should a perpetrator of an act that resulted in the patient being offered the choice of forgoing life sustaining treatment be considered the actual and proximate cause of a death that would have been avoided or postponed if the patient had opted for treatment? What is the extent of tort liability that arises out of an act that results in a patient being offered the choice of forgoing treatment? Is a grossly negligent motorist who injures a Jehovah's Witness guilty of vehicular homicide when his victim dies even though the death could have been avoided through a (refused) blood transfusion? Is the motorist relieved of the tort liability that is attributable to the "unnecessary" death under the same circumstances?

Finally, the courts have yet to address consistently the question of how any right to forgo life sustaining treatment that might be possessed by

5. Of course, the Supreme Court has been willing to allow states to draw this line as a matter of state policy (in distinguishing physician assisted death from the removal of life sustaining medical treatment). See Washington v. Glucksberg, 521 U.S. 702 (1997) and Vacco v. Quill 521 U.S. 793 (1997).

6. See e.g., Margaret Battin, The Least Worst Death, 13 Hastings Center Rep. 16

(April 1983); see also § 6–11, for a discussion of "informed refusal".

7. At least one Justice has assumed that the law "do[es] not prohibit doctors from providing patients with drugs sufficient to control pain...." Washington v. Glucksberg, 521 U.S. 702, 790 (Breyer, J., concurring).

competent patients could be protected by the judiciary. Is a civil process appropriate? If so, which civil process? Under what circumstances is it necessary to seek judicial review, and under what circumstances is such review unnecessary?

E. THE RIGHT TO FORGO LIFE SUSTAINING TREATMENT AND INCOMPETENT ADULTS

1. Principles of Proxy Decisionmaking

§ 16–16. The Right to Forgo Life Sustaining Treatment and Incompetent Adults: Proxy Decisionmaking

The right to choose to forgo life sustaining treatment is a manifestation of a patient's autonomy interest. Obviously, it is much more difficult to vindicate that interest in the case of an incompetent patient than in the case of a patient who is competent. Incompetent patients, by definition, cannot make treatment choices. Any choice regarding treatment must be made by someone other than the patient, such as a proxy decisionmaker. The law must address three significant issues that determine the form and outcome of proxy decisionmaking for incompetent patients: (1) the selection of the proxy decision maker; (2) the substantive principles that must guide that decision maker; and (3) the process that must be followed when the proxy decision maker is appointed and the decision is made.

§ 16–17. Proxy Decisionmaking: Selection of the Proxy

The proxy decision maker is most often a member of the patient's family. The decision maker could be, however, the family acting as a whole, a specially determined level of family members (such as adult children or siblings), a good friend, someone else specifically nominated by the patient, a corporate body (such as a private guardianship organization), a state agency (such as a public guardian), the physician, an institutional ethics committee, a judge, or some combination of all of these potential decision makers. Jurisdictions differ as to whom the court or physician may call upon to act as a proxy.

In most circumstances physicians may reasonably depend upon the unanimous decision of the patient's family to make decisions regarding the termination of life sustaining treatment. There has been no formal disagreement with this practice articulated in the law; it is, as the President's Commission pointed out, a practice so common in medicine over the last century that it has been impliedly accepted by law.[1] Over the past several years most states have also encorporated the principles of proxy decisionmaking in their statutes, which generally provide a hierarchy of proxy decisionmakers upon which healthcare providers can depend.[2]

§ 16–17

1. President's Commission for the Study of Ethical Problems in Medicine and Biomedical and Behavioral Research, 1 Making Health Care Decisions 57–60 (1982).

2. See Section 16–23, below, on family consent statutes.

§ 16–18. Proxy Decisionmaking: Substantive Decisionmaking Principles

There is agreement on the substantive principles to be applied by proxy decision makers. Because the purpose of the appointment of a proxy decision maker is to vindicate the autonomy interest of the patient, that decision maker must apply the values and interests of the patient, not his own values and interests.[1] Ideally, the proxy decision maker would make exactly the decision that the patient, if competent, would make. Such decisionmaking employs the principle of "substituted judgment."[2] The success of any attempt at applying "substituted judgment" depends on the sensitivity of the decision maker and the amount and specificity of the information left by the incompetent patient about the kind of treatment he would desire. There are few cases where the "substituted judgment" choice is simple. For example, it is rare that a patient would be able to anticipate exactly the treatment choice that would follow his incompetency and direct in writing what that choice should be.[3] In reality, most cases are fraught with the uncertainty that naturally arises out of decisions about which we all have some ambivalence.

In cases where the patient has never been competent, the application of the principle of "substituted judgment" is logically impossible. An alternative standard must be applied by the decision maker. This alternative, the "best interest" standard, requires that the proxy make the choice that she believes is in the best interest of the patient, without regard to the inquiry into what choice the patient would make.[4] Such decisionmaking, however, cannot be intended to serve the interest of the patient's autonomy. It serves the interest of beneficence, which becomes the guiding principle only where there is no possibility of vindicating the autonomy interest.[5]

§ 16–18

1. In making this subjective determination, courts usually consider a patient's statements prior to his incapacity. For example, the Washington Supreme Court held that, "prior statements may be probative in determining the wishes of an incompetent patient, with the age and maturity of the patient, the context of the statements, and the connection of the statements to the debilitating event being factors to be weighed," in making a substituted judgment decision. Matter of Welfare of Colyer, 660 P.2d 738, 748 (Wash.1983). The Uniform Health Care Decisions Act, approved by the National Conference of Commissioners on Uniform State Laws in 1994, requires that one making a health care decision on behalf of another act "in accordance with the principal's individual instructions, if any, and other wishes to the extent known to the agent. * * * In determining the principal's best interest, the agent shall consider the principal's personal values to the extent known to the agent." Uniform Health Care Decisions Act, §§ 2(e), 5(f).

2. See e.g., Foody v. Manchester Memorial Hospital, 482 A.2d 713 (Conn.Super.1984); In re Severns, 425 A.2d 156 (Del.Ch.1980); In re Estate of Longeway, 139 Ill.Dec. 780, 549 N.E.2d 292 (Ill.1989).

3. But see, In re Storar, 438 N.Y.S.2d 266, 270, 420 N.E.2d 64, 68 (N.Y.1981).

4. See Rasmussen v. Fleming, 741 P.2d 674, 689 (Ariz.1987) (holding that the best interest standard requires that a surrogate decision maker assess such broad and undefined factors "as relief from suffering, the preservation or restoration of functioning, and quality and extent of sustained life"); Conservatorship of Drabick, 245 Cal.Rptr. 840 (Cal.App.1988).

5. Some commentators have proposed that the best interest standard should be applied in all cases in order to protect against self-serving motives of a substituted decisionmaker. See e.g., Louise Harmon, "Falling Off the Vine: Legal Fictions and the Doctrine of Substituted Judgment," 100 Yale L.J. 1 (1990). Some courts have declared the appropriate standard to be the "best interest" standard, but then interpreted that standard to be the same as the substituted judgment standard, "The best interests of the ward is a standard that attempts in the first instance to replicate the decisions that the ward herself would make in the circumstances present, if she did not suffer from diminished mental capacity or physical incapacity." In the Matter of Gordy, 658 A.2d 613, 618 (Del.Ch.1994).

§ 16–19. Proxy Decisionmaking: The Decisionmaking Process

Different states impose different procedures upon proxy decision makers. Although many states provide by statute for the procedure to be followed in the appointment of the decision maker and, where necessary, the judicial confirmation of that choice, these same statutes generally do not specify any procedure to be followed by the proxy decision maker in making the decision itself.[1]

2. Formerly Competent Patients

§ 16–20. Formerly Competent Patients: Anticipatory Decisionmaking and Advance Directives

Where an incompetent patient has been competent and possessed discernible values and interests, the proxy decision maker is obliged to apply the patient's values and interests in an attempt to make the decision that the patient would have made if she were, at that moment, competent. This task is made easier when the patient has left an indication of her values and interests, or, better still, when the patient has addressed the kinds of treatment she would desire if she were to become incompetent. A number of devices have been developed to facilitate efforts by competent people who wish to plan for their medical decision making should they become incompetent. These include the "living will" or "right to die" statement (now called an "individual instruction" under the Uniform Health Care Decisions Act); the durable power of attorney for health care decisionmaking; and the values history. These documents, often called "advance directives," have been given a range of formal legal effects in different jurisdictions.[1] In addition, patients are increasingly encouraged to talk with their physicians, family members, and others likely to be present for any decision that must be made when the patient becomes incompetent. The courts have increasingly recognized the significance of statements made under these circumstances, even if they do not have the formal legal effect of written advance directives.

§ 16–21. Living Wills

The Karen Quinlan[1] case gave rise to legislative activity in a host of state capitals, and within two years of the first press reports of that case, several states had adopted statutes that formally recognized some forms of written directives describing some circumstances in which certain kinds of medical care could be terminated. These statutes were sometimes denominated "living will" acts, sometimes "right to die" acts, and occasionally "natural death" acts;[2] they are all known colloquially as living will statutes. Because of the

§ 16–19

1. Compare Utah Code Ann. 1953, 75–2–1107 with W.Va. Code, 16–30B–8.

§ 16–20

1. While most states have promulgated different statutes to deal with these different documents, the trend is to combine living will, durable power and family consent laws into a single statute. See Ariz.Rev.Stat. § 36–3201 through 36–3252; Fla.Stat.Ann. § 765.101–.401; Md.Code, Health–General, § 9–601

through 9–618, and Va.Code 1950, § 54.1–2981 through 54.1–2993.

§ 16–21

1. In re Quinlan, 355 A.2d 647 (N.J.1976) cert. denied sub nom. Garger v. New Jersey, 429 U.S. 922, 97 S.Ct. 319, 50 L.Ed.2d 289 (1976).

2. Some states also have passed legislation which specifically provides for withdrawal of life sustaining treatments for patients who have not executed a living will and are diag-

apparent urgency created by the specter of Karen Quinlan deteriorating on a ventilator (and, later, on tube feeding), state legislatures felt the need to act quickly to create something that resembled a living will statute, even if it meant failing to reach any real agreement on the substance of a proposed statute. In addition, several interest groups, including the right to die and right to life lobbies, spent a considerable amount of energy attempting to help shape the statutes. Today, virtually every state has produced a living will statute. The statutes vary widely from state to state; some allow for the creation of very powerful documents, and others are little more than political window dressing without any substantive value.

A Uniform Rights of the Terminally Ill Act was promulgated in 1989, but it has had only scant effect in state legislatures: no legislature has adopted the Act in the form in which the Commissioners issued it. The Uniform Health Care Decisions Act ("UHCDA"), which was approved in 1994, would substantially recast the living will. Under that uniform act, an "individual instruction" may direct virtually any health-care decision. As of 1999, only three states have adopted this uniform act.[3]

An analysis of the meaning of the variety of living will statutes promulgated by the states requires an inquiry into several discrete issues.

—*Who can execute living wills?*

In some states, living wills are available only to competent adults.[4] In Virginia living wills can be executed on behalf of children, but only following a prescribed judicial process.[5] Some states do not permit a terminally ill person to execute a document, apparently out of fear that the terminal illness itself puts the patient's competence (or thoughtfulness, at the least) at risk.[6]

—*When does a living will become effective?*

In most cases a living will becomes effective immediately after it is executed. Sometimes, however, a waiting period—analogous to a commercial sales cooling off period—delays the effective date of the document.[7] Under the Uniform Rights of the Terminally Ill Act, the document becomes "operative" when it is communicated to the attending physician and the patient is both terminally ill and incompetent.[8] In many states and under the Uniform Rights of the Terminally Ill Act, the living will is suspended during the term of a pregnancy, at least as long as the fetus might be born alive if life sustaining treatment is continued.[9] Such attempts to extend narrower statutory "right to die" protection to pregnant women than to others may be ineffective because they may violate the equal protection clause of the fourteenth amendment, or

---

nosed as comatose with no reasonable possibility of recovery. See e.g., Conn. Gen. Stat.Ann. §§ 19a–570 to 19a–575 (Connecticut Removal of Life Support Systems Act); Elizabeth D. McLean, Living Will Statutes in Light of Cruzan v. Director, Missouri Department of Health: Ensuring that Patient's Wishes Will Prevail, 40 Emory L.J. 1305, 1319 n.61 (1991).

3. Maine, Mississippi, and New Mexico.

4. See e.g., Iowa Code Ann. § 144A.3(1).

5. See Va. Code 1950, §§ 54.1–2981 to 54.1–2992; see also V.T.C.A., Health & Safety Code § 672.006.

6. See e.g., N.H. Rev. Stat. Ann. 137–H:1 to 137–H:16.

7. See e.g., Minn. Stat.Ann. § 145B.05.

8. Unif. Rights of the Terminally Ill Act, § 3, 9B U.L.A. 118 (Supp. 1993).

9. See Unif. Rights of the Terminally Ill Act, § 6(c), 9B U.L.A. 121 (Supp. 1993); see also Gregory Gelfand, Living Will Statutes: The First Decade, 1987 Wis. L.Rev. 737, 816–17 (1987).

equal protection provisions of state constitutions;[10] this issue has yet to be litigated.

—When does the living will expire?

Under most statutes, a living will never expires (although, of course, it may be revoked or changed). Under other statutes, however, a living will has a finite life, and it must be renewed periodically or it will expire.[11] The time limit on the survival of living wills is a legal anachronism that arose out of the fear that people would execute such documents and then have a change of values but forget to alter their living wills; the statutory language, however, has survived the demise of this fear.

—To what conditions does the living will apply?

Living wills generally apply in the case of terminal illness. What constitutes a terminal illness is variously defined,[12] or not defined at all. The Uniform Rights of the Terminally Ill Act applies in the case of a "terminal condition"[13] (rather than a terminal illness), which is defined as a condition that is "incurable and irreversible."[14] Moreover, following the discussion generated by *Cruzan*, some states amended their statutes to make it clear that living wills applied to some non-terminal conditions such as "irreversible coma"[15] or "persistent vegetative state"[16] as well as to terminal conditions.

—To what kind of treatment does the living will apply?

Living will statutes do not apply to all forms of treatment. In some states the statute applies only to life sustaining treatment[17] or to maintenance medical care, terms that are often defined (if at all) in ambiguous or circular ways. Identical terms sometimes have varied definitions in different states.[18] About half of the states explicitly exclude nutrition and hydration from the list of treatments that may be withdrawn. Excluding Missouri, the state courts that have addressed this issue have ignored or sidestepped these legislative exceptions by assuming that the statutory exceptions were meant to apply only to non-medical feeding, not to the provision of nutrition and hydration through medical apparatus.[19] In any case, there is some question

10. See Elizabeth Carlin Benton, Note, The Constitutionality of Pregnancy Clauses in Living Will Statutes, 43 Vand. L. Rev. 1821 (1990). While most states address the issue of pregnancy in their living will statutes, several states avoid serious constitutional questions by adopting more flexible pregnancy provisions.

11. See e.g., West's Ann.Cal. Health & Safety Code § 7189.5 (living will is only valid for five years); see also Gelfand, supra note 9, at 765.

12. Colorado's statute defines terminal condition as "an incurable or irreversible condition for which the administration of life-sustaining procedures will serve only to postpone the moment of death." West's Colo. Rev. Stat. Ann. § 15–18–103(10). The Wisconsin living will statute defines "terminal illness" as one "that a reasonable medical judgment finds would cause death imminently." Wis. Stat. Ann. 154.01(8). Hawaii and Montana use the phrase "within a relatively short period of time." Haw. Rev. Stat. § 327D–2; Mont. Code Ann. 50–9–102(7).

13. Unif. Rights of the Terminally Ill Act, § 3, 9B U.L.A. 170 (Supp. 1999).

14. Unif. Rights of the Terminally Ill Act, § 1, 9B U.L.A. 163 (Supp. 1999).

15. La. Stat. Ann.–Rev.Stat. 40:1299.58.210.

16. Idaho Code § 39–4503(3); Haw.Rev. Stat. § 327D–2; Tenn.Code Ann. § 32–11–103(9). Ohio and Arkansas extend the application of their living will statutes to patients in a permanent unconscious state. See Ohio Rev. Code § 2133.01(u); Ark.Code Ann. § 20–17–201(11).

17. See e.g., Tenn. Code Ann. § 32–11–103(5).

18. See Gelfand, supra note 9, at 750 n.49.

19. McConnell v. Beverly Enterprises–Connecticut, Inc., 553 A.2d 596 (Conn.1989); Cor-

about the constitutional validity of such exclusions, especially after the *Cruzan* case.[20] The Uniform Health Care Decisions Act is the broadest form of advance directive statute; it applies to any health-care decision.

—What formalities are required to execute a living will?

The formalities to execute a living will also vary from state to state and they generally do not follow the requirements for executing a will. There is usually some kind of witness requirement, and some states disqualify some witnesses, including health care workers and potential heirs.[21] These requirements were based on the fear that the hospital or nursing home staff and the patient's heirs might conspire to coerce a patient to sign a living will, or simply lie in order to take the financial fruits of the patient's death. Unfortunately, such a limitation excludes exactly those individuals who would be most likely to talk to a patient about the living will and help him execute the document. Furthermore, some statutes provide living will forms that are mandatory;[22] in those states no other form has any legal validity. Other statutes provide nonmandatory (i.e., sample) form documents.

Statutes in some states (and both the Uniform Rights of the Terminally Ill Act and the Uniform Health Care Decisions Act) expressly provide that any document executed in one state and in compliance with the law of that state is valid outside that state under at least some circumstances. In some of these states nothing more than a directive properly executed under the laws of the place of execution is required; in at least one state it is valid only if it "substantially complies" with the laws of the state in which it is to be enforced as well.[23] No court has yet evaluated whether a living will executed in one state in conformity with that state's laws must be enforceable in another state in the absence of such a statute. Arguably, the full faith and credit clause of the United States Constitution requires every state to give the effect to such documents that they would be given in the state in which they were executed.

—How is a living will revoked?

The process for revoking a living will varies from state to state. Often a living will can be revoked in the same manner as a will. Most states also provide other, easier ways for a patient to revoke a living will because of the concern that the patient may be locked into a health care decision that was made years before. Some statutes make virtually any indication that a patient

---

bett v. D'Alessandro, 487 So.2d 368, 370–71 (Fla.App.1986).

20. See Gelfand, supra note 9, at 750–751 n.49.

21. Virtually all states require that at least two adult witnesses verify the living will and its signatories. See e.g., Iowa Code Ann. § 144A.3(1); Vernon's Ann. Mo. Stat. § 459.015(3); Mont. Code Ann. 50–9–103(3). Eight states, Arkansas, Connecticut, Iowa, Maine, Missouri, Montana, New Mexico, and New York do not require anything more than two witnesses. The remaining states have qualifications and prerequisites regarding how many witnesses are required or who those witnesses may be. See Gelfand, supra note 9, at 757–58. The Uniform Health Care Decisions

Act takes a more liberal approach; it does not require witnesses and the individual instruction may be oral or in writing. UHCDA, § 2(a).

22. See e.g., Iowa Code Ann. § 144A.1.–11; California, West's Ann. Cal. Health & Safety Code §§ 7185–7195. Those in favor of a strict form requirement believe that it provides clarity and consistency, and it simplifies the duties of doctors who must interpret the living will.

23. See Unif. Rights of the Terminally Ill Act, § 12, 9B U.L.A. 127 (Supp. 1993). Haw. Rev. Stat. § 327D–25 ("A document executed in another state will be considered valid for purposes of this chapter if the document and the execution of said document substantially complies with the requirements of this chapter.").

wishes to revoke the document an effective revocation; under the Uniform Rights of the Terminally Ill Act "[a] declarant may revoke a declaration at any time and in any manner, without regard to the declarant's mental or physical condition."[24]

—*What is the effect of a living will?*

The consequences of a living will also vary from state to state. Few states actually require health care workers to carry out the formal legal requests of the patient. As a general matter, statutes permit health care workers to carry out the patient's requests without fear of other legal consequences, including criminal and civil liability.[25] Most statutes also provide that taking actions permitted by the document does not constitute suicide for any purpose, and that the physician's (and others') cooperation in the process does not constitute assisting suicide. Finally, many statutes require physicians who do not wish to carry out the requests of the patient to transfer the patient to another health care provider who will.

Some statutes contain professional, civil, or criminal sanctions.[26] Failure to transfer a patient to someone who will carry out the wishes expressed in the living will may give rise to professional action,[27] including licensing action, against the offending health care worker. Coercing someone to sign a living will, destroying or hiding someone's living will, forging another person's living will, and concealing a patient's revocation of a living will (and, sometimes, the failure to record the existence of the living will, or conditioning medical care or health insurance coverage on the existence of a living will) may give rise to ordinary civil or criminal liability.[28] There is, however, no reported civil or criminal case in which any health care professional has been sanctioned for any action taken with regard to a living will.[29]

—*What if a patient has a living will that is not consistent with the formalities of state statutory requirements?*

Even when living wills do not comply with the formalities of state law, they are treated as significant written statements and are highly persuasive to courts called to decide upon the wishes of a patient without a formally valid advance directive.[30] Indeed, the very fact that a patient would want to execute such a document—whether formally valid or not—constitutes evidence of the patient's serious consideration of this issue. As the Florida Supreme Court pointed out while evaluating a technically invalid living will, "[i]f * * * a person, while competent, had executed a so-called 'living' or 'mercy' will, that will would be persuasive evidence of that incompetent person's intention and it should be given great weight."[31] Thus, technically and formally invalid living wills are not legally irrelevant to decision making concerning life sustaining processes; they are likely to be extremely significant, albeit like any other relevant independent statements of the patient.

24. Unif. Rights of the Terminally Ill Act, § 4, 9B U.L.A. 173 (Supp. 1999).

25. See e.g., Haw. Rev. Stat. § 327D–18.

26. See e.g., Mont. Code Ann. 50–9–206(1); Tenn. Code Ann. § 32–11–108. See also Gelfand, supra note 9, at 777.

27. See e.g., Utah Code Ann. 1953, 75–2–1112(3).

28. See e.g., Official Code Ga. Ann. § 31–32–10.

29. See Gelfand, supra note 9, at 776.

30. See e.g., In re Eichner, 438 N.Y.S.2d 266, 420 N.E.2d 64 (1981), cert. denied 454 U.S. 858, 102 S.Ct. 309, 70 L.Ed.2d 153 (1981).

31. John F. Kennedy Memorial Hosp., Inc. v. Bludworth, 452 So.2d 921, 926 (Fla.1984).

§ 16–22. Durable Powers of Attorney for Health Care

A durable power of attorney is a document executed by a competent person to appoint another to make health care decisions for him when he becomes incompetent to make them himself. As a matter of course, any competent adult may be appointed an agent under durable power statutes. A principal may appoint an agent, and then also name an alternate to act if the agent is unavailable or unwilling to serve.

Durable powers generally may be limited in time, scope, or method of decision making, at the discretion of the principal executing the document. Thus, a principal may designate a person to make only decisions concerning life sustaining treatment, or only decisions that do not involve life sustaining treatment, or any other subclass of decisions. A principal may require the agent to consult with designated others (a spouse, child, or religious authority, for example) before making health care decisions or to apply principles that are explicitly set out in the power itself. While agents are expected to apply principles of substituted judgment when making health care decisions, and thus to make the decisions that the principal would make if she were competent, durable powers may specify other bases of decision, at the discretion of the principal. There are virtually no practical limits to the restrictions and conditions that may be placed on agents in durable powers of attorney for health care decisionmaking.

In the early 1990s, the durable power of attorney quickly became the preferred form of advance directive. In Justice O'Connor's separate opinion in the *Cruzan* decision, she approved of durable powers of attorney and commented that "the practical wisdom" of such documents had been recognized by several states.[1] She also suggested that durable powers, which she described as "valuable additional safeguard[s] of the patient's interest in directing his medical care,"[2] might have Constitutionally protected status: "Today's decision * * * does not preclude a future determination that the Constitution requires states to implement the decisions of a patient's duly appointed surrogate."[3]

It is not hard to understand why durable powers for health care decision making have become accepted so quickly by ethicists, physicians, medical institutions, and the law. A durable power allows the patient, whose autonomy is at stake, to decide who shall make her health care decisions. This, in turn, allows the patient to choose the decisionmaker most likely to understand and apply the patient's values. Because it does not require a patient to anticipate with any precision the treatment that she may need when incompetent, a durable power is much less likely to give rise to questions and concerns over the possibility that a patient has changed her mind than is a living will. Further, because it creates a particular decisionmaker rather than a particular decision, the durable power allows physicians and family members to participate in discussions about the proposed treatment when the decision is proposed; it allows for more engagement in the process than does a living will.

§ 16–22

1. Cruzan v. Director, Missouri Dept. of Health, 497 U.S. 261, 290, 110 S.Ct. 2841, 2857, 111 L.Ed.2d 224 (1990) (O'Connor, J., concurring).

2. Id. at 291–292, 110 S.Ct. at 2857–59.

3. Id.

Although a durable power is not inconsistent with a living will—a principal could instruct an agent to follow the wishes expressed in a living will—it is usually a far broader document that can apply to all health care decision making, not just to those narrow categories recognized by living will statutes.[4]

No court has addressed the question of whether an agent appointed by a durable power of attorney would prevail if he made a health care decision inconsistent with that directed by a living will. While the specificity of the conditions to which the living will apply would seem to give it priority over the more general power, the dynamic nature of the durable power suggests that the appointed agent should have priority. In any case, of course, the agent must consider the existence of the living will when making his decision on the part of the principal.

Powers of attorney have been recognized at common law for centuries.[5] At common law, however, all such powers became invalid upon the incapacity of the principal, who was expected to supervise the activities of the agent.[6] Thus, at common law a power of attorney could not be employed to make health care decisions—if the principal were competent he would not need the power, and if he were not competent the power would be ineffective. It was not until the last half of this century that it became apparent—probably as a consequence of an increasing number of elderly individuals with variable competency who depended upon others to manage their financial affairs—that the utility of powers of attorney could be increased if they could be made to continue in effect (or even become effective) upon the incapacity of the principal. As a response to this recognition, certain provisions of the Uniform Probate Code were designed to modify the common law rule and allow the principal to choose whether the power of attorney would become effective, remain in effect, or terminate upon his or her incapacity.[7] Some version of the Uniform Probate Code provision creating durable powers has now been adopted by most of the states, and the rule that the power of attorney is always revoked by the incapacity of the principal has been changed by statute in every state.[8]

There is great variety in the durable power statutes promulgated specifically for health care purposes. Some of the earliest statutes—like California's—are very narrow and restrictive;[9] while others are as broad as the

4. For more detailed discussions about durable powers of attorney, see David A. Peters, Advance Medical Directives: The Case for the Durable Power of Attorney for Health Care, 8 J. Legal Med. 437 (1987); Susan R. Martyn & Lynn Balshone Jacobs, Legislating Advance Directives for the Terminally Ill: The Living Will & Durable Power of Attorney, 63 Neb. L. Rev. 779 (1984).

5. Jeffrey Kolb, Indiana Power of Attorney Act, 25 Ind. L. Rev. 1345, 1347–48 (1992); Evan R. Collins et al., Drafting the Durable Power of Attorney—A System's Arrival 5 (2d ed. 1991); Martyn & Jacobs, supra note 4, at 795–96.

6. See, Restatement (Second) of Agency § 120 cmt. a (1958) ("[T]o the extent that agency is a consensual relation, it cannot exist after the death or incapacity of the principal or

the agent. This was the common law viewpoint and consistent with the older theory as to contractual relations to the effect that the minds of the parties must 'meet' before a contract can be made. From this point of view, an agreement that an agency should continue after the death [or incapacity] of a principal is a legal impossibility.")

7. See William M. McGovern, Jr., Trusts, Custodianship, and Durable Powers of Attorney, 27 Real Prop., Prob. & Tr. J. 1, 18 (1992).

8. David M. English, The UPC and the New Durable Powers, 27 Real Prop., Prob. & Tr. J., 333, 337 (1992).

9. See West's Ann. Cal. Civ. Code § 2433 (enumerating strict requirements for form of durable power of attorney for health care).

Uniform Probate Code provision.[10] Some statutes provide sample forms, while others provide mandatory forms.[11] Moreover, a few state statutes require that a named agent agree to serve in that capacity.[12] Although most statutes (and the Uniform Probate Code) do not require that the agent formally accept his authority, it is certainly the better practice to seek the agreement of the agent when the durable power is executed. If nothing else, seeking that acceptance allows the principal and the named agent to talk about the principal's expectations and the agent's intentions.

§ 16–23.   Family Consent Laws

Most incompetent patients facing decisions concerning the termination of life sustaining treatment have not executed living wills or durable powers of attorney. In fact, the vast majority of Americans have not made any formal advance directives.[1] While there are a number of reasons for this—including the preference most people have not to think about the events that require such documents—many people are confident that such documents are unnecessary because they believe that their family members would make proper decisions on their behalf without the need for intervening formalities. Indeed, physicians (and the courts) have been relying on families to make such health care decisions for most of the last century, despite the absence of any legal basis for the practice.[2] In 1983, the President's Commission assumed (without citation to any authority) that such a longstanding practice must have gained legal acceptance, and the Commission pointed out five reasons that deference to family members is appropriate:

> (1) The family is generally most concerned about the good of the patient. (2) The family will usually be the most knowledgeable about the patient's goals, preferences, and values. (3) The family deserves recognition as an important social unit that ought to be treated, within limits, as a responsible decision-maker in matters that intimately affect its members. (4) Especially in a society in which many other traditional forms of community have eroded, participation in a family is often an important dimension of personal fulfillment. (5) Since a protected sphere of privacy

10. According to the Uniform Probate Code,

A durable power of attorney is a power of attorney by which a principal designates another his attorney in fact in writing and the writing contains the words "This power of attorney shall not be affected by subsequent disability or incapacity of the principal, or lapse of time," or "This power of attorney shall become effective upon the disability or incapacity of the principal," or similar words showing the intent of the principal that the authority conferred shall be exercisable notwithstanding the principal's subsequent disability or incapacity, and unless it states a time of termination, notwithstanding the lapse of time since the execution of the instrument.

Unif. Probate Code § 5–501, 8 U.L.A. 420 (1996).

11. "A written power of attorney for health care shall provide no other authority than the authority to make health care decisions on behalf of the principal and shall be in the following form * * *." Or. Rev. Stat. § 127.530 (emphasis added). For detailed analysis of statutory forms, see English, supra note 8, at 363–76.

12. See e.g., Mich. Comp. Laws Ann. § 700.496(6); Or. Rev. Stat. § 127.525.

§ 16–23

1. In 1995 the General Accounting Office reported, "Surveys indicated that, in general, only 10 to 25 percent of Americans have documented their end-of-life choices or appointed a health care agent ... (with some estimates as low as 5 percent.)" GAO/HEHS 95–135 Aug.28, 1995, WL 522873 (F.D.C.H.)

2. See Marshall B. Kapp, Who's The Parent Here? The Family's Impact on the Autonomy of Older Persons, 41 Emory L. J. 773, 774 (1992).

and autonomy is required for the flourishing of this interpersonal union, institutions and the state should be reluctant to intrude, particularly regarding matters that are personal and on which there is a wide range of opinion in society.[3]

Physicians and institutions may have been particularly disposed to accept family members' decisions because those who made the decisions were also the ones generally authorized to bring any subsequent informed consent action on behalf of the patient. Thus, accepting family members' decisions made malpractice actions based on those decisions unlikely.

Growing concern over the formal legal status of family decision making in the 1980s caused many state legislatures to recognize the practice and regulate it by statute.[4] These "family consent" statutes vary from state to state. Some have been added to state living will statutes to provide a back-up mechanism for making decisions regarding life sustaining treatment on behalf of those who did not execute any advance directive; others are free-standing statutes that either apply to life sustaining treatment or health care decisions generally.[5] While most statutes discourage families and health care workers from seeking judicial review of the vast majority of health care decisions made under the statutes,[6] some require judicial confirmation of decisions which result in the death of the patient.[7]

Despite their differences, family consent statutes have many common attributes. They become effective only when the patient is incompetent, and some require a certificate that the patient is incompetent before the family is authorized to make any health care decision. They authorize designated close family members to act on behalf of the patient, although the procedure for designation of the family member varies from state to state. All of the statutes prescribe a hierarchy of family members. No state prescribes precisely the same hierarchy as that recognized for purposes of intestate succession in the state's probate code because state legislatures have recognized that the purposes of the probate code are not reflected in the need for surrogate decision makers, and an alternative hierarchy is appropriate.[8] Because some

3. President's Commission for the Study of Ethical Problems in Medicine and Biomedical and Behavioral Research, Deciding to Forego Life–Sustaining Treatment: A Report on the Ethical, Medical, and Legal Issues in Treatment Decisions 127–28 (1983).

4. See generally Jan Ellen Rein, Preserving Dignity and Self–Determination of the Elderly in the Face of Competing Interests and Grim Alternatives: A Proposal for Statutory Refocus and Reform, 60 Geo. Wash. L. Rev. 1818 (1992).

5. One federal court has interpreted the Cruzan decision as constitutionally requiring that states follow laws on substituted judgment when they are available. Woodland v. Angus, 820 F.Supp. 1497, 1517 (D.Utah 1993) (stating that Missouri had fulfilled the due process requirement by applying its own living will statute, and that Utah was required to do the same by applying the substituted judgment provision of the state's informed consent statute to an incompetent prisoner refusing medication). Thus, under this interpretation of

Cruzan, any state with a substitute decision making provision within a general informed consent statute may be required to apply the statute to all medical treatment decisions, including those concerning life sustaining procedures.

6. See e.g., W.Va. Code § 16–30B–7 (providing that court approval is not required); see also In re Lawrance, 579 N.E.2d 32 (Ind.1991); DeGrella v. Elston, 858 S.W.2d 698 (Ky.1993) (stating that court approval is intrusive upon a private matter and unnecessarily expensive).

7. See e.g., Ohio Rev. Code Ann. § 2123.08 (requiring probate court approval before withdrawing artificial nutrition and hydration). In addition, Maryland's Attorney General interpreted the former Maryland statute as requiring court approval for the termination of life-sustaining procedures. 73 Op. Att'y Gen. 162 (Md. October 17, 1988).

8. The typical hierarchy is as follows: 1) Guardian of the person; 2) the person's spouse;

statutes recognize that family members may not be available for these decisions, close friends are included in the hierarchy, typically at the lowest level.[9] In addition, instead of a rigid hierarchy, Colorado simply grants authority to a person who has a close relationship and who is most likely to be currently informed of the patient's wishes regarding medical treatment.[10] Two states provide that the decision making power rests with the physician, not the family, although the physician must consult with the family before deciding to terminate life sustaining treatment.[11] All family consent statutes provide that a patient's specific designations of health care decisionmakers (through a durable power of attorney, for example) or of particular decisions (through a living will, for example) take priority over a family member exercising authority under the statute.[12] Thus, there can be no conflict between a living will or durable power and a family member's decisions: the decisions made in the living will, or by the agent appointed by the durable power, prevail over the family member's decisions.

Like living will statutes, family consent laws usually are permissive, not mandatory, upon health care providers. Family members and health care providers who act in accordance with consent given under the terms of the acts are relieved of liability for depending on such consent.[13] Some family consent statutes formally recognize the principle of substituted judgment and require authorized family members to attempt to discover what the patient would wish if competent.[14]

Because the common law status of family decision making remains unclear, it is difficult to know whether a family consent statute necessarily preempts all nonstatutory family decision making, or whether the family consent statute operates only within the sometimes very limited scope of the statute itself. These statutes have been the subject of very little litigation, perhaps because they do no more than bring formal recognition to an arrangement which is so clearly based in common sense and which has been accepted in fact for so long.

3) any adult child of the person; 4) either parent of the person; 5) any adult sibling of the person; 6) any adult grandchild of the person. Since the parents and siblings (ancestors and collaterals) take precedence over grandchildren (issue), this cannot follow any intestacy scheme. See e.g., West's Fla. Stat. Ann. § 765.07. However, the Arkansas statute does, atypically, provide for "heirs at law" as a last resort. Ark. Code Ann. § 20–17–214.

9. See Ariz. Rev. Stat. § 36–3231 (also providing for a domestic partner); Ill. S.H.A. 755 ILCS 40/1; W.Va. Code, 16–30B–7; see also D.C. Code 1981, § 21–2210 (providing for a religious superior). Under the Uniform Health Care Decisions Act, a patient may orally designate any person he wishes to be at the top of his priority list by communicating that choice to his supervising health-care provider. See Uniform Health Care Decisions Act, § 5(b).

10. West's Colo. Rev. Stat. Ann. § 15–18.5–101.

11. Conn. Gen. Stat. Ann. § 19a–571; Haw. Rev. Stat. § 327D–21.

12. See e.g., N.C. Gen. Stat. § 90–322 (b) (requiring that no advance directive exist in order for the family to have decision making authority, and placing an appointed health care agent in the first class of the hierarchy, above guardian of the person, thereby allowing the health care agent to go beyond the written powers of attorney, but not contrary to its instructions, in order to act as a surrogate decision maker where the document is unclear).

13. See e.g., West's Fla. Stat. Ann. § 765.10.

14. See e.g., W.Va. Code § 16–30B–8 (providing that the surrogate shall make decisions in accordance with the patient's wishes and religious and moral beliefs as well as in accordance with the patient's best interest).

§ 16–24. Common Law and Proxy Decisionmaking in the Absence of Governing Statutes or Advance Directives

When there is no advance directive, and when there is no family consent (or similar) statute applicable to provide for decision making for an incompetent patient, courts have attempted to serve the principle of autonomy by allowing others to make health care decisions on behalf of incompetent patients. Because the guiding principle is that the wishes of the patient should be carried out, courts attempt to apply a substituted judgment test in these cases.[1] Unfortunately, it is often difficult to know with any certainty what kind of treatment a patient would desire in any particular instance.[2]

Typically, it is only possible to know precisely what a patient would desire in the rare instance when the patient recently and reliably described exactly what he would want under the very circumstances in which he is subsequently found.[3] For example, in *In re Eichner*,[4] the New York Court of Appeals was willing to accept a decision to terminate life sustaining treatment made on behalf of a Catholic priest when the decision was based on statements made and repeated by the priest, when those statements were consistent with his religious life and the tenets of his religion, and when he was in exactly the medical condition that he had addressed in his statement. The priest, who had taught bioethics and knew the area well, was in a condition identical to that of Karen Quinlan, on whose case he had commented.

Even if the level of seriousness, consideration, and depth of thought that was attributed to the patient in *Eichner* were attributed to others, it is hard to imagine how most people for whom decisions about life sustaining medical treatment must be made could anticipate their subsequent condition with such specificity. The variety of diagnoses and prognoses that could give rise to the need to make such decisions is so broad that even those well versed in the medical possibilities could not be expected to make statements that would anticipate all situations. To require such specificity effectively eliminates the possibility of substitute decisionmaking in the vast majority of cases, and for that reason, even the New York Court of Appeals would not require that the patient foresee precisely his own diagnosis and the exact treatment proposed for him.[5]

§ 16–24

1. See e.g., Woodland v. Angus, 820 F.Supp. 1497, 1517 (D.Utah 1993).

2. See In Matter Westchester County Medical Center on Behalf of O'Connor, 534 N.Y.S.2d 886, 531 N.E.2d 607 (N.Y.1988).

3. Id.

4. 438 N.Y.S.2d 266, 420 N.E.2d 64 (N.Y. 1981).

5. In re Westchester County Medical Center on Behalf of O'Connor, 534 N.Y.S.2d 886, 531 N.E.2d 607 (N.Y.1988), holding, "We do not mean to suggest that to be effective, a patient's expressed desire to decline treatment must specify a precise condition and a particular treatment," Id. at 893, 531 N.E.2d at 614. Rather, the test is "whether the infirmities she was concerned with and the procedure she eschewed are qualitatively different than those now presented." Id. See Sol Wachtler, A Judge's Perspective: the New York Rulings, 18 Law, Medicine, & Health Care 60 (1990) (suggesting that the O'Connor opinion was largely based on the individual facts that the patient was conscious, was not terminally ill, was able to feel pain, and had a disputed prognosis; Wachtler distinguishes O'Connor from Cruzan in that O'Connor did not involve a patient in a persistent vegetative state); see also Stewart Pollock, Identifying Appropriate Decision–Makers and Standards for Decision, 18 Law, Medicine, & Health Care 63 (1990).

As a consequence, virtually all courts (except, arguably, those in New York[6], Missouri[7] and Michigan[8]) now permit substitute decision making for formerly competent patients in broader circumstances. The decision maker (sometimes a family member, sometimes someone else appointed by the court, sometimes the court itself) must look to all potentially trustworthy sources of information and determine, with sufficient reliability, what decision the patient would make if that patient were competent.

§ 16–25. Statements of the Patient

While courts have identified a variety of appropriate sources of information upon which a decision maker may rely to formulate substitute decisions, all agree that the most important basis for such decision making is found in the statements of the patient made when the patient was competent. These statements are considered more reliable under the following circumstances:

- if they are made on serious occasions (or, in the words of the *Eichner* court, are "solemn pronouncements"),[1]

- if they are consistently repeated,[2]

- if they are made by a mature person who understands the underlying issues,[3]

- if they are consistent with values demonstrated in other aspects of the patient's life (including the patient's religion, which appears to be significant to a great number of courts),[4]

- if they are made shortly before the need for the treatment decision,[5] and

- if they address with some specificity the actual condition of the patient.[6]

§ 16–26. Other Sources of Information About the Health Care Choices of the Patient

A patient's statements are not the only source of information about what health care decisions an incompetent patient would make if that patient were competent. Except in Missouri, Michigan and New York, which arguably still adhere to the narrow view that any decision to terminate life sustaining treatment must be based on the statement of the patient herself,[1] courts

6. In re Westchester County Medical Center on Behalf of O'Connor, 534 N.Y.S.2d 886, 531 N.E.2d 607 (N.Y.1988).

7. Cruzan v. Harmon, 760 S.W.2d 408 (Mo. 1988).

8. In re Martin, 538 N.W.2d (Mich. 1995).

§ 16–25

1. In re Eichner, 420 N.E.2d 64, 72, 438 N.Y.S.2d 266, 274 (N.Y.1981); In re Conroy, 486 A.2d 1209, 1230 (N.J.1985); In re Westchester County Medical Center on Behalf of O'Connor, 534 N.Y.S.2d 886, 892, 531 N.E.2d 607, 613 (N.Y.1988).

2. In re Westchester County Medical Center on Behalf of O'Connor, 534 N.Y.S.2d 886, 531 N.E.2d 607 (N.Y.1988).

3. Id.
4. Id.
5. Id.
6. Id.

§ 16–26

1. See Cruzan v. Harmon, 760 S.W.2d 408 (Mo.1988), cert. granted 492 U.S. 917, 109 S.Ct. 3240, 106 L.Ed.2d 587 (1989); In re Westchester County Medical Center on Behalf of O'Connor, 534 N.Y.S.2d 886, 892, 531 N.E.2d 607, 613 (N.Y.1988) (stating that inquiries beyond a patient's expressed intent conflict with

attempt to serve the autonomy interest of the patient by looking beyond the formal articulations of the patient to find any relevant evidence of what health care decision the patient would make if confronted, when competent, with the question that now confronts the patient's surrogate. There are several possible sources of such information aside from the statements of the patient directly addressing the issue:

- the religious convictions, and other deeply held beliefs, of the patient,[2]

- the values expressed in the activities of the patient through her competent life,[3]

- the patient's general attitude about health care and the health care system, and the patient's reactions to previous encounters with the health care system,[4]

- the patient's attitude toward disease and health,[5]

- the patient's reaction to others (perhaps friends or family members) undergoing similar experiences,[6] and

- the patient's relationship with her family and the impact of the treatment on the family.[7]

In some cases these additional sources of a patient's values will provide a rich and convincing source of information about what choice a patient would make about a particular health care decision; in other cases they reveal very little.

§ 16–27. The Values History

Perhaps the best model for a source of information that can contribute to decision making concerning life sustaining treatment is the "values history," a kind of declaratory, non-mandatory advance directive.[1] Unlike other similar documents, the "values history" generally is not limited to specific questions about whether a person would want particular kinds of medical intervention; the answer to any such question depends on too great a variety of contingencies. Although many people would not want ventilator support if it were unlikely to return them to a cognitive state, most people would want to be placed on a ventilator under some conditions. Instead, the values history asks questions about those values, general interests, desires, fears, and expectations that are most likely to be significant when a surrogate must make a decision about life sustaining treatment. It provides the information necessary to make a reasonable and thoughtful decision; it does not purport to be the

the court's "fundamental commitment to the notion that no person or court should substitute its judgment as to what would be an acceptable quality of life"), In re Martin, 538 N.W.2d 399 (1995)(requiring an analysis of the articulated desires of the patient).

2. See e.g., Brophy v. New England Sinai Hosp., Inc., 497 N.E.2d 626, 631 (Mass.1986). A religious advisor to the patient may be able to help the court determine whether an incompetent patient would choose to forgo life sustaining medical treatment even if that advisor has not spoken to the patient about that issue. See In Re Tavel, 661 A.2d 1061 (Del.1995).

3. Id.

4. See e.g., In re Jobes, 529 A.2d 434 (N.J. 1987).

5. Id.

6. Id.

7. See e.g., Brophy v. New England Sinai Hosp., Inc., 497 N.E.2d 626, 631 (Mass.1986).

§ 16–27

1. See, Ben A. Rich, The Values History: A New Standard of Care, 40 Emory L.J. 1109, 1141–80 (1991).

decision itself.[2] The values history is likely to be extraordinarily useful to thoughtful surrogate decision makers, and thus, it is likely to be well respected by most courts as a source of relevant information about the patient's likely decision.

§ 16–28. Applying the Evidence of the Patient's Desires: Subjective, Limited Objective, and Pure Objective Standards

The most influential opinion describing the standard to be applied in terminating life support treatment for patients without advance directives was the 1985 decision in *In re Conroy*.[1] The New Jersey Supreme Court explained and broadened that decision in a trio of cases two years later.[2] The New Jersey Supreme Court suggested that the standard should sometimes be a subjective one, sometimes an objective one, and sometimes a combination of the two, depending on the strength and certainty of the articulation of the patient when that patient was competent, and the current condition of the patient.

The New Jersey Supreme Court adopted a purely subjective standard that carries out the patient's wishes "when it is clear that the particular patient would have refused the treatment under the circumstances involved. * * * [The surrogate decision maker should] do under the circumstances * * * what the particular patient would have done if able to choose for himself."[3] Recognizing that it will not often be clear just what the patient would have chosen, the New Jersey Supreme Court would apply some version of a "best interests" test—an objective test—in other cases.

First, in describing what the court denominated the "limited objective" test, the court held that (1) when there is some trustworthy evidence that the patient would refuse the life sustaining treatment, and (2) when it is clear that the burden of the treatment exceeds the benefit of the continued life to the patient, the treatment may be withheld or withdrawn.[4] This test thus is applied only for patients who had expressed desires, but not "unequivocally," and for whom the net suffering that is a consequence of continued treatment (i.e, "the pain and suffering of life with the treatment less the amount and duration of pain that the patient would likely experience if the treatment were withdrawn") "markedly outweigh[s]" any physical, emotional or intellectual pleasure that may be derived from life.[5] Finally, the New Jersey Supreme Court would apply what it denominated the "pure objective" test to allow the discontinuation of life sustaining treatment (1) when there is no reliable evidence of the patients desires (or no evidence whatsoever), but (2) (a) "the net burdens of the patient's life with the treatment * * * clearly and markedly outweigh the benefits that the patient derives from life," and (b) "the recurring, unavoidable and severe pain of the patient's life with the

2. Thus, a values history is designed to promote patient autonomy. See, e.g., Pam Lambert et al., The Values History: An Innovation in Surrogate Medical Decision Making, 18 Law, Med., & Health Care 202 (1990).

§ 16–28

1. 486 A.2d 1209 (N.J.1985).

2. In re Jobes, 529 A.2d 434 (N.J.1987); In re Peter, 529 A.2d 419 (N.J.1987); In re Farrell, 529 A.2d 404 (N.J.1987).

3. In re Conroy, 486 A.2d 1209, 1229 (N.J. 1985).

4. Id. at 1232.

5. Id.; see also In re Guardianship of Grant, 747 P.2d 445 (Wash.1987).

treatment [is] such that the effect of administering life sustaining treatment would be inhumane."[6]

Thus, the court, in one of the most frequently cited cases dealing with this subject, provided that the "clear" and "unequivocal" desires of the patient to terminate treatment must be carried into effect. Where the desire of the patient is either unclear or equivocal, however, the apparent desire for the termination of treatment will be carried into effect only if the burdens of continued life "clearly" outweigh the benefits of treatment. Where the patient has never made any expression about whether life sustaining treatment should be continued, such treatment must be continued unless it would be inhumane to do so.

While the New Jersey analysis has been generally welcomed by commentators, it was explicitly rejected by the Michigan Supreme Court.[7] That Court pointed out that "[a]ny move from a purely subjective standard to an analysis that encompasses objective criteria is grounded in the state's parens patriae power, not in the common law right of informed consent or self determination,"[8] and thus any move from the subjective standard must be accompanied by the consideration of other state-determined values, including the value of maintaining life. In effect, the Michigan rule permits the state to deny the patient's decisionmaker the authority to terminate life sustaining medical treatment unless the patient had unequivocally announced her own view with regard to the treatment in question before she became incompetent.

§ 16–29. The Special Case of Patients in a Persistent Vegetative State

Although bold for its era in liberalizing the circumstances under which life sustaining treatment could be terminated, the *Conroy* case soon appeared to be too narrow in its approach to patients with some medical conditions—notably, to those patients in a persistent vegetative state. This condition

describes a body which is functioning entirely in terms of its internal controls. It maintains temperature. It maintains heartbeat and pulmonary ventilation. It maintains digestive activity. It maintains reflex activity of muscles and nerves for low level conditioned responses. But there is no behavioral evidence of either self-awareness or awareness of the surroundings in a learned manner.[1]

Both Karen Quinlan and Nancy Cruzan were in persistent vegetative states when their cases came to the judiciary—although this condition was most commonly called "irreversible coma"[2] when the court decided the *Quinlan* case. A person in a persistent vegetative state has no chance of return to a

6. In re Conroy, 486 A.2d 1209, 1232 (N.J. 1985).

7. In re Martin, 538 N.W.2d 399 (Mich. 1995).

8. Id. At 408.

§ 16–29

1. In re Jobes, 529 A.2d 434, 438 (N.J. 1987).

2. Even though Quinlan's cognitive abilities were irreversibly lost due to the destruc-

tion of the cognitive part of her brain, she was not "brain dead" according to the criteria established by the Ad Hoc Committee of the Harvard Medical School. See Matter of Quinlan, 355 A.2d 647 (N.J.1976); see also In re Conroy, 486 A.2d at 1227. The phrase "irreversible coma" has been used inconsistently to describe both brain death (see Chapter 15) and persistent vegetative state. In order to avoid confusion, this phrase is generally avoided today.

cognitive state, although the body of a patient with this condition can be maintained—sometimes without the use of a ventilator—for many years, and in some cases for decades. While it is impossible to know from experience if there is any pain, pleasure, satisfaction, or joy that can be felt by patients in a persistent vegetative state, the medical presumption is that all such feelings are non-existent in these patients.

Do the "limited-objective" and "pure-objective" tests announced in *Conroy* make sense in such cases? Neither would ever permit the termination of life sustaining treatment in the case of a patient in a persistent vegetative state, because the burdens of providing continuing treatment to such a patient (which are nonexistent because the patient has absolutely no sensation of any kind) cannot possibly markedly outweigh the benefits (which are also nonexistent). In essence, the *Conroy* test seems to be too difficult a test to meet when the patient is in a persistent vegetative state; it makes it impossible to terminate treatment unless the patient has made it clear, while competent, that the patient would refuse the treatment under the circumstances involved.

The New Jersey Supreme Court recognized this only two years after it decided *Conroy*, and it determined that the two forms of the objective test should not be applied to patients in a persistent vegetative state.[3] As the court pointed out, the subjective test of *Conroy* must be applied if that is possible. If it is not possible to do so, however, "the right of a patient in an irreversibly vegetative state to determine whether to refuse life-sustaining medical treatment may be exercised by the patient's family or close friend."[4] This right is not subject to any burdens-benefits balancing, as it is with patients who are not in a persistent vegetative state. This very liberal (and, some would say, less protectionist) approach to patients in a persistent vegetative state has been accepted in theory by many states that have faced the question. As Justice Stevens points out in his *Cruzan* dissent, every court which had faced a request to terminate life sustaining treatment for a patient in a persistent vegetative state had ultimately approved the request except the *Cruzan* court itself.[5]

§ 16–30. The Presumption In Favor of Treatment

In determining how to evaluate requests to terminate life-sustaining treatment for incompetent patients, courts have often articulated the principle that "it is best to err, if at all, in favor of preserving life."[1] The United States Supreme Court, in *Cruzan*, explicitly noted the constitutionality of incorporating such a principle in state law.[2] Effectively, many courts have set the continuation of life (and thus the continuation of treatment) as the default position; unless there is a substantial amount of evidence supporting the position that the patient would elect the termination of treatment, it is to be presumed that the patient would elect to have treatment continued.

---

3. In re Jobes, 529 A.2d 434 (N.J.1987).

4. Id. at 447.

5. Cruzan v. Director, Missouri Dept. of Health, 497 U.S. 261, 348–49, 110 S.Ct. 2841, 2888, 111 L.Ed.2d 224 (1990) (Stevens, J., dissenting).

§ 16–30

1. In re Conroy, 486 A.2d 1209, 1233 (N.J. 1985).

2. Cruzan v. Director, Missouri Dept. of Health, 497 U.S. 261, 283, 110 S.Ct. 2841, 2854, 111 L.Ed.2d 224 (1990).

There are several problems with this default position. First, of course, there is no factual basis for it. As the dissent points out in *Cruzan*, the goal of the court ought to be to correctly evaluate the patient's wishes, not to evaluate the best way to err in performing that evaluation.[3]

Second, the oft-repeated argument that it is always better to err on the side of life may substantially underestimate the various kinds of cost of such an error. The continuation of life-sustaining treatment in the case of a terminally ill patient in great pain does little more than continue the discomfort and its accompanying indignity. Erring on the side of requiring such a patient to prolong his pain for additional weeks or months does not seem to be an appropriate default position, and furthermore, it is hard to understand how such unnecessary agony is "susceptible of correction." Similarly, the financial cost of a final illness may represent resources the patient worked for a lifetime to be able to pass on to her children; refusing her the opportunity to do so because of the state's interest in erring on the side of life seems cruel. Finally, the indignity that maintenance of life-sustaining treatment can bring is substantial.

While there are cases in which it is appropriate to err on the side of maintaining life, it may be too great an oversimplification of medical facts and ethical theory to argue that the error always ought to be on that side. Where the patient is terminally ill, where the patient is in terrible pain, and where the patient is in a persistent vegetative state, there is good reason to believe that there should be no default position; an error in favor of maintaining treatment is likely to have consequences that are as drastic as the consequences of a decision in favor of terminating treatment.

3. *Patients Who Have Never Been Competent*

§ 16–31. Patients Who Have Never Been Competent

When a patient has never been competent—when, for example, the patient is profoundly mentally disabled and has been so since birth—it is extremely difficult to apply the substituted judgment standard to determine what kind of life sustaining treatment that patient would want under any particular circumstances. For this reason, courts are divided over whether a subjective standard, based on the individual patient's wishes and desires, should be applied to evaluate the appropriate treatment for adults who have never been competent, or whether an objective standard should be applied.

As the Supreme Judicial Court of Massachusetts pointed out in one of the earliest and most influential cases involving the decision to forgo life sustaining treatment, "we recognize a general right in all persons to refuse medical treatment in appropriate circumstances. The recognition of that right must extend to the case of an incompetent, as well as a competent, patient because the value of human dignity extends to both."[1] That court went on to explain that in any case in which a competent (or formerly competent) person would

---

3. 497 U.S. at 320–21, 110 S.Ct. at 2873–74   (Mass.1977).
(Brennan, J., dissenting).

§ 16–31

1. Superintendent of Belchertown State School v. Saikewicz, 370 N.E.2d 417, 427

be entitled to make a choice, a choice must be made as well for a person who has been incompetent from birth. Such a choice, the court suggested, is not to be made by asking unquestioningly what a majority of competent people would choose under similar circumstances, but rather "to determine with as much accuracy as possible the wants and needs of the individual involved."[2] In the end, the decision is to be the choice "which would be made by the incompetent person, if that person were competent, but taking into account the present and future incompetency of the individual as one of the factors which would necessarily enter into the decision-making process of the competent person."[3]

Other courts have been less concerned with the autonomy and dignity interests of those who have been severely mentally disabled since birth, and some have suggested that an objective "best interest" standard should be applied under such circumstances. Indeed, the New York Court of Appeals, which has narrowly defined even competent patients' right to forgo life sustaining treatment, has declared that adults incompetent since birth should be treated like children.[4] Such an approach to the mentally disabled, once advanced as a means to provide protective services for needy adults but now rejected by disability advocacy groups, led the New York Court of Appeals to establish a default position that requires treatment in virtually every case. For example, that court ordered blood transfusions for a severely mentally disabled adult with terminal cancer.[5] Although acknowledging that the transfusions were painful, the court did not find that they were "excessively" painful. The court justified its decision by analogizing any attempt to deny treatment to the 52–year–old man to an attempt to deny a child a necessity of life. As the court pointed out, "[a] parent or guardian has a right to consent to medical treatment on behalf of an infant. * * * The parent, however, may not deprive a child of life saving treatment, however well intentioned."[6]

F. THE RIGHT TO FORGO LIFE SUSTAINING TREATMENT AND CHILDREN

1. Parental Rights and Authority

§ 16–32. The Right to Forgo Life Sustaining Treatment and Children: General Principles

In law, children have traditionally been treated as legally incompetent to make most significant decisions, including decisions regarding their own health care. On the other hand, children are not in the same position as comatose (or many otherwise incompetent) adults. In some ways they are likely to be far better at making health care decisions—for example, they can sense and evaluate information provided to them—and in some ways they may be less well equipped to make those decisions—for example, they have

---

2. Id. at 430.

3. Id. at 431. Of course, even patients institutionalized as mentally retarded may be competent to make some health care decisions, and they "should be given every opportunity to make their own ... decisions," including those that might be made through the execution of

an advance directive. Halderman v. Pennhurst 1997 WL 835412 (E.D.Pa.1997).

4. See In re Storar, 438 N.Y.S.2d 266, 420 N.E.2d 64 (N.Y.1981).

5. Id.

6. Id. at 275, 420 N.E.2d at 73.

not had the maturity of a lifetime to develop the values that a substituted judgment is expected to carry to fruition. As a consequence, courts have treated children as a class of patients different from both competent adults and incompetent adults for the purpose of making decisions concerning life sustaining treatment. Further, while such decisions for newborns are governed by federal regulations, decisions for other children are most generally guided by principles of common law that vary from state to state.

§ 16–33. Parental Authority to Make Health Care Decisions

As a general matter, parents are legally authorized to make important decisions for their children. This authority is founded on the nature and significance of the family, and it is based on the presumption that parents are both the most likely to know the incipient interests and values of their children (which are sometimes presumed to be those of the parents) and that parents are the most likely to act in the best interest of their children. Thus, the rule that permits parents to make decisions on behalf of their children is consistent with both the substituted judgment standard and the best interest standard. As the Supreme Court has pointed out, parents "possess what a child lacks in maturity, experience and capacity of judgment required for making life's difficult decisions."[1]

The parents' authority to make decisions for their children is recognized as a matter of United States constitutional law, state constitutional and statutory law, and prevailing state common law. The United States Supreme Court has declared that the "primary role of the parents in the upbringing of their children is now established beyond debate as an enduring American tradition."[2] This enduring American tradition was declared to be one protected by the Constitution as early as 1944 in *Prince v. Commonwealth of Massachusetts*,[3] and the significance of the role of parents in making such

---

§ 16–33

1. Parham v. J.R., 442 U.S. 584, 602, 99 S.Ct. 2493, 2504, 61 L.Ed.2d 101 (1979). The rules for infants under one year are not necessarily the same as those that apply to children generally. Following the much publicized Baby Doe case in 1984, when a newborn with Down Syndrome was allowed to die after its parents refused consent to life sustaining surgery unrelated to the Down Syndrome, the Department of Health and Human Services promulgated regulations which attempted to limit the circumstances under which such treatment could be denied. Although one set of regulations was found to exceed the powers of the Department, Bowen v. American Hospital Association, 476 U.S. 610, 106 S.Ct. 2101, 90 L.Ed.2d 584 (1986), and a new statutory authorization for such regulations was ultimately modified, the Department does maintain a set of current regulations which ties a state's receipt of some federal child abuse prevention funds to the maintenance of procedures for dealing with reports of the medical neglect of infants. The regulations define "medical neglect" as including "the withholding of medically indicated treatment from a disabled infant with a life threatening   condition."   45   C.F.R.

§ 1340.15(b)(1). Further, the regulation provides that the

> "withholding of medically indicated treatment" means the failure to respond to the infant's life-threatening conditions by providing treatment (including appropriate nutrition, hydration, and medication) which in the treating physician's * * * reasonable medical judgment will be most likely to be effective in ameliorating or correcting all such conditions. * * *

45 C.F.R. § 1340.15(b)(2). The regulation does not apply when the infant is "chronically and irreversibly comatose," when the treatment would "merely prolong the dying" of the infant and not ameliorate or correct the underlying medical problem (and thus be futile), or when the treatment would be "virtually futile" and "inhumane." Id. The regulation also discusses the nature of appropriate state reaction to reports of medical neglect of infants. 45 C.F.R. § 1340.15(c).

2. Wisconsin v. Yoder, 406 U.S. 205, 232, 92 S.Ct. 1526, 1541–2, 32 L.Ed.2d 15 (1972).

3. 321 U.S. 158, 166, 64 S.Ct. 438, 442, 88 L.Ed. 645, rehearing denied 321 U.S. 804, 64

decisions for their minor children has been repeated often during the last half century.

In some states, legislatures have formally acknowledged family authority in their statutes.[4] All courts also recognize that, as a matter of common law, parents have the right to make health care decisions for their minor children.[5] Indeed, a physician's attempt to perform any medical procedure on a child without a parent's consent is likely to constitute a battery.[6]

§ 16–34. Limitations on Parental Authority to Make Health Care Decisions for Children

The parents' right to make health care decisions for their child is not unrestrained. First, some courts have permitted older children who otherwise can meet the standard of competence for adults (see § 17–14, above) to make their own decisions under the "mature minor"[1] doctrine. Even when children are not permitted to make their own health care decisions, they may be permitted to participate in those decisions in a formal way that appropriately recognizes their level of maturity and understanding. For example, federal regulations provide that under some circumstances children must "assent" to participation as subjects in medical research; while their parents maintain the legal right to consent (and thus there can be no participation without parental agreement), the children maintain an effective veto on their participation.[2] Similarly, it is difficult to imagine a court allowing the termination of life sustaining treatment in the case of a child who objected to the termination, even if the parents were to request it.

Second, in those rare cases in which the parents disagree over what constitutes appropriate treatment for their child, courts simply cannot carry out the wishes of the parents. By carrying out the directions of one parent, the court necessarily would be rejecting the directions of the other.[3] Indeed, it is hard to envision a court rejecting the request of a custodial parent who wants to have his child's treatment continued to satisfy the wishes of a parent who wants to have the treatment withdrawn.[4] When either of the parents or the child wishes to have life sustaining treatment maintained, courts have not been willing to reject the default position that treatment should be continued,

---

S.Ct. 784, 88 L.Ed. 1090 (1944) (stating "[i]t is cardinal with us that the custody, care and nurture of the child reside first in the parents, whose primary function and freedom include preparation for obligations the state can neither supply nor hinder.")

4. See e.g., Del. Code Tit. 10, § 902(a) (the preservation of the family is "fundamental to the maintenance of a stable, democratic society. * * *"); and Del. Code Tit. 16, § 901 (abuse, neglect reporting statute designed to ensure strength of "parental care.").

5. See e.g., Newmark v. Williams, 588 A.2d 1108, 1115 (Del.1991).

6. Id.; see William L. Prosser & Page Keeton, The Law of Torts § 18 at 114 (5th ed. 1984) ("The common law recognizes that the only party capable of authorizing medical treatment for a minor in 'normal' circumstances is usually his parent or guardian.")

§ 16–34

1. See e.g., In re E.G., 139 Ill.Dec. 810, 815–16, 549 N.E.2d 322, 327–28 (Ill.1989); In re Application of Long Island Jewish Med. Ctr., 557 N.Y.S.2d 239, 243 (Sup.1990) (both upholding a minor's decision regarding his or her own medical care, but only when the child presented clear and convincing evidence that he or she was mature enough to exercise an adult's judgment and to understand the consequences of the decision).

2. See e.g., 45 C.F.R. § 46.408.

3. See In re Doe, 418 S.E.2d 3 (Ga.1992). See also In re Baby "K", 16 F.3d 590 (4th Cir.1994).

4. Id.

however those same courts would allocate decisionmaking authority among the parents and the child under other circumstances.

The most significant limitation on parental authority to control the health care decisionmaking of their children is found in state child abuse and neglect statutes. Under the statutes of virtually every state, parents may not act so as to deprive their children of the basic necessities of life, including food, housing, clothing, education, and medical care. Parents who deny their children adequate medical care neglect their children, and the state is authorized to exercise its *parens patriae* authority and to take custody of the children to assure that all of their basic needs (including their needs for medical care) are met. The question for many courts, thus, has been whether a parental decision to terminate life sustaining treatment for a child constitutes the denial of necessary medical care to that child: if it does, the state must take custody of the child and order treatment; if it does not, the parental decision must be carried into effect.

There are two ways in which courts have gone about deciding whether parental decisions to terminate life sustaining treatment constitute child neglect. Some courts have concluded that any decision denying life sustaining treatment to a child is *per se* an act of neglect of that child. These courts, which often assume that anything a physician has to offer must be provided to a child, are deferential to medical testimony. They perceive the issue solely as a medical one, not one that involves the application of important values to medical facts.[5]

Other courts have applied a more sophisticated balancing test to determine when the denial of life sustaining treatment for a child constitutes neglect of that child. These courts, following the Massachusetts Supreme Court decision in *Custody of a Minor*[6] *and the useful opinion of the Delaware Supreme Court in Newmark* balance the interests of the parents, the child, and the state.[7] In so doing, the courts consider three factors:

(1) the prognosis without treatment;

(2) the prognosis with treatment;

(3) the invasiveness of the treatment and the pain that it necessarily imposes on the child.

If the prognosis without treatment is good—if the child's condition is not a life threatening one, for example—the courts are very unlikely to intervene and order treatment inconsistent with that desired by the parents.[8] When the prognosis with treatment is very good—when treatment promises a virtually certain cure to what would otherwise be a terminal condition—the courts will

---

5. See In re Hamilton, 657 S.W.2d 425 (Tenn.App.1983) (ordering necessary medical treatment for a child against her father's wishes). Some believe that this is the presumption of the Baby Doe regulations, which govern treatment decisions for severely ill infants under one year of age.

6. 379 N.E.2d 1053 (Mass.1978).

7. See Newmark v. Williams, 588 A.2d 1108, 1114–17 (Del.1991).

8. Id. at 1117; see also In re Green, 292 A.2d 387, 392 (Pa.1972) (refusing to authorize corrective spine surgery on a minor); In re Seiferth, 127 N.E.2d 820, 823 (N.Y.1955) (refusing to authorize the parent to correct a cleft palate and harelip on a fourteen-year-old minor); but cf. In re Sampson, 317 N.Y.S.2d 641, 657–58 (Fam.Ct.1970), affirmed 328 N.Y.S.2d 686, 278 N.E.2d 918 (N.Y.1972) (authorizing corrective surgery on a minor where the parents' only objection was a blood transfusion).

usually order treatment, even if that is inconsistent with the parents' desires.[9] For example, courts routinely order blood transfusions for children of Jehovah's Witnesses when there is medical testimony that such transfusions—which are relatively quick, painless, and involve comparatively little intrusion—offer the only hope of survival for the patient. If the prognosis with treatment, however, is only somewhat better than the prognosis without treatment, the court will not intervene without also considering the third factor—the pain and invasiveness of the proposed treatment.[10] For example, when the proposed treatment is "highly invasive, painful, involve[s] [possibly] terrible temporary and potentially permanent side effects, pose[s] an unacceptably low * * * [risk] of success, and a high risk that the treatment itself would cause * * * death,"[11] the court will not order the treatment over the objections of the parents, whether those objections are based on religious grounds or any others.[12]

Similarly, courts are reluctant to order chemotherapy for children with childhood cancers when the treatment requires a long course of very painful and debilitating infusions, even if chemotherapy provides the only hope for survival.[13] Furthermore, courts will rarely order intervention to provide treatment that is inconsistent with the parents' wishes with regard to conditions that would not be fatal or severely disabling to the child in the absence of the proposed treatment.[14]

Parental objection to treatment is not itself irrelevant to the balancing undertaken by the most thoughtful courts that have addressed these issues. First, family support for the patient is well recognized in medicine as an important factor in achieving the medical success of the treatment. A proposed treatment for a child is more likely to be successful if the family and the child together decide that they want to pursue that treatment.[15] In addition to the immeasurable benefit that comes to the child in knowing that her parents are supporting her course of treatment, the actual participation of the parents in the day to day treatment routine may be absolutely necessary, especially in long courses of treatment, such as many chemotherapy protocols.[16] While theoretically a child could be removed from his parents and placed in an institution or with a foster family until his treatment is completed, it would be hard for any court to order a child facing death who must undergo

9. See Application of President & Directors of Georgetown College, Inc., 331 F.2d 1000, 1007 (D.C.Cir.1964), rehearing denied 331 F.2d 1010, cert. denied 377 U.S. 978, 84 S.Ct. 1883, 12 L.Ed.2d 746 (1964) (finding a greater than 50% change of saving patient's life with a blood transfusion); Jehovah's Witnesses In State of Washington v. King County Hospital Unit No. 1, 278 F.Supp. 488, 503 (W.D.Wash.1967) affirmed 390 U.S. 598, 88 S.Ct. 1260, 20 L.Ed.2d 158 (1968) (authorizing a blood transfusion where it was deemed "safe" and necessary); In re Cabrera, 552 A.2d 1114, 1115 (Pa.Super.1989) (finding a blood transfusion 90% effective to treat the patient's illness); People in Interest of D.L.E., 645 P.2d 271, 275 (Colo. 1982) (authorizing medication for the patient to prevent epileptic seizures); Muhlenberg Hospital v. Patterson, 320 A.2d 518, 521 (N.J.Super.Law Div. 1974), New Jersey v. Perricone, 181 A.2d 751, 759 (N.J.1962), cert. denied 371 U.S. 890, 83 S.Ct. 189, 9 L.Ed.2d 124 (1962); People v. Labrenz, 104 N.E.2d 769, 774 (Ill. 1952) (each of the last three cases dealt with a court authorized blood transfusion for the patient).

10. See e.g., Newmark v. Williams, 588 A.2d 1108, 1117 (Del.1991); In re Burns, 519 A.2d 638, 645 (Del.1986).

11. Newmark, 588 A.2d at 1119.

12. Id.

13. Id. at 1118.

14. Id. at 1117.

15. See id. at 1115.

16. See Newmark v. Williams, 588 A.2d 1108, 1119 n. 10 (Del.1991).

excruciating treatment to be removed from a loving family to spend what may be his last days in an institution or with a family he has never known; such an order would appear as cruel to the court as it would to the child.

In addition to considering the effect of family support on the medical prognosis of the child, some courts also consider the effect of ordering treatment over parental objections on the rest of the family.[17] After all, protecting and supporting the integrity of the family is itself one of the goals of the law. It hardly serves society to remove one child from a family for a marginally valuable treatment process when that could create serious problems for the whole family and, thus, adversely affect other children (and the parents), who could not benefit from the treatment.

§ 16–35. Potentially Inconsistent Presumptions Governing Parental Decisionmaking for Children: The Presumption for Life Sustaining Treatment and the Presumption of the Integrity of Parental Decisionmaking

There are two overarching presumptions that color all cases involving health care decision making for children, one makes a court more willing to order treatment despite the wishes of the parents and the other makes a court less likely to intervene. First, as is the case in making such decisions for incompetent adults, there is a presumption in favor of treatment whenever the absence of treatment would result in the death of the child. This presumption is especially strong when the patient is a child because the state traditionally has had an obligation to protect the lives of children and a right to intervene to protect them.

On the other hand, there is a presumption that the state should not intervene in the parent-child relationship except where there is a compelling need to do so.[1] Indeed, child abuse and neglect statutes generally require "clear and convincing evidence" of abuse or neglect before the state may take custody. The United States Supreme Court has announced that this higher standard of proof is Constitutionally required, at least when a court permanently removes parental rights.[2] These two overarching legal presumptions—the presumption of treatment and the presumption of the integrity of parental decisionmaking—are, obviously, often inconsistent with each other. Over the past few years each has been heavily criticized. The first is an anachronism that fails to recognize that death is sometimes preferable to continued existence and the second is based on an unrealistic notion of the integrity of families which seems less and less descriptive of American life each year. It is likely that the discussion of these cases will be advanced when both of these presumptions, each with its own default position, are more carefully evaluated by the judiciary.

17. Id.; see e.g., Strunk v. Strunk, 445 S.W.2d 145 (Ky.1969).

§ 16–35

1. See e.g., Newmark, 588 A.2d at 1115 ("We have repeatedly emphasized that the pa-

rental right is sacred which can be invaded for only the most compelling reasons.").

2. Santosky v. Kramer, 455 U.S. 745, 102 S.Ct. 1388, 71 L.Ed.2d 599 (1982).

2. Remedies Available Where Parents Refuse Necessary Treatment for Their Children

§ 16–36. Remedies Available Where Parents Refuse Necessary Treatment For Their Children: An Overview

Different kinds of judicial actions are available in different states to test the propriety of a parental decision to withhold or withdraw life sustaining treatment from a child. Most states that have addressed the issue have been willing to consider whether children denied life sustaining treatment are neglected under child protective services statutes. Some states have permitted the issue to be raised in the course of guardianship actions outside of the scope of child protective services statutes. Some states have permitted the issue to be raised through declaratory judgment actions or other actions based in the general common law jurisdiction of the courts. Finally, a few states have commenced criminal actions against parents who have effectively denied their children access to life sustaining treatment.

§ 16–37. Child Protective Services Actions

Every state provides a statutory framework to assure the state's protection to abused or neglected children. Such statutes generally permit the state to seek custody of a child when there is reason to believe that the child meets certain statutorily defined criteria. Significantly, the state is permitted (or, in some cases, required) to take custody of children who are being denied the necessities of life, including housing, clothing, food, education, and medical care.[1] Thus, a child who is denied necessary medical care is a neglected child and subject to being placed in the custody of the state to assure that the child is provided adequate medical care.

Child protective services statutes generally require that others (for example, physicians, other health care workers, teachers, social workers, and sometimes anyone who knows of a case of neglect) report neglect to a state agency. Some of these statutes impose penalties for failing to meet the obligation to report;[2] virtually all protect those who do report in good faith from subsequent legal actions.[3] All statutes provide that the reports are confidential.[4] Thus, those who know of parents who refuse to provide potentially necessary health care to their children are encouraged (and, in many cases, required) to report those cases. On the one hand, this allows physicians and others to report cases that need to be investigated without fear of legal liability, and, arguably, without the adverse consequences that might otherwise attend the doctor-patient relationship if the physician were to report the family. There is value, therefore, in allowing (or requiring) the physician, and others with contact with the child, to serve as police informers.

---

§ 16–37

1. See e.g., N.M.Stat.Ann.1978, § 32–1–2; Mass. Gen. Laws Ann. ch. 119 § 1. This provides the basis for the Baby Doe regulations, which limit the scope of nontreatment for seriously ill infants under one year of age. 45 C.F.R. § 1340.15. See also Chapter 4.

2. See e.g., N.M. Stat. Ann.1978, § 32A–4–3; Mass. Gen. Laws Ann. c. 119, §§ 51E, 51F.

3. See e.g., N.M. Stat. Ann. § 32A–4–3.

4. See e.g., N.M. Stat. Ann.1978, § 31–25–5; Mass. Gen. Laws Ann. c. 119, § 51F.

On the other hand, the fact that physicians have such obligations may discourage parents from seeking any medical help for their children. They may worry that the failure to complete the medical course required by the doctor will result in a legal action in which the state will attempt to remove the child from their custody. This worry is likely to be especially great where the parents are members of a community that is aware of the reporting obligation—for example, the Christian Science or Jehovah's Witness community. Thus, these parents may be especially careful to avoid any contact between their sick children and medical authorities. In other words, there also is a real risk in having physicians and others serve as police informers.

§ 16–38. Guardianship Actions

Another way to raise the issue of medical neglect is to seek a guardian for the child, with the special instruction from the court that the guardian consent to the designated medical treatment. In most states, guardianships are available on the petition of any person (including physicians, friends, neighbors, hospitals, and other natural and fictional persons) for the protection of any person without legal capacity to protect herself.[1] Children, by definition, lack that legal capacity.

Parents are the natural guardians of their children, and courts will not appoint a guardian in derogation of the parents' natural rights unless there is a good reason to replace the parents. The "good reason" is most likely to be one found in the child protective services statute. Thus, a guardianship case is likely to reduce itself to the same substantive issues as an action under the child protective services statute. The guardianship procedures will be different, however, and depending on the terms of state statutes, the procedures may have advantages (or disadvantages) compared to those offered in a child protective services action.

§ 16–39. Declaratory Judgment and Other Common Law Actions

Courts may address the question of when life sustaining treatment should be terminated within their ordinary common law jurisdiction or under a declaratory judgment act.[1] While the substantive issues that would arise in such common law actions would be identical to those that would arise in child protective services and guardianship actions, there are procedural advantages to declaratory and common law actions. They are flexible actions, with procedures that can be tailored to meet the needs of the parties in individual cases. Unlike other actions, they do not require a petitioner to allege that the parents are unfit or are otherwise neglecting their child—a highly charged accusation which creates an adversarial environment.

For example, when Atlanta Scottish Rite's Hospital Bioethics Committee determined that treatment should be discontinued (or, at the least, de-escalated) for a 13–year–old terminally ill child, but the parents did not agree that it was proper to modify the treatment, the hospital sought a declaratory

§ 16–38

1. See e.g., Sup. Ct. R. 10–305; N.M. Stat. Ann. § 32A–4–31; Mass. Gen. Laws Ann. c. 201, § 34.

§ 16–39

1. See e.g., N.M. Stat. Ann.1978, §§ 44–6–1 to 44–6–15; Mass. Gen. Laws Ann. c. 231A, §§ 1 to 9.

judgment. The Supreme Court of Georgia[2] ultimately decided that the hospital was entitled to a declaratory judgment under the relevant Georgia statute. The state had argued that the action should be dismissed for lack of jurisdiction and refiled in the juvenile court. The Georgia Supreme Court did not conclude that the juvenile court would be without jurisdiction; it merely concluded that the juvenile court would not have exclusive jurisdiction. As the supreme court pointed out,

> [this] * * * action did not seek to terminate the legal parent-child relationship or to wrest custody or control from Jane Doe's parents. Further, Jane Doe was not a 'deprived child,' because both parents actively sought the best available care and treatment for her.[3]

Indeed, the more dispassionate approach and the less accusatory form of a declaratory or general civil action (when compared to allegations of abuse, neglect or deprivation that commence a child protective services proceeding, the unwieldy nature of a guardianship action, and the highly accusatory nature of a criminal proceeding) suggest that the resolution of these issues may be better achieved through these broader forms of action than through trying to stretch other narrower causes of action, which were originally developed to resolve very different kinds of disputes, into something appropriate for these cases.

§ 16–40. Criminal Actions

In several cases, prosecutors have commenced criminal actions for homicide or child neglect resulting in death against parents who did not seek or permit necessary medical care for their children.[1] These actions usually have been commenced against parents whose decisions were motivated by their religious views, when their child, who had been denied appropriate medical treatment, died as a result of the denial of treatment. Parents have been charged with murder, voluntary or involuntary manslaughter, criminally negligent homicide, child abuse or neglect resulting in death, child endangerment, and a host of less heinous offenses. Such criminal prosecutions were very rare until the 1990s, in part because of uncertainty over the effect of state and federal laws exempting the spiritual healing of children from abuse and neglect statutes and the criminal law. Over the last decade, however, there have been several convictions and there appears to be a new interest in undertaking the prosecution of such cases. To be successful in such prosecutions, the state, as it does in all criminal prosecutions, must show that the parents perpetrated the *actus reus* of a crime while possessing the *mens rea* for that crime.

2. In re Doe, 418 S.E.2d 3 (Ga.1992).

3. Id. at 5 n. 3.

§ 16–40

1. See e.g., Hermanson v. State, 570 So.2d 322 (Fla.App.1990), reversed 604 So.2d 775 (Fla.1992) (Christian Science parents provided prayer-based treatment and were charged with involuntary manslaughter after their child died); Commonwealth v. Twitchell, No. 89–210 (Mass. Dist. Ct. 1989), reversed 617 N.E.2d 609 (Mass.1993) (child died of an obstructed bowel after her Christian Science parents relied on spiritual healing to treat illness). See generally Deborah Sussman Steckler, A Trend Toward Declining Rigor In Applying Free Exercise Principles: The Example of State Courts' Consideration of Christian Science Treatment For Children, 36 N.Y.L. Sch. L. Rev. 487 (1991).

a. Actus Reus

The state must first prove the *actus reus*. While acts, not omissions, are generally required for this purpose, an omission may constitute an *actus reus* when the actor is required by law to act but fails to do so. Because parents are required to provide their children with the necessities of life, including all necessary medical care, the failure to provide such care may constitute the *actus reus* for a crime.[2] This element has caused little trouble for prosecutors in recent prosecutions.

b. Mens Rea

The state must also show that the parents possessed a culpable *mens rea* coincident with the *actus reus*. This element has proven more difficult to analyze. The *mens rea* for the highest degree of homicide—murder or its equivalent—generally requires malice aforethought and that requirement is met when there is an intent to kill. Further, the law presumes that a person intends the ordinary and natural consequences of his acts. The parents' knowledge, therefore, that an omission to provide medical care will result in the death of a child may be enough to meet the *mens rea* requirement of murder. In addition, the parent may be presumed to have the knowledge that would be possessed by a reasonable person in the position of the defendant. Thus, if a reasonable parent would know that denial of treatment would lead to the death of a child, the parent-defendant may be deemed to have that knowledge. If the question of the existence of the *mens rea* is left to a jury (which may be prejudiced against the unusual religious views of the defendant), it is easy to imagine the question being answered in the affirmative. In many states the *mens rea* requirement for murder may also be satisfied if the defendant acts with a "depraved heart," i.e., if the defendant acts with wanton disregard for life. Again, it is not hard to imagine a jury, disgusted by the apparently needless death of a child, finding that the child's parents possessed such a culpable *mens rea*.

In fact, however, no jury has found parents guilty of murder or its equivalent under these circumstances. Instead, juries have tended to treat the parents' failure to act as reckless (the required *mens rea* for involuntary manslaughter or its equivalent) or criminally negligent (the required *mens rea* for criminally negligent homicide or its equivalent). Because these levels of culpability are generally measured by objective rather than subjective standards, they can be evaluated without any attention to the motivating religious views of the parents. Juries have been willing to return guilty verdicts to charges of involuntary manslaughter, criminally negligent homicide, or reckless homicide against parents who have denied necessary medical care to their children.[3]

The *mens rea* for child abuse or neglect resulting in death is usually nothing more than the general intent necessary for the abuse or neglect—i.e., the intent to do the act (or, as here, where an omission serves as the *actus reus*, the intent not to do an act) that itself constitutes the abuse or neglect. Because the defendants often readily agree that they intentionally did not get

---

2. See e.g., State v. Mahurin, 799 S.W.2d 840 (Mo.1990) (en banc) (parents convicted of endangering welfare of child and involuntary manslaughter when they failed to seek medical attention for malnourished child).

3. See Walker v. Superior Court, 253 Cal. Rptr. 1, 763 P.2d 852 (Cal. 1988); Bergmann v. State, 486 N.E.2d 653 (Ind.App.1985).

medical care for their child (because of their religious views, for example), the culpable mental state for this crime often follows directly from the act itself.

c. Causation

In addition to proving the *actus reus* and the *mens rea* necessary for the crime, the prosecution must prove that the death was actually caused by the *actus reus*; the prosecution must prove that the death of the child was caused by the parents' failure to obtain necessary medical care. This element is not always an easy one for the prosecution to meet; after all, there must have been some underlying disease or injury that necessitated the proposed medical care. If the defense can raise a reasonable doubt about whether death would have ensued even with the treatment, the criminal prosecution for homicide should fail.

d. Sentencing

If the death of a child is not the most severe penalty a parent could suffer for an omission, then a declaration that the parent is culpable for the death surely is. Recognizing this, the courts have generally imposed sentences that serve to warn other parents and protect the defendant's remaining children, rather than to punish the parent. Although the charges may carry the possibility of long terms of imprisonment, no court has imprisoned a parent who acted on religious or other principled motivation to deny a child necessary medical treatment. Instead, courts have imposed long periods of probation, and have conditioned the probation on the parents arranging for regular medical treatment (including regular well child visits) for their remaining children.[4]

e. Policy Considerations

Many prosecutors have rejected the opportunity to commence criminal actions against parents whose child has died because those parents, acting in good faith, denied him life sustaining treatment. There are many reasons that a prosecutor might choose to forgo criminal action.[5] First, there are problems of proof; it is not easy to establish the appropriate *mens rea* and *actus reus* in such cases, and it is often difficult to prove that the parents' omission to act was the cause of the death of the child. Second, in criminal actions, every element of the crime must be proven beyond a reasonable doubt; these same matters can often be better handled through some other form of proceeding with a lower burden of proof. Third, parents who have recently lost a child may be sympathetic defendants; it may not be worth the risk of the loss of what will be a high profile case to drag those parents through the courts. Finally, adding a criminal prosecution to the agony suffered by parents who are mourning the loss of a child is cruel by any standard.

On the other hand, those who have prosecuted these actions believe that they are justified. First, they argue, it is important that the community know that the state will protect the integrity of its children, and that the state's protection will extend to those children in families with unusual religious beliefs with as much vigor as it extends to others. Second, they point out that

---

4. See e.g., Commonwealth v. Twitchell, No. 89–210 (Mass. Dist. Ct. 1989), reversed 617 N.E.2d 609 (Mass.1993); Hermanson v. State, 570 So.2d 322 (Fla.App.1990), reversed 604 So.2d 775 (Fla.1992).

5. See Barry Nobel, Religious Healing in the Courts: the Liberties and Liabilities of Patients, Parents, and Healers, 16 U. Puget Sound L.Rev. 599, 655–668 (1993).

the recent prosecutions have had a substantial deterrent effect on others who may put their families at risk. Third, prosecutors argue that it is no more cruel to prosecute a parent whose child has died after the denial of adequate medical treatment than it is to prosecute a parent whose reckless driving resulted in the death of another's child. While, in some sense, the first potential defendant may have suffered a great deal without the intervention of the criminal law, that person is culpable under the criminal law and that culpability is not ameliorated because of the close personal relationship to the victim.

Finally, some prosecutors suggest, there may be no alternative way for the legal system to evaluate the propriety of a parental decision to deny life sustaining treatment to children, at least in the case of Christian Scientists and others who object to any form of medical care. Jehovah's Witness's children are regularly brought to medical facilities; their parents object only to blood transfusions, not to other forms of medical treatment. Doctors, social workers, officers of health care institutions, and others know they can seek judicial review through child protective services actions, guardianship actions, declaratory judgment actions, and other common law forms of action when a child needs a blood transfusion but is being denied one by the parents. Christian Scientists, however, may reject virtually all medical intervention and may be unwilling to bring their children into the health care system at all. If criminal actions are not pursued in these cases, some argue, the rights of these children to receive adequate health care would be left entirely without a remedy.

G. RELIGION AND THE RIGHT TO FORGO LIFE SUSTAINING TREATMENT

§ 16–41. Religion and the Right to Forgo Life Sustaining Treatment: An Introduction

There are several religious groups with tenets that prohibit the application of some forms of medical care, or any medical care at all.[1] The most well known are the Jehovah's Witnesses, which prohibit taking blood (and, thus, receiving blood in transfusion or other form),[2] and the Church of Christ, Scientist (Christian Science), which prohibits virtually all forms of medical

---

§ 16–41

1. See generally Barry Nobel, Religious Healing in the Courts: The Liberties and Liabilities of Patients, Parents and Healers, 16 U. Puget Sound L. Rev. 599 (1993).

2. Jehovah's Witnesses believe, based on the following Bible passages, that the act of receiving blood or blood products precludes them from resurrection and everlasting life:

As for any man of the house of Israel or some alien resident who is residing as an alien in your midst who eats any sort of blood, I shall certainly set my face against the soul that is eating the blood, and I shall indeed cut him off from among his people. Leviticus 17:10.

You must not eat the blood of any sort of flesh, because the soul of every sort of flesh is its blood. Anyone eating it will be cut off. Leviticus 17:14.

Only flesh with its soul—its blood—you must not eat. Genesis 9:4.

[K]eep yourselves free from things sacrificed to idols and from blood. * * * Acts 15:20.

See In re McCauley, 565 N.E.2d 411, 412 (Mass.1991); see generally, Julie A. Koehne, Witnesses on Trial: Judicial Intrusion Upon the Practices of Jehovah's Witness Parents, 21 Fla. St. U.L.Rev. 205 (1992).

care and depends instead upon spiritual healing.[3] The Christian Science movement grew out of the widespread Nineteenth Century interest in natural healing, and, given the limited success of medical practitioners only a century ago, it is likely that any movement that discouraged such treatment saved a great many lives. Today, despite claims to the contrary, there is some evidence that those who subscribe to Christian Science teachings have somewhat higher mortality and morbidity than the rest of the population.[4]

Christian Science was not the only religious group to arise out of the nineteenth century fascination with "natural" non-medical cures. For example, the "Peculiar People" and their progeny in England have presented the British courts with the same questions as the Christian Scientists have in the United States.[5] In addition, a diversity of other faiths, many of them sects with adherents who believe that God will provide any cure that is appropriate, have developed during this century.

Adherents within a faith may interpret the requirements of their faith differently. For example, some forms of medical treatments are acceptable to some Christian Scientists, and some Jehovah's Witnesses find some kinds of procedures involving blood to be tolerable. The courts, however, may not arbitrate disputes over the "true" religious belief of such faiths; the resolution of such disagreements is always beyond the courts' jurisdiction. Rather, the court must accept the adherent's sincere views of what is required by his religion, and even the inquiry into "sincerity" is a limited one. In any case, a decision concerning the discontinuation of life sustaining treatment that is based upon a religious requirement is now treated like any other decision. The fact that a "right to die" decision (or any other) is based in religion (vel non) should be beyond the consideration of the court. Thus, whether a patient's reasoning is religiously based, whether the religious basis is a "correct" interpretation of religious dogma, and whether the religious dogma itself is "correct" (or even "reasonable") all become properly irrelevant.

1. Adults

§ 16–42. Religion and the Right to Forgo Life Sustaining Treatment: The General Rule for Adults

The law is now well established that a competent adult may forgo life sustaining treatment for any reason, or for no reason at all.[1] The fact that a competent adult believes that the decision is required by his religion is irrelevant; as a Constitutional matter, religious justifications may not be given greater or lesser weight than other reasons for making the same decision. Nonetheless, some courts search for reasons to deny competent adults the opportunity to carry out religiously based decisions when those courts are

3. See generally, Mary B. Eddy, Manual of the Mother Church, 17–19 (1935). See also Nathan A. Talbot, The Position of the Christian Science Church, in Freedom and Responsibility: Christian Science Healing for Children 12, 18–19 (1989).

4. W.F. Simpson, Comparative Longevity in a College Cohort of Christian Scientists, 262 JAMA 1657 (1989).

5. See Regina v. Senior, All ER Rep 511 (1895–9) (upholding manslaughter conviction of member of the "Peculiar People" sect for death of infant due to failure to provide medical attention).

§ 16–42

1. See § 16–15, above.

unsympathetic to the underlying religions. These reasons fall into several categories, none of which is able to survive serious scrutiny.

§ 16–43. An Adult's Competency to Forgo Life Sustaining Treatment on Religious Grounds

Some courts have argued that patients facing death are necessarily so overcome by the prospect that they cannot be sufficiently competent to make life and death decisions. This potential incompetency is made even more likely, some courts have suggested, when it is caused by the need for blood (most usually the case with Jehovah's Witness patients).[1] While it is true that the trauma or illness that makes a person confront death may change that person, there is no reason to conclude that it limits that person's decisional capacity; indeed, it may enhance it. Many people claim that an encounter with death makes clearer what is truly important in life.

Further, while the need for blood itself may affect the patient's reasoning capacity, there is no reason to conclude that it does so more than other forms of trauma. Finally, courts routinely accept the decisions of religiously motivated patients who consent to life saving blood transfusions or other forms of treatment. It is inconsistent with fundamental principles underlying the notion of autonomy to accept the decisions of these patients to undergo treatment, but to deny their decisions to forgo it. A patient cannot be competent to consent to a proposed treatment, yet incompetent to deny consent to that same treatment.

§ 16–44. Distinguishing Consensual Transfusions From Court Ordered Transfusions

In reviewing treatment decisions of Jehovah's Witnesses, some courts have announced that the tenets of the Jehovah's Witness faith require its adherents to deny consent for blood transfusions: they do not forbid the transfusions themselves. As Judge Skelly Wright pointed out in the controversial *Georgetown College* case, "I asked * * * [the Jehovah's Witness patient] whether she would oppose the blood transfusion if the court allowed it. She indicated, as best I could make out, that it would not then be her responsibility."[1] Some courts have gone so far as to suggest that the correct reading of Jehovah's Witness religious dogma requires only that patients deny consent for blood transfusions, not that they refuse to accept those transfusions when imposed upon them.[2]

§ 16–43

1. See e.g., Application of the President and Directors of Georgetown College, Inc., 331 F.2d 1000, 1007 (D.C.Cir.1964) (ordering blood transfusion for woman presumably weakened by her loss of blood despite her barely audible declaration to the judge that it is "against my will."). But see In re Brooks' Estate, 205 N.E.2d 435 (Ill.1965); Mercy Hospital, Inc. v. Jackson, 489 A.2d 1130 (Md.App.1985), vacated on other grounds 510 A.2d 562 (Md.1986) (affirming denial of petition to appoint a guardian to consent to Jehovah's Witness blood transfusion during C-section where fetus was not at risk); In re Osborne, 294 A.2d 372 (D.C.App.1972).

§ 16–44

1. Application of the President and Directors of Georgetown College, Inc., 331 F.2d 1000, 1007 (D.C.Cir.1964).

2. Id. at 1009.

§ 16–45. Judicial Efforts to Help Providers Avoid Civil and Criminal Liability and Ethical Culpability When a Patient Refuses Life Sustaining Treatment on Religious Grounds

Some courts have been willing to ignore religious objections to medical treatment to spare physicians and other health care institutions the risk of criminal and civil liability for failure to provide treatment, and to spare them from acting inconsistently with the ethical requirements of their profession.[1] Now that it is established that providing treatment contrary to the expressed wishes of a competent patient is ethically inappropriate and may yield civil and criminal liability for battery, this argument is left without force. In any case, when an action comes before the court for a formal determination of the propriety of respecting a patient's decision to forgo treatment, the court is in a unique position; its very decision in the case effectively cuts off civil, criminal and professional recourse against those who carry out the decision.

§ 16–46. The Judicial Presumption in Favor of Life When a Patient Refuses Life Sustaining Treatment on Religious Grounds

When reviewing an individual's decision to refuse life sustaining treatment for religious reasons, the court is usually obliged to act quickly and without full opportunity for argument and reflection. Under such circumstances, some courts have argued, it is better to err on the side of preserving life—especially if the patient's decision is based in religion.[1] This argument has all of the shortcomings of other arguments founded in the premise that it is better to err on the side of the preservation of life, and it adds an additional questionable presumption—that religiously motivated actions are subject to special scrutiny. In reality, of course, there is reason to believe that religiously based decisions represent more deeply and continuously held values of patients than do other kinds of decisions,[2] not that they represent transient values that ought to be accorded little deference. The law ought not discount religious views (and especially those of religions on the margins of society) as inadequate bases for decisions to forgo medical care.

§ 16–47. Judicial Efforts to Protect Children of Parents Who Refuse Life Sustaining Treatment on Religious Grounds

Finally, some courts have accepted an argument that parents have a special obligation to accept life sustaining treatment despite their religious views, and that courts have an obligation to impose that treatment on those patients. This argument stems from the premise that children are entitled to

§ 16–45

1. See Application of the President and Directors of Georgetown College, Inc., 331 F.2d 1000, 1009 (D.C.Cir.1964) ("The hospital doctors had the choice of administering the proper treatment or letting [the patient] die in the hospital bed, thus exposing themselves, and the hospital, to the risk of civil and criminal liability in either case.").

§ 16–46

1. See Application of the President and Directors of Georgetown College, Inc., 331 F.2d 1000 (D.C.Cir.1964).

2. See Matter of Tavel, 661 A.2d 1061 (Del. 1995) and In re Eichner, 438 N.Y.S.2d 266, 420 N.E.2d 64 (N.Y.1981).

be raised by two healthy parents. While all courts are quick to admit that this is a difficult premise to enforce as a general matter, some courts have argued that they are authorized to do what they can to bring it to fruition.

Parents are obliged by child abuse and neglect laws to provide their children with all of the necessities of life, including adequate housing, clothing, nutrition, medical care and education. A dead parent cannot provide these necessities to her children, and, thus, some courts have said that a parent has a legal obligation to stay alive for the benefit of her children. The courts have a correlative obligation, under this theory, to act in the best interest of the children and, thus, to order that the parents be given the treatment that keeps them alive.[1] As Judge Wright announced in the *Georgetown* case when he ordered a blood transfusion for a questionably competent Jehovah's Witness mother,

> The state, as parens patriae, will not allow a parent to abandon a child, and so it should not allow this most ultimate of voluntary abandonments. The patient had a responsibility to the community to care for her infant. Thus the people had an interest in preserving the life of this mother.[2]

Presumably, a pregnant woman would have the same obligation to accept treatment—whether or not the fetus is viable—to protect and advance the health of her fetus.[3] Some courts have characterized the interest in assuring that parents provide adequately for their children as a "compelling state interest," one that can overcome even an otherwise constitutionally protected right to make health care decisions.

This argument, used to justify judicial decisions which ignore competent parents' decisions to forgo life sustaining treatment, is based on the court's assumption that it can intervene to protect children from their parents. Taken to its extreme, it would permit courts to prohibit parents from undertaking dangerous professions or hobbies, from living in risky neighborhoods, from giving up well paid jobs to take more satisfying ones, from moving to a community with inferior schools, or from serving too many high-fat meals. It would allow the court to usurp the basic authority that defines the role of the parent. In addition, a serious application of this argument would require the court to evaluate how good the parent had been at providing the necessities of life before the medical decision arose (might the child live a *better* life with a relative or in a foster family?) and also to evaluate the provisions the parent had made for care of the child after the parent's death. A court that adopted this theory would be required to order treatment for a parent (and, presumably, for a legal guardian), even when that court would

§ 16–47

1. See, Application of the President and Directors of Georgetown College, Inc., 331 F.2d 1000, 1008 (D.C.Cir.1964). Some courts, however, in deciding whether to order life-saving treatment for a person with children, will consider the child's support system in the event of the death of the parent. If the children would not be abandoned if the parent were to die, these courts will not compel the parent to undergo the treatment. See Norwood Hosp. v. Munoz, 564 N.E.2d 1017 (Mass.1991); Public Health Trust of Dade County v. Wons, 541

So.2d 96 (Fla.1989); In re Dubreuil, 603 So.2d 538 (Fla.App.1992), reversed 629 So.2d 819 (Fla.1993) (ordering blood transfusion because estranged husband and family would be unable to care for the minor children).

2. Georgetown, 331 F.2d at 1008.

3. See e.g., Application of Jamaica Hosp., 491 N.Y.S.2d 898, 900 (N.Y.Sup.1985) (ordering a blood transfusion for a woman who was 8 months pregnant); see also Fosmire v. Nicoleau, 536 N.Y.S.2d 492 (N.Y.App.Div.1989).

not order the same treatment for a person without children, or for a person whose children had reached majority.

Finally, this argument dismisses the significance of the religion itself to the family. As one justice of the Florida Supreme Court announced in accepting a young mother's decision to forgo a blood transfusion that would save her life,

> [W]e must not assume from her choice that [this mother] was not considering the best interests of her children. * * * As a parent, however, she also must consider the example she sets for her children, how to teach them to follow what she believes is God's law if she herself does not. The choice for her cannot be an easy one, but it is hers to make. It is not for this Court to judge the reasonableness or validity of her beliefs. Absent a truly compelling state interest to the contrary, the law must protect her right to make that choice.[4]

2. Children

§ 16–48. A Child's Right to Forgo Life Sustaining Treatment for Religious Reasons: The General Rule

Courts routinely intervene to require treatment for children whose parents deny consent for life saving medical intervention for religious reasons. While competent adults may choose to follow the tenets of their religion, including the right to forgo life sustaining treatment, they must permit their children to grow old enough to become competent adults and make these decisions themselves. Courts can intervene in a number of different kinds of formal proceedings to assure that children are provided adequate medical care, and there is not a single recent case in which a court has allowed a child to die because a parent, for solely religious reasons, refused consent to a treatment that virtually all other parents would have accepted for their children.

Of course, the fact that a parent refuses to consent to treatment for religious reasons does not mean that the court, *ipso facto*, will order the treatment in question. In dealing with cases in which a parent denies consent to life sustaining treatment for a child, some courts now apply the following analysis. First, they determine whether any reasonable parent might withhold consent to the proposed treatment, whatever the motivation for that action. If one might, the court will defer to the wishes of the parent (and refuse to order treatment), whatever the parent's motivation.[1] On the other hand, if no reasonable parent would refuse consent to the proposed treatment, the court will order the treatment even if the parent does object on religious or other grounds.

4. Public Health Trust of Dade County v. Wons, 541 So.2d 96, 102 (Fla.1989) (Ehrlich, J., concurring).

highly invasive and painful treatment having only a 40% rate of success).

§ 16–48

1. See Newmark v. Williams, 588 A.2d 1108, 1118 (Del.1991) (denying court order for

§ 16–49.   State Statutory Exemptions for Spiritual Healing

Most states have adopted statutes providing that a child shall not be considered abused or neglected because that child is being treated "solely by spiritual means" in accord with the tenets of a "recognized church" by a "duly accredited practitioner" of that church.[1] Although the statutes are generally similar, some of them also exclude such children from the scope of the otherwise mandatory abuse and neglect reporting statutes, and some provide immunity for criminal liability to all of those who participate in the spiritual treatment.

After active lobbying by the Christian Science Church, most states adopted these statutes in the 1970s.[2] The fact that the statutes apply only to "recognized" churches and to "accredited practitioners" of those churches (both terms used to describe the structure of the Church of Christ, Scientist) reveals their origin.[3] The Christian Science lobbyists were also successful on the federal level, and by the mid–1970s states were required to have statutes providing this special protection for Christian Science parents in order to receive any distribution under the largest of the federal programs designed to provide aid to states in dealing with abused and neglected children.[4] While the language of these statutes supports the decision of Christian Science parents who wish to deny consent to necessary medical care for their children, the statutes are almost certainly unconstitutional as violations of the establishment clause of the first amendment[5] and the equal protection clause of the fourteenth amendment[6] to the United States Constitution. In many states

§ 16–49

1. Forty-seven states and the District of Columbia have enacted some form of spiritual treatment exemption to their child abuse and neglect laws; Hermanson v. State, 604 So.2d 775, 776–77 n. 1 (Fla.1992) (listing statutes). See also, Jennifer L. Hartsell, Mother May I . . . Live? Parental Refusal of Life–Sustaining Medical Treatment For Children Based On Religious Objections, 66 Tenn.L.Rev. 499 (1999).

2. See David Margolick, In Child Deaths, A Test for Christian Science, N.Y. Times, Aug. 6, 1990, at 1.

3. See Walker v. Superior Court, 253 Cal. Rptr. 1, 24, 763 P.2d 852, 875 (Cal.1988) (Mosk, J., concurring), cert. denied 491 U.S. 905, 109 S.Ct. 3186, 105 L.Ed.2d 695 (1989) (pointing out that since Christian Scientists sponsored the spiritual treatment exception to California's abuse and neglect law it was "more than a fortuity that the word 'practitioner' " appeared in the state's spiritual healing statute).

4. To carry out the Child Abuse Prevention and Treatment Act of 1974, the Department of Health, Education and Welfare (HEW) promulgated what is now the federal spiritual healing exemption. 45 C.F.R. § 1340.2. The current federal regulation provides that "[n]othing in this part should be construed as requiring or prohibiting a finding of negligent treatment or maltreatment when a parent practicing his or her religious beliefs does not, for that reason

alone, provide medical treatment for a child. * * * " 45 C.F.R. § 1340.2(d)(2)(ii). Moreover, states were required to pass statutes similar to this regulation in order to qualify for federal funds. See Danna K. LeClair, Comment, Faith Healing and Religious Treatment Exemptions to Child Endangerment Laws: Should Parental Religious Practice Excuse the Failure To Provide Necessary Medical Care To Children?, 13 U. Dayton L.Rev. 79, 96–7 (1987).

5. See Walker v. Superior Court (People), 253 Cal.Rptr. 1, 25, 763 P.2d 852, 876 (Cal. 1988) (Mosk, J., concurring), cert. denied 491 U.S. 905, 109 S.Ct. 3186, 105 L.Ed.2d 695 (1989) ("[H]ere the accommodation reflects nothing less than a denominational preference in the face of indistinguishable religious conduct."). For a thorough discussion of this issue, see Ann MacLean Massie, The Religion Clauses and Parental Health Care Decisionmaking for Children: Suggestions for a New Approach, 21 Hastings Con.L.Q. 725 (1994).

6. An Ohio State Court ruled that the statutory exemption to the criminal abuse and neglect statute violated both the establishment clause and the equal protection clause of the fourteenth amendment. State v. Miskimens, 490 N.E.2d 931, 933–36 (Ohio 1984). The Miskimens court found that the statute "hopelessly involve[d]" the state in issues involving religious beliefs and thus served no "legitimate purpose" for the state. Id. at 934.

these statutes also violate the religious protection clauses of the state constitutions. The establishment clause of the first amendment prohibits any governmental action that advances or inhibits religion in general, or any religion in particular, or which creates "excessive entanglement" between the church and the state. A statute designed to provide special status to the Church of Christ, Scientist, advances that religion and, thus, violates the establishment clause.

In addition, any statute that would require a state to determine which religions are "recognized" religions (and which, thus, requires states to "recognize" some religions) both improperly advances religion and improperly entangles the state with the potentially recognized religions. As the United States Supreme Court has pointed out, the "clearest command of the Establishment Clause is that one religious denomination cannot be officially preferred over another."[7] Because the statute only exempts from medical care those children treated by practitioners "duly accredited" by the church, it also has the effect of delegating state power to church accrediting authorities—yet another violation of the establishment clause.[8]

At least one state supreme court justice has also found a statutory exemption for spiritual healing to be a violation of the equal protection clause of the fourteenth amendment. The statute treats decisions of parents who are members of a recognized church differently than it treats religious decisions of parents who belong to an "unrecognized" church, who have made their decision for entirely secular reasons, or who decide to have their child treated by a practitioner who is not accredited by the church.[9] Because the underlying right is a fundamental right protected by the First Amendment, these classifications drawn by the statute can be justified under the fourteenth amendment only if the statute serves a "compelling state interest."[10] There is little reason to believe that the classification serves any governmental interest, much less a compelling one.

H. JUDICIAL PROCESS IN CASES INVOLVING DECISIONS TO FORGO LIFE SUSTAINING TREATMENT

§ 16–50. Introduction: The Propriety of Judicial Involvement in "Right to Die" Cases and the Role of the Court

There is no consensus as to when, if ever, the court must participate in decision making concerning the refusal of life sustaining treatment. On the

7. Larson v. Valente, 456 U.S. 228, 244, 102 S.Ct. 1673, 1683, 72 L.Ed.2d 33 (1982) rehearing denied 457 U.S. 1111, 102 S.Ct. 2916, 73 L.Ed.2d 1323 (1982) (holding that statutory provisions that discriminate "among religions" are subject to strict scrutiny and must further a compelling government interest).

8. See Walker, 763 P.2d at 874–78 (Mosk, J., concurring).

9. Walker, 763 P.2d at 875 (Mosk, J., concurring). See also State v. Miskimens, 490 N.E.2d 931 (Ohio 1984).

10. Larson v. Valente, 456 U.S. 228, 246, 102 S.Ct. 1673, 1684, 72 L.Ed.2d 33, rehearing denied 457 U.S. 1111, 102 S.Ct. 2916, 73 L.Ed.2d 1323 (1982) (stating that statutes that "grant * * * denominational preferences of the sort consistently and firmly deprecated in our precedents * * * must be invalidated unless [they are] justified by a compelling governmental interest").

one hand, judicial involvement in the termination of life sustaining treatment provides protection of different sorts to the patient, the family, and to the medical community which would otherwise be providing treatment. Conversely, its involvement adds a level of government and bureaucracy to a decision that is usually intensely personal and private. Despite the American interest in involving the courts in all phases of life, decisions to forgo life sustaining treatment are better made by patients, families and physicians acting together, without the involvement of any judicial apparatus. Requiring judicial involvement in every "right to die" decision would not only intolerably burden families and medical institutions, but it would swamp the courts as well.

A few states have formally recognized this, and courts in those states have announced that there is no need for judicial intervention in most cases. For example, the Washington Supreme Court has announced that there is no need for resort to the judiciary where there is total agreement among the "immediate family, the treating physicians, and the prognosis committee * * * as to the course of medical treatment."[1] The Massachusetts Supreme Judicial Court formally abandoned its earlier view requiring judicial confirmation of all decisions to forgo life sustaining treatment,[2] the Uniform Health Care Decisions Act[3] and some other statutes explicitly provide that there need not be any judicial action before a decision to discontinue life sustaining medical treatment is carried out, and, as a matter of practice, most decisions to forgo life sustaining treatment never find their way into the legal system in any state.

Judicial willingness to avoid this kind of decisionmaking also stems from a recognition that the adversary process may be a particularly inappropriate way to make such intimate decisions, especially when the court is called upon to create an adversarial relationship that would not otherwise exist. As Justice Stevens pointed out in his dissent in Cruzan,

> [i]t may reasonably be debated whether some judicial process should be required before life-sustaining treatment is discontinued; this issue has divided the state courts. I tend, however, to agree * * * that the intervention of the State in these proceedings as an adversary is not so much a cure as it is part of the disease.[4]

As any family member who has been called upon to participate in making a decision to terminate life sustaining treatment will attest, the last thing that the family and the physician need is the artificial creation of an adversary relationship. Better decisionmaking is more likely to result from the development of true and thoughtful consensus, not the invention of disagreement where none would otherwise exist.

§ 16–50

1. In re Guardianship of Hamlin, 689 P.2d 1372, 1377 (Wash.1984).

2. See In re Spring, 405 N.E.2d 115 (Mass. 1980) (requiring judicial intervention only in limited circumstances).

3. Uniform Health Care Decision Act, section 4.

4. Cruzan v. Director, Missouri Dept. of Health, 497 U.S. 261, 341, n. 13, 110 S.Ct. 2841, 2884 n. 13, 111 L.Ed.2d 224 (Stevens, J., dissenting).

§ 16–51. Forms of Actions in Cases Involving Decisions to Forgo Life Sustaining Treatment

Judicial actions testing the propriety of decisions to forgo life sustaining treatment have taken a variety of forms, depending on the nature of the case, the initiating party, the reason for undertaking the litigation, and the procedural rules of the state in which the action is filed. Actions are commonly commenced by health care authorities concerned about carrying out a patient's (or a patient's family's) wish that treatment be discontinued, or by those patients or their families when their physicians or health care institutions refuse to carry out their wishes. Actions may also be commenced by public authorities, including district attorneys and state nursing home ombudsmen, or by family members or hospital employees who disagree with the position taken by the consensus of others involved in the process.

The form of the action is virtually entirely dependent upon state procedural rules, and the technical structure of the pleadings is relevant only in so far as it permits a court which does not want to decide the case to dismiss it on technical or jurisdictional grounds. The various possible forms of actions include: special statutory proceedings under living will statutes; guardianship proceedings under general or special guardianship statutes;[1] civil rights actions under state or federal statutes and invoking state or federal constitutional provisions;[2] extraordinary writs (including writs of habeas corpus, and, where the health care institutions are public entities, mandamus);[3] ordinary civil actions seeking damages or injunctive relief; and declaratory judgment actions under the virtually universal statutes that permit such actions.[4] In addition, the actions of patients, their families and health care workers can be reviewed after the fact in litigation for payment for medical services (where the family objects to payment for life sustaining treatment provided after the patient objected to such treatment, for example);[5] in battery or other tort actions against providers who continue life sustaining treatment after there has been objection to it[6], and through criminal actions against those who have terminated life support systems.

§ 16–52. The Burden of Proof in Cases Involving Decisions to Forgo Life Sustaining Treatment

a. The "Clear and Convincing Evidence" Standard

§ 16–51

1. See e.g., Rasmussen v. Fleming, 741 P.2d 674 (Ariz.1987).

2. See 42 U.S.C.A. § 1983. Of course, civil rights action require a substantive basis. Most courts invoking federal or state constitutions to support an individual's right to remove or refuse life-sustaining treatment (whether or not in the context of a civil rights action) have relied on the fundamental constitutional right to privacy. See e.g., In re Welfare of Colyer, 660 P.2d 738 (Wash.1983); Bouvia v. Superior Ct., 225 Cal.Rptr. 297 (Cal.App.1986). Alternatively, courts have relied on the liberty interest protected by the due process clause of the Fourteenth Amendment. See e.g., Cruzan v. Director, Missouri Department of Health, 497 U.S. 261, 110 S.Ct. 2841, 111 L.Ed.2d 224 (1990); McKay v. Bergstedt, 801 P.2d 617 (Nev. 1990).

3. See Bouvia v. Superior Ct., 225 Cal.Rptr. 297 (Cal.App.1986).

4. See Cruzan v. Harmon, 760 S.W.2d 408 (Mo.1988) (en banc).

5. Grace Plaza of Great Neck v. Elbaum, 588 N.Y.S.2d 853 (N.Y.App.Div.1992), affirmed 603 N.Y.S.2d 386, 623 N.E.2d 513 (1993).

6. See e.g., Anderson v. St. Francis–St. George Hosp., 671 N.E.2d 225 (Ohio 1996) (largely unsuccessful action for battery, negligence and "wrongful living"); Bartling v. Glendale Adventist Medical Ctr., 229 Cal.Rptr. 360 (Cal.App.1986) (battery).

Virtually all courts that have addressed the issue have concluded that whoever requests that life sustaining treatment be discontinued in the case of a currently incompetent patient must prove that he is entitled to this relief by "clear and convincing evidence," the highest burden of proof imposed upon plaintiffs in civil actions.[1] Courts have rejected an application of both lower (preponderance of the evidence) and higher (beyond a reasonable doubt) standards.[2]

Indeed, the majority of the Supreme Court treated the Cruzan case as if the central issue were nothing more than the constitutionality of the state's decision to impose this burden of proof, and the Chief Justice announced his holding very succinctly: "[A] state may apply a clear and convincing evidence standard in proceedings where a guardian seeks to discontinue nutrition and hydration of a person diagnosed to be in a persistent vegetative state."[3]

Of course, the "clear and convincing evidence" standard is not a symmetrical one; it applies to one seeking to terminate treatment, not to one seeking to maintain that treatment. Really, the application of a strict "clear and convincing evidence" standard to these cases serves primarily to recognize a policy that it is better to err on the side of maintaining life than terminating it. This is not, however, a universally accepted policy. As the Michigan Supreme Court has pointed out, "[t]o err either way has incalculable ramifications. To end the life of a patient who still derives meaning and enjoyment from life or to condemn persons to lives from which they cry out for release is nothing short of barbaric."[4]

b. The Nature and Amount of Evidence Required to Meet the "Clear and Convincing Evidence" Standard

There is considerable difference from state to state as to how much evidence is required to meet the "clear and convincing evidence" standard. In New York, for example, where the burden of proof is effectively a complete bar to the petitioner's success, much more is needed to satisfy the standard than in New Jersey, California, or other states in which the burden of proof is not a complete bar. For instance, the New York Court of Appeals announced that

> the "clear and convincing" evidence standard requires proof sufficient to persuade the trier of fact that the patient held a firm and settled commitment to the termination of life supports under the circumstances like those presented. As a threshold matter, the trier of fact must be convinced, as far as is humanly possible, that the strength of the individual's beliefs and the durability of the individual's commitment to those beliefs makes a recent change of heart unlikely.[5]

This is an exceptionally rigorous standard, unique among the states; even the generally higher "beyond a reasonable doubt" standard applied in criminal

§ 16–52

1. See e.g., In re Jobes, 529 A.2d 434, 441 (N.J.1987).

2. See e.g., McConnell v. Beverly Enterprises–Connecticut, Inc., 553 A.2d 596 (Conn. 1989).

3. Cruzan v. Director, Missouri Dept. of Health, 497 U.S. 261, 284, 110 S.Ct. 2841, 2854, 111 L.Ed.2d 224 (1990).

4. In re Martin, 538 N.W.2d 399, 401 (Mich.1995).

5. In re Westchester County Med. Ctr., 534 N.Y.S.2d 886, 892, 531 N.E.2d 607, 613 (N.Y. 1988) (emphasis added).

cases does not require that ancillary issues—here, the likelihood that a patient would not have changed her mind—be proven with a conviction that goes "as far as is humanly possible."

In fact, the application of this standard by the New York Court of Appeals suggests that the required conviction must extend beyond what is "humanly possible." Some New York Court of Appeals judges have said that no petitioner will ever be able to meet the standard established by the court. Judge Hancock described that standard as "unrealistic, often unfair or inhumane and, if applied literally, totally unworkable,"[6] and, as he points out, "[t]he rule posits, as the only basis for judicial relief, the court's finding by clear and convincing proof of a fact which is inherently unknowable. * * * What the rule literally demands is an impossibility."[7] Judge Simons, concurring in the same case, added that the use of this burden of proof, as applied in New York, "for all practical purposes foreclose[s] any realistic possibility that a patient, once rendered incompetent, will have his or her wishes to forego life-sustaining treatment enforced."[8]

Other courts have adopted more modest descriptions of what constitutes "clear and convincing evidence," even if those other courts also set the default position as the preservation of life. In New Jersey, for example, evidence in "right to die" cases is "clear and convincing" when it "produce[s] in the mind of the trier of fact a firm belief or conviction as to the truth of the allegations sought to be established * * *."[9] Of course, uncontroverted evidence, even if sufficient to meet the "preponderance of the evidence" standard, is not necessarily clear and convincing. Thus, the mere fact that there is some admissible evidence that a patient would choose to discontinue treatment does not mean that a court must require that the treatment be discontinued, even if there is no contrary evidence. Weak but consistent testimony about the patient's desires (from distant relatives, for example), therefore, may not justify the termination of life sustaining treatment, even outside of New York.

§ 16–53. Evidence Relevant and Thus Admissible in Cases Involving the Decision to Forgo Life Sustaining Treatment: General Principles

General rules of evidence govern the admissibility of evidence in "right to die" cases. Evidence is relevant if it "makes the existence of any fact that is of consequence to the determination of the action more probable or less probable than it would be without the evidence."[1] Different courts, though, have accorded different weight to different kinds of evidence. Given the "clear and convincing evidence" burden in these cases, as well as the fact that, as a matter of logic, no evidence can be truly definitive on the issue of what an incompetent person would want were that person competent, the subjective

---

6. Id. at 895, 531 N.E.2d at 616 (Hancock, J. concurring).

7. Id.

8. Id. at 895, 531 N.E.2d at 619 (Simon, J., concurring). Only New York imposes a standard that is effectively impossible to meet. Missouri and Michigan, however, come close. Compare Cruzan v. Harmon, 760 S.W.2d 408 (Mo.1988), reversed 497 U.S. 261, 110 S.Ct.

2841, 111 L.Ed.2d 224 (1990) and In re Warren, 858 S.W.2d 263 (Mo.App.1993). See also In re Martin, 538 N.W.2d 399 (Mich.1995).

9. In re Jobes, 529 A.2d 434, 441 (N.J. 1987).

§ 16–53

1. Fed. R. Evid. 401.

decisions about the weight to be accorded the evidence produced in "right to die" cases often will be determinative.

§ 16–54. Written Statements as Evidence of the Patient's Wishes

Courts are more receptive to written documents (including living wills and durable powers of attorney, whether technically valid under the state law or not) than to witnesses' recollections of oral statements. This respect for written statements stems from the greater probability that such statements actually were made by the patient, from the increased seriousness that generally attends the production of written documents, and from the increased likelihood that anyone making a written statement that might be used by others for these purposes would formally rescind the statements if there were a change of heart about the sentiments there expressed.[1] The courts' preference for written statements seems to extend to cases where the issue is the choice of a surrogate as well as those where the issue is the actual decision that would be made by the patient.[2]

§ 16–55. Oral Statements as Evidence of the Patient's Wishes

Of course, oral statements should be admissible also. As the Michigan Supreme Court has pointed out, "While a written directive would provide the most accurate evidence of the patient's decisions, and we strongly urge all persons to create such a directive, we do not preclude consideration of oral statements, made under the proper circumstances."[1] Some courts, however, have severely discounted oral statements made in reaction to news of another's "unnecessarily prolonged death,"[2] as "casual remarks"[3] or mere chatter not sufficiently "solemn" to be significant in a legal proceeding requiring the production of "clear and convincing evidence."[4] The Michigan court, for example, asserts that,

> The amount of weight accorded prior oral statements depends on the remoteness, consistency, specificity, and solemnity of the prior statement. The decisionmaker should examine the statement to determine whether it was a well thought out, deliberate pronouncement or a casual remark made in reaction to the plight of another. Statements made in response to seeing or hearing about another's prolonged death do not fulfill the clear and convincing standard.[5]

§ 16–54

1. "The ideal situation is one in which the patient's wishes were expressed in some form of writing, perhaps a 'living will,' while he or she was still competent. The existence of a writing suggests the author's seriousness of purpose and ensures that the court is not being asked to make a life-or-death decision based upon casual remarks." In re Westchester County Med. Ctr., 534 N.Y.S.2d 886, 892, 531 N.E.2d 607, 613 (N.Y.1988). See also In re Martin, 538 N.W.2d 399 (Mich.1995) and In re Tavel, 661 A.2d 1061 (Del.1995).

2. See In re Martin, 538 N.W.2d 399 (Mich. 1995).

§ 16–55

1. Id. At 410.

2. In re Westchester County Med. Ctr., 534 N.Y.S.2d 886, 531 N.E.2d 607, 614 (N.Y.1988).

3. Id. at 613.

4. Id. at 614; see also In re Eichner, 438 N.Y.S.2d 266, 274, 420 N.E.2d 64, 72 (N.Y.1981)(distinguishing between remarks made about one's religious beliefs and those made at a social gathering).

5. In re Martin, supra at 410–411.

Other courts have dismissed as irrelevant statements made about diagnoses, prognoses, or treatments even slightly different from those which the speaker subsequently confronted.

As a general matter, such oral statements are probably far more significant than they are credited to be. While judges may be used to announcing their opinions in signed and certified form, most of the rest of society is not. Discussions with family members and friends, often spurred on by a news event or the travails of another friend, provide the setting for the most serious and important statements that most people make; to trivialize and discount those statements is to trivialize and discount the lives of the people who utter them, and it effectively makes it impossible for those people, should they become incompetent, to exercise a right to forgo life sustaining treatment.

§ 16–56. The Guardian Ad Litem in Cases Implicating the Decision to Forgo Life Sustaining Treatment

A guardian ad litem is not a guardian, and the similarity in title has confused judges as well as those who have been appointed to serve in these two distinct roles. A guardian (sometimes called a "conservator" when the authority extends only to property) is appointed to protect the patient and act on his behalf in ways defined by order of the court. For example, a guardian may be appointed to make a decision concerning the discontinuation of life sustaining treatment on behalf of the patient. A guardian ad litem is a lawyer (or, increasingly commonly, an organization which employs a lawyer) who acts as legal counsel during the course of the litigation on behalf of the subject of the litigation.[1] A guardian may have responsibilities beyond the litigation, both in time and scope; the obligations, responsibility, and authority of a guardian ad litem, however, generally cannot extend beyond the litigation itself. Any competent adult may be appointed guardian, and there is no reason to believe that lawyers are particularly adept at this function. A guardian ad litem, who represents the patient in court, must be admitted to practice (or employ someone who is).

The guardian ad litem may not have the only independent pair of eyes looking out for the interests of the patient. Under some state statutes, under some circumstances, a court visitor is appointed to serve this same purpose.[2] In addition, the federal statute requiring states to have nursing home ombudsmen effectively creates another independent source of evaluation in cases involving people protected by that statute.[3] Court visitors and nursing home ombudsmen need not be lawyers, however, and their role is generally an investigational one, not the representational one of the guardian ad litem.

§ 16–56

1. For an excellent discussion of the various roles of guardians ad litem, see Susan Goldberg, Of Gametes and Guardians: The Impropriety of Appointing Guardians Ad Litem for Fetuses and Embryos, 66 Wash.L.Rev. 503, 505–509 (1991).

2. Id. at 509.

3. 42 U.S.C.A. § 3012.

I. CIVIL LIABILITY FOR FAILING TO RECOGNIZE A DECISION TO FORGO LIFE SUSTAINING TREATMENT

§ 16–57. Civil Liability for Failure to Recognize a Decision to Forgo Life Sustaining Treatment: Introduction

Physicians and health care institutions often claim that the reason for their refusal to terminate life sustaining treatment is their fear of civil and criminal liability. This fear is an irrational one, based more on medical legend and emergency room folklore than on any history of such lawsuits. There has been only one case in which physicians have been charged with criminal conduct for the termination of such treatment, and the physicians were ultimately vindicated in that case.[1] There has yet to be a single successful reported civil action brought against health care providers for the inappropriately early termination of life sustaining treatment, although, in theory, such actions should be available in the form of common law damage actions or wrongful death actions, depending on whether the patient actually dies as a result of the allegedly inappropriate nontreatment.

§ 16–58. Tort Liability for Failure to Recognize a Decision to Forgo Life Sustaining Treatment

If the threat of legal action provides any incentive to health care providers in cases involving the discontinuation of life sustaining treatment, it ought to be the incentive to discontinue treatment. In theory, courts do recognize that the continuation of treatment (whether life sustaining or not) after consent for such treatment has been properly denied or withdrawn constitutes an actionable battery.[1] Because a plaintiff—either the patient or the patient's estate—will be successful if the battery is proved by a "preponderance of the evidence," a lower standard than the "clear and convincing evidence" required in some other forms of litigation involving the termination of life sustaining treatment, battery actions against health care providers for failure to terminate life sustaining treatment may someday constitute a particularly fertile field in which patients and their families may test providers' decisions. In addition, because such actions are common law or statutory wrongful death actions for damages, plaintiffs will be entitled to trial by jury, an opportunity foreclosed in guardianship actions and other actions seeking injunctive relief. The public abhorrence of such over-treatment of the terminally ill and those in persistent vegetative state, and the widespread public fear of being kept alive against one's will, may make the possibility of trial by jury a very attractive one to potential plaintiffs and their counsel.

On the other hand, such tort actions have not proven as successful in fact as they should be in theory. In one Ohio case[2], the court evaluated the propriety of a battery and "wrongful living" action commenced on behalf of an 82 year old man who was admitted to the hospital complaining of chest pains. He told his physician that he did not want to be resuscitated, and "No Code Blue" was marked in his chart. Despite this, when he needed defibrilla-

---

§ 16–57

1. Barber v. Superior Court, 195 Cal.Rptr. 484 (Cal.App.1983).

§ 16–58

1. See e.g., Estate of Leach v. Shapiro, 469 N.E.2d 1047 (Ohio App.1984)("A physician who treats a patient without consent commits a battery, even though the procedure is harmless or beneficial"). But see Anderson v. St. Francis-St. George Hospital, 671 N.E.2d 225 (Ohio 1996).

2. Anderson v. St. Francis-St. George Hospital, 671 N.E.2d 225 (Ohio 1996).

tion he was revived by an attending nurse. Two days after his resuscitation he suffered a stroke and remained extremely debilitated and virtually helpless for the two years until his death. The court found that there was no cause of action for the wrongful administration of life-sustaining treatment, and that there were no compensable damages suffered as a result of the resuscitation. While the court found that the nurse's action did constitute a battery, the court found that the stroke and its consequences were not causally related to the nurse's action. Thus, while the patient could recover in tort, he would be limited to nominal damages.[3]

§ 16–59. Damages for Failure to Recognize a Decision to Forgo Life Sustaining Treatment

Although actions against health care providers for failure to terminate life sustaining treatment are, in most senses, ordinary tort actions, they do pose one significant and unique problem: how are damages to be measured in such cases? Obviously, such damages could include any medical expenses incurred as a result of the improper treatment. Damages could also include the pain, suffering, mental anguish and indignity suffered by the patient on account of the continued treatment, and, in the view of at least one court, the pain, suffering and mental anguish of the patient's close relatives as well.[1] Of course, any damages in tort actions for failure to terminate life sustaining treatment must be based on the premise, still unacceptable to some courts[2], that death is reasonably preferable to continued life under some circumstances, and that continued life per se can warrant damages. As this principle grows in acceptance it may become easier for courts to award damages in cases where health care providers have improperly continued life sustaining treatment.

§ 16–60. Attempts by Health Care Providers to Recover in Contract for Services Rendered Inconsistently With a Request That Life Sustaining Treatment Be Discontinued

Health care providers who continue life sustaining treatment after there has been a request that it be terminated face one other potential loss. Any such treatment that is improperly provided is not "necessary" treatment, and thus the patient (and his third party payer) are not obliged to pay for it. As a matter of logic, treatment which legally may not be provided, and for which the patient refuses consent, cannot be "necessary" treatment. Except for palliative care requested by or on behalf of the patient, virtually any treatment that is provided after the patient properly requests the termination of life sustaining treatment is "unnecessary," and thus not within the terms of the implicit contract between the patient and the health care provider or the

3. One subsequent Ohio case questioned the propriety of even a battery action under similar circumstances. See Allore v. Flower Hospital, 699 N.E.2d 560 (Ohio App. 1997). For an account of the way tort law could be applied in these cases, see John Donohue, "Wrongful Living": Recovery for a Physician's Infringement on an Individual's Right to Die, 14 J. Contemp. Health L. & Pol'y 391 (1998).

§ 16–59

1. See Estate of Leach v. Shapiro, 469 N.E.2d 1047 (Ohio App.1984). But see Anderson v. St. Francis-St. George Hospital, 671 N.E.2d 225 (Ohio 1996).

2. See, e.g., Anderson v. St. Francis-St. George Hospital, 671 N.E.2d 225 (Ohio 1996).

explicit contract between the third party payer (whether an insurance company, government payer, or other health plan) and the patient or the provider.

The only court to consider this issue ultimately required the family of a patient who was treated against his family's request to pay the nursing home a substantial fee for treatment rendered after the patient's family asked that treatment be stopped and that he be allowed to die.[1] In reaching its result, the New York Court of Appeals reasoned that it was inappropriate to deny payment to a medical institution on the basis of a surrogate decision made by one without authority, under New York law, to make that health care decision. Given the unusually narrow New York law authorizing surrogate decisionmaking, it seems unlikely that this case will be persuasive in other jurisdictions.

J. HOMICIDE LIABILITY AND THE DECISION TO FORGO LIFE SUSTAINING TREATMENT

§ 16–61. Homicide Liability and the Decision to Forgo Life Sustaining Treatment: Introduction

Even if the risk of conviction for a homicide is small, the fear caused by the prospect of defending such an action may greatly affect the decisionmaking of physicians who are asked to terminate life sustaining treatment. In fact, the technical law of homicide in many jurisdictions puts physicians who terminate such treatment at risk of prosecution. Despite this, outside of the Kevorkian case[1], which involved euthanasia rather than the removal of life sustaining medical treatment, there has been only one such prosecution, and that was unsuccessful.[2] Indeed, there have been few prosecutions for "mercy killings," i.e., killings designed to mercifully end the victim's suffering, even when there is active intervention by someone who does not purport to be practicing medicine.[3]

§ 16–62. Structure of Homicide Statutes

Homicide statutes take different forms in different states, although most provide for at least two degrees of murder (or, in many states, "intentional homicide"), some lower degree of intentional homicide (historically called "voluntary manslaughter"), and a form of criminally or grossly negligent homicide.[1] At common law, murder is distinguished from other forms of homicide by the presence of "malice aforethought," which requires either the intent to kill or an act demonstrating such little regard for human life that the act can be said to be the product of a malignant heart.[2] Notwithstanding

§ 16–60

1. Grace Plaza of Great Neck, Inc. v. Elbaum, 588 N.Y.S.2d 853 (N.Y.App.Div.1992), affirmed 603 N.Y.S.2d 386, 623 N.E.2d 513 (N.Y. 1993).

§ 16–61

1. For a discussion of the Kevorkian case, see section 16–68, below.

2. Barber v. Superior Court, 195 Cal.Rptr. 484 (Cal.App.1983.)

3. Ann Alpers, Criminal Act or Palliative Case? Prosecutions involving the Case of the Dying, 26 J.L. Med & Ethics 308 (1998).

§ 16–62

1. See generally, Wayne R. LaFave, S. Austin, W. Scott, Jr. et al., Criminal Law, § 7.7B7.11 (2d ed. 1986).

2. Id.

this definition of "malice aforethought," which bears only slight relationship to the ordinary meaning of the word "malice," a killing committed in the heat of passion upon adequate provocation is deemed to have been committed without malice aforethought.[3] Such killings, and, in some states with more recently adopted penal codes, killings committed by those with diminished capacity, constitute voluntary manslaughter.[4] Unintentional killings generally are criminal only if they are committed with recklessness or extraordinary negligence; they constitute what the common law called "involuntary manslaughter."[5]

§ 16–63. Applying Homicide Statutes to the Termination of Life Sustaining Treatment

When a physician intentionally removes a respirator or a feeding tube from a patient to hasten that patient's death, the physician will have committed the crime of murder if the physician can be said to have acted with "malice aforethought," which, as we've seen, requires no more than the intent to kill. Further, if the actor knows that his act will cause death he will be deemed to have intended the death because all human actors are deemed to have intended the natural and probable consequences of their intentional acts.[1] Physicians who intentionally terminate life sustaining treatment know that their act is likely to cause the death of their patient; it is implicit in the definition of "life sustaining treatment." Thus, if discontinuing life sustaining treatment constitutes homicide at all, it is likely to constitute murder and not some lesser degree.[2]

In addition, the highest degree of murder is generally distinguished from other degrees by the presence of "premeditation."[3] A murder is premeditated if the perpetrator has contemplated his act, even for a moment, before performing it.[4] Physicians who terminate life sustaining treatment are presumed to have given the matter full thought and consideration. To avoid malpractice liability, for example, they must admit to having considered the nature and consequences of their acts. Thus, if their acts constitute homicide, they constitute murder (or its equivalent); further, if their acts constitute murder, they constitute the highest degree of murder, premeditated murder.

§ 16–64. Potential Defenses in Homicide Cases Based Upon Termination of Life Sustaining Treatment

The defenses that seem the most obvious in these cases are not available. For example, while it is tempting to argue that the termination of life sustaining treatment does not cause death but merely hastens the death that

3.   Id.

4.   Id.

5.   Id.

§ 16–63

1.   See e.g., Wayne R. LaFave et al., Criminal Law, § 7.7 (2d ed. 1999 Supp.) One defense potentially available to physician-defendants in these cases is "the doctrine of double effect," which provides that if a physician intends only to relieve the suffering of a patient, the physician is not deemed to have intended to cause the death of the patient, even where the death is a natural and probable consequence of the physician's act. This defense is generally raised when a physician is providing palliative care that hastens the patient's death. For a further discussion of the doctrine of double effect, see § 16–68.

2.   Id.

3.   Id.

4.   Id.

was sure to come in any case, that is all any murderer does. We are all going to die; criminal courts can only ask whether someone has hastened the victim's death. It is, thus, no defense to a murder charge that the provider merely hastened the patient's death.

It is similarly unsatisfactory to argue that the patient's death was caused by the underlying illness, not the termination of life sustaining treatment. While the Quinlan [1] court and others have suggested that the termination of life sustaining treatment does not cause the death of the patient for this reason, such an argument is broad enough to exculpate even a killer who sneaks into a hospital and disconnects the life sustaining equipment from a patient he wants to murder. The termination of life sustaining treatment is an act that causes death under all traditional legal approaches to homicide law.

Equally unavailing is the defense that the termination of life sustaining treatment is merely an omission, not an act, and thus cannot constitute the actus reus of any homicide crime. While normally only acts and not omissions can constitute the actus reus of homicide crimes, omissions are adequate to serve this function when there is a legal duty to perform the omitted act.[2] The physician has a well established legal duty to provide adequate care to his patient.[3] If he fails to provide adequate care, and that failure causes the death of the patient, his failure does constitute the actus reus of homicide.

These defenses were all rejected by the California Court of Appeal in Barber v. Superior Court,[4] the only reported criminal prosecution lodged against a physician for terminating a patient's life sustaining treatment. The court agreed that the defendant physicians' omissions could have been breaches of their duty to act to provide proper medical care for their patient, and thus could have constituted the actus reus of murder (with which they were charged).[5] In California, however, murder is the "unlawful killing of a human being, * * * with malice aforethought".[6] The court was thus called upon to determine whether the physician's actions were "unlawful." Ultimately, the court concluded that California law permitted physicians to remove life sustaining treatment from incompetent patients, at least under some circumstances, upon the request of the families of those patients.[7] The physicians in Barber acted with the consent of the patient's wife, who was qualified to make the surrogate decision under California law (or who would have been qualified had she sought judicial approval, a distinction apparently unimportant to the California court), and the family was unified in its position and was acting with good faith.[8] The court therefore concluded that the physicians had acted lawfully in terminating the treatment that resulted in the patient's death.[9] Thus, the court held, the physicians' act could not satisfy the "unlawfulness" element of the crime of murder.[10] In the end, the Barber case depends upon

§ 16–64

1. Matter of Quinlan, 355 A.2d 647 (N.J. 1976).

2. See e.g., Wayne R. LaFave, S. Austin, W. Scott, Jr., Criminal Law § 3.3 (1986).

3. Id.

4. 195 Cal.Rptr. 484 (Cal.App.1983).

5. Id.

6. Id. at 486 (citing the West's Ann.California Penal Code § 187)(emphasis added).

7. Barber v. Superior Court, 195 Cal.Rptr. 484 (Cal.App.1983).

8. Id.

9. Id.

10. Id.

the language of the California law, which apparently exculpates actors engaged in activities that are otherwise lawful, even if those activities cause the death of another.

As a general matter, once the state has presented a prima facie case of homicide, the only defenses available are those recognized as justifications and excuses.[11] Justifiable homicides are those committed in self defense, in defense of family or country, or, in narrow circumstances in some jurisdictions, in defense of property.[12] Excusable homicides are those that are accidental as well as those committed by defendants who are insane, or, in some cases, by those who are acting under duress.[13] Although family members who have committed mercy killings of the terminally ill or those in intractable pain have been found not guilty by reason of temporary insanity,[14] a verdict available uniquely in American jurisdictions and very rarely invoked, it seems unlikely that any formally recognized justification or excuse will be available to physicians charged with homicide crimes arising out of their acts terminating life sustaining treatment.

§ 16–65. Impropriety of Applying Homicide Law to the Termination of Life Sustaining Treatment

The antiquated homicide law, which would commonly treat the termination of life sustaining treatment as murder, is especially out of place in this context. Fortunately, except in California, there has been no interest in commencing criminal actions against doctors who recognize "right to die" statements of their patients or those patients' families.[1] There are several reasons for this. First, most prosecuting attorneys recognize that it is a political liability, not an advantage, to prosecute these cases; the public is strongly supportive of the physicians who would be charged. Second, in some cases it may be difficult for the prosecution to meet the "beyond a reasonable doubt" standard of proof imposed in all criminal cases. Third, even in otherwise strong cases, the prosecution must face the real possibility of jury nullification; "mercy killing" cases provide the largest class of cases in which it is obvious that juries (and even judges) have simply ignored evidence in order to acquit the defendants.[2] In addition, when there is a conviction in a mercy killing case, the penalty imposed is usually trivial.[3]

---

11. See e.g., Wayne R. LaFave, S. Austin, W. Scott, Jr., Criminal Law § 5 (1986).

12. Id.

13. Id.

14. See e.g., People v. Waskin (unreported), Chicago Tribune, Aug. 10, 1967 (Defendant found not guilty by reason of insanity for the killing of his terminally ill mother who had been suffering great pain); People v. Zygmanik (unreported), (Super. Ct. N.J.1973) (Defendant found not guilty by reason of insanity of first degree murder of quadriplegic brother.)

§ 16–65

1. Even in California the interest in such actions seems to be on the wane. See, Thor v. Superior Court, 21 Cal.Rptr.2d 357, 855 P.2d 375, 386 (Cal.1993) (holding that a competent adult patient may refuse treatment and such

non-treatment will not subject the physician to civil or criminal liability).

2. For a general discussion of jury acquittals in these circumstances, see I. Horowitz, The Effect of Jury Nullification Instruction on Verdicts and Jury Functioning in Criminal Trials, 9 Law & Hum. Behav. 25, 29B30 (1985).

3. See e.g., People v. Sallander, (unreported), Houston Chronicle, Jan. 23, 1986 (defendant pleaded guilty to murder and was sentenced to five years probation); People v. Healy (unreported), Ass'd Press Report, June 1984 (71–year-old woman pleaded guilty to voluntary manslaughter after she killed her bedridden husband to end his misery; she was sentenced to 5 years probation, a $10,000 fine, and 1,000 hours of community service work). For a full account of the extremely lenient approach prosecutors, grand and petit juries, and judges

Finally, there are much better ways to test the propriety of the termination of life sustaining treatment than through criminal prosecution of the physician after the patient's death. Most health care institutions provide an ethics committee to facilitate discussions about the proper way to treat terminally or irreversibly ill patients. If such discussions are not fruitful, the family, physician, institution, district attorney, or, in many cases, anyone else may institute any one of a host of civil actions before the life sustaining treatment is terminated in order to test its propriety.

K. PHYSICIAN ASSISTED DEATH

§ 16–66. Physician Assisted Death—Introduction

The role, if any, that a physician may (and should) play in the death of a patient has become the subject of a great deal of discussion over the past several years. While there has been a consensus that the physician is not obliged to keep a patient alive at all costs and under all circumstances, without regard to the wishes of the patient,[1] there has not yet emerged a consensus as to what role the physician (or other health care provider) may play in actually hastening the death of a patient. As is often the case, the language used to describe the question may dictate the answer to that question. Those who argue for the propriety of a physician assisted death often argue in favor of "death with dignity," as if anyone would actually support the requirement that death be undignified. Those on all sides of the issue support "death with dignity," even if there is no consensus as to what it means. Similarly, those opposed to physician assisted death may refer to it as physicians killing patients or "euthanasia," which is a far less accepted process than "death with dignity." Because the use of language has played such an important role in the development of the law and public policy in this area, it is worth considering the meaning of the words that are most commonly used.

§ 16–67. Euthanasia and Suicide Distinguished

Euthanasia (Greek for "good death") generally refers to an act in which one person kills another at the request of, and for the benefit of, the one who dies.[1] Some have distinguished "active euthanasia," where there is an affirmative *actus reus* that causes the death of another, from "passive euthanasia," where it is an omission which results in the death.[2] Today "euthanasia" generally is used to describe only "active" euthanasia, not the process of allowing another to die.[3] Suicide is the taking of one's own life. Assisted

have taken towards "mercy killers" at every level of the criminal proceedings, in the United States and elsewhere, see Margaret Otlowski, Legal Aspects of Voluntary Euthanasia in Australia, 139–143 (1992).

§ 16–66

1. See section 16–61, above.

§ 16–67

1. Euthanasia is also defined as the act of "bringing about the death of a person who suffers from an incurable disease or condition, especially a painful one, for reasons of mercy." Blacks Law Dictionary 575 (7th ed. 1999).

2. See e.g., Lawrence O. Gostin, Drawing a Line Between Killing and Letting Die: The Law and Law Reform on Medically Assisted Dying, 21 J.Law, Med. & Ethics 94 (1993); see also, Blacks Law Dictionary 575 (7th ed. 1999).

3. Id.

suicide may constitute euthanasia if there is a close enough causal relationship between the assistance and the death.

§ 16–68. The Current Legal Status of Physician Assisted Death in the United States

a. Background

1. Euthanasia

Because consent is not a defense to homicide crimes, and because the law makes no distinction between a "good death" and any other kind of death, euthanasia is criminal homicide in every state and in almost every country, whether it is committed by a physician, another health care worker, a family member, or anyone else. Over the past several years, there have been some suggestions that this should change, and that euthanasia should be permitted by law. These calls for change have arisen from the development of well respected and legally unchallenged medical practices that appear to be indistinguishable from euthanasia.[1]

The most obvious of these practices in the United States is the current practice of physicians prescribing sufficient pain medication to assure that terminally ill patients are kept comfortable in their last few days of life.[2] Sometimes the very medication provided for pain relief also depresses breathing in these patients, who already may be extremely debilitated, and this may result in the hastening of the patient's death by a few hours or more.[3] When the physician administering the medication knows that it is likely to cause the patient's breathing to be depressed, and thus the patient's death to be hastened, she will be presumed to intend that result, and, if death is thus hastened, she will have committed the crime of murder.[4]

In traditional legal analysis, there is simply no way to square the formal law of homicide with these generally approved attempts to keep patients comfortable in their last hours or days of life. The practice of providing large doses of pain medications under these circumstances is one, albeit limited, form of euthanasia that is now so well accepted in medicine that it has been accepted in American law as well. Attempting to finesse this exception to the rule that euthanasia is prohibited, some commentators have called it "indirect euthanasia," or argued that "palliative care" can never constitute criminal activity. Of course, it cannot be distinguished from other forms of euthanasia on the ground that its primary purpose is to ameliorate the patient's suffering; that is, by definition, the purpose of any act of euthanasia. One commentator has argued that "[t]here is a tacit understanding that prosecution would never be undertaken, even if causal connection between the analgesic and death could be established. * * * [M]edical practice has won de facto legal acceptance because of widespread acknowledgement of its humane grounding."[5]

§ 16–68

1. See Lawrence Gostin, Drawing a Line Between Killing and Letting Die: The Law and Law Reform on Medically Assisted Dying, 21 J.Law, Med. & Ethics 94 (1993).

2. For a general discussion, see Margaret A. Somerville, The Song of Death: The Lyrics of Euthanasia, 9 Contemp. Health L. & Policy (1993).

3. Id.

4. Id.

5. Norman Cantor, Legal Frontiers of Death and Dying 35 (1987).

Over the past few years legal commentators have settled on justifying this practice of hastening patients' deaths by referring to the "doctrine of double effect," a theological doctrine originally used to justify the practice within the Catholic church. Under this doctrine, the actor is not deemed to intend to cause the death of the patient if the actor's only intent is to eliminate suffering. The secondary effect of the act may be the death of the patient, but the one causing the death does not have to bear the moral burden of causing that death if the intent were the permissible one of relieving suffering. The legal acceptance of the doctrine of double effect was assumed in Washington v. Glucksberg[6], where Justice O'Connor pointed out that "[t]he parties and amici agree that ... a patient who is suffering from a terminal illness and who is experiencing great pain has no legal barriers to obtaining medications, from qualified physicians, to alleviate that suffering, even to the point of causing unconsciousness and hastening death."[7] She was willing to join in the majority because "[t]here is no dispute that dying patients ... can obtain palliative care, even when doing so would hasten their deaths."[8]

2. Suicide and Assisted Suicide

Suicide and assisted suicide are analyzed differently from euthanasia. Although suicide was punishable under the common law in England for the past two centuries, it was not a crime in that country until 1854.[9] The common law of the American states is hardly monolithic on the issue of suicide. While all states have abrogated laws making suicide a crime (and they were hardly enforceable in any case), most states (but not all) do prohibit aiding or assisting the suicide of another. Some treat assisting suicide rather harshly; in Illinois and Ohio it has been treated as murder. Hawaii and Indiana only prohibit causing suicide, not assisting it.[10] A few states have no laws against causing or assisting suicide and there are very few prosecutions under those statutes that proscribe participation in another's suicide in any event.[11]

While the United States Supreme Court had indicated in the Cruzan case that state statutes criminalizing assisting suicide were constitutional,[12] a position subsequently confirmed in Washington v. Glucksberg,[13] there was no interest in enforcing criminal sanctions against physicians assisting suicide until Dr. Jack Kevorkian began his campaign publicizing and using his "suicide machine," which allowed patients—sometimes young, relatively healthy patients, in his case—to terminate their own lives. In the early 1990s Dr. Kevorkian chose Michigan as the venue for the operation of his machine

6. Washington v. Glucksberg 521 U.S. 702, 117 S.Ct. 2258(1997).

7. Id. At 737, 117 S.Ct. at 2302. (Opinion of O'Connor, J.).

8. Id. At 737, 117 S.Ct. at 2303.

9. For a general historical discussion, see Wilbur Larremore, Suicide and the Law, 17 Harv. L. Rev. 331 (1904). For a comprehensive account of current statutory law, see Catherine Bjorck, Physician–Assisted Suicide: Whose Life Is It Anyway? 47 S.M.U.L.Rev. 371, 378–383 (1994).

10. See Wayne R. LaFave and Austin W. Scott Jr., Criminal Law, 2nd Ed., § 7.8–7.12 (1986); George Smith, Final Choices: Autonomy in Health Care Decisions (1989).

11. For a good history of the statutes and case law enforcing assisted suicide statutes, see George P. Smith, All's Well That Ends Well: Toward a Policy of Assisted Rational Suicide or Merely Enlightened Self–Determination?, 22 U.C. Davis L. Rev. 275, 290–91 (1989) and George P. Smith, Final Choices: Autonomy in Health Care Decisions (1989).

12. Cruzan v. Director, Missouri Dept. of Health, 497 U.S. 261, 110 S.Ct. 2841, 111 L.Ed.2d 224 (1990).

13. Washington v. Glucksberg 521 U.S. 702, 117 S.Ct. 2258(1997).

because it was one of the states that did not make aiding or assisting suicide a crime. Ultimately, after several successful legal defenses in criminal cases arising out of his assisted suicides, he performed a euthanasia that was recorded and subsequently televised nationally. He unwisely decided to represent himself in the criminal action that followed, and he was convicted of second degree murder. He is currently serving a 22 year sentence as a result of that conviction.

As a general matter, the remarkable Kevorkian phenomenon aside, courts are not anxious to intervene when doctors help terminally ill patients in intractable pain take their own lives. When Dr. Timothy Quill wrote in the *New England Journal of Medicine* in 1991 describing the process of providing barbiturates and instructions on how to use them to one of his patients, his confession was regarded as a statement of his sensitivity, not the admission of a crime.[14] A Rochester grand jury decided against indicting him for assisting his patient's suicide, saving the prosecutor from the dilemma of having to proceed against a doctor who had served the fundamental values of his profession but who had been required to violate the letter of the criminal law to do so.[15]

The Ethics and Health Policy Council of the American Medical Association has taken a very narrow approach and determined that "[d]eeply rooted medical traditions and the guiding principles of medical practice" dictate physicians should not assist the suicide of even hopelessly ill patients.[16] As the AMA Council notes, however, this position is not the unanimous view of American physicians.[17] Some physicians view assisting the death of a patient in an appropriate case as being within the appropriate role of a physician dedicated to caring for, as well as curing, the patient.[18]

b. The Supreme Court Decisions in Washington v. Glucksberg and Quill v. Vacco

In 1997 two cases involving claims that the Constitution protected individual acts of physician assisted death, at least under some circumstances, came before the Supreme Court. The first was a review *Compassion in Dying v. Washington,*[19] in which the Court of Appeals had held that Washington's ban on physician-assisted suicide violated the Due Process Clause of the Fourteenth Amendment. The Ninth Circuit, sitting en banc, found a "... liberty interest in choosing the time and manner of one's death ...", and thus concluded that "... prohibiting physicians from prescribing life-ending medication for use by terminally ill patients who wish to die violates the patients' due process rights."[20] The second was *Quill v. Vacco,*[21] in which the Second Circuit held that New York's statutory ban on assisted suicide violated the

14. See Timothy Quill, Death And Dignity: A Case of Individualized Decision Making, 324 New Eng. J. Med. 691 (1991). For a response to Dr. Quill, see Robert J. Blendon et al., Should Physicians Aid Their Patients in Dying? 267 JAMA 2658 (1992).

15. William Kates, Grand Jury Clears Doctor Who Aided Patient's Suicide, Boston Globe, July 28, 1991, National/Foreign at 2.

16. See David Orentlicher, Physician Participation in Assisted Suicide, 262 JAMA 1844 (1989). See also Thomas Marzen, Out, Out Brief Candle: Constitutionally Prescribed Sui-

cide for the Terminally Ill, 21 Hastings Con. L.Q. 799 (1994).

17. See Orentlicher, supra note 16.

18. See Sidney Wanzer et al., The Physician's Responsibility Toward Hopelessly Ill Patients: A Second Look, 320 N. Eng. J. Med. 844 (1989).

19. 79 F.3d 790 (9th Cir.1996).

20. Id. at 728.

21. 80 F.3d 716 (2nd Cir. 1997).

Equal Protection Clause of the Fourteenth Amendment. The Second Circuit reasoned that "... New York does not treat similarly circumstanced persons alike: those in the final stages of terminal illness who are on life-support systems are allowed to hasten their deaths by directing the removal of such systems; but those who are similarly situated, except for the previous attachment of life-sustaining equipment, are not allowed to hasten death by self-administering prescribed drugs."[22]

The Supreme Court, unanimous in its result but divided in the reasons for it, reversed both the Ninth and Second Circuits. In *Washington v. Glucksberg*[23] the Court held that Washington's ban on assisted suicide did not violate the Due Process Clause. Chief Justice Rehnquist, writing for the Court, announced that the Due Process Clause protects those rights and liberties which are "... deeply rooted in this nation's history and tradition."[24] The Court then concluded neither suicide nor assisted suicide has been well accepted in this society, and that it could not meet this "deeply rooted" test. The Court continued by stating that Washington has a state interest in the preservation of human life which would justify its limitation of assisted suicide in any case.

Ultimately the Court determined that this was a political issue best left to the legislative branches, not to the Federal judiciary; the determination of whether physician assisted death ought to be countenanced was to be left to the legislature of each state. As the Chief Justice concluded, "[t]hroughout the nation, Americans are engaged in an earnest and profound debate about the morality, legality and practicality of physician assisted suicide. Our holding permits this debate to continue, as it should in a democratic society."[25] Several concurring Justices suggested that they might reconsider this issue if physician assisted death were necessary to allow a patient to avoid arbitrary and severe suffering, but, because both Washington and New York permitted all necessary palliative care to be provided, that issue was not before the Court.[26]

In *Vacco v. Quill*[27] the Supreme Court found that New York's ban on assisted suicide did not violate the Equal Protection Clause because there is a distinction between hastening death by withdrawing life support and hastening death by assisted suicide. The Court explained that "[t]he distinction between letting a patient die and making that patient die is important, logical, rational and well established...."[28] Because of this distinction, the Court reasoned, no one is treated inappropriately differently under the law. "Everyone, regardless of physical condition, is entitled, if competent, to refuse unwanted lifesaving medical treatment; no one is permitted to assist suicide."[29]

c.   The Oregon Death With Dignity Act

The legislatures of several states have considered statutes that would have offered legal recognition to physician assisted death under some circum-

22. Id. at 728.

23. 521 U.S. 702, 117 S.Ct. 2258 (1997).

24. Id. at 2268.

25. Id. At 735, 117 S.Ct. 2258.

26. See Opinions of O'Conner, Stevens, Ginsburg and Breyer.

27. 521 U.S. 793, 117 S.Ct. 2293 (1997).

28. Id. at 2295.

29. Id.

stances. Until 1994 all were unsuccessful. However, in 1994 the Oregon electorate approved an initiative that created the Oregon Death with Dignity Act[30] by a margin of 51% to 49%.

Less than two weeks before the Act was to go into effect, the United States District Court issued a preliminary injunction against its operation, reasoning that the initiative violated the Equal Protection Clause because it discriminated against the physically and mentally disabled and others.[31] The Ninth Circuit vacated the judgment of the district court upon a finding that federal courts lacked jurisdiction over the matter[32], and the Supreme Court refused to hear the matter. In 1997 the Oregon Legislature returned the issue to the electorate for a second vote and the Act was upheld by a margin of 60% to 40%.

The Oregon Death with Dignity Act provides for a physician to prescribe a lethal dose of medication to a patient; the patient must then take the medication herself.[33] The Act prohibits a physician from directly acting in a way that would end the patient's life, thus prohibiting active euthanasia. A patient seeking assistance under the Act must be diagnosed with a terminal illness—defined as one that will lead to death within six months—by two physicians. The Act also requires that either physician must refer the patient to counseling if the physician believes the patient to be suffering from a mental disorder or depression that would cause impaired judgment. No life-ending medication may be prescribed until the patient is no longer suffering from such a condition.

A patient seeking to employ the Death With Dignity Act must be over the age of eighteen and a resident of Oregon. The patient must be capable of communicating health care decisions. The Act requires that the patient make two verbal requests for the prescription from her physician separated by at least 15 days, and at least one written request, which must be made at least 48 hours before the prescription is written. The Act does not allow a patient to qualify solely based upon age or disability.

The Act requires that the Oregon Health Division create a reporting system to collect information on physician assisted suicide. The first report, studying the first year of actual operation of the Act, was released in February, 1999. During the 1998 reporting year, twenty-three terminally ill patients received prescriptions. Fifteen of these patients died after taking the lethal medication, six died of underlying illnesses and two were alive at the time the data was collected. The mean age of the twenty-one patients now deceased was 69 years of age. Eleven of the patients were male; ten were female. Four of the twenty-one patients were referred to counseling and were ultimately found competent to receive the prescription.

The report further revealed that patients who chose physician-assisted suicide in 1998 were similar with respect to age, race and sex to all Oregonians who died of similar underlying illnesses. There was no statistical relationship between patients who chose physician-assisted suicide and income, education, insurance status or access to hospice care. This finding suggests that

30. Or. Rev. Stat. §§ 127.800–.897 (1995).

31. Lee v. Oregon 891 F.Supp. 1429 (D.Or. 1995).

32. Lee v. Oregon 891 F.Supp. 1439 (D.Or. 1995).

33. See Or.Rev.Stat. §§ 127.800–.897.

patients in lower income brackets and the uneducated will not be forced by their conditions to choose physician assisted suicide at a higher rate than their educated and wealthier counterparts. Similarly, a patient's fear of the financial impact of the illness was not significantly related to the patient's choice regarding physician-assisted suicide. However, loss of autonomy and bodily functions were associated with the choice of physician assisted suicide.[34]

Those who oppose physician assisted death have been concerned with the Oregon experiment, and some have sought to have Congress pass legislation that would make it impossible for Oregon to carry out the provisions of the Death With Dignity Act. For example, such legislation could make it illegal to prescribe drugs regulated by the Drug Enforcement Agency (DEA) to cause the death of a patient.

§ 16–69. Physician Assisted Death: The Arguments

a. *Reasons for Dissatisfaction With Current Law*

There are some types of physician assisted death that are now well accepted in medicine and law. Many factors have combined to create this more flexible approach to euthanasia: the ascendancy of the principle of autonomy and the respect for human dignity that comes with it; the recognition that what is morally required ought to be, at the very least, legally permitted; a widespread concern and fear over the possibility that physicians can wrest control of a patient's destiny from that patient and force the patient to continue to live as a virtual corpse; and, perhaps, an increased interest in the use of health resources. At least where a well informed competent patient who is terminally ill and in intractable pain thoughtfully and repeatedly requests medical intervention to end her life, most people believe that medicine and law ought to allow for that aid. Indeed, the arguments for permitting euthanasia under some circumstances seem so persuasive and so well accepted in this country that the burden of maintaining the law has fallen to those defending the current legal structure.

b. *Reasons for Maintaining the Current Absolute Ban on Euthanasia*

Several arguments are made against the case for euthanasia.[1] These arguments fall into six categories.

(1) Misdiagnosis. If euthanasia were permitted, a mistake in the diagnosis of a patient could result in the quick and comparatively unconsidered

---

34. A.E. Chin et al., Legalized Physician Assisted Suicide in Oregon—The First Year's Experience, 340 N.Eng.J.Med. 577 (1999). The experience during the second year was largely parallel to that of the first year, although more people (33) received prescriptions for lethal medication during the second year, and more (26, plus one who had received the prescription the previous year) used the lethal medication to cause their deaths. By the end of the second year it had become clear that the primary reasons patients chose physician assisted death were loss of autonomy (79%) and the inability to participate in activities that make life enjoy-

able (77%). Only about one in five patients suggested that inadequate pain control was a factor contributing to the decision to seek a physician assisted death. Amy Sullivan, Katrina Hedberg and David Fleming, Legalized Physician Assisted Suicide in Oregon—The Second Year, 342 N.Eng.J.Med. 598 (2000).

§ 16–69

1. Many of these arguments can be found in more detail in a special supplement on Mercy, Murder and Morality: Perspectives on Euthanasia, 19 Hastings Center Rep. (Jan./Feb. 1989).

death of the patient. This risk, which is avoided when we are required to allow death to take its natural course, outweighs any benefit that euthanasia may bring with it.

(2) Involuntariness. It is very difficult to determine whether the application of euthanasia in any particular case is truly voluntary. When is the person who volunteers for death doing so freely and when is that person doing so because he believes (rightly or wrongly) that he is a financial or social burden upon his family, or upon the community?

(3) The Slippery Slope. While at first euthanasia may be permitted only for those in terrible pain, or those who are terminally ill, or those for whom it is otherwise appropriate, the pressure of the allocation of health care resources will inevitably enlarge the class for whom euthanasia is deemed appropriate. Every society has a group that is deemed to be socially unworthy and members of that group—the uneducated, the unemployed and the disabled, for example—will become good candidates for euthanasia. The only way to avoid slipping down this slope is to refuse to permit euthanasia in any case.

(4) Disrespect for the Disabled. Presumably, those severely disabled people who choose death would be physically unable to accomplish it by their own means. Thus, the disabled would be the most likely to take advantage of any socially permitted euthanasia. Allowing euthanasia which disproportionately affects this portion of the population is tantamount to promulgating a social policy that says that we should rid ourselves of the disabled, that the disabled are less worthy of life than the able-bodied.

(5) Change in the Role of Medicine. Permitting euthanasia would turn doctors who practice it into killers, and this would change the relationship between the medical profession and the community. Doctors, who generally are esteemed and trusted in the community, would no longer be viewed exclusively as care givers but instead would also be viewed as takers of life. This additional role as executioner would adversely affect the ability of the profession to serve in its helping role.

(6) Promoting the Right to Refuse Life Sustaining Treatment. It has been a difficult political road to achieve the right to refuse treatment, a right recognized in one form or another in most states and in most countries. The fear that the right to refuse treatment would lead to euthanasia has always been a major argument against the right to refuse treatment itself. To argue in favor of euthanasia now would be to give credence to those arguments and would slow the very important development of the right to refuse treatment.

§ 16–70. Proposals for Reform—The Dutch Model

The only nation to formally legally tolerate euthanasia, under some circumstances, is the Netherlands. Euthanasia still constitutes a *prima facie* case of homicide under the 1886 Dutch Penal Code provision that outlaws killing another "at that other person's express and serious request."[1] However, the Dutch Supreme Court has determined that the defense of *force majeure* is available to a physician who takes affirmative acts that result in the death of a patient when those acts are required by the ethical precepts

§ 16–70
1. Penal Code § 293 (Netherlands).

that define the good practice of medicine.[2] Thus, while the practice of euthanasia does constitute homicide, it is excusable homicide if certain conditions are met.[3]

Appropriately, given the nature of the defense, the conditions which justify the exercise of euthanasia have been developed through formal and informal interchange between the Dutch courts, which have addressed the question in several cases, and the Royal Dutch Medical Association. In essence, the conditions are:

(1) that the request for euthanasia come from a competent patient;

(2) that the request for euthanasia be entirely voluntary, without any coercion or incentive;

(3) that the request for euthanasia be repeated over time, i.e., that it be a "durable" request;

(4) that the requesting patient be enduring unacceptable suffering (whether that suffering be due to pain or to indignity that does not otherwise impose pain), and

(5) that the physician consult with another physician about the propriety of engaging in euthanasia.[4]

In order to fully articulate all of the principles guiding the appropriate use of Euthanasia in the Netherlands, the government appointed a State Commission on Euthanasia in 1982.[5] The Commission's 1985 report recommended several, mostly minor, changes to the Dutch Penal Code to allow doctors to practice active voluntary euthanasia on patients who are in hopeless situations without any reasonable possibilities of change.[6] In order to get reliable data, in 1990 the government commissioned the Remmelink Committee to survey physicians throughout the Netherlands. The Remmelink Committee Report, which was released in 1992, did little to quiet the Dutch debate about whether the law should be formally changed, although it did confirm that in 1990, 2300 deaths (just under 2% of all deaths in the Netherlands) resulted from physician assistance, and that these were most often carried out by family practitioners, and only very rarely by nursing home doctors.[7] Because physician assisted death is still technically illegal (even if excused) under Dutch law, there has been a concern that physicians have underreported its practice.

Whether euthanasia is "legal" in the Netherlands is a jurisprudential question; it is not formally permitted by statute, but those who perform euthanasia are excused from criminal culpability if they follow articulated substantive standards and reporting requirements. Indeed, some Dutch com-

---

2. For a general discussion, see B. Sluyters, Euthanasia in the Netherlands, 57 Medico–Legal J. 34 (1989).

3. Id.

4. Royal Dutch Medical Association, Vision on Euthanasia 3, 8–11 (1986).

5. The Commission was charged with advising the government on its future policy toward active voluntary euthanasia and rendering assistance in self-killing.

6. Report of the Netherlands State Commission on Euthanasia, 167.

7. P. Van der Maas, et al., Euthanasia and Other Medical Decisions Concerning The End of Life, 338 Lancet 669 (1991); G. Van der Wal et al., Euthanasia and Assisted Suicide: How Often Practiced By Family Doctors in the Netherlands? 9 Family Practice 130 (1992); G. Van der Wal et al., Euthanasia and Assisted Suicide: II. Do Dutch Family Doctors Act Prudently? 9 Family Practice 135 (1992).

mentators have argued that euthanasia is no more common in the Netherlands than in other Western countries; the difference is that the medical and
legal communities in the Netherlands are the only ones willing to talk about it
openly and honestly.[8] In early 2000 there was speculation that the Dutch
Parliament would reconsider the current legal structure upholding physician
assisted death with an eye to making it formally legal (rather than merely
tolerated), in part in the hope that such a legal change would improve the
regularity of reports of its practice.

L.   SPECIAL ISSUES IN TERMINATING PARTICULAR KINDS OF LIFE SUSTAINING TREATMENT

§ 16–71.   Special Issues in Terminating Particular Kinds of Life Sustaining Treatment: Introduction

As a general matter, the same rules and principles apply to the withholding and withdrawing of all types of medical treatment. For example, competent adult patients can accept or refuse any kind of medical treatment, and
the characterization of the kind of medical treatment is irrelevant. Thus, the
principles discussed in this chapter have been applied to the termination of
ventilator support, the discontinuation of dialysis, the decision not to commence chemotherapy (or other forms of cancer) treatment, the discontinuation of nutrition and hydration, the decision to forgo surgery, the determination not to hospitalize a patient, the discontinuation of antibiotics, the entry
of a "do not resuscitate" order, and almost every other imaginable form of
treatment offered by medicine. While the attributes of the proposed treatment
will be significant in determining how appropriate principles of law are
applied, differing treatment modalities do not attract the application of
different principles.

Despite the general rule that all forms of treatment are to be evaluated in
terms of the same principles, some theologians, philosophers, courts, and
legislatures have suggested that particular forms of therapy warrant special
evaluation, outside of the scope of the rules articulated for general cases. For
example, some have sought to distinguish between "active" and "passive"
conduct that results in the death of the patient and "withholding" and
"withdrawing" medical treatment.[1] In addition, since the Papal statement on
termination of life sustaining treatment was issued in 1957, theologians and
others have attempted to distinguish between "ordinary" and "extraordinary" medical means. Further, in the 1980s many legislatures sought to draw
a distinction between the principles that should apply to the termination of
nutrition and hydration and the principles that should apply to the termination of all other forms of medical care. Some state legislatures, including
that in New York, have sought to distinguish the entry of "do not resuscitate"

---

8. H. Leenen, Dying With Dignity: Developments in the Field of Euthanasia in the Netherlands, 8 Med. & Law 517, 525 (1989).

Language of Euthanasia and Causing, 1 J. Cul.
Ethics 268 (1990).

§ 16–71

1. For a general discussion of the distinctions drawn, see R. Devettere, The Imprecise

orders from all other decisions regarding life sustaining treatment.[2] Finally, many people—in philosophy, medicine and law—have begun to wonder whether patient requests for medically futile treatment should be treated differently from patient requests for the continuation of otherwise medically indicated treatments.

§ 16–72. The Distinction Between "Active" and "Passive" Treatment

The distinction between "active" and "passive" treatment has become an anachronism in law, just as it has become an anachronism in ethical discussions of "right to die" issues. Whatever meanings might be attributed to the terms "active" and "passive" in other circumstances, they are ambiguous when applied to most forms of medical care. Virtually any form of medical care can be characterized as "active" or "passive," depending on the interests of the one making the characterization. As the New Jersey Supreme Court asked in the *Conroy* case,

> [W]ould a physician who discontinued nasogastric feeding be actively causing [the death of a person kept alive by that process] by removing her primary source of nutrients; or would he merely be omitting to continue the artificial form of treatment, thus passively allowing her medical condition, which includes [the] ability to swallow, to take its natural course?[1]

Similarly, the "active" conduct of removing a ventilator from a patient may be characterized as the "passive" conduct of allowing the patient to forgo breathing support, and the "passive" conduct of not resuscitating a patient may be characterized as the "active" conduct of writing a "do not resuscitate" order.

§ 16–73. The Distinction Between "Withholding" and "Withdrawing" Treatment

The distinction between "withholding" and "withdrawing" treatment partakes of the same fallacy as does the distinction between "active" and "passive" conduct. While there is some emotional attraction to the argument that we have a greater obligation to finish a job than to start it, there is no rational basis to this argument, and the consequences of the adoption of such a principle could be truly dire. As Justice Brennan pointed out in his dissent in *Cruzan*,

> [t]here may be considerable danger that [forbidding the withdrawal of treatment] would impair rather than serve any interest the state does have in sustaining life. Current medical practice recommends use of heroic measures if there is a scintilla of a chance that the patient will recover, on the assumption that the measures will be discontinued should the patient improve. When the President's Commission in 1982 approved the withdrawal of life support equipment from irreversibly vegetative patients, it explained that "[a]n even more troubling wrong occurs when

2. N.Y.—McKinney's Public Health Law § 2962. See § 16–76, below.

§ 16–72

1. In re Conroy, 486 A.2d 1209, 1233–34 (N.J.1985).

a treatment that might save life or improve health is not started because the health care personnel are afraid that they will find it very difficult to stop the treatment if, as is fairly likely, it proves to be of little benefit and greatly burdens the patient."[1]

Indeed, there is some evidence that emergency medical technicians do not commence life sustaining treatment when they believe it is likely to be unsuccessful yet they think that hospital physicians will be obliged to continue it indefinitely.[2]

§ 16–74. The Distinction Between "Ordinary" and "Extraordinary" Treatment

This distinction, recognized at least since its theological articulation in 1957 as a way of justifying the termination of treatment under some circumstances, was originally embraced by the judiciary but has now virtually disappeared as a meaningful element in cases involving the decision to forgo life sustaining treatment. As the Massachusetts Supreme Court recognized in 1986, "while * * * the distinction between extraordinary and ordinary care is a factor to be considered, the use of such a distinction as the sole, or major, factor of decision tends * * * to create a distinction without meaning."[1]

The problem with attempting to distinguish between "ordinary" and "extraordinary" treatment is that such a characterization depends upon the medical facilities available at the time and place the decision is made as well as the diagnosis and prognosis of the patient. What was extraordinary a few years ago is ordinary now, and what is extraordinary in the bush of Alaska may be perfectly ordinary in central Seattle. Ventilator support, for example, cannot be described as either "ordinary" or "extraordinary" treatment. It is certainly appropriate (and thus, apparently, "ordinary" under the standards of those who would draw this distinction) when it is a short term treatment designed to allow a trauma victim to fully recover (i.e., for a patient with a good prognosis); it is extraordinary when applied to one who is brain dead.

§ 16–75. Discontinuation of Nutrition and Hydration

The issue of withdrawing nutrition and hydration has become especially contentious since it found its place on some political agendas. Generally, courts have concluded that the termination of nutrition and hydration is no different from the termination of other forms of mechanical support. As one federal court pointed out, "[a]lthough an emotional symbolism attaches itself to artificial feeding, there is no legal difference between a mechanical device that allows a person to breathe artificially and a mechanical device that allows a person nourishment. If a person has right to decline a respirator, * * * then a person has the equal right to decline a gastrostomy tube."[1] This view echoes the perspective of the Florida Court of Appeals: "We see no reason to

§ 16–73

1. Cruzan v. Director, Missouri Dept. of Health, 497 U.S. 261, 314, 110 S.Ct. 2841, 2870, 111 L.Ed.2d 224, 264 (1990).

2. D. Johnson and W. Maggiore, Resuscitation Decisionmaking by New Mexico Emergency Medical Technicians, 11 Am. J. Emergency Med. 139 (1993).

§ 16–74

1. Brophy v. New England Sinai Hospital, Inc., 497 N.E.2d 626, 637 (Mass.1986).

§ 16–75

1. Gray v. Romeo, 697 F.Supp. 580, 587 (D.R.I.1988).

differentiate between the multitude of artificial devices that may be available to prolong the moment of death."[2]

In 1990, a majority of the Supreme Court (the four dissenters and concurring Justice O'Connor) in *Cruzan* agreed that nutrition and hydration were merely forms of medical care, to be treated like any other kind of medical care. As Justice O'Connor pointed out, "[a]rtificial feeding cannot readily be distinguished from other forms of medical treatment. * * * Whether or not the techniques used to pass food and water into the patient's alimentary tract are termed 'medical treatment,' it is clear they all involve some degree of intrusion and restraint."[3] She concluded that "the liberty guaranteed by the due process clause must protect, if it protects anything, an individual's deeply personal decision to reject medical treatment, including the artificial delivery of food and water."[4]

Nonetheless, as several courts have recognized, even if the provision of nutrition and hydration is logically and philosophically no different from the provision of any other kind of care, there are emotional and symbolic differences between the provision of nutrition and hydration and other life sustaining treatments. In the words of the New Jersey Supreme Court, "[a]s infants, we could breathe without assistance, but we were dependent on others for our lifeline of nourishment."[5] There is no more obvious symbol of compassionate care than the provision of food.

The emotional and symbolic significance of food and water is increased by the presumption that death through the absence of nutrition and hydration—death by "starvation and thirst"—would be exceptionally painful. In fact, there is no reason to believe that a person in persistent vegetative state (for whom this question is most likely to arise) would feel pain under any circumstances, and the administration of nutrition and hydration in a medical setting may itself be highly intrusive and even painful to those who are not in persistent vegetative states. While the medical literature is spare on this issue, there has been a suggestion that death through removal of nutrition and hydration may be far less painful than the alternative for many patients.

In any case, those who argue that nutrition and hydration are different from other medical treatment forget that the medical process for the delivery of nutrition and hydration is far different from spooning raspberry jello into a patient's mouth. One good description of the process is found in Justice Brennan's dissenting opinion in *Cruzan*:

> The artificial delivery of nutrition and hydration is undoubtedly medical treatment. The technique to which Nancy Cruzan is subject—artificial feeding through a gastrostomy tube—involves a tube implanted surgically into her stomach through incisions in her abdominal wall. It may obstruct the intestinal tract, erode and pierce the stomach wall, or cause leakage of the stomach's contents into the abdominal cavity. * * * The tube can

2. Corbett v. D'Alessandro, 487 So.2d 368, 371 (Fla.App.1986).

3. Cruzan v. Director, Missouri Dept. of Health, 497 U.S. 261, 288, 110 S.Ct. 2841, 2857, 111 L.Ed.2d 224 (1990) (O'Connor, J., concurring).

4. Id. More recently the Missouri Court of Appeals declared that the Missouri Supreme Court's decision in *Cruzan* was necessitated by its determination that nutrition and hydration were not medical treatment. In re Warren, 858 S.W.2d 263 (Mo.App.1993).

5. In re Conroy, 486 A.2d at 1236.

cause pneumonia from reflux of the stomach's contents into the lung. * * * Typically, and in this case, commercially prepared formulas are used, rather than fresh food. * * * The type of formula and method of administration must be experimented with to avoid gastrointestinal problems. * * * The patient must be monitored daily by medical personnel as to weight, fluid intake and fluid output; blood tests must be done weekly.[6]

Thus, the suggestion that denying a patient nutrition and hydration is indistinguishable from forcing that patient to die of starvation or thirst is polemic. We do not describe the removal of a ventilator as a process designed to kill by asphyxiation, or the termination of dialysis as a process designed to kill by poison; similarly, describing the removal of a feeding tube as the commencement of the starvation of the patient mischaracterizes the issue.

Many state legislatures have amended their living will legislation to provide a special status to the provision of nutrition and hydration, and some have absolutely prohibited the withdrawal of nutrition and hydration under any circumstances.[7] To avoid the potentially draconian consequences of such provisions, however, courts have simply ignored them, usually by construing them so narrowly that they do not apply to medical food preparations. For example, the Supreme Court of Connecticut authorized the withdrawal of feeding by a gastrostomy tube despite a statute that appeared to say that under such circumstances "nutrition and hydration must be provided."[8] The court reasoned that the nutrition and hydration that was implicated in the statute was that provided by "a spoon or a straw," and that the legislature could not have intended that feeding by gastrostomy tube should be treated any differently than any other mechanical or electronic medical intervention.[9]

§ 16–76. Cardiopulmonary Resuscitation

There may be some reason to treat cardiopulmonary resuscitation (CPR) differently from the way we treat other forms of life-sustaining therapy. CPR is the only form of life-sustaining treatment that is provided routinely without consent of the patient, and it may be the only medical treatment of any sort that is generally initiated without an order of a physician.[1] CPR generally is provided unless a formal "Do Not Resuscitate" (DNR) order is entered in the patient's chart. Remarkably, even patients in hospitals are infrequently asked to make their own decisions on cardiopulmonary resuscitation.[2] One startling study of over 9000 patients, conducted over several years, revealed that fewer than half of the physicians with seriously ill patients in the hospital knew

6. Cruzan v. Director, Missouri Dept. of Health, 497 U.S. 261, 307, 110 S.Ct. 2841, 2866, 111 L.Ed.2d 224 (1990) (Brennan, J., dissenting).

7. See Alan Meisel, The Right to Die (2d ed. 1995 and 1999 Supp.), section 11.12.

8. McConnell v. Beverly Enterprises–Connecticut, Inc., 553 A.2d 596 (Conn.1989).

9. Id.

§ 16–76

1. William G. Bartholome, "Do Not Resuscitate" Orders, Accepting Responsibility, 148 Arch.Intern.Med. 2345 (1988).

2. See Stuart J. Youngner et al., Do Not Resuscitate Orders, Incidents and Implications in a Medical Intensive Care Unit, 253 JAMA 54 (1985). For a general account of the underlying medical-legal issues, see Tracy E. Miller, Do Not Resuscitate Orders: Public Policy and Patient Autonomy, 17 L., Med. & Health Care 245 (1989).

whether their patients wanted CPR, and almost half of the patients with DNR orders had them entered within two days of their deaths. That study also showed that intensive intervention to explain the likely outcome of CPR to physicians and improve the communication between the health care providers and the patients had virtually no effect on whether the patients were provided CPR.[3]

Why don't doctors talk to patients about CPR? The long medical tradition of not discussing CPR was exacerbated by the mid–1980s fear among physicians that they would be liable for damages if they did not resuscitate whenever it was possible to do so, even when attempts at resuscitation were futile or inconsistent with the desires of the patient.[4] These factors gave rise to "slow codes" or "pencil DNRs" in which the hospital staff was instructed to provide certain patients with resuscitation under circumstances that would guarantee that the resuscitation would fail (by delaying the commencement of the treatment, for example). Sometimes the hospital staff was instructed in a more straightforward way to avoid resuscitation, but the instruction was provided in some form that would leave no record: it was written in the chart in pencil or, in New York, indicated by the placement of a removable purple dot on the patient's file.

The reaction to this transparently dishonest process was the development of formal hospital policies that provided for honest and open decision making on DNR.[5] Today generally accepted principles of medical ethics require that hospitals maintain such policies, and many hospitals have delegated the authority to draft and review these policies to their institutional ethics committees. Indeed, any hospital without a policy governing DNR orders could face legal liability for its absence should it inappropriately resuscitate (or fail to resuscitate) a patient because of the uncertain reaction of a nurse or physician within the institution.

These institutional developments were accompanied by a more formal legal analysis of the problems of hospital decisionmaking in this area, and in 1986 the New York State Task Force on Life and the Law proposed legislation on Do Not Resuscitate orders. A statute similar to that recommended by the Task Force was adopted in New York in 1987.[6] The statute is remarkable for its precision, and, some might say, for the bureaucracy it has brought to making one kind of treatment decision.[7] Ironically, the statute, which was promulgated because of the worry of overuse of CPR, has been criticized because it may require CPR in cases where it would be inappropriate—for example, even where such treatment would be futile[8]—unless a DNR order has been entered. The statute also provides for a very narrow therapeutic

3. A Controlled Study to Improve Care for Seriously Ill Hospitalized Patients–The Study to Understand Prognoses and Preferences for Outcome and Risks of Treatment (the "SUPPORT" study), 274 JAMA 1591 (1995).

4. See e.g., R.M. Veatch and C.M. Spicer, Medically Futile Care: The Role of the Physician in Setting Limits, 18 Am. J. L. & Med. 15 (1992).

5. See e.g., Committee on Policy for DNR Decisions, Yale–New Haven Hospital, Report on Do Not Resuscitate Decisions, 47 Conn. Med. 478 (1983); Robert Levine and Kathleen Nolan, Editorial, Do Not Resuscitate Decisions, A Policy, 47 Conn. Med. 511 (1983).

6. N.Y.—McKinney's Public Health Law § 2962.

7. Id.

8. See section 16–79, below.

privilege[9], and it imposes a cumbersome and formal procedure on those entering a DNR order.

Other states promulgating DNR statutes generally have avoided the bureaucratic thicket created by the original New York statute. Some of the subsequent statutes permit the patient to sign an advance directive that CPR not be provided, while others provide a streamlined process by which a physician can enter a DNR order. A few states require witnesses on DNR advance directives or orders, some include DNR forms, some provide for virtually no formalities. Some statutes apply only in designated institutions (hospitals and nursing homes, for example), some apply specifically to prehospital treatment by paramedics, and some apply under all circumstances. Frequently DNR provisions are part of advance directive statutes, although sometimes they are codified elsewhere, and sometimes (most commonly in the case of prehospital orders) they are included in regulations promulgated by an administrative agency.[10]

§ 16–77. Requests for Continuation of Futile Treatment

Beginning in the early 1990s, hospitals and nursing homes occasionally have been confronted with requests that they continue medical treatment even when the medical staffs of those institutions believe it is scientifically futile or ethically inappropriate to do so. A treatment is scientifically futile when it can not achieve the medical result expected by the patient or her family; it is ethically inappropriate when it may achieve a specific result but that result is not within the purview of medicine.[1] For example, some families may believe that health care providers should give laetrile or other unproven drugs to treat their relative's cancer; such treatment is scientifically futile because, as a scientific matter, it cannot help mitigate the disease. Other families believe that institutions should continue ventilator support or tube feeding when, in the view of the health care providers, such treatment will do nothing more than extend the patient's persistent vegetative state or otherwise delay the patient's inevitable death—results which those health care providers may believe are inappropriate and inconsistent with their ethical obligations to treat their patient with dignity.

As a general matter, patients need not be offered or provided scientifically futile treatment; health care providers must offer patients only that range of treatments that is medically indicated under the circumstances. Thus, if the provision of ventilator support cannot possibly extend the life of the patient or affect the quality of that life, no provider is obliged to accede to requests for that treatment, just as physicians need not provide laetrile therapy to cancer patients or appendectomies to those with myopia—even if the patients inappropriately, in the eyes of the provider, seek those therapies.

It is more difficult to assess the provider's obligation to offer or give the patient treatment which is not scientifically futile but which the provider believes is ethically inappropriate. A family might desire a treatment that will

9. See section 16–73, above.

10. For a general discussion, see Paul Sorum, Limiting Cardiopulmonary Resuscitation, 57 Alb. L. Rev. 617 (1994).

§ 16–77

1. See e.g., Baruch Brody, Special Ethical Issues in the Management of PVS Patients, 20 L., Med. and Healthcare 104 (1992).

keep the patient's body aerated and nourished, even if it does nothing more; providers may believe that the continuation of mere corporeal existence is not within the proper goals of medicine. Under such circumstances, the family views the life sustaining treatment as effective (in keeping the patient alive) while the provider sees the treatment as ineffective (in serving the goals of medicine).[2]

The Council on Ethical and Judicial Affairs of the American Medical Association has expressed a concern that the use of the term "futility" has obscured this issue rather than cast light upon it. The Council has determined that "[p]hysicians are not ethically obliged to deliver care that, in their best professional judgment, will not have a reasonable chance of benefiting their patients. Patients should not be given treatments simply because they demand them. Denials of treatment should be justified by reliance on openly stated ethical principles and acceptable standards of care, ... not on the concept of " 'futility," which cannot be meaningfully defined."[3]

In one celebrated 1991 case a Minnesota hospital sought (but did not receive) formal judicial authority to replace a patient's surrogate decision maker on the sole ground that the decision maker, who was the patient's husband, insisted upon the continuation of life sustaining treatment for an elderly patient in persistent vegetative state.[4] The doctors argued that the continued treatment of the patient would be futile and they sought a guardian more likely to agree with their position. The issue for the court, then, was whether the guardian should be replaced. The decision of the probate court denying the request for the appointment of a new guardian was correct as a technical legal matter because there was no reason to believe that anyone would be better able than the husband to determine what decisions that patient, if competent, would make under the circumstances. The Minnesota court was not forced to confront the question of whether the health care provider was required to offer the patient's surrogate the choice of continued life sustaining treatment. If the provider had sought a declaratory judgment on the propriety of discontinuing treatment, or if the lawsuit were commenced by the guardian and sought an order requiring the hospital to continue life sustaining treatment, it would have provided the court with a chance to address the difficult ethical question.[5]

M. THE PATIENT SELF–DETERMINATION ACT

§ 16–78. The Patient Self–Determination Act: Introduction

In the late 1980s many members of Congress were looking for a way to join the "right to die" bandwagon without having Congress take a substantive

2. For a general discussion of the issue of futility, see Judith Daar, Medical Futility and Implications for Physician Autonomy, 21 Am. J. L. and Med. 221 (1995), R. Schwartz, Autonomy, Futility and the Limits of Medicine, 2 Camb. Q. Healthcare Ethics 159 (1992), and Daniel Callahan, Medical Futility, Medical Necessity: The Problem–Without–A–Name, Hastings Center Rep. 30 (July–August 1991).

3. Council on Ethical and Judicial Affairs, American Medical Association, Current Opin-

ion 2.035 ("Futility"), Code of Medical Ethics (1998–99 ed.).

4. In Re Wanglie, No. PX–91–283 (Minn. D. Ct. June 28, 1991).

5. See e.g., David H. Johnson, Helga Wanglie, Revisited: Medical Futility and the Limits of Autonomy, 2 Cambridge Q. Healthcare Ethics 161 (1993).

position on any of the thorny underlying issues. One way to achieve this end appeared to be through the Patient Self Determination Act of 1990,[1] which was designed primarily to require health care institutions to inform patients about their rights to execute advance directives and to otherwise control their own health care under state law—whatever that law might be—without actually requiring states to adopt any particular substantive law. Although the bill had much support in Congress, it was opposed by the American Hospital Association, the American Bar Association, the Health Care Financing Administration and the American Medical Association (even though individual doctors were exempted from its requirements). After hearings on the bill in 1990, it was presumed dead. In what was a surprise to virtually everyone following the bill, it was resurrected as a part of the Omnibus Budget Reconciliation Act of 1990 and it passed in that form virtually without debate. While the Act contemplated enforcing regulations, they were not promulgated in final form by the Health Care Financing Administration until 1995.[2]

§ 16–79. The Patient Self–Determination Act: Coverage

The Act has an extremely broad coverage. It binds all hospitals, nursing facilities, home health agencies, hospice programs, and health maintenance organizations that receive any funding through the Health Care Financing Administration.[1] Thus, virtually all institutional providers that receive any Medicare or Medicaid funding are covered by the statute.[2] The only substantial group of providers not covered by the statute are non-institutional providers who practice outside of health maintenance organizations.[3]

The statute applies to patients in hospitals and nursing facilities upon their admission to those facilities, to clients of home health care and hospice prior to their receipt of care, and to members of health maintenance organizations at the time that their membership becomes effective.[4] The general language of the statute, however, allows providers some leeway in determining the most sensible (and sensitive) time to carry out their obligations.

§ 16–80. The Patient Self–Determination Act: Requirements

a. Health Care Providers

The statute requires that each of those covered by the act provide every patient with written information describing that person's rights under state law "to make decisions concerning * * * medical care, including the right to accept or refuse medical treatment or surgical treatment and the right to formulate advance directives."[1] The state law that must be described to

§ 16–78

1. 42 U.S.C.A. §§ 1395(a)(1)(Q), 1395cc(f), 1395mm(c)(8), 1396a(a)(57) & (58), 1396a(w).

2. 42 C.F.R., parts 417, 430–31, 434, 483–84, 489.

§ 16–79

1. 42   U.S.C.A.   §§ 1395cc(f)(1)(A), 1396a(w)(1)(A).

2. Id.

3. Id.

4. Id.

§ 16–80

1. 42 U.S.C.A. § 1395 cc(a)(1)(F)(1)(A). Under the Assisted Suicide Funding Restriction Act, 42 U.S.C.A. section 14406, this need not include information related to the right, under state law, to engage in "assisted suicide, euthanasia or mercy killing."

patients is not just state statute law; the explanation given to patients must include a description of the law "recognized by the courts of the State"[2] as well as an explanation of any right to die statute, durable power of attorney statute, or other relevant statute.[3]

Covered providers must also give all of their patients written documents explaining the provider's own policies with regard to these rights.[4] The fact that the providers must provide a written explanation of their policies with regard to right to die issues means that the provider must *have* such policies. Thus, one of the most significant consequences of the Patient Self Determination Act is that it indirectly requires virtually all health care institutions in the United States to develop formal written policies that deal with the termination of life sustaining treatment.[5]

Although the statute is silent on whether the families of patients must be given the information when the patient is incompetent, most good providers give the information to whoever has decisional authority under state law, and to whoever is likely to be seriously involved in making the health care decision on behalf of the patient.[6] The statute does not require that the information be distributed by any particular person, although health care providers should provide the information under circumstances that encourage discussion of advance directives, and they should provide easy access to someone—most commonly a specially trained nurse, social worker or a pastoral counselor—to answer any questions that arise.[7]

The Act also requires that every patient's record must indicate whether or not that patient has signed an advance directive of any kind—a requirement that necessitates an interaction between the provider and each patient about that patient's wishes concerning life sustaining treatment.[8] All covered providers also must assure that the state laws are followed within their organizations, and they must provide education about advance directives to their organizational staff as well as to the public.[9]

b. *Government Agencies*

In order to help providers carry out the Act, state and federal governments are also given responsibilities. State governments must develop written descriptions of their state laws, and the Department of Health and Human Services is required to conduct a nationwide education program on advance directives, and to provide additional substantive material about advance directives to all Social Security and Medicare recipients.[10] Of course, to the extent that government agencies are also covered health care providers, they are bound by the same requirements that bind other providers.

2. 42 U.S.C.A. § 1396a(a)(58).

3. For valuable accounts of the way the Act has been applied, see Thaddeus Pope, The Maladaptation of Miranda to Advance Directives: A Critique of the Implementation of the Patient Self Determination Act, 9 Health Matrix 139 (1999), and Henry Glick et al., Advanced Medical Directives in U.S. Hospitals and Nursing Homes: The Implementation and Impact of the Patient Self Determination Act, 14 Pol. & Life Sci. 47 (1995).

4. 42   U.S.C.A.   §§ 1395cc(f)(1)(A), 1396a(w)(1)(A).

5. 42 U.S.C.A. §§ 1395cc(f)(1), 1396a(w)(1).

6. Id.

7. Id.

8. 42   U.S.C.A.   §§ 1395cc(f)(1)(B), 1396a(w)(1)(B).

9. 42   U.S.C.A.   §§ 1395cc(f)(1)(E), 1396a(w)(1)(E).

10. 42 U.S.C.A. § 1396a(a)(58).

§ 16–81. The Patient Self–Determination Act: Sanctions

Each covered health care provider is required to give a formal assurance to the Secretary of Health and Human Services that it is complying with all applicable sections of the Patient Self–Determination Act. The statute requires the Secretary to cut all Medicaid and Medicare funding to any institution that fails to make the proper assurance. This penalty is mandatory, and the Secretary is given no discretion to ameliorate what is, effectively, the economic death penalty for any non-complying institution.[1]

Although the statutory penalty technically applies only to those institutions that do not provide the required assurance, it would, presumably, also apply to any institution that filed a false assurance. The harshness of this sanction suggests that it will not be applied except in the most egregious circumstances. In other words, as long as the provider tries to implement the Act in good faith, the Secretary is unlikely to require more.

The cut-off of federal funding remains the only remedy available under the Act. Attempts to claim private causes of action under the Patient Self–Determination Act have been unsuccessful,[2] although the facts that give rise to such claims may separately state causes of action under state law.

§ 16–81

1. 42 U.S.C.A. § 1395cc(b).

2. See Asselin v. Shawnee Mission Medical Center, 894 F. Supp. 1479 (D. Kan. 1995).

Chapter 17

WRONGFUL BIRTH, WRONGFUL LIFE AND WRONGFUL CONCEPTION

Table of Sections

Research References

Am Jur 2d, Prenatal Injuries; Wrongful Life, Birth, or Conception §§ 89–180
ALR Index: Wrongful Birth
ALR Digest: Physicians and Surgeons § 29.6
Am Jur Legal Forms 2d, Physicians and Surgeons §§ 202:121–202:141
Am Jur Pleading and Practice Forms (Rev), Negligence § 105; Physicians, Surgeons, and Other Healers § 614; Products Liability §§ 194, 204, 205
22 POF3d 1, Health Care Provider's Liability for Brain–Damaged Infant
16 Am Jur Trials 471, Defense of Medical Malpractice Cases; 15 Am Jur Trials 373, Discovery and Evaluation of Medical Records

§ 17–1. Distinguishing Wrongful Birth, Wrongful Life and Wrongful Conception

Although at times courts have used these terms differently (and interchangeably), "wrongful birth," "wrongful life" and "wrongful conception" have come to describe identifiably different kinds of actions.[1] An action for

---

§ 17–1

1. Some have argued that the use of these terms obscures the real harm involved in these cases and have recommended against their us-

age. See Viccaro v. Milunsky, 551 N.E.2d 8, 10 n. 3 (Mass.1990). See Mark Strasser, Misconceptions and Wrongful Births: A Call for a Principled Jurisprudence, 31 Ariz. St. L. J. 161

wrongful birth is one commenced by the parents (or the legal representative) of a child with serious birth anomalies who claim that if they had been given sufficient information they would have chosen not to conceive, or to abort, the child.[2] Thus, for example, when parents bring an action against a physician for negligent genetic counseling, claiming they would not have conceived a child if they had been given adequate information,[3] or when parents bring an action against an obstetrician for failing to diagnose a condition of the fetus in utero or the mother during pregnancy, claiming that they would have aborted the fetus if they had been properly informed of the risks,[4] they are making wrongful birth claims. The basis of a wrongful birth claim is that the parents negligently were denied a procreative choice they should have enjoyed, and, as a consequence, a seriously ill child was born.[5]

An action for wrongful life is one commenced by a child born with serious anomalies against a physician who negligently provided information that resulted in the child's conception or birth.[6] Thus, although it stems from a distinct duty and is governed by some different policy considerations, a wrongful life claim is a wrongful birth claim with a different plaintiff. If the parents are the plaintiffs, the action is one of wrongful birth, whereas if the child is the plaintiff, it is denominated one in wrongful life.[7]

An action for wrongful conception (sometimes called an action for wrongful pregnancy) is one commenced by a healthy child's parents against a defendant whose negligence resulted in the conception of the child.[8] Thus, a wrongful conception case may be commenced against a physician who negligently performs a tubal ligation,[9] for example, or a pharmacist who negligently dispenses birth control drugs or devices.[10] An action for wrongful conception is distinguished from actions for wrongful birth and wrongful life by the health of the child who is the subject of the litigation. If the plaintiffs claim that a healthy child would not have been born except for the negligence of the defendant, the action is one in wrongful conception; if they claim that a seriously ill child would not have been born except for that negligence, the action is one in wrongful birth or wrongful life (depending on the identity of the plaintiff). Like the basis of wrongful birth and wrongful life cases, the basis of a wrongful conception case is that the parents were denied a reproductive choice they otherwise would have been afforded.[11]

(1999); Alexander Capron, Tort Liability in Genetic Counseling, 79 Colum. L. Rev. 618, 634, n.62 (1979); Michael Kelly, The Rightful Position in "Wrongful Life" Actions, 42 Hastings L. J. 505, 506, n.4 (1991).

2. Smith v. Cote, 513 A.2d 341 (N.H.1986).

3. See Becker v. Schwartz, 413 N.Y.S.2d 895, 386 N.E.2d 807 (N.Y.App.1978); See generally Capron, supra note 1.

4. See e.g., James G. v. Caserta, 332 S.E.2d 872 (W.Va.1985).

5. See generally Capron, supra note 1.

6. Kelly, supra note 1, at 506; Turpin v. Sortini, 182 Cal.Rptr. 337, 643 P.2d 954 (Cal. 1982).

7. See Kelly, supra note 1 at 506.

8. See e.g., James G. v. Caserta, 332 S.E.2d 872 (W.Va.1985). Some commentators have suggested that wrongful conception is a subset of wrongful pregnancy, and the two should be distinguished. See Mark Strasser, Misconceptions and Wrongful Births: A Call for a Principled Jurisprudence, 31 Ariz. St. L. J. 161 (1999). But see C.S. v, Nielson, 767 P.2d 504 (Utah 1988).

9. Lovelace Medical Center v. Mendez, 805 P.2d 603 (N.M.1991).

10. See e.g., Troppi v. Scarf, 187 N.W.2d 511, (Mich.App.1971) (pharmacist negligently filled prescription for contraceptives with tranquilizers).

11. See Michael A. Berenson, Comment, The Wrongful Life Claim—The Legal Dilemma of Existence Versus Nonexistence: "To Be or Not to Be," 64 Tul. L. Rev. 895, 899 n.15 (1990).

Wrongful birth, wrongful life and wrongful conception cases are classic negligence actions which are subject to the rules of pleading and proof, and the substantive law, of other negligence actions. In order to succeed, the plaintiff must show that the defendant owed a duty to the plaintiff, that the defendant breached this duty, and that the breach was the actual and proximate cause of some demonstrable and ascertainable damage. As a matter of general course, wrongful birth, wrongful life and wrongful conception cases present special problems only with regard to the element of damages;[12] other elements of the tort of negligence are analyzed just as they would be in any other case alleging medical negligence.

Although there has been a spirited academic and judicial debate over the propriety of wrongful birth, wrongful life and wrongful conception cases,[13] they seem consistent with the underlying purposes of the law of torts and it would be a substantial departure from the ordinary rule of tort law to fail to recognize these actions.[14] Tort law is designed to serve several purposes. Among them are deterrence, justice, edification, and cost spreading,[15] all of which are served by the existence of this genre of litigation. First, the existence of such actions should deter negligent genetic counseling, prescription dispensing, and other potentially harmful conduct.[16] Second, justice requires that, as between the perpetrator and the victim, the one who negligently imposes damages on another ought to bear the burden of those damages.[17] Third, the edification function of tort law is served by articulating a formal policy mandating that health care providers be liable for all of their negligent acts; ultimately this will assure continued respect for the health care system and improve the quality of provider-patient interactions.[18] Finally, a family with an unexpected additional (and, in wrongful birth and wrongful life cases, usually extremely expensive) child should not bear the full cost of the special medical, educational, and other needs of that child. Through malpractice litigation that cost can be spread over the entire medical community, and, through that community, over virtually the entire population of patients—i.e., over all of society.

§ 17–2. State Statutory Limits on Wrongful Life, Wrongful Birth, and Wrongful Conception Cases

The development of wrongful birth, wrongful life, and wrongful conception actions opened new areas of malpractice liability. That, combined with

---

12. See Kelly, supra note 1 at 512; Lisa A. Podewils, Note, "Traditional Tort Principles and Wrongful Conception Child–Rearing Damages," 73 B.U.L. Rev. 407 (1993).

13. Compare Kurtis J. Kearl, Note, Turpin v. Sortini: Recognizing the Unsupportable Cause of Action for Wrongful Life, 71 Calif. L. Rev. 1278 (1983) with Note, Wrongful Birth Actions: The Case Against Legislative Curtailment, 100 Harv. L. Rev. 2017 (1987).

14. Harbeson v. Parke–Davis, Inc., 656 P.2d 483 (Wash.1983) (stating that wrongful birth is a logical and necessary development of tort law). For a strong argument that all of these cases ought to be treated like ordinary malpractice cases, see Strasser, supra note 1.

15. See Kelly, supra note 1, at 508–509; Podewils, supra note 12, at 418.

16. See Troppi v. Scarf, 187 N.W.2d 511, 517 (Mich.App.1971) (stating that liability was necessary to encourage contraception providers to exercise great care); Podewils, supra note 12, at 419 (stating that liability in wrongful conception will cause physicians to practice at the same level of care in sterilizations as in other medical procedures); Kelly, supra note 1, at 510 (stating that liability encourages genetic counselors to "take precautions in order to avoid careless mistakes").

17. Kelly, supra note 1, at 510.

18. See Kelly, supra note 1, at 511.

the fact that these and similar actions are premised on the availability of abortion, caused most state legislatures to consider bills that would limit these kinds of lawsuits. One state legislature expressly recognized wrongful birth and wrongful life actions,[1] and several others have expressly prohibited them.[2]

Most of the states that have taken this second course have done so to avoid legal recognition of the right of abortion.[3] For example, the Minnesota statute, which is typical, provides that "no person shall maintain a cause of action or receive an award of damages on the claim that but for the negligent conduct of another, a child would have been aborted."[4] One consequence of the language of the Minnesota statute is that actions based on the allegation that a child would never have been conceived in the absence of the defendant's negligence are still permitted; it is only when the negligence comes too late to avoid conception, but early enough to permit abortion, that the subsequent tort action is barred. The Minnesota Supreme Court narrowly upheld this statute in 1986 in an action brought by a 34–year–old woman who gave birth to a child with Down Syndrome.[5] The mother alleged that the defendant physician negligently discouraged her from having a test that would have revealed the Down Syndrome and would have resulted in the abortion of the fetus.[6] The Supreme Court found there was no state action (and, thus, the fourteenth amendment of the United States Constitution was not implicated), and even if there were state action, the statute did not impermissibly burden the plaintiff's right to an abortion.[7]

Despite the failure of the challenge to the Minnesota statute, statutes that prohibit wrongful birth, wrongful life and wrongful conception legislation remain subject to constitutional attack on federal and state due process and equal protection grounds, and perhaps on other grounds as well in states with strong state constitutional provisions that assure open access to the courts and the preservation of common law remedies.[8] In any case, the legislative attempts to curtail these actions appear to have been premature attempts to deal with a genre of malpractice litigation that has not grown so rapidly as to pose much of an economic threat to medical practitioners. Since the late 1980s, legislative interest in limiting wrongful birth, wrongful life, and wrongful conception cases by statute has waned, and legislatures have left it to the courts to determine the contours of this area of malpractice.

§ 17–2

1. Me. Rev. Stat. Ann. Tit. 24, § 2931.

2. See e.g., Idaho Code § 5–334; Minn. Stat. Ann. § 145.424; Mo. Rev. Stat. § 188.130; N.D. Cent. Code § 32.03–43; 42 Pa. Cons. Stat. § 8305; S.D. Codified Laws § 21–55–1 et. seq., and Utah Code § 78–11–24.

3. See Michael A. Berenson, Comment, The Wrongful Life Claim—The Legal Dilemma of Existence Versus Nonexistence: "To Be or Not To Be", 64 Tul. L. Rev. 895, 900–901.

4. Minn. Stat. Ann. § 145.424(2).

5. Hickman v. Group Health Plan, Inc., 396 N.W.2d 10 (Minn.1986).

6. Id.

7. Id. at 10. For an alternative view of whether this statute is constitutional and whether a state court's application of a state statute constitutes state action for purposes of the due process clause, See Note, Wrongful Birth Actions: The Case Against Legislative Curtailment, 100 Harv. L. Rev. 2017, 2026 (1987).

8. At least thirty-six states have constitutional provisions prohibiting the legislature from removing a recognized legal remedy. Thus, in states which already recognize these actions, the legislature may be bound by the judiciary's determination. See Note, supra note 7, at 2023 n.35.

§ 17–3. Existence and Breach of Duty

a. *The Existence of a Duty*

In wrongful birth, wrongful life and wrongful conception cases, negligence standards are applied in determining if a defendant owed a duty to the plaintiff and if that duty was breached. Often, however, the conduct that results in a wrongful birth, wrongful life or wrongful conception case can best be characterized as an omission rather than an act—the omission to tell a patient that she could become pregnant despite a medical procedure, for example. Normally a mere omission (rather than an affirmative act) is insufficient to constitute a breach of duty for purposes of the law of negligence, but an omission may constitute a breach of duty when the defendant has a legally recognized special relationship with the plaintiff and a consequent duty to act. Health care providers maintain a special relationship with their patients, and they have a well recognized legal duty to provide adequate care (including the duty to provide adequate information) to their patients; effectively, medical omissions are treated exactly like medical acts once the provider-patient relationship is established. Thus, health care professionals may breach a duty to their patient when they fail to provide information to that patient, whether that failure is characterized as an act or a mere omission.

Thus, often the very possibility of a wrongful birth, wrongful life, or wrongful conception case hinges upon the establishment of the provider-patient relationship. In the cases of an obstetrician who is sued by a pregnant woman he attended, a genetic counselor sued by a couple she advised, or a pharmacist sued by a client for whom she incorrectly filled a prescription, such a relationship is easily established. However, the existence of the relationship is less obvious in other cases: while an obstetrician clearly owes a duty to the woman who is an immediate patient, does she also owe a duty to the father of the child to be born[1] (who may be another wrongful birth or wrongful conception plaintiff), or, more significantly, to the child herself (who may be a wrongful life or wrongful conception plaintiff)?[2]

It may make little difference if the father is considered a patient for tort purposes; any action the father could bring would be available to the mother as well. It does, however, make a difference if the unborn child is treated as the patient. First, the child's separate action includes some heads of damages arguably unavailable to the parents.[3] Second, the statute of limitations may be longer for the child.[4] Indeed, at least one court has recognized that this is the primary reason to allow the child to bring an action that otherwise would have been available to her parents, and that it is a justifiable reason to do so.[5]

Previously, it was thought that children could not sue for negligence that resulted in their conception because no defendant could be found to owe a duty to a plaintiff who did not exist at the time of the alleged negligence.

---

§ 17–3

1. Michael Kelly, The Rightful Position in Wrongful Life Actions, 42 Hast. L.J. 505, 508 n.13 (1991).

2. See id.; Timothy J. Dawe, Note, Wrongful Life: Time for a "Day in Court", 51 Ohio St. L. J. 473, 477 (1990).

3. Dawe, supra note 2, at 479.

4. Id. at 476.

5. Procanik v. Cillo, 478 A.2d 755 (N.J. 1984).

However, the law does recognize such a duty under other circumstances. As one legal scholar has pointed out, a defendant surely could be liable in tort if he placed a time bomb in a newborn nursery and set it to go off in a year when it would injure a child who had not even been conceived at the time of the tortious act,[6] and a provider may be liable in negligence to a child conceived some time after that provider treated the child's mother.[7] In addition, most courts now recognize that children born alive (and, in some cases, those who are not) may sue tortfeasors whose negligence or intentional acts occurred before birth, whether the injury manifested itself in utero or later.

b. Standard of Care

The standard of care in wrongful birth, wrongful life and wrongful conception cases is determined the same way that the standard of care is determined in all other cases of medical negligence. Physicians, nurses, genetic counselors, and others whose conduct may give rise to these actions must exercise the care that others of similar training and experience would exercise under the same or similar circumstances. Thus, an obstetrician is held to a different (and, in most relevant ways, higher) standard than is a general practitioner. A physician who holds himself out as a genetic counselor will be held to the standard of a physician with training and experience in genetic counseling,[8] and a nurse who holds himself out as a genetic counselor will likewise be held to the standard of a nurse with that training and experience.[9]

§ 17–4. Causation

Defendants in wrongful life, wrongful birth, and wrongful conception cases frequently argue that they cannot be liable in negligence because their actions cannot be said to be the actual or proximate cause of the injury.[1] First, in wrongful birth and wrongful life cases they argue that it was the disease process, not any act of the provider, that caused the birth anomaly in the child. It was the mother's German measles that caused so much damage in the fetus, they argue, not any action (or, for that matter, any inaction) of the provider; similarly, it was the normal genetic action that caused the pain of Tay–Sachs disease, they argue, not the allegedly negligent laboratory's failure to properly screen the amniotic fluid. Indeed, the plaintiff's complaint in a wrongful birth or wrongful life case must acknowledge, at least implicitly, that the birth anomaly would have been present even if the defendant healthcare provider never existed.[2]

---

6. John Robertson, Toward Rational Boundaries for Tort Liability for Injury to the Unborn: Prenatal Injuries, Preconception Injuries, and Wrongful Life, 1978 Duke L. J. 1401.

7. See e.g., Renslow v. Mennonite Hosp., 10 Ill.Dec. 484, 367 N.E.2d 1250 (Ill.1977).

8. Thomas Rogers, Wrongful Life and Wrongful Birth: Medical Malpractice in Genetic Counseling and Prenatal Testing, 33 S.C.L. Rev. 713, 732–733 (1982); Harbeson v. Parke–Davis, Inc., 656 P.2d 483, 496 (Wash.1983).

9. Rogers, supra note 8, at 732; Harbeson, 656 P.2d at 496.

§ 17–4

1. Pitre v. Opelousas General Hosp., 530 So.2d 1151 (La.1988); Smith v. Cote, 513 A.2d 341 (N.H.1986). See Mark Strasser, Misconceptions and Wrongful Births: A Call for a Principled Jurisprudence, 31 Ariz. St. L. J. 161 (1999).

2. See Thomas Rogers, Wrongful Life and Wrongful Birth: Medical Malpractice in Genetic Counseling and Prenatal Testing, 33 S.C.L. Rev. 713 (1982).

This causation argument misunderstands the nature of the injury in wrongful birth and wrongful life. The real injury is not the birth of the child with anomalies, but the loss of the parent's ability to make informed reproductive decisions about the birth of that child.[3] The mother with German measles does lose the ability to make informed reproductive decisions about her child when her disease is misdiagnosed or she is not informed that German measles imposes a risk on her fetus. Similarly, the couple with the Tay–Sachs child loses the ability to make an informed decision about the birth of that child when they are negligently informed that the child will not have Tay–Sachs disease. Although the birth of the child may be a consequence of the loss of this choice, it is entirely derivative of the primary injury—the loss of an ability to make informed procreative decisions.

Some defendants in wrongful conception cases, and in wrongful life and wrongful birth cases where the negligence is alleged to have occurred before conception, argue that any negligence on the part of the provider is superseded by the act of sexual intercourse, which is thus the real cause of the injury.[4] They argue that any causal chain is broken by such a substantively important act. This causation argument misses the basic point, though: the parents sought the counseling, screening, or medical care to find out whether they could safely engage in sexual intercourse without risk of (or to) offspring. To say that the parents who engaged in procreation, not the healthcare provider who previously provided negligent advice, are the cause of the birth is equivalent to saying that the person driving a car with its newly repaired brake system is at fault for the accident caused by brake failure, not the person who negligently repaired the brakes.

§ 17–5. Damages

a. Classes of Damages

Once the causation problem is overcome, the greatest difficulty that wrongful birth, wrongful life, and wrongful conception cases have presented to the courts is the determination of damages. Indeed, courts that have denied absolutely recovery in these cases have done so on the grounds that there are no damages, or on the grounds that any damages are necessarily too speculative to permit any action in tort.[1] Plaintiffs may claim any of several classes of damages in these cases, depending on the identity of the plaintiff (parents, guardian, or child), the identity of the cause of action (wrongful birth, wrongful life, or wrongful conception) and the claimed alternatives to the birth of the child.[2] The plaintiff may claim that the alternative to the injury

3. Id. at 734; Timothy J. Dawe, Note, Wrongful Life: Time for a "Day in Court," 51 Ohio St. L. J. 473, 478 (1990).

4. Bishop v. Byrne, 265 F.Supp. 460 (S.D.W.Va.1967).

§ 17–5

1. See Mark Strasser, Misconceptions and Wrongful Births: A Call for a Principled Jurisprudence, 31 Ariz. St. L. J. 161 (1999); Michael Kelly, The Rightful Position in "Wrongful Life" Actions, 42 Hastings L. J. 505, 506 n. 4 (1991); Lisa A. Podewils, Note, Traditional

Tort Principles and Wrongful Conception Child–Rearing Damages, 73 B.U.L. Rev. 407 (1993); Note, Wrongful Birth Actions: The Case Against Legislative Curtailment, 100 Harv. L. Rev. 2017 (1987).

2. See F. Allan Hanson, Suits for Wrongful Life, Counterfactuals, and the Nonexistence Problem, 5 S. Cal. Interdis. L. J. 1 (1996); Michael A. Berenson, Comment, The Wrongful Life Claim—The Legal Dilemma of Existence Versus Nonexistence: "To Be or Not To Be," 64 Tul.L.Rev. 895, 897–900 (1990).

sustained would have been additional contraceptive precautions (when the claim follows a doctor's failure to reveal that a tubal ligation failed, for example),[3] a healthy child (when the claim follows a doctor's failure to identify an illness treatable in utero, for example),[4] choosing to avoid conception (when the claim follows a doctor's failure to inform the parents about a prospective genetic condition before conception, for example),[5] or an abortion (where a doctor fails to reveal a genetic or other illness of a child after conception but before birth).[6]

Courts commonly have determined the propriety of awarding damages on a class by class basis.[7] The classes of damages that may be sought by parents in a wrongful birth or wrongful conception case include the expenses of the pregnancy itself (including the medical expenses, lost earnings of the pregnant woman, and other actual expenses), the extraordinary medical and educational expenses of a seriously impaired child (including the domestic care given to the child by family members), the value of the parent's emotional burden that is a consequence of the birth of a child, all of the costs of raising the child (including ordinary expenses), and the "insult" damages that arise out of denying the parents their reproductive choice.[8] In a wrongful life or wrongful conception case the child may seek damages to compensate for the child's "impaired childhood," i.e., a childhood impaired as a direct consequence of any avoidable serious illness with which the child is born, or that impaired as an indirect consequence of the effect the birth had on the child's parents and the child's family.[9] Any damages to which the plaintiff is otherwise entitled may be reduced or eliminated if the plaintiff fails to mitigate damages, and all damages are subject to the "benefits" rule[10] that, some argue, provides that any benefit incidentally provided to the plaintiff by the defendant must be offset against the damages.[11]

b. Damages in Wrongful Birth Cases

No court has refused to entertain a wrongful birth action because of the difficulty of assessing damages since *Roe v. Wade* was decided in 1973. On the other hand, courts have been reluctant to allow all of the classes of damages generally alleged by plaintiffs in those cases. While claims for the extraordinary costs associated with the medical care and education of a seriously ill child are now universally permitted in such cases,[12] and claims for the costs associated with a pregnancy that otherwise would not have occurred are generally recognized,[13] courts have been reluctant to permit the recovery of

---

3. Lovelace Medical Center v. Mendez, 805 P.2d 603 (N.M.1991).

4. Smith v. Cote, 513 A.2d 341 (N.H.1986).

5. Kelly, supra note 1, at 513, n.35; Naccash v. Burger, 290 S.E.2d 825, 827 (Va.1982).

6. Smith v. Cote, 513 A.2d 341 (N.H.1986).

7. See Kelly, supra note 1, at 518; Berenson, supra note 2, at 904; see also Turpin v. Sortini, 182 Cal.Rptr. 337, 339, 643 P.2d 954, 956 (Cal.1982).

8. Podewils, supra note 1, at 408.

9. Timothy J. Dawe, Note, Wrongful Life: Time for a "Day in Court," 51 Ohio St.L.J. 473 (1990); Kelly, supra note 2, at 517.

10. Restatement (Second) of Torts § 920 (1979).

11. Burke v. Rivo, 551 N.E.2d 1, 6 (Mass. 1990); Troppi v. Scarf, 187 N.W.2d 511, 517 (Mich.App.1971); Strasser, supra note 1; Kelly, supra note 1; Podewils, supra note 1.

12. Troppi v. Scarf, 187 N.W.2d 511, 517 (Mich.App.1971). Ron Weiss, Wrongful Birth and Wrongful Life Actions: In Search Of A Logical Consistency, 1987 Ann.Surv. Am. L. 507, 513 (1989). See Strasser, supra note 1.

13. See e.g., Siemieniec v. Lutheran Gen. Hosp., 111 Ill.Dec. 302, 317, 512 N.E.2d 691, 706 (Ill.1987); Smith v. Cote, 513 A.2d 341, 349–50 (N.H.1986).

other damages. In particular, courts generally have not permitted plaintiffs to recover any compensation for the emotional damage that accompanies the birth of an unnecessarily ill child,[14] and most commonly they have not permitted the recovery of the cost of raising a "normal" child.[15] No court has yet formally awarded damages for the injury to the parents' loss of their reproductive decision making.[16]

The current majority view of the judiciary that damages in wrongful birth cases should be limited to the extraordinary costs of raising the seriously ill child, and not include the ordinary costs associated with raising "normal" children, does not bear logical scrutiny. The distinction has been defended primarily on grounds of fairness and proportionality. First, some courts have suggested, parents have chosen to keep the children who are the subject of the litigation even though those parents could have offered them for adoption. While courts are unwilling to apply the "avoidable consequences" rule in any way that requires that parents give away the children they find too expensive to raise, courts have found that permitting the recovery of the costs associated with raising a "normal" child would constitute an unfair windfall for the parents, even if permitting the recovery of extraordinary costs would not.[17]

Presumably, the distinction between extraordinary costs (which are compensable in damages) and ordinary costs (which are not) is relevant because the parents were willing to undertake the costs of raising a normal child when they decided to incur the pregnancy, but they were not then willing to undertake the costs of raising a seriously ill child. As some courts and commentators have recognized, denying parents the recovery of the costs of raising a normal child stems from the application of the concept of expectancy damages in contract in this tort context.[18] Under this theory, because of the defendant's negligence, the parents did not get the normal child they expected. Thus they should be compensated in such a way that they will be put in the position they would have been in if they did get the child they expected. Such compensation includes all costs exceeding what they had expected to pay for the child they desired and expected—i.e., the extraordinary cost of raising their child. This importation of contract principles into an area of classic tort law remains unjustified by legal principle. Although some medical malpractice law has its origin in both contract and tort law,[19] wrongful birth, wrongful life and wrongful conception cases do not; they are pure negligence actions in tort.

14.   See e.g., Siemieniec, 111 Ill.Dec. at 318, 512 N.E.2d at 707; see also, Duplan v. Harper, 188 F.3d 1195 (10th Cir.1999).

15.   But see Phillips v. United States, 575 F.Supp. 1309, 1317–19 (D.S.C.1983); see generally Gregory G. Sarno, Annotation, Recoverability of Compensatory Damages for Mental Anguish or Emotional Distress for Tortiously Causing Another's birth, 74 A.L.R. 4th 798 (1989).

16.   Cf. Lovelace Medical Center v. Mendez, 805 P.2d 603, 610 (N.M.1991).

17.   Smith v. Cote, 513 A.2d 341 (N.H. 1986); Berman, 404 A.2d at 14. See also Strasser, supra note 1.

18.   See e.g., Sullivan v. O'Connor, 296 N.E.2d 183 (Mass.1973)(court held surgeon liable for expectancy damages as measured by out-of-pocket expenses, worsening of patient's condition, and pain and suffering for future corrective operations). For another challenge to the operation of tort law in this area, see Philip Peters, Rethinking Wrongful Life: Bridging the Boundary Between Tort and Family Law, 67 Tul. L. Rev. 397 (1992). For an argument that ordinary tort law ought to apply, see Strasser, supra note 1.

19.   See Sullivan v. O'Connor, 296 N.E.2d 183 (Mass.1973).

States are divided on whether the emotional costs associated with the birth of a seriously ill child are recoverable.[20] States which generally permit recovery for the negligent infliction of emotional distress ought to permit this head of damages in these cases as well, as long as the requirements for that tort are satisfied. Some cases have drawn the analogy between parents' claims for emotional distress that arise out of the death of their children and parents' wrongful birth claims.[21] Although the cases are not identical, we can expect states that have permitted recovery in the first of these classes of cases to permit it in the second.[22]

c. *Damages in Wrongful Life Cases*

Even though actions for wrongful life are not substantively different from actions for wrongful birth, they have been far less successful in the courts. The judiciary has been reluctant to find that one can sustain damages merely by being born alive.[23] A majority of states that have considered the issue have recognized wrongful birth, but not wrongful life, actions,[24] although some now recognize both.[25]

There are four reasons that courts which do recognize actions for wrongful birth choose not to recognize actions for wrongful life. First, there is some question about whether the defendant owes a duty to the child (who may not even have been conceived at the time of the negligent act) even when it is clear that the defendant owes a duty to the parents.[26] The other three reasons for denying recognition to wrongful life claims all grow out of the nature of potential damages in those cases. Some courts have concluded that there can be no injury (and thus there are no damages) in being born,[27] concluding that they cannot recognize damages for being born alive because no one can ever know whether non-existence is preferable to existence; if this is inherently unknowable, it is argued, it can not be the basis of a damages action.[28] Some courts have concluded that any damages that might be awarded in such circumstances are too speculative to be permitted in tort actions;[29] and some have argued that awarding damages for being born with a disability sends an inappropriate message that the society believes that handicapped lives are worth less than other lives.[30]

20. Thomas Rogers, Wrongful Life and Wrongful Birth: Medical Malpractice in Genetic Counseling and Prenatal Testing, 33 S.C.L. Rev. 713, 751 n.290; Kelly, supra note 1, at 507, n.9, 514, n.39.

21. See generally Sarno, supra note 15.

22. Cf. Kush v. Lloyd, 616 So.2d 415 (Fla. 1992) (citing emotional distress damages being available in other torts, such as defamation and invasion of privacy, as reason for allowing these damages in a wrongful conception case).

23. Becker v. Schwartz, 413 N.Y.S.2d 895, 386 N.E.2d 807 (N.Y.App.1978).

24. Lori B. Andrews, "Torts and the Double Helix: Malpractice Liability for Failure to Warn of Genetic Risks," 29 Hous. L. Rev. 149 (1992).

25. See Turpin v. Sortini, 182 Cal.Rptr. 337, 643 P.2d 954 (Cal.1982), Procanik v. Cillo, 478 A.2d 755 (N.J.1984), and Harbeson v. Parke–Davis, Inc., 656 P.2d 483 (Wash.1983).

26. But see Renslow v. Mennonite Hosp., 10 Ill.Dec. 484, 367 N.E.2d 1250 (Ill.1977)(defendant doctor liable to child born to a woman several years after the doctor negligently gave a woman with RH-positive blood a transfusion of RH-negative blood).

27. Smith v. Cote, 513 A.2d 341 (N.H. 1986); Bruggeman v. Schimke, 718 P.2d 635, 640–42 (Kan.1986).

28. Joel Feinberg, Comment: Wrongful Conception and The Right Not To Be Harmed, 8 Harv. J.L. & Pub. Policy 57 (1985).

29. Becker v. Schwartz, 413 N.Y.S.2d 895, 900, 386 N.E.2d 807, 812 (N.Y.App.1978); Dumer v. St. Michael's Hospital, 233 N.W.2d 372, 375–76 (Wis.1975).

30. Siemieniec v. Lutheran Gen. Hosp., 111 Ill.Dec. 302, 308, 512 N.E.2d 691, 697 (Ill. 1987); Kelly, supra note 1, at 536.

Once courts determine that damages are allowable in wrongful life actions, a determination of which damages should be awarded ought to be governed by the same principles that apply in wrongful birth cases. There is little question that such damages, if allowed at all, include the extraordinary medical, educational, and care costs associated with the disability of the plaintiff.[31] They may also include the ordinary costs associated with raising a child[32] and the damages for the "impaired childhood" of the plaintiff.[33] This last class of damages could include damages sustained by the child directly because of her inability to participate in the normal joys of childhood, and the damages sustained by the child as a result of the adverse effect the child's disability has upon her parents and her family.[34]

d. *Damages in Wrongful Conception Cases*

Wrongful conception cases are virtually always successful in recovering the costs directly associated with the pregnancy, such as medical expenses and lost earnings during a portion of the pregnancy.[35] Wrongful conception cases which have sought to recover the cost of raising the healthy child, however, have run into the same barriers that have faced wrongful birth and wrongful life actions seeking recovery for these ordinary child-rearing expenses. Until the 1990s, every court which considered the issue rejected any attempt to collect the cost of raising a healthy child born as a result of medical negligence. Over the last several years, however, a few courts have allowed the plaintiff to recover the cost of raising the normal child.[36] The emerging (but still minority) rule appears to be that such damages—usually far smaller than the extraordinary costs of caring for a child born with serious problems—are fully recoverable.

Courts faced with wrongful conception cases have addressed arguments that the cost of raising a healthy child is too speculative to be recoverable, that such actions amount to "medical paternity" actions that are inappropriate because they violate notions of proportionality, that actions seeking damages for a healthy birth are inherently debasing of the sanctity of life, that the child who is the subject of such actions will suffer psychological harm upon finding out that her parents thought that her birth was a damage, and that doctrines of mitigation of damages and set off ultimately reduce the damage in such cases to nothing.[37]

First, however, damages in wrongful conception cases are not difficult to quantify. Government agencies publish accounts of the costs of raising children from birth to majority, and expert economists called to testify in such cases are likely to disagree only on the margins. According to the Department of Agriculture, the average cost of raising a child born in 1998 to majority will

31. Smith v. Cote, 513 A.2d 341 (N.H. 1986).

32. Marciniak v. Lundborg, 450 N.W.2d 243 (Wis.1990).

33. Rogers, supra note 20, at 728; Curlender v. Bio–Science Laboratories, 165 Cal.Rptr. 477, 489 (Cal.App.1980).

34. Kelly, supra note 1, at 517–18.

35. See e.g., O'Toole v. Greenberg, 488 N.Y.S.2d 143, 477 N.E.2d 445 (N.Y.App.1985), Lovelace Medical Center v. Mendez, 805 P.2d 603 (N.M.1991); Hartke v. McKelway, 707 F.2d 1544 (D.C.Cir.1983).

36. Marciniak v. Lundborg, 450 N.W.2d 243 (Wis.1990); Burke v. Rivo, 551 N.E.2d 1 (Mass.1990) (recovery permitted where parents sought to avoid pregnancy for financial reasons); Lovelace Medical Center v. Mendez, 805 P.2d 603 (N.M.1991). See Strasser, supra note 1.

37. See generally Podewils, supra note 1; see also Rogers, supra note 23, at 718; Marciniak, 450 N.W.2d at 245–47.

be $313,380 for a middle income family.[38] Indeed, such damages are considerably easier to quantify than many of the items of damages courts are routinely called upon to evaluate in wrongful death and other tort actions.[39]

Second, wrongful conception actions are not analogous to paternity actions, even if some items of damages may be the same in each type of case. Negligent motorists who cause their victims to need constant medical care are not described as defendants in "motorist paternity" actions, and, in any case, physicians are not held responsible for the welfare of the children born as a result of their negligence. They are simply required to pay for the cost incurred as a direct result of their negligence. Third, such damages are as proportional to the fault of the medical practitioner as are damages in any negligence action, and all of the functions of tort law are served by allowing full recovery of damages in these cases.

Fourth, there is no reason to believe that recognizing wrongful conception cases debases the apparent value of life. It simply recognizes that there are costs associated with a child, and that even parents who love their healthy children must bear those costs. Fifth, there is no reason to believe that wrongful conception cases have adverse effects (or, for that matter, any nonfinancial effects) on their subjects, despite claims that such actions could turn children into "emotional bastards" when they learn about them.[40] Nobody knows how many children were "mistakes," at least in terms of their parents' original intentions, but the number surely is in the millions. There is no evidence that such children are less loved or respected after birth than are other children, and there is no evidence that the knowledge that they were not initially desired has any adverse effect on the children. In any case, a court fearful that the discovery of the litigation will disturb the child who is its subject has other ways to address that problem. That court can close the hearing and seal the file, for example, if it really believes access to the proceedings will injure the child; it is not necessary to dismiss the action and deny the parent's recovery in order to preserve the child's emotional integrity.

e. Defenses to Damages Claims in Wrongful Birth, Wrongful Life, and Wrongful Conception Cases: Mitigation and the Benefits Rule

1. Mitigation of Damages

No court has found that a parent in a wrongful birth, wrongful life or wrongful conception case has the obligation to mitigate damages by obtaining an abortion or abandoning the child for adoption. The doctrine of mitigation of damages requires only that the plaintiff take "reasonable" actions to limit the damages that accrue as a result of the defendant's negligence, and courts have universally found that such actions are not reasonable under the circumstances.[41]

---

38. U.S. Department of Agriculture, Center for Nutrition Policy and Promotion, Expenditures on a Child by Families, 1998. For lower class families, the cost will be $230,040, and for upper class families $457,380. Id.

39. Kelly, supra note 1, at 517; Troppi v. Scarf, 187 N.W.2d 511, 520–21 (Mich.App. 1971).

40. Id.

41. Id. at 247.; Troppi v. Scarf, 187 N.W.2d 511, 519–20 (Mich.App.1971). See also Strasser, supra note 1.

2. The Benefits Rule

Defendants have been far more successful in raising the defense of "the benefits rule," which permits defendants to take, as an offset against damages, some kinds of benefits conferred by the tortious conduct that also resulted in the damages.[42] Following this rule, many courts have been willing to allow the joy and satisfaction that come with having a child as an offset against damages otherwise recoverable.[43] When the court also finds these benefits to be so speculative that they cannot be meaningfully evaluated, it may conclude that no damages can be recoverable.[44] If it is impossible to know how much should be offset, these courts reason, it is impossible to know how much damages should be awarded, even if the plaintiff can prove damages with certainty.[45] Some courts have gone further and determined, as a matter of law, that the value of the joy and pleasure that come with having an additional child must exceed the plaintiff's damages, at least in wrongful conception cases.[46]

When thus applied, the "benefits rule" is a camouflage for other policy arguments that recovery should be denied in these cases. There are two reasons that the application of the "benefits rule" increasingly has been rejected over the last few years, at least in wrongful conception cases. First, as the Restatement (Second) of Torts points out, "[d]amages resulting from the invasion of one interest are not diminished by showing that another interest has been benefitted."[47] Thus, financial losses (including medical and educational expenses, whether characterized as ordinary or extraordinary) cannot be offset by any purely nonfinancial benefit characterized as the joy of having the child. In addition, when the plaintiff's financial losses are determinable with certainty, it seems unfair to deny the plaintiff recovery because the defendant cannot meet his burden of showing the value of the offset with equal precision.

Second, the "benefits rule" may not be applied to force the plaintiff to accept an unwanted benefit. In wrongful birth, wrongful life, and wrongful conception cases, of course, the alleged benefit—the joy of raising the child—is an unwanted benefit. Indeed, the reason the parent-plaintiffs sought the medical care which they allege was negligently provided was to avoid exactly this "benefit." Defendants who argue that the "benefits rule" forbids any recovery in these cases are taking the ironic position that their negligent conduct is better for the plaintiff than their non-negligent conduct would have been.

42. Restatement (Second) of Torts, § 520 (1979) ("When the defendant's tortious conduct has caused harm to the plaintiff or to his property and in so doing has conferred a special benefit to the interest of the plaintiff that was harmed, the value of the benefit conferred is considered in mitigation of damages, to the extent that it is equitable.")

43. See Marciniak v. Lundborg, 450 N.W.2d 243, 247–48 (Wis.1990).

44. See id. at 248; Burke v. Rivo, 551 N.E.2d 1, 6 (Mass.1990).

45. Kelly, supra note 1, at 519; Podewils, supra note 1, at 420.

46. Troppi v. Scarf, 187 N.W.2d 511 (Mich. App.1971).

47. Restatement (Second) of Torts § 920 (1979).

Chapter 18

ABORTION

Table of Sections

Research References

    Am Jur 2d, Abortion and Birth Control §§ 1 et seq.
    ALR Index: Abortion
    ALR Digest: Death § 10; Physicians and Surgeons § 29.6
    Am Jur Legal Forms 2d, Physicians and Surgeons §§ 202:137–202:141
    Am Jur Pleading and Practice Forms (Rev), Abortion §§ 1 et seq.; Depositions and Discovery § 571; Physicians, Surgeons, and Other Healers §§ 266–274
    1 POF 15, Abortion and Miscarriage
    15 Am Jur Trials 373, Discovery and Evaluation of Medical Records

§ 18–1. Introduction

During the last quarter of this century, no legal and political issue has so divided the United States as the issue of abortion. The question of abortion has been regularly debated in both houses of Congress, in virtually every state legislature, by the governing bodies of all relevant medical associations, by the American Bar Association as well as state and local bar associations, and by every other public or quasi-public agency that might conceivably make any decision that arguably could affect the legality or availability of abortions. The Supreme Court receives piles of amicus briefs in every abortion case, and the Court is flooded with letters from protagonists on both sides of abortion issues. The public has forced the United States Senate to scrutinize all potential Supreme Court nominees' records for any imaginable hints about how they might evaluate abortion related issues.

The Supreme Court itself reflects the uncompromising political battle that has been joined over this issue in the more political spheres. Before *Planned Parenthood of Southeastern Pennsylvania v. Casey*[1] was decided in 1992, the Supreme Court had addressed three consecutive abortion cases without the ability to muster any majority opinion. Even in *Casey*, the majority is concocted by bringing together Justices who believe that the result is required by the Constitution with those who believe that the moral authority of the Court itself could be at risk if the Court overtly and formally overruled *Roe v. Wade*,[2] which established a woman's right to an abortion under some circumstances, nineteen years before. There is no other area of law where the tone of the Supreme Court opinions is so acrimonious, disrespectful, and, occasionally, even personally spiteful.[3]

Suggestions that the judiciary should simply exit the abortion arena and leave the matter for state legislatures seem doomed, at least in the short run. Similarly, suggestions that the Supreme Court should apply the Constitution to eliminate virtually all state regulation of abortion seems extremely unlikely to be brought to fruition, although that did not seem impossible only twenty-five years ago.[4] Although some Justices clearly favor this first path,[5] and some seem to favor the second, it appears that the Supreme Court will remain an uncertain umpire in the annual state legislative battles between those who want to restrict access to abortions and those who want to maintain or increase ease of that access.[6]

The legal questions surrounding abortion do not remain intractable just because the political and social questions remain so. Ultimately, there can be no resolution of the legal issues until there is a resolution of the underlying philosophical issues and there can be no resolution of the underlying philosophical issues until there is a determination of the point at which human stock—the conjunction of human sperm and ovum—becomes a person entitled to legal respect. While some believe that a new human being is entitled to all

§ 18-1

1. 505 U.S. 833, 112 S.Ct. 2791, 120 L.Ed.2d 674 (1992).

2. 505 U.S. 833, 112 S.Ct. 2791, 2814–2816(1992) (overruling Roe would "seriously weaken the Court's capacity to exercise the judicial power and function as the Supreme Court of a Nation dedicated to the rule of law"); Roe v. Wade, 410 U.S. 113, 93 S.Ct. 705, 35 L.Ed.2d 147 (1973).

3. See e.g., Casey, 505 U.S. at 984, 112 S.Ct. at 2876 (Scalia, J., dissenting).

4. See Roe, 410 U.S. at 155, 93 S.Ct. at 728 (stating that abortion is a fundamental right and that all regulation should be narrowly drawn and submitted to a strict scrutiny standard of review).

5. See Casey, 505 U.S. at 1001, 112 S.Ct. at 2885 (Scalia, J., dissenting).

6. Id. at 911, 112 S.Ct. at 2838 (Stevens, J., concurring in part and dissenting in part) and 2843 (Blackmun, J., concurring in part, concurring in the judgment in part, and dissenting in part).

the respect accorded human beings from the point of conception, others put the point somewhat later—at the point of pregnancy (when the embryo has implanted in the uterine wall), when there is cell differentiation, when the neural tube (the precursor of the central nervous system) develops, at quickening, at the end of the first or second trimester of pregnancy, when the soul enters the fetus, at viability, at the termination of the ceremonio de umbligado, at birth, or some point after birth (when the child first develops self consciousness, for example).[7] Some believe that there is some point at which all of the attributes of personhood are conferred on a new person, while others believe that those rights accrete to the new person over some period of time, perhaps over 3 months, 9 months, or 18 years. Obviously, the "right" answer to these questions will not be discovered through more medical research, closer analysis of the law or public opinion surveys. It is hardly surprising that we are no closer to finding the "right" answers now than we were twenty-five (or 2500) years ago. The question is one of basic and essentially spiritual values. It is not one the courts are particularly well suited to address, although it is one the courts must answer to be able to resolve the cases that come before them.

For purposes of legal development, the history of abortion in the United States may be divided into three periods: (1) before *Roe v. Wade* was decided in 1973, (2) after *Roe* was decided but before *Casey* was decided in 1992, and (3) the current, post-*Casey* law on abortion. Because the law was so substantially redefined and recharacterized by the Supreme Court in 1992, and, perhaps, because no legal principles in an area this politically and emotionally charged can be (or should be) simple and easy to apply mechanically, the current law is easy to articulate in principled terms, but uncertain in its application. It is worth discussing the first two of these periods briefly before describing the current state of the American law of abortion.

A. THE CONSTITUTIONAL FRAMEWORK

§ 18–2. The Constitutional Framework Before Roe v. Wade

Most of the statutes outlawing abortion can be traced to the last half of the nineteenth century.[1] Before that, abortion was generally available as a legal matter, although it must not have been an inviting prospect before the development of effective anesthesiology and antiseptic techniques. By the middle of this century all states had statutes that imposed substantial legal restrictions on abortion,[2] and in many states virtually all abortions (except those necessary to preserve the life of the pregnant woman) were prohibited.[3] As a general matter, physicians performing abortions were subject to the criminal law, which provided that performing an abortion constituted a felony. Physicians were also subject to licensing sanctions. Under some statutes, the pregnant mother herself was also subject to criminal penalties, although state courts sometimes interpreted these statutes narrowly to allow

---

7. Sylvia Law, Abortion Compromise Inevitable and Impossible, 1992 U. Ill. L. Rev. 921.

§ 18–2

1. Roe v. Wade, 410 U.S. 113, 138, 93 S.Ct. 705, 719, 35 L.Ed.2d 147 (1973).

2. See id. at 139, 93 S.Ct. at 720.

3. Id. at n. 34.

their application only to those performing the abortion.[4]

By 1973, when *Roe v. Wade* was decided by the United States Supreme Court, a few states had begun to liberalize their laws to permit abortion when it was necessary to preserve the health of the pregnant women. In addition, the laws prohibiting any abortions were being routinely ignored by some physicians.[5] Well informed and sufficiently wealthy women would go to those states with more permissive laws, or to foreign countries, to obtain abortions prohibited in their own states. Moreover, statutory exceptions to the bans on abortions were being interpreted very broadly. Thus, when the Supreme Court first addressed the issue of abortion, the United States was covered by a web of highly restrictive abortion statutes that had lost much of their medical and moral authority and that were just beginning to be changed through the state legislative process.[6]

§ 18–3. The Rule of Roe v. Wade

In this landmark 7–2 decision the Supreme Court found that the due process clause of the fourteenth amendment to the Constitution protected the right to privacy, which included the right of a pregnant woman to choose to have an abortion, at least under some circumstances.[1] While the Supreme Court had suggested that there was a right to privacy implicit in the Constitution in cases concerning state restrictions on contraception, before *Roe v. Wade* no majority had clearly announced that its source was the fourteenth amendment.

Because, according to *Roe v. Wade*, the right to privacy (including the right to an abortion) is a fundamental right, it can be limited by the state only when the limitation is necessary to serve a compelling state interest.[2] The Court found that there were two potentially compelling state interests that could justify regulation of a woman's fourteenth amendment right to choose to have an abortion: (1) the interest in protecting the life and health of the pregnant woman, and (2) the interest in protecting the potential human life of the fetus.[3] The Court determined that this first interest would become compelling at the point at which it becomes more dangerous for the pregnant woman to have an abortion than to give birth to the child. Because the Court found that through the first trimester of pregnancy an abortion posed less of a threat to a pregnant woman than did continuing the pregnancy and childbirth, the Court determined that regulations designed to protect the life or health of the pregnant woman after the first trimester could be Constitutional, even if they limited some pregnant women's opportunities to have abortions. The Court held that the second interest became compelling at the point of viability, because "the fetus then presumably has the capability of meaningful life outside of the mother's womb."[4] Because the Court found that the

4. Id. at 151 n. 49, 93 S.Ct. at 726 n. 49.

5. Roe v. Wade, 410 U.S. at 143–44, 93 S.Ct. at 722–23 (outlining the changing position of the AMA and other health organizations).

6. Id. at 140 n.37, 93 S.Ct. at 720 n.37 (listing 14 states that had adopted a version of the American Law Institute's statute liberalizing abortion laws).

§ 18–3

1. Id. at 152–155, 93 S.Ct. at 726–728, 35 L.Ed.2d at 174–75.

2. Id. at 155, 93 S.Ct. at 728, 35 L.Ed.2d at 175.

3. Id. at 162, 93 S.Ct. at 731, 35 L.Ed.2d at 182.

4. Id. at 163, 93 S.Ct. at 732, 35 L.Ed.2d at 183.

point of viability occurred at the beginning of the third trimester,[5] it found that virtually any state regulation of abortion during the last trimester, including the absolute prohibition of all abortions except those necessary to preserve the life or health of the pregnant woman, could be Constitutional.[6]

The opinion of the Court in *Roe v. Wade* provided a template against which all regulation of abortion could be measured:

> (a) For the stage prior to approximately the end of the first trimester, the abortion decision and its effectuation must be left to the medical judgment of the pregnant woman's attending physician.[7]

> (b) For the stage subsequent to approximately the end of the first trimester, the State, in promoting its interest in the health of the mother, may, if it chooses, regulate the abortion procedure in ways that are reasonably related to maternal health.[8]

> (c) For the stage subsequent to viability, the state in promoting its interest in the potentiality of human life may, if it chooses, regulate and even proscribe, abortion except where it is necessary, in appropriate medical judgment, for the preservation of the life or health of the mother.[9]

Roe v. Wade immediately became a political touchstone for people on both sides of the abortion controversy. While the Supreme Court never formally repudiated *Roe*, the 7–2 majority in *Roe* began to wither, becoming a 6–3 majority a few years later,[10] and bare 5–4 majority by 1986.[11] In 1989 and 1990 the Supreme Court addressed the abortion question in three major cases, and it was unable to find a majority to join any opinion of the Court in abortion cases.[12] In 1991, prior to Justice Thomas's appointment, the Court appeared to be evenly divided, with four Justices favoring the continued recognition of some form of the *Roe v. Wade* analysis,[13] and four Justices favoring overturning Roe absolutely.[14] The Supreme Court finally directly confronted the continuing validity of *Roe v. Wade* in 1992,[15] when it provided a new template

---

5. The *Roe* court left the question of when viability occurred in individual cases to physicians, but pointed out that a fetus was generally viable at 28 weeks. See 410 U.S. at 160, 93 S.Ct. at 730, 35 L.Ed.2d at 181. See also Mark Woltz, Note, A Bold Reaffirmation? Planned Parenthood v. Casey Opens the Door for States to Enact New Laws to Discourage Abortion, 71 N.C.L. Rev. 1787 (1993).

6. Roe v. Wade, 410 U.S. 113, 163–64, 93 S.Ct. 705, 732–33, 35 L.Ed.2d 147, 183 (1973).

7. Id. at 164, 93 S.Ct. at 732, 35 L.Ed.2d at 183.

8. Id.

9. Id. at 164–65, 93 S.Ct. at 732, 35 L.Ed.2d at 183.

10. Akron v. Akron Center for Reproductive Health, Inc., 462 U.S. 416, 103 S.Ct. 2481, 76 L.Ed.2d 687 (1983).

11. Thornburgh v. American College of Obstetricians & Gynecologists, 476 U.S. 747, 106 S.Ct. 2169, 90 L.Ed.2d 779 (1986).

12. Webster v. Reproductive Health Services, 492 U.S. 490, 109 S.Ct. 3040, 106 L.Ed.2d 410 (1989); Ohio v. Akron Center for Reproductive Health, 497 U.S. 502, 110 S.Ct. 2972, 111 L.Ed.2d 405 (1990); Hodgson v. Minnesota, 497 U.S. 417, 110 S.Ct. 2926, 111 L.Ed.2d 344 (1990).

13. Justices Stevens, Blackmun, O'Connor, and Souter.

14. Justices Scalia, White, and Kennedy and Chief Justice Rehnquist.

15. Planned Parenthood of Southeastern Pennsylvania v. Casey, 505 U.S. 833, 112 S.Ct. 2791, 120 L.Ed.2d 674 (1992). Prior to this case, some had proposed that Webster effectively overruled Roe v. Wade. Webster, 492 U.S. at 532 (Scalia, J., concurring); Webster, 492 U.S. at 538 (Blackmun, J., dissenting); Sylvia Law, Abortion Compromise—Inevitable and Impossible, 1992 U. Ill. L. Rev. 921, 932.

against which any state regulation of abortion is to be measured.[16]

§ 18–4. The Rule of Planned Parenthood of Southeastern Pennsylvania v. Casey

In *Casey* a majority of the Supreme Court, speaking through the joint opinion of Justices O'Connor, Kennedy and Souter, formally reaffirmed what it called the "essential holding" of *Roe*, but reinterpreted it to allow substantially more room for the states to regulate abortion.[1] The Court retreated from the notion that there was a fundamental right to an abortion and abandoned *Roe*'s trimester test, under which different Constitutional limitations were placed upon state regulation of abortion during each trimester, replacing it with a two part test in which different Constitutional limitations are placed upon state regulation of abortion before and after viability.

a. *Reaffirming Roe While Rejecting Its Substance*

First, the Court avoided reference to the "fundamental right" to an abortion and the necessity that any state limitation be justified by a "compelling state interest." While the opinion of the Court mentioned the fact that this right would now be accorded a lower level of scrutiny than had been the case under *Roe*,[2] the Chief Justice called special attention to this development in his impassioned dissent favoring overruling *Roe v. Wade* altogether.[3]

Second, the Supreme Court explicitly rejected the trimester framework that many thought was the foundation upon which *Roe v. Wade* was constructed,[4] while retaining the last of the three trimester principles of *Roe*: states are still permitted to impose virtually any limitation, including a complete proscription on abortions, except those necessary to preserve the life or health of the pregnant woman, after viability.[5] After *Roe*, there had been some question as to whether the point at which the state's interest in the life of the fetus became compelling was at the beginning of the third trimester or at the point of viability. While these points coincided at 28 weeks at the time of *Roe* in 1973, advances in neonatal medicine had pushed the point of viability back a few weeks, perhaps to as early as 23½ or 24 weeks, by 1992.[6] Although in 1983 the Court had suggested that the trimester limitations were the Constitutionally significant time boundaries under *Roe*,[7] in *Casey* the Supreme Court made it clear that the Constitutionally relevant line would

---

16. Casey at 878, 112 S.Ct. at 2821.

§ 18–4

1. Planned Parenthood of Southeastern Pennsylvania v. Casey, 505 U.S. 833, 112 S.Ct. 2791, 120 L.Ed.2d 674 (1992) (Joint opinion of O'Connor, Kennedy and Souter, JJ.)

2. Planned Parenthood of Southeastern Pennsylvania v. Casey, 505 U.S. 833, 875, 112 S.Ct. 2791, 2820, 120 L.Ed.2d 674 (1992) (stating that the Roe standard "undervalues the State's interest in the potential life within the woman" and replacing strict scrutiny with undue burden as the appropriate standard of review of state regulation).

3. Id. at 953, 112 S.Ct. at 2860 (Rehnquist, C.J., dissenting).

4. Id. at 873, 112 S.Ct. at 2818 ("We reject the trimester framework, which we do not consider to be part of the essential holding of Roe.").

5. Id. at 877–878, 112 S.Ct. at 2821.

6. Id. at 860, 112 S.Ct. at 2811–12. The point of viability has not been pushed much further back since then; barring a substantial technological development like the creation of an artificial womb, the 23 or 24 week limit appears to be a natural limit.

7. See Akron v. Akron Center For Reproductive Health, Inc., 462 U.S. 416, 103 S.Ct. 2481, 76 L.Ed.2d 687 (1983).

now be viability, not the beginning of the third trimester.[8] In *Casey* the Court also announced that the state interest in the protection of the life of the fetus, as well as the health of the pregnant woman, now extended from the point of conception to the point of birth;[9] either interest can now justify state regulation of abortion during the first and second, as well as the third, trimester.[10]

b. *The Undue Burden Rule*

In place of the *Roe* holding with regard to abortions during the first two trimesters of pregnancy, the Court offers the "undue burden" rule, which outlaws any state regulation which imposes an "undue burden" on a woman's right to obtain the abortion of a nonviable fetus.[11] This rule grows out of the principle that "[o]nly where state regulation poses an undue burden on a woman's ability to make this decision does the power of the state reach into the heart of the liberty protected by the Due Process Clause."[12] The question, then, becomes when is the burden imposed on a woman by a state statute regulating abortion "undue"? As the Court points out, "[a] finding of an undue burden is a shorthand for the conclusion that a state regulation has the purpose or effect of placing a substantial obstacle in the path of a woman seeking an abortion of a nonviable fetus."[13] Thus, a state statute is illegal if it unduly burdens a woman's decision to have an abortion, and it unduly burdens that decision when it puts a substantial obstacle in the way of a woman who desires an abortion.

In addition to its certain and admitted retreat from *Roe v. Wade* and its announcement of the undue burden/substantial obstacle test, *Casey* made three important points which clarify the bases of the new rules to be applied to evaluate state regulation of abortion. First, as the opinion points out, "[w]hat is at stake is the woman's right to make the ultimate decision, not a right to be insulated from all others in doing so."[14] Thus, the Court is not likely to find any state statute regulating abortion of nonviable fetuses to be an undue burden on a woman's right to choose to have an abortion as long as the decision is ultimately the woman's, however fettered it might be. The state is free to announce its preference for childbirth over abortion and do all that it wishes to do to encourage women to choose that state preferred option. It is only where the statute effectively takes the ultimate decision away from the woman that it is likely to be found to be a substantial obstacle.

Second, a state regulation will be found to be an undue burden on a woman's right to have an abortion when the Court finds that it has the "purpose *or* effect" of placing a substantial obstacle in the path of a woman's choice.[15] This "purpose or effect" test, which seems to be borrowed from other

---

8. Casey, 505 U.S. at 878–879, 112 S.Ct. at 2821.

9. Id. at 876–877, 112 S.Ct. at 2820.

10. Id. at 879, 112 S.Ct. at 2821.

11. Planned Parenthood of Southeastern Pennsylvania v. Casey, 505 U.S. 833, 876–877, 112 S.Ct. 2791, 2820, 120 L.Ed.2d 674 (1992) (joint opinion of Souter, O'Connor, & Kennedy, JJ.). Although Justices Blackmun and Stevens did not join in the undue burden analysis, preferring the strict scrutiny standard of Roe, Justice Stevens pointed out that he would find several provisions unconstitutional even under

the joint opinion's own analysis. See Casey at 917–920, 112 S.Ct. at 2841–43 (Stevens, J., concurring in part and dissenting in part); see also Forum, The Impact of Casey, 1992 Wis. L. Rev. 1331.

12. Id. at 874, 112 S.Ct. at 2819.

13. Id. at 877, 112 S.Ct. at 2821.

14. Planned Parenthood of Southeastern Pennsylvania v. Casey, 505 U.S. 833, 877, 112 S.Ct. 2791, 2821, 120 L.Ed.2d 674 (1992).

15. Id. at 877, 112 S.Ct. at 2820.

areas of Constitutional jurisprudence, suggests that the Court will not tolerate obstacles in the path of a woman seeking an abortion, even if the obstacles themselves can be overcome, if they were placed there by the state for no other purpose than to be obstacles. The state may instruct, educate, cajole, entice, and encourage a woman so that she will choose to have her baby rather than to abort her fetus, but it may not impose a burden on her that is not rationally justified as serving some state interest related to the abortion itself. A special tax on abortions, for example, would seem to be a violation of the undue burden test, even if the tax were low enough that it did not exclude women who otherwise wanted them from obtaining abortions. As Justice Stevens points out in his concurring and dissenting opinion, "[a] burden may be 'undue' either because the burden is too severe or because it lacks a legitimate, rational justification."[16]

Third, the determination of whether a state imposed burden is undue may be fact-based.[17] Thus, while the Court is willing to conduct facial evaluations of statutory schemes that present obstacles to women seeking abortions, attacks on those schemes are much more likely to be successful if those challenging them can establish, as a matter of fact, that they effectively deny some women the ultimate decision over whether they will have an abortion or carry their fetus to term.[18] Further, in evaluating the nature of the burden under the *Casey* standard, the Court seems willing to consider both facts presented as evidence to the trial court and more general legislative facts contained in social science research.

B. PARTICULAR LIMITATIONS AND RESTRICTIONS ON ABORTION

§ 18–5. An Introduction to Particular Limitations and Restrictions Placed on Abortion

Ever since *Roe* was decided in 1973 state legislatures have been testing the Constitutional limits on their authority to impose restrictions on abortions. Every year the courts are faced with new statutes that test every frontier left open by the Supreme Court's decisions in this area. While the scope of these statutes is virtually unlimited, the most significant forms of attempted restriction have fallen into several identifiable categories: parental consent or notification requirements, spousal or partner consent or notification requirements, limitations on government funding and use of government facilities, regulation of the informed consent process, and regulation of the medical process for the performance of the procedure.

§ 18–6. Laws Requiring Parental Consent or Notification

The most common restriction on abortion is one that requires a minor wishing to have an abortion to notify or obtain the consent of a parent before

---

16. Casey, 505 U.S. at 921, 112 S.Ct. at 2843 (Stevens, J., concurring in part and dissenting in part).

17. See id. at 876–877, 112 S.Ct. at 2820.

18. For an excellent account of the limited availability of facial attacks upon statutes that restrict abortions, see Ruth Burdick, The Casey Undue Burden Standard: Problems Predicted and Encountered, and the Split Over the Salerno Test, 23 Hastings Const. L. Q. 825 (1996).

the abortion can be performed. Parental consent and notification statutes meet Constitutional muster as long as they except true emergencies where such consent would be impossible and they provide for an adequate judicial bypass which allows the pregnant girl to substitute judicial consent for parental consent under some circumstances.[1] Indeed, the Supreme Court invented the "undue burden" test, subsequently applied to all state limitations on abortion, to uphold a parental notification statute in 1990,[2] and one-parent consent and notification statutes were routinely upheld even before the change in the Constitutional analysis that came with *Casey* in 1992.[3]

The Court has upheld statutes that allow for judicial consent (in lieu of consent by the parent or guardian) when the pregnant girl can show that an abortion is in her best interest[4] or that she is mature enough to make the decision herself,[5] at least when the Court also finds that she has made an informed decision.[6] Although the by-pass process is justified by the argument that merely notifying or seeking consent from a parent may be harmful to a pregnant girl in some cases, courts have generally not required that girls seeking judicial approval in lieu of parental approval prove that they would be at risk if their parents were notified.

In *Casey* the Court also upheld requirements that the parent's consent be informed under processes defined by statute, and that it be subject to a 24 hour waiting period.[7] The Court had upheld a 48 hour waiting period for minors in *Hodgson*.[8] Since the *Casey* opinion was rendered, the Supreme Court has not addressed any statute that would require consent or notification of both parents, although at least one Circuit has upheld a two-parent consent requirement which was designed to increase "reflection and deliberation in the decisionmaking process. That court also pointed out that if one parent were to deny consent the other could go to court in support of the child.[9]

The legislative debate over parental notification and consent statutes has been characterized by the unreflective and dogmatic positions taken by each side. On the one hand, state legislators who support parental consent statutes note that the law of informed consent generally requires unemancipated children to have a parent's consent before any medical procedure may be

§ 18–6

1. See Akron v. Akron Center for Reproductive Health, Inc., 462 U.S. 416, 103 S.Ct. 2481, 76 L.Ed.2d 687 (1983); Bellotti v. Baird, 443 U.S. 622, 99 S.Ct. 3035, 61 L.Ed.2d 797 (1979); Planned Parenthood of Central Missouri v. Danforth, 428 U.S. 52, 96 S.Ct. 2831, 49 L.Ed.2d 788 (1976).

2. See Hodgson v. Minnesota, 497 U.S. 417, 110 S.Ct. 2926, 111 L.Ed.2d 344 (1990); Ohio v. Akron Center for Reproductive Health, 497 U.S. 502, 110 S.Ct. 2972, 111 L.Ed.2d 405 (1990).

3. See Planned Parenthood Association of Kansas City, Mo., Inc. v. Ashcroft, 462 U.S. 476, 103 S.Ct. 2517, 76 L.Ed.2d 733 (1983); Akron v. Akron Center for Reproductive Health, 462 U.S. 416, 103 S.Ct. 2481, 76 L.Ed.2d 687 (1983); Bellotti v. Baird, 443 U.S. 622, 99 S.Ct. 3035, 61 L.Ed.2d 797 (1979).

4. Akron at 439–40, 103 S.Ct. at 2497.

5. Id.

6. See also Planned Parenthood Association of Kansas City, Mo., Inc. v. Ashcroft, 462 U.S. 476, 103 S.Ct. 2517, 76 L.Ed.2d 733 (1983); Bellotti v. Baird, 443 U.S. 622, 99 S.Ct. 3035, 61 L.Ed.2d 797 (1979).

7. Casey, 505 U.S. at 879–888, 112 S.Ct. at 2822–26.

8. Hodgson v. Minnesota, 497 U.S. 417, 448, 110 S.Ct. 2926, 2944, 111 L.Ed.2d 344 (1990) (holding that a judicial bypass saved the constitutionality of the 48–hour waiting period for minors).

9. See Barnes v. Mississippi, 992 F.2d 1335 (5th Cir. 1993).

performed—for example, a physician must obtain consent of a parent before she performs a non-emergency appendectomy. They argue that it is inconsistent to require parental consent before an appendectomy is performed, but require neither consent nor notification before the same physician performs an abortion upon the same girl—especially if the reason for treating abortion differently from other medical procedures is the extraordinary significance of the decision to have an abortion. On the other hand, it seems equally inconsistent to require a girl who the state believes is too immature to make the decision to have an abortion to become a mother instead. Whatever maturity and judgment is required to make the abortion decision, even more is required to provide maternal care for a child, and the law never requires parental consent or notification (nor could it, as a practical matter) before a girl becomes a mother.

The debate for and against parental consent and notification requirements reveals an even deeper debate about the role of the family in contemporary life. The virtually universal view that a teenager's abortion decision should be made in consultation with her parents rests upon several assumptions: that the daughter's disclosure of her pregnancy will not trigger family abuse, that the daughter lives with her parents or, at the least, has easy access to them, and, most significantly, that her parents will act in their daughter's best interest.[10] Unfortunately, some of these assumptions may be based on an idealized view of contemporary family life. While many children are brought up in healthy families and most parents want what is best for their children, as one Justice of the California Supreme Court has pointed out, "[n]ot every pregnant adolescent has parents out of the comforting and idyllic world of Norman Rockwell."[11]

§ 18–7. Laws Requiring Spousal or Partner Consent or Notification

The Supreme Court has refused to countenance any requirement that the pregnant woman's husband (or the father of the fetus, if not the husband) consent to, or even be notified of, the woman's intent to have an abortion. In 1976 the Court found unconstitutional a Missouri statute that required a husband's consent to an abortion under most circumstances, because such a statute "granted the husband 'a veto power exercisable for any reason whatsoever or for no reason at all.' "[1] In *Casey* the Court invalidated a spousal notification statute, pointing out that "[a] husband has no enforceable right to require a wife to advise him before she exercises her personal choices."[2] One new legislative attempt to get around the constitutional limitation on

---

10. Casey, 505 U.S. at 971, 112 S.Ct. at 2869 (Rehnquist, C.J., dissenting) ("In our view, it is 'entirely rational and fair for the state to conclude that, in most instances, the family will strive to give a lonely or even terrified minor advice that is both compassionate and mature,' " quoting Justice Kennedy's concurrence in Ohio v. Akron Center for Reproductive Health, 497 U.S. 502, 110 S.Ct. 2972, 111 L.Ed.2d 405 (1990)). See also Planned Parenthood of Central Mo. v. Danforth, 428 U.S. at 91, 96 S.Ct. at 2851 (Stewart, J., concurring).

11. American Academy of Pediatrics v. Lungren, 912 P.2d 1148 (Calif. 1996)(Kennard, J., dissenting), vacated 940 P.2d 797 (1997).

§ 18–7

1. Planned Parenthood of Southeastern Pennsylvania v. Casey, 505 U.S. 833, 972, 112 S.Ct. 2791, 2870, 120 L.Ed.2d 674 (1992) (Rehnquist, C.J. dissenting, quoting Danforth, 428 U.S. at 71, 96 S.Ct. at 2842).

2. Id. at 898, 112 S.Ct. at 2831.

spousal consent and notification requirements has been to permit the abortion without regard to the spousal consent, but to impose civil liability on any physician who would perform an abortion under those circumstances. At least one court has found this liability provision to be indistinguishable from requiring spousal consent, and thus unconstitutional.[3]

§ 18–8. Limitations on Government Funding and the Use of Government Facilities

The Supreme Court has been willing to accept virtually any limitation that a federal or state agency wishes to impose upon the use of its funds or facilities to perform abortions.[1] In 1977 the Court upheld state Medicaid plans that refused to cover non-therapeutic abortions[2] as well as a city restriction on the performance of publicly funded non-therapeutic abortions at municipal hospitals.[3] Three years later in the landmark case of *Harris v. McRae*[4] the Court upheld the Hyde amendment, which provided that federal funds could not be used for virtually any abortion. Responding to the argument that this effectively removed the possibility of an abortion from indigent women, the Court pointed out that Congress's decision to restrict the use of such funds left "an indigent woman with at least the same range of choice in deciding whether to obtain a medically necessary abortion as she would have had if Congress had chosen to subsidize no health care at all."[5] Congress has thus far gone only so far as to proscribe the use of federal funds for the purposes of abortion, and some states have continued to provide for abortions as part of their Medicaid state plans. In those states Medicaid abortion services (unlike all other Medicaid services) are provided exclusively with state funds. Indeed, state constitutional provisions or state legislation may require the state Medicaid agencies to provide abortion services to the same extent that they provides other necessary health care.[6]

In 1989 in *Webster v. Reproductive Health Services*[7] the Supreme Court upheld a Missouri statute which not only outlawed the use of any public facility for the performance of any abortion not necessary to save the mother's life, but also made it illegal for any public employee, acting within the scope of that person's employment, to "perform or assist" any abortion that was not required to save the life of the mother.[8] The Court had less difficulty upholding this statute than the Hyde amendment because the lack of the availability of public facilities and physicians "is more easily remedied, and thus considerably less burdensome, than indigency * * *;"[9] the patient mere-

---

3. Planned Parenthood of Southern Arizona v. Woods, 982 F.Supp. 1369 (D. Ariz. 1997).

§ 18–8

1. See e.g., Thornburgh v. American College of Obstetricians and Gynecologists, 476 U.S. 747, 106 S.Ct. 2169, 90 L.Ed.2d 779 (1986); Maher v. Roe, 432 U.S. 464, 97 S.Ct. 2376, 53 L.Ed.2d 484 (1977).

2. Beal v. Doe, 432 U.S. 438, 97 S.Ct. 2366 53 L.Ed.2d 464 (1977).

3. Poelker v. Doe, 432 U.S. 519, 97 S.Ct. 2391, 53 L.Ed.2d 528 (1977).

4. 448 U.S. 297, 100 S.Ct. 2671, 65 L.Ed.2d 784 (1980).

5. Harris, 448 U.S. at 317, 100 S.Ct. at 2688.

6. See N.M. Right to Choose/NARAL v. Johnson, 975 P.2d 841 (N.M. 1998), Women of Minnesota v. Gomez, (Minn. 1993), and Women's Health Center of W. Va. v. Panepinto, 446 S.E.2d 658 (W.Va.1993).

7. 492 U.S. 490, 109 S.Ct. 3040, 106 L.Ed.2d 410 (1989).

8. Id. at 507, 109 S.Ct. at 3050.

9. Id. at 509, 109 S.Ct. at 3052.

ly had to choose a private physician and private health facility. The Court went on to point out that "[n]othing in the Constitution requires States to enter or remain in the business of performing abortions. Nor * * * do private physicians and their patients have some kind of Constitutional right of access to public facilities for the performance of abortions."[10] Effectively, in both *Harris* and *Webster* the Supreme Court found that the absence of government resources did not constitute a government imposed burden on a woman seeking an abortion; a government does not impose a roadblock on the way to an abortion by failing to build or maintain the road.

§ 18–9. Regulation of the Consent Process

As long as such regulation does not impose an "undue burden" on a pregnant woman seeking an abortion, the state may prescribe not only the kind of information that must be given to her before she can consent to the abortion, but also the circumstances and conditions surrounding her grant of consent. It is in evaluating states' attempts to regulate the process of gathering informed consent to abortion that the *Casey* approach is most obviously narrower than its predecessor. Before 1992, the Supreme Court had found several state attempts to prescribe informed consent processes for abortion cases to violate the Constitution because they constituted, in the Court's view, nothing more than "outright attempt[s] to wedge the [states'] message discouraging abortion into the privacy of the informed-consent dialogue between the woman and her physician."[1] In *Casey*, however, the Court overruled those cases and the plurality announced that it does not violate the Constitution for the government to require that particularly designated "truthful, non-misleading information about the nature of the procedure, the attendant health risks and those of childbirth, and the 'probable gestational age' of the fetus," be provided to the pregnant woman before she consents to the procedure.[2]

States may require that informed consent to abortion be in writing,[3] and they may require that a woman acknowledge in writing that she has been told about other sources of information.[4] In addition, a state may require that information necessary for informed consent to an abortion be provided to the pregnant woman by a physician rather than some other person;[5] the plurality in *Casey* said that such a requirement was consistent with the authority the states have to limit certain kinds of functions to designated licensed professionals, and, in any case, there was no evidence that such a requirement imposed any substantial obstacle on pregnant women seeking abortions.[6]

In evaluating the Pennsylvania informed consent requirements in *Casey* the Supreme Court had the greatest trouble with the requirement that there be a 24–hour waiting period between providing the statutorily required

10. Id. at 510, 109 S.Ct. at 3052.

§ 18–9

1. Thornburgh v. American College of Obstetricians and Gynecologists, 476 U.S. 747, 762, 106 S.Ct. 2169, 2179, 90 L.Ed.2d 779 (1986).

2. Planned Parenthood of Southeastern Pennsylvania v. Casey, 505 U.S. 833, 882, 112 S.Ct. 2791, 2823, 120 L.Ed.2d 674 (1992).

3. Planned Parenthood of Central Missouri v. Danforth, 428 U.S. 52, 96 S.Ct. 2831, 49 L.Ed.2d 788 (1976).

4. Casey, 505 U.S. at 882, 112 S.Ct. at 2823.

5. Id. at 883, 112 S.Ct. at 2824.

6. Id. at 883, 112 S.Ct. at 2824.

information and performing the abortion. The Court overruled its previous determination that such a waiting period, obviously designed to dissuade a woman from having an abortion, was *per se* a violation of the Constitution.[7] Indeed, the Court recognized that the waiting period, which requires that a woman have at least two visits with a physician before an abortion can be performed, did "increas[e] the cost and risk of delay of abortions,"[8] and that it would be, in the words of the District Court in that case, "particularly burdensome" in some cases.[9] The plurality found, however, that the waiting period was justifiable as a way to encourage reflection about a very serious decision and "a reasonable measure to implement the State's interest in protecting the life of the unborn."[10] Thus, the Court concluded that, as burdensome as it was, a one day waiting period did not constitute an undue burden in violation of the Constitution.[11]

§ 18–10.   Regulation of Medical Techniques and Facilities for Use in Performing Abortion

The Supreme Court has not been receptive to statutorily imposed limitations on the medical process of abortion, although no cases involving such limitations have come before the Court since it adopted the looser *Casey* standard in 1992. In *Casey* the Supreme Court announced that, "[a]s with any medical procedure, the State may enact regulations to further the health or safety of a woman seeking an abortion. Unnecessary health regulations that have the purpose or effect of presenting a substantial obstacle to a woman seeking an abortion impose an undue burden on that right."[1]

While questions relating to regulation of the medical processes used in providing an abortion have not been revisited by the Supreme Court since *Casey* was decided, the Supreme Court had found the requirement that second trimester abortions be performed in a hospital—which is a comparatively expensive venue for such procedures, but provides premature babies with better care—to be unconstitutional;[2] on the other hand, the Court had upheld some less substantial (and less expensive) restrictions and limitations on the location of second trimester abortions.[3] In addition, most attempts to limit the medical discretion of physicians performing abortions have been found to violate the Constitution. The state has not been able to prohibit the use of a particular procedure, as Missouri attempted to do by banning saline amniocentesis, in order to increase the chance that an abortion procedure will result in a live birth.[4] More generally, the state has not been able to require the

---

7. Akron v. Akron Center for Reproductive Health, 462 U.S. 416, 450, 103 S.Ct. 2481, 2503, 76 L.Ed.2d 687 (1983).

8. Planned Parenthood of Southeastern Pennsylvania v. Casey, 505 U.S. 833, 887, 112 S.Ct. 2791, 2825, 120 L.Ed.2d 674 (1992).

9. Id.

10. Id.

11. Id.

§ 18–10

1. Planned Parenthood of Southeastern Pennsylvania v. Casey, 505 U.S. 833, 878, 112 S.Ct. 2791, 2821, 120 L.Ed.2d 674 (1992).

2. Akron v. Akron Center for Reproductive Health, 462 U.S. 416, 103 S.Ct. 2481, 76 L.Ed.2d 687 (1983); Planned Parenthood of Kansas City, Mo. v. Ashcroft, 462 U.S. 476, 103 S.Ct. 2517, 76 L.Ed.2d 733 (1983).

3. Simopoulos v. Virginia, 462 U.S. 506, 103 S.Ct. 2532, 76 L.Ed.2d 755 (1983).

4. Planned Parenthood of Central Missouri v. Danforth, 428 U.S. 52, 79, 96 S.Ct. 2831, 2845, 49 L.Ed.2d 788 (1976).

physician to employ the abortion technique that is most likely to result in the live birth of the fetus.[5] While the Court had refused to allow a state to require the attendance of a second physician at a post-viability abortion to assure that adequate post-natal care is given in a live birth, it suggested that a properly drawn "second physician" requirement could pass the standard of *Roe*.[6] State legislation that requires abortions be provided only by licensed physicians has generally been upheld because the scope of medical licensing is a matter within the state police power.[7] Statutes providing for the "humane" disposition of the fetus have also been found to violate the *Roe* standard.[8] Presumably, all of these statutory schemes will some day have to be revisited by the Court as it applies the "undue burden" standard.

In the late 1990s the major flash point on abortion in state legislatures and in Congress was the propriety of the "dilation and extraction" process, also known as the "partial birth abortion." Many states promulgated legislation outlawing this rarely used medical procedure for late term abortions, and Congressional legislation designed to have the same effect nationally was vetoed by President Clinton every year beginning in 1997. Litigation challenging "partial birth" abortion bans has been commenced against most of the state statutes, and the courts have generally found the statutes to be unconstitutional, either as a violation of the "undue burden" test of *Casey*, or as unconstitutionally vague criminal legislation.[9] The Fourth Circuit, striking down the bans in Nebraska, Iowa and Arkansas, found that the vague definitions of "partial birth abortion" could be extended beyond the dilation and extraction abortion to the dilation and evacuation process, which remains the most common form of second trimester abortion.[10] Because the legislative ban could be read to outlaw this commonly used process, it imposed an "undue burden" on a woman's choice to have an abortion. The Seventh Circuit, sitting en banc, concluded 5–4 that the Illinois and Wisconsin statutes banning "partial birth abortions" could be read constitutionally because the states–by legislative or judicial means–could interpret them to apply only to dilation and extraction processes, and not to dilation and evacuation procedures.[11] Beyond this, the Seventh Circuit held that the statutes, which permitted exceptions to save the life but not the health of the mother, were consistent with *Casey* because they left open many other "safe options" for

---

5. Colautti v. Franklin, 439 U.S. 379, 99 S.Ct. 675, 58 L.Ed.2d 596 (1979). See also Thornburgh v. American College of Obstetricians and Gynecologists, 476 U.S. 747, 106 S.Ct. 2169, 90 L.Ed.2d 779 (1986).

6. Thornburgh at 769–771, 106 S.Ct. at 2183–2184 (a second physician requirement could be constitutional if it provided an exception where the health of the mother is endangered by delay in the arrival of the second physician).

7. See. E.g., Armstrong v. Mazurek, 906 F.Supp. 561 (D.Mont.1995), vacated 94 F.3d 566 9th Cir.1996), cert. granted, judgment reversed 520 U.S. 968, 117 S.Ct. 1865, 138 l.Ed.2d 162 (1997).

8. Casey, 505 U.S. at 949–950, Akron v. Akron Center for Reproductive Health, 462 U.S. 416, 103 S.Ct. 2481, 76 L.Ed.2d 687 (1983).

9. See, e.g., Planned Parenthood v. Verniero, 41 F.Supp.2d 478 (D.N.J.1998); Richmond Medical Center for Women v. Gilmore, 11 F.Supp.2d 795 (E.D.Va.1998), stay grated 144 F.3d 326 (4th Cir.1998); Hope Clinic v. Ryan, 995 F.Supp. 847 (N.D.Ill.1998).

10. Carhart v. Stenberg, 192 F.3d 1142 (8th Cir. 1999), decided along with Planned Parenthood of Greater Iowa v. Miller, 195 F.3d 386 (8th Cir. 1999) and Little Rock Family Planning Services v. Jegley, 192 F.3d 794 (8th Cir. 1999). See also Womens Medical Professional Corporation v. Voinovich, 130 F.3d 187 (6th Cir. 1997).

11. Hope Clinic v. Ryan, 195 F.3d 857 (7th Cir. 1999)(Judge Easterbrook writing for the majority; Judge Posner, joined by Judges Rovner, Wood and Evans, dissenting).

abortion

women seeking third trimester abortions. Some state "partial birth abortion" laws are pending adjudication, and some have yet to be challenged. Just before this book went to press early in 2000, the Supreme Court granted certiorari to review the constitutional status of legislation banning partial birth abortion.[12]

§ 18–11. Record Keeping Requirements

The Court has permitted most record keeping requirements that arguably can lead to medically valuable generalized data and that do not disclose the identity of the women undergoing the abortion.[1] Several years before *Casey*, the Court announced that it would uphold such provisions that are "[1] reasonably directed to the preservation of maternal health and that [2] properly respect a patient's confidentiality and privacy."[2] In *Casey* itself the Court expanded the first condition to include provisions that relate to health generally[3] and upheld a statute that required the maintenance of abortion-by-abortion data, including the identity of the physician performing the abortion (but not the identity of the pregnant women).[4]

§ 18–12. Other Abortion Related Litigation and Regulation

There seems to be no limit on the circumstances that can give rise to litigation over abortion. Some states have acted to impose legal burdens on abortion providers that are designed more to drive those providers out of business than to impose any medically meaningful regulation. In Louisiana, for example, a statute that provided for civil damage actions on behalf of aborted fetuses and their mothers for "all special and general damages which are recoverable in [tort, including wrongful death actions]" was found to place an undue burden on women seeking abortions because it was written to force providers away from this medical endeavor.[1] The court also found that the statute was unconstitutionally vague because it made it impossible for a doctor to know what kinds of information to provide to a patient before the performance of an abortion.

A few cases have arisen over the right of prisoners to abortions.[2] The Third Circuit has determined in separate cases both that a prisoner has a right to an abortion that cannot be limited by the requirement of a court ordered "release" for that purpose[3] and that a prisoner cannot be required to arrange her own financing to have an abortion if doing so would effectively deny her access to an abortion.[4]

Courts also have been called upon to make or allow substituted judgments concerning abortions on behalf of incompetent patients, and one state

12. Stenberg v. Carhart, 2000 WL 241054, reviewing 192 F.3d 1142 (8th Cir. 1999).

§ 18–11

1. Planned Parenthood of Central Missouri v. Danforth, 428 U.S. 52 , 96 S.Ct. 2831, 49 L.Ed.2d 788 (1976).

2. Planned Parenthood of Southeastern Pennsylvania v. Casey, 505 U.S. 833, 400, 112 S.Ct. 2791, 2832, 120 L.Ed.2d 674 (1992).

3. Id.

4. Id. at 900, 112 S.Ct. at 2832–33.

§ 18–12

1. Okpalobi v. Foster, 190 F.3d 337 (5th Cir. 1999), rehearing en banc granted 201 F.3d 353, (5th Cir. 2000).

2. See e.g., Monmouth County Correctional Institutional Inmates v. Lanzaro, 834 F.2d 326 (3d Cir.1987).

3. Id. at 337.

4. Id. at 340–44.

supreme court authorized an abortion for a profoundly retarded woman suffering from a seizure disorder and cerebral palsy, whose pregnancy was the result of a sexual assault, even though her mother (who was also her guardian) objected.[5] In the course of a non-statutory informed consent case, the Oklahoma Supreme Court determined that a physician did not breach the standard of care by failing to tell his patient that she could go to another state to abort her 23 or 24 week hydrocephalic fetus, which was arguably viable and thus not subject to an abortion in Oklahoma.[6] Given the depth of interest in the subject and the strength of the national division over the propriety of abortion under any circumstances, it is remarkable that there have been so few civil liability cases involving abortion.

C. ACTIONS TO PROTECT WOMEN SEEKING ABORTIONS AND ABORTION PROVIDERS

§ 18–13. The Freedom of Access to Clinic Entrances Act of 1994

As the focus of the challenge to abortion practices moved from the courts to the state legislatures in the early 1990s, and as the issue became a more formally political one, many clinics which provided abortion services became the subject of protests, prayer vigils, marches and other demonstrations. In a few cases, violence erupted and some physicians who provided abortion services were murdered. Many clinic employees feared for their own safety and the safety of their patients, some of whom felt harassed as they entered the medical facilities. The protesters argued that they were doing nothing more than exercising their first amendment rights, and that they were exercising them in those ways most likely to make them effective–by dissuading patients from having abortions.

In response to the most egregious acts of violence, Congress passed the Freedom of Access to Clinic Entrances Act of 1994. This Act made it a federal crime to intentionally injure, intimidate or interfere with any person by force, threat of force or by physical obstruction because that person is seeking reproductive health services (including abortion services).[1] The statute provides harsher penalties for repeat offenders and more lenient treatment of those cases "involving exclusively a nonviolent intrusion."[2] It covers conduct virtually anywhere an abortion can be performed, including hospitals, clinics and doctors' offices. The Act can also be enforced by the Attorney General and attorneys general of the states through civil actions, and it expressly provides that it does not prohibit any expressive conduct otherwise protected by the first amendment.[3]

There has been substantial litigation involving the limits the first amendment places upon state restrictions imposed on abortion protesters. Trial courts have issued injunctions routinely where judges thought it was neces-

---

5. In re Jane Doe, 533 A.2d 523 (R.I.1987).

6. Spencer v. Seikel, 742 P.2d 1126 (Okl. 1987).

2. Id., section 248(b).

3. Id., section 248(d)(1).

§ 18–13

1. 18 U.S.C.A. section 248(a).

sary to do so to protect the rights of the clinic patients. In 1997 the Supreme Court upheld an injunction which created a 15–foot protected "bubble zone" around the doorways and driveways of a clinic offering abortion services, and it upheld a limit on the number of people who could "counsel" a woman entering the clinic.[4] The Court also decided that those seeking to dissuade a woman from entering the clinic could be required to desist when the patient asked them to do so, although the Court found that a moveable bubble zone that followed patients as they entered the clinics would violate the free speech clause of the first amendment.

§ 18–14. Actions for Damages and Other Legal Protection for Abortion Providers

The Freedom of Access to Clinic Entrances Act is not the only weapon provided to those who are concerned about the effects of demonstrations around clinics that provide abortions. Ordinary tort, nuisance and trespass actions are available against those who come upon the clinic's property or seek to intimidate or harass the clinic's patients, and many lawsuits seeking to restrain abortion protesters have raised both federal statutory and state common law claims. In addition, in 1994 the Supreme Court determined that the federal Racketeer Influenced and Corrupt Organization Act ("RICO") could be applied against those who violate laws to blockade clinics, even if there is no economic motivation for the defendants' conduct. This created the possibility of substantial civil damage awards against organizations and individuals that participate in illegal activities to dissuade women from visiting the clinics.[1] In order to obtain a civil judgment under this statute, a plaintiff must demonstrate that the defendant, through the commission of two or more acts constituting a pattern of racketeering activity, directly or indirectly invests in, or maintains an interest in, or participates in an enterprise the activities of which affect interstate or foreign commerce.[2] Further, a plaintiff may recover treble damages if the defendant injures the plaintiff in his business or property under the terms of the statute.[3]

Both the Freedom of Access to Clinic Entrances Act and RICO were implicated in 1999 when an Oregon federal court jury returned a verdict of more than $100 million against twelve individuals, the American Coalition of Life Activists and the Advocates for Life Ministries, for maintaining a web site that threatened those who performed abortions. The site, called "The Nuremberg Files," listed physicians who performed abortions, drew lines through those who had been murdered, and listed those who had been wounded by would-be assassins in gray. The defendants also published old West style "wanted" posters with the names and pictures of physicians who performed abortions. The defendants claimed a first amendment right to publish the web site and the wanted posters, and some first amendment analysts were con-

4. Schenck v. Pro–Choice Network, 519 U.S. 357, 117 S.Ct. 855 (1997).

§ 18–14

1. National Organization of Women v. Schiedler, 510 U.S. 249 (1994).

2. 18 U.S.C.A. § 1962; see also Town of West Hartford v. Operation Rescue, 915 F.2d 92, 100 (2d Cir.1990).

3. 18 U.S.C.A. § 1964(c).

cerned about the potential chilling effect of such a large judgment on the publication of unpopular political views.[4]

Until 1993, many civil actions were prosecuted against those who were alleged to have interfered with a woman's right to have an abortion under a Reconstruction era civil rights statute.[5] Under this statute, originally passed in response to Ku Klux Klan interference with the rights of African Americans, a remedy is available for any person or class of persons who has been deprived, through a conspiracy, of "equal protection of the laws or of equal privileges and immunities under the laws."[6] The Supreme Court rejected the position that this statute could be used to redress interference with the right to an abortion in *Bray v. Alexandria Women's Health Clinic.*[7] First, the Supreme Court held, women seeking abortions did not constitute a class for purposes of the statute,[8] and, while the defendants' actions were primarily aimed at women, they were not directed at women as a class.[9] Thus, the Supreme Court concluded, the plaintiff had failed to demonstrate a class-based animus. Second, the Court held that blocking access to abortion clinics, even to out-of-state residents, does not impede the plaintiffs' claimed right to interstate travel because that interference is a local action non-discriminatorily aimed at both residents and non-residents.[10] The Court held that the statute would be violated only if there were a conscious objective to impair the right in question, and since the defendant's objective was to prevent abortions rather than interfere with interstate travel, this "conscious objective" element also could not be met.[11] Finally, the Court held that the statute did not apply to the entirely private defendant in *Bray.*[12]

4. In another case that raised the first amendment rights of those opposed to abortion, in 1999 the Supreme Court denied review of a Third Circuit decision that a public transit authority could not deny advertising space to a group that wanted to place signs that said, "Women who choose abortion suffer more and deadlier breast cancer." The agency had accepted other abortion related advertising, and, thus, had created an open forum on abortion related issues.

5. 42 U.S.C.A. § 1985(3).

6. 42 U.S.C.A. § 1985(3).

7. 506 U.S. 263, 113 S.Ct. 753, 122 L.Ed.2d 34 (1993).

8. Id. at 269, 113 S.Ct. at 759.

9. Id.

10. Id. at 276–277, 113 S.Ct. at 763.

11. Id.

12. Bray v. Alexandria Women's Health Clinic, 506 U.S. 263, 113 S.Ct. 753, 122 L.Ed.2d 34 (1993). Following *Bray*, it appeared that the federal civil rights statutes were essentially foreclosed as an available remedy to women seeking abortions. In *Town of West Hartford v. Operation Rescue*, 915 F.2d 92 (2d Cir. 1990), however, the Second Circuit read the *Bray* holding to be limited to the specific facts in question on the issue of animus toward women as a class. As a result, the court remanded to the district court for a specific determination on whether the defendant had the required class-based animus in the case at bar. Presumably, if plaintiffs could demonstrate this factual element, then this statute would be available to them. In addition, *Bray* did not directly address the second clause of 42 U.S.C.A. § 1985(3), which prohibits private conspirators from preventing or hindering state or local authorities from giving or securing all persons the equal protection of the laws.

Chapter 19

POTENTIAL FETAL–MATERNAL CONFLICTS

Table of Sections

Research References

Am Jur 2d, Abortion and Birth Control § 26
ALR Index: Abortion; Conflict of Interest
ALR Digest: Physicians and Surgeons § 29.6
Am Jur Pleading and Practice Forms (Rev), Abortion § 34.2

§ 19–1. Introduction

There are times when the decisions or actions of a pregnant women are alleged to be in conflict with the interests of her fetus, or with a state interest in protecting the life or health of the fetus. There are three situations which most commonly give rise to these alleged conflicts: health care decisionmaking by the pregnant woman, lifestyle decisionmaking by the pregnant woman, and employment choices made by the pregnant woman, each of which may put the life or health of the pregnant woman's fetus at risk. For example, a pregnant woman's decision to refuse a blood transfusion necessary to save the life of the fetus (or her own life) is arguably inconsistent with the fetus's interest in

941

being born or the state's interest in protecting the life of the fetus.[1] Similarly, a pregnant woman's addiction to drugs[2] or heavy use of alcohol[3] during pregnancy is arguably inconsistent with the fetus's interest in being born healthy or the state's interest in protecting the health of the fetus. Finally, a pregnant woman's decision to work in an area with a high lead concentration is arguably inconsistent with her fetus's interest in normal fetal development and the state's general interest in the welfare of children.[4]

True conflicts between pregnant women and their fetuses are extremely rare. There are few relationships, if any, that engender a greater sense of responsibility than carrying a fetus. As one obstetrician pointed out in a statement ultimately quoted by an appellate court, "most of the women [I see] 'would cut off their heads to save their babies.' "[5]In evaluating potential fetal-maternal conflicts, the courts should avoid being pulled into apparent but false conflicts between the interests of the pregnant woman and the interests of the fetus. These apparent conflicts between pregnant women and their fetuses may really be conflicts between the pregnant woman's evaluation of what is best for the fetus and the evaluation of a doctor or prosecuting authority. Allegations of fetal-maternal conflict sometimes are merely the assertion of power (of physicians over patients, for example) or attempts by ambitious prosecutors to exploit the politically rich field of child abuse and neglect. There may be real conflicts, however, and it is difficult to imagine a charge of greater moral culpability than the allegation that a woman is putting the life or health of her fetus at risk to satisfy her own selfish desires.

Of course, the mere fact that such conduct is morally culpable does not mean that it is also illegal. Not all immoral conduct is illegal. Those kinds of arguably culpable conduct that are most politically charged, most personal, and about which there is most ethical disagreement, are, appropriately, the least likely to be subject to legal restraint. In addition, while the law forbids child abuse or neglect, it also tolerates conduct that virtually everyone would consider bad parenting because the law is reluctant to intervene in the family. Finally, the law rarely intervenes to stop a person from taking an action, however immoral it may be deemed, that does not affect other people. For the law to intervene and to require a pregnant woman to take some action (or to refrain from taking some action) to protect her fetus, the court must determine that the pregnant woman has the *legal* obligation to do so.

§ 19–2. Medical Decisionmaking by a Pregnant Woman

a. Introduction: The Question of Balancing Maternal and Fetal Interests

Many forms of medical treatment performed upon a pregnant woman affect her fetus, and all forms of medical treatment performed upon a fetus

§ 19–1

1. See e.g.,In re Fetus Brown, 689 N.E.2d 397 (Ill.App.1997); Raleigh Fitkin–Paul Morgan Memorial Hospital v. Anderson, 201 A.2d 537 (N.J.1964).

2. See e.g., Appeal in Pima County Juvenile Severance Action No. S–120171, 905 P.2d 555 (Ariz.App.1995); In re Valerie D., 613 A.2d 748 (Conn.1992); In re Stefanel Tyesha C., 556 N.Y.S.2d 280 (N.Y.App.Div.1990).

3. Matter of Milland, 548 N.Y.S.2d 995 (N.Y.Fam.Ct.1989).

4. See e.g., Automobile Workers v. Johnson Controls, 499 U.S. 187, 111 S.Ct. 1196, 113 L.Ed.2d 158 (1991). See § 19–5, below.

5. In re A.C., 573 A.2d 1235, 1245 (D.C.App.1990).

affect the pregnant woman because it is always necessary to go through the pregnant woman to get to the fetus. Thus, medical decisionmaking by a pregnant woman frequently affects her fetus, and it is at least theoretically possible for the pregnant woman to have an interest that is in conflict with the best interest of her fetus. Two kinds of cases have given rise to the bulk of the non-criminal litigation involving potential fetal-maternal conflicts: first, a pregnant woman's refusal, usually on religious grounds, to consent to a blood transfusion arguably necessary to save her own life or that of the fetus; and second, a pregnant woman's refusal, sometimes on religious grounds, to consent to a caesarean delivery arguably necessary to save her life or health, or to assure the live birth or health of the fetus.[1] As techniques for fetal therapy are developed and improved, a new class of potential fetal-maternal conflicts will also arise: a pregnant woman may refuse to consent to other forms of therapy—such as fetal surgery or prenatal drug therapy—that are arguably necessary to maintain the health of the fetus but inconsistent with her values, interests, or desires.

State courts that have considered these issues have been divided over when, if ever, judicial intervention is appropriate to order a pregnant woman to undergo a medical procedure for the benefit of her fetus. Early cases almost universally resulted in decisions that the pregnant woman must follow the health regimens prescribed by their physicians.[2] The tide of legal and medical writing critical of those cases, however, has resulted in considerable judicial reevaluation. It now seems less likely that a court would require a pregnant woman to undergo any treatment without her truly voluntary consent.[3]

The theoretical question upon which this issue depends is whether the court should balance the interests of the mother against the interests of the fetus (or the state's interest, which is usually denominated the interest in protecting the fetus), or whether such balancing is unnecessary.[4] If a court determines that the interests of the mother always prevail, there is no reason to engage in balancing. Similarly, if a court were to determine that the interest of the fetus always were to prevail—a position no court has taken— there would be no need to engage in balancing. If a court determines that

§ 19–2

1. See e.g., Raleigh Fitkin–Paul Morgan Memorial Hospital v. Anderson, 201 A.2d 537 (N.J.1964) (ordering a pregnant Jehovah's Witness to undergo a blood transfusion to save her "unborn child"); In re Application of Jamaica Hospital, 491 N.Y.S.2d 898 (N.Y.Sup.1985) (blood transfusion ordered to save a fetus not yet viable); Pemberton v. Tallahassee Memorial Regional Medical Center, 66 F.Supp.2d 1247 (N.D.Fl. 1999) (finding no constitutional defect in a state court order requiring mother to undergo a caesarian section against her will); Jefferson v. Griffin Spalding County Hospital Authority, 274 S.E.2d 457 (Ga.1981) (ordering a mother to undergo a caesarean section against her religiously motivated wishes when her physician argued the caesarean was necessary to save both the mother and fetus). But see In re Fetus Brown, supra note 1 (Jehovah's

Witness mother not required to receive blood transfusion necessary to save her own life and that of her fetus) and In re Baby Boy Doe, 632 N.E.2d 326 (Ill.App.1994)(mother not ordered to have caesarean even though her failure to do so would be harmful to her fetus).

2. Jefferson v. Griffin Spalding County Hospital Authority, 274 S.E.2d 457 (Ga.1981); Raleigh Fitkin–Paul Morgan Memorial Hospital v. Anderson, 201 A.2d 537 (N.J.1964).

3. See In re A.C., 573 A.2d 1235 (D.C.App. 1990). See also In re Fetus Brown, 689 N.E.2d 397 (Ill.App.1997) and In re Baby Boy Doe, 632 N.E.2d 326 (Ill.App.1994). But see Pemberton v. Tallahassee Memorial Regional Medical Center, 66 F. Supp.2d 1247 (N.D.Fl.1999).

4. In re A.C., 573 A.2d 1235 (D.C.App. 1990).

neither interest is absolute, and that there are some (even if limited) circumstances under which the court may intervene to order a pregnant woman to undergo medical treatment without her voluntary consent, that court must then determine the principles and the procedures under which it will balance the interests of the pregnant woman and the fetus. In some early cases courts did, in fact, attempt to balance the interests of the pregnant woman and the fetus, even though the process was not always described as such.[5] Most recent cases addressing this issue directly, however, have concluded that there is no balancing to be done because the only interest to be considered is that of the pregnant woman.[6]

b. Why the Interests of the Pregnant Woman Must Prevail: Reasons Not to Balance

Courts that have rejected the balancing approach have concluded either that (1) Federal constitutional principles prohibit that balancing, or (2) ordinary principles of health care decisionmaking apply to pregnant women, just as those principles apply to anyone else, or both.[7] These principles provide that the patient herself must give truly voluntary consent to any form of medical treatment, and that if the patient is incompetent, a surrogate should apply the principle of substituted judgment to determine what form of treatment the patient, if competent, would desire. There are several reasons to reject any kind of balancing of interests when making these kinds of health care decisions.

First, a woman does not give up any constitutional or other rights upon becoming pregnant.[8] If a non-pregnant woman would be authorized to make a health care decision (about undergoing a blood transfusion, for example), a pregnant woman should be able to do so also.

Second, even assuming that the fetus is considered a person for legal purposes, the law does not recognize any circumstance when a person must undergo a medical procedure for the benefit of another person. There is simply no legal obligation on any person to rescue another, even a relative, by providing medical care. Courts have never required relatives to give tissue for transplantation, for example, even when the tissue sought is renewable and the life of the potential recipient depends upon it.[9] Parents have no legal

5. See e.g., In re Application of Jamaica Hospital, 491 N.Y.S.2d 898 (N.Y.Sup.1985); Raleigh Fitkin–Paul Morgan Memorial Hospital v. Anderson, 201 A.2d 537 (N.J.1964).

6. See and In re Baby Boy Doe, 632 N.E.2d 326 (Ill.App.1994)(explicitly rejecting any form of balancing). For the seminal case taking this position, see In re A.C., 573 A.2d 1235 (D.C.App.1990). But see Pemberton v. Tallahassee Memorial Regional Medical Center, 66 F.Supp.2d 1247 (N.D.Fl. 1999) ("In anything other than the extraordinary and overwhelming case, the right to decide would surely rest with the mother, not with the state. But * * * this was an extraordinary and overwhelming case * * *").

7. Id.

8. See e.g., and In re Baby Boy Doe, 632 N.E. 2d 326,332 (Ill. App. 1994):

[A[woman's right to refuse invasive medical treatment, derived from her rights to privacy, bodily integrity, and religious liberty, is not diminished during pregnancy. The woman retains the same right to refuse invasive treatment, even of lifesaving or other beneficial nature, that she can exercise when she is not pregnant. The potential impact upon the fetus is not legally relevant, to the contrary....

See also Matter of Fletcher, 533 N.Y.S.2d 241, 243 (N.Y.Fam.Ct.1988) (noting "an expectant mother, just like any other person, is protected by a constitutional right to privacy and bodily integrity which the state may not violate without showing a compelling state interest.")

9. McFall v. Shimp, 10 Pa.D. & C.3d 90 (Pa.Com.Pl., Allegheny County Ct. 1978) (refusing to order a person to donate bone mar-

obligation to provide tissue for their children; there can be no greater legal obligations on pregnant women to serve the interests of their fetuses than there are on parents to serve the interests of their already-born children. The law of rescue is the classic tort law area where ethical obligations are not translated into legal ones. While pregnant women may have a moral obligation to protect their fetuses, that obligation is not a legal one.

Third, judicial balancing of the interests of pregnant women and their fetuses, and the consequent possibility of judicial intervention to require pregnant women to undergo medical treatment against their will, adversely affects the doctor-patient relationship and may discourage some pregnant women from seeking the health care they need. As the American Public Health Association has pointed out with regard to court ordered caesarean births:

> Rather than protecting the health of women and children, court-ordered caesareans erode the element of trust that permits a pregnant woman to communicate to her physician—without fear of reprisal—all information relevant to her proper diagnosis and treatment. An even more serious consequence of court-ordered intervention is that it drives women at high risk of complications during pregnancy and childbirth out of the health care system to avoid coerced treatment.[10]

Thus, a court may conclude, the public health consequences of court ordered treatment, which may scare women with high risk pregnancies away from prenatal care, are not justified by the advantages of intervention in any particular case.

Fourth, there is a history of incorrect prognoses where physicians claim that the life or health of a fetus depends upon treatment the pregnant woman wishes to refuse. Treating physicians seem ready to testify that intervention is necessary even when the prognosis without intervention is uncertain. Well meaning physicians may unconsciously color their testimony in such cases to make what is doubtful appear certain, and to assure that their own judgment of what is in the best interest of the patient ultimately will prevail. For example, there is a series of cases in which doctors have testified that caesarean sections were necessary to protect the lives or health of fetuses or pregnant women (or both), in which the pregnant women have "escaped" and had normal vaginal births without the predicted complications.[11] As bioethicist Joseph Fletcher has pointed out, "[f]orced fetal therapy on the basis of misdiagnosis would constitute an ethical megadisaster."[12]

Fifth, the difficulty in prognosis is compounded by the inadequate judicial procedure available to courts to resolve these questions. Hearings generally have to be conducted immediately, before the pregnant woman has much of an opportunity to find, hire, and instruct legal counsel, before a guardian ad

row necessary to save the life of his cousin.); Curran v. Bosze, 566 N.E.2d 1319 (Ill.1990) (refusing to order child to donate bone marrow to half sibling); see also In re Baby Boy Doe, 632 N.E. 2d 326,332 (Ill. App. 1994)("A woman is under no duty to guarantee the mental and physical health of her child at birth, and thus cannot be compelled to do or not to do anything merely for the benefit of her unborn child.")

10. Amicus Curiae Brief of American Public Health Assoc., in In re A.C., 573 A.2d 1235 (D.C.App.1990).

11. For several examples, see Joseph Fletcher, Drawing Moral Lines in Fetal Therapy, 29 Clin. Obstetrics & Gynecology 595 (1986).

12. Id. at 599.

litem can be appointed to represent the fetus, and before expert witnesses other than the treating physicians can become familiar with the condition of the pregnant woman and the fetus.[13] The judicial process is particularly inadequate to illuminate and resolve these kinds of potential conflicts.

Finally, there is no adequate way of enforcing a judgment that a woman must undergo medical treatment which she has refused. Even those who believe that it is appropriate to balance the interests of the pregnant woman and the fetus are appalled by the prospect of the marshall being called to manacle a pregnant woman so that she can be forcibly subjected to a blood transfusion or a caesarean section.[14]

c. Why the Interests of the Fetus or the State May Prevail: Reasons to Balance

A few judges and commentators continue to take the position that the interests of the pregnant woman must be balanced against the fetus's interest in being born (or being born healthy), and the state's derivative interest in protecting the lives and health of children (and, directly or indirectly, fetuses).[15] Those who take this position argue that the fetus—at least from the point of viability—is a person for other medical and common law purposes and, thus, is entitled to be treated like any other person for purposes of medical decisionmaking.[16] In all jurisdictions, the tort law recognizes actions brought on behalf of children born alive for injuries they received in utero.[17] Health care providers now recognize that when they treat pregnant women they have two patients—the pregnant woman and the fetus. The fact that health care providers must treat them both as patients is recognized in the codes of professional organizations.[18] Tort law, too, recognizes that health care providers may be liable to a child for injuries sustained when the health care provider was treating the pregnant woman.[19] It appears inconsistent to impose liability on the providers under these circumstances and yet to prohibit those providers from doing what is necessary to preserve the life and health of the fetus if another one of the provider's patients—the pregnant woman—objects.

Those who argue in favor of balancing also reject the analogy to the rescue theory in tort.[20] The pregnant woman-fetus relationship is unique, they argue, and it should not be governed by the principles that apply to relationships between strangers, or even by the principles that apply to relationships between other family members.[21] After all, the pregnant woman was a party, and usually a willing party, to the creation of the pregnancy.[22] In cases where

13. Id.

14. See In re A.C., 573 A.2d 1235 (D.C.App. 1990).

15. Id. at 1253 (Belson, J., concurring in part and dissenting in part). This is also the position, at least in "extraordinary" cases, taken by the court in Pemberton v. Tallahassee Memorial Regional Medical Center, 66 F.Supp. 1247 (N.D.Fl.1999).

16. In re A.C., 573 A.2d at 1255.

17. W. Page Keeton et al., Prosser and Keeton on the Law of Torts, 5th Ed., 368 (1984).

18. Ethics Committee of the American College of Obstetrics and Gynecologists Opinion

No. 55: reads, "[t]he welfare of the fetus is of the utmost importance to the majority of women; thus only rarely will a conflict arise."

19. In re A.C., 573 A.2d 1235, 1255–56 (D.C.App.1990) (Belson, J., concurring in part and dissenting in part).

20. See, In re A.C., 573 A.2d 1235, 1253 (D.C.App.1990) (Belson, J., concurring in part and dissenting in part).

21. In re A.C., 573 A.2d 1235, 1256 (D.C.App.1990) (Belson, J., concurring in part and dissenting in part, attributes this to the unique dependence of the fetus upon the mother).

22. Id.

the fetus has reached viability, the pregnant woman has chosen to continue the pregnancy even though she had a legal right to terminate it. As one judge pointed out in a forced caesarean case,

> A woman carrying a viable unborn child is not in the same category as a relative, friend, or stranger called upon to donate bone marrow or an organ for transplant. Rather, the expectant mother has placed herself in a special class of persons who are bringing another person into existence, and upon whom that other person's life is totally dependent. Also, uniquely, the viable unborn child is literally captive within the mother's body. No other potential beneficiary of a surgical procedure on another is in that position.[23]

d. How to Balance the Relevant Factors

Those who favor balancing the pregnant woman's interest against the interest of the fetus or the interest of the state in protecting the fetus must define the way in which the balancing is to be done. In fact, no court has announced a coherent and complete formula for performing this balancing act, although several have defined factors that ought to be considered. First, on the side of the pregnant woman, the court must consider the autonomy interest of that woman in choosing her own health care and in avoiding unwanted medical intrusion upon her body.[24] The strength of this interest will depend, in part, upon the nature of the intrusion upon the pregnant woman that is necessary to provide health care for the fetus and the certainty with which the pregnant woman articulates her opposition to the proposed medical intervention.[25] In addition, any potential physical or mental danger to the pregnant woman that might be a consequence of the proposed intervention must be weighed in the balancing calculus.[26]

The other side of this balancing fulcrum bears the weight of the value of life and health to the fetus, modified by the chance that the proposed intervention actually will yield the life or health of the fetus after birth. While some courts view this interest as one that belongs to the fetus,[27] others view the preservation of the life and health of the fetus as a state interest,[28] and those courts may also consider the value of the message that intervention gives to the rest of society about the state's respect for life.

Two factors that may be relevant in performing the balance deserve special consideration: (1) the right of the pregnant woman to abort the fetus, and (2) the determination of whether the fetus will, in fact, be born alive, whether or not it is viable at the time of the proposed intervention. In some ways the debate over the propriety of requiring a woman to undergo medical treatment for the benefit of her fetus is analogous to the debate over abortion. It would be strange indeed if the law could require a woman to undergo special medical treatment to preserve the life and health of her fetus when she possesses a Constitutionally protected right to terminate the pregnancy

---

23. Id.

24. Id. at 1258.

25. Id.

26. In re A.C., 573 A.2d 1235, 1258 (D.C.App.1990) (Belson, J., concurring in part and dissenting in part).

27. Id.

28. See Jefferson v. Griffin Spalding County Hospital Authority, 274 S.E.2d 457 (Ga. 1981). See also Pemberton v. Tallahasee Memorial Regional Medical Center, 66 F.Supp. 1247 (N.D.Fl.1999) (analogizing to the third trimester balancing required by Roe v. Wade).

without substantial restriction. For this reason, there is no meaningful legal argument that the pregnant woman's decision can be outweighed by that of a fetus which she legally may choose to abort,[29] and the balancing approach must be abandoned for these cases. Of course, if the Constitutional law changes and states are permitted to impose more substantial restrictions on abortions performed before viability, the law may also permit greater legal intrusions on the pregnant women's medical decisionmaking before viability.

Some bioethicists have argued that the significant point in determining whether the pregnant woman's interest can be outweighed by some other interest is not the point of viability or the point at which a woman is legally entitled to seek and obtain an abortion but, rather, the point at which the pregnant woman decides that she will carry the fetus to term, even if that decision is made very early in the course of the pregnancy.[30] According to these bioethicists, once the pregnant woman decides that she will carry the fetus to term, the interests of the fetus, viable or not, become the interest of a person who will be born alive.[31] In effect, this argument is that a yet-to-be-born person is entitled to greater legal respect than a mere fetus who may yet be aborted.

§ 19–3.   Lifestyle Decisionmaking by a Pregnant Woman

Medical decisionmaking is not the only way that a pregnant woman arguably may put her fetus at risk. A pregnant woman who smokes, drinks alcohol, uses drugs, over exercises, under–exercises, rides a motorcycle, skis, or engages in a host of other activities, may risk the life or health of her fetus. While participation in some of these activities is hardly within the truly free choices of the pregnant woman (as when an addict uses drugs or cigarettes), a pregnant woman's moral obligation to her fetus may well extend beyond the realm of medical decisionmaking to decisionmaking about lifestyle choices.

There is disagreement about whether this moral obligation ought to be enforceable in law as well, and the important question appears to be whether such conduct is otherwise illegal. Thus, there have been only a few attempts to use the law to prohibit a woman from drinking alcohol during her pregnancy,[1] even though this is probably the single most dangerous activity available to pregnant women: fetal alcohol syndrome is now the leading known cause of mental retardation in the United States. Conversely, some courts have applied laws that prohibit the use of drugs in order to protect fetuses from the harm that may come from *in utero* exposure to those drugs,[2] even though it may be more dangerous to the fetus for the mother to withdraw from drugs during the pregnancy than to continue their use.

The prospect of the courts deciding how women should spend their pregnancies and the specter of a new kind of judicially required confinement have chilled interest in using the law to define what constitutes acceptable

---

29. But see, In re Application of Jamaica Hospital, 491 N.Y.S.2d 898 (N.Y.Sup.1985) (blood transfusion ordered to save a fetus who was not yet viable).

30. See John A. Robertson and Joseph D. Schulman, Pregnancy and Prenatal Harm to Offspring: The Case of Mothers With PKU, 17 Hastings Center (4) Rep. 23 (1987).

31. Id.

§ 19–3

1. See Matter of Milland, 548 N.Y.S.2d 995 (N.Y.Fam.Ct.1989).

2. In re Stefanel Tyesha C., 556 N.Y.S.2d 280 (N.Y.App.Div.1990).

prenatal parenting.[3] Some courts that have considered the issue have determined that their abuse, neglect and dependency statutes, whether written as criminal statutes or as statutes to provide civil protection for children, are not designed to protect fetuses and that they cannot be applied to fetuses.[4] Some of these statutes explicitly do include fetuses within their definition of "children," however, and a few courts in other states also have been willing to extend their abuse and neglect statutes to include fetuses,[5] at least in those cases where the challenged conduct amounts to medical decisionmaking directly related to the pregnancy—for example, in forced caesarean and blood transfusion cases.[6] The greatest problem for those who wish to be able to control a pregnant woman's lifestyle choices, ostensibly to protect her fetus, is the choice of an appropriate legal remedy.

§ 19–4. Remedies for Potential Fetal–Maternal Conflicts Arising Out of Medical and Lifestyle Decision-making of Pregnant Women

a. Introduction

It has been a difficult search for those seeking legal remedies to enforce the pregnant woman's moral obligation to her fetus because it is hard to construct appropriate legal remedies to vindicate a breach of such a moral obligation. Courts and commentators, however, have discovered a number of legal remedies that are available to encourage or require women to take actions consistent with the courts' perceptions of the interest of their fetus, or to punish them if they do not.[1] These remedies fall into three categories: civil remedies, criminal remedies, and various forms of non-criminal commitment.

b. Civil Remedies

1. Mandatory Injunctions and Child Protective Services Actions

Except in tort actions, civil remedies in potential fetal-maternal conflict cases inevitably take on the appearance of mandatory injunctions directed to the conduct of the pregnant woman.[2] Some courts have simply denominated them as such, and other courts have attempted to enter orders in the form prescribed in child protective services actions.[3] When the remedy applied by the court comes out of a protective services action, it normally requires that the state (or some designated private agency) take custody of the allegedly

3. For a interesting and well supported account of the range of activities–legal and illegal—through which a pregnant woman can harm her fetus, see Reinesto v. Superior Court, 894 P.2d 733, 736–37 (Ariz.App.1995).

4. See e.g., People v. Morabito, 580 N.Y.S.2d 843 (N.Y.City Ct.1992); Reinesto v. Superior Court, 894 P.2d 733, 736–37 (Ariz. App.1995); Appeal in Pima County Juvenile Severance Action No. S, 905 P.2d 555 (Ariz. App.1995).

5. See In re Ruiz, 500 N.E.2d 935 (Ohio Com.Pl.1986); see also Matter Concerning Baby X, 293 N.W.2d 736 (Mich.App.1980).

6. See e.g., Raleigh Fitkin–Paul Morgan Memorial Hospital v. Anderson, 201 A.2d 537

(N.J.1964); Jefferson v. Griffin Spalding County Hospital Authority, 274 S.E.2d 457 (Ga. 1981).

§ 19–4

1. See e.g., Bonte v. Bonte, 616 A.2d 464 (N.H.1992).

2. See e.g., In re A.C., 573 A.2d 1235 (D.C.App.1990); Jefferson v. Griffin Spalding County Hospital Authority, 274 S.E.2d 457 (Ga.1981).

3. See e.g., Matter of Stefanel Tyesha C., 556 N.Y.S.2d 280 (N.Y.App.Div.1990). See also In re Fetus Brown, 689 N.E.2d 397 (Ill.App. 1997) and In re Baby Boy Doe, 632 N.E.2d 326 (Ill.App.1994).

abused, neglected, or dependent child.[4] When the child is a fetus, as is alleged in actions involving potential fetal-maternal conflict, the normal form of the remedy, therefore, would require the state to take custody of the fetus. Of course, it is impossible to take custody of a fetus without taking custody of the pregnant woman in whom the fetus lives, and any order directed at the fetus in a child protective services case necessarily will require that the state also take custody of the pregnant woman. It is for this reason that the use of child protective services proceedings seems inappropriate in most potential fetal-maternal conflict cases.

There is one subgroup of potential fetal-maternal conflict cases in which the use of child protective services proceedings seems justified— when the pregnant woman is herself a minor. There is a high correlation between teenage drug and alcohol abuse and teenage pregnancy, just as there is a high correlation between those forms of substance abuse and high risk pregnancy. Arguably, the behavior of the pregnant girl which puts her own fetus at risk (whether through the use of alcohol or drugs, or other dangerous behavior) is evidence that she herself is neglected and, thus, subject to state intervention. In a proper child protective services proceeding, the state could take custody of the pregnant minor in order to provide her with protection and adequate supervision, and, thus, indirectly assure that she provides an adequate environment for her fetus. This would require the state to prove that the pregnant girl had been neglected, though, and even if the neglect of her fetus were evidence that she had not been adequately supervised by her parents, this evidence may not be sufficient, without other supporting evidence, to justify the state's assumption of custody.

2. *Tort Actions*

In all states children born alive can commence actions against those whose tortious conduct injured them *in utero*.[5] Further, some states have abrogated their doctrines of family immunity, which made it impossible for children to bring actions against members of their families whose tortious conduct had injured them.[6] Thus, in those states which no longer recognize the defense of family immunity, at least, a child may have an action against his mother for negligently failing to provide him with an adequate prenatal environment, provided that the common law recognizes a duty that runs from the pregnant woman to her fetus.[7]

---

4. Id.

5. W. Page Keeton et al., Prosser and Keeton on the Law of Torts, 5th Ed., 368 (1984).

6. W. Page Keeton et al., Prosser and Keeton on the Law of Torts, 5th Ed., 907 (1984).

7. See e.g., Grodin v. Grodin, 301 N.W.2d 869 (Mich.App.1980); Bonte v. Bonte, 616 A.2d 464 (N.H.1992) (infant born with brain damage brought negligence suit against mother for failing to take reasonable care in crossing street and not using crosswalk. Mother was struck and infant was born prematurely with brain damage. New Hampshire Supreme Court held that child born disabled has cause of action against mother for mother's negligence that caused injury to child in utero). But see Stallman v. Youngquist, 126 Ill.Dec. 60, 531 N.E.2d 355 (Ill.1988) (Illinois Supreme Court reversed Court of Appeals decision allowing infant to bring suit against mother for prenatal injury incurred in automobile accident, holding that mother is not liable for negligent infliction of prenatal injury) and Chenault v. Huie, 989 S.W.2d 474 (Tex.App.1999)(Texas appellate court finds that a child may not bring a tort action against mother for injury negligently caused by the mother while she was pregnant). See, generally, Ron Beal, "Can I Sue Mommy?" An Analysis of a Woman's Tort Liability for Prenatal Injuries to her Child Born Alive, 21 San Diego L. Rev. 325 (1984) and Joseph Badger, Stallman v. Youngquist, "No, You Can't Sue Mommy in Illinois," 11 N. Ill. U. L. Rev 409 (1991).

The existence of such a duty is undercut by the pregnant woman's legally protected option of abortion before the fetus becomes viable; it makes little sense to say that a pregnant woman has a legal duty to preserve the health of a fetus she has the legal right to abort. On the other hand, the virtual prohibition on abortion during the last trimester in some states suggests that the law is more likely to recognize a duty that runs from the mother to her fetus after the fetus is viable. Further, applying the analysis suggested above, the duty of the mother to the fetus may attach as soon as the pregnant woman decides that she will bear the child, whether that decision occurs before or after viability. If the common law recognizes that such a duty does indeed attach, tort liability may follow.

Children bring actions against their parents to obtain payment from the insurers that have written personal liability, homeowner's, general umbrella, or other policies of broad coverage for their parents.[8] Indeed, such actions commonly are commenced by the parents on the child's behalf. It is to avoid exactly this kind of potential collusion that states previously applied doctrines of family immunity. The judicial abrogation of that defense amounts to a determination that the value of the risk spreading function of insurance (which cannot be served if plaintiffs are kept out of court by arbitrary defenses like that of family immunity) outweighs the adverse consequences of such potentially collusive lawsuits.[9]

c. Criminal Remedies

Since the late 1980s, there have been a raft of criminal prosecutions against pregnant women for conduct arising out of the pregnancy. Most of these actions have been commenced against pregnant women who use drugs and, thus, "deliver" or "provide" these drugs to their fetuses during the course of their pregnancy in violation of criminal statutes designed to be enforced against drug pushers. Some prosecutors have argued, usually unsuccessfully, that a fetus is a "person" for purposes of these statutes.[10] In one case the Florida Supreme Court reversed a lower court finding that after the child left the womb, but before the umbilical cord was cut, the child was a person who could be delivered drugs through the cord in violation of the criminal law.[11]

There are other potential criminal actions against women who make medical or lifestyle decisions that put their fetuses at risk, although they remain largely untried. States do impose criminal penalties on parents who abuse or neglect their children, and, to the extent that a fetus may be a person for purposes of such statutes, a pregnant woman will have committed

---

8. In one New Hampshire case, for example, a child injured in utero collected $100,000 from a motorist's insurer and $850,000 from the child's mother's uninsured/underinsured motorist insurer. The child also sought $300,000 more from the mother's homeowner's insurer (and more from the mother's employer, as well as the lessee of the premises where she worked). Bonte v. American Global Insurance Company, 618 A.2d 825 (N.H.1992).

9. See Keeton, supra note 5, at 905.

10. See e.g., People v. Hardy, 469 N.W.2d 50 (Mich.App.1991). For a general criticism of the use of the criminal law in this way, see Margaret P. Spencer, Prosecutorial Immunity: The Response to Prenatal Drug Use, 25 Conn. L.Rev. 393 (1993); Lisa Ikemoto, The Code of Perfect Pregnancy: At the Intersection of the Ideology of Motherhood, the Practice of Defaulting to Science, and the Intervention Mindset of Law, 53 Ohio St.L. 1205 (1992).

11. Johnson v. Florida, 602 So.2d 1288 (Fla.1992), reversing 578 So.2d 419 (Fla.App. 1991).

a criminal offense if she abuses or neglects her fetus. Thus, because forcing a child to consume drugs or alcohol could constitute abuse, providing drugs or alcohol to a fetus may as well.[12] Similarly, because the failure to obtain adequate medical care itself constitutes neglect, a pregnant woman who fails to consent to a caesarean section or a blood transfusion when necessary to preserve the life or health of the fetus may be liable in the criminal law. Of course, such an interpretation of the criminal law could turn any pregnant woman who did not follow all of her doctor's advice, and thus neglected some element of her fetus's health, into a criminal. Indeed, if the fetus were to die, the pregnant woman could be liable for some form of homicide.

d. Non–criminal Commitment

Finally, remedies of civil commitment may be available under some state statutes to protect fetuses from abuse by mentally incapacitated, drug abusing, or alcoholic pregnant women. The availability of commitment and the commitment process for each of these conditions varies from state to state. As a general matter state statutes, read consistently with Constitutional limitations, require that the person committed be found to be a danger to herself or others, that the commitment be for the treatment of the designated condition, and that every element necessary for commitment be proven by "clear and convincing evidence," the highest standard applied in civil cases.[13] No court has addressed the question of whether a fetus could be an "other" whose danger could subject the pregnant woman to commitment. In any case, the use of civil commitment processes against pregnant women who pose a risk to their fetuses possesses most of the difficulties of the application of the slightly harsher criminal law, and it is unlikely to be undertaken frequently.

§ 19–5. Employment Decisionmaking by a Pregnant Woman: Employer Fetal Protection Policies

One's employment may affect one's offspring in many ways. Although workplace exposure to toxic chemicals can have an affect on the offspring of both men and women at the workplace, many employers presume that some toxic chemicals are more likely to have an affect on a child if the child is regularly exposed to the chemicals *in utero* than if the child's father is exposed to them before conception. For altruistic reasons—to protect the offspring of their employees—and for less altruistic reasons—to avoid tort liability and adverse publicity and to minimize the cost of employer paid health insurance—some employers used to promulgate "fetal protection" policies which prohibited fertile women from filling certain jobs at some work sites. In 1991 in *Automobile Workers v. Johnson Controls*,[1] the United States Supreme Court found that such policies violate Title VII of the Civil Rights Act of 1964 and the Pregnancy Discrimination Act, and thus all such policies promulgated by employers covered by those statutes are now illegal and unenforceable. In addition, at least one state has found such policies to be illegal as a matter of state law.[2]

12. For an unsuccessful attempt at such a prosecution, see Reinesto v. Superior Court, 894 P.2d 733 (Ariz.App.1995).

13. Addington v. Texas, 441 U.S. 418, 99 S.Ct. 1804, 60 L.Ed.2d 323 (1979).

§ 19–5

1. 499 U.S. 187, 111 S.Ct. 1196, 113 L.Ed.2d 158 (1991).

2. Johnson Controls, Inc. v. California Fair Employment and Housing Commission, 267 Cal.Rptr. 158 (Cal.App.1990).

In *Johnson Controls*, the Supreme Court found that the employer's policy, which excluded fertile women but not fertile men from certain jobs in a battery manufacturing plant with high lead levels, discriminated on the basis of sex. The policy was discriminatory on its face, and the fact that it discriminated only against fertile women (and not against all women) was irrelevant to the Court's Civil Rights Act analysis.[3] If there had been any question about the propriety of such discrimination under the Civil Rights Act, the Court pointed out that the uncertainty was removed by the Pregnancy Discrimination Act, which explicitly includes discrimination "because of or on the basis of pregnancy, childbirth, or related medical conditions" as discrimination "on the basis of sex" under Title VII.[4]

The more difficult question for the Court was whether such discrimination was permitted under the Civil Rights Act because sex was a "bona fide occupational qualification reasonably necessary to the normal operation of that particular business or enterprise."[5] The Court refused to change the well established case law that this exception applies only "to instances in which sex or pregnancy actually interferes with the employee's ability to perform the job."[6] Because "[f]ertile women * * * participate in the manufacture of batteries as efficiently as anyone else,"[7] the defense was unavailable to the employer.

3. Automobile Workers v. Johnson Controls, Inc., 499 U.S. 187, 197, 111 S.Ct. 1196, 1203, 113 L.Ed.2d 158 (1991).

4. Id. at 198, 111 S.Ct. at 1203.

5. Id. at 200, 111 S.Ct. at 1204.

6. Id. at 204, 111 S.Ct. at 1206.

7. Id. at 206, 111 S.Ct. at 1207.

Chapter 20

ASSISTED REPRODUCTION

Table of Sections

Research References

    Am Jur 2d, Prenatal Injuries; Wrongful Life, Birth, or Conception §§ 24, 25
    ALR Index: Artificial Insemination; Reproduction; Reproductive Organs
    ALR Digest: Physicians and Surgeons § 29.6
    Am Jur Legal Forms 2d, Physicians and Surgeons §§ 202:81–202:110

§ 20–1. Introduction

We are both blessed and cursed to live in an era of unprecedented options in the means of conceiving a child; blessed with a dazzling new array of reproductive technology and cursed by the extraordinarily complex relationships and conflicts that result. Reproductive technologies now offer previously unimagined means of creating both traditional and nontraditional families in response to rising infertility, delayed child-bearing, and non nuclear family choices.

However, there are risks. Not only the physical and emotional risks of the medical procedures, but economic and legal risks which arise directly from the still developing technologies and uncertain legal relationships of the various parties to any collaborative reproductive process. Where reproduction was once an extremely private event with potential parenting conflicts limited to those between the biological parents, the process of assisted reproduction now may include a number of persons, each of whom may later wish to establish some formal and legally recognized relationship with the child, forcing a complete redefinition of "parenthood." The once biological definition of parenthood first evolved legally to recognize nurturing parents as sometimes having superior legal rights over mere biology. Now, when a child may have four or five potential "parents," with differing basis for their claims, the law must consider and resolve disputes as to which persons are the "lawful" parents with rights and obligations.

From time immemorial, fertility and reproduction have been primal concerns of human beings. Fertility gods were vital to ancient civilizations, and rites imploring higher powers to bless crops and bring rain and children are still practiced in many societies. Historically, fertility has not only been associated with survival, but has also served as a measure of human worth. A parent with many sons, for example, is held in high esteem in many cultures, while a childless woman may be looked upon as cursed or worthless. Whether these perspectives are vestiges of rural eras when survival depended upon large families or are rooted in ancient systems of inheritance and land ownership, their current impact on child-bearing decisions of women world-wide is still powerful.

Even in the United States, where women enjoy a degree of choice about child-bearing rivaled in few areas of the world, child-bearing issues still dominate many women's lives. Infertility is a significant problem for both women and men in the United States,[1] and its increase over recent years may be the result of birth control methods such as the Dalkon Shield IUD, congenital problems, infections, or, possibly, environmental exposures. Finally, some women who have delayed child-bearing for economic reasons or to establish careers are discovering the negative impact of age on their ability to conceive. Many potential parents are simultaneously discovering that their health insurance refuses coverage on infertility procedures such as assisted reproduction and that the cost is beyond their means, raising societal issues of access to such procedures and whether only those with vast financial resources will have meaningful access to remedy their infertility problems[2].

Complex issues of multiple legal parenthood are no longer speculative, and are now painfully real, as dramatically reflected in the recent California case of *In re Marriage of Buzzanca*[3]. In *Buzzanca*, young Jaycee was born with five potential "parents." She is the genetic child of an anonymous egg donor and an anonymous sperm donor, and her gestational mother was a surrogate for her two intended parents. When the intended father filed for a divorce shortly before Jaycee's birth, he stated that there were "no children born of the marriage." His ongoing claim in the litigation that followed was essentially that he had no legal obligation of child support since he was not biologically related to Jaycee. The trial court concluded that the child was "a legal orphan" despite the affirmative acts of five persons involved in bringing her into the world. On appeal, that holding was reversed on the rational that the husband had intended to create and parent a child. The appellate court framed its legal analysis around the undisputed fact that Jaycee would never

§ 20–1

1. See Office of Technology Assessment, 100th Cong., 2d. Sess., Infertility: Medical & Social Choices (Comm. Print 1988). Infertility affects over eight percent of Americans during their childbearing years, and the chances of having infertility problems increase with age. Over a quarter of women between the ages of thirty-five and forty-four may suffer from problems with fertility. Id. See also Lori Andrews and Lisa Douglass, Alternative Reproduction, 65 S.Cal.L.Rev. 623, 626 (1991).

2. For on going summary, see Edward L. Raymond, Jr., Annotation, Coverage of Artificial Insemination Procedures Or Other Infertility Treatments By Health, Sickness Or Hospitalization Insurance, 80 A.L.R.4th 1058 (1990).

3. 72 Cal.Rptr.2d 280 (App. 1998).

have been born but for the intended parents' agreement to have a fertilized egg implanted in a surrogate. His intent, as reflected in the agreement with the surrogate, and his affirmative act of proceeding were conclusive "parenthood" under the common law doctrine of estoppel. The court concluded that by his consent to the medical procedures that resulted in the birth of Jaycee, the intended father was later estopped from taking a position denying legal responsibility for his actions.

This case epitomizes not only double donor participation, but use of a surrogate as well and the painful aftermath that results when circumstances change by divorce. As assisted reproduction becomes ever more complex and widely utilized, because the process itself can require years of intrusive infertility treatments, the prolonged stress, medication and financial drain can surely contribute to the breakdown of a marriage. The *Buzzanca* divorce, rather than being an unusual legal turn, may well signal an increasing need for contingency agreements because the infertility treatment context may carry a higher then normal risk of divorce.

Although many legal issues have yet to be resolved, it is clear that advances in reproductive technology have irreversibly altered the field of child-bearing. As drafters of the Uniform Status of Children of Assisted Conception Act[4] observe, "Medical technology has produced many miracles that have been feared and rejected at first * * * [but] advances developed by human ingenuity are here to stay. Once out, the genie never returns to the bottle. Our responsibility is to acknowledge the reality of these forces, and with wisdom and prudence, order and design their use for the good of humanity."[5] Not only has the genie not returned to the bottle, but rapidly expanding international access to the internet is now making available to potential parents a vast network of reproductive technology information and links to specific facilities, making rapid growth of the technology most likely.

§ 20–2. Redefining Family and Parenthood

At the heart of the legal debate over the utilization of assisted conception technology lies a fundamental question: What constitutes a family? As new family structures emerge that bear little resemblance to the stereotypical nuclear family, societal pressures build for the law to recognize and protect these less traditional family relationships. Many states now provide, for example, for stepparent visitation in the event of a divorce, recognizing that although no biological relationship exists, a parenting relationship may warrant legal recognition.[1] Grandparents are also increasingly granted visitation rights under some state statutes, and some case law recognizes the right of same gender parents to visitation once their non-legal union dissolves, on a theory of best interests of the child. Taking an even more significant step, some jurisdictions and employers are also beginning to recognize same-gender

---

4. 9B U.L.A. 135 (1993 Supp.).

5. Robert Robinson & Paul Kurtz, Uniform Status of Children of Assisted Conception Act: A View from the Drafting Committee, 13 Nova L. Rev. 491 (1989).

§ 20–2

1. See e.g., Minn. Stat. Ann. § 6257.022 (visitation permitted when child has lived with

the one seeking visitation for more than two years). See generally John Gregory, Peter Swisher and Sheryl Scheible, Understanding Family Law, § 10.05[d] (1993); see also, ABA Family Law Section Committee Draft, Proposed Model Assisted Reproductive Technologies Act (1999), § 1.07.

partnerships, in lieu of marriages, for purposes such as extending spousal health and other benefits.[2]

Just as the smaller nuclear family gradually replaced the traditional extended family of past generations in response to lifestyle changes, the evolution of the family continues. As increasing numbers of Americans become single parents, live in same-gender partnerships, or assemble family units of children from various marriages, the stereotypical nuclear family is steadily vanishing. The trend is both voluntary and involuntary. While some women, for example, choose to be single parents, others find themselves reluctantly in that role, following a death, divorce, or abandonment. While courts and legislatures have developed processes to accommodate the break-up of nuclear families, e.g., custody and child support guidelines, they are just beginning to address the complex issues raised by new family forms. These include various constitutional issues, such as right to privacy and right to make child-bearing decisions, interpretation of existing statutes involving related matters, and public policies regarding termination of parental rights and the role of financial compensation in assisted conception.

As the definition of family has expanded to include greater diversity, the legal issue of who is a child's parent first became a battlefield between those who believe that biology should be completely determinative and those who believe that parenting is defined by nurturing, not biology.[3] Recently, the issue of biological or genetic relation has taken on a new complexity as many children born of assisted conception have multiple biological parents. This increasing uncertainty regarding the appropriate role of biology in defining parenthood casts an uncertain shadow over persons considering assisted conception involving donors or surrogates in states without clear guidelines. In artificial insemination, the biological father may be a sperm donor or a willing friend; in in vitro fertilization, a woman may be receiving both donated sperm and a donated egg; of course, in surrogacy, the gestational mother is often, although not always, the biological mother. As reproductive technology has increased in developing sophisticated means of conception, the need for legal resolution of issues surrounding parentage has escalated.[4]

In recent years, the debate over recognition of parental rights in the assisted conception context has been constantly in the news, from the rights of sperm donors, to the custody or disposition of frozen embryos, and the implications of surrogacy agreements. Virtually the entire nation followed the bitter surrogacy custody fight in New Jersey between Baby M's biological father (and his wife) and Baby M's surrogate/biological mother.[5] In that case, the fact that the surrogate mother was also the biological mother was given great weight by the court, and it appeared to be determinative in allowing the

---

2. As this book went to press, the United States Supreme Court was considering whether state grandparent visitation statutes violated the constitutional rights of parents. Troxel v. Granville, U.S.S.Ct., No. 99–138 (1999–2000 term), reviewing In re Custody of Smith, 969 P.2d 21 (Wash.1998). With regard to judicial extension of benefits to domestic partners, see Baker v. Vermont, 744 A.2d 864 (Vt. 1999). See also Understanding Family Law, supra note 1, § 1.02[b] (1993).

3. For an exhaustive review of the issues involved in this debate, see John Hill, What Does It Mean To Be A "Parent"? The Claims Of Biology As The Basis For Parental Rights, 66 N.Y.U. L. Rev. 353 (1991).

4. See e.g., ABA Family Law Section Committee Draft, Proposed Model Assisted Reproductive Technologies Act (1999).

5. In the Matter of Baby M, 537 A.2d 1227 (N.J.1988).

mother visitation rights (after finding, under the "best interests of the child" standard, that the biological father and his wife should have custody). This is in sharp contrast to the recent denial, by a California court, of a surrogate mother's petition for parental rights where she was not biologically related to the child she carried.[6]

The United States Supreme Court has addressed the issue of biological versus nurturing parenthood on several occasions, usually in cases where an unwed father sought to establish parental rights. However, no case of multiple biological claims has yet reached the Court. In 1989, in *Michael H. v. Gerald D.*, a divided Court upheld the constitutionality of a century old California law which rejected an apparent biological father's attempt to establish his paternity because the child was conceived while the mother was married to another man with whom she shared a household.[7]

This opinion is revealing in its deference to the marital relationship over biology and in the divergent views held by various justices. Writing a plurality opinion, Justice Scalia noted that "California law, like nature itself, makes no provision for dual fatherhood." He concluded that since "inquiries into the paternity of the child would be destructive of family integrity and privacy," the state was justified in refusing to allow the apparent biological father to prove his paternity.[8] Ignoring the fact that the mother had lived off and on with the man who fathered her child outside of her marriage (and whom the child called Daddy), the Court waxed eloquent about the sanctity that should be accorded the married couple's rocky relationship.

In dissent, three Justices argued that many children these days have dual fathers because they often live primarily with a stepfather and continue a relationship with their biological father.[9] Moreover, the dissenters argued that enduring "family" relationships which develop in unconventional settings may be entitled to constitutional protection. The dissenters pointed out that due to technological advances, paternity determinations no longer involve unacceptably intrusive investigations into marital practices, but are virtually always resolved by blood testing. Characterizing the plurality's view as an out of touch "rhapsody on the 'unitary family,' "[10] the dissenters argued that the constitutional analysis should have focused on the relationship sought to be preserved between biological father and child rather than the marital relationship.

Following the early legal debates surrounding biology versus nurturing, the relevant factual difficulties increased dramatically. With virtually no specific legal response during the early years from legislatures, the perception of a gap and need for regulation resulted in numerous uniform and model proposals from professional organizations.

In 1974, when the only assisted reproduction procedure widely used was artificial insemination, the Uniform Parentage Act was developed and it has now been fairly widely adopted. This Act clarifies paternity under the specific circumstances of artificial insemination. The Act is now in the process of

6. Johnson v. Calvert, 19 Cal.Rptr.2d 494, 851 P.2d 776 (Cal.1993).

7. 491 U.S. 110, 109 S.Ct. 2333, 105 L.Ed.2d 91 (1989).

8. Id. at 118.

9. Justices Brennan, Marshall, and Blackmun. Id. at 136.

10. Id. at 145.

being revised and it is uncertain whether it will continue to contain assisted conception provisions. In 1989, the Uniform Status of Children of Assisted Conception Act was drafted, providing even more detailed guidelines. Each of these statutes denies some elements of biology as the legally determinative criteria of parenthood, and the acts suggest a general trend in the law recognizing that the contributors of the genetic material for a child are not the only ones with legitimate claims to a formal parenting relationship with that child; indeed, intent is emerging as the primary analysis for determining legal parenthood.

In 1978, in vitro fertilization became a successful reality, triggering excitement and fear as the technology became more and more effective. As in vitro fertilization became widely used, it in turn generated a second generation of related procedures and possibilities, from pre-implantation genetic screening and gender selection to the freezing of pre-embryos for future implantation. For the first time, the possibility of assisted conception outside of the intended mother's womb became a reality, generating renewed interest in surrogacy.

As reproductive technology has matured into a very sophisticated medical field, legal aspects have lagged behind, forcing many courts to grapple with complex issues of parental rights and obligations with no legal guidance other than general principles of family law such as "best interests of the child," common law estoppel principles, contract law, proposals from professional organizations, proposed uniform and model acts, and a plethora of commentary in journals and legal seminars. For example, the American Bar Association is developing a Model Assisted Reproductive Technologies Act which should be available in the near future and the National Conference of Commissioners on Uniform State Laws is in the process of rewriting the Uniform Parentage Act. The questions are fascinating and the stakes high. As new reproductive technologies are appearing faster than legal ethics or legislatures can respond, what was once science fiction has rapidly become commonplace, but the legal response is still emerging.

§ 20-3. Artificial Insemination

Artificial insemination is the placement of semen in the vagina or cervical canal by means other than a penis. The sperm source produces the semen through masturbation and ejaculation, which is then put into a syringe and injected directly into the woman who intends to become pregnant. This process using fresh semen need not be a medical procedure; it can be done successfully at home by anyone who understands the underlying biological principles. Ideally, the insemination is done at about the time of ovulation, a time that can be determined with increasing accuracy through home ovulation prediction tests. Artificial insemination is typically used when the woman's tubes and uterus are fine, but either her partner has fertility problems, or she is proceeding without a partner.

Medically performed artificial insemination now generally employs frozen semen rather than fresh semen. Donors may be drawn from a variety of sources, and generally potential donors to sperm banks are asked to provide basic family medical information to screen out transmittable infections or genetic problems. Although freezing semen permits subsequent tests upon the donor to determine the presence of any latent contaminant, such as HIV, the freezing process is medically difficult and thus relatively expensive. The semen is mixed with a preservative before it is frozen, and it must be carefully thawed before it is used. Once the semen is frozen, however, it is unlikely to undergo substantial deterioration; one estimate is that the risk of genetic mutation will double if the semen is kept frozen for 5,000 years. In 1990, a Seattle man successfully inseminated his wife with semen he deposited in a New York sperm bank fourteen years earlier. The man, who became sterile after his deposit, paid $50 a year to keep his deposit on ice.[1]

Statistics vary depending on source; however, there is no doubt that there are now a very large number of births utilizing artificial insemination by unrelated donors at medical clinics each year in the United States (and an undetermined number who are inseminated at home). Hundreds of doctors throughout the country provide the service to thousands of patients each year, with the cost varying widely. In many large urban areas, sperm banks provide listings of sperm donors with brief descriptions to aid in selection, and many will ship orders (on dry ice) to women or physicians outside their immediate area. In addition, specialized information is now widely available on the internet as to providers.

Although at one time artificial insemination was considered unnatural, scandalous, and some said it constituted adultery, as reproductive technology has advanced, artificial insemination has become the least legally and morally controversial of assisted conception procedures. The now relatively long period of use of artificial insemination makes it most likely to be addressed by state statutes and case law.[2]

The most frequently litigated issue in the absence of statutory guidelines is who should be recognized as the legal father of the child.[3] If the woman is married and uses her husband's sperm, no issues of paternity are raised by the procedure, since the biological parents are the only potential parents of any child that is conceived. On the other hand, when a child is born of a married woman through insemination with the sperm of a donor who is not the husband, the donor is the biological father, while the husband has no genetic link to the child. The Uniform Parentage Act of 1974 provides that when donor insemination is done under the supervision of a licensed physician with the husband's written consent, the husband is treated in law as if he were the natural father of the child conceived.[4] Some states have modified this provision to eliminate the requirement that the insemination be done by a physician.[5] Given the variety of conditions required to make the provisions

§ 20-3

1. The long life of frozen semen raises other issues that are yet to be litigated. What is the family relationship of a deceased donor to a child born of his sperm, for example? While it is not impossible for a naturally procreated child to be born following the death of his father, of course, the development of cryogenic technology allows that child to be born years, or even centuries, after the death of the sperm donor. At least two jurisdictions, France and California, have determined that posthumous insemination per se does not violate public policy. For a discussion of the French case, Parpalaix v. CECOS, see I. Kennedy and A.

Grubb, Principles of Medical Law (1998). For a discussion of the California case, see Hecht v. Superior Court, 20 Cal.Rptr.2d 275 (Cal.App. 1993).

2. See generally, Michael Yaworsky, Annotation, Rights And Obligations From Human Artificial Insemination, 83 A.L.R.4th 295 (1991).

3. Id.

4. 9B U.L.A. 3 (1993 Supp.).

5. See Robert Robinson and Paul Kurtz, Uniform Status of Children of Assisted Conception Act: A View From the Drafting Committee, 13 Nova L. Rev. 491, 498 (1989).

of the Uniform Parentage Act applicable, a great number of women inseminated every year are not covered by the Act either because they did not do the insemination through a physician, they are not married, or they live in a state that has not adopted that provision of the Uniform Parentage Act.

The Uniform Status of Children of Assisted Conception Act,[6] twelve years after introduction, has been adopted in only three jurisdictions. The Act substantially resolves most legal paternity issues raised by artificial insemination.[7] The Act reflects a broader presumption that a husband is the legal father of a child born to his wife by assisted conception than does the Uniform Parentage Act. The Uniform Status of Children of Assisted Conception Act not only establishes a rebuttable presumption of consent on the part of the husband, but it also does not require supervision by a licensed physician. The Act further specifies that a sperm donor is not the legal father, at least by virtue of the donation alone, when the donor and woman to be inseminated are not married to each other.[8] This effectively resolves an issue previously addressed only by common law.

In jurisdictions which have not adopted either the Uniform Parentage Act or the Uniform Status of Children of Assisted Conception Act, and where a situation is not otherwise covered by statute law, common law and public policy will govern the relative parental rights in artificial inseminations by donor. Early case law should be approached with caution, however, because first impression cases heard when assisted reproduction was new are riddled with outdated declarations of inseminations as adultery and automatic deference to the principle of biology as controlling. Given the rapid changes in both social acceptance of assisted conception and legal analysis of the issues, early case law in this area is not necessarily persuasive any more. Some early courts considering the issue of the parental rights of the sperm donor, for example, treated the sperm donor as the legal father with all of the attendant rights and obligations, while other courts have held to the contrary.[9]

Recent case law appears to be moving toward integrating the principles articulated in the uniform acts into the common law even where the uniform acts have not yet been adopted. In 1991, for example, a husband argued that he should not be liable for child support because he failed to give written consent to his wife's artificial insemination, as required by statute, and therefore he was not legally the father of the child. The Texas appellate court upheld the trial court's finding of ratification where the husband had given oral consent to the donor insemination, participated in the process, acknowledged the child and held him out as his son.[10] This holding is consistent with the Uniform Status of Children of Assisted Conception Act and other recent opinions which all favor a presumption of consent by husbands to donor insemination of their wives.[11]

6. 9B U.L.A. 135 (1993 Supp.).

7. The Comment to Section 1 of the Act specifies that the definition of "assisted conception" includes artificial insemination.

8. 9B U.L.A. 135, Section 4(a) (1993 Supp.).

9. Compare Gursky v. Gursky, 242 N.Y.S.2d 406 (N.Y.Sup.1963) (child born of artificial insemination by donor is illegitimate) with In re Adoption of Anonymous, 345 N.Y.S.2d 430 (N.Y.Sur.1973); See also, ABA Family Law Section Committee Draft, Proposed Model Assisted Reproductive Technologies Act (1999), § 1.075 and § 1.08.

10. K.B. v. N.B., 811 S.W.2d 634 (Tex.App. 1991).

11. See e.g., In re Marriage of Adams, 124 Ill.Dec. 184, 528 N.E.2d 1075 (Ill.App.1988), reversed on other grounds 141 Ill.Dec. 448, 551

A considerable number of single women, after recognizing the simplicity of artificial insemination procedures, have entered into formal or informal agreements with friends to act as sperm donors and have successfully conceived children. Since few of these agreements have resulted in litigation over parental rights, it can only be assumed that in the vast majority of cases the issue is generally resolved to the satisfaction of the two biological parents. Although using a known donor carries the risk that the donor may assert his own parental rights, some single women welcome the acknowledgement of paternity, and see it as beneficial for the child. A married woman, in contrast, may see the potential assertion of paternity as a threat, although some marital partners have jointly selected a known donor. Despite the risks, the advantages of a known donor are readily apparent: the woman or potential parents can select someone with desired genetic qualities, and health related information presumably would be more easily available from a known donor.

The use of an anonymous donor by either a single or married woman raises other legal issues. For example, the degree of preinsemination health screening of anonymous donors may vary depending on whether the mother uses a sperm bank or a private doctor's donors. Suits have been brought against physicians for using semen in artificial insemination that was later discovered to carry the HIV virus.[12] Other suits have arisen over the erroneous provision of the wrong person's semen (such as providing a wife with semen from a person other than that of her husband, who had preserved semen prior to becoming infertile).[13] There is still considerable legal uncertainty over issues such as the appropriate standard of care that sperm banks and physicians should meet, although the American Fertility Society and the American Association of Tissue Banks are attempting to set standards for sperm bank operation and donor criteria.[14]

In addition to health screening issues, the question of who should have access to artificial insemination remains a difficult one. Due to the considerable expense involved in safely screening and freezing semen, the cost of the semen is beyond the reach of many women who would otherwise use the procedure. This problem is compounded by the fact that many health insurance policies have excluded fertility procedures from coverage.[15] Many physicians are also imposing their own personal screening criteria to deny patients access to donors. Marital status, sexual orientation, evidence of drug or

N.E.2d 635 (Ill.1990). For an analysis of a sperm donor's constitutional rights to maintain a relationship with the child when the woman promised she would permit such a relationship, see McIntyre v. Crouch, 780 P.2d 239 (Or.App.1989), affirmed 784 P.2d 1100 (Or. 1989).

12. Brown v. Shapiro, 472 N.W.2d 247 (Wis.App.1991).

13. See e.g., Creed v. United Hospital, 600 N.Y.S.2d 151 (N.Y.App.Div.1993).

14. Sally Squires, Ensuring Safe Artificial Insemination, Washington Post, Feb. 11, 1992, at Z13. In any case involving potential liability of clinics or semen donors, these organizations should be consulted to obtain current recommended guidelines. See also ABA Proposed Model Artificial Reproductive Technologies Act

§ 1.04 and § 1.05 (1999), on issues of confidentiality and disclosure respectively.

15. Most companies now exclude fertility procedures explicitly, although historically some companies denied coverage under many circumstances on the grounds that the infertility treatment provided in those cases was "experimental". See e.g., Reilly v. Blue Cross and Blue Shield United of Wisconsin, 846 F.2d 416 (7th Cir.1988). See also Annotation, Coverage of Artificial Insemination or Other Infertility Treatments by Health, Sickness or Hospitalization Insurance, 80 A.L.R. 4th 1059; See ABA Family Law Section Committee Draft, Proposed Model Assisted Reproductive Technologies Act (1999), § 1.10.

alcohol abuse, HIV status, and welfare status are among the attributes considered by physicians in determining whether to provide insemination. Although states have not attempted to address this issue directly, such restrictions raise civil rights issues that cannot be lightly dismissed. To the extent that a medical facility providing insemination is covered by local, state, or federal civil rights statutes that prohibit discrimination on the basis of race, ethnicity, marital status, or sexual orientation, for example, that facility cannot apply criteria that directly or effectively discriminate on those grounds in determining eligibility for clinic services. Discrimination on these grounds may also pose constitutional questions in appropriate cases.

§ 20–4. In Vitro Fertilization Related Procedures

In 1978, a quiet stirring in a petri dish in England sent ripples around the world, as science fiction became reality. First came the amazement, as Louise Brown was conceived outside the human body and then returned to her mother's womb. Then came an extraordinary proliferation of in vitro fertilization (IVF) clinics throughout the world, followed by an outpouring of ethical, religious, and practical questions.

Despite trepidation on the part of some physicians and attorneys, IVF has been eagerly embraced by the patients it seeks to serve. When the first IVF clinic opened in 1981, 3,000 people rushed to sign up, despite a reported success rate of only two percent, and by the mid-nineties there were more than 220 IVF programs in the United States alone.[1] The medical cost of these processes approaches or exceeds $10,000 per ovulation cycle in most jurisdictions, with multiple cycles needed for many women. While many infertile couples are thus priced out of in vitro fertilization, it may be the only process available to women whose fallopian tubes cannot accommodate the fertilization process and to others with determined or undetermined causes of infertility. Thousands of children have been born through these procedures.

In vitro (literally, "in glass") fertilization is a highly technical medical intervention. Unlike artificial insemination, it cannot be performed at home. In the normal in vitro case, an ovum that is ready to be released from the ovary is identified through laparoscopy or ultrasound and removed from the ovary by surgery or, more commonly, by a nonsurgical procedure. The ovum (or ova, there usually is an attempt to get more than one) is placed in a container with the appropriate amount of semen containing fertile sperm. The fertilized ovum is then placed in the woman's uterus, where it is permitted to implant and develop.[2]

In the United States clinics conducting in vitro fertilization programs try to remove several eggs so that many will be fertilized in vitro and more than one can be replaced in the uterus to attempt implantation. In many cases there is no fertilization or inadequate fertilization in vitro, and, thus, no return to the uterus. Even when fertilized ovum are placed in the uterus, there is a relatively high chance of miscarriage. The rate of miscarriage for in vitro fertilization pregnancies is about twice the rate of spontaneous miscar-

§ 20–4

1. A. Bonnicksen, In Vitro Fertilization: Building Policy From Laboratories to Legislatures, 23–24 (1989).

2. See Lori Andrews and Lisa Douglass, Alternative Reproduction, 65 So.Cal.L.Rev. 623 (1991), for a good brief discussion of the various medical alternatives.

riages in other pregnancies. While the "take home baby" rate varies widely by process, maternal age of ovum source, maternal age of womb, and other factors, in 1989, in vitro fertilization resulted in a pregnancy in eighteen percent of the cases, and it resulted in a live birth in fourteen percent.[3] Current statistics vary widely, but are generally higher as the technology has become more sophisticated. The perinatal (i.e., birth) and neonatal (i.e., newborn) mortality rates for in vitro fertilization babies are higher than for others, and the rate of caesarean section births is much higher for in vitro fertilization babies than for babies conceived in other ways.

Because the chances of success are substantially increased if several fertilized ova are returned to the uterus, and because of the high cost of repeating the procedure, women undergoing in vitro fertilization are generally given drugs to increase the number of ova that become ripe and ready for release and fertilization in one cycle. While this "superovulation" increases the chances of successful fertilization and implantation, inducing ovulation itself may have adverse side effects. In addition, the simultaneous placement of multiple fertilized ova results in a high rate of multiple births; one study found that almost one fourth of successful in vitro fertilization pregnancies resulted in multiple births.[4]

The development and now relatively common use of in vitro fertilization has given rise to several other related procedures and some variations on the original process. In gamete intrafallopian transfer (GIFT), the ova are collected just as they would be for in vitro fertilization, but both the ova and the semen containing fertile sperm are then injected into the fallopian tubes, where fertilization takes place. Zygote intrafallopian transfer (ZIFT) is described as "an intermediate procedure between GIFT and standard IVF."[5] If the problem is the inability of the sperm to penetrate the wall of the ovum, a physician may try Intracytoplasmic Sperm Injection (ICSI), in which a single sperm is injected into an ovum. If the problem arises because the ovum cannot break free of its "shell" and implant in the uterus, physicians can use an "assisted hatching" technique, AZH, and cut into the shell with a hard object, a laser, or an acid solution.

In addition, it is now possible to freeze ova either before or after fertilization. This permits evaluation of the genetic structure of the ova or preembryo before it is thawed and implanted. While the insertion of the fertilized ovum may be the most difficult portion of the procedure from a medical point of view, the removal of the ovum is the most difficult process from the point of view of the woman. Thus, removing extra ova and freezing them, either before or after they are fertilized, may save an additional retrieval process if the first insertion is unsuccessful. While cryopreservation of ova is a comparatively new technology, it is quite commonly employed with fertilized ova. About half of frozen embryos are capable of use upon thawing, although the long term medical consequences of freezing embryos remains unknown.

---

3. Id. at 644. This figure seems a bit more promising when one considers that the "success" rate for conjugal intercourse has been estimated to be about 20 to 25 percent per cycle.

4. Id. at 652.

5. Id. at 643, citing S. Silber et al., New Treatment for Infertility Due to Congenital Absence of Vas Deferens, 1987 Lancet 850.

There has been a remarkable lack of litigation involving IVF considering the initially controversial nature of the procedure and the large numbers of potential parents who have been through the process. That is not to say that the legal issues raised have not provoked commentary; a very large number of law review articles, for example, have appeared on the complex conflicts presented by parental disputes over the disposition of frozen preembryos.

IVF procedures generate many of the same issues raised by artificial insemination. In IVF, as in artificial insemination, where a married couple use their own egg and sperm to conceive a child, there are no issues as to legal parentage. The only legally significant issue for married couples undergoing IVF without donors is their relative authority regarding disposition of any frozen preembryos they create.

Far more complicated are situations where either an unmarried woman or a married couple use an outside egg source or sperm source, or both. Responding to the need for legal certainty regarding the parentage of children with various potential parents, the Uniform Status of Children of Assisted Conception Act[6] provides that the husband of a married woman is the legal father of any child born to his wife though assisted conception such as IVF.[7] The Act establishes a rebuttable presumption of consent by the husband; it provides that the husband is the legal father "unless within two years after learning of the child's birth he commences an action in which the mother and child are parties and in which it is determined that he did not consent to the assisted conception." Under the Act, in both the marital or non-marital context, a donor of either an egg or sperm has no parental rights,[8] and the woman giving birth to a child through assisted conception is declared the legal mother, with certain specified exceptions for surrogates.[9]

§ 20–5.　The Status of Frozen Preembryos

Due to both the physical and financial costs associated with the removal of eggs from a woman and the in vitro creation of a fertilized egg, it is most common for a physician to create more fertilized pre-embryos than will be used in one particular cycle of attempted implantation. As a result, an entire industry has developed that freezes and stores pre-embryos for future use. Increasing knowledge has enabled potential parents to store their reproductive genetic material (sperm or eggs) prior to cancer or other medical treatments that may render them infertile, or participate in sequential attempted implantation without repeating the difficult first stage. The ability of potential parents to now gestate children who are the genetic product of a deceased spouse or a divorced spouse is causing an understandable debate regarding who has the right to make decisions about disposition of the pre-embryos.[1]

Two states have addressed these issues in depth to date: Tennessee and New York. In 1992, *Davis v. Davis* was decided by the Tennessee Supreme Court. At issue was the relative rights of divorcing couples who disagree as to the disposition of frozen preembryos that they have created through IVF. In

---

6.　9B U.L.A. 122.

7.　Id., Section 3.

8.　Id., Section 4.

9.　Id., Section 2.

§ 20–5

1.　For proposed disposition provisions see, ABA Family Law Section Committee Draft, Proposed Model Assisted Reproductive Technologies Act (1999), § 1.06.

that case,[2] the trial court treated the parties' seven frozen preembryos as children, and awarded custody to the potential mother, Mary Sue Davis, because her intent to attempt implantation was in the preembryo's best interest. The Court of Appeals reversed, finding that the potential father, Junior Davis, had a constitutionally protected right not to beget a child where no pregnancy had yet occurred, and that the state had no compelling interest which could justify ordering implantation against the wishes of either potential parent.

Mary Sue Davis then appealed to the Tennessee Supreme Court, which affirmed the Court of Appeals but disagreed with its reasoning. It articulated a balancing test to be applied in such legal conflicts. As a preliminary matter, the court noted a significant change in the posture of the case: Mary Sue was no longer seeking control of the preembryos to attempt conception herself, but instead wished to donate them for implantation. Junior's position had also shifted; his prior uncertainty had by then cemented into an adamant refusal to become a father against his will.

The Tennessee Supreme Court began by considering the debate that occurred during trial over what the fertilized ovum should be called and noted the importance of that issue in avoiding erroneous analysis. After considering the testimony of various expert witnesses on the subject, the court concluded that "preembryo" rather than "embryo" was the accurate term.[3]

Turning to the issue of whether preembryos should be considered persons or property under the law, the court concluded that preembryos were not "persons" within the meaning of either state or federal law, and therefore were not entitled to independent legal rights. In so finding, the court rejected the trial court's "custody award" under the best interests of the child standard. The court also rejected the concept of preembryos as property, preferring instead to adopt a characterization offered by the American Fertility Society: preembryos are not persons, but because of their potential to become persons, they are entitled to special respect. Without discussing what the adoption of such a standard implied, the court characterized the progenitors' interests as "an interest in the nature of ownership, to the extent that they have decisionmaking authority concerning disposition of the preembryos."[4]

The Davis court ultimately affirmed the lower appellate court, and set forth the following sequential inquiry for resolution of such disputes: First, the court looks to see if the preferences of the parties as to disposition can be reconciled; if not, then the court will enforce any prior agreement as to disposition. If no prior agreement exists, then the relative interests of the parties must be weighed, with the party objecting to becoming a parent ordinarily being given greater weight, assuming that the party who wants to proceed has other options. Based upon this analysis, the court awarded

2. Davis v. Davis, 842 S.W.2d 588 (Tenn. 1992).

3. The court cited both the American Fertility Society's June 1990 report on Ethical Considerations of the New Reproductive Technologies and John Robertson, In the Beginning: The Legal Status of Early Embryos, 76 Va. L. Rev. 437 (1990), on the biologic differences between a preembryo and an embryo. See also John Robertson, Prior Agreements for Disposition of Frozen Embryos, 51 Ohio St. L.J. 407 (1990) and Mario Trespalacios, Comment, Frozen Embryos: Towards an Equitable Solution, 46 U. Miami L.Rev. 803 (1992).

4. Davis, 842 S.W.2d at 597.

dispositional control to the husband who had objected to becoming a father under the changed circumstances of divorce.

While the Tennessee Supreme Court determined that preembryos are neither persons nor property, that is not the only potential legal perspective. One state has enacted legislation specific to frozen preembryos: in Louisiana, the intentional destruction of a preembryo is prohibited, and disputes between parties are to be governed by a best interests of the preembryo standard.[5] In effect, Louisiana has chosen to treat preembryos as children rather than property. On the other hand, *York v. Jones*[6] involved a dispute between a fertility clinic and a married couple over whether the clinic would transfer a frozen preembryo to another clinic when the couple moved. The court treated the matter as one involving property of the couple which had been left for bailment with the clinic. This unexamined assumption that the preembryo was "property" is in sharp contrast to the *Davis v. Davis* trial court's assumption that the preembryos were something greater than that.[7]

Not long after *Davis*, the New York courts turned to similar issues in Kass v. Kass[8]. In 1995, the New York trial court heard a divorce dispute to determine disposition of five frozen pre-zygotes that were created by the parties through in vitro fertilization. The wife was awarded the pre-zygotes to attempt implantation on the rationale that a husband's procreative rights in the in vitro fertilization context terminate at the moment of conception, with the wife having ongoing discretion. The Appellate Division reversed after finding it was legal error to equate a pregnant woman's right to exercise control over the disposition of a nonviable fetus with her rights over a frozen pre-zygote. Instead, the court concluded that the intentions of the parties must be determined and carried out if possible. The court relied upon the intent of the parties as memorialized in their informed consent document with the in vitro fertilization clinic, which specified that in the event that the parties could not agree on disposition, the pre-zygotes would be retained by the clinic for research. Consequently, the court held that the former written expression of intent would govern the issue and the wife was denied "custody" of the pre-zygotes.

The Court of Appeals of New York then affirmed the Appellate Division, issuing a well reasoned opinion that returns to the heart of the issue: what was the mutual intention of the potential parents at the time they created the pre-zygotes, and what was their expressed intention for any contingency in which they could not agree? Where an unambiguous agreement exists that sets forth the parties' mutual intent, it will govern the difficult issues that arise when one intended parent wishes to proceed and the other is opposed to becoming a parent, at least when there are changed circumstances such as divorce.

The development of state statutes to give certainty to the issue of disposition of frozen pre-embryos has been extremely slow, perhaps due to the sensitivity of the issues involved. Only a few states have enacted statutes that

5. La. Stat. Ann.–Rev.St. 14:87.2.

6. 717 F.Supp. 421 (E.D.Va.1989).

7. Cf. Hecht v. Superior Court, 20 Cal. Rptr.2d 275 (Cal.App.1993) (finding that a decedent maintained a property interest in his cryogenically preserved sperm, and that the probate court could thus maintain jurisdiction over its distribution).

8. Kass v. Kass, 696 N.E.2d 174, 673 N.Y.S.2d 350 (N.Y.App.1998).

specifically set forth the state's unique perspective. In Louisiana, for example, a pre-zygote "must" be implanted, while Florida, in contrast, simply requires written agreements setting forth dispositional intent. Meanwhile, issues of pre-embryo disposition are being resolved by various approaches outside of the United States. Britain, the mother country of the first successful in vitro fertilization birth, in 1990 enacted the Human Fertilization and Embryology Act, which mandates that unclaimed abandoned pre-embryos must be destroyed within five years after creation unless there are instructions from the intended parents. Germany has outlawed the freezing of pre-embryos. Australia, in response to the well publicized death of an American couple in an airplane accident, leaving frozen embryos in an Australian clinic, enacted the Infertility Treatment Act of 1984, which also mandates destruction of pre-embryos after a period of time when there are no instructions from the donors. These embryos may be made available to other women if the donors consent.

In the United States, the American Medical Association[9] has proposed guidelines that allow the creators of the pre-embryos to use them, thaw them, permit research upon them, or donate them to another woman, but not to sell them. The guidelines encourage advance agreements that clarify the potential parent's intent in the event of various contingencies, but curiously, the AMA guidelines propose that such advance agreements not be made mandatory. The American Bar Association, Section of Family Law, in their proposed Model Assisted Reproductive Technologies Act, has similar provisions regarding payment for pre-embryos.[10]

§ 20–6. Surrogacy

a. Introduction

Long before the medical miracles of reproductive technology were even imagined, couples who could not bear children occasionally turned to other women who acted as surrogate mothers. In ancient times, when inheritance and blood lines were considered paramount concerns, a man who was married to an infertile woman might turn to a woman who could provide him an heir. Given the quasi-property status that many women were considered in ancient cultures, the insemination was most likely not artificial, which perhaps helps explain some of the vehement opposition to surrogacy by some persons who claim that the participation is rarely voluntary in the true sense. This historical use of surrogacy is also a possible source of some contemporary concerns regarding whether the surrogate's ultimate relinquishment of her child is truly voluntary. For example, Genesis tells of Abraham's servant Hagar bearing a child to be raised by the genetic father, Abraham, and his wife Sarah.[1] The image of a servant "voluntarily" relinquishing her child to her master falls short of truly uncoerced consent, and it suggests some of the concern that survives today.

9. See Council on Ethical and Judicial Affairs, American Medical Ass'n., Code of Medical Ethics: Current Opinions with Annotations, Op. 2.141 (1998–99 ed.)

10. ABA Family Law Section Committee Draft, Proposed Model Assisted Reproductive Technologies Act (1999), § 1.09.

§ 20–6

1. Genesis 16:1—16.

Although fertilization may take place through normal coitus, as was the case with Hagar, in recent times it typically occurs through artificial insemination, in vitro fertilization, or embryo transfer. While the genetic father is often the husband of the woman who expects to raise the child, that need not be the case. Similarly, while the genetic mother is usually the pregnant woman, that need not be the case either. It is now technologically possible to take the sperm from one source and the ovum from another, to place the subsequently developed embryo in the uterus of a third person, and then to have the child raised by two biologically unrelated persons.[2] In the most common kinds of surrogacy arrangements today, the child is the biological offspring of the intended father, and sometimes of the intended mother, and a biological connection with one of the intended parents is required for approval of a surrogacy contract under the Uniform Status of Children of Assisted Conception Act.[3]

Surrogacy arrangements currently provide the only way for a woman without a uterus to be the genetic mother of a child (through embryo transfer) or to become the mother of a child whose genetic father is her husband (through artificial insemination of the surrogate with the husband's sperm). In addition, the arrangement allows women who must avoid pregnancy because it poses a physical or emotional risk to them to become mothers. Finally, surrogacy could be used by women to avoid the inconvenience of pregnancy.[4] As reproductive technology has matured in recent years, various forms of surrogacy have emerged, raising additional legal issues related to distinguishing the potential rights and obligations that may result from differing forms of surrogacy. As the early cases reveal, the fact that the surrogate was giving birth to her own biologically related child forced the courts to accelerate their analysis of the already changing definition of "legal parent." Then, once in vitro fertilization became available, surrogates sometimes became "gestational" or birth mothers only, carrying a child to term that was implanted after the pre-embryo was created. The pre-embryo, in turn, might or might not have a biological relationship to its intended parents, but no genetic connection existed with the fetus' birth mother, who offers her womb but no genes.

Surrogacy raises several kinds of significant legal issues, although they generally fall into two categories: whether contractual arrangements between the parties entered into prior to the conception are legally enforceable, and what parental rights and obligations the various participants have in regard to the child. In evaluating these two primary questions, the distinction between gestational surrogacy, where the child is not genetically related to the woman carrying him, and biological surrogacy, where the surrogate is also the genetic mother, may be legally significant. The law also must address the degree to which persons other than the surrogate should be allowed to profit

---

2. As one of the drafters of the Uniform Status of Children of Assisted Conception Act notes, this raises the possibility of the child having five "parents." The legal uncertainties inherent in such a situation are cited as one of the primary reasons for the drafting of the Act, to unequivocally vest the child with certainty as to his or her legal parentage. See Robert Robinson & Paul Kurtz, Uniform Status of Children of Assisted Conception Act: A View from the Drafting Committee, 13 Nova L. Rev. 491 (1989).

3. Section 1(3).

4. Although the specter of surrogacy being used for convenience has been raised, no incident of such surrogacy has been reported.

from surrogacy arrangements, what psychological and genetic screening is appropriate for the surrogate, what screening criteria, if any, is appropriate for the intended parents, and whether surrogacy may be restricted to married heterosexual couples.[5]

The early ambiguity surrounding the legal rights and obligations of parties to surrogacy is slowly being replaced by state statutes and case law addressing surrogacy, declaring such agreements void or voidable, or declaring them enforceable when they are drawn consistently with statutorily provided requirements. Perhaps it is a measure of the strong reactions people have to surrogacy that states are moving more quickly to place legal parameters on surrogacy than on any other form of assisted reproduction. The fact that a majority of the first states to legislate on the issue have declared surrogacy agreements invalid may not be as significant as it first appears, since those states strongly opposing surrogacy may have felt compelled to act quickly, while other states are content to allow surrogacy agreements to find their way to the courts. What is apparent, however, is that there exists a wide divergence of state perspectives amongst the relatively small number of states that have codified their policies.

b. *Arguments For and Against Permitting Surrogacy*

The primary reason for permitting surrogacy is that it serves the utilitarian interest of allowing infertile women to have children who are genetically related to their husbands, or, in the case of gestational surrogacy, to themselves. This allows people who would otherwise be unable to have genetically related children to lead a more fulfilling life and to participate in one of the great joys of life, one that would otherwise be denied to them. Those who believe that society should tolerate or foster surrogacy arrangements point out that it is easy for parents without fertility problems to cavalierly dismiss the yearnings of those who suffer those problems. Indeed, there are few more basic desires than the desire to bear and raise children, and it seems irrational to require childless couples to remain that way when a surrogate is willing to provide them with the child they want.[6]

The argument that willing intending parents and willing surrogates should be able to enter freely negotiated contracts is based in libertarian theories of individual freedom. It is also supported by arguments based in Constitutional law, and one leading scholar has argued that the right to enter surrogacy contracts is protected as a part of the right to procreate. Because this is a fundamental right, it can be limited only when there is a compelling state interest in its limitation.[7] Those who support permitting surrogacy point

---

5. See e.g. ABA Family Law Section Committee Draft, Proposed Model Assisted Reproductive Technologies Act § 1.02 and § 1.03 (1999) discussing issues of informed consent and mental health screening and counseling.

6. See e.g., Carmel Shalev, Birth Power: The Case for Surrogacy (1989); Marjorie M. Schultz, Reproductive Technology and Intent–Based Parenthood: An Opportunity for Gender Neutrality, 1990 Wis.L.Rev.297. For a discussion of the notion that basic principles of eco-

nomics also argue that such practices should be allowed, see William M. Landes and Richard A. Posner, The Economics of the Baby Shortage, 7 J. Leg.Stud. 323 (1978).

7. See John Robertson, Embryos, Families and Procreative Liberty: The Legal Structure of the New Reproduction, 59 So.Cal.L.Rev.939 (1986); John Robertson, Procreative Liberty and the Control of Conception, Pregnancy, and Childbirth, 69 Va. L. Rev. 405 (1983).

out that the research shows there are very few adverse consequences on the surrogate or the child.[8]

There are three primary arguments against permitting surrogacy arrangements, at least when payment is involved. First, some argue, it amounts to the economic exploitation of poor, fertile women who will be enticed into surrogacy because of the insubstantial economic alternatives available to them. Some also argue that this could lead to the creation of a caste of women, defined in economic, and, perhaps, racial terms, who bear children for society's wealthy.

Second, they argue, such a change in the nature of reproductive processes dehumanizes the surrogate mother and harms the relationship between the child and the mother. This leads to the commodification of babies, who are treated as a market commodity not substantially different from sofas, pork bellies, or anything else that can be traded for money. In addition, they argue, surrogacy will give rise to such market features as baby traders and surrogacy brokers.

Finally, those opposed to these arrangements argue, the real psychological consequence of forcing a woman to relinquish a baby she gestated for adoption may be much greater than we now believe. Without further information on the consequences upon the surrogates, who are generally poor and powerless, the process and its potentially devastating results should not be tolerated.[9]

The legal position against tolerating surrogacy is based in the common law argument that, for the reasons described in the last three paragraphs, it is contrary to public policy. If the practice is contrary to public policy, contracts to engage in the practice should be either void or unenforceable. In addition, some have argued that surrogacy arrangements violate the Constitutional rights of the surrogate either by forcing her to give up her child after birth without affording her the protections otherwise afforded to women who do so, or by treating her effectively as a slave in violation of the thirteenth amendment.[10]

c. The Uniform Status of Children of Assisted Conception Act Approach

The Uniform Status of Children of Assisted Conception Act[11] resolves the current debate over whether surrogacy contracts should be valid by offering alternatives that either (1) provide detailed guidelines for surrogacy agreements and render them enforceable when those guidelines are met, or (2) declare all such agreements to be void. Virginia, for example, has adopted the Act's alternative which requires judicial review and approval of the surrogacy agreement, appointment of a guardian ad litem to protect the interests of the unborn child, and supervision of the surrogacy arrangements through the first

---

8. Lori Andrews and Lisa Douglass, Alternative Reproduction, 65 So. Cal. L. Rev. 623, 673–79 (1991).

9. For a discussion of these policy considerations, see Margaret Radin, Market Inalienability, 100 Harv. L. Rev. 1849 (1987), and New York State Task Force on Life and the Law, Surrogate Parenting: Analysis and Rec-

ommendations for Public Policy (1988). For the best brief judicial evaluation of these positions and the literature supporting them, see Johnson v. Calvert, 19 Cal.Rptr.2d 494, 509, 851 P.2d 776, 791–793 (Cal.1993)(Kennard, J., dissenting).

10. See Radin, supra note 9.

11. 9B U.L.A. 135 (1993 Supp.).

six months of the child's life.[12] North Dakota, in contrast, has adopted the Act's alternative which declares surrogacy arrangements void and states that a birth mother is the legal mother of any child she bears.[13]

The purpose of the Act is not to provide detailed regulation of any of the reproductive technologies it encompasses, but rather to clarify the legal status and parentage of children born through such procedures. The regulatory alternative surrogacy provisions, however, do provide comprehensive criteria for creating a legally enforceable surrogacy arrangement. The intended parents, for example, must be a heterosexual couple, married to each other, with at least one of them donating genetic material to the child carried by the surrogate.[14] Further restricting the use of surrogacy, the Act requires that the intended mother be "unable to bear a child or [be] unable to do so without unreasonable risk to an unborn child or to the physical or mental health of the intended mother or child," a finding that must be supported by medical evidence.[15] In addition, to obtain judicial approval, the intended parents must "meet the standards of fitness applicable to adoptive parents" in the applicable state.[16]

The surrogate, in turn, must be an adult[17] who has had at least one pregnancy and delivery, and who can provide medical evidence that bearing another child will not pose an unreasonable physical or mental risk to the surrogate or the unborn child.[18] If the surrogate is married, her husband must be a party to the agreement,[19] and both must meet the same standard of fitness applicable to adoptive parents in the state.[20] To further insure that the interests of the unborn child are considered, the court is required to appoint a guardian ad litem, and may appoint counsel for the surrogate until such time as the agreement receives court approval.[21]

Procedurally, the intended parents and the surrogate file a petition with the court for approval of a surrogacy agreement.[22] Following a hearing, the court may issue an order approving the surrogacy agreement for a period of twelve months upon finding that: (1) the court has jurisdiction; (2) there is evidence that the intended mother is unable to bear a child; (3) home study reports by the state child welfare agency have been filed with court; (4) the intended parents and surrogate (and spouse where applicable) meet state adoption standards; (5) the parties understand the agreement and are voluntarily entering into it; (6) there is evidence of the surrogate's prior delivery and lack of medical risk; (7) there are psychological reports confirming that all parties have received counseling and are capable of entering into and fulfilling the agreement; (8) all reports of any genetic, medical or psychological testing agreed to by parties or required by law have been provided; (9) there is adequate provision for payment of reasonable health care costs, including responsibility if agreement is terminated; and (10) the agreement will not be substantially detrimental to the interests of any of the affected individuals.[23]

---

12. Va. Code 1950, §§ 20–159 to 20–160.

13. N.D. Cent. Code 14–18–02, 14–18–05.

14. 9B U.L.A. 135 (1993 Supp.) Section 1(3).

15. Id., Section 6(b)(2).

16. Id., Section 6(b)(4).

17. Id., Section 1(4).

18. Id., Section 6(b)(6).

19. Id., Section 5(a), 6(a).

20. Id., Section 6(b)(4).

21. Id., Section 6(a).

22. Id., Section 6(a).

23. Id., Section 6(b)(1–10).

Under the Act, parties who have entered into a judicially approved surrogacy contract may still terminate that contract. After entry of an order approving the surrogacy contract, but before conception, any of the parties, or the court for cause, may terminate the agreement by giving written notice to all other parties and the court.[24] After conception, if the surrogate is also the egg donor, the surrogate may terminate the agreement within 180 days[25] after the last insemination pursuant to the agreement. A hearing follows notice to all parties, and if the court finds that the surrogate is voluntarily terminating the agreement, the court vacates its prior order.[26] Upon termination of the contract, the Act provides that the surrogate is recognized as the mother of the resulting child, and if she is married and her husband was a party to the agreement, he is recognized as the father. If she is unmarried, or her husband was not a party to the agreement, paternity is governed by applicable state law, such as the Uniform Parentage Act, where adopted.[27]

Upon the birth of a child to a surrogate under an approved surrogacy agreement the intended parents are the legal parents of the child.[28] After receipt of a formal notice of the birth, the court orders the birth certificate to be reissued in the name of the intended parents, and the original one sealed.[29] If the intended parents and the surrogate do not follow the procedural requirements for obtaining judicial approval of their agreement under the Act, the agreement will be void, and the surrogate will be considered the mother of the resulting child.[30] If the surrogate is married and her husband was a party to the agreement, he will be considered the father. If she is not married, or he was not a party to the agreement, paternity is governed by applicable state law,[31] such as the Uniform Parentage Act, where adopted.

d. *Other State Statutory Developments*

To date, nineteen states have adopted statutes expressly addressing surrogacy agreements, with many in the last two years.[32] Two efforts at enacting federal laws to limit or prohibit surrogacy arrangements have failed.[33] In states that have affirmatively addressed the issue of surrogacy, a dramatic spectrum of positions has emerged, raising additional issues of forum shopping and resulting conflict of law disputes if residents of one state enter into surrogacy contracts in a different, more tolerant state, then the birth occurs in the state of intended residency. If one wishes to enter into an

---

24. Id., Section 7(a).

25. This period roughly parallels the surrogate's constitutional right to abort the fetus. See Chapter 18.

26. Id., Section 7(b).

27. Id., Section 8(2).

28. Id., Section 8(1).

29. Id., Section 8(3).

30. Id., Section 5(b).

31. Id.

32. Ala.Code §§ 26–10A–33 to 26–10A–34 (1992); Ariz. Rev. Stat. Ann. § 25–218 (1991 & Supp. 1997); Ark. Code Ann. §§ 9–10–201 to 202 (Michie 1998); Fla. Stat. Ann. §§ 742.14 to 742.17 (West. 1997); Ky. rev. Stat. Ann. §§ 199.950(20), 199.590(4), 199.990 (Michie/Bobbs–Merrill 1995); La. Rev. Stat. Ann.

§ 9:2713 (West 1991); Mich. Comp. Laws Ann. §§ 722.851 to 722.863 (West 1993); Neb. Rev. Stat. § 25–21, 200 (1996); Nev. Rev. Stat. Ann. § 126.045 (Supp. 1997); N.H. Rev. Stat. Ann. §§ 168–B:1 to 168–B:32 (1994 & Supp. 1995); N.J. Rev. Stat. Ann. §§ 9:3–41, 9–17–44 (West 1993 & Supp. 1998); N.Y. Dom. Rel. Law §§ 121–124 (Consol. 1993 & Supp. 1998); N.D. Cent. Code §§ 14–18–01 to 14–18–07 (1997); Or. Rev. Stat. Ann. §§ 109.239, 109.243, 109.247 (1997); utah Code ann. § 76–7–204 (1995); Va.Code Ann. §§ 20–156 to 20–165 (Michie 1995 Supp. 1998); Wash. Rev. Code Ann. §§ 26.26210 to 26026.260 (West 1997); W.Va. Code § 48–4–16 (1998).

33. H.R.275, 101 Cong. (1989), and H.R. 576, 101 Cong (1989).

enforceable and legal surrogacy contract, the best states would currently include New Hampshire, Florida, Arkansas, and Virginia, although the requirements differ. Other states prohibit certain aspects of payment to the surrogate, such as Washington, Louisiana, Kentucky and Nebraska. One would definitely want to avoid Michigan where surrogacy is a felony, and presumably New York, Arizona, Utah and North Dakota, where such contracts are void and unenforceable. In general, those states codifying surrogacy regulation require informed consent, counseling, a formal contract and certain rights afforded the surrogate, and certain provision for either termination of the birth mother's rights, or assertion of those rights. Some states, such as Virginia, require judicial participation prior to the entering of a surrogacy contract. The lack of distinction between gestational surrogates and genetic or traditional surrogates may ultimately require revision in many early statutes, unless the trend toward an intent based analysis of parental recognition overcomes all biological based claims.

e. Caselaw Prior to or in the Absence of Surrogacy Statutes

While often suggesting that they would prefer to leave the issue to the legislature, courts have addressed surrogacy contracts in a number of different ways[34]. In one of the first cases to directly confront the issue, the Kentucky Supreme Court held that brokering surrogacy contracts does not constitute baby selling, which is outlawed by Kentucky statute.[35] Against a vigorous dissent, the majority held that outlawing surrogacy contracts would not serve any of the purposes of the baby selling prohibition.

Surrogacy contracts had been found to be unenforceable by an appellate court in Michigan[36] and voidable by a lower court in New York[37] when the Baby M case came before the New Jersey Supreme Court in 1988.[38] In that plenary consideration of the issue of the legal status of for-pay surrogacy contracts, the court invalidated the contract, finding that it was inconsistent with public policy and law. The court pointed out that while it recognized "the depth of the yearning of infertile couples to have their own children," it was required to conclude that "the payment of money to a 'surrogate' mother [is] illegal, perhaps criminal, and potentially degrading to women."[39] The court ultimately granted custody to the commissioning father, basing its determination for custody purposes on the best interests test that it rejected as a basis for the determination of parentage. Thus, under the court's order, the child was entitled to live with her intending parents, although the surrogate, who was recognized as the legal mother of the child, was entitled to liberal visitation. The court went on to say that gratuitous surrogacy would not violate the public policy of the state, as long as the surrogate was not compelled by contract to give up the child upon its birth.

---

34. For a summary of ongoing caselaw on the issue of surrogate contracts, See, Danny R. Veilleux, Annotation, Validity And Construction Of Surrogate Parenting Agreement, 77 A.L.R.4th 70 (1990).

35. Surrogate Parenting Associates v. Commonwealth, ex rel. Armstrong, 704 S.W.2d 209 (Ky.1986).

36. Doe v. Kelley, 307 N.W.2d 438 (Mich. App.1981), cert. denied 459 U.S. 1183, 103 S.Ct. 834, 74 L.Ed.2d 1027 (1983).

37. In re Adoption of Baby Girl L.J., 505 N.Y.S.2d 813 (N.Y.Sur.1986).

38. In the Matter of Baby M, 537 A.2d 1227 (N.J.1988).

39. Id. at 1227.

The issue of gestational surrogacy was considered by the California Supreme Court in 1993.[40] In a fight between the intending mother (who was also the source of the ovum, and whose husband was the source of the sperm) and the gestational mother over custody of the child, the court determined that the rights of the parties could not be finally determined by reference to the Uniform Parentage Act, as adopted in California.[41] Although that statute provides that the mother-child relationship may be established by proof of birth, it also provides that it may be established in other ways permitted by law, presumably by genetic testing.[42] Thus, the statute was read to be ambiguous as between the rights of the birth mother and the genetic mother, and the court rejected the proposal of an amicus that both be declared to be the child's mothers.[43]

The court rejected arguments that gestational surrogacy contracts violated the public policy found in the adoption statutes, that it violated the state or federal constitution, that it exploited women, and that it violated the procreative liberty of the surrogate. It concluded that "[a]lthough the Act recognizes both genetic consanguinity and giving birth as a means of establishing a mother and child relationship, when the two means do not coincide in one woman, she who intended to procreate the child, that is, she who intended to bring about the birth of a child that she intended to raise as her own, is the natural mother under California law."[44] This approach rejects the suggestion that the placement of the child should be based on the child's best interests.[45] This intention-based approach was subsequently affirmed by the California Court of Appeals in the *Buzzanca* case, which the California Supreme Court declined to review.[46]

§ 20–7.　Assisted Reproduction: Is there an Emerging Consensus?

As the field of reproductive technology has matured in the last two decades, is any consensus emerging from the early alarm and confusion? Perhaps the only accurate answer is both yes, and no. Given the vast diversity of cultural, religious and even geographical perspectives on family and change, the nationwide response is not a uniform one. With issues of family law generally deferred to the states, unless the health/reproductive aspects eventually are found to warrant federal attention, there promises to be great diversity in perspectives. The spectrum of differences varies, depending partly on the degree of controversy the procedure triggers. Artificial insemination has been widely accepted over the years, with legal issues of paternity relatively clear in most jurisdictions. Donors are generally, by their intent to not become parents, no longer held to parental obligations or entitled to parental rights.

40. Johnson v. Calvert, 19 Cal.Rptr.2d 494, 851 P.2d 776 (Cal.1993).

41. West's Ann. Cal. Civ. Code § 7000 et seq.; now recodified as West's Ann. Cal. Fam. Code § 7600 et seq.

42. The court pointed out that the statute provided that its provisions with regard to the father-child relationship were to apply to the mother-child relationship also, as far as possible. Since the father-child relationship could be determined by genetic testing, the mother-child relationship could be established in that way, too. See Johnson, 851 P.2d at 780.

43. Johnson, 851 P.2d at 781.

44. Id. at 782.

45. Id. at 788 (Kennard, J., dissenting.)

46. *In re Marriage of Buzzanca*, 72 Cal. Rptr.2d 280 (App. 1998). For a discussion of the Buzzanca case, see section 20–1, above.

In vitro fertilization has become less controversial as a procedure outside of the mother's body, yet the relationships created by the child having multiple biological and intended parents continues to create anguish, as epitomized by the *Buzzanca* case. The related issues of disposition of frozen preembryos also raise widely differing responses. Surrogacy, in turn, whether gestational or traditional typically adds a third potential parent to the roster.

The encouraging development that is emerging from case law and many statutory guidelines is the weight being given to the intent of the participants to assisted reproduction. Donors are generally acknowledged as *not* intending to become parents, at least to the extent their relationship to the transaction is limited to their usually anonymous genetic donation. The *Davis*, *Kass*, and *Buzzanca* courts looked to written intent, affirmative acts expressing intent, and estoppel as precluding an intended parent from changing his mind after he had "brought" a child into the world through his affirmative acts. Where intent is impossible to determine or the intent of the parties is inconsistent, courts now agree that a balancing of interests should apply, such as with preembryo disposition. It is a reasonable presumption that this judicial consensus, focusing on intent of the parties, will eventually be codified in state statutes.

Over the last two decades, the initial fear and alarm over new reproductive technology has largely given way to issues of regulation and acceptance. What was once science fiction has become nearly commonplace. The concept of preembryos squirming in a glass dish on a laboratory counter no longer horrifies and fascinates—it is now simply an option for infertile persons to consider. Having perhaps finally exhausted the first waves of commentary and debate over in vitro fertilization and surrogacy, some commentators are now turning to speculation as to cloning and embryo fusion as the next frontier[1]. The only certainty is that what was once science fiction is now reality and the law must respond to each new wave of technology with integrity to build a foundation for the even more perplexing legal issues that will surely come.

---

1. See Lee M. Silver & Susan R. Silver, Confused Heritage and The Absurdity of Genetic Ownership, 11 Harv. J. Law & Tech 593 (1998), in which a professor of molecular biology at Harvard and an attorney explore possibilities on the horizon.

Chapter 21

REGULATION OF RESEARCH UPON HUMAN SUBJECTS

Table of Sections

Research References

Am Jur 2d, Health § 53
ALR Index: Medical Experiments or Tests; Medical Research; Medical Treatment
ALR Digest: Physicians and Surgeons §§ 29–45
Am Jur Legal Forms 2d, Physicians and Surgeons §§ 202:151–202:180
15 POF2d 711, Physician's Failure to Obtain Informed Consent to Innovative Practice or Medical Research

§ 21–1. Introduction and History

The shocking horrors that superbly qualified scientists can perpetrate under the guise of necessary medical experimentation became apparent to the world through the Nazi war crimes trials which resulted in the prosecution of several prominent German physicians at Nuremberg. These trials unveiled conduct ignominious under any circumstances. For example, they brought to light medical research in which "volunteers," usually concentration camp inmates, were exposed to extremely low atmospheric pressure until they died in order to help the German Air Force prepare for high altitude military

977

operations. Additionally, the trials revealed that subjects were forced to drink seawater or breathe mustard gas, were exposed to epidemics such as malaria, jaundice, and typhus, or were placed in ice water until they froze. Several of the experiments were "open" to a wide range of concentration camp inmates, while others were limited to Jews, Gypsies, Polish priests, or other "special" groups.

The perpetrators did not perceive the experimentation as an abuse of medicine. Remarkably, it was sometimes perceived as appropriate conduct, done in the name of healing, and considered consistent with the Hippocratic Oath.[1] Most of the twenty physicians accused of participating in or directing this experimentation were convicted, and some were hanged. A few were acquitted and one escaped. In one of the tribunal's most significant and ultimately most important judgments, the court of three allied judges sitting in Nuremberg promulgated a set of principles to be applied to determine when medical experimentation is appropriate. These principles have provided the basis for all subsequent discussions of the substantive limitations to be put upon research involving human subjects, and they provide the basis for the current federal regulation of research involving human subjects.[2] In particular, they provide that, as a first principle, "voluntary consent of the human subject is absolutely essential." They also provide that the studies should be scientifically and socially necessary, that they should be based on the results of animal or other non-human experimentation, that they should avoid unnecessary burdens on the subjects, that they should be conducted by qualified researchers who are willing and able to stop the research at any point when that becomes appropriate, and that the subjects must be able to withdraw from the research at any time.

Nazi Germany does not provide the only example of grotesque medical experimentation. Research in the United States has also been tainted by racially and politically motivated selection of subjects for medical investigation. The most famous twentieth century American breach of research ethics was the Tuskegee Syphilis Study. In this study, hundreds of African American men in the South were studied so that the United States Public Health Service could develop an understanding of the natural history of syphilis. The Public Health Service justified its choice of poor, rural, African Americans as subjects in two ways: (1) the agency cited the difficulty African Americans might have in seeking treatment for syphilis, and (2) the agency deemed that African Americans would be more likely to benefit from the research because it was thought that African Americans were more sexually active and physically and mentally weaker than whites. The USPHS believed that the objective of the study could only be achieved if the subjects went untreated, even in the face of successful treatments for syphilis. The United States Public Health Service continued this research for forty years. Even when penicillin, the first effective treatment for syphilis, became available, the Public Health Service physicians failed to offer that treatment to most of their subjects, and many were regularly discouraged from obtaining other forms of treatment. The study came to public light in 1972 and was the topic of federal administrative

§ 21–1

1. For an account of the professional role of physicians in the Nazi policy of extermination, see R.J. Lifton, The Nazi Doctors (1986).

2. See generally Robert Levine, Ethics and Regulation of Clinical Research (2d ed. 1986).

and Congressional hearings in 1973. While participants in the study successfully sued the Public Health Service for compensation, no criminal actions
arose out of the case.[3]

The Tuskegee Syphilis Study is not a unique example of American
medical research's failure to respect individual subjects. Other publicized
cases include the Jewish Chronic Disease Hospital case, in which live cancer
cells were injected into patients without their knowledge, and the Willow-
brook State Hospital hepatitis study, in which children admitted to a state
hospital rife with hepatitis were given the disease as a condition of admission.
In addition, in early 1994 the United States government revealed previously
withheld information about radiation studies, conducted over the course of
decades, some of which were carried on without the consent, or even the
knowledge, of those who were made subjects of the studies. In each of these
cases, as in the Nazi experiments, the only authorities determining whether
the subjects were properly selected were the medical investigators themselves.[4]

In 1974, one year after the public disclosure of the Tuskegee Syphilis
Study, Congress enacted the National Research Act establishing the National
Commission for Protection of Human Subjects of Biomedical and Behavioral
Research. The Commission's mission was to, "conduct a comprehensive
investigation and study to identify basic ethical principles" that should
underlie the conduct of research involving human subjects. In recognition of
the interdisciplinary nature of the issue, the Act also required the establishment of institutional review boards (IRBs) at institutions under contract with
the Department of Health, Education and Welfare. By 1975, when the
Department of Health, Education and Welfare issued its "Policy for the
Protection of Human Research Subjects," virtually every university, medical
school, and research hospital had established IRBs that operated within the
requirements of both federal and state regulations. The federal regulations
were revised by what had become the Department of Health and Human
Services (DHHS) in 1981 to remove the necessity of IRB reviews from some
low-risk research and to provide for informal consent procedures in some
cases. The regulations have been further revised, in less significant ways,
since then. Every year in the United States, hundreds of IRBs will review
thousands of research protocols. No research involving human subjects funded
by the Department of Health and Human Services—and virtually no other
research involving human subjects—may be carried out at an institution
without that institution's IRB approval.

§ 21-2.   Scope of Federal Regulations Governing Research Involving Human Subjects

The Federal Regulatory scheme governing research involving human
subjects, entitled the "Basic Department of Health and Human Services
Policy for Protection of Human Research Subjects," governs all research that
is at least partly funded by the Department of Health and Human Services.[1]

---

3. For a complete account of this tawdry
episode in American medical history, see J.
Jones, Bad Blood (1981).

4. For further commentary on these infa-
mous studies and a more comprehensive dis-

cussion of selection of subjects, see Levine supra note 2 at 67–93.

§ 21-2

1. 45 C.F.R. § 46.101(a), (f). From time to
time there is a call to reform these regulations

Because the Department of Health and Human Services, through the National Institutes of Health and its many other programs, provides a substantial amount of resources for medical research, it maintains genuine authority over the manner in which human subjects are selected for medical research protocols. To that end, the department ties institutional adherence to the Federal Regulations to its funding.[2] The correlative Food and Drug Administration regulations requiring IRB review parallel the Department regulations.[3] They apply to all research done to support applications to the Food and Drug Administration.[4]

Until 1981, it was unclear whether the Federal Regulations applied only to that research funded by the Department, or whether they applied to all research at institutions that received any funding from the Department. In 1981 the regulations were amended to make it clear that their application only extends to those research protocols funded by the Department. The amended regulations also provided that any institution which receives Department funds must supply the Department with an assurance that all research protocols involving human subjects conducted at that institution would be reviewed to determine the propriety of the use of the human subjects.[5] Thus, while institutions receiving federal funds are required only to apply the federal regulations to their Department funded research, they are required by federal mandate to maintain procedures for reviewing all of their research involving human subjects, whether or not the Department funds that research. Rather than maintain two separate processes for approval of research involving human subjects—one for federally funded research and another for other research—most institutions receiving federal funds have chosen to meet the "assurance" requirement by informing the Department of Health and Human Services that they will apply the process mandated by the federal regulations to all research protocols involving human subjects. Because virtually all institutions that do meaningful medical research receive some research funds from the Department of Health and Human Services, virtually all research institutions in the United States have assured the Department of Health and Human Services that they will apply the federal regulations to all of their research involving human subjects, whether or not that research is federally funded. Thus, despite the narrow, formal applicability of the regulations to research funded by the Department, in fact, they govern virtually all research involving human subjects in the United States.

The regulations define "research" as "a systematic investigation designed to develop or contribute to generalizable knowledge."[6] "Research" is thus

to provide stricter control on research involving human subjects. For example, see Dept. of Health and Human Services, Office of the Inspector General, Institutional Review Boards: A Time for Reform (Washington, 1988), Jonathan Moreno et al., Updating Protections for Human Subjects Involved in Research, 280 JAMA 1951 (1998).

2. See generally Robert Levine, Ethics and Regulation of Clinical Research (2d ed.1986) 19–36.

3. 21 C.F.R. §§ 56.101 et seq. Subsequent text in this chapter cites to the Department of Health and Human Services version; in each

case, though, there is a correlative citation in the Food and Drug Administration regulations. A host of other federal departments and agencies have also adopted parallel regulations. See e.g., 28 C.F.R. § 46.101 et seq. (Department of Justice), 32 C.F.R. § 219.101 et seq. (Department of Defense), and 34 C.F.R. § 97.101 et seq. (Department of Education).

4. 21 C.F.R. §§ 56.101(a), 56.103.

5. 46 C.F.R. § 46.103.

6. 45 C.F.R. § 46.102(e).

distinguished from experimentation, which is usually defined as an untried deviation from the standard treatment, employed for therapeutic purposes. The use of a new medical procedure in an individual case does not qualify as "research" under the regulations unless it is a "systematic investigation" and it is undertaken to yield "generalizable knowledge". For example, a surgeon's decision to use a new technique in a single case does not constitute "research" if she applies the technique entirely for therapeutic purposes; on the other hand, if she intends to write it up for the medical literature, it would constitute "research" under the federal regulations, even if it were also undertaken for therapeutic purposes.

The regulations provide a broad definition of "human subject."[7] It includes anyone about whom the researcher seeks (1) data through intervention or interaction with the individual, or (2) identifiable private information.[8] "Intervention" and "interaction" are broadly defined and "private information" includes that information about which an individuals has a reasonable expectation of privacy, i.e., it includes that information that the individual reasonably believes is not being observed or recorded, or that the individual reasonably believes will not be made public.[9]

The regulations specifically exclude some categories of low risk research from their coverage[10] and they grant wide authority to the Secretary of the Department of Health and Human Services to vary the applicability of the requirements. The Secretary has final authority to determine which research is covered by the regulations.[11]

§ 21–3. The Creation, Authority, and Membership of Institutional Review Boards (IRBs)

The cornerstone of the federal regulatory process is the Institutional Review Board (IRB). Every covered institution must maintain an IRB to review research conducted at that institution. Although the federal regulations prescribe outside limits on the membership and process of the IRBs, they operate in accord with the policies of their local institutions. Thus, IRBs at different institutions may differ with respect to their size, professional composition, meeting schedule, review procedure, accessibility, the availability of their records, and in a host of other ways.[1] Institutional Review Boards are a successful example of highly decentralized federal regulatory decision-making.

No federally funded research (and, as previously described, usually no research) may be conducted at an institution without the approval of that institution's IRB.[2] The IRB must render its decisions in writing and provide an opportunity for researchers whose protocols have been rejected to respond to the reasons for disapproval.[3] The IRB is also permitted to conduct "con-

7. 45 C.F.R. § 46.102(f).

8. Id.

9. The regulations explicitly provide that a medical record is an example of "private information" which an individual can reasonably expect will not be made public. Id.

10. 45 C.F.R. § 46.101(b).

11. 45 C.F.R. § 46.101(c).

§ 21–3

1. Their names also vary: some are called Human Subjects Boards, some Research Review Boards, some Subject Protection Committees, and most have yet other names.

2. 45 C.F.R. § 46.109(a).

3. 45 C.F.R. § 46.109(b).

tinuing review" of the research they have approved, and they must review each continuing research protocol at least once each year.[4] If in the course of their review the IRB determines that the research is "not being conducted in accordance with the IRB's requirements" or that the research has been "associated with unexpected serious harm to subjects," the IRB may suspend or terminate its approval of the research. If the IRB does terminate approval, it must inform the researcher, "appropriate institutional officials," and the Secretary of the Department of Health and Human Services.[5]

IRBs are intended to reflect local conditions and values. They may have as few as five members or as many as the institutions wish to place on the Board; some have dozens of members. The boards should be composed of persons of "varying backgrounds" who are diverse racially and culturally. The members should exhibit "sensitivity to such issues as community attitudes," and members should have scientific, legal, and professional competence to review the research protocols that come before them.[6] Moreover, the IRB must have a gender and professional mix,[7] it must include one non-scientist,[8] and it must include at least one person who is not "affiliated" with the institution (and has no immediate family member who is affiliated).[9] In addition, if the IRB "regularly reviews" research protocols with an identifiable category of vulnerable subjects (for example, patients at mental hospitals), the IRB is required to have at least one member who is "primarily concerned with the welfare of the subjects."[10] The IRB may also add members with special competence when it is necessary to review particularly complex protocols, although those special members do not become voting members of the IRB.[11] Finally, the regulations explicitly provide that a member of the IRB may not participate in the review of any protocol where the member has a conflict of interest.[12]

Members are appointed to the institutional review board in accord with the process determined by the institution itself, and the membership may be changed whenever the institution determines that such a change is warranted. Thus, there is the risk that an institutional administration, concerned about the income generated by federally funded research protocols, might seek to construct a toothless IRB. In fact, this has not happened—perhaps because of the altruistic and sincere concerns of institutional administrators, perhaps because of the fear of adverse publicity and potential litigation, and perhaps because of the regular audits of local institutional review boards conducted by the Office of Protection from Research Risks of the Department and Health and Human Services.

§ 21–4. Criteria for IRB Approval of Research

To approve a research protocol the IRB must make seven findings:

(1) The risk to subjects must be minimized;

4. 45 C.F.R. § 46.109(c).

5. 45 C.F.R. § 46.113.

6. 45 C.F.R. § 46.107(a).

7. 45 C.F.R. § 46.107(b).

8. The regulations suggest a lawyer, ethicist, or member of the clergy. 45 C.F.R. § 46.107(c).

9. 45 C.F.R. § 46.107(d).

10. 45 C.F.R. § 46.107(a).

11. 45 C.F.R. § 46.107(f).

12. 45 C.F.R. § 46.107(e).

(2) The risk to subjects must be "reasonable in relation to anticipated benefits, if any, to subjects and the importance of the knowledge that may reasonably be expected to result;"

(3) The selection of subjects must be equitable;

(4) Each prospective subject must give adequate informed consent;

(5) The informed consent must be appropriately documented;

(6) There must be adequate monitoring of the data; and

(7) There must be adequate provisions to protect the privacy of subjects and to maintain the confidentiality of data.[1]

Of these seven requirements, the requirements related to informed consent[2] and the requirement that the risk/benefit ratio be acceptable are the two that are most thoroughly considered and debated by Institutional Review Boards. The "risk/benefit ratio" requirement demands that the IRB determine if the risks to the subjects are reasonable in relationship to (1) benefits to the subjects and (2) "the importance of the knowledge that may reasonably be expected to result."[3]

The regulations also provide a catch-all provision that applies when the research subjects for a particular protocol "are likely to be vulnerable to coercion or undue influence." In cases where the human subjects are "persons with acute or severe physical or mental illness, or persons who are economically or educationally disadvantaged," for example, the IRB must provide for any safeguards it believes necessary to protect the subjects.[4]

§ 21–5. Inclusion of Women and Minorities in Research

In 1994, the regulations were revised so that women and minorities would not be excluded from participation as subjects in medical research. The revisions came in response to concern from both women's health care advocates and minority groups who presented substantiated charges that women and minorities were underrepresented in medical studies.[1] The policy challenged and eliminated the widespread practice of disqualifying all women of child bearing age from participating in what is, at times, therapeutic medical research. Additionally, it forced researchers to think seriously about the repercussions of homogenous research on a diverse population and to recruit subjects accordingly. For example, almost all patients react similarly to penicillin, but certain diet-pills increase blood pressure in women and not men, and many African Americans require less lithium than others to control mania.[2] The 1994 guideline specifically requires the investigator to review the data to determine if there is likely to be a difference in the way an alternate treatment would affect different gender and racial or ethnic subgroups. A

§ 21–4

1. 45 C.F.R. § 46.111(a).
2. See § 21–5, below.
3. 45 C.F.R. § 46.111(a)(2).
4. 45 C.F.R. § 46.111(b).

§ 21–5

1. For a thorough discussion of the historical catalysts that prompted revision, see Karen L. Baird, "The New NIH and FDA Medical Research Policies: Targeting Gender, Promoting Justice," 24 J. Health Pol. Pol'y & L. 531 (1999).

2. See Jonathan M. Eisenburg, "NIH Promulgates New Guidelines for the Inclusion of Women and Minorities in Medical Research. 10 Berkeley Women's L.J. 183 (1995).

subgroup is defined as "a readily identifiable subset of the U.S. population which is distinguished by either, racial, ethnic and/or cultural heritage."[3] If the data "strongly indicates" a significant difference of clinical or public health importance, the "design of the study must specifically accommodate this." If the data "strongly indicates" no such difference, then gender and race or ethnicity need not be considered (although inclusion of subgroups "is still strongly encouraged.")[4] If there is no indication of any difference or similarity by subgroup, the research must include all relevant subgroups, although the research need not "provide high statistical power for each subgroup."[5]

§ 21–6. Informed Consent to Participate in Research as a Human Subject

a. Substantive Requirements

The regulations require that a researcher obtain legally effective informed consent. Because state law governs the doctrine of informed consent, research done consistently with the federal regulations will adhere to the informed consent law of the state where consent is obtained.[1] In addition, the federal regulations augment state law requirements in several ways. The circumstances of consent must give the subject "sufficient opportunity to consider whether or not to participate" and they must "minimize the possibility of coercion or undue influence."[2] In addition, the regulations explicitly require that the information provided to the subject be in language understandable to that subject.

The regulations also require that the consent document not include any "exculpatory language through which the subject or the representative is made to waive or appear to waive any of the subject's legal rights, or releases or appears to release the investigator, the sponsor, the institution or its agents from liability for negligence."[3] While many exculpatory clauses are unenforceable under state law in any case, the federal regulation prohibits language by which the subject waives any legal right. Thus, for example, apparently a research subject could not be required to submit any negligence claim arising out of the research to arbitration because such an agreement would constitute a waiver of the subject's legal right to a jury trial.

In addition to articulating the general requirements of informed consent, the regulations provide for eight "basic elements of informed consent" that must be provided to each research subject:

(1) A statement that the study involves research, an explanation of the purposes of the research and the expected duration of the subject's participation, a description of the procedure to be followed, and identification of any procedures which are experimental;

3. 59 FR 14508.
4. Id.
5. Id.

2. 45 C.F.R. § 46.116.
3. Id.

§ 21–6
1. See Anderson v. George H. Lanier Memorial Hospital, 982 F.2d 1513 (11th Cir.1993).

(2) A description of any reasonably foreseeable risks or discomforts to the subject;

(3) A description of any benefits to the subject or to others which may reasonably be expected from the research;

(4) A disclosure of appropriate alternative procedures or courses of treatment, if any, that might be advantageous to the subject;

(5) A statement describing the extent, if any, to which confidentiality of records identifying the subject will be maintained;

(6) For research involving more than minimal risk, an explanation as to whether any compensation and an explanation as to whether any medical treatments are available if injury occurs and, if so, what they consist of, or where further information may be attained;

(7) An explanation of whom to contact for answers to pertinent questions about the research and research subjects' rights and whom to contact in the event of a research-related injury to subject; [and]

(8) A statement that participation is voluntary, refusal to participate will involve in no penalty or loss of benefits to which the subject is otherwise entitled, and the subject may discontinue participation at any time without penalty or loss of benefits to which the subject is otherwise entitled.[4]

While most of these requirements are consistent with the state law of informed consent, not all of this information is otherwise required in every state. One important provision, added after the regulations were originally promulgated, requires that the researcher provide the subject with information stating whether compensation or medical treatment will be provided if an injury occurs to the subject in the course of medical treatment. This provision, which applies only to that research involving more than minimal risk,[5] does not require a researcher to provide any compensation or medical treatment; it only requires disclosure of whether the subject will (or will not) receive such compensation.

In addition, the final requirement for informed consent imposes a substantive obligation upon the researcher. Because the proposed subject may refuse participation with "no penalty or loss of benefits to which the subject is otherwise entitled," neither a physician nor an institution engaged in research may refuse to see a patient or terminate the professional relationship with a patient just because that patient fails to consent to participation in medical research.[6]

Finally, the regulation permits the IRB to waive or change some of the requirements of informed consent, at least with regard to research involving no more than a minimal risk, when it is necessary to do so in order to carry

---

4. 45 C.F.R. § 46.116(a). The regulations provide for six additional elements of informed consent under some circumstances. 45 C.F.R. § 46.116(b).

5. Research involves more than minimal risk to a subject when the "risks of harm anticipated in the proposed research are * * * greater considering probability and magnitude, than those ordinarily encountered in daily life or during the performance of routine physical or psychological examinations or tests." 45 C.F.R. § 46.102(g)(definition of "minimal risk").

6. See Chapter 6 on the maintenance of the patient-physician relationship.

out the research, when the change will not "adversely affect the rights and the welfare of the subjects," and where the "the subjects will be provided with additional pertinent information after participation."[7] The authority to waive or change informed consent requirements is used sparingly.

b. Requirements of Documentation of Consent

As a general matter, research involving human subjects provides one of very few contexts in which informed consent must be in writing under American law. The regulations provide that a researcher must secure written informed consent from each subject in each protocol covered by the regulations unless (1) the consent form would be "the only record linking the subject and the research," "the principal risk would be potential harm resulting from a breach of confidentiality," and the subject has decided that she does not want documentation, or, alternatively, (2) written consent would not be required in a therapeutic context, given the nature of the medical intervention, and the research involves less than minimal risk.

§ 21–7. Access to Institutional Review Board Records

Recently some litigants, most commonly plaintiffs in malpractice cases, have sought access to IRB records. Patient records maintained by individual review boards are accorded the same level of confidentiality as medical records maintained elsewhere in the institution. However, the status of IRB records that are specific to research protocols, but not to individual patients, is less certain. While Institutional Review Boards are established pursuant to federal regulation, they are not federal agencies within the definition of the Freedom of Information Act[1] and thus their records may not be obtained under that statute. State hospitals and state universities frequently operate state IRBs, however, and those institutions may come within the scope of state public records acts.

It may also be possible to obtain IRB records through ordinary discovery in litigation, depending on the discovery rules of the jurisdiction. While the records of the IRB and any information about the process of the IRB may be privileged under some peer review privilege statutes, most such statutes would not extend to IRB considerations because of the mandated diversity of IRB membership.[2] One recent case determined that the Minnesota peer review statute did not extend to IRBs.[3] The court concluded that the purpose of IRBs is not peer review; "[l]ike peer review statutes around the nation, the Minnesota statute concerns the protections afforded by peer review."[4] Therefore, the Court held that the protections afforded by peer review statutes do not extend to IRB records.[5] Moreover, the Court also suggested that any attempt by Minnesota to apply its statute to the IRB might be preempted by the federal regulations, which were described as "part of a highly regulated scheme designed to protect the rights and safety of human subjects."[6]

7. 45 C.F.R. § 46.116(d).

§ 21–7

1. 5 U.S.C.A. §§ 551 et seq.

2. See § 21–3, supra.

3. Konrady v. Oesterling, 149 F.R.D. 592 (D.Minn.1993).

4. Id. at 597.

5. Id.

6. Id.

§ 21-8. Regulation of Research Performed Upon Special Groups of Subjects

a. Children

In 1983 the Department of Health and Human Services promulgated regulations which provide supplementary protection to children who are research subjects. These regulations divide research that includes children into three categories: "research not involving greater than minimal risk," "research involving greater than minimal risk but presenting the prospect of direct benefit to the individual subjects," and "research involving greater than minimal risk and no prospect of direct benefit to individual subjects, but likely to yield generalizable knowledge about the subject's disorder or condition."[1] In all cases, IRB approval is dependent upon a showing that, "adequate provisions are made for soliciting the assent of the children and permission of their parents or guardians."[2]

The regulations place additional limitations on research involving "[c]hildren who are wards of the state or any other agency, institution, or entity."[3] The regulations attempt to discourage researchers from using these easy marks as subjects, and their use as subjects is prohibited unless the research is "related to their status as wards" or is conducted in such a way that most of the children who are subjects are not wards.[4]

b. Fetuses and Embryos

The most controversial federal regulations governing research are those that severely limit fetal research.[5] These regulations divide fetal research into two categories: research done upon fetuses *in utero*, and research done upon fetuses *ex utero*. Therapeutic research is permitted on a fetus *in utero* only if the risk is minimized. Non-therapeutic research is permitted on a fetus *in utero* only if the risk is minimized and the research is intended to result in "the development of important biomedical knowledge, which cannot be obtained by other means."[6]

Viable fetuses *ex utero* are treated as children, of course, and non-viable fetuses *ex utero* may be subjects in research only if "(1) vital functions of the fetus will not be artificially maintained except where the purpose of the activity is to develop new methods for enabling fetuses to survive to the point of viability, (2) experimental activities which of themselves would terminate the heartbeat or respiration of a fetus will not be employed, and (3) the purpose of the activity is the development of important biomedical knowledge which cannot be obtained by other means."[7] Both the mother and father (unless he is unavailable or the pregnancy is the result of rape) must consent to the research before a fetus can be a subject of such research.[8]

Opponents of these limitations believe that this effective prohibition on research upon human fetuses slows the development of medical treatment

§ 21-8

1. 45 C.F.R. §§ 46.404, 46.406.

2. 45 C.F.R. § 46.408.

3. 45 C.F.R. § 46.409.

4. Id. For a thorough analysis of research involving children as human subjects, see Robert Levine, Ethics and Regulation of Clinical Research 235–256 (2d ed. 1986).

5. Id. at 297–320.

6. 45 C.F.R. § 46.208.

7. 45 C.F.R. § 46.209.

8. Id.

which could help many non-viable fetuses reach the point of viability and which could help viable fetuses live longer and happier lives. Proponents contend that the unique vulnerability of the fetus requires special protection by government regulation. Of course, the debate over the appropriate limitations on research involving fetal tissue is not unrelated to the debate over the propriety of abortion. Some fear that giving physicians the authority to do research upon fetal tissue will inevitably result in their acquisition of that tissue through encouraged or solicited abortions. This fear resulted in a 1988 ban (called a "moratorium") on all federal funding of research in which human fetal tissue from induced abortions is transplanted into humans. After five years of continual opposition from ethicists and medical researchers, President Clinton lifted the ban in 1993.

c. Prisoners

Other classes of subjects have been deemed to require special protection through regulation. For example, limitations have been placed upon research involving prisoners[9] because "prisoners may be under constraints because of their incarceration, which could affect their ability to make a truly voluntary and uncoerced decision[10] whether or not to participate as subjects in research."[11] These regulations concerning the use of prisoners as subjects require that any IRB which approves research involving prisoner–subjects have at least one prisoner or prisoner representative and that a majority of the IRB be unassociated with the prison.[12] Generally, research upon prisoners is now limited to criminal behavior, prison conditions and other issues of potential special value to prisoners.[13] In addition, the approval of research involving prisoners requires assurances that the prisoner-subjects will not receive substantially better treatment or early parole as gratuity for their participation in the research, and that the selection of the prisoner-subjects will be "fair" and "immune from arbitrary intervention by prison authorities or prisoners."[14]

d. Mentally Disabled

Among those for whom additional research protections have been proposed but not adopted are those institutionalized as mentally disabled.[15] While the unadopted regulations have no legal consequence, the public discussion that followed the proposal to severely limit the use of institutionalized mentally disabled subjects has had a real effect on the research community; researchers now avoid this class of subjects if others are available.

---

9. "In the 1950's, American inmates were intentionally infected with live-cancer cells, herpes, ringworm, hepatitis, and syphilis, all in the name of medical research." When those and, "other experiments were brought to light in the 1970's, they were stopped and research in prisons was banned in some states and severely curtailed in others." More recently, a panel of experts drafted preliminary guidelines for medical experimentation upon prisoners in response to inmates infected with HIV and hepatitis C who wish to again be included in medical research. David Rising, "New Guidelines on Inmate Research", Associated Press, October, 15, 1999.

10. The drafters of the proposed changes, which intend to again allow inmate access as subjects to medical research, promise not to repeat past mistakes. David Rising, "New Guidelines on Inmate Research", Associated Press, October, 15, 1999.

11. 45 C.F.R. § 46.302.

12. 45 C.F.R. § 46.304.

13. 45 C.F.R. § 46.306.

14. 45 C.F.R. § 46.305.

15. 43 Fed. Reg. 53950 (1978). For a discussion of this class of research subjects, see Levine, supra note 4 at 257–276.

§ 21–9. Application of Federal Regulations to Emergency Research

Prior to the 1996 amendments to the federal regulations, researchers expressed concern that the regulations effectively eliminated the possibility that they could carry out necessary emergency room research. For example, prior to the amendments, emergency room physicians were confronted with a choice of highly promising but unproven alternative medications that could be of use to unconscious patients who arrive after suffering a heart attack or a stroke. However, because these patients would not be competent to consent, they could not be employed as subjects in research to prove the efficacy of the newly developed treatments. Therefore, under the pre-1996 regulations, it would always be impossible to do randomized clinical trials of any promising treatment used in an emergency situation to treat patients who were not competent. This limitation fettered doctors' abilities to treat individual patients and to accrue clinically sound research on innovative emergency treatments.

In 1996, the the federal regulations were amended to take into account this conundrum and to provide for an exception to the rule that a subject must supply informed consent to be properly included in a clinical study approved by an IRB.[1] The amended regulations provide that research upon a subject who is in a life-threatening situation is permitted "when available treatments are unproven or unsatisfactory" and the research is "necessary to determine what particular intervention is most beneficial."[2] Moreover, the prospective researcher must show that the subjects will be unable to provide consent as a result of their medical condition and that the proposed intervention must be administered before it would be feasible to have a legal representative grant consent.[3] Also, there must not be a reasonable means of identifying those who could appropriately serve as subjects prior to the subjects' arrival at the emergency room,[4] and the research must be in the best interest of the subjects.[5] Finally, there must be consultation with the community from which the subjects will be drawn and the public must receive disclosure of proposed research and the results of the research.[6]

§ 21–10. Liability

Researchers may be liable for negligence, for fraud, or for breach of the fiduciary duty they owe their subjects. In one case, the California Supreme Court was presented with a patient/subject who sought damages against his physicians for a failure to secure informed consent, a breach of fiduciary duty, and a conversion of tissue.[1] Initially, the patient's physicians convinced him

§ 21–9

1. 21 C.F.R. § 50.24
2. Id.
3. Id.
4. Id.
5. Id.
6. Id.

§ 21–10

1. Moore v. Regents of the University of California, 793 P.2d 479 (Calif. 1990). There are other cases where researchers have been found to have profited inappropriately from their research. Drs. Condie and Najarian were accused of making very substantial profits from the sales of ALG, an antirejection drug they developed to assist in organ transplantation. Dr. Condie pled guilty to a charge that grew out of failure to seek proper FDA licensing of ALG, and, while Dr. Najarian was acquitted at trial, the University of Minnesota refused to reinstate him as head of the surgery department because it found him unfit for such

that the removal of his cancerous spleen was necessary to save his life. For seven years following the removal, the patient regularly returned to the hospital where the surgery took place — 1000 miles away from his home — for aftercare procedures that his physicians claimed could only performed at their hospital. The patient was subjected to the taking of blood, blood serum, skin, bone marrow and sperm. Unbeknownst to the patient, his physicians used his tissue to develop and patent a commercially valuable cell line. The patient alleged that the physicians concealed from him the fact that they would "benefit financially" by continuing the doctor-patient relationship. Ultimately the Court determined that the patient stated a cause of action for failure to obtain informed consent and for breach of fiduciary duty, but not for conversion of tissue.

General liability theories may apply against IRBs as they apply against other defendants. Thus, an IRB may be liable for negligence if it fails to exercise due care and a patient (or someone else, consistent with principles of tort law) is injured as a result of its failure. While some IRBs at state institutions may enjoy the sovereign immunity of their sponsor, there is no independent immunity which arises out of the role of the IRB as a creature of the federal law. In addition, an IRB may be subject to an action or an injunction when it improperly refuses to approve research or improperly refuses to allow a subject to participate.[2] Of course, if an IRB were to be found to engage in fraud, it could be liable under ordinary principles applied to such cases, also.[3] There is no precedent for imposing liability upon individual members of an Institutional Review Board because of the decision of that board and, presumably, their individual liability would be analogous to the individual liability of members of a corporate board of directors for actions of that board.

§ 21–11. Using Third World Subjects as Research Subjects: The African AIDS Trials

The roles of international research organizations, and American researchers doing research abroad, were called into question as a consequence of a series of perinatal HIV transmission studies done in Africa and Asia in the mid–1990s.[1] There is a particular need for treatment for HIV-positive pregnant women in some African and Asian countries, where the HIV infection rate is far higher than it is in most of the developed world. There are more than a half million HIV infected babies born each year, most in the developing world, and the United Nations has put a high priority on finding some genuinely feasible way of dealing with this increasingly pervasive problem.

As a general matter, between 17% and 25% of pregnant women who are infected with HIV will give birth to an HIV-positive baby. In the United

a position. For an interesting opinion arising from this litigation upholding FDA regulations against the claim that they are too vague to give rise to criminal allegations, see United States v. Najarian, 915 F.Supp. 1460 (D.Minn. 1996).

2. See Mason v. Institutional Review Board for Human Research, Medical University of South Carolina, 953 F.2d 638 (4th Cir.1992)(action dismissed as moot).

3. See Anderson v. George H. Lanier Memorial Hospital, 982 F.2d 1513 (11th Cir.1993).

§ 21–11

1. For one summary account of the results of the studies, see Lawrence Altman, Spare AIDS Regime Is Found To Reduce Risks to Newborns, New York Times, February 2, 1999, at A–1.

States, an HIV-positive mother will be offered AZT during her last six weeks of pregnancy and intravenous medication during delivery, and the baby will be treated for six weeks after birth. This protocol, which decreases the transmission rate to about 8%, is too expensive (at more than $1000) for use in developing countries, where any use of a needle may also be too risky. As a consequence, the United Nations AIDS program, along with the United States National Institutes of Health, the Centers for Disease Control and others, sponsored research in which mostly impoverished HIV-positive women in poor countries were randomized to a few different relatively inexpensive courses of treatment. Some women were also randomized to a placebo. While the investigators sought the consent of those who participated in the study, it was not always provided in writing, and, given the alternative–no treatment at all– some believe that it was inherently coerced consent. The purpose of the research was to find some cheap and safe way of treating HIV-positive pregnant women in very poor countries; of course, the beneficiaries of the research could include the HIV-positive pregnant women (and third party health care payers) in the United States and the rest of the developed world, too.

Some criticized the studies as improper research involving human subjects, and attempts to modify the Declaration of Helsinki to accommodate this kind of research were strongly opposed by the Health Research Group of Ralph Nader's Public Citizen and other medical researchers.[2] First, they argued, modification of the Declaration to permit such research would change the current ethical requirement that a new therapeutic intervention be tested against the best current treatment, not against a placebo. They argued that changing this requirement so that the new treatment would need to be tested against the best treatment "that would otherwise be available" to the subjects, not the best treatment, would endanger the poor, who routinely could be offered a second class alternative to the research treatment being tested. As the Health Research Group argued, "[p]articularly in countries like the United States, which does not have universal health coverage, it is inevitable that this principle will ultimately be used to deny uninsured or underinsured persons access to medical care in human experiments." That group also opposed changes in the Declaration of Helsinki that would permit the use of placebos where "the outcome measures are neither death nor disability," that would allow medical journals to publish research that was done in violation of the Declaration if the editors had "consider[ed] carefully" the reasons for the variances, and that would permit informed consent to be oral (rather than written) in cases of "slight risk" or when the medical intervention would not ordinarily require a written document.

2. For the full text of Public Citizen's letter criticizing proposed changes in the Declaration of Helsinki, see http://www.citizen.org/hrg/WHAT'SNEW/1777.htm. See, generally, Marcia Angell, The Ethics of Clinical Research in the Third World, 337 N. Eng. J. Med. 847 (1997) and H. Varmus and D. Satcher, Ethical Complexities of Conducting Research in Developing Countries, 337 N. Eng. J. Med. 1003 (1997).

Appendix

RESEARCHING HEALTH
LAW ON WESTLAW®

Analysis

Section 1. Introduction

Health Law provides a strong base for analyzing even the most complex problem involving health law. Whether your research requires examination of case law, statutes, expert commentary or other materials, West books and Westlaw are excellent sources of information.

To keep you abreast of current developments, Westlaw provides frequently updated databases. With Westlaw, you have unparalleled legal research resources at your fingertips.

Additional Resources

If you have not previously used Westlaw or have questions not covered in this appendix, call the West Group Reference Attorneys at 1–800–REF–ATTY (1–800–733–2889). The West Group Reference Attorneys are trained, licensed attorneys, available 24 hours a day to assist you with your Westlaw search questions.

Section 2.   Westlaw Databases

Each database on Westlaw is assigned an abbreviation called an *identifier*, which you use to access the database. You can find identifiers for all databases in the online Westlaw Directory and in the printed *Westlaw Database Directory*. When you need to know more detailed information about a database, use Scope. Scope contains coverage information, lists of related databases and valuable search tips. To access Scope, **click Scope** after you access the database.

The following chart lists Westlaw databases that contain information pertaining to health law. For a complete list of health law databases, see the online Westlaw Directory or the printed *Westlaw Database Directory*. Because new information is continually being added to Westlaw, you should also check Welcome to Westlaw and the Westlaw Directory for new database information.

Selected Health Law Databases on Westlaw

Database	Identifier	Coverage
Federal Case Law		
Federal Health Law–Cases	FHTH–CS	Begins with 1789
Federal Health Law–Supreme Court Cases	FHTH–SCT	Begins with 1790
Federal Health Law–Courts of Appeals Cases	FHTH–CTA	Begins with 1891
Federal Health Law–District Courts Cases	FHTH–DCT	Begins with 1789
National Disability Law Reporter	NDLRPTR	Begins with 1990
State Case Law		
Multistate Health Law Cases	MHTH–CS	Varies by state
Individual State Health Law Cases	XXHTH–CS (where XX is a state's two-letter postal abbreviation)	Varies by state
National Disability Law Reporter	NDLRPTR	Begins with 1990
Federal Statutes and Regulations		
Federal Health Law–U.S. Code Annotated	FHTH–USCA	Current data
United States Public Laws	US–PL	Current data
Arnold & Porter Legislative History: Health Security Act– 103rd and 104th Congress	HEALTH103–4–LH	Full history
Federal Health Law–Code of Federal Regulations	FHTH–CFR	Current data
Federal Health Law–Federal Register	FHTH–FR	Begins with July 1980

Database	Identifier	Coverage
State Statutes and Regulations		
State Statutes–Annotated	ST–ANN–ALL	Varies by state
Individual State Statutes–Annotated	XX–ST–ANN (where XX is a state's two-letter postal abbreviation)	Varies by state
Multistate Legislative Service	LEGIS–ALL	Varies by jurisdiction
Individual State Legislative Service	XX–LEGIS (where XX is a state's two-letter postal abbreviation)	Varies by jurisdiction
ENFLEX State Environmental, Health and Safety Regulations	ENFLEX–STATE	Current data
ENFLEX Individual State Environmental, Health and Safety Regulations	ENFLEX–XX (where XX is a state's two-letter postal abbreviation)	Current data
International Regulations		
ENFLEX International Environmental, Health and Safety Regulations	ENFLEX–INT	Current data
ENFLEX Brazil Environmental, Health and Safety Regulations	ENFLEX–BR	Current data
ENFLEX European Union Environmental, Health and Safety Regulations	ENFLEX–EU	Current data
ENFLEX France Environmental, Health and Safety Regulations	ENFLEX–FR	Current data
ENFLEX Indonesia Environmental, Health and Safety Regulations	ENFLEX–IO	Current data
ENFLEX Italy Environmental, Health and Safety Regulations	ENFLEX–IT	Current data
ENFLEX Mexico Environmental, Health and Safety Regulations	ENFLEX–MX	Current data
ENFLEX Spain Environmental, Health and Safety Regulations	ENFLEX–SP	Current data
ENFLEX United Kingdom Environmental, Health and Safety Regulations	ENFLEX–UK	Current data
Federal Administrative Decisions		
Federal Health Law–FDA Enforcement Report	FHTH–FDA	Begins with May 1984
Federal Health Law–Health and Human Services Decisions	FHTH–HHS	Begins with March 1974
Federal Health Law–Health Care Financing Administration Rulings	FHTH–HCFA	Begins with 1990

Database	Identifier	Coverage
Federal Health Law–Provider Reimbursement Review Board Hearing and Appeals Decisions	FHTH–PRRB	Provider Reimbursement Review Board: begins with 1994; Health Care Financing Administration: begins with 1996
National Disability Law Reporter	NDLRPTR	Begins with 1990
United States Department of Agriculture Decisions	USDA	Begins with 1977

State Administrative Decisions

New York Department of Health Administrative Review Board	NYDOH–ARB	Begins with 1990

Litigation Reports

Andrews AIDS Litigation Reporter	ANAIDSLR	Begins with November 1996
Andrews Health Care Fraud Litigation Reporter	ANHCFLR	Begins with November 1996
Andrews Health Law Litigation Reporter	ANHLLR	Begins with November 1996
Andrews Pharmaceutical Litigation Reporter	ANPHARLR	Begins with November 1996
Mealey's Emerging Drugs and Devices	MLREDD	Begins with January 1996
Mealey's Emerging Insurance Disputes	MEINSD	Begins with January 1996
Mealey's Emerging Toxic Torts	METT	Begins with January 1993
Mealey's Litigation Reports: Asbestos	MLRASB	Begins with January 1993
Mealey's Litigation Reports: Biotechnology	MLRBT	Begins with September 1996
Mealey's Litigation Reports: Breast Implants	MLRBI	Begins with January 1993
Mealey's Litigation Reports: Fen–Phen/Redux	MLRFPR	Begins with November 1997
Mealey's Litigation Reports: Insurance	MLRINS	Begins with January 1993
Mealey's Litigation Reports: Insurance Supplement	MLRINSSUP	Begins with March 1995
Mealey's Litigation Reports: Tobacco	MLRTOBAC	Begins with May 1995
Mealey's Managed Care Liability Report	MLRMCLR	Begins with January 1997

News, Daily Reports, Current Developments and Legal Directories

American Political Network–American Health Line	APN–HE	Begins with March 1992
BNA Health Care Daily	BNA–HCD	Begins with October 1992
BNA's Health Care Policy Report	BNA–HCP	Begins with March 1993

Database	Identifier	Coverage
BNA's Health Law Reporter	BNA–HLR	Begins with September 1992
BNA's Medicare Report	BNA–MED	Begins with November 1991
California Health Law Monitor	SMCAHTHLM	Begins with January 1997
Health Care Services Industry News	WNS–HC	Varies by publication
Health News	HTHNEWS	Varies by source
Health News Daily	HND	Begins with January 1990
Medical Malpractice Law and Strategy	MEDMALLST	Begins with March 1995
Medico–Legal Watch	ANMEDLW	Begins with January 1997
MediConf: Medical Conferences & Events	MEDICONF	1993–2013
New York Health Law Update	SMNYHTHLU	Begins with January 1997
United Kingdom Current Awareness Food and Health	UKCA–FOOD	Most recent 90 days
Westlaw Topical Highlights–Health	WTH–HTH	Current data
West Legal Directory®–Health	WLD–HTH	Current data

Expert Witness Materials

ExpertNet	EXPNET	Current data
Forensic Services Directory	FSD	Current data
National Expert Transcript Service	NETS	Begins with April 1993

Legal Texts and Periodicals

Health Law–Law Reviews, Texts & Bar Journals	HTH–TP	Varies by publication
American Journal of Law & Medicine	AMJLM	Selected coverage begins with 1989 (vol. 15); full coverage begins with 1993 (vol. 19, no. 3)
American Jurisprudence Legal Forms 2d	AMJUR–LF	Current through June 1999 supplement
American Jurisprudence Pleading and Practice Forms Annotated	AMJUR–PP	Current through March 1999 supplement
American Jurisprudence Proof of Facts	AMJUR–POF	Current through July 1998 supplement
American Jurisprudence Proof of Facts and Trials Combination	AMJUR–POFTR	Current through July 1998 supplements
American Jurisprudence Trials	AMJUR–TRIALS	Current through July 1998 supplement
American Law Reports	ALR	Current data
Annals of Health Law	AHTHL	Selected coverage begins with 1992 (vol. 1); full coverage begins with 1994 (vol. 3)

Database	Identifier	Coverage
DePaul Journal of Health Care Law	DPLJHCL	Full coverage begins with 1996 (vol. 1)
Florida Legal and Business & Pleading and Practice Forms Combined	FL–LFPP	*Florida Jur Forms Legal and Business*: current through October 1999 supplement; *Florida Pleading and Practice Forms*: current through March 1999 supplement and 1999 replacement volumes
Florida Jur Forms Legal and Business	FL–LF	Current through October 1999 supplement
Florida Pleading and Practice Forms	FL–PP	Current through March 1999 supplement and 1999 replacement volumes
Food and Drug Law Journal	FOODDLJ	Selected coverage begins with 1989 (vol. 44)
Guidelines for State Court Decision Making in Life–Sustaining Medical Treatment Cases	LSMTCS	Revised Second Edition
Health Lawyer	HTHLAW	Selected coverage begins with 1990 (vol. 4–SUM)
Health Care Fraud	HTHCRFRD	Current through Release No. 5, 1999
Health Matrix: Journal of Law–Medicine	HTHMTX	Selected coverage begins with 1991 (vol. 1); full coverage begins with 1993 (vol. 3, no. 2)
Issues in Law and Medicine	ISSULM	Selected coverage begins with 1985 (vol. 1)
Journal of Contemporary Health Law & Policy	JCHLP	Selected coverage begins with 1985 (vol. 1); full coverage begins with 1993 (vol. 10)
Journal of Health Care Law & Policy	JHTHCLP	Full coverage begins with 1998 (vol. 1)
Journal of Health Politics, Policy & Law	JHPPL	Selected coverage begins with 1990 (vol. 15); full coverage begins with 1994 (vol. 19)
Journal of Law & Health	JLHEALTH	Selected coverage begins with 1985 (vol. 1)
Journal of Law, Medicine & Ethics	JLMEDETH	Full coverage begins with 1998 (vol. 26)
Journal of Legal Medicine	JLEGMED	Selected coverage begins with 1992 (vol. 13); full coverage begins with 1994 (vol. 15)
Medicine and Law	MEDLAW	Full coverage begins with 1997 (vol. 16)
New York Forms Legal and Business	NY–LF	Current through November 1999 supplement and 1999 edition of Tables volume
Occupational Safety and Health Law	OSHL	Current through 1999

Database	Identifier	Coverage
Ohio Forms Legal and Business	OH–LF	Current through September 1999 supplement and 1999 revised volumes
Ohio Jurisprudence Pleading and Practice Forms	OH–PP	Current through 1998 supplement
Ohio Legal and Business & Pleading and Practice Forms	OH–LFPP	*Ohio Forms Legal and Business*: current through September 1999 supplement and 1999 revised volumes; *Ohio Jurisprudence Pleading and Practice Forms*: current through 1998 supplement
Quinnipiac Health Law Journal	QHTHLJ	Full coverage begins with 1996 (vol. 1)
Risk: Health, Safety & Environment	RISKHSE	Selected coverage begins with 1990 (vol. 1)
Texas Forms Legal and Business	TX–LF	Current through November 1999 supplement and 1999 edition of Tables volume
Texas Jurisprudence Pleading and Practice Forms 2d	TX–PP	Current through November 1998 supplement and 1999 replacement volumes
Texas Legal and Business & Pleading and Practice Forms	TX–LFPP	*Texas Forms Legal and Business*: Current through November 1999 supplement and 1999 edition of Tables volume; *Texas Jurisprudence Pleading and Practice Forms 2d*: Current through November 1998 supplement and 1999 replacement volumes
West's® McKinney's® Forms	NY–FORMS	Current data
West's McKinney's Forms– All Forms Indices	NYFORMSIDX–ALL	Current through January 1999

Section 3.   Retrieving a Document with a Citation: Find and Hypertext Links

3.1   Find

Find is a Westlaw service that allows you to retrieve a document by entering its citation. Find allows you to retrieve documents from anywhere in Westlaw without accessing or changing databases. Find is available for many documents, including case law (state and federal), the *United States Code Annotated®*, state statutes, administrative materials, and texts and periodicals.

To use Find, simply access the Find service and type the citation. The following list provides some examples:

To Find This Document	Access Find and Type
Your Home Visiting Nurse Services, Inc. v. Shalala 119 S. Ct. 930 (1999)	**119 sct 930**
42 U.S.C.A. § 1395dd	**42 usca 1395dd**
42 C.F.R. § 405.1885	**42 cfr 405.1885**
Cal. Welf. & Inst. Code § 14105.98	**ca wel & inst 14105.98**
Minn. Stat. Ann. § 147A.02	**mn st 147a.02**

For a complete list of publications that can be retrieved with Find and their abbreviations, consult the Publications List after accessing Find.

3.2 Hypertext Links

Use hypertext links to move from one location to another on Westlaw. For example, use hypertext links to go directly from the statute, case or law review article you are viewing to a cited statute, case or article; from a headnote to the corresponding text in the opinion; or from an entry in a statutes index database to the full text of the statute.

Section 4. Searching with Natural Language

Overview: With Natural Language, you can retrieve documents by simply describing your issue in plain English. If you are a relatively new Westlaw user, Natural Language searching can make it easier for you to retrieve cases that are on point. If you are an experienced Westlaw user, Natural Language gives you a valuable alternative search method.

When you enter a Natural Language description, Westlaw automatically identifies legal phrases, removes common words and generates variations of terms in your description. Westlaw then searches for the concepts in your description. Concepts may include significant terms, phrases, legal citations or topic and key numbers. Westlaw retrieves the 20 documents that most closely match your description, beginning with the document most likely to match.

4.1 Natural Language Search

Access a database, such as Multistate Health Law Cases (MHTH–CS). In the text box, type a Natural Language description such as the following:

can a patient file a claim against a hospital under the emergency medical treatment and active labor act

4.2 Next Command

Westlaw displays the 20 documents that most closely match your description, beginning with the document most likely to match. If you want to view additional documents, use the Next command.

4.3 Natural Language Browse Commands

Best Mode: To display the best portion (the portion that most closely matches your description) of each document in your search result, click the **Best Selection** arrow at the bottom of the window or page.

Standard Browsing Commands: You can also browse your Natural Language search result using standard Westlaw browsing commands, such as citations list, Locate and term mode. When you browse your Natural Language search result in term mode, the five portions of each document that are most likely to match your description are displayed.

Section 5. Searching with Terms and Connectors

Overview: With Terms and Connectors searching, you enter a query, which consists of key terms from your issue and connectors specifying the relationship between these terms.

Terms and Connectors searching is useful when you want to retrieve a document for which you know specific details, such as the title or the fact situation. Terms and Connectors searching is also useful when you want to retrieve documents relating to a specific issue.

5.1 Terms

Plurals and Possessives: Plurals are automatically retrieved when you enter the singular form of a term. This is true for both regular and irregular plurals (e.g., **child** retrieves *children*). If you enter the plural form of a term, you will not retrieve the singular form.

If you enter the nonpossessive form of a term, Westlaw automatically retrieves the possessive form as well. However, if you enter the possessive form, only the possessive form is retrieved.

Automatic Equivalencies: Some terms have alternative forms or equivalencies; for example, *5* and *five* are equivalent terms. Westlaw automatically retrieves equivalent terms. The *Westlaw Reference Manual* contains a list of equivalent terms.

Compound Words, Abbreviations and Acronyms: When a compound word is one of your search terms, use a hyphen to retrieve all forms of the word. For example, the term **along-side** retrieves *along-side, alongside* and *along side.*

When using an abbreviation or acronym as a search term, place a period after each of the letters to retrieve any of its forms. For example, the term **f.d.a.** retrieves *fda, f.d.a., f d a* and *f. d. a.* Note: The abbreviation does *not* retrieve *Food and Drug Administration*, so remember to add additional alternative terms to your query such as **"food and drug administration"**.

The Root Expander and the Universal Character: When you use the Terms and Connectors search method, placing the root expander (!) at the end of a root term generates all other terms with that root. For example, adding the ! to the root *treat* in the query

treat! /5 patient

instructs Westlaw to retrieve such terms as *treat, treated, treating* and *treatment.*

The universal character (*) stands for one character and can be inserted in the middle or at the end of a term. For example, the term

withdr*w

will retrieve *withdraw* and *withdrew.* Adding three asterisks to the root *elect*

elect*

instructs Westlaw to retrieve all forms of the root with up to three additional characters. Terms such as *elected* or *election* are retrieved by this query. However, terms with more than three letters following the root, such as *electronic,* are not retrieved. Plurals are always retrieved, even if more than three letters follow the root.

Phrase Searching: To search for an exact phrase, place it within quotation marks. For example, to search for references to *health maintenance organization*, type "**health maintenance organization**". When you are using the Terms and Connectors search method, you should use phrase searching only if you are certain that the terms in the phrase will not appear in any other order.

5.2 Alternative Terms

After selecting the terms for your query, consider which alternative terms are necessary. For example, if you are searching for the term *admissible*, you might also want to search for the term *inadmissible*. You should consider both synonyms and antonyms as alternative terms. You can also use the Westlaw thesaurus to add alternative terms to your query.

5.3 Connectors

After selecting terms and alternative terms for your query, use connectors to specify the relationship that should exist between search terms in your retrieved documents. The connectors are described below:

Use:	To retrieve documents with:	Example:
& (and)	both terms	**c.o.b.r.a. & medicare**
or (space)	either term or both terms	**doctor physician**
/p	search terms in the same paragraph	**inspect! /p hospital**
/s	search terms in the same sentence	**assist! /s suicide**
+s	the first search term preceding the second within the same sentence	**burden +s prov! proof**
/n	search terms within "n" terms of each other (where "n" is a number)	**risk /3 assum!**
+n	the first search term preceding the second by "n" terms (where "n" is a number)	**managed +3 care**
" "	search terms appearing in the same order as in the quotation marks	**"american medical association"**

Use:	To exclude documents with:	Example:
% (but not)	search terms following the % symbol	**laminectomy %"work! compensation"**

5.4 Field Restrictions

Overview: Documents in each Westlaw database consist of several segments, or fields. One field may contain the citation, another the title, another the synopsis and so forth. Not all databases contain the same fields. Also depending on the database, fields with the same name may contain different types of information.

To view a list of fields for a specific database and their contents, see Scope for that database. Note that in some databases not every field is available for every document.

To retrieve only those documents containing your search terms in a specific field, restrict your search to that field. To restrict your search to a specific field, type the field name or abbreviation followed by your search terms enclosed in parentheses. For example, to retrieve an Illinois case entitled *Baksh v. Human Rights Commission,* access the Illinois Health Law Cases database (ILHTH–CS) and search for your terms in the title field (ti):

ti(baksh & "human rights")

The fields discussed below are available in Westlaw databases you might use for researching health law issues.

Digest and Synopsis Fields: The digest (di) and synopsis (sy) fields, added to case law databases by West's attorney-editors, summarize the main points of a case. The synopsis field contains a brief description of a case. The digest field contains the topic and headnote fields and includes the complete hierarchy of concepts used by West's editors to classify the headnotes to specific West digest topic and key numbers. Restricting your search to the synopsis and digest fields limits your result to cases in which your terms are related to a major issue in the case.

Consider restricting your search to one or both of these fields if

- you are searching for common terms or terms with more than one meaning, and you need to narrow your search; or
- you cannot narrow your search by using a smaller database.

For example, to retrieve state cases that discuss liability for false positive test results for HIV, access the Multistate Health Law Cases database (MHTH–CS) and type the following query:

sy,di(false! /p positive /p h.i.v. immun*-deficien!)

Headnote Field: The headnote field (he) is part of the digest field but does not contain topic numbers, hierarchical classification information or key numbers. The headnote field contains a one-sentence summary for each point of law in a case and any supporting citations given by the author of the opinion. A headnote field restriction is useful when you are searching for specific statutory sections or rule numbers. For example, to retrieve headnotes from federal cases that cite 42 U.S.C.A. § 1395dd, access the Federal Health Law Cases database (FHTH–CS) and type the following query:

he(42 +5 1395dd)

Topic Field: The topic field (to) is also part of the digest field. It contains hierarchical classification information, including the West digest topic names and numbers and the key numbers. You should restrict search terms to the topic field in a case law database if

- a digest field search retrieves too many documents; or
- you want to retrieve cases with digest paragraphs classified under more than one topic.

For example, the topic Drugs and Narcotics has the topic number 138. To retrieve state cases that discuss a drug manufacturer's liability for failing to provide warning of side effects, access the Multistate Health Law Cases database (MHTH–CS) and type a query like the following:

to(138) /p manufactur! /p fail! /5 warn! /p side-effect

To retrieve cases classified under more than one topic and key number, search for your terms in the topic field. For example, to retrieve cases discussing a health care facility's liability to a person contracting an infectious disease on the premises, which may be classified to Damages (115), Hospitals (204), Limitation of Actions (241), Physicians and Surgeons (299) or Workers' Compensation (413), among other topics, access the Multistate Health Law Cases database (MHTH–CS) and type a query like the following:

to(infect! disease) /p contract! /p hospital clinic facility

For a complete list of West digest topics and their corresponding topic numbers, access the Key Number Service or the Key Number Center.

> *Note*: Slip opinions, cases not reported by West and cases from topical services do not contain the digest, headnote and topic fields.

Prelim and Caption Fields: When searching in a database containing statutes, rules or regulations, restrict your search to the prelim (pr) and caption (ca) fields to retrieve documents in which your terms are important enough to appear in a section name or heading. For example, to retrieve federal statutes relating to emergency medical care, access the Federal Health Law–U.S. Code Annotated database (FHTH–USCA) and type the following:

pr,ca(emergency /s medical health /s care treatment service)

5.5   Date Restrictions

You can use Westlaw to retrieve documents *decided* or *issued* before, after or on a specified date, as well as within a range of dates. The following sample queries contain date restrictions:

da(1995) & "living will"

da(aft 1998) & "living will"

da(7/30/1999) & "living will"

You can also search for documents *added to a database* on or after a specified date, as well as within a range of dates. The following sample queries contain added-date restrictions:

ad(aft 1995) & "living will"

ad(aft 2–1–1999 & bef 2–17–1999) & "living will"

Section 6.   Searching with Topic and Key Numbers

To retrieve cases that address a specific point of law, use topic and key numbers as your search terms. If you have an on-point case, run a search using the topic and key number from the relevant headnote in an appropriate database to find other cases containing headnotes classified to that topic and key number. For example, to search for cases containing headnotes classified under topic 204 (Hospitals) and key number 6 (Management of institution) access the Multistate Health Law Cases database (MHTH–CS) and enter the following query:

204k6

For a complete list of West digest topic and key numbers, access the Key Number Service or the Key Number Center.

Note: Slip opinions, cases not reported by West and cases from topical services do not contain West topic and key numbers.

Section 7. Verifying Your Research with Citation Research Services

Overview: A citation research service is a tool that helps you ensure that your cases are good law; helps you retrieve cases, legislation or articles that cite a case, rule or statute; and helps you verify that the spelling and format of your citations are correct.

7.1 KeyCite

KeyCite is the citation research service from West Group.

KeyCite for cases covers case law on Westlaw, including unpublished opinions.

KeyCite for statutes covers the *United States Code Annotated* (USCA®), the *Code of Federal Regulations* (CFR) and statutes from all 50 states.

KeyCite Alert monitors the status of your cases or statutes and automatically sends you updates at the frequency you specify when their KeyCite information changes.

KeyCite provides the following:

- Direct appellate history of a case, including related references, which are opinions involving the same parties and facts but resolving different issues
- Negative indirect history of a case, which consists of cases outside the direct appellate line that may have a negative impact on its precedential value
- The title, parallel citations, court of decision, docket number and filing date of a case
- Citations to cases, administrative decisions and secondary sources on Westlaw that have cited a case
- Complete integration with the West Key Number System® so you can track legal issues discussed in a case
- Links to session laws amending or repealing a statute
- Statutory credits and historical notes
- Citations to pending legislation affecting a federal statute

• Citations to cases, administrative decisions and secondary sources that have cited a statute or federal regulation

7.2 Westlaw As a Citator

For citations not covered by KeyCite, including persuasive secondary authority such as restatements and treatises, use Westlaw as a citator to retrieve cases that cite your authority.

For example, to retrieve state cases citing the law review article "Litigating Life and Death," 102 Harv. L. Rev. 375, access the Multistate Health Law Cases database (MHTH–CS) and type a query like the following:

102 +5 375 /s life /s death

Section 8. Researching with Westlaw—Examples

8.1 Retrieving Law Review Articles

Recent law review articles are often a good place to begin researching a legal issue because law review articles serve 1) as an excellent introduction to a new topic or review for a stale one, providing terminology to help you formulate a query; 2) as a finding tool for pertinent primary authority, such as rules, statutes and cases; and 3) in some instances, as persuasive secondary authority.

Suppose you need to gain background information on the use of experimental drugs.

Solution

• To retrieve recent law review articles relevant to your issue, access the Health Law–Law Reviews, Texts & Bar Journals database (HTH–TP). Using the Natural Language search method, enter a description like the following:

use of experimental drugs

• If you have a citation to an article in a specific publication, use Find to retrieve it. For more information on Find, see Section 3.1 of this appendix. For example, to retrieve the article found at 1 Alb. L.J. Sci. & Tech. 131, access Find and type

1 alb l j sci & tech 131

• If you know the title of an article but not which journal it appeared in, access the Health Law–Law Reviews, Texts & Bar Journals database (HTH–TP) and search for key terms using the title field (ti). For example, to retrieve the article "Investigational Treatments: Coverage, Controversy, and Consensus," type the following Terms and Connectors query:

ti(investigat! & treatment & coverage & controversy)

8.2 Retrieving Case Law

Suppose you need to retrieve Illinois case law dealing with wrongful birth actions.

Solution

- Access the Illinois Health Law Cases database (ILHTH–CS). Type a Natural Language description such as the following:

wrongful birth

- When you know the citation for a specific case, use Find to retrieve it. (For more information on Find, see Section 3.1 of this appendix.) For example, to retrieve *Williams v. University of Chicago Hospitals*, 667 N.E.2d 738 (Ill. App. 1996), access Find and type

667 ne2d 738

- If you find a topic and key number that is on point, run a search using that topic and key number to retrieve additional cases discussing that point of law. For example, to retrieve cases containing headnotes classified under topic 299 (Physicians and Surgeons) and key number 18.110 (Damages), type the following query:

299k18.110

- To retrieve cases written by a particular judge, add a judge field (ju) restriction to your query. For example, to retrieve cases written by Judge Murray that contain headnotes classified under topic 299 (Physicians and Surgeons), type the following query:

ju(murray) & to(299)

8.3   Retrieving Statutes and Regulations

Suppose you need to retrieve federal statutes and regulations specifically addressing lead poisoning.

Solution

- Access the Federal Health Law–U.S. Code Annotated database (FHTH–USCA). Search for your terms in the prelim and caption fields using the Terms and Connectors search method:

pr,ca(lead! & poison!)

- When you know the citation for a specific statute or regulation, use Find to retrieve it. For example, to retrieve 40 C.F.R. § 745.87, access Find and type

40 cfr 745.87

- To look at surrounding sections, use the Table of Contents service. Click a hypertext link in the prelim or caption field, or click the **TOC** tab in the left frame. You can also use Documents in Sequence to retrieve the section following § 745.87, even if that subsequent section was not retrieved with your search or Find request.

- When you retrieve a statute on Westlaw, it will contain a message if legislation amending or repealing it is available online. To display this legislation, click the hypertext link in the message.

> Because slip copy versions of laws are added to Westlaw before they contain full editorial enhancements, they are not with Update. To retrieve slip copy versions of laws, access the United States Public Laws database (US–PL) or a state's legislative service database (XX–LEGIS, where XX is the state's two-letter postal abbreviation). Then type **ci(slip)** and descriptive terms, e.g., **ci(slip) & lead**. Slip copy documents are replaced by the editorially enhanced versions within a few working days. Update also does not retrieve legislation that enacts a new statute or covers a topic that will not be incorporated into the statutes. To retrieve this legislation, access US–PL or a legislative service database and enter a query containing terms that describe the new legislation.

8.4 Using KeyCite

Suppose one of the cases you retrieve in your case law research is *Northern Trust Co. v. Upjohn Co.*, 572 N.E.2d 1030 (Ill. App. 1991). You want to determine whether this case is good law and to find other cases that have cited this case.

Solution

- Use KeyCite to retrieve direct history and negative indirect history for *Northern Trust*.

- Use KeyCite to display citing references for *Northern Trust*.

8.5 Following Recent Developments

As the health law specialist in your firm, you are expected to keep up with and summarize recent legal developments in this area of the law. How can you do this efficiently?

Solution

One of the easiest ways to stay abreast of recent developments in health law is by accessing the Westlaw Topical Highlights–Health database (WTH–HTH). The WTH–HTH database contains summaries of recent legal developments, including court decisions, legislation and materials released by administrative agencies in the area of health law. Some summaries also contain suggested queries that combine the proven power of West's topic and key numbers and West's case headnotes to retrieve additional pertinent cases. When you access WTH–HTH you will automatically retrieve a list of documents added to the database in the last two weeks.

Table of Cases

A

Albain v. Flower Hosp., 50 Ohio St.3d 251, 553 N.E.2d 1038 (Ohio 1990)—§ **4–35, n. 11; § 7–2, n. 1; § 7–4; § 7–4, n. 10, 32; § 7–8, n. 9.**

Albany Medical College v. McShane, 499 N.Y.S.2d 376, 489 N.E.2d 1278 (N.Y. 1985)—§ **5–10, n. 40.**

Alberts v. Schultz, 126 N.M. 807, 975 P.2d 1279 (N.M.1999)—§ **6–7, n. 18.**

Albertsons, Inc. v. Kirkingburg, 527 U.S. 555, 119 S.Ct. 2162, 144 L.Ed.2d 518 (1999)— § **4–23, n. 14.**

Albrecht v. Herald Co., 390 U.S. 145, 88 S.Ct. 869, 19 L.Ed.2d 998 (1968)—§ **14–2, n. 6; § 14–17, n. 47.**

Alessi v. Raybestos–Manhattan, Inc., 451 U.S. 504, 101 S.Ct. 1895, 68 L.Ed.2d 402 (1981)—§ **8–3, n. 5.**

Alexander v. Choate, 469 U.S. 287, 105 S.Ct. 712, 83 L.Ed.2d 661 (1985)—§ **10–19; § 10–19, n. 6, 9; § 12–6; § 12–6, n. 11.**

Alexander v. Margolis, 921 F.Supp. 482 (W.D.Mich.1995)—§ **3–23, n. 14.**

Alexander v. Rush North Shore Medical Center, 101 F.3d 487 (7th Cir.1996)—§ **4–23, n. 11.**

Aliessa v. Whalen, 181 Misc.2d 334, 694 N.Y.S.2d 308 (N.Y.Sup.1999)—§ **12–3, n. 6.**

All Care Nursing Service, Inc. v. High Tech Staffing Services, Inc., 135 F.3d 740 (11th Cir.1998)—§ **14–32, n. 33.**

Allen v. Mansour, 681 F.Supp. 1232 (E.D.Mich. 1986)—§ **12–6, n. 8.**

Allen v. Utah Dept. of Health, Div. of Health Care Financing, 850 P.2d 1267 (Utah 1993)—§ **12–4, n. 6.**

Allentown Hospital–Lehigh Valley Hosp. Center v. Board of Assessment Appeals, Lehigh County, 148 Pa.Cmwlth. 422, 611 A.2d 793 (Pa.Cmwlth.1992)—§ **2–3, n. 16.**

Alliance for Healthcare, Inc., State v., 1991 WL 290818 (Me.Super.1991)—§ **14–25, n. 8.**

Allied Tube & Conduit Corp. v. Indian Head, Inc., 486 U.S. 492, 108 S.Ct. 1931, 100 L.Ed.2d 497 (1988)—§ **14–2, n. 49; § 14–13, n. 5, 7, 10.**

Allison v. Centre Community Hosp., 145 Pa. Cmwlth. 495, 604 A.2d 294 (Pa.Cmwlth. 1992)—§ **4–4, n. 15.**

Allore v. Flower Hosp., 121 Ohio App.3d 229, 699 N.E.2d 560 (Ohio App. 6 Dist.1997)— § **16–58, n. 3.**

Allstate Ins. Co. v. Horowitz, 118 Misc.2d 787, 461 N.Y.S.2d 218 (N.Y.City Civ.Ct.1983)— § **5–26, n. 6.**

Almonte v. New York Medical College, 851 F.Supp. 34 (D.Conn.1994)—§ **4–34, n. 33.**

Alonso v. Hospital Authority of Henry County, 175 Ga.App. 198, 332 S.E.2d 884 (Ga.App. 1985)—§ **4–4, n. 2; § 4–10, n. 18.**

Alston, D.M.D., P.C., United States v., 974 F.2d 1206 (9th Cir.1992)—§ **14–24, n. 7; § 14–25, n. 4; § 14–29, n. 6.**

Altenheim German Home v. Turnock, 902 F.2d 582 (7th Cir.1990)—§ **1–16, n. 16, 22.**

Altieri v. Cigna Dental Health, Inc., 753 F.Supp. 61 (D.Conn.1990)—§ **8–5, n. 6.**

Aluminum Co. of America, United States v., 148 F.2d 416 (2nd Cir.1945)—§ **14–20, n. 2.**

Alvarado Community Hosp. v. Shalala, 155 F.3d 1115 (9th Cir.1998)—§ **11–14, n. 12.**

Amaral v. Gordon, No. 126484 (Cal.Sup.Ct. 1990)—§ **4–34; § 4–34, n. 66.**

American Academy of Dermatology v. Department of Health & Human Services, 118 F.3d 1495 (11th Cir.1997)—§ **11–27, n. 38.**

American Academy of Ophthalmologists, 108 F.T.C. 25 (1986)—§ **14–12, n. 12.**

American Academy of Ophthalmology, 101 F.T.C. 1018 (1983)—§ **14–10, n. 19.**

American Academy of Optometry, Inc., 108 F.T.C. 25 (1986)—§ **14–10, n. 5.**

American Academy of Pediatrics v. Lungren, 51 Cal.Rptr.2d 201, 912 P.2d 1148 (Cal. 1996)—§ **18–6, n. 11.**

Americana Healthcare Corp. v. Schweiker, 688 F.2d 1072 (7th Cir.1982)—§ **1–16, n. 2, 23, 27.**

American Council of Certified Podiatric Physicians and Surgeons v. American Bd. of Podiatric Surgery, Inc., 185 F.3d 606 (6th Cir.1999)—§ **14–14; § 14–14, n. 3.**

American Drug Stores, Inc. v. Harvard Pilgrim Health Care, Inc., 973 F.Supp. 60 (D.Mass. 1997)—§ **8–3; § 8–3, n. 41, 55.**

American Healthcorp, Inc., United States ex rel. Pogue v., 914 F.Supp. 1507 (M.D.Tenn. 1996)—§ **13–9, n. 41.**

American Hosp. Ass'n v. N.L.R.B., 499 U.S. 606, 111 S.Ct. 1539, 113 L.Ed.2d 675 (1991)—§ **4–15, n. 4.**

American Hosp. Ass'n v. N.L.R.B., 899 F.2d 651 (7th Cir.1990)—§ **4–15, n. 1.**

American Hosp. Ass'n v. Schweiker, 721 F.2d 170 (7th Cir.1983)—§ **10–16, n. 2.**

American Institute of Certified Public Accountants, In re, Dkt. No. C–3297 (1990)—§ **14–9, n. 11.**

American Medical Ass'n v. Bowen, 857 F.2d 267 (5th Cir.1988)—§ **11–23, n. 6.**

American Medical Ass'n v. F.T.C., 638 F.2d 443 (2nd Cir.1980)—§ **14–2, n. 35; § 14–9, n. 1; § 14–10, n. 19.**

American Medical Ass'n v. Heckler, 606 F.Supp. 1422 (S.D.Ind.1985)—§ **11–23, n. 5.**

American Medical Ass'n v. United States, 317 U.S. 519, 63 S.Ct. 326, 87 L.Ed. 434 (1943)—§ **14–2, n. 45; § 14–9, n. 3; § 14–18; § 14–18, n. 1; § 14–28, n. 5.**

American Medical Ass'n v. United States, 130 F.2d 233, 76 U.S.App.D.C. 70 (D.C.Cir. 1942)—§ **14–9, n. 6; § 14–26, n. 2, 3.**

American Medical Ass'n, In re, 94 F.T.C. 701 (1979)—§ **5–10, n. 14; § 14–7, n. 10; § 14–9, n. 4, 10; § 14–10, n. 1, 2, 3.**

American Medical Centers of Michigan, Ltd., People v., 118 Mich.App. 135, 324 N.W.2d 782 (Mich.App.1982)—§ **13–15, n. 22.**

American Medical Intern., Inc., 104 F.T.C. 1 (1984)—§ **14–44, n. 1; § 14–45, n. 1, 2; § 14–52, n. 36; § 14–54, n. 6, 9, 10.**

American Medical Intern., Inc. v. Scheller, 590 So.2d 947 (Fla.App. 4 Dist.1991)—§ **4–11, n. 15.**

D

E

F

H

Long v. Houston Northwest Medical Center, Inc., 1991 WL 19837 (Tex.App.-Hous. (1 Dist.) 1991)—§ 4–4, n. 3.

Long, United States ex rel. v. SCS Business & Technical Institute, Inc., 173 F.3d 890, 335 U.S.App.D.C. 351 (D.C.Cir.1999)—§ 13–4, n. 28.

Long, United States ex rel. v. SCS Business & Technical Institute, Inc., 173 F.3d 870, 335 U.S.App.D.C. 331 (D.C.Cir.1999)—§ 13–4, n. 27.

Longeway, In re Estate of, 133 Ill.2d 33, 139 Ill.Dec. 780, 549 N.E.2d 292 (Ill.1989)— § 16–18, n. 2.

Long Island Jewish Medical Center, Application of, 147 Misc.2d 724, 557 N.Y.S.2d 239 (N.Y.Sup.1990)—§ 16–34, n. 1.

Long Island Jewish Medical Center, United States v., 983 F.Supp. 121 (E.D.N.Y.1997)— § 14–49; § 14–49, n. 8, 10; § 14–52, n. 32.

Lopez v. Aziz, 852 S.W.2d 303 (Tex.App.-San Antonio 1993)—§ 6–1, n. 18.

Lopez v. Central Plains Regional Hosp., 859 S.W.2d 600 (Tex.App.-Amarillo 1993)—§ 7–4, n. 23.

Lopez v. Medford Community Center, Inc., 384 Mass. 163, 424 N.E.2d 229 (Mass.1981)— § 5–18, n. 2.

Lopez v. New Mexico Bd. of Medical Examiners, 107 N.M. 145, 754 P.2d 522 (N.M. 1988)—§ 3–12, n. 1; § 3–14, n. 1.

Lopez–Soto v. Hawayek, 175 F.3d 170 (1st Cir.1999)—§ 10–5, n. 4.

Lorain Ave. Clinic v. Commissioner, 31 T.C. 141 (Tax Ct.1958)—§ 2–3, n. 5.

Lorenzo, United States v., 768 F.Supp. 1127 (E.D.Pa.1991)—§ 5–30, n. 4; § 13–4, n. 6.

Los Angeles, County of v. Superior Court, 224 Cal.App.3d 1446, 274 Cal.Rptr. 712 (Cal. App. 2 Dist.1990)—§ 4–26, n. 21.

Loss v. Song, M.D., S.C., 1990 WL 159612 (N.D.Ill.1990)—§ 10–5, n. 5; § 10–10, n. 5.

Love v. Cramer, 414 Pa.Super. 231, 606 A.2d 1175 (Pa.Super.1992)—§ 6–4, n. 3.

Lovelace Medical Center v. Mendez, 111 N.M. 336, 805 P.2d 603 (N.M.1991)—§ 17–1, n. 9; § 17–5, n. 3, 16, 35, 36.

Luby v. Teamsters Health, Welfare, and Pension Trust Funds, 944 F.2d 1176 (3rd Cir. 1991)—§ 8–6, n. 10.

Lucas v. South Carolina Coastal Council, 505 U.S. 1003, 112 S.Ct. 2886, 120 L.Ed.2d 798 (1992)—§ 1–17, n. 21.

Lucas v. United States, 757 S.W.2d 687 (Tex. 1988)—§ 6–21; § 6–21, n. 42.

Lugenbuhl v. Dowling, 96-1575 La. 10/10/97, 701 So.2d 447 (La.1997)—§ 6–9, n. 6; § 6–9, n. 18.

Lugo v. Simon, 426 F.Supp. 28 (N.D.Ohio 1976)—§ 10–15, n. 3.

Lupo v. Human Affairs Intern., Inc., 28 F.3d 269 (2nd Cir.1994)—§ 8–4, n. 23; § 8–5, n. 28.

Lurie, Commonwealth v., 524 Pa. 56, 569 A.2d 329 (Pa.1990)—§ 13–15, n. 21.

Lussier v. Dugger, 904 F.2d 661 (11th Cir. 1990)—§ 4–21, n. 21.

Lynch v. Dawson, 820 F.2d 1014 (9th Cir. 1987)—§ 12–15, n. 13.

Lynch v. John M. Redfield Foundation, 9 Cal. App.3d 293, 88 Cal.Rptr. 86 (Cal.App. 2 Dist.1970)—§ 5–14, n. 1; § 5–15, n. 5.

Lyness v. Commonwealth, State Bd. of Medicine, 529 Pa. 535, 605 A.2d 1204 (Pa. 1992)—§ 3–17; § 3–17, n. 3.

M

MacDonald v. Clinger, 84 A.D.2d 482, 446 N.Y.S.2d 801 (N.Y.A.D. 4 Dept.1982)—§ 4–33, n. 11.

Machovec v. Council for Nat. Register of Health Service Providers in Psychology, Inc., 616 F.Supp. 258 (E.D.Va.1985)—§ 14–12, n. 20, 22.

Mackey v. Lanier Collection Agency & Service, Inc., 486 U.S. 825, 108 S.Ct. 2182, 100 L.Ed.2d 836 (1988)—§ 8–3; § 8–3, n. 5, 13, 63.

Mackey v. National Football League, 543 F.2d 606 (8th Cir.1976)—§ 14–2, n. 43.

Macombs Pharmacy, Inc. v. Wing, 1998 WL 696008 (S.D.N.Y.1998)—§ 12–15, n. 4.

Madden v. Kaiser Foundation Hospitals, 131 Cal.Rptr. 882, 552 P.2d 1178 (Cal.1976)— § 7–10, n. 5.

Madison–Hughes v. Shalala, 80 F.3d 1121 (6th Cir.1996)—§ 10–19, n. 17.

Madrid v. Lincoln County Medical Center, 121 N.M. 133, 909 P.2d 14 (N.M.App.1995)— § 4–23, n. 31.

Magee, In re, 87 N.C.App. 650, 362 S.E.2d 564 (N.C.App.1987)—§ 3–12, n. 2; § 3–13, n. 1.

Maggipinto v. Reichman, 481 F.Supp. 547 (E.D.Pa.1979)—§ 6–2, n. 90.

Mahan v. Bethesda Hosp., Inc., 84 Ohio App.3d 520, 617 N.E.2d 714 (Ohio App. 1 Dist. 1992)—§ 6–3, n. 12.

Maher v. Roe, 432 U.S. 464, 97 S.Ct. 2376, 53 L.Ed.2d 484 (1977)—§ 12–6, n. 24; § 18–8, n. 1.

Mahmoodian v. United Hosp. Center, Inc., 185 W.Va. 59, 404 S.E.2d 750 (W.Va.1991)— § 4–4, n. 3, 15; § 4–5, n. 9; § 4–6, n. 5, 10; § 4–7, n. 1.

Mahon v. Cyganiak Planning, Inc., 41 F.Supp.2d 910 (E.D.Wis.1999)—§ 8–4, n. 18.

Mahurin, State v., 799 S.W.2d 840 (Mo.1990)— § 16–40, n. 2.

Maine v. Thiboutot, 448 U.S. 1, 100 S.Ct. 2502, 65 L.Ed.2d 555 (1980)—§ 12–15, n. 3, 12.

Maine Heart Surgical Associates, P.A., State v., 1996 WL 773330 (Me.Super.1996)—§ 14–44, n. 3.

Majca v. Beekil, 183 Ill.2d 407, 233 Ill.Dec. 810, 701 N.E.2d 1084 (Ill.1998)—§ 6–7, n. 38, 39.

Majebe v. North Carolina Bd. of Medical Examiners, 106 N.C.App. 253, 416 S.E.2d 404 (N.C.App.1992)—§ 3–7, n. 1, 6.

Major v. Memorial Hospitals Assn., 84 Cal. Rptr.2d 510 (Cal.App. 5 Dist.1999)—§ 4–11, n. 7.

T

W

*

Table of Statutes

UNITED STATES CODE ANNOTATED
26 U.S.C.A.—Internal Revenue Code

Sec.	This Work Sec.	Note
105	9–5	
105(h)	9–5	34
501(c)	2–1	
501(c)	2–12	
501(c)	5–21	
501(c)(3)	2–1	
501(c)(3)	2–2	
501(c)(3)	2–3	
501(c)(3)	2–4	
501(c)(3)	2–5	
501(c)(3)	2–6	
501(c)(3)	2–8	
501(c)(3)	2–11	
501(c)(3)	2–12	
501(c)(3)	2–13	
501(c)(3)	2–13	1
501(c)(3)	2–13	10
501(c)(3)	2–14	
501(c)(3)	2–15	
501(c)(3)	2–15	3
501(c)(3)	5–11	
501(c)(3)	5–11	7
501(c)(3)	5–21	
501(c)(3)	10–1	
501(c)(4)	2–12	1
501(e)	2–9	8
501(m)	2–13	1
508(e)(1)(B)	5–11	8
512(b)	2–9	8
513(e)	2–9	8
704(b)	5–32	8
721(a)	5–42	5
1361(b)(1)	5–9	8
1401(b)	11–1	3
3101(b)	11–1	3
3111(b)	11–1	3
4958	2–4	
4958	2–6	
4958	2–8	
4958(a)(1)	2–6	2
4958(a)(2)	2–6	3
4958(b)	2–6	4
4958(c)(1)(A)	2–6	1
4980B	9–6	1

28 U.S.C.A.—Judiciary and Judicial Procedure

Sec.	This Work Sec.	Note
1331	11–27	
1346(b)	7–1	16
2671—2680	7–1	16

29 U.S.C.A.—Labor

Sec.	This Work Sec.	Note
101	14–28	2
152(3)	14–28	3
157	4–18	3
158(d)	4–18	2
158(g)	4–19	3

UNITED STATES CODE ANNOTATED
29 U.S.C.A.—Labor

Sec.	This Work Sec.	Note
183(a)	4–19	3
185	8–4	9
206(d)	4–20	2
621—630	9–5	31
621 et seq.	4–20	5
623(f)(2)(B)(1)	9–5	33
630(b)	9–5	31
630(l)	9–5	32
651 et seq.	4–23	30
702(b)	10–20	3
706(8)(D)	4–23	17
721(b)	10–20	6
791(b)	4–20	6
793	4–20	6
794	4–20	6
794	4–21	18
794	4–21	19
794	4–23	4
794	10–20	1
794(a)	4–23	5
794(a)	10–20	5
1002(1)	8–2	5
1002(3)	8–2	5
1002(6)	8–2	21
1002(7)	8–2	20
1002(16)(A)	8–2	23
1002(16)(B)	8–2	22
1002(21)(A)	8–2	24
1002(32)	8–2	2
1002(33)	8–2	3
1003(a)	8–2	1
1003(b)(1)	8–2	2
1003(b)(2)	8–2	3
1022	8–1	
1022	8–8	3
1022(b)	9–2	4
1103(b)(3)	8–2	4
1104	8–7	
1104(a)	8–1	
1109	8–7	
1109(a)	8–6	
1132	7–13	4
1132(a)	8–1	
1132(a)	8–7	
1132(a)(1)	8–4	1
1132(a)(1)	8–6	14
1132(a)(1)(B)	7–13	4
1132(a)(1)(B)	8–1	3
1132(a)(1)(B)	8–5	2
1132(a)(2)	8–7	
1132(a)(3)	8–4	1
1132(a)(3)	8–6	15
1132(a)(4)	8–4	1
1132(c)	8–8	24
1132(e)	8–4	12
1133	8–1	
1133	8–6	3
1140	8–7	9
1144(a)	7–13	2
1144(a)	8–3	
1144(a)	8–4	
1144(a)(1)	8–1	
1144(b)(2)(A)	8–3	42

UNITED STATES CODE ANNOTATED
29 U.S.C.A.—Labor

Sec.	This Work Sec.	Note
1144(b)(2)(B)	8–3	61
1144(b)(4)	8–3	42
1144(b)(4)	8–3	64
1144(b)(5)	8–3	22
1144(b)(5)	8–3	42
1144(b)(6)	8–3	42
1144(b)(7)	8–3	42
1144(b)(8)	8–3	42
1161—1168	9–6	1
1161	9–6	3
1162(1)	9–6	14
1162(2)	9–6	8
1162(2)(A)(ii)	9–6	9
1162(2)(B)	9–6	10
1162(2)(C)	9–6	10
1162(2)(D)	9–6	10
1162(3)	9–6	16
1162(3)	9–6	18
1162(4)	9–6	13
1162(5)	9–6	12
1163	9–6	6
1163(2)	9–6	5
1163(6)	9–6	7
1164	9–6	16
1164(2)	9–6	17
1164(3)	9–6	18
1167(3)	9–6	4
1167(3)(C)	9–6	7
1169(c)	8–9	3
1169(d)	8–9	4
1181	8–9	
1181(a)(1)	9–7	2
1181(a)(2)	9–7	3
1181(a)(3)	9–7	4
1181(a)(3)	9–7	5
1181(b)(1)(B)	9–4	49
1181(c)	9–7	5
1181(d)	9–7	6
1181(f)(1)	9–7	3
1181—1182	9–7	1
1182	8–9	
1182(a)	9–7	7
1182(a)(1)(F)	9–4	50
1182(a)(2)	8–9	1
1182(a)(2)	9–7	8
1182(b)	9–7	7
1182(b)(2)	8–9	1
1185	8–9	
1185(a)	9–7	15
1185(b)	9–7	16
1185a	8–9	
1185a(a)	9–7	17
1185a(b)	9–7	18
1185a(c)(2)	9–7	18
1185a(e)(4)	9–7	18
1185a(f)	9–7	18
1185b	8–9	
1185b	9–7	17
1444(d)	8–3	42

31 U.S.C.A.—Money and Finance

Sec.	This Work Sec.	Note
3729	13–4	

UNITED STATES CODE ANNOTATED
31 U.S.C.A.—Money and Finance

Sec.	This Work Sec.	Note
3729(a)	13–4	
3729(a)	13–4	4
3730(b)(1)	13–4	
3730(b)(2)	13–4	9
3730(b)(3)	13–4	12
3730(d)	13–4	15
3730(d)	13–4	16
3730(d)(4)	13–4	17
3730(h)	13–4	18
3730(h)	13–4	26
3731(c)	13–4	2
3801—3812	13–4	40

42 U.S.C.A.—The Public Health and Welfare

Sec.	This Work Sec.	Note
263a	1–7	1
263a	1–15	7
263a(a)	1–15	8
263a(b)	1–14	2
263a(e)	1–4	29
263a(e)	1–15	10
263a(h)	1–17	6
280(c)	7–6	8
290dd–3	4–32	3
291	10–15	1
291c(e)(2)	10–15	2
291i	10–17	7
300(c)	7–6	8
300aa–1 et seq.	6–24	16
300bb–1 to 300bb–8	9–6	1
300bb–1	9–6	3
300bb–2(1)	9–6	14
300bb–2(2)	9–6	8
300bb–2(2)(A)(ii)	9–6	9
300bb–2(2)(B)	9–6	10
300bb–2(2)(C)	9–6	10
300bb–2(2)(D)	9–6	10
300bb–2(3)	9–6	16
300bb–2(3)	9–6	18
300bb–2(4)	9–6	13
300bb–2(5)	9–6	12
300bb–3	9–6	6
300bb–3(2)	9–6	5
300bb–4	9–6	16
300bb–4(2)	9–6	17
300bb–4(3)	9–6	18
300bb–8(3)	9–6	4
300e to 300e–17	9–10	2
300e	9–10	7
300e(b)(1)	9–10	5
300e(b)(1)	9–10	6
300e(b)(1)(C)	9–10	6
300e(b)(2)	9–10	6
300e(b)(3)	9–10	3
300e(b)(4)	9–10	4
300e–1(8)	9–10	6
300gg(a)(1)	9–7	2
300gg(a)(2)	9–7	3
300gg(a)(3)	9–7	4
300gg(a)(3)	9–7	5
300gg(b)(1)	9–4	49

UNITED STATES CODE ANNOTATED

42 U.S.C.A.—The Public Health and Welfare

Sec.	This Work Sec.	Note
1395ww(b)(3)(B)(i)	11–10	7
1395ww(d)	11–10	1
1395ww(d)(1)(B)	11–10	3
1395ww(d)(1)(B)	11–17	2
1395ww(d)(3)(A)(j)	11–10	7
1395ww(d)(3)(E)	11–11	8
1395ww(d)(5)(A)	11–12	1
1395ww(d)(5)(B)	11–12	2
1395ww(d)(5)(C)	11–12	6
1395ww(d)(5)(D)	11–12	4
1395ww(d)(5)(F)	11–12	3
1395ww(d)(5)(G)	11–12	5
1395ww(d)(5)(I)	11–12	7
1395ww(d)(5)(J)	11–12	7
1395ww(d)(7)	11–14	1
1395ww(d)(7)	11–27	19
1395ww(d)(8)	11–11	6
1395ww(d)(10)	11–11	7
1395ww(f)(2)	13–11	
1395ww(j)	11–16	1
1395ww(j)(7)	11–27	22
1395x(a)	11–5	2
1395x(aa)	11–6	7
1395x(aa)	11–6	38
1395x(aa)(5)	11–6	10
1395x(aa)(5)	11–6	13
1395x(b)(6)	11–5	5
1395x(b)(7)	11–5	5
1395x(bb)	11–6	33
1395x(cc)	11–6	39
1395x(cc)(2)(I)	11–8	5
1395x(dd)	11–5	10
1395x(e)	1–4	20
1395x(e)	11–9	
1395x(f)	11–9	
1395x(ff)	11–6	4
1395x(ff)	11–6	43
1395x(g)	11–6	6
1395x(gg)	11–6	14
1395x(hh)	11–6	10
1395x(hh)	11–6	16
1395x(i)	11–5	6
1395x(i)	11–5	7
1395x(ii)	11–6	15
1395x(jj)	11–6	20
1395x(m)	11–5	12
1395x(m)	11–5	14
1395x(m)	11–5	15
1395x(m)	11–6	35
1395x(mm)(3)	11–6	41
1395x(n)	11–6	28
1395x(n)	11–22	1
1395x(n)	11–22	3
1395x(nn)	11–6	21
1395x(o)(7)	11–8	5
1395x(p)	11–6	6
1395x(p)(4)(A)(v)	11–8	5
1395x(pp)	11–6	19
1395x(q)	11–6	2
1395x(qq)	11–6	24
1395x(rr)	11–6	22
1395x(s)(1)	11–6	2
1395x(s)(2)	11–6	4

UNITED STATES CODE ANNOTATED

42 U.S.C.A.—The Public Health and Welfare

Sec.	This Work Sec.	Note
1395x(s)(2)(A)	11–6	3
1395x(s)(2)(C)	11–6	5
1395x(s)(2)(D)	11–6	6
1395x(s)(2)(E)	11–6	7
1395x(s)(2)(F)	11–6	8
1395x(s)(2)(G)	11–6	9
1395x(s)(2)(H)	11–6	10
1395x(s)(2)(I)	11–6	11
1395x(s)(2)(J)	11–6	12
1395x(s)(2)(K)	11–6	13
1395x(s)(2)(L)	11–6	14
1395x(s)(2)(M)	11–6	15
1395x(s)(2)(N)	11–6	16
1395x(s)(2)(O)	11–6	17
1395x(s)(2)(P)	11–6	8
1395x(s)(2)(P)	11–6	18
1395x(s)(2)(Q)	11–6	23
1395x(s)(2)(R)	11–6	19
1395x(s)(2)(S)	11–6	24
1395x(s)(2)(T)	11–6	23
1395x(s)(3)	11–6	25
1395x(s)(4)	11–6	26
1395x(s)(5)	11–6	27
1395x(s)(6)	11–6	28
1395x(s)(7)	11–6	29
1395x(s)(8)	11–6	30
1395x(s)(9)	11–6	31
1395x(s)(10)	11–6	32
1395x(s)(11)	11–6	33
1395x(s)(12)	11–6	34
1395x(s)(13)	11–6	20
1395x(s)(14)	11–6	21
1395x(s)(15)	11–6	22
1395x(u)	11–8	2
1395x(v)(1)(A)	11–17	3
1395y(a)(1)	11–7	3
1395y(a)(9)	11–5	8
1395y(a)(9)	11–7	13
1395y(a)(14)	11–11	2
1395y(b)	9–2	27
1395y(b)	11–28	1
1395y(b)(2)	11–28	2
1395y(b)(4)	11–28	3
1395y(e)	13–11	1
1395y(e)(1)(B)	13–11	2
1395yy(e)	11–16	2
1395yy(e)(8)	11–27	22
1396a	12–7	
1396a(2)(A)(i)	12–2	32
1396a(10)(E)(i)	12–5	37
1396a(a)	1–6	2
1396a(a)	12–3	4
1396a(a)(1)	12–6	18
1396a(a)(1)—(a)(58)	12–12	1
1396a(a)(3)	12–14	1
1396a(a)(4)(B)	12–6	19
1396a(a)(8)	12–3	13
1396a(a)(8)	12–6	1
1396a(a)(10)(A)	12–5	33
1396a(a)(10)(A)(i)(I)	12–2	2
1396a(a)(10)(A)(i)(II)	12–2	11
1396a(a)(10)(A)(i)(II)	12–2	13
1396a(a)(10)(A)(i)(III)	12–2	16

REVISED MODEL NON–PROFIT CORPORATION ACT

Sec.	This Work Sec.	Note
6.30(a)	5–18	4
6.30(a)(i)	5–18	8
6.30(a)(ii)	5–18	9
6.30(c)	5–18	7
8.30	5–15	16
8.30(a)	5–15	18
8.30(a)(3)	5–16	17
8.30(e)	5–14	5
8.30, Official Comment	5–15	16
8.31(d)	5–16	17
8.31, Official Comment	5–16	24
8.32	5–16	19
8.32, Official Comment	5–16	20
10.03	5–11	11
10.21	5–11	11
14.06	5–21	6
14.06(7)	5–21	5

REVISED UNIFORM LIMITED PARTNERSHIP ACT

Sec.	This Work Sec.	Note
101(6)	5–38	2
101(7)	5–38	1
101(11)	5–38	2
201(b)	5–38	5
301(b)(1)	5–39	7
302	5–39	5
303(a)	5–40	3
303(b)	5–40	2
303(b)(6)	5–39	5
304	5–38	5
401	5–39	7
403	5–39	7
405	5–39	4
503	5–39	1
702	5–39	2
1001	5–39	9
1105	5–37	1

REVISED UNIFORM PARTNERSHIP ACT

Sec.	This Work Sec.	Note
103	5–32	7
103(b)	5–35	19
103(b)(4)	5–35	5
306	5–36	2
307	5–36	2
307(d)	5–36	6
404(b)	5–35	18
404(c)	5–35	4
404(e)	5–35	19
506(a)	5–36	6

SHERMAN ACT

Sec.	This Work Sec.	Note
1	5–49	16

SHERMAN ACT

Sec.	This Work Sec.	Note
1	14–2	
1	14–4	
1	14–6	
1	14–8	
1	14–17	
1	14–19	
1	14–20	
1	14–21	
1	14–23	
1	14–25	
1	14–30	
1	14–31	
1	14–32	
1	14–34	
1	14–47	
2	14–2	
2	14–20	
2	14–23	
2	14–31	
2	14–33	
2	14–34	
2	14–36	
2	14–43	

SOCIAL SECURITY ACT

Sec.	This Work Sec.	Note
Tit. V	13–4	
Tit. XIX	12–2	
Tit. XVIII	11–1	
Tit. XVIII	11–2	
Tit. XX	13–4	
205(h)	11–27	
209(b)	12–2	
209(b)	12–2	27
209(b)	12–4	
209(b)	12–4	8
209(b)	12–4	15
1801	11–2	
1818	11–2	

TAX REFORM ACT

Sec.	This Work Sec.	Note
89 (repealed)	9–5	34

UNIFORM COMMERCIAL CODE

Sec.	This Work Sec.	Note
2–315	7–3	

UNIFORM HEALTH CARE DECISIONS ACT

Sec.	This Work Sec.	Note
1(3)	16–14	6
2(a)	16–21	21
2(e)	16–18	1
4(2)	16–4	1
5(b)	16–23	9

UNIFORM HEALTH CARE DECISIONS ACT

Sec.	This Work Sec.	Note
5(f)	16–18	1

UNIFORM LIMITED PARTNERSHIP ACT

Sec.	This Work Sec.	Note
5(a)(1)	5–38	3
6(2)	5–37	1
6(2)	5–37	1
9(1)	5–39	6
19(1)	5–39	2

UNIFORM PARTNERSHIP ACT

Sec.	This Work Sec.	Note
6(1)	5–32	2
7(2)	5–32	3
7(3)	5–32	3
7(4)	5–32	3
9	5–34	5
9(3)	5–34	6
9(4)	5–34	7
13—15	5–36	2
16	5–32	6
17	5–36	5
18(a)	5–34	2
18(a)	5–34	4
18(b)	5–34	3
18(e)	5–32	7
18(e)	5–33	1
18(f)	5–34	1
18(g)	5–33	2
18(h)	5–33	1
18(h)	5–33	3
20	5–32	8
20	5–32	15
21	5–32	15
21	5–35	6

UNIFORM PROBATE CODE

Sec.	This Work Sec.	Note
5–501	16–22	10

UNIFORM STATUS OF CHILDREN OF ASSISTED CONCEPTION ACT

Sec.	This Work Sec.	Note
1(3)	20–6	3
1(3)	20–6	14
1(4)	20–6	17
1, Comment	20–3	7
5(a)	20–6	19
5(b)	20–6	30
6(a)	20–6	19
6(a)	20–6	21
6(a)	20–6	22
6(b)(1)—(b)(10)	20–6	23
6(b)(2)	20–6	15
6(b)(4)	20–6	16

UNIFORM STATUS OF CHILDREN OF ASSISTED CONCEPTION ACT

Sec.	This Work Sec.	Note
6(b)(4)	20–6	20
6(b)(6)	20–6	18
7(a)	20–6	24
7(b)	20–6	26
8(1)	20–6	28
8(2)	20–6	27
8(3)	20–6	29

STATE STATUTES

ALABAMA CODE

Sec.	This Work Sec.	Note
6–5–60(a)	14–2	55
6–5–333	4–28	9
6–5–484	6–10	7
6–5–484	6–12	7
6–5–485	6–21	22
10–2A–73	5–6	9
10–2A–301(1)(b)	5–9	6
10–4–389	5–28	3
10–12–3	5–44	1
10–12–4	5–44	2
10–12–14(a)	5–42	2
10–12–14(b)	5–42	2
16–22–309	6–21	8
22–4–1 to 22–4–17	1–20	3
22–21–260(5)	1–20	6
26–10A–33 to 26–10A–34	20–6	32
27–21A–23(a)	5–10	36
27–53–2	9–4	42
34–19–4	3–6	18

ALASKA STATUTES

Sec.	This Work Sec.	Note
08.64.170	3–10	4
08.64.170	3–10	7
08.65.050	3–6	16
09.55.556(b)(2)	6–15	9
10.06.485	5–7	20
10.45.140(a)	5–29	1
10.45.210	5–28	3
10.45.220	5–28	3
18.07.031—18.07.111	1–20	3
18.20.080(a)	1–4	14
18.20.310(a)(6)	1–17	8
21.54.100	9–4	47

ARIZONA CONSTITUTION

Art.	This Work Sec.	Note
2, § 8	16–4	8

ARIZONA REVISED STATUTES

Sec.	This Work Sec.	Note
10–032	5–3	4
10–905	5–30	2
10–905	5–30	13

WEST'S COLORADO REVISED STATUTES ANNOTATED

Sec.	This Work Sec.	Note
7–80–406	5–42	8
10–3–1104.7	9–4	44
10–16–102(23)	9–10	11
10–16–324	5–22	1
10–16–324	5–22	20
10–17–125(3)	7–11	1
12–36–106	3–7	8
12–36–106	3–10	9
12–36–106(5)(a)	3–10	1
12–36–117(1)(r)	3–23	49
12–36–134	5–10	3
12–36–134(1)(d)	5–27	3
12–36–134(1)(f)	5–27	3
12–36–134(1)(g)	5–30	2
12–36–134(1)(g)	5–30	8
12–36–134(1)(g)	5–30	9
12–36–134(3)	5–29	3
12–36–134(5)	5–29	6
12.3605–101 et seq.	14–2	59
13–1–111.6	6–21	11
13–22–401 to 13–22–409	6–21	19
13–64–403	6–21	22
15–18.5–101	16–23	10
15–18–103(10)	16–21	12
25–1–801	4–31	10
25–1–802	4–31	10
25–3–108	1–17	15
25–3–109(4)(a)	4–26	50

CONNECTICUT GENERAL STATUTES ANNOTATED

Sec.	This Work Sec.	Note
4–104	4–31	10
17B–99	13–15	2
17B–99	13–15	13
19a–17b	4–26	7
19a–408.031—19a–408.0455	1–20	3
19a–486a	5–22	29
19a–524 to 19a–528	1–17	9
19a–542	1–2	10
19a–570 to 19a–575	16–21	2
19a–571	16–23	11
19a–630	1–20	3
19a–638—19a–639d	1–20	3
20–7a	13–9	5
Ch. 370, § 20–8	3–6	13
20–12a(a)(7)	3–10	8
20–12a(b)(1)	3–2	8
20–86c	3–6	18
33–182	5–30	13
33–447(d)	5–11	4
38a–226d	9–9	27
38a–816	9–4	47
53A–290—53A–296	13–15	2
53a–290(3)	13–15	7
53a–290(4)	13–15	7
188	5–22	1

DELAWARE CODE

Tit.	This Work Sec.	Note
6, § 17–102(3)	5–38	3
6, § 1515(b)	5–45	2
8, § 102(b)(7)	5–3	6
8, § 102(b)(7)	5–6	7
8, § 102(b)(7)	5–8	1
8, § 102(b)(7)	5–8	2
8, § 144	5–7	3
8, § 145	5–6	3
8, § 145(a)	5–8	10
8, § 145(a)—(d)	5–8	9
8, § 145(g)	5–8	11
8, § 607	5–29	5
8, § 608	5–30	5
8, § 610	5–27	2
8, § 615	5–28	4
8, § 618	5–26	1
10, § 902(a)	16–33	4
16, § 901	16–33	4
16, §§ 2501—2517	16–4	1
16, § 9112	5–10	36
16, §§ 9301—9311	1–20	3
16, § 9303	1–20	10
18, § 6865	6–21	6
24, § 1703	3–10	1

DISTRICT OF COLUMBIA CODE

Sec.	This Work Sec.	Note
2–1345	6–5	49
6–1921	16–12	2
21–2210	16–23	9
28–4509(a)	14–2	54
29–304(6)	5–7	19
32–505	4–26	47
32–551 to 32–560	5–22	1
32–1412	1–17	15

WEST'S FLORIDA CONSTITUTION

Art.	This Work Sec.	Note
1, § 23	16–4	6

WEST'S FLORIDA STATUTES ANNOTATED

Sec.	This Work Sec.	Note
322.126	4–34	6
381.004(3)	4–34	55
381.701—381.7155	1–20	3
381.711	1–20	42
381.714	1–20	42
381.04065	14–45	5
385.202	4–34	6
395.016	4–30	9
395.018	4–32	6
395.019	4–8	1
395.041(11)	4–28	6
395.0115(5)	4–28	9
395.0115(7)	4–26	33
395.0115(8)(a)	4–28	19
395.0193(7)	4–26	29

WEST'S FLORIDA STATUTES ANNOTATED

Sec.	This Work Sec.	Note
395.3025	4–34	10
400.022(i)(p)	1–13	26
400.126	1–17	15
408.02	6–21	17
409.913	13–15	7
409.913(1)(a)	13–15	8
409.913(15)	13–15	11
409.913(15)	13–15	19
409.920	13–15	2
409.920	13–15	3
409.920(5)	13–15	23
415.101	4–34	21
415.511	4–34	20
458.327(2)(c)	13–9	6
458.331(1)(gg)	13–9	6
458.331(1)(i)	5–10	47
458.331(1)(j)	3–23	49
458.331(1)(j)	3–23	56
458.331(j)	3–23	34
607.0202	5–3	1
608.401 et seq.	5–42	1
608.405	5–42	3
626.9541(g)	9–4	12
626.9707	9–4	40
641.19(13)	9–10	11
641.227	9–10	18
641.228	9–10	18
641.3901	9–10	19
641.3903	9–10	19
742.14—742.17	20–6	32
765.07	16–23	8
765.10	16–23	13
765.101—765.401	16–20	1
766.103(4)	6–16	1
766.303	6–24	5
768.13	6–5	95
768.60	7–3	19

OFFICIAL CODE OF GEORGIA ANNOTATED

Sec.	This Work Sec.	Note
4–11–100 to 4–11–1109	5–44	10
14–2–727	5–3	4
14–9–303	5–40	5
14–11–201	5–44	1
31–6–1 to 31–6–70	1–20	3
31–6–2(5)	1–20	16
31–6–42	1–20	34
31–6–43	1–20	26
31–6–44	1–20	28
31–6–44	1–20	33
31–6–44(i)	1–20	40
31–6–47(4)	1–20	6
31–6–47(16)	1–20	8
31–7–3(b)	1–4	14
31–7–7	4–5	17
31–7–89.1	5–22	1
31–7–400 to 31–7–412	5–22	1
31–7–400(2)(A)	5–22	12
31–9–6.1	6–12	5
31–32–10	16–21	28
33–18–17	9–11	4
33–20–1 et seq.	5–21	9

OFFICIAL CODE OF GEORGIA ANNOTATED

Sec.	This Work Sec.	Note
33–30–23(b)(3)	9–11	23
33–30–23(b)(4)	9–11	23
33–30–23(b)(5)	9–11	25
33–30–24	9–11	21
33–46–4(1)	9–9	19
33–46–4(2)	9–9	9
33–46–5(b)(3)	9–9	6
38–723(g)	4–34	58
43–1B–1 to 43–1B–8	13–9	6
43–9–16	3–5	7
43–34–1 (repealed)	3–5	22
43–34–37(a)(9)	3–5	17
51–1–29.1	6–5	95
51–12–1	6–21	11
88–2906.1(b)(2)	6–16	1

GEORGIA REGULATIONS

Reg.	This Work Sec.	Note
120–2–44–.05(3)	9–11	24

HAWAII REVISED STATUTES

Sec.	This Work Sec.	Note
323D–1 to 323D–12	5–22	1
323D–41—323D–83	1–20	3
323D–43	1–20	13
323D–54(2)	1–20	7
323D–71–83	1–20	20
323D–76	5–22	25
323D–77	5–22	21
324–34	4–32	6
327D–2	16–21	12
327D–2	16–21	16
327D–18	16–21	25
327D–21	16–23	11
327D–25	16–21	22
346–43.5	13–15	2
393–7(c)(6)(C)	1–4	15
415–48.5	5–8	4
415A–11	5–30	11
415B–70	5–16	19
432C–3	5–22	30
453–2	3–7	7
453–2(4)	3–10	7
622–58	4–30	9
624–25(a)	4–26	32
671–11 to 671–20	6–21	19
671D–12	4–28	19

IDAHO CODE

Sec.	This Work Sec.	Note
5–334	17–2	2
39–1392c	4–28	8
39–4305	6–16	1
39–4502	16–4	2
39–4503(3)	16–21	16
48–101	14–2	51
48–102	14–2	51

IDAHO CODE

Sec.	This Work Sec.	Note
54–1402(d)	3–8	3
54–1804(f)	3–7	8

ILLINOIS COMPILED STATUTES

Ch.	This Work Sec.	Note
20 ILCS 305/8–102	4–32	8
20 ILCS 3960/1—3960/19	1–20	3
210 ILCS 5/3	1–1	3
210 ILCS 45/3–503	1–17	15
215 ILCS 5/370h	9–11	16
215 ILCS 5/370m	9–11	31
215 ILCS 125/4–7	9–10	18
225 ILCS 47/1 et seq.	6–11	89
225 ILCS 47/20(b)(7)	6–11	89
225 ILCS 60/9	3–2	1
225 ILCS 60/22	3–20	3
225 ILCS 60/22(5)	3–20	11
225 ILCS 60/22(7)	3–20	9
225 ILCS 60/22(16)	3–20	12
225 ILCS 60/22(17)	3–20	8
225 ILCS 60/22(20)	3–20	19
225 ILCS 60/22(23)	3–20	13
225 ILCS 60/22(32)	3–20	6
225 ILCS 60/22(36)	3–20	14
225 ILCS 60/22(38)	3–20	11
225 ILCS 60/49	3–5	16
225 ILCS 65/25	3–20	3
225 ILCS 65/25	3–20	7
225 ILCS 65/25(b)(4)	3–20	4
225 ILCS 65/25(b)(7)	3–20	11
225 ILCS 65/25(b)(8)	3–20	8
225 ILCS 65/25(b)(9)	3–20	9
225 ILCS 65/25(b)(9)	3–23	21
225 ILCS 65/25(b)(10)	3–20	10
225 ILCS 65/25(b)(12)	3–20	13
225 ILCS 65/25(b)(14)	3–20	5
225 ILCS 95/4	3–10	7
305 ILCS 5/8–7(b)	13–15	15
305 ILCS 5/8–7.1	13–15	8
305 ILCS 5/8A–3	13–15	4
305 ILCS 5/8–A–7(b)	13–15	14
735 ILCS 5/8–2101	4–34	11
740 ILCS 110/12	4–34	35
740 ILCS 110/15	4–32	6
740 ILCS 140/1	3–23	40
755 ILCS 40/1	16–23	9
805 ILCS 5/2.10	5–3	1
805 ILCS 10/4	5–26	3
805 ILCS 10/7	5–29	5
805 ILCS 10/8	5–26	3
805 ILCS 10/8	5–30	7
805 ILCS 10/10	5–27	3
805 ILCS 10/11	5–27	2
805 ILCS 105/108.85	5–11	4
805 ILCS 105/112.16	5–21	5
805 ILCS 180/30–5	5–42	9

ILLINOIS REVISED STATUTES

Ch.	This Work Sec.	Note
23, para. 8A–3(d)	13–15	5

ILLINOIS REVISED STATUTES

Ch.	This Work Sec.	Note
23, para. 8A–7(c)	13–15	19
111, para. 4405	6–5	95
607–14.5	6–21	8

WEST'S ANNOTATED INDIANA CODE

Sec.	This Work Sec.	Note
16–9.5–2–2	6–21	12
16–21–2–5	5–6	23
16–29–1–1 to 16–29–5–1	1–20	3
16–182	5–23	5
16–915–1–4	6–1	43
20–12–30–5.7	1–4	15
23–1.5–2–1	5–26	2
23–1.5–2–5	5–29	5
23–1–37–9	5–3	5
23–1–39–1	5–3	18
25–22.5–1–1.1	3–5	1
27–8–11–3	9–11	12
27–8–11–3(b)	9–11	16
27–8–17–11	9–9	8
27–8–17–11(9)	9–9	9
27–8–17–12(c)	9–9	9
27–8–17–14	9–9	27
27–13–1–19	9–10	11
28–9–11–4	9–11	25
34–3–15.5–1 et seq.	4–36	3

IOWA CODE ANNOTATED

Sec.	This Work Sec.	Note
135.61—135.83	1–20	3
135.64	1–20	34
135.66	1–20	26
135.66(3)(b)	1–20	30
135.67	1–20	27
135B.11	5–6	23
135J.2	1–4	14
144A.1—144A.11	16–21	22
144A.3(1)	16–21	4
144A.3(1)	16–21	21
147.135	4–26	14
147.135	4–26	50
147.137	6–10	16
147.137	6–12	5
490A.1501	5–44	3
490A.1501	5–44	5
490A.1502	5–44	4
490A.1507	5–44	6
490A.1512	5–44	9
504A.27	5–16	19
514.21	7–8	19
619.18	6–21	9

KANSAS STATUTES ANNOTATED

Sec.	This Work Sec.	Note
65–2872a	3–6	8
65–4925(a)(2)	4–27	1
77–202	15–4	3

KANSAS STATUTES ANNOTATED

KANSAS LAWS

KENTUCKY REVISED STATUTES

LOUISIANA STATUTES ANNOTATED— REVISED STATUTES

MAINE REVISED STATUTES ANNOTATED

MAINE REVISED STATUTES ANNOTATED

MARYLAND ANNOTATED CODE

MARYLAND CODE, CORPORATIONS AND ASSOCIATIONS

MARYLAND CODE, HEALTH–GENERAL

MARYLAND CODE, HEALTH OCCUPATIONS

Sec.	This Work Sec.	Note
1–301—1–306	13–9	6
8–601	3–9	9
14–102	3–7	7

MASSACHUSETTS GENERAL LAWS ANNOTATED

Ch.	This Work Sec.	Note
30A	1–8	1
111, §§ 25B–25H	1–20	3
111, § 204(b)	4–27	2
111, § 205(b)	4–27	1
112, § 7	3–7	7
118E, §§ 21A–21G	13–1	10
118E, §§ 39—46A	13–1	10
119, § 1	16–37	1
119, § 51E	16–37	2
119, § 51F	16–37	4
176I, § 2	9–11	32
176I, § 3(a)	9–11	23
176I, § 3(b)	9–11	21
176I, § 4	9–11	15
182, §§ 1–14	5–25	1
201, § 34	16–38	1
201D, § 2	16–12	2
231, § 85W	5–8	5
231A, §§ 1 to 9	16–39	1

CODE OF MASSACHUSETTS REGULATIONS

Tit.	This Work Sec.	Note
211, § 51.04(h)	9–11	31
211, § 51.07(7)(j)	9–11	29
211, § 51.07(8)	9–11	28
211, § 51.07(9)	9–11	36

MICHIGAN COMPILED LAWS ANNOTATED

Sec.	This Work Sec.	Note
333.21054s	9–10	19
333.21054t	9–10	19
333.21515	4–26	10
333.21702 et seq.	1–13	26
333.22203(11)	1–20	16
333.22205	1–20	5
333.22227	1–20	10
333.22229	1–20	24
333.22231(1)(c)	1–20	38
333.22231(2)	1–20	39
333.22232(2)	1–20	31
333.22243	1–20	17
400.607	13–15	2
450.226	5–30	13
450.2209	5–8	6
500.3405	9–11	24
500.3631	9–11	24
550.55	9–11	25
550.56	9–11	32
600.5040 et seq.	6–5	99
600.6307	6–21	10

MICHIGAN COMPILED LAWS ANNOTATED

Sec.	This Work Sec.	Note
700.496(6)	16–22	12
722.851 to 722.863	20–6	32
750.428	13–5	6
750.520b(1)(f)(iv)	3–23	30

MINNESOTA STATUTES ANNOTATED

Sec.	This Work Sec.	Note
62J.09	14–2	60
62J.34(3)	6–21	17
62J.34(3)(a)	6–2	45
62M.06.2	9–9	11
144.34	4–34	17
144.335	4–31	11
145.61(5)	4–26	17
145.413	4–34	18
145.424	17–2	2
145.424(2)	17–2	4
145B.05	16–21	7
147.091(1), subd. 1(i)	3–5	17
147.091, subd. 1(i)	3–10	1
147.091, subd. 1(p)	13–5	6
147.091, subd. 1(p)(3)	13–9	6
147A.09	3–10	12
302A.181	5–3	17
302A.251(1)	5–15	1
319A.03	5–44	2
322B.20	5–42	10
325D.53	14–2	51
549.25	6–21	10
604.05	6–5	50
609.342(1)(g)	3–23	30
6257.022	20–2	1

MISSISSIPPI CODE

Sec.	This Work Sec.	Note
41–7–171 to 41–7–209	1–20	3
41–7–191(1)(d)	1–20	16
41–7–197(2)	1–20	31
41–9–65	4–31	12
41–41–201 to 41–41–229	16–4	1
41–83–9(1)(a)	9–9	10
41–83–9(1)(b)	9–9	7
41–83–9(1)(d)	9–9	5
41–83–17	9–9	5
41–83–23	9–9	13
43–13–13	13–15	2
43–13–129	13–15	2
43–13–205	13–15	2
43–13–207	13–15	3
43–13–213	13–15	2
43–13–217	13–15	2
43–13–225	13–15	11

VERNON'S ANNOTATED MISSOURI STATUTES

Sec.	This Work Sec.	Note
188.130	17–2	2

VERNON'S ANNOTATED MISSOURI STATUTES

NEW JERSEY STATUTES ANNOTATED

Sec.	This Work Sec.	Note
26:6A–5	15–7	2
30:4D–17(c)	13–15	4
30:4D–17(c)	13–15	5
30:4D–17(f)	13–15	16
42:3–9 to 42:3–11	5–25	1
45:9–22.5	13–9	6

NEW MEXICO STATUTES ANNOTATED

Sec.	This Work Sec.	Note
14–6–2A	4–31	20
14–6–2c	4–31	21
24–1–5.2(A)(1)(b)	1–17	8
24–1–5.2(A)(1)(e)	1–17	8
24–1–5.2(A)(2)	1–17	9
24–7a–1 to 24–7a–18	16–4	1
30–44–4—30–44–8	13–15	2
30–44–5	13–15	6
30–44–7	13–15	3
30–44–8(C)	13–15	17
31–25–5	16–37	4
32–1–2	16–37	1
32A–4–3	16–37	2
32A–4–3	16–37	3
32A–4–31	16–38	1
44–6–1 to 44–6–15	16–39	1
61–6–15(D)(16)	13–5	6

NEW YORK, MCKINNEY'S CONSTITUTION

Art.	This Work Sec.	Note
X, § 4	5–25	1
X, § 4	5–25	2

NEW YORK, MCKINNEY'S BUSINESS CORPORATION LAW

Sec.	This Work Sec.	Note
71	5–6	3
723	5–3	5
1505(a)	5–30	5
1508	5–27	3

NEW YORK, MCKINNEY'S CIVIL PRACTICE LAW

Sec.	This Work Sec.	Note
5031–5039	6–21	10

NEW YORK, MCKINNEY'S DOMESTIC RELATIONS LAW

Sec.	This Work Sec.	Note
121—124	20–6	32

NEW YORK, MCKINNEY'S EDUCATION LAW

Sec.	This Work Sec.	Note
6509	3–20	1
6509(2)	3–20	4
6509(2)	3–20	5
6509(3)	3–20	9
6509(5)	3–20	7
6509(5)(b)	3–20	10
6509(6)	3–20	6
6509(6)	3–20	15
6509(6)	10–1	7
6509(9)	3–20	11
6542	3–10	9

NEW YORK, MCKINNEY'S EXECUTIVE LAW

Sec.	This Work Sec.	Note
296 et seq.	4–20	2

NEW YORK, MCKINNEY'S GENERAL BUSINESS LAW

Sec.	This Work Sec.	Note
340	14–2	54

NEW YORK, MCKINNEY'S NOT–FOR–PROFIT CORPORATION LAW

Sec.	This Work Sec.	Note
623(a)	5–18	4
623(d)	5–18	7
716	5–16	19
717(a)	5–15	7
720	5–18	1
720a	5–8	5
720a	5–8	6

NEW YORK, MCKINNEY'S PENAL LAW

Sec.	This Work Sec.	Note
Ch. 40, § 175.35	13–15	1

NEW YORK, MCKINNEY'S PUBLIC HEALTH LAW

Sec.	This Work Sec.	Note
230(11)(a)	3–19	16
230(17)—(18)	3–23	24
238–a	13–9	6
2101	4–34	16
2782(4)(a)	4–34	58
2782(4)(b)	4–34	58
2801–b	4–2	7
2801–b	4–5	17
2801–b	4–8	3
2801–c	4–8	4
2802	1–20	3
2803	1–20	3
2805–b(1)	10–13	2
2805–b(2)	10–13	3

NEW YORK, MCKINNEY'S PUBLIC HEALTH LAW

Sec.	This Work Sec.	Note
2805–b(2)(a)	10–13	4
2805–j	4–28	9
2805–m	4–26	48
2810(2)(b)	1–17	24
2901—2907	1–20	3
2962	16–71	2
2962	16–76	6
4165	4–30	8

NORTH CAROLINA GENERAL STATUTES

Sec.	This Work Sec.	Note
55–8–31	5–7	3
57c–2–01	5–44	2
58–50–55	9–11	13
58–65–70	9–4	40
59–45	5–36	2
90–14(a)(6)	3–6	6
90–322(b)	16–23	12
131E–138(g)	1–4	14
131E–175 to 131E–199	1–20	3
131E–183	1–20	34
131E–185(a1)(2)	1–20	30
131E–185(a1)(4)	1–20	29
131E–188	1–20	33
131E–188	1–20	40

NORTH DAKOTA CENTURY CODE

Sec.	This Work Sec.	Note
10–19.1–89(c)	5–7	20
10–19.1–89(d)	5–7	20
10–31–02.1	5–44	3
14–18–01 to 14–18–07	20–6	32
14–18–02	20–6	13
14–18–05	20–6	13
26.1–26.4–04	9–9	27
26.1–47–02	9–11	28
26.1–47–03	9–11	21
26.1–47–03	9–11	26
26.1–47–03[1][b]	9–11	22
32.03–43	17–2	2

OHIO REVISED CODE

Sec.	This Work Sec.	Note
109.34(b)	5–22	16
109.35	5–22	1
109.99	5–22	1
1329.10(B)	5–32	1
1701.03	5–10	3
1701.60	5–7	3
1707.03(o)(2)	5–26	7
1751.10—1751.71	9–8	24
1751.28	9–13	4
1785.07	5–27	3
2123.08	16–23	7
2133.01(u)	16–21	16
2913.40	13–15	2

OHIO REVISED CODE

Sec.	This Work Sec.	Note
3701.351	4–8	1
3701.351	4–8	2
3702.51—3702.68	1–20	3
3727.02(a)	1–4	14
3727.21	14–2	60
3727.21—3727.24	14–45	5
3999.16	9–4	16
4112 et seq.	4–20	2
4730.02(D)	3–10	8
5111.03(B)(4)	13–15	17
5111.03(D)	13–15	16

OKLAHOMA STATUTES ANNOTATED

Tit.	This Work Sec.	Note
56, § 1007(A)(3)	13–15	17
63, §§ 1–851—1–859	1–20	3
63, §§ 1–880.1—1–880.11	1–20	3

OREGON REVISED STATUTES

Sec.	This Work Sec.	Note
41.675	4–26	9
58.185	5–30	13
58.185(7)	5–30	10
61.530	5–21	5
65.369	5–8	5
65.800—65.815	5–22	1
65.803(a)(i)	5–22	10
65–811	5–22	22
109.239	20–6	32
109.243	20–6	32
109.247	20–6	32
127.525	16–22	12
127.530	16–22	11
127.800—127.897	16–68	30
127.800—127.897	16–68	33
192.525	4–31	11
441.057	4–28	6
442.015—442.347	1–20	3
442.015(14)	1–20	5
646.715(2)	14–2	51
677.097(2)	6–15	11
677.190(5)	4–33	16
677.515(1)(b)	3–10	10
685.010 et seq.	3–6	8
743.531(2)(b)	9–11	4

PENNSYLVANIA STATUTES

Tit.	This Work Sec.	Note
35, §§ 448.101—448.712	1–20	3
35, § 448.603(e)	1–20	41
35, § 448.603(f)	1–20	41
35, § 448.701	1–20	13
35, § 448.702(b)	1–20	26
35, § 448.702(e)(1)	1–20	39
35, § 448.702(f)(2)	1–20	32
35, § 448.702(j)	1–20	24
35, § 448.704	1–20	31

PENNSYLVANIA STATUTES

Tit.	This Work Sec.	Note
35, § 448.707	1–20	34
35, §§ 448.901—448.904b	1–20	3
35, § 449.8(a)	10–13	2
35, § 449.8(a)	10–13	4
35, § 5641	6–12	6
62, § 1407(a)(8)	13–15	9

PENNSYLVANIA CONSOLIDATED STATUTES ANNOTATED

Tit.	This Work Sec.	Note
10, § 371–85	5–23	6
10, § 375	5–23	7
15, § 513	5–8	2
15, § 1106	5–3	3
15, § 2925	5–30	7
42, § 8305	17–2	2
59, § 512	5–38	4
63, § 425.4	4–28	10

PENNSYLVANIA ADMINISTRATIVE CODE

Tit.	This Work Sec.	Note
31, § 152.4	9–11	36
152.102—152.105	9–11	27

RHODE ISLAND GENERAL LAWS

Sec.	This Work Sec.	Note
7–5.1–3	5–28	1
23–15–1 to 23–15–10	1–20	3
23–15–6	1–20	25
23–17.12–8	9–9	27
23–17–14	5–22	7
23–17.14–1 to 23.17.14–31	5–22	1
23–17.14–6(a)(21)	5–22	23
23–17.14–19	5–22	19
23–17–23	4–5	17
40–8.2–3	13–15	5
40–8.2–3(a)(3)	13–15	6

SOUTH CAROLINA CODE

Sec.	This Work Sec.	Note
33–8–310	5–7	3
33–55–210	6–5	95
38–70–20(c)(1)	9–9	8
44–7–190	1–20	37
44–7–200	1–20	29
44–7–210(B)	1–20	30
44–7–210(D)	1–20	33
44–29–90	4–34	61

SOUTH DAKOTA CODIFIED LAWS

Sec.	This Work Sec.	Note
21–3–11	6–21	14
21–55–2	17–2	2

SOUTH DAKOTA CODIFIED LAWS

Sec.	This Work Sec.	Note
36–4A–22	3–10	4
47–11A–8 to 47–11A–12	5–30	9
47–11B–17 to 47–11B–21	5–30	9
47–11C–17 to 47–11C–21	5–30	9
47–23–29	5–8	5
47–24–17	5–22	1

TENNESSEE CODE ANNOTATED

Sec.	This Work Sec.	Note
32–11–103(5)	16–21	17
32–11–103(9)	16–21	16
32–11–108	16–21	26
56–6–705(a)	9–9	27
56–6–705(a)(4)(C)	9–9	11
63–6–219(b)(2)	4–28	9
63–6–219(c)	4–27	1
68–10–101	4–34	61
68–11–101 to 68–11–125	1–20	3
68–11–102(5)(B)(iii)	1–20	6
68–11–106(a)(4)	1–20	16
68–11–106(a)(7)	1–20	23
68–11–304	4–31	1
68–11–305(a)	4–31	20
68–11–804	1–17	9

VERNON'S ANNOTATED TEXAS CIVIL STATUTES

Art.	This Work Sec.	Note
21.402	9–4	46
4495b	4–8	1
4495b, § 5.08(h)(7)	4–34	8
4512i	3–6	16

V.A.T.S., BUSINESS CORPORATIONS ACT

Art.	This Work Sec.	Note
3.02	5–3	2

V.A.T.S., INSURANCE CODE

Art.	This Work Sec.	Note
21.58A, § 4(i)	9–9	20
21.58A, § 5(1c)	9–9	21
21.58A, § 14(e)	9–9	7
29.06(a)	14–28	10
29–09(b)	14–28	10

V.T.C.A., CIVIL PRACTICE AND REMEDIES CODE

Sec.	This Work Sec.	Note
101.021	7–1	15

V.T.C.A., HEALTH AND SAFETY CODE

Sec.	This Work Sec.	Note
314.001—314.008	14–45	5
576.002	16–12	2
672.006	16–21	5

TEXAS ADMINISTRATIVE CODE

Tit.	This Work Sec.	Note
25, § 13.11–20	5–23	6
28, § 3.3703	9–11	24
28, § 3.3703	9–11	30
28, § 3.3703(1)	9–11	13
28, § 3.3703(1)	9–11	14
28, § 3.3703(2)	9–11	19
28, § 3.3703(3)	9–11	27

UTAH CODE ANNOTATED

Sec.	This Work Sec.	Note
16–10a–841	5–8	4
31A–22–617(4)	9–11	36
31A–22–618	9–11	13
48–2b–125	5–42	7
48–2b–131(1)	5–42	9
56–44a–301	3–6	18
58–12–22	3–6	8
75–2–1107	16–19	1
75–2–1112(3)	16–21	27
76–7–204	20–6	32
78–11–24	17–2	2

VERMONT STATUTES ANNOTATED

Tit.	This Work Sec.	Note
12, § 519	6–5	51
18, § 9403 et seq.	6–2	47

VERMONT LAWS

Year	This Work Sec.	Note
1992, c. 160, § 9409	14–2	60

VIRGINIA CODE

Sec.	This Work Sec.	Note
13.1–110	5–44	4
13.1–1002	5–42	4
13.1–1100	5–44	3
13.1–1102	5–44	5
13.1–1109	5–44	7
13.1–1118	5–44	8
20–156 to 20–165	20–6	32
20–159 to 20–160	20–6	12
32.1–102.1—32.1–102.12	1–20	3
32.1–122.01—32.1–122.08	1–20	3
32.1–138.14	9–9	29
32.1–310—32.1–321	13–1	10
38.2–3407	9–11	18
54.1–2900 et seq.	5–44	5

VIRGINIA CODE

Sec.	This Work Sec.	Note
54.1–2952	3–8	8
54.1–2952	3–10	4
54.1–2972	15–4	2
54.1–2981—54.1–2993	16–20	1
54.1–2981—54.1–2992	16–21	5
54–276.12	6–5	95
55–531 to 55–533	5–22	1
55–531	5–22	10

WASHINGTON CONSTITUTION

Art.	This Work Sec.	Note
XII, § 5	5–25	1
XII, § 5	5–25	2

WEST'S REVISED CODE OF WASHINGTON ANNOTATED

Sec.	This Work Sec.	Note
18.36A.010 et seq.	3–6	8
18.36A.040	3–6	8
18.71A.020(2)	3–10	7
26.26210 to 26.26260	20–6	32
70.38.015 to 70.38.920	1–20	3
70.38.025	1–20	5
70.38.105(4)(d)	1–20	18
70.38.111(1)	1–20	11
70.38.115(7)	1–20	24
70.44.007	5–22	1
70.44.300	5–22	1

WEST VIRGINIA CODE

Sec.	This Work Sec.	Note
16–2D–1 to 16–2D–13	1–20	3
16–2D–3(b)	1–20	23
16–2D–4(b)	1–20	11
16–2D–4(c)	1–20	17
16–2D–6	1–20	34
16–2D–9(c)	1–20	38
16–2D–9(d)	1–20	38
16–2D–13	1–20	41
16–5B–6a	5–12	2
16–30B–7	16–23	6
16–30B–7	16–23	9
16–30B–8	16–19	1
16–30B–8	16–23	14
30–3–16(b)	3–10	10
30–3–16(g)	3–10	10
30–3–16(l)	3–10	13
30–3C–2	4–28	9
30–3C–3	4–26	7
30–3C–3	4–26	31
30–3C–3	4–26	33
48–4–16	20–6	32

WISCONSIN STATUTES ANNOTATED

Sec.	This Work Sec.	Note
50.35	5–22	1

WISCONSIN STATUTES ANNOTATED

Sec.	This Work Sec.	Note
146.024(2)(a)	10–22	19
146.024(4)	10–22	19
150.01—150.86	1–20	3
154.01(8)	16–21	12
165.40	5–22	1
165.40(3)(b)	5–22	14
250	14–2	60
448.03	3–7	7
448.08	5–10	3
609.15	9–11	33
609.20(1)	9–11	26
609.20(2)	9–11	22
628.36.2(b)[2]	9–11	19
631.89	9–4	47

WISCONSIN ADMINISTRATIVE CODE

Sec.	This Work Sec.	Note
3.3705	9–11	28

WYOMING STATUTES

Sec.	This Work Sec.	Note
17–15–103	5–44	1
17–15–106	5–42	3
17–15–121(a)	5–42	6
26–22–503	9–11	12
26–22–503(b)	9–11	27
33–26–402(a)(vii)	3–23	48

FEDERAL RULES OF CIVIL PROCEDURE

Rule	This Work Sec.	Note
11	14–22	16
16	14–22	16
16(f)	14–22	16
26	4–31	22
26	14–22	16
26(g)	14–22	16
34	4–31	23
37	14–22	16

FEDERAL RULES OF EVIDENCE

Rule	This Work Sec.	Note
401	16–53	1
803	4–31	29
803(4)	4–31	28
803(6)	4–31	27
803(18)	6–2	88
804	4–31	29

SUPREME COURT RULES

Rule	This Work Sec.	Note
10–305	16–38	1

TREASURY REGULATIONS

Sec.	This Work Sec.	Note
1.501(c)(3)–1(a)	2–2	1
1.501(c)(3)–1(b)	2–2	2
1.501(c)(3)–1(b)(1)(iii)	2–9	11
1.501(c)(3)–1(b)(3)	2–1	5
1.501(c)(3)–1(b)(4)	2–2	3
1.501(c)(3)–1(c)	2–2	4
1.501(c)(3)–1(c)(1)	2–9	11
1.501(c)(3)–1(c)(2)	2–2	5
1.501(c)(3)–1(c)(3)	2–1	5
1.501(c)(3)–1(d)(2)	2–1	5
1.501(c)(3)–1(d)(2)	2–3	1
1.501(c)(3)–1(e)	2–9	11
1.513–1	2–8	1
1.513–1	2–9	1
1.513–1(b)	2–9	4
1.513–1(d)(2)	2–8	2
1.513–1(d)(2)	2–8	3
1.513–1(d)(2)	2–9	2
1.513–1(d)(2)	2–9	3
301.7701.1	5–43	1
301.7701–2(a)(1)	5–43	1
301.7701–2(a)(2)	5–25	3

CODE OF FEDERAL REGULATIONS

Tit.	This Work Sec.	Note
16, § 1.3	14–2	63
16, § 1.7	14–2	30
16, § 1.22	14–2	30
16, § 50.6	14–2	64
20, §§ 404.509—404.512	11–24	4
20, §§ 404.900—404.999(d)	11–26	2
20, §§ 404.967—404.982	11–26	14
21, § 50.24	21–9	1
21, § 56.101 et seq.	21–2	3
21, § 56.101(a)	21–2	4
21, § 56.103	21–2	4
26, §§ 1–105–5–1–105–11(c)	9–5	34
26, § 1.501(c)(3)–1(c)	2–11	1
28, § 36.104	10–22	3
28, § 36.202	10–22	4
28, § 36.208	10–22	7
28, § 36.302	10–22	5
28, § 46.101 et seq.	21–2	3
29, § 103.30	4–15	3
29, § 1604.10	9–5	26
29, Pt. 1604, App.	9–5	27
29, Pt. 1604, App.	9–5	28
29, § 1625.10	9–5	33
29, § 1630.2(r)	4–23	27
29, § 1630.4(f)	9–5	4
29, § 1630.16(f)	9–5	8
29, Pt. 1630, App.	9–5	8
29, § 2510.3–1(j)	8–2	
29, § 2520.102–3	9–2	4
29, § 2560.503–1	8–6	3
29, § 2560.503–1	8–6	4
29, § 2560.503–1(j)	8–6	4
29, § 2560.503–1	8–6	5
32, § 219.101 et seq.	21–2	3
34, § 97.101 et seq.	21–2	3
41, § 489.24	11–8	11

CODE OF FEDERAL REGULATIONS

CODE OF FEDERAL REGULATIONS

INDEX

Management Summary. List the recommendations in broad terms and describe the impact that implementation of the recommendations will have on the organization. This section should not be longer than two pages.

Introduction. Describe the background (Investigation Guidelines 1, 2, and 3) for writing the report.

Benefits of Manuals. Describe the benefits in general terms (as discussed in Section 1.2) and give specific examples found in your organization.

Alternative Solutions. Present each alternative plan. For example:

1. A full manuals program for the organization
2. A partial program (for one or more departments)
3. A few selected manuals
4. No manuals

Costs. Present the costs associated with each alternative. Don't forget that there are costs associated with having no manuals. They may be difficult to quantify, but they do exist. (Sections 1.1, 1.4, and 1.5)

Recommendations. Choose the solution which best fits the needs of the organization, and offer reasons for your recommendation.

Implementation. Present an implementation plan which fits the recommendations. Options may also be considered. For example, if Alternative Solution 2—a partial program—was chosen for this year, with a view to implementing a full program by next year, then draw up a schedule to reflect this.

INVESTIGATION GUIDELINES FOR
REPORT B
(the organization that has manuals but has no centralized manuals program or manuals standards)

These guidelines should be followed before preparing your report.

1. Collect copies of all manuals in the organization and compare them. Consider the following:

   - Are the manuals housed in a uniform manner; for example, binders, tab dividers, etc.? See Chapter 7.
   - Is there adequate instruction regarding the use and maintenance of the manuals? See Chapter 3.
   - Are there adequate retrieval devices in the manual—alphabetic subject index, forms index, table of contents? Are these retrieval devices up-to-date? See Chapter 3.
   - Is the numbering system used in the manual simple? Can Subjects be added, deleted, and amended without disrupting other content? See Chapter 3.

- Is the writing style simple? Use one of the writing formulas described in Chapter 4 to find out.
- Are appropriate layouts used to present data? See Chapter 5.
- Is print quality good?
- Is the reading line of the text too long? (4½ inches is recommended)
- Are there sufficient illustrations to support subject matter? Have all the forms mentioned in every Subject been illustrated? Have all the forms been indexed?
- Have standards been set and maintained for typing? See Chapter 6.
- Is there a critique process? See Chapter 6.
- Is there an approvals procedure? See Chapter 6.
- Is the page design functional, simple, and attractive? See Chapter 2.

2. Do a spot audit to see if users are keeping their manuals up-to-date. See Chapter 9.
3. Perform a user test to determine retrieval costs and reading costs. Refer to Section 1.4 for details of this test.
4. Send out a user questionnaire. Ask the following questions:

- How often do you reference your manual?
- Is there subject matter in the manual which needs to be revised?
- Is there subject matter missing?
- Are there adequate illustrations in the manual?
- What is the average time it takes to find a required Subject?
- When you find the required Subject, can you understand the text?

OUTLINE FOR
REPORT B

A report prepared for an organization that has manuals but no centralized manuals program should contain the following information.

Management Summary. Describe, in general, the recommendations made and the impact that implementation of the recommendations will have on the organization. This section should be about 1 or 2 pages in length.

Introduction. Describe the organization's requirements for manuals and the history of manuals in the organization.

Report Objectives. These may be as follows: to judge the effectiveness of existing manuals, to assess whether improvements can be made, etc.

Method of Review. Describe the methods used to review the manuals. Develop an organization chart that shows existing manuals, manuals under development, and their relationships to one another.

Review Findings. Describe each of your investigative findings.

Alternative Solutions. Describe alternatives to correct the problems discovered. For example: